Encyclopedia
of the
Confederacy

Ex Libris

Editorial Advisers

Encyclopedia of the Confederacy

RICHARD N. CURRENT, Editor in Chief
Emeritus, University of North Carolina, Greensboro

Editorial Board

PAUL D. ESCOTT
Wake Forest University

LAWRENCE N. POWELL
Tulane University

JAMES I. ROBERTSON, JR.
Virginia Polytechnic Institute and State University

EMORY M. THOMAS
University of Georgia

Volume 2

S I M O N & S C H U S T E R
A Paramount Communications Company

New York   London   Toronto   Sydney   Tokyo   Singapore

Simon & Schuster
Academic Reference Division
15 Columbus Circle
New York, New York 10023

Printed in the United States of America

printing number
1 2 3 4 5 6 7 8 9 10

Library of Congress Cataloging-in-Publication Data

Encyclopedia of the Confederacy

Richard N. Current, Editor in Chief; editorial board, Paul D.
Escott . . . [et al.].
p.   cm..

Includes bibliographical reference and index (p.).
ISBN 0-13-275991-8 (set: alk. paper)
1. Confederate States of America—Encyclopedia.
I. Current, Richard Nelson.

E487.55 1993   973.7'13—dc20   93-4133 CIP

ISBN 0-13-275991-8 (set)
ISBN 0-13-276023-1 (v. 2)

*Acknowledgments of sources, copyrights, and
permissions to use previously printed materials
are made throughout the work.*

*The paper used in this publication meets the minimum requirements of
American National Standard for Information Sciences—Permanence
of Paper for Printed Library Materials ANSI Z39.48-1984.*

Abbreviations and Symbols Used in This Work

A.D. *anno Domini*, in the year of the (our) Lord
Adj. Gen. adjutant general
Adm. admiral
Ala. Alabama
A.M. *ante meridiem*, before noon
Ariz. Arizona
Ark. Arkansas
b. born; beam (interior measurement of width of a ship)
B.C. before Christ
brig. brigade
Brig. Gen. brigadier general
c. *circa*, about, approximately
Calif. California
Capt. captain
cf. *confer*, compare
chap. chapter (pl., chaps.)
cm centimeters
Col. colonel
Colo. Colorado
Comdr. commander
Como. commodore
Conn. Connecticut
Cpl. corporal
C.S. Confederate States
C.S.A. Confederate States of America, Confederate States Army
CSS Confederate States ship
cwt. hundredweight (equals 772 lbs.)
d. died
D.C. District of Columbia
Del. Delaware
diss. dissertation

div. division
dph. depth of hold
ed. editor (pl., eds.); edition; edited by
e.g. *exempli gratia*, for example
Eng. England
enl. enlarged
Ens. ensign
esp. especially
et al. *et alii*, and others
etc. *et cetera*, and so forth
exp. expanded
f. and following (pl., ff.)
1st Lt. first lieutenant
fl. *floruit*, flourished
Fla. Florida
frag. fragment
ft. feet
Ga. Georgia
Gen. general
Gov. governor
HMS Her Majesty's ship
ibid. *ibidem*, in the same place (as the one immediately preceding)
i.e. *id est*, that is
Ill. Illinois
Ind. Indiana
Kans. Kansas
km kilometers
Ky. Kentucky
l. length
La. Louisiana
lb. pound (pl., lbs.)
Lt. lieutenant
Lt. Col. lieutenant colonel

Lt. Comdr. lieutenant commander
Lt. Gen. lieutenant general
m meters
M.A. Master of Arts
Maj. Major
Maj. Gen. major general
Mass. Massachusetts
mi. miles
Mich. Michigan
Minn. Minnesota
Miss. Mississippi
Mo. Missouri
Mont. Montana
n. note
N.C. North Carolina
n.d. no date
N.Dak. North Dakota
Neb. Nebraska
Nev. Nevada
N.H. New Hampshire
N.J. New Jersey
N.Mex. New Mexico
no. number (pl., nos.)
n.p. no place
n.s. new series
N.Y. New York
Okla. Oklahoma
Oreg. Oregon
p. page (pl., pp.)
Pa. Pennsylvania
pdr. pounder (weight of projec tile in pounds; pl., pdrs.)
pl. plural, plate (pl., pls.)
P.M. *post meridiem*, after noon
Pres. president
pt. part (pl., pts.)

Pvt. private
r. reigned; ruled; river
Rear Adm. rear admiral
regt. regiment
Rep. representative
rev. revised
R.I. Rhode Island
S.C. South Carolina
S.Dak. South Dakota
sec. section (pl., secs.)
2d Lt. second lieutenant
Sen. senator
ser. series
Sgt. sergeant
sing. singular
sq. square
supp. supplement; supplementary
Tenn. Tennessee
Tex. Texas
trans. translator, translators; translated by; translation
U.S. United States
USS United States ship
Va. Virginia
var. variant; variation
vol. volume (pl., vols.)
Vt. Vermont
Wash. Washington
Wis. Wisconsin
W.Va. West Virginia
Wyo. Wyoming
° degress
' feet; minutes
" inches; seconds
£ pounds
? uncertain; possibly; perhaps

Key to Map Symbols

	Troops, Confederate		Trees
	Troops, Union		Marsh
	Cavalry, Confederate		Elevation
	Cavalry, Union		River
	Tactical Movement, Confederate		Railroad
	Tactical Movement, Union		Unfinished Railroad
	Strategic Movement, Confedederate		Road
	Strategic Movement, Union		State Boundary
	Retreat		
	Engagement		
	Artillery		Building
	Encampment		Church
	Headquarters		Village
	Fortifications		Town, Strategic
	Entrenchments		Town, Tactical
	Casemate Ironclad		Pontoon Bridge
	Gunboat		Bridge
	Monitor		
	Warship		

Encyclopedia
of the
Confederacy

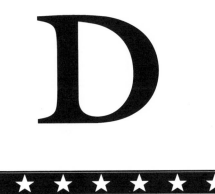

D

DAHLGREN PAPERS. Following the aborted Kilpatrick-Dahlgren cavalry raid on Richmond (February 28–March 3, 1846), Col. Ulric Dahlgren was killed while attempting to return to Union lines. Soon after Dahlgren's death young William Littlepage, a local schoolboy, searched Dahlgren's pockets and discovered papers that produced a storm of controversy. They contained various inflammatory statements, including references to burning Richmond and killing President Jefferson Davis and his cabinet.

The publication of the Dahlgren papers in the Richmond newspapers fanned the flames of hatred and prompted cries for retribution. Eventually Gen. Robert E. Lee wrote to Gen. George G. Meade, asking him if his government had approved or sanctioned the violent actions proposed in the captured letters. Meade disavowed the statements but wrote his wife of "collateral evidence in my possession," suggesting he believed the papers genuine.

Dahlgren's supporters quickly sprang to his defense and insisted the papers were either forged or planted on the fallen warrior. All those intimately involved in the raid, including its leader Gen. Judson Kilpatrick, denied the published statements concerning the burning of Richmond and the killing of Davis and the Confederate cabinet. Others claimed the transposition of the *h* and *l* in Dahlgren's signature on one of the documents proved they were forgeries.

Any impartial investigation into the controversy became frustratingly difficult because none of the original Dahlgren papers survived. During the 1950s, however, historian V. C. Jones thoroughly reviewed the issue and refuted theories that claimed the papers were false because of Dahlgren's name being misspelled. He noted that of the three separate papers concerning the raid, the two with the most damning statements had no signature. To establish the papers' authenticity he documented a chain of possession and offered testimony from virtually every prominent Confederate authority who claimed to have seen the documents. His findings are still valid today.

[*See also* Kilpatrick-Dahlgren Raid.]

BIBLIOGRAPHY

Dahlgren, Admiral John A. *Memoir of Ulric Dahlgren.* Philadelphia, 1872.
Jones, Virgil Carrington. *Eight Hours before Richmond.* New York, 1957.

MICHAEL J. ANDRUS

DALLAS, MOSES (1840–1874), Confederate naval pilot and Union soldier. Dallas, a twenty-three-year-old Duval County, Florida, slave, joined the Union navy in 1863 but soon changed sides and became the chief coastal pilot for the Confederacy's beleaguered Savannah Squadron. Although the circumstances surrounding Dallas's defection are unclear, the Confederacy rewarded him handsomely for his services. On May 31, 1863, Comm. William A. Webb of CSS *Atlanta* felt "compelled to increase the pay of Moses Dallas from $80 to $100 per month in order to retain him." Considered the "best inland pilot on the coast," Dallas remained in Confederate service for more than a year and apparently enjoyed the full trust of white Southern officers.

His loyalty received its greatest test on the night of June 2–3, 1864, when he led a force of 132 Confederate sailors in a daring attack on the Union gunboat *Water Witch,* anchored near the mouth of the Ogeechee River. Dallas accompanied the expedition's commander in the first of seven open boats that approached within two ship-lengths of the Union vessel before their presence was discovered. Amid volleys of gunfire and sharp hand-to-hand fighting, Confederates boarded and subdued the enemy ship, believing that their black pilot had died gallantly during the initial moments of the attack.

In fact, Dallas had exploited the confusion in order to escape, and on March 9, 1865, he enlisted in Company E of the 128th U.S. Colored Infantry at Beaufort, South Carolina. Mustered out with the rank of corporal in October 1866, he rejoined his family in Jacksonville, Florida, where he remained until his death eight years later.

BIBLIOGRAPHY

Mohr, Clarence L. *On the Threshold of Freedom: Masters and Slaves in Civil War Georgia.* Athens, Ga., 1986.
Valuska, David Lawrence. "The Negro in the Union Navy, 1861–1865." Ph.D. diss., Lehigh University, 1973.

CLARENCE L. MOHR

DALTON, GEORGIA. Located on the Western and Atlantic Railroad, eighty miles north of Atlanta and thirty miles southeast of Chattanooga, Dalton was the site of Gen. William Tecumseh Sherman's opening offensive of the 1864 Atlanta campaign against Gen. Joseph E. Johnston and his Army of Tennessee.

Since the Confederate defeat at Missionary Ridge the previous November, the Army of Tennessee had been camped near Dalton protected by nearly impregnable defensive works on top of 1,500-foot-high Rocky Face Ridge, which ran about three miles north and south and was located just west of the city. Sherman's army was made up of the 60,000-man Army of the Cumberland under Gen. George H. Thomas, the 23,000-man Army of the Tennessee under Gen. James B. McPherson, and the 17,000-man Army of the Ohio under Gen. John M. Schofield. Sherman also had with him 254 pieces of artillery and a division of cavalry commanded by Gen. Hugh Judson Kilpatrick.

At Dalton during the winter of 1863–1864, Johnston, who had inherited the remains of Gen. Braxton Bragg's Army of Tennessee when that officer asked to be relieved after Missionary Ridge, had recruited and refitted this 40,000-man force, which consisted of two corps, one commanded by Gen. William J. Hardee and the other by Gen. John Bell Hood. After Johnston requested additional troops from the government in Richmond, President Jefferson Davis ordered the 15,000-man Army of Mississippi commanded by Gen. Leonidas Polk to join Johnston in early May. Rounding out his troop strength were 124 field pieces and the cavalry of Gen. Joseph Wheeler.

The Army of the Cumberland, screened by Kilpatrick's cavalry, advanced from its position at Ringgold, Georgia, on the morning of May 7 and by afternoon was in position from Mill Creek Gap on Rocky Face Ridge north to Tunnel Hill, which it occupied after driving out the Confederate troops

stationed there. The Army of the Ohio marched south from Cleveland, Tennessee, and, after some minor skirmishing with Wheeler's cavalry, connected with the left of Thomas's command near Tunnel Hill that same day. Off to the west, the Army of the Tennessee was moving around and to the south of Rocky Face Ridge through Snake Creek Gap with the intention of getting in the rear of Johnston's weak left flank and cutting off his railroad supply lines at Resaca, about ten miles south of Dalton. By May 8, McPherson occupied Snake Creek Gap, and the whole of the Union force was in place.

Meanwhile, Johnston, alerted by his cavalry scouts of Sherman's movements, ordered his army into positions along Rocky Face Ridge and its gaps. Sherman was well aware that he could not take Johnston by direct assault against the impenetrable ridge. His actual intent was a feint by the Army of the Cumberland and the Army of the Ohio against the Confederate stronghold in order to give McPherson time to flank the Southern left undetected.

At Mill Creek Gap, the Confederate engineers had dammed the creek, creating a small lake, and on May 8, Thomas made three unsuccessful attacks on the dam with the intention of destroying it so that the Federals could move through the gap. In the afternoon a division of the Army of the Cumberland led by Gen. John W. Geary attacked Dug Gap south of Mill Creek without success. On May 9, two divisions of Schofield's army battled the Confederates at Crow Valley north of Mill Creek and for the third time there was no gain. For the next several days the Federals kept up their pressure so that Sherman could achieve his real objective of getting McPherson to Resaca and destroying the Confederate supply lines and, consequently, the Army of Tennessee.

No casualty figures are available for the Dalton action, other than 357 Union men reported lost by Geary.

BIBLIOGRAPHY

Bailey, Ronald H. *Battles for Atlanta: Sherman Moves East.* Alexandria, Va., 1985.
Miles, Jim. *Fields of Glory: A History and Tour Guide of the Atlanta Campaign.* Nashville, Tenn., 1989.
U.S. War Department. *War of the Rebellion: A Compilation of the Official Records of the Union and Confederate Armies.* Washington, D.C., 1880–1901. Ser. 1, vol. 38, pts. 1–5.

WARREN WILKINSON

DANIEL, JUNIUS (1828–1864), brigadier general. Daniel was born in Halifax County, North Carolina, June 27, 1828. He trained as a soldier, graduating from West Point in 1851. After serving seven years in the U.S. Army, he resigned to take charge of his father's plantations in Louisiana.

JUNIUS DANIEL.   LIBRARY OF CONGRESS

When North Carolina seceded on May 20, 1861, Daniel enlisted in Northampton County, in the Fourteenth Regiment, North Carolina Troops. He was appointed colonel of this regiment and served with it until elected colonel of the Forty-fifth Regiment in April 1862. In May a brigade consisting of three North Carolina regiments was formed under Daniel's command and rushed to Drewry's Bluff, south of Richmond. This brigade saw action during the Seven Days' Battles, and two more regiments were added to it. He was appointed brigadier general to date from September 1, 1862.

During the winter of 1862 Daniel's brigade saw service in North Carolina. In May 1863 the brigade was transferred back to Virginia in time to participate in the Gettysburg campaign and battle, where the command suffered the greatest losses of any brigade in Robert Rode's division. Daniel greatly distinguished himself. He and his brigade continued to fight in the Mine Run campaign and the Wilderness battles until May 12, 1864, at Spotsylvania where Daniel was mortally wounded while striving to recapture the Confederate works at the tip of the Bloody Angle. Daniel died the following day. His body was taken back to Halifax, North Carolina, where he was buried in an old churchyard.

BIBLIOGRAPHY

Jordon, Weymouth T., Jr., and Lewis H. Manerin. *North Carolina Troops, 1861–1865: A Roster.* Vols. 5 and 11. Raleigh, N.C., 1975, 1987.

Warner, Ezra J. *Generals in Gray: Lives of the Confederate Commanders.* Baton Rouge, La., 1959.

JOHN R. WOODARD

DANVILLE, VIRGINIA. Located in south-central Virginia, less than five miles from the North Carolina border, the city of Danville was a primary supply center for the Confederacy during the Civil War. From a population of 3,689 (1,674 white; 1,466 slave; 202 free black; 347 other) in 1860, the city expanded to almost 6,000 by the end of the war. In the decade before the war the major economic activity of the region was tobacco, and by 1860 Danville had become the third largest processing center of the crop in the state. Moreover, because it was the only urban center in the county, the city contained a variety of other businesses—shoes, clothing, blacksmith, flour and meal—to sustain the needs of the townspeople and the neighboring countryside.

Its citizens, like the vast majority of Southerners, were conservative in their outlook on life. To get ahead they advocated hard work and frowned on consumption of liquor, so much so that they banned its sale within city limits. The city council also instituted a slave patrol to control the black population and limit their access to the city.

In 1861 the majority of the city's residents opposed secession, believing that the South could best defend its rights by remaining in the Union. When Virginia called for a convention to decide the issue, the people elected William T. Sutherlin, a moderate Unionist, to represent them. To many in Danville the argument for or against secession revolved around its economic consequences. In the end, they opposed Virginia leaving the Union because they believed that secession would bring disruption and chaos to the local economy. Lincoln's call for troops changed the disposition of the townspeople, however, and thereafter they willingly supported the Confederate cause.

The fear that the local economy would decline proved to be unfounded. In fact, the city became a major economic beneficiary of the conflict. The war caused existing manufacturers, especially of shoes and clothing, to expand their production dramatically, and it led to the development of new industries—munitions, coal, and fertilizer—as well. A primary factor in this increased productivity was the city's strategic location. Situated far behind the front lines, businesses could operate without fear of enemy interference. This security led several manufacturing companies in Richmond and Petersburg to transfer their operations to Danville. The city had direct rail connections with Richmond, and in May 1864 the War Department completed construction on a railway that connected the city with Greensboro, North Carolina, which facilitated the transportation of supplies from the Deep South.

In the last two years of the war the morale of the

townspeople declined considerably, with numerous individuals failing to meet their responsibilities. In January 1864 the citizens petitioned the War Department to have Union prisoners removed from the city. Danville served as the last capital of the Confederacy from April 3 to April 10, 1865, when President Jefferson Davis transferred the government there after the fall of Richmond.

BIBLIOGRAPHY

Ballard, Michael. *The Long Shadow*. Jackson, Miss., 1988.

Davis, William C. *Jefferson Davis: The Man and His Hour*. New York, 1991.

Hattaway, Herman, and Archer Jones. *How The North Won: A Military History of the Civil War*. Urbana, Ill., 1983.

Siegel, Frederick F. *The Roots of Southern Distinctiveness: Tobacco and Society in Danville, Virginia, 1780–1865*. Chapel Hill, N.C., 1987.

MICHAEL G. MAHON

DARDEN, STEPHEN HEARD (1816–1902),

colonel and congressman from Texas. Born in Mississippi on November 19, 1816, Darden moved to Texas in 1836 to join the Texas Revolution. That fall he served briefly as a clerk for the comptroller of the new republic. After returning home for a time, he acquired land near Gonzales, Texas, and began farming there in the late 1840s. He participated in the American party during the mid-1850s and served in the Texas house of representatives from 1853 to 1856. Although reluctant about secession, he won election to the Texas senate in 1861. The following year he joined the Fourth Texas Infantry of Hood's Brigade as captain of a company and fought in the Seven Days' Battles, at Second Manassas, and at Sharpsburg. In the fall he went back to Texas in poor physical condition, but in 1863 returned to duty as colonel of the Fifth Infantry Regiment of the Texas state troops defending the coast.

After the death of Congressman John A. Wilcox in 1864, Darden was elected to his seat. In the Confederate Congress he served on the naval affairs committee and supported such military measures as expansion of the army and designation of a commander in chief as well as additional funding. Yet he favored individual and state control of economic activities including slave labor.

After Reconstruction, the state Democratic party elected him Texas comptroller for 1874–1881. In the 1880s he served in other minor state offices. He became active in the Texas Veterans' Association before his death on May 16, 1902, at Wharton.

BIBLIOGRAPHY

Daniell, L. E. *Personnel of the Texas State Government*. Austin, Tex., 1889.

Simpson, Harold B. *Hood's Texas Brigade*. 4 vols. Waco, Tex., 1968–1977.

Warner, Ezra J., and W. Buck Yearns. *Biographical Register of the Confederate Congress*. Baton Rouge, La., 1975.

Webb, Walter Prescott, and H. Bailey Carroll, eds. *The Handbook of Texas*. 2 vols. Austin, Tex., 1952.

Winkler, Ernest William, ed. *Platforms of Political Parties in Texas*. Austin, Tex., 1916.

ALWYN BARR

DARGAN, E. S. (1805–1879), congressman from

Alabama. Born April 15, 1805, in Wadesboro, North Carolina, Edmund Strother Dargan became self-supporting at an early age when his father died. Self-educated, he learned English, Latin, and Greek while working as a farm laborer. In 1823 he moved to Washington, Alabama, where he taught school, practiced law, and served as justice of the peace. He moved to Montgomery in 1833, and the legislature elected him to the Circuit Court in 1840. He was elected to the Alabama Senate in 1844, to the U.S. House of Representatives as a Democrat in 1845, and to the Alabama Supreme Court in 1847. He became chief justice two years later, a position he retained until 1852, when he resigned to resume his law practice in Mobile.

He was elected to the Alabama secession convention, where he voted for the ordinance in January 1861. Soon after he was sent to the First Confederate Congress, where he supported President Jefferson Davis, served on the Judiciary Committee, and opposed impressment of private property for Confederate use. His efforts led to the 1863 order limiting Confederate impressment of private goods. According to fellow Congressman E. A. Pollard, Dargan responded to derogatory remarks by Congressman Henry S. Foote by accosting Foote with a bowie knife. Later information revealed that Dargan was holding the pen with which he had been writing when verbally attacked. He declined reelection and returned to his law practice in Mobile, where he lived until his death in 1879.

Some published sources contain several errors about Dargan's life. He never served as mayor of Mobile, as has been suggested. His middle name was Strother, not Spann, and he died November 24, 1879, not November 22. The latter errors occurred in his obituary in the *Mobile Weekly Register* of November 29, 1879. The paper printed a correction on December 6.

BIBLIOGRAPHY

Owen, Thomas McAdory. *History of Alabama and Dictionary of Alabama Biography*. 4 vols. Chicago, 1921.

Thornton, J. Mills, III. *Politics and Power in a Slave Society: Alabama, 1800–1860*. Baton Rouge, La., 1978.

Wakelyn, Jon L. *Biographical Directory of the Confederacy*. Edited by Frank E. Vandiver. Westport, Conn., 1977.

Warner, Ezra J., and W. Buck Yearns. *Biographical Register of the Confederate Congress.* Baton Rouge, La., 1975.

SARAH WOOLFOLK WIGGINS

DAVIDS. The torpedo boat *David* gave its name to other torpedo boats of the same or similar specifications. The name derived from its size relative to Goliath-sized Union ships. Its mission was to glide in under the guns of a blockader and detonate a spar torpedo beneath the waterline. Using such a ship was exclusively a Confederate tactic—though Union Lt. William B. Cushing destroyed *Albemarle* from a launch carrying a spar torpedo. The psychological effect of the Davids upon Union blockaders and the resulting restriction on their movements greatly outweighed actual losses.

The prototype *David* was built in Charleston in 1863 by the Southern Torpedo Company, a group of private investors who later gave control of the ship to the Confederate navy. Its mission determined the design. A 50-foot keel, 6-foot beam, and 5-foot draft satisfied requirements for a small craft. The essential design feature was a 10-foot metal spar extending from the prow; to this was fixed a spar torpedo armed with 60 or more pounds of powder capable of damaging or sinking the largest ship.

A steam engine propelled the cigar-shaped hull at five to seven knots as the ship darted through the Union fleet, seeking its target. Iron plating furnished protection both from attacking ships and from its own exploding torpedo. *David* offered a very low profile because tanks in the hold could be filled to submerge the hull up to the pilot's cabin and smokestack; thus the ship could be almost entirely concealed beneath the water's surface.

On October 5, 1863, *David* attacked the 3,486-ton ironclad *New Ironsides,* a ship of immense symbolic significance to the entire Union as well as the Charleston blockading fleet. Lt. William Glassel commanded, Engineer James H. Tomb manned the engines, Seaman James Sullivan managed the spar, and Walker Cannon piloted *David* to the target. *New Ironsides* was not sunk, but the exploding torpedo badly damaged both the ship and the fleet's morale. The design and its initial success drew praise from U.S. Adm. John A. Dahlgren.

David's success fueled interest in manufacturing more such ships. In a construction system where standardized design and parts were virtually unknown, some attempt was made to issue uniform specifications for a David: 30-, 46-, or 50-foot length and 5- to 6-foot draft. The one exception was a 160-foot David "Number Six" at Charleston. Of about fifteen vessels built, most were at least partially ironclad. The spar on later versions was usually longer by several feet than *David*'s 10-foot spar.

Of four wooden Davids built at Richmond for service on the James—*Hornet, Scorpion, Wasp,* and *Squib*—the latter was made famous when Lt. Hunter Davidson commanded an attack on USS *Minnesota* at Newport News. He

DAVID. The torpedo boat off the U.S. Naval Academy at Annapolis, Maryland, during the late 1860s.

NAVAL HISTORICAL CENTER, WASHINGTON, D.C.

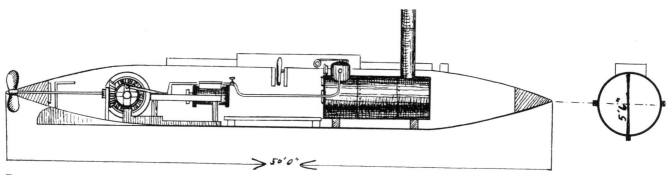

DAVID-CLASS TORPEDO BOAT.   Line drawing of internal layout.

NAVAL HISTORICAL CENTER, WASHINGTON, D.C.

failed to sink the ship but was promoted to commander for his daring.

At Charleston in March and April 1864, Engineer Tomb commanded a David against USS *Memphis* and USS *Wabash*. Though neither attack inflicted damage on the ships, the psychological effect was devastating. As ships in Charleston anchored close alongside within protective nets, blockade runners moved more freely. *Torch, Midge,* and eight unnamed Davids were also laid down at Charleston.

In January 1865, *St. Patrick,* built at Selma, Alabama, seriously alarmed the crew of USS *Octorara* and other blockaders at Mobile. At the Columbus (Georgia) Naval Iron Works, *Viper* transported men fleeing the last battle of the war in April 1865. Victorious Union men captured numerous Davids, regarding them as a curiosity. *Midge* was transported to the Brooklyn Navy Yard and another to Annapolis as trophies of war.

[*See also* Spar Torpedoes.]

BIBLIOGRAPHY

Perry, Milton F. *Infernal Machines: The Story of Confederate Submarine and Mine Warfare.* Baton Rouge, La., 1965.

Scharf, J. Thomas. *History of the Confederate States Navy from Its Organization to Surrender of Its Last Vessel.* New York, 1887. Reprint, New York, 1977.

Silverstein, Paul H. *Warships of the Civil War Navies.* Annapolis, Md., 1989.

Turner, Maxine. *Navy Gray: A Story of the Confederate Navy on the Chattahoochee and Apalachocola Rivers.* University, Ala., 1988.

MAXINE TURNER

DAVIDSON, ALLEN T.

DAVIDSON, ALLEN T. (1819–1905), congressman from North Carolina. Born on May 9, 1819, in Haywood County, North Carolina, Davidson attended the local schools and worked in his father's general store before studying law. He was admitted to the bar in 1845 while serving as clerk and master of equity for Haywood County.

In 1846 he moved to Cherokee County and became its solicitor. By 1860 he was president of the Miners and Planters Bank, the owner of two slaves and an estate valued at $21,800, and a leading Whig in the North Carolina mountain district.

Davidson was elected as a Unionist to the state convention in February 1861 but never served, since the convention was rejected in a referendum. He was also a member of the convention that adopted the ordinance of secession on May 20, 1861. Shortly afterward, he was elected by the convention to the Provisional Congress, narrowly defeating secessionist Nicholas W. Woodfin. He supported many of the early war measures of the Davis administration, including the issuance of Treasury notes and the levying of a war tax to support their redemption, but he opposed administration efforts to centralize control over state troops.

In November 1861 Davidson was elected to the First Congress, defeating secessionist William H. Thomas. There he became a vocal opponent of the administration, particularly on military issues. He voted against the Conscription Act and supported a policy of liberal exemptions. He also opposed suspension of the writ of habeas corpus and other measures that he believed infringed on state rights and individual liberties. On the other hand, he apparently accepted the idea of a permanent Confederate nation, and in September 1862 he voted with the secessionists in the North Carolina delegation to table a bill urging President Jefferson Davis to begin peace negotiations.

Davidson's opposition to the burgeoning peace movement made him vulnerable to challenge by more radical advocates of a negotiated settlement. By 1863, when he announced as a candidate for reelection, he was an acknowledged member of the Conservative party, which a year earlier had driven the secessionists from power in North Carolina and had elected his cousin, Zebulon Vance, to the governorship. Although united in opposition to the centralizing policies of the Davis administration, the Conservatives were bitterly divided in their attitude toward the war. In Davidson's district three Conservatives, along with secession Democrat Marcus Erwin, joined the race. With Erwin siphoning off Democratic votes that might otherwise have gone to Davidson and with ex-Whig John D. Hyman cutting into his support among pro-war Conservatives, Davidson lost the election to George Washington Logan, who had closely identified himself with William W. Holden's peace movement.

After the expiration of his term, Davidson was appointed by Vance to the Council of State, which served as the governor's advisory board. As agent for the North Carolina Commissary Department, he was instrumental in providing supplies to families of Confederate soldiers in the mountain district.

After the war Davidson resumed his law practice. Although an influential figure in the postwar Conservative (later Democratic) party, he never again held public office. He died in Asheville, North Carolina, on January 24, 1905.

BIBLIOGRAPHY

Alexander, Thomas B., and Richard E. Beringer. *The Anatomy of the Confederate Congress: A Study of the Influences of Member Characteristics on Legislative Voting Behavior, 1861–1865.* Nashville, Tenn., 1972.

Kruman, Marc W. *Parties and Politics in North Carolina, 1836–1865.* Baton Rouge, La., 1983.

Powell, William S. *Dictionary of North Carolina Biography.* 4 vols. to date. Chapel Hill, 1979–.

Wakelyn, Jon L. *Biographical Dictionary of the Confederacy.* Edited by Frank E. Vandiver. Westport, Conn., 1977.

Warner, Ezra J., and W. Buck Yearns. *Biographical Register of the Confederate Congress.* Baton Rouge, La., 1975.

THOMAS E. JEFFREY

DAVIDSON, HENRY BREVARD (1831–1899),

brigadier general. Born in Tennessee and a graduate of West Point, Davidson was a captain in the U.S. Army on the eve of the Civil War. When the fighting erupted, he resigned his commission and offered his services to the Confederacy.

Davidson spent the first year of the war in the West, as a staff officer to Simon Bolivar Buckner, John B. Floyd, and William Whann Mackall. He also served as Buckner's chief of artillery during the defense of Fort Donelson but managed to escape before the garrison surrendered. His freedom did not last long. Captured at Island Number 10, he was held prisoner at Fort Warren, Massachusetts, until exchanged on August 27, 1862. Promoted to colonel, he spent the next year as post commander at Staunton, Virginia.

In August 1863, Davidson was promoted to brigadier general and sent west to command a brigade in the cavalry corps of Nathan Bedford Forrest. He fought at Chickamauga and was an integral part of Forrest's advance against Chattanooga the following day. Transferred to Joseph Wheeler's command a short time later, Davidson participated in a cavalry raid into Tennessee, but his primary responsibility was to protect the Western and Atlantic Railroad from enemy cavalry raids. From September 1864 to March 1865, he commanded a brigade of cavalry under Jubal Early in the Shenandoah Valley, seeing action at Cedar Creek and Waynesboro.

For the two years immediately following the war, Davidson served as deputy sheriff of New Orleans. Later, he held the position of inspector of U.S. public works at San Pedro, California (1878–1886), and in 1887 he was appointed deputy secretary of the state of California.

BIBLIOGRAPHY

Henry, Robert Selph. *"First with the Most" Forrest.* Indianapolis, 1944. Reprint, Westport, Conn., 1974.

Porter, James D. *Tennessee.* Vol. 8 of *Confederate Military History.* Edited by Clement A. Evans. Atlanta, 1899. Vol. 10 of extended ed. Wilmington, N.C., 1987.

U.S. War Department. *War of the Rebellion: A Compilation of the Official Records of the Union and Confederate Armies.* Washington, D.C., 1880–1901. Ser. 1, vol. 31, pt. 3, p. 638; ser. 1, vol. 43, pt. 2, pp. 880, 914; ser. 2, vol. 4, p. 438.

MICHAEL G. MAHON

DAVIDSON, HUNTER (1827–1913), navy com-

mander. Davidson, who was born in the District of Columbia, entered the Confederate navy from Virginia. He had been appointed midshipman on December 29, 1841, as a member of the second class of Annapolis cadets. His assignments in the Confederate navy ranked him among the foremost technical innovators of the time.

An early assignment to *Virginia* involved him in the battle of the ironclads in March 1862. More significant was his apprenticeship to Matthew Fontaine Maury; in June 1862 Davidson's command on the James River, the steam tug *Teaser,* became the first ship to lay mines in the Civil War. Also aboard *Teaser* was another innovation, an observation balloon pieced together from old silk frocks.

After *Teaser* was captured, Davidson continued mining the James aboard *Torpedo.* When Maury went abroad, Davidson succeeded him in the work of improving and deploying these new weapons. They proved so successful that the Naval Submarine Battery Service was formed in October 1862 under Davidson's command.

Davidson was promoted to commander for "gallant and meritorious conduct" when he commanded the *David*-class torpedo boat *Squib* that detonated a fifty-pound spar

HUNTER DAVIDSON.   NAVAL HISTORICAL CENTER, WASHINGTON, D.C.

torpedo against the hull of the steam frigate *Minnesota* at Newport News.

Davidson ended the war commanding the blockade runner *City of Richmond* in an effort to convoy the ironclad *Stonewall* from Europe to the Confederacy. Following the war he joined that group of technically competent but professionally displaced officers who served in South American navies. Davidson settled in Paraguay, where he died in 1913.

BIBLIOGRAPHY

Perry, Milton F. *Infernal Machines: The Story of Confederate Submarine and Mine Warfare.* Baton Rouge, La., 1965.
Registry of Officers of the Confederate States Navy, 1861–1865. Washington, D.C., 1931.
Scharf, J. Thomas. *History of the Confederate States Navy from Its Organization to the Surrender of Its last Vessel.* New York, 1887. Reprint, New York, 1977.
Wuerlich, David P. *Admiral of the Amazon: John Randolph Tucker, His Confederate Colleagues, and Peru.* Charlottesville, Va., 1990.

MAXINE TURNER

DAVIS, GEORGE (1820–1896), congressman from North Carolina and attorney general. Davis was born March 1, 1820, at Porter's Neck, New Hanover County, North Carolina, on his father's plantation. His forebears included two governors of South Carolina. He graduated at the head of his class from the University of North Carolina in 1838 and was admitted to the bar two years later. He established his practice in Wilmington and acquired a reputation for eloquence at the bar and for brilliance as a historical scholar and lecturer.

Politically, he was identified with the Whig party until that party's demise. He joined the Constitutional Union party in 1860, prompted by his dedication to the Union and the party's policy of reconciliation. A member of the Washington peace conference of February 1861, he deplored the conference's failure to arrive at mutually acceptable terms, but felt constrained to join the secession movement.

Davis was chosen in June 1861 by moderate secessionists as a delegate-at-large from North Carolina to the Provisional Congress. But three months later he was elected for a two-year term in the Confederate Senate, where he distinguished himself as one of his state's strongest nationalists. After he was defeated for a second term in September 1863, he was named by Jefferson Davis on the last day of the year as attorney general. He served in that office with distinction until the Confederacy's collapse.

Perhaps his most important contribution as a cabinet member was the friendly advice he gave to Jefferson Davis in an effort to improve the thin-skinned president's relations with his critics and Congress.

After the war he was imprisoned for several months at Fort Hamilton, New York, and then paroled on January 2, 1866. In greatly reduced circumstances, Davis devoted himself to restoring his law practice and his career as a railroad lawyer. Although declining to seek public office, he threw his weight against the radicals' proposed constitution of 1868. When it was approved nevertheless, Davis and others of like mind labored successfully to have it reformed in 1875. He died February 23, 1896, and was buried in the Wilmington, North Carolina, Oakdale Cemetery.

BIBLIOGRAPHY

Ashe, Samuel A. *Biographical History of North Carolina.* Vol. 2. Greensboro, N.C., 1907.
Powell, William S., ed. *Dictionary of North Carolina Biography.* Vol. 2. Chapel Hill, N.C., 1986.

RICHARD BARDOLPH

DAVIS, JEFFERSON (1807 or 1808–1889), U.S. senator, U.S. secretary of war, and president of the Confederate States of America. Davis was born on June 3, probably in 1807 (he sometimes put it in 1808), in Christian County (present-day Todd), Kentucky, the son of Samuel and Jane (Cook) Davis. In about 1811 the family settled near Woodville, Mississippi. After two years at St. Thomas College, near Springfield, Kentucky, Davis entered Jefferson College in Mississippi and later transferred to Wilkinson County Academy. He joined the junior class at Transylvania University, Lexington, Kentucky, in the fall of 1823. Influenced by his elder brother, Joseph E. Davis, Jefferson entered the U.S. Military Academy in September 1824. Cadet Davis compiled a good academic record as well as a fairly large number of demerits. He ranked twenty-third out of thirty-three in the graduating class and was commissioned brevet second lieutenant of infantry on July 1, 1828.

Routine assignments took him to various frontier posts and to some Indian fighting. In September 1832 he received the surrender of the famed Sauk chief Black Hawk and escorted his prisoner from Prairie du Chien, Wisconsin Territory, to Jefferson Barracks, Missouri. Promoted to first lieutenant of dragoons, May 10, 1834, Davis led several expeditions into hostile Kiowa and Wichita villages. A year later on May 12, 1835, he submitted his resignation from the army.

Davis married Sarah Knox Taylor (daughter of Zachary Taylor) on June 17 at her aunt's house near Louisville, Kentucky. The couple went immediately to Mississippi, where brother Joseph had provided Jefferson eight hundred acres to clear, build on, and on which to start a planter's life. Both Jefferson and "Knoxie" contracted a severe fever in late August or early September, and on September 15, 1835, she died. Desolate and gravely ill, Davis traveled to Havana, Cuba, in the winter to recover. He returned to Mississippi via New York and Washington. He lived in seclusion—working on his plantation (Brierfield), reading, and learning his brother's views on slave management, which were considered comparatively liberal. Gradually he became a knowledgeable and successful planter whose slaves are reported to have held him in high regard.

Nearly ten years passed before Davis emerged from his seclusion. When he did, he entered Mississippi politics and married again. Varina Howell, a Natchez girl not twenty when she married Davis on February 25, 1845, became the mainstay of his life. Independent, sometimes willful, Varina irritated Davis at first, but after a period of adjustment, she shared his trials and triumphs, fought battles for him, bore him four sons and two daughters, and loved him always.

Davis was elected to Congress that year and when the Mexican War began he was elected colonel of a volunteer regiment from Vicksburg. With it he joined his former father-in-law's army at Carmargo, Mexico. General Taylor advanced against Monterrey, and Davis's Mississippi regiment played an important role in the campaign. Davis and his Mississippians remained with Taylor while much of his army joined Gen. Winfield Scott's campaign from Vera Cruz to Mexico City. Mexico's leader, Gen. Antonio Lopez de Santa Anna, attacked Taylor in the expectation of anni-

hilating a weakened American force. At the victorious Battle of Buena Vista, Davis and his Mississippi riflemen did heroic duty. Wounded, Davis returned to the United States to find himself a hero.

The Mississippi legislature presented him a sword of honor and appointed him in 1847 to fill out an unexpired Federal senatorial term. Reelected in 1850, Democrat Davis went on to prominence in the Senate and in Federal affairs. He became chairman of the Military Committee of the Senate and proved to be a bureaucrat with remarkably progressive ideas—new weapons always caught his attention and he remembered the success of the new percussion rifles he had provided for his Mississippians. During his term Davis's cultural interests led him to take a leading role in developing the Smithsonian Institution.

Senator Davis could be heard expressing the Southern position on national issues often and eloquently. He disliked the Compromise of 1850 and favored extension of the Missouri Compromise line to the Pacific as a solution to the slavery problem.

In the 1850s Davis came to inherit the mantle of John C. Calhoun as the leading Southern spokesman. But party and doctrinal loyalty led him to resign his Senate seat in 1850 to enter, belatedly, the governor's race in Mississippi against Henry S. Foote. Foote took a moderate stance toward the Great Compromise and seemed to be riding a rising feeling of Unionism. Davis had once before been in a raucous campaign for a forlorn hope, but had usually held appointive office and had not really been a cracker-barrel politician; now he disciplined himself to doff his natural hauteur and stump as much of the state as time and his precarious health permitted. He talked of the need for a united South, one committed to protecting its rights within the Union; he reached for votes from the poor whites, a class long ignored under a Mississippi oligarchy. He lost, by barely a thousand votes, and returned, in his words, to "quiet farm-labors, until the nomination of Franklin Pierce, when I went out to advocate his election." Davis became President Pierce's secretary of war.

His penchant for innovation, already seen during his Senate stint, grew with his new position. Convinced by experience that western military operations required new methods, Secretary Davis brought in camels for use in the desert. He introduced new infantry tactics, pushed the substitution of iron for wooden gun carriages, increased the number of rifles and rifled muskets capable of using the new minié cartridge, and modernized the ordnance at some of the coastal forts.

He had long advocated a transcontinental military railroad and, as secretary of war, surveyed various routes for that line. During his secretaryship he had charge of expanding the U.S. Capitol and sometimes served as acting navy secretary.

Mississippi returned Davis in March 1857 to a Senate

JEFFERSON DAVIS.   Pre–Civil War portrait by Mathew Brady, c. 1860.

facing serious national problems. Davis viewed the future with increasing gloom. The Kansas-Nebraska Act of 1854 had repealed the Missouri Compromise and opened lands west of Missouri to local option on slavery. A protracted war between pro- and antislavery settlers in Kansas Territory dragged on through the 1850s until the whole country lamented "Bleeding Kansas." This crisis finally disrupted the party system as the Whig party expired and the anti-South and antislavery Republican party took its place.

Increasingly the cotton South turned to Davis as adviser and defender. He made no apologies for slavery since he considered it the best adjustment of capital to labor, far better than the industrial system of the North where laborers were subjected to "humiliation and suffering." Davis saw slavery in the South as "moral, a social and political blessing." Protecting slavery meant, also, protecting sovereign state rights in the Union. Davis's defense of the South threw him into combat with the "Black Republican" party. Seeking to preserve the Democratic party as the last national forum of compromise between the sections, he opposed Stephen A. Douglas's popular sovereignty doctrine enshrined in the Kansas-Nebraska Act. Initially a proponent of the act, Davis came to see it as a snare and a delusion, since "squatter sovereignty," as he called it, would allow territories to pass laws annulling Southerners' constitutional property rights.

From a constitutional issue, slavery rose to become a moral issue, and political rhetoric inflamed the national conscience. Davis spoke often on the slave issue. And he hewed hard to his love for the Union. As late as the spring of 1860 he thought the Union safe but felt, rightly enough, that danger came not from differences but from politics and politicians.

He knew, after 1858, that preserving the Union would be difficult in 1860, an election year that might see the Republicans winning and ensconcing an "abolition president" in the White House. He considered that tantamount to ending the nation—the South could not live under an abolitionist administration because constitutional protection would disappear.

Jefferson Davis came to his views on Southern rights through reading, discussion, and iron logic. Devoted to the nation by lineage, history, and patriotism, Davis nonetheless believed in the compact theory of the Union, which held that the states were sovereign, that they had yielded sovereignty by joining the Union, and that they could reclaim it by seceding. As pressure built against slavery and against the cotton system through the 1850s, Davis became louder in his calls for Southern rights within the Union, but he urged moderation and restraint to save the Republic.

Appointed in December 1860 to the Senate Committee of Thirteen charged with finding a solution to the crisis, Davis saw little hope and reluctantly advised secession and the formation of a Southern confederacy.

Anguished, ill, and weary, Davis made a farewell speech to the Senate on January 21, 1861, which stated clearly the South's position and reasons for leaving the Union. He and his family left Washington for Brierfield Plantation on January 22. Back in Mississippi he accepted a commission as major general of state troops, but at Brierfield he received word of his election as president of the Provisional Government of the Confederate States of America.

He did not want the job. He felt better qualified for military command, but dutifully accepted the political post. Why his reluctance about the presidency? He knew the problems ahead for the new Confederacy—the probability of war and the South's unreadiness—and he disliked the kind of politicking the presidency required. Was he the right man? Yes. On balance, the South called its best to lead its quest for independence. Davis had national, even interna-

JEFFERSON DAVIS. The official presidential portrait by John Robertson, completed in the Confederate White House in 1863, where it hung for the duration of the war. The painting traveled with Davis to England in 1868 and remained there for the next four and a half decades. In 1925 it was recovered by the Museum of the Confederacy and returned to the restored White House. It hangs there to this day, just yards away from its original location. Photograph by Katherine Wetzel.

THE MUSEUM OF THE CONFEDERACY, RICHMOND, VIRGINIA

tional, renown, the respect of friends and foes, a judiciousness valuable in raucous times, a balancing realism, a need to be needed, and proper presidential probity.

In his inaugural address at Montgomery, Alabama, on February 18, 1861, Davis spoke of his hope for peace, described the South's course to secession, stressed the Confederacy as a product of evolution, not revolution, announced Southern dedication to agriculture and to free trade, and made a firm declaration: "We have entered upon the career of independence, and it must be inflexibly pursued." He urged creation of a national army and navy and spoke prophetically of his own future:

> Experience in public stations . . . has taught me that care and toil and disappointment are the price of official elevation. You will see many errors to forgive, many deficiencies to tolerate, but you shall not find in me either a want of zeal or fidelity to the cause that is to me highest in hope and of most enduring affection.

An expected state rights advocate, Davis became almost immediately an unexpected Confederate nationalist. A constitutionalist, he used that document to strengthen the central government. A national army that superseded the state militias became the main bastion of his administration. When the government took control of military operations within Confederate borders, the states lost more power than they guessed.

Davis picked his cabinet with an eye toward state representation, toward old political lines, and toward ability. His first picks were not uniformly good, notably the secretary of war, Alabamian Leroy P. Walker; the secretary of state, Georgia's Robert Toombs; and the secretary of the treasury, South Carolinian Christopher G. Memminger. His two best appointees were Louisianan Judah P. Benjamin who as attorney general headed the new Department of Justice, and Floridian Stephen R. Mallory as secretary of the navy. Benjamin would become a close presidential confidant and Mallory an innovative, resourceful navy builder.

Through early negotiations with Abraham Lincoln's government about Federal property in the South, Davis learned quickly that diplomacy, far from being a gentlemanly enterprise, was a practice in deceit. Failure of negotiations led to the Fort Sumter crisis in April 1861. That fort athwart Charleston Harbor boasted old ordnance and a small garrison, but its Union banner flouted Confederate sovereignty. Davis made a decision, over some cabinet objections, and Confederate guns began firing at Fort Sumter on April 12, 1861. War began.

Davis organized his armies with skill, although critics suggested that he meddled with generals too much and stuck by such controversial cronies as Gen. Braxton Bragg and Commissary Gen. Lucius B. Northrop beyond reason. To some extent Davis served as his own war secretary—

that six men filled that title indicates problems—and, like most chief executives, he relied on people he knew to get things done. If he did hold a tight rein on some generals, many of them needed it; to generals he trusted, such as Robert E. Lee, he gave help and scant advice.

He understood morale building and, in order to weld Virginia to the Confederacy, moved the capital to Richmond in late May 1861.

From the start he offered a hard war program to a laissez-faire Congress. His urging produced a Conscription Act in 1862 that saved the Confederate armies as first enlistments expired; he supported an impressment program that generated much public resentment as the armies commandeered supplies for the men and animals; despite his own predilections he urged tough taxes on land, cotton, and slaves, and endorsed a unique tax-in-kind to be paid with food, forage, cloth, or animals; he accepted also the produce loan, which was designed to extract more staples in return for Confederate paper. But neither he nor Congress could condone the truly draconian taxes needed in a new and warring nation.

Necessity brought Davis to varied innovations. As war eroded his country and its people, he forced himself to become a much more public figure, spoke often, made several "swings around the Confederacy" to rekindle flagging faith, and maintained a prodigious correspondence with critics, friends, and restive governors. Toward the last he even proposed limited slave emancipation in return for national service.

Some things he ought to have done he could not bring himself to do. Although Congress provided authority virtually to nationalize the railroads, Davis did not press its enforcement—it smacked too much of federalism. Nor did he deal harshly with an increasingly critical press. Where Lincoln suppressed seditious publications, Davis did not; he stuck by freedom of expression. He suspended the writ of habeas corpus only under congressional authority, never under assumed war powers.

As the war ran against his country, Davis worked harder for longer hours, pushed his wretched health beyond limits, and became estranged from Congress and from most of the public. He found the state rights policies of many governors almost inconceivable in a period of crisis and frowned on cajoling reluctant patriots. Congress often balked at the president's war program, but grudgingly followed his lead. His own dedication was sometimes seen as haughty aloofness, but a close reading of his state papers and his letters shows his fiery devotion unflagging to the end.

As president he had the task of devising a national strategy for victory, and he adopted the offensive-defensive as the best way to use interior lines and inferior Southern resources against Northern strength. Under this plan, Southern armies would conserve men and matériel, retreat in the face of superior forces (if state rights governors permitted), and wait for a moment of Southern superiority. He applied this strategy in Maryland and Kentucky in 1862 and in the West. When he found that old-fashioned command structures failed under the vastness of the war, he tried a new theater-command idea that might well have worked had Joseph E. Johnston, the general picked for the command, been bold.

At the end, his dream of independence fading, Davis remained first and last the foremost Confederate. When General Lee evacuated Richmond on April 2, 1865, Davis led a refugee government to Danville, Virginia, and then moved southward in hopes of getting across the Mississippi and continuing the struggle. He was captured at Irwinville, Georgia, on May 10, 1865.

He had done as well as anyone could to create a Southern nation. Although he lacked Lincoln's facility with language, at times he approached eloquence in talking of the cause he nearly won. He created a revolutionary state, and when the dream was lost and his country gone, he could take some consolation in a legacy of honor.

Davis served a harsh two-year prison stint at Fort Monroe while awaiting a treason trial and achieved at last a mite of martyrdom. Varina's ceaseless efforts to free him, combined with those of many others in the North and South, finally succeeded. Released from prison on bail in May 1867 (he was never brought to trial), Davis continued his life in the Confederacy. Never wavering in his belief in the cause, never admitting error, he continued to argue the constitutional right of secession and the legitimacy of the Confederacy. Financially strapped, he worked at tasks that friends provided, tried various business schemes that failed, and at last found refuge at Beauvoir, a charming house belonging to a lifelong friend near Biloxi, Mississippi. There he spent his last years writing his history of the war and his country. In June 1881, Davis's two-volume *Rise and Fall of the Confederate Government* appeared. A heavy, badly organized book, product of Davis and several collaborators, it was Davis's view of the whole Confederate experience and decidedly his book as he flayed his enemies and praised his friends: Joseph E. Johnston and P. G. T. Beauregard ranked as villains, while Bragg and Northrop came off well. Davis's second book, *Short History of the Confederate States,* published in 1889, lacked anger, presented a more balanced view of the war, and showed real literary quality.

Personal tragedy dogged much of Davis's life. Not only did he lose his first wife early, but also his four sons died before him. One of them, Joseph Evan, was killed in a fall from a White House balcony on April 30, 1864.

In his last years, Davis became a hero, seen as a long-neglected symbol. On his rare public appearances he came increasingly to advocate reunion and reconciliation. He died on December 5, 1889, aged eighty-two, survived by Varina and two daughters, Margaret and Varina Anne ("Winnie").

[*See also* Beauvoir; Davis Bend; Presidency.]

BIBLIOGRAPHY

Davis, Jefferson. *The Rise and Fall of the Confederate Government.* 2 vols. New York, 1881.

Davis, Varina H. *Jefferson Davis, Ex-President of the Confederate States of America: A Memoir by His Wife.* 2 vols. New York, 1890.

Davis, William C. *Jefferson Davis: The Man and His Hour, A Biography.* New York, 1991.

Dodd, William E. *Jefferson Davis.* Philadelphia, 1907.

Eaton, Clement. *Jefferson Davis.* New York, 1977.

Monroe, Haskell M., James T. McIntosh, Lynda L. Crist, Mary S. Dix, and Richard Beringer, eds. *The Papers of Jefferson Davis.* 7 vols. to date. Baton Rouge, La., 1971–.

Patrick, Rembert W. *Jefferson Davis and His Cabinet.* Baton Rouge, La., 1944.

Rowland, Dunbar, ed. *Jefferson Davis, Constitutionalist: His Letters, Papers, and Speeches.* 10 vols. Jackson, Miss., 1923.

Strode, Hudson. *Jefferson Davis.* 3 vols. New York, 1955–1964.

Woodworth, Steven E. *Jefferson Davis and His Generals: The Failure of Confederate Command in the West.* Lawrence, Kans., 1990.

FRANK E. VANDIVER

DAVIS, JOSEPH E. (1784–1870), Mississippi planter and elder brother and adviser to Jefferson Davis. Born in Georgia the eldest of ten children of whom Jefferson was the youngest, Joseph Emory Davis grew to manhood in Kentucky and read law in Mississippi. As a prosperous Natchez lawyer Davis accumulated land and in midlife moved to Hurricane, a large cotton plantation on the Mississippi River below Vicksburg where he became one of the wealthiest planters in the state. He was known for his innovative slave management, establishing a slave jury to decide disputes and allowing workers to keep what they earned beyond their worth as field hands.

Davis served as a father figure for his brother. He gave him land adjacent to Hurricane on which to develop a cotton plantation and, as an active Democrat, fostered Jefferson's political career. Shortly after the outbreak of the Civil War, Joseph, at Jefferson's request, went to Richmond to assist the Confederate president and his family. But after a few weeks he returned to Mississippi to attend to his and his brother's plantations. He continued to send Jefferson his opinions of Confederate generals and the conduct of the war.

In April 1862 Joseph Davis and his family fled from Hurricane when Federal raiders looted and burned the plantation. Officers of the Union navy, then the army, and finally the Freedmen's Bureau attempted to set up a model community for freed slaves at Davis Bend, the 11,000-acre loop of land that had contained the plantations of the Davis brothers and John A. Quitman, ex-governor of Mississippi. They enjoyed only modest success. For the next three years the elderly Davis was a refugee struggling to provide for his many dependents, as the armies swept back and forth across Mississippi. After the war Davis spent the last five years of his life seeking to rebuild his fortunes.

[See also Davis Bend.]

BIBLIOGRAPHY

Davis, Jefferson. The Papers of Jefferson Davis. Vol. 1. Edited by Haskell M. Monroe, Jr., and James T. McIntosh. Vols. 2–3. Edited by James T. McIntosh. Vols. 4–6. Edited by Lynda Laswell Crist. Baton Rouge, La., 1971–1989.

Hermann, Janet Sharp. Joseph E. Davis, Pioneer Patriarch. Jackson, Miss., 1990.

Hermann, Janet Sharp. The Pursuit of a Dream. New York, 1981.

JANET SHARP HERMANN

DAVIS, JOSEPH ROBERT

DAVIS, JOSEPH ROBERT (1825–1896), brigadier general. Nephew of the Confederate president, Davis was born January 12, 1825, at Woodville, Mississippi. He graduated from Miami University in Ohio and established a law practice in Madison County, Mississippi. Elected to the state senate in 1860, Davis the following year "was among the first to answer his country's call," a state historian wrote. "Not only did he contribute freely of his means, but his voice was raised in many eloquent appeals" on behalf of the Southern cause.

Davis entered the army as captain of Company I, Tenth Mississippi. He became lieutenant colonel of the regiment during service in Florida and then joined his uncle's staff as a colonel. Promotion to brigadier general came on September 15, 1862, after a Confederate Senate fight that saw charges of nepotism leveled and the nomination at first rejected. The Mississippian, described by a Virginia adjutant as "a very pleasant and unpretending gentleman," took command of a brigade as brave and inexperienced as himself. One of Davis's four regiments (Fifty-fifth North Carolina) did not contain a man over the age of thirty.

At Gettysburg, Davis's brigade was shattered. The commander lost two of his regiments in the first day's action by improper disposition. Controversy surrounds Davis's role in the Pickett-Pettigrew charge. The brigadier contracted fever thereafter and was absent from duty, but he returned and led his troops creditably at the Wilderness and during the siege of Petersburg.

After the war Davis resumed his law practice. Following his death on September 15, 1896, he was buried in Biloxi, Mississippi.

BIBLIOGRAPHY

"General Joseph R. Davis." Confederate Veteran 5 (1897): 63. Reprint, Wilmington, N.C., 1985.

Hooker, Charles E. Mississippi. Vol. 7 of Confederate Military History. Edited by Clement A. Evans. Atlanta, 1899. Vol. 9 of extended ed. Wilmington, N.C., 1987.

JAMES I. ROBERTSON, JR.

DAVIS, NICHOLAS (1825–1874 or 1875), congressman from Alabama and lieutenant colonel. Born on January 14, 1825, in Athens, Alabama, Davis enrolled in the law school of the University of Virginia. Before graduating, however, he volunteered for duty in the Mexican War and saw service as a lieutenant in the Thirteenth U.S. Infantry Regiment. Returning home, he completed his studies and opened a private law practice in Athens, Limestone County, northern Alabama.

In 1851 Nicholas was elected to the Alabama House of Representatives and in 1853 moved to Huntsville. He was elected solicitor in 1855 and remained in office until 1860. That year he campaigned for Democrat Stephen A. Douglas for president and actively opposed the secessionist movement throughout northern Alabama. Elected to the Alabama secession convention, Nicholas argued against withdrawing from the Union, maintaining that such action could not be taken without a vote of the people. When the convention passed the ordinance of secession, however, he vowed to protect his home state.

Although he did not stand for election to the Provisional Congress of the Confederacy, when Dr. Thomas Fearn resigned his seat, Davis was chosen as his successor and took his seat on April 29, 1861. He attended few sessions and did not seek election to the First Congress. Nicholas was offered a commission as a lieutenant colonel of the Nineteenth Alabama Infantry Regiment, but he declined to assume command of a battalion. His military career was short-lived.

When the fighting ended, Nicholas refused to take an oath of allegiance to the United States; however, he did resume his law practice. Nicholas died in Huntsville and was buried in Maple Hill Cemetery. Some list his year of death as 1874, but his grave marker indicates November 3, 1875.

BIBLIOGRAPHY

Brewer, W. Alabama: Her History, Resources, War Record, and Public Men from 1540 to 1872. Montgomery, Ala., 1872.

Fleming, Walter L. Civil War and Reconstruction in Alabama. New York, 1905.

Moore, Albert B. History of Alabama and Her People. Chicago, 1927.

Owen, Thomas M. History of Alabama and Dictionary of Alabama Biography. 4 vols. Chicago, 1921.

MARK LEA (BEAU) CANTRELL

DAVIS, REUBEN (1813–1890), brigadier general of Mississippi state troops and congressman from Mississippi. Davis was born January 18, 1813, in Winchester, Tennessee. His father was a frontier Baptist preacher who carried his family into the wild country of northern Alabama in 1818. There Davis grew up, received a sporadic backwoods education, and, at his father's insistence, studied medicine with a brother-in-law. Davis's ambitions, however, lay in the law, and he soon trained himself in that field.

In 1834 Davis opened a law office in Aberdeen, Mississippi, and proceeded to gain immediate fame and prosperity. At the age of twenty-two he became a district attorney and in 1838 was an unsuccessful candidate for the U.S. Congress. At twenty-nine he was appointed to the Mississippi High Court of Errors and Appeals but, after serving only a few months, resigned to return to private practice.

Davis served as a brigadier general in the state militia, and during the Mexican War in 1846, he was elected colonel of the Second Mississippi Regiment. He saw no fighting, however, for like hundreds of other volunteers, he suffered from bad health. He became so ill he was near death when he was brought home. (His Second Regiment lost three times as many men from sickness as Jefferson Davis's First Mississippi Regiment lost from injury in the battle at Monterrey.)

In the secession crisis of 1850–1851, precipitated by the issue of the extension of slavery into the territory acquired from Mexico, Davis, though a Democrat, stood for the Union. If war came, he predicted, it would bring in its train "desolation of the most fearful and terrific character that

REUBEN DAVIS.   *HARPER'S PICTORIAL HISTORY OF THE GREAT REBELLION*

has ever been inflicted upon any people or any country." Nevertheless, despite his objections to disunion at this point, Davis was a state rights Democrat, and later he grew more pugnacious on the subject of slavery. Although he did not favor reopening the slave trade, he was determined to protect the institution itself.

In 1858 Davis entered the U.S. Congress. By then, he believed so firmly in the likelihood of war that he became known as a fire-eater. He claimed that if a Republican was elected president in 1860, the South would bring upon the world "bankruptcy and ruin, famine and pestilence, lamentation and mourning," and it would "tear this Constitution in pieces, and look to [its] guns for justice and right against aggression and wrong." He warned that if the North persisted in not admitting Kansas into the Union as a slave state, the "South will resist with arms—resist to the dissevering of the last ties that bind these States together—resist to the pulling down of this grand political fabric of ours to its foundation." In 1861, he resigned from the House of Representatives in the midst of his second term, and when his home state seceded, he and his Mississippi colleagues left Washington.

Davis again pursued his earlier avocation—the military. In 1861, leading two regiments and a battalion of state troops, he was sent to Kentucky to serve under Gen. Albert Sidney Johnston. Davis was to supervise the fortification of the town of Bowling Green. His command escaped active engagement, but the snow, intense cold, lack of adequate protection, and an epidemic of measles took their toll. After a standard tour of sixty days, the regiments disbanded.

In November 1861 Davis was named to the Confederate Congress. Throughout his tenure, he opposed President Jefferson Davis's conduct of the war. He was critical of the administration's support of conscription and even tried to abolish his own Committee on Military Affairs. During his term, in 1863, he ran for governor of Mississippi on a platform critical of the way the Confederacy was running the war. He had very strong opposition: Charles Clark was a Confederate general who had been severely wounded in service, and A. M. West was a brigadier general in the state. Clark received 16,428 votes; West, 4,863; and Davis, 2,009. Apparently his opposition to Jefferson Davis's policies did not sit well with the voters. In 1864, he resigned from Congress in protest.

During Reconstruction Davis worked for the overthrow of the Republican regime that controlled the state. In his later years he returned to the practice of criminal law, a field in which he enjoyed considerable success. In 1878 he ran again for the U.S. Congress but without success. He then turned his energies to writing and produced one of the best memoirs by a Mississippian in the nineteenth century. His *Recollections of Mississippi and Mississippians* spans more than fifty years of the state's history and is still a primary source for that eventful era.

BIBLIOGRAPHY

Alexander, Thomas B., and Richard E. Beringer. *The Anatomy of the Confederate Congress: A Study of the Influences of Member Characteristics on Legislative Voting Behavior, 1861–1865.* Nashville, Tenn., 1972.

Davis, Reuben. *Recollections of Mississippi and Mississippians.* New York, 1889.

Warner, Ezra J., and W. Buck Yearns. *Biographical Register of the Confederate Congress.* Baton Rouge, La., 1975.

RAY SKATES

DAVIS, VARINA HOWELL (1826–1906), first lady of the Confederacy. It is one of the Civil War's rich ironies that Varina Howell Davis became First Lady of the Confederacy, for she was unsuited by personal background and political inclination for the role. Born into the planter class in Mississippi in 1826, she received an excellent education at a girls' academy in Philadelphia and at home

VARINA HOWELL DAVIS. Miniature by John Wood Dodge, 1849. Watercolor on ivory, 6.5 by 5.3 centimeters.

NATIONAL PORTRAIT GALLERY, SMITHSONIAN INSTITUTION, WASHINGTON, D.C.

with a private tutor. Her father, William B. Howell, was an active member of the Whig party, and she grew up in a household where people took politics seriously and discussed them with gusto. She was a straightforward, candid, and outspoken girl, and her personality was always at odds with the role of the Southern "lady."

When she met Jefferson Davis at a Christmas party in 1843, she was a tall seventeen-year-old with large expressive eyes, and she was already known for her dry wit. Davis was a rich widower in his mid-thirties who had only recently recovered from the death of his first wife, Knox Taylor Davis. Her impressions of Davis were mixed: she thought he was arrogant and aloof, but also handsome, well-spoken, and cultivated. Her initial doubts gradually faded, however, and she fell in love with him. He also fell in love, attracted to her fine mind and good looks. The couple married on February 26, 1845.

The marriage was charged with struggle from the beginning, starting with an inheritance dispute. Joseph E. Davis, Jefferson's older brother and manager of the family's large estate, devised a will that excluded Varina from inheriting any of the Davis property. She protested immediately, but to no avail—Jefferson told her to accept his brother's decision. She felt further alienated from her husband when he enlisted in the army to fight in the Mexican War without consulting her. It was becoming clear that Jefferson simply accepted the sex roles of his era and expected her to do what he told her to do. By the time he returned from war in 1847, the couple had become estranged. When he was appointed to the U.S. Senate, he left her at home in Mississippi for almost a year to punish her.

Somehow the Davises reconciled and she went to Washington, but other conflicts plagued the marriage, often because Jefferson Davis continued to make arbitrary decisions without consulting his wife. He controlled the family's finances and even decided whether Varina could visit her relatives. In what became a typical pattern in the relationship, she would protest his decisions and then eventually acquiesce. She had no other choice. If she wanted a divorce—which she never mentioned in writing—it would have been almost impossible to obtain under Mississippi law. Moreover, she had no income of her own, and it would have been difficult to return to her parents because by the late 1840s her father was going bankrupt. In the 1850s the Davises had four children, but they were never able to resolve their power struggles.

Varina Davis retained her Whiggish sympathies through the 1850s, even though her husband was a Democrat, and like many Southern Whigs she was alarmed by the secession crisis of 1860 and 1861. She told several close friends and relatives that it was foolish for Southern states to leave the Union and that the Confederacy would never survive. After her husband became president, she reluctantly joined him in Richmond to spend what she later called four of the worst years of her life.

Few people seem to have known of her opposition to secession, but she nonetheless became a controversial figure. Members of Richmond's society called her direct manner crude and unrefined; the First Lady was not deemed to be a proper lady. Some politicians, surprised by her astute understanding of contemporary issues, accused her of meddling in the president's decisions. In fact she seems to have exercised little political influence over her husband, but her extraordinary behavior was enough in and of itself to draw criticism.

The First Lady got off to a bad start in the summer of

LETTER FROM VARINA HOWELL DAVIS. Dated August 12, 1866, and addressed to "Mrs. Nelly."   GORDON BLEULER

1861 by appearing at public receptions when she was visibly pregnant, something that very few politicians' wives did in the nineteenth century. She could also be blunt-spoken, according to a man who met her in Richmond in 1862. He described her as "very smart, . . . quite independent, says what she pleases and cuts at people generally." Furthermore, Varina Davis had an acute sense of the ridiculous, which got her into trouble. At a dinner party she attended, a general's wife remarked that the underdrawers for an entire Confederate regiment had mistakenly been made with two right legs. She burst out laughing, much to the horror of the other guests.

As the war ground on, Varina Davis continued to depart from the traditional female role. As early as 1862, she envisioned a hard life after the war and told her husband she would take a paying job outside the home if necessary. She also began selling off her personal possessions—clothing, china, and books—to build up cash reserves. Her personal life was further marred by the tragic death of her young son Joseph, who died in a freak accident in 1864 when he broke his neck in a fall. As she told one of her friends, she was relieved when the Confederacy collapsed and the war ended in 1865.

Yet the postwar era was also filled with challenges for Varina Davis. Her husband served two years in federal prison, and after he was released in 1867 he was never able to support his family. Continually at the edge of destitution, the Davises never again owned a home. Varina Davis gradually took over the management of their household affairs as her husband's health declined. After he died in 1889, she moved to Manhattan, where she lived for the rest of her life. Still fending off poverty, she nonetheless created an interesting life, writing for newspapers and magazines. Many of her publications focused on the war, and they often reflected her conviction that secession had been a terrible mistake. It certainly cast a long shadow over her life, even though she had never wanted to be the Confederate First Lady.

BIBLIOGRAPHY

Cashin, Joan E. "Varina Howell Davis." In *Portraits of American Women.* Edited by G. B. Barker-Benfield and Catherine Clinton. New York, 1991.

Davis, Jefferson. *The Papers of Jefferson Davis.* 6 vols. Edited by James T. McIntosh, Lynda L. Crist, Mary Seaton Dix, et al. Baton Rouge, La., 1971–1986.

Evans, Eli N. *Judah P. Benjamin: The Jewish Confederate.* New York, 1988.

Rable, George C. *Civil Wars: Women and the Crisis of Southern Nationalism.* Urbana, Ill., 1989.

Woodward, C. Vann, ed. *Mary Chesnut's Civil War.* New Haven, 1981.

JOAN E. CASHIN

DAVIS, WILLIAM GEORGE MACKEY

(1812?–1898), brigadier general. Davis was born in Portsmouth, Virginia. Most authorities accept May 9, 1812, as his date of birth, but in April 1863 he wrote that he was fifty-two years old. His year of birth would, therefore, have been 1810 or 1811, depending on whether he referred to his last birthday or to his next. He ran away from home when he was seventeen, worked as a sailor, and eventually settled in Apalachicola, Florida. There he prospered as a lawyer and speculator in cotton.

In 1861 Davis helped finance, raise, organize, and equip the First Florida Cavalry Regiment. After brief service in the ordnance department in Tallahassee, he became colonel of the First Florida Cavalry. He commanded for a few months in eastern Florida and then was sent with his regiment to eastern Tennessee, where he served at various times as a regimental, brigade, post, departmental, and district commander until May 1863. He participated in the 1862 Kentucky campaign with the forces under Maj. Gen. E. Kirby Smith. For a while he was post commander at Knoxville.

On November 4, 1862, Davis was promoted to brigadier general. Almost five months later he resigned for reasons of health and to provide for his family and care for his personal affairs. Davis then engaged in blockade running.

After the war he lived in Jacksonville, Florida, and Washington, D.C., where he practiced law. He died March 11, 1898, and is buried in the Tackett-Burroughs-Davis Cemetery, Remington, Virginia.

BIBLIOGRAPHY

Davis, William C. "William George Mackey Davis." In *The Confederate General.* Edited by William C. Davis. Vol. 2. Harrisburg, Pa., 1991.

Warner, Ezra J. *Generals in Gray: Lives of the Confederate Commanders.* Baton Rouge, La., 1959.

RICHARD M. MCMURRY

DAVIS BEND.

Site of the adjoining plantations of Jefferson Davis, his older brother Joseph E. Davis, and Mississippi Governor John A. Quitman, Davis Bend was an 11,000-acre loop of land on the Mississippi River about twenty-five miles down the river from Vicksburg in Warren County.

In 1818 Joseph Davis began acquiring land on Davis Bend and settled there in 1827. His Hurricane Plantation (named after an 1825 storm) was situated on the western end of the loop. The land (some 5,000 acres), crops, and his personal property made him one of the wealthiest men in Mississippi by 1860. Hurricane House, built in the 1830s, was a three-story mansion famed for its size, elegance, and conveniences. Numerous outbuildings and spectacular grounds and gardens completed the estate, including a replica Greek temple for the owner's office and library.

Brierfield, located on the southwestern curve of Davis Bend, comprised about 1,800 acres and was named for the dense tangle of greenery that had to be cleared when Jefferson Davis moved there in 1835. His house, completed about 1850, was smaller and plainer than Hurricane, a rambling wooden one-story structure designed by the owner with a classic central hall, capacious rooms and fireplaces, and traditional galleries front and rear.

In April 1862 both plantations were abandoned and Hurricane was burned by Union forces in June. The Freedmen's Department (a precursor of the Freedmen's Bureau) used the Davis plantations beginning in 1863. Four years later they were sold by Joseph Davis (Jefferson Davis was then a Federal prisoner) to Benjamin Montgomery, his former slave. Isolated after the river changed Davis Bend to Davis Island in 1867 and plagued by flooding, the property was difficult to farm and manage, leading the Montgomery family to default. After years of litigation following Joseph Davis's death, Jefferson Davis regained control of Brierfield in 1878; Brierfield House survived until destroyed by fire in 1931. Hurricane remained in the Davis family until 1897 and Brierfield until 1953.

BIBLIOGRAPHY

Davis, Jefferson. *The Papers of Jefferson Davis.* 7 vols. to date. Baton Rouge, La., 1971–.

Everett, Frank E., Jr. *Brierfield: Plantation Home of Jefferson Davis.* Hattiesburg, Miss., 1971.

Hermann, Janet Sharp. *Joseph E. Davis, Pioneer Patriarch.* Jackson, Miss., 1990.

Hermann, Janet Sharp. *The Pursuit of a Dream.* New York, 1981.

LYNDA LASSWELL CRIST

DAWKINS, JAMES BAIRD

(1820–1883), congressman from Florida. Dawkins was born in Union District, South Carolina, graduated from the University of South Carolina in 1840, and practiced law in his hometown until the mid-1840s when he moved to Gainesville, Florida. Like most newcomers from the Palmetto State, Dawkins was a radical Southern Democrat, and he voted for secession at the convention in January 1861.

Elected delegate from eastern Florida to the First Confederate Congress, he served on the Elections, Military Transportation, and Naval Affairs committees. He proposed that a railroad connecting Florida to Georgia be constructed, a measure that might have eased the military situation for the Confederacy at the Battle of Olustee had the bill passed. He supported the Davis administration during his brief term, but returned to Florida in 1862 and served as a circuit judge for the duration of the war.

After the surrender, Dawkins resumed his Gainesville law practice and, as a Bourbon or Conservative Democrat, was excluded from public office during Reconstruction. From 1877 until his death in 1883, he served as judge of the Fifth Judicial Circuit at Gainesville, Florida.

BIBLIOGRAPHY

Sifakis, Stewart. *Who Was Who in the Civil War*. New York, 1988.

Wakelyn, Jon L. *Biographical Dictionary of the Confederacy*. Edited by Frank E. Vandiver. Westport, Conn., 1977.

Warner, Ezra J., and W. Buck Yearns. *Biographical Register of the Confederate Congress*. Baton Rouge, La., 1975.

ARCH FREDRIC BLAKEY

DEARING, JAMES (1840–1865), brigadier general.

Dearing, born April 25, 1840, was a native Virginian who attended the U.S. Military Academy. He was performing well academically in his third year at West Point, despite a generous ration of demerits, when his native state seceded and he resigned. Dearing was commissioned as lieutenant in a Louisiana artillery unit just days before First Manassas and served in that capacity for seven months. A Virginia battery selected Dearing as its captain early in 1862. He led that company with notable valor at Williamsburg and Seven Pines, where Gen. James Longstreet commended his "conspicuous courage and energy." Dearing also played a brief role near the climax of Second Manassas.

In January 1863, Dearing won promotion to major and command of an artillery battalion in George E. Pickett's division. His guns supported the division's famous charge on July 3 at Gettysburg. Early in 1864, Dearing left artillery service to command a cavalry detachment under Pickett with rank of colonel. His successful role in the 1864 operations near the coast of North Carolina earned Dearing the wreath of a brigadier general on April 29, 1864, four days after his twenty-fourth birthday. The new general fought with distinction at Drewry's Bluff and Petersburg in May and June. For much of 1864 his mixed brigade of Georgia and North Carolina units served at widely separated points, sometimes independently and sometimes as part of a division. Near the end of the war Dearing assumed command of the noted Laurel Brigade of Virginia cavalry. He was mortally wounded at its head on April 6, 1865, and died seventeen days later. Dearing was one of the youngest Confederate generals and the last to die from battle wounds. He is buried in Lynchburg, Virginia.

BIBLIOGRAPHY

Dearing, James. Papers. Virginia Historical Society, Richmond; Historical Society of Pennsylvania, Philadelphia; University of Virginia, Charlottesville.

Halsey, Don P. *Historic and Heroic Lynchburg*. Lynchburg, Va., 1935.

Parker, William L. *General James Dearing*. Lynchburg, Va., 1990.

ROBERT K. KRICK

DEAS, ZACHARIAH CANTEY (1819–1882), brigadier general.

Born in Camden, South Carolina, October 25, 1819, Deas was educated there and at Caudebec in Calvados, Rouen, France. He moved with his family to Mobile, Alabama, in 1835. He served in the Mexican War and prospered as a cotton broker.

In 1861 Deas joined the staff of Gen. Joseph E. Johnston, with whom he served through the First Battle of Manassas. He then raised the Twenty-second Alabama Regiment, of which he was elected colonel (commissioned October 25, 1861). He and the regiment served briefly on the Gulf coast and then joined what became the Army of Tennessee.

At Shiloh (April 6–7, 1862) Deas was severely wounded, but he recovered in time for the Kentucky campaign of 1862. In December he was appointed brigadier general.

Deas commanded a brigade through 1863, winning acclaim for his performance at Chickamauga (September 19–20). Illness often kept him away from the army in 1864, but he served in parts of the Atlanta campaign and the Franklin and Nashville campaign. Slightly wounded at Franklin, he took command of the division after Nashville when Maj. Gen. Edward Johnson was captured. In 1865 Deas participated in the Carolinas campaign until March when sickness again forced him away from the army. He was paroled May 12, 1865, at Meridian, Mississippi.

A Democrat, Deas lived in New York City after the war and resumed his brokerage business. He died in New York, March 6, 1882, and was buried there in Woodlawn Cemetery.

BIBLIOGRAPHY

Hewitt, Lawrence. "Zachariah Cantey Deas." In *The Confederate General*. Edited by William C. Davis. Vol. 2. Harrisburg, Pa., 1991.

Wheeler, Joseph. *Alabama*. Vol. 4 of *Confederate Military History*. Edited by Clement A. Evans. Atlanta, 1899. Vol. 8 of extended ed. Wilmington, N.C., 1988.

RICHARD M. MCMURRY

DEATH AND MOURNING.

One of the most famous images to come out of the South's wartime experience was of the funeral of a young Confederate officer. William D. Washington's 1864 painting *The Burial of Latané* immortalized the mourning ritual for twenty-nine-year-old Capt. William Latané, a Virginian killed in a skirmish near Richmond in June 1862. His brother John, who was with him when he died, took the body to a nearby plantation for burial. With the men away at war, the women, slaves, and children of the area fulfilled their promise to John Latané to give his brother a proper burial. A former editor for the *Southern Literary Messenger,* John R. Thompson, wrote a poem about the incident, and a verse from it appears on the marker over Latané's grave: "A brother bore his body from the field . . . / but woman's voice read over his hallowed / dust the ritual of the dead." Washington's painting, frequently reproduced in the postbellum South, came to symbolize the Lost Cause and Southerners' response to the loss of so many of its young men.

Death and mourning were pressing matters to people experiencing a bloodbath. The casualty rate made Southerners acutely aware of mortality. Out of a potential military population of about a million, 750,000 soldiers served in the Confederate armies, and approximately 250,000 died during the war—about one in four Southern white men of military age in contrast to the Northern rate of one in ten. Individual battles, such as those at Sharpsburg, Shiloh, and Gettysburg, resulted in death on a scale that Americans had never seen before. In addition to battle deaths, disease killed both soldiers and civilians in unprecedented numbers; the ratio of those dying from disease to those killed in battle was close to two to one. Infectious diseases of childhood, such as mumps and measles, were killers of young country boys newly exposed to them. Camp diseases, including malaria, dysentery, and diarrhea, proved fatal to many soldiers as well.

Southerners of the mid-nineteenth century were accustomed to death. Growing up mostly in rural places, they were used to the slaughtering of livestock and the hunting of animals. Infant mortality rates were high and the death of family members not uncommon. But despite this familiarity, the scale of wartime carnage, the bullets and cannonballs tearing comrades apart, the sights and sounds and smells of mortality, hit soldiers hard. Death often came suddenly and left its memory in blood on survivors. Soldiers saw gruesome scenes of mutilated bodies and swollen corpses.

The men dealt with the psychological trauma in a number of ways. Some adopted a public attitude of indifference. Others went into despair, often developing hardened attitudes to inure them to the brutalities around them. Many engaged in grim humor, displaying a plain folk realism. During the siege of Petersburg, one wizened veteran cooking bacon was almost hit by a minié ball that disturbed his fire, and he complained: "Plague take them fellows. I 'spect they'll spile my grease yet before they stop their foolishness." A story told in the Confederate ranks was that one Yankee body would kill an acre of land but a Southerner's bones would fertilize it forever.

Most typically, Confederate soldiers accepted fatalistically the hard realities of death in war. Coming mainly from evangelical Protestant homes, they looked upon death as part of God's plan, and godliness became a protective armor. Imbued with the confidence of holy warriors at the beginning of the conflict, they trusted God to protect individual soldiers. But the length of the war and its bloodiness undermined this attitude. The good died all too often. It was hard enough to accept the death of an individual at home, but battle deaths eluded their understanding. How could such grotesque deaths be part of a divine plan, they wondered.

Fear of death was connected to the widespread revivalism in Confederate armies. As the casualty rates mounted and the war stretched on year after year, these soldiers in an evangelical age tried "to get right with God," to gain the assurance of salvation. As many as 150,000 soldiers may have professed religion during the war. Denominations encouraged revivalism by distributing death-focused tracts with such titles as *Prepare for Battle* and *A Word of Warning for the Sick Soldier. Sufferings of the Lost* predicted an eternity of fire and brimstone for the unrepentant, but *Mother's Parting Words to Her Soldier Boy,* issued to nearly 250,000 soldiers, promised hope after death; in heaven, home and family would be reunited.

Soldiers drew strength from this reassurance of an afterlife but feared an impersonal death. They saw comrades die anonymously and rest in unmarked graves, and they were worried that their deaths would go unreported to their loved ones at home, that their remains would be treated with disrespect. Some soldiers pinned their names on their uniforms before battles; others carried letters from wives who could be notified of their death. But some men avoided attempts at identification, fearing that to prepare for death was to invite it.

Soldiers seeking an honorable, decent death tried to invest it with meaning by facing death with bravery and sacrificial gallantry. In recounting the tales of battle, much attention was given to the context in which the death occurred and whether the deceased had died illustrating the manly ideal. Burial carried an especially heavy burden of meaning. A Confederate soldier who suffered through the Battle of Gettysburg recalled that "the worst of all was we did not get to bury our dead."

Letters of condolence were a vital part of the mourning process. Soldiers clung to memories of home; writing of a friend's death, they often explicitly evoked scenes of childhood happiness in their letters. Soldiers typically avoided dwelling on death in their correspondence, both to save their home folks worry and to boost their own morale. But when they had to write in sympathy to a family about a comrade's death, the letter became a battlefront obituary. The writer would give the mourning family details of the casualty, including where and when the soldier fell, whether the death was instantaneous or prolonged, and what had happened to the remains. He would end with praise for the soldier's character and courage.

The rising tide of the dead as the war continued weakened morale, perhaps even more on the home front than on the battlefield. Confederate rhetoric taught that women as well as men had to sacrifice for the cause. Once the protectors of family, women now had to give up husbands and fathers, brothers and sons, for the Confederacy. Alone at home, they themselves faced the fear of death from illness, childbirth, and attacks on civilian populations. Bread riots hit Southern cities near the end of the war, led by women facing death by starvation for themselves and their children.

Women not only made sacrifices but also celebrated their martyred men. They transformed mourning from a private ceremony to a ritual with public meaning; by sanctifying the men who fought and died for the Confederacy, they sanctified the cause itself. But as the war dragged on and demands on soldiers and their families increased, women who faced the deaths of their loved ones in battle and at home became alienated. "My husband is my country," wrote one woman. "What is country to me if he be killed?" In the last year of the war, its emotional toll mounted, and, ironically, mourning seemed to lose its intensity. "People do not mourn their dead as they used to," wrote diarist Kate Stone in the spring of 1864. Soldiers had become hardened to the fighting and the death around them, and military hospitals were seen as places treating the injured and the dead with little respect.

Historians who argue for a collapse of the Confederate will to fight as a factor in its defeat can point to the accumulated effects of Southerners living with death as part of that collapse.

[*See also* Burial of Latané; Funerals.]

BIBLIOGRAPHY

Faust, Drew Gilpin. "Altars of Sacrifice: Confederate Women and the Narratives of War." *Journal of American History* 76 (1990): 1200–1228.
Mitchell, Reid. *Civil War Soldiers: Their Expectations and Their Experiences.* New York, 1988.
Wiley, Bell I. *The Life of Johnny Reb.* Indianapolis, 1943.

CHARLES REAGAN WILSON

DE BOW'S REVIEW. *See* Magazines, *article on* De Bow's Review.

DEBRAY, XAVIER B. (1819–1895), colonel and acting brigadier general. DeBray, a native of Epinel, France, attended the French Military Academy and at age twenty-nine immigrated to Texas. After holding a number of jobs, he became a translator in the General Land Office. When Texas seceded, he was elected a lieutenant in Thomas Green's rifle regiment, and almost simultaneously, Governor Francis R. Lubbock appointed him as a military aide.

In September 1861, DeBray was commissioned a major in the Second Texas Infantry, and in December he was selected to become colonel of the Twenty-sixth Texas Cavalry. Given command of the eastern district of Texas in July 1862, DeBray was responsible for the defense of Galveston. When that city fell to a Federal naval attack later that year, DeBray was extremely active in the fighting. His gallantry during the Confederate attack on January 1, 1863, that drove the Federal forces out received a special commendation by Gen. John B. Magruder. In 1864 DeBray's regiment was ordered to join Gen. Richard Taylor's forces in the Red River campaign, and Taylor personally commended both DeBray and his unit in the after-action reports on the Battles of Mansfield and Pleasant Hill, Louisiana. Gen. E. Kirby Smith appointed DeBray brigadier general (never recognized formally by the Confederate government) on April 13, 1864, and gave him command of a brigade consisting of three Texas cavalry regiments. DeBray was a superb cavalry commander. In 1864, DeBray's unit was one of the few not to be dismounted, proof of the high regard his superiors held for his command. He led his brigade until March 24, 1865, when the unit was discharged.

After the surrender of the Trans-Mississippi Department, DeBray returned to Texas, ultimately resuming his position as translator in the Land Office. He died in Austin on January 6, 1895.

BIBLIOGRAPHY

DeBray, Xavier B. *A Sketch of the History of DeBray's Twenty-Sixth Regiment of Texas Cavalry.* Austin, Tex., 1884.
Roberts, O. M. *Texas.* Vol. 11 of *Confederate Military History.* Edited by Clement A. Evans. Atlanta, 1899. Vol. 15 of extended ed. Wilmington, N.C., 1989.

ROY R. STEPHENSON

DEBT. Debts within the Confederacy fell into four categories: those of the Confederate government, those of the states, those of local governments, and the obligations of private individuals to Northerners. The governmental debts were all repudiated after the war; private debts frequently proved impossible to collect as many Southern firms and citizens went bankrupt in 1865.

Confederate Debt. The Confederacy started out with no debt, but the outbreak of war in April 1861 forced the government to borrow heavily by issuing Treasury notes, bonds, and certificates of indebtedness payable on demand. These debts rapidly mounted.

At the end of the Provisional government on February 17,

Amount of State-Issued Treasury Notes

STATE	AMOUNT IN MILLIONS
Alabama	$4.6
Arkansas	$2.8
Florida	$2.2
Georgia	$17.8
Louisiana	$8.5
Mississippi	$8.0
Missouri	$4.0
North Carolina	$5.2
Texas	$8.2
Virginia	$4.2
Total	$65.5

1862, the total debt was $163.3 million of which $95.8 million was represented by Treasury notes, $41 million by loans, and $26.4 million in overdue army pay and other obligations. By January 1, 1863, the debt equaled $605.8 million, of which $410 million was in Treasury notes, $145 million in bonds, and $50 million in unpaid bills.

The debt expanded geometrically during 1863. Total indebtedness by January 1864 came to $1,340 million of which $791 million was in Treasury notes, $537 million in foreign and domestic bonds, and $150 million in past due army payments. Despite belatedly passed tax laws, the Confederate debt by October 31, 1864, had risen to $1,863 million. Treasury notes fell to $709 million, and the funded debt was $804 million, with over $350 million of unpaid obligations. Economists generally agree that the primary cause of this rapid increase in the public debt lay in the absence of a productive internal revenue system.

State Debts. At the start of secession, the acknowledged debts of the eleven Confederate states were approximately $98 million. Since the states, particularly at the beginning of the war, were actively levying troops, their expenses were heavy. The states also furnished small-denomination notes as a substitute for hoarded silver coins and provided relief to soldiers' families and to the cotton planters, who were unable to export their produce.

Moreover, the state governments, pandering to the public opposition to the war tax, paid this levy on behalf of their citizens. They did so by selling state bonds for Confederate Treasury notes, which were paid over to the Confederacy.

So far as the prewar bonds were concerned, the states generally allowed the interest to accumulate on them until after the war, when the state finances had to be completely reorganized. This unpaid interest accounts in most cases for the reported increase in state debts in 1865.

Figures for the additional funded debt emitted during the war are not readily available. State governments did sell some bonds. The total funded indebtedness of the Southern states incurred on behalf of the Confederate cause was probably over $50 million.

War expenses, coupled with a limited borrowing ability and a reluctance to raise enough taxes to cover anything like the current expenses, inevitably resulted in the issue of large quantities of state Treasury notes. Total issues outstanding in 1865 exceeded $65 million, although because of funding operations and redemptions, the total amount issued may well have exceeded $100 million.

City and County Debts. Very few records of local government expenditures have survived from the Confederate era. Cities other than New Orleans, the South's largest metropolis, had limited credit. Consequently, to judge by the few surviving specimens in the numismatic market today, city and county bond issues were neither numerous nor in large amounts. Bond issues in even the richest Louisiana parishes frequently came to less than $15,000 and were used largely for arming and organizing local military units.

The note issues of towns and counties are better known, largely because many of them were approved by the state governments. There are also many surviving notes, which are sold to collectors today.

The largest issues of such currency occurred in Virginia, Louisiana, and Texas where practically all the counties and parishes issued notes and many of the cities and towns did so. The total in Virginia alone was $2.5 million. In South Carolina, which forbade local government scrip, such issues were practically confined to Charleston, while in other states only a handful of towns and about 15 percent of the counties emitted notes. The total of such issues came to about $12.5 million as compared to about $3 million of local government bonds.

State Bond Issues, 1861–1865

STATE	AMOUNT IN MILLIONS
Alabama	$6.5
Arkansas	$2.5
Florida	$0.5
Georgia	$6.0
Louisiana	$7.0
Mississippi	$1.5
Missouri	$0.5
North Carolina	$16.0
South Carolina	$3.8
Tennessee	$6.0
Texas	$1.0
Virginia	$2.5
Total	$53.8

Private Debts. As was typical of a quasi-colonial economy, the South depended for its commercial liquidity upon funds borrowed from outside the region. These were usually used by the local businessmen who lent the planters money in anticipation of the harvest to move the crops in the fall and import goods in the spring. In early 1861, the crop advances had been paid off and the usual $60 million of credits on merchandise had been curtailed to only $40 million by uneasy Northern lenders.

In addition, Northerners had made permanent investments in the South by purchasing government bonds and bank and railroad securities and by mortgage lending. Thus when the Federal government decreed the confiscation of Southern assets held in the North, the Confederate Congress retaliated in kind. The congressmen thought that as Northerners owned 30 percent of all Southern corporate capital and debt (which they valued at $300 million, although the number was nearer to $100 million), the sale of these investments and the collection of debts due Northerners would result in at least $100 million of cash for the Confederate Treasury. But these calculations proved to be wildly optimistic.

Leaving aside the unrealistic estimate, there were a variety of reasons the Confederacy managed to collect only $12 million from this program. Many Southerners wanted to maintain their Northern business relationships. Consequently, the New Orleans banks paid off $4 million of Northern debts after the war began, and many persons refused to report their obligations or Northern holdings in their corporations. Some also foresaw that if they paid such funds over to the Confederacy, they might have to pay twice in the event of a Union victory.

If anyone in the South had supported secession with a view to evading payment of their debts, the final outcome was a great disappointment. The war not only destroyed the value of all Confederate-related assets but left the Southerners obligated to pay their Northern creditors both the principal of what they owed and a four-year accumulation of interest as well.

The rapid and irresponsible accumulation of Confederate and state debts adversely affected government credit and the economy at large. A bloated currency led to hyperinflation, shortages of goods, and a general collapse of morale, military and civilian. By 1862, the public began to fear that the burgeoning debt would be completely or partially repudiated. Thus farmers refused to sell their crops to the Confederate agents. The army then resorted to seizing goods under impressment laws. Since owners were paid little or nothing for their crops, such actions alienated the victims while discouraging the production and distribution of food. Thus the growing public debt was among the factors contributing to Confederate defeat.

[*See also* Bonds; Confiscation; Currency; Impressment; Taxation.]

BIBLIOGRAPHY

Ball, Douglas B. *Financial Failure and Confederate Defeat.* Urbana, Ill., 1991.

Hawk, Emory Q. *Economic History of the South.* New York, 1934.

Schwab, John Christopher. *The Confederate States of America, 1861–1865.* New York, 1901.

Todd, Richard Cecil. *Confederate Finance.* Athens, Ga., 1954.

DOUGLAS B. BALL

DECLARATION OF IMMEDIATE CAUSES.

The Declaration of the Immediate Causes of Secession was adopted by the South Carolina secession convention to explain the reasons for the state's withdrawal from the Union. The declaration was drafted by a special committee of the convention, chaired by Christopher G. Memminger, a longtime South Carolina congressman and future Confederate secretary of treasury.

The declaration represented the views of the more moderate members of the convention. Another document, the Address to the People of South Carolina, drafted by a committee chaired by Robert Barnwell Rhett, Sr., reflected the philosophy of the radical faction in the convention.

The declaration stated that South Carolina and other states had asserted their rights of freedom and sovereignty in the Declaration of Independence, the peace treaty signed with Great Britain in September 1783, and the Federal Constitution ratified in 1788. The declaration noted that in recent years the Northern states had refused to fulfill their constitutional obligations to the Southern states, especially in regard to fugitive slaves. The election of a president whose opinions and purposes were hostile to the Southern institution of slavery left South Carolina no recourse but to dissolve the union existing between the states and to resume its position as a separate and independent state.

The declaration was debated by the convention on December 24, 1860. An effort by Maxcy Gregg, a member of the radical faction, to table was defeated by a 124 to 31 vote, and the convention, after some minor amendments, passed the declaration.

[*See also* Appendix *for the complete text of the declaration.*]

BIBLIOGRAPHY

Channing, Steven A. *A Crisis of Fear: Secession in South Carolina.* New York, 1970.

Journal of the Convention of the People of South Carolina Held in 1860, 1861, and 1862, Together with the Ordinances, Reports, Resolutions. Columbia, S.C., 1862.

May, John Amasa, and Joan Reynolds Faunt. *South Carolina Secedes.* Columbia, S.C., 1960.

Wooster, Ralph A. *The Secession Conventions of the South.* Princeton, N.J., 1962.

RALPH A. WOOSTER

DE CLOUET, ALEXANDRE (1812–1890), congressman from Louisiana and colonel. Born on June 9, 1812, in St. Martin Parish, Louisiana, de Clouet was orphaned at an early age. He studied at Bardstown, Kentucky, and graduated from Georgetown College in 1829. After briefly studying law, he devoted his energies to managing his sugar plantations and acting as a director of the New Orleans, Opelousas, and Great Western Railroad Company. A Whig, de Clouet was elected to the Louisiana legislature in 1837 and made an unsuccessful bid for governor in 1849. Following the disintegration of the Whig party, he joined the Democrats, serving in the state constitutional convention of 1852. Elected to the Louisiana secession convention, de Clouet supported leaving the Union.

De Clouet was elected as a representative-at-large to the Provisional Congress in 1861. He sat on the Commercial Affairs and Accounts committees and regularly attended the sessions. Generally, however, he remained silent. A member of the committee to write the Confederate Constitution, de Clouet was author of Article V concerning the calling of conventions. He signed the Constitution and voted to sustain President Jefferson Davis's veto of the African slave trade. In November 1861, he lost a senatorial election to Thomas Semmes.

During the war, de Clouet served as a brigadier general in the Louisiana militia. He helped organize and outfit the Twenty-sixth Louisiana Volunteers, of which he was elected colonel. The regiment was stationed at New Orleans until the fall of that city. In May 1862, de Clouet commanded the regiment in the defense of Vicksburg. Ill health forced him to resign his command on November 10, 1862.

After the war, de Clouet slowly rebuilt his fortune and supported the Home Rule faction. Following the end of Reconstruction, he retired from public life. He died on June 26, 1890, at his plantation on Bayou Vermilion.

BIBLIOGRAPHY

Booth, Andrew B. *Records of Louisiana Soldiers and Louisiana Confederate Commands.* New Orleans, La., 1920.
Hall, Winchester. *The Story of the 26th Louisiana Infantry.* N.p., c. 1890. Reprint, Gaithersburg, Md., 1984.
Warner, Ezra J., and W. Buck Yearns. *Biographical Register of the Confederate Congress.* Baton Rouge, La., 1975.
Yearns, Wilfred B. *The Confederate Congress.* Athens, Ga., 1960.

KEVIN S. FONTENOT

DECORATIONS. *See* Medals and Decorations.

DE JARNETTE, DANIEL C. (1822–1881), congressman from Virginia. Born at Spring Grove Manor, in Caroline County, Virginia, Daniel Coleman de Jarnette became a wealthy planter and slave owner before the war. He won election to the Virginia legislature as a Democrat and served from 1853 until 1858 when he won election to the U.S. House of Representatives. He was reelected but did not take his seat because, an early and ardent secessionist, he followed Virginia out of the Union. (In February 1861 he told the House that the union "exists no longer.") He won election to the Confederate House of Representatives in 1861 and reelection in 1863. Unfazed by the irony, this fervent believer in state rights strongly supported the central government in his sentiments and votes throughout his legislative service as a member of the Foreign Affairs, Medical Department, and Conference committees.

In 1864 de Jarnette was embroiled in a dispute with a Richmond newspaper editor who alleged that the congressman advocated exempting Marylanders from the draft because his district benefited so much from smuggling across the Potomac. Only the arrest of both men averted a duel. In early 1865 de Jarnette made a bizarre speech—after which Mary Boykin Chesnut called him "that fool"—suggesting that France's interference in Mexico might offer an opportunity for the United States and the Confederacy jointly to enforce the Monroe Doctrine.

Although de Jarnette never held public office after the war, he did serve as an arbitrator in 1871 in settling a boundary dispute between Virginia and Maryland. He died at White Sulphur Springs, West Virginia, on August 20, 1881, and is buried at Spring Grove.

BIBLIOGRAPHY

Biographical Directory of the United States Congress, 1774–1989. Washington, D.C., 1989.
Wakelyn, Jon L. *Biographical Dictionary of the Confederacy.* Edited by Frank E. Vandiver. Westport, Conn., 1977.
Warner, Ezra J., and W. Buck Yearns. *Biographical Register of the Confederate Congress.* Baton Rouge, La., 1975.

NELSON D. LANKFORD

DE LAGNEL, JULIUS ADOLPH (1827–1912), lieutenant colonel and inspector of arsenals. De Lagnel was born near Newark, New Jersey, on July 24, 1827. He received a commission as second lieutenant in the Second U.S. Artillery March 8, 1847, and was promoted to first lieutenant January 26, 1849.

The year 1861 found de Lagnel attached to Company D, Second U.S. Artillery, stationed at the U.S. Arsenal, Fayetteville, North Carolina. After the secession of that state, the arsenal surrendered to state forces April 23, 1861, and personnel left for Fort Hamilton, New York. After arriving there, de Lagnel resigned from the Federal army May 17, 1861, and returned to his adopted state, Virginia. There he tendered his services to the Confederacy and accepted a captain's commission in the army.

His first major action was at the Battle of Rich Mountain, July 11, 1861, in present-day West Virginia. Serving as chief of artillery on the staff of Brig. Gen. Robert S. Garnett, he was badly wounded, captured, and subsequently exchanged. Upon return to duty, he received a promotion to major and was assigned to the Twentieth Battalion of Virginia Artillery.

De Lagnel had been recommended to Col. Josiah Gorgas, chief of ordnance, as a member of the growing Ordnance Department, an organization desperate for professional cadre. De Lagnel accepted the assignment, having refused appointment to the rank of brigadier general, and joined the Ordnance Department headquartered in Richmond.

Promoted to lieutenant colonel, he returned to the arsenal at Fayetteville to command the major ordnance works situated on Hay Mount overlooking the town. After six months, during which the production of rifles on the machinery captured at Harpers Ferry came on line, he was reassigned to field duty and appointed inspector of arsenals, which required his constant travel to arsenals throughout the Confederacy. Colonel de Lagnel spent the remainder of the war in this capacity.

After the war, de Lagnel became involved in the Pacific steamship service with some success. He died June 3, 1912, in Washington, D.C., and was buried in Alexandria, Virginia.

BIBLIOGRAPHY

U.S. War Department. *War of the Rebellion: A Compilation of the Official Records of the Union and Confederate Armies*. Washington, D.C., 1880–1901. Ser. 1. Vol. 1, pp. 478–479; vol. 2, pp. 242–278; vol. 4, p. 670; vol. 9, pt. 1, p. 69; vol. 1, pt. 2, pp. 534, 802; vol. 9, pt. 3, pp. 384–385; vol. 13, p. 874; vol. 32, pt. 3, p. 592.

Vandiver, Frank E. *Ploughshares into Swords: Josiah Gorgas and Confederate Ordnance*. Austin, 1952.

Warner, Ezra J. *Generals in Gray: Lives of the Confederate Commanders*. Baton Rouge, La., 1959.

RUSS A. PRITCHARD

DELAWARE. *See* Border States.

DEMOCRATIC PARTY. The American party system that emerged in the 1830s took deep root in the South as it did elsewhere in the country. The system was a highly mobilized, deeply divided one, in which Democrats and Whigs regularly confronted each other in intense election and legislative battles. In the Southern states, both parties competed effectively on a regionwide basis (with the exception of South Carolina, where the two-party system never developed). In the 1830s and 1840s the Democrats enjoyed their greatest Southern support in Mississippi, Alabama, Texas, Arkansas, and Florida, but they were closely competitive in the rest of the region as well.

In addition to their electoral strength, Southerners, such as James K. Polk, John C. Breckinridge, Howell Cobb, John Slidell, Jefferson Davis, and the editor Thomas Ritchie, also played significant roles in the national party, shaping its outlook, articulating its perspective, managing its activities, and advancing its policies. Between 1836 and 1860, Southerners appeared on every Democratic presidential ticket.

The party's commitment to limited government included nonintervention with slavery where it existed and resistance to demands, when they arose, that slavery be abolished or its extension limited. Although Southerners were a minority within the party as a whole, their interests, when different from those of other Democrats, were safeguarded by such procedural devices as the need of a candidate to garner two-thirds of a national convention's votes before a nomination for president could be made.

When the crisis over the expansion of slavery into new territories began in the mid-1840s, the Democrats repeatedly demonstrated their commitment to leaving the South to pursue its own practices in peace and to sustaining its claim to equal treatment in the new territories. Democrats defended Southern rights and values within the Union even at the ultimate cost of Northern votes. And as the party became identified with appeasing Southerners in the matter of slavery extension, some Northerners reacted violently enough to contribute to a fundamental electoral realignment that severely weakened the party as a national force.

Many Northern Democrats resisted Senator Stephen A. Douglas's successful attempt in 1854, at Southern insistence, to repeal the Missouri Compromise prohibition of slavery in the federal territories above the line of 36° 30' north latitude. Three years later the Democratic administration of President James Buchanan, again at Southern insistence, demanded that Congress accept Kansas's proslavery Lecompton Constitution. Douglas believed the Lecompton Constitution to be fraudulently ratified and a corruption of the notion of popular sovereignty, and he refused to accept any further moves by the party to guarantee slavery in the territories. A bitter and devastating internal party fight followed, and a significant number of Northern Democrats left their party in disagreement and disgust.

As a result, while keeping its national status and role, in the 1850s the center of gravity of the Democracy shifted South. This meant that, in addition to traditional Democratic policy preferences on economic development and issues of the role and power of government, the Democratic attitude toward slavery expansion became more favorable to Southern interests and more aggressive in its support for them. The Republican party built itself as a major political force by stressing how far the Democrats had become a tool of Southern interests.

There continued to be ideological congruence on a range of traditional Democratic policies among the factions. But they could not resolve their differences over how far to guarantee the right of slaveholders to take their property into new territories under Federal protection. In 1860, the fatal split led to two different Democratic candidates contesting for the surviving Democratic vote: Douglas, the national candidate, and Breckinridge, the candidate of the Southern wing. This catastrophic national breach was the prelude to the secession crisis in which Southern Democrats divided between strong Southern rights men who led the secession movement, on the one hand, and on the other, various factions of administration supporters and more pro-Union types, including some who still followed Douglas despite his hostility toward the notion of a territorial slave code.

After secession and the establishment of the Confederacy, Democrats played important political roles in the new nation. The Confederacy's top leadership—Jefferson Davis and such cabinet members as Robert M. T. Hunter and Judah P. Benjamin, among many others—were all prominent prewar Democrats who continued to dominate the policies and politics of their homeland. The Democratic commitment to limited government remained a hallmark of their policies as well. Although wartime exigencies inevitably led to the centralization of power in the Confederacy, its very strong state rights tradition more than echoed prewar Democratic advocacy in a way that Whiggery did not.

Political divisions within the Confederacy were persistent and bitter in constitutional conventions and state legislatures, in Congress, and ultimately in the electoral arena. Although formal partisanship and party organization was discouraged and never officially existed, partisan memories and differences, under other names and in fragmented fashion, often affected policies, attitudes, and behavior in the Confederate States. And there was a Whig-dominated revulsion against the Democratic leaders of the Southern nation expressed in state and congressional elections in the upper South in 1862 and 1863. But all of this remained localized and unsustained in the absence of formal national institutions of electoral and policy mobilization and management: caucuses, partisan newspapers, national committees, and regular conventions.

In the North during the Civil War, the Democratic party remained strong and vigorous, although it was now the minority party there, owing to the loss of its Southern wing. Generally, most Northern Democrats supported the war against secession, but though hostile to the Confederacy,

"GRAND NATIONAL DEMOCRATIC BANNER." An 1864 presidential campaign banner with the portraits of Democratic candidates George B. McClellan and George H. Pendleton. Lithograph with watercolor on wove paper. Published by Currier and Ives, New York, 1864.   LIBRARY OF CONGRESS

they provided continuous and sturdy opposition to the Lincoln administration, challenging what they believed to be Republican lust for revolutionary changes in American society, including the end of slavery. At the same time, an important peace wing in the party fought strenuously to end the war and allow the South to do as it wished. They were strong enough to include a peace plank in their national platform in 1864. Confederate leaders hoped for Democratic victory in the nation, but their hopes were in vain. Although the racism and tenacious, crabbed conservatism of many Democrats attracted hundreds of thousands of votes in the North, their search for peace without victory and their willingness to appease the South allowed the Republicans to brand all Democrats as Southern sympathizers, even traitors to the Union in time of peril. One Republican newspaper, the *New York Evening Post,* blasted them, not untypically, as the party of "Dixie, Davis and the devil."

This war-induced Southern coloration of the Democratic

party remained a potent issue in national politics for more than a generation after Appomattox. "Waving the Bloody Shirt" of Unionism against Democrats was standard Republican practice into the 1890s. Although a "solid South" favorable to the Democrats also ultimately was a product of the Civil War and its aftermath, the pro-Southern tone of the party over the course of America's most dramatic and defining episode as a nation severely handicapped Democratic efforts to regain control of national politics until well into the twentieth century.

[See also Bleeding Kansas; Copperheads; Election of 1860; Fugitive Slave Law; and biographies of numerous figures mentioned herein.]

BIBLIOGRAPHY

Alexander, Thomas P., and Richard E. Beringer. *The Anatomy of the Confederate Congress: A Study of the Influences of Member Characteristics on Legislative Voting Behavior, 1861–1865.* Nashville, Tenn., 1972.

Escott, Paul. *After Secession: Jefferson Davis and the Failure of Confederate Nationalism.* Baton Rouge, La., 1987.

Freehling, William W. *The Road to Disunion: Secessionists at Bay, 1776–1854.* New York, 1990.

Johannsen, Robert. *Stephen A. Douglas.* New York, 1973.

Kruman, Marc. *Parties and Politics in North Carolina, 1836–1865.* Baton Rouge, La., 1983.

Nichols, Roy F. *The Disruption of the American Democracy.* New York, 1948.

Silbey, Joel H. *A Respectable Minority: The Democratic Party in the Civil War Era, 1860–1868.* New York, 1978.

JOEL H. SILBEY

DESERTION. Although desertion was as prevalent in the Union army as in the Confederate forces, the North's overwhelming superiority in numbers made such defections a comparatively minor annoyance for the Union, whereas for the South they were disastrous. In the spring of 1862 Confederate desertion had progressed alarmingly, and by the latter half of the war hundreds of regiments could not muster so much as half of their paper strength. In the wake of the Battle of Sharpsburg (September 17, 1862), Gen. Robert E. Lee told President Jefferson Davis that deserters and stragglers had deprived him of a third to a half of his effective force and "were the main cause of . . . retiring from Maryland."

The War Department's official estimate disclosed that there were by June 30, 1863, 136,000 absent from the three Confederate armies of Lee, Braxton Bragg, and John C. Pemberton; and in September 1864, Davis told a Macon, Georgia, audience that two-thirds of the army was absent without leave. If half of them would return, he said, victory would be within the Confederacy's grasp. The gravity of the statistics becomes clear when it is recalled that the entire effective strength of the Confederate army never exceeded 500,000 at any one time, and that at Gettysburg (July 1–3, 1863) the Confederacy's troops numbered only 75,000.

Thirty years after Appomattox, North Carolina's future chief justice Walter Clark became editor of the five-volume *Histories of the North Carolina Regiments.* The individual authors of its regimental histories made almost no reference to desertion as a factor in the war, but Clark himself candidly wrote that "the evil became so great that it overcame all bounds and together with the breakdown in the finances of the Confederacy it was the cause of its overthrow."

As the war progressed, attitudes of both soldiers and civilians toward deserters softened from vociferous outrage to grudging tolerance and not infrequently to unconcealed sympathy. In midsummer of 1863 a conscription official in South Carolina reported to the Richmond government that "it is no longer a reproach to be known as a deserter," and early in 1865, Gen. John S. Preston, superintendent of the Confederate Bureau of Conscription, declared that "so common is the crime, it has in popular estimation lost the stigma which justly pertains to it, and [deserters] are everywhere shielded by their families and by the sympathies of many communities."

It is, of course, impossible to establish with precision the motives that prompted any particular soldier to abandon the Confederate colors, but much can be learned from letters written by troops in the ranks now reposing in private collections, public and private libraries, archives, and museums; from wartime newspapers; and from the *Official Records of the War of the Rebellion.* The latter contains hundreds of dispatches by Federal commanders in which data drawn from interviews with Southern defectors were transmitted to Union headquarters, as well as quantities of letters in which Confederate officers and civilians discuss the causes of the flight from duty.

Some soldiers were by temperament, experience, or for reasons of health less able than their comrades to cope with hunger, cold, rain, sleeplessness, disease, wounds, and exposure. Many were pitifully ignorant of the war's issues; many were depressed by dispiriting letters from home; and some, as they contemplated the plight of their families on hardscrabble farms in the rural hinterlands felt that they were choosing between deserting the army or deserting their families in a cause they only dimly understood. The more pious troopers found it hard to bear the sights and sounds of wickedness that offended their eyes and ears at every turn, and others were more grievously distressed than their tentmates by news from home about the depredations of marauding bands of deserters, vandals, and Confederate cavalrymen who "borrowed" their poultry and livestock for food.

Perhaps the most frequent complaints were the scarcity

of rations, the sporadic payment of their paltry wages, the unavailability of furloughs, and the news of peace meetings on the home front. The rigors of campaigning and of combat were, of course, a severe trial, to say nothing of the tedium of inactivity during the long winter months, which was hard on rustics pining for a furlough that never came, ignorant of their military obligations. Mystified by the rules of discipline and the Articles of War, they had little understanding of the gravity of their offense. There were, in fact, men in all social ranks who were—at least from time to time—far from convinced that the cause was worth the compulsory military service they were called upon to perform in what many considered a "rich man's war and a poor man's fight."

Official response to the problem included measures to prevent desertions; to return escapees to the ranks; to round up draft dodgers; and to punish wrongdoers both to deter other runaways and to penalize defections. The authorities confronted a dilemma in the desperately outnumbered Confederacy. If deserters were severely punished, they could not be immediately, if at all, returned to duty; and if the draft laws were aggressively enforced in seriously disaffected areas, loyalty to the cause would falter. But if a policy of leniency were pursued, regiments in the field would be seriously thinned.

Efforts to raise the enlisted man's morale and ease his hardships included the provision of food and other necessities to his hard-pressed family, supplemented by appeals to those at home not to write gloomy letters to men in the army. Generals also ordered regimental commanders to read to the troops at assembly the sections of the Articles of War that bore upon straggling, desertion, and insubordination.

In times of heightened discouragement, following hard fighting, exhausting marches, exposure to hunger and weather, and disheartening news of defeats, the Confederacy made such efforts as its meager means permitted to scour the country for additional rations and supplies (notably shoes and blankets), to distribute occasional rations of whiskey, and to improve opportunities for recreation and for worship.

But when, despite these efforts, desertion continued unabated, the authorities would experiment briefly with the tightening of discipline. A few particularly incorrigible offenders might be publicly executed, furloughs virtually suspended, and even minor offenses punished with unaccustomed vigor. But such strategems did little to reduce disaffection and were periodically abandoned until another surge of exasperation prompted another attempt.

To prevent troops from dropping out of line, commanders published stringent orders regulating such conduct, and frequent roll calls, sometimes three or four in an hour, kept a check upon soldiers' whereabouts. The most severe command issued by General Lee to curb desertion and straggling was his general order (perhaps never seriously enforced) instituting a system of "file closers," assigning to every tenth man on the march the duty of keeping a fixed bayonet and loaded pistol at the ready to cut down men who showed evidence of breaking from the ranks. The object, Lee sadly explained, was to "make the avoidance of duty more dangerous than its performance."

Sometimes the granting of furloughs was suspended altogether, either because the men simply could not be spared or because furloughed men all too frequently failed to return. The number of furloughs was often tied to the number of men present for duty, a policy calculated to give every aspirant for a leave a stake in the whole regiment's attendance record. To tighten controls further, an order might stipulate that a regimental commander must accompany a certificate of furlough with his affirmation "that none are absent without leave since the publication of this order."

Until the critical summer of 1863, newspapers throughout the Confederacy were crowded with paid notices calling for the return of specifically named deserters, carefully identified as to regiment and company, and offering thirty dollars for each runaway apprehended. The tactic was eventually abandoned as a failure, for it yielded almost no harvest. In some tragic instances soldiers published as deserters were in fact not runaways at all but were discovered to have been killed in action or to have died of wounds or disease.

Several times a conciliatory policy was undertaken whereby the government offered amnesty to soldiers who would return by a specified date and pledged that they would not be punished. When the offer brought little response, the date was extended, but even this indulgence proved unavailing in the end. Contemporary records do show, however, that thousands of absentees went home fully intending to return to duty after looking to the spring plowing and planting and did in fact drift back to their units.

When efforts to prevent desertion and to persuade recusants to return disappointed official hopes, the Confederate authorities turned increasingly to more aggressive measures by stricter enforcement of military regulations, the Articles of War, and state laws forbidding civilians to harbor or assist runaways. The twentieth Article of War prescribed that troops who were "convicted of having deserted . . . shall suffer death, or such other punishments as, by sentence of a court martial, shall be inflicted." In addition the Confederacy assigned to various civil and military agencies the duty of hunting down and capturing fugitives to be returned to their units for trial and sentencing.

Because the Articles of War did not clearly distinguish between "desertion" and "absence without leave," those charged with enforcement were disposed to shrink from relentlessly pursuing absentees and dealing out the full penalties. Desertion, literally construed, was the abandonment of military service with *intent not to return*—a point all but impossible to establish. In short, hunting deserters was always a sprawling, widespread, but unsuccessful enterprise.

Not infrequently deserters chose not to return to their own homes where they might encounter official pursuers, but congregated in mountainous or wooded regions where enthusiasm for the Confederacy was at best grudging. When militia units were dispatched to duty in such "deserter country," it was by no means unusual to discover that their quarry were more numerous and better organized and armed than they themselves were. Not a few Confederate deserters chose to cross over to Union lines where, in relative comfort and safety, they were separately interviewed for military information to be forwarded to Union headquarters.

Runaways who were apprehended and convicted by courts-martial were subjected to various punishments, among them detention in military prisons, subjection to ball-and-chain confinement, bread and water diets, stoppage of pay, branding with the letter D, hanging by the thumbs, and "bucking and gagging." More severe were the infliction of a stipulated number of lashes (usually thirty-nine or fifty, "well laid on") and long prison terms at hard labor. Most fearful of all was the death penalty, in nearly all cases by firing squad but occasionally by hanging. The records of courts-martial in the National Archives confirm the conclusion that only a relatively small number of deserters sentenced to death actually suffered the extreme penalty. The court-martial's proceedings were sent upward through the chain of command to the secretary of war for review and then to President Davis for final determination. In hundreds of cases, death sentences stopped there and were mercifully revoked by the president and replaced by lesser penalties.

By modern standards, however, the death penalty was by no means rare. A special study of its application to the men of North Carolina's regiments has disclosed that approximately two hundred of the state's convicted deserters were executed while their assembled comrades were compelled to look on as a warning not to bring the same fate upon themselves. Because North Carolina supplied approximately a fifth of enlistments, it may perhaps be assumed that the total Confederate executions approached a thousand.

Only a small fraction of the Confederacy's deserters were in fact apprehended and sentenced, and it seems safe to say that a similarly small proportion of those convicted were actually put to death. There can be little doubt that capital punishment was resorted to not primarily to punish the transgressor but to afford examples for those contemplating defection. There is, moreover, no evidence to suggest that the imposition of the death penalty was in any significant degree more effective than lesser penalties in curbing the propensity of a surprising number of Civil War soldiers, North and South, to yield to the impulse to abandon their more steadfast comrades.

[*See also* Class Conflict; File Closers; Military Justice; Morale.]

BIBLIOGRAPHY

Bardolph, Richard. "Confederate Dilemma: North Carolina Troops and the Desertion Problem." *North Carolina Historical Review* 66 (January and April 1989): 61–86; 179–210.

Dodge, David. "The Cave-Dwellers of the Confederacy." *Atlantic Monthly* 68 (1891): 514–521.

Lonn, Ella. *Desertion during the Civil War*. New York, 1928. Reprint, Gloucester, Mass., 1966.

Martin, Bessie. *Desertion of Alabama Troops from the Confederate Army*. New York, 1932.

Moore, Albert B. *Conscription and Conflict in the Confederacy*. New York, 1924. Reprint, New York, 1963.

Robertson, James I., Jr. *Soldiers Blue and Grey*. Columbia, S.C., 1988.

Wiley, Bell I. *The Life of Johnny Reb*. Baton Rouge, La., 1971.

RICHARD BARDOLPH

DESHLER, JAMES (1833–1863), brigadier general. Deshler was born February 18, 1833, in Tuscumbia, Alabama. He attended West Point and graduated in the class of 1854. He then began a career with the U.S. Army, serving in the western territories of California, Utah, and Colorado, and at the Carlisle Barracks in Pennsylvania. Deshler was in Colorado when the Civil War broke out, and he was soon appointed captain of artillery in the regular Confederate service.

Deshler, who was much admired by his fellow officers and men for his bravery and dedication, served in western Virginia, North Carolina, and Arkansas Post. On December 13, 1861, he was wounded in both thighs at the Battle of Alleghany Summit. Deshler was captured at Arkansas Post in January 1863. Upon his release, he was promoted to brigadier general, July 28, 1863, and was assigned an infantry brigade in Patrick Cleburne's division, Army of Tennessee.

Deshler's brigade went into the Battle of Chickamauga on September 19, 1863, and suffered light casualties the first day. Col. Roger Q. Mills described Deshler's death on the second day: "About noon our supply of ammunition began to give out and I sent a courier to Brigadier General Deshler to inform him of the fact and to [ask] where we could get more. A few minutes later, after I saw him coming toward my right, some forty paces from me he was struck by a shell in the chest and his heart literally torn from his bosom." His body was removed to his native Alabama and buried in Tuscumbia's Oakwood Cemetery.

BIBLIOGRAPHY

Walker, Robert Sparks. "The Pyramids of Chickamauga." *Chattanooga Sunday Times*, August 23, 1936.
Warner, Ezra J. *Generals in Gray: Lives of the Confederate Commanders*. Baton Rouge, La., 1959.

JOHN F. CISSELL

DEWITT, WILLIAM H. (1827–1896), congressman from Tennessee. A Unionist member of the Tennessee secession convention, DeWitt, a former school teacher and attorney, was elected in August 1861 to the Provisional Congress from Tennessee's Fourth District. This was an old Whig stronghold which he had represented a few years earlier in the state legislature and whose constituents generally had opposed secession until President Abraham Lincoln's call for volunteers. A reluctant Confederate who later claimed to have been swept away by the "blighting influences" of the "great storm of secession," DeWitt played a relatively minor role during the six months he was in Richmond, serving on the Printing and the Territories committees. He took a strong position in favor of issues related to the raising and equipping of an army, but did not support as a retaliatory measure the sequestration of property belonging to Unionist citizens. In his final official act as congressman, on February 12, 1862, he voted against the appointment of Lucius B. Northrop as commissary-general of the army.

DeWitt's Confederate career was, as he himself admitted, "as brief as it was inglorious." Not a candidate for election to the Regular Congress, he returned to his native Smith County, Tennessee, in mid-February 1862, "staying at home all the time and [remaining] quiet." After abandoning all sympathy and cooperation with the Confederacy, he took an oath of allegiance to the United States in early 1863. He never held an elected political office again, practicing law in Carthage, Tennessee, until 1875 and afterward in Chattanooga.

BIBLIOGRAPHY

Amnesty File. William H. DeWitt. Microcopy M1003, Roll 49. Record Group 94. National Archives, Washington, D.C.
Obituary. *Chattanooga Times*, April 12, 1896.
Journal of the Congress of the Confederate States of America, 1861–1865. Washington, D.C., 1904–1905.
Speer, William S., ed. *Sketches of Prominent Tennesseans*. Nashville, Tenn., 1988.
Warner, Ezra J., and W. Buck Yearns. *Biographical Register of the Confederate Congress*. Baton Rouge, La., 1975.

R. B. ROSENBURG

DIARIES, LETTERS, AND MEMOIRS. No event in American history has provoked more extensive and heated commentary on the part of participants than the Civil War. Recognized, even before it began, by people on both sides as a historic—for some a missionary—confrontation to determine the future course and identity of the United States, the war seemed to demand that those who had lived through it record their experience and reflect upon its larger significance. But for those who had lived within or fought for the Confederate States of America, the significance was greater yet. The defeat of the Confederacy and emancipation of the slaves, followed by the abolition of slavery, bequeathed a special and uniquely conflicted legacy to the white and black residents of the erstwhile seceding states.

Personal or firsthand accounts of life within the Confederacy and of the war to defend it abound and take a variety of forms. Diaries and journals kept during the war interweave the experiences of specific individuals with the vicissitudes of the struggle. In varying degree, depending upon the sophistication of the author, these are crafted literary documents, some of which were revised for publication by the author, others of which have been rescued from oblivion by editors and historians who have recognized their special value. Letters, written during the war and subsequently published, normally embody greater spontaneity, since their authors usually had no thought of publication. Memoirs, which most often were written after the cessation of hostilities and explicitly intended for publication, tend to subordinate representations of the author to an evaluation of the events the author observed or participated in. Memoirs, too, frequently served to justify the author's evaluation of battles, strategies, policies, or events, and, if relevant, the author's role in them.

Chronicling Momentous Events. Before the news of Abraham Lincoln's election to the presidency raced through the Southern states, white Southerners of both sexes and all ages put pen to paper to record their private experience of what they sensed would prove momentous events. At the beginning of June 1860, Catherine Ann Devereux Edmonston, in Halifax County, North Carolina, began the diary that she would keep throughout the war, noting that although she had previously commenced diaries, she had always left off, "perhaps from weariness, perhaps from an absolute dearth of events."

Beginning in 1860, she and other Southerners had a plethora of events to reflect upon and record. At an accelerating rate, the war forced itself into the most isolated and previously uneventful lives. In the most common pattern, men were drawn into politics and battles while women remained at home to cope with the management of rural households, hostile troops and marauders, the ever more burdensome dearth of supplies, and, eventually, the upheaval of emancipation. But the lines between men's and women's experience of the war were never entirely neat. Some women participated directly in the political and military circles of Richmond and other cities. Others, who founded and staffed hospitals for the wounded and dying, lived intimately with the human cost of the conflict. As the Union's war effort broadened into William Tecumseh Sherman's policy of systematic devastation, women found themselves the direct objects of military attack. And all women were vulnerable to the disruptions and deprivations that followed in the wake of mobilization, military conflict, and, ultimately, defeat. Nor were men, notwithstanding their special concern with military events, impervious to or isolated from the disruption of civilian life.

The four years of the Civil War and the Confederacy decisively shaped Southern life and consciousness for the ensuing century and beyond. White Southerners initially turned to diaries and journals because they knew themselves to be living during a momentous historical epoch, to be living through revolutionary events. Fighting for Southern independence and the preservation of slavery as a social system, they knew that the outcome of the struggle would result in the recognition of a new nation or in their subjugation. So they wrote of their experience in the knowledge that even its most mundane details would one day be of interest to others.

If white Southerners kept their diaries and journals while uncertain of the outcome, they published them when the outcome had been decided. The shadow of defeat thus hangs over the Southern accounts of the war and the Confederacy that we read today. Consider the case of Mary Boykin Chesnut, the most celebrated Confederate diarist of all. Born into one political family of the slaveholding elite and having married into an even more influential and wealthy one, she spent much of the war in the company of the innermost circles of the Confederacy. Her published diary appropriately begins on February 18, 1861, the day of Jefferson Davis's inauguration as provisional president of the Confederacy. The concluding entry, July 26, 1865, begins, "I do not write often now—not for want of something to say, but from a loathing of all I see and hear. Why dwell upon it?"

Between 1865 and her death on November 22, 1886, Mary Chesnut turned periodically to revising her diary for publication. In her case, thanks to the scholarship of Elisabeth Muhlenfeld and C. Vann Woodward, we can follow the progress of successive revisions and, accordingly, recognize at least some of the considerations that led her subtly but tellingly to rewrite her account under the influence of unfolding events. Revisions similar to, if not as extensive and self-conscious as Mary Chesnut's, almost certainly shaped the published diaries and journals of others as well.

Mary Chesnut's diary especially reveals the tension that permeates most, if not all, Confederate diaries and journals between the writer's concern to provide a chronicle of events and his or her concern to provide an autobiographical portrait. Thus she interweaves accounts of conversations among influential or not-so-influential participants and descriptions of life in various parts of the Confederacy with reflections upon herself—her role in events, other people's reactions to her, her character, and her feelings. In this respect, the diaries and journals of the Confederacy normally embody interpretations of the struggle on the part of those who are desperately assessing the consequences of defeat, attempting to justify their own actions and roles, worrying about their own and their region's future place in the newly consolidated Union, or trying to construct from the bitterness of defeat a history or memory in which future generations of Southerners might take comfort and pride. But if all the diaries and journals, in greater or lesser degree, reflect their writer's concern with self-portraiture and the worthiness of their section's cause, many also provide invaluable information on the waging of the struggle at the front, in political circles, and at home.

Women's Diaries. For obvious reasons, women's diaries provide the most extensive information about life on the home front, although letters from absent husbands frequently include information—and, not infrequently, directives—on how things should be done. Women from different parts of the South and with different levels of income detailed discrete versions of a general story of hardship and, as the years passed, deprivation and devastation. As a young woman, Lucy Rebecca Buck in Front Royal, Virginia, lived through several periods of occupation by both Union and Confederate troops. She especially registered the destruction of the fences upon her family's farm and the demands to feed the occupiers. Like Lucy Buck, Kate Stone, from a well-to-do Louisiana slaveholding family, experienced the war as a young woman. As the fighting around Vicksburg intensified and the forts and cities around it fell, Federal gunboats and soldiers came to dominate their lives. In resistance, Kate's mother burned twenty thousand dollars worth of cotton rather than allow the invaders to capture it. Supplies of food and clothing dwindled, relations with slaves deteriorated, and in 1863 the family, like many others of the region, migrated with 130 slaves and what possessions they could salvage to Tyler, Texas, where they spent the remainder of the war.

Parthenia Hague spent the war as a schoolteacher on a large plantation in southern Alabama. As the blockade of the coast between Mobile and New Orleans tightened, especially after the capture of Ship's Island in September 1861, she and the family with whom she was living began to feel the pinch of dwindling imports. In her diary, published in 1888, she proudly recounted her own and the other white women's ingenuity in devising substitutes for the luxuries they had previously enjoyed. She described in especially loving detail their growing skill in the production of cloth and clothing, from spinning and weaving to dyeing and sewing. Since, before the war, elite white women were unlikely to have used walnuts for brown dye or even to have known that they could, we may assume that she and her friends received invaluable instruction from slave women, who had been dyeing cloth for "Sunday clothing" for their own families throughout the antebellum period.

Because of shortages caused by the blockade, the escalating inflation of the Confederate dollar, the failure and devastation of crops, and the depredations of enemy troops, unaccustomed economic hardships permeated white Southern women's experience and recollections of the war. As a result, many others like Parthenia Hague also wrote of the ways in which they were forced to make do and the goods they had to do without.

But while women's lives on farms and plantations ranged from uncomfortable to dangerous, some women's lives in the cities assumed a cast of frenetic gaiety, characterized by the feeling that one should dance tonight for tomorrow one may die. Years later, Thomas Cooper De Leon published his recollections of those days and that mood. In a diary that was never published, Meta Morris Grimball worried about the effect that the new laxness in social mores would have upon her daughters. And after the war, Emma Holmes still wrote disapprovingly of the festive mood that had prevailed in Charleston as late as 1865.

Other women, however, lived intimately, as nurses, with the more somber face of the war. Throughout the South many, such as Virginia Davis Gray in Arkansas, sewed clothes for soldiers and nursed the wounded in their own homes or in hospitals. Phoebe Yates Pember, who served as a hospital matron in Richmond, provided a careful account of hospital organization and nursing activities.

Most diarists focused upon what they considered the most dramatic aspects of their experience, notably the arrival of enemy troops, the burning of plantations and farms, and the departure of slaves. Mary Sharp Jones and her pregnant daughter, Mary Sharp Jones Mallard, kept a journal of their harrowing experience of the ruthlessness of Sherman's soldiers who pillaged and occupied their plantation, Montevideo, during the March to the Sea. Eliza Frances Andrews, who edited the diary of her youth for publication in 1908, described her growing fear of the Northerners as she traveled in late 1864 and early 1865 across the route of Sherman's march through Georgia. What she saw redoubled her fears of the enemy: "Yankee, Yankee, is the one detestable word always ringing in Southern ears. . . . They thwart all my plans, murder my friends, and make my life miserable." As a seventeen-year-old, Emma LeConte personally experienced the terror of Sherman's approach. After

surviving the destruction and pillaging of Columbia, South Carolina, she wrote of feeling unconquered and of hating the Federals more than ever, viewing the very name *Yankee* as "a synonym for *all* that is *mean, despicable* and *abhorrent.*"

Other women, like Elizabeth Hardin who described the confusion that overtook Nashville after the fall of Fort Donelson, penned their own accounts of civilians' direct encounters with military activities. Burning cities, scorched countryside, and looted plantations indeed brought the war into Southern homes—although none so much as the news of a dead or wounded friend, cousin, father, brother, husband, or son.

For many slaveholding women the response of their own former slaves to the news of the Emancipation Proclamation seemed the irreducible moment of truth—the final destruction of the world they had known and the devastating knowledge that they might never have understood the slaves they had thought they knew well. One diarist after another has her own example of disillusionment—of the slave, frequently a trusted house servant whom she had considered virtually a member of the family, who took off without so much as a good-bye. Mary Chesnut was taken aback when, in 1865, her friends the Martins left Columbia "and their mammy, the negro woman who had nursed them, refused to go with them. That daunted me."

Many slaveholding women found it hard to accept the simple fact that their former slaves wanted to be free, and even those who acknowledged the desire for freedom had great difficulty in understanding what freedom meant. Diaries teem with women's accounts of their problems with the former slaves who did remain, but now had to be treated like the free laborers they were. Ella Gertrude Clanton Thomas had an especially difficult time in coming to terms with those of her former slaves who stayed. On the other hand, Catherine Edmonston was frankly relieved to be free of the responsibility for hers. Since men's absence had forced many women to assume unaccustomed responsibilities of farm and plantation management, their difficulties with former slaves concerned labor in the fields as well as service in the house. The departure of slaves confronted many former slaveholding women with the desperate situation women on small farms had contended with throughout the war. And what slaveholding women registered as unimaginable burdens, former slave women embraced as new, if uncertain, opportunities.

Letters. Like diaries and journals, letters between friends or family members provide an immediate impression of the confusion and challenges of everyday life and the mounting problems during the final years of the conflict. Robert Manson Myers's edition of the letters of the men and women of the family of Charles Colcock Jones, a Presbyterian minister and the owner of large slaveholdings in

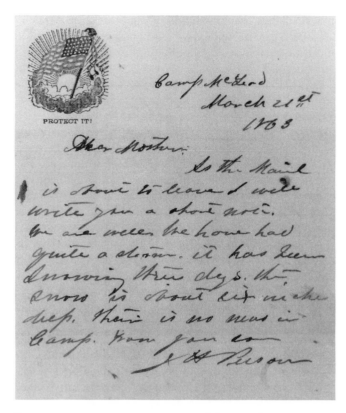

LETTER ON CAPTURED STATIONERY.   Confederate soldier J. H. Pee-son wrote this letter to his mother on stationery seized from Union troops. The note is dated March 21, 1863.

CIVIL WAR LIBRARY AND MUSEUM, PHILADELPHIA

Liberty County, Georgia, conveys the immediate response of the members of a highly educated elite family to the disasters that were falling upon them.

Throughout the war, Southerners wrote to friends and kin in the North about their views and experiences. In March 1861, Sue Sparks Keitt of South Carolina explained the decision to secede to a Northern friend, denouncing the intentions of the "Black Republicans." And Sarah Lamb, whose husband was the commanding officer of Fort Fisher, North Carolina, wrote regularly to her parents in Providence, Rhode Island, about life in the blockade-running city.

Letters became a lifeline that bound those who were separated by the fighting. Typically, soldiers wrote to the parents, siblings, wives, or sweethearts they had left at home of the travails of life at the front, and those at home wrote of their growing difficulties. Winston Stevens of the Second Florida Cavalry and his wife, young Octavia, who remained to cope with their plantation in Florida, corresponded about the hardships they both confronted and, toward the end, worried about the departure of the slaves and the threat of insurrection. In a similar vein, Isaac Hall, a private from Bienville Parish, Louisiana, and his wife,

Mary, exchanged accounts of their respective problems. Many yeoman men, like William Stoker of Texas, worried about their wives and their farms. Stoker knew that enemy soldiers might mistreat women whose husbands were away; he also knew that women could be unfaithful. And like so many small farmers, he was especially aware of how hard it would be for women to plant and harvest crops or find help for doing so.

More than diaries and journals, which were primarily written by those who had education and leisure, letters permit us to glimpse the experiences and perceptions of less affluent and less well educated Southerners who found the time and the words to communicate with the family members and friends from whom they were separated. Leander Huckaby, who served in the Eleventh Mississippi Infantry in the Peninsular campaign and who spelled pneumonia "new monia," wrote to his wife of his experiences and his concern for the maintenance of their farm. Letters such as these, by ordinary people whose words usually would not have been preserved, bring alive the suffering, discomfort, and physical danger that were a daily reality for innumerable Southerners.

Freedmen's Bureau Papers. African American Southerners—whether slaves, escaped slaves, free blacks, or emancipated slaves—were even less likely than the less affluent whites to keep journals and diaries, to write letters, or to have their letters preserved. But from the start—although at an accelerating rate following the news of the Emancipation Proclamation—more and more black Southerners came in contact with the agents of the Freedmen's Bureau, who received letters from and about them, took affidavits from them, and generally monitored their situation.

Although the papers of the Freedmen's Bureau obviously differ from those of private individuals, they nonetheless offer direct testimony to at least some of the experiences and aspirations of those who were attempting to extricate themselves from slavery—those who were claiming their freedom. In this respect, the edition of the papers of the Freedmen's Bureau for the war years contributes an essential dimension to an understanding of the Confederacy. What some Southerners experienced as a traumatic defeat, other Southerners experienced as the dawn of a new era.

A Political Diary. From the beginning, life in the Confederacy unfolded under the shadow of mobilization for and conduct of a war. The business of war dominated the operations of the Confederate government, which was born of the determination to defend Southern independence and died with Southern defeat on the battlefield. J. B. Jones, who, four days before the firing on Fort Sumter, fled South from Philadelphia, where he had been editing a proslavery newspaper, the *Southern Monitor,* spent the years of the

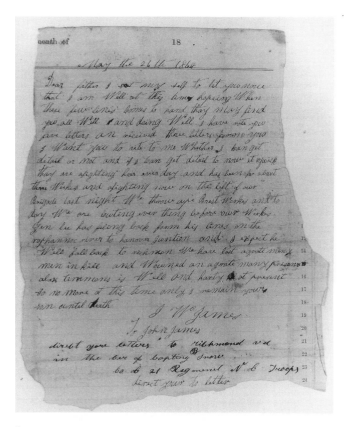

LETTER WRITTEN ON MUSTER ROLL FORM. By the end of the war, paper had become so scarce that soldiers would write home on any scraps they could find. This letter, dated May 26, 1864, is from John W. James to his father, John James. At the bottom the writer directs return mail to Richmond, Virginia, care of the Twenty-first Regiment North Carolina Troops.

CIVIL WAR LIBRARY AND MUSEUM, PHILADELPHIA

war in Richmond as clerk to the five successive Confederate secretaries of war. During those years, Jones, an accomplished professional writer, kept an extensive diary of the events and personalities he witnessed at first hand.

Jones's diary captures the quality of life in Richmond, the intrigues and tensions that frequently pervaded the civilian and military leadership of the Confederacy, and the ways in which the war pervaded the consciousness of Confederate purpose. Sitting in the War Office, he was always among the first to learn of military successes, defeats, and shortages. He was also privy to the jockeyings for position and what he sometimes took to be the failure to appreciate talent. In March 1862, for example, he noted, "Price, Beauregard, Walker, Bonham, Toombs, Wise, Floyd, and others of the brightest lights of the South have been somehow successively obscured. And Joseph E. Johnston is a doomed fly, sooner or later, for he said, not long since, that there could be no hope of success as long as Mr. [Judah P.] Benjamin was Secretary of War." Since the words had been spoken at

a dinner table, he observed, they would reach the ears of the secretary. And three days later he penned the deadpan entry, "Mr. Benjamin has been promoted. He is now Secretary of State."

Even as the pace of events accelerated and Southern prospects looked ever less hopeful, Jones retained his cool, understated tone. In the fall of 1864, he dispassionately recorded, "Sherman left a burning Atlanta at his back and started his 'March to the Sea.'" Two days later, noting that the Confederate Senate had passed a resolution requesting that Jefferson Davis limit the number of exemptions from military service that governors might grant, he wryly added, "This will, perhaps, startle Governor Smith of Virginia, who has already kept out of the army at least a thousand." Perhaps, Jones reflected, "it will hit Governor Brown of Georgia, also; but Sherman will hit him hardest."

A passionate and occasionally acerbic Confederate, Jones was a proslavery man and a Southern nationalist. His diary, published in 1866 shortly after the Confederate defeat and before the more self-consciously crafted diaries that appeared during the final decades of the nineteenth century, ranks among the most illuminating and comprehensive accounts of the day-by-day progress of the Confederacy.

Military Memoirs and Diaries. Although a civilian, Jones's experience in the War Department afforded him a special position from which to appreciate the constant encroachment of the war effort on every aspect of Southern life. Gen. Edward Porter Alexander spent those same years upon the field of battle with the Army of Northern Virginia, participating in both Manassas campaigns, as well as the Sharpsburg campaign, the Battles of Fredericksburg and Chancellorsville, and the Gettysburg campaign. During the final year of the war, he was present at Wilderness, Spottsylvania, the siege of Petersburg, and Appomattox. Not until 1897 did Alexander, at his children's prompting, begin to write the story of his experience. After completing a massive manuscript, he began to polish sections, which he published to great acclaim in 1907 as *Military Memoirs of a Confederate.* The more personal sections, which he kept back, were not identified, collected, and published until 1989, when they appeared as *Fighting for the Confederacy.*

Alexander's *Military Memoirs,* which were admired by President Theodore Roosevelt and countless historians, stand as a model of an objective, almost scholarly account of the Army of Northern Virginia as seen by a participant, in keeping with Alexander's own ambition to tell the story professionally. For that very reason, the *Military Memoirs* excluded many of his personal responses and, especially, his candid assessment of other participants. *Fighting for the Confederacy* breaks that silence, permitting readers to glimpse, for example, a complex portrait of Gen. Robert E. Lee as not merely a brilliant commander but a man of humor, frustration, anger, and his share of pettiness. More

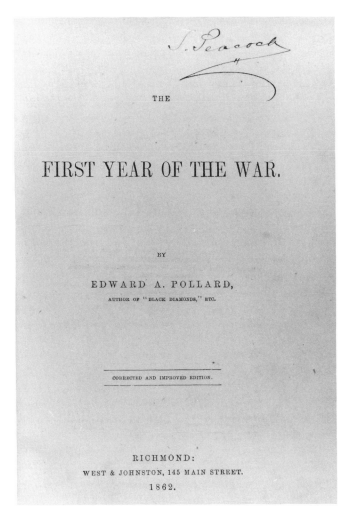

THE

FIRST YEAR OF THE WAR.

BY

EDWARD A. POLLARD,

AUTHOR OF "BLACK DIAMONDS," ETC.

CORRECTED AND IMPROVED EDITION.

RICHMOND:
WEST & JOHNSTON, 145 MAIN STREET.
1862.

TITLE PAGE TO *THE FIRST YEAR OF THE WAR.*   Written by Gen. Edward A. Pollard and published in Richmond in 1862, this memoir was the first account of the war produced by a Confederate in the field.   CIVIL WAR LIBRARY AND MUSEUM, PHILADELPHIA

important, it offers an immediate and wonderfully detailed picture of army life that is all the more gripping for being told by a man who had firsthand knowledge of the business of war—of the importance of terrain, of supplies, of chains of command, of railroads, and all the rest. And even at his most candid, Alexander retains the responsible commander's respect for those with whom he was working and fighting. The point of his book is the immediate evocation of experience, not an after-the-fact ascription of blame.

Alexander's *Fighting for the Confederacy,* while an exemplary narrative of life on the Confederate battlefront, does not stand alone. The writings of innumerable ordinary soldiers who attempted, in memoirs, diaries, or letters, to capture their personal experience in specific battles or locations may now be seen as so many small pieces in an immense mosaic of collective memory. Leonidas Torrence,

a corporal in the Twenty-third (formerly Thirteenth) North Carolina Infantry, penned his own account of the Peninsular, Sharpsburg, Chancellorsville, and Gettysburg campaigns, including the bout of measles that kept him, like so many others, out of action for a period. John Tucker, a sergeant in the Fifth Alabama Infantry, wrote of many of the same campaigns, including accounts of how he provisioned his troops with help from civilians by plundering Union camps and by foraging. John Johnston, who served in the Seventh and Fourteenth Tennessee cavalries and participated in the Confederate withdrawals from Tennessee, Mississippi, and Georgia, later recalled the experience of being under fire, when the tension mounted so high that the hours went by like minutes. The feeling dissipated as one became "indifferent to time and danger." But after the fighting had ceased, he and his comrades experienced an indescribable feeling of delight and relief.

Even as the war was raging, soldiers and civilians alike expressed criticism of its general conduct and frequently of Jefferson Davis or specific commanders. Edwin Hedge Fay, who served first as a sergeant in Webb's (Louisiana) Cavalry Company and then as captain of the Office of the Chief of the Topographical Bureau, District of West Louisiana and Arkansas, had scant patience with the war or the army, which he constantly schemed to leave so as to go home to his family. Valerius Cincinnatus Giles, a captain in the Fourth Texas Infantry, wondered in his diary about Gen. Braxton Bragg's failure to follow up the victory at Chickamauga with a pursuit of Gen. William S. Rosecrans's army. Sam Watkin's well known memoir, *"Co. Aytch" Maury Grays,* is similarly very critical of Bragg's generalship throughout the war. Thomas Jewett Goree, captain in the First Corps of the Army of Northern Virginia and aide-de-camp to Gen. James Longstreet, never spared other officers in his letters and even ranked them according to their drinking habits. He deplored President Davis's failure to take Washington after the First Battle of Manassas and reproached him for his misunderstanding of his generals, especially Joseph E. Johnston.

Memoirs as Apologia. The generals had their own quarrels with one another that were born in the bitterness of mounting reverses and festered long after the war. Gen. John Bell Hood's memoir of the Army of Tennessee, which he commanded, began as a report to the Confederate Congress on his failure in the Franklin and Nashville campaign but, by 1880, had grown into a full-fledged book, which Gen. P. G. T. Beauregard arranged to have published as part of his own continuing struggle with Jefferson Davis and Gen. Joseph E. Johnston. Johnston had already aired his position, to which Hood was responding, in his *Narrative of Military Operations* (1874). In 1891, Beauregard followed up Hood's counterattack with his own commentary, justifying the wisdom of his actions and his role in the army.

Gen. James Longstreet, bitter over the criticism of his alleged failure at Gettysburg, used his memoirs published in 1896 to defend his record.

For all the bitterness among the former generals of the Confederacy, Robert E. Lee escaped virtually unscathed and avoided the elaborate self-justifications so many of the others indulged in. His posthumously collected *Wartime Papers* offer an extensive picture of his relations with the military and civilian leaders of the Confederacy as well as with his own family. Jefferson Davis did not get off so lightly. On his shoulders fell the principal responsibility for the entire government of the Confederacy, including much of the burden for the conduct of the war. In keeping with the magnitude of that responsibility, Davis cast his apologia as a defense of the Confederacy itself, acknowledging by his choice of subject that his life and reputation would remain inextricably tied to the office he had held. His two-volume work, *The Rise and Fall of the Confederate Government* (1881), provided an extensive exploration of constitutional issues and governmental policies, but it remained, above all, a monumental effort of self-justification.

Long before Davis began, much less finished, his account, others had taken up the work of justification. Well before Appomattox, Albert Taylor Bledsoe had begun his classic justification for secession, *Is Davis a Traitor, or Was Secession a Constitutional Right Previous to 1861?* (1866). Bledsoe was not alone in his concern to justify something larger than personal reputation. General Lee himself is said to have admonished Bledsoe in the wake of Appomattox, "Doctor, you must take care of yourself; you have a great work to do; we all look to you for our vindication." The overwhelming magnitude of the Civil War as a political and military crisis led many other Southerners to reflect upon it as a judgment upon their society and values.

Religion and the Lost Cause. During the war, in letters and diaries, Southerners explored their consciences and sought to understand the ways in which the crisis through which they were living might reflect a divine judgment. Few doubted the legitimacy of their cause, or even the legitimacy of slavery, but they did worry that they must strive to live their chosen lives as better Christians than they had in the past. Col. David Lang, who served in the Eighth Florida Infantry at Gettysburg, Cold Harbor, and Petersburg, wrote approvingly in his letters of the revivalism that he saw sweeping the Army of Northern Virginia in September 1863. His and others' concerns echoed those of the Southern divines who, throughout the war, had preached Fast Day sermons calling their people to account and urging them to justify their actions by their faith.

Even after defeat, Southerners generally perpetuated this religious commitment in their recollections of the faith that had animated the troops. In January 1892, Basil Gildersleeve, the eminent classical scholar who had served in the Confederate army until he was wounded in 1864, warmly recalled the deep religious feeling of the army and its leaders in the *Atlantic Monthly*. His recollections seconded the firsthand accounts that Rev. J. William Jones had collected and published in *Christ in the Camp* (1888).

Others, however, experienced defeat as a direct challenge to the faith that had informed their conviction of the righteousness of their cause. On October 8, 1865, Ella Gertrude Clanton Thomas wrote in her diary that the abolition of slavery had forced her to acknowledge "how intimately my faith in revelations and my faith in the institution of slavery had been woven together." Following emancipation and the defeat of the Confederacy, her "faith in God's Holy Book was terribly shaken." Even prayer could not assuage her doubts, for when she opened the Bible "the numerous allusions to slavery mocked me. Our cause was lost. Good men had had faith in that cause. Earnest prayers had ascended from honest hearts—Was so much faith to be lost? I was bewildered—I felt all this and *could not* see God's hand."

Gertrude Thomas did not publish the diary in which she recorded the doubts that wracked her in the wake of defeat. Shaken at the collapse of her world, she set herself to putting her life back together as best she could. Others throughout the South did the same. And most of them made their peace with defeat as an expression of God's will without repudiating their previous certainty that they had fought for his cause against the Antichrist. But soul-searching and moments of doubt there were, even as the struggle to reconstruct private lives merged with a larger struggle to reconstruct sectional pride. Men like Bledsoe and Lee recognized the importance of reclaiming the righteousness and legitimacy of the Confederacy, if only to justify the sacrifices that the war had extracted from so many. Davis and his generals believed that they must defend their reputations before the bar of history. Many private citizens with no public honor to defend had a harder time of it. At least in the short run, the devastation of their lives seemed to swamp their concerns about the meaning of the struggle.

But as the South began to recover and lives resumed some semblance of a normal pattern, Southern men and women began to collect and sort their memories. And as they did, they began to reclaim their own experience of the past. Since the 1880s, the publication of diaries, journals, memoirs, and letters that capture the events and meaning of the war to those who, on the front or at home, participated in it has continued virtually unabated. Taken together, the disparate personal records of those who lived in and through the Confederacy—from the memoirs of generals to the letters of ordinary soldiers, from the diaries of elite ladies to the plaintive letters of farm wives, from the letters and affidavits of slaves and former slaves to the reflections of ministers and intellectuals—constitute the living witness, if not necessarily the "vindication" that Lee feared the South might lack, a testimonial to the spirit and conviction of those who survived and those who did not.

[*For further discussion of letters from the war front, see* Soldiers. *See also biographies of numerous figures mentioned herein.*]

BIBLIOGRAPHY

Diaries and Journals

Andrews, Eliza Frances. *The War-Time Journal of a Georgia Girl.* Edited by Spencer Bidwell King, Jr. Macon, Ga., 1960.

Breckinridge, Lucy Gilmer. *Lucy Breckinridge of Grove Hill: The Journal of a Virginia Girl, 1862–1864.* Edited by Mary D. Robertson. Kent, Ohio, 1979.

Buck, Lucy Rebecca. *Sad Earth, Sweet Heavens: The Diary of Lucy Rebecca Buck during the War between the States, Front Royal, Virginia, December 25, 1861–April 15, 1865.* Edited by William P. Buck. Birmingham, Ala., 1973.

Burge, Dolly Sumner Lunt. *Diary.* Edited by James I. Robertson, Jr. Athens, Ga., 1962.

Chesnut, Mary Boykin. *Mary Chesnut's Civil War.* Edited by C. Vann Woodward. New Haven, 1981.

Coleman, Ann Raney. *Victorian Lady on the Texas Frontier: The Journal of Ann Raney Coleman.* Edited by C. Richard King. Norman, Okla., 1971.

Crossley, Martha Jane. "A Patriotic Confederate Woman's War Diary, 1862–1863." Edited by H. E. Sterkx. *Alabama Historical Quarterly* 20 (1958): 611–617.

Dawson, Sarah Morgan. *A Confederate Girl's Diary.* Edited by James I. Robertson, Jr. Bloomington, Ind., 1960.

Edmonston, Catherine Ann Devereux. *Journal of a Secesh Lady: The Diary of Catherine Ann Devereux Edmonston, 1860–1866.* Edited by Beth Gilbert Crabtree and James W. Patton. Raleigh, N.C., 1979.

Gray, Virginia Davis. "Life in Confederate Arkansas: The Diary of Virginia Davis Gray, 1863–1865." Edited by Carl H. Moneyhon. *Arkansas Historical Quarterly* 42 (Spring 1983): 47–85; 42 (Summer 1983): 134–169.

Grimball, Meta Morris. Journal. Grimball Family Papers. Southern Historical Collection. University of North Carolina Library.

Hague, Parthenia Antoinette. *A Blockaded Family: Life in Southern Alabama during the Civil War.* Edited by Elizabeth Fox-Genovese. Lincoln, Neb., 1991.

Hardin, Elizabeth Pendleton. *The Private War of Lizzie Hardin: A Kentucky Confederate Girl's Diary of the Civil War in Kentucky, Virginia, Tennessee, Alabama, and Georgia.* Edited by G. Glenn Clift. Frankfort, Ky., 1963.

Holmes, Emma. *The Diary of Miss Emma Holmes, 1861–1866.* Edited by John F. Marszalek. Baton Rouge, La., 1979.

Ingraham, Mrs. Alfred. "The Vicksburg Diary of Mrs. Alfred Ingraham (May 2–June 13, 1863)." Edited by W. Maury Darst. *Journal of Mississippi History* 44 (May 1982): 148–179.

Jones, J. B. *A Rebel War Clerk's Diary.* Edited by Earl Schenck Miers. New York, 1961.

Jones, Mary Sharp, and Mary Sharp Jones Mallard. *"Yankees a' comming": One Month's Experience during the Invasion of Liberty County, Georgia, 1864–1865.* Edited by Haskel Monroe. Tuscaloosa, Ala., 1959.

Kean, Robert G. H. *Inside the Confederate Government.* New York, 1957.

LeConte, Emma. *When the World Ended: The Diary of Emma LeConte.* Edited by Earl Schenck Miers. New York, 1957.

Morgan, Sarah. *The Civil War Diary of Sarah Morgan.* Edited by Charles East. Athens, Ga., 1991.

Pember, Phoebe Yates. *A Southern Woman's Story: Life in Confederate Richmond, Including Unpublished Letters Written from the Chimborazo Hospital.* Edited by Bell Irwin Wiley. Jackson, Tenn., 1959.

Smedes, Susan Dabney. *Memorials of a Southern Planter.* Edited by Fletcher M. Green. New York, 1965.

Stone, Kate. *Brokenburn: The Journal of Kate Stone, 1861–1868.* Edited by John Q. Anderson. Baton Rouge, La., 1955.

Thomas, Ella Gertrude Clanton. *The Secret Eye: The Journal of Ella Gertrude Clanton Thomas, 1848–1889.* Edited by Virginia Ingraham Burr. Chapel Hill, N.C., 1990.

Torrence, Leonidas. "The Road to Gettysburg: The Diary and Letters of Leonidas Torrence of the Gaston Guards." Edited by Haskell Monroe. *North Carolina Historical Review* 36 (October 1959): 476–517.

Tucker, John S. "The Diary of John S. Tucker: Confederate Soldier from Alabama." Edited by Gary Wilson. *Alabama Historical Quarterly* 43 (1981): 5–33.

Letters

Barr, James Michael, ed. *Confederate War Correspondence of James Michael Barr and Wife Rebecca Ann Dowling Barr.* Taylors, S.C., 1963.

Glover, Robert W., ed. "The War Letters of a Texas Conscript in Arkansas." *Arkansas Historical Quarterly* 20 (1961): 355–387.

Goree, Langston James, ed. *The Thomas Jewett Goree Letters.* Vol. 1. Bryan, Tex., 1981.

Groene, Bertram H., ed. "Civil War Letters of Colonel David Lang." *Florida Historical Quarterly* 54 (1976): 340–366.

Herd, Elmer Don, Jr., ed. "Sue Sparks Keitt to a Northern Friend, March 4, 1861." *South Carolina Historical Magazine* 62 (April 1961): 82–87.

Hodges, Ellen E., and Stephen Kerber, eds. "Children of Honor: Letters of Winston and Octavia Stephens, 1861–1862." *Florida Historical Quarterly* 56 (1977): 45–74.

Hodges, Ellen E., and Stephen Kerber, eds. " 'Rogues and Black Hearted Scamps': Civil War Letters of Winston and Octavia Stephens, 1862–1863." *Florida Historical Quarterly* 57 (1978): 54–82.

McInty, Garnie W., ed. "The Human Side of War: Letters between a Bienville Parish Civil War Soldier and His Wife." *North Louisiana Historical Association Journal* 13, nos. 2–3 (1982): 59–81.

Reynolds, Donald E., ed. "A Mississippian in Lee's Army: The Letters of Leander Huckaby." *Journal of Mississippi History* 36 (February 1974): 53–67; 36 (May 1974): 165–178; 36 (August 1974): 273–288.

Thomas, Cornelius M. Dickinson, ed. *Letters from the Colonel's Lady: Correspondence of Mrs. (Col.) William Lamb Written from Fort Fisher, N.C., C.S.A., to Her Parents in Providence, R.I., U.S.A., December 1861 to January 1865.* Winnabow, N.C., 1965.

Wiley, Bell Irwin, ed., with Lucy E. Fay. *This Infernal War: The Confederate Letters of Edwin H. Fay.* Austin, Tex., 1958.

Memoirs

Alexander, Edward Porter. *Fighting for the Confederacy: The Personal Recollections of General Edward Porter Alexander.* Chapel Hill, N.C., 1989.

Alexander, Edward Porter. *Military Memoirs of a Confederate: A Critical Narrative.* New York, 1907.

Beauregard, P. G. T. *A Commentary on the Campaign and Battle of Manassas.* New York, 1891.

Davis, Jefferson. *The Rise and Fall of the Confederate Government.* 2 vols. New York, 1881.

De Leon, Thomas Cooper. *Belles, Beaux, and Brains of the '60s.* New York, 1909.

De Leon, Thomas Cooper. *Four Years in Rebel Capitals: An Inside View of Life in the Southern Confederacy, from Birth to Death.* Edited by E. B. Long. New York, 1962.

Gildersleeve, Basil. "The Creed of the Old South." *Atlantic Monthly* 69 (January 1892): 75–87.

Giles, Val C. *Rags and Hope: The Recollections of Val C. Giles, Four Years with Hood's Brigade, Fourth Texas Infantry, 1861–1865.* Edited by Mary Lasswell. New York, 1961.

Hood, John Bell. *Advance and Retreat: Personal Experiences in the United States and Confederate Armies.* Edited by Richard N. Current. Bloomington, Ind., 1959.

Johnston, John. "The Civil War Reminiscences of John Johnston, 1861–1865." Edited by William T. Alderson. *Tennessee Historical Quarterly* 13 (1954): 65–82, 156–178, 244–276, 329–354; 14 (1955): 43–81, 142–175.

Johnston, Joseph E. *Narrative of Military Operations.* New York, 1874.

Jones, Rev. J. William. *Christ in the Camp; or, Religion in Lee's Army.* Richmond, Va., 1888.

Lee, Robert E. *The Wartime Papers of Robert E. Lee.* Edited by Clifford Dowdey and Louis H. Manarin. Boston, 1961.

Longstreet, James. *From Manassas to Appomattox: Memoirs of the Civil War in America.* Philadelphia, 1896. Reprint, edited by James I. Robertson, Jr. Bloomington, Ind., 1960.

Watkins, Sam R. *"Co. Aytch" Maury Grays: First Tennessee Regiment; or, A Side Show of the Big Show.* Nashville, Tenn., 1882. Reprint, edited by Bell I. Wiley. Jackson, Tenn., 1952.

Collections and Secondary Sources

Berlin, Ira, Barbara J. Fields, Thavolia Glymph, Joseph P. Reidy, and Leslie Rowland, eds. *The Destruction of Slavery.* Ser. 1, vol. 1 of *Freedom: A Documentary History of Emancipation, 1861–1867.* [Freedmen's Bureau papers.] New York, 1985.

Elliott, Colleen Morse, and Louise Armstrong Moxley Easley, eds. *The Tennessee Civil War Veterans Questionnaires.* Compiled by Gustavus W. Dyer and John Trotwood Moore. Columbia, S.C., 1985.

Harwell, Richard Barksdale, ed. *The Confederate Reader.* New York, 1957.

Horn, Stanley F., ed. *Tennessee's War, 1861–1865: Described by Participants.* Nashville, Tenn., 1965.

Jones, Katharine M. *Ladies of Richmond, Confederate Capital.* Indianapolis, Ind., 1955.

Jones, Katharine M., ed. *Heroines of Dixie: Confederate Women Tell Their Story of the War.* Indianapolis, Ind., 1955.

Rawick, George P., ed. *The American Slave: A Composite Autobiography.* 19 vols. Westport, Conn., 1972.

Rawick, George P., ed. *The American Slave: A Composite Autobiography.* Supplement. 12 vols. Westport, Conn., 1977.

ELIZABETH FOX-GENOVESE

DIBRELL, GEORGE GIBBS

DIBRELL, GEORGE GIBBS (1822–1888), brigadier general and U.S. congressman. Dibrell was born at Sparta, Tennessee, on April 12, 1822. Reared and educated in Tennessee, he briefly attended the East Tennessee University in Knoxville. Afterward, Dibrell engaged in numerous occupations: clerk in the Bank of Tennessee, justice of the peace and clerk of White County, merchant, and planter. He was elected to the Tennessee House of Representatives in 1861 and to the state secession convention.

Although he personally opposed Tennessee's leaving the Union, Dibrell joined the Confederate army as a private once secession became an accomplished fact. Subsequently, he recruited and became colonel of the Eighth Tennessee Cavalry, serving with distinction under Brig. Gen. Nathan Bedford Forrest in the latter's mid-December 1862 raid into western Tennessee. Although given the command of a brigade under Forrest, Dibrell did not actually receive a promotion until January 28, 1865.

Following service with Forrest in 1863, he joined the cavalry command of Maj. Gen. Joseph Wheeler. Near the end of the war, Dibrell fought in North and South Carolina. He joined President Jefferson Davis in the latter's retreat from Richmond in 1865. Dibrell's command provided an escort for the fleeing Confederate entourage. He remained with Davis until the party disbanded near Washington, Georgia. Subsequently, Dibrell received a parole on May 9, 1865.

Following the war, Dibrell had a distinguished career as a merchant, financier, and member of Congress (1874–1884); he was also president of the Southwestern Railroad and principal developer of the Bon Air coal mines. He remained in Sparta, Tennessee, until his death on May 9, 1888.

BIBLIOGRAPHY

Johnson, Allen, and Dumas Malone, eds. *Dictionary of American Biography.* New York, 1937–1964.

Speer, William S. *Sketches of Prominent Tennesseans.* Easley, S.C., 1978.

Wills, Brian Steel. *A Battle from the Start: The Life of Nathan Bedford Forrest.* New York, 1992.

Wyeth, John Allan. *Life of General Nathan Bedford Forrest.* New York, 1899. Reprint, Baton Rouge, La., 1989.

BRIAN S. WILLS

DICKINSON, JAMES SHELTON (1818–1882),

congressman from Alabama. Born January 18, 1818, in Spotsylvania County, Virginia, Dickinson moved with his family to Clarke County, Alabama, in 1821 and attended school in Grove Hill before returning to Virginia to attend law school at the University of Virginia. After graduation in 1844 he opened a law practice in Grove Hill. Dickinson was elected to the Alabama Senate in 1853 as a Democrat; he served one term. In 1860 he was a presidential elector pledged to John C. Breckinridge. When the war began in 1861, he raised and equipped at his own expense an infantry company for the Confederacy. In 1863 he was elected to the Second Confederate Congress, where he was a member of the Claims, Commerce, and Conference committees. Unlike opponents of the war elected from Alabama in 1863, he supported legislation to strengthen the Confederate central government. He voted to double the tithe on agriculture and to requisition state governors for soldiers absent without leave. He served one term and then returned to Grove Hill, where he resumed his law practice. He died there on July 23, 1882.

BIBLIOGRAPHY

Owen, Thomas McAdory. *History of Alabama and Dictionary of Alabama Biography.* 4 vols. Chicago, 1921.

Wakelyn, Jon L. *Biographical Directory of the Confederacy.* Edited by Frank E. Vandiver. Westport, Conn., 1977.

Warner, Ezra J., and W. Buck Yearns. *Biographical Register of the Confederate Congress.* Baton Rouge, La., 1975.

SARAH WOOLFOLK WIGGINS

DIPLOMACY.

From the outset of the Civil War Confederate leaders sought to exercise the prerogatives of nationhood by securing European recognition and, through direct negotiations, to tap whatever foreign interests might exist in the perpetuation of an independent Southern republic. As early as March 1861 President Jefferson Davis, with the approval of the Confederate Congress, appointed William Lowndes Yancey, Pierre A. Rost, and A. Dudley Mann as commissioners to Great Britain, France, Russia, and Belgium, empowering them with the authority to establish diplomatic relations with those countries. Their instructions, prepared by Secretary of State Robert Toombs, emphasized the need to confirm the South's legitimacy as an independent nation—its long and careful deliberations that had led to separation, its constitutional government, its strength and determination to defend its political integrity. The Confederacy's free trade and liberal navigation policies, Toombs added, would ensure accessible and profitable markets for the manufactures of Europe. Toombs instructed the commissioners to propose treaties of friendship, commerce, and navigation with the nations of Europe when they received official recognition.

Early Optimism for Recognition. Confederate leaders had reason to anticipate the triumph of their diplomacy. Britain's powerful conservative classes, long cynical toward the democratic experiment in America, saw clearly that the Civil War placed democratic institutions on trial. The United States itself had passed beyond the control of the Old World, but if the American people were determined to demonstrate the failure of their political institutions, reactionary Europe could encourage them in their effort so that the work of destruction might triumph. In July 1861 *Blackwood's Magazine* declared: "It is precisely because we do *not* share the admiration of America for her institutions and political tendencies that we do not now see in the impending change an event altogether to be deplored." Even much of Britain's liberal sentiment turned instinctively against the North. Sympathetic to the idea of self-determination, it questioned Washington's right to employ force in repressing the will of a minority that preferred independence. Many British liberals, moreover, were attracted to the South's free trade principles. Édouard de Stoeckl, the Russian chargé d'affaires in Washington, observed that British leaders anticipated the elimination of an Atlantic rival. "The Cabinet in London," he reported, "is watching attentively the internal dissensions of the Union and awaits the result with an impatience which it has difficulty in disguising."

During April 1861 the Confederate objective of securing Europe's recognition seemed propitious. If many in Britain favored the breakup of the American Republic for moral, political, and economic reasons, French emperor Napoleon III understood that his dream of a colonial empire in Mexico would face far less challenge from an independent Confederacy than from a reconstructed Union. Shortly after the Fort Sumter crisis in April, Henri Mercier, the French minister in Washington, proposed to British minister Lord Lyons that they seek authority to recognize the Confederacy at the appropriate moment. The United States had recognized other countries without regard to their revolutionary origins. Lyons agreed in principle but believed that their governments should carry the responsibility for determining the time and mode of the decision, especially since recognition would damage British relations with the government in Washington. For Stoeckl the rupture between North and South was irrevocable; strict impartiality between the warring sections would serve no European interest. "The recognition of the Southern Confederacy by France and England," he wrote on April 14, "will offer us a very natural excuse to follow their example in recognizing a *fait accompli.*"

Conscious of Confederate weakness on the high seas as well as the North's immense shipping trade, President Davis, on April 17, issued a proclamation offering letters of marque and reprisal for privateers to prey on Northern commerce. Two days later President Abraham Lincoln, determined to deprive the Confederacy of all foreign imports, announced a blockade of the entire Southern coast. Lincoln, with the overwhelming support of the North, recognized but one objective: the reforging of the Union. Secession was unacceptable. Unless the North retreated from its demand for Southern capitulation, Confederate vice president Alexander H. Stephens responded, "no power on earth can arrest or prevent a most bloody conflict." Pursuing uncompromisable goals, the North and South after the firing on Fort Sumter faced total war. Lincoln's secretary of state, William H. Seward, reaffirmed the North's determination when, on April 23, he informed the governor of Maryland that the United States, under no circumstances, would permit the issues between North and South to be settled by foreign arbitrament. Any Anglo-French effort at mediation, he warned Mercier and Lyons, would constitute unwarranted intervention calling for total resistance.

Seward had warned Lyons earlier that, if war came, Britain would need to forgo the importation of Southern cotton for a time. The British minister observed that his country required Southern cotton and would obtain it one way or another. With news of the war, however, Queen Victoria, on May 13, issued a proclamation of neutrality, recognizing the South as a belligerent. France, Spain, the Netherlands, Brazil, and other maritime states followed the British lead. The Lincoln administration, joined by congressional leaders, resented deeply the European recognition of Southern belligerency. Seward responded by informing the British and French governments that the conflict between North and South was not war but a local insurrection of no legitimate concern to foreign powers. Seward instructed U.S. diplomats abroad to prevent any European recognition of the Confederate States of America. Lincoln added that Confederate privateering was piracy and all engaged in it would be treated as pirates.

Mann reached London on April 15; Yancey and Rost two weeks later. On May 3 they gained an informal interview with British foreign minister Lord John Russell. The commissioners argued the legitimacy of the Confederacy's existence, its determination to survive under its Constitution, and its intention to cultivate peaceful and mutually profitable relations with other countries. Such evidences of nationhood, they said, merited recognition. Russell declared that the matter rested with the cabinet; meanwhile he would not comment. Rost moved on to Paris where Count

de Morny, a confidant of Emperor Louis Napoleon, informed him that France and England had agreed to pursue identical policies toward the Confederate States, but that recognition was merely a matter of time. Britain and France, he said, understood their interests in Southern independence. In mid-July the commissioners reported that British opinion was undergoing an encouraging change, more and more convinced that the North could not subdue the South.

Washington discovered during April that the Confederate government had dispatched commissioners to the European capitals. Seward warned the French government that the United States would regard any communication between it and the Southern agents as injurious to American dignity and honor. When he learned that Lord Russell in London had received the commissioners informally, he prepared a letter, his famed Number 10 of May 21, so menacing that Lincoln modified some passages and eliminated others. Even in revised form the dispatch was little less than an ultimatum, suggesting that the United States would break diplomatic relations if Russell persisted in seeing the Southern envoys. Charles Francis Adams, the new U.S. minister, arrived in Britain on May 13, the day of the queen's proclamation. A few days later, in an interview with Russell, he condemned the British decision. Then on June 10 Adams received Seward's dispatch of May 21. He now informed Russell that any further relations between the British government and the Confederate commissioners, whether official or not, would constitute a manifestation of hostility toward the United States. Russell assured Adams that conversation was not recognition, and that he had no intention of seeing the Confederates again. Throughout the summer of 1861 Seward condemned the British and French governments for behaving as if the United States were at war. The country, he argued, faced a domestic disturbance that it would dispose of in its own way.

The Failure of King Cotton. What gave the South its presumption of success in its quest for European recognition was the alleged power of cotton. Toombs reminded the commissioners in March that the annual yield of British manufacturing based on Southern cotton totaled $600 million. "The British Ministry," he observed, "will comprehend fully the condition to which the British realm would be reduced if the supply of our staple should suddenly fail or even be considerably diminished." *De Bow's Review* predicted that the blockade would be "swept away by the English fleet of observation hovering on the Southern coasts to protect . . . the free flow of cotton to English and French factories." If cotton was king, the South had only to embargo that commodity to force Britain to destroy the blockade. The Confederate Congress refused to establish a formal embargo, but Committees of Public Safety in the Southern seaports effectively halted the export of cotton to Europe. Having burned much of the 1861 cotton crop, the

South had little to sell. The Confederacy gambled that the shortage of cotton would destroy British adherence to the blockade. The added realization that the blockade, maintained largely by lightly armed merchant vessels, was ineffective reinforced this conviction. The Treaty of Paris (1856) had declared not only that a neutral flag covers enemy goods, except contraband, but also that a blockade, to be legally binding, must also be effective. Still the British government, ignoring the blockade's weakness as well as its doubtful legality, treated it with great circumspection. The dearth of cotton for shipment not only failed to eliminate the blockade but also created resentment and the unwanted impression that the blockade was effective. The huge surplus of raw cotton in British and French warehouses merely compounded the evidence of King Cotton's weakness.

In September President Davis, with congressional support, assigned separate commissioners to the principal governments of Europe. He appointed Mann to Brussels, James M. Mason to London, and John Slidell to Paris. The new secretary of state, Robert M. T. Hunter of Virginia, instructed Mason to explain to the British government the true position of the Confederate States as an independent, permanent, and constitutional nation. The North, Hunter added, had rejected peaceful separation and then subjected the South to a barbarous, uncivilized war. In taking up arms the Confederate States appealed to the world, not for aid and alliances, "but for the moral might which they would derive from holding a recognized place as a free and independent people." Six months of fighting, including the Confederate victory at Manassas in July, had demonstrated the South's capacity and determination to maintain its independence. If recognition must finally come, it appeared the duty of nations to place their moral weight immediately on the side of peace.

The *Trent* Affair and the U.S. Blockade. Mason and Slidell, with secretaries George Eustis and James Macfarland, left Charleston on October 12, ran the Union blockade, and made their way to Havana. There, on November 7, they embarked on *Trent,* a British mail steamer bound for England. On the following day Capt. Charles Wilkes of USS *San Jacinto* removed them and their secretaries from the British vessel, permitting *Trent* to continue on its voyage. Wilkes took the Confederates to Fortress Monroe and then to Boston. Confederate officials and writers took hope from the realization that Wilkes had defied international law and insulted the British flag. Hunter assumed that the British, in protecting the right of asylum, would avenge the insolence. Britain, declared the Confederate press, would suffer an unmitigated insult or go to war. "If the insult goes unresented," the *Southern Literary Messenger* advised, "another too flagrant to be borne will inevitably follow."

From London the Confederate commissioners reported a wave of anger and resentment. They reminded Russell on November 27 that the Federal action was a violation of international law, not justified under any treaty between Britain and the United States. If Confederate citizens merited the protection of the British flag, the cabinet had no

JAMES M. MASON AND JOHN SLIDELL. Mason (at left) and Slidell, the Confederate commissioners to Europe seized aboard the British mail steamer *Trent*.

HARPER'S PICTORIAL HISTORY OF THE GREAT REBELLION

choice but to demand the restoration of Mason and Slidell to their former positions. In his response of December 7 Russell declined to enter into any discussion of the *Trent* case, but the British government had already demanded the instant restitution of the captured Confederate leaders; unless the North yielded, Rost observed, war was certain. Seward recognized the justice of the British case, as well as the warlike mood of the British people, and brought the controversy to a deliberate end. With the release of Mason and Slidell, Yancey predicted, the British government would maintain a "frigid neutrality" toward the Confederacy. As the year ended, the Confederate commissioners could only lament the apparent control that Seward and Adams exerted over European policy.

Mason, Slidell, and their secretaries reached London on January 29, 1862. Slidell and Eustis departed for Paris the following morning. Mason found himself surrounded by Confederate sympathizers, but the ministry, he reported, remained reticent on the questions of blockade and recognition. In late January the British Foreign Office submitted to Europe's governments the Union practice of clogging harbors by sinking ships loaded with stones; all agreed that the damage to Charleston Harbor was an outrage. The British government complained to Washington but in no way challenged the legitimacy of the Federal blockade. On February 7 Mason requested and received an interview with Lord Russell; it resolved nothing. Mason concluded that the British cabinet would act on the blockade if pressed by the House of Commons, but the debates of early March convinced him that Parliament would never force any change in British policy. Indeed, on February 11 Russell informed Lyons that as long as the Federal government maintained ships in sufficient numbers, not to prevent access to any harbor, but merely to render entering or leaving dangerous, Britain would regard the blockade as effectual under international law.

Slidell, on February 5, asked French minister Antoine Édouard Thouvenel for an interview. Thouvenel informed Rost that the French government would welcome a discussion of the blockade but was not prepared to entertain the question of recognition. If the Federal blockade was so ineffective, Thouvenel asked Slidell, why did so little cotton reach neutral ports? French merchants had asked Slidell that same troubling question. Slidell explained that the blockade runners were generally small vessels; for them turpentine provided greater profit than an equal volume of cotton. Slidell acknowledged that the blockade, despite its ineffectiveness, still managed to eliminate large neutral vessels whose owners preferred to avoid risks. In reporting his interview Slidell advised Hunter that "two or three steamers arriving at Havre with cotton on French account, after having run the blockade, would go further to convince people here of its inefficiency than all the certified lists from our customhouses." Slidell added that France was sympathetic to the Confederate cause and would challenge the blockade if Britain, with its greater interests, would take the initiative. Unfortunately, Slidell observed in March, British policy was not promising. Russell's definition of a blockade, he complained to French officials, merely resuscitated the discarded notion of paper blockades.

Confederate Public Relations Efforts and Pro-Southern Sympathies. Confederate leverage in seeking European recognition required not only the power to compel attention but also popular sympathy for the Southern cause. In large measure the Confederate commissioners carried the burden of informing Europe's political and business leaders of the validity, strength, and promise of the Southern independence movement. But in November 1861 Hunter dispatched Henry Hotze, a young and able journalist, to direct the Confederacy's educational program in Europe. In London Hotze detected not only the North's near monopoly of the news but also the strange capacity of its agents to antagonize through exaggerated claims to power. Hotze quickly gained access to the *London Post* and by April 1862 was writing editorials for the *Standard* and the *London Herald,* a leading opposition paper. In May he established his own journal, the *Index.* Determined to influence British leaders, Hotze avoided giving offense. His fair and accurate reporting of battles and commercial opportunities won respect and a wide British following.

Meanwhile President Davis sent Edwin de Leon to France as a Confederate agent. De Leon failed from the outset. Slidell denied him the support required to gain access to French leaders of importance. With de Leon's dismissal in late 1863, Hotze took up the Confederacy's educational program in France. His fairness again gave him access to important news agencies. He won widespread support among French officials, merchants, shipbuilders, and others who favored the Confederacy, but he could not undermine French liberal attachment to the United States. However pervasive Europe's pro-Confederate sympathies, they had no bearing on the decisions of the European governments.

For many Europeans Northern industrial and financial advantages had at first created doubts that the South could sustain even a defensive war. But the rout of the Union forces at Manassas in July 1861 dispelled the illusion of a certain and easy Northern victory. The Southern commissioners reported that the Confederate triumph produced a powerful sensation in Europe. Benjamin Moran, assistant secretary in the U.S. legation in London, lamented: "This defeat will have a bad effect for the North in Europe, & will raise the hopes of the rebels." On August 14 the commissioners reminded Lord Russell that Britain had recognized countries that had demonstrated far less capacity to maintain their independence than had the Confederacy at Manassas. Russell offered no response.

Yet so lacking in energy and purpose was the Northern war effort that foreign observers now questioned the capacity of the Union to reconquer the South. Not even the Federal capture of Fort Henry, Fort Donelson, and New Orleans between February and April 1862 convinced the British of Northern superiority. "All the successes of the North," Lord Russell observed in April, "do not persuade me they can conquer the South." The Federal capture of New Orleans challenged the illusion of Confederate power, but Gen. George B. McClellan's retreat from Richmond in early July confirmed the widespread conviction among European observers that the Union was doomed. "It is plain," declared the *Times* (London), "that the time is approaching when Europe will have to think seriously of its relations to the two belligerents in the American war." In Parliament William S. Lindsay advocated British mediation to end the apparently interminable and pointless struggle. Lindsay withdrew the motion when Prime Minister Lord Palmerston warned Parliament that mediation meant war.

Mason noted in June that the gradual exhaustion of the cotton supply was driving British sentiment toward the Confederacy. He described the impact on Lancashire:

The cotton *famine* (as it is now every where termed), prevailing and increasing in the manufacturing districts, is attracting the most serious attention. Parochial relief . . . is found utterly inadequate to prevent *actual starvation* of men, women, and children, who, from such causes, are found dead in their houses. Private contributions . . . do not and cannot remove the sufferers from the starvation point; and very soon they must be left to die, unless aid is afforded from the treasury.

Clearly British policies that deprived the mills of Southern cotton were becoming matters of public concern, especially as the Lancashire mills in 1862 began to deplete the stores of raw cotton in British warehouses. By July Britain's stock of 1.2 million bales had declined to 200,000; by September only 100,000 remained, with the mills consuming 30,000 bales a week. This proved to be the climax of the cotton famine, although unemployment and destitution among the mill workers continued. During 1863 both the cotton supply and employment began to recover, partially from successful blockade running in the South and partially from increased imports of raw cotton from India, China, Brazil, and Egypt. In France the cotton famine and recovery corresponded to that of Great Britain.

By July 1862 the high cost of British neutrality and the Confederate successes in the field had convinced Mason and Slidell that the time had come to demand formal recognition as a matter of right. But under strong advice from friends in Parliament, they agreed to await a more opportune occasion. Responding to the news of Confederate successes in Virginia, Slidell, on July 20, gained an interview at Vichy with the French emperor, who stressed his troubles in Mexico and fear of a collision with the United States. Slidell then argued the Confederate case for immediate recognition in a long letter to Thouvenel. The Confederate States, he wrote, now stood before the world as an established nation meriting immediate recognition. During their conversation on July 23, Thouvenel advised Slidell to withhold his demand. "In a few weeks," said the French minister, "when we shall have further news from the seat of war, we can better judge the expediency of so grave a step, and the English Government may perhaps then be prepared to cooperate with us, which they certainly are not now." When Slidell urged mediation and assured Thouvenel that the South would welcome it, Thouvenel responded that both Mercier and Lyons insisted that an offer of mediation would create exasperation in the North and achieve nothing. In London, on July 24, Russell explained British reluctance to offer mediation by observing that neither the North nor the South would compromise its objectives. Mason responded that all Europe understood the finality of the separation; Britain's refusal to grant recognition merely prolonged a ruinous and hopeless war. Russell observed that the ultimate outcome of the American war remained uncertain. When the South had finally resisted all efforts to conquer it, other countries might justly recognize its independence. That time had not arrived.

In September Mason and Slidell assured Judah P. Benjamin, Confederate secretary of state since March, that the British and French governments were reconsidering their previous decisions to avoid any involvement in American affairs. In mid-September the earl of Shaftesbury, returning from a vacation in the south of France, visited Slidell in Paris to inform him that Britain was fast approaching a decision to intervene. The British ministry, encouraged by the South's victory in the Second Battle of Manassas in late August, had taken up the question of mediation. Palmerston, responding to Second Manassas, penned a note to Russell on September 14: "The Federals . . . got a very complete smashing. . . . Even Washington and Baltimore may fall into the hands of the Confederates. If this should happen, would it not be time for us to consider whether in such a state of things England and France might not address the contending parties and recommend an arrangement upon the basis of separation?"

The Confederacy's Opportunity Passes. On September 14 and 15 Gen. Robert E. Lee moved his forces into Maryland. When the news of Lee's costly battle at Sharpsburg and the Confederate retreat across the Potomac reached Europe in late September, Slidell predicted that the Northern success in checking the Southern advance would serve as another pretext for British procrastination. Indeed, on October 2 Palmerston reminded Russell that mediation based on separation would benefit the South; the North, therefore, would resist such interference until additional

Southern victories compelled it to capitulate. Ignoring Palmerston's caution, William E. Gladstone, chancellor of the exchequer, declared at Newcastle on October 7: "Jefferson Davis and other leaders have made an army, and are making, it appears, a navy, and they have made what is more than either, they have made a nation." Supported by Gladstone, Russell in mid-October prepared a memorandum arguing for mediation; the cabinet, including Palmerston, rejected it.

In Paris Slidell, on October 26, informed the new French minister, Édouard Drouyn de Lhuys, that the British cabinet, except for Gladstone, stood firm against mediation. If the French government favored the Confederacy, as the emperor insisted it did, the time had come for France to act alone. Two days later the emperor called Slidell to St. Cloud and again expressed his sympathy for the South. To act without Britain, however, would render France vulnerable to British policy and expose it to Washington's wrath. He informed Slidell, however, that on October 15 the king of Belgium had advocated a joint French-British-Russian proposal for a six-month armistice with a lifting of the Federal blockade. Slidell doubted that Britain and Russia would accept mediation; nor was he convinced that the emperor would act. Yet on November 8 Mason reported that Britain and Russia had received such a proposal. On that day the Russian government informed the British Foreign Office that it had rejected the emperor's strategy. On November 12 the British cabinet, convinced that the North would reject mediation, reached the same decision. With good reason Richmond's dismay over the failure of mediation was profound; never again would the European powers consider such a direct involvement in the American war.

In January 1863 Mason, responding to Benjamin's repeated instructions, pressed Lord Russell on the issue of the blockade. Mason protested the British refusal to explain why, in its modification of the doctrine of blockade, it denied the Confederacy the historic rights of belligerency. Russell repeated what he had written to Lord Lyons in February 1862, that the Declaration of Paris did not demand that a port be blockaded so that no vessel could gain access, whatever its size or the prevailing conditions. Storms and winds, he argued, could not render a blockade nonbinding on neutrals. Mason responded in February that nowhere did the Declaration of Paris refer to winds or storms or the nature and size of vessels engaged in blockade running. One vessel, wrote Mason, had evaded the blockade at Charleston thirty times. Russell terminated the exchange on February 27 by asserting that he had explained the British position and did not care to discuss it further. In Paris Slidell took hope from assurances that French sentiment continued to favor the South. The emperor, he wrote in January, would pursue mediation again, either alone or with the concurrence of Britain and Russia. As the weeks passed, Mann in mid-March expressed his growing disillusionment:

> So far as I can judge . . . the chances for an early European recognition of our independence, have not increased in the slightest degree. . . . The Emperor of the French seems to be just as far as ever from taking the initiative in this regard.

No longer did Confederate successes in the field—the victory at Fredericksburg in December or even that at Chancellorsville in May—seem to matter.

Naval Purchases Abroad. Even as the British government rejected Southern appeals for recognition or any direct intervention in the American war, it enabled the Confederacy to achieve remarkable successes on the high seas. As early as May 1861 Confederate Secretary of the Navy Stephen R. Mallory instructed James D. Bulloch of Georgia to buy or order six vessels in England to prey on Northern commerce. At the same time the Confederate Congress appropriated funds for the purchase of two ironclads and dispatched James H. North to procure them in France under the assumption that the French government favored the destruction of the blockade. Bulloch, finding no cruisers available, contracted for the construction of two vessels. North discovered that France was not prepared to sell ironclads. Eventually, in May 1862, he arranged for the construction of a giant ironclad by the Thompson works of Glasgow. In July Bulloch contracted with the Laird Brothers of Birkenhead for two rams.

As early as February 1862 the U.S. consul in Liverpool, Thomas H. Dudley, reported to Adams that Liverpool shipbuilders were constructing a Confederate cruiser, *Oreto*. Lord Russell insisted that an Italian company had ordered the ship. *Oreto* cleared for Palermo but sailed to the Bahamas where, armed and equipped, it became the Confederate commerce raider *Florida*. During April Adams learned that another Confederate cruiser, *No. 290,* was under construction in Liverpool. Too late Russell ordered the vessel stopped. It departed suddenly in July, acquired armament in the Azores, and became the famed Confederate raider *Alabama*.

Despite Adams's continued warnings that one day the United States would demand compensation for the damage wrought by British-made Confederate commerce raiders, the British permitted additional vessels to escape during the early months of 1863. But in September Adams threatened the British government with war if it permitted the Laird rams, then in the water, to escape. In seizing them the British government terminated the Confederate acquisition of British-made vessels. Cruisers already in the Atlantic continued their devastating assaults on Northern commerce. Later Russell, in conversation with Adams, condemned the South for making Britain the base of its maritime operations.

Final Diplomatic Efforts. As late as June 1863 Slidell continued to press the French government for recognition, arguing that the capacity of the Confederate States to maintain their independence was beyond question. He informed the emperor that the British cabinet denied recognition not because it doubted the South's eventual success but because it desired the breakup of the Union and was confident of a Confederate victory. France could stop the prolonged conflict by recognizing the Confederacy. The emperor responded that any proposal for recognition submitted to the London government to stop the war would reach Washington and expose an isolated France to U.S. retribution. At risk was not only French commerce but also the entire French effort in Mexico. France could not afford to move without Britain. Again, during the parliamentary debates of July, Palmerston, supported in his judgment by the Union victories at Vicksburg and Gettysburg, refused to budge. Concluding that Britain would never recognize Mason, Benjamin on August 4 instructed him to conclude his mission and, with his secretary, withdraw from London.

Mason received Benjamin's letter on September 21 and informed Russell of his impending departure. Russell, in a brief note, observed that he had explained the British refusal to recognize him on previous occasions. "These reasons," he concluded, "are still in force, and it is not necessary to repeat them." Having lost faith in Britain, Benjamin turned to France for support in breaking the blockade; the French government, still refusing to act unilaterally, rejected responsibility for Europe's acceptance of the blockade as well as any intention of courting trouble by challenging it.

Throughout 1864 Confederate leaders hoped that their assertions of ultimate victory would still bring the needed European support. By summer the Confederacy's fate in the courts of Europe hinged on the success or failure of Gen. Ulysses S. Grant's assault on Richmond. Mason, now in London under a broad commission to serve the Confederacy wherever he might be effective, reported optimistically in June that a Southern victory in Virginia would still compel the British ministry to act. In Paris Slidell complained that the French emperor was too concerned with his problems elsewhere, but still agreed with Mason that a decisive Confederate victory at Richmond would lead to Anglo-French intervention.

To reassure Europe of the South's determination to win, the Confederate Congress, on June 14, issued a manifesto to the governments of Europe, which declared that the South, in its quest for immunity against external interference, committed its cause to "the enlightened judgment of the world." In his final appeal to Europe on December 27, 1864, Benjamin wondered why Britain and France, despite the South's continued resistance, had refused to recognize its independence. Concluding at last that the explanation lay in slavery, he dispatched Duncan F. Kenner, a member of Congress from Louisiana, on a secret mission to convey to Mason and Slidell his offer of emancipation in exchange for recognition. In Paris the emperor informed Slidell that such an offer would not have influenced his decision. Mason returned to London where, on March 14, 1865, Palmerston presented an identical response. Britain's earl of Donoughmore observed that two years earlier the offer might have mattered; in March 1865 Grant's campaign had eliminated the issue.

Lee's surrender terminated the Confederacy's diplomatic effort in Europe. Richmond's perennial pursuit of European recognition and trade was a major element in the entire Confederate war effort. Europe's recognition of Southern independence would have created diplomatic havoc in Washington. European defiance of the Federal blockade would have opened the South to the massive imports the Confederate war effort required. That Washington escaped such potentially costly external challenges was a measure of Seward's success in convincing the European governments that, whatever their interests in Southern independence, they could not intervene diplomatically without risking war. Europe's disinclination to fight the United States bound any European support of the Confederacy to the conviction that the South could triumph on its own. That conviction was never realized.

[*See also* Blockade, *overview article;* Canada; France; Great Britain; Laird Rams; Mexico; Monroe Doctrine; Propaganda; Russia; Spain; State Department; Trent Affair; *and biographies of numerous figures mentioned herein.*]

BIBLIOGRAPHY

Adams, Ephraim Douglas. *Great Britain and the American Civil War.* 2 vols. New York, 1925.

Callahan, James Morton. *Diplomatic History of the Southern Confederacy.* New York, 1901.

Case, Lynn M., and Warren F. Spencer. *The United States and France: Civil War Diplomacy.* Philadelphia, 1970.

Crook, David Paul. *The North, the South, and the Powers, 1861–1865.* New York, 1974.

Ellison, Mary L. *Support for Secession: Lancashire and the American Civil War.* Chicago, 1973.

Ferris, Norman B. *The Trent Affair: A Diplomatic Crisis.* Knoxville, Tenn., 1977.

Jordan, Donaldson, and Edwin J. Pratt. *Europe and the American Civil War.* Boston, 1931.

Meade, Robert Douthat. *Judah P. Benjamin: Confederate Statesman.* New York, 1943.

Merli, Frank J. *Great Britain and the Confederate Navy, 1861–1865.* Bloomington, Ind., 1970.

Owsley, Frank Lawrence. *King Cotton Diplomacy: Foreign Rela-*

tions of the Confederate States of America. Revised by Harriet Chappell Owsley. Chicago, 1959.

NORMAN A. GRAEBNER

DIRECT TAX ACT. At the time the Confederacy was established in February 1861, there had been no direct taxation of real estate or personal property in the United States since the War of 1812. Instead, the chief fiscal tool of the Federal government had been import duties. With a view to getting rid of the protective tariffs, some Southerners had proposed the abolition of the customs houses and the imposition of direct taxation. But fearful of any system in which the taxpayers knew how much they were paying, Congress retained the customs dues.

The Provisional Constitution of the Confederacy provided either that direct taxes could be apportioned among the states, each state to pay a fixed amount based on the last census (the old Federal system), or that the Confederacy, in the absence of a census, could levy a tax based on a fixed percentage of the assessed value of all property. Because the Confederacy never took a census of its own and refused to use the Federal census of 1860, and because the Permanent Constitution had no alternative provision for levying and collecting such a tax, the power of levying direct taxes expired to all practical purposes with the end of the provisional government on February 18, 1862.

In the congressional session on May 8, 1861, Secretary of the Treasury Christopher G. Memminger sought authorization to impose a direct tax on the Southern people. But lacking a letter of support from President Jefferson Davis for this radical measure, Congress tabled Memminger's request and asked him to furnish a report on direct taxes at its next session in July 1861.

In preparing this report, the secretary discovered that each state used a system unique to itself, so that Congress would have to devise its own program. He therefore proposed that $25 million be raised through a tax of fifty-four cents on each hundred dollars of assessed property. To be taxed were real estate, slaves, and personal property such as stocks, bonds, cattle, and merchandise.

Resistance to the war tax authorized by the act of August 19, 1861, was noisy and prolonged. Unable to attack this proposal on legal grounds, opponents claimed that a tax equal to only 2.5 percent of the South's Gross National Product would provoke armed resistance and the collapse of the Confederacy. The plain fact was that both within and outside Congress most owners of large slaveholdings expected to have their $3.5 billion stake in slavery protected without their having to make any sort of contribution for that purpose. They also assumed that the war would be short and Southern independence secured at little or no cost to themselves. Secretary Memminger inadvertently assisted such delusions by failing to make clear the direct connection between inadequate taxation and defeat. Gazeway B. Lamar, a Georgia banker, presciently observed that the Southern people must be prepared to pay heavy taxes. Otherwise, they might as well surrender immediately and hand over their slaves for emancipation by the Federal authorities.

Yet the law as finally enacted was riddled with exemptions that reduced tax yields by a third. Moreover, lacking prior experience in such measures, Congress made numerous drafting errors. Collection and assessment times were put off to too distant a day. No provisions were made for paying the assessors and collectors, for reimbursing them for their expenses, or for securing the cooperation of sheriffs, who held the state tax records. Moreover, in the interest of economy, too few personnel were provided for, so that the effectiveness of the tax depended upon the integrity of the taxpayer.

As finally passed, the act called for the appointment of a chief collector in each state and a collector in each county assisted by at least two assessors. Each citizen was to furnish a list of taxable property by a specified date. The necessity of collecting the tax directly from the public might be avoided if a state assumed the tax. In that case, the state would receive a 10-percent rebate on the amount it paid. Payment had to be in specie or Confederate Treasury notes only.

As a fiscal measure, this tax was not a success. There were long delays getting suitable persons to fill the various posts. The state governments issued their own currency in exchange for Confederate notes, thereby frustrating the whole purpose of the tax, which was to reduce inflation by retiring some of the excess Treasury notes. Assessments and checking the veracity of property declarations were hindered by states' giving encouragement to their sheriffs not to cooperate with the Confederate assessors. Moreover, because there was no centralized guidance from Richmond, appraisals varied widely from state to state. This was particularly true of slaves, whose average declared prices were much too low.

Texas and Mississippi, in the hope of evading payment entirely, refused to assume the tax, and the Treasury had to collect directly from the citizens. Only South Carolina took the Confederate records and collected the tax from its own citizens. Without doubt, however, the greatest deficiencies of the act were its failure to impose the tax each year for the duration of the war and its failure to demand a larger revenue of at least $40 million to $80 million a year.

BIBLIOGRAPHY

Ball, Douglas B. *Financial Failure and Confederate Defeat.* Urbana, Ill., and Chicago, 1991.
Schwab, John Christopher. *The Confederate States of America,*

1861–1865: A Financial and Industrial History of the South during the Civil War. New York, 1901.

Todd, Richard C. *Confederate Finance.* Athens, Ga., 1954.

DOUGLAS B. BALL

DISCOGRAPHY. Commercially recorded record albums featuring music of the Civil War date back to the 1940s, but it was only in the 1960s that recordings were issued that had some element of authenticity and were accompanied with adequate annotations. With the coming of compact discs in the late 1980s, many of these albums were reissued in digital sound. This discography deals with recordings that are widely available to a general audience. The issue number refers to the compact disc (CD) release unless otherwise indicated; most commercial companies have discontinued vinyl long playing (LP) versions of their albums.

Some albums attempt to include a cross section of the war's different types of music, and others feature a specific type or genre. One of the most faithful attempts to re-create the parlor music and sentimental songs of the age is New World Records' *Songs of the Civil War* (CD 202–2). Since parlor music especially was equally popular in the South and the North, the album relates to the Confederacy as much as the Union and contains rare recordings of popular songs like Will S. Hays's "Drummer Boy of Shiloh," as well as splendid notes and song texts. A related collection, though more focused on Northern songs, is *Who Shall Rule This Nation (Songs of Henry Clay Work,* Nonesuch LP 71317).

Far fewer of the original Confederate band books survived the conflict than did their Northern counterparts, but the 1st Brigade Band has recorded several albums of Southern band music. The 1st Brigade Band, perhaps the best-known of the modern groups re-creating the sound of the brass band, uses authentic period instruments and arrangements from the old books. Their various tapes and LPs are issued through the Heritage Military Music Foundation in Milwaukee. One of their most interesting is *Gen. Rob't E. Lee's Favorite 26th N.C. Band* (vol. 8, cassette only), a collection of quicksteps, marches, and dance tunes taken from the books of the Twenty-sixth North Carolina Band. *Band Music of the Confederacy* (vol. 4, LP only) celebrates and re-creates the music of the legendary Eleventh Mississippi Infantry Regimental Band, thought by some to be the best in the Confederacy. A third collection, *Dixie's Land* (vol. 7, cassette only), contains more concert and marching fare from various sources, as well as occasional vocals.

There is no authentic comprehensive collection of traditional or folk music from the South, but Confederate camps were filled with the sound of ballad singing and fiddle playing. During the 1930s and 1940s, the Library of Congress recorded in the field dozens of folk songs and tunes, but many of these are available only at the Archive of Folk Culture in Washington. A sample of them may be found on an LP issued by the Library of Congress, *Songs and Ballads of American History and the Assassination of Presidents* (AFS L29); this contains "Booth Killed Lincoln," "The Southern Soldier," and "The Battle of Antietam Creek," all taken from vintage field recordings. Less authentic but well interpreted is a larger collection of folk music, Folkways' *Songs of the Civil War* (SFW 5717, 2 cassettes), designed to accompany Irwin Silber's book of the same name; artists include Pete Seeger, the New Lost City Ramblers, and others. The fiddle tunes of the era are presented in two tapes on the Pearl Mae label by instrumentalist Jim Taylor and fiddler Bruce Green; these are *Falls of Richmond* and *Little Rose Is Gone.* Both tapes have good annotations and are full of tunes that either were known in the war or have associations with the Confederacy.

Several popular recordings feature modern interpretations of songs from the conflict. These often fail to use authentic settings or styles, but they are more accessible to modern listeners. One of the best is *Tennessee Ernie Ford Sings Songs of the Civil War* (Capitol, 2 CDs, C2 95705), a compilation of two LPs (*Songs of the North* and *Songs of the South*) originally issued in 1961. Framed by spare, modern arrangements, Ford's booming baritone lends itself well to "Stonewall Jackson's Way" and "Bonnie Blue Flag," among others. A more recent set of interpretations is *Songs of the Civil War* (Col. CK-CD 48607, CD or cassette), drawn from a PBS television show by the same name. The Southern half of the set features modern country and bluegrass singers like John Hartford, Waylon Jennings, Hoyt Axton, and Kathy Mattea, often in sparse, appealing settings featuring acoustic instruments. Sweet Honey in the Rock, based in Washington, adds several good renditions of spirituals. A series of cassettes beginning with *Songs of the CSA* has been produced by Birmingham singer and songwriter Bobby Horton, and it has the distinction of being one of the few series devoted exclusively to songs of the Confederacy.

Several recent collections offer a cross section of all sorts of music, from folk to popular to military. The first of these was the CBS/Legacy set *The Confederacy* (CB 47123), an opulent set issued in the 1960s and containing elaborate photographs and song notes. Produced by classical expert Goddard Leiberson, the set features formal singers and heavily orchestrated backgrounds that had little resemblance to the actual music of the 1860s. Mercury's set *Music of the Civil War* (LP, SR12–7701) contained a wider selection of music but was marred by sound effects and narration. Perhaps the most popular recent Civil War set is the sound track to the Ken Burns PBS television series, *The Civil War* (Elektra Nonesuch 9 79256–2, CD or cassette). Though the famous theme song for the series, "Ashokan Farewell," is a modern composition dating from 1984, many other pieces on the album are evocative, well performed, and authentic. Many vocal tunes, however, are heard only as piano solos.

The most elaborate attempt to recapture the actual sound of the music of the age is Time-Life Music's *The Civil War Music Collector's Edition* (R–103–12, CD or cassette). Drawing on performers both known and unknown, the producers have assembled fifty performances on three CDs. They include not only parlor songs, band music, and folk music but also spirituals, fife and drum music from camp duty, and minstrel show music. A large booklet accompanies the set and chronicles just how rich and complex the music of the age was.

With the increasing popularity of spoken word recordings ("audio books") in the late 1980s, a number of Civil War books have become available in this format. Recorded Books, Inc., of Prince Frederick, Maryland, has issued a number of such tapes, including Adrian Cronauer's reading of *Andersonville Diary* (5 cassettes, RBI 88090). Dick Estell's reading of James I. Robertson, Jr.'s, biography *General A.P. Hill: The Story of a Confederate Warrior* is one of the most polished of these performances, available from Books on Tape (10 cassettes, BOT 2455). Bierce's famous "Occurrence at Owl Creek Bridge" is available on a number of tape editions, including that of Mark Hammer (RBI, 2 cassettes, 82041). Noteworthy too is Alan Bergreen's reading of Bruce Catton's *The Civil War: A Short History* (RBI, 5 cassettes, 85440).

CHARLES K. WOLFE

DISEASE. *See* Health and Medicine, *articles on* Sickness and Disease *and* Medical Treatments.

DIVORCE. *See* Marriage and Divorce.

DIXIE. The most popular song associated with the Confederate cause, "Dixie," had its origins in a term that had been used to denote the South since the 1850s. The ultimate source of *Dixie,* the term, is obscure, but two favorite explanations for it are the popularity of the term *Mason-Dixon Line* and the use by the Citizens' Bank and Trust Company of Louisiana of its own currency notes in which the ten-dollar notes bore the French word for "ten," *dix*. Whatever its origin, by the end of the 1850s, *Dixie* was being used to denote the South.

The song itself originally bore the title "I Wish I Was in Dixie's Land" and was composed, ironically, in the heart of New York City. One rainy day in April 1859, in an old, chilly boardinghouse, a forty-four-year old minstrel singer named Dan Emmett was struggling to produce a new song for the troupe he was with, Bryant's Minstrels. A native of Mount Vernon, Ohio, Emmett had earlier been an army fife player and a circus band musician, but by the 1840s he was writing songs for the new type of entertainment springing up, the minstrel show. His "Old Dan Tucker" had become a favorite in these new shows, and since then he had written dozens of others. Now he had to come up with a finale for Bryant's show.

Emmett later recalled that as he started to work out a new song, the phrase "I wish I was in Dixie" kept running through his mind; his wife had used the phrase to complain about northern winters. He picked up a tin whistle and began to work out a melody and in less than an hour had the first verse and chorus. The song had its formal debut at Mechanics Hall in New York on April 4, 1859. "It made a tremendous hit," Emmett recalled, "and before the end of the week everybody in New York was whistling it." Sheet music publication soon followed—in 1860 by Firth, Pond and Company, and later by dozens of unauthorized companies. By the fall of 1860, the song had made its way into the South and was even used as the basis for an anti-Lincoln campaign song. Though it continued to be popular in the North, by 1861 the South had made it its own. It was played at Jefferson Davis's inauguration in Montgomery in 1861, and Gen. George E. Pickett ordered it played at the famous charge at Gettysburg. Since the original text of the song had little in it about the war or war issues, Albert Pike added some new words with a refrain that concluded, "To arms! To arms! And conquer peace for Dixie!"

In later years, controversy arose as to whether Emmett had really composed the song. A Louisville publisher insisted that two of his writers had made the song by fitting new words to an older folk tune known by Southern blacks, and others argued that the song first came from black stevedores on the Mississippi River. No effective proof of this ever surfaced, though, and Emmett's claim is generally accepted today.

By the end of the nineteenth century, "Dixie" had become a favorite anthem at various Confederate reunions and a staple in fiddling contests throughout the South. Often accompanied by rebel yells and the waving of the Confederate banner, by the mid-twentieth century the song had become popular with high school bands who used it as a rally song at local football games. The song's connotations and association with the Lost Cause were still so powerful that by the 1980s the playing of the song at high school games became mired in controversy, and many school administrators banned it from school events.

[*See also* Mason-Dixon Line.]

Dixey

Southerners hear your country call you
if less worse than death before you
　　　　　　To arms to arms in dixey
Though all the lincolns fire is lited

then at peace and crowned with glory
hear your chilldren tell the story
　　　　　　to arms to arm in dixey
Advance the flag of dixey ho ra
ho ra for dixeys land I take my stand
to live or die for dixey　　　　to arms
to and conquer peace for dixey
8 If the love owns weap in sadness
victory soon shall bring them gladness
　　　　　　to arms to arms in dixey
~~exalte~~
exalent pride will banish sorrows
smiles chase tears a way tomorrow
　　　　　　to arms to arms in dixey
　　　Advance the flag of dixey ho ra
ho ra for dixeys land I take my
stand to live or die for dixey
to arms and conquer peace for dixey

EARLY VERSION OF "DIXIE." From a manuscript titled "Dixey."

GORDON BLEULER

BIBLIOGRAPHY

Harwell, Richard B. *Confederate Music*. Chapel Hill, N.C., 1950.
Heaps, Willard A., and Porter W. Heaps. *The Singing Sixties: The Spirit of Civil War Days Drawn from the Music of the Times*. Norman, Okla., 1960.

CHARLES K. WOLFE

DOCKERY, THOMAS PLEASANT (1833–1898),

brigadier general. A prosperous planter before the war, Dockery commanded the Fifth Arkansas State Troops at the Battle of Oak Hills, Missouri, August 10, 1861, leading the charge that swept the Federals from the field. When this regiment's enlistment expired, Dockery raised and equipped the Nineteenth Arkansas Infantry at his own expense. Elected colonel, he briefly commanded a brigade in the Army of the West during the summer of 1862. A jolly, imperturbable man, he led his regiment into battle at Farmington, Iuka, Corinth, Hatchie Bridge, and Champion's Hill, Mississippi, with a reckless élan that won him frequent citations for gallantry.

Dockery succeeded to brigade command during the siege of Vicksburg, when a Federal sharpshooter killed Brig. Gen. Martin Edwin Green on June 27, 1863. Paroled with the surrender of the garrison, he was appointed brigadier general on August 10 and sent to the Trans-Mississippi Department to reorganize and reequip Arkansas troops who had gone home after the fall of Vicksburg.

The brigade of mounted infantry Dockery raised was part of an army Maj. Gen. Sterling Price pitted against Union Maj. Gen. Frederick Steele during the Red River campaign. Ordered to intercept Steele's wagon train, Dockery rode all night, but his decision to stop so his men could feed their horses forced another brigade to bear the brunt of the savage fighting at Marks's Mill, Arkansas, April 25, 1864.

Reassigned to organize the Arkansas State Reserves in September 1864, Dockery never held another important field command and surrendered the Confederate troops in southern Arkansas in June 1865. He moved to Texas after the war, where he worked as a civil engineer.

BIBLIOGRAPHY

Harrell, John M. *Arkansas*. Vol. 10 of *Confederate Military History*. Edited by Clement A. Evans. Atlanta, 1899. Vol. 14 of extended ed. Wilmington, N.C., 1988.
Reynolds, A. H. "Vivid Experiences at Champion Hill, Miss." *Confederate Veteran* 18 (January 1910): 21–22.

DAVID EVANS

DOCTORS. *For discussion of the role of doctors in the Confederacy, see* Medical Departments *and the various articles under* Health and Medicine. *For discussion of related topics, see* Hospitals; Nursing. *For biographies of individual doctors, see* Duke, Basil C.; Jones, Joseph; Moore, Samuel Preston; Stout, Samuel Hollingsworth.

DOLES, GEORGE PIERCE (1830–1864),

brigadier general. A native of Milledgeville, Georgia, Doles was born May 14, 1830, and displayed an early affinity for the military. He was a teenager when he attempted to run away and join the army, then at war in Mexico, but was apprehended while waiting for the stagecoach and returned home. Doles subsequently exercised his martial propensities with the "Baldwin Blues," a local company that he captained and which "attained a state of efficiency not surpassed by any volunteer company in the land," according to historian A. B. Caldwell.

In April 1861 Doles bade farewell to a prosperous mercantile business and marched away with the Blues, which became part of the Fourth Georgia Infantry. He was elected its colonel. The regiment left for Virginia on May 2 and for the next year was stationed at Norfolk, away from hostile fire. When the men met the enemy for the first time at Seven Pines, their formation and alignment brought admiring glances from veteran troops. On one occasion during the Seven Days' Battles, a newspaperman reported that the "Fourth Georgia fought like devils."

Doles was wounded at Malvern Hill but returned to duty in time to fight conspicuously at South Mountain and Sharpsburg. He was appointed brigadier general on November 1. After the Battle of Fredericksburg, D. H. Hill reported that Doles was a "tried veteran and brigade commander," under whose leadership "the men always do well." Doles's brigade was at the forefront of Thomas J. ("Stonewall") Jackson's attack that rolled up Joseph Hooker's flank at Chancellorsville. For his performance there, Doles was cited for his "great gallantry and efficiency."

On July 1, 1863, Doles's brigade was the first to enter Gettysburg. In this engagement, he was cited by Robert Rodes for handling "his men with a skill and effect truly admirable, exhibiting marked coolness and courage." At both Chancellorsville and Gettysburg, Doles had a horse shot from under him.

Doles was killed on June 2, 1864, while supervising the entrenchment of his line near Bethesda Church. He was buried in Milledgeville.

BIBLIOGRAPHY

Compiled Military Service Records. George Pierce Doles. Microcopy M331, Roll 77. Record Group 109. National Archives, Washington, D.C.
Derry, Joseph T. *Georgia*. Vol. 6 of *Confederate Military History*. Edited by Clement A. Evans. Atlanta, 1899. Vol. 7 of extended ed. Wilmington, N.C., 1987.

"General R. E. Rodes' Report of the Battle of Chancellorsville." *Southern Historical Society Papers* 2 (1876): 148, 171. Reprint, Wilmington, N.C., 1990.

Northen, William J. *Men of Mark in Georgia.* 7 vols. Atlanta, Ga., 1906. Reprint, Spartanburg, S.C., 1974.

LOWELL REIDENBAUGH

DON. The fourth, and best known, twin-screw steamer built by the shipyard of John and William Dudgeon in London, was launched as *Diana* on May 24, 1863, and then sold and renamed *Don* shortly after its trial trip. Twin-screw steamers used a pair of propellers to provide unprecedented speed and maneuverability. The first, *Flora,* had been so successful as a blockade runner that the company received orders for seventeen similar ships before the war ended. *Don* was one of eight iron sisterships measuring 425 tons, 165 feet in length, 22 feet in beam, and 13 feet in depth of hold. Two boilers produced steam to power two twin-cylinder horizontal direct-acting engines, one per propeller shaft. Several features made *Don* difficult for blockaders to detect: the two-masted schooner rig was hinged to lower flat against the deck, the funnel was designed to lower telescope-fashion, and the ship was painted haze gray as camouflage.

Don was owned by Alexander Collie and Company of London. The company, in a potential breach of British neutrality, hired a Royal Navy officer on inactive status to command the ship. Capt. Augustus Charles Hobart-Hampden, operating under the assumed name "Captain Roberts," guided *Don* through the blockade between Wilmington and Nassau or Bermuda ten times before turning command over to another captain. On the next trip, March 4, 1864, *Don* was captured off Beaufort, North Carolina, by USS *Pequot.* Condemned by the Boston prize court and purchased by the U.S. Navy, *Don* became a Union blockader, serving in the Potomac Flotilla until the end of the war.

After the war *Don* stayed active in the North Atlantic Squadron until decommissioned May 18, 1868, and was sold in August to R. M. Funkhauser, an American commercial shipowner. The new owner continued to operate the ship under the name *Don* until 1871, when he sold it to Spanish owners. The former blockade runner continued in service in the Caribbean as *Cantabro* into the 1880s.

BIBLIOGRAPHY

"Don." In *Dictionary of American Naval Fighting Ships.* Vol. 2. Washington, D.C., 1963.

Hobart-Hampden, Augustus C. *Sketches from My Life.* New York, 1887.

Wise, Stephen R. *Lifeline of the Confederacy: Blockade Running during the Civil War.* Columbia, S.C., 1988.

KEVIN J. FOSTER

DONELSON, DANIEL SMITH (1801–1863), major general. Donelson was born in Sumner County, Tennessee, and graduated from West Point in 1825. After less than a year in the Third Artillery he resigned to pursue a career as a planter, politician, and state militia officer. In 1861 Donelson, Speaker of the state legislature, was an ardent secessionist.

Appointed adjutant general of state troops, Donelson chose the defensive posts known as Fort Donelson, named for him, on the Cumberland River and Fort Henry on the Tennessee River. In July 1861 he was appointed brigadier general in the Confederate army and was sent to western Virginia, where he commanded a brigade in the Cheat Mountain campaign. In December 1861 his unit was ordered to the South Carolina coast to guard against potential Union amphibious attacks. In April 1862 Donelson's two Tennessee regiments moved to Corinth, Mississippi, where they joined Gen. B. Franklin Cheatham's division and were combined with three more Tennessee regiments.

During Gen. Braxton Bragg's Kentucky campaign of October 1862, Donelson led his brigade into battle at Perryville and routed a Union brigade in what Gen. Leonidas Polk described as "one of the most heroic and brilliant movements of the war." At Murfreesboro, in

DANIEL SMITH DONELSON.   LIBRARY OF CONGRESS

December, Donelson led his Tennesseeans against the Round Forest (also known as "Hell's Half Acre," an area of mature hardwoods along the Nashville and Chattanooga Railroad held by Union Gen. Thomas Crittenden) and was repulsed with heavy casualties, although several of his regiments pushed a Union brigade out of its position in the cedar woods. Bragg praised Donelson for being "conspicuously gallant" and suggested his promotion to major general.

In January 1863 Donelson took command of the Department of East Tennessee based at Knoxville. He found a scattered command that was disorganized and poorly disciplined. Donelson struggled to organize his command and launch raids into Kentucky but suffered from personal illness and departmental conflicts. On April 17, 1863, he died, probably at Montvale Springs, Tennessee. Ironically the Confederate Congress, unaware of his death, promoted him to major general on April 22.

BIBLIOGRAPHY

Hewitt, Lawrence L. "Daniel Donelson." In *The Confederate General*. Edited by William C. Davis. Vol. 1. Harrisburg, Pa., 1991.

Porter, James D. *Tennessee*. Vol. 8 of *Confederate Military History*. Edited by Clement A. Evans. Atlanta, 1899. Vol. 10 of extended ed. Wilmington, N.C., 1987.

U.S. War Department. *War of the Rebellion: A Compilation of the Official Records of the Union and Confederate Armies*. Washington, D.C., 1880–1901. Ser. 1. Vol. 6, pt. 1, pp. 349, 433; vol. 16, pt. 1, pp. 1109–1111; vol. 20, pt. 1, pp. 689–690, 710–714; vol. 23, pt. 2, pp. 621, 626, 705, 787.

CHARLES M. SPEARMAN

DORSEY, SARAH ANNE (1829–1879), writer.

Dorsey is best remembered not for her literary efforts but for her relationship with Jefferson Davis. She belonged to a tiny elite of powerful southwestern slaveholders and boasted an unusually aristocratic lineage: she was descended from Rouths, Ellises, and Percys—all prominent nabobs of Natchez, where she was born February 16, 1829. Between 1862 and 1877 she published six novels, none of which was memorable but all of which revealed a woman of considerable intellectual range. Most important was her biography of a wartime Louisiana governor, her friend and neighbor in Tensas Parish—*Recollections of Henry Watkins Allen* (1865). It was marked by a vivid description of her own flight from Elkridge Plantation to Texas during the war, insightful reflections on military action in the Southwest, and a deep understanding of the considerable merits and forgivable weaknesses of her subject.

After the death of her well-born husband, Samuel Worthington Dorsey, in 1875, she established herself at Beauvoir, a waterfront property at Biloxi. Looking for a place to write his memoirs, Jefferson Davis worked out an agreeable arrangement with Dorsey over the protests of his wife, Varina Davis, then suffering from ill health in Europe. When Dorsey died of cancer on July 4, 1879, Davis discovered that she had bequeathed all her property to him, modest though her fortune had become by then. Her motive, she claimed, was to demonstrate the gratitude toward the former Confederate leader that his own Southern people had failed to express. Family members sued Davis on the grounds of his supposed influence over a mentally vulnerable woman. The courts, however, dismissed the suit, and eventually Beauvoir became known as the Jefferson Davis Shrine.

[*See also* Beauvoir.]

BIBLIOGRAPHY

Smallwood, J. B. "Dorsey, Sarah Anne." In *Lives of Mississippi Authors, 1817–1967*. Edited by James B. Lloyd. Jackson, Miss., 1981.

Wyatt-Brown, Bertram. *The House of Percy: Power and Creativity in a Southern Family*. Forthcoming.

BERTRAM WYATT-BROWN

DORTCH, WILLIAM THEOPHILUS (1824–

1889), congressman from North Carolina. Dortch was born August 23, 1824, near Rocky Mount on his father's plantation. He studied law under Bartholomew Moore and opened his first law office in Nashville, North Carolina, but moved in 1848 to Goldsboro when that city became the Wayne County seat. Besides practicing law, he served as county attorney and engaged in planting.

In 1852 and 1854 Dortch was elected to the North Carolina House of Commons as a Democrat and subsequently served two more terms from 1858 to 1861, the latter year as Speaker of the House. Although associated with the faction favoring immediate secession after Abraham Lincoln's election, he repeatedly acknowledged a firm attachment to "the Union as it was," a predilection that was in part responsible for his selection by the Whig-dominated legislature as a compromise for a seat in the Confederate Senate.

Dortch occupied a somewhat pivotal position because of his close friendship with cabinet member Judah P. Benjamin and his role as a mediator between Benjamin and Governor Zebulon Vance. A man of retiring disposition, his voting record nevertheless was that of a strong Confederate nationalist, and he was noted for his opposition to proposals that President Jefferson Davis send out peace feelers to the Lincoln administration. He also supported efforts to have the Confederate government pay more for impressed goods, to give fuller effect to the writ of habeas corpus, and to improve anti-inflationary measures. Dortch was chairman of the Senate's Committee on Engrossment and Enrollment.

The end of the war found him close to bankruptcy, but he gradually rebuilt his law practice and his planting operations. After 1878 he returned for six years to the state senate, serving in 1879 as its president and in 1883 as chairman of its Judiciary Committee. As a director of the state-owned North Carolina Railroad, he unsuccessfully opposed the sale of the road to Northern investors. He also served in 1881 to 1883 as chairman of a commission that revised the North Carolina Code to accommodate the far-reaching legal changes precipitated by the war and its aftermath. Dortch suffered a stroke and died November 21, 1889.

BIBLIOGRAPHY

Dowd, Jerome. *Sketches of Prominent Persons Living in North Carolina.* Raleigh, N.C., 1888.
Powell, William S., ed. *Dictionary of North Carolina Biography.* Vol. 2. Chapel Hill, N.C., 1986.

RICHARD BARDOLPH

DRAYTON, THOMAS F. (1808–1891), brigadier
general. Drayton was the scion of a distinguished South Carolina family and brother of Percival Drayton, who commanded a U.S. Navy vessel in the 1861 bombardment of Port Royal. Born August 24, 1808, probably at Charleston, Thomas Drayton graduated from the U.S. Military Academy in 1828. He ranked twenty-eighth in a class of thirty-three in which Jefferson Davis finished twenty-third and with whom Drayton formed a lasting friendship. After two years of garrison duty in St. Louis and Newport, Kentucky, Drayton was assigned to topographical duty. In this role he figured in the unsuccessful project to build a Charleston, Louisville, and Cincinnati railroad, first as assistant surveyor and then as resident engineer. He resigned from the army, August 15, 1836.

Having acquired a plantation in St. Luke's Parish, South Carolina, Drayton cultivated its acres until the start of the Civil War. During this same period, he was captain of a militia company, a member of the state Board of Ordnance, a state senator, and president of the Charleston and Savannah Railroad.

Drayton was fifty-three in 1861 when he was commissioned a brigadier general. For several months he commanded military districts in the South. In July 1862, he was sent to Virginia where his brigade saw action at Thoroughfare Gap, Second Manassas, South Mountain, and Sharpsburg. Transferred to Arkansas in August 1863, Drayton was put in charge of a brigade in Sterling Price's division. Later he was given command of a subdivision in Texas. His last service to the Confederacy was as president of a court of inquiry investigating Price's Missouri expedition.

Hints of Drayton's ineffectiveness as a commander dot his record almost from the beginning of the war. At one point Robert E. Lee notified Jefferson Davis that "he is a gentleman and a soldier in his own person, but seems to lack the capacity to command."

After the war, with his plantation damaged by Union soldiers and partly confiscated by the Federal government, Drayton went to Dooly County, Georgia, where he tried to develop a farm with the help of a bequest from his brother Percival. When this venture failed, Drayton became an agent for the Southern Life Insurance Company. In 1878 he was appointed president of the South Carolina Immigrant Society. He died February 18, 1891, in Florence, South Carolina, and was buried in Charlotte.

BIBLIOGRAPHY

Capers, Ellison. *South Carolina.* Vol. 5 of *Confederate Military History.* Edited by Clement A. Evans. Atlanta, 1899. Vol. 6 of extended ed. Wilmington, N.C., 1987.
Warner, Ezra J. *Generals in Gray: Lives of the Confederate Commanders.* Baton Rouge, La., 1959.

LOWELL REIDENBAUGH

DRED SCOTT DECISION. As the slave of army
surgeon John Emerson, Dred Scott had lived on a military base in Illinois and at Fort Snelling, in Wisconsin Territory, which was made free by the Missouri Compromise. In 1850 a St. Louis court, following Missouri precedents dating from 1824, found Scott had become free while living outside Missouri, a slave state, and once free, he remained free despite his return to Missouri. In 1852 the Missouri Supreme Court, articulating the proslavery ideology and hostility to the North that would eventually lead to secession, rejected its own long-standing precedents:

> Times are not as they were when the former decisions on this subject were made. Since then not only individuals but States have been possessed of a dark and fell spirit in relation to slavery, whose gratification is sought in the pursuit of measures, whose inevitable consequence must be the overthrow and destruction of our government. Under such circumstances it does not behoove the State of Missouri to show the least countenance to any measure which might gratify this spirit.

In 1854 Scott began a new suit in the U.S. District Court against John F. A. Sanford, a New Yorker who had recently become the executor of Emerson's estate after Emerson's widow, and initial executor, had remarried. Scott argued he was a citizen of Missouri and sued Sanford in federal court because there was a diversity of citizenship between the two parties. Sanford answered that blacks, whether free or in bondage, could *never* sue as U.S. citizens in a federal court.

"THE POLITICAL QUADRILLE: MUSIC BY DRED SCOTT." Satire of the impact of the Dred Scott decision on the 1860 presidential election. The four candidates dance with caricatures of their supposed constituencies while Dred Scott fiddles. In the upper left, Southern Democrat John C. Breckinridge cavorts with ally James Buchanan, depicted as a goat (a reference to his nickname, "Buck"). At upper right, Republican Abraham Lincoln dances with an African American woman, a reference to his party's abolitionist leanings. At lower right, Constitutional Unionist John Bell dances with an Indian, alluding to his brief attentions to Native American interests. At lower left, National Democrat Stephen A. Douglas jigs with an Irishman, whose cross may refer to Douglas's backing among Irish immigrants and to his own alleged Catholicism. Lithograph on wove paper, published in 1860, possibly in Cincinnati, Ohio.   LIBRARY OF CONGRESS

Judge Robert W. Wells ruled that *if* Scott was free, then he was a citizen of Missouri for purposes of federal diversity jurisdiction. After a trial, however, Judge Wells ruled that Scott was still a slave. Scott then appealed to the U.S. Supreme Court. At issue was more than the status of Scott and his family: the Missouri Supreme Court's decision challenged Congress's authority to prohibit slavery in any federal territory. The central political issue of the 1850s was now before the Supreme Court.

The end of the Mexican-American War had left the nation in possession of vast amounts of land (known as the Mexican Cession) including the present-day states of New Mexico, Arizona, California, Utah, and Nevada. Much of this land was below the Missouri Compromise line, and thus theoretically open to slavery. With the acquisition of this territory and the rise of proslavery thought and Southern nationalism, Southerners were no longer content to be shut out of the western territories. The Kansas-Nebraska Act (1854), which partially repealed the Missouri Compromise by allowing slavery in the territory immediately to the west of Missouri under a concept of popular sovereignty, led to a mini-civil war in Kansas and the formation of the Republican party in the North. In the 1856 presidential election this two-year-old party, pledged to stop the spread of slavery into the territories, carried all but five Northern states.

The avidly proslavery Chief Justice Roger B. Taney of Maryland used *Dred Scott v. Sandford* [sic] (1857) to decide these pressing political issues in favor of the South. Taney's two most controversial points were (1) that the Missouri Compromise was unconstitutional because Congress could not legislate for any federal territories acquired after 1787 and because freeing slaves in the territories constituted a taking of property without due process, in violation of the Fifth Amendment; and (2) that blacks, even those in the North with full state citizenship, could never be U.S. citizens. Taney asked: "Can a negro, whose ancestors were imported into this country, and sold as slaves, become a member of the political community formed and brought into existence by the Constitution of the United States, and as such become entitled to all the rights, privileges, and immunities guaranteed by that instrument to the citizens?" Rigorously applying a jurisprudence of original intent, Taney answered with a resounding no. In an analysis that was historically incorrect and shocking to the North, Taney asserted that when the Constitution was adopted blacks were universally considered "beings of an inferior order, and altogether unfit to associate with the white race, either in social or political relations; and so far inferior, that they had no rights which the white man was bound to respect; and that the negro might justly and lawfully be reduced to slavery for his benefit."

In dissent Justice Benjamin Robbins Curtis, of Massachusetts, noted that in 1787 free blacks were citizens of five states and thus they were also citizens of the United States when the Constitution was adopted. Curtis also argued that under a "reasonable interpretation of the language of the Constitution" Congress had the power to regulate slavery in the federal territories. This dissent heartened Northerners like Horace Greeley who wrote that Taney's decision was an "atrocious," "wicked," "abominable," "false," "detestable hypocrisy" built on "shallow sophistries." The *Chicago Tribune* expressed the reaction of many Northerners: "We scarcely know how to express our detestation of its inhuman dicta, or to fathom the wicked consequences which may flow from it."

But, not all Northerners opposed the decision. Northern Democrats hoped the decision would destroy the Republican party by essentially declaring its "Free-Soil" platform to be unconstitutional and once and for all end the national debate over slavery in the territories. In the words of the New York *Journal of Commerce*, the decision was an "authoritative and final settlement of grievous sectional issues."

The decision also undermined Northern Democrats, however, whose strength had been grounded in the party's appeal to popular sovereignty. Under popular sovereignty settlers would decide for themselves if they wanted slavery in a territory. This system appealed to American concepts of democratic rule and Northern negrophobia. Northern Democrats hoped popular sovereignty would keep both slaves and blacks out of the territories. At the same time,

however, popular sovereignty allowed Northern Democrats to appease their Southern colleagues who opposed restrictions on slavery in the territories.

Just as Taney's decision undermined Republican Free-Soil politics, so it undermined Democratic popular sovereignty. Under *Dred Scott* the settlers of a territory, like the Congress, were precluded from restricting slavery. This made popular sovereignty meaningless and took away from Northern Democrats their most potent weapon. Stephen A. Douglas, the most prominent proponent of popular sovereignty, told his Illinois constituents that settlers could still keep slavery out of most of the territories by not passing laws that would protect slave property. This led Southern Democrats to demand a federal slave code for the territories and helped set the stage for the split within the Democratic party in 1860.

Taney doubtless thought his powerful fifty-four-page decision would finally open all the territories to slavery while undermining the Republican party. "Taney's opinion," historian Don Fehrenbacher has written, "proves to be a work of unmitigated partisanship, polemical in spirit though judicial in its language, and more like an ultimatum than a formula for sectional accommodation. Peace on Taney's terms resembled . . . a demand for unconditional surrender." The decision was, as historian Harry Jaffa has written, "nothing less than a summons to the Republicans to disband."

But instead of disbanding, Republicans successfully made Taney and the decision the focus of their 1858 and 1860 campaigns. In his "house divided" speech (1858) Abraham Lincoln argued that Taney's opinion was part of a proslavery conspiracy to nationalize slavery and a prelude to future proslavery jurisprudence. He warned of "another Supreme Court decision, declaring that the Constitution of the United States does not permit a *state* to exclude slavery from its limits." He told the voters in Illinois, and by extension the entire North, that "we shall *lie down* pleasantly dreaming that the people of Missouri are on the verge of making their state *free;* and we shall *awake* to the *reality,* instead, that the Supreme Court has made *Illinois* a *slave* state."

Such arguments, combined with such other issues of the day, led a majority of Northerners to vote Republican in 1860; that in turn led to secession and the creation of the Confederacy.

[*See also* Bleeding Kansas; Compromise of 1850; Democratic Party; Fugitive Slave Law; Kansas-Nebraska Act; Missouri Compromise; Republican Party; Sumner, Caning of; Wilmot Proviso.]

BIBLIOGRAPHY

Erlich, Walter. *They Have No Rights: Dred Scott's Struggle for Freedom.* Westport, Conn., 1979.

Fehrenbacher, Don E. *The Dred Scott Case: Its Significance in American Law and Politics.* New York, 1978.

Finkelman, Paul. *An Imperfect Union: Slavery, Federalism, and Comity.* Chapel Hill, N.C., 1981.

Jaffa, Harry V. *The Crisis of the House Divided: An Interpretation of the Issues in the Lincoln-Douglas Debates.* New York, 1959.

Potter, David M. *The Impending Crisis: 1848–61.* New York, 1976.

PAUL FINKELMAN

DREWRY'S BLUFF, VIRGINIA.

Also called Fort Darling, the fortified position atop Drewry's Bluff overlooking the James River played a vital role in defending the water approaches to Richmond, about seven miles away.

As the Union Army of the Potomac under Maj. Gen. George B. McClellan prepared to blast the Confederates out of their defenses at Yorktown in May 1862, Gen. Joseph E. Johnston determined to evacuate the Yorktown line and retreat farther up the Virginia Peninsula toward Richmond. In doing so, however, he compelled the evacuation of Norfolk. To prevent the capture of the Confederate ironclad *Virginia,* its crew destroyed the ship, leaving the James River open to ascent by the Union navy.

The Federals naturally determined to take advantage of *Virginia's* absence, and in mid-May the Union ironclads *Monitor* and *Galena* escorted three wooden warships upriver. The best place to challenge this small fleet of Union vessels was at Drewry's Bluff. The high ground would afford Confederate artillery with a clear field of fire and be difficult to hit from the river below. The narrowness of the river at that point and the installation of sunken vessels as obstructions would further hinder the Federals. Gen. Robert E. Lee sent a brigade of infantry to support the position, while the crew from *Virginia* arrived to serve the heavy guns in the works.

Although the Confederates carried out their improvements in haste, the natural advantages of the position soon became apparent. When the Federal fleet arrived on May 15, 1862, neither of the ironclads could elevate its guns sufficiently to return the Confederate fire. Furthermore, the obstructions prevented them from attempting to run past the fort. As the Southern crews watched from above, all the while pouring fire into the vessels below, *Monitor* and *Galena* maneuvered futilely. As the fighting continued, *Galena* began to suffer damage from the Confederates' heavy shells. After four hours of battle, the Union ships moved off. *Galena* sustained more damage and casualties than any of the other vessels, but limped to safety. Still, the Confederates at Drewry's Bluff had thwarted the Federal attack.

On May 16, 1864, Drewry's Bluff again became the scene of fighting. A Union landing at Bermuda Hundred earlier in the month threatened to leave the Confederate capital and the city of Petersburg below it vulnerable to attack. Union Maj. Gen. Benjamin F. Butler, commanding the 39,000-man Army of the James, failed to press his advantage, however. He lost precious time as he cautiously moved along the peninsula of land between the James and Appomattox rivers. The Confederates had time enough to concentrate their forces and stop Butler's advance, whereupon the Union commander retreated to Bermuda Hundred.

Butler's position was too strong to be attacked directly, but Gen. P. G. T. Beauregard was willing to pit his 20,000 men against them in the open. Hoping to bring Butler out of his defenses, Beauregard sent Maj. Gen. Robert Frederick Hoke to Drewry's Bluff. This was enough to convince the Federals to leave their lines.

On May 12, Butler advanced almost half of his force toward Drewry's Bluff, leaving behind enough infantry to hold his defenses. On the next day, the Federals attacked the Confederate works with some success, but once again, rather than following up his initial success, Butler vacillated. He formed a defensive line with Maj. Gens. Quincy A. Gillmore and William F. Smith on the left and right, respectively.

In the meantime, Beauregard reached Drewry's Bluff and received welcome reinforcements. He hoped to launch an attack of his own, now that he had succeeded in luring Butler away from his defenses. Early on the morning of May 16, Confederates under Maj. Gen. Robert Ransom, Jr., slammed into the Union right flank. The Southerners enjoyed great initial success, but as the fighting progressed in the early morning fog, the attack became disjointed.

The assault soon spread along the broad front of the opposing forces, but the poor visibility continued to disrupt the attacking columns. The Federals managed to launch a counterattack that stymied any further Confederate inroads. By midmorning, the fighting had begun to slacken, and despite a half-hearted attempt by the Southerners to strike at Butler as he retreated to his defenses, the battle was over. The fighting had cost the Federals almost twice as many men as the Confederates—4,160 to 2,506—and had ended Butler's threat to Richmond and Petersburg. By the end of the next day, May 17, Beauregard had put the "cork" in the "bottle" and sealed Butler into his lines at Bermuda Hundred, where he could do no further harm.

BIBLIOGRAPHY

Johnson, Robert U., and C. C. Buel, eds. *Battles and Leaders of the Civil War.* 4 vols. New York, 1887–1888. Reprint, Secaucus, N.J., 1982.

Robertson, William Glenn. *Back Door to Richmond: The Bermuda Hundred Campaign, April–June 1864.* Baton Rouge, La., 1987.

U.S. Naval War Records Office. *Official Records of the Union and Confederate Navies in the War of the Rebellion.* Washington, D.C., 1894–1927. Ser. 1, vol. 7, pp. 269–270, 352–370.

U.S. War Department. *War of the Rebellion: A Compilation of the Official Records of the Union and Confederate Armies.* Ser. 1, vol. 11, pt. 1, p. 636; ser. 1, vol. 36, pt. 2, pp. 6–269.

BRIAN S. WILLS

DUBOSE, DUDLEY MCIVER (1834–1883), brigadier general and U.S. congressman.

In 1863 and 1864 heavy casualties cost the Army of Northern Virginia progressively more of its experienced regimental and brigade commanders. Officers with little or no experience leading troops in combat were temporarily assigned, or promoted, to replace them. Though in many instances these new officers were ill-suited for command, some succeeded so well that they were later assigned permanently or promoted again. Dudley McIver DuBose is an excellent example of such an officer.

Born in Shelby County, Tennessee, on October 28, 1834, DuBose graduated from the University of Mississippi and practiced law in Tennessee and Georgia before the war. Most of his early Confederate service, through 1862, was as a captain on the staff of his father-in-law, Robert Toombs. In January 1863 DuBose, though he had no experience commanding a regiment, was appointed colonel of the Fifteenth Georgia Infantry.

DuBose's first battle as a colonel was at Gettysburg, where he led his regiment in the fight at the Devil's Den on July 2, 1863. He was wounded, though not seriously, at Chickamauga. In May 1864, after Henry Benning was wounded at the Wilderness, DuBose succeeded to temporary command of the brigade and performed well until Benning's return to duty in November. Promoted to brigadier general on November 16, 1864, DuBose was assigned to command another Georgia brigade in the army's First Corps. He was captured, with most of his brigade, at Sayler's Creek on April 6, 1865.

DuBose practiced law in Georgia and served a term in the U.S. House of Representatives after the war. He died in Washington, Georgia, on March 4, 1883.

BIBLIOGRAPHY

Compiled Military Service Records. Dudley M. DuBose. Microcopy M331, Roll 80. Record Group 109. National Archives, Washington, D.C.

Derry, Joseph T. *Georgia.* Vol. 6 of *Confederate Military History.* Edited by Clement A. Evans. Atlanta, 1899. Vol. 7 of extended ed. Wilmington, N.C., 1987.

J. TRACY POWER

DUELING.

The duel was an important element of life in the Confederacy, with roots going back to the antebellum period. Although widely outlawed in the region before the Civil War—in Virginia as early as 1776 and even in South Carolina by 1812—dueling had been invested with great significance by those antebellum Southerners who continued the practice, closely tying it to concepts of honor and social position. After dueling largely disappeared from the North during the early national period, it also became a symbol of a distinctively Southern way of life. Thus, as white Southerners confronted the questions of honor and nationalism brought on by the war, dueling took on a notable role in the Confederate states.

Although it is impossible to say how many duels were fought during the war, many contemporary observers believed that the crisis increased the incidence of dueling. It infiltrated army life, as officers resorted to duels to settle private scores. The most noted such duel resulted in the 1863 killing of Ransom Calhoun, a nephew of John Calhoun, by Alfred Rhett, the son of fire-eater Robert Barnwell Rhett. And it entered Confederate politics and government, as vitriolic debate brought challenges, threats, and sometimes combat between political figures or between those in government and, especially, their journalistic critics.

After the war, dueling declined rapidly. Although a few duels were fought and challenges issued into the 1890s, these were isolated affairs that met with increasing public disapproval. The culture of honor having been eclipsed, its most visible manifestation could no longer be sustained.

BIBLIOGRAPHY

Chesnut, Mary Boykin. *Mary Chesnut's Civil War.* Edited by C. Vann Woodward. New Haven, 1981.

Coulter, E. Merton. *The Confederate States of America, 1861–1865. A History of the South*, vol. 7. Baton Rouge, La., 1950.

Wyatt-Brown, Bertram. *Southern Honor: Ethics and Behavior in the Old South.* New York, 1982.

DICKSON D. BRUCE, JR.

DUKE, BASIL C. (1815–?), physician and brigadier general.

Born near Orangeburg, Mason County, Kentucky, on March 31, 1815, Basil C. Duke was educated in private schools and studied under Dr. N. R. Smith before graduating from the University of Maryland's Medical School in 1834. Afterward he opened a private practice in Mayslick, Kentucky. A Whig, Duke actively supported the Constitutional Union party in the presidential election of 1860. He later became a staunch Democrat.

Although not an ardent secessionist, Duke at the outbreak of the Civil War enlisted as a private in the Fifth Kentucky Volunteer Infantry commanded by Col. John S. Williams. Commissioned as the regiment's surgeon, Duke was promoted to brigadier general. Throughout the remainder of the war, he served on the medical staff of Confederate organizations along the border states. He was named chief of the medical staff of the Army of Eastern Kentucky in 1861, and the following year he was made the medical director of Southwestern Virginia, East Tennessee, and Eastern Kentucky, which was commanded by Humphrey Marshall. Duke saw action with Kentucky troops at Middle Creek, Kentucky; Princeton, Virginia; during the Kanawah valley, West Virginia, campaign; and throughout Virginia and Tennessee between 1861 and 1865.

When the war ended, Duke returned to Mayslick, resumed his medical practice, and became a leading Kentucky physician.

BIBLIOGRAPHY

Mosgrove, George D. *Kentucky Cavaliers in Dixie: The Reminiscences of a Confederate Cavalryman.* Jackson, Tenn., 1957.
Warner, Ezra J. *Generals in Gray: Lives of the Confederate Commanders.* Baton Rouge, La., 1959.

KENNY A. FRANKS

DUKE, BASIL WILSON (1838–1916), brigadier general and historian. Duke was born May 28, 1838, in Scott County, Kentucky. After he earned a law degree at Transylvania University, he opened a law practice in St. Louis, Missouri. In June 1861, he married Henrietta Hunt Morgan, sister of John Hunt Morgan.

Active in the Missouri secessionist movement, Duke was sentenced to death in absentia by a secessionist vigilance committee. He was elected a first lieutenant in Morgan's Lexington Rifles, a part of the Second Kentucky Cavalry; after promotion to colonel, Duke commanded the regiment. He was wounded at Shiloh, but recovered to participate in Morgan's great Ohio raid in 1863, where he was captured along with the rest of Morgan's command. A prisoner of war for a year before being exchanged, he returned to Confederate service, was promoted to brigadier general in September 1864, and commanded a cavalry brigade that served in Kentucky and Virginia until Appomattox. With Robert E. Lee's surrender, Duke was ordered to provide Jefferson Davis's escort as he fled Richmond. He was captured during a decoy mission to lead Federal troops away from Davis.

After the war, Duke resumed his law practice in Louisville and was elected to the Kentucky House of Representatives in 1869. He wrote, among other works, *A History of Morgan's Cavalry* (1867) and *The Reminiscences of General Basil W. Duke, C.S.A.* (1911), and edited *Mid-Continent* and *Southern* magazines. Duke died on September 16, 1916.

BIBLIOGRAPHY

Brown, Dee Alexander. *The Bold Cavaliers.* Philadelphia, 1959.
Mosgrove, George D. *Kentucky Cavaliers in Dixie: The Reminiscences of a Confederate Cavalryman.* Jackson, Tenn., 1957.

Warner, Ezra J. *Generals in Gray: Lives of the Confederate Commanders.* Baton Rouge, La., 1959.

PAUL F. LAMBERT

DUNCAN, JOHNSON K. (1827–1862), brigadier general. Johnson Kelly Duncan was born in York, Pennsylvania, March 19, 1827. Appointed to West Point from Ohio, he graduated fifth out of forty-nine in the class of 1849 and entered the army as a brevet second lieutenant, Second Artillery. Promoted to second lieutenant, Third Artillery, October 31, 1849, and to first lieutenant, December 24, 1853, Duncan fought the Seminoles in Florida and explored the Northwest, searching for a route for the Northern Pacific Railroad. He resigned his commission January 31, 1855, to become superintendent of government construction in New Orleans. When he cast his lot with his adopted state in 1861, he held the post of chief engineer of the Board of Public Works of Louisiana.

Appointed a colonel of artillery, Duncan assumed command of the defenses of New Orleans, including Forts Jackson and St. Philip downriver. Promoted to brigadier general January 7, 1862, Duncan had about five hundred men and eighty guns at the two forts to oppose the Union fleet, which anchored below them in April. After bombarding the forts for six days, the Union fleet successfully steamed past on April 24 and captured New Orleans the following day. With the city lost and Union infantry closing in from the rear, most of Duncan's men mutinied, and he was compelled to surrender.

After his release, Duncan served as chief of staff to Gen. Braxton Bragg. His new assignment proved of short duration, however. He died of fever at Knoxville, Tennessee, December 18, 1862. He was buried in McGavock Cemetery at Franklin, Tennessee.

BIBLIOGRAPHY

Dufour, Charles L. *The Night the War Was Lost.* Garden City, N.Y., 1960.
Duncan, Johnson K. "Bombardment of Forts Jackson and St. Philip." *Confederate War Journal* 1 (1893): 181–189.

LAWRENCE L. HEWITT

DUNOVANT, JOHN (1825–1864), colonel and temporary brigadier general. A native of South Carolina, Dunovant began his military career fighting with the Palmetto Regiment in the Mexican War. Following the Treaty of Guadalupe-Hidalgo, he received a commission as captain of the Tenth Infantry in the U.S. Army. In 1861 he resigned that position and became a major in the state militia. At Fort Moultrie, he participated in the first battle

JOHN DUNOVANT.   LIBRARY OF CONGRESS

of the Civil War. Later, he became colonel of the First South Carolina Regulars.

Though he was a trained and experienced soldier, Dunovant encountered difficulty with the rigid regulations of army life. While stationed on St. John's Island in 1862, he was court-martialed and dismissed from service for drunkenness and frequent absences during muster. But shortly thereafter, perhaps because he had proven an able soldier, or because the Confederacy badly needed trained men, Governor Francis W. Pickens appointed Dunovant colonel of the Fifth South Carolina Cavalry.

As a colonel in Gen. Matthew Calbraith Butler's brigade, he reestablished his reputation as a dependable soldier. In 1864 his regiment received orders to report to Virginia, where he earned praise for his participation in the bloodbath at Cold Harbor. Following the battle, President Jefferson Davis suggested to Robert E. Lee that Dunovant receive the temporary rank of brigadier general. He took command of a brigade in Wade Hampton's division in August 1864.

Following the capture of Fort Harrison, Dunovant re-

ceived a mortal wound from a Union bullet. He died October 1, 1864, near the James River.

BIBLIOGRAPHY

Capers, Ellison. *South Carolina*. Vol. 5 of *Confederate Military History*. Edited by Clement A. Evans. Atlanta, 1899. Vol. 6 of extended ed. Wilmington, N.C., 1987.

Warner, Ezra J. *Generals in Gray: Lives of the Confederate Commanders*. Baton Rouge, La., 1959.

JENNIFER LUND

DUPRÉ, LUCIEN JACQUES (1822–1869), congressman from Louisiana. Born in St. Landry Parish on April 18, 1822, Dupré came from a prominent Louisiana political family, his grandfather having served as governor of the state. Dupré received law degrees from both the University of Virginia and the University of Louisiana (now Tulane University). He practiced law in Opelousas before the war and was elected Fifteenth Judicial District judge in 1853. A secessionist Whig, Dupré attended the 1861 Louisiana secession convention (where he voted for secession) and the constitutional convention.

Dupré enlisted as a private in the Eighteenth Louisiana Infantry, but resigned in November 1861, following his election to the Confederate Congress. He was reelected in 1863, defeating two opponents. A strong supporter of the Davis administration, Dupré felt that Congress should allow the president to handle military matters without interference. While in Congress, Dupré sat on the Judiciary and Indian Affairs committees and chaired the Committee on Printing. He also headed a special committee on military economy. Dupré was a fiscal conservative and demonstrated his leanings by fighting against higher taxes and regulation of speculation. He also advocated equalization of salaries and proposed that Treasury notes be made legal tender, a move he hoped would curtail inflation. Dupré also opposed conscription, a stand fueled by his belief that the Union had captured New Orleans because of the lack of Confederate troops in Louisiana. He constantly supported military measures to regain New Orleans.

Following the war, Dupré, bankrupt and disheartened, resumed his law practice until his death in Opelousas on March 5, 1869.

BIBLIOGRAPHY

Warner, Ezra J., and W. Buck Yearns. *Biographical Register of the Confederate Congress*. Baton Rouge, La., 1975.

Winters, John D. *The Civil War in Louisiana*. Baton Rouge, La., 1963.

Yearns, Wilfred B. *The Confederate Congress*. Athens, Ga., 1969.

KEVIN S. FONTENOT

EARLY, JUBAL (1816–1894), lieutenant general. Early was one of the Confederacy's most able corps commanders and an architect of the cult of the Lost Cause. "Old Jube" fought in most of the major campaigns of the Army of Northern Virginia and held an independent command in the Shenandoah Valley late in the war. Although he should be considered just behind Thomas J. ("Stonewall") Jackson and James Longstreet in ability, Early's reputation suffered because of losses to Union Maj. Gen. Philip Sheridan in 1864 and because of a cantankerous personality that won from Robert E. Lee the fond epithet of "my bad old man" but also created friction with fellow officers.

Jubal Anderson Early was born November 3, 1816, in Rocky Mount, Franklin County, Virginia, the third of ten children. His father was a prominent farmer, his mother from a family with large slaveholdings. Young Jubal entered the U.S. Military Academy at West Point in 1833, performing better in academics than in discipline and graduating eighteenth of fifty in the class of 1837, which included Joseph Hooker, John C. Pemberton, and John Sedgwick. Commissioned second lieutenant July 1, 1837, Early as part of Company E, Third Artillery, participated in the Seminole War in Florida (1837–1838) and then went to Tennessee to assist with Indian removal. Before learning of his promotion to first lieutenant, to date from July 7, 1838, Early had begun the process of resigning from the army, effective July 31, 1838.

Returning to Rocky Mount, Early studied law and set up practice in 1840. He became active in the Whig party, representing Franklin County for a term in the Virginia General Assembly. In 1843, Early was appointed commonwealth's attorney for Franklin, a post he held until 1852. In between came service in the Mexican War. As major of the First Virginia Regiment, he performed garrison duty in northern Mexico under Zachary Taylor, seeing no combat but contracting the rheumatism that afflicted him throughout his life. He was honorably discharged August 3, 1848.

When the secession crisis came, Early won a seat as delegate to the Virginia secession convention, which convened in Richmond on February 13, 1861. Franklin County voters selected Early, a staunch Unionist, presumably because of the county's tobacco ties with markets in the North. Early's cautious approach earned him the nickname "the Terrapin from Franklin." Even after the climactic events at Fort Sumter and the Federal call for troops to put down the rebellion, Early voted on April 17 with the fifty-five delegates hoping to remain in the Union. When the ordinance passed, he barely hesitated before offering to help with the military defenses of Virginia, claiming that the U.S. Constitution still prevailed but that "that does not prevent our State authorities from repelling invasion." After the war, Early wrote that any doubts about secession "were soon dispelled by the unconstitutional measures of the authorities at Washington and the frenzied clamor of the people of the North for war upon their former brethren of the South."

For the next four years, the man called "Old Jube" or "Old Jubilee" by his troops would assert his forceful character on the battlefield. Named colonel on May 16, 1861, he led the brigade at First Manassas that turned the tide of battle late in the day on the Confederate left. For these efforts he was promoted to brigadier general, to date from July 21. At the Battle of Williamsburg on May 5, 1862, he was severely wounded in the shoulder but recuperated in time to rejoin the army at Malvern Hill on July 1. Commanding a brigade under Richard Ewell in Jackson's wing of the army, Early fought at Cedar Mountain, Second Manassas, and Harpers Ferry. Old Jube's performance at Sharpsburg garnered the praise of Lee and Jackson for

JUBAL EARLY.   LIBRARY OF CONGRESS

repelling withering Federal assaults on the Confederate left near the Dunkard Church. At the Battle of Fredericksburg on December 13, Early's men again sealed a breach during a crucial moment in the Union attack on the Confederate right.

By the end of 1862, Early had also proved himself to be one of the true characters in the army. He had a knack for challenging superiors without repercussion. While marching to Fredericksburg in late November, Jackson questioned why he saw so many stragglers in the rear of Early's column. Early cracked that Jackson witnessed the straggling "probably because he rode in the rear of my Division." The severe Jackson reportedly only smiled at the blunt reply. Early also was one of the few people who could swear in front of Lee, who overlooked such indiscretions because of Early's talents for command. Others, however, did not so readily forgive his acerbic nature. Brig. Gen. G. Moxley Sorrel wrote that Early's "irritable disposition and biting tongue made him anything but popular," and Confederate soldier Henry Kyd Douglas found him "arbitrary, cynical," and "personally disagreeable." Both, however, offered high praise for his abilities. Early himself knew the impression he had on others, but did not care.

In appearance, Early was considered striking with dark piercing eyes and a gray patriarchal beard broken at times by a smile like that of a possum. He rode into battle wearing a slouch hat topped by a black ostrich plume. Rheumatism bent his six-foot frame, making him appear shorter and older than he was. He punctuated a piping, nasal voice (which one person likened to an old woman's) with streams of tobacco juice and stinging oaths that impressed many with their originality. Arriving at Lynchburg, Virginia, in 1864, he raised himself in the saddle to yell to Federal cavalry: "No buttermilk rangers after you now, you God-damned Blue-Butts!"

Promotion to major general did not come until January 17, 1863. At that time he was also confirmed as permanent commander of Ewell's former division. As Lee and Jackson outmaneuvered Union Maj. Gen. Joseph Hooker at Chancellorsville (May 1–3), Early guarded Marye's Heights above Fredericksburg against Maj. Gen. John Sedgwick. The Union forces proved too much for Old Jube's smaller command, but the Confederates on May 4 regrouped with Lee's army to push Sedgwick back over the Rappahannock.

In June 1863, Lee steered his army northward to conduct a raid that culminated at Gettysburg. With the death of Jackson at Chancellorsville, Ewell had ascended to command of the Second Corps, which included Early's division. To them fell the task of clearing the Union Eighth Corps under Maj. Gen. Robert H. Milroy from Winchester, Virginia. On June 14, Early's men successfully stormed a Federal fort northwest of town in what became the Second Battle of Winchester. Early's men continued through the Cumberland Valley into Pennsylvania, brushing aside the minimal resistance from emergency militia and traveling to the Susquehanna River at Wrightsville until receiving the call from Lee to concentrate toward Gettysburg. The march fortuitously placed Early's men on the enemy's right flank in the late afternoon of July 1, just in time to help shatter the Eleventh Corps under Maj. Gen. O. O. Howard and chase it through town toward Cemetery Hill.

What happened next became one of the great "what ifs" of the Civil War. Lee ordered Ewell to take Culp's Hill, if practicable. Early and Ewell both believed their men too disorganized to seize the moment. After the war, Early and Longstreet waged a bitter war of words over this and other actions at Gettysburg in some of the most celebrated articles written about the conflict. Each blamed the other for contributing to Confederate defeat. Some historians believe Ewell (and secondarily Early) acted appropriately based on information of the time. Nonetheless, Early overstated Longstreet's culpability in an attempt to absolve Lee from criticism.

Early continued to show promise for higher command, although his progress was not unblemished. He took part in a disaster at the Rappahannock Bridge on November 7, 1863, but performed better in the Mine Run campaign at the end of November, leading the Second Corps when Ewell fell ill. In December, he was sent to western Virginia to disrupt rail lines of the Baltimore and Ohio and canvass the countryside for supplies. At the Wilderness on May 5 and 6, 1864, Early refused to launch a flank attack on the Federal right because he believed an enemy force would prevent the maneuver (despite testimony to the contrary from John B. Gordon). Although Lee needed to prod Early to make the successful attack, he valued his lieutenant enough to give him the Third Corps at Spotsylvania when A. P. Hill fell ill. Early returned briefly to divisional command before taking over the Second Corps when Lee removed Ewell.

The new lieutenant general, with promotion to date from May 31, 1864, shortly received exciting orders. Union forces under Maj. Gen. David A. Hunter were advancing up the Shenandoah Valley with the ultimate destination of Lynchburg. If the railroad link in that town were severed, and the Valley controlled by the Federals, then a vital granary and invasion route would be lost. On June 12, Lee ordered a twofold mission: clear Hunter and his army out of the Valley and then head north to threaten Baltimore and Washington in the hope that Ulysses S. Grant would divert troops from the Richmond-Petersburg theater. With his small Army of the Valley, numbering from 8,000 to never more than 14,500, Early from June to November marched more than 1,600 miles while fighting seventy-five battles and skirmishes. His men chased Hunter from the valley in mid-June, raided Maryland, collected levies of $220,000 from Hagerstown and Frederick, defeated a scratch force under Lew Wallace at Monocacy Junction on July 9, and threatened to enter Washington, D.C., on July 11. Many criticized Early for failing to take the city, but the fight at the Monocacy River had delayed the advance, allowing two divisions of the Union's Sixth Corps to file into the defenses and limit the chances of success. Early's campaign nevertheless had caught Grant by surprise and forced the diversion of the Sixth and Nineteenth Corps that would have faced the Army of Northern Virginia.

Grant now ordered Philip Sheridan to assemble an Army of the Shenandoah to deny Lee the Valley's resources. In three battles—Third Winchester on September 19, Fisher's Hill on September 22, and Cedar Creek on October 19—Sheridan defeated the Confederates. At Cedar Creek, however, Early had conducted a surprise flank attack that routed two corps and forced another to withdraw until Sheridan delivered a decisive counterattack later that day.

Many Southerners blamed Early for the loss of the Valley, although it is doubtful anyone else could have prevented it. He made errors in the placement of his troops but overall conducted an excellent campaign that rivaled Jackson's performance of 1862. The fall defeats, however, removed the area from the Confederates and contributed to a turn in Northern morale that ensured President Abraham Lincoln's reelection in November.

After a defeat of his thousand-man force on March 2, 1865, at Waynesboro, Early finally was removed by Lee, who still had faith in his lieutenant but recognized his "bad old man" had lost the confidence of soldiers and authorities. Artillerist E. Porter Alexander after the war wrote that Early had "proved himself a remarkable corps commander," adding that his "greatest quality perhaps was the fearlessness with which he fought against all odds & discouragements."

After Lee's surrender, Early fled first to Texas and then to Mexico, finally arriving in Canada in July 1866 where he wrote his memoirs. He returned to the United States in 1869, after President Andrew Johnson pardoned former Confederates, and settled in Lynchburg to practice law. In 1877 he became a commissioner of the Louisiana State Lottery, which allowed him to pursue his lecture tours and writing for various Confederate military studies. The former Unionist became an unreconstructed rebel who wore only gray and never apologized for his actions, including the burning of Chambersburg, Pennsylvania, on July 30, 1864, which he ordered as retribution for Union destruction in the Shenandoah Valley.

As an officer in both the Association of the Army of Northern Virginia and the Southern Historical Society, Early had an enormous influence on the writing of Civil War history. He helped fashion the cult of the Lost Cause, elevating Lee to saintlike status and arguing that the agrarian South never lost a battle but only succumbed to overwhelming numbers churned out by a greedy, industrial North. As long as Old Jube lived, wrote historian Robert Stiles, "no man ever took up his pen to write a line about the great conflict without the fear of Jubal Early before his eyes."

Early maintained his cantankerous ways until 1894. On February 16, he took a fall from which he never recovered and finally died on March 2. He was buried in Spring Hill Cemetery in Lynchburg.

BIBLIOGRAPHY

Bushong, Millard K. *Old Jube: A Biography of General Jubal A. Early.* Boyce, Va., 1955. Reprint, Shippensburg, Pa., 1988.

Early, Jubal Anderson. *Autobiographical Sketch and Narrative of the War between the States.* Philadelphia, 1912. Reprint, Wilmington, N.C., 1989.

Early, Jubal A. *A Memoir of the Last Year of the War for Independence, in the Confederate States of America, Containing an Account of His Commands in the Years 1864–1865.* Toronto, 1867.

Freeman, Douglas S. *Lee's Lieutenants: A Study in Command.* 3 vols. New York, 1942–1944. Reprint, New York, 1986.

Osborne, Charles C. *Jubal: The Life and Times of Jubal A. Early, CSA, Defender of the Lost Cause.* Chapel Hill, N.C., 1992.

Stiles, Robert. *Four Years Under Marse Robert*. New York, 1903. Reprint, Dayton, Ohio, 1977.

WILLIAM ALAN BLAIR

EARLY'S WASHINGTON RAID.

With about 14,000 men, Lt. Gen. Jubal Early in July 1864 raided Maryland, defeated a small force at Monocacy Junction, threatened to enter Washington, D.C., and forced the Union to divert the better portion of two corps that would have been pitted against the Army of Northern Virginia. Early lost about 700 and the Federals 1,300 of their roughly 7,000 men during the major action of the campaign at the Monocacy River on July 9.

Early conducted the raid as the second half of a two-part plan by Gen. Robert E. Lee first to clear the Shenandoah Valley of Union soldiers and then to threaten Washington and Baltimore to compel Ulysses S. Grant to siphon troops from Petersburg. Recently promoted to command the Second Corps of the Army of Northern Virginia, "Old Jube" started for Lynchburg on June 13 to prevent Union Maj. Gen. David A. Hunter from seizing the town and severing a vital east-west rail link. Although Hunter commanded 18,000 men against Early's 12,000, the Union general apparently lost his nerve, retreated to the west on June 19, and handed the valley to the Confederates.

Early seized the chance Hunter's departure presented; by July 5, the vanguard of the newly christened Army of the Valley had begun crossing the Potomac at Shepherdstown. Complicating Early's advance was a vaguely defined scheme to free Confederate prisoners of war at Point Lookout,

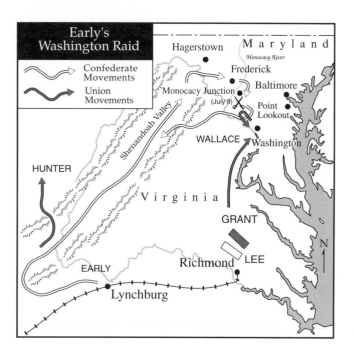

below Baltimore. Lee wanted Early to incorporate the men into the Army of the Valley but could supply his lieutenant with few details on how the escape would be managed. Early sent cavalry toward Baltimore to cut rail lines and be in position to aid the escaped Confederates—something that never occurred because Federals learned of the escape plan. With the remainder of the army, Early traveled through many of the sites of the 1862 Maryland campaign. At Hagerstown and Frederick he forced levies totaling $220,000.

Union Maj. Gen. Lew Wallace, meanwhile, had used his own initiative to establish a force at Monocacy Junction, several miles south of Frederick, where he could protect roads leading to Baltimore and Washington as well as a rail line of the Baltimore and Ohio. To bolster his force of reserves, Wallace received last-minute reinforcement from seasoned veterans of James B. Rickett's division of the Sixth Corps. Wallace stationed most of his men where they could guard two bridges—a wooden structure for the Georgetown Road and an iron one for the Baltimore and Ohio rail line a half mile to the north. He also sent a portion of his troops two miles farther to the north to protect the Baltimore Pike from Robert Rodes's Confederate division.

After testing the Union positions with artillery and a demonstration that Wallace repulsed, Early concluded that he would have to ford the Monocacy to flank the Union position. John McCausland's cavalry fortuitously provided the way when the men crossed the river roughly a mile below the bridge and ran into the Union left. Early decided that Dodson Ramseur's division would hold the center while John B. Gordon's division followed the cavalry's path to attack the Federal left. Gordon advanced with three brigades, attacking en echelon from the right under brigadiers Clement A. Evans, Zebulon York, and William Terry. After emerging from woods seven hundred yards from the Union soldiers, Gordon's men needed to mount three charges across a field choked with shocks of wheat and broken by a stream to force the Federals from three positions along wooden fences, a stone fence, and finally the cuts along the Georgetown Road. General Evans went down with a serious wound early in the attacks. By 4:30 P.M. the work was done; Wallace's men retreated toward Baltimore and the road to Washington lay open to Early's men.

Shortly after noon on July 11, Early scanned the outer defenses of Washington while the remainder of his army finished an arduous march in extreme heat along dust-choked roads. Early correctly judged his men to be too fatigued to attack works manned by 100-day men, invalids, and heavy artillery. The delay, however, proved fateful. During the night, the remainder of the Sixth Corps under Maj. Gen. Horatio G. Wright filed into the defenses. They would soon be bolstered by the Nineteenth Corps under William H. Emory. Wallace's defense at the Monocacy had delayed Early's men just enough to allow reinforcements to arrive.

Early spent July 12 skirmishing with Union soldiers, but decided to withdraw rather than risk an attack that would have proved far too costly, even if successful. The Confederates recrossed the Potomac at White's Ford, July 13 and 14, having raided the North successfully and having forced Grant to part with troops that could have helped in the campaign against Lee.

BIBLIOGRAPHY

Cooling, B. Franklin. *Jubal Early's Raid on Washington: 1864.* Baltimore, 1989.

Gallagher, Gary W., ed. *Struggle for the Shenandoah: Essays on the 1864 Valley Campaign.* Kent, Ohio, 1991.

Vandiver, Frank E. *Jubal's Raid: General Early's Famous Attack on Washington in 1865.* New York, 1960.

Worthington, Glenn. *Fighting for Time; or, The Battle that Saved Washington and Mayhap the Union.* Baltimore, 1932.

WILLIAM ALAN BLAIR

EASTPORT. The Confederates purchased the swift, 700-ton, 280-foot-long steamer *Eastport* October 31, 1861, and took it up the Tennessee River to Cerro Gordo, Tennessee. Workmen began converting it into an ironclad, but when Fort Henry fell April 6, 1862, they scuttled the vessel. Had it been finished, its superiority over Union gunboats would have substantially bolstered Confederate defenses.

After reaching Cerro Gordo on February 7, 1862, Union Lt. Samuel Ludyard Phelps's flotilla crew raised *Eastport* and sent the ship and the abandoned materials necessary to finish it to Cairo, Illinois. Phelps received command of the eight-gun ironclad when it was commissioned in August. Transferred from the War to the Navy Department January 9, 1863, *Eastport* headed for Vicksburg in February but struck a sandbar; after a four-month delay for repairs, it began patrolling the Mississippi River.

When the Union fleet steamed up the Red River on March 12, 1864, *Eastport* led the way. It cleared the obstructions below Fort De Russy and then bombarded the fort until its surrender two days later. Pushing on to Alexandria, the fleet took sixty hours to get *Eastport* over the rocky falls. But an obstruction blocked the ships at Shreveport Landing on April 10, and the expedition started downstream.

Eastport hit a torpedo and sank below Grand Ecore on April 15. Raised on the twenty-first, it covered fifty-two miles and grounded seven times before finally foundering on April 26. Later that day, following the removal of personnel and equipment, *Eastport* was blown up.

BIBLIOGRAPHY

Johnson, Ludwell H. *Red River Campaign: Politics and Cotton in the Civil War.* Baltimore, Md., 1958.

Still, William N., Jr. *Iron Afloat: The Story of the Confederate Armorclads.* Nashville, Tenn., 1971.

LAWRENCE L. HEWITT

ECHOLS, JOHN (1823–1896), brigadier general. A prominent Virginian but somewhat obscure Confederate officer, Echols was born March 20, 1823, in Lynchburg. At his 1840 graduation from Washington College in Lexington, he and twenty of his classmates established the alumni association of that institution. Echols studied law at Harvard and started a legal practice in Staunton. He successively became commonwealth attorney, member of the state's general assembly, and delegate to the Virginia secession convention.

Appointed lieutenant colonel of the Twenty-seventh Virginia, Echols led the regiment at First Manassas. Promotion to colonel occurred shortly after. At Kernstown, Echols suffered a severe arm wound, but his gallantry brought an April 16, 1862, advance to brigadier general. A huge man (six feet, four inches tall, 260 pounds), he served most of the remainder of the war in western Virginia. He was in the action at Droop Mountain and commanded the Confederate right at New Market. In both Jubal Early's raid on Washington and the second Shenandoah Valley

JOHN ECHOLS.   NATIONAL ARCHIVES

campaign, Echols's troops played a support role. He was in command of southwestern Virginia at Robert E. Lee's surrender. Echols guarded President Jefferson Davis on his flight from Danville to Augusta.

Echols had an impressive postwar career. He became a prominent Staunton businessman, served on the Committee of Nine in the restoration to the Union of his native state, and was instrumental in the expansion of the old Virginia Central Railroad into the Chesapeake and Ohio rail system. Echols served on the board of visitors of both Washington and Lee University and Virginia Military Institute. He died May 24, 1896, of Bright's disease in Staunton, where he is buried.

BIBLIOGRAPHY

"Gen. John Echols." *Confederate Veteran* 4 (1896): 316–317. Reprint, Wilmington, N.C., 1985.
Hotchkiss, Jedediah. *Virginia.* Vol. 3 of *Confederate Military History.* Edited by Clement A. Evans. Atlanta, 1899. Vol. 4 of extended ed. Wilmington, N.C., 1987.

JAMES I. ROBERTSON, JR.

ECHOLS, JOSEPH HUBBARD (1816–1885),

congressman from Georgia. Echols was born into a wealthy planter family in Washington, Georgia, on December 26, 1816. He attended Randolph-Macon College in Virginia and the University of Georgia, where he graduated in 1838, after taking two months off to serve in the army supervising Cherokee removal in northern Georgia. Echols's family had then moved to nearby Lexington, Georgia, where he read law and was admitted to the bar in 1841. In 1845, he became a Methodist minister and spent the next five years as a circuit preacher. In 1851, he was appointed professor of mathematics at the female college in Madison, Georgia. He also served as president of the college from 1852 until 1856, when his father died and he returned to Lexington to manage the large cotton plantation he had inherited.

Though Unionist in sentiment in 1861, he was elected to the state senate after Georgia's secession and served until October 1863, when he was elected to represent the Sixth District in the House of Representatives. Adhering to Governor Joseph E. Brown's state rights stance, he decisively defeated incumbent William W. Clark, a strong supporter of Jefferson Davis's administration. Once he reached Richmond, though, Echols's concerns were similar to those of Clark. He pushed for greater relief to soldiers' families and more flexibility in the collection of the tax-in-kind from them. He favored the sale of government cotton to pay the Confederate debt and supported cotton broker interests by urging that price regulations be limited only to cotton sold to the government. As a minister, he made his most memorable impression on Congress by proposing that military policy adhere to stricter observance of the Sabbath.

Echols supported congressional efforts to negotiate a peace settlement with the Lincoln administration. He was so disappointed by the failure of the Hampton Roads peace conference in February 1865 that he returned home from Richmond, never to return to Congress.

Echols spent the postwar years managing his plantation in Lexington, participating in an Augusta cotton exchange, and continuing his ministry through Methodist circuits until his death in 1885.

BIBLIOGRAPHY

Knight, Lucian Lamar. *Standard History of Georgia and Georgians.* New York, 1917.
Smith, Florie Carter. *History of Oglethorpe County, Georgia.* Washington, Ga., 1970.
Warner, Ezra J., and W. Buck Yearns. *Biographical Register of the Confederate Congress.* Baton Rouge, La., 1975.

JOHN C. INSCOE

ECONOMY. The Confederate States of America faced many problems during its four-year existence, and many if not most of them were related to mobilizing and paying for the war effort. During the war, the Southern economy underwent many permutations. Most scholars agree that Confederate fiscal and monetary policies weakened the Southern economy and thus hastened, if not caused, eventual Southern defeat. Nevertheless, despite the many flaws in economic policy-making, the Confederate economy did manage to support the war effort for four years. In the process, the Southern economy was transformed from its antebellum roots.

In 1861, the eleven states that formed the Confederacy contained 9 million people, of which close to 4 million were bondsmen. These inhabitants lived in an overwhelmingly agricultural economy: cotton was indeed king and represented almost 70 percent of all U.S. exports. The vast majority of Southerners farmed, and those who realized profits usually plowed them back into land and slaves.

Still, many Southerners had, during the decade immediately preceding the firing on Fort Sumter, awakened to the perils of a staple crop economy. Commercial conventions and the press began trumpeting the need to diversify as early as the 1840s. In the beginning, the voices of J. D. B. De Bow, William Gregg, and Daniel Pratt appeared to be voices in the South's agrarian wilderness, but by the 1850s, these stalwart boosters of economic diversification began to attract an audience. During the 1850s, their boosterism bore fruit, as Southerners began to invest in nonagricultural pursuits. Southerners increased railroad mileage almost 300 percent; they poured millions into industrial establishments such as cotton and rolling mills; and they improved the value of the products they produced by close to 300 percent. By 1860, the South contained over 20,000 manufacturing establishments, which employed over 110,000 workers and represented a capital investment of $95,974,585—an increase of more than 100 percent over 1850 totals.

But despite such impressive totals, the Southern states still lagged well behind the more industrialized North. Indeed, the South's share of national manufacturing actually dropped between 1850 and 1860. Moreover, the growth was uneven: some states in the Deep South contained few industrial establishments and even fewer rail lines, while states such as Virginia and Georgia housed most of the factories and about one-third of the railroads. (These figures are based upon the *Statistical View of the United States . . . Compendium of the Seventh Census,* 1850, and the *Eighth Census of the United States: Manufactures,* 1860. The census takers used different categorizations for manufacturing and other pursuits; consequently, there may be slight variations. These figures are drawn for the Southern states, defined as the eleven states of the future Confederacy.) In short, the South expanded dramatically, but the rest of the nation grew even more rapidly. Consequently, when the Confederate States formed, they produced one-twentieth the amount of pig iron and had one-twenty-fourth the number of locomotives and one-seventeenth the amount of cotton and woolen goods that the North had.

This nation of farmers was undaunted by the task it faced. Though many in Montgomery (and later Richmond) realized that the Confederacy faced formidable handicaps, most were confident that indigenous resources and foreign purchases could provide all the nascent country needed to defeat the Union.

Foreign Trade

Initially, both Union and Confederate officials concentrated upon European sources for supply. This was not unusual: though the North had an established manufacturing base, it, like the South, was woefully deficient in war matériel. Consequently, the first skirmishes between the two sides took place in the financial and manufacturing centers of England and the Continent.

Until about 1862, Confederate procurement policies abroad were marked by their haphazard nature. To be sure, Confederate purchasing agents were dispatched to Europe to buy, usually on credit, badly needed war goods. For the first year and a half, foreign purchases were paid for with specie, foreign bills of exchange, and credit. Eventually, the Treasury Department relied upon Confederate bonds and cotton certificates to pay for foreign goods.

Finding adequate sources of funds and credit were

problems for the Confederacy's foreign agents, but they were by no means the only ones. Most of the agents represented different bureaus within the Confederate government. As a result, competition ensued between the Ordnance and Navy departments, and others. This competition hindered Confederate purchasing efforts and gradually led to an overhaul of the system. Colin McRae became the Confederacy's sole government agent in 1863. After that year, McRae apportioned funds for foreign goods among the various departments and oversaw the general financing of war matériel with cotton. Had this reorganization taken place sooner, Confederate financial and purchasing operations abroad would have been enhanced significantly.

Davis and others within the Congress realized that the new nation needed foreign goods, but they also believed that Europe needed Southern cotton more. Consequently, they were confident that a self-imposed blockade on cotton shipments abroad would force Britain and France to intervene to secure an uninterrupted flow of cotton. This policy was endorsed by the press, planters, factors, and other businessmen involved in the production and shipment of cotton. Although Congress never passed a law prohibiting cotton exports, the states and localities passed restrictive measures that had the desired effect. These measures were enforced by local committees of public safety.

The states and localities that enacted restrictive legislation lifted those restrictions beginning in 1862. By the time the Confederacy did this, the Union's naval blockade was in place. Davis and others assumed that the existence of a "paper blockade" in defiance of international law would force Britain and France to intervene to break the Union blockade, but such was not the case. Nor did the Confederate government make an effort initially to circumvent the Union cordon and thus send 400,000 stockpiled bales of cotton overseas. Instead, Davis encouraged private firms to do so. Nonetheless, Confederate purchasing agent Caleb Huse bought four steamers for the government to use in running the blockade. These vessels ran the gauntlet forty-four times without a loss.

The continued competition between Confederate agents overseas and the success of these Confederate blockade runners convinced the South's European emissaries and chief agent McRae that the government should become actively involved in blockade running. Congress finally acceded to the request and passed a law in 1863 requiring all blockade-running vessels to carry at least one-third to one-half of their cargo on government account. Congress grudgingly followed up on this law a year later when it passed an initiative that prohibited the importation of luxuries and gave Davis the authority to regulate all cotton shipments sent out of the Confederacy. The results of this experiment in state socialism were impressive: Davis reported that all the problems with the old system of individual runners had been eliminated. Cotton was being shipped to Europe where it played a key role in financing purchases of badly needed war matériel and in boosting Confederate credit overseas. Had this government oversight been undertaken sooner, there is no doubt that the South would have been able to obtain more supplies and would have been able to finance its foreign operations more efficaciously.

Mobilizing for War

President Jefferson Davis initially may have misjudged the extent of the Union blockade, but he did not underestimate the North's war-making capacity. Indeed, Davis placed top priority on obtaining arms, ammunition, and other accoutrements of war for his armies. The War Department's Ordnance Bureau rose to the challenge of equipping the Southern armies.

The chief of the Ordnance Bureau was Josiah Gorgas. This Pennsylvania-born officer was a godsend to the Confederacy; he worked miracles. He knew that the whole Confederacy contained only two mills capable of rolling and rerolling iron. He immediately contracted with the Tredegar Iron Works and the Atlanta Rolling Mill (later renamed the Confederate Rolling Mill) for badly needed iron bar and plate. With government aid in the form of lucrative advances to firms that would convert to government production, and with the establishment of Confederate arsenals, depots, an ammunition laboratory, and powderworks, Gorgas succeeded in creating what one scholar has termed a military-industrial complex. Gorgas himself noted in his diary that "where three years ago we were not making a gun, pistol, nor a sabre, no shot or shell [except at the Tredegar Iron Works]—a pound of powder—we now make all these in quantities to meet the demands of our large armies." Statistics bear out Gorgas's statement. The Atlanta Rolling Mill produced almost 400,000 pounds of sheet iron for the Confederate Navy Department in 1862 alone. The Augusta Powder Works churned out, among other things, 110 twelve-pound guns, 4.6 million lead balls, over 10 million small arms cartridges, and 174 gun carriages. The Tredegar Iron Works produced over 200 pieces of heavy siege, field, and seacoast ordnance a year and, in 1862 alone, manufactured 351 such guns.

Gorgas also drew upon the expertise of smaller manufacturers. The Ordnance Bureau directed local and regional arsenals to let contracts with interested parties to produce assorted accoutrements for the War Department. The response was immediate. Hardware shops, gunsmiths, and others converted existing facilities into small factories to produce war matériel.

The Quartermaster Department oversaw the mobilization of the economy for the supply of the armies. The first quartermaster general, Col. Abraham C. Myers, was not as capable as Gorgas, nor did he have enough supplies on hand—uniforms, blankets, tents, and the like—to clothe and equip all the soldiers who took up Confederate arms. Consequently, Myers offered cash bonuses to those who initially supplied their own. He then placed advertisements in newspapers throughout the South soliciting contracts for uniforms, clothing, blankets, and tents. The response to these entreaties was immediate. Established textile firms and budding entrepreneurs took advantage of lucrative contracts to produce for the Quartermaster Department.

The euphoria among the manufacturers soon waned, however, and the department found itself with less goods than anticipated. The problem lay in the system: competitive bidding led manufacturers to sell more goods on the open market where greater profits could be made. Those manufacturers then reneged altogether on government contracts. These problems were soon exacerbated by the loss of two key quartermaster depots in Nashville and New Orleans. To compensate, Myers directed local agents to impress needed raw materials for government factories, and he saw to it that factories kept their workers via draft exemptions.

Myers was soon faced with the necessity of reorganizing the bureau. He did not survive the reorganization: he was replaced by Brig. Gen. Alexander R. Lawton in 1863. Lawton went even further than Myers. He renegotiated all contracts and lowered the profit ceiling from 75 percent to 33⅓ percent. He kept manufacturers with government contracts faithful by making them dependent upon the department for raw materials and labor exemptions. Though accounts are fragmentary, it appears that all factories with quartermaster contracts were required to earmark two-thirds of their output for the department.

The early successes of the Ordnance and Quartermaster bureaus were gradually forgotten after 1863. From that year until the end of the Confederacy, all Confederate bureaus were increasingly faced with problems that did not go away and that reflected graver problems in the Confederate economy. As time passed, machinery and spare parts wore out and could not be replaced because raw materials were lacking. Replacement parts and supplemental goods could not be obtained because the Union blockade's increased effectiveness cut down on the amount of cargo that could be garnered from outside sources. Indigenous sources of raw materials were slowly but steadily lost as the Union military continued its conquest of the Southern heartland. When raw materials were obtained it was often to little effect. In 1864, Davis and the War Department issued General Order No. 77, which rescinded exemptions for virtually all detailed laborers. Consequently, all private firms lost their skilled workers to the Confederate army. (It should be noted, however, that the Ordnance and Niter and Mining bureaus successfully appealed this ruling and were able to maintain, with only a slight reduction, their work force.) Some factories went bankrupt because the government could not pay for contracted goods. Quartermaster General Lawton estimated that his bureau owed factories with government accounts over $5 million by 1865.

Other problems in production were related to other weaknesses within the Confederate economy. The breakdown of the Southern transportation system proved decisive in the final demise of the Confederate war effort. The South's failure to maintain its limited rail network doomed most supply efforts: both raw materials destined for factories producing war goods and foodstuffs bound for the armies or urban centers were often left at the depot for want of transportation. So too, the South's failure to create an adequate credit system to buy supplies from domestic and foreign sources seriously handicapped the Confederacy's ability to support its war effort completely.

Despite these problems, the Confederacy's military mobilization should still get high marks. The South did manage to expand its antebellum manufacturing base enough to sustain its field armies, for the most part, for four years. But this was achieved at a high cost: the government's mobilization policies profoundly affected the domestic economy and resulted in much hardship for the Southern people.

Fiscal Policy

Jefferson Davis vested the task of overseeing the Confederate economy with Christopher G. Memminger, a lawyer from South Carolina who had only limited experience in business and financial affairs. The secretary of the treasury enumerated several measures to finance the war effort during the early months of the Confederacy, including war taxes, tariffs, the floating of bonds, and the acquisition of overseas credit. Few of these initiatives proved adequate to sustain the economy's war-making capabilities.

From the beginning, Memminger and the Treasury Department relied upon loans to finance the war effort. As early as February 28, 1861, Congress passed the Act to Raise Money for the Government and to Provide for the Defence of the Confederate States of America. This loan, the so-called $15 million loan, instructed Memminger to issue $15 million in bonds or stock certificates bearing 8 percent interest, paid semiannually in specie. The loan was to be paid for with an export duty on cotton. Unfortunately, the loan proved difficult to administer: all banks within the Confederacy had suspended specie payments almost immediately after secession. This merely compounded the more serious problem of a general dearth of hard currency in the Confederacy to pay the interest on the bonds subscribed. In order to solve this problem, Memminger altered the loan

subscription policies slightly to allow payment in bank notes of exchange. This loan was fully subscribed and did aid the Confederacy in its early days. Still, as most knew, it was not enough. Consequently, the Treasury Department turned to other types of loans.

Produce Loans. The most successful and longest lived loans were produce loans, which Congress authorized on May 16, 1861, at Memminger's request. Fifty million dollars worth of twenty-year bonds were, according to the law, to be sold for "specie, military stores, or for the proceeds of sales of raw produce or manufactured articles, to be paid in the form of specie or with foreign bills of exchange." The act also directed the Treasury to issue $20 million in Treasury notes that were to be used by the people to pay all taxes. Antebellum newspaper editor and tireless Southern booster J. D. B. De Bow was placed in charge of the loan's administration.

The Southern people reacted favorably to the loan. In fact, so many people subscribed that it was extended by $100 million more in August 1861. This extension was funded by a war tax on property and was designed to continue to bolster Confederate credit overseas and help curb the inflationary nature of the currency by taking excess Treasury notes out of circulation. Over time, however, the enthusiasm for the produce loans began to wane. Many agricultural producers disliked the government's call to pay for the bonds on a set day—it implied the government could choose a day when agricultural prices were very low, thus forcing farmers to sell at a loss. These complaints led many farmers to urge Congress to pass legislation guaranteeing them relief. Some went so far as to urge the government to buy all crops. These plans for state subsidies and government control of produce died quietly.

Congress followed the produce loans with the issue of more Treasury notes: an April 18, 1862, law called for $250 million in Treasury stocks, notes, and bonds to be issued. At Memminger's request, the law allowed individuals to exchange goods in kind for the notes. These regulations were further refined less than a month later, when the Treasury Department instructed bond officials to buy only cotton with the bonds.

Subscribers to the produce loan were also urged to pay their subscriptions, especially since cotton was selling well on the open market. Here, however, many farmers and planters balked, for they believed that the price of cotton differed in various parts of the Confederacy. Farmers also demanded that payment for their cotton be made in Treasury notes, a negotiable form of de facto legal tender, instead of non-negotiable Confederate bonds with a lengthy term of maturity.

The Treasury's renewed emphasis on cotton was understandable. Cotton was garnering good prices, and many believed it could be used to finance more foreign purchases.

Consequently, Memminger began to issue cotton certificates. These were to be offered in Europe as collateral for any war purchases made by Southern agents.

The Erlanger Loan. Many disagreed with the stockpiling of cotton to finance foreign purchases; with the Union blockade reducing exports, it appeared more and more unlikely that the South would be able to get all its warehoused cotton to Europe. Still, that cotton was to serve as the collateral on the Confederacy's $15 million Erlanger loan.

The Erlanger loan was negotiated October 28, 1862, between Confederate agent John Slidell and the French banking house of Emile Erlanger and Company. The final agreement (completed in January 1863) called for the Erlanger House to float a $15 million loan. The Confederate Congress was to borrow 75 million francs, using 7 percent bonds based on cotton as collateral. The Erlanger loan was an initial success, but the military fortunes of Confederate armies soon dampened enthusiasm for the loan. Indeed, news of Confederate defeats depressed the market in 1863, but renewed successes in 1864 buoyed it back up. By February 1865, almost all the loan had been sold for $7.7 million—just over half its face value. Still, the Erlanger loan played a pivotal role in Confederate financial operations, for it restored Southern credit abroad and allowed Southern agents to contract for more war matériel.

As might be expected, the resort to loans and the printing press created unprecedented levels of inflation. As the stock of money increased, so too did price levels. The urban populations were especially hard hit by prices that seemed to spiral out of control. Indeed, by the end of 1863, the general price index in the eastern Confederacy was over two thousand times what it had been in January 1861; by the beginning of 1865, that index was over five thousand times the 1861 levels. State and local governments did attempt to address this problem by fixing prices and by establishing city stores for the poor. But often these initiatives merely added to the inflationary spiral by encouraging hoarding.

Taxation. High prices and charges of speculation and hoarding were heard throughout the Confederate South. Again, government programs did little to arrest these problems; in fact, they may have exacerbated them. In an ongoing effort to feed the Southern troops and ensure that farmers and planters did their share for the Confederate cause, Congress passed the Impressment Act on March 26, 1863, and the Tax-in-Kind Acts on April 24, 1863. Secretary of the Treasury Memminger urged the passage of a tax-in-kind for several reasons: it would help provide subsistence for the army; it would keep the Confederate government from having to impress needed agricultural goods from the civilian population; it would remove the government from the marketplace for food, thus increasing the amount available for civilian consumption; it would

relieve the flood of currency in circulation; and it would be a tax easy to collect and less easy to evade. The tax-in-kind called for all Southern farmers and planters to contribute one-tenth of their agricultural products and one-tenth of their slaughtered hogs to the Treasury and War departments, the chief administrators of the tax. Government agents, known derisively as T.I.K. men, would assess the value of farm products and tell the producers what their tax would be. The goods would then be collected and funneled to district-level administrators who would see that the food was forwarded to the armies.

The tax-in-kind proved to be one of the most unpopular measures ever passed. All farmers resisted the assessment process and argued that the agricultural tithe was merely a euphemism for impressment. Farmers were also plagued by phony agents who stole goods at random. Finally, many of the goods destined for the troops never reached them because the overburdened Confederate railroads could not transport them; tons of produce rotted at government depots as a result. The chorus of protest against the law resulted in its eventual amendment. In February 1864, Congress allowed farmers to pay the tax on sweet potatoes in cash, and those who had a relative in the ranks were exempted altogether. By 1865, all individuals had the option to pay the tithe in cash.

The Confederate Congress passed the Impressment Act also in 1863. It was born out of the Commissary and Quartermaster departments' need to acquire food, transportation, and slave labor to build fortifications, drive wagons, and assist in the general war effort. One historian has noted that the act merely legalized what the armies and the bureaus were already practicing: the seizure of goods to support the armies at the front lines. Again, the Southern people resisted—and resented—the law because it allowed the army to impress food and other supplies at government-fixed prices that were often 50 percent below the prevailing market rates. Farmers and merchants, when they were reimbursed by impressment agents, were paid in badly depreciated Confederate scrip. As with the tax-in-kind, the impressment process encouraged individuals to hoard goods—despite stiff penalties for those found evading the law. It also contributed to the downward trend of civilian morale. Fear of seizures, the lack of confidence in Confederate money, and the perception that the government was becoming a centralized tyranny created popular bitterness and resentment, which only added to the malaise that dominated the home front by the beginning of 1864.

The Confederacy's resort to such measures as the tax-in-kind and impressment reflected the government's failure to develop an adequate tax system. In 1861, most Confederate officials believed that the war would be short and thus could be financed through import and export duties. In February 1861 the Provisional Congress passed a temporary tariff based upon the 1857 U.S. tariff. The next month, Congress levied additional duties on imports of iron, coal, cheese, lumber, and paper and placed a tax on all ships passing into Southern ports. Unfortunately for Secretary Memminger, these duties amounted only to approximately $3.5 million because of the increased effectiveness of the Union's naval blockade.

Memminger saw the failure of this policy and began to advocate the levying of a direct tax on real property. The tax would be used to pay the interest on foreign loans and would reduce the redundancy of the currency because it would be paid in Treasury notes. Memminger pleaded his case in May 1861, but Congress and the president balked: both feared the people would resent the intrusion of government and the cost of a direct tax. Memminger was also stymied by the Confederate Constitution, which mandated that all taxes be apportioned according to population, a stipulation that required a census. Given the instability occasioned by the war, the taking of a census was manifestly impossible. Congress did incorporate tax provisions in its 1861 loan acts, including one that levied a tax of one-half of 1 percent on all Southern taxable wealth. Memminger estimated that $26 million could be realized from this levy. To sweeten the law—and to obviate the need to establish a national tax-gathering mechanism—the law allowed the states to decrease the tax by 10 percent if the state assumed the tax for its residents. As might be expected, the states followed the law as they interpreted it. Most floated state bonds to pay for the tax instead of adding the half of 1 percent tax to state taxes. Ultimately, about $18 million was collected under these provisions.

The failure to tax in adequate measure continued to force the Confederate government to rely on notes, loans, and bonds. But by 1863, this policy had created a debt so huge that the government could not even pay the interest on it. As bonds and notes continued to be printed, inflation spiraled. Consequently, many people began to lobby for the enactment of a general tax law. Congress responded and on April 24, 1863, passed the nation's first comprehensive tax: it placed an 8 percent ad valorem tax on all farm products and established a list of license, occupational, income, and profit taxes. The law did not tax income from earnings or profits from land, because these items were covered under the Tax-in-Kind Act.

Opposition to the tax law surfaced immediately. Many found its provisions complicated and inequitable. Most could evade it altogether if they chose to do so. In the end, the law raised only approximately $82 million, which could not begin to cover all the Confederacy's debts.

Given the shortcomings of the 1863 tax law, President Davis and Congress decided to levy a direct tax—in violation of the constitutional mandate of a census. On February 17, 1864, Congress provided for a 5 percent tax to be levied on all real and personal property. The act also called for levies on profits, jewelry, and other luxury items. Taxes on land and slaves were to be based on 1860 values. Once again, the people protested, and the collection of the tax was largely stymied.

Impact of Failed Economic Policy

The failure to develop an adequate tax law, continued inflation, a spiraling debt, redundant currency, and other financial problems forced Memminger to resign in June of 1864. In his place, Davis appointed a man who was no stranger to financial circles: businessman George Trenholm of the well-known Charleston firm of Fraser and Trenholm. Trenholm immediately set out to reduce the amount of money in circulation and thus stop inflation. Trenholm also advocated that duties be paid on exports and imports. The Congress endorsed his funding measures but refused to implement his recommendation on trade duties.

The desperate situation of Confederate finances did not go away as the new year of 1865 dawned. Trenholm was forced to tell Congress that he had to have at least $500 million in order to keep the government and the war effort going for the first six months of 1865. Davis, too, urged the Congress to pass some supplemental tax law so the Confederacy could continue to exist, but Congress merely increased the rates of the 1863 law. This expedient could not save the Confederacy; Gen. Robert E. Lee surrendered before any more money was collected for the nation's coffers.

There is no doubt that the Southern economy during the Civil War was a decisive factor in the Confederacy's defeat. Misguided policies during the early months of the conflict and later resistance to needed initiatives doomed the Confederacy. The South's rejection of taxes and the government's inability to communicate the need for sacrifice and certain specific financial measures created a vicious cycle. The failure to enact a comprehensive and long-term economic policy that would distribute the economic burden equally created hardships behind the lines and popular fears of government tyranny. Bureaucratic and congressional mistakes and the resulting domestic hardship did much to destroy civilian support for the war effort.

On the other hand, mobilization policies did not fail the South. The Confederate bureaus were able to take a small manufacturing base and convert it to war production. The success of the War Department's efforts in particular proved that good management and far-seeing entrepreneurs could make a difference.

Although Confederate economic policies get mixed marks and economic weaknesses proved crucial in the South's defeat, there is little doubt that the war years unleashed a revolution in the economic life of the nation. Government encouraged and took over needed war industries; people converted small shops and larger factories to war-related production; they lobbied for tax and poor relief from the government; and all were subjected to forcible seizures of products deemed essential for the war effort. The Southern economy, overwhelmingly agrarian in 1860 was, in five short years, transformed into an industrial one. For the first time, many individuals embraced and encouraged a more balanced, diversified economy; many others saw the need for far-reaching policies and programs; still others embraced the notion of activist government. The Confederacy may have self-destructed economically in 1865, but the road to that self-destruction left a legacy that would be called upon in the postwar era.

[*See also* Banking; Blockade; Bonds; Bread Riots; Civil Service; Cotton; Currency; Debt; Extortion; Farming; Impressment; Inflation; Labor; Lead; Mining; New Plan; Ordnance Bureau; Poverty; Plantation; Public Finance; Quartermaster Department; Rice; Salt; Saltpeter; Slavery; Speculation; State Socialism; Substitutes; Sugar; Taxation; Textile Industry; Tobacco; Transportation; Treasury Department; *and biographies of numerous figures mentioned herein.*]

BIBLIOGRAPHY

Ball, Douglas B. *Financial Failure and Confederate Defeat.* Urbana, Ill., 1991.

Coulter, E. Merton. *The Confederate States of America, 1861–1865.* A History of the South, vol. 7. Baton Rouge, La., 1950.

DeCredico, Mary A. *Patriotism for Profit: Georgia's Urban Entrepreneurs and the Confederate War Effort.* Chapel Hill, N.C., 1990.

Dew, Charles B. *Ironmaker of the Confederacy: Joseph R. Anderson and the Tredegar Iron Works.* New Haven, 1966.

Goff, Richard. *Confederate Supply.* Durham, N.C., 1969.

Lerner, Eugene M. "Inflation in the Confederacy." In *Studies in the Quantity Theory of Money.* Edited by Milton Friedman. Chicago, 1956.

McPherson, James M. *Battle Cry of Freedom.* New York, 1988.

Owsley, Frank L. *King Cotton Diplomacy: Foreign Relations of the Confederate States of America.* 2d ed. Chicago, 1959.

Thomas, Emory M. *The Confederate Nation, 1861–1865.* New York, 1979.

Todd, Richard Cecil. *Confederate Finance.* Athens, Ga., 1954.

MARY A. DeCREDICO

ECTOR, MATTHEW DUNCAN

ECTOR, MATTHEW DUNCAN (1822–1879), brigadier general. Born in Georgia and trained as a lawyer, Ector began his military career by serving in a regiment from his native state during the Mexican War. Attracted to the Southwest, Ector moved to Texas in 1849 and six years later served in the state legislature. When his adopted state seceded, the erstwhile soldier abandoned politics and enlisted in the army.

Ector served in the South Kansas–Texas Regiment as an adjutant to Acting Brig. Gen. Elkanah Brackin Greer at the Battles of Wilson's Creek and Elkhorn Tavern, and commanded Company B at the Battle of Chustenahlah in the Cherokee Nation. In 1862, Ector was elected colonel of the Fourteenth Texas Dismounted Cavalry and was promoted to brigadier general on August 23.

Ector first led his regiment into combat at Richmond, Kentucky, on August 30, 1862, and two months later he was given command of a brigade. On the last day of the year, Ector, commanding the First Brigade, Maj. Gen. John P. McCown's division, Army of East Tennessee, led a successful attack against the Federal right at the Battle of Murfreesboro, Tennessee, driving the enemy back two and a half miles before being forced to withdraw.

In May 1863, Ector was ordered to Mississippi to join forces with Gen. Joseph E. Johnston in an attempt to lift the siege of Vicksburg. With his brigade incorporated into Maj. Gen. W. H. T. Walker's division, Ector remained with Johnston until rejoining Gen. Braxton Bragg prior to the Battle of Chickamauga. There Ector and his men served as part of the reserve corps for the Confederate right wing. After the battle the brigade went back to Mississippi, where it remained until ordered to Georgia in May 1864.

During the early summer of 1864, Ector's brigade participated in Johnston's attempt to stop Federal forces from seizing Atlanta. On July 27, while observing counter-battery fire from inside a redan west of the city, Ector was wounded in the left thigh by an exploding Federal shell. He was removed from the field and his leg amputated. His brigade went on to participate in the Battles of Franklin and Nashville, as well as the defense of Mobile, but there is no evidence that Ector ever fought again.

Ector returned to Texas after the war and practiced law. He was the presiding justice of the Texas Court of Appeals when he died in Tyler.

BIBLIOGRAPHY

Hewitt, Lawrence L. "Matthew Duncan Ector." In *The Confederate General.* Edited by William C. Davis. Vol. 2. Harrisburg, Pa., 1991.

Roberts, O. M. *Texas.* Vol. 11 of *Confederate Military History.* Edited by Clement A. Evans. Atlanta, 1899. Vol. 15 of extended ed. Wilmington, N.C., 1989.

Wakelyn, Jon L. *Biographical Dictionary of the Confederacy.* Edited by Frank E. Vandiver. Westport, Conn., 1977.

Warner, Ezra J. *Generals in Gray: Lives of the Confederate Commanders.* Baton Rouge, La., 1959.

ALAN C. DOWNS

EDGED WEAPONS

EDGED WEAPONS. [*This entry contains two articles:* Edged Weapons in the Army *and* Edged Weapons in the Navy.]

Edged Weapons in the Army

Edged weapons were already obsolete by the mid-nineteenth century, made so by the rifle-musket, breech-loading carbine, and revolver. Swords, however, were still considered a badge of rank by officers and a necessary inconvenience for cavalry and mounted artillery. Foot artillery needed short swords as camp tools and for clearing fields of fire. Bayonets were useful to infantry as digging implements, candle holders, and spits for cooking meats. Such weapons were infrequently used in combat.

Confederate edged weapons came from various sources. Without doubt the largest numbers were captured from Federal installations in the South or gleaned from the battlefield during the early months of the conflict. The most popular model, and the most functional, was the U.S. model 1860 cavalry saber. Surprising numbers of this model with strong Confederate provenance exist today in the collections of the Museum of the Confederacy at Richmond, Virginia. Many Confederates who had previously been career officers in the U.S. Army carried their prewar service swords, model 1850 foot officer's and model 1850 staff and field officer's types. Gens. Robert E. Lee and Thomas

J. ("Stonewall") Jackson are notable individuals who did so. It was a popular practice to carry war trophies, engraved or presentation Federal swords taken in action from an adversary.

Importation of edged weapons from England and the Continent greatly supplemented the South's supply of swords, sabers, cutlasses, bayonets, and knives. England supplied a considerable number of iron-mounted pattern 1853 sabers, and some brass-mounted variations made by Robert Mole are sometimes encountered. Model 1822 officer's swords were also imported in some quantity. In some cases blades were etched with Confederate motifs and hilt decoration altered in similar fashion. Soligen, Germany, also supplied many thousands of blades to the American market, both North and South. French models were imported in lesser quantities. Gen. J. E. B. Stuart is known to have carried a French saber made by Devisme of Paris, as did Lee at the close of the war.

The smallest number, but certainly the most interesting, are those rare weapons made within the Confederacy. These were handmade in limited numbers. Surviving specimens exhibit the whole spectrum of quality and craftsmanship. With the beginning of hostilities, dozens of companies

EDGED WEAPONS.   Pictured pointing right are, from top to bottom, Marshall cavalry saber (in scabbard); foot artillery short sword; d-guard side knife and scabbard; Fayetteville saber bayonet; Boyle, Gabble staff and field officer's sword (in scabbard); and naval cutlass. Pictured pointing left are Raleigh Bayonet Factory socket bayonet and scabbard; side knife and scabbard.   SIDE KNIFE AND D-GUARD SIDE KNIFE COURTESY OF BENJAMIN P. MICHEL; NAVAL CUTLASS COURTESY OF JOHN A. CLEVELAND; ALL OTHER ITEMS COURTESY OF RUSS A. PRITCHARD began manufacture of edged weapons in Alabama, Georgia, Louisiana, North and South Carolina, Tennessee, and Virginia. No makers have been positively identified in Arkansas, Florida, Mississippi, or Texas, but there are many unmarked specimens whose maker and place of fabrication are unknown. The majority of these swords were copies of existing Federal patterns, but there were some notable exceptions.

The firm of Thomas, Griswold, and Company, New Orleans, designed and manufactured some of the finest swords made in the South. The masterpiece produced by this shop is the sword made for Gen. Sterling Price now in Richmond's Museum of the Confederacy. The heavily gilt guard bears the coat of arms of the state of Missouri; the grip is ivory in the form of an ear of corn. Aguider Dufilho, also of New Orleans, made blades of exceptional quality. One of his designs features a pelican feeding its young between the raised letters *CS* cast in the brass guard. The pelican was part of the state seal of Louisiana. Both Dufilho and Thomas, Griswold ceased production with the Federal occupation of New Orleans in 1862.

Nashville, Tennessee, boasted two extensive sword manufacturers who shared expertise. In their short period of operation, the Nashville Plow Works, also known as Sharp and Hamilton, and the College Hill Arsenal produced a variety of distinctive edged weapons. Similarities of manufacture and the commonality of component parts turned out by the two firms indicate their degree of cooperation. Leech and Rigdon, also known as the Memphis Novelty Works, operated in Memphis until the capture of the city. This firm produced at least four different models of edged weapons for officers and enlisted men. The company also made sword belts, sword belt plates, and spurs. The loss of Louisiana and Tennessee deprived the Confederacy of some of its finest and most distinctive sword makers.

The most prolific sword manufacturer in the Confederacy was the firm of Boyle, Gamble, and MacFee of Richmond and its affiliated companies of Boyle and Gamble and Company, and Mitchell and Tyler. These firms produced a wide variety of officer's swords and sabers, some exceptional quality pieces with etched blades, enlisted men's sabers, saber bayonets, and artillery short swords. Surviving specimens indicate a large and diverse operation. The company also repaired swords, etched blades, and furnished replacement scabbards for those damaged in the field.

The Confederate States Armory, a private enterprise run by Louis Froelich in Kenansville, North Carolina, produced a most distinctive sword of his own pattern with the letters *CSA* cut out within the cast brass guard. Froelich made several other types of swords, an unusual cavalry saber, and a considerable number of cutlasses, side knives, and short swords of his own design. Also in North Carolina was the Raleigh Bayonet Factory, a major source of Confederate-made socket and saber bayonets. Although none is marked or has been positively identified, surviving correspondence indicates that the operation was not a small one.

Kraft, Goldschmidt, and Kraft in Columbia, South Carolina, produced a variety of high-quality edged weapons and fitted some early double-edged European blades to cavalry hilts, resulting in an unusual saber.

The companies of E. J. Johnston and William J. McElroy in Macon, Georgia, were closely allied with the ordnance complex at that location. Both firms are known for their officer's swords, although their quality seems to vary from sword to sword. Louis Haiman and Brother and A. H. DeWitt were located in Columbus, Georgia, and were also allied with the ordnance complex there. The Haiman products are quite varied, almost as if the swords were made to order. The basic patterns are unique to the firm and usually follow no known Federal pattern. Few products of DeWitt have survived, although documentation suggests that the firm made several edged weapons.

The company of James Conning, in Mobile, Alabama, produced a significant number of edged weapons, most of them utilitarian, although some were fine copies of antebellum U.S. swords. Before the war Conning had been a jeweler, and the quality of many of his officer's swords is evidence of his trade.

Also surviving today are numerous unmarked swords and sabers, obviously made in very limited numbers, some by competent swordsmiths but more by untrained small cutlers and blacksmiths. It must be realized that there was no single existing sword foundry in the South when the war commenced. Tremendous effort and enthusiasm were required to produce the wide range of edged weapons that remain. Total production of many firms may have numbered only a few thousand swords or even a few hundred or less. Any Confederate edged weapon is relatively rare today.

[*See also* Joe Brown's Pikes.]

BIBLIOGRAPHY

Albaugh, William A., III. *Confederate Edged Weapons.* New York, 1960.

Albaugh, William A., III. *Photographic Supplement of Confederate Swords.* Washington, D.C., 1963.

Albaugh, William A., III. *Photographic Supplement of Confederate Swords with Addendum.* Orange, Va., 1979.

Albaugh, William A., III, and Richard D. Steuart. *Handbook of Confederate Swords.* Harriman, Tenn., 1951.

Edmunds, Frederick R. "Collecting Confederate Swords: The Mystique." *Bulletin of the American Society of Arms Collectors,* no. 52 (1985): 9–23.

Edmunds, Frederick R. "The Edged Weapons of Kenansville, North Carolina." *Bulletin of the American Society of Arms Collectors,* no. 54 (1986): 11–24.

RUSS A. PRITCHARD

Edged Weapons in the Navy

Edged weapons prescribed by naval ordnance instructions for shipboard use included boarding pikes, cutlasses, battle axes, and bayonets for use with shoulder arms. In addition, officers carried swords purchased at their own expense. Sheath knives were forbidden, but jackknives, useful tools aboard ship, were allowed.

Sizable numbers of edged weapons fell into Confederate hands at the beginning of the war. At Gosport Navy Yard in Norfolk, Virginia, retreating Federals left behind 2,111 pikes and 411 battle axes. These were later supplemented by locally made weapons and by imports from Europe, particularly Britain.

Intended for use in repelling boarders, the boarding pike consisted of a seven-inch-long iron tip attached to the end of an eight-foot-long hardwood staff. The pattern in Federal use in 1861 was the model 1816, and the few surviving Confederate-made naval pikes follow this design, although some substitute brass for iron.

Probably the most distinctive of naval weapons, the cutlass was a short sword used primarily in boarding operations. Most Southern-made cutlasses were either imitations of the straight-bladed U.S. model 1841 or variations that closely resembled the artillery short sword. Cook & Brother and Thomas, Griswold & Company of New Orleans produced some of the South's finest cutlasses, and Robert Mole of Birmingham, England, manufactured many of those imported through the blockade. When supplies were short and the need immediate, the navy typically improvised: at New Orleans, one hundred machetes were purchased, apparently for use as cutlasses.

The navy issued battle axes to designated members of crews for use in cutting through boarding nets and rigging or for fire fighting. Though no contracts are known to have been issued for the manufacture of battle axes, the navy did purchase similar civilian tools such as shingling hatchets as substitutes. Naval crews used a wide variety of bayonets, the kind depending on the shoulder arm the man carried. One type, the British Enfield navy cutlass bayonet used with the short Enfield sea-service rifle, served two purposes, as its name implies.

The Confederate government commissioned a naval officer's sword to be manufactured by Robert Mole in England. The sword bears a distinctive pommel cap in the shape of a dolphin head, a brass guard containing the seal or arms of the Confederate navy, and etchings of tobacco and cotton leaves on the blade. It is often found with the markings of Firmin & Sons and Courtney & Tennant, British military outfitters and Confederate importers, respectively. Another popular model was the L. Haiman & Brothers sword made in Columbus, Georgia. In addition, many officers who had previously served in the U.S. Navy continued to carry their U.S. model 1852 naval officer's sword throughout their Confederate service.

BIBLIOGRAPHY

Albaugh, William, III. *Confederate Edged Weapons.* New York, 1960.

Albaugh, William, III. *A Photographic Supplement of Confederate Swords.* Washington, D.C., 1963.

Brown, Rodney H. *American Pole Arms, 1526–1865.* New Milford, Conn., 1967.

Lord, Francis. *Civil War Collector's Encyclopedia.* Vol. 1. New York, 1965.

Todd, Frederick P. *American Military Equipage, 1851–1872.* New York, 1980.

A. ROBERT HOLCOMBE, JR. and CHARLES V. PEERY

EDUCATION. [*This entry contains four articles:*
Primary and Secondary Education
Higher Education
Military Education
Women's Education.
See also Childhood; Slavery, *article on* Slave Life; *and entries on numerous biographical figures mentioned herein.*]

Primary and Secondary Education

Although antebellum Southerners generally accepted the value of an education and responsibility for the schooling of orphans and children of the indigent, few were willing to endorse, much less fund, widespread public schooling. Communities instead relied upon denominational schools, private academies, or, for the well-to-do, family tutors. To their supporters, such insular schools possessed several advantages: they were devoid of bureaucratic interference, closely reflected local mores, and were easily formed, or disbanded, as circumstances warranted.

And yet by 1860 several prominent Southerners had spoken out in favor of wider educational opportunities. Christopher G. Memminger of South Carolina, Thomas R. R. Cobb and Joseph E. Brown of Georgia, and especially the Reverend Calvin H. Wiley of North Carolina were outspoken proponents of state-supported schools. Thus despite legislative inertia and a general suspicion that such a system would be both abolitionist and socialist, several state assemblies by 1861 had initiated literary funds through which communities received financial aid. Louisiana, for example, funded free schools as early as 1847 despite strong protest by the state's Catholic community, and Virginia by 1860 enjoyed a fund sufficient to defray tuition and books for some fifty thousand indigent children scattered throughout 3,197 primary schools. Several of the larger cities, too—Charleston, Mobile, New Orleans, and Norfolk, for instance—adopted their own local tax-supported institutions. Private classrooms nevertheless continued to dominate, effectively denying a large segment of the population a basic education. Whereas several literary funds might allow children one or two dollars toward tuition expenses at nonpublic institutions, schools such as Virginia's Danville Female Academy charged twenty-five dollars per session for courses of instruction.

Whatever the type of school, resentment of Northern methods was nearly universal. Much of the dislike reflected the South's dependence on outside sources for educational materials. Even basic school equipment had to be purchased elsewhere. As for the many Northern teachers throughout the South, "Let us in no instance," one observer commented, "employ raw Yankee teachers. Let them all be watched, and let them know they are objects of suspicion." Books, however, attracted the loudest protests. There were few textbooks published in the South, and thus educators were constantly reacting to what they perceived to be biased passages and interpretations. *De Bow's Review,* for example, protested that whereas a basic geography text devoted two pages to Connecticut onions and broom corn, the Louisiana sugar industry rated only ten lines. Several Northern publishers worsened the situation by adding surcharges to titles shipped South, disguising offensive books by merely replacing the title page, or marketing editions with only a few pages or passages removed or obliterated.

The war provided an opportunity to start anew. But Confederate textbooks were often too difficult for the age group for which they were intended; others were only slight revisions of standard Northern texts; and all of them suffered from a lack of skilled printers and adequate supplies of paper. The South did produce a variety of titles, but as economic conditions deteriorated, the region increasingly turned back to those Northern books that survived.

It was not long before teachers and students were in short supply as well. In the first rush of patriotism, academies lost many of their students to the army. In a Blount County, Alabama, school, for instance, twenty-two of the twenty-three boys over sixteen volunteered. Girls, too, were eager to help the cause. Sallie Eola Reneau attempted to form a company of "Mississippi Nightingales," complete with military uniforms and sidearms; in Columbia, South Carolina, schoolgirls organized benefits to raise money for Hampton's Legion; and the *Nashville American* reported on the little girl who remarked to a passing soldier that she would study hard "if you will whip the Yankees good for us."

Like their pupils, many teachers left for the army. In an effort to retain instructors, the Confederate government in 1862 exempted from the draft all male teachers with at least twenty students and two years' experience. Unfortunately, the public-service gesture attracted more derision than praise. That combined with the declining state of the schools led instructors to lament, "Away with the thought that teaching is an easy life," for "in no occupation is labor—exhausting, nervous labor—more demanded." Such conditions, continued enlistments, and the public's declining perception of educators in time led to a severe shortage of qualified teachers. North Carolina, for example, in 1860 included 2,164 licensed male teachers, but in 1863 only 525. Women refugees filled some slots, and disabled veterans took others, but it was not enough. Alabama authorities were hardly alone in resorting to teacher competency examinations, nor were they unique in having to admit that leniency was necessary in many cases "where peculiar hardships would exist if the above provisions were rigidly enforced."

Schools had to adapt as best they could. For example, female boarding academies in Morehead City, North Carolina, and Huntsville, Alabama, cleverly offered situations "secure from danger, either of epidemics or war's alarms." Others fought for professional standards, banding together in statewide organizations or within the Confederate States Educational Association, formed in 1861 and still active in the last months of the war. Teachers did their part as well. In the face of rocketing inflation, a Vicksburg teacher, Madge Brown, readily accepted "wood and potatoes, butter and pumpkins" for pay.

By 1863, however, teachers and administrators increasingly had to defend their school's very existence in the face of greater national need. Jefferson Davis expressed his support of continued school terms, but many publicly funded institutions disappeared as local and state governments reallocated scarce funds. Louisiana managed as late as 1865 to retain its literary fund, whereas Florida, Texas, and Virginia withheld varying amounts to sustain the war effort. To retain public support, some schools took on expanded roles. In Raleigh, the North Carolina Institution for the Deaf and Dumb and the Blind instructed its students in the manufacture of rifled-musket cartridges. But as the war progressed, and defeat appeared more certain, the schools' primary function took on new meaning. In 1863 Eliza Burleson Sivley instructed her son "to content yourself to remain at school for an education is about all we can give you and can't be taken from you and will do you more good than wealth."

Supporters also pointed out that eliminating schools only accomplished at home what the enemy was attempting on the battlefield, the destruction of Southern society; schools, after all, were "where the young mind and heart of the State are trained for virtuous and useful enterprise, imbued with patriotic sentiments and fitted for the grave responsibilities which devolve upon the citizens of a free country." In the end, though, declining enrollments, teacher shortages, low morale, inadequate funds, scarce supplies, and adverse public opinion combined to defeat the best efforts of Southern educators. As diarist Mary Boykin Chesnut commented, "wait until you have saved your country before you make preachers and scholars."

[*See also* Textbooks.]

BIBLIOGRAPHY

Kennerly, Sarah Law. "Confederate Juvenile Imprints: Children's Books and Periodicals Published in the Confederate States of America, 1861–1865." Ph.D. diss., University of Michigan, 1956.

Parrish, T. Michael, and Robert M. Willingham, Jr., comps. *Confederate Imprints: A Bibliography of Southern Publications from Secession to Surrender.* Austin, Tex., and Katonah, N.Y., 1987.

Stillman, Rachel Bryan. "Education in the Confederate States of America, 1861–1865." Ph.D. diss., University of Illinois at Urbana-Champaign, 1972.

Weeks, Stephen B. *Confederate Text-Books: A Preliminary Bibliography.* Washington, D.C., 1900.

EDWARD D. C. CAMPBELL, JR.

Higher Education

Prior to the Civil War, higher education found a significant measure of support among the white population of a number of the states eventually forming the Confederacy. The impetus for the development of Southern higher education grew out of the region's increasing isolationist tendencies fueled by powerful economic, cultural, intellectual, political, and religious forces. As the abolitionist cries intensified and the sectional crisis deepened throughout the 1840s and 1850s, a strong sentiment emerged among the region's wealthiest and most influential families that Southern students needed to be educated in their own region away from what they perceived to be the unsympathetic, radical, and seditious intellectual influences of the North. As the South became increasingly suspicious of nonindigenous intellectual currents, there was a corresponding increase in efforts to establish new academies and colleges. Colleges were seen as vital elements for the preservation of a Southern culture and way of life.

Impeding the development of higher education, however, was the inability of the region to develop a system of preparatory (elementary and secondary) schools. This absence of preparatory schools forced the region's institutions to devote considerable resources to elementary and secondary-level instruction. Thus many of the colleges founded in the antebellum South were by late-nineteenth-century standards actually primary or secondary schools. Even the best Southern colleges were forced to offer extensive preparatory programs. Although the quality of many Southern institutions that called themselves colleges was necessarily suspect, their numbers are impressive. There were only nine colleges in America at the time of the Revolution; by 1850 there were approximately 240 with almost half of them in the South. In the middle of the nineteenth century, the South led the nation in the number of colleges, faculty members, and college students in proportion to its population. Specific enrollment contrasts are enlightening: in 1860 the South had one college student for every 247 white inhabitants; the North counted one student for every 703 residents.

On the eve of the Civil War, South Carolina College (antecedent of the University of South Carolina) reported an enrollment of 184, and East Tennessee University (later renamed the University of Tennessee) enrolled approximately 110 students each year, although about 66 percent of these students were in a preparatory or precollege-level department. The University of Mississippi at Oxford registered approximately 100 students each year, and the University of North Carolina counted 461 students from nearly half the states of the nation. A similar situation existed in Athens, Georgia, where enrollment in the late 1850s reached 159. A law school was established there, and the faculty grew in size and stature, boasting of such distinguished scholars as Joseph and John LeConte and William Louis Jones, all recognized leaders in the nation's scientific and academic communities. These figures compare favorably with Northern institutions. In the 1860–1861 school year, Rutgers enrolled 124, Princeton 314, and Michigan, one of the largest American institutions, 614 students. At the University of Wisconsin the enrollment surpassed 300 only twice during the entire decade of the 1850s.

In the years immediately preceding the war, Wake Forest College in North Carolina was a comfortable if not prosperous institution. Unencumbered by debt, it possessed an endowment and physical plant valued at $100,000. In Spartanburg, South Carolina, Wofford College experienced a steady expansion. In the six years following its founding in 1854, enrollment increased from 24 to 79 and plans were under way to increase its endowment of $69,000 to $200,000. Its library contained 1,000 volumes, and a museum was on the drawing boards.

Thus the antebellum period was, for Southern higher education, a period of both material prosperity and intellectual advancement. Individual institutions experienced modest expansion of financial support and enrollment. Faculties, in general, were academically respectable and included a number of nationally recognized scholars.

The Civil War drastically altered the situation, as students and faculty were scattered and physical plants damaged or destroyed. In September 1861, the University of Tennessee attempted to open but could do so only for a few weeks before suspending operations; most of its students had joined the military and its buildings had been commandeered by the Confederate army. By January of 1862 the army had turned the buildings into a lodging for the wounded. From September 1863 to June 1865 Union forces expropriated the university, and during this occupation one of its seven buildings, as well as the library and scientific equipment, was destroyed. The grounds of the university were also substantially damaged by Union troops, with trees and shrubs removed to make way for ramparts and other fortifications. The university reopened on March 1, 1866, but could find only students in need of preparatory work. It was not until 1868 that the university enrolled a freshman class of 11 students.

The wartime suspension of operations and the experiences of the University of Tennessee were not unique among the colleges of the Confederacy. By the summer of 1861, 75 of the 123 students enrolled at the University of Georgia were in the military, and the university struggled to remain open. As the military fortunes of the Confederacy declined, additional students and faculty entered military service, and during the fall of 1863 the university suspended operations. Its buildings were converted to war use and were subsequently utilized as a hospital for Confederate soldiers, as a refugee camp for families displaced by the fighting, and ultimately as headquarters for Union troops, who remained until the fall of 1865. For the most part, however, the buildings escaped the most severe damages of war, and on January 6, 1866, the university reopened with 78 students.

The University of Mississippi in Oxford, although forced to suspend operations in the fall of 1861, suffered virtually no damage during the war, and just three months after the surrender at Appomattox it reopened with 193 students. Conditions were less favorable at the University of Alabama, which had to suspend operations for most of the war. Virtually all its buildings had been burned and most of the library lost. An attempt to reopen in 1865 was aborted when only one student arrived for classes. The situation was also bleak at Wofford College; its endowment—which had been loyally invested in the Confederate government—evaporated. Similarly Wake Forest College suspended operations in 1862 and saw its $100,000 in assets reduced to about $11,000. When it finally reopened in 1866, its buildings were badly in need of repair, and it could count only 22 of 67 students as at the college level; the remainder were in preparatory classes.

Emory in Atlanta suspended operations in the fall of 1861 and remained closed for the duration of the war, as did South Carolina College, which closed during the early months of 1862. The College of Charleston also closed for the war. It reopened in 1866, but it was not until 1878 that enrollment reached 50, a figure comparable to the ante-

bellum period. The conflict virtually destroyed the University of the South in Sewanee, Tennessee. With prewar assets in excess of $500,000, the university had aspired to be an educational center for the entire South. It emerged from the war with its buildings burned, its founder, Bishop Polk, dead, and its assets greatly devalued.

At the conclusion of the war, 4,000 Union soldiers occupied the village and campus of the University of North Carolina at Chapel Hill. The university possessed $200,000 in worthless securities and debts of over $100,000. Closed for the war, the university attempted to reopen in 1868, but lacking adequate financial support it closed again in 1871. It resumed instruction in 1875 with a faculty of 7 and about 70 students, considerably reduced from its 1857–1858 enrollment of over 400 students in nine departments.

The war profoundly effected the colleges and universities of the Confederacy. Colleges that prospered in the antebellum era were forced to suspend operations during a conflict that saw endowments lost, the tax base weakened, students and faculty in disarray, and facilities often in ruins. It was not until decades later that a revitalized South witnessed (with the exception of efforts long under way at the University of Virginia) real attempts to build true universities in Nashville, Chapel Hill, and Durham that would eventually rank with the best in the nation.

BIBLIOGRAPHY

Cartter, Allan M. "The Role of Higher Education in the Changing South." In *The South in Continuity and Change.* Edited by John C. McKinney and Edgar T. Thompson. Durham, N.C., 1965.

Coulter, E. Merton. *College Life in the Old South.* 2d ed. Athens, Ga., 1983.

Dyer, Thomas G. *The University of Georgia: A Bicentennial History, 1785–1985.* Athens, Ga., 1985.

Hollis, D. W. *University of South Carolina.* 2 vols. Columbia, S.C., 1951, 1956.

Montgomery, James Riley, Stanley J. Folmsbee, and Lee Seifert Greene. *To Foster Knowledge: A History of the University of Tennessee, 1794–1970.* Knoxville, Tenn., 1984.

Sansing, David G. *Making Haste Slowly: The Troubled History of Higher Education in Mississippi.* Jackson, Tenn., 1990.

JOSEPH M. STETAR

Military Education

Military academies were established in the south starting in 1839 with the Virginia Military Institute (VMI) at Lexington and the South Carolina Military Academy at the Citadel in Charleston in 1842. By 1861, these two famous colleges had been joined by similar institutions in all the Confederate states. Either through state sponsorship of public colleges or through state donations to private colleges, military education was flourishing in the South at the time of secession. The antebellum South led the nation in military academies per capita, prompted in part by the martial traditions of plantation slave society. The Federal government had also encouraged this kind of education by sending army officers as advisers to various college campuses, both military and civilian.

During the 1840s and 1850s, military colleges continued to spring up across the South. Col. Robert T. P. Allen founded the Kentucky Military Institute in 1845. Maj. George Alexander started the Arkansas Military Institute at Tulip, Arkansas, in 1850. That same year, Jefferson College in Natchez, Mississippi, resumed its military training, the state providing muskets and accoutrements. In 1851, Col. Arnoldus Brumby, West Point class of 1835, started the Georgia Military Institute in Marietta, which was later donated to the state of Georgia. In Tennessee, the Western Military Institute at Tyree merged with the economically troubled University of Nashville to become the Nashville Military Institute. South Carolina added another campus, the Arsenal, at Columbia. Maj. D. H. Hill, later a Confederate lieutenant general, opened the North Carolina Military Institute at Charlotte in 1859. Louisiana State Seminary of Learning and Military Academy opened at the same time, under Superintendent William Tecumseh Sherman. Colonel Allen left Kentucky and opened the Texas Military Institute at Bastrop in 1860.

Alabama led the South in the number of military colleges with two private academies at Glenville and La Grange. Both received generous state support. In 1860, Alabama made martial training compulsory at the University of Alabama, making it a military academy of sorts.

The military institutes trained the students in tactics and drill. The manual of arms and the school of the soldier were emphasized, as were parade ground formations. Formal dress parades were frequent. Everyday life at the schools was harsh, regimented, and run on the West Point model. Cadets wore their uniforms at all times; civilian clothes were forbidden. The men lived four to a room, which was typically furnished by each cadet with an iron bedstead, a pine table, a mirror, a wash basin and foot tub, a bucket and dipper, a washstand, and a candlestick. Games of chance, including checkers, chess, and backgammon, were barred. Reading was restricted to course materials. In the classroom, cadets learned engineering, mathematics, tactics, architecture, French, English, natural and experimental philosophy, history, chemistry, rhetoric, and the law of nations. In many states, including Alabama and Georgia, at least one scholarship was awarded to a student from each county. This practice spread military education and militarism throughout the state.

These colleges produced hundreds of officers and noncommissioned officers for the Confederacy, with the Virginia Military Institute leading the way. In 1861, VMI claimed 433 living graduates and 654 nongraduates. That

year, Virginia raised 64 regiments of infantry, heavy artillery, and cavalry, and VMI graduates commanded 22. An additional 790 commissioned officers of other ranks came from VMI. Of the 1,902 students who attended VMI from its opening to 1865, 1,781 served in the Confederate army. Though neither of the national service academies was in the South, 294 West Point graduates served the Confederacy, 144 as generals. The Citadel also contributed: of its 224 living graduates prior to 1860, 193 served the Confederacy. These included 4 generals, 17 colonels, 10 lieutenant colonels, 22 majors, 58 captains, 62 lieutenants, and 20 noncommissioned officers. Of these men, thirty-nine died in combat.

At the beginning of the war, many cadets of the various military academies served as drill instructors. High-ranking officers who were unschooled in formal tactics submitted to the training of teenaged students as the Confederacy built its army. Sometimes as individuals, other times as a company, cadets could be found at many of the principal training camps in the South during the opening months of the war. Protected from conscription in most states, cadets continued their studies until the proximity of battle intervened.

When the time came, the cadets also fought. Many simply left school on their own and joined the army. On other occasions, however, cadet battalions were deployed as units. A unit of cadets from the Citadel claimed to have fired the first shot on Fort Sumter in Charleston Harbor on April 12, 1861. In May 1864, the 177 cadets of the Georgia Military Institute (GMI) turned out to repel Sherman's invasion. Still dressed in their flashy school uniforms, these boys came under fire for the first time at Resaca on May 14. Later attached to the Georgia Militia Division under Maj. Gen. Gustavus Smith, the GMI students fought around Atlanta and opposed Sherman's march to Savannah. In all, over a dozen GMI cadets were killed or wounded.

The most famous instance of cadets fighting was at the Battle of New Market, Virginia, on May 15, 1864. Some 247 students from VMI joined Confederate Maj. Gen. John C. Breckinridge's ad hoc force to repel a Union invasion of the Shenandoah Valley. Ten cadets died and 47 were wounded in the fighting.

The Southern military academies also produced famous faculty members. Besides the aforementioned Hill and Sherman, Lt. Gen. Thomas J. ("Stonewall") Jackson taught at VMI. Bushrod Rust Johnson, military superintendent of the University of Nashville, became a Confederate major general. Colonel Allen led Texas troops in Virginia, Arkansas, and Louisiana.

The Civil War destroyed most of these schools. Union troops razed the buildings of VMI and GMI. The loss of students and faculty also hampered school operations. By the end of Reconstruction, all Southern military schools had disappeared save for the Citadel and Virginia Military Institute. The Southern military education tradition was upheld in postbellum years by state agricultural and mechanical colleges established under the Morrill Land Grant Act.

[See also Citadel, The; Georgia Military Institute; Louisiana State Seminary and Military Institute; Virginia Military Institute.]

BIBLIOGRAPHY

Baker, Gary R. *Cadets in Gray: The Story of the Cadets of the South Carolina Military Academy and the Cadet Rangers in the Civil War.* Columbia, S.C., 1989.

Conrad, James Lee. "Training in Treason." *Civil War Times Illustrated* 30 (September–October 1991): 22–29, 62–64.

Franklin, John Hope. *The Militant South.* Cambridge, Mass., 1956.

Napier, John Hawkins, III. "Military Schools." In *The Encyclopedia of Southern Culture.* Edited by Charles Reagan Wilson and William Ferris. Chapel Hill, N.C., 1989.

Wise, Henry A. *Drawing Out the Man: The VMI Story.* Charlottesville, Va., 1978.

DONALD S. FRAZIER

Women's Education

The fortunes of the Confederacy had a decisive impact on women's education only in the long run. The vicissitudes of war frequently affected specific schools, academies, and colleges, but the wartime education of Southern women did not differ significantly from the education they had received before.

Throughout the antebellum period, many elite Southern women had received a remarkably sophisticated education in literature, history, languages, art, and music, although typically they spent only a few years at school. As a result of the slow development of public schools in the South, girls of wealthy families mainly received their early education at home from their mothers, a governess, or a tutor. Less affluent white women, especially those who lived in the countryside without access to a town, might receive some basic education from their mothers or in an old field or Sabbath school. Slave women, who received no formal education, were not supposed to learn to read, although some did, usually taught by a slaveholding woman.

During the 1850s, the number of female academies and colleges in the South expanded dramatically, testifying to a broad interest among the elite in women's education. Indeed, during the decade the South outpaced the North in the chartering of women's colleges. Many, although not all, of these institutions were closely associated with one of the Protestant denominations, most commonly the Methodists, and were directed by ministers. Many academies encouraged religion among their students. Instruction at Judson College in Alabama included the Bible and other religious texts, and once a semester the college held a series of revival services. Ella Gertrude Clanton Thomas regarded her conversion as one of the high points of her stay at Wesleyan College.

Whether religious or secular, schools invariably embodied a strong commitment to the education of women in Christian morals and were designed to prepare students for their distinct roles as women. Even those that prided themselves on offering an extensive and rigorous education that might include geography, mathematics, Latin, and rudimentary science firmly opposed what they perceived as a Northern tendency to encourage an interest in women's rights. Politics was discussed, sometimes hotly, in women's seminaries and colleges, but nowhere do we find evidence that the young women strayed far, if at all, from the views considered appropriate to a slave society. The South resisted the Northern and midwestern trend toward coeducation and discouraged women of "good" families from becoming teachers.

As early as June 1861, alarm over the mobilization for war led parents to withdraw their daughters from the highly respected Salem College in North Carolina, so that during that summer the school had empty places for the first time in recent memory. But as the war progressed, parents came to believe that their daughters would be safer in Salem than at home, especially if home was in a war-torn region. By 1862, girls were streaming into Salem, which became more crowded than ever and remained so throughout the rest of the war. Wesleyan College in Macon also stayed open throughout the war, except for a few weeks, although during the final year the school dropped its requirement that students master French as a second language, presumably because of a decline in the number of teachers.

Many academies and colleges suffered the loss of teachers, some of whom returned to the North or chose to serve the Confederacy as soldiers or nurses. Others closed because their buildings were requisitioned for the war effort. The Auburn Masonic Female College in Auburn, Alabama, which occupied a fine new brick house, became a hospital for Confederate soldiers; during the latter part of the war the Montevallo Female Institute in Montevallo, Alabama, quartered the soldiers camped in the town. After the war, both institutions eventually returned to their educational missions, although the Auburn Masonic Female College served for a brief period as a furniture factory before becoming a school for girls and boys. The Tuscumbia Female Academy in Tuscumbia, Georgia, which had been founded in 1826, did not survive the war. Having been closed during the hostilities, the building was eventually used for the Public School of Tuscumbia.

The abiding consequences of the defeat of the Confederacy pushed Southern women's education in new directions. Most dramatic was a growing acceptance of women as teachers. The collapse of their fortunes forced many families to rely, at least in part, on income that women could earn, and teaching offered the most acceptable occupation. The gradual emergence of a comprehensive public school system also generated a need for teachers and new opportunities for women. Thus, during the final quarter of the nineteenth century, the South began to follow the path of the feminization of teaching that had characterized the North before the war.

Formal education for former slave women emerged during the war. The establishment of schools for freed women and men on the Sea Islands during those years was a response as much to the desires of the former slaves themselves as to the missionary zeal of the Northerners who taught them and testified to their eagerness for education. Following the war, Southern African Americans struggled to create schools, educating their women as fully as possible and increasingly training them to become teachers for the next generation.

Although the Confederacy promoted no distinct new developments in women's education, it proved remarkably successful in perpetuating the tradition of educating elite women that had prevailed before the war. The defeat of the Confederacy, however, ensured the emergence of new educational opportunities for poor white and former slave women and new possibilities for all Southern women to take up careers as teachers.

BIBLIOGRAPHY

Blandin, I. M. E. *History of Higher Education of Women in the South prior to 1860.* Washington, D.C., 1975.

Griffin, Frances. *Less Time for Meddling: A History of Salem Academy and College.* Winston-Salem, N.C., 1979.

Swint, Henry Lee. *The Northern Teacher in the South, 1862–1870.* New York, 1967.

Young, Elizabeth Barber. *A Study of the Curricula of Seven Selected Women's Colleges of the Southern States.* New York, 1932.

ELIZABETH FOX-GENOVESE

ELECTION OF 1860. The election of 1860 led to the secession of some of the states that formed the Confederate States of America, but to this day historians are not sure why. The platform of the victorious Republican party dropped its 1856 denunciation of slavery as a "relic of barbarism" comparable to polygamy, and instead pledged the "maintenance inviolate of . . . the right of each state to order and control its own domestic institutions." Though the platform opposed slavery's expansion into the territories and the reopening of the African slave trade, many

knowledgeable Southerners doubted the West would sustain slave agriculture and many opposed the slave trade agitation. The Republican candidate, Abraham Lincoln, carried a consistent antislavery record, but he was so little known outside Illinois and so widely regarded as a nonentity sure to be controlled by others that he, personally, could hardly have weighed as a factor. Honoring regnant political custom, he did not campaign or offer any remarks for publication from his nomination on May 18 to his election on November 6.

The Constitutional Union party, embracing conservative Whig remnants, on May 9 had nominated John Bell of Tennessee with no platform. The Democratic party had convened their national nominating convention in Charleston, South Carolina, in April, but no candidate was nominated until June. Southern delegates wanted a platform pledging Congress and the executive to protect slave property in the territories. The minority platform, drafted by Democrats who supported the nomination of Stephen A. Douglas of Illinois, left it to the Supreme Court to decide what power Congress or territorial legislatures held over slave property in the territories. After the minority platform was adopted by the full convention, the Alabama delegation led those of Mississippi, Louisiana, South Carolina, Florida, Texas, Georgia, and some delegates from Delaware and Arkansas out of the convention.

The Democrats reconvened in Baltimore on June 18. When they refused to let bolting Southern delegates back in, the Virginia, North Carolina, and Tennessee delegations withdrew along with parts of the Maryland, Kentucky, Missouri, Arkansas, California, and Oregon delegations. Douglas gained the nomination. On the next day the (mostly) Southern Democrats nominated John C. Breckinridge of Kentucky on a platform that demanded federal protection of slave property in the territories until statehood. It also urged the acquisition of Cuba and the building of a Pacific railroad while condemning the acts of state legislatures that frustrated execution of the Fugitive Slave Act.

The party contest for popular votes that ensued, though lively, did little to inform or educate voters. The political campaign of that summer was bewildering. Despite the critical issues looming in the sectional party split, the Republicans, drawing on their old Whig heritage, somehow set the tone by running a copy of the old Harrison log-cabin-and-hard-cider campaign of the 1840s. The Republicans ran what has been called a "hurrah" campaign, characterized more by spectacle and vociferous cheering for their candidate than by emphasis on or explanation of the planks in their platform. They slighted issues and scoffed at threats of disunion. The other parties scurried to match the Republicans' marching clubs and torchlight parades.

Essentially the contest boiled down to a Breckinridge-Bell struggle in the South and a Lincoln-Douglas struggle in the

Presidential Election of 1860

	REPUBLICAN	DEMOCRAT	SOUTHERN DEMOCRAT	CONSTITUTIONAL UNION
ALABAMA	0	13,651	48,831	27,875
ARKANSAS	0	5,227	28,732	20,094
DELAWARE	3,815	1,023	7,337	3,864
FLORIDA	0	367	8,543	5,437
GEORGIA	0	11,590	51,889	42,886
KENTUCKY	1,364	25,651	53,143	66,058
LOUISIANA	0	7,625	22,681	20,204
MARYLAND	2,294	5,996	42,282	41,760
MISSISSIPPI	0	3,283	40,797	25,040
MISSOURI	17,028	58,801	31,317	58,372
NORTH CAROLINA	0	2,701	48,539	44,990
SOUTH CAROLINA	Did not hold a popular vote for presidential electors.			
TENNESSEE	0	11,350	54,709	69,274
TEXAS	0	Fused with Bell	47,548	15,438
VIRGINIA	1,929	16,290	74,323	74,681

North. Voters learned little about the candidates from the other section of the country except what the candidates from their own section wanted them to hear. Perceptions of Lincoln and Douglas in the South were terrifyingly distorted. Breckinridge's image in the North was equally skewed. Breckinridge made one speech in the campaign, breaking with tradition, but Douglas shattered tradition altogether, campaigning throughout the North in the summer and venturing into the upper South late in the summer. After news from the states that held their gubernatorial elections in October showed that Lincoln would win Pennsylvania and Indiana and with them the presidential election, Douglas plunged into the Deep South in the autumn. Most historians have written admiringly of his attempts to save the Union in this campaign by warning the South against secession in the event of Lincoln's election.

Like all elections up to that time in American history, the election of 1860 was a collection of state elections, and party strategies varied from state to state. Some Southern radicals hoped for Republican victory in order to bring about secession all the faster. Naturally, in the upper South, an area likely to become the bloody doormat over which armies marched in the event of disunion and civil war, the Breckinridge forces stressed their Unionism (and downplayed its conditional quality). In the Deep South they

especially urged Southern unity—perhaps to extract concessions from the Republicans, perhaps to start the process of secession and independence. Motives varied greatly and are difficult for historians to assess. Most Breckinridge leaders seem to have doubted they could win. Few put much faith in achieving victory ultimately by throwing the election into the House of Representatives. And both Bell and Breckinridge forces depicted themselves as the best guarantors of slavery's survival; the former maintained that the best chances lay *within* the Union.

Despite the fatalism of many Southern politicians about the outcome on November 6, voting totals rose in every Southern state—in some by great margins. Estimates of voter turnout are not available for the South, but it appears to have been good there and may have been as high as 82 percent in the North.

Breckinridge carried all the future states of the Confederacy except Virginia (which included the Unionist area that would secede to form West Virginia in three years) and Tennessee, both of which went to Bell. Most historians have been quick to point out, however, that Breckinridge's opposition, if united, carried 55 percent of the Southern vote.

Secessionist Democrats emerged from the election with unity sufficient to take the Deep South out of the Union. Republican victory thus prompted secession in several

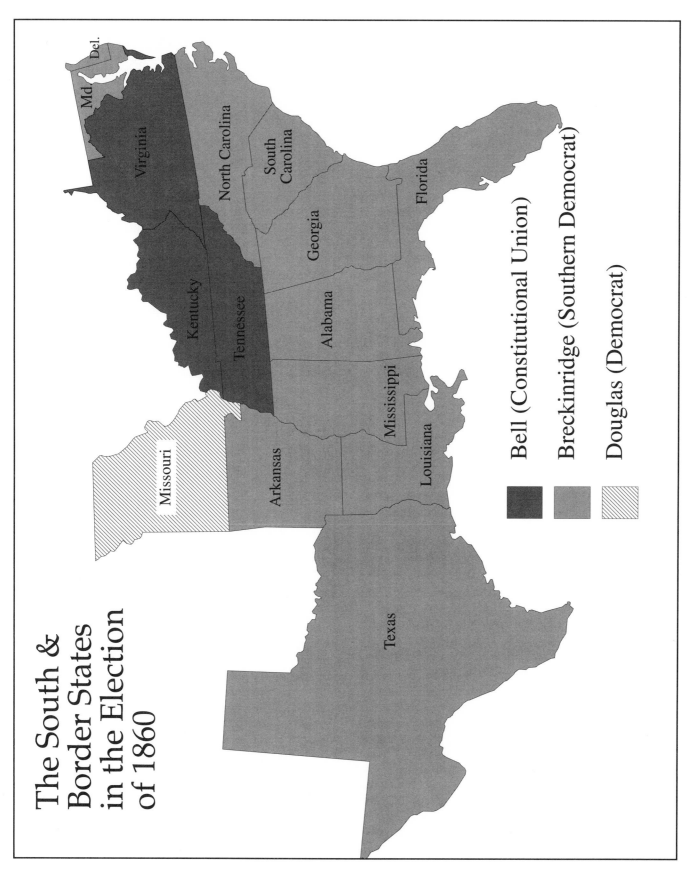

The South &
Border States
in the Election
of 1860

Bell (Constitutional Union)

Breckinridge (Southern Democrat)

Douglas (Democrat)

states, but only the threat of military coercion after the firing on Fort Sumter provoked the secession of some of the states that formed the Confederacy.

[*See also* Constitutional Union Party; Democratic Party; Lincoln, Abraham, *article on* Image of Lincoln in the Confederacy; Republican Party; *and entries on particular states.*]

BIBLIOGRAPHY

Crenshaw, Ollinger. *The Slave States in the Presidential Election of 1860.* Baltimore, 1945.

Historical Statistics of the United States: Colonial Times to 1970. 2 vols. Washington, D.C., 1975.

Johannsen, Robert W. *Lincoln, the South, and Slavery: The Political Dimension.* Baton Rouge, La., 1991.

Potter, David M. *The Impending Crisis, 1848–1861.* New York, 1976.

MARK E. NEELY, JR.

ELECTION OF 1863. This election, coming on the heels of serious military reverses in the summer of 1863, changed the nature of Confederate politics. On July 4 Gen. Robert E. Lee withdrew from Gettysburg after defeat there. On the same day Gen. John C. Pemberton surrendered his army and the city of Vicksburg to Gen. Ulysses S. Grant. In June, Gen. Braxton Bragg had been maneuvered out of his base at Tullahoma, Tennessee, and withdrew his army to Chattanooga, which he soon abandoned.

Although the Confederate armies bounced back to win some victories, notably at Chickamauga in September 1863, the morale of the home front deteriorated under the impact of the military setbacks, combined with inflation, conscription, impressment, and long casualty lists. Pathetic letters from home to soldiers at the front painted graphic pictures of starvation, fears of slave unrest, and marauding bands of deserters from both armies. Many soldiers, responding to these letters, returned home and were among the voters in 1863. In some locations, discontent was channeled into action by various peace societies, some of which even ran candidates.

Almost 40 percent of the 137 members of the Second Congress were new to that body, for many incumbents who had been secessionists in 1860 and 1861 were turned out of office. Among the new congressmen, over two-thirds had opposed secession in 1861. The results had party implications: in 1861 Democrats had tended to be secessionists, and former Whigs, Unionists; three-fifths of the new congressmen in 1863 had once been Whigs. These men had gone with the Confederacy once the decision for secession was made; but their initial hesitation seemed to recommend them to the voters in the crisis of 1863. Moreover, some of the new members composed a "peace party," bringing a fresh ideological stance into Congress. Some desired a restoration of the Union; others believed that peace with independence could still be won at the conference table if President Jefferson Davis were not too stubborn to negotiate.

This political change was not confined to Congress. Former Whigs (mostly former Unionists) increased their strength in almost every Confederate state legislature, and some were elected governors. In Alabama the voters picked a former Whig in the gubernatorial election for the first time in the state's history—even though the Whig party itself was long dead.

The Second Congress, meeting in its initial session May 2, 1864, presented a striking contrast to the First Congress. Almost two-thirds of the members of the first House had been Democratic or secessionist; in the second House the balance was about even. Not counting areas where normal elections could not be held because of the presence of Federal troops, the voters elected former Unionists to replace secessionists in fifteen districts and returned incumbent former Unionists in another sixteen. Most of these thirty-one seats in the second House represented districts in the Appalachians and the adjacent Piedmont.

Much of the change was due to peace sentiment. Jehu A. Orr of Mississippi told the electorate during his campaign that he would do his best to achieve an honorable peace and that he believed secession had been a great mistake. The contraction of Confederate-controlled territory also resulted in legislative turnover. Many of the reelected secessionists came from "phantom constituencies," districts that were controlled by the Union army. For such areas, notably Kentucky, Missouri, and much of Tennessee, ballots could be cast only by soldiers and refugee civilians. Had normal elections been held throughout the Confederacy, the result would probably have been a resounding defeat for those who had originally favored secession.

The North Carolina contingent in the Second Congress included eight newcomers, some of them apparently elected through the influence of peace societies. The Tarheel delegation was now composed of ten former Union Whigs and only two former secession Democrats (one a holdover senator and the other an incumbent who reclaimed his seat by a mere ten-vote margin). Some Confederates were so alarmed by Tarheel behavior that they feared a second revolution, and in fact much of the change in voting behavior in the Second Congress was due to bloc voting by the North Carolina delegation. James Madison Leach of North Carolina, for example, declared that he had opposed secession for twenty years; James T. Leach, North Carolina, avowed that he was an early advocate of reconstruction; and another North Carolinian frankly admitted that he ran for the Second Congress because he opposed Davis's war measures and wanted to stay out of the military.

For the most part, the Unionists in the Second Congress were opposed to the rigorous policies of the Davis administration, which they thought were encroaching upon their constitutional rights. The new congressmen and their incumbent allies were less willing than other congressmen to curtail draft exemptions and more willing to restrict the zeal of quartermasters who impressed supplies for the army and paid less than market prices for what they took. The impact of the 1863 elections was especially notable on the issue of the suspension of the writ of habeas corpus. By 1864 suspension was being used to prevent the emasculation of the draft law by judges who would issue writs to get soldiers out of the army. Some legislators who opposed conscription attacked it indirectly by appealing to the individual's right to be free of arbitrary detention by government authority. Similarly, the new congressmen were less willing to use slaves as soldiers than were their more experienced colleagues. In contrast, those voting for draconian measures in support of the war effort usually represented occupied districts, notably Missouri, Kentucky, and parts of Tennessee and Virginia. These delegates could vote in full confidence that their constituents would not feel the effects of harsh impressment, sweeping conscription, or suspension of the writ of habeas corpus.

The turnover in membership also meant that the Second Congress would be less unified than its predecessor. Although political parties never developed in the Confederacy, the change in the composition of the membership in the Second Congress, the legislative issues of the last Congress, and the stress of a losing war effort exacerbated political divisions and led to the development of factions that might have become the basis of a two-party system if the Confederacy had survived. Analysis of legislative voting in the Second Congress reveals deep cleavage between former Union Whigs and former secession Democrats. More important, however, legislative behavior in the Second Congress was closely correlated with the location of a congressman's home in relation to the Union army.

In short, by the fall of 1863, Confederate-controlled territory had diminished and the cost of secession had become apparent to Confederate voters, who turned away from original secessionists. Even so, the new members—though differing in attitude from the old—were generally familiar to the voters. There was no electoral revolution; most of the new members were simply familiar names whose previous behavior was more symbolic of caution than that of the men they displaced.

[*See also* Conscription; Habeas Corpus; Impressment; *and entries on particular states.*]

BIBLIOGRAPHY

Alexander, Thomas B., and Richard E. Beringer. *The Anatomy of the Confederate Congress: A Study of the Influences of Member Characteristics on Legislative Voting Behavior, 1861–1865.* Nashville, Tenn., 1972.

Beringer, Richard E. "A Profile of the Members of the Confederate Congress." *Journal of Southern History* 33 (November 1967): 518–541.

Beringer, Richard E. "The Unconscious 'Spirit of Party' in the Confederate Congress." *Civil War History* 18 (December 1972): 312–333.

"Proceedings of the Confederate Congress." *Southern Historical Society Papers* 44–52 (1923–1959). Reprint, Wilmington, N.C., 1991–1992.

Yearns, Wilfred B. *The Confederate Congress.* Athens, Ga., 1960.

RICHARD E. BERINGER

ELKHORN TAVERN, ARKANSAS. Also known as the Battle of Pea Ridge, the fighting in Benton County, Arkansas, on March 7 and 8, 1862, secured Union control of Missouri. The Confederates suffered around

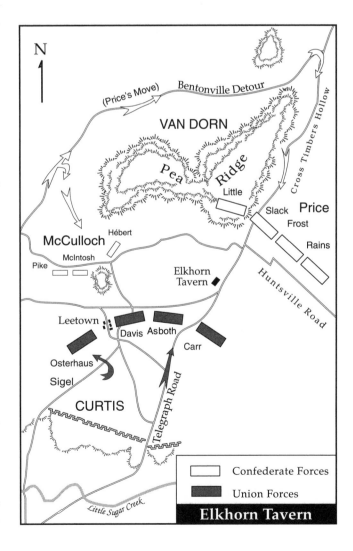

Elkhorn Tavern

1,500 men killed, wounded, and missing, and the Federals lost slightly less than 1,400.

Pro-Confederate Missourians under Maj. Gen. Sterling Price had been trying to gain the upper hand in their home state since the summer of 1861. After Union Brig. Gen. Nathaniel Lyon was killed in August in the Wilson's Creek campaign to drive them out of the state, Price had moved into the interior where the pro-Southern Missouri State Guard had captured Lexington. Price, however, was unable to capitalize on his victory and had been forced to retreat into Missouri's southwest corner where he established his base at Springfield.

Price hoped that he could gain enough support from Richmond to move back into Missouri and had been trying to persuade Brig. Gen. Ben McCulloch, who commanded Confederate troops in northwest Arkansas, to help him. But the two men disagreed over how this could be accomplished; as a result of this dispute, the government created the Trans-Mississippi District of Department No. 2 and placed Maj. Gen. Earl Van Dorn in command. Van Dorn arrived at Little Rock, Arkansas, late in January and began plans for an invasion of Missouri that he expected to culminate in the capture of St. Louis.

To oppose the Confederates, the Union government had appointed Brig. Gen. Samuel R. Curtis over the newly created Southwestern District of Missouri. Curtis's objective was to protect the state from the Confederates and if necessary drive them farther south. He took command of the Army of the Southwest, which consisted of the First Division under Brig. Gen. Franz Sigel, the Second under Brig. Gen. Alexander S. Asboth, the Third under Brig. Gen. Jefferson C. Davis, and the Fourth under Col. Eugene A. Carr. Sigel, however, was second in command of the entire army; therefore, his division was actually under Col. Peter J. Osterhaus. After arriving at Rolla, Curtis began to move his 10,250 men, and on February 13, 1862, his army marched into Springfield, taking the town without a battle.

The Confederates retreated before him; Price had joined McCulloch in the Boston Mountains near Fayetteville in northwestern Arkansas. Van Dorn arrived on March 2 and divided his new Army of the Southwest, numbering around 16,500, into two divisions. Price still headed the Missourians, while McCulloch oversaw two brigades of Texas, Arkansas, and Louisiana troops, with the infantry under Col. Louis Hébert and cavalry under Brig. Gen. James McQueen McIntosh. In addition, Brig. Gen. Albert Pike, who commanded Indians from the Five Southern Tribes, was summoned from the Indian Territory. On March 4 Van Dorn had his army on the move and reached Little Sugar Creek two days later.

Curtis, learning of the Confederate advance, pulled back to a defensive position where Telegraph Road, which ran north and south, crossed the creek. His line, just below the Missouri border, was near an inn known as Elkhorn Tavern and three miles south of a 150-foot-high plateau called Pea Ridge. Believing that the attack would come from the direction of Fayetteville, Curtis closed Telegraph Road with felled trees and dug earthen fortifications in the Little Sugar Creek valley, making any attack from the south or southwest perilous.

Van Dorn recognized the futility of an assault on such a strong position. Therefore, he decided to envelop the Federal army and hit it in the rear, destroying Curtis's link with Missouri Unionists and breaking his supply line. During the night the Confederates moved around Curtis's right flank down a local road that paralleled Telegraph Road, the Bentonville Detour. But the Confederates had been on the march for three days, and by the morning of March 7 the men were tired and cold. Price's Missourians reached the crossing of the Bentonville Detour and Telegraph Road first; the roads met in Cross Timber Hollow just over three miles north of the tavern. But since McCulloch's Confederates lagged behind, Van Dorn decided to split the attack. Price's Missourians would move straight down Telegraph Road, while McCulloch would hit Curtis several miles west of Elkhorn Tavern near the tiny village of Leetown. This decision meant that the engagement became two battles.

Curtis was not deceived; he knew the Confederates had moved around his flank and had turned much of his army to the rear facing north. Without waiting for Van Dorn to attack him, he pushed his army forward. Osterhaus's and Davis's divisions encountered McCulloch's men just north of Leetown while Carr met Price's advance down Telegraph Road. Van Dorn's decision to split his army proved to be a bad one, as McCulloch and McIntosh were killed near Leetown and Hébert was captured. This left one wing of the battle without a leader, and by midafternoon the remnants of McCulloch's division retreated to the Bentonville Detour. In the meantime Van Dorn accompanied Price's division through Cross Timbers Hollow toward Pea Ridge. After Southern artillery weakened the Federal position on the plateau, Confederates climbed the embankment west of Elkhorn Tavern and drove the Federals back. The fighting ended as night fell with the Confederates holding the tavern and key positions on Telegraph and Huntsville roads. Survivors from the Leetown fight joined Van Dorn at this location and waited to renew the battle the next day.

On the morning of March 8 the two armies had consolidated their troops. Curtis deployed his four divisions facing north while Van Dorn formed a defensive line near the tavern. But Van Dorn was short of ammunition, and when the battle opened, the Confederates fell back under heavy artillery fire and soon began to scatter. By 11:00 A.M. the battle was over, and Curtis could claim a well-deserved and decisive victory.

The Battle of Elkhorn Tavern was one of the few major engagements in the Trans-Mississippi. The Confederate defeat ensured that the Union would retain control over Missouri, and Van Dorn, who significantly outnumbered the Federals, must be faulted for his failure to adapt to the situation as it developed. Moreover, the defeat may have influenced Richmond's decision to relegate the Trans-Mississippi to a secondary role in the war; Van Dorn's army was transferred to the east side of the Mississippi River at the end of the month. This decision had far-reaching consequences, as it appeared that the Confederate government was abandoning the Trans-Mississippi. Although there would be future Confederate raids into Missouri, this engagement proved the pivotal battle for control of the state.

BIBLIOGRAPHY

Bearss, Edwin C. "The First Day at Pea Ridge, March 7, 1862." *Arkansas Historical Quarterly* 17 (Summer 1958): 132–154.

Brown, Walter L. "Pea Ridge: Gettysburg of the West." *Arkansas Historical Quarterly* 15 (Spring 1956): 3–16.

Castel, Albert. "A New View of the Battle of Pea Ridge." *Missouri Historical Review* 62 (January 1968): 136–151.

Hartje, Robert George. *Van Dorn: The Life and Times of a Confederate General.* Nashville, Tenn., 1967.

Hughes, Michael A. "A Forgotten Battle in a Region Ignored. Pea Ridge, or Elkhorn Tavern, Arkansas—March 7–8, 1862." *Blue & Gray Magazine* 5 (January 1988): 8–36.

Pea Ridge National Park. "The Battle of Pea Ridge, 1862." Pamphlet. Rogers, Ark., n.d.

Shea, William L., and Earl J. Hess. "Pea Ridge." In *The Civil War Battlefield Guide.* Boston, 1990.

Shea, William L., and Earl J. Hess. *Pea Ridge: Civil War Campaign in the West.* Chapel Hill, N.C., 1992.

ANNE J. BAILEY

ELLERSON'S MILL, VIRGINIA. *See* Mechanicsville, Virginia.

ELLET, HENRY T. (1812–1887), member of the Mississippi secession convention.

Born in Salem, New Jersey, on March 8, 1812, Ellet attended the Latin School in Salem and graduated from Princeton College. Admitted to the bar in 1833, he opened a law office in Bridgeton, New Jersey. Ellet moved to Port Gibson, Claiborne County, Mississippi, in 1837 and became active in Democratic politics. On January 12, 1846, he was appointed captain of the Claiborne Guards and organized Claiborne County volunteers for service in the Mexican War. When Jefferson Davis resigned from the U.S. Congress in 1846, Ellet was elected to succeed him. He served in Congress from January until March 1847. Declining to seek reelection, he returned to his law practice.

Ellet was elected to the Mississippi State Senate in 1853 and served until 1862. He was a member of the Mississippi convention of 1849, which defended state sovereignty. He represented Mississippi at the Nashville Convention in 1850, which restated the South's position on slavery and the extension of slavery into the territories. In 1854 Ellet was appointed by the Mississippi Supreme Court to serve on a commission to rewrite the state's legal code, which was adopted by the legislature in 1857. In 1856 he also acted as a Democratic presidential elector for James Buchanan.

Ellet was a member of the Mississippi secession convention in 1861. Temporary chairman of the meeting, he also served on the committee that drafted the Mississippi ordinance of secession. In February 1861, Davis appointed Ellet postmaster general of the Confederacy, but he declined the post.

In 1865 Ellet was elected judge of the Mississippi High Court of Appeals and Errors. After resigning on October 1, 1867, he moved to Memphis, Tennessee, the next year and resumed his legal practice. In 1886, Ellet was elected chancellor of the Twelfth Division of Tennessee.

Ellet died in Memphis on October 15, 1887, while delivering a welcoming address for President Grover Cleveland.

BIBLIOGRAPHY

Roland, Dunbar. *History of Mississippi: The Heart of the South.* 4 vols. Chicago, 1925.

Roland, Dunbar. *Military History of Mississippi, 1803–1898.* Spartanburg, S.C., 1978.

Roland, Dunbar. *Mississippi.* 3 vols. Atlanta, 1907.

KENNY A. FRANKS

ELLIOT, STEPHEN, JR. (1830–1866), brigadier general.

Elliot was born at Beaufort, South Carolina, October 26, 1830. After attending Harvard for a short time, he graduated from South Carolina College in 1850 and became a plantation owner on Parris Island, South Carolina. He was a member of the state legislature and captain of a militia company, the Beaufort Volunteer Artillery Company.

When the state called for volunteers, Elliot's company joined the Eleventh South Carolina Infantry, serving in the Charleston area and fighting at Pocataligo. Elliot attached himself briefly to another unit in order to participate in the bombardment of Fort Sumter. He also took part in the defense of Port Royal in November 1861, earning a reputation as a daring raider. He served as major and lieutenant colonel of the artillery in South Carolina for three years, as chief of artillery for various districts, and for a short time as commander of Fort Sumter.

Appointed colonel commanding Holcombe's South Carolina Legion, Elliot was transferred to Virginia during the spring of 1864. Promoted to brigadier general to date from May 24, he was assigned to command Gen. Nathan Evans's old brigade on the Petersburg lines. Part of his brigade was blown up by a Federal mine during the Battle of the Crater, July 30. Elliot was seriously wounded while trying to organize a counterattack. After a lengthy recovery, he was given command of a brigade in the Department of South Carolina, Georgia, and Florida from January 2 to April 9, 1865. In April he was commanding a brigade in Anderson's Division, Stewart's Corps, Army of the Tennessee. Joining Gen. Joseph E. Johnston's army near Bentonville, North Carolina, he was wounded for the second time. He eventually surrendered with Johnston's army.

After the war, he was elected to the South Carolina legislature "but exhausted by wounds and exposure, survived only a few months." He died of his wounds at Aiken, South Carolina, February 21, 1866. He was buried in the Episcopal Churchyard in Beaufort.

BIBLIOGRAPHY

Crute, Joseph H., Jr. *Units of the Confederate Army.* Midlothian, Va., 1987.

Sifakis, Stewart. *Who Was Who in the Civil War.* New York, 1988.

Warner, Ezra J. *Generals in Gray: Lives of the Confederate Commanders.* Baton Rouge, La., 1959.

JOHN R. WOODARD

ELLIOTT, GILBERT (1843–1895), naval shipbuilder. Born in Elizabeth City, North Carolina, young Elliott was one of the most prolific builders of warships in the Confederacy. At the beginning of the war he was employed as a lawyer's clerk in the office of William F. Martin. Acting as agent for Gen. James G. Martin, eighteen-year-old Elliott negotiated a contract with the C.S. Navy Department on October 22, 1861, for the construction of a sail and steam gunboat at Elizabeth City. This contract was followed by one on January 13, 1862, for three Maury gunboats (small, inexpensive, and easily constructed gunboats meant to operate in squadrons of about fifteen ships and attack larger enemy ships en masse), and another contract on April 16 for a small ironclad. All three of these contracts went unfulfilled because of Union inroads in the areas where the construction was taking place: Norfolk and its vicinity were evacuated by the Confederates in May 1862, and Elizabeth City was captured early that same year. After the destruction of the vessels prior to their completion, Elliott briefly served in the Seventeenth North Carolina Infantry before taking leave to resume naval construction.

Again working with Martin, Elliott contracted on September 17, 1862, for a small two-gun ironclad to be built at Tarboro, North Carolina. A later addendum provided for the construction of a sister ironclad at nearby Edward's Ferry. Although the threat of capture forced the burning of the Tarboro vessel before its completion, the Edward's Ferry ironclad was finished in April 1864 as the famous *Albemarle.* The two contractors also completed a small four-gun floating battery at about the same time. Another ironclad being built by Elliott, with P. E. and W. H. Smith, was nearing completion at Edward's Ferry when hostilities ceased.

Following the war Elliott practiced law in Norfolk, St. Louis, and New York. He died May 9, 1895, at Fort Wadsworth, Staten Island, and is buried in Greenwood Cemetery, Brooklyn.

BIBLIOGRAPHY

Elliott, Gilbert. "The Ram *Albemarle:* Her Construction and Service." In *Histories of the North Carolina Troops.* Vol. 5. Edited by Walter Clark. Goldsboro, N.C., 1901.

Elliott, Robert G. *A Tarheel Confederate and His Family.* Daytona Beach, Fla., 1989.

Jones, Virgil Carrington. *The Final Effort.* Vol. 3 of *The Civil War at Sea.* New York, 1962. Reprint, Wilmington, N.C., 1990.

A. ROBERT HOLCOMBE, JR.

ELLIOTT, JOHN MILTON (1820–1879), congressman from Kentucky. Elliott spent most of his life in the rugged, mountainous eastern corner of his state, a section with few slaves, no plantation crops, and a strong tradition of Southern Unionism. Eastern Kentucky's marginal identification with the Confederacy possibly explains Elliott's lackluster record in the Confederate Congress.

Born in Virginia, Elliott moved to Morgan County, Kentucky, as a child and received his basic education there. He later graduated from Virginia's Emory and Henry College, read law, and passed the Kentucky bar in 1843. After establishing a practice in Prestonsburg, Kentucky, in 1847, he was elected to represent Floyd County in the Kentucky House of Representatives. Five years later Elliott ran successfully as a Democrat for the U.S. House of Representatives. He served three consecutive terms, returned to Prestonsburg to practice law in 1859, and was reelected to the Kentucky legislature.

In December 1861, Elliott was expelled from the Kentucky House of Representatives because of his pro-Southern leanings. His secessionist views, however, led to his appointment by the Provisional Government of Kentucky to the Provisional Congress from the Ninth District. He subsequently was elected to two terms from the Twelfth District in the Confederate House of Representatives. He served on the Enrolled Bills, Indian Affairs, and Post Offices and Post Roads committees. Elliott's Confederate congressional career reflected the condition of his isolated and militarily moribund constituency. Early in the war he opposed granting the president the power to remove home guards from remote sections of the South. Later Elliott objected to heavy taxation policies that he feared would discriminate against expatriate Kentuckians.

Following Appomattox, Elliott practiced law in Prestonsburg, served as circuit judge, and was appointed a justice on the Kentucky Court of Appeals. In 1879 he was assassinated by a disgruntled defendant.

BIBLIOGRAPHY

Quisenberry, A. C. "The Alleged Secession of Kentucky." *Register of the Kentucky State Historical Society* 15 (1917): 15–32.

Wakelyn, Jon L. *Biographical Dictionary of the Confederacy.* Edited by Frank E. Vandiver. Westport, Conn., 1977.

Warner, Ezra J., and W. Buck Yearns. *Biographical Register of the Confederate Congress.* Baton Rouge, La., 1975.

JOHN DAVID SMITH

ELLIS, JOHN W. (1820–1861), governor of North Carolina. Born on a plantation in eastern Rowan County, Ellis graduated from the University of North Carolina, read law, and established his practice in Salisbury in 1842. Elected three times to the North Carolina House of Commons in the 1840s, he was chosen a state superior court judge by the General Assembly in 1848. Returning to politics ten years later, he was easily elected governor in 1858 as a Democrat and secured reelection in 1860 with little difficulty. An ardent secessionist, Ellis had become convinced as early as 1854 that slavery interests were jeopardized within the Union. Following the election of Abraham Lincoln, he urged that North Carolina convene a Southern consultative conference to be followed by a state secession convention. He also called for a militia reorganization. The General Assembly acted promptly on his military recommendations, voting an appropriation of $300,000 and appointing a military commission to help him administer it. Badly divided, the legislators stalled on the convention issue until late January 1861. They then submitted it to a popular referendum in which it was rejected by 651 votes.

In the meantime Ellis in January had declined a request by a delegation from Wilmington to have state forces seize Forts Caswell and Johnston on lower Cape Fear before they could be garrisoned by Federal troops. When local forces seized the forts anyway, he detached the Thirtieth North Carolina Militia to restore them to Federal control because the state had not yet seceded. He then informed President James Buchanan of his action and received assurances that no Federal reinforcements would be sent to the Cape Fear region.

Following the firing on Fort Sumter, Ellis refused Lincoln's call for troops, denouncing what he called "this war upon the liberties of a free people." Instead he asked for thirty thousand volunteers to defend against invasion and promptly seized all Federal military installations within the state. Calling the General Assembly into special session on May 1, he also asked President Jefferson Davis to visit North Carolina. At Ellis's instigation the General Assembly quickly passed a convention bill. When that body met on May 20 it just as promptly adopted a secession ordinance by unanimous vote. Ellis meanwhile had already begun to muster in state troops under assembly authorization to prepare them for transfer to the Confederacy. Prior to adjournment the legislature voted its thanks to the governor for his efforts in preparing the state for war. Ellis now made a quick trip to Richmond to confer with Confederate authorities and resolve problems over the transfer of state troops. Then, with his health rapidly failing owing to consumption, Ellis sought rest at Red Sulphur Springs, Virginia, in late June. But he had worked himself to exhaustion, and he died there on July 7.

BIBLIOGRAPHY

Barratt, John G. *The Civil War in North Carolina.* Chapel Hill, N.C., 1963.

Barratt, John G. "North Carolina." In *The Confederate Governors.* Edited by W. Buck Yearns. Athens, Ga., 1985.

Tolbert, Noble J., ed. *The Papers of John Willis Ellis.* 2 vols. Raleigh, N.C., 1964.

WILLIAM E. PARRISH

ELZEY, ARNOLD (1816–1871), major general. Upon graduating from the U.S. Military Academy in 1837, Arnold Elzey Jones changed his name. There were a multitude of Joneses in the army, but not so many Elzeys, and he wanted to set himself apart. He spent his early adulthood as a soldier fighting Seminoles in Florida and Mexicans south of the border, earning the respect of his superior officers. In 1847 the General Assembly of Maryland offered official thanks to Elzey for "gallantry, bravery and good conduct" as an American soldier.

Fourteen years later, when Confederates fired on Fort Sumter, Elzey commanded the U.S. arsenal at Augusta, Georgia. He unhesitatingly turned the arsenal over to Confederate forces, resigned his commission, and traded his blue uniform for Confederate gray. A native Marylander, Elzey soon assumed colonelcy of the First Maryland Infantry.

On July 21, 1861, at the Battle of First Manassas, when his brigadier commander, E. Kirby Smith, fell wounded, Elzey became responsible for his entire brigade. He rose to the occasion and aided in repulsing Federal troops in the first major engagement of the war. A letter in the *Richmond*

ARNOLD ELZEY.   NATIONAL ARCHIVES

Dispatch described Gen. P. G. T. Beauregard rushing up to Elzey and proclaiming him the "Blücher of the day." President Jefferson Davis purportedly promoted Elzey on the spot to brigadier general. In any event, promotion did come and Elzey continued as brigadier under Maj. Gen. Thomas J. ("Stonewall") Jackson in the famed Valley campaign of 1862. At the Battle of Port Republic, Elzey's horse fell wounded beneath him and he received a slight leg injury. But his fighting spirit had not waned, and he continued in active duty through the early weeks of the Peninsular campaign. At the Battle of Gaines' Mill on June 27, 1862, Elzey sustained a near fatal bullet wound to his skull. The injury prevented him from again taking field command, and the Confederacy lost a dependable fighter. On December 4, 1862, he returned to duty, newly promoted to major general, to serve as head of the Department of Richmond. Elzey retained this post through 1864, organizing defenses for the often-threatened Confederate capital.

In March 1863, Gen. Robert E. Lee recommended Elzey for the position of chief of artillery in the Army of Northern Virginia, but apparently Elzey's continued weakened condition prevented him from accepting the post. A year and a half later, he did become chief of artillery in the Army of Tennessee, though records do not indicate his participating in the invasion of Tennessee late in 1864. Relief from duty came on February 17, 1865. The man once hailed as the "Blücher" of the Confederacy no longer had a place in the army.

When the war ended, Elzey returned to Maryland to spend quietly the remainder of his years as a farmer.

BIBLIOGRAPHY

Freeman, Douglas S. *Lee's Lieutenants: A Study in Command.* 3 vols. New York, 1942–1944. Reprint, New York, 1986.

Johnson, Bradley T. *Maryland.* Vol. 2. of *Confederate Military History.* Edited by Clement A. Evans. Atlanta, 1899. Vol. 2 of Extended ed. Wilmington, N.C., 1987.

"Men of Maryland Specially Honored by the State or the United States." *Maryland Historical Magazine* 12, no. 3 (September 1917): 215–216.

Warner, Ezra J. *Generals in Gray: Lives of the Confederate Commanders.* Baton Rouge, La., 1959.

LESLEY JILL GORDON-BURR

EMANCIPATION PROCLAMATION. In the Preliminary Emancipation Proclamation of September 22, 1862, President Abraham Lincoln declared that, as of January 1, 1863, "all persons held as slaves within any State, or designated part of a State, the people whereof shall then be in rebellion," would be "forever free." In the final Emancipation Proclamation of January 1, 1863, he designated all of the Confederacy as still in rebellion except for certain Louisiana parishes and Virginia counties and the entire state of Tennessee. Most of the excepted areas were those under the presumed control of Federal forces. Eastern Tennessee was not yet under such control but could hardly be considered "in rebellion," since its people were overwhelmingly pro-Union. Lincoln justified the proclamation as "a fit and necessary war measure," and so he could not logically have applied it to the border slave states or to the Federally occupied portions of the South—areas in which his government was not waging war.

Newspapers in the Confederacy ridiculed Lincoln's action. They accused him of leaving the slaves in bondage where he had the power to free them and pretending to emancipate them where he had no power to do so. Yet the papers also denounced the proclamation as a call upon the slaves to revolt. Especially worrisome were its clauses advising freed slaves to "abstain from all violence, unless in necessary self-defense," and stating that "such persons" would be "received into the armed service of the United States."

The Confederate government took steps to retaliate. In a January 12, 1863, message to his Congress, Jefferson Davis characterized the proclamation as "a measure by which millions of human beings of an inferior race" were being

EMANCIPATION PROCLAMATION.   The entire text of the Proclamation is printed inside the oval and dated September 22, 1862. The names of Confederate and Federal states are linked together in a chain surrounding the oval. At the bottom, freed slaves pray under the inscription "Give thanks all ye people, give thanks to the Lord."

"encouraged to a general assassination of their masters." He recommended dire punishment for captured white officers of black troops. Congress responded with a joint resolution containing the following provisions: such officers were to be tried by military courts, which could impose the death penalty; black soldiers, if formerly slaves, were to be handed over to state governments for return to their previous owners.

The Davis government was temporarily strengthened by the popular reaction to Lincoln's policy, which at first had a unifying effect on Confederate citizens. Even the most persistently anti-Davis newspaper, the *Richmond Examiner,* endorsed Davis's stand, charging Lincoln with "the most startling political crime in American history." The preliminary announcement disheartened Unionists in eastern Tennessee and caused Thomas A. R. Nelson and other leaders to switch their loyalty from Lincoln to Davis. Andrew Johnson, the Unionist governor of Tennessee, feared that still others would go over to the Confederate side, and he was much relieved when Lincoln excluded the entire state from the final proclamation.

The Confederacy was seriously weakened, however, by the long-term effects of Lincoln's emancipation policy. Early on, Davis feared that it would handicap Confederate efforts to gain recognition and intervention from abroad. His diplomatic and propaganda agents overseas, aware of "the universal hostility of Europe to slavery," also worried that Lincoln's action would draw European sympathy and support away from the Confederacy. To counteract this threat of the proclamation, Confederate propagandists included in the June 11, 1863, issue of their periodical, the *Index,* an "Address to Christians throughout the World," in which a number of prominent Southern preachers testified that the abolition of slavery would be "an interference with the plans of Divine Providence." Eventually the Confederates indicated a willingness to issue their own emancipation decree if, by doing so, they could be assured of foreign recognition. Their failure to obtain such recognition was due, at least in part, to Lincoln's proclamation.

For the Confederacy, the proclamation had even more disastrous consequences through its influence on the slaves. Though nearly all of them were illiterate, they soon learned about the promise of freedom to come on January 1, 1863. Some Mississippi militiamen in Confederate service requested permission to go home before then—"as the negroes are making their brags that by the first of January they will be free as we are and a general outbreak is expected about that time." Here and there throughout the South the rumor ran that slaves were preparing to rise on the appointed day. To strengthen control over them, Congress amended the Conscription Act on October 11, 1862, so as to exempt one man as owner or overseer for every twenty slaves on a plantation (the Twenty-Slave Law). Actually,

slaves responded to the proclamation not by attempting to revolt but by heading for the nearest Union army camp. They were already fleeing in that direction; now, with freedom as the lure, the numbers increased. Approximately 100,000 from the Confederate states (along with other blacks from the Northern and border states) sooner or later joined the Union army.

By stimulating the movement of laborers and soldiers to the Union side, the proclamation threatened to worsen the already serious manpower shortage of the Confederacy. As early as January 10, 1863, Gen. Robert E. Lee warned the secretary of war about the consequences of the "savage and brutal policy" that Lincoln recently had proclaimed. There is an "absolute necessity," Lee wrote, "to increase our armies, if we desire to oppose effectual resistance to the vast numbers that the enemy is now precipitating upon us." It proved impossible to increase the armies sufficiently, however, and a year later Gen. Patrick Cleburne concluded that the South was losing the war because it lacked the manpower of the North. As a result of the proclamation, Cleburne said, "slavery, from being one of our chief sources of strength," had become "one of our chief sources of weakness." He therefore suggested that the Confederacy take the drastic step of recruiting its own army of slaves. When Congress finally authorized such a step, on March 13, 1865, the earlier joint resolution concerning the proclamation was revised. Instead of warning the North against recruiting "negroes," the resolution now warned only against recruiting "our negro slaves."

At the Hampton Roads peace conference, on February 3, 1865, the proclamation emerged as an issue in the discussion between Lincoln and representatives of the Confederacy. Vice President Alexander H. Stephens (according to his own account) asked Lincoln what permanent effect, if any, the proclamation would have on the slaves. "Would it be held to emancipate the whole, or only those who had, at the time the war ended, become actually free under it?" Lincoln (again, according to Stephens's account) replied that this was a question for the courts. "His own opinion was, that as the proclamation was a *war measure,* and would have effect only from its being an exercise of the war power, as soon as the war ceased, it would be inoperative for the future." Doubting, as he did, the postwar validity of the proclamation, Lincoln helped to bring about the adoption of the Thirteenth Amendment, which made the question moot.

Whether or not the proclamation would have conferred legal and lasting freedom on any slave, it certainly brought at least a degree of practical freedom to the multitudes that it encouraged to escape from bondage. By thus depleting the human resources of the Confederacy, while also helping to deter foreign intervention, the proclamation contributed mightily to the Confederacy's ultimate defeat.

[*See also* African Americans in the Confederacy; African American Troops in the Union Army; Contraband; Juneteenth; Slavery; Thirteenth Amendment.]

BIBLIOGRAPHY

Coulter, E. Merton. *The Confederate States of America, 1861–1865.* A History of the South, vol. 7. Baton Rouge, La., 1950.
Franklin, John Hope. *The Emancipation Proclamation.* Garden City, N.Y., 1963.
Wiley, Bell I. *Southern Negroes, 1861–1865.* Baton Rouge, La., 1938. Revised ed., Baton Rouge, La., 1974.

RICHARD N. CURRENT

ENCHANTRESS AFFAIR.

The brig *Enchantress* was taken by the Confederate privateer *Jeff Davis* on July 6, 1861, off the coast of Delaware. A prize master and five seamen from the Confederate vessel attempted to take the prize into a Southern port. But sixteen days after her capture, *Enchantress* was retaken by the Union warship *Albatross.* The six Confederates were imprisoned in Philadelphia, tried for piracy (October 22–28, 1861), and convicted.

When an international conference meeting in 1856 had agreed to declare privateering illegal, the United States had declined to sign the agreement. Nevertheless, in 1861 the U.S. government decided to accept the argument that privateering was piracy, and the *Enchantress* affair gave it the opportunity to do so. The five members of the brig's crew were sentenced to death as pirates.

The sentence, however, was never carried out. Confederate president Jefferson Davis threatened retaliation for what he described as "a practice unknown to the warfare of civilized man, and so barbarous as to disgrace the nation which shall be guilty of inaugurating it." If any Confederate privateersmen were executed, he said, captured Union officers would be treated in accordance with the disposition of the imprisoned crew. Ultimately, the captured privateersmen and the prize muster were declared prisoners of war, and many were eventually exchanged.

The *Enchantress* case was one of several involving captured Confederate privateers that persuaded Lincoln's government to drop its decision to treat their crews as pirates.

[*See also* Privateers.]

BIBLIOGRAPHY

Coulter, E. Merton. *The Confederate States of America.* A History of the South, vol. 7. Baton Rouge, La., 1959.
Robinson, William. *The Confederate Privateers.* Columbia, S.C., 1990.

WILLIAM N. STILL, JR.

ENGINEER BUREAU.

The Confederate Engineer Bureau was born with the recognition that precautionary measures needed to be taken by the new Confederacy to protect itself in the event of attack. Although the Confederate Congress formally authorized the formation of the Engineer Bureau on March 7, 1861, by designating an engineer force of a number of commissioned officers together with one hundred "sappers and miners and pontoniers," the bureau, as a central authority, played little or no role in Confederate engineering in the early stages of the war. What engineering was done to secure the defenses at Charleston Harbor, Savannah, Mobile Bay, Pensacola, the Mississippi River, the North Carolina coast, the river approaches in Tennessee and Kentucky, and the Virginia coast and peninsulas was accomplished by departmental commanders and their own staff engineers, not by any coordinated effort from the Engineer Bureau.

From the inception of the bureau until the late summer of 1861 Maj. Josiah Gorgas, chief of the Ordnance Department, served as its unofficial head. On August 3, 1861, Maj. Danville Leadbetter of Alabama was ordered to Richmond to assume command of the bureau. Although Leadbetter remained in titular command of the bureau until the fall of 1862, he was unable to render efficient service as bureau chief. Sent to Chattanooga in November 1861, Leadbetter never returned to Richmond.

On September 24, 1862, Lt. Col. Jeremy Francis Gilmer was named chief of engineers. The date of Gilmer's appointment marked the true emergence of the bureau as a central agency. Gilmer set about trying to coordinate engineering efforts in the far-flung Confederacy by making frequent inspections of important defensive installations. In spite of Gilmer's tremendous efforts, the bureau was hampered by chronic shortages of manpower and matériel as well as finances. Like the Ordnance and Commissary departments, the Engineer Bureau required a large budget to finance the construction of forts, earthworks, bridges, railroads, and mobile engineering and construction equipment. As the war progressed, finances dwindled, crippling the bureau's efforts to provide necessary defenseworks and to supply armies in the field with necessary equipment.

Although the South had relied upon slave labor for its economic survival up to and through the war, the Engineer Bureau was never able to use slave labor to augment manpower shortages in any systematic manner. The very limited natural resources of the South further reduced the bureau's attempts to build railroads, bridges, and fortifications. Even its efforts to unify major railroad lines inside the Confederacy failed, owing to lack of manpower, iron rails, and government support for the control of the otherwise privately owned railroad lines.

Among the responsibilities assigned to the Engineer Bureau was the preparation of maps. In the field, most

PONTOON BRIDGE.

mapmaking was performed by staff topographers in the respective armies. But in countless engagements in all theaters of war, the lack of adequate maps hampered the armies. The central mapmaking efforts of the Engineer Bureau, however, were not very successful. The bureau assigned numerous survey teams to the peninsula, Richmond, northern Virginia, Fredericksburg, Chattanooga, Vicksburg, the Trans-Mississippi, and other locations, but to little avail. The lack of adequate manpower and the unavailability of necessary supplies, including paper, hampered the effort from the beginning.

It was not until the end of 1862 that the Confederacy recognized the need for organizing engineer regiments with pioneer and bridge equipment. Of all the efforts of the bureau, the initiative to organize these regiments met with the greatest success. Gilmer had suggested forming such units in the Army of Northern Virginia as early as the fall of 1862. Although not enthusiastic about the idea, Gen. Robert E. Lee finally agreed to the formation of an engineer regiment in his army. Such an organized engineer command accompanied the Army of Northern Virginia on its invasion

of Pennsylvania in the summer of 1863, laying pontoon bridges across the Potomac at Falling Waters. A similar engineer regiment was formed in the Army of Tennessee in early 1863, and other engineer commands were formed in western Virginia, the Department of the Carolinas, Georgia, and Florida, and the Department of the Trans-Mississippi.

It was the organized First Regiment of Engineers of the Army of Northern Virginia that helped Lee rapidly establish his defense works at Spotsylvania Court House in May 1864 and Cold Harbor in June 1864. The efforts of the First Engineers at laying pontoon bridges over the James River at Chaffin's Bluff near Richmond, building and strengthening the defense works at Petersburg, and maintaining the rail lines in and out of Richmond and Petersburg helped Lee defend the capital city longer than it otherwise could have been done. The First Regiment of Engineers surrendered at Appomattox Courthouse with the rest of Lee's army.

The Third Regiment of Engineers accompanied the Army of Tennessee throughout the campaign from Dalton, Georgia, to the fall of Atlanta, laying bridges and overseeing the construction of fortifications and the maintenance of railroads. The regiment was divided after the fall of Atlanta, a portion following Gen. John Bell Hood's advance into Tennessee and a portion remaining with Gen. William J. Hardee and, ultimately, Gen. Joseph E. Johnston.

Although the Engineer Bureau represented an attempt to centrally coordinate the defense of the Confederacy, coordination never occurred. Partly because the war had progressed too far before the bureau itself became coordinated and partly because of the lack of manpower, matériel, and finances, the bureau was unable to perform effectively the task it was assigned. As well, in a Confederacy where central authority was politically abhorrent, the bureau's task was thwarted by uncooperative private interests and departmental commanders who jealously guarded their own territories of command.

Aside from the success of the bureau in forming engineer regiments that served in the major theaters of war and in providing critical bridging and railroad maintenance work, the most notable engineering efforts in the Confederacy were performed by departmental and local commanders and their staff engineers without the direction of the Engineer Bureau.

[See also Gilmer, Jeremy Francis; Forts and Fortifications; Leadbetter, Danville; Transportation.]

BIBLIOGRAPHY

Nichols, James L. *Confederate Engineers.* Tuscaloosa, Ala., 1957.
Thomas, Emory M. *The Confederate Nation, 1861–1865.* New York, 1979.

KENT MASTERSON BROWN

EPISCOPAL CHURCH. During the sectional crisis most of the 11 bishops and 450 ministers in the South's Episcopal church defended their region. Among themselves, however, they divided on doctrine and liturgical practice. Although the church was once a hierarchical and eucharistically centered faith, to survive in the antebellum South many Episcopalians became low church or evangelical. They stressed adult renewal of faith, a simplified liturgy to allow more preaching, and revivalism. Throughout the period their numbers remained small; the majority clustered along the Atlantic seaboard from Maryland to South Carolina. As the Oxford or Anglo-Catholic movement spread from England during the 1840s, a high church revival led many Episcopalians back to a eucharistically centered form of worship. High church leaders sought to restore the importance of the baptismal covenant and apostolic succession. On the eve of the Civil War, the divided church had spread into the southwest, enlarging its numbers to perhaps 25,000 communicants.

Many church members came from old, established Southern families; they held high political office and owned slaves, plantations, and wealth far in excess of their small numbers. The Episcopal clergy and laity staunchly supported the slave regime and the formation of the Confederacy.

After the war began, Bishops Leonidas Polk and Stephen Elliott argued that state political activities determined church loyalty, and in 1862, at a special convention, they formed the Confederate States Protestant Episcopal church. If apprehensive about internal theological divisions and worried over Northern anger at their actions, most of the clergy preached on behalf of the Confederate cause. Bishops founded pro-Confederate diocesan newspapers and published a separate Confederate States Book of Common Prayer and a hymnal. At least one hundred clergy became chaplains, and a few entered the army. The West Point graduate Bishop Leonidas Polk, a close friend of Episcopal convert President Jefferson Davis, held a major command in the western military theater. Bishops Stephen Elliott and James Otey also baptized and confirmed a number of famous Confederate generals.

Institutional and hierarchical beliefs kept many Episcopalians loyal to the Confederacy throughout the war. But after prolonged military losses and devastation of lands, people, and property in the upper South, evangelical Bishop John Johns of Virginia and other low church leaders began to preach about God's denial of grace to the Confederacy. The old split in the Episcopal church resurfaced during the war, and the resultant loss of morale among low churchmen no doubt affected support for the cause.

During the war the clergy proselytized among the slaves and advocated reforms with hopes of converting them to the church, but they had little success. Perhaps because the Episcopal church lacked a preaching tradition, or because so many slaves identified the church with conservative slaveholders, those few blacks who had belonged to the church soon left it after the war. Most of them joined the African Methodist Episcopal church.

The white clergy, however, had no difficulty reuniting their institutional bonds with the once hostile Northern church. Episcopal ministers assumed the lead in the Lost Cause movement. They used the image of Robert E. Lee's support for Southern values and traditions to create a vision of an idyllic Old South of conservative leaders and faithful retainers. The Episcopal minister William N. Pendleton, an ex-Confederate general, traveled throughout the South to preach about God's support for the Southern way of life. But because of lasting tensions between the evangelical and hierarchical factions, the Episcopal church failed to become a dominant force in the New South of religious piety and fundamentalism.

BIBLIOGRAPHY

Chesire, Joseph Blount. *The Church in the Confederate States.* New York, 1912.

Clebsch, William A., ed. *Journal of the Protestant Episcopal Church in the Confederate States of America.* Austin, Tex., 1962.

DuBose, William Porcher. *Turning Points in My Life.* New York, 1912.

Lee, Susan Pendleton. *Memoirs of William Nelson Pendleton.* Philadelphia, 1893.

London, Lawrence Foushee, and Sarah McCulloh Lemmon, eds. *The Episcopal Church in North Carolina, 1701–1959.* Raleigh, N.C., 1987.

Jon L. Wakelyn

ERLANGER LOAN. Negotiated between the Confederate States of America and Emile Erlanger and Company of Paris, the Erlanger Loan was issued on March 19, 1863, in five European cities and raised £1,759,894 ($8,535,486 gold value) for Confederate use in Europe. It was secured by government-owned cotton in the Confederacy and provided that cotton would be delivered in the Confederacy to the bondholders on demand.

The Erlanger family had become prominent in banking in Germany in the early nineteenth century under the leadership of Raphael Erlanger. By midcentury, the family, originally Jewish, had converted to Christianity, and Raphael Erlanger had become a baron. He sent his son, Frederick Emile, to establish a branch of the family business in Paris. The firm issued railroad and government bonds, and Emile became friendly with the emperor, Louis Napoleon.

John Slidell, Confederate commissioner to France, cultivated the friendship of many businessmen, bankers, and others with connections to the emperor. Slidell was aware that by mid-1862, the Confederacy was severely restricted in its ability to place funds in Europe to pay for its shipbuilding and munitions-purchasing programs. The Confederacy had, during the first year of the war, sent to Europe nearly all of the bills of exchange that had accumulated in the South before the Federal blockade stopped all normal shipping in early June 1861. Although numerous small vessels ran the blockade, only small amounts of cotton were carried to Europe during the first year to earn new exchange. The Confederate government was slow to develop a blockade-running program of its own and hesitated to risk shipping the limited amounts of gold and silver that it held. Confederate paper money had, of course, no value in Europe. When Emile Erlanger and Company proposed a bond issue for the Confederacy, Slidell highly recommended it, not only as a means of meeting the financial crisis, but also for political purposes, since Erlanger was influential with the emperor. It may have been relevant also that Slidell's daughter and Emile Erlanger were soon to become engaged to be married.

Erlanger's original offer to issue £5 million at 8 percent interest, with the Confederacy receiving 70 percent of the face value and paying a commission of 5 percent to the firm, was rejected by the Richmond authorities as much too expensive. They agreed to allow the firm to issue £3 million, at 7 percent interest with the South receiving 77 percent and paying a 5 percent commission, only because they hoped that it would increase Slidell's ability to elicit favorable decisions from Louis Napoleon. A provision that bondholders could convert their bonds into cotton in the Confederacy with the right to export it was an important incentive for investors, since the price of cotton in Europe was quite high.

The firm issued the bonds at 90 percent of face value in London, Liverpool, Paris, Amsterdam, and Frankfurt, and the issue was an immediate success. Within two weeks, however, the price sagged to 87 and Erlanger feared that subscribers might not make the remainder of their installment payments. The firm secretly bought in the market to sustain the price and induced the Confederates to provide funds to continue the effort. The price was sustained and all payments were made, but the Confederates had bought back nearly half of the loan. During the next year, Erlanger was able to resell many of these bonds, and the Confederates were able to use many others in payment of debts. In the end, the Confederate government had sold bonds with a face value of £2,391,000 and had raised £1,759,894 in Europe at an effective annual interest rate of a little over 12 percent. The price of the bonds became an indicator of European estimates of the likelihood of Confederate independence.

It is impossible to determine whether the bond issue increased Slidell's influence at the court of Louis Napoleon. The Erlanger loan was successful, however, in providing funds in Europe to continue Confederate military and naval purchases in 1863.

BIBLIOGRAPHY

Ball, Douglas B. *Financial Failure and Confederate Defeat.* Chicago, 1991.

Gentry, Judith Fenner. "A Confederate Success in Europe: The Erlanger Loan." *Journal of Southern History* 36 (May 1970): 157–188.

Lester, Richard I. *Confederate Finance and Purchasing in Great Britain.* Charlottesville, Va., 1975.

Owsley, Frank Lawrence. *King Cotton Diplomacy: Foreign Relations of the Confederate States of America.* 2d ed., rev. Chicago, 1959.

Thompson, Samuel Bernard. *Confederate Purchasing Operations Abroad.* Chapel Hill, N.C., 1935.

Judith Fenner Gentry

ESPIONAGE. [*This entry is composed of three articles:* Confederate Secret Service, *which overviews the organization and operations of Southern espionage efforts;* Federal Secret Service, *which discusses Northern espionage during the Civil War; and* Confederate Military Spies, *which* *profiles notable Southern espionage agents. For further discussion of Confederate attempts to influence the war and Northern opinion through espionage, see* Copperheads; Lincoln, Abraham, *article on* Assassination of Lincoln; Northwestern Conspiracy; *and* Propaganda. *For further examination of Confederate innovations in the field of espionage, see* Signal Corps *and* Torpedoes and Mines. *See also biographies of numerous figures mentioned herein.*]

Confederate Secret Service

According to records discovered as recently as 1990, the Confederacy spent approximately $2 million in gold on Secret Service activities—a princely sum for those days and many times the amount spent by the Union for similar purposes. The Confederate Secret Service covered a wide range of operations from classic espionage penetration of the Federal government in Washington to the development of secret weapons for use behind enemy lines. Secret Service operations also included assistance to Gen. Robert E. Lee and other field commanders in the collection of tactical intelligence and an ambitious attempt to capture President Abraham Lincoln as a hostage. Most important of all, the Secret Service engaged in a serious clandestine political effort to create a peace movement in the North.

The Confederate Secret Service, like the modern American intelligence community, comprised a group of organizations created at different times for distinct purposes and originally with no unifying concept of operations. Experience, however, was an active teacher, and before the war's end legislation was introduced into the Confederate Congress to bring the diverse activities together into a Special and Secret Service Bureau—the Confederate version of a central intelligence agency.

In early 1861, while the Confederate government was still in Montgomery, Alabama, Jefferson Davis began to employ secret agents for political missions abroad. The most successful early espionage operation, however, appears to have been organized by Virginia before that state had formally joined the Confederacy. The most notorious agent of this effort was a Washington hostess, Rose O'Neal Greenhow, who used her social connections and her sexual attractions to elicit a flow of useful information about Federal military preparations in the Washington area. Her greatest success was to alert the Confederates in northern Virginia to Gen. Irvin McDowell's movement from Washington toward the railroad junction at Manassas, which resulted in the Union defeat at the 1861 battle there.

The Confederate espionage network in Washington that included Greenhow continued throughout the war to supply intelligence in support of the government in Richmond, and the network also provided direct support to General Lee's Army of Northern Virginia. Its information enabled Lee to anticipate General Grant's Wilderness campaign and even informed him of Grant's basic strategy of making a flanking maneuver after each frontal encounter. Lee thus was able to prepare roads in order to get ahead of and stop Grant's moves.

The War Department also assigned skilled Secret Service agents to various Confederate generals for specific campaigns. For example, Lt. Henry Thomas Harrison was assigned to Gen. D. H. Hill in North Carolina in early 1863 and later to Gen. James Longstreet for the Gettysburg campaign. Harrison was credited with alerting Longstreet to George Meade's movements into Pennsylvania that resulted in the battle.

Conventional wisdom says that the North was industrial and the South agricultural, but the war brought a spate of technical innovations from Southern inventors. Some of these inventions were weapons like underwater mines that could be used more effectively if they and their technology could be kept secret. As a result, a number of activities, like mine laying and the development of timed detonators for sabotage, were considered by the Confederates as Secret Service activities and protected by special security arrangements.

Similarly, the Confederate Signal Corps, another innovation, depended on the security of its signaling and the cipher systems used for important messages. As a result, it did not seem illogical to the Confederates to charge their Signal Corps with the mission of managing a secret courier line between Washington and Richmond for the delivery of

CONFEDERATE SECRET SERVICE CODING DISK. Photograph by Katherine Wetzel.   THE MUSEUM OF THE CONFEDERACY, RICHMOND, VIRGINIA

important messages from Confederate agents in the North. Once the Signal Corps was involved in clandestine operations via the secret line, it was a small step to have both the Signal Corps and the War Department espionage apparatus managed by the same people.

The idea of using signal flags to send messages over the battlefield was first advanced before the war by surgeon Albert James Myer of the U.S. Army. The Confederates used the system in time to help win the First Battle of Manassas, but the Union army failed to implement the idea until the Confederates had demonstrated its success. The Confederate Signal Corps also ran its secret line between Richmond and Washington continuously throughout the war. It was still in operation when General Lee surrendered on April 9, 1865.

The practical use of underwater explosives was first demonstrated in the James River near Richmond in the summer of 1861 by Comdr. Matthew Fontaine Maury, who had established an enviable reputation as a scientist through his work on oceanography. The use of mines was further developed by the Confederate War Department's Torpedo Bureau, under Gen. Gabriel J. Rains, and by the Navy Department's Submarine Battery Service under first Maury and then Lt. Hunter Davidson.

The Confederates also organized groups of saboteurs, called Strategic Corps, to plant explosives at depots, factories, bridges, river shipping facilities, and other targets behind Union lines. Their chief success was the destruction of the Union army's main supply base at City Point, Virginia, on August 9, 1864. A Strategic Corps team planted a bomb on a ship at the dock, which caused several other ships loaded with ammunition to explode, showering Ulysses S. Grant's neighboring headquarters with debris and inflicting widespread damage. Other teams burned ships on the Mississippi and Ohio rivers and attacked logistics targets in the rear of Union armies.

The most important Secret Service operation of the entire Confederate effort was the attempt to turn widespread disaffection with the war and the Lincoln administration into an effective peace movement. Preparations for this operation began in 1863, and it was launched in April 1864 when Jefferson Davis approved the allocation of $1 million in gold to Jacob Thompson, a former U.S. secretary of the interior who had been selected to head the operation. Thompson's overt mission was to serve as a Confederate commissioner in Canada to search for peace with the U.S. government. (Since Canada was a British possession and Britain did not recognize the Confederacy, Thompson could not be appointed as a minister or ambassador; therefore, the title "commissioner" meant only that the Confederates had commissioned him to act on their behalf.)

There was a covert side to Thompson's mission, however. If no progress was made toward peace, Thompson was to attack the Union war effort by clandestine operations from Canada. To provide him with the technical means necessary for such operations, Clement C. Clay, a former U.S. senator, was also appointed a commissioner. Clay apparently represented the interests of the War Department.

The Confederates promoted an existing secret political group, the Knights of the Golden Circle, as a means of organizing the opposition to the war. Many local chapters of the Knights operated on a quasi-military basis, and some were armed and willing to consider a revolt to express their disaffection. The Confederates tried to induce the Copperheads, as they were called, to take coordinated action against the war. The primary focus was to be Chicago where the Copperheads and a cadre of Confederates infiltrated from Canada were to free the thousands of Confederate prisoners of war held there. The target date was August 1864, and the attack was to be accompanied by revolts or demonstrations in other cities in Illinois, Indiana, and Ohio. The copperheads, however, could never be brought to act, and the operation was eventually penetrated by Federal agents who arrested several of the key plotters in November 1864.

In the meantime, other operations were attempted by the Confederates in Canada. One of the leading Secret Service operatives, John Y. Beall, tried to free the Confederate prisoners on Johnson Island in the harbor of Sandusky, Ohio, but was frustrated when his supporting team got cold feet. Another team, led by Lt. Bennett H. Young, tried to burn St. Albans, Vermont, and made off with over $200,000 in U.S. currency and negotiable paper.

The Confederates in Canada also apparently recruited John Wilkes Booth in July 1864 to organize an attempt to abduct President Lincoln. Booth had help from Richmond but appears to have been directed primarily from Canada. He tried once to capture Lincoln in March 1865, but failed. At that point, Richmond apparently decided it was too late to try again and planned instead to blow up the White House to disrupt coordination between Grant and William Tecumseh Sherman. An explosives expert was sent to assist Booth, but he was captured on his way into Washington. In the absence of his technical adviser and unable to contact knowledgeable superiors, Booth apparently decided to approximate the damage that would be caused by an explosion by attacking simultaneously several officials who would likely have been involved in such an explosion. The result of Booth's decision was the assassination of Lincoln and the wounding of Secretary of State William H. Seward on April 14, 1865. None of the other targets was attacked. Booth was assisted in his escape by several elements of the Secret Service, but he was caught and killed by Union cavalry on April 26, 1865.

The end of the war found the Confederate espionage net in Washington and the Signal Corps' secret line still in operation. More important, the Confederate apparatus in Canada, now under the direction of Gen. Edwin Grey Lee,

EXECUTION OF THE LINCOLN CONSPIRATORS.   Execution of Mary E. Surratt, Lewis T. Powell, David E. Herold, and George A. Atzerodt, the four people condemned as conspirators in the Lincoln assassination. Photograph by Alexander Gardner, July 7, 1865.

NATIONAL ARCHIVES

who had replaced Thompson, was still intact and had Secret Service money to operate with. For several months Lee and his colleagues acted almost like a Confederate government in exile, turning out propaganda denying Confederate complicity in the Lincoln assassination and defending individuals accused of crimes by the Federal government.

Like all clandestine operations, the Confederate Secret Service had failures as well as successes, but on the whole, the efforts were imaginative and made contributions to the Confederate war effort that have never been recognized.

BIBLIOGRAPHY

Bakeless, John. *Spies of the Confederacy*. Philadelphia and New York, 1970.

Baker, Gen. L[afayette] C. *History of the United States Secret Service*. Philadelphia, 1867.

Nelson, Larry. *Bullets, Bayonets, and Rhetoric: Confederate Policy for the United States Presidential Contest of 1864*. University, Ala., 1980.

Perry, Milton F. *Infernal Machines*. Baton Rouge, La., 1965.

Stern, Philip Van Doren. *Secret Missions of the Civil War*. New York, 1959.

Tidwell, William A., with James O. Hall and David Winfred Gaddy. *Come Retribution: The Confederate Secret Service and the Assassination of Lincoln*. Jackson, Miss., and London, 1988.

WILLIAM A. TIDWELL

Federal Secret Service

As in the new Confederacy, intelligence and espionage in the Union emerged more out of necessity, accident, and experimentation than from any organized plan. Indeed, many in the Northern high command still held to the eighteenth-century notion that spying was a contemptible practice beneath the dignity of soldiers. No systematic attempt was made during and immediately after secession to gather reliable military information. Instead, the Union leaders simply relied upon what came to them via rumor and exaggerated newspaper claims. When Gen. Irvin McDowell led his army into Northern Virginia in the campaign culminating in humiliating defeat at Manassas on July 21, 1861, he did not even have a good map of the countryside.

In fact, the first—admittedly ineffective—attempts to arm Abraham Lincoln's armies with information came from the agents of a civilian detective, Allan Pinkerton. Lincoln had known him prior to the war, and it was Pinkerton who discovered a plot to assassinate Lincoln during his trip to Washington to be inaugurated. Foiling the plot endeared Pinkerton to Lincoln, and also called his name to the attention of another former acquaintance, Gen. George B. McClellan. First in western Virginia, and then in Washington, when McClellan replaced the hapless McDowell, Pinkerton was called on to use his stable of "detectives" to provide information on contract. At McClellan's behest, Pinkerton, though always a civilian, organized what he chose to call the U.S. Secret Service, though in fact it never held any official military or governmental status or sanction.

Pinkerton's was a twofold mission: in Washington he was to keep an eye on Confederate sympathizers and ferret out spies; when McClellan's Army of the Potomac was on campaign, Pinkerton would serve on his staff without official rank and manage the efforts of spies and scouts in collecting information about enemy troops. At the former task Pinkerton proved to be rather effective. He caught noted Southern agent Rose O'Neal Greenhow and saw her imprisoned, and had a number of other suspected traitors either arrested or driven out of the city.

In the field, however, Pinkerton proved to be one of the war's notable failures. He knew nothing of military intelligence—few did—nor of how to interpret what information he acquired. From his Chicago detective agency and elsewhere he assembled a small corps of agents, all civilians, whom he sent behind enemy lines charged with learning whatever they could of Confederate numbers, positions, morale, equipment, and anticipated movements. The value of Pinkerton's reports was in the first place predicated on the quality of what was sent to him. His agents were sometimes effective, like Timothy Webster, who operated in the Confederacy for months under cover before being caught and hanged. But they were not trained military men and women who knew the value or import of what they saw. Moreover, they all were prone to accept rumor as fact. And when their reports came back to Pinkerton, he compounded the problem by apparently devising a formula of his own for converting *reported* numbers of troops into *actual* numbers—which always

came out much higher. Thus, in April 1862 when only 17,000 Southerners faced McClellan at Yorktown, Pinkerton told the general that there were 120,000! Even when Pinkerton succeeded in enumerating every unit in the army facing McClellan that summer, he still tripled their actual numbers in his reports. In part this may have been because Pinkerton read his man McClellan very well, and the general always preferred to believe himself too heavily outnumbered to risk a fight. When McClellan was finally eclipsed in the fall of 1862, Pinkerton disappeared from the war with him.

Despite the lack of an organized beginning to Federal espionage and intelligence gathering, many generals besides McClellan employed their own agents, though usually for limited times and specific purposes. Moreover, once Union armies began to occupy Confederate territory, information started coming into the camps on its own, chiefly from Union sympathizers seeking protection and from runaway slaves, or "contrabands," who flocked to the Federal banners in the thousands. Each commander dealt with such information as he chose, although most turned responsibility for it over to the army provost marshal general, who was already charged with managing the fugitives themselves.

The first attempt at a systematic military gathering of information emerged in the western theater, under the guidance of Ulysses S. Grant. In October 1862, as he was planning his overland drive toward Vicksburg, Grant selected Brig. Gen. Grenville M. Dodge for command of a division in his army, with authority for organizing and operating a spy network to provide Grant with intelligence on enemy numbers and movements. Dodge was a perfect choice, having already built and commanded the First Tennessee Cavalry, a regiment of mounted scouts operating in Missouri and Arkansas. He also operated another regiment of loyal western Tennesseeans who provided information on the enemy in their region.

Upon receiving the assignment from Grant, Dodge went to work and quickly produced something far more effective and efficient than Pinkerton's dime novel–style operation. Secrecy was a byword. Only Dodge knew the identity of all of his agents, most of them civilians; they were frequently noted in dispatches only by numbers. He equipped them with Confederate money for their work behind enemy lines and paid them for their services with profits from the sale of confiscated cotton. Although the total number of his agents may never be known, at least 117 would serve him at one time or another, and his network would, by the end of the war, include operatives in almost every Confederate state east of the Mississippi except Florida.

Any kind of information was of interest to Dodge. Given the deplorable quality of road and terrain maps of the Southern states, Dodge—himself an engineer—constantly used information from his people to update the charts he provided to Grant. During the Vicksburg campaign itself, Dodge kept Grant constantly informed of Confederate numbers and positions, allowing the Federals to apply numerical superiority where it counted, while ignoring lesser enemy forces that Pinkerton and McClellan would have exaggerated into legions. Dodge even gave his operatives bogus information about Federal movements as gifts for Confederate commanders in order to win their confidence, thus inaugurating counterintelligence and double agents. Not only did Dodge's network gather information. It also collected Southern spies, constantly thwarting Confederate operatives, including the capture and eventual execution of Sam Davis, the boy spy later virtually canonized in the Lost Cause pantheon for dying rather than revealing the names of his fellow spies.

Dodge managed his small intelligence empire, while still leading his combat division, until he was wounded in the Atlanta campaign. Thereafter it functioned largely on its own under the hand of William Tecumseh Sherman, having already set a model for effectiveness as the most widely flung and far-reaching intelligence network of the war.

Meanwhile, spy work in the eastern theater had progressed at a more leisurely and less professional pace. Following the disappearance of Pinkerton in November 1862, espionage floundered without firm management until the spring of 1863 when Gen. Joseph Hooker engaged Col. George H. Sharpe to head the newly formed Bureau of Military Information in March. A Rutgers and Yale graduate, Sharpe was colonel of the 120th New York Infantry, but more likely it was his proclivity for drinking and high living that grabbed the equally fun-loving Hooker's attention. Yet if he was a bit of a dissipate, Sharpe was also a born spy master. In his first major task, providing Hooker with data on Robert E. Lee's army prior to the Chancellorsville campaign, Sharpe assessed Confederate numbers down to less than one-fourth of 1 percent—a margin of error of only 150 men out of some 60,000. He performed nearly as well during the Gettysburg campaign, but then commenced his most dramatic service when Grant came east in 1864.

Through contacts as yet unknown, Sharpe managed to get through to Samuel Ruth, Union-sympathizing superintendent of the Richmond, Fredericksburg, and Potomac Railroad, and Elizabeth Van Lew, both operating in the Confederate capital itself. Ruth furnished information on troop movements, supplies, and the condition of the South's rail network, and helped escaped Federal prisoners find their way to safety. He even sent information for Federal raiding parties who destroyed portions of his own rail line when it carried valuable matériel for the Southern war effort. Van Lew, a woman regarded as odd and therefore not suspected by her high society Richmond friends and neighbors, was Ruth's associate in some of this work.

LAFAYETTE C. BAKER.   Chief of the National Detective Police in Washington, D.C.
FRANK LESLIE'S ILLUSTRATED FAMOUS LEADERS AND BATTLE SCENES OF THE CIVIL WAR

"Crazy Bet" visited Northern prisoners in Richmond's prisons and then conveyed military information gleaned from them through the lines to Sharpe. From these and other sources, many of them Confederate officers whom she flattered into indiscreet revelations, Van Lew derived a mass of information that she wrote in code on onionskin paper and hid inside empty eggshells, sending them in the keeping of her servants to Union lines. Upon the fall of Richmond in April 1865, one of Grant's first calls was at the Van Lew mansion to extend his thanks.

While Sharpe assumed the field intelligence role once performed by Pinkerton, the duty of keeping an eye on traitors and spies within Washington itself, and much of the North, fell to the National Detective Police, created in 1863 under the management of Lafayette C. Baker. His counterintelligence efforts, for the most part effective, were sometimes crude and brutal, including midnight arrests, incarceration without habeas corpus, and involuntary confessions.

Even as late as 1865 there was no uniform coordination of all Union intelligence activities. Baker reported to the secretary of war; Sharpe to George G. Meade or Grant; Dodge's network to Sherman's staff; and a host of other operatives to their individual employers. As a result methods and effectiveness varied widely, but in the main, by mid- or late 1863 Union armies across the map were getting good information and using it well. At the same time they were successfully subverting most Confederate efforts at gathering good intelligence and performing acts of espionage behind Federal lines.

BIBLIOGRAPHY

Baker, Lafayette C. *History of the United States Secret Service.* Philadelphia, 1867.

Fishel, Edwin. "The Mythology of Civil War Intelligence." *Civil War History* 10 (1964).

Hirshson, Stanley P. *Grenville M. Dodge.* Bloomington, Ind., 1967.

Pinkerton, Allan. *The Spy of the Rebellion.* New York, 1888.

Time-Life Books. *Spies, Scouts and Raiders.* Alexandria, Va., 1985.

WILLIAM C. DAVIS

Confederate Military Spies

The Confederate spies who were successful at their missions and never bragged about their successes remain largely unknown. We know the most about those spies who either were caught in the act or talked at some point about their wartime experiences.

The men and women who served as spies supporting the Confederate military effort were a diverse group representing many aspects of Southern society. The two attributes that come closest to describing them as a group were their commitment to the Southern cause and their lack of qualification for combat service. Even this second attribute is not completely descriptive, however, for though many of the spies were women, physically disabled men, or wounded veterans no longer able to serve in the field, the young soldiers who served as cavalry scouts proved to be so capable at collecting information under pressure that a number of them were drawn into the clandestine world of espionage.

When the Confederates began to create the institutions that were needed for combat, they had the help of a number of men who knew clandestine operations to the extent that it was known by the U.S. government before the war. In addition, a number of immigrants in both the North and the South had had personal experience in the clandestine activities associated with various republican revolutions in Europe in the decades before the Civil War. The Confederates may also have had some help from British or French intelligence agents who saw the weakening of the United States as one possible outcome of a Confederate victory. The net effect was that the Confederates had available nearly all the know-how then in existence to help them organize the collection of information they needed to defend themselves against the Northern armies.

Confederate spies belonged to a number of different organizations that together formed the Confederate Secret Service. Scholars are still trying to piece together the history of these organizations, but some parts of the story are well known.

Rose O'Neal Greenhow. The first Confederate spy to gain widespread recognition was Rose O'Neal Greenhow, widow of a respected agent of the U.S. State Department. She was noted for her intelligence and had a great deal of political experience—much more than was usual for a woman in those days. She had lived in Mexico and California and had known most of the American presidents and cabinet officers from the time of Andrew Jackson down to Abraham Lincoln's predecessor, James Buchanan. The great spokesman for the Southern point of view, John C. Calhoun, had been her friend and tutor. As an active member of Washington society and a successful hostess, Greenhow knew or was acquainted with nearly everybody of any consequence in the American government before the arrival of Lincoln.

When the leading Southerners left Washington in early 1861 to begin the organization of the Confederate government, it would have been only natural for them to think of Rose Greenhow as somebody who might be able to help them gather information about the activities of the Northerners who remained behind. She was recruited into an espionage organization by Thomas Jordan of the provisional army of Virginia. Jordan taught her a simple cipher system for her communications and arranged a courier network to deliver her reports to the Virginia forces across the Potomac River. When the Virginia forces were incorporated into the Confederate army in June 1861, Jordan became a member of the staff of Gen. P. G. T. Beauregard, the Confederate commander, and continued to manage Greenhow and the other members of the espionage organization to which she belonged.

Greenhow exploited her contacts among government officials, particularly her friendship with Senator Henry Wilson of Massachusetts, who had succeeded Confederate President Jefferson Davis as chairman of the Senate Military Affairs Committee. In July she was able to send a message to Jordan alerting him to the plans of Union Gen. Irvin McDowell for an advance into Virginia. McDowell's venture ended with Union defeat at the First Battle of Manassas, and Greenhow was widely credited in Confederate circles with having provided the information that made victory possible.

Greenhow's chief drawbacks were her flamboyant personality and her ardent belief in the Southern cause. Combined, these attributes kept her from maintaining the low profile that would have been more suitable for a successful spy. She was arrested by Union detectives on August 23, 1861, and kept under house arrest or in prison until mid-1862 when she and two other Confederate women spies were freed and sent to the Confederacy.

Greenhow, while in prison, continued to contact some of her informants and to forward their information, but after her release the Confederates sent her to England to promote sympathy for the Southern cause. On her return to the Confederacy in October 1864, she was drowned while trying to reach shore from her stranded blockade runner.

Augusta Morris and Catherine Baxley. The other women sent south with Rose Greenhow were Augusta Hewitt Morris and Catherine Virginia Baxley. These two women did not achieve the notoriety that surrounded Greenhow, but they had longer careers in espionage.

Morris apparently returned to the North using the alias "Mrs. Mason" and continued to work for the Confederacy. One of the leading Confederates in Washington was Thomas Green, who lived in a mansion only three blocks from the White House. In 1863 Green was reported by Union detectives to be working with a Mrs. Mason and traveling to Baltimore two or three times a week in order to mail information to Richmond. (The Confederates used the U.S. mails heavily in their courier system. A report in a double envelope would be mailed to a collaborator who would remove the outer envelope and hand the inner one to a courier who would carry it across the Potomac and deliver it in Richmond.)

On May 3, 1864, Morris was given $10,500 from the Incidental and Contingent Expenditures fund of the Confederate War Department. This was a large sum for those days and probably represented a payroll for an espionage organization such as the one reporting to Green.

Baxley also returned to the North and was provided with a cipher system for communication with the Confederate State Department and the South's clandestine organization in Canada. Her mission probably involved carrying information and messages between Canada and Richmond through Union territory. She was arrested again by the Union in early 1865 and remained in prison until the war was over.

Belle Boyd. Another woman who achieved some notoriety as a Confederate spy was a young Virginian named Belle Boyd. During 1861 around Martinsburg, Virginia (present-day West Virginia), and in 1862 near Front Royal, Virginia, Boyd served as a courier and spy for the Confederate forces in the area. She appears to have had little or no training in the craft of espionage and exposed herself unnecessarily to arrest by the Federal forces, but she talked her way out of a number of close calls and managed to provide Col. Turner Ashby and Gen. Thomas J. ("Stonewall") Jackson with some extremely useful information on Federal troop movements and strengths. She was arrested in June 1862 and confined in the Old Capitol Prison in Washington. In August of the same year she was sent south in an exchange of civilian prisoners. She returned to Martinsburg, was arrested again, and sent south once more.

On May 8, 1864, Boyd sailed from Wilmington, North Carolina, on a blockade runner, carrying dispatches for Confederate agents in Europe. Her ship, *Greyhound,* was captured, and Boyd (who had destroyed the dispatches in her care) was sent to the North for interrogation. She was finally released by her captors and sent to Canada.

On June 12, 1864, Miss Belle Boyd and maid checked into the St. Lawrence Hall Hotel in Montreal and were assigned rooms 136 and 137. On June 15, the Reverend Stuart Robinson, a Presbyterian minister from Louisville, Kentucky, who was assisting the Confederate clandestine organization in Canada, checked into the same hotel and was assigned room 138. It would appear that the Confederates were anxious to keep track of Boyd and to verify her continued loyalty to the Confederacy.

In due course Boyd went on to England where she was married on August 25, 1864, to Ensign Samuel Hardinge, recently of the U.S. Navy. He had commanded the prize crew that had taken *Greyhound* into port and had fallen in love with Boyd. Unfortunately, he did not live long thereafter, and Boyd became a widow at twenty-one. After the war, she spent the remainder of her life as an actress and lecturer trading on her notoriety as a former Confederate spy.

Other Female Agents. There were several other female spies who provided outstanding service to the Confederacy. Early in the war, Antonia Ford of Fairfax County, Virginia, added to the information provided by Rose Greenhow, and later after the Confederate partisan Col. John S. Mosby began his operations in northern Virginia, Ford provided him with valuable tactical information. Sarah Slater and Josephine Brown worked between Richmond and Canada, mostly during 1864 and 1865. The sisters Ginnie and Lottie Moon were raised in Ohio by a Virginia father. When war came, they went south and found useful employment in gathering information and carrying messages for the Confederates in Kentucky and Tennessee and in the Trans-Mississippi area. After the war, they continued their unconventional activities, working for women's suffrage and other causes.

Still other women worked for the Confederate clandestine effort in a variety of circumstances, but there were also a number of men who provided invaluable information to the Confederacy.

Daniel Lucas. A good example of male espionage agents who were not qualified for combat was Daniel Bedinger Lucas of Jefferson County, Virginia (present-day West Virginia). Lucas was a graduate of the University of Virginia and a lawyer. In 1861 he served on the staff of Gen. Henry A. Wise, a former governor of Virginia, in his campaign in western Virginia, but Lucas suffered from a congenital deformity that prevented him from engaging in the physical activity demanded by field duty. He returned to Richmond where he was active in the management of espionage and other secret operations. In late 1864 he went to Canada to assist Gen. Edwin Grey Lee who had been sent there to change the direction of the clandestine activities being organized against the North.

After the war, Lucas practiced law in West Virginia, was appointed to a short term as a U.S. senator from that state, and became a justice of the West Virginia Supreme Court of Appeals. He was discreet in conversation and writings about his wartime clandestine experiences, and as a result, the details of his years with the Confederate Secret Service are not known.

John Palmer. One of the most successful of the Confederate spies was John Williamson Palmer, a correspondent for the *New York Tribune*. Palmer had impeccable credentials and freedom of access behind Union lines. His dispatches, printed under the byline "Altamont," were widely read and exceptionally perceptive concerning Confederate strategy. What was not so obvious was that he was in an excellent position to report on Union strategy and to make sure that his interpretation of Confederate strategy represented the view the Confederates wanted the Union to have. Palmer played this difficult and dangerous game for about two years, but finally he gave it up—possibly because of the nervous strain involved—and spent the final years of the war in Richmond writing letters carrying Confederate propaganda. These letters were put into the Union mail system for delivery, thus appearing to have originated in the North.

Thomas Conrad. Another successful Confederate spy was Thomas Nelson Conrad, who operated a boys' school in connection with the Dumbarton Avenue Methodist Church in Georgetown in the District of Columbia. At the beginning of the war, Conrad helped the Confederate clandestine organization in Washington—probably the same one to which Rose Greenhow belonged. In 1862, however, Conrad was arrested and sent south in an exchange of civilian prisoners. Conrad went to work for the Secret Service of the Confederate War Department and made numerous trips into Union territory. In 1863 he was in Montgomery County, Maryland, just north and west of the District of Columbia, and from that point he observed the movements of the Union army north toward Gettysburg.

The youthful Captain Conrad took great delight in devising disguises that would fool enemy detectives, and he chose to try them out on the Confederates protecting Richmond to prove their effectiveness. The Confederate provost marshals, however, did not like being fooled. One of their ledgers, now in the U.S. National Archives, was used to record persons clearing the provost checkpoint on entering or leaving Richmond. It contains a list of aliases known to have been used by Captain Conrad—they were on the lookout for him.

Later Conrad, as a lay Methodist preacher, became a chaplain in the Third Virginia Cavalry and served at the same time as one of Gen. J. E. B. Stuart's cavalry scouts. In the spring of 1864 he was sent by Jefferson Davis to report on the movements and destination of the corps being assembled near Annapolis, Maryland, by Northern Gen. Ambrose Burnside:

The following September he was sent to Washington as head of a small team to observe the movements of President Lincoln and determine if it would be feasible to capture Lincoln as a hostage. While in Washington, Conrad stayed at the home of Thomas Green, who had worked with Augusta Morris. Conrad reported that Lincoln's capture was possible. In November 1864 he was sent back to the Potomac River to organize an espionage line, paralleling the existing secret line of the Confederate Signal Corps, in order to report information pertinent to the operation to abduct Lincoln. He was captured by the Union navy on the night of April 16, 1865, and kept in prison for some weeks.

After the war, Conrad held various teaching positions and served as the first president of the institution that later became the Virginia Polytechnic Institute and State University.

Henry Harrison. Another highly successful Confederate spy was Henry Thomas Harrison of Mississippi who worked as a scout and spy against Ulysses S. Grant's forces in Tennessee and Mississippi. For a time he operated under the direction of Thomas Jordan, who had directed Rose Greenhow before being transferred to the Confederate Army of Tennessee.

Later Harrison moved to the eastern area to work against the Union forces in North Carolina and Virginia. He was particularly successful in providing information to Gen. James Longstreet during the Gettysburg campaign. Later Harrison was assigned to duty behind Union lines in New York City, but the nature of his mission there is not known.

Sam Davis. A less successful Confederate scout in the Army of Tennessee was young Sam Davis of the First Tennessee Infantry. He was recruited by Capt. Henry Shaw, who operated under the alias of Coleman, to join a group of scouts collecting information for Gen. Braxton Bragg, then in command. The group successfully collected a great deal of important information behind Union lines and then scattered to make their way individually back to Confederate territory. Davis was picked to carry the essential papers; the other members of the group would not have anything incriminating on them if caught.

As it transpired, Davis, Shaw, and other members of the group were captured, but only Davis could be proved to be working for the Confederate Secret Service. His Union captors pressed him to identify "Coleman," but he refused. He was tried as a spy, although he had been captured in uniform. He was sentenced to be hanged and at the last moment was offered a pardon if he would tell where Coleman could be found. Although Coleman was a fellow prisoner, Davis refused to point him out and gave his life for the cause.

John Wilkes Booth. Another ardent supporter of the Southern cause was John Wilkes Booth, whose sister, Asia Booth Clark, wrote that her brother had told her that he was a spy for the Confederacy. A good deal is known about Booth's activities in 1864 and 1865 while he was trying to organize the capture of President Lincoln as a hostage, but very little is known about his activities before he was drawn into that plot.

Booth appears to have been recruited to head the team for the capture operation in late July 1864. He abandoned his other activities for the Confederate Secret Service and in August and September wound up an oil venture and other personal affairs. He recruited several people to help in the operation and in October 1864 went to Canada, where he met leading members of the Confederate Secret Service in Montreal. A trip to Washington in November overlapped with Captain Conrad's stay for a few days. In late November and December Booth made trips to southern Maryland to organize the route his team would take when they had captured Lincoln. Finally, in March 1865, the team set out to seize the president but were frustrated when Lincoln changed his itinerary.

The Confederates then sent Lt. Thomas F. (Frank) Harney, an explosives expert, to Washington in a scheme to blow up the White House during a meeting of key officials in order to disrupt coordination between Grant's and Sherman's armies. Harney, however, was caught on his way into Washington, and Booth took it upon himself to approximate the damage that would have been caused by an explosion. He tried to organize simultaneous attacks against Lincoln, Vice President Andrew Johnson, Secretary of State William Seward, and Secretary of War Edwin Stanton. As it turned out, only Lincoln was murdered and Seward injured by his attacker.

Booth escaped through southern Maryland, but Union troops caught and killed him on April 26, 1865. Four of his associates were hanged in June of that year, and several others served prison sentences of varying lengths.

P. C. Martin. A Confederate spy of a radically different type was P. C. Martin, an importer and liquor dealer from Baltimore. Martin left Maryland early in the war to es-

JOHN WILKES BOOTH.   Confederate espionage agent and assassin of Abraham Lincoln.

HARPER'S PICTORIAL HISTORY OF THE GREAT REBELLION

cape arrest for his pro-Southern activities. He settled in Montreal where he became the leader of the Confederate clandestine activity in that city.

He helped organize an ambitious plan to free the Confederate prisoners of war held on Johnson Island in the harbor of Sandusky, Ohio, but the plan was frustrated when word of it got out. After Booth's departure in October 1864, Martin took the actor's theater wardrobe on a ship down the St. Lawrence to run the blockade into the Confederacy. The ship was wrecked and Martin was drowned. Booth's wardrobe was recovered in 1865.

LEWIS PAYNE. An accomplice of John Wilkes Booth, Payne attacked Secretary of State William H. Seward on April 14, 1865.

NATIONAL ARCHIVES

Walter Bowie. One of the most intriguing Confederate spies was Walter Bowie of Prince George's County, Maryland. Bowie was a prominent young lawyer in Upper Marlboro, Maryland, when the war broke out. He went south to volunteer his services to the Confederacy and served for some months in a staff position in Richmond. In 1862, he returned to Maryland to take charge of the courier and reporting system supporting the Confederate espionage organization in Washington that Rose Greenhow had belonged to. He was apprehended and imprisoned in the Old Capitol Prison in Washington, but he managed to escape with the help of the Confederate underground organization in that city.

Bowie acquired a reputation as a guerrilla operating in southern Maryland and eventually joined the partisan unit in northern Virginia commanded by John S. Mosby, but his reputation appears to have been based on a confusion of identities. There were three Walter Bowies in the Confederate army in Virginia, and their records were sometimes mixed up (they still are today). During the Civil War when news was often circulated by word of mouth, there was ample opportunity for one Walter Bowie to be credited with the actions of another. One of the other Walter Bowies, for instance, was a graduate of the Virginia Military Institute who spent several months operating in southern Maryland as the head of a raiding team belonging to the Confederate volunteer navy. It is likely that his activities were credited to the Walter Bowie from Prince George's County.

One of Bowie's duties in managing the espionage network was to prepare summaries of information collected by the entire organization. A summary that has survived among the papers of Col. Charles Venable of Robert E. Lee's staff shows that in April 1864 Bowie reported to Lee General Grant's preparations for the campaign of 1864. Bowie's report was quite accurate and even outlined the tactic of repeatedly moving to the flank of Lee's army that Grant employed when the campaign opened in May 1864.

Mosby's force had become well established in northern Virginia, and Bowie was sent to join his unit where he found that Walter Bowie of the volunteer navy had preceded him. Mosby took over the task of maintaining contact with the Confederate clandestine organization in Washington while the Maryland Bowie, as a lieutenant of one of Mosby's companies, was sent with a small team to southern Maryland with the ostensible mission of seizing the governor of Maryland. This mission coincided in time with Conrad's mission to investigate the possibility of capturing Lincoln and was probably related to it.

Bowie moved through southern Maryland, passed around Washington to the north, and tried to return to Virginia through Montgomery County north and west of the District of Columbia. In the course of that passage Bowie's party was ambushed by local citizens, and Bowie was killed.

Robert Coxe. A different type of agent was Robert Edwin Coxe of Georgia. Coxe was a wealthy planter who had lived in Europe for several years before the war. In 1863 he moved his family to Canada and established himself in St. Catharines, Ontario, near Niagara Falls. The proximity to Niagara provided excellent cover for the meeting of clandestine agents. A museum (which still exists) on the Canadian side of the falls kept a book in which visitors recorded their signatures. An agent could visit the museum and sign the book without attracting attention. Somebody at the museum or another visitor would inspect the book periodically and, when an expected signature appeared, send word to St. Catharines. In due course a representative of the Confederate Secret Service would turn up to meet the visiting agent at a prearranged location. Under cover of tourist traffic, this arrangement lasted through the remainder of the war without being discovered.

In June 1864, the former U.S. senator Clement C. Clay, one of the Confederate commissioners in Canada, moved into Coxe's house in St. Catharines along with the former

U.S. consul Beverly Tucker. Clay and Tucker conducted a number of clandestine operations from this location while Coxe went to Maine, then to Poughkeepsie, New York, and finally to Washington, D.C. After the assassination of Lincoln, Coxe was arrested, but he was later released for lack of evidence.

In addition to the people mentioned above, there were a number of others known to have been involved in Confederate clandestine operations, but we have little information about them. These include Benjamin Franklin Stringfellow, who served as a cavalry scout and was in Washington to deliver a diplomatic message when the war ended; Channing Smith, another cavalry scout who was commissioned in late 1864 and sent for some special assignment with Mosby; Emile Longmare, who worked with the copperheads in the North to promote an antiwar movement; Vincent Camalier, who worked as a smuggler of contraband and crossed the lines with word of impending Union movements; Augustus Howell of Prince George's County, Maryland, who was almost caught up in Booth's assassination operation; and Thomas Harbin, an agent of the Confederate War Department who worked with Booth and his team.

The dedication of these and other Confederate spies is obvious. Many of them received no money for their pains, and most who were paid received little more than their expenses. They were individuals doing what they could for the cause in which they believed.

BIBLIOGRAPHY

Bakeless, John. *Spies of the Confederacy.* Philadelphia and New York, 1970.

Foster, G. Allen. *The Eyes and Ears of the Civil War.* New York, 1963.

Grimes, Absalom. *Absalom Grimes: Confederate Mail Runner.* Edited by M. M. Quaife. New Haven, 1926.

Kane, Harnett T. *Spies for the Blue and Gray.* New York, 1954.

Ross, Ishbel. *Rebel Rose.* New York, 1954.

Stern, Philip Van Doren. *Secret Missions of the Civil War.* New York, 1959.

Tidwell, William A., with James O. Hall and David Winfred Gaddy. *Come Retribution: The Confederate Secret Service and the Assassination of Lincoln.* Jackson, Miss., 1988.

WILLIAM A. TIDWELL

EVANS, AUGUSTA JANE (1835–1909), author.
Born on May 8, 1835, in Columbus, Georgia, to Matt and Sarah Howard Evans, Augusta Jane Evans began life in comfortable conditions. By 1839, however, economic reversals had forced her father into bankruptcy, and in 1845 the family moved to Texas, and in 1849 to Mobile, Alabama, to recoup their fortunes.

Although Evans had little formal schooling, apparently because of persistent ill health, she received an extensive education from her mother, who encouraged her daughter's love of learning. Shortly before Evans turned twenty, she completed a novel, *Inez, A Tale of the Alamo,* which drew upon her own Texas experiences. In 1855, *Inez* was published, but never earned its author the financial rewards or literary reputation she craved. But her next novel, *Beulah,* published in 1859, sold widely, making Evans a wealthy woman and establishing her reputation as a novelist.

Although neither *Inez* or *Beulah* explicitly focused on the defense of slavery that characterized many Southern women's novels of the period, both manifested Evans's ardent Southern nationalism. On the eve of the War, she was contemplating an engagement to James Reed Spaulding, an editor of the New York *Morning Courier and Enquirer,* who had written a flattering review of *Beulah.* But with the outbreak of war, Evans, an ardent secessionist, broke the engagement because of Spaulding's unacceptable Northern views and turned her energies to serving the Southern cause. During the war, she organized a soldiers' hospital near Mobile, worked tirelessly as a nurse for the wounded, and corresponded extensively with Confederate statesmen and military men, notably J. L. M. Curry and Gen. P. G. T. Beauregard, to whom she offered advice on politics and warfare. She also wrote her third novel, *Macaria; or, Altars of Sacrifice,* in which she simultaneously defended female independence and the Southern cause.

Composed on scraps of paper as Evans sat by the beds of wounded soldiers and dedicated to "the Army of the Southern Confederacy," *Macaria* was explicitly intended to serve the Southern war effort, both by moving Southern women to serve that cause and by demonstrating the ways in which women's efforts were indispensable to the Confederacy. At least one Federal general, G. H. Thomas, recognized the novel's value as Confederate propaganda, pronouncing it "contraband and dangerous," banning it among Federal troops, and burning all the copies he found. In the South, however, the novel became immensely popular—a wartime best-seller with twenty thousand copies in print.

After the war, Evans published *St. Elmo* (1867), the most popular of all of her novels and, in 1868, married a wealthy sixty-year-old widower, Lorenzo Madison Wilson. His wealth, together with her own, ensured Evans an extremely comfortable life and the ability to help others. Although she continued to produce a novel almost every decade until her death on March 9, 1909, she devoted much of her time to family, close friends, and favorite charities.

BIBLIOGRAPHY

Evans, Augusta J. *Beulah.* Edited by Elizabeth Fox-Genovese. Baton Rouge, La., 1992.

Evans, Augusta J. *Macaria; or, Altars of Sacrifice.* Edited by Drew G. Faust. Baton Rouge, La., 1992.

Fidler, William. *Augusta Evans Wilson: A Biography.* University, Ala., 1951.

ELIZABETH FOX-GENOVESE

EVANS, CLEMENT A.

EVANS, CLEMENT A. (1833–1911), brigadier general. Born in Stewart County, Georgia, and educated in local public schools, Clement Anselm Evans earned a law degree in Augusta and was licensed to practice law in 1852 at the age of nineteen. Throughout the remainder of the decade he served with distinction as a lawyer and judge and in 1859 was elected to the state senate.

Soon after the election of Abraham Lincoln, Evans helped organize a local militia company, but he did not serve with it. Instead he enlisted in the Thirty-first Georgia Infantry as a private and was elected its major. Although he had little formal military training, he showed early leadership ability. Wounded five times during the war, Evans served with his regiment under Thomas J. ("Stonewall") Jackson through Chancellorsville. He also led his regiment at Gettysburg and a year later was under Jubal Early's command in the raid on Washington and the subsequent Shenandoah Valley campaign.

CLEMENT A. EVANS.   LIBRARY OF CONGRESS

Already a brigadier general in May 1864, Evans was given command of John B. Gordon's old division in November after the latter was appointed a corps commander. Throughout the remainder of the Petersburg campaign, Evans's division engaged in several failed assaults on Federal positions. Prior to his retreat from Petersburg, he was promoted to acting major general.

Before Evans's division surrendered at Appomattox, it had the distinction of being the last Confederate force to achieve a victory over Federal units: on the morning of April 9 Evans and his men beat back an enemy force, capturing equipment and prisoners.

Soon after his parole Evans made good his promise during the war to enter the Methodist Episcopal ministry. He served the church until his retirement in 1892, when he moved to Atlanta. His scholarly interests led to his editorship of the twelve-volume *Confederate Military History* (1899) and involvement in several related studies of the war. An active member of the United Confederate Veterans, he was also appointed to several boards and commissions during his last years.

BIBLIOGRAPHY

Clement A. Evans, ed. *Confederate Military History.* 12 vols. Atlanta, 1899. Extended ed. in 19 vols. Wilmington, N.C., 1987–1989.

Stephens, Robert G., Jr. *Intrepid Warrior, Clement Anselm Evans.* Dayton, Ohio, 1992.

FRITZ P. HAMER

EVANS, NATHAN ("SHANKS")

EVANS, NATHAN ("SHANKS") (1824–1868), brigadier general. Born in Marion, South Carolina, Evans was a controversial officer whose early success at First Manassas was obscured by disputes with subordinates and superiors alike throughout the war. After graduating from West Point in 1848, Evans was appointed to a cavalry regiment and sent west where he gained renown as an Indian fighter. When South Carolina seceded, he was appointed colonel of state troops and eventually went to Virginia to join the Confederate army.

At First Manassas, Evans, with the assistance of Barnard E. Bee and Wade Hampton, took the initiative without prior orders to hold off a Federal force of about 17,000 trying to outflank the Southerners near the Stone Bridge. Evans's determined defense with a force of barely 5,000 saved the Confederate left, allowing the Southern forces to win the battle. Commended for his courage and skill by superiors, Evans appeared to have a bright future. After his brigade routed Federal troops at Ball's Bluff, he was promoted to brigadier general and placed in command of the Third Military District. He subsequently served at Second Manassas, South Mountain, and Sharpsburg, and in the Vicksburg campaign.

Despite his initial successes, Evans by late 1862 had become involved in disputes over his conduct. At the Battle of South Mountain, subordinates accused him of drunkenness and cowardice under fire. Evans had his accusers arrested and court-martialed with inconclusive results. He himself was court-martialed for disobeying orders but was acquitted. In spring 1863 his superiors reported unfavorably on the conditions of his brigade in North Carolina. P. G. T. Beauregard finally removed him from command, calling him incompetent. Although he later returned to duty, he remained in obscurity for the rest of the war.

After the war, Evans became principal of a high school in Midway, Alabama, where he died. He is buried in Cokesbury, South Carolina.

BIBLIOGRAPHY

Freeman, Douglas S. *Lee's Lieutenants: A Study in Command.* 3 vols. New York, 1942–1944. Reprint, New York, 1986.

Warner, Ezra J. *Generals in Gray: Lives of the Confederate Commanders.* Baton Rouge, La., 1959.

FRITZ P. HAMER

EWELL, RICHARD S. (1817–1872), lieutenant general. One of seventeen men to attain the rank of lieutenant general in the Confederate military, Richard Stoddard Ewell was a key figure in the eastern campaigns. He served as a division commander under Gen. Thomas J.

RICHARD S. EWELL.

HARPER'S PICTORIAL HISTORY OF THE GREAT REBELLION

("Stonewall") Jackson early in the war and then replaced Jackson after his death as head of the Second Corps in Gen. Robert E. Lee's Army of Northern Virginia.

A native of Virginia, Ewell graduated thirteenth in the West Point class of 1840, and served mostly in the Far West with the cavalry during the twenty years prior to the Civil War. He saw limited action in the Mexican War.

Ewell entered Confederate service in April 1861. He commanded a brigade at the Battle of First Manassas but was not directly involved in the combat.

In March 1862 Ewell (now leading a division) went to the Shenandoah Valley to join Jackson in his campaign against Union Gen. Nathaniel Banks. Though Jackson was the overall commander, Ewell's men did most of the fighting. His troops engaged and routed the Federals in the opening battle at Front Royal on May 23, 1862. Two days later, moving against Banks at Winchester, Ewell made the initial attack, and one of his brigades under Gen. Richard Taylor led a final charge that routed the enemy. After Jackson retreated to avoid a pincer by Federal Gens. John C. Frémont and James Shields that threatened his rear, Ewell personally planned, directed, and won a battle with Frémont at Cross Keys on June 8, 1862. When Jackson attacked Shields early the next morning, Ewell led the men who captured a Federal artillery battery on the coaling ground above Port Republic, resulting in a Southern victory.

In June 1862, Ewell moved with Jackson to Richmond to join Lee in defending the Confederate capital under siege by Union Gen. George B. McClellan. He fought in only one of the five battles (Gaines' Mill, June 27, 1862); after taking terrible losses in an unsuccessful attack against an entrenched enemy, he held his tenuous line until Southern reinforcements came up to make the final, victorious charge.

Ewell moved north with Jackson after the Seven Days' Battles to confront Federal Gen. John Pope leading the newly formed Army of Virginia. After defeating the leading Union element under Banks at Cedar Run on August 9, 1862, Jackson and Ewell raced north on a flanking march to Pope's rear. They opened the Battle of Second Manassas at Groveton on August 28, 1862, where Ewell was shot in his right knee. The wound resulted in the amputation of his leg.

While Jackson continued the campaign, moving with Lee into Maryland, Ewell returned to Richmond to recuperate. He was nursed by the sweetheart he had lost to another during his youth, Lizinka Campbell Brown, who was now a wealthy widow.

In May 1863, just as Ewell was well enough to return to duty, Jackson was wounded at Chancellorsville. Jackson died on May 10, 1863, and Ewell was named as his replacement to head Lee's Second Corps. Prior to his rejoining the army, Ewell married Lizinka on May 24 and they enjoyed a brief honeymoon. He then led his corps north toward Pennsylvania.

Marching down the Shenandoah Valley, Ewell stopped to engage Union Gen. Robert Milroy at Winchester. He gained a spectacular victory on June 14, 1863, and then moved northward, intent on capturing Harrisburg, the capital of Pennsylvania. Just prior to his attack, Lee recalled Ewell to Gettysburg, where the enemy under Gen. George Meade was concentrating.

Ewell attacked the Northern flank on July 1, 1863, and drove the Federals from the field. Although Ewell has been criticized by some for not continuing to assault the enemy, who had retired to Cemetery Hill, this assertion ignores the facts. The Federals' position was strongly manned. Had he charged the heights, Ewell would have been easily repelled and would have suffered devastating losses to his command. The next day Lee attacked the Union left with Gen. James Longstreet's corps. Late in the day, when Meade drew men from his right (fronting Ewell) to hold off this threat, the chance arose for Ewell to drive a wedge into the Northern line. But he was not ready, and his delayed charge, mounted piecemeal, failed.

Following their defeat at Gettysburg, Lee and his army retreated back to Virginia. Ewell spent the winter of 1863–1864 along the Rappahannock River. Not completely recovered from the amputation of his leg, he considered relinquishing command, but Lizinka (who had joined him that winter) would not hear of it. She took the unprecedented step of assuming charge of his affairs while he rested to regain his strength.

In May 1864, Gen. Ulysses S. Grant led the Federals south against Lee. Ewell made initial contact with the enemy in the Wilderness on May 5, 1864, showing consummate skill as he fought off the repeated Federal charges. Grant, facing a stalemate, took his army around Lee's right, and the two met again at Spotsylvania. At first the battle was inconclusive. Thinking that Grant would once again maneuver, Lee started to withdraw Ewell's artillery just as the Northerners renewed their assault at sunrise on May 12, 1864. Without his guns, Ewell was quickly overrun, losing half his corps before he finally restored his line. He was so distraught over the casualties to his command, however, that he became sick and was forced to go on leave. When he reported for duty on May 31, Ewell found that Lee had replaced him with Jubal Early.

Assigned to Richmond, Ewell managed the city's defenses above the James River. After repeated unsuccessful attempts to regain a field command, Ewell became so disillusioned that when Lizinka proposed in late December that she take the oath of allegiance to the Union in order to regain her properties in the North, Ewell agreed to assist her in committing treason. She left Richmond for St. Louis on March 24, 1865. Less than two weeks later, Ewell led his ragtag assortment of troops after Lee toward Appomattox. He was captured on April 6 during the Battle of Sayler's Creek and imprisoned at Fort Warren in Boston Harbor.

Released in July 1865, Ewell retired to Spring Hill, Tennessee, where Lizinka owned a large plantation. He became a gentleman farmer. During the winter of 1872, Ewell fell ill with pneumonia. When his spouse attempted to nurse him back to health, she contracted the disease and died on January 22. Forty-eight hours later, Ewell joined his wife in death.

BIBLIOGRAPHY

Hamlin, Percy. *The Making of a Soldier*. Richmond, Va., 1935.
Hamlin, Percy. *Old Bald Head*. Strasburg, Va., 1940.
Martin, Samuel J. *The Road to Glory: Confederate General Richard S. Ewell*. Indianapolis, Ind., 1991.

SAMUEL J. MARTIN

EWING, GEORGE WASHINGTON (1808–1888), congressman from Kentucky. Ewing was one of the most prominent Kentuckians to serve in the Confederate Congress. Descended from a pioneer Virginia settler, and the son of a general in the War of 1812, he was born near Adairville in Logan County, Kentucky. He was educated first in Russellville, Kentucky, and later at Princeton College before embarking on a legal career in Russellville. In 1860 Ewing owned twenty-two slaves, marking him as one of Logan County's more substantial planters. Before the Civil War, he served seven terms as a Whig in the Kentucky legislature.

Ewing became a Democrat in 1860 and, in 1862, was appointed by the Provisional Government of Kentucky to the Provisional Confederate Congress from the Fourth District. He served only the last three days of the Provisional Congress but was elected from the Fourth District to the next two congresses. Because Ewing served concurrently in the Kentucky and Confederate legislatures, he resided for much of the war in the commonwealth. In Richmond he served on the Territories and Public Lands and Claims committees. Though he generally supported the administration, Ewing advised President Jefferson Davis to make changes in civilian and military command and responded coolly to the expansion of the president's appointive powers. Early in 1865 he advocated an invasion of Kentucky to oust the Union government.

Ewing is best known for his vitriolic January 1865 resolutions underscoring the rift between congressmen from districts overrun by Union troops and those still under Confederate control. Ewing asked rhetorically whether or not representatives from constituencies then in enemy hands were entitled to retain their seats. If not, he argued, troops raised from these jurisdictions should be discharged immediately. Congressmen from occupied regions of the South would then "organize under our own banner and with our brave soldiers march upon the soil of our own States and there live or die freemen." This resolution was, according to historians Ezra J. Warner and W. Buck Yearns, "largely a matter of self-interest" and proved "intensely embarrassing to the whole government." It was tabled permanently.

After the war, Ewing relocated in Greensboro, North Carolina, before moving back to his farm near Adairville. He never again held public office.

BIBLIOGRAPHY

Alexander, Thomas B., and Richard E. Beringer. *The Anatomy of the Confederate Congress: A Study of the Influences of Member Characteristics on Legislative Voting Behavior, 1861–1865.* Nashville, Tenn., 1972.

Quisenberry, A. C. "The Alleged Secession of Kentucky." *Register of the Kentucky State Historical Society* 15 (1917): 15–32.

Warner, Ezra J., and W. Buck Yearns. *Biographical Register of the Confederate Congress.* Baton Rouge, La., 1975.

JOHN DAVID SMITH

EXPANSIONISM IN THE ANTEBELLUM SOUTH.

The myth of a monolithic, unchanging slave South distorts the history of the slavocracy. Thus the Civil War supposedly matched the entire South against the North. But, in fact, the four border states never left the Union, West Virginia seceded from Virginia, and over 100,000 Confederate residents joined Abraham Lincoln's army. So too, before the Civil War, the South supposedly massed unanimously behind the so-called positive good of perpetual slavery. But, in fact, most upper South residents considered slavery a temporary evil. They hoped to remove blacks and slaves from their half of the South. Meanwhile, important lower South clergymen considered slavery short on Christian blessings. They urged state legislatures to protect slaves' families and access to Christianity. Most owners derided such suggestions as meddling interference, not proslavery Christianity.

These divergent viewpoints within the South, involving the pivotal matters of whether slaveholders' absolute power should be perpetuated, limited, or removed to other locales, put into perspective another fundamental Southern intramural contest, that concerning whether slavery should be expanded into new territories. According to the standard account, Southerners combated only Northerners in pre-Civil War controversies over territorial expansion, with "expand or perish" the Southerners' persistent motto. So when Abraham Lincoln won the presidency in 1860 pledging no expansion of slavery, Southerners supposedly concluded that the Union, not slavery, must perish.

The expand-or-perish interpretation, while concentrating the causes of secession into three vivid words, actually reduces a complex phenomenon to a caricature. The oversimplification is useful only to warn all who study Southern slaveholding that variations over time and space must be noticed. Southern beliefs about the *economic* necessity for expansion especially fluctuated. Convictions about slaveholders' *political* need for expansion flourished more consistently—with some important exceptions. The exceptions predominated in the climactic 1850s, when expand-or-perish thinking was particularly erratic. As the Civil War approached, South Carolina's planters, who feared they might perish without disunion, worried that Southern territorial expansion, especially into the Caribbean, might remove slavery from their state. In contrast, New Orleans merchants, who thought they might perish without Caribbean expansion, believed that disunionism could cripple expansionism. The border South's prosperous residents, who often supported territorial expansion as a way to remove slavery from their area, still hoped that expansionism would perish if disunion resulted.

Just as Southern attitudes about territorial expansion changed from one place to another, so the expansion issue changed from one era to another. Southern drives for more territory accelerated from 1793 to the mid-1830s, met opposition in the 1840s, and turned around again in the 1850s, as the Southern economy veered from half recession to unrelieved depression to almost universal prosperity. A paradox illuminates the point: the fallacious myth of universal Southern enthusiasm for expansion during the era of sectional controversy, from 1844 to 1860, fits the facts—*before* 1844. As for the period before 1793, then Southern zeal for expansion could scarcely be found.

From 1793 to 1843, Southern expansionists were making up for earlier Southern generations' characteristic lack of desire for new territorial acquisitions, but they had not yet developed the fears of later generations that exotic territorial adventures could destroy old cultural stabilities. During the eighteenth century, the slave South had been predominantly a seaboard civilization, usually (though not always) uninterested in spreading west of the coastal colonies. Native Americans—Creeks, Choctaws, Seminoles, and Cherokees—had cultivated some of what became upland South Carolina and Georgia, northern Mississippi and Alabama, and western Tennessee. Non-English peoples had controlled the rim of the Anglo lower South, including the French-owned areas of what became Louisiana and Arkansas, and the Spanish-owned areas of what became Texas, Florida, and southern Alabama and Mississippi.

Eighteenth-century entrepreneurs did not yet covet what became the southernmost tier of the United States, because they could not conceive of a lucrative crop suitable for North America's westward, noncoastal tropics. They considered lower South latitudes too tropical for the upper South's staple crop, tobacco, and not tropical enough for South America's staple crops, sugar and coffee. Only the South Carolina and Georgia coastal malarial swamps could support the colonial lower South's most coveted crop, rice; and only the Sea Islands near the coast could support the secondary staple, silky Sea Island cotton. West of the coast, some colonial South Carolinians grew indigo for a limited market, lost after the American Revolution. Other Carolinians produced the cheaper grades of cotton, also commercially limited without a then-uninvented gin to separate seeds from fibers. So while black slaves outnumbered white citizens more than eight to one in Georgia and especially South Carolina coastal areas, almost four out of five North American slaves toiled north of the future cotton kingdom. Slaves especially peopled the upper South tobacco belts, although whites still outnumbered blacks.

Southern Consensus for Expansionism

Eli Whitney's invention of the cotton gin in 1793 at last sent lower South entrepreneurs swarming to southwestern frontiers soon densely populated by slaves. Two simultaneous economic and political developments accelerated the population surge from the oldest South to the new cotton frontier. Almost at the moment when the cotton kingdom required more slaves, Congress abolished the African slave trade (1807). And almost at the moment when the newer South's economy ascended, the older South's economy declined. In upper South tobacco belts, debilitated soil and poor prices produced chronic stagnation. In South Carolina's coastal rice swamps, land was more worn and profits less fabulous than in colonial times; and in that state's up-country area, the first cotton spree had yielded the first cotton-exhausted soil. Throughout these eastern locales, struggling planters needed to shrink their operation or lose their property. Out in the southwestern cotton kingdom, buoyant developers, now legally barred from buying slaves from Africa, competed for contracting slaveholders' unneeded bondsmen. As a result, some 750,000 blacks were relocated from 1790 to 1860. The lower South's share of slaves in the United States leapt from 21 to 59 percent over these years.

In the wake of slavery's spread over previously uncultivated tropical regions, slave sellers in older areas had the cash to finance a modest postboom survival economy. Slave buyers in new cotton areas had the laborers to produce a post–eighteenth century bonanza. The process of paying leaner Peter to fatten hungry Paul, however, served more than economic desires. Among planters who wanted to preserve slavery, slave buying was the key to consolidating slavery's lower South empire. Among Southerners who wanted to remove slavery and blacks from their area, slave selling was the key to producing an all-white upper South.

That antislavery rationale for an expansion of slavery even came to appeal to some Southern opponents of slavery who had earlier opposed slaveholder expansionism. In the eighteenth century, before the cotton expansion, Thomas Jefferson of Virginia had considered slavery's expansion wrong. But by 1820, after the cotton kingdom was well established, Jefferson called expansionism right. If slavery were to be bottled up in old areas, he thought, fearful whites would never free the densely concentrated blacks. If slavery were to be "diffused" into new areas, on the other hand, whites would more readily emancipate the scattered slaves. "Diffusion" was the key word. It united Southerners who hoped to remove all slaves from their declining area with Southerners who wanted more slaves to proceed toward their advancing area.

That unanimity imperiled both Native American landowners inside the lower South's domain and foreign landowners just outside. Newly expansive slave owners, while wishing the lower South swept of alien whites and Native Americans, especially sought to remove neighbors who encouraged slave resistance. The most menacing resistance came not from the few groups of slave insurrectionists, who always were quickly quashed, but from the more numerous individual runaways, who ultimately helped defeat Confederate armies. During the Civil War, runaways increased when slaveholders' enemies massed close by; and in the early nineteenth century, foreigners and Native Americans were uncomfortably close to the new cotton kingdom.

In Spanish Florida, for example, some Spaniards, Seminoles, and an occasional Englishman encouraged Georgia and South Carolina slaves to flee. In the face of this unrest, slaveholders argued that either the government must protect property or property holders must protect themselves. Farther north, on the Tennessee frontier, Andrew Jackson had become a vivid symbol of that maxim. In 1818, President James Monroe ordered General Jackson to chastise some Seminoles who were troubling whites on the United States side of the Spanish Florida border. Jackson did more. He chased Seminoles over the Spanish border, seized their fort, killed several of their chieftains, hanged two Englishmen said to be their accomplices, and expelled a Spanish garrison from Pensacola.

Southern statesmen, in a pattern that would become crucial in the 1850s, divided along geographic lines on the wisdom of such adventuring as Jackson's. Southwestern frontiersmen cheered Jackson's raid. But South Carolina's John C. Calhoun (privately) and Kentucky's Henry Clay (publicly) deplored private raids that arguably exceeded governmental authorization. Nevertheless, southwesterners, South Carolinians, and border Southerners alike urged public government to oust aliens and make private assaults unnecessary. After the Missouri controversy of 1819 through 1821, slaveholders' motivations were increasingly political as well as economic. More lower South land would mean more Southern states and thus more defenders of slavery in Congress.

Safer Southern frontiers would also mean safer American frontiers. That nationalistic reason for expansion southward especially prevailed before the Missouri controversy but lingered long after. Such patriotism enabled Southern leaders to rally a national consensus to evict foreigners and Native Americans from the entire lower South during the first four decades of the nineteenth century. In 1803, President Thomas Jefferson, as part of the Louisiana Purchase, bought the future slave states of Louisiana, Arkansas, and Missouri from the French. In 1819, another Virginian president, James Monroe, taking advantage of the Spanish weakness that Jackson's raid had revealed, purchased the future state of Florida and southern areas of Mississippi and Alabama from Spain. In the 1830s, yet another Southern president, Jackson himself, deported Native Americans to reservations across the Mississippi River. And in 1844, the last antebellum president from Virginia, John Tyler, brought four decades of unanimous Southern zeal for expansion to a climax—and to an end—with his insistence that the Union annex Texas. That republic had secured its independence from Mexico in 1836, which had secured its independence from Spain in 1819.

President Tyler sought a national consensus to make the United States the latest nation with sovereignty over the vast Texas acreage. He thus did not emphasize one aim of fellow Southern expansionists: increasing the South's power in Congress. He did, however, reemphasize slaveholders' problems with neighbors perceived as hostile. If neighboring enemies incited slaves, Jackson had said and Tyler now repeated, slaveholders must be able to control the contiguous land. Jackson had worried about allegedly slave-inciting Spaniards, Englishmen, and Seminoles in Spanish Florida, which abutted Georgia. Tyler thought that English antislavery influence might eventually prevail in the Texas Republic, which abutted Louisiana and Arkansas. Better to annex another area contiguous to the lower South, Tyler declared with the aging Jackson's support, than to expose the slavocracy to antislavery neighbors.

Tyler reiterated not only Jackson's determination to take over contiguous areas but also Jefferson's desire to acquire outlets for relocation of slaves. A new economic slump throughout the South, moreover, lent urgency to Jefferson's old argument for diffusing slaves away. In the 1840s the adolescent southwestern cotton kingdom, no less than the aging colonial South, endured economic crisis. Cotton prices, which had averaged 16.4 cents a pound in 1835 and 1836, plunged in the 1840s, after the devastating panic of 1837, to an average of 7.9 cents a pound. Only an exorbitant yield could compensate for these 50 percent lower prices,

and only virgin lands could spawn 50 percent higher yields. Not even the relatively undeveloped Southwest now seemed sufficiently unscarred. An unspoiled Texas would provide an economic safety valve, said Tyler, to drain redundant slaves away from decaying slaveholding areas.

This newest safety valve argument continued to promise racial as well as economic relief. If no Texas outlet was secured, annexationists warned, the black population would swell in states suffering economic decline. If economic depression then persisted, whites would flee from excess blacks. Were Texas to be annexed, on the other hand, slaveholders would be able to sell unneeded slaves through the outlet. Here, in pristine form, was the agrarians' expand-or-perish argument. Unless slavery could spread into new areas, the slaveholders' depressed economy would collapse and the South's racial order would crumble. Add to this formula for disaster the possibility that English abolitionists in Texas, right across the Louisiana-Arkansas border, would incite blacks to flee or pillage or worse. This logic yielded a clear choice: increase the number of Southern congressional seats and double the lower South's land by adding Texas to the Union or expect a racial inferno. That exclusively Southern reason for national expansion, however, made Northerners increasingly resistant to American Manifest Destiny, slaveholder-style.

Collapse of the Southern Consensus

If the Southern expand-or-perish argument had remained unchallenged in the mid-1840s and had pervaded the 1850s, no historian would be able to deny that a monolithic South had been united behind slave diffusion. But in Texas annexation times, the expansionists' diffusion argument inspired, in dialectical fashion, the first Southern breach over the question of slavery's expansion. In 1844, Southern Democrats, with rare border South exceptions, massed behind the expand-or-die thesis. When Southern Democrats thus insisted, reluctant Northern Democrats almost had to appease their party brethren, for the Democratic party was always stronger in the South than in the North. In contrast, when Northern Whigs insisted, Southern Whigs could hardly defy their party allies, for Whiggery was always stronger in the North than in the South. In 1844, after Southern Democrats relentlessly demanded Texas and after Northern Democrats reluctantly acquiesced and Northern Whigs contemptuously disapproved, Southern Whigs were driven to ask whether slavery would in fact perish unless the institution could diffuse into Texas.

That query undercut lower South unanimity on the expand-or-perish dogma. How, after all, could the single new slave state of Texas save slavery, in or out of Congress, if the institution drained out of eight border and upper South states and out of South Carolina too? Furthermore, how could cotton production in virgin Texas rescue the cotton South from a depression caused by cotton over-production? Annexation, warned Whig South Carolina Congressman Waddy Thompson, would "very soon" remove slavery from "Maryland, Virginia, North Carolina, Tennessee, and Kentucky." Even in aging South Carolina, he feared, slavery would become "an incumbrance which we shall be glad to get rid of; and . . . it will afford me very little consolation in riding over my fields, grown up in broom-sedge and washed into gullies, to be told that . . . slavery still exists and is prosperous" in Texas.

Kentucky's Henry Clay, Whig nominee for president in 1844, reversed Waddy Thompson's lower South logic. Although a large border South slaveholder himself, Clay looked for the day when the South could rid itself both of slaves and of free blacks. He declared Texas annexation desirable in the abstract, because more slaves would then be diffused from the upper South. But he saw diffusion as not worth either a foreign war or a sectional controversy. A statesman's "paramount duty," he declared, was "preserving the Union," not saving slavery, a "temporary institution."

Slavery a "temporary institution"! Preserving the Union the "paramount duty"! With those four words, Henry Clay underscored, as if in Civil War blood, the difference between the border and lower Souths in their priorities about slavery, expansionism, and Unionism. But if the lower South's Waddy Thompson, hoping to keep slaves in South Carolina, and the border South's Henry Clay, hoping to keep all Americans in the Union, rejected annexation for contrary Whig reasons, the Whigs' alliance against Texas almost killed expansionism. Three months after the Democrats' ultra-expansionist James K. Polk defeated Clay in the November 1844 presidential election, the U.S. Senate nearly rejected the admission of Texas into the Union. The margin for Texas was thin, 27–25, because only three of fifteen Southern Whigs joined with the unanimously pro-Texas Democratic senators. Despite continued Whig opposition, the Democrat–led administration and Congress annexed Mexican territories from Texas to the Pacific, including California, in the Mexican Cession of 1848.

In the half century since the invention of the cotton gin, U.S. expansionism in lower South latitudes had swept across the continent. That omnivorous territorial expansion, achieved in the 1840s despite increasing Southern opposition and greater Northern opposition, bid fair to override all obstacles once again in the 1850s. During that presecession decade, Southern attempts to control Kansas, California, New Mexico, Arizona, Cuba, Nicaragua, and Mexico periodically convulsed the nation, helped provoke the election of Abraham Lincoln in 1860, and helped lead to the formation of the Confederacy. Yet all latter-day Southern expansion efforts failed, in part because Northerners

massed powerfully against them, and in part because Southerners failed to mass unanimously for them.

The lack of unanimous Southern zeal for expansion in the 1850s stemmed, first of all, from expansionism's very success. During the presecession decade, there was no way slaveholders could cultivate all the Texas, Arkansas, and California acres previously acquired. There was also no way most Southerners could still think that the slave South would perish economically. As the 1840s ended, so did the post-1837 depression. The prosperity of Southerners in the 1850s, with the exception of South Carolina rice farmers, exceeded pre-1837 levels. Cotton prices, which had averaged under 8 cents a pound in the 1840s, averaged 11 cents a pound in the 1850s. The lower South now needed more slaves to exploit unused land, not more outlets for unneeded slaves. Meanwhile, the upper South, also enjoying better times, no longer needed to sell slaves to survive. So lower South demand for slaves exceeded the supply, and the price of slaves soared 70 percent between 1850 and 1860.

One remarkable proposed solution demonstrated how completely times had changed. In the 1840s, many declining Southerners, growing too much cotton on too many tired acres, had sought fresh lands as a way to export excess blacks. In the 1850s, some booming Southerners, growing too little cotton with too few laborers, sought to import Africans as a way to develop excess land. A lower South movement to reopen the African slave trade grew with stunning rapidity in the mid-1850s. By buying slaves from Africa, ran one rationale for the proposed panacea, the lower South could expand its cotton kingdom continually without contracting the upper South's number of slaves counterproductively. With the upper South keeping its slaves while the lower South consolidated a hemisphere-wide empire, went the dream, Southern states, ever more numerous in Congress, would transcend the debilitating divisiveness of Texas annexation.

But the proposal caused a worse divisiveness. In the upper South, angry slave sellers noted that by seeking to reopen the African slave trade, slave buyers in the lower South were seeking to slice prices, even to cut U.S. sellers out of the market altogether. Reopening the trade would also defy Federal laws, enrage the North, and lead to disunion. After this upper South outcry, the lower South proposal sank almost as fast as it had arisen. But by urging that the South had overly abundant territory and insufficient slaves, the lower South finished off the Texas-outlet logic.

In yet another indication that the economic side of the planters' expand-or-perish rationale had become past history, the only remaining group of economically perishing planters tended now to oppose territorial expansion. South Carolina coastal rice aristocrats suffered through a crippling economic slide in the 1850s, with the value of the rice

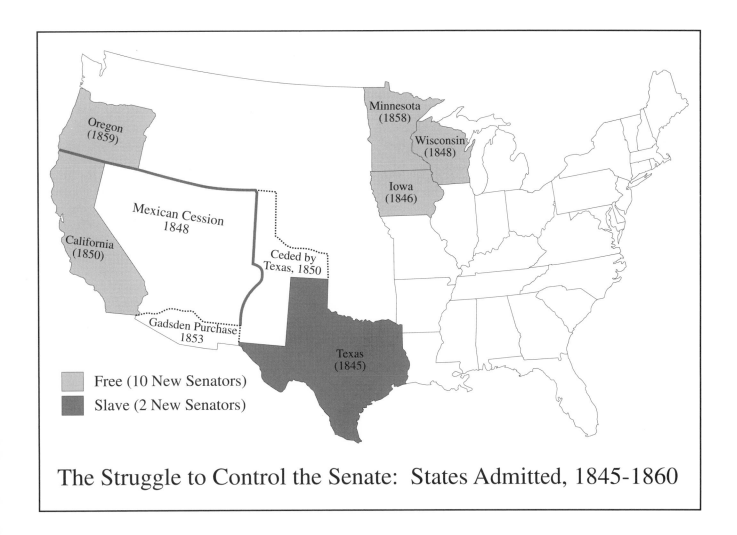

Oregon
(1859)

Minnesota
(1858)

Wisconsin
(1848)

Iowa
(1846)

Mexican Cession
1848

California
(1850)

Ceded by
Texas, 1850

Gadsden Purchase
1853

Texas
(1845)

Free (10 New Senators)

Slave (2 New Senators)

The Struggle to Control the Senate: States Admitted, 1845-1860

crop sinking 25 percent below 1840s levels. South Carolina up-country cotton producers fared better, but their economic recovery was less spectacular than Southwesterners'. Some 7,000 whites and 70,000 South Carolina blacks departed for the cotton frontier in the 1850s, preserving that stagnating state's distinction as the only slave-exporting lower South state. The state also retained its distinction as the only declining eighteenth-century locale of slavery that exported slaves and still crusaded to keep slavery forever.

That singular determination to retain departing slaves turned most South Carolinians against tropical meccas. Waddy Thompson had put it well in Texas times: who would stay in depleted Carolina if they could go to virgin El Dorados? John C. Calhoun came around to a similar attitude in 1846, opposing a southwestern drive to acquire all of Mexico. Leading South Carolinians continued to harbor such views of proposed Caribbean expansion in the 1850s. Mexico seemed full of non-American peons, Cuba full of free blacks, and the Southwest full of coarse frontiers-

men. "It is not by bread alone that man liveth," intoned South Carolina's revered Francis Sumter in 1859. "We want some stability in our institutions."

Many South Carolinians opposed a supposedly destabilizing Caribbean empire because they favored a supposedly stabilizing disunion revolution. These disunionists hoped that outside the Union and beyond unsettling Northern attacks, a settled South could flourish. They feared that if the Union did acquire vast tropical lands, restless southwesterners would never decide to secede. Still, a taste for staying home and distaste for expansionism swept up the powerful South Carolina Unionist, U.S. Senator James Henry Hammond, just as it did the secessionists. "I do not wish," said Hammond, "to remove from my native state and carry a family into the semibarbarous West."

While South Carolinians, the most avid disunionists, usually considered slaveholder expansion into raw land the semibarbarous road toward extinction, New Orleans businessmen, the most important proponents of Caribbean expansion, also cared little about acquiring new agricultural land. These avid imperialists instead longed for new urban markets. New York City and other northeastern urban centers were routing New Orleans in the competition for midwestern trade. In response, New Orleans merchants dreamed of commanding South American trade from U.S. ports in the Caribbean. It was not planters but the South's most expansive merchants who feared they might perish unless the North American republic spread over South America.

New Orleans merchants, as capitalist as any Northerner, and South Carolina planters, more anticapitalist than any other Americans, clashed not only over whether capitalistic hustle was salutary but also over the most effective means of Southern survival. Most South Carolinians favored disunion as a way to escape the materialistic North. Most New Orleans capitalists favored the Union as a means to acquire a materialistic empire. If we exert enough pressure on Northern Democrats, New Orleans newspapers editorialized, the party will use the Union's power to acquire first Cuba's harbors and then other lucrative Caribbean ports. If we fail to leave the Democratic party and the Union, responded many South Carolinians, we will be left hopelessly behind in a riotously expansive nation.

That climactic Southern intramural war undercuts an important latter-day explanation for slaveholder expansionism. The Southern slave labor system, runs some historians' argument, generated less efficient laborers and less entrepreneurial owners than the Northern free labor system; and hence, without constant expansion to fresh lands, Southerners supposedly feared that their allegedly anachronistic system would perish. Evidence for that interpretation derives from the Texas annexation struggle in the 1840s, when the cotton South was staggering economically. But during the climactic struggle over Caribbean expansion in the 1850s, when cotton growers were booming, up-to-date New Orleans capitalists became the avid Southern territorial expansionists, South Carolina's not-very-capitalistic planters generally became anti-expansionists, and southwestern slaveholders, whatever they thought of Cuba, were seeking more slaves so they could pile up higher profits than Northern employers of free laborers could muster.

With the economic aspect of agrarians' expand-or-perish conception now vanished, and with economic expand-or-perish imperatives now impelling only the nonagrarian merchants, the political taproot of Southern agriculturalists' expansion became preeminent. Throughout the eras when Southerners sought more land, then more safety valves, and then more markets and more slaves, defensive defiance was these slaveholders' political style. Slaveholders' aggressive defensiveness usually took the form of drives for more congressional seats and especially for more

secure borderlands, lest Northerners overwhelm slaveholders from without and corrode hinterlands from within. The old concern about slaveholders' vulnerable outposts, however, shifted in the 1850s from lower South to border South latitudes. True, near the Mexican border, lower South expansionists continued to complain about Mexican seduction of fugitive slaves. That argument helped impel abortive efforts to acquire Mexico in the 1850s. Near the Gulf of Mexico, other lower South expansionists focused on Cuba. They claimed that English abolitionists wished to emancipate (or, as the word went, "Africanize") Cuba, just as Englishmen had wished to emancipate Texas. An "Africanized" island commanding the Gulf, ninety miles from Florida, could not be tolerated. But Southerners farther from the Gulf considered English-inspired "Africanization" less creditable than in Texas times.

With a lower South reaching from the Atlantic to the Pacific now acquired, the greater border menace seemed to be northward, where more Northerners seemed to be helping slaves escape from the border South. This shift in the direction of greatest Southern concern created a revealing phenomenon: Southern congressmen cared less about California and Cuba, on the one hand, than about the Fugitive Slave Law and Kansas, on the other. During the crisis of 1850, Southerners demanded the opportunity to make California a slave state; and especially in southern California, cotton plantations would have enjoyed fabulous yields. But Southerners in Congress surrendered California to the North in exchange for a new Fugitive Slave Law. That edict was especially designed to protect the border South, where less plantation slavery was possible. Four years later, Southern drives to acquire Cuba and to open up Kansas to slavery came to a climax at practically the same moment. Cuba, already a slave island and more tropical than the most tropical lower South, possessed even more fertile land for slaveholders than did California. In contrast, Kansas, difficult to win for slavery and located northward in the border South temperate zone, could never sustain cotton and offered less potential for other plantation crops as well. Yet in 1854, Southern congressmen fought harder for the Kansas-Nebraska Act than for Cuba. Subsequently, Southern congressmen more insistently demanded that the Union admit Kansas than that the nation acquire Cuba.

These Southern priorities exasperated William Marcy, a New York Democrat and Franklin Pierce's secretary of state. The South's demand for Kansas, wrote Marcy, "has sadly shattered our party in all the free states," depriving "it of that strength which . . . could have been more profitably used for the acquisition of Cuba." Marcy's irony could as easily have been applied to 1850, when the South's insistence on a dubiously enforceable Fugitive Slave Law ruptured Southern sympathy in the North and deflected

Southern energies from southern California, which was so highly adaptable to slaveholding.

Such priorities were less bizarre than Marcy thought. A now land-rich South understandably put lower priority on the acquisition of California and Cuba, both lush but neither located on a slaveholder's porous border. The higher priority involved consolidation of the vulnerable border South. Inside that embattled middle ground between the free labor North and the heavily slaveholding South, many inhabitants often hoped that their relatively few slaves would drain southward. Meanwhile, some Northern neighbors hoped to entice border fugitive slaves northward. The border slave state of Missouri, already surrounded on two sides by free labor Illinois and Iowa, could not save slavery, so Missouri slaveholders said, if a free labor Kansas menaced it from a third border. With this critical argument for the Kansas-Nebraska Act, Missourians reemphasized one constant in the changing story of Southern expansionism. Whether in Louisiana in 1803 or Florida in 1819 or Texas in 1844 or Kansas in 1854, Southerners feared slaves would flee from borderlands unless land could be seized from enemies over the border.

But if the entire South put its highest priority on controlling the Kansas borderlands, southwestern congressmen continued to support the lesser priority of Cuba. As U.S. Senator Albert Gallatin Brown of Mississippi put it, "I want Cuba, and I know that sooner or later we must have it, . . . for the planting or spreading of slavery" and to expand slaveholders' congressional power. Presidents Franklin Pierce (1853–1857) and James Buchanan (1857–1861), both Northern Democrats, tried to meet this demand by buying Cuba from Spain. When Spain would not sell, Pierce's ministers to Spain, England, and France issued the famous Ostend Manifesto (1854), warning that if Spanish possession of Cuba endangered America, "by every law, human and divine, we shall be justified in wresting it."

Spain would not be bullied, whereupon Caribbean expansionists embraced so-called filibustering. Antebellum Americans used that term (linguistically derived from *freebooter*) to connote private armies that hoped to sail from a U.S. port, land in a Caribbean nation, lead an allegedly popular revolution, and annex the supposedly liberated nation to the United States. Such private invasions, which arguably culminated in John F. Kennedy's Bay of Pigs fiasco in Cuba in the 1960s, bore a resemblance to Andrew Jackson's incursion into Florida in 1818. A disproportionate percentage of 1850s filibusterers came from Jackson's Tennessee frontier. The most successful filibusterer, Tennessee's William Walker, briefly captured Nicaragua in the mid-1850s. The Jackson-Walker raiding spirit found its perfect financial complement in the New Orleans mercantile community's worried imperialism.

The combination of New Orleans cash and Tennessee

adventurism might have been lethal to Caribbean nations—if the U.S. government had failed to enforce the Neutrality Law of 1818, which forbade U.S. citizens from invading foreign nations. But Northerners would have condemned any president who allowed lawless Southerners to capture a slaveholder's empire (and hence gain more congressional votes). Northern Democrats always preferred to appease the South a good deal while standing firm against Southern demands a little, thus keeping the party electable in the North and overwhelming in the South. In pursuit of that politic goal, Northern presidents sought legal purchase of Cuba while imprisoning illegal filibusterers. Only a relentlessly unified South might have budged Presidents Pierce and Buchanan from that seemingly balanced statecraft.

Southerners could not muster unanimous support for illicit private raids on Caribbean nations any more than they could for reopening the African slave trade or for Jackson's 1818 strike on Florida. Just as John C. Calhoun had considered Jackson an enemy of hierarchy and order, so most South Carolinians usually considered the filibusterers to be disorderly pirates who were seeking to seize disorderly nations. Just as Henry Clay had feared that Jackson's raid (and, later, Texas annexation) would disrupt the Union, so many upper South Democrats declared piracy in Cuba not worth disunion in America. With Southerners fighting Southerners, Northern Democratic presidents could follow Northern constituents' desires. Thus, Federal judges and naval officers blocked critical filibuster expeditions before invasions reached the targeted nations, aborting especially the plot of former Mississippi governor John Quitman to capture Cuba in 1855 and the assault by William Walker on Nicaragua in 1857.

Although Southerners were as badly divided on filibustering as on reopening the African slave trade, they were more united on the issue of Kansas. Yet irresolution plagued even this main Southern expansionist effort of the 1850s. By securing the Kansas-Nebraska Act in 1854, Southerners acquired the right to race Northern settlers to Kansas. Instead of speeding to Kansas, however, most migrants to the Southwest headed for more tropical virgin lands in Texas and Arkansas. With more Northerners peopling Kansas, not even determined Southern congressmen could pressure enough Northern Democrats to admit Kansas as a slave state in defiance of most Kansans' wishes.

Not enough Northerners appeased the South because too many Southerners deserted. In 1858, the House of Representatives rejected Kansas as a slave state by a vote of 120–112. If the six upper South ex-Whigs who voted "no" had voted "yes," the South would have had its sixteenth slave state. Southern opposition, having almost defeated Texas, had blocked the acquisition of Kansas for the South. The only southward expansion to triumph in the 1850s was the Gadsden Purchase (1853) of a strip of lower California—an acquisition aimed at building railroads, not planting cotton.

The frenetic Southern expansion efforts of the 1850s, which upset most Northerners yet acquired not one slave state, contrasted dismally with the sustained expansion efforts of 1793 to 1843, which had distressed few Northerners and had secured a lower South empire. But back in the heady pre-Texas days, all Southerners had cherished expansionist objectives, even if some had winced at Jackson's methods. With Southern unanimity over expansionist goals dissolving and Northern protests rising, Southerners were fortunate that Texas squeaked through; and no luck could thereafter win further expansion of the slavocracy. Even in Kansas, despite the Kansas-Nebraska Act, late antebellum slave society's demands eventually outran its power. Disunited Southerners could not forever successfully defy the more numerous and, in the end, equally resolute Northerners.

Northern Republicans of the 1850s would have dismissed the notion that Southern division hindered Southern expansion. They believed in that decade that everywhere they looked, whether toward Cuba or Nicaragua or Kansas or Mexico, Southerners were seeking to take over the Union and the hemisphere. Moreover, whenever Republicans called slavery too immoral to be allowed to spread, Southerners responded that Republicans must silence their hateful slander.

Republicans were right that *some* Southerners wanted every inch of New World space in the 1850s and that *no* Southerner could abide Northern insult. By calling slavery too barbarous to spread, Republicans took the expansion issue beyond pragmatic considerations, such as whether Caribbean acquisitions would depopulate South Carolina, to patriotic considerations, especially whether Southerners were respectable people. Republican moral condemnation generated a charged Southern vocabulary: would Southerners "submit" or "resist"? In this white man's egalitarian nation, white males could not "submit" to charges of moral inferiority without surrendering their self-respect and honor. Indeed, a failure to "resist" moral condemnation itself had practical consequences in a Southern world still divided on the morality of permanent slavery. If border Southerners submitted to Republican insult, these disbelievers in slavery's permanence would be lost to the slavocracy. Waverers must instead be rallied to resent the Republicans. If clergymen who criticized slaveholders' Christian imperfections saluted Republicans' antislavery morality, no Southerner would listen to them. Internal reformers must instead castigate outside agitators. All factions of Southern opinion thus had a pragmatic stake in condemning Northern critics.

This verbal aggressiveness once again illuminated the most constant aspect of Southern expansionism, whatever the changing economic motives: besieged Southerners' defiance of detractors, whether by rebutting insult or by seeking additional congressional seats or by fortifying vulnerable hinterlands. And curse the Republicans they constantly did. Along with their scorn came expansionist proposals, each more extreme than the last, and all of them, taken together, giving off the illusion of a consolidated civilization, even of a conspiratorially united slavocracy. But if resentment of Republican condescension was almost universal, support of filibusterers or endorsement of reopening of the African slave trade or a move to Kansas was not. So, too, in the secession crisis, while the necessity of resisting Lincoln's antislavery criticism was acknowledged almost universally, the necessity of resisting only outside the Union was not. After anti-expansionist South Carolinians precipitated disunion, pro-expansionist Louisianians felt compelled to follow their lower South brethren. But border Southerners felt a countervailing compulsion: to save the Union. Here again, the Southern politics of the 1850s, so often aimed at making border areas more Southern than Northern, had failed.

The resulting Southern disunity would prove to be even more fatal to Confederate armies than it had been to Caribbean filibusterers, the reopening of the African slave trade, and the securing of Kansas. In war even more than in peace, the infuriated Southerner was an awesome force. But not even the South's fabled courage could ultimately defeat the more numerous Northerners, plus the border South third of Southern white folk, plus the runaway sixth of Southern black folk. And fugitive slaves, by fleeing toward Northerners during the Civil War, proved that prewar Southern expansionists' fears of nearby "aliens" had been all too prescient.

[*See also* Bleeding Kansas; Compromise of 1850; Democratic Party; Fugitive Slave Law; Imperialism; Kansas-Nebraska Act; Missouri Compromise; Wilmot Proviso.]

BIBLIOGRAPHY

Brown, Charles H. *Agents of Manifest Destiny: The Lives and Times of the Filibusterers.* Chapel Hill, N.C., 1980.

Freehling, William W. *Secessionists at Bay, 1776–1854.* Vol. 1 of *The Road to Disunion.* New York, 1990.

Horsman, Reginald. *Race and Manifest Destiny: The Origins of American Racial Anglo-Saxism.* Cambridge, Mass., 1981.

Lander, Ernest M., Jr. *Reluctant Imperialists: Calhoun, the South Carolinians, and the Mexican War.* Baton Rouge, La., 1980.

May, Robert E. *The Southern Dream of a Caribbean Empire, 1854–1861.* Baton Rouge, La., 1973.

Merk, Frederick. *Manifest Destiny and Mission in American History: A Reinterpretation.* New York, 1963.

Potter, David. *The Impending Crisis, 1848–1861.* New York, 1976.

Rauch, Basil. *American Interest in Cuba: 1848–1855.* New York, 1948.

Remini, Robert V. *Andrew Jackson and the Course of American Empire, 1767–1821*. New York, 1977.

Smith, Justin H. *The Annexation of Texas*. New York, 1911.

Takaki, Ronald T. *A Pro-Slavery Crusade: The Agitation to Reopen the African Slave Trade*. New York, 1971.

Urban, C. Stanley. "The Idea of Progress and Southern Imperialism: New Orleans and the Caribbean, 1845–1861." Ph.D. diss., Northwestern University, 1943.

Walker, William. *The War in Nicaragua*. Mobile, Ala., 1860.

WILLIAM W. FREEHLING

EXTORTION. As part of their effort to unite the South around a coherent set of ideals, Confederate cultural and political leaders struggled to identify the particular virtues of the South and to purge themselves of any accompanying vices. Wanting to consider themselves morally superior to the greed they claimed had overwhelmed the economic system of the North, leading Confederates hoped to root out their own greediest practices.

Foremost among those was what Southerners called extortion. As historian Drew Gilpin Faust has pointed out, since the eve of secession, "southerners had been citing the growing materialism of American, and especially northern, society as a fundamental justification for independence." Religious and political speakers drew on the South's heritage of republican ideology to claim that special economic privilege threatened to undermine the region's particular virtues of self-sufficiency, personal independence, and mutual respect among the classes. Southerners defined extortion as using a position of power to make unfair profits. Under this heading fell such practices as creating monopolies on goods, speculating on cotton and food crops, hoarding goods to raise prices, and setting prices on necessities beyond reasonable limits. To Southerners who believed that their society adhered to values of personal integrity and respect rather than those of a faceless marketplace, these were offenses against public morality and suggested that the South was becoming too much like the North. The practices mocked Southerners' claim to have a country based on religious principles and to understand the basic truths of political economy.

People who manipulated the economy for selfish purposes had long faced criticism in the South, but the opportunities the war presented for both production and marketing intensified economic developments that were well underway. In the 1850s far more Southerners than ever were turning to commercial agriculture, and those with money were investing in a wide range of commercial ventures, especially manufacturing and the railroads. Accusing fellow Southerners of extortion was a way to raise general concerns about the growing importance of a commercial economy, and then to blame the problem on the region's most obvious offenders. Accusations of extortion could thus serve a cathartic function for much of society.

The issue became most heated over food shortages and increases in food prices. Households unable to support themselves were newly dependent on local stores. A main problem with food supplies was impressment by the military. After the Confederate Congress passed the impressment law, farmers lived in fear of getting less than market prices for crops seized by the government. The impressment agents then became the enemies, appearing to work in tandem with corrupt marketers to deprive farmers of a just return on their goods and consumers of a just price. General store owners who hoarded food and raised prices seemed especially offensive in a time of sacrifice. In towns and cities from Richmond to Mobile, women mounted protests and then riots against the unfairness of high food prices and the unavailability of basic items. As historian Paul Escott has noted, the general popularity of the goals of these riots shows how fully most Southerners had accepted the idea that government and financial interests were working together unfairly.

As the war dragged on and Confederate troops met failure after failure, Southerners looked in many directions for scapegoats. With unseen forces apparently sapping the region's economic fortunes, many Southerners blamed Jewish bankers and immigrant merchants. This tendency continued the long-standing fear held by native-born Protestant Southerners that outsiders came to the South only to cheat them out of their money. Jews offered obvious targets for numerous reasons. Along with their historical stereotype as Shylocks, many did not work in the fields, many owned stores, and they were not part of the Protestant churches that were so important as agents of community life. Congressman Henry S. Foote wildly estimated that Jews made up nine-tenths of the region's merchants and speculated that they would own most of the wealth in the South by the end of the war.

Southerners generally agreed that too many were taking advantage of the war. As a Montgomery, Alabama, newspaper noted, "the whole country is ringing with denunciations of the extortioners." Some claimed that the profiteering followed economic logic and saw no reason to try to stop it, but they were the minority. The difficulty lay in what to do about extortion. The Confederate Senate debated a bill to restrict overpricing and excessive speculation, and seven states passed laws against those practices. A law in South Carolina set a 75 percent limit on the amount of profit resalers could make, and other states passed similar laws. The vagueness of the issue and the fear of stifling production limited such laws to symbolic importance, but that should not minimize their significance. By condemning the various forms of extortion so frequently, Southerners could believe that they were fighting for ideals far higher than money.

[*See also* Bread Riots; Speculation.]

BIBLIOGRAPHY

Escott, Paul D. *Many Excellent People: Power and Privilege in North Carolina, 1850–1900.* Chapel Hill, N.C., 1985.

Faust, Drew G. *The Creation of Confederate Nationalism: Ideology and Identity in the Civil War South.* Baton Rouge, La., 1988.

Silver, James W. *Confederate Morale and Church Propaganda.* New York, 1967.

Thomas, Emory M. *The Confederate Nation: 1861–1865.* New York, 1979.

TED OWNBY

F

FAGAN, JAMES F. (1828–1893), major general. Fagan was born in Kentucky March 1, 1828. His father moved the family in 1838 to the newly formed state of Arkansas. When the Mexican War broke out in 1846, Fagan joined the military as a volunteer and returned at war's end a lieutenant. With the emergence of the Confederacy, the Arkansas secession convention, in an unusual move, commissioned Fagan a colonel and commander of the First Arkansas Infantry Regiment.

Fagan remained with the unit in the early years of warfare in Virginia and Tennessee and was cited by his men for his distinguished service as "their indomitable leader" at the Battle of Shiloh in April 1862. In July Fagan resigned from the military to return to Arkansas to tend to his family. In September, however, he was commissioned a brigadier general, attached to the Trans-Mississippi Department. In December Fagan fought in the Battle of Prairie Grove, Arkansas, where he again won a citation for distinguished service. In 1863, serving under Gen. Sterling Price, Fagan became increasingly involved in the defense of Arkansas. In April 1864 he took part in forcing Union Maj. Gen. Frederick Steele's retreat from the town of Camden. Gen. E. Kirby Smith commended him for his role in Steele's repulse and commissioned Fagan a major general on April 24.

In September, Fagan joined Sterling Price's raid deep into Missouri in a last failing effort to seize the border state. Price cited Fagan's "unabated gallantry and ardor." When the Confederacy collapsed, Fagan was commanding the District of Arkansas. He and his men held out for more than two months after Robert E. Lee's surrender, not capitulating until June 14, 1865.

After the war, Fagan returned to planting and politics, serving as an official of the Federal government in Arkansas under President Ulysses S. Grant. He died in Little Rock on September 1, 1893.

BIBLIOGRAPHY

Hammock, John C. *With Honor Untarnished: The Story of the First Arkansas Infantry Regiment, Confederate States Army.* Little Rock, Ark., 1961.

Nichols, James L., and Frank Abbott, eds. "Reminiscences of Confederate Service by Wiley A. Washburn." *Arkansas Historical Quarterly* 35, no. 1 (1976): 47–90.

Warner, Ezra J. *Generals in Gray: Lives of the Confederate Commanders.* Baton Rouge, La., 1959.

JAMES F. FAGAN.　　　　NATIONAL ARCHIVES

FREDERICK SCHULT

FAIR OAKS, VIRGINIA. *See* Seven Pines, Virginia.

FAMILY LIFE. In Southern culture, kin relationships were central to an individual's self-image and standing in the community. More than any other region, the South placed the family at the center of social life; it was the chief forum for socialization, education, and community.

White Families

Southern white families during the Confederacy lived in an agrarian society with few cities. Many farmed land they did not own, and most had few or no slaves; only a small proportion cultivated large plantations with many slaves. The economic responsibilities on these family farms varied with the wealth of the family, but their structures were similar. Nuclear, extended, or augmented families had male heads and reinforced the patriarchal culture.

Patriarchy defined both the Northern and the Southern family, but the patriarchal nature of Southern society, unlike that in the North, was primarily agrarian. In a farming community, everyone in the household worked at producing food and daily necessities, and the father was in charge. Of course, differences in family structure and functions of family members varied according to economic status. But scholars no longer accept the old mythology of a bifurcated distinction between a white aristocratic family with a strong paternalistic father and a poor white family whose father was more interested in alcohol and fishing than his home. Actually, Southern families, rich and poor, held many values in common. Notions of honor and virtue, of parental priority in the family, of the importance of religion, were shaped and shared by varied groups of white Southerners.

Southern culture held children in high regard; they were a major source of pride and satisfaction for their parents. In wealthy families, childhood was a time to play and to study under a tutor or private schoolteacher. Poorer rural families could not afford the luxuries and concentrated attention that planters gave their children. Nevertheless, they worked together daily, and, with the seasonal rhythms of farm life, rainy days, Sundays, and holidays, the family had some recreational time together. Close bonds developed, and family members demonstrated strong feelings of affection for one another.

Southern society consisted of farms dispersed throughout neighborhoods, which were usually networks of interlocking families. Many white Southerners were born, married, had children, and were buried, all within a family context in an area of ten to twenty miles. Intermarriage within families heightened the significance of kinship bonds. In many instances among rich and poor whites, brothers in one family married sisters in another. This pattern of sibling exchange is often confused with cousin marriage. Wealthy clans formed interlocking relationships through marriage. Family linkages, important factors in political alliances and allegiances, often led to an individual's acquiring a leadership role in the community, the state, or ultimately the Confederacy.

It was men from these kinship networks who rushed off to defend their families and communities when the Confederacy called for troops. The family and kinship nature of neighborhoods initially gave an advantage to the Southern soldiers. Local men formed companies identified by county and neighborhood. Brothers, cousins, and in-laws stood shoulder to shoulder. Some entire companies were made up of relatives, often with a single surname. For example, Company I of the Twentieth South Carolina Volunteers, raised in 1862, had thirty-four men whose surnames were "Gunter," and most of the others were nephews, uncles, and cousins. Fighting with one's family strengthened a man's courage and helped ease the massive dislocation he felt upon leaving home for the first time. Moreover, he felt constrained not to let down his family by deserting or running in the face of danger.

The Civil War, of course, caused great disruption in the Southern family. So many men of military age, sometimes as much as 70 percent of those eighteen to forty-five years of age, were absent from Southern communities. Even some boys as young as thirteen and men as old as sixty left for the battlefront. The family lost moral authority over the boys in the army; moreover, in Southern society, where masculinity was associated with power, children at home sometimes used the opportunity of their father's absence to test their mother's control. Initially many of the men going off to war rushed through whirlwind courtships and quick marriages. With so many casualties and some survivors' deferring marriage, the birthrate declined significantly during the war years.

The Civil War brought separation, economic distress, and death, and family life reflected these changes. Physical closeness and family togetherness no longer maintained a sense of community, so news reports, letters, fleeting visits, and a vague notion of a common purpose had to take their place. The absence of fathers created great stress, which is reflected in correspondence among Southern family members. Wives mediated between fathers and children, writing to their husbands about home life and their offspring. Letters of some elite families indicate strained marriages.

Although divorce was illegal in some Southern states, one study suggests that before the war some wealthier women sought divorce and accused their husbands of abuse, particularly blaming "Demon Rum." During the war armies attracted camp followers, and prostitution flourished at winter camps. And too, nonslaveholding men, many of them serving as soldiers, accused their wives of adultery and sought divorce. Prior to the war, Southern churches traditionally were very involved in the personal lives of members. Church committees monitored the conduct of their members and helped with domestic problems, and some churches formally accused men of physical abuse of their families. These discipline committees became less active as the war continued.

Just as concern for family led to large initial enlistments, concern for the family may have ultimately led to Confederate defeat. As family and kin in a given unit were replaced by men from other areas as the war went on, the neighborhood meaning of the war was diluted. Also, when the wealthy used their family influence to get safer positions such as in home guards, class tensions caused morale problems. More important, Southern fighting men ultimately were compelled to weigh duty to country against love of family. Hunger on the home front forced many to place the welfare of their families above loyalty to the cause. Because the Confederate government failed to provide sufficient relief for the families of soldiers, many men deserted to keep their families from starving. When the government could no longer provide families with subsistence levels of food, Confederate women desperately petitioned officials for food and furloughs for their husbands. Some of these women, moreover, encouraged their menfolk to desert.

Men also felt the need to protect their families from the growing crime on the home front. Crime of all sorts increased as bandits, guerrillas, and soldiers roamed the countryside. Women left alone were particularly vulnerable. Scholars have argued that the heavy desertion rate, particularly in the last year, was one reason the South lost the war. But scholars have not fully explored the war's impact. Children bore a heavy burden of responsibility on family farms, working long hours beside their mothers and other relatives; poorer white children worked in war industries. Approximately every third white family lost a father, son, or brother, and many children were orphaned. In the face of death, families provided support and love, and nearly every Southern family sheltered disabled veterans.

One of the most important roles of Southern women was their willingness to sacrifice their loved ones to the Confederate cause. But they also found that the exigencies of war enabled them to make a more substantial contribution to family and community life than they had previously had the opportunity to make. Women ran farms, businesses, and their communities with increasing confidence as the war progressed. These changes in their lives, however, were probably short-lived, as after the war they returned to their more limited antebellum roles.

Demographers have cited a "male gap" in the South during and after the war. In 1870 in Georgia, for instance, white women outnumbered men by thirty-six thousand. Thus, some women never married. The mother-child ratios indicate that significantly fewer children were born during the 1860s. The demographic stability of the North after the war is explained by the continuing inflow of immigrants; however, preliminary analysis of the white South reveals that demographic stability quickly returned to that region as well, even without immigration. The Civil War brought to the white families of the South their most traumatic moment, but despite its effects, most of the structures and values of Southern white families survived.

Black Families

If the Civil War was traumatic for Southern white families, who, for the most part, enthusiastically supported the Confederacy, it was even more traumatic for African Americans already vulnerable under slavery. War necessarily entailed anxiety and apprehension. Then, with the defeat of the Confederacy, came freedom, citizenship, and the legal recognition of marriage and family.

Despite debate among historians on the nature of the slave family, strong evidence suggests that monogamous marriage was the norm. Planters' records often list slaves in family units. The demographic vitality of the slave population of the southern United States required a social base—stable families that provided physical, emotional, and cultural support for childbirth and child rearing. And, despite the most difficult circumstances, the slave family in the South was typically a male-dominated nuclear family (father, mother, and children), the prevailing form the world over.

Families provided economic benefits through family gardens and also, to some extent, shielded their members emotionally from the hardships of slavery. Having a spouse to love, to accompany, and to grow old with was important in the difficult circumstances of slavery. Slave children worked alongside parents daily, and on Sundays families traveled to and from church together. Slave children played games and listened to the folktales of parents and extended family members.

Slave owners saw slave families as a means to increase the labor force and also to enhance their control and plantation stability. For example, family ties and responsibilities deterred slaves from running away. Some planters offered incentives for slaves to marry and ritualized slave marriages; others merely allowed them. Nevertheless, slave marriages were acknowledged by the community if not by the law. Divorce also was acknowledged, and children born out of wedlock carried no stigma.

Slave families were inescapably vulnerable to separation at someone else's whim. Although most masters sanctioned slave marriages, some owners separated families, even while proclaiming they did not want to. A master's vacation or extended visit included his personal slaves, who might have preferred to remain at home with their own families. Slaves were rented, willed, given, sold, and purchased according to the needs of owners, and the slaves' desire for family autonomy counted for nothing. While the ideology of paternalism moved some masters to decline profitable sales in order to avoid breaking up slave families, this same ideology led to the sale of some slaves in order to maintain social control through the threat of additional sales in the future.

The Civil War immediately separated families, both black and white, although demographic patterns were not as dramatic for African Americans as for Southern whites. White refugees often took their slaves when they moved, thereby disrupting slave families. Slaves feared the evacuation of plantations as they had estate dispersals. Husbands and wives owned by different masters were particularly apprehensive about relocation during the Civil War.

Just as white soldiers left their homes to join regiments, some slaves had to go with their masters to the front lines to act as valets and cooks. Slaves could not or were not allowed to write, but often sent messages to loved ones with travelers or in the slave owners' letters. Even more slaves were separated from their families when impressed to work on fortifications. The standard of living for most of these African Americans, generally men, was at best minimally adequate. In an occasional military or industrial job, however, slaves could do extra work to earn income for their families at home or to purchase transportation for visits. Sometimes slaves hired out to the government were given leaves of absence to visit families, and employers sometimes linked family visitation to overtime work.

Free blacks had a different role during the Civil War. While early in the war some Southern states permitted free blacks to muster into local or state militia units, none allowed African Americans to serve as regular soldiers. Yet some light-skinned free blacks became "honorary white men" and actually enlisted and fought for the Confederacy. Families of Confederate free blacks, whether volunteers or impressments, were not eligible for even the meager aid furnished to whites by state and local governments.

Although the war was hard on the African American families whose husbands and sons were forced into Confederate service, the war decidedly benefited the black family by increasing its autonomy. Freedom for slaves did not await the Emancipation Proclamation. Especially in more remote rural areas, as institutional control and close personal supervision of slaves lessened, slave families attained greater personal freedom. While masters were away at war, slaves took advantage of the situation. They expanded their own garden spots and traditional space around their cabins, and black women spent more time with their own families and in their own homes. Parental authority, especially of the father, increased when the white boss was away at the front. In many cases slaves refused to submit to punishment, demanded wages from owners, slipped away to become Union "contraband," or enlisted in the Federal army.

During the last two years of war, church reformers in the South argued that slave marriages must be legalized and not violated by whites. As slaves were liberated by Union forces or escaped to federal lines, many were eager to "legitimize" their marriages and have their children formally baptised and recognized.

The Civil War also altered escape patterns; before the war it was solitary young men who had run away. During the Civil War the number of families who escaped together noticeably increased. As the war and Union troops presented a real opportunity for slaves, more families and kin groups, sometimes even entire plantation communities, attempted to gain their liberty. Family commitment among slaves, however, also worked to deter escape; some slaves opted to remain at home rather than risk losing contact with their family.

The Confederacy may arguably have lost the Civil War because of the commitment of African Americans to family. Union black troops made a significant difference in the manpower of the Union army. Runaway slaves and free African Americans understood that the Union Army offered them an opportunity to rescue family and kin still slaves in the South. The white commander of the black First South Carolina Volunteers explained that his men "had more to fight for than whites. Besides the flag and the Union, they had home and wife and child." According to one Union recruiter, when he asked a group of African Americans at St. Helena Island to enlist "to fight for themselves [and] . . . protect their wives and children from being sold away from them, and told of the little homes which they might secure to themselves and their families in after years, they all rose to their feet, the men came forward and said 'I'll go,' the women shouted, and the old men said 'Amen.' "

African American families suffered a higher percentage of lost loved ones. Black Union soldiers were treated as traitors and not as prisoners of war by Confederates. Confederate soldiers often took no quarter when facing black troops. The gruesome massacre after the surrender at Fort Pillow vividly illustrates the racism and dangers that black soldiers faced. Two-thirds of all black soldiers were killed, some literally crucified and burned.

Defeat for the Confederacy certainly did not mean defeat for all Southerners. States with a majority black population actually won the Civil War. With freedom wrought by the Civil War, former slaves immediately began the search for family members sold and separated during slavery. Slave families demanded valid and legal marriages. Even as many Southern whites began restricting freedom for former slaves, they saw the need to allow black families. One newspaper quoted a typical comment: "Freedom from being sold on the block and separated from his wife and children is all the freedom he ought to have."

African Americans celebrated their newfound freedom by keeping and strengthening their family life. The black family and demographic stability of the African-American community held firm.

[*See also* Children; Marriage and Divorce; Morale; Slavery, *article on* Slave Life.]

BIBLIOGRAPHY

Bleser, Carol, ed. *In Joy and in Sorrow: Women, Family, and Marriage in the Victorian South.* New York, 1991.

Burton, Orville Vernon. *In My Father's House Are Many Mansions: Family and Community in Edgefield, South Carolina.* Chapel Hill, N.C., 1985.

Bynum, Victoria E. *Unruly Women: The Politics of Social and Sexual Control in the Old South.* Chapel Hill, N.C., 1992.

Censer, Jane Turner. *North Carolina Planters and Their Children, 1800–1860.* Baton Rouge, La., 1984.

Escott, Paul D. " 'The Cry of the Sufferers': The Problem of Welfare in the Confederacy." *Civil War History* 23, no. 3 (1977): 228–240.

Gutman, Herbert G. *The Black Family in Slavery and Freedom, 1750–1925.* New York, 1976.

Kenzer, Robert C. *Kinship and Neighborhood in a Southern Community: Orange County, North Carolina, 1849–1881.* Knoxville, Tenn., 1987.

Mohr, Clarence L. *One the Threshold of Freedom: Masters and Slaves in Civil War Georgia.* Athens, Ga., 1986.

Rable, George C. *Civil Wars: Women and the Crisis of Southern Nationalism.* Urbana, Ill., 1989.

ORVILLE VERNON BURTON

FARMING. On the eve of the Civil War, farming in the South had assumed a patchwork quality. There were, of course, thousands of large plantations employing mainly slave labor in the river bottoms of the Old Southwest and on the South Atlantic coast. But tens of thousands more small farmers, mostly white, cultivated the uplands, some of whom farmed for a subsistence and a surplus of cotton, corn, tobacco, or hogs, while still others were content to avoid markets altogether. Within these crop cultures, there labored many others, not properly called farmers, but without whom crops could not be planted or harvested. Most conspicuously, women labored in the home to raise children, make cloth, prepare food, and produce commodities for local trade in their truck gardens, milking barns, and chicken pens.

These various kinds of farming arose not from personal preference but from a conflict over the shape of Southern agriculture that had begun in the 1830s and would end only with the Populist revolt in the 1890s. As plank roads, river improvements, and later railroads connected the Southern interior to northeastern and midwestern markets, large farmers seized the opportunity to make ever greater profits. In some but not all parts of the South, they used the power of state and local government to require others to fence their animals in place of enclosing crops and to hunt game and range hogs only in designated places, thus limiting access to what had been common lands. Developers also required by means of cash taxes that small farmers help build and pay for an infrastructure of roads, cotton weighing platforms, and other public buildings that made commercial farming profitable. In the early 1840s, these development measures had begun to place commercial growers and subsistence farmers in conflicting positions.

By 1860, then, three kinds of farmers labored on the land in the Old South—large planters who produced a staple crop, mostly cotton, with slave labor for sale in distant markets; large commercial farmers who employed tenants and day laborers to produce livestock, corn, and wheat, also for distant markets; and smaller farmers and the women and children in their households who produced a subsistence for themselves and sometimes a surplus, usually for sale or for barter in the neighborhood. This tripartite social formation also produced two distinct classes of dependents, slaves on the one hand and poor white tenants and laborers on the other. When the war began, secessionists supposed that the South's farmers would rise as one to defend the new nation, but that was not the case. The war, in fact, exacerbated differences among farmers as well as disrupting the production of agricultural products.

Farmers in the Confederacy first felt the impact of the war during the financial crisis of late 1860 and early 1861. As secession became nearly a certainty, creditors began to call in their debts due from Southern commercial farmers, both large and small, and after secession credit disappeared entirely. At the same time, trade in farm commodities ground to a halt as banks began to hoard specie after the Union blockade of the Southern coast took hold. Cotton and wheat lay on docks and in barns, and a new Confederate war tax on property forced farmers to either borrow scarce money or sell crops at ruinously low prices. Those farmers who had most thoroughly committed themselves to supplying markets outside the South took the first blow in the conflict.

Smaller semisubsistence farmers did not begin to feel the pinch until the fall of 1861. By that time, the first wave of volunteers had served in summer campaigns after having taken care to plant their crops the previous spring. In the fall, however, as the fighting continued, soldiers could not return home to help harvest those crops. The task fell to women and children who found themselves both short-handed and without animals to haul crops from the fields to barns or to markets; the Confederate army had purchased or impressed thousands of horses, mules, and oxen in the summer of 1861. Moreover, it became nearly impossible to preserve pork in December because the price of salt had skyrocketed—by a factor of twelve in Savannah between May and October 1861. Before the war, salt had been imported mainly as ballast in ships that would carry away cotton, ships that in 1861 remained blockaded in Southern ports. The result was a subsistence crisis on many Southern farms during the first winter of the war. Between November 1861 and March 1862, six Confederate states approved legislation for the relief of indigent families left behind by men serving in either state militias or the Confederate army.

In April 1862, the Confederate government's Conscription Act began a massive and forced removal of labor from the countryside at the worst possible moment. But the act did not effect everyone equally. On small farms, young men between the ages of eighteen and thirty-five, both heads of households and agricultural laborers, were unable to plant spring wheat and corn, thereby leaving their families at the mercy of local markets in foodstuffs. At the same time, large planters, being exempt themselves from the draft, instructed their slaves to plant corn and wheat and beans instead of cotton, thus ensuring not only a subsistence for slaves but also a large marketable crop in foodstuffs that would command premium prices among the poor during the next fall and winter. Moreover, a severe drought that summer parched the crops and reduced yields for all farmers, and the Confederate army itself consumed a large portion of the South's foodstuffs and cloth. It also commandeered much of the best pasture land in the Shenandoah Valley and the Tennessee River basin to graze horses used by the cavalry and the quartermaster corps. Finally, the war itself disrupted planting in many parts of the Confederacy, especially on the South Atlantic coast where Union raiders regularly penetrated one hundred miles or more inland, and in parts of middle Tennessee, the Mississippi delta, and southern Louisiana occupied by Union armies.

By the fall of 1862, the price of corn, produced now mainly on large plantations, had risen to $2.50 per bushel, well beyond the purchasing ability of ordinary farm families. Confederate soldiers received only about eleven dollars per month, and part of that paid the soldiers' own expenses: a uniform, shoes, and tobacco. Not surprisingly, many of those soldiers deserted and returned home to harvest what little had been planted the previous spring. As one farmer in Mississippi wrote in December 1862, "We are poor men and are willing to defend our country but our families first and then our country." The crops had failed, however, and many were forced to purchase corn at inflated prices. In a Mississippi county, for example, one local notable wrote that

six hundred families there had a father or son in the army and could not afford to eat. "The Bread is here," he argued, "but owing to the High price is beyond the reach of these poor people."

Many blamed speculators for the scarcity and high price of foodstuffs, but small farmers themselves had contributed to the inflated prices, especially of corn. Confederate taxes, unlike most local taxes, had to be paid in cash, and therefore many converted their corn, rye, wheat, and barley into liquor, which, being easily transportable and in great demand as usual, could be sold in distant cities and to Confederate soldiers for specie. Yet the Confederate government remained the real culprit in these difficulties. Its conscription laws had confiscated the labor supply on small farms and its new taxes had the effect of converting foodstuffs into a marketable luxury.

As a result, many small farmers began to organize actively against not only military service but also the Confederacy itself; both had undercut the independent economy that they had gone to war to preserve in the first place. Farmers in the mountains barricaded themselves in hollows; others in Piedmont North Carolina closed the borders of several counties against Confederate recruiting agents; and many in Tennessee, Arkansas, and northern Alabama organized themselves into guerrilla bands. Moreover, many Southern communities included disaffected yeoman families who hid male relatives by day and fed and comforted them by night. But that strategy only preserved the men; it did not make their labor available to their families.

In 1863, inflation destroyed any hope the Confederate government might have had of mobilizing smaller farmers in its favor. The continued absence of labor on small Southern farms meant that little had been planted in the spring of 1863, and less harvested the following fall. Farmers in Virginia harvested only about one-third of their normal crop. In addition, the spring wheat in Georgia and Alabama suffered from rust and the corn from a severe drought. The price of corn rose that summer from three dollars to ten dollars per bushel. Moreover, the supply of cloth dwindled in the countryside. Southern textile mills diverted all their efforts to the production of uniforms, blankets, and tents for the army, leaving little or nothing for a population that was still wearing clothing manufactured three years earlier. Farmers' wives found it impossible to make their own cloth, mainly as a result of a shortage of cards with which to straighten cotton and wool fibers. For small farmers and their families food and clothing had become not just pricey, but impossible to obtain or even to produce at home.

In the spring of 1863, poor women in the South took the matter directly to the authorities. In a dozen or more places in the Confederacy, women rioted for fair prices that would enable poor men and women to acquire the common necessities of everyday living. In Salisbury, North Carolina, women working in government textile mills invaded stores and offered what they called "government prices" for flour, bacon, and molasses; these were prices that had been set by a local board under the terms of the Impressment Act and had lagged behind inflation. When their demands were refused, the women simply seized the items they needed. In Richmond, more than a thousand women met at the capitol building and then looted downtown stores of food and clothing. Poor men and women in the countryside did much the same when they threatened "to organize and commence operations" if food and clothing did not soon become available. As one farmer in Bladen County, North Carolina, put it: "Some of us has been traveling for the last month with the money in our pockets to buy corn & tryd men that had plenty & has bin unable to buy a bushel." Planters were "holding on for a better price . . . so as to take all the soldiers wages for a fiew bushels," and that was not fair. "The time has come," he concluded, "that we the comon people has to hav bread or blood & we are bound boath men & women to hav it or die in the attempt."

But the worst was yet to come. In 1864, inflation placed all commodities of any kind out of the reach of ordinary farmers. In February of that year, flour sold in Richmond for $250 per barrel, corn for $30 per bushel, and bacon for $6.50 per pound. Moreover, the Confederate government began to impress at a government price much below market prices all goods of any use to the army. Farmers located near railroads typically lost all their grain and livestock, and large portions of eastern North Carolina were commandeered as pasture for the Army of Northern Virginia's cavalry because pastures in the Shenandoah Valley were now both worn out and vulnerable to Union attack. The final blow came with Union advances into southern Virginia, the Mississippi delta, Tennessee, and northern Alabama, and with William Tecumseh Sherman's march through Georgia and the Carolinas. The devastation of farms in the Confederacy was complete.

In the end, the war to preserve the Southern countryside had transformed it. It had bankrupted commercial farmers and destroyed their capital for a generation. It had turned many poor white farmers against both the Confederate government and neighboring planters. And it had freed the slaves who, after the war, would compete with white farmers for scarce land and credit and later flood the Southern market for agricultural labor, thereby driving down wages. But the war had also created new possibilities. Southern farm men and women who had protested the imposition of unjust prices during the war would do so again in the Southern Alliance and the Populist party. And Southern commercial farmers who had struggled against the deadweight of slavery before 1860 would seize the opportunity to produce a New South rooted in highly commercialized investment agriculture.

[*See also* Bread Riots; Class Conflict; Conscription; Cotton; Desertion; Food; Impressment; Inflation; Plain Folk; Rice; Slavery; Substitutes; Sugar; Taxation; Tobacco.]

BIBLIOGRAPHY

Ash, Stephen A. *Middle Tennessee Society Transformed, 1860–1870: War and Peace in the Upper South.* Baton Rouge, La., 1988.

Auman, William Thomas. "Neighbor against Neighbor: The Inner Civil War in the Central Counties of Confederate North Carolina." Ph.D. diss., University of North Carolina, 1988.

Hahn, Steven. *The Roots of Southern Populism: Yeoman Farmers and the Transformation of the Georgia Upcountry, 1850–1890.* New York, 1983.

Ramsdell, Charles W. *Behind the Lines in the Southern Confederacy.* Baton Rouge, La., 1944.

Simkins, Francis Butler, and James Welch Patton. *The Women of the Confederacy.* Richmond, Va., 1936.

WAYNE K. DURRILL

FARRAND, EBENEZER (1803–1873), naval captain. A New York native, Farrand entered the U.S. Navy in 1823 as a midshipman. He had obtained the rank of commander by the time of his January 21, 1861, resignation from Federal service to follow the Southern cause. Appointed immediately to the same rank in the Confederate navy, Farrand served in rapid succession at Warrington Navy Yard as a member of a commission to purchase or contract for the building of gunboats, as chief of the Light House Bureau, and as commander of the Evansport, Virginia, batteries. From late 1861 through early 1862 he superintended the construction of gunboats at Jacksonville and Milton, Florida, before brief assignment to the Savannah Station.

Farrand was in command of the James River defenses at Drewry's Bluff May 15, 1862, when an attack led by USS *Monitor* was repulsed. For his part in this action he received a joint resolution of thanks from Congress. In July he served as a member of the General Court Martial that absolved Josiah Tattnall of blame in destroying the ironclad *Virginia.*

The following September Farrand was ordered to Alabama to construct ironclad warships. There, he established naval yards, negotiated contracts, and supervised construction at Selma, Oven Bluff, Montgomery, and Mobile. He was promoted to the rank of captain January 7, 1864. With the capture of Adm. Franklin Buchanan at Mobile Bay August 5, 1864, Farrand assumed command of the remaining naval forces afloat in Alabama. He surrendered this small fleet at Nanna Hubba Bluff, on the Tombigbee River, May 4, 1865.

Farrand settled after the war in Montgomery, where he sold insurance. In poor health, he moved to the northeastern Alabama village of Attalla in 1871 and managed a hotel for the Alabama Great Southern Railroad until his death on March 16, 1873.

BIBLIOGRAPHY

Bergeron, Arthur W., Jr. *Confederate Mobile.* Jackson, Miss., 1991.

Martin, Will I. "The Little Known Story of Commodore Farrand." *Gadsden Times,* January 28, 1947.

Register of Officers of the Confederate States Navy, 1861–1865. Washington, D.C., 1931. Reprint, Mattituck, N.Y., 1983.

Still, William N. *Iron Afloat: The Story of the Confederate Armorclads.* 2d ed. Columbia, S.C., 1985.

A. ROBERT HOLCOMBE, JR.

FARROW, JAMES (1827–1892),

congressman from South Carolina. Born April 3, 1827, at Laurens, South Carolina, Farrow was the son of Samuel Farrow, lieutenant governor and state legislator. He graduated from South Carolina College in 1847 and read law in Laurens. He began practicing law in Spartanburg in 1849. An early secessionist, Farrow supported Robert Barnwell Rhett's Bluffton movement in 1844. In 1856 he was elected to the state legislature and served until 1861. He joined James L. Orr's National Democratic faction and was a delegate to the Democratic National Convention in 1856.

After Abraham Lincoln's election in 1860, Farrow supported separate state secession. In 1861 he was elected to Congress from the Fifth District and was reelected in 1863. He served on the Claims and Medical Department committees, and in his second term he also served on the Accounts, Commerce, and Deceased Soldiers' Claims committees. Farrow supported the powers of the central government, except in extreme cases, such as the suspension of the writ of habeas corpus. But he also defended the equality of Congress with the president in setting policy in time of war. He worked to secure adequate care and furloughs for wounded soldiers and backed proposals to allow manufacturers to pay taxes-in-kind, to recruit foreign soldiers, and to excuse women clerks from giving their ages.

In 1865 Farrow was elected to the U.S. Congress, but was refused his seat. He moved to Missouri and served as city judge in Kansas City. In 1875 he became president of Laurens Female College. He served one term in the legislature before his death in 1892.

BIBLIOGRAPHY

Wakelyn, Jon L. *Biographical Dictionary of the Confederacy.* Edited by Frank E. Vandiver. Westport, Conn., 1977.

Warner, Ezra J., and W. Buck Yearns. *Biographical Register of the Confederate Congress.* Baton Rouge, La., 1975.

A. V. HUFF, JR.

FAST DAYS.

Jefferson Davis proclaimed nine days of fasting between June 1861 and March 1865. Along with national fasting days, the governors and legislatures of several states proclaimed occasional days of either thanksgiving or humiliation. Most stores closed, and, when possible, military companies suspended drills. With roots deep in American religious history, fast days have long sounded a call for sacrifice and unity in the name of a high religious goal. Denying themselves food to show religious and political unity may well have held a special meaning for people being asked to sacrifice food for the war effort. Fast days were also times for collecting money for the cause: the call for self-denial served as a call for contributions.

Official days of fasting were part of the effort by Confederate leaders to create the national unity necessary to fight a long and difficult war. Fast-day preachers and secular speakers proclaimed that Southerners were fighting a holy war that pitted a people of high moral standards against a people driven by greed and consumed by immorality. Linking the religious mission of the Confederacy to the stories of the Old Testament, they claimed to represent a new chosen people. One church periodical asserted that military success at Manassas, Chancellorsville, and Chickamauga had followed specific days of fasting.

Preachers used the occasion to castigate Southerners for a host of sins that seemed to stand in the way of the military effort and of the purity of their cause. Drunkenness and adultery seemed especially tempting to men away from their homes, dishonest financial dealings seemed too available with the economic disruption of the war years, the possibility of corruption among political officials seemed more likely with the new powers the government was assuming, and the abuse of slaves seemed more of a problem with opportunities for escape increasing.

On days of fasting, Southerners were urged to examine whether they were living up to the highest of their ideals and to consider the consequences of failure. As Georgian Charles Colcock Jones, Jr., wrote from an army camp, "the nation must be brought to feel their sins and their dependence upon God, not only for their blessings but for their actual salvation from the many and huge dangers which surround us."

It is not easy to determine how fully white Southerners answered the calls for fasting and humiliation. Discussions of the fasts appear often in the letters and diaries of the wealthy, but they are much harder to find in the documents left by the ordinary folk. For example, the diaries of South Carolina farmer David Golightly Harris mentioned the first of the Confederacy's nine fast days, but not the other eight. The call for public fasting ran up against two important Southern traditions. One was a religious tradition that stressed individual conversion rather than group rituals. The second was a political tradition that stressed personal independence rather than obedience to central authority. Despite their less than complete acceptance, however, the fast days were important examples of calls for self-examination and sacrifice.

BIBLIOGRAPHY

Chesebrough, David B., ed. *"God Ordained This War": Sermons on the Sectional Crisis.* Columbia, S.C., 1991.

Daniel, W. Harrison. "Protestantism and Patriotism in the Confederacy." *Mississippi Quarterly* 24 (1971): 117–134.

Faust, Drew G. *The Creation of Confederate Nationalism: Ideology and Identity in the Civil War South.* Baton Rouge, La., 1988.

Myers, Robert Manson, ed. *The Children of Pride: A True Story of Georgia and the Civil War.* New Haven, 1972.

Racine, Philip N., ed. *Piedmont Farmer: The Journals of David Golightly Harris, 1855–1870.* Knoxville, Tenn., 1990.

Silver, James W. *Confederate Morale and Church Propaganda.* New York, 1967.

TED OWNBY

FEARN, THOMAS (1789–1863), congressman from Alabama.

Born in Danville, Virginia, on November 15, 1789, Fearn entered Washington College, Lexington, Virginia, in 1806 and graduated from the Old Medical College at Philadelphia in 1810. He settled in Huntsville, Alabama, where he practiced medicine from 1810 until 1818 when he traveled to Europe to further his medical education. He studied surgery in European hospitals from 1818 to 1820, and became a member of the Royal College of Surgeons in London before returning to his practice in Huntsville. Fearn refused numerous offers to teach at prestigious medical schools. He served in the Alabama House of Representatives from 1822 to 1829. His other activities included service as a surgeon in the Creek Wars, 1812–1814, presidential elector in 1824, trustee of the University of Alabama, trustee of Green Academy in Huntsville, and builder of a canal from the Tennessee River to Huntsville.

In 1861 Fearn served in the Alabama secession convention although he opposed secession. After he took his seat in the Provisional Confederate Congress on February 8, 1861, he announced that he now believed secession necessary. He served on the Public Lands, Special, and Territories committees. Fearn resigned on April 29 because of ill health. He practiced medicine until his death in Huntsville on January 16, 1863.

BIBLIOGRAPHY

Owen, Thomas McAdory. *History of Alabama and Dictionary of Alabama Biography.* 4 vols. Chicago, 1921.

Thornton, J. Mills, III. *Politics and Power in a Slave Society: Alabama, 1800–1860.* Baton Rouge, La., 1978.

Wakelyn, Jon L. *Biographical Directory of the Confederacy.* Edited by Frank E. Vandiver. Westport, Conn., 1977.

Warner, Ezra J., and W. Buck Yearns. *Biographical Register of the Confederate Congress.* Baton Rouge, La., 1975.

SARAH WOOLFOLK WIGGINS

FEATHERSTON, WINFIELD SCOTT (1820–1891), U.S. congressman and brigadier general.

The son of pioneers from Virginia, Featherston was born near Murfreesboro, Tennessee, on August 8, 1820, and developed a taste for armed conflict at an early age. He was attending school in Columbus, Georgia, in 1836 when he abruptly abandoned his studies to help fight the Creek Indians. Later he studied law and was admitted to the bar in Houston, Mississippi, in 1850. Featherston attained prominence in Democratic circles while living in Holly Springs, Mississippi. He served as a U.S. congressman from 1847 to 1851. When war clouds started to gather in 1860, Featherston was sent by his state to Kentucky to consult with authorities there over the issue of secession.

At the outbreak of the war, Featherston was elected colonel of the Seventeenth Mississippi Infantry Regiment. He saw action at First Manassas and Ball's Bluff, where his thunderous voice eclipsed the roar of artillery as he shouted: "Charge, Mississippians, Charge! Drive them into the Potomac or into eternity!" His men did a lot of both. Of commanding presence, standing over six feet in height and known as "Old Swet" to his men, Featherston was promoted to brigadier, March 4, 1862. He was wounded in the Seven Days' campaign but took part in all the battles in Virginia for the remainder of the year.

Relieved of command in early 1863, Featherston was transferred to the western theater at his own request. There he joined W. W. Loring's division in the operations around Vicksburg. When Loring was cut off from John C. Pemberton within the city, the troops marched eastward and joined Joseph E. Johnston's army, thereby escaping capture when Vicksburg fell. Featherston's brigade was in the Battle of Resaca as well as the fighting at Atlanta and southern Tennessee. When Leonidas Polk was killed and Loring assumed temporary command of the corps, Featherston took charge of the division. Featherston accompanied Johnston into the Carolinas and was included in the surrender of the army.

Featherston resumed his law practice after the war and, in 1874, was president of a state taxpayers' convention. He occupied a seat in the state legislature from 1876 to 1878 and again from 1880 to 1882. He led the fight to overthrow the carpetbagger regime of Governor Adelbert Ames. In 1887 he was named judge of the second judicial circuit. Featherston's last public service was as a member of the judiciary committee in the constitutional convention of 1890. He died at Holly Springs, May 28, 1891, and was buried in Hill Creek Cemetery.

BIBLIOGRAPHY

Holien, Kim Bernard. *Battle at Ball's Bluff.* Orange, Va., 1985.

Hooker, Charles E. *Mississippi.* Vol. 7 of *Confederate Military History.* Edited by Clement A. Evans. Atlanta, 1899. Vol. 9 of extended ed. Wilmington, N.C., 1987.

McCaleb, E. Howard. "Featherstone-Posey-Harris Mississippi Brigade." *Southern Historical Society Papers* 32 (1904): 332–334. Reprint, Wilmington, N.C., 1991.

LOWELL REIDENBAUGH

FELTON, REBECCA LATIMER (1835–1930),

journalist and reformer. Born on June 10, 1835, in Decatur, Georgia, Felton, like her siblings, was encouraged by her liberal parents to pursue independence, competitiveness, and scholarship. Felton graduated from Madison Female College in 1852, and a year later married William Harrell Felton. Although they opposed secession from the Union, the Feltons became staunch supporters of the Confederacy once the war started.

For Rebecca Felton, the war proved to be a test of character, strength, and perseverance. Already grieving over the death of her only daughter, she lost both her sons to measles and malaria before the war ended. The trainloads of wounded passing through Carterville after the Battle of Chickamauga also left an indelible mark, and when William Tecumseh Sherman rode through Georgia, the Feltons took refuge in a run-down farmhouse in Macon, where they were terrorized by Union troops. When the Feltons returned to their farm, they found it gutted and overgrown. The experience convinced Felton that women and children were the victims when governments were run by "stupid, cruel men."

After the war, her husband served in the U.S. Congress and the state legislature, with Felton managing his campaigns. She was active in the temperance crusade, lobbied for women's rights, fought for public school funding, and from 1899, wrote a column for the *Atlanta Journal* for twenty years. In 1922, Felton was appointed to fill out the term of U.S. Senator Thomas E. Watson. Since his successor would be elected before Congress convened, it was merely an honorary appointment, but she became the first woman to be seated in the U.S. Senate, if only for a day. Throughout her life, Felton employed a sharp tongue to skewer those she opposed. In her column, she railed against African Americans, Catholics, and Jews, although she defended others whom she believed to be at a disadvantage. She died on January 24, 1930.

BIBLIOGRAPHY

James, Edward T., ed. *Notable American Women: A Biographical Dictionary.* Cambridge, Mass., 1971.

Talmadge, John E. *Rebecca Latimer Felton: Nine Stormy Decades.* Athens, Ga., 1960.

CHRISTINE A. LUNARDINI

FERGUSON, SAMUEL WRAGG (1834–1917),

brigadier general. Born in Charleston, South Carolina, November 3, 1834, Ferguson graduated from the U.S. Military Academy in 1857 (nineteenth of thirty-eight in his class). Until he resigned March 1, 1861, to join the Confederacy, he was a lieutenant in the First U.S. Dragoons.

On March 6, 1861, Ferguson, commissioned captain in the South Carolina army, joined the staff of Brig. Gen. P. G. T. Beauregard. He received the formal surrender of the Federal garrison at Fort Sumter and raised the first Confederate flag over that captured post. He remained on Beauregard's staff until the spring of 1862, but he did transfer to the Confederate army in which he was commissioned lieutenant. When the Twenty-eighth Mississippi Cavalry was organized, Ferguson became the regiment's lieutenant colonel. In 1863 he was briefly colonel of the Fifth South Carolina Cavalry.

For two years Ferguson served in the cavalry in Mississippi, helping to defend that state, winning praise from a superior for his "gallantry, energy, and good service," and being condemned by others for insubordination. On July 28, 1863, he was promoted to brigadier general (with rank to date from July 23). In the spring of 1864 his command was transferred to Georgia, and he helped oppose the Federal advance on Atlanta, Savannah, and through the Carolinas. On May 10, 1865, after serving as part of the escort for the fleeing Jefferson Davis, the command disbanded at Forsyth, Georgia.

Ferguson then practiced law in Greenville, Mississippi. In the 1870s and 1880s he served on government agencies that controlled engineering projects on the Mississippi River. On February 3, 1917, he died in Jackson, Mississippi, and is buried in Greenwood Cemetery there.

BIBLIOGRAPHY

Bergeron, Arthur W., Jr. "Samuel Wragg Ferguson." In *The Confederate General.* Edited by William C. Davis. Vol. 2. Harrisburg, Pa., 1991.

Warner, Ezra J. *Generals in Gray: Lives of the Confederate Commanders.* Baton Rouge, La., 1959.

RICHARD M. McMURRY

FIELD, CHARLES W. (1828–1892), major general.

The Field family had but recently migrated from Virginia to Woodford County, Kentucky, when Charles William Field was born on April 6, 1828. After graduating from West Point in 1849, he served six years in Albert Sidney Johnston's Second U.S. Cavalry. Field was a professor of cavalry tactics at his alma mater for the five years prior to his May 30, 1861, resignation from the army.

His initial Confederate service was as colonel of the Sixth Virginia Cavalry. On March 9, 1862, he received promotion to brigadier general and took command of an infantry brigade consisting of the Fortieth, Forty-seventh, Fifty-fifth, and Sixtieth Virginia. The brigade, part of A. P. Hill's Light Division, led the attack at Mechanicsville that opened the Seven Days' campaign. For the next two months Field was in the thick of the fighting in Virginia. The brigadier's leadership prompted Hill to state: "His gallant bearing and soldierly qualities gave him unbounded influence over his men, and they were ever ready to follow where he led." Stocky, affable, and humorous, "Charlie" Field was a congenial officer with neither ostentation nor driving ambition.

At Second Manassas he received such a severe wound in the leg as to lead some postwar writers to assert falsely that the limb was amputated. The injury kept Field out of action for months. During much of that time, he served in a thankless role as superintendent of the Bureau of Conscription. On February 12, 1864, Field was promoted to major general and assigned to command John Bell Hood's veteran division in James Longstreet's corps. Field hobbled back to duty and became, in the words of Longstreet's chief of staff, "an active and capable commander . . . [of] unquestioned valor."

Field was conspicuous in the May 6, 1864, counterattack in the Wilderness. Four days later, his troops beat back all-day Union assaults in front of Spotsylvania. At Cold Harbor, Fort Harrison, and throughout the Richmond-Petersburg siege, Field provided dependable leadership. He was among the handful of Confederate generals who surrendered with the army on April 9, 1865, at Appomattox. Later that day, Field and his staff received badly needed food as a personal gift from his close friend from prewar days, Federal Gen. John Gibbon.

An extremely varied career followed in the post–Civil War years. Field pursued business ventures for a time and then spent a period as an officer in the Egyptian army. Upon his return to the United States, he served first as doorkeeper of the U.S. House of Representatives and next as a civil engineer for the federal government. His final post was superintendent of the Hot Springs, Arkansas, reservation. Following his death on April 9, 1892, Field was buried in Baltimore's Loudon Park Cemetery.

The Kentuckian was not a flashy commander of troops. Solid rather than brilliant, a professional soldier to the core, Field was the kind of general who was always with his troops and never disappointing.

BIBLIOGRAPHY

Field, Charles W. "Campaign of 1864 and 1865." *Southern Historical Society Papers* 14 (1886): 542–563. Reprint, Wilmington, N.C., 1990.

Freeman, Douglas S. *Lee's Lieutenants: A Study in Command.* 3 vols. New York, 1942–1944. Reprint, New York, 1986.

Johnston, J. Stoddard. *Kentucky.* Vol. 9 of *Confederate Military History.* Edited by Clement A. Evans. Atlanta, 1899. Vol. 11 of extended ed. Wilmington, N.C., 1988.

JAMES I. ROBERTSON, JR.

FILE CLOSERS. The main assault formation used by Civil War soldiers, North and South, was well over two hundred years old when the war began. Based on a system invented by Gustavus Adolphus in the mid-1600s, Civil War assault formations were generally linear to take advantage of the firepower of the musket. Soldiers, facing their enemy, lined up shoulder to shoulder in lines that were two deep, one directly behind the other. These lines, separated by thirteen inches, were called ranks. A file was the formation that resulted from positioning one soldier behind the other. Officers and noncommissioned officers—for instance, the commanding officer and first sergeant or sergeant major—took their places as prescribed by regulations.

The tactical manuals of the day stated: "The remaining officers and sergeants will be posted as file closers, and two paces behind the rear rank." The file closers were to ensure that the formation stayed in strict alignment as it advanced. When casualties occurred, as they inevitably did in Civil War assaults, and men dropped out of formation, the file closers ordered men in their vicinity to move to the right or left to fill the hole the casualty created.

As the Civil War came to its bloody close and discipline broke down in the Confederate armies, file closers were given another, far more deadly, assignment. On February 22, 1865, Gen. Robert E. Lee issued General Order Number 4, directing that file closers on the march were to prevent straggling and that in action they were always to have "loaded guns and fixed bayonets." They were to maintain discipline and

use such degree of force as may be necessary. If any refuse to advance, disobey orders, or leave the ranks to plunder or to retreat, the file-closer will promptly cut down or fire upon the delinquents.

Lee's harsh order giving peremptory execution authority to file closers was generally ignored. In an army where comradeship was more important than military discipline, for one Confederate soldier to shoot or bayonet another was more than even General Lee could ask for from his men.

FILE CLOSERS AT SHARPSBURG, MARYLAND.

THE SOLDIER IN OUR CIVIL WAR

BIBLIOGRAPHY

Hardee, William J. *Rifle and Light Infantry Tactics.* Philadelphia, 1855.

Mahon, John K. "Civil War Infantry Assault Tactics." In *Military Analysis of the Civil War.* Millwood, N.Y., 1977.

Scott, H. L. *Military Dictionary.* New York, 1864.

U.S. War Department. *War of Rebellion: Official Records of the Union and Confederate Armies.* Washington, D.C., 1880–1901. Ser. 1, vol. 46, pt. 2, pp. 1249–1250.

P. NEAL MEIER

FILM AND VIDEO. [*This entry consists of two articles,* Documentary Film and Video *and* Fictional Presentations.]

Documentary Film and Video

At most only several minutes long, the first motion pictures depended heavily on instantly recognizable and popular subjects such as the Civil War to attract audiences. Newsreels of current events—the earliest form of documentary—were especially suitable. The activities of the Grand Army of the Republic and other Northern veterans' groups dominated most of the first productions, but the South, too, provided material for scores of brief silent documentary films. Universal Film's Animated Weekly, International News, Mutual Weekly, Reel Life, Screen Telegram, and the Selig-Tribune recorded Confederate veterans' reunions at Macon (1912), Arlington National Cemetery (1913), Gettysburg (1913), Atlanta (1914), Richmond (1915), Birmingham (1916), Washington, D.C. (1917), Corinth (1926), Tampa (1927), Little Rock (1928), and Charlotte (1929). A 1925 Pathe Weekly news short of a Dallas reunion even featured eighty-two-year-old veteran A. B. Willy introducing his new bride to his former compatriots.

Besides showing the usual parades and encampments, these early films occasionally included interviews with former Confederate soldiers, with the spoken words printed on cards. The productions also included insights into the sometimes unreconstructed Southern mind-set. A 1914 Animated Weekly news film depicted a delegation of United Confederate Veterans preparing to urge Congress to add the Cross of Saint Andrew to the U.S. flag. More remarkable, the Gaumont Weekly series filmed reunions of former slaves and their former masters in Birmingham (1913) and Washington, D.C. (1916).

There were far more instances, however, of sectional reconciliation. A 1909 Columbia Photograph Company newsreel featured President William Howard Taft meeting with assembled Confederate and Union veterans in Petersburg, Virginia. Several films (1914, 1917, 1923) recorded Woodrow Wilson reviewing veterans' parades or greeting members of the United Daughters of the Confederacy. Perhaps most moving to audiences both North and South were the documented returns of captured battle flags to Confederate or Union groups or representatives.

Many of the silent shorts, especially those marking the war's fiftieth anniversary, emphasized how quickly the past was fading. A 1911 Powers Studio film featured veterans' distant reminiscences; in 1912 the Edison company depicted disabled veterans at Hampton, Virginia; the Lubin company in 1913 presented elderly former Confederate and Union soldiers reunited at Gettysburg. Still later, in 1923, several newsreel companies recorded the U.S. Marines' reenactment of Pickett's Charge, watched by veterans too infirm to do more than feebly stand aside and cheer. An Urban-Kineto production, *Romantic Richmond* (1924), presented a city filled with both wartime memories and old soldiers.

The various film companies also captured the increasingly strong Southern urge to memorialize the Lost Cause. A 1918 Universal Animated Weekly newsreel recorded Virginia governor Henry Carter Stuart gratefully accepting the sword of the late Camille J. Polignac, a French nobleman and esteemed Confederate major general. Monument dedications in cities large and small were frequent subjects, but none more so than the Confederate Memorial at Stone Mountain, Georgia. International News featured sculptor Gutzon Borglum three times in 1924, his angry destruction of the models the next year, the appointment of a successor, Augustus Lukeman, in 1926, and scenes of the dedication (with a separate version distributed only in Atlanta) in 1928.

But while those productions recorded current news events, several film companies, government agencies, and corporations also began experimenting with retrospective views. The Mutual Film Corporation, for example, in 1916 included tours of Chattanooga, Chickamauga, Gettysburg, Montgomery, Vicksburg, and the Richmond defenses in its *See America First* series. A ten-minute 1921 Ford Motor Company documentary was among the first to explore Civil War personalities and causes. And in another innovation, the U.S. Army Signal Corps produced several training films utilizing Confederate and Union troop movements, including *Concentrations for the Battle of Gettysburg* (1924).

With the advent of sound recording in the late 1920s, film's dramatic possibilities increased. The Signal Corps, for instance, recorded Marshall Foch's 1936 visit to Richmond where he reviewed Civil War veterans. A year later, the Virginia Conservation Commission financed *Richmond under Three Flags,* which featured the Confederate Memorial Institute's Battle Abbey shrine. The Smithsonian Institution in 1934 filmed archaeological excavations at the Shiloh National Monument in Tennessee, and the National Park Service funded *Heart of the Confederacy* (1937) and

They Met at Gettysburg (1938), the latter featuring Confederate veteran William H. Jackson's tour of the battlefield. Southern military history furnished especially useful lessons during World War II. The U.S. Army's 1941 animated eight-minute training film, *The Battle of Chancellorsville,* presented basic strategic and tactical concepts to inductees.

Controlling production, distribution, and theaters, too, the major Hollywood studios during the 1930s produced the most documentaries—mostly as brief fillers to accompany their major releases. More travelogue than documentary, Warner Brothers' *The Blue and the Gray* and *Dixieland* (both 1935) presented tours of Southern monuments. The studio's Vitaphone subsidiary in 1937 presented *Under Southern Stars,* an account of Lee and Jackson at Chancellorsville. Sometimes feature films were severely recut as documentaries. MGM's *Tennessee Johnson,* released in 1942, provided enough footage five years later for two educational films: *Jefferson Davis Declares Secession* and *Johnson and Reconstruction.* Newsreels also remained popular, in the 1930s and 1940s featuring centenarian Confederate veterans, reunions in Biloxi (1930) and Chattanooga (1942), the famed 1938 Gettysburg reenactment, and a remarkable 1942 Movietone News short of aged veterans beside army trainees at Fort Oglethorpe, Georgia.

By the 1950s changes in audience demographics and the Federal government's antitrust actions dismantling the studios' long-time monopoly of all phases of film production and presentation caused a decline in commercial documentary filmmaking. Besides, there were few veterans left alive to film. The government, however, continued production: the U.S. Navy in 1958 and 1959 produced studies of the maritime war; the army in 1957 completed a brief film on Civil War photography; and the Defense Department in 1956 sponsored four thirty-minute films on the struggle to end slavery. Corporations such as E. I. du Pont Nemours, McGraw-Hill, and Nationwide Insurance also funded several films.

The rapid growth of television, especially network news divisions, fostered scores of dramatized documentaries. The CBS News *You Are There* series narrated by Walter Cronkite included programs on the Emancipation Proclamation (1955), death of Stonewall Jackson (1955), capture of John Wilkes Booth (1956), the Appomattox surrender (1956), and the attack on Fort Sumter (1957). The NBC network countered with *Gentleman's Decision* (1961), a dramatization of Lee's surrender. A St. Louis television station in 1955 produced *The War between the States* and *The War's Aftermath* for its *Young USA* program.

Animated maps and period photography dominated documentary and educational films in the post-1945 years. Productions such as MGM's *The Battle of Gettysburg* (1959) emphasized military maneuver, a tendency particularly evident in the site-specific films produced during and after the Civil War Centennial for battlefield parks, historic sites, and museums. Coronet Instructional Films, the Encyclopaedia Britannica, and Film Associates of California were among the few educational film producers that attempted any analysis of Confederate economic, geographic, social, and political conditions. In the 1970s television, too, retreated from Civil War topics; producer David Wolper's re-creation of the trial of Henry Wirz, commander of Andersonville prison, was among the rare exceptions.

Two recent productions—*The Divided Union* (1987) and *The Civil War* (1990)—in effect have carried documentary explorations of the Confederacy to the extreme in both length and variety of period images. Produced and written by Ken Burns, Ric Burns, and Geoffrey C. Ward for PBS affiliate WETA, of Washington, D.C., the nine-part *Civil War* won more than a dozen awards, including two Emmys and a George Foster Peabody citation. Although less familiar, the five-hour *Divided Union,* created by English producer-director Peter Batty, also balances period photography and artwork, newsreel footage, and excerpts from Civil War letters, diaries, and personal reminiscences in a presentation of both Confederate and Union military history. *The Divided Union* differs, though, in that it also includes considerable footage of reenactments by living-history interpreters, a recently popular and rapidly expanding mode of quasi-documentary film that includes, for example, introductions to Civil War era weaponry, battlefield and site tours, and histories of various engagements. Companies such as Time-Life, which distributes *The Video History of the Civil War,* produce the films primarily for home distribution.

BIBLIOGRAPHY

Fielding, Raymond. *The American Newsreel, 1911–1967.* Norman, Okla., 1972.

Jacobs, Lewis, comp. *The Documentary Tradition.* New York, 1979.

Spehr, Paul C., comp. *The Civil War in Motion Pictures: A Bibliography of Films Produced in the United States since 1897.* Washington, D.C., 1961.

EDWARD D. C. CAMPBELL, JR.

Fictional Presentations

David O. Selznick hesitated to purchase the film rights to Margaret Mitchell's *Gone with the Wind.* Knowing the odds against any Civil War movie earning a profit, particularly after the recent disaster, *So Red the Rose,* Selznick had to be repeatedly prodded into action. The Civil War required a heavy investment in props, costumes, and complex settings, and such movies required deftly handled, inoffensive stories that could play in theaters both North and South.

The same factors had influenced the production of silent films, but the early motion pictures' briefer format helped alleviate several cost factors. More important, because the war remained such a vivid event for most audiences, fictional films in many instances served as exciting retrospectives. Hundreds of these early films featured Southern stories. Produced by studios such as Biograph, Broncho, Champion, Edison, New York Motion Picture, Triangle, and Universal, the films often revolved around themes of sectional reconciliation. In *A Reconstructed Rebel,* for example, a former Confederate fights as a U.S. Marine in Honduras. Thomas H. Ince produced perhaps the most outlandish of the type, *A Southern Cinderella* (1913), with the beautiful Southern Cinderella left under the care of her wicked Yankee stepmother. Vitagraph's *The Carpenter; or the Stranger in Gray* (1914) was the most extreme example of the genre: a mysterious Christ-like carpenter brings peace to a family divided by the war.

The Kalem studio's *Southern Boy of '61* (1911) was one of numerous stories in which a Confederate spares a blue-uniformed family member encountered in battle. Many more Civil War plots were, however, more overtly Southern in tone. In D. W. Griffith's *In Old Kentucky* (1909), the protagonist abandons his family rather than listen to Unionist sentiment; in *The Flag of His Country* (1910), a Southern wife deserts her husband after his enlistment in the Federal army. A few were more ambivalent. In Griffith's *The Honor of His Family* (1910), a Confederate officer kills his son for desertion under fire and then to spare the family reputation places the body among his fallen Southern comrades. Other productions harped on the sometimes violent hatreds spawned by the war. In the Selig studio's *Brother against Brother* (1909), rival siblings try to murder one another; in *The Boomerang* (1913), a Union soldier kills his father, a Confederate officer who had deserted him years before; and in *A Rose of the South* (1916), two lifelong friends kill each other in battle, determined to die true to their respective causes. Wartime events and legends furnished several early movie plots; *Barbara Frietchie,* for example, became a staple for several studios, with productions released in 1908, 1911, 1915, and 1924.

Usually presented as loyal slaves and acted by whites in blackface, African American characters were a prominent part of numerous Confederate stories. In both *The Confederate Spy* (1910) and *The Informer* (1912), "happy, contented, and well cared for" blacks defend their masters' homes against Union troops. Uncle Wash, in *Hearts and Flags* (1911), protects his mistress from foragers. The famous minstrel performer Lew Dockstader, playing the title role in *Dan* (1914), rescues his master from Union captors. D. W. Griffith's *His Trust* and *His Trust Fulfilled* (both 1911) tell of the slave Old George, charged with protecting the plantation during the war. After his master's

FROM *THE WARRENS OF VIRGINIA*, 1915. Raymond Hatton as the Spy in Cecil B. DeMille's film adaptation of the play by William C. deMille, later remade in 1924.   THE MUSEUM OF MODERN ART, FILM STILLS ARCHIVE, NEW YORK

death in battle, it is George who cares for his owner's child—and his sword.

Several directors attempted large-scale productions years before D. W. Griffith's *Birth of a Nation* (1915). Thomas H. Ince, for example, completed an expensive five-reel epic, *The Battle of Gettysburg* (1913), approximately an hour long and complete with special bookings and advance tickets. Released the same year, the Kalem studio's *Shenandoah* included hundreds of extras in Virginia battle scenes. Almost as many reels in length, it was cut at the last moment, as the studio feared no one would sit through so long a picture. Griffith had no such fears. Adapted from clergyman Thomas Dixon's novel and successful play *The Clansman*, Griffith's monumental epic was, in fact, a second attempt at filming the story. The Kinemacolor studio had initiated a color version of Dixon's story shot at

authentic Southern locations, but the company eventually ran afoul of financial and technical problems.

Griffith also ran short of money but remained determined that his production be realistic in every detail. Although his interpretation of the war and black-white relations aroused strident protests, his depictions of military life were universally praised. Griffith studied minute details of uniform types, weapons, and fortifications, often arriving on locations with a stack of books under one arm and his pockets overflowing with scribbled notes. In his earlier films such as *The Battle* (1911), Griffith had already experimented with filming swirling scenes of combat; thus for *Birth of a Nation* he was able to stage elaborate scenes of combat so exciting that even Northern audiences found themselves sometimes cheering for the besieged Confederates.

FROM *BIRTH OF A NATION*, 1915. *Above:* Ben ("Little Colonel") Cameron, played by Henry B. Walthall, at left, baptizes the cross of fire during a Ku Klux Klan ceremony in the woods. W. D. Griffith's use of racial stereotypes in his portrayal of African Americans and his assertion that the Klan was heroic drew heavy protest from many film audiences. *Below:* Cameron being pulled wounded into Union trenches at Petersburg by boyhood friend Phil Stoneman, played by Elmer Clifton.   THE MUSEUM OF MODERN ART, FILM STILLS ARCHIVE, NEW YORK

FROM *SECRET SERVICE,* 1919.   Union spy being questioned at a Confederate telegraph station. During and after World War I, the American public became increasingly frightened and intrigued by espionage. The motion picture industry responded accordingly. Three versions of this film alone were produced in sixteen years.   THE MUSEUM OF MODERN ART, FILM STILLS ARCHIVE, NEW YORK

Still studied and debated for its interpretation of the antebellum and postwar South, *Birth of a Nation* also deserves attention for its view of the war itself. Griffith and his technicians attempted to evoke the conflict's massive sweep, variety, and losses on a scale that has never been repeated. Facing financial constraints himself, David Selznick did not even seriously consider adding such large-scale combat scenes to *Gone with the Wind*. Released only a week after *Birth of a Nation,* Cecil B. DeMille's *The Warrens of Virginia* was produced on a smaller scale but was equally biased in its scenes of African American unrest, Confederate dead, and the destroyed Southern landscape. (The film was remade in 1924 with less success.)

Buster Keaton's *The General* (1926), based on James J. Andrews and his Union raiders' attempt to destroy a Confederate rail route, used the war as a comic foil. The Kalem studio had used the same plot for *The Railroad Raiders of '62* (1911); Walt Disney would again in 1956. Filmed in Oregon, Keaton's masterpiece, despite its farcical spirit, included several well-directed battle scenes and a period narrow-gauge railway. Moreover, Bert Haines and Devereaux Jennings provided a cinematography that captured much of the feeling of Mathew Brady's Civil War images. In 1939, an elderly Keaton appeared in yet another Civil War film, *Mooching through Georgia.*

By the advent of sound films in the late 1920s, studios had found the Civil War an increasingly awkward subject. Although movies about the prewar South provided escapist entertainment, productions on the Confederacy itself tended to alienate the predominantly non-Southern moviegoer. One way around the impasse was to rely on spy stories, stories that audiences perceived more as mysteries than as sectional dramas. *Secret Service* (1931), for example, first produced as a silent film in 1915 and again in 1919,

FROM *BARBARA FRIETCHIE*, 1924.   Florence Vidor, center, in the title role. Frietchie's legend was a favorite in Hollywood, where it served as the basis for four separate film versions. The 1924 release was adapted from the play by Clyde Fitch and directed by Lambert Hillyev.

THE MUSEUM OF MODERN ART, FILM STILLS ARCHIVE, NEW YORK

depicted a Union infiltrator at work in Richmond; *Operator 13* (1934) starred Marion Davies as a disguised mulatto spy. Also safe were musicals such as *The Littlest Rebel* (1935) starring Shirley Temple and Bill ("Bojangles") Robinson.

Hollywood nevertheless occasionally ventured into more serious plots. The 1928 version of *The Little Shepherd of Kingdom Come* (first adapted from the John Fox, Jr., novel in 1920) starred Richard Barthelmess as a Kentucky-raised lad torn between secession and the Union. Hardly as ambivalent was Paramount's *So Red the Rose* (1935), loosely adapted from a Stark Young novel. Simultaneously premiered in each of the former Confederate capitals and with advertisements to "see the Old South ride again," it was a box-office disaster. The movie's setting was so romanticized and its characters so stereotyped, even within the context of films made in the 1930s, that black actor

Daniel Haynes at first refused to work in Hollywood again, and director King Vidor, a Southerner, avoided even mentioning the film in his later autobiography. Small wonder David Selznick was nervous in adapting Margaret Mitchell's *Gone with the Wind*.

GWTW, as it became popularly known, consumed at least seven script writers, including F. Scott Fitzgerald, as well as six directors but opened in Atlanta at last in December 1939. It proved so popular that the South's smaller and fewer movie theaters often had to delay showings so that Selznick and the film's distributor, Metro-Goldwyn-Mayer, could meet the demand of larger audiences elsewhere. Like *Birth of a Nation*, *GWTW*'s scenes were carefully researched. Griffith served as his own expert; Selznick hired his, including Atlanta historian Wilbur G. Kurtz. And although, like Griffith's film, the Civil War scenes comprised the shortest portion of *GWTW*, the

FROM *THE GENERAL*, 1926. *Above:* Buster Keaton riding the engine *Texas* in pursuit of his own engine, *The General*, earlier stolen by Confederates. Keaton is attempting to throw a railroad tie at obstructions placed on the tracks by the fleeing Southerners. *Below:* Keaton peers out of a Western & Atlantic Railroad car attached to the wrecked engine *Texas*. The same car had been used earlier in the film as a U.S. Military Railroad car (note the initials "U.S.M.R.R." visible beneath the initials "W.&.A.R.R"). After the film was completed, the engine and car sat in the river for fifteen years, until they were sold for scrap in 1941 during the metal drives in World War II.

THE MUSEUM OF MODERN ART, FILM STILLS ARCHIVE, NEW YORK

FROM *SO RED THE ROSE,* 1935. Margaret Sullavan, at left, recovers the body of the family's son for burial.

overcrowded hospitals, the battlefield covered with dead, the panic at the fall of Atlanta, seemed even starker in contrast.

Despite *Gone with the Wind*'s enormous success, few similar films followed, in part because Confederate themes hardly complied with the government's World War II restrictions that films comport with Allied war aims to free suppressed peoples. *Dark Command* and *Virginia City* (both 1940), Civil War westerns, were permissible, in large part because of their more neutral setting. Studios eventually produced scores of such western films, including *Escape from Fort Bravo* (1953), Sam Peckinpah's *Major Dundee* (1965), the Italian-made *The Hills Run Red* (1967), *The Outlaw Josie Wales* (1976), and *The Long Riders* (1980). Similarly, *The Raid* (1954), directed by Argentinian Hugo Fregonese, depicted an attack by Confederate marauders on a small Vermont town. Although set in the South, *Tap*

Roots (1948) and *Shenandoah* (1965) were acceptable, as both depicted families opposed to the war; *Band of Angels* (1957) seemed more a vehicle for its star (Clark Gable) than its setting; and *The Horse Soldiers* (1959), directed by John Ford, focused on its Union protagonists.

Television has provided a middle ground, with miniseries that move characters and incidents between the opposing sides. The CBS network touted the eight-hour *The Blue and the Gray* (1982) as an educational production, and ABC advertised its twelve-hour *North and South* Civil War segments (1986) as a "novel for television." Like many of their precursors, both films were elaborate costume romances with ample chances for fictional characters to encounter historical personalities, reconfirming that the genre presents not so much significant historical events interpreted with incidental stories as the reverse—fiction embellished with period detail.

BIBLIOGRAPHY

Campbell, Edward D. C., Jr. *The Celluloid South: Hollywood and the Southern Myth.* Knoxville, Tenn., 1981.

Cassidy, John M. *Civil War Cinema: A Pictorial History of Hollywood and the War between the States.* Missoula, Mont., 1986.

Spears, Jack. *The Civil War on the Screen and Other Essays.* New York, 1977.

Spehr, Paul C., comp. *The Civil War in Motion Pictures: A Bibliography of Films Produced in the United States since 1897.* Washington, D.C., 1961.

EDWARD D. C. CAMPBELL, JR.

FINEGAN, JOSEPH (1814–1885), brigadier general.

A native of Clones, Ireland, Finegan was born November 17, 1814, and migrated to America while still in his twenties. After establishing himself as a lawyer and planter, he built and operated a lumber mill in Jacksonville, Florida. Later he moved to Fernandina where he was involved in railroad construction with U.S. Senator David L. Yulee.

Finegan was a member of the secession convention and was appointed by Governor John Milton early in the war to command the military district of middle and eastern Florida. He was commissioned brigadier general on April 5, 1862.

Finegan's most significant achievement in his home state occurred at the Battle of Olustee in February 1864. When Federal forces invaded Florida, hopeful of a resounding victory that would hasten the state's return to the Union, Finegan, though inexperienced in war, met the enemy's superior forces at Olustee, sixty miles west of Jacksonville. Fighting in a pine forest, the Confederates routed the enemy and terminated Northern efforts to proselytize the state. In acknowledging the victory, the Confederate Congress adopted a resolution expressing thanks to Finegan "and the officers and men of his command for the skill and gallantry displayed" at Olustee.

In May 1864, Finegan was sent to Virginia at the head of a brigade that had been consolidated with that of Edward A. Perry. Finegan's regiments immediately enhanced their reputation as fighters. When Federals broke through a weak spot in John C. Breckinridge's line at Cold Harbor, Finegan rushed his men into the breach and, in a desperate struggle, drove back the assailants with heavy losses. Finegan remained with the Army of Northern Virginia until March 1865 when he was reassigned to Florida.

After the war, Finegan returned to his law practice and won a seat in the state senate (1865–1866). He was also a cotton broker in Savannah, Georgia. His closing years were spent in Rutledge, Georgia, where he died October 29, 1885. He was buried in Old City Cemetery in Jacksonville.

BIBLIOGRAPHY

Beauregard, P. G. T. "Battle of Ocean Pond, Florida." *Southern Historical Society Papers* 9 (1881): 116–120. Reprint, Wilmington, N.C., 1990.

Dickison, J. J. *Florida.* Vol. 11 of *Confederate Military History.* Edited by Clement A. Evans. Atlanta, 1899. Vol. 16 of extended ed. Wilmington, N.C., 1989.

Rice, J. G. "The Battle of Olustee." *Confederate Veteran* 22 (1914): 244–245. Reprint, Wilmington, N.C., 1985.

Warner, Ezra J. *Generals in Gray: Lives of the Confederate Commanders.* Baton Rouge, La., 1959.

LOWELL REIDENBAUGH

FINGAL. See entry on the ship Atlanta.

FINLEY, JESSE JOHNSON (1812–1904), brigadier general, U.S. congressman, and judge.

Born November 18, 1812, in Wilson County, Tennessee, Finley studied law and in the 1830s served against the Seminole Indians in Florida. A popular, peripatetic man, Finley moved to Arkansas in 1840, where he was elected to the state senate the next year. In 1842 he moved to Memphis and was elected mayor in 1845. He then moved in 1846 to Marianna, Florida, where in 1850 he won election to the Florida senate. A Whig presidential elector in 1852, he was appointed circuit judge of the Western District of Florida in 1853.

Finley labored to bring about Florida's secession. Resigning from the (then Confederate) court in 1862, he joined the Sixth Florida Infantry. He was elected captain and, after a few months, colonel of the regiment. His unit joined the Army of Tennessee. Finley distinguished himself at Chickamauga (September 19–20, 1863), and in November he was appointed brigadier general. He was assigned to command the Florida Brigade in the Army of Tennessee.

Twice wounded in the 1864 Atlanta campaign, Finley did not recover in time to rejoin the army. Late in the war he served briefly with Maj. Gen. Howell Cobb in Georgia and surrendered there.

Finley lived in Lake City and Jacksonville, Florida, after the war. He served in the national House of Representatives (1875–1879) and as circuit court judge (1887–1903). He died in Lake City, November 6, 1904, and is buried in Evergreen Cemetery, Gainesville, Florida.

BIBLIOGRAPHY

Dickison, J. J. *Florida.* Vol. 11 of *Confederate Military History.* Edited by Clement A. Evans. Atlanta, 1899. Vol. 16 of extended ed. Wilmington, N.C., 1988.

Jones, Terry L. "Jesse Johnson Finley." In *The Confederate General.* Edited by William C. Davis. Vol. 2. Harrisburg, Pa., 1991.

RICHARD M. MCMURRY

FIRE-EATERS.

FIRE-EATERS. Southern proslavery and state rights extremists were termed the fire-eaters in the two decades before the Civil War. The image evoked by the term was that of swaggering hotheads intent on breaking up the Union in their defense of slavery and Southern rights. The most famous of the fire-eaters were Edmund Ruffin of Virginia, an agricultural reformer; Robert Barnwell Rhett, Sr., of South Carolina, an editor and low-country planter; and William Lowndes Yancey of Alabama, a lawyer and gifted orator.

The fire-eaters were the ideologues of secession. They identified the ownership of slaves as the most fundamental of all Southern rights and insisted that Southern honor and equality could accept no outside interference with the institution of slavery. They pushed traditional state rights doctrines to the logically extreme position that states could peacefully withdraw from the Union.

Too impatient and scornful of compromise to be entrusted with positions of political power, the fire-eaters turned to agitation to spread their message that Southern honor and security demanded separate nationhood. Through speeches, pamphlets, editorials, and committees of correspondence they popularized secession as a constitutional right among the Southern white masses.

Although blocked in their secessionist efforts during the sectional crisis over the Compromise of 1850, the fire-eaters played a key role in the secession movement of 1860 and 1861. They were instrumental in the breakup of the national Democratic party over the issue of Federal protection of slavery in the territories and fully exploited Southern fears over Abraham Lincoln's election. Nevertheless, they were soon shunted aside as more moderate politicians assumed control of the new Confederate government.

BIBLIOGRAPHY

Barney, William L. *The Road to Secession.* New York, 1972.
Craven, Avery. *Edmund Ruffin, Southerner.* New York, 1932.
DuBose, John. *The Life and Times of William Lowndes Yancey.* Birmingham, Ala., 1892.
McCardell, John. *The Idea of a Southern Nation: Southern Nationalists and Southern Nationalism.* New York, 1979.
White, Laura A. *Robert Barnwell Rhett: Father of Secession.* New York, 1931.

WILLIAM L. BARNEY

FISHER'S HILL, VIRGINIA.

FISHER'S HILL, VIRGINIA. Called a "Gibraltar" by some Confederate soldiers, this hill overlooking Strasburg, Virginia, in the Shenandoah Valley was the site of the defeat of Lt. Gen. Jubal Early's Army of the Valley by Maj. Gen. Philip Sheridan's Union forces on September 22, 1864. Early lost 1,300 men (most of them captured) out of a force of under 10,000 while Sheridan's 35,000 suffered fewer than 500 casualties.

The battle served as a sequel to the Third Battle of Winchester on September 19, when Sheridan's Army of the Shenandoah, after a stubborn, day-long fight, forced the Confederates up the Valley Pike roughly twenty miles south to Fisher's Hill. Early believed that if he did not hold at Fisher's Hill, he would have to give ground to gaps in the Blue Ridge Mountains, at Charlottesville or at Gordonsville. He also hoped the ground offered enough natural defenses to discourage a Federal attack.

In August, "Old Jube" had positioned his army at Fisher's Hill while testing the mettle of his opponent. Acting somewhat cautiously then, Sheridan had earned the disdain of Early. But the Confederate general soon learned that the circumstances of August had changed.

The way Early positioned his troops has provoked repeated and justified criticism. To cover a line along Tumbling Run from the North Fork of the Shenandoah on the right to the Little North Mountain on the left, Early needed to stretch his command over nearly four miles—too much for his meager numbers. In order from the right, he placed the divisions of Gabriel Wharton, John B. Gordon, John Pegram, and Dodson Ramseur. This left a mile-long gap to Little North Mountain, which Early filled with only a thin line of dismounted cavalry under Brig. Gen. Lunsford Lindsay Lomax. These troopers consisted of poorly equipped, ill-disciplined, and demoralized men. Such an array squandered manpower where they were needed least—protecting the imposing Fisher's Hill which one Vermonter called "a huge, high-fronted billow of earth and rocks, which . . . became strangled between these two mountains and held still, with its frowning crest looking northward."

Sheridan took his time studying the Confederate position and crafting his battle plan. He decided to send cavalrymen up the Luray Valley to the east of Early to work their way behind the Confederates and cut off an escape, while the Eighth Corps under Maj. Gen. George Crook marched along Little North Mountain to launch the major attack on the Confederate left. Horatio G. Wright's Sixth Corp and William H. Emory's Nineteenth would occupy the Confederate center and right. Sheridan hoped to surprise the Southerners and wanted Crook's troops to mask their movements as much as possible from the Confederate observers on Three Top Mountain. A future president of the United States, Col. Rutherford B. Hayes, commanded one of the two divisions that would make the attack. The Eighth Corps moved into camp at night on September 21 and before dawn the next day began the advance through the woods, ravines, and cedar thickets of Little North Mountain.

For Early's men, September 22 dawned with the popping of gunfire among pickets that lasted until midday. At 1:00

P.M., a portion of the Federals in front of Ramseur's division stabbed at the Southern lines but stopped after clearing out skirmishers. Old Jube apparently began to have second thoughts about the ability of his troops to hold their ground and sometime between 2:00 and 3:00 P.M. issued orders for a withdrawal that night. But it was not to be an orderly departure. About 4:00, the divisions of Hayes and Col. Joseph Thoburn burst from the woods on the Confederate flank like "a western cyclone" and scattered Lomax's cavalry. Early attempted to shift troops, but only created more confusion as the lines melted in the general advance joined by the Sixth and Nineteenth Corps. Artillery covered the fleeing Southerners, which saved some lives while costing fourteen guns.

Early's army eluded the Union cavalry and staggered up the valley, reaching Waynesboro on September 28. The attack may have been a turning point in the confidence the soldiers had in their lieutenant general. Sheridan, meanwhile, spent the next few weeks in the valley systematically destroying crops and facilities in what residents called "The Burning." The Confederates, however, were not completely defeated. Early's army launched one more attack on Sheridan's forces at Cedar Creek on October 19, only to suffer a final rout that wrested the valley from Confederate control.

BIBLIOGRAPHY

Early, Jubal A. *Autobiographical Sketch and Narrative of the War between the States.* Philadelphia, 1912. Reprint, Wilmington, N.C., 1989.

Gallagher, Gary W., ed. *Struggle for the Shenandoah: Essays on the 1864 Valley Campaign.* Kent, Ohio, 1991.

Wert, Jeffry D. *From Winchester to Cedar Creek: The Shenandoah Campaign of 1864.* Carlisle, Pa., 1987.

Williams, T. Harry. *Hayes of the Twenty-third: The Civil War Volunteer Officer.* New York, 1965.

WILLIAM ALAN BLAIR

FITZHUGH, GEORGE (1806–1881), proslavery polemicist and Treasury clerk. Born on the Brenttown tract in Prince William County, Virginia, Fitzhugh became one of the Old South's most interesting, but hardly its most popular or important, defender of slavery. With relatively little formal schooling and claiming, perhaps questionably, descent from Virginia's distinguished Fitzhughs, he set up a law practice in Port Royal, Caroline County, in 1829. Never very successful at law or in providing a sufficient income to support his wife and nine children, Fitzhugh turned to lecturing and writing on slavery, the failures of capitalism, the conditions of labor in free society, and a perfected slaveholding South.

In his first book, *Sociology for the South; or the Failure of Free Society* (1854), he seized upon a growing body of literature critical of the condition of labor in industrialized England and America to defend slaveholding as a beneficent system. In his next book, *Cannibals All! or, Slaves without Masters* (1857), he carried the attack further afield by suggesting that degraded free labor or "wage slaves" would be better cared for if they were placed under responsible slavemasters. In these and all of Fitzhugh's writings, he took an intriguing idea—a provocative and potentially useful insight—and proceeded to sensationalize it beyond reason. He did this so consistently in virtually all of his writings that he was never taken seriously by his contemporaries and was virtually forgotten after the Civil War until he was rediscovered by historians in the twentieth century.

Fitzhugh, nevertheless, used his trenchant pen to borrow liberally from thinkers ranging from Adam Smith to Karl Marx, Carlyle to Comte, and particularly from a growing group of Southern intellectuals (Albert Taylor Bledsoe, George F. Holmes, James H. Hammond) to illustrate his steady stream of articles and publications. While serving briefly after 1856 as an attorney in the land claims office of the U.S. attorney general, he came to know James D. B. De Bow, publisher of *De Bow's Review* in New Orleans. Between 1857 and 1867, Fitzhugh was one of De Bow's most faithful and constantly published contributors. *De Bow's Review* became Fitzhugh's single reliable outlet for his fertile imagination.

While Fitzhugh continuously flirted with cutting-edge fashions in political economy, philosophy, and sociology and sometimes avoided racial justifications for slavery, he eventually embraced the racial doctrines of the American school of ethnology. When the work of these pseudoscientific theorizers came to be popularized in the late 1850s by such disparate proponents as French Count Joseph Arthur de Gobineau and New York physician Dr. John H. Van Evrie, Fitzhugh accepted the notion that the Negro was a separate species that had to be treated differently from the Caucasian. Such presumed separate physical characteristics and capacities made it all the easier for Fitzhugh to lay out a hierarchical conception for Southern society.

On the eve of the Civil War he was hoping that President James Buchanan and the large body of conservatives in the North would overwhelm what Fitzhugh called "anarchists" and Republicans to save the Union. Then he suggested that the South should not trade with the North, thereby creating "disunion within the Union." Next he urged secession, thinking that Virginia would become the New England of the Confederacy and that New York City would see that its best interests lay in joining the new nation. He thought finally that war was a necessity that would purify and elevate its participants. Whereas he saw the American Revolution as a mere war for independence, he looked upon the Civil War as a conservative revolution rolling back excesses of the Reformation and the French Revolution. By 1863 he was arguing that the Confederacy substituted "for Liberty, Equality, Fraternity . . . Slavery, Subordination, and Government." His play on ideas and words ended only when, with the death of De Bow in 1867, he could no longer find a reliable publisher.

Fitzhugh and his family remained at Port Royal until early 1862, when the town became vulnerable to Union forces. Fitzhugh moved his family to Richmond, where he became a clerk in the auditor's office of the Confederate Department of the Treasury. Within months after Appomattox, Fitzhugh had become a court agent for the Freedmen's Bureau. He served as a judge of the Freedman's Court until the end of 1866. With the onset of Radical Reconstruction Fitzhugh returned to Port Royal, where he attempted briefly to continue his writing career—still obsessed with the role of African Americans in Southern society. He died in 1881 without notice or comment.

Fitzhugh's provocative style of expression has consistently led historians to the conclusion that he represented one or another extreme position in the Old South. While one historian might view him as pre- or anticapitalist, another might just as easily interpret his theory as principally racial in nature. His method of writing made him a most quotable—if not an entirely notable—Southern intellectual.

BIBLIOGRAPHY

Fitzhugh, George. *Cannibals All! or, Slaves without Masters.* Edited by C. Vann Woodward. Cambridge, Mass., 1960.

Genovese, Eugene D. *The World the Slaveholders Made.* New York, 1969.

Wish, Harvey. *George Fitzhugh, Conservative of the Old South.* Charlottesville, Va., 1938.

Wish, Harvey. *George Fitzhugh: Propagandist of the Old South.* Baton Rouge, La., 1943. Reprint, Gloucester, Mass., 1962.

LARRY E. TISE

FIVE CIVILIZED TRIBES. *For discussion of Confederate relations with the Five Civilized Tribes, see* Indians; Indian Territory. *See also* Cherokees; Chickasaws; Choctaws; Creeks; Seminoles.

FLAGS. [*This entry contains three articles:* The Confederate Flag, Military Flags, *and* State Flags.]

The Confederate Flag

During its four years of existence, the Confederacy adopted three official flags. The first was adopted on March

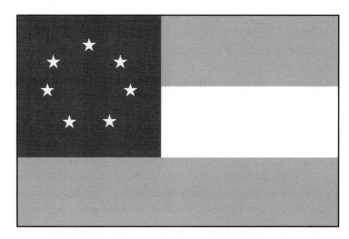

FIRST CONFEDERATE FLAG. Nicknamed the "Stars and Bars," this flag was adopted by the Provisional Congress as the official Confederate national banner on March 14, 1861. The circle of seven stars represented the seven states that had joined the Confederacy at the time of the flag's adoption. The darker shaded areas in the above illustration would have appeared blue; the lighter shaded areas, red.   APPLIED ACADEMIC SERVICES

14, 1861, by the Provisional Congress then meeting in Mobile, Alabama. Its design, credited to Nichola Marschall of Marion, Alabama, combined a field consisting of three equal horizontal bars (red, white, and red) with a blue canton or union (the top quarter of the flag nearest the staff or halyards) in the upper hoist corner extending through the upper red and center white bars. (The hoist is the part of the flag along the flagstaff and also refers to its height or width; the fly is the distance from the flag staff to the end of the flag and also refers to its length.) The canton bore a circle of white stars equal to the number of states in the Confederacy. When first adopted, seven states were represented. By year's close, as additional states seceded, the number grew to thirteen. This flag came to be nicknamed the "Stars and Bars."

No official proportions were established for this flag, although the first ordered for Congress was proportioned 9 to 14, hoist (width) to fly (length). Lacking specifications, flag makers set their own proportions. The most common among surviving flags are 2 to 3, 3 to 5, 5 to 9, 3 to 4, and 1 to 2 (all hoist to fly). Similar discretion was permitted in the arrangement of stars. Although a circle of stars was the most common arrangement, many flags were made with a central star as well, often larger than those in the ring of the circle. Star patterns other than circular were also tolerated.

Because of its deliberate similarity to the Stars and Stripes, the Stars and Bars was judged inadequate. After an initial, unsuccessful attempt to modify the flag by eliminating the white bar and all but four of the stars, on April 19, 1862, the Flag Committee of the new Congress proposed an

SECOND CONFEDERATE FLAG. The "Stainless Banner" was adopted by Congress on May 1, 1863. The first flag made in this design was used to enshroud the body of Gen. Thomas J. ("Stonewall") Jackson after his death at Chancellorsville on May 2, 1863. Hence it is also known as the "Jackson Flag." The darker shaded areas would have appeared blue; the lighter shaded areas, red.

APPLIED ACADEMIC SERVICES

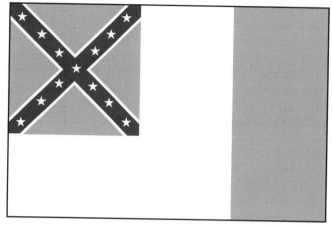

THIRD CONFEDERATE FLAG. The third national banner was designed by Maj. Arthur L. Rogers of the Confederate States Artillery and adopted by Congress on March 4, 1865. The darker shaded areas would have appeared blue; the lighter shaded areas, red.

APPLIED ACADEMIC SERVICES

BIBLIOGRAPHY

Cannon, Devereaux D. *The Flags of the Confederacy: An Illustrated History.* Memphis, Tenn., 1986.

Madaus, Howard Michael. "Rebel Flags Afloat: A Survey of the Surviving Flags of the Confederate States Navy, Revenue Service, and Merchant Marine." *Flag Bulletin* 25, nos. 1–2 (1986): 1–78.

Preble, George Henry. *Origin and History of the American Flag.* Philadelphia, 1917.

Thian, Raphael. *Documentary History of the Flag and Seal of the Confederate States of America, 1861–'65.* Washington, D.C., 1880.

HOWARD MICHAEL MADAUS

alternate design, consisting of a red field traversed by a white St. Andrew's cross having at its center a blue shield bearing a golden sunburst. This proposal, however, died in the House, and nearly a year later (April 22, 1863), the committee proposed another design. This design combined a field of three horizontal bars (white, blue, and white) with a square canton extending two-thirds of the hoist, having as its design the Southern Cross battle flag of the eastern Confederate armies. On May 1, this design was amended by eliminating the central blue bar and was adopted by both houses. This new national flag was soon nicknamed the "Stainless Banner" for its dominating white field.

Although the congressional proposal called for proportions of 1 to 2 (hoist to fly), both the navy and the Quartermaster Department of the army quickly modified the flags made for those services to the more practical proportions of 2 to 3. Variations were also produced by nongovernmental makers. These included variants made in Mobile devoid of the canton's central star and several made in Mississippi without the white border to the St. Andrew's cross of the canton.

In calm weather, however, a limply hanging Stainless Banner was often mistaken for a flag of truce. Accordingly, on March 4, 1865, Congress revised the design by adding a red vertical bar to the fly end of the field equal in width to the white portion next to the canton, and at the same time they proportioned the flag 2 to 3. Although the new flag was also to have its canton reproportioned 3 to 5, nearly all surviving examples are simply modified second national flags and accordingly have square cantons. The last national flag was short-lived, as the surrender of Confederate ground forces in April and May ended the Confederacy.

Military Flags

The national and state flags of the Confederacy identified political entities, and early in the war many of both types were presented to military units. The inadequacy of these flags for distinguishing battlefield combatants resulted in the development of another class of flags for the use of army units. The evolution of these military battle flags took different directions in each of the main theaters of operation.

East of the Appalachians, the most famous of the battle flags, that of the Army of Northern Virginia, was devised in September 1861. As a result of confusion over flags at First Manassas, the senior officers of the major field armies, Gens. P. G. T. Beauregard and Joseph E. Johnston, modified a design that had been submitted as a national flag by William Porcher Miles of South Carolina. Miles's design consisted of a rectangular red field traversed by a blue St.

Andrew's cross edged in white and bearing white stars equal to the number of Confederate states. Beauregard added a border, and Johnston altered the proportions to square.

The initial 120 flags of this design were made from silk, but shades of pinks were used, owing to a shortage of red silk in Richmond. The borders were yellow, and, reflecting Kentucky's neutrality, only twelve stars graced the cross. Subsequent issues of this flag were manufactured from bunting seized at Norfolk or later imported through the blockade. Although interior dimensions and materials could vary, the basic design was uniform in the east throughout the war. The bunting flags were square, with a red field traversed by a dark blue St. Andrew's cross edged with a narrow strip of white. After 1861, thirteen white five-pointed stars decorated the arms of the cross. Except for two issues made in early 1862 with orange borders, all were bordered in white. Although intended to be made in three sizes (2½, 3, and 4 feet square respectively for cavalry, artillery, and infantry), in practice, the smallest size was quickly discontinued, the cavalry using infantry flags instead. Significantly, the design of this flag was never officially promulgated by the War Department; rather the design was carried to the western theater by Beauregard and Johnston when they were transferred.

When Beauregard arrived in the western theater in early 1862, he found three other battle flag designs had been adopted by units in the Army of the Mississippi Valley (later the Army of Tennessee). Two forces had adopted rectangular blue battle flags while in Kentucky: William J. Hardee's corps a flag bordered in white and bearing a white central disk, and Leonidas Polk's corps a flag traversed by a red St. George's cross, edged in white and bearing eleven to thirteen white stars. Earl Van Dorn's corps (the Army of the West) brought from the Trans-Mississippi theater a flag featuring a rectangular red field bordered in yellow and bearing thirteen scattered white stars and a white crescent in the upper hoist corner. Only Braxton Bragg's corps from the Florida coast had arrived without a distinctive flag. Beauregard furnished this corps with a battle flag that differed from its eastern counterpart only by having twelve six-pointed stars and pink or yellow borders.

The absence of uniformity of battle flags in the western army was partly corrected in 1864. After Johnston took command, he reinstated the design of the eastern battle flag, now rectangular in configuration and without exterior borders. A new army corps added to the Army of Tennessee in May 1864 from the Department of Mississippi and East Louisiana brought battle flags of similar shape and pattern but bearing only twelve stars. Johnston's desire for uniformity, however, was frustrated when Patrick Cleburne's division was permitted to retain its battle flags featuring a blue field bordered in white and bearing a white central disk.

FLAG OF THE ARMY OF NORTHERN VIRGINIA. After the Battle of First Manassas, Gens. P. G. T. Beauregard and Joseph E. Johnston adopted this flag design for their troops. It was later adopted by many other Confederate military units. The darker shaded areas in the above illustration would have appeared blue; the lighter shaded areas, red.   APPLIED ACADEMIC SERVICES

After Van Dorn's departure from the Trans-Mississippi Department, little effort was made to institute battle flags there until 1864. A few conforming to the eastern theater's design were presented to units, but they were usually rectangular, bore neither exterior borders nor edging on the blue cross, and frequently had a central star larger than those on the arms of the cross. A variant of this design, blue with a red cross, served as the battle flag for John G. Walker's Texas Division in 1864. Sterling Price's Missouri Division also received battle flags in 1864 featuring a blue field bordered on three sides in red and bearing a white Latin cross. This design copied a similar pattern that had been made in early 1863 for the Missouri Brigade in Mississippi and which, shortly before Vicksburg's surrender, was modified by Gen. John C. Pemberton by changing the field color to red and the borders to white.

BIBLIOGRAPHY

Crute, Joseph H., Jr. *Emblems of Southern Valor: The Battle Flags of the Confederacy.* Louisville, Ky., 1990.

Madaus, Howard Michael, and Robert D. Needham. *The Battle Flags of the Confederate Army of Tennessee.* Milwaukee, Wis., 1976.

Madaus, Howard Michael, and Robert D. Needham. "Unit Colors of the Trans-Mississippi Confederacy." *Military Collector &*

Historian 41, nos. 3–4 (1989): 123–141, 172–182; 42, no. 1 (1990): 16–21.

Todd, Frederick P. "Confederate Colors and Flags." In *American Military Equipage, 1851–1872.* Providence, R.I., 1972.

HOWARD MICHAEL MADAUS

State Flags

The Southern states, in seceding, were claiming to resume their status as independent republics, and accordingly many adopted distinctive national flags. These fell into three broad categories.

Prior to the war, only the state militias had consistently required flags. Most conformed to the flag known between 1796 and 1841 as the "national standard," which consisted of a blue field emblazoned with the coat of arms of the United States. As early as 1839 South Carolina had substituted the palmetto tree for the U.S. symbols on the flags for its militia. After toying with other variations, on January 28, 1861, its legislature adopted a similar blue flag, having a white palmetto in its center and a white crescent in the upper hoist corner.

Shortly after seceding, Virginia followed South Carolina's example, and on April 30, 1861, the Virginia convention adopted a flag consisting of a blue field fringed in white on its fly and bearing the state's coat of arms in its center in full color. Scrolls over and below the figures bore the state's name and its motto *sic semper tyrannis* ("thus always to tyrants").

Although South Carolina and Virginia were the only Southern states to adopt state flags adapted from the old national standard, unofficial flags having blue fields with the state's coat of arms were made and presented to Confederate volunteers from Maryland, North Carolina, Georgia, and Louisiana in 1861. The Confederate-allied Missouri State Guard also adopted a blue field with the Missouri coat of arms in gold in its center the same year.

In those states with minimal militia traditions, the flags tended to follow a different model: the flag of the United States. Although Florida on September 13, 1861, adopted a state flag modeled after the first Confederate national flag, an earlier state flag, selected on January 13, 1861, had combined a field of thirteen red and white horizontal stripes with a blue canton bearing a white five-pointed star. Louisiana followed Florida's earlier example and adopted a state flag on February 11, 1861, that joined thirteen horizontal stripes alternating blue, white, and red with a red canton bearing a yellow five-pointed star. The single stars on these little-used flags bore a common kinship with another group of Southern state flags: those that emphasized the single five-pointed star as a symbol of independence.

In 1861, a flag consisting of a blue field bearing a white five-pointed star was popularized in the Southern states through the song "The Bonnie Blue Flag." Although historical precedents for this flag existed in the 1810 flag of the Republic of East Florida and the Texan independence flags of 1836 and 1839, there is little evidence of a direct lineage from these earlier flags. Rather, the idea of the design seems to have emanated from the Flag Act of 1818, which stipulated that a star be added to the U.S. flag on the Fourth of July after the admission of a new state to the Union. Conversely the flags with a single star would symbolize the withdrawal of a state from the Union.

Several Confederate states adapted this concept in 1861. Alabama's unofficial flag featured its name in white above a white star set in a blue field. Mississippi, on January 26, 1861, adopted a flag with a field of white bordered and fringed in red and bearing a full-color magnolia tree in its center. The design was completed by the addition of a blue canton containing a white star. Texas, upon seceding in February, unofficially revived its 1839 independence flag, which joined a vertical blue bar bearing a white star to two horizontal bars (white over red). North Carolina's flag, adopted on June 22, 1861, copied many elements of the Texas flag. The Carolina flag also consisted of two horizontal bars (blue over white) joined to a red vertical bar on the hoist. The red bar bore a white five-pointed star surrounded by the dates of the state's Mecklenburg Resolution and of its secession, both in white.

Despite their emphasis on state rights, the Southern states made little effort to promote their flags. Only Virginia and North Carolina provided state flags to their volunteer forces during the conflict. Indeed, three Confederate states, Arkansas, Kentucky, and Tennessee, never adopted flags, though the last made an abortive effort in 1861 to adopt one that simply substituted the state's coat of arms for the stars of the Confederacy's first national flag.

BIBLIOGRAPHY

Cannon, Devereaux D. *The Flags of the Confederacy: An Illustrated History.* Memphis, Tenn., 1986.

Hubbs, G. Ward. "Lone Star Flags and Nameless Rags." *Alabama Review* 39, no. 4 (1986): 271–301.

Smith, Whitney. *The Flag Book of the United States.* New York, 1970.

HOWARD MICHAEL MADAUS

FLANAGIN, HARRIS (1817–1874), governor of Arkansas. Born in Roadstown, New Jersey, Flanagin taught school in Pennsylvania and Illinois. He also studied law and after being admitted to the bar moved to Clark County, Arkansas, in 1839. He prospered not through the law but through real estate speculation and became associated with the Whig party. He served in the legislature in the 1840s and also enrolled in the Arkansas militia during the Mexican War but retired from state politics in the 1850s. Elected to the 1861 secession convention, Flanagin made speeches there indicating his reservations about the issue. But when the war began he accepted a captaincy in the Second Arkansas Mounted Rifles and became its colonel following the Battle of Elkhorn Tavern, Arkansas.

While he was on duty in Tennessee in the fall of 1862, friends nominated him to contest the reelection of Governor Henry M. Rector, who had had a tumultuous two years in office. The popular Flanagin won handily. He inherited a bankrupt government and a deteriorating military situation. Handicapped by his strict constructionist views, Flanagin provided only flaccid leadership, even though he was supported by an activist legislature. With the abandonment of Little Rock in September 1863, his became an administration on the run. Plagued by complaints from all sides, Flanagin barely managed to hold his administration together until the Confederacy collapsed in the spring of 1865. When his proposals of cooperation with federal authorities were rejected, he retired unmolested to his home in Arkadelphia. He later served in the 1874 constitutional convention that ended Republican rule, but he died shortly thereafter.

BIBLIOGRAPHY

Dougan, Michael B. "Arkansas." In *The Confederate Governors.* Edited by W. Buck Yearns. Athens, Ga., 1985.

Dougan, Michael B. *Confederate Arkansas: The People and Policies of a Frontier State in Wartime.* University, Ala., 1976.

Kerby, Robert L. *Kirby Smith's Confederacy: The Trans-Mississippi South, 1863–1865.* New York, 1972.

Newberry, Farrar. "Harris Flanagin." *Arkansas Historical Quarterly* 17 (1958): 3–21.

WILLIAM E. PARRISH

FLETCHER, THOMAS

FLETCHER, THOMAS (1815–1880), acting governor of Arkansas. Born in Nashville, Tennessee, Fletcher graduated from the University of Tennessee in 1836 and then studied law with his father Thomas H. Fletcher for two years. Following his admission to the bar, he moved to Natchez, Mississippi, where he had a successful practice. Elected probate judge in 1843, he received an appointment as U.S. marshal for southern Mississippi two years later. In 1850 Fletcher moved to the vicinity of Red Fork in Desha County, Arkansas, where he acquired a sizable plantation.

Taking an active interest in Democratic politics, he was elected to the state senate in 1858 and served there through the Civil War. Although considered a potential candidate for governor in 1860, he declined to run. Chosen by his colleagues as senate president three times, Fletcher was in line to assume the governorship on November 4, 1862, when Governor Henry M. Rector resigned in disgust over having been defeated for reelection. Fletcher served as governor until November 15 when the newly elected Harris Flanagin was inaugurated. Following the war, he returned to his law practice and remained active in politics. He was considering making a bid for the position of secretary of state when he died on a business trip to Little Rock.

BIBLIOGRAPHY

Donovan, Timothy P., and Willard B. Gatewood, eds. *The Governors of Arkansas: Essays in Political Biography.* Fayetteville, Ark., 1981.

Dougan, Michael. "Arkansas." In *The Confederate Governors.* Edited by W. Buck Yearns. Athens, Ga., 1985.

Dougan, Michael. *Confederate Arkansas: The People and Politics of a Frontier State in Wartime.* University, Ala., 1976.

WILLIAM E. PARRISH

FLORIDA

FLORIDA. With votes split in the 1860 election among Southern Democrat John C. Breckinridge (8,543), Constitutional Unionist John Bell (5,437), and Democrat Stephen A. Douglas (367), the state of Florida seceded from the Union on January 10, 1861. Out of a population of 140,424 (77,746 white, 61,745 slaves, and 932 free African Americans), the state contributed roughly 15,000 soldiers to the Confederate cause. Approximately 1,200 white Floridians and nearly as many African Americans served in the Union armies. At least a third of the Florida soldiers in the Confederate armies lost their lives in battle or from disease.

Contributions to the Confederacy. Although the number of soldiers furnished by Florida was relatively modest, the state made significant contributions to the Confederate cause in military leadership and in valuable foodstuffs. Among the major leaders from Florida was Stephen R. Mallory, the Confederate secretary of navy. Despite a shortage of conventional ships and weapons, Mallory was ahead of Union Secretary of Navy Gideon Welles in recognizing the changes that were taking place in naval warfare. Mallory utilized shell guns, screw propellers, torpedoes, armored ships, and even submarines in naval combat. A crude submarine, *H. L. Hunley,* claimed the sinking of the blockader *Housatonic* outside Charleston Harbor in February 1864, the first such sinking in history.

Another military leader from Florida was Gen. W. W. Loring, who, when he surrendered with Gen. Joseph E. Johnston in April 1865, was the senior major general on field duty with the Confederate armies. The colorful E. Kirby Smith, another Floridian, commanded Confederate forces west of the Mississippi River and was the last Confederate general in the field when he surrendered to Gen. E. R. S. Canby on May 26, 1865.

The production of salt was a major Florida contribution

FORT PICKENS, PENSACOLA, FLORIDA.   Front view of the fort.

to the Confederacy. The industry was concentrated around St. Andrews Bay (near present-day Panama City) and in Taylor County along the Gulf of Mexico (Apalachee Bay). Great kettles of seawater were evaporated over large furnaces to obtain salt used to preserve meat for Robert E. Lee's armies. The product was so important that Floridians were exempted from conscription to manufacture it.

After the surrender of Confederate forces at Vicksburg in 1863, another of Florida's strengths came into play. Cattle driven from the open ranges in the state compensated in large part for the Confederate loss of Texas cattle and helped the South carry on the war for two more years. Florida supplied Confederate armies with more than 25,000 cattle and 10,000 hogs in 1864.

The state also provided sugar, syrup, and hides to the Confederate cause, and its inland rivers and inlets served as harbors for blockade runners throughout the war. New Smyrna in East Florida and Apalachicola in West Florida became bases from which smuggled goods were distributed.

Secession and the War in Florida. In January 1861, rural Florida faced a new national existence with no cities or factory system, and with only about four hundred miles of railroads and a thousand free skilled laborers within its borders. On February 4, delegates from Florida and other seceding states met at Montgomery, Alabama, and agreed upon a provisional government for the Confederate States of America, with a constitution to be returned to the states for ratification. The Florida secession convention reassembled on February 26 and unanimously adopted the Constitution.

Governor Madison S. Perry quickly ordered the seizure of all Federal arsenals by state militia troops. The men occupied arsenals at Chattahoochee, Fort Marion at St. Augustine, and Fort Clinch at Fernandina, but failed to dislodge Federals at Fort Pickens on Santa Rosa Island in Pensacola Bay and the fifty troops in Fort Taylor at Key West. The Union commander at Fort Barrancas at Pensacola was Lt. Adam Slemmer of the First Artillery. When a large Confederate force prepared to attack the fort, Slemmer, with no orders or authorization from the Union command in Washington, ordered his force of eighty-one men to move to Fort Pickens at the western extremity of Santa Rosa Island. This contingent held the fortress until President Abraham Lincoln was inaugurated and subsequently sent reinforcements. Strategic Pensacola Harbor became a Union command post for capture of Confederate blockade runners. Fort Taylor, located on the west shore of the Key West island, remained in Union hands throughout the war. Since the townspeople of Key West were mostly Confederate sympathizers, Union intelligence officers stationed at Fort Taylor collected information here about Confederate military operations to send to Washington.

John Milton, inaugurated in October 1861 as Florida's wartime governor, was pleased with Confederate plans for defense of the approaches to Apalachicola, the harbor and railroad terminus at Fernandina, the port of Jacksonville, and other coastal towns. But in February 1862, Governor Milton was dismayed when these plans were abandoned. Pressures from Federal forces in Tennessee and Kentucky brought a sweeping order to the Florida department to send all men and supplies northward to defend the northwestern border of the Confederacy. A month later only two thousand Confederate troops remained in the state. Coastal defenses were dismantled and military ordnance was moved into the interior. Governor Milton reflected the temper of Floridians when he wrote to President Jefferson Davis that "the Confederacy has abandoned most of Florida to the mercy and abuse of the Lincoln government." Nevertheless,

Milton, according to Davis biographer Rembert Patrick, was among the most loyal and cooperative state rights governors in his dealings with Davis.

The movement of Confederate troops inland enabled the Federal navy to gain effective control of and occupy at will the east coast of the United States extending from Port Royal, South Carolina, to Key West, Florida. This in turn enabled blockade squadrons to keep watch on the Florida-based blockade runners. On March 3, 1862, the Federals took control of Fernandina and Fort Clinch on Amelia Island, and a Federal garrison occupied Fort Clinch for the duration of the war. In that same month Union forces moved southward to occupy Jacksonville and St. Augustine. Incapable of effective resistance, Confederate sympathizers moved into the interior, where the Federals followed them. The Northerners conducted raids, freed slaves to obtain army recruits, destroyed military stores, and then withdrew. They returned to Jacksonville in October 1862 and March 1863 for the same purposes. Raiders coming in from the gulf destroyed the saltworks at Cedar Key and Apalachicola on several occasions, but the Confederate workers soon returned and resumed their saltmaking.

Florida's interior—the area between the St. Johns and Apalachicola rivers and including the capital city of Tallahassee—remained in Confederate hands throughout the war. Capt. John Jackson Dickison, a legendary Civil War hero in Florida, deployed a little band of old men and young boys in guerrilla warfare in defense of the state's interior. Dickison, a middle-aged, well-to-do plantation owner at Orange Springs, Florida, when the war began, organized a cavalry unit known as the Leo Dragoons. His militia unit was assigned as home guards defending the west bank of the St. Johns River, gateway to the interior. He deployed his little band of cavalry to strategic positions for ambushing Northerners who ventured west of the St. Johns River.

Throughout the summer and fall of 1863 and January of 1864, Florida enjoyed almost a year of respite from significant Federal attacks. This virtual armistice was broken in February 1864 when five thousand Federal troops from lower South Carolina and upper Georgia embarked aboard transports for an invasion of northeast Florida. Union objectives were to stop the flow of cattle and other foodstuffs from moving northward to General Lee's armies, to free the slaves, and to enlist them in the Union armies. The Federal forces reached Jacksonville on February 7 and moved westward in the direction of Lake City. Despite critical need for troops elsewhere, General Lee ordered reinforcements to assist Gen. Joseph Finegan, commander of the East Florida Military District, in repelling the invaders.

General Finegan withdrew his small force ahead of the Union advance until he received the reinforcements and found a strong defensive position near the village of Olustee located thirteen miles east of Lake City. His men took up position on a line about a mile and a half long running between Ocean Pond on the north and a large cyprus swamp on the south and waited for the advancing Union army. Gen. Truman A. Seymour, the Union commander, had added about five hundred ex-slaves to his original force. Around the middle of the day on February 20, the two forces engaged in the Battle of Olustee. Repeated assaults by the Union forces were repelled at very close range by the Confederates artillery and small arms. By a little after six in the evening the Confederates had forced the Union men to retreat, which was made easier by the fact that General Seymour had failed to bring all of his forces to the battle.

Olustee, though a minor battle with respect to the number of men involved, had the highest percentage of casualties, both Union and Confederate, of any battle in the war. The Union lost 40 percent of its force in dead, wounded and missing men while the Confederate forces reported casualties of 20 percent. Though the Confederates were unable to follow up their victory, it was decisive. Seymour's army departed from Florida; the interior and the supply lines for shipment of foodstuffs to the Confederate armies remained secure. Historian Rembert Patrick contends that the Olustee victory may well have enabled the South to carry on the war for an added year.

The Home Front. Floridians were asked to endure hardships and make sacrifices to solve wartime problems. The state budget averaged $500,000 per year during the war. Previously it had never exceeded $50,000 per year. Because tax collections were sometimes suspended and tax payments were irregular, especially in the enemy-held areas of Florida, the only way for the state to pay for war expenditures was to borrow money. The legislature authorized treasury notes and twenty-year bonds, but the bonds did not sell well and were used to pay creditors who would take them. The total amount of treasury notes issued during the war was $2,236,640.38, of which only $397,370.36 was redeemed. The Civil War cost Floridians $2,225,000 in addition to the capital that had been invested in some 65,000 slaves.

The Confederate government, in order to meet financial obligations, assessed Florida and other states a tax according to the population. More painful and of more direct affect on Floridians was the Confederate Impressment Act of 1863, which permitted Confederate or state officials to enter homes, seize surplus foods and items needed for war, and leave IOUs for payment to the occupants.

Outfitting the troops with arms, ammunition, clothing, and equipment soon became a major problem. Florida's legislature first appropriated $100,000 for this purpose, but this was just a drop in a very large bucket. The Confederate government provided no help. Consequently, some troops were not provided with even basic equipment, which lowered morale. Wealthy planters organized military units and provided some of the equipment, and often they were elected as the units' officers. The Ladies Military Aid Societies were given $10,000 worth of material, appropriated by the Florida legislature, to make uniforms, but there was never enough clothing, shoes, and blankets. Hospitals, doctors, and nurses were also in short supply. To ease the situation, Florida opened the Howard Grove Hospital in Richmond to care for its sick and wounded fighting on the Virginia front. It was supported by contributions of food and money from Floridians and an appropriation of $30,000 from the legislature.

With four-fifths of Florida men absent from their homes, women who lived on plantations and depended on slave labor found their lives greatly changed. In the early years of the war, slaves often stayed on the plantations, but eventually they left, leaving their mistresses to do the tasks they had performed. The plantation women had to learn how to fell trees, roll logs, clear fields, and plant crops. They also continued their traditional tasks of weaving, knitting, and canning foods.

Military supplies for the Confederacy were brought to Florida by blockade runners—small boats that slipped out of Florida bays and inlets often at night to evade capture by Federal gunboats. In the first year of the war the business of running the blockade was usually conducted through legal channels with clearance papers approved by the Confederate customs or military officials. Sponsors of these enterprises promised to import supplies for government use in return for permission to export cotton, tobacco, and naval stores. But as the war progressed and Federal forces strengthened the blockade, dwindling supplies and increased demand encouraged the runners to import consumer goods without authorization. Catherine Cooper Hopley, an English tutor on Governor Milton's plantation, wrote of profiteers who sold scarce imported goods at exorbitant prices both to consumers and to the Confederate government. Quinine, used for many medical purposes, sold for $20 an ounce. Flour that would have brought $10 a sack upon arrival was sold to the Confederate government in the quartermaster's depot for $30 to $50. Rum, purchased in Cuba for 17 cents a gallon, was sold in Florida for $25 a gallon. Governor Milton, in his letters to President Davis, complained that goods manufactured in the North were shipped to the Bahamas, covered with English stamps, and then sold at a profit in Florida. Milton argued that this profiteering did damage to Confederate morale that outweighed any good for consumers, and in 1864 he asked that the Confederacy halt the approval of papers for the runners. The Confederate government, however, did not agree. The Confederacy, in fact, encouraged the trade with Northern markets and toward the end of the conflict tried to reserve as much cargo space as possible with the blockade runners.

Regardless of the Confederate success in defending the interior of Florida, the day of the Confederacy was soon over. Lee surrendered on April 9, 1865, and Johnston on April 26. On May 10, Gen. E. M. McCook reached Tallahassee and accepted the surrender of the capital and the eight thousand Confederate troops remaining in Florida. Governor Milton, in a message to the Florida legislature, declared that "death would be preferable to reunion," and asserted that this was "the sentiment of all true Southern men." These were not idle words: the governor took his own life on April 1, 1865. The majority of war-weary Floridians did not share Milton's view. A few went into exile in Latin America, but most shared the feeling of a returning veteran who said, "Thank God, it is over, one way or another."

[*For further discussion of battles and cities in Florida, see* Fort Pickens, Florida; Olustee, Florida; Tallahassee, Florida. *See also biographies of numerous figures mentioned herein.*]

BIBLIOGRAPHY

Davis, William Watson. *The Civil War and Reconstruction in Florida.* New York, 1913.
Hopley, Catherine C. *Life in the South from the Commencement of the War.* London, 1863.
Johns, John E. *Florida during the Civil War.* Gainesville, Fla., 1963.
Tebeau, Charlton. *A History of Florida.* Coral Gables, Fla., 1980.

MERLIN G. COX

FLORIDA. The wooden cruiser *Florida* was 192 feet long and displaced 700 tons. Its all-rifle armament consisted of two 7-inch Blakely rifles and six 6-inch Blakely rifles. The ship had a screw propeller that could be lifted out of the water when under sail. Although *Florida*'s speed averaged 9½ knots, its maximum speed was 12 knots. The crew's size varied but averaged 100 men and 20 officers. A sister ship to *Alabama,* it was the first cruiser constructed in England. It was built from the modified plans of a Royal Navy gunboat by William C. Miller and Sons of Liverpool, and the engines were the work of Fawcett and Preston, also of Liverpool. In order to conceal the ship's real identity, it was built under the name of *Oreto,* supposedly for the Italian government. Construction on *Florida* began in June 1861, and it sailed for Nassau on March 22, 1862, posing as an ordinary merchant ship.

After some difficulty the ship left Nassau under command of Lt. John N. Maffitt, who could not begin his cruise immediately because *Florida* lacked an adequate crew and critical parts of armament. In addition, some men aboard had yellow fever. Maffitt, trying unsuccessfully to complete his equipment and roster of men in Cuba, took *Florida* on a daring daylight run through the Union blockade into

CSS *FLORIDA*. The Confederate clipper pursuing the Federal ship *Jacob Bell*, which it captured and burned in the Atlantic on February 12, 1863. Lithograph by J. H. Bufford, 1863. NAVAL HISTORICAL CENTER, WASHINGTON, D.C.

Mobile on September 4, 1862. The need for tedious repairs prevented the ship's departure until January 17, 1863.

During the first cruise *Florida* captured twenty-five ships, nineteen of which were destroyed and six were bonded. The practice of bonding referred to a form of ransom where the owner agreed to pay a specified amount after the war to the Confederacy for not burning his ship. Three prizes were outfitted as cruisers, and these vessels, *Tacony, Clarence,* and *Lapwing,* captured twenty-two more ships. Of these captures, fifteen were destroyed, six were bonded, and one, *Archer,* was recaptured by Union forces. Directly or indirectly *Florida* captured forty-seven prizes during the first cruise. Lt. C. W. Read commanded one prize used as a cruiser. Read ended his cruise by capturing the armed revenue cutter *Caleb Cushing* at Portland, Maine, and blowing it up.

After months at sea, *Florida* was refitted at Brest, France, remaining there from August 23, 1863, until February 10, 1864. By this time, Maffitt, ill and exhausted, asked to be relieved of his duty. While the ship was at Brest, Comm. J. N. Barney took over its command and supervised the repairs. Ill health, however, prevented his continuing, and he was replaced by Lt. Charles M. Morris. *Florida's* second cruise, considerably less successful than the first, accounted for the capture of thirteen prizes, eleven of which were destroyed and the other two bonded. The crew found far fewer enemy ships this time out, in part because many U.S. ships were either tied up in port or had been transferred to foreign flags.

Florida was captured in the neutral port of Bahia, Brazil, on October 7, 1864, by the U.S. warship *Wachusetts,* a sister ship of *Kearsarge,* which had already sunk *Alabama. Wachusetts* commander Napoleon Collins sailed *Florida* to Hampton, Virginia, where it sank.

BIBLIOGRAPHY

Boykin, Edward. *Sea Devil of the Confederacy: The Story of the Florida and Her Captain John Newland Maffitt.* New York, 1959.

Bulloch, James D. *The Secret Service of the Confederate States in Europe or How the Confederate Cruisers Were Equipped.* 2 vols. New York, 1883.

Owsley, Frank L. *The C.S.S. Florida: Her Building and Operations.* Tuscaloosa, Ala., 1987.

FRANK LAWRENCE OWSLEY

FLOYD, JOHN B. (1806–1863), politician and brigadier general. Born June 1, 1806, in Montgomery County, Virginia, John Buchanan Floyd served as governor from 1848 to 1852. His political service to the Democratic party secured his appointment as President James Buchanan's secretary of war (1857–1860). After bitter criticism by Northern politicians and the press for alleged transfer of arms and equipment from Northern to Southern arsenals and contractor indiscretions within the War Department, he was commissioned a Confederate brigadier in 1861. He served in the West Virginia campaign under Robert E. Lee, being involved in small battles at Cross Lanes, Carnifix Ferry, and Gauley Bridge. Sent west in December 1861 with his brigade of Virginia troops, he joined Albert Sidney Johnston's forces in western Kentucky.

As senior brigadier, Floyd assumed command on the Cumberland River at Fort Donelson, Tennessee, in February 1862 just as Ulysses S. Grant's joint army-navy expedition invested the work (having captured nearby Fort Henry on the Tennessee River a week before). Although hampered by divided leadership (there were three brigadiers besides himself), unclear and conflicting orders from

Command: Factions and Ideas in Confederate Strategy. Baton
Rouge, La., 1973.

Warner, Ezra. Generals in Gray: Lives of the Confederate Commanders. Baton Rouge, La., 1959.

B. Franklin Cooling

FOLK NARRATIVES. Folklorists study three
types of folk narratives: myths, legends, and folktales.
Myths are those narratives set in a prehistoric past that deal
with the actions of gods and supernatural beings. *Legends*
are stories set in the historic past and told to convey what
the teller feels is truth; or, at least, they allow for an element
of belief or disbelief. *Folktales* are fictional stories told
primarily for entertainment, although they may contain a
moral or illustrate some generally accepted truth. There are
four broad categories of folktales that have been distinguished by folklorists. These include animal tales (such as
"The Tar Baby"), wonder tales (such as "The Smith
Outwits the Devil"), jokes and anecdotes, and formula tales
(such as "The Old Woman and Her Pig" or "The House
That Jack Built"), which are cumulative, catch, or endless
tales. Viewed from this stance, there are no myths about the
Confederacy. It is true, as scholar Richard M. Dorson has
suggested, that the war left no coherent body of folk sagas
in its wake; nevertheless, legends and folktales were
abundant on both sides of the conflict.

Although Confederate soldiers told both legends and
folktales, their activity in this regard is, for a variety of
reasons, less well known than the narrative traditions
concerning the Confederacy that have lingered on to the
present. One of the chief reasons is that, because of the
ongoing conflict, folklorists at the time of the war were not
collecting folk narratives from soldiers on either side. Even
if conditions had permitted, there likely would have been
little interest in such collections, because most nineteenth-
century folklorists were concerned with the traditions of
American Indians, African Americans, or other groups
considered to be outside of mainstream society. Thus, only
through perusal of diaries, journals, and newspaper articles
or from orally preserved accounts can one discover what
traditional stories Confederate soldiers told. The interests
of American folklorists have expanded considerably since
the Civil War. Consequently, a great deal more is known
about the folk narrative traditions that lingered on after
1865 pertaining to the war than about the narrative
traditions that existed during the war.

Available information suggests that the folk narratives
told by soldiers consisted mainly of legends and jokes. Many
of the legends dealt with famous personalities such as
Abraham Lincoln. One characteristic Southerners persistently attached to the president was that he was a drunk,
and many stories circulated around campfires that pur-
ported to give the truth about his legendary binges. But just

JOHN B. FLOYD.   LIBRARY OF CONGRESS

Johnston, a jealous but largely untested army of over fifteen thousand men, and an untenable static defense
position, Floyd stymied Union forces for three days while
Johnston conducted a retreat of the main army from
Bowling Green to Nashville. Nonetheless, in a comedy of
errors, fouled communications, amateurish tactical bun-
gling, and loss of nerve, Floyd and his fellow officers (Gideon Pillow, Simon Bolivar Buckner, Bushrod Rust Johnson) relinquished the initiative, failed to extricate their
army, and were forced to surrender to Grant. In a famous opéra bouffe scene of passing command, Floyd and
Pillow fled with the Virginia brigade (and miscellaneous
portions of the garrison), thereby earning the enmity
and scorn of friend and foe alike for the remainder of
the war.

Floyd subsequently escaped to Nashville and aided in
restoration of order and transfer of army supplies from the
city. But because he had deserted his command, he was
subsequently removed from other positions of command in
the Confederate service. Active as a Virginia militia major
general in southwestern Virginia, Floyd organized partisan
bands to combat Union incursions, but his health broke,
resulting in his early death in August 1863 near Abingdon,
Virginia. Known to posterity for the Fort Donelson disaster,
Floyd represented the typical nineteenth-century political
general whose ambitions exceeded his military talents to the
detriment of the Confederacy.

BIBLIOGRAPHY

Barnwell, Robert W. "General John B. Floyd." Confederate Veteran
39 (April 1931): 141–142.

Connelly, Thomas Lawrence, and Archer Jones. The Politics of as often the tales told by fighting men dealt with less well-known personalities. Stories about hairbreadth escapes by rank-and-file soldiers became the stuff of legends, as did yarns about the hardships of war. Other favorite legend topics included the activities of guerrillas, haunted burial grounds, and battlefields.

Jokes were numerous and extremely varied and often conveyed the toll of the war on an individual level. Typical is a humorous tale recorded in the *Memorial Reminiscences of the Confederate Women of Arkansas*. According to this yarn, a tired and war-weary Confederate was cooling his feet in a stream and trying to mend his ragged coat when he was visited by a mounted Union soldier who said, "Hi, there, Johnny Reb. I've got you this time." To this the Confederate soldier replied: "Yes, and a hell of a git you got." Often the jokes that were told had nothing to do with the war or its personalities. Ribald jokes were especially popular with the troops but are even less well documented than other forms of folk narrative. Some famous persons, such as Governor Zebulon Vance of North Carolina, achieved renown among the troops and the general populace for their skill at telling jokes, and many widely traveled yarns became attached to them. One widely known tale attributed to Vance concerned a rabbit that sprang from the bushes during the Battle of Malvern Hill. The rabbit darted in front of the troops who called out, "Run, run, run!" An officer then asked Vance if he should shoot the animal. Vance replied no and called out, "Run, little cottontail! I'd run too if I wasn't governor of North Carolina." Other personalities, in particular Lincoln, were the subject of jokes, both ribald and "clean."

Those people left at home related the same types of narratives that were told by those in the ranks, but the civilians' stories encompassed a broader range. Animal tales and wonder tales, for example, were commonplace on the home front but rarely told in military camps. Many of the narratives related by civilians, though, dealt with the war; the activities of guerrillas, known in many communities as jayhawkers, were one of the most frequent subjects of legends. Indeed, a whole series of episodic cycles has grown up around Beanie Short, a guerrilla who operated in the Cumberland region of northern Tennessee and southern Kentucky. These narratives focus on his raiding activities, his treacherous death, and his buried treasure. If legend is to be believed, most guerrillas amassed sizable treasures, which they buried and have never been found.

Some traditional stories told during the Confederacy were related from the viewpoint of African Americans. The most widely told dealt with the freedom of blacks, their abilities as soldiers, and humorous comments on race relations. In Virginia a black woman was asked if she had run away from her master, to which she replied no, saying her master had run away from her. In Vicksburg, a black boy stood still while a shell landed almost at the feet of his party, which consisted of himself, a Catholic nun, and a convalescent Confederate soldier. After the soldier leaped to safety, the boy threw the smoldering shell away just before it exploded. When asked by the nun why he did not act earlier, he answered that he had too much respect for white people to do something like that while a white gentleman was standing there. Of course, such tales were also told by some whites.

Most Confederate folk narratives were short, consisting of a single episode, and were relatively uncomplicated. Exceptions would be the wonder tales and some of the animal stories, but these had no connection with the war and were commonplace before the 1860s. Legends were told by most people, but folktales were likely related by only a few star narrators. Both types of narratives differed in one other important way—namely, the manner of their telling. Both legends and folktales were told anywhere two people congregated but legends were related in a matter-of-fact, relatively undramatic style whereby the narrator let the text speak for itself and did not attempt to improve the story with dramatic flourishes. Folktale narrators, on the other hand, were usually more animated and dramatic when delivering their yarns. The difference in presentation styles was, of course, mainly due to the manner in which the narrators and their audiences regarded legends and folktales. Those telling the former generally thought of themselves as merely relaying factual information, whereas those telling the latter viewed their task as one of providing entertainment.

BIBLIOGRAPHY

Aarne, Antti, and Stith Thompson. *The Types of the Folk-Tale.* Helsinki, Finland, 1928. Reprint, Bloomington, Ind., 1964.

Botkin, B. A. *A Civil War Treasury of Tales, Legends and Folklore.* New York, 1960.

Dorson, Richard M. *America in Legend: Folklore from the Colonial Period to the Present.* New York, 1973.

Roberts, Leonard W. *Up Cutshin and Down Greasy: Folkways of a Kentucky Mountain Family.* Lexington, Ky., 1959.

Roberts, Nancy. *Civil War Ghost Stories and Legends.* Columbia, S.C., 1992.

Wiley, Bell Irvin. *The Common Soldier in the Civil War: The Life of Johnny Reb.* Indianapolis, Ind., 1943. Reprint, Baton Rouge, La., 1986.

Wilgus, D. K., and Lynwood Montell. "Beanie Short: A Civil War Chronicle in Legend and Song." In *American Folk Legend: A Symposium.* Edited by Wayland D. Hand. Berkeley, Calif., 1971.

W. K. McNeil

FOOD. In the Confederacy, food varied from plentiful to inadequate, depending on what could be produced, acquired, and transported. People who could afford staples and luxury items or lived where the war had little physical impact ate relatively well. But shortages of food were common and many soldiers, refugees, urban dwellers, people living near battlefields, and poor farmers suffered hunger or malnutrition by the latter half of the war.

In 1860, the South produced an adequate amount of food to feed its citizens, especially rice, wheat, corn, pork, sugar, sweet potatoes, peas, and beans. But once the war started, spoilage, inadequate and disrupted transportation systems, impressment, poor weather, destruction of crops, a shortage of producers, and the occupation of food-producing regions by Federal troops caused many Southerners to experience hunger.

Food shortages hit the Confederacy almost as soon as the war began. Coffee, tea, salt, and sugar disappeared, and by 1863, meat, butter, and lard were also in limited supply. Military rations proved inadequate after the early months of war. Food was a daily concern for Confederate soldiers and a major topic in letters they wrote home. Some feared hunger more than the enemy. In their writings, they bemoaned Spartan helpings, spoiled meat, and persistent shortages of pork, butter, coffee, fruits, vegetables, and flour. Insufficient food fostered desperation, depression, lethargy, and often an inability to fight and survive disease and battle wounds. Nutritional deficiencies led to night blindness, and rancid food, unripened fruit, and polluted water caused dysentery, worms, and typhoid.

The Confederate Subsistence Department contracted with Southern farmers for grains and meat to feed the army, but the department was the most poorly organized of all governmental agencies. Adding to its problems were speculators who overcharged the government and farmers who hoarded food. Orders often were ignored. Rations might sit at food depots for days because there was no way to transport them.

Typical military fare included hardtack (crackers), corn meal, fresh beef, and sometimes rice, field peas, or potatoes. Soldiers drank coffee substitutes, alcohol, and water, though the latter often had to be purified, disguised, or drunk with one's eyes closed. Initially, the army specified generous rations for infantry and officers based on U.S. Army rations. Rarely were specifications met, however, and rations declined significantly as the war dragged on—so much so that by 1864 soldiers often ate a day's food supply at one meal.

The men became resourceful in locating outside sources of food and less picky about what they ate and how it was prepared. Soldiers foraged for additional supplies in the countryside, purchased affordable extras when near a town or farm, and sometimes stole from a farmer's field. They hunted deer, possums, muskrats, squirrels, and wild fowl to add variety and protein to their diet. Men cooked a dough mixture of flour, grease, and water. Pieces of meat were skewered on sticks and held over the fire, since cooking implements were scarce. When wood was unavailable, they ate their food raw. During active campaigning, they either cooked prior to marching or ate nothing more than crackers and water. A few regiments had black slaves as cooks, but most men managed on their own. Occasionally, a bakery or central kitchen provided breads and foods for several regiments, but usually rations were distributed as needed.

More fortunate soldiers had other sources of food. Some received food boxes or trunks from relatives or soldiers' or ladies' aid societies. From family larders and fields came hams, turkeys, pickles, vinegar, cakes, catsup, and breads. But as the war progressed, limited or disrupted transportation made it increasingly difficult to deliver such food to the designated recipient without a personal agent. Occasionally soldiers purchased home-cooked foods and fresh vegetables at wayside stands, but these were rare.

While all soldiers suffered hunger or consumed inedible fare at one time or another during their military service, some men had an especially miserable time of it. Braxton Bragg's Army of Tennessee faced desperate hunger during 1863. His soldiers moved southward from Murfreesboro through land that had been picked clean by Federal and Confederate troops and commissary agents. Though Florida beef and corn meal rations were available, Robert E. Lee's Army of Northern Virginia had priority before the Army of Tennessee. Troops at Fort Donelson in 1862, D. H. Hill's division during the 1862 spring campaign, and the soldiers defending Vicksburg in the spring and early summer of 1863 faced near starvation. The Army of Northern Virginia was well fed marching north into Pennsylvania but famished on its retreat from Gettysburg. During the Virginia campaign of 1864, Lee's army was described as "half clothed, half fed." No longer could that state provide enough food for the military, and supplies had to be secured from the Deep South. By June 1864, four crackers and a quarter-pound of meat a day comprised rations in Lee's army. Marching toward Appomattox, his men became even more desperate. Some did not eat for days, and others consumed corn kernels intended for the horses.

Officers ate better than the average soldier, although Lee reportedly was abstemious in his eating habits. Most generals exhibited some sensitivity to their hungry troops, and leaders like Bragg repeatedly demanded more and better provisions. Yet piles of rations spoiled at depots when orders were misunderstood, railroad cars and wagons were unavailable to transport the food, or armies changed their marching plans and missed intended supplies.

Hospital food ranged from nourishing to inedible, depending on supplies from local farmers and the presence of female nurses who were sensitive to patients' needs. Chimborozo Hospital in Richmond had its own bakeries, slaughterhouse, and kitchens to feed thousands of patients. Ladies' aid societies often prepared hams, turkeys, biscuits, and pies for the wounded. Nevertheless, soldiers complained about hospital meals, and those who could travel preferred home care where food was tastier, cleaner, and more plentiful.

The diet of civilians varied significantly but generally was better than that of the common soldier. Residents of middle Georgia, Alabama, South Carolina, and Texas were not significantly affected until Federal troops moved in and destroyed food supplies, crops, farm tools, and animals. The wealthy of Richmond, Augusta, Mobile, and the low-country plantations rarely experienced hunger until the end of the war. They could afford the staples and delicacies that made it through the blockade; their main complaints were high prices and unscrupulous speculators. Wealthy families continued to enjoy oysters, bacon, fresh shrimp and crab, tea, vegetables, fruits, a bit of sugar, and even fine flour for cakes. Varina and Jefferson Davis were criticized for eating extremely well while thousands in Richmond went hungry.

Yet more typical behavior was scrimping, preserving, and developing greater self-sufficiency. A new sense of asceticism developed even among some of the privileged. The lower and middle classes tightened their belts. Some Southerners ate only two meals a day, and mothers often sacrificed their own food to feed thin and hungry children. Torrential rains and droughts in several Southern states spoiled or burned out corn and vegetable crops in 1862 and 1863. Many urban and rural poor fell victim to inflation, as it put what little was available out of reach. Many urban women begged or scavenged.

In addition, food shortages prevailed for civilians because military needs came first. As farmers entered the army and became consumers rather than producers and women took charge of planting, less food was available. The shortages, high prices, and hunger fostered great discontent on the home front, and women wrote letters complaining to the Confederate government and begging husbands and sons to come home. So desperate were some women in towns in North and South Carolina, Alabama, and Georgia that they took to the streets to protest or riot. To counter the growing unease, public support for hungry soldiers' families was essential. States such as North Carolina, Georgia, and Louisiana enacted laws to distribute rations or cash payments to malnourished families.

Other issues concerning food fostered further discontent on the home front. Confederate agents ordered and purchased food to feed the soldiers, but farmers became increasingly reluctant to sell when promissory notes failed to be paid and severe inflation ate into any funds they received. Impressment laws, enacted in 1863, were unpopular. Fearing the seizure of their produce, farmers often refused to market their crops in some cities despite the growing need for food. When families failed to cooperate with the government, agents often took food with or without paying.

Farmers faced other problems, too. Given limited transportation, they found it increasingly difficult to reach markets to sell or purchase food. State laws encouraged farmers to grow corn rather than cotton, but some ignored such demands. Fearing that cotton or corn crops might fall into Federal hands, Southerners burned fields as enemy troops approached. Confederate soldiers from Lee's army journeyed to the North Carolina mountains in search of new food sources and stole what they needed from local farms.

Refugees crowding into Southern cities put more pressure on limited urban resources, especially food supplies. Few refugees could carry food when they fled their homes, and those who moved in with friends or into crowded boarding houses found food supplies scarce and expensive.

Owing to the increasing shortage of grains, some states enacted prohibition laws during the war. Yet such laws usually were ignored or, at least, were difficult to enforce. Alcohol was a pleasurable indulgence for many, especially war-weary soldiers, and its medicinal uses made it essential.

The greatest food shortage in the Confederacy was salt, which, before the outbreak of war, had been imported primarily from Europe and the Northern states. The blockade exacerbated the limited supply, and Federal troops gradually occupied the areas containing the Confederacy's sources of salt; only Saltville, Virginia, remained an important mine throughout the four years. Because salt was essential for preserving meat and for seasoning, its shortage caused both the Confederate and the state governments to search for other sources, including seawater, new salt mines, and artesian wells. So desperate was the need for salt that states exempted from military service those who labored in the mines. Families often begged soldiers serving near the coast to send them salt. Others resorted to a primitive means of extracting and reusing the salt from dirt floors of smokehouses. High prices and scarcity forced many to abandon salt as a preservative; instead they dried their meat, experimented with other spices, or restricted themselves to fresh meat when it was available.

Coffee was sorely missed, and no substitute adequately replaced it. Southerners concocted alternative brews from parched corn, wheat, acorns, okra seed, chicory, dandelions, persimmon seeds, and even potato peelings. Tea also became scarce. Women substituted sassafras or strawberry leaves, boiled grasses, or drank plain hot water with milk. Little sugar was available once Federal troops occupied Louisiana, and Southerners substituted molasses, maple syrup, sorghum, honey, or fruit syrups as sweeteners—or did without.

Because of the shortage of pork and beef, civilians ate

more fish and fowl. Thus, ironically, those Southerners who *were* adequately fed probably, in some respects, consumed a better diet during the war than before it, with less fat, sugar, and red meat, and more vegetables and legumes in their daily fare. Meals improved in summer and early fall with the appearance of fresh vegetables and fruits and the harvesting of corn and wheat. Fortunate families expanded the size of their gardens and orchards if they could obtain seeds. Lucky Southerners who owned a cow enjoyed milk and butter. Wheat flour, especially finely ground, disappeared, and cooks used other grains such as corn and rice. Some whites observed that their food resembled what slaves had always consumed.

Women became resourceful cooks and meal planners. They scavenged for fresh berries and roots, baked mock apple pie made with crackers instead of apples, and learned how to revive rancid butter. The urban poor rummaged through discarded garbage for tidbits. Newspapers carried stories providing advice on how to cook with available foods. *The Confederate Receipt Book,* compiled in 1863, testifies to the creative use of scarce foods. Privileged Southerners sometimes did without, holding "starvation parties" where no food was served.

Slaves' diets changed little during the war since they had always depended on corn, pork, field peas, biscuits, and molasses. They too faced shortages and consumed less meat and fresh foods, but most ate better than the average Confederate soldier. Many continued to fish, hunt, and garden to supplement their meal offerings. Probably many worked fewer hours in the absence of male masters and therefore perhaps had lighter caloric needs. And because some masters could no longer afford to feed their slaves, more were rented out.

Food, then, was a matter of daily concern for soldiers and civilians during the four long years. Thousands went hungry on the battleground and the home front. Some historians feel that the will of the South would have been stronger had sufficient food been available for everyone. Some even argue that food ultimately affected the war's outcome.

[*See also* Bread Riots; Extortion; Farming; Impressment; Inflation; Salt; Speculation; Substitutes; Tax-in-Kind.]

BIBLIOGRAPHY

Confederate Receipt Book: A Compilation of over One Hundred Receipts, Adapted to the Times. Richmond, Va., 1863. Reprint, with introduction by E. Merton Coulter. Athens, Ga., 1960.

Gates, Paul W. *Agriculture and the Civil War.* New York, 1965.

Goff, Richard D. *Confederate Supply.* Durham, N.C., 1969.

Lonn, Ella. *Salt as a Factor in the Confederacy.* New York, 1933.

Massey, Mary Elizabeth. *Ersatz in the Confederacy.* Columbia, S.C., 1952.

Stevens, John K. "Hostages to Hunger: Nutritional Night Blind-

ness in the Confederate Armies." *Tennessee Historical Quarterly* 48 (1989): 131–143.

Taylor, Robert A. "Rebel Beef: Florida Cattle and the Confederate Army, 1862–1864." *Florida Historical Quarterly* 67 (1988): 15–31.

Wiley, Bell I. *The Life of Johnny Reb.* Baton Rouge, La., 1971.

SALLY G. MCMILLEN

FOOTE, HENRY S. (1804–1880), Tennessee governor and congressman. Historians who have mentioned Henry Stuart Foote at all have not been kind to his memory. Charles S. Sydnor viewed him as the Clement L. Vallandigham of the South, and E. Merton Coulter said he was "choleric," "excitable," "incorrigible," "eccentric," "irascible," "voluble," and "restless." Clement Eaton described him as "a little man, always barking and snapping, . . . a consummate demagogue." But worse still, most historians have done what Foote would have abhorred: they have ignored him. Thomas Hart Benton swore not even to mention his name in his *Thirty Years' View.* When others have referred to him, the comments have been negative. His only biographer, John Edmond Gonzales, suggests that he was a "political chameleon"—aligning himself with first one political party and then another.

Contemporaries had little better to say of him. Jefferson Davis, a fellow Mississippian, found him a thorn in his side in both the U.S. Senate and the Confederate presidency;

HENRY S. FOOTE.   NATIONAL ARCHIVES

Davis, who fought him physically and verbally, denounced him as "a constitutional liar." A colleague in the Confederate Congress described him as a "nuisance" whose conduct on the floor of Congress often was "disgraceful," and a Richmond newspaper editor said he was a "loose and inaccurate thinker."

On the other hand, his Nashville postwar law partner, Arthur S. Colyar, saw him as "one of the brightest intellects on the American continent," but also observed that he was "the most changeable of men." A Mississippian, writing some fifteen years after Foote's death, regarded him as a "foeman worthy of the steel of the ablest opponent of whatever cause espoused." No one questioned his skill at debate and repartee. He had a good basic knowledge of law; indeed, the Nashville Bar Association declared at the time of his death that he had had no equal as a trial lawyer. As a journalist, lawyer, writer, and lawmaker, he was successful. As a politician, he won—perhaps—his share of the contests. Always on the move, he was respected if not loved whether in Alabama, Mississippi, California, Texas, Tennessee, Richmond, or Washington.

Foote was born in Fauquier County, Virginia, February 28, 1804. After graduation from Washington College at the age of fifteen, he studied law and was admitted to the bar at Richmond when nineteen. During his lifetime he established residence and practiced law in half a dozen states and the District of Columbia, in addition to residing for some months in exile in England and Canada.

Foote first settled in Tuscumbia, Alabama, in 1823, where he married, practiced law, and edited a newspaper. His vitriolic journalistic style soon led to a duel with John A. Winston, later governor of Alabama. Neither man was hurt, but Foote was barred from the practice of law in Alabama for three years. Undaunted, he gathered up his family and moved to Mississippi, living and practicing law successively in Jackson, Natchez, and Vicksburg. His support of Andrew Jackson made him known throughout much of Mississippi, and he was elected to the legislature in 1837. At about the same time, he developed a strong interest in the independence movement in Texas and, after paying an extended visit to that new republic, published in 1841 a two-volume work, *Texas and the Texans*.

But his primary interest was politics, not law and journalism, and he aligned himself with the Democratic party in Mississippi, becoming one of the party's most respected leaders. He served, with Jefferson Davis, as a presidential elector in 1844 and vigorously supported James K. Polk because of Polk's willingness to annex Texas. In 1847 he was elected to the U.S. Senate.

In Washington, Foote became one of the architects of the Compromise of 1850, although his colleague Davis, and indeed all of the Mississippi House delegation, bitterly opposed the measure. But he saw the compromise as a means of preserving the Union; as a strong Union supporter in a state where secession already was being discussed, he risked his political future to work for the measure's passage. In 1851, boldly heading the Union Democrats, he announced for governor and was elected by a small majority over Davis, a state rights Democrat—a feat attributable to his oratorical abilities and his powers of persuasion.

He was unhappy as governor because his interests lay primarily in national politics. He had supported Franklin Pierce for president and hoped for a cabinet post but received "a cruel blow" when the president ignored him and appointed Jefferson Davis secretary of war. He offered his candidacy for U.S. Senate in 1854, but the legislature, controlled in large measure by state rights Democrats, elected Albert Gallatin Brown. Soon, in typical Foote fashion, he resigned the governorship a few days before he had finished one term and moved to San Francisco, where he joined his two sons-in-law in the practice of law. By the end of the decade, however, he had returned to Mississippi and again entered politics with vigor. In 1859, he announced for Congress, but because of his Unionist proclivities, he received little encouragement. He withdrew and by midsummer had established a residence and law practice in Nashville.

Foote had been in Nashville less than six weeks when he became aligned with the Democratic party with a view to exerting influence in the presidential election of 1860. Months before Democrats assembled in Charleston to nominate a presidential candidate, Foote had announced his support for Stephen A. Douglas. Alarmed at the Republicans' gains in 1856 and viewing that party as a prime instigator of disunion, he predicted that the Southern states would secede should a Republican be elected. The Illinois Democrat, he said, was the only person who could satisfy all sections and maintain peace.

Douglas's defeat was upsetting to Foote, and he confidently predicted that Abraham Lincoln would bring secession and war. Remembering the Southern convention of 1850, he urged Governor Isham G. Harris and other Tennessee Democrats to call a conference of representatives from the Southern states to meet in Nashville. The fifteen slaveholding states should attempt to secure certain guarantees from the Republicans, he said; that failing, they should declare the Union at an end and withdraw in concert. The last thing they should do, he asserted, was to secede in piecemeal fashion. But these efforts failed, and Foote turned his attention to Tennessee. He worked with Governor Harris and the secessionist Democrats to accomplish separation in the Volunteer State, becoming one of the many former sincere Unionists who gave up hope for a peaceful settlement after Lincoln was inaugurated.

In the early fall of 1861, Foote became a candidate for the Confederate Congress from the Fifth District. He won handily over two opponents, and in early February 1862, he departed for Richmond. He wasted no time in leading the opposition to the administration and soon was at war with Davis and most of the cabinet. He accepted with difficulty the fall of Forts Henry and Donelson and the occupation of Nashville, calling for the dismissal and censure of Secretary of War Judah P. Benjamin and Naval Secretary Stephen R. Mallory. Benjamin, he said, was unfit to hold a cabinet post and Mallory was "utterly incompetent." But he saved most of his invective for his old nemesis, President Davis; he was a person, Foote said, who would establish a dictatorship to serve his own ends, who had only "power for mischief," who was basically corrupt, and who might best serve his country if placed in a mental institution. (He had characterized Thomas Hart Benton in roughly these same terms a decade earlier when both served in the U.S. Senate.)

Foote's propensity for fighting anyone and everyone got him into serious trouble in Richmond, and he occasionally despaired of his life. He had remembered Washington as a place where he had been threatened with fists and guns, but men of the Deep South also fought with knives and clubs. He had only to refer to Alabama Congressman E. S. Dargan as a "damned rascal" when the Alabamian lunged at him with a bowie knife. When Foote ridiculed a congressman from Arkansas, the two came to blows before being separated. When a Richmond editor called upon Congress to censure and expel him for his general conduct, he reacted in such a manner that the editor threatened to kill him. The editor persuaded Congressman William G. Swan to carry a written challenge to Foote, but the irascible Nashvillian responded so violently that Swan stabbed him with the only weapon at hand—an umbrella. The two were arrested and placed under a peace bond by a Richmond magistrate.

Foote referred to himself as the champion of the people against the aggressions of a selfish administration. As such, he boasted that he carefully read all bills introduced, and he presented a large number himself. He bitterly opposed the suspension of the writ of habeas corpus by Earl Van Dorn around the Vicksburg area and attacked Braxton Bragg for imposing martial law in Atlanta. He insisted upon a careful investigation after each battle the Confederacy lost, and he frequently criticized the Davis administration for withholding information on the conduct of the war. He investigated the commissary and cited the waste and profiteering he uncovered. Generally anti-Semitic, he wanted to expel all Jewish traders from the South and constantly urged Davis to dismiss Benjamin from his cabinet. He urged people to accept Confederate paper money, wanted Congress to make it legal tender, and publicly declared that anyone who refused to accept Confederate notes was "deserving of the Penitentiary."

Foote was disturbed that the new government was not accepted in Europe, and on this matter he and President

Davis agreed. Davis was critical of both France and England because they appeared to be "unfriendly," and Foote introduced a resolution urging Davis to recall the Southern envoys from every country that had not granted recognition by May 1, 1863.

Foote and Davis also agreed on the wisdom of trying to persuade the states of the Old Northwest to withdraw from the war. Southern Illinois, Indiana, and Ohio, in large measure, had been settled by migrants from Confederate states, and their sentimental attachment to the land of their birth remained strong. The Northwest was tied to the South by the vast Mississippi River system, and common economic bonds. Also, the peace element in the Democratic party in those states had won important victories in the fall 1862 elections. Both Foote and Davis urged leaders in those states to force Lincoln to make peace and recognize the independence of the South. The matter became one of the many subjects upon which Foote repeatedly addressed Congress.

If there was one characteristic that Foote consistently displayed, it was his inconsistency. Invariably, in matters affecting his political life he fled when the going got rough. So it was with his relationship with the Confederacy. Early in his congressional career he had predicted a short war and an early victory for the South. Always impatient, he urged that the war be taken to the enemy; he would expend a million men and $2 billion, if need be, to take the war into the North and rake those states with fire and sword. It was the Northern people who must be made to feel the harshness of war, he said; their "cupidity" and "semi-barbarous and insatiable lust for . . . domination had started the war," and they must be made to suffer.

He rejoiced in his first few months in Richmond that the Southern people daily became "more enthusiastic and resolute and far more confident as to the ultimate outcome of the struggle." So encouraged was he with victories in the East in the late fall of 1862 that he suggested that commissioners be sent to Washington to propose terms of a just and lasting peace guaranteeing Southern independence. He believed the South had so much support among the common folk of the North that a refusal by the administration would result in a revolt of such magnitude that Lincoln would be deposed. But as Northern armies took Tennessee, the West, and much of the Southwest and ultimately closed in on Atlanta and on Lee in Virginia, he turned to Washington to beg for peace at almost any price.

When Congress convened in November 1864 after a brief recess, Foote expressed a belief that the Confederacy could not hold on beyond spring of the next year. He had given up on Southern independence but believed that a negotiated peace might at least preserve slavery. Congress, however, published a manifesto declaring that the Confederacy would never give up short of independence and then enacted a measure making negotiation with the enemy punishable by fine and imprisonment.

Foote nevertheless was determined to sound out the Federal authorities. He and his wife secretly fled toward Union lines but were overtaken on January 10, 1865, by Confederate troops some thirty-seven miles beyond the picket lines and within five miles of Union troops. Mrs. Foote was permitted to proceed, but Foote was briefly confined in Fredericksburg and then permitted at his request to return to Congress in Richmond. As his colleagues debated censure and expulsion, he fled again—this time successfully—and on January 28 was received across enemy lines and imprisoned. Although he wrote letters to Lincoln, the press, and some of the cabinet members, he was in large measure ignored.

When Andrew Johnson became president, he ordered Foote to either leave the country within forty-eight hours or stand trial for treason and rebellion. Foote fled to Montreal, from where he wrote numerous letters pleading not for the Confederacy but for his own liberty and the right to live in the United States. He wrote Johnson of his hope for peace and prosperity for America and to affirm that he was ready to take the oath of allegiance. To fellow Tennesseans, he wrote advising them to ratify the Thirteenth Amendment and swear allegiance to the United States. Finally, in late August 1865, Johnson permitted him to return to the country. By that time he had taken the oath of allegiance, publicly endorsed black suffrage, and assured all that he would not become involved again in politics.

After Foote paid an extended visit to his daughter and her husband, William M. Stewart, a U.S. senator from Nevada, he lived in St. Louis for a year, writing and speaking. By the summer of 1867, he was back in Nashville and had become affiliated with the conservative Democrats. He campaigned for the Democratic presidential candidate in 1868, and, though the Radical Republicans won the presidency, the conservatives in Tennessee were returned to power. Foote apparently had little confidence in Ulysses S. Grant, but he urged Tennesseans to support the president—another instance of his ambivalence and opportunism.

Writing had been not only a profitable venture for Foote but therapeutic. Early in 1866, Harper and Brothers published his *War of the Rebellion,* a lengthy work covering the colonial period through 1864 but emphasizing the past fifteen years. He saw nothing "irrepressible" about the conflict, but attributed it to a "blundering generation" of the fifties and sixties—the "sectional factionists." In 1873 he moved to Washington where he practiced law and wrote a series of articles for a Washington newspaper. These were collected and published as *Casket of Reminiscences* in 1874. Then, in 1876, he published his last book, *The Bench and Bar of the South and Southwest;* critics complimented the "new" Foote for the absence from this work of the usual vitriolic comments about people he did not like.

By the time his last book circulated, he was back in Tennessee and affiliated with the Republican party, the same party he had vilified since its formation in 1854. Republicans composed the minority party in the Volunteer State, and leaders welcomed him gladly. They named him an elector for the state at large, and he used his position to describe Democrats repeatedly as "unscrupulous men," dishonest and corrupt. Rutherford B. Hayes's victory in 1876 was pleasing to Foote, who for the next four years divided his time between Nashville and Washington. In 1878 he was elected permanent president of the Republican State Convention, and a few men even talked of him for governor. He was seventy-four by that time, however, and a Nashville newspaper described him as "a decrepit old gentleman with a fiery red head, almost entirely bald, . . . leaning heavily on a stout gold-headed cane."

Late in 1878, Hayes appointed him superintendent of the U.S. Mint at New Orleans, where he was well received. By the end of the following year he had become seriously ill and departed in April 1880 for Nashville, where he died on May 19. Former governor Joseph E. Brown of Georgia attended his funeral, and Gen. William Brimage Bate and former Confederate congressmen Robert Looney Caruthers and Arthur Colyar were pallbearers. He was buried in Mt. Olivet Cemetery.

BIBLIOGRAPHY

Chambers, William Nisbet. *Old Bullion Benton: Senator from the New West.* Boston, 1956.

Coulter, E. Merton. *The Confederate States of America, 1861–1865.* A History of the South, vol. 7. Baton Rouge, La., 1950.

DeBerry, John H. "Confederate Tennessee." Ph.D. diss., University of Kentucky, 1969.

Eaton, Clement. *Jefferson Davis.* New York, 1977.

Gonzales, John Edmond. "The Public Career of Henry Stuart Foote, 1804–1880." Ph.D. diss., University of North Carolina, 1957.

Warner, Ezra J., and W. Buck Yearns. *Biographical Register of the Confederate Congress.* Baton Rouge, La., 1975.

ROBERT E. CORLEW

FORAGING. In its proper military context, foraging was defined in H. L. Scott's *Military Dictionary* (1861) as "the collection of forage (food for animals) or other supplies systematically in towns and villages, or going with an escort to cut nourishment for horses in the field. . . . The word foraging is sometimes inaccurately used for marauding." By the end of the Civil War foraging would have a far more devastating definition.

When the war began, foraging was a routine means of resupply covered by standard military operating procedures. The foraging command was to contact local leaders and levy demands for supplies upon them. If the requested supplies were not forthcoming, then the unit was to take them by force, an operation also covered by strict military procedure. To ensure accountability, the commander was to divide the areas to be foraged into subsections. Detachment commanders were to operate only in their assigned areas. Guards were to arrest any foragers who became unruly. In addition, individuals whose property was taken were to be reimbursed, paid in kind, or given a voucher. These procedures were to be used in both friendly and enemy territory.

For the Federals, the war changed the nature of foraging from a military necessity used to resupply a unit to an offensive operation designed to punish the South. One of the first instances of the new use of foraging occurred in Virginia in June 1862. Shortly after taking command of the newly formed Federal Army of Virginia, Maj. Gen. John Pope issued a directive stipulating that his army would live off the surplus of Virginia's farms. General Order No. 5 further directed that only loyal citizens of the United States would be issued vouchers for their confiscated goods. By not mentioning how Confederate farmers were to be treated, Pope had unwittingly authorized the theft of Southern property by his foragers. Pope later reclaimed General Order No. 5 and issued more explicit instructions to his men, but not before the genie of total war had been let loose. For waging war against civilians Pope was labeled a "miscreant" by Gen. Robert E. Lee.

The Confederate armies also used foragers to supply themselves, in both the South and the North. For instance, after the Battle of Second Manassas, the Confederate mapmaker Jedediah Hotchkiss wrote: "The soldiers are very bad, stealing everything eatable they could lay their hands on, after trying to buy it." Both the buying and the stealing would have been done principally by men who considered themselves to be foraging. In the North, the Army of Northern Virginia operated under strict orders to pay for supplies taken, but there were numerous tales of Confederate soldiers being "attacked" by Yankee pigs and chickens that had to be shot in self-defense. Naturally, once dead, such an animal could not go to waste and had to be cooked and eaten.

In 1863 foraging became a standard offensive operation for Federal armies in the West. Gen. Ulysses S. Grant in his Vicksburg campaign began a practice that culminated in Gen. William Tecumseh Sherman's devastating Georgia campaign and March to the Sea. During the march there was no Federal resupply and Sherman's men foraged an eighty-mile-wide path of destruction through Georgia. His foragers earned the nickname "bummers" for their activities, and the name was later applied to all of Sherman's soldiers. Sherman continued to use foraging as an offensive operation in South and North Carolina.

As bad as the destruction was in Georgia, Federal Gen. Philip Sheridan's 1864 Shenandoah Valley campaign was worse. General Grant had ordered Gen. David Hunter to have his soldiers "eat out Virginia clear and clean as far as they go, so that crows flying over it for the balance of the season will have to carry their provender with them." The inept Hunter was defeated in the valley, but Sheridan was different. He also had been ordered to clean out the valley and so he did, burning two thousand barns and seventy mills in the process.

Foraging became one of the most feared of Federal tactics in the South for it left great areas without food for civilians and fodder for any farm animals the armies left. What started as a method of resupply for hungry armies became the keystone of total war.

[See also Bummers.]

BIBLIOGRAPHY

Hotchkiss, Jedediah. *Make Me a Map of the Valley*. Dallas, Tex., 1973.

Scott, H. L. *Military Dictionary*. New York, 1861.

McFeely, Mary D., and William S. McFeely, eds. *Memoirs and Selected Letters: Ulysses S. Grant*. New York, 1990.

Sherman, William T. *Memoirs of General William T. Sherman*. New York, 1873.

U.S. War Department. *War of the Rebellion: A Compilation of the Official Records of the Union and Confederate Armies*. Washington, D.C., 1880–1901. Ser. 1. Vol. 2, p. 50; vol. 12, pt. 3, p. 573; vol. 27, pt. 3, pp. 912–913.

P. NEAL MEIER

FORD, ANTONIA (1838–1871), spy. The daughter of a prominent merchant in Fairfax Court House, Virginia, Ford began her career as a spy in 1861 by passing information she gathered from Union forces in her hometown to Confederate leaders Col. J. E. B. Stuart and Gen. P. G. T. Beauregard. Although the exact nature of Ford's espionage activities is unclear, they seem to have been appreciated by Stuart, who rewarded Ford, on October 7, 1861, with a commission as an honorary aide-de-camp.

Gen. Lafayette C. Baker, chief of Union counterintelligence, was aware of Ford's reputation: in March 1863, in the wake of Col. John S. Mosby's famous capture of Gen. Edwin H. Stoughton in Fairfax Court House, Baker placed a female counterspy in Fairfax to entrap Ford. Ford allegedly revealed to the counterspy that she had aided Mosby, and as a result, she was arrested on March 13, 1863, and committed to Old Capitol Prison in Washington, D.C. A few months later, Ford was released and sent on to Richmond as part of a prisoner exchange. Mosby in later years adamantly maintained that Ford had nothing to do with the Stoughton incident.

A year after Ford's arrest, on March 10, 1864, she married the Union officer who had arrested her, Maj. Joseph C. Willard. The couple settled in Washington, D.C., where Antonia Ford died in 1871.

BIBLIOGRAPHY

Bakeless, John. *Spies of the Confederacy.* Philadelphia, 1970.
Kane, Harnett T. *Spies for the Blue and Gray.* New York, 1954.

ELIZABETH R. VARON

FORD, SAMUEL HOWARD (1819–1905), congressman from Kentucky. English-born Samuel H. Ford played a brief and rather inconsequential role in the Confederate Congress and had at best a tangential relationship to his Kentucky constituency. The son of a Baptist minister who immigrated first to Illinois and then to Missouri, Ford graduated from the University of Missouri in 1843. Though licensed to preach three years earlier, he also was ordained a Baptist minister in 1843. During the antebellum period Ford held pastorates in Jefferson City, St. Louis, and Cape Girardeau, Missouri, in Memphis, Tennessee, and in Louisville, Kentucky. A religious scholar, he authored *Origin of Baptists* (1860) and edited *Ford's Christian Repository* and the Missouri *Baptist*.

Late in 1861 Ford left Louisville and sided with the Provisional Government of Kentucky, which appointed this "obscure Baptist minister" to the Provisional Congress from the Seventh District. Ford attended only the last six weeks of the Provisional Congress and served on the Inauguration Committee. During his short tenure in office, he generally favored the prerogatives of the states over the Davis administration but supported centralization when local interests were not jeopardized. Ford did not stand for election to the First Congress, but he did serve briefly as chaplain of the House of Representatives. He soon after returned to the life of a pastor, encouraging congregations in Memphis, Tennessee, and Mobile, Alabama, to support the Confederacy.

Following the war, Ford returned to Memphis and renewed publication of the *Christian Repository*. He later moved to St. Louis, where he continued to edit his newspaper and write religious history.

BIBLIOGRAPHY

Alexander, Thomas B., and Richard E. Beringer. *The Anatomy of the Confederate Congress: A Study of the Influences of Member Characteristics on Legislative Voting Behavior, 1861–1865.* Nashville, Tenn., 1972.
Quisenberry, A. C. "The Alleged Secession of Kentucky." *Register of the Kentucky State Historical Society* 15 (1917): 15–32.
Warner, Ezra J., and W. Buck Yearns. *Biographical Register of the Confederate Congress.* Baton Rouge, La., 1975.

JOHN DAVID SMITH

FOREIGNERS. Contrary to popular myth, the Confederate States of America was not an entirely homogeneous society. The eleven states of the Confederacy had a white population of almost 5.5 million, of whom nearly a quarter of a million, or about 4 to 5 percent, were alien. The foreign-born percentages in two states were surprisingly high—Texas, over 7 percent, and Louisiana, over 11 percent—and Florida and Virginia each had more than 2 percent. In all Confederate states except Texas, the Irish were more numerous than any other ethnic group, followed by the Germans and the English.

The Home Front. The Germans created a German belt of sorts in south-central Texas where by their very numbers and geographic isolation they were able to reconstruct much of their Old World culture. In Texas and Virginia, the immigrants cultivated distinctive Texas-German and Shenandoah-German dialects, agricultural practices, housing styles, arts and crafts, food preparations, and folkways. The rural Germans, like other groups of immigrants living in the backcountry of Alabama, Tennessee, and North Carolina, did not significantly affect the balance of Confederate political power. In fact, most rural immigrants in the Confederacy largely eschewed politics, turning instead to their own institutions, and thus provided no challenge to the Confederacy's insistence on slavery and a conservative social order.

On the other hand, immigration did have a major effect upon the Confederacy's urban life. In many ways, the presence of immigrants in Southern cities made those urban areas less Southern and more Northern in appearance. Ethnic churches, presses, musical societies, theaters, beer gardens, and fraternal organizations took their places within the heart of the Confederacy. Through such port cities as New Orleans; Galveston, Texas; Mobile, Alabama; Savannah, Georgia; and Charleston, South Carolina, many hopeful immigrants arrived. But because of poverty, disease, or circumstance they often remained in the poorest neighborhoods near the wharves and warehouses. As their numbers grew in these cities and in such river cities as

Percentage of Foreigners in State Population in 1860

	IRISH	GERMAN	ENGLISH	TOTAL FOREIGN
Ala.	.59	.27	.12	1.28
Ark.	.30	.26	.09	.86
Fla.	.60	.34	.23	2.36
Ga.	.62	.23	.11	1.10
La.	3.98	3.48	.56	11.44
Miss.	.49	.25	.11	1.08
N.C.	.09	.08	.07	.33
S.C.	.70	.38	.11	1.42
Tenn.	1.12	.35	.18	1.91
Tex.	.58	3.40	.28	7.19
Va.	1.03	.66	.26	2.19

Memphis and Louisville, an immigrant-related political backlash emerged.

On the eve of the Civil War the immigrant population in the urban South decidedly changed the size, character, and composition of the working classes in Southern cities. The foreign-born became the major source of free labor in all key Confederate river and port cities. As the immigrants assumed positions in drayage, smithing, fitting shops, and taxi and hotel services, they drove blacks into manual labor and the resulting economic competition created additional strains in race relations.

The poverty of the immigrants and their tenuous relationship with Southern blacks made them suspect in the eyes of native-born white Southerners. Southern politicians viewed the immigrants as a danger to the urban social order and thus supported the enlarging of police forces—often ironically by hiring the foreign-born themselves—to control immigrant and black behavior. Nativism emerged, directed especially at the Irish Catholics who were accused of rowdyism, drunkenness, and consorting with blacks (even though they competed with them for jobs). Confusing causes with consequences, when disease and epidemic broke out in the poorest sections of Southern cities, white Southerners immediately concluded that immigrants threatened their region. Election riots involving Irish immigrants only fanned the fires of nativism. Defenders of the Confederacy proclaimed that the presence of immigrants in the South only brought to Southern cities all the social, economic, political, and cultural ills of the North.

Nevertheless, nativism did not consume Southern cities as it did those in the North because most immigrants remained either apolitical or staunchly supportive of slavery and the Confederate cause. Urban politicians eventually even acknowledged the immigrant presence by adding German and Irish names to the ballot, but Southern immigrants remained as yet too unorganized to create an effective political base.

The Military. Foreigners in the Confederacy occupied virtually every socioeconomic category. Some rose to prominence as politicians, lawyers, editors, or doctors, and many found their calling in military service. As might be expected, significant foreign companies were raised from areas with diverse, cosmopolitan populations such as Mobile, Alabama, and New Orleans, Louisiana. Various units comprised men of Irish, German, Scottish, French, Spanish, Mexican, Italian, and Chinese backgrounds.

Many of these men enlisted in the colorful regiments known as Zouaves. Organized in 1831 in Algeria, the Zouaves eventually admitted Europeans into their ranks. Like their namesakes, the Confederate Zouaves were noted for their gaudy dress of baggy trousers, short open jackets with extravagant embroidery, white gaiters, and turban headdresses. Perhaps most famous among the Confederate Zouaves were the Louisiana Zouaves, a name given to at least three regiments commonly known as the Tigers. Composed mainly of French, Italians, and creoles, the Louisiana Tigers were recruited from the most undisciplined and irreverent elements of New Orleans. Although they had a reputation as chronic troublemakers, their performance on the battlefields was impressive.

Another group of foreigners in the Confederate army was the European Brigade. Formed in February 1862 as the Union army advanced into Louisiana, the brigade was composed mostly of Europeans living in New Orleans. Among its numbers were 2,500 Frenchmen, 800 Spaniards, 500 Italians, 400 Germans, Dutchmen, and Scandinavians, and 500 Swiss, Belgians, Englishmen, Slavonians, and Austrians. The European Brigade performed yeoman duty

Louisiana Tigers. In New Orleans, 1861.

during the Federal capture of New Orleans. With few Confederate troops left in the city, Mayor J. T. Monroe called upon the brigade, under Col. Paul Juge, to maintain law and order in the Crescent City. When Confederates threatened to burn the city rather than submit to Union control, the European Brigade suppressed the movement. Mayor Monroe prevailed upon Juge, who had planned to retire, to keep his men under arms until order was restored and the transition to Federal control was completed. The European Brigade disbanded in May 1862. It was given much credit by the mayor and the citizens of the city for maintaining the public order and preventing wanton destruction of life and property during very frightening times. Much like native-born Confederates the foreign-born served in the home guards to provide local defense, to preserve order, to guard property and commissary stores, to stand guard at prison camps, and to do provost duty in general.

Only two foreign-born Confederates attained the rank of major general. Irish-born Patrick Cleburne distinguished himself at the Battles of Shiloh; Richmond, Kentucky; and Franklin. His British military background, discipline, and charm earned him the respect of his men and admiration of his superiors despite opposition from some Southerners because of his foreign birth. The Frenchman Camille J. Polignac fought at the Battles of Shiloh and Corinth and in the Red River campaign. When he died in 1913 he was the longest surviving Confederate major general. The dashing Prussian-born cavalryman Heros von Borcke was perhaps the most widely known foreigner in the Confederate army. Chief of staff and close friend to Gen. J. E. B. Stuart, von Borcke participated in all of Stuart's campaigns and flamboyantly carried into battle what was reputedly the largest sword in the Confederacy.

[See also Cleburne, Patrick; Germans; Irish; Louisiana Tigers; Polignac, Camille J.; Population.]

BIBLIOGRAPHY

Jones, Terry L. *Lee's Tigers: The Louisiana Infantry in the Army of Northern Virginia.* Baton Rouge, La., 1987.
Lonn, Ella. *Foreigners in the Confederacy.* Chapel Hill, N.C., 1940. Reprint, Gloucester, Mass., 1965.
Silverman, Jason H. *Beyond the Melting Pot in Dixie: Immigration and Ethnicity in Southern History.* Lexington, Ky., forthcoming.
Silverman, Jason H. "Stars, Bars, and Foreigners: The Immigrant and the Making of the Confederacy." *Journal of Confederate History* 1 (1988): 265–285.

JASON H. SILVERMAN

FORMAN, THOMAS MARSH

FORMAN, THOMAS MARSH (1809–1875), congressman from Georgia. Thomas Forman was born Thomas Forman Bryan on his father's plantation on Wilmington Island near Savannah, Georgia. His father, Joseph Bryan, died when his son was three, and Thomas moved to Maryland with his mother, where he was adopted by his maternal grandfather. He later made Forman his last name in order to comply with stipulations in his grandfather's will. He was educated at St. Mary's College in Baltimore and returned to manage the Bryan plantation on Wilmington Island until he sold it in 1831. He bought another a few miles south on Broughton Island in McIntosh County, the first of several tracts of land that made him by 1860 one of coastal Georgia's wealthiest planters.

Other than a single term in the state legislature in 1847 and 1848, Forman never held public office until he was elected to fill the vacancy in the Provisional Congress created by the death of Francis S. Bartow at First Manassas. Forman served from August 1861 to February 1862. He actively represented cotton interests by urging a policy of free trade with any nation not engaged in war with the Confederacy and by advocating that the government buy the entire 1861 cotton crop at 1860 market prices. Congress's failure to enact such legislation led to the defeat of Forman and other congressmen who sought reelection in November 1861 to the First Congress. Forman's reelection bid was also hurt by his failure to win special port of entry status for Savannah. He spent the rest of the war raising funds for the Georgia State Navy and continuing to lobby for policies favorable to cotton prices and trade.

Forman suffered serious financial setbacks as a result of the war and emancipation, and he spent his final decade attempting to recoup those losses on his various plantations. In 1875, Forman died at his plantation in Brunswick, Georgia.

BIBLIOGRAPHY

Knight, Lucian Lamar. *Standard History of Georgia and Georgians.* New York, 1917.
Warner, Ezra J., and W. Buck Yearns. *Biographical Register of the Confederate Congress.* Baton Rouge, La., 1975.

JOHN C. INSCOE

FORNEY, JOHN HORACE

FORNEY, JOHN HORACE (1829–1902), major general. Forney, who was born August 12, 1829, at Lincolnton, North Carolina, was the younger brother of Brig. Gen. William Henry Forney. The family moved to Alabama in 1835, and in 1852 Forney graduated from West Point, twenty-second out of forty-three. He served on the frontier and participated in the Mormon campaign.

When the secession crisis began, he was teaching at West Point and resigned on January 23, 1861. Forney was placed in command of Alabama artillery and ordered to Pensacola. On March 16, 1861, he transferred to the Confederate service and was commissioned a captain. Forney joined

Braxton Bragg's staff and remained there until he became colonel of the Tenth Alabama Infantry on June 4, 1861. He served in the Shenandoah Valley and led E. Kirby Smith's brigade after Smith was wounded at First Manassas. Forney himself suffered a severe wound in his arm at Dranesville in December 1861. The next year, he was promoted to brigadier general on March 10 and to major general on October 27. He commanded the Department of Southern Alabama and West Florida and then the District of the Gulf, Department No. 2. Forney commanded a division in Mississippi early in 1863 and was at Vicksburg when John C. Pemberton surrendered. In 1864 he was transferred to the Trans-Mississippi Department where he took command of John G. Walker's Texas Infantry Division. Many of the Texans were opposed to serving under Forney, however, for they regarded him as too strict. As a result, he did not assume command until September and was subsequently replaced by the popular Walker in May 1865.

After the war, Forney returned to Alabama. He died September 13, 1902, in Jacksonville, Alabama, and is buried there.

BIBLIOGRAPHY

Daugette, Annie Forney. "The Life of Major General John H. Forney, Written by His Daughter." *Alabama Historical Quarterly* 9 (1947): 361–383.

Henderson, Harry McCorry. *Texas in the Confederacy.* San Antonio, Tex., 1955.

Parks, Joseph H. *General Kirby Smith, C.S.A.* Baton Rouge, La., 1954.

ANNE J. BAILEY

FORNEY, WILLIAM HENRY (1823–1894), brigadier general and U.S. congressman.

In the first months of 1865 the Confederacy prepared its armies for the spring campaign. Regiments reenlisted, a public debate raged over arming blacks to fight for the South, and many badly needed promotions were made. Forney, who had served in the Army of Northern Virginia since 1861 and had commanded a brigade for several months, received one of those last-minute appointments to brigadier general.

He was born in Lincolnton, North Carolina, on November 9, 1823. After his family moved to Alabama he graduated from the University of Alabama in 1844, practiced law, and served as a lieutenant in the Mexican War. Forney entered Confederate service as a captain in the Tenth Alabama Infantry, the regiment commanded by his brother John Horace Forney. William was promoted to major and then to lieutenant colonel, and he was wounded and captured at Williamsburg on May 5, 1862.

After his exchange a few months later Forney was promoted to colonel and led the Tenth Alabama in the Fredericksburg and Chancellorsville campaigns. He was wounded three times—the last severely—on July 2, 1863, at Gettysburg and was again captured. Though he served the rest of the war on crutches, Forney commanded an Alabama brigade in the army's Third Corps from his return to duty in November 1864 to the war's end. He was promoted to brigadier general on February 15, 1865; his brigade was one of the largest in Robert E. Lee's army when it surrendered at Appomattox.

Forney practiced law in Alabama after the war and served in the U.S. House of Representatives from 1875 to 1893. He died in Jacksonville, Alabama, on January 16, 1894.

BIBLIOGRAPHY

Compiled Military Service Records. William H. Forney. Microcopy M331, Roll 96. Record Group 109. National Archives, Washington, D.C.

Wheeler, Joseph. *Alabama.* Vol. 7 of *Confederate Military History.* Edited by Clement A. Evans. Atlanta, 1899. Vol. 8 of extended ed. Wilmington, N.C., 1987.

J. TRACY POWER

FORREST, FRENCH (1796–1866), naval officer.

Born in St. Mary's County, Maryland, Forrest entered the U.S. Navy as a midshipman in June 1811. He was aboard USS *Hornet* when it fought HMS *Peacock* in 1813 and claimed service in the Battle of Lake Erie. Rising to the rank of captain in 1844, he commanded the landing operations of Gen. Winfield Scott's American army at Vera Cruz during the Mexican War. From 1855 to 1856 he was the head of the Washington Navy Yard.

Resigning his commission after Virginia's secession, Forrest joined the state navy of Virginia as a captain in April 1861. He accepted a commission at the same rank in the Confederate navy in June, making him its third-ranking officer. He had commanded the navy yard at Norfolk while in Virginia service, and he remained in that position when he entered the Confederate navy. His primary task was the reconstruction of the ineffectively scuttled USS *Merrimack* into the ironclad ram CSS *Virginia*. Command of the vessel, however, went to Franklin Buchanan, much to Forrest's disappointment. Forrest was replaced at Norfolk three months after the Battle of Hampton Roads to become the head of the Office of Orders and Details. There he was responsible for ensuring the flow of correspondence and orders within the Confederate Naval Department.

In March 1863 he took command of the James River Squadron. Frustrated by this squadron's relative inactivity, Secretary of the Navy Stephen R. Mallory replaced him with Commdr. John K. Mitchell in May 1864. Since his name disappears from the roster of Confederate naval officers by June, he apparently was dismissed from the service. After

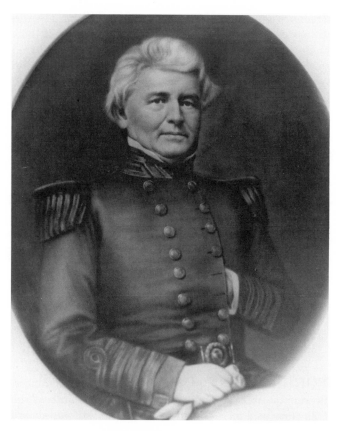

FRENCH FORREST. Pre–Civil War portrait of Forrest in a Union uniform.   NAVAL HISTORICAL CENTER, WASHINGTON, D.C.

the war, he returned to his home in Alexandria, Virginia, and died in Washington, D.C., in November 1866.

BIBLIOGRAPHY

Forrest, Douglas French. *Odyssey in Gray: A Diary of Confederate Service, 1863–1865.* Richmond, Va., 1979.

Johnson, Allen, and Dumas Malone, eds. *Dictionary of American Biography.* New York, 1931.

Still, William N., Jr. *Iron Afloat: The Story of the Confederate Armorclads.* Nashville, Tenn., 1971.

ROBERT S. BROWNING III

FORREST, NATHAN BEDFORD (1821–1877), lieutenant general. Forrest was born in Chapel Hill, Tennessee, on July 13, 1821. Although he had barely six months' formal education, Forrest assumed responsibility for his family at the age of sixteen following his father's death. Life in the Southern backcountry, the demands of Southern honor, and a constant struggle for control conditioned his life.

Forrest supported his family until 1842, when he moved to Hernando, Mississippi, to go into business with an uncle.

In 1851, he relocated to Memphis, Tennessee, where he engaged extensively in the slave trade, establishing one of the largest such operations in the region. With the money he obtained, he rose from semisubsistence to planter status, acquiring substantial plantation property in Coahoma County, Mississippi. Throughout his prewar years, Forrest held various public offices and positions of authority: constable in Hernando; coroner in DeSoto County, Mississippi; lieutenant in the DeSoto Dragoons (Fifty-first Regiment, Mississippi Militia); and alderman in Memphis from 1858 to 1859 and in 1860.

Following Tennessee's secession from the Union, Forrest enlisted as a private in Capt. Josiah White's Tennessee Mounted Rifles (Seventh Tennessee Cavalry) with his youngest brother and fifteen-year-old son. Shortly afterward, the governor of Tennessee summoned him to Memphis and authorized him to raise a battalion of mounted troops, which later became known as the Third Tennessee Cavalry Regiment. As a lieutenant colonel, Forrest recruited and equipped his command, mostly at his own expense. In his first substantial combat experience at Sacramento, Kentucky, on December 28, 1861, he demonstrated the traits that characterized him as a soldier throughout the war by employing envelopment tactics and engaging the enemy personally.

In February 1862, Forrest established a reputation for boldness when he led his men out of Fort Donelson before its surrender, after having participated actively in its defense. Following his election as colonel, the cavalry commander fought at Shiloh, suffering a severe wound during the final phase of that battle. Subsequently, he assumed a new command, later known simply as Forrest's cavalry brigade, and promptly won promotion to brigadier

NATHAN BEDFORD FORREST.   NATIONAL ARCHIVES

general following a daring raid against the Union garrison at Murfreesboro, Tennessee, on July 13, 1862.

In mid-December 1862, Forrest crossed the Tennessee River into the western part of the state on a raid designed to sever Maj. Gen. Ulysses S. Grant's supply lines. For two and a half weeks, Forrest's cavalrymen used bluff and bluster to capture railroad depots, burn supplies, and disable miles of track and trestlework. Forrest succeeded in eluding his pursuers until December 31, when he fought a pitched battle at Parker's Crossroads. He was on the verge of winning the battle when a second Union force appeared, at which point he was fortunate just to extricate the bulk of his command. Nevertheless, Forrest succeeded in crippling Grant's supply lines and thwarting that general's initial assault against Vicksburg, Mississippi.

On February 3, 1863, Forrest's command suffered a defeat at Dover, Tennessee, while under the overall command of Maj. Gen. Joseph Wheeler. Then, following redeeming victories at Thompson and Brentwood, Tennessee, Forrest successfully halted a raid in April and May 1863 by Union Col. Abel Streight against the Western and Atlantic Railroad. In the climax to his pursuit, the Confederate cavalryman again used psychology and deception to compel a numerically superior force to surrender to him. Forrest was a master of this kind of warfare. In the case of his confrontation with Abel Streight, he employed false couriers from phantom units and moved the minimal number of troops at hand so as to artificially inflate his command.

Forrest's cavalry participated in Braxton Bragg's retreat from central Tennessee, his evacuation of Chattanooga, and the subsequent battle along Chickamauga Creek, Georgia. Following the victory over William S. Rosecrans's Federals at Chickamauga, Forrest urged but failed to convince Bragg to pursue the defeated enemy. Angry at his superior's ineptitude and resenting Bragg's previous treatment of him, Forrest bitterly denounced Bragg and won a transfer to an independent command in Mississippi.

For the third time in his military career, Forrest raised a command, known simply as Forrest's cavalry corps, with new recruits and conscripts joining a small nucleus of veterans. Promoted to major general on December 4, 1863, he led raids against Federal communications and supply lines in Tennessee and Alabama and blunted various Union raids into Mississippi throughout 1864. In April, he conducted a raid into western Tennessee that culminated in the capture of Fort Pillow. In the latter stages of that battle, Forrest lost control of his men, who killed members of the black Tennessee Unionist garrison who should have been spared.

In June, Forrest ably defeated and routed a superior force of Union infantry and cavalry at Brice's Cross Roads. In July, he helped turn back another Federal invasion force at Tupelo, although he suffered a temporarily disabling wound while directing the pursuit of the retreating Union troops. After recovering from his wound, Forrest engaged in a generally successful effort to destroy the railroads of northern Alabama and central Tennessee and decimated the river supply depot at Johnsonville, Tennessee. He cut short the Johnsonville expedition to march with John Bell Hood in that general's disastrous Tennessee campaign in November and December 1864. Forrest's outstanding conduct of the rear guard in Hood's retreat from Nashville, Tennessee, saved the Army of Tennessee from further destruction.

Forrest returned to Mississippi to reorganize his cavalry command. During this period he received a promotion to lieutenant general to date from February 28, 1865. In the closing months of the war, Forrest attempted to restore the condition of his command to resist further Union advances. Despite his preparations, he was unable to prevent a vastly superior force under Brig. Gen. James Harrison Wilson from dispersing his command and capturing Selma, Alabama, in March and April 1865. Forrest regrouped his men a final time before surrendering them at Gainesville, Alabama, in May.

Following the war, Forrest struggled to regain control over his life during Reconstruction and in the face of a series of business failures. For some years, he served as president of and worked diligently to promote the Selma, Marion, and Memphis Railroad. Contrary to his avowal at the end of the war to remain quietly at home, he embraced the budding Ku Klux Klan and assumed the role of first grand wizard of the secret organization. Never completely adjusting to the new realities of the postwar years, Forrest helped restore white Conservative Democrats to power and sought to reassert white supremacy in the South. He died in Memphis on October 29, 1877, having failed to recoup his prewar fortune.

Nathan Bedford Forrest stands as one of the foremost cavalry raiders of the war. His ferocity as a warrior was almost legendary. His claim to have slain one more enemy soldier in personal combat than the twenty-nine horses killed beneath him only added to the legend. Forrest fought by the simple maxim "Forward men, and mix with 'em." He understood, perhaps better than most, the basic premise of war: "War means fighting and fighting means killing."

BIBLIOGRAPHY

Henry, Robert Selph. *"First with the Most" Forrest.* Indianapolis, 1944.

Jordan, Thomas, and J. P. Pryor. *The Campaigns of Lieut. Gen. N. B. Forrest, and of Forrest's Cavalry.* New Orleans, 1868.

Lytle, Andrew. *Bedford Forrest and His Critter Company.* New York, 1931.

Mathes, J. Harvey. *General Forrest.* New York, 1902.

Wills, Brian Steel. *A Battle from the Start: The Life of Nathan Bedford Forrest.* New York, 1992.

Wyeth, John Allan. *Life of General Nathan Bedford Forrest.* New York, 1899. Reprint, Baton Rouge, La., 1989.

BRIAN S. WILLS

FORREST'S RAIDS. Gen. Nathan Bedford Forrest conducted three principal cavalry raids against Federal garrisons and supply lines in his native state of Tennessee during the Civil War. He undertook forays behind Union lines throughout his career, but those in July 1862 against the Union garrison at Murfreesboro, in December 1862 and January 1863 against Union lines in western Tennessee, and in November 1864 against the Union depot and storage facility at Johnsonville, established his reputation as one of the South's foremost cavalry raiders.

The first of these raids occurred in July 1862, when Colonel Forrest, already recommended for promotion to brigadier general for his conduct at Fort Donelson and Shiloh, took his cavalry command across the Tennessee River. At McMinnville he received reinforcements and prepared for a push on the Union garrison at Murfreesboro. Arriving at the town early on July 13, Forrest divided his men into three groups. The first was to attack the nearest Union camp of the Ninth Michigan Infantry and the Seventh Pennsylvania Cavalry, the second was to storm the town, and the third was to hit the camp of the Third Minnesota on the farthest side of Murfreesboro.

Forrest expected the operation to proceed smoothly, but complications developed. The Federals in the town surrendered, but the others quickly rallied after the surprise attack and put up a stubborn defense. Forrest led his men against the Minnesotans, capturing their camp and some prisoners. As his troopers pinned down these Federals, he rode off to supervise the fighting in the other camp. When one of his officers recommended that they break off the raid before Union reinforcements arrived, Forrest answered characteristically, "I did not come here to make half a job of it. I mean to have them all."

Through the astute use of bluff, Forrest soon convinced both of the remaining Union commanders to surrender. His victory netted the Confederates 1,200 prisoners and substantial stores of weapons and equipment. He had inflicted casualties of 29 killed and 120 wounded while sustaining losses of 25 killed and 40 to 60 wounded.

Forrest's second major raid into Tennessee took place between December 11, 1862, and January 2, 1863. In compliance with orders to destroy the Union supply lines in western Tennessee, Brigadier General Forrest set out from Columbia, Tennessee, on December 11 to wreck the track and trestlework of the Mississippi Central and the Mobile and Ohio Railroads.

The Southerners reached the Tennessee River crossing at Clifton on December 15, pushing across the river on flatboats by late the next night. As the Confederates moved toward Jackson, Tennessee, they encountered Union troops under Col. Robert G. Ingersoll. The two forces clashed, with the Southerners routing and capturing much of Ingersoll's command, including the colonel, 147 men, and two 3-inch Rodman cannons.

Forrest then used several ploys to deceive Brig. Gen. Jeremiah C. Sullivan into believing that the Confederates were in front of Lexington in superior numbers. Sullivan obliged Forrest by concentrating his forces and conceding the countryside to the Southerners. Forrest seized the opportunity to dispatch forces to attack depots and destroy track and bridges north and south of the town. He left a thin screen of horsemen to maintain the deception and rode on to capture Humboldt and Trenton.

On December 23, Forrest took Union City and continued to destroy rail lines in the region. In his December 24 report, he noted with satisfaction: "We have made a clean sweep of the Federals and [rail]roads north of Jackson." On Christmas Day, Forrest moved his command to the southeast, with an eye to returning to Confederate lines. Finding that Federal gunboats and burned bridges on the Obion River blocked his path, he located an old, unstable bridge the Federals had ignored, had his men shore up the structure, and pushed his command across the river.

Forrest faced a final obstacle before he could reach the safety of Confederate lines. Union Col. Cyrus Dunham had placed his brigade onto the Confederates' path at Parker's Cross Roads. On December 31, Forrest decided to strike these Federals, capture them if possible, and proceed. Using his artillery and flanking attacks to great advantage, Forrest had almost succeeded when other Federals appeared in his rear, and he was fortunate just to extricate his command from the trap. His men escaped the pincers and reached the crossing at Clifton. Brushing aside a final effort to stop him, Forrest had his men across the river by January 2, 1863.

Despite the rough handling at Parker's Cross Roads, Forrest's western Tennessee raid was a success. Coupled with Brig. Gen. Earl Van Dorn's capture of Maj. Gen. Ulysses S. Grant's forward supply base at Holly Springs, Mississippi, Forrest's actions crippled Grant's initial assault on Vicksburg.

The third of his Tennessee raids began on October 24, 1864, when Major General Forrest's cavalry command left their base at Jackson, Tennessee. On October 28, the Confederates reached the Tennessee River near Fort Heiman and placed batteries along the bank, concealing them from view. For the next two days, their artillery sparred with Union gunboats and steamers. The Southerners succeeded in capturing and temporarily converting

FORREST'S RAIDERS ATTACKING IRVING PRISON.   During Forrest's 1864 raid on Memphis, Tennessee.

the Union gunboat *Undine* and the steamer *Venus* to Confederate service. Although Forrest lost both ships in subsequent fighting, his crews managed to escape capture and his plans for an attack on the massive depot and storage facility at Johnsonville remained intact.

In the meantime, Forrest began to deploy his troops and artillery across the river from the depot. His cannoneers wrestled their guns into place and concealed them. By 2:00 P.M. on November 4, all was ready. The Confederate gunners, their weapons targeted from as close a range as the terrain would permit, blasted the Union supply base with devastating effectiveness. By nightfall, the entire bank was ablaze.

In the Johnsonville raid, Forrest's men had destroyed four Union gunboats, fourteen transports, twenty barges, and an estimated $6.7 million worth of Federal property. Sherman noted stoically, "That devil Forrest was down about Johnsonville, making havoc among the gunboats and transports." Forrest was also, as in his previous Tennessee raids, enhancing his reputation as a raider.

BIBLIOGRAPHY

Henry, Robert Selph. *"First with the Most" Forrest.* Indianapolis, 1944.
Jordan, Thomas, and J. P. Pryor. *The Campaigns of Lieut.-Gen. N. B. Forrest, and of Forrest's Cavalry.* New Orleans, 1868.
Morton, John Watson. *The Artillery of Nathan Bedford Forrest's Cavalry.* Nashville, Tenn., 1909.
Wills, Brian Steel. *A Battle from the Start: The Life of Nathan Bedford Forrest.* New York, 1992.
Wyeth, John Allan. *Life of General Nathan Bedford Forrest.* New York, 1899. Reprint, Baton Rouge, La., 1989.

BRIAN S. WILLS

FORSYTH, JOHN (1812–1879), peace commissioner, mayor of Mobile, Alabama, colonel, journalist, and editor. As a member of the Confederate peace commission to Washington, Forsyth endeavored to obtain U.S. recognition of his government, establish friendly relations, and negotiate on all questions in order to avoid war. But when he found the Lincoln administration unreceptive, Forsyth concluded that a just peace was unlikely and advised President Jefferson Davis to prepare for war.

Elected mayor of Mobile in 1860, Forsyth continued in that office until 1866 and planned the city's defenses. He also spent considerable time with Confederate troops. He campaigned in Kentucky with Gen. Braxton Bragg in 1862, and in 1864 he received a hip wound at Spotsylvania, when he accompanied an Alabama brigade in its attempt to recapture breastworks at the Bloody Angle.

Under Forsyth's direction the *Mobile Daily Advertiser*

and Register became one of the most influential and often-quoted newspapers in the lower South. As such it reflected Forsyth's devotion to the cause to the bitter end. The *Register* opposed secession until after Abraham Lincoln's election, but thereafter Forsyth became a strong supporter of the Davis administration. The *Register* tirelessly drummed up support for the war effort and heaped abuse upon grumblers and croakers. In 1864 Forsyth belittled William Tecumseh Sherman's successes in Georgia, and in 1865 he castigated those who flirted with the peace movement. He even went so far as to offer to duel the renegade editor Nathaniel S. Morse of the *Augusta Chronicle* for publishing defeatist and pro-peace sentiments.

After the war, Forsyth converted the *Register* into a voice of opposition to Federal Reconstruction legislation.

BIBLIOGRAPHY

Andrews, J. Cutler. *The South Reports the Civil War*. Princeton, N.J., 1970.

Owen, Thomas McAdory. *History of Alabama and Dictionary of Alabama Biography*. 4 vols. Chicago, 1921.

CHARLES MCARVER

FORT DARLING, VIRGINIA. *See* Drewry's Bluff, Virginia.

FORT DELAWARE PRISON. Fort Delaware was a fortification built of cut stone on Peapatch Island to control the navigation of the Delaware River. The fort was near the New Jersey side of the river opposite Delaware City, Delaware. Just after the war's start, the United States used it to hold political and naval prisoners. In the spring of 1862, to handle the growing number of Confederate army prisoners, the Federals built shed barracks inside the fort intended for two thousand men. During the period of exchange under the cartel of July 22, 1862, the fort often served as a way station for officers and enlisted men en route to City Point, Virginia. With the breakdown of exchange in 1863, the Federal authorities declared Fort Delaware to be a regular prison depot and built outside the walls of the original fort additional barracks intended to hold five thousand prisoners.

From 1863 to 1865, the commanding officer of Fort Delaware was Brig. Gen. Albin Francisco Schoepf. A refugee of Austrian-Polish birth, he had received military training in Europe and was a protégé of Joseph Holt, the powerful judge advocate general of the army. Prisoners' complaints against him sometimes reflected antiforeign prejudices, but since Schoepf tried to be verbally conciliatory, especially to captive officers, they often deflected their grievances to his adjutant, Capt. George W. Ahl, whom they blamed for much

of what they disliked about the prison. Ahl headed a unit formed from Confederate deserters who supplemented the militia that made up the principal guard force. These ex-Confederates were inevitably a prominent target of the hatred of the prisoners, who charged them with deliberate cruelty.

Officer prisoners, who were carefully segregated from enlisted men, complained, but they recognized that their housing and usual ability to buy additional food from the civilian provisioner meant that their condition was better than that of the common soldiers. As in other prisons, officers could entertain themselves by reading, holding informal classes and minstrel shows, gambling, and even preparing a manuscript newspaper. But all prisoners complained that the rations of bread and meat served in mess halls were inadequate in both quality and quantity. Even the water was deficient; that used for cleaning came from ditches and the river and was polluted by the fort's own sewage. Drinking water brought in by boat from nearby Brandywine Creek was marginally less noxious. Complaints of dampness in a prison barely above river level were endemic, and indeed in July 1863, the new barracks sank into the mud and several threatened to tip over.

Ill health, including typhoid fever, was to be expected, and in September 1863, 327 men died out of 8,822. A month later, smallpox broke out, yet the U.S. commissary general of prisoners rejected the complaint even of the surgeon general that the fort was not a suitably healthy prison site. And in fact the monthly death toll did decline in 1864, even though the prison reached a maximum population of 9,174. Because literate, vocal officers were among the prisoners, conditions at Fort Delaware elicited frequent denunciations by the Confederate government and newspapers, and the fort became one of the more dreaded prisons in Southern eyes.

Fort Delaware's location convenient to the warring lines guaranteed that it would continue to be used when exchange resumed in 1865, and it was not finally abandoned as a military prison until August 1865. The fort itself was used in the Spanish-American and other wars and then became a Delaware state park. The prison's most significant monument is on the New Jersey shore: the 2,436 Confederate graves in the Finns Point National Cemetery.

BIBLIOGRAPHY

Byrne, Frank L. "Prison Pens of Suffering." In *Fighting for Time*. Edited by William C. Davis. Vol. 4 of *The Image of War, 1861–1865*. Garden City, N.Y., 1983.

Hesseltine, William B. *Civil War Prisons: A Study in War Psychology*. Columbus, Ohio, 1930. Reprint, New York, 1964.

Rich, Edward Robins. *Comrades!* Easton, Md., 1898.

Wilson, W. Emerson. *Fort Delaware*. Newark, Del., 1987.

FRANK L. BYRNE

FORT DONELSON, TENNESSEE. *For discussion of the fall of Fort Donelson, see* Henry and Donelson Campaign.

FORT FISHER, NORTH CAROLINA. Situated at the mouth of the Cape Fear River, Fort Fisher guarded the approaches to the port of Wilmington, North Carolina. A mammoth earthwork, the fort assumed strategic importance late in the war because Wilmington, a favorite base for blockade runners, remained the last major port open for the Confederacy. In December 1864 and January 1865 the Federal command launched two attacks on Fort Fisher that featured a huge number of ships and massive artillery bombardments. On January 15, the fort fell to combined sea and land assaults.

Work began on Fort Fisher in April 1861. In July 1862 Col. William Lamb assumed command and continued the construction of the largest earthwork in the Confederacy and one of the largest in the world. Shaped like a letter L, with the angle pointing in a northeasterly direction out to sea, the fort placed its long side toward the seacoast and threw its short side across a narrow peninsula. Forty-eight guns looked out from behind sandbagged and revetted walls that stood twenty feet high and twenty-five feet thick. Heavy traverses lay between the gun chambers and thus protected gunners from explosions nearby. A shallow ditch, a log palisade, and a mine field further protected the land approach to the fort.

Several other forts lined the Cape Fear River, but Fort Fisher was the key installation. Its size and big guns had kept the Union fleet several miles out at sea. So much hard labor, by slaves and conscripts, had gone into the making of the fort that during Reconstruction, Republicans angled for votes among poorer whites and blacks by warning that the Democrats planned to rebuild it.

On September 2, 1864, U.S. Secretary of the Navy Gideon Welles won approval for his proposal to attack Fort Fisher. After Rear Adm. David Farragut declined command of the naval expedition because of illness, the assignment was given to Rear Adm. David D. Porter. Gen. Benjamin F. Butler headed the troops of the Federal army that would attack following a bombardment. On the Confederate side, Gen. Braxton Bragg was in overall command at Wilmington, with Gen. W. H. C. Whiting immediately responsible for the defense of the city and its approaches. Colonel Lamb commanded the Confederates at the fort. Fifty-six vessels, the largest U.S. armada assembled to that time, sailed to the fort and anchored in a semicircle one-half mile away. Twenty-five hundred Federal troops landed to assault fewer than eight hundred Confederates in the fort.

The first attack began on the night of December 23 as Federal sailors towed an old ship laden with powder and

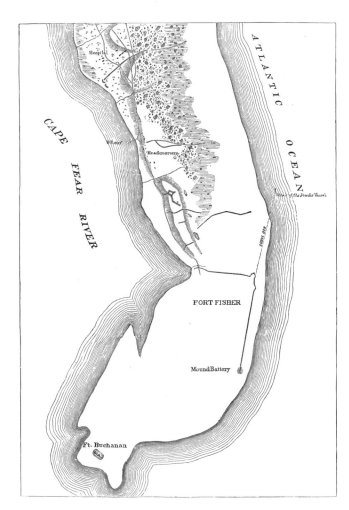

MAP OF FORT FISHER, NORTH CAROLINA.

Harper's Pictorial History of the Great Rebellion

explosives to within three hundred yards of Fort Fisher. General Butler had conceived this idea, believing that a huge explosion could do great damage, but the blast was without consequence. So also was a tremendous bombardment on the twenty-fourth. "Never since the invention of gunpowder," wrote Colonel Lamb, "was there so much of it harmlessly expended as in the first day's attack on Fort Fisher." Another huge bombardment on Christmas Day prepared the way for Butler's ground attack, but when his men had come to within fifty yards of the fort, he ordered a retreat, and the first attack was over.

Admiral Porter asked Gen. Ulysses S. Grant for the same troops and a different commander, and on January 13, 1865, the second battle began with Maj. Gen. Alfred H. Terry landing 8,000 Federal troops against 1,500 Confederates in the fort. Two days of bombardment that General Whiting characterized as "beyond description" did considerable damage to the fort, wounded many of its defenders, and led the Confederate commanders to call for reinforcements from Bragg. Only 350 men arrived. On January 15 a Federal force of 6,000 stormed the fort, now manned by about 1,200 Confederates. Vicious hand-to-hand fighting wavered both ways, but precise support from the navy's guns helped ensure a Federal victory. About 10:00 P.M. on January 15 the Confederates surrendered, having received no effective relief from General Bragg, who had at hand 6,000 troops under Gen. Robert Frederick Hoke and three artillery batteries.

The fall of Fort Fisher deprived the Confederacy of its last connection with the rest of the world. In the second attack Federal forces had lost 670 soldiers and about 400 sailors. The Confederates suffered approximately 500 casualties, including General Whiting (who later died in prison) and Colonel Lamb. Fifteen hundred Confederates were taken as prisoners. Admiral Porter, who wrote that "no one could form the slightest conception of these works . . . who had not seen them," estimated that his fleet expended fifty thousand shells in its attack. In February Federal forces followed up their victory by moving against General Hoke's forces and on February 22 captured Wilmington.

[See also Wilmington, North Carolina.]

BIBLIOGRAPHY

Barrett, John G. The Civil War in North Carolina. Chapel Hill, N.C., 1963.

Gragg, Rod. Confederate Goliath: The Battle of Fort Fisher. New York, 1991.

PAUL D. ESCOTT

FORT HARRISON, VIRGINIA.

Located on the northern side of the James River south of Richmond in an area known as Chaffin's Bluff, Fort Harrison constituted one of the outer defense works protecting the Confederate capital. The fort contained several pieces of large artillery, but only about 150 men when, on September 29 and 30, 1864, Federal troops took possession of it. Both sides incurred substantial losses in the process.

Strategically, an attack on Fort Harrison could benefit the Union in several ways. Federal troops either would gain possession of the fort, enabling them to initiate an attack on Richmond from north of the James River, or would draw Confederate troops away from Robert E. Lee's defenses at Petersburg, which would benefit Ulysses S. Grant in his siege of that city.

At 9:00 P.M. on September 28, the Tenth and Eighteenth Corps of the Union army received orders to move, and by 3:00 A.M. the next morning, they had crossed the James River. As the sun began to rise they met Confederate pickets, but progressed rapidly for two or three miles through a wooded area until they encountered open ground.

The troops halted three-quarters of a mile from the garrison, moved into formation, and then received the order to attack.

After briefly halting at the base of the fort, Northern troopers stormed over the walls amidst a blaze of artillery. The 150 soldiers stationed in the fort could not withstand the attack of an entire division. Union men captured fifteen pieces of artillery and fifty prisoners, but not without suffering substantial losses themselves.

As the Southerners retreated, Union soldiers followed them to Fort Gilmer, four miles from the capital, where the Confederates repulsed another attack. By nightfall, the Federals had retreated to Fort Harrison and spent the night enclosing the fortification and reinforcing it.

Upon hearing of the capture of Fort Harrison, General Lee requested that Gen. Richard S. Ewell retake the garrison. Lee felt that the fort, which guarded the waterway into Richmond, was strategically too important to surrender to the enemy. Ewell arrived at Chaffin's Bluff on the afternoon of the twenty-ninth with Charles W. Field's and Robert Frederick Hoke's divisions to assist in an advance the next day.

The Confederates attacked at 2:00 P.M. on September 30. Vicious fighting ensued, and both sides suffered heavy losses. The Confederates, however, were unable to regain the fort. Poor communications between Confederate commanders and the numerical superiority of the Federal troops plagued the mission. At 8:10 P.M., General Lee reported to Secretary of War James A. Seddon that the attack had failed. The Union remained in control of Fort Harrison for the remainder of the war.

Ultimately, Union troops did not use the acquisition of Fort Harrison as a point from which to thrust Federal soldiers into the Confederate capital. Nor did the attack divert enough Southern troops away from Petersburg to allow Grant to take the city. The capture of Fort Harrison, however, enabled the Union to establish new lines extending to the north and south of the fort, and it forced the Confederates to re-form new lines of defense.

By the close of 1864 the Confederacy suffered a severe shortage of manpower. No reserves existed to replace their casualties. Following the heavy losses at Fort Harrison, Confederate commanders became wary of taking an offensive position unless they felt success was possible.

BIBLIOGRAPHY

Clay, Cecil. A Personal Narrative of the Capture of Fort Harrison. Washington, D.C., 1891.

Freeman, Douglas Southall. Lee's Lieutenants: A Study in Command. 3 vols. New York, 1942–1944. Reprint, New York, 1986.

Hotchkiss, Jed. Virginia. Vol. 3 of Confederate Military History. Edited by Clement A. Evans. Atlanta, 1899. Vol. 4 of extended ed. Wilmington, N.C., 1987.

Sommers, Richard J., and Frank E. Vandiver. *Richmond Redeemed: The Siege at Petersburg.* Garden City, N.Y., 1981.

JENNIFER LUND

FORT HENRY, TENNESSEE. *For discussion of the fall of Fort Henry, see* Henry and Donelson Campaign.

FORT HILL. The South Carolina plantation home of American statesman John C. Calhoun was originally named Clergy Hall when it was built in 1803 and served as a Presbyterian manse during the early settlement of the old Cherokee Indian boundary. Calhoun acquired the property in 1825 through his mother-in-law, although while serving as vice president, he continued to live in the Georgetown section of the District of Columbia. Financial and domestic considerations hastened a decision to return to the South, and he moved his family to Clergy Hall the following year.

Calhoun renamed the house Fort Hill and transformed the original structure of vernacular up-country design into a Greek Revival plantation home of commanding presence, with broad views of the surrounding 1,100-acre estate. Fort Hill allowed Calhoun to indulge his avocation of agriculture. It did not, however, distract him from the political events of the day. In the summer of 1831 the nullification controversy was developing into a national crisis. From his office, located behind the main house, Calhoun wrote the "Fort Hill Address," which gave intellectual focus to the gathering forces of Southern nationalism.

Fort Hill remained a Calhoun family property for nearly forty years after Calhoun's death in 1850. Plantation lands were under cultivation throughout the Civil War, and after the conflict, crops were tended by former Calhoun family slaves working as paid laborers.

Fort Hill came through the Civil War unscathed. After the war, there were Federal troops in the nearby town of Pendleton, but their few acts of vandalism were confined to the town itself. Since 1889, Fort Hill has been the site of Clemson University, a legacy of Calhoun's son-in-law, Thomas Green Clemson.

BIBLIOGRAPHY

Cook, Harriet Hefner. *Fort Hill: John C. Calhoun Shrine.* Revised by Carol C. Brannon. Clemson, S.C., 1970.

Freehling, William W., ed. *The Nullification Era: A Documentary Record.* New York, 1967.

Wilson, Clyde N., and W. Edwin Hemphill, eds. *The Papers of John C. Calhoun.* 20 vols. to date. Columbia, S.C., 1977–.

ROBERT T. BARRETT

FORT PICKENS, FLORIDA. One of three forts that guarded the entrance to Pensacola Bay, Florida, Fort Pickens almost became the site of the first shots of the Civil War. Early in January 1861 a combination of quick thinking by the Federal commander and Southerners' hesitation saved the fort from Confederate capture. By April 16, 1861, the Union had a thousand men and four warships at Fort Pickens, and its possession was never seriously challenged. With the Union forces firmly entrenched in the bay, Confederates could not fully utilize the Pensacola Navy Yard, and by the spring of 1862 all of Pensacola was in Union control.

Secession winter, 1860–1861, found the small Union force at Pensacola threatened with isolation. Fort Pickens along with Forts McRee and Barrancas were key positions for defense of the harbor and the valuable Pensacola Navy Yard. During December and early January, Alabama militia joined Florida secessionists at Pensacola to aid in wresting the forts from U.S. control. But on January 10, the same day that Florida seceded from the Union, Federal forces at Fort Barrancas abandoned their position for the more formidable location at Fort Pickens on the western tip of Santa Rosa Island. This stone garrison contained numerous cannons, thousands of projectiles, loose shot, and several pounds of powder. The Federal lieutenant had only eighty-one men, and the fort, unused since the Mexican War, had fallen into disrepair. Southerners attempted to obtain a peaceful surrender over the next few days, but the small contingent of Federals stood firm. A confrontation seemed only a matter of time.

Confederates soon received word that the warship *Brooklyn* was en route to reinforce Pickens with two hundred men. Two former U.S. senators quickly moved to forestall the outbreak of hostilities. Stephen R. Mallory and John Slidell joined other leaders of the soon-to-be-formed Confederacy in determining that "the possession of the Fort was not worth one drop of blood to us." They approached President James Buchanan with a simple compromise. If he called off the Federal expedition, the state troops that had massed at Pensacola would not attack. Buchanan agreed. On January 29, 1861, *Brooklyn* dropped anchor in the harbor and waited.

After Abraham Lincoln's inauguration in March, the situation began to change. Denying the validity of the quasi armistice, Lincoln sent orders on March 12 to land the company and reinforce the fort, but the ship's commander delayed the landing for a month. Finally, on April 12, the same day Confederates fired on Fort Sumter, two hundred Union men with supplies and ammunition disembarked at Fort Pickens. They were soon joined by an additional eight hundred men.

Between April 12, 1861, and May 9, 1862, five engagements occurred, including incidents of burning, attempted infantry invasions, and artillery duels. In early October Brig. Gen. Braxton Bragg sent a thousand men to make a

FORT PICKENS, PENSACOLA, FLORIDA. View of the flagstaff bastion with the American flag.

HARPER'S PICTORIAL HISTORY OF THE GREAT REBELLION

clandestine attack on the fort. The resulting Battle of Santa Rosa Island ended with Confederates in full retreat and Federals shaken by the surprise. Both sides claimed victory, but the battle left the same stalemate in place that had existed since early spring. On May 9, 1862, the Confederates burned and abandoned their position at Pensacola.

BIBLIOGRAPHY

Bearss, Edwin, "Civil War Operations in and around Pensacola." *Florida Historical Quarterly* 36 (1957): 125–165; 39 (1961): 231–255.

Dickison, J. J. *Florida.* Vol. 11 of *Confederate Military History.* Edited by Clement A. Evans. Atlanta, 1899. Vol. 16 of extended ed. Wilmington, N.C., 1989.

Tilley, John Shipley. *Lincoln Takes Command.* Chapel Hill, N.C., 1941.

LESLEY JILL GORDON-BURR

FORT PILLOW MASSACRE. The Confederates originally constructed the earthwork fortification on the

Mississippi River, north of Memphis, to protect the water approaches to that city. Fort Pillow was situated on a high bluff on the eastern bank, overlooking the river. After the Confederates evacuated the fort in 1862, it became part of the chain of Federal garrisons employed to protect communications and supply lines in the region. In 1864, Maj. Lionel F. Booth commanded a garrison there, variously estimated at between 557 and 580 black and white troops of the Thirteenth Tennessee Cavalry, the Eleventh U.S. Colored Troops, and Battery F of the Fourth U.S. Colored Light Artillery.

In March and April 1864, Maj. Gen. Nathan Bedford Forrest determined to attack the isolated Union garrison as part of a raid into western Tennessee and Kentucky. The first Confederates arrived before Fort Pillow in the early morning hours of April 12, under the command of Brig. Gen. James R. Chalmers. Chalmers succeeded in driving the Federals into their innermost entrenchments and deployed his men. Forrest arrived at 10:00 A.M. to find Fort Pillow virtually surrounded, with Confederate sharpshooters situated on high ground, enabling them to fire directly into the

FORT PILLOW MASSACRE.

fort. Forrest reconnoitered and placed additional sharp-shooters.

These sharpshooters had already profoundly affected the fighting at Fort Pillow. At 9:00 A.M., Confederate fire had struck Booth in the chest as he stood near one of the earthwork's portholes. Maj. William F. Bradford assumed command, although he continued to use Booth's name in negotiations with the Confederates.

Under this covering fire, Forrest's men seized a row of Union barracks and outlying rifle pits. This success convinced the Confederate general that he was now in a position to storm the fort. But, typically, Forrest preferred to take the fort through negotiation, if possible. To that end, at 3:30 P.M., he sent in a demand for the unconditional surrender of the garrison, warning, "Should my demand be refused, I cannot be responsible for the fate of your command."

Bradford insisted upon having an hour to consult with his officers. Forrest, worried that he might use the time to obtain reinforcements, granted him twenty minutes. The Confederate commander also dispatched troops to the riverbank to prevent an approaching Union transport vessel from landing and impatiently rode to the scene of the truce

negotiations. Finally, Bradford declared that he would not surrender. Forrest rode back to his lines and issued orders for an assault.

The Confederates rushed across the relatively short distance to the fort and scaled the parapet. As they swarmed into Fort Pillow, firing point-blank into the defenders, the Federal garrison retreated. In such an eventuality, the Union commanders had planned to rely upon the gunboat *New Era* to drive off the pursuing Southerners and thereby enable the garrison to escape. As the garrison broke for the riverbank below, however, the fighting became chaotic and Bradford was unable to execute the plan. Many of the Federals tried to surrender. Others ran for their lives. Still others fired as they withdrew, apparently hoping to prolong the defense until help could arrive.

Remaining outside Fort Pillow, Forrest lost control of events inside the fort and on the riverbank below. Pent-up anger and racial animosity led some of the Confederates to give their opponents no mercy. Casualty figures demonstrate that members of the fort's garrison, especially black troops, suffered an inordinately high number of deaths. Although the Confederates were the attacking party, they lost just 14 killed and 86 wounded, while the Federal defenders lost 231 killed, 100 wounded, and 226 captured. The victorious Southerners took prisoner only 58 of the 262 black troops engaged.

The Northern press immediately labeled the events at Fort Pillow a "massacre." A U.S. congressional committee investigated the affair, calling witnesses and accumulating often gruesome testimony. The committee determined that a massacre had occurred at the fort. Forrest denied the charges, but the exertions that he and other Confederate officers had to take to prevent unnecessary killings are the most telling testimony that such slaughter took place and that, for however long, he was powerless to prevent it. In any event, as commander of the troops on the scene, Forrest was responsible.

BIBLIOGRAPHY

Castel, Albert. "The Fort Pillow Massacre: A Fresh Examination of the Evidence." *Civil War History* 4 (1958): 37–50.

Cimprich, John, and Robert C. Mainfort, Jr. "The Fort Pillow Massacre: A Statistical Note." *Journal of American History* 76 (December 1989): 830–837.

Cimprich, John, and Robert C. Mainfort, Jr. "Fort Pillow Revisited: New Evidence about an Old Controversy." *Civil War History* 28 (December 1982): 293–306.

Maness, Lonnie E. "The Fort Pillow Massacre: Fact or Fiction." *Tennessee Historical Quarterly* 45 (Spring 1986): 287–315.

Wills, Brian Steel. *A Battle from the Start: The Life of Nathan Bedford Forrest.* New York, 1992.

BRIAN S. WILLS

FORT PULASKI, GEORGIA. The Confederate surrender of Fort Pulaski, following an intense two-day Union artillery bombardment (April 10–11, 1862), eliminated Savannah, Georgia, as a blockade-running seaport. Located on Cockspur Island and named for Count Casimir Pulaski, the Polish hero of the American Revolution, this pentagonal masonry fort made of 25 million bricks was completed in 1847. On January 6, 1861, it was seized by the Georgia militia.

Union plans for a naval blockade of the Confederacy included the capture of Fort Pulaski. By November Northern troops had landed on nearby Tybee Island, with Capt. Quincy A. Gillmore designated commander of the projected bombardment. Gillmore's men began erecting eleven batteries containing 36 heavy guns and mortars at ranges varying between 1,650 and 3,400 yards. Fort Pulaski mounted 48 cannons with a garrison of 385 officers and men commanded by Col. Charles H. Olmstead. Brig. Gen. Robert E. Lee, who years earlier had sited and begun building the fort and who now commanded Confederates in Georgia, South Carolina, and eastern Florida, believed Fort Pulaski to be invulnerable.

After sunrise on April 10, 1862, Olmstead confidently rejected Gillmore's surrender summons, saying, "I am here to defend this Fort, not to surrender it." Union artillery opened fire at 8:15 A.M. Fort Pulaski replied shortly after. By evening the beginnings of a breach were plainly visible in the southeast wall. Incoming harassment fire throughout the night hampered repairs. Exchange of fire resumed the second morning. Northern gunners exploited the expanding breach by aiming shells through it and across the parade ground to strike the fort magazine. With sixteen cannon dismounted and his defenders endangered by the probable explosion of 40,000 pounds of gunpowder, Olmstead at 2:00 P.M. hoisted a bedsheet and Gillmore rowed over to receive a formal surrender.

During the two-day bombardment 5,275 shot and shell had been hurled against Fort Pulaski. Mortars proved ineffectual. The decisive breach had been cut almost entirely by three large rifled cannon, which led Northern artillerists to predict correctly that rifled ordnance would "revolutionize such warfare."

BIBLIOGRAPHY

Bryan, T. Conn. *Confederate Georgia.* Athens, Ga., 1953.

Gillmore, Quincy A. "Siege and Capture of Fort Pulaski." In *Battles and Leaders of the Civil War.* Edited by Robert U. Johnson and C. C. Buel. Vol. 2. New York, 1888. Reprint, Secaucus, N.J., 1982.

Lawrence, Alexander A. *A Present for Mr. Lincoln: The Story of Savannah from Secession to Sherman.* Macon, Ga., 1961.

DENNIS KELLY

FORTS AND FORTIFICATIONS. [*This entry is composed of two articles that discuss the use of coastal fortifications, tower defenses, frontier forts, and field fortifications in the Confederacy:* An Overview *and* Field Fortifications. *For further discussion of the construction, armament, and management of these forts and fortifications, see* Artillery *and* Engineer Bureau. *For further discussion of their role in the Civil War, see* Fort Fisher, North Carolina; Fort Harrison, Virginia; Fort Pickens, Florida; Fort Pulaski, Georgia; Fort Stedman, Virginia; Fort Sumter, South Carolina; Fort Wagner, South Carolina; *and entries on the numerous battles and campaigns mentioned herein.*]

An Overview

At the onset of the Civil War, the Confederacy found itself in possession of a wide range of formerly Federal coast defense and frontier forts. These installations and others built during the war would play a major role in the defense of the Confederate States.

Fortification building was not an arcane science; the U.S. Army had a long history of developing fortified installations, dating back to before the American Revolution. The standard guide of the time was *A Complete Treatise on Field Fortification,* written in 1836 by Dennis H. Mahan, professor of military and civil engineering at the U.S. Military Academy. Mahan's engineering doctrine was the dominant influence in the development of fortifications, addressing all aspects including permanent and field (temporary) defenses, establishing clear lines of fire, planning for defense, trenches, revetments (support facings for ramparts), and the like. Mahan's work effectively served as the bible on the subject and was widely used by both sides during the war. Indeed, in the preface Mahan stated that his work was "a book not for study alone, but one which the officer can take with him into the camp, and consult at any moment." Though the clouds of sectional violence had already been long gathering by the time Mahan's work was published, few could imagine that its tenets would be followed by Americans fighting Americans.

The development of fortifications normally required the efforts of trained engineers. During the prewar period the Corps of Engineers was the elite branch of the army, receiving the top graduates of West Point. Among their ranks were several officers who would later find fame while serving in the Confederate army. Superintending engineer from 1848 to 1849 for the construction of Fort Gaines, on Dauphin Island at the entrance to Mobile Bay, was Capt. P. G. T. Beauregard. Fort Alafia, an 1849 temporary defense erected in Polk County, Florida, was built under the supervision of 1st Lt. John C. Pemberton, Fourth U.S. Artillery. Army Engineer Lt. Col. Robert E. Lee designed the plans for Fort De Soto, a major coastal defense on Mullet Key in Tampa Bay, Florida; when the fort was finally built in 1898, Lee's original plans were utilized. The lessons learned by these and other future Confederate staff and field officers were well applied during the Civil War.

At the start of the war there was some hesitation on both sides over the employment of fortifications. One major reason was that no one believed the war would last long enough to require serious fortification programs; both South and North fully expected to sweep the battlefield of the foe at the first opportunity, quickly bringing the conflict to an end. It was also felt that these structures were not appropriate as devices of modern civilized warfare. The violence of the combat and effectiveness of modern weaponry quickly disabused the participants of this notion.

As the war intensified, it became apparent that often the combatants felt secure only if they were dug in somewhere. Southern field commanders quickly recalled that the use of fortifications, whether of earth, logs, rails, or other material, gave the advantage to the defense. A standard axiom of the time was that good troops would be able to hold the line against three times their number. As a result, throughout the war much time and energy was spent by both sides digging trenches and erecting fortifications.

The fortifications utilized by the Confederate States during the war generally fell into the categories of coastal fortifications, field forts, tower defenses, and frontier forts.

Coastal Fortifications

The earliest seacoast defenses of the United States were built of varying designs, utilizing earth, stone, brick, and other natural materials. There had been two recognized periods of construction before 1816, when a board established by President James Madison planned and oversaw the construction of the third phase of seacoast defenses. The board was headed by a French military engineer, Simon Bernard, who followed the work of Marquis de Vauban, a fortification engineer who revolutionized fort design and construction in France. Bernard designed several forts that would later be used by the Confederacy, including Fort Morgan at the entrance of Mobile Bay. Another member of the board, Bvt. Lt. Col. (later Brig. Gen. and Chief of Engineers) Joseph G. Totten, was responsible for several other installations that rank as some of the most impressive harbor defenses ever produced. These included Forts Sumter, Pickens, and Pulaski.

The board recommended that nearly two hundred new forts and batteries be built, but only a few were actually constructed, with some effort spent on upgrading existing installations. The resulting works were known as the "Third System." Several examples of these permanent forts were acquired by the Confederacy in 1861. The Third System forts were of uniform brick and stone construction, designed to withstand the current threat of wooden sailing ships armed with smoothbore cannons possessing a range of about one mile. The forts were massive, vertical-walled structures, normally polygonal in plan with from four to seven faces. They combined a strong, durable structure with a high concentration of armament and substantial firepower. The method used to multiply the available firepower was the extensive use of casemated gun emplacements, which provided additional protection to the guns and crews, enabled more aiming flexibility, and permitted multiple tiers of guns to be installed. Depending upon the size and location of the defense, the planned armament could run from fewer than fifty guns up to nearly four hundred.

Following secession, the majority of the existing coastal defense forts along the southern Atlantic seaboard and Gulf coast were quickly captured or turned over to state forces. For his part, the outgoing president James Buchanan made no real effort to reinforce the Union forts remaining in the seceding states. In several cases state militias simply marched in and took possession, as occurred during the first week of January 1861 when Governor Thomas O. Moore

FORT PULASKI. Situated on Cockspur Island in the Savannah River, the fort commanded the entrance to the river and the city of Savannah.

THE SOLDIER IN OUR CIVIL WAR

ordered Louisiana troops to seize the Federal forts in that state. Alabama state troops seized Forts Morgan and Gaines on Mobile Bay that same week.

The first Federal shots of the war came in Pensacola, Florida, on the night of January 8 when a guard at Fort Barrancas, immediately west of the Pensacola Navy Yard, fired at a group of men who approached the fort and failed to respond to challenges. Shortly afterward the Federal troops ferried across Escambia Bay under the command of 1st Lt. Adam Slemmer and occupied Fort Pickens on Santa Rosa Island. The Southerners successfully occupied the Navy Yard, Fort Barrancas, and nearby Fort McRee, but Pickens remained in Union hands, effectively denying the use of Pensacola to the Confederacy.

Where the Confederates were able to seize well-maintained forts, they found strong, lasting defenses. One example was Fort Jackson, built by the United States on the Mississippi River below New Orleans between 1822 and 1832 on the former site of Spanish Fort Bourbon. A star-shaped pentagon, the fort's walls were twenty-five feet above the water line of a moat that completely surrounded it. The walls were constructed of red brick to a thickness of twenty feet, with reinforced gun foundations of red and gray granite. In the center of the fort was a defensive barracks intended as a bombproof shelter capable of accommodating five hundred men. The entire structure rested on foundations made of three layers of cypress logs, topped by cypress two-by-fours used as a leveling device and all made airtight by being submerged in water.

Many of the coastal forts, however, had been unoccupied for several years or at best had seen only small maintenance garrisons. A number of the forts acquired by the Confederacy were in deplorable condition after several years of neglect. Foundations had shifted, walls were collapsing, the wind and rain had washed away parapet platforms, and fittings had rotted away. Lacking guns and facilities for personnel to return these acquisitions to service, the Confederate engineers faced a stiff test in readying the defenses.

When possible the coastal fortifications were reinforced with supporting installations. At major seaports these additional placements became rather extensive, a prime example being the Savannah River approaches in Georgia. The two existing masonry forts acquired by the Confederate defenders were Forts Jackson and Pulaski; additional defenses included Forts Beaulieu, Boggs, Brown, Lee, McAllister, Mercer, and Rose Dew, and Battery Jones. This pattern of enhancing the defenses was regularly repeated elsewhere.

The Confederacy's strongest forts had been designed to

handle extended shelling by smoothbore artillery and naval guns. Indeed, the Union fleet's bombardment and running of Forts Jackson and St. Phillip below New Orleans in late April 1862 did only superficial damage. But the Union's introduction of rifled guns at Fort Pulaski, Georgia, that same month made these forts effectively obsolete. Following the Federal bombardment of Fort Sumter in April 1863, General Beauregard, commander of the Charleston defenses, noted in an official report that the use of rifled guns and ironclads on masonry forts had irrevocably changed the defensive equation.

Surprisingly, it turned out that the fortification material best suited for defense against the Northern rifled cannon was any sort of yielding substance that could be shoveled back into place easily, such as sand. Union Brig. Gen. Quincy Gillmore, the engineer who devised the assaults on Fort Pulaski and later on the Charleston defenses, reported that though his cannons had holed Fort Pulaski, causing its surrender, an even larger bombardment had negligible effect on Fort Wagner outside Charleston. Wagner, built of sand, survived multiple attempts at breaching, as the sand would fall back into the area that had been displaced.

Forts that were of primarily earthen construction lent themselves to even longer survival. Fort McAllister of the Savannah defenses was bombarded by the Federal navy on January 27, February 1, and March 3, 1863. Each time, the defenders dug their cannons out of the dirt that had been piled up by the shelling and resumed firing. In the case of Fort Sumter, which was assaulted regularly from April 1863 to February 1865, the breaches in the walls were packed with gabions (wickerwork filled with stones and dirt), sand, cotton bales, and rubble. The fort held, but like the few other remaining permanent forts in Confederate hands, it was doomed by the overwhelming manpower of the North and the collapse of the Confederacy itself.

Field and Semipermanent Forts

The prewar emphasis had been on large masonry installations, but the Civil War witnessed a widespread use of entrenchments and earthen fortifications built by soldiers as the need arose. Early in the hostilities, the idea of digging trenches and doing earthwork was frowned upon, the prevailing feeling being that the manual labor required was beneath the dignity of soldiers. Those who did engage in fortification work were often given the epithet of "dirt-diggers." Throughout the war the South relied primarily on slave labor when available to build its forts and trenches.

Although the Confederates made little use of earthworks during the earlier campaigns, they increasingly utilized earthen fortifications, often enabling them to hold the field, even when they were outnumbered. By war's end, the field fortifications were the most common type to be found, owing to their relative ease of construction and applicability to changing defensive needs. By Appomattox the Confederates had built thousands of earthen fortifications throughout the South, ranging from quickly erected battlefield defenses to major networks protecting whole cities, transport routes, and waterways.

The basis for field fortifications was the trench, which, if necessary, could be built rapidly while under fire or, if time permitted, could be rather extensive. As men worked to excavate the trench, the dirt was piled up in front, providing a parapet, or defensive platform. As time permitted, parapets would be raised, strong-point redoubts (rectangular earthworks) and redans (triangular earthworks) erected, and defensive ditches built in front of the earthworks. Bombproofs against artillery fire were often constructed at forts by leaning timbers against the inner walls and covering them with earth. If there was no timber, the parapets might be made as much as fifteen feet thick to stop artillery fire. A head log, under which the men could fire, was frequently utilized with some sort of skid or device placed to ensure that the log wouldn't roll back on the defenders if struck by a projectile.

Individual gun batteries were usually earthen and were erected for the purpose of supporting major installations or defending a specific approach. These battery positions required extensive work, including laying floor planking and providing protective space for the gun crews. They were normally equipped with only one or two cannons, and sandbags and gabions were often used to build up the shoulders of the gun embrasures to provide the gun crews with more cover. In the field, battery positions were usually not very substantial, owing to their temporary nature, and often they were built hurriedly wherever possible with whatever materials were at hand. One example was Battery or Fort Powell, one of the Confederate defenses of Mobile Bay, which was erected on a sandbar off Cedar Point at the western entrance of the bay.

In advance of the defense, trees would be felled with their tops facing the direction of the enemy and the tips of the branches sharpened into spikes, resulting in devices called abatis. Closer to defense (if time allowed), sharpened sticks were placed in the ground, again facing the enemy, giving the appearance of a picket fence laid almost on its side. Known as palisades, or chevaux-de-frise, these served the same purpose as abatis but gave the defending riflemen a clearer view of the approaching enemy.

In the field, the Confederates quickly learned the value of fortifications. Immediately following their victory at First Manassas, a network of trenches and redoubts was constructed to allow them to preserve their position. This included the substantial use of "Quaker guns," logs that were shaped and blackened to appear like emplaced artillery. With George B. McClellan's move for Richmond via the peninsula, the Confederates evacuated their Manassas

BARRICADES AT ALEXANDRIA, VIRGINIA.   Union Brig. Gen. Herman Hampt erected these stockades to protect railroads entering Washington from Confederate raiders. Photograph by Mathew Brady, 1861.   NATIONAL ARCHIVES

battlefield fortifications and starting working on a string of defenses in advance of the Union army, which included the utilization of Lord Cornwallis's old defenses in the vicinity of Yorktown. These field forts served the purpose admirably, causing no end of delays for McClellan and forcing him to bring heavy siege guns up the peninsula with great difficulty. The Southerners continued a pattern of building defenses and then falling back, first through Williamsburg and then to the outskirts of Richmond. When the Confederate army broke out during Lee's Seven Days' campaign, it was the Federals who were forced to rely on rapidly erected defenses, building them and then withdrawing, for protection.

Later in the war, during William Tecumseh Sherman's Atlanta campaign, practically every foot from Ringgold to Atlanta was entrenched, fortified, and laced with obstructions by the Southern defenders. One singular earthen fortification type developed for this series of defenses was the "Shoupade" redoubt, named for its designer, Brig. Gen. Francis Shoup, chief of artillery for Gen. Joseph E. Johnston. Shoup designed the redoubts to follow the lay of

the land along the north bank of the Chattahoochee River and provide supporting fire to one another. The fortifications were of triangular design, built of logs and earth ten to twelve feet high in front, with each to be defended by a company of about eighty men. The structures were placed roughly eighty feet apart, linked by heavy palisades with two artillery pieces between each strong point. The resulting line was effectively impregnable and, most important, gave Johnston much flexibility in moving the body of his army behind the line to repel any crossing.

The Federals nevertheless managed to cross the river in several locations on the night of July 8, 1864, and Johnston once again traded terrain for position. Over General Shoup's opposition, the Army of Tennessee was pulled back from the Chattahoochee River line, and these unique structures were not combat-tested. Johnston's army withdrew into Atlanta, where boundary defenses had already been erected.

As with Atlanta, lengthy strings of more permanent earthen defenses were erected at numerous important locations across the South, including Vicksburg, Mobile,

CHEVAUX-DE-FRISE, FORT MAHONE, VIRGINIA. Crack appears in original glass negative.   NATIONAL ARCHIVES

Charleston, Petersburg, and Richmond. At locations like Charleston, the new defenses were erected to work in concert with the established masonry forts. At the inland cities, the defensive lines were built from scratch.

Richmond was the initial primary target of the Union army, and under the auspices of General Lee, the Confederates started fortifying the city in July 1861. The first hastily constructed defenses were completed in 1862 at Drewry's Bluff overlooking the James River (these being subsequently reinforced). The James was further fortified below the mouth of the Appomattox River, with additional defenses placed at Jamestown Island, Hardin's Bluff, Mulberry Island, and Day's Point. When possible, civilian and both slave and free black labor was utilized, but the work proceeded very slowly and the Richmond defenses were not effectively completed until the summer of 1864.

As originally planned, the fortification line was to include eighteen closed or semiclosed forts with seven supporting outerworks equipped with 218 heavy guns. As completed, the defenses included an outer line located about ten miles from the capital, stretching for over sixty-five miles around the city. Key earthen forts included Fort Harrison, Fort Darling (on Drewry's Bluff), Fort Hoke, Fort Johnson, and Fort Stephens. Toward the end of the war, these substantial defenses were bolstered by the emplacement of mines and ship hulks sunk in the channel of the James. The Confederate fortifications in defense of Petersburg to the south were similarly substantial, including Forts Baldwin, Gregg, Whitworth, Mahone, and Walker, and Battery 45 and Battery Pegram. Taken together, the Richmond and Petersburg defenses made the region one of the more heavily defended portions of the Confederacy, but the loss of Petersburg in the spring of 1865 made Richmond's defenses superfluous.

In the western theater, Maj. Samuel H. Lockett, chief engineer under Lt. Gen. John C. Pemberton, erected a similar network on a smaller scale for the defense of Vicksburg, Mississippi. Lockett took advantage of the natural lay of the bluffs rising above the Mississippi River, erecting an effectively impregnable series of fortifications and earthworks on the last continuous ridge around the town, linked by trenches and rifle pits. These defenses included Square Fort (Fort Garrott), Fort Hill, the Second Texas Lunette, Third Louisiana Redan, Salient Works, Railroad Redoubt, South Fort, and others.

Less permanent installations were still erected when needed to fulfill short-term defensive requirements or to counter an expected move by the enemy. During a two-week span in March 1863, a Confederate detachment out of Vicksburg under the command of Brig. Gen. W. W. Loring erected seven earthen forts in the vicinity of Greenwood, Mississippi, in order to prevent the Union from running gunboats and transports down to the Yazoo River. The primary defense was Fort Pemberton, erected at a point where the Tallahatchie and Yazoo rivers closed to within two hundred yards of each other. Equipped with one 32-pounder and three 12-pounder rifles, one 3-inch Whitworth, one 10-pounder Parrott rifle, one 20-pounder Parrott rifle, and one 8-inch naval gun, Pemberton was supported by six other defenses ranging along the Tallahatchie and Yalobusha rivers: Forts Ann, LeFlore, Moore, and Texas, and Middle Fort and Lower Fort. Assisting in the defense was the steamer *Star of the West* (of Fort Sumter fame), which was sunk in the Tallahatchie River.

One of the key strategies for the North during the prosecution of the war was the policy of coordination between the Union army and the fleet. In response, the Confederacy found it imperative to continue the development of semipermanent fieldworks at obvious choke points and on commanding ground, throughout both the western and the eastern theaters. Examples include the fortifications erected at Island Number 10, Fort Henry, and Fort

Donelson in the west. Fort Donelson, on the Cumberland River in Tennessee, covered some ninety-seven acres with earthworks, rifle trenches and water batteries.

The Fort Blakely–Spanish Fort complex on Mobile Bay was equally impressive. Blakely consisted of a four-mile-long barricade of pine logs covered with mud and sand and fronted with dense abatis. The fort boasted nine lunettes (crescent-shaped earthworks) and was armed with thirty-five artillery pieces in addition to siege mortars; its flanks were covered by the marshes of the Appalachee River. Spanish Fort, historically a defensive position for Mobile, was equally impressive. Located seven miles from the Confederate city, it consisted of three redoubts (Spanish Fort, Fort Alexis, and Red Fort), linked by rifle pits that stretched some 2,500 yards from the Appalachee River to Bayou Minette. At the base of the works was a deep ditch six feet in width, with the inner side next to the forts protected by telegraph wire fencing, an elaborate chevaux-de-frise, and a line of thick abatis, all backed up by heavy artillery.

Charleston, South Carolina, was considered the single most heavily armed and best defended port on the Atlantic seaboard. The main defenses included Third System masonry Fort Sumter and Fort Moultrie (Sullivan's Island) as well as the earthworks of Battery Gregg and Battery Wagner, both of which were located on Cumming's Point. To back up the midharbor defenses, the Confederates built several batteries in Charleston proper, including White Point (or "South") Battery, between the Cooper and Ashby rivers. The inner harbor defenses never saw action, as the Union fleet never penetrated the harbor.

At Mobile Bay and other locations, earthen coastal-inlet fortifications served an additional purpose: providing protection for blockade runners. These riverine defenses often employed combinations of rafts, mines, booms, pilings, and fire vessels to further obstruct the rivers and outlets. Fort Forrest, a Confederate seven-gun redoubt opposite Roanoke Island, North Carolina, was placed to take advantage of a double line of sixteen sunken vessels and a system of pilings in the Croatan Sound.

The single strongest earthworks complex of the Confederacy was Fort Fisher, the key to the Cape Fear defenses in North Carolina. Expansion of the existing Battery Boles commenced in July 1863 on timbers stacked fifteen to twenty-five feet thick, with sand covering and marsh grass planted over the resulting structure. An L-shaped fort evolved, with its angle pointing northeast out to sea. The eastern face, running 1,900 yards down the beach, was the vertical arm. At its southern tip was the massive Mound Battery, equipped with two long-range guns. About a mile from the mound and near the tip of Confederate Point on the river side was Battery Buchanan. A line of rifle pits protected the rear of the fort in case of an attack from the river. Located below Wilmington, Fort Fisher staunchly protected the approaches to that port, making Wilmington the last major Confederate port available to blockade runners.

Tower Defenses

One final form of fixed fortification that saw limited use in the Confederate States was the tower defense. Earlier tower defenses had been built under the Federal Third System, primarily in the South. Either rectangular or circular in plan, these multistory structures mounted a few weapons arranged in such a way as to provide fire in all directions. These fixed-point defenses were commonly referred to as Martello towers, after a similar structure on the Bay of Martello in Corsica.

Notable examples included Tower Dupre (otherwise known as Battery Dupre) and a similar structure near Proctorsville, both constituting part of the New Orleans defenses. Dupre was located about four miles below the mouth of Bayou Bienvenue on Lake Borgne; hexagonal in shape, it had loopholes in the first floor for riflemen, and embrasures, or slotlike openings, on the second floor adequate for six cannons. Other five 24-pounder cannons were placed in a lunette water battery at the base of the tower.

The tower defense at Proctorsville was lower down on Lake Borgne and protected the terminus of the Mexican Gulf Railroad. A square, three-floored structure about forty-eight feet high, the top floor of the defense had embrasures for four cannons, the second floor had loopholes and embrasures for rifles, and the ground floor contained quarters and the magazine. Though this structure was considered important enough to be manned during 1861 by Company B, Twenty-first Louisiana Infantry, neither it nor Dupre played a role in Confederate operations in the New Orleans vicinity.

Frontier Forts

Although the last form of defensive works employed by the Confederates were called forts, they were not truly developed fortifications. The numerous frontier installations covering the western approaches to the United States were normally open posts, consisting of several buildings, stables, barracks, guardhouse, and the like, built out of whatever materials were available (stone, adobe, sticks). Built during the 1840s and 1850s to guard the frontier as American settlers pushed westerly (or as conflicts with Indians arose), these dragoon and cavalry outposts and camps were themselves continually abandoned with new posts being built farther west.

As with the major permanent installations in the East, the western forts had been poorly manned and maintained because of insufficient regular army personnel. For those that remained in active service in Texas and New Mexico

Territory, the secession of the Southern states created a serious problem. Brig. Gen. David E. Twiggs, the Federal commander in Texas (and later a Confederate general), surrendered all the Federal property under his command to the Confederates in April and May 1861, leaving most of the forts unmanned. State militia forces immediately occupied a few. Ironically, one of the posts that was garrisoned by the Confederates was Fort Davis in southwestern Texas, which had been named in 1854 for Secretary of War Jefferson Davis. But a serious lack of manpower and materials, combined with a need to defend the Trans-Mississippi Confederacy, left the majority of the frontier forts unoccupied by the South.

Some did see Confederate use during the war, although they were employed primarily as frontier supply bases and protection against Indians. Fort Bliss, Texas, for example, served as headquarters for Confederate activities in the far Southwest until August 1862. A few of the remaining Spanish presidios were also occasionally utilized by the Confederates, one being the Presidio of Nuestra Señora del Pilar y Gloriosa San José, also known as the Presidio of San Elizario, about twenty-five miles below El Paso.

The Confederates also built several new installations along the Gulf coast, notably in the vicinity of the major ports of Corpus Christi and Galveston, as well as at the entrances of major tributaries. An example of the latter was Fort Sabine, erected to defend the approaches of the Sabine River. It was successfully defended by a force under the command of Lt. Dick Dowling on September 8, 1863 (in the process, the thrown-together Confederate force managed to sink two Union gunboats). As the North closed down river accesses to Texas, these forts, too, were abandoned.

Armament

The early armament used by the Confederates in their fortifications was primarily 24- and 32-pounders. When possible, the Southerners used whatever was left behind at the former Federal posts; field fortifications relied upon regular field artillery. In general, though, providing defensive weaponry for the Confederacy remained a catch-as-catch-can proposition throughout the war and often led to an eclectic mix of firepower. An example was Battery Beauregard, built on Sullivan's Island as part of the Charleston defenses. By the end of the war, it was equipped with one 10-inch Columbiad smoothbore, one 8-inch Columbiad which had been rifled and banded, three 8-inch seacoast howitzers, three 32-pounders rifled and banded, two 24-pounders rifled and banded, one 6-pounder smoothbore, and one 6-pounder rifled.

Even when field commanders received cannons, there was no guarantee that the weapons would contribute to the success or strength of the fort. Early in the war the commander of the Louisiana defenses submitted a request for guns to the Confederate War Department. The secretary of war replied that 125 32-pounders had been ordered from the Norfolk Navy Yard for shipment to New Orleans. By the end of the year, only 95 of these guns had been delivered, and they had arrived without sufficient amounts of powder.

Even if powder had been provided, these guns were still of limited use; the War Department had neglected to send carriages, chassis, or implements. The pattern was repeated elsewhere: Fort Pulaski, built for 146 pieces, had only 20 installed. Fort Sumter had about 60 of its 135 in place. Fort Cobb, a battery located below Elizabeth City in Pasquotank County, North Carolina, utilized 4 guns taken from a sunken ship. Moreover, there was practically no reserve of heavy cannons available to replace those that might be damaged in service or to arm the temporary works being erected.

At no time during the war was the Confederate arms industry able to adequately supply the medium and heavy guns and accoutrements required for the defenses. Both sides suffered from this problem initially, but the North's industrial strength provided increasing supplies of adequate artillery for its fixed and field fortifications as the war progressed, whereas the Confederacy's inadequacies only worsened.

As the fighting went on, the South's temporary fortifications were steadily abandoned in the face of an overpowering Union army. Many of the permanent forts went earlier, as the North attained control of the Atlantic seaboard, Gulf coast, and inland waterways. The defenders of Vicksburg held out for forty-seven days, withstanding two assaults by Ulysses S. Grant's army, before General Pemberton surrendered the "Gibraltar of the Confederacy." Fort Fisher lasted until January 1865, finally succumbing to a combined Union land and naval assault that saw more than 2 million pounds of ordnance thrown at the structure. The two attacks on the fort constituted the single heaviest land-sea battle of the war.

The last to fall was Fort Tyler, Georgia, overlooking the town of West Point on the Chattahoochee River. Described as a "strong bastioned earthwork" thirty-five yards square, surrounded by a ditch twelve feet wide and ten feet deep, the fort was protected by an abatis and mounted two 32-pounders and two fieldpieces. On Easter Sunday, April 16, 1865, Fort Tyler (under the command of Brig. Gen. Robert Charles Tyler) was attacked by a Federal brigade. The fort surrendered following Tyler's death. Thus ended Confederate use of permanent and field fortifications.

BIBLIOGRAPHY

Bergeron, Arthur W. "Confederate Coastal Defenses in Louisiana." *Periodical: Journal of the Council on America's Military Past* 13, no. 4 (1985): 29–39.

Biggs, Greg. "The 'Shoupade' Redoubts: Joseph E. Johnston's

Chattahoochee River Line." *Civil War Regiments: A Journal of the American Civil War* 1, no. 3 (1991): 82–93.

Coleman, James C., and Irene S. Coleman. *Guardians of the Gulf: Pensacola Fortifications, 1698–1980.* Pensacola, Fla., 1982.

Holden, W. C. "Frontier Defense in Texas during the Civil War." *West Texas Historical Association Yearbook* 4 (1928): 16–31.

Hunt, O. E., ed. *Forts and Artillery.* Vol. 5 of *A Photographic History of the Civil War in Ten Volumes.* New York, 1911. Reprint, New York, 1957.

Lewis, Emanuel Raymond. *Seacoast Fortifications of the United States: An Introductory History.* Annapolis, Md., 1970.

Mahan, D. H. *A Complete Treatise on Field Fortification.* New York, 1836. Reprint, New York, 1968.

Peterson, Harold L. *Forts in America.* New York, 1964.

Prucha, Francis Paul. *A Guide to Military Posts of the United States, 1789–1895.* Madison, Wis., 1964.

Roberts, Robert B. *Encyclopedia of Historic Forts: The Military, Pioneer, and Trading Posts of the United States.* New York, 1988.

Young, Rogers W. "The Construction of Fort Pulaski." *Georgia Historical Quarterly* 20 (1936): 41–51.

MARK MORGAN

Field Fortifications

Rifle pits, trenches, and breastworks—field fortifications—were unknown to eager volunteers rushing to the colors in the first eight months of 1861. Until the 1850s, the foot soldier's standard firearm was a percussion musket with an effective range of 70 yards, a figure no greater than the Brown Bess and Charleville flintlock muskets carried by his grandfather in the Revolutionary War. The infantry advanced, halted, fired, and charged in the linear formations perfected by Napoleon Bonaparte, the century's foremost soldier.

The rifle-musket adapted by the U.S. Army in the mid-1850s and destined to be the Civil War's standard infantry weapon had an effective range of 600 yards. Although a muzzle loader, a trained soldier utilizing it could fire two aimed rounds a minute. This giant leap forward in weapons technology doomed the linear tactics of Napoleon, in which artillery was the queen of battle and a mass charge of cavalry, boot to spur, usually determined the victor. This revolution in weaponry gave a decided tactical advantage to

MAKING FASCINES AND GABIONS. The Seventy-seventh Pennsylvania Regiment making fortifications for breastworks.

the defenders, and as the war progressed field fortifications became increasingly sophisticated and significant.

In 1861 and through the Battle of Shiloh (April 6–7, 1862), soldiers North and South frowned on the use of field fortifications. It was believed that the labor required to throw them up was undignified, unworthy of a volunteer, and would sap morale. Many officers argued that masked batteries and trenches were uncivilized, and advocates of entrenching were labeled "dirt-diggers." Gen. Robert E. Lee, an early champion of construction and use of earthworks for defense of ports and harbors against amphibious attack, was derisively called the "King of Spades."

In the months before Shiloh, the Confederacy, determined to fight a defensive war, devoted much effort by both soldiers and impressed slaves to the construction of earthen fortifications to cover the approaches to their Centreville and Manassas Junction encampments. These included batteries (emplacements for one or more cannons); redoubts (enclosed works with four angles and four fronts); redans (works with two fronts and three angles); lunettes (works with three or more angles, their rear open to interior lines); and trenches (ditches with the soil thrown up front), fronted by an abatis, usually of felled timber or sharpened stakes. When Maj. Gen. George B. McClellan arrived on the peninsula in the first week of April 1862 and began his march on Richmond, he found his way barred by the Yorktown-Warwick line. The Confederate left was anchored on the 1781 British Yorktown works, their parapets greatly thickened and the ditches widened and deepened, with their center posted behind the Warwick River, dammed at four points to create water barriers, and their right on Skiff Creek. The dams and other points where the river could not be flooded were covered by earthen batteries and entrenchments. These defensive works caused McClellan to pause from April 5 to May 4 to construct breaching batteries, seriously compromising his campaign.

At Williamsburg, on May 5, the Confederates used previously constructed redoubts and batteries to batter McClellan's vanguard and were enabled then to undertake a successful retrograde into the Richmond defenses. As they closed on the eastern approaches to Richmond, Union engineers marked out and soldiers constructed earthworks, from which McClellan, a former Corps of Engineers officer, proposed to invest the city. These works served the Union well when they were assailed by the Confederates at Seven Pines (May 31–June 1) and in the Seven Days' Battles (June 26–July 1). At Seven Pines, Ellerson's Mill (June 26), and Gaines' Mill (June 27), these works shielded the defenders as they inflicted disproportionate losses in killed and wounded on the attacking Southerners. At Gaines' Mill the Federals, because of time constraints, sheltered themselves behind fence rails, knapsacks, and blanket roll barricades.

In the East, except for the Harpers Ferry siege (September 12–15, 1862) when the defenders employed previously

FASCINES IN THE CONFEDERATE TRENCHES AT PETERSBURG, VIRGINIA.   NATIONAL ARCHIVES

prepared earthworks, neither the Army of the Potomac nor the Army of Northern Virginia again made more than limited use of field fortifications until mid-December at Fredericksburg. At the latter fight, the Confederates, sheltered in rifle pits and trenches and behind stone walls, supported by artillery emplaced behind earthen parapets, inflicted frightful casualties on the attackers.

At Forts Henry, Donelson, and Pillow, and Island Number 10 in the West, defensive earthwork perimeters were thrown up by the Confederates on lines laid out by their engineers to cover the approaches to heavy batteries commanding the rivers at these key strongholds. These entrenched camps, along with the large defending forces at Donelson and Island Number 10, were captured by the Union.

After Shiloh, Maj. Gen. Henry W. Halleck hastened to the front and directed the advance on Corinth (April 28–May 30, 1862). He pushed ahead continually, but his troops entrenched after every forward movement and invaluable time was lost throwing up trenches, when vigorous scouting and patrolling would have revealed that they would be of little use.

At Murfreesboro (December 31, 1862–January 2, 1863), both beligerents entrenched and underscored the vital role that ''dirt-diggers'' played when the armies assumed defensive stances. The breastworks erected by Maj. Gen. George H. Thomas's wing shielding the Lafayette Road (September 19–20) facilitated his stand ''like a rock'' at Chickamauga. Confederate engineers delineated three lines of earthworks at Missionary Ridge, but the topography was against them and they were stormed by Thomas's troops on November 25. Both at Vicksburg and at Port Hudson in the late spring of 1863, Confederates posted in the trenches defending the perimeters of these bastions hurled back their attackers with prohibitive losses. In early July, Vicksburg and Port Hudson, cut off from reinforcements, surrendered to investing Union armies.

In the East in 1863, Maj. Gen. Joseph Hooker, after gaining General Lee's flank at Chancellorsville, lost confidence and pulled back into the Wilderness and entrenched, which proved his undoing. At Gettysburg neither army made a concerted effort to entrench. Union soldiers for the most part utilized man-made and natural features. Later the same year, at Mine Run (November 26–December 2), both armies made extensive use of field fortifications as they marched, maneuvered, and skirmished.

The war roared toward a bloody and terrible climax in 1864. With Ulysses S. Grant in charge and the implementation of his sustained offensive strategy, soldiers in the two major Union army groups, and the Confederate Army of Tennessee in the West and the Army of Northern Virginia in the East now maneuvered with ''a rifle-musket in one hand and a shovel in the other.'' All levels of command from

general to private now knew that breastworks gave a decisive edge to the defenders. It was recognized that veteran troops shielded by field fortifications could fight off at least three times their number of attackers. Units, on coming into the presence of the enemy, habitually deployed from column into line, and their commanders sent out skirmishers. Experienced officers examined the terrain to locate the best ground for entrenching, and the soldiers turned to. They stacked arms, secured tools from the wagons, or, if under fire, made use of bayonets, mess plates, or cups to entrench their section of the line.

In woods, trees were felled, positioned, and covered with earth. If no timber was available, the superior slopes of the parapet, if artillery was a hazard and there was sufficient time, were given a thickness of fifteen to twenty-two feet. Against small arms fire, two feet sufficed. Head logs positioned on skids were commonplace.

These field works—trenches and rifle pits—were thrown up by the rank and file with little oversight from field officers. During the war's final year, the soldiers, whenever they halted in the presence of the enemy, entrenched before kindling fires or preparing food. These improvised works were abandoned with the same unconcern with which they were erected. European officers visiting the armies were surprised at seeing average infantrymen accomplishing what in their armies was the province of engineer and sapper battalions.

In Virginia from the Rapidan to Richmond and on to Petersburg, General Lee's veterans fighting from behind earthworks savaged their assailants. From the time Maj. Gen. George G. Meade's Army of the Potomac crossed the Rapidan on May 4 until it crossed the James on June 14 through 16, Grant's losses nearly equaled the strength of Lee's army encountered in the Wilderness (May 5–6). At Petersburg and on the eastern approaches to Richmond during the next nine months, Union losses in killed, wounded, and prisoners were only slightly less than the total defending force on March 29, 1865.

William Tecumseh Sherman's experience with field fortifications in the Atlanta campaign that carried his army from Ringgold Gap across the Chattahoochee (May 7–July 8) was similar, but his losses were far less than those suffered by Grant's eastern army. Unlike Grant, Sherman skillfully used the terrain and superior numbers to first probe and then maneuver Gen. Joseph E. Johnston's Confederates out of ten successive lines of earthworks. Only at Kennesaw Mountain on June 27 did Sherman launch a frontal assault on Johnston's field fortifications, but he soon called off the attack and went back to outflanking the foe.

The realities of the technological revolution in weaponry and the response of the Civil War soldier to it through the use of field fortifications are as much a part of survival in warfare today as 130 years ago. The much-boasted initiative of the American soldier impressed itself in no aspect of military art more than in the development and construction of earthworks during the Civil War.

BIBLIOGRAPHY

Fieberger, G. J. *A Textbook on Field Fortifications.* New York, 1900.
Hogane, James T. "Reminiscences of the Siege of Vicksburg." *Southern Historical Society Papers* 2 (November 1883): 223–227, 291–297, 484–489. Reprint, Wilmington, N.C., 1990.
Hunt, O. E. *Entrenchments and Fortifications.* Vol. 5 of *The Photographic History of the Civil War.* Edited by Francis Trevelyn Miller. 10 vols. New York, 1911.
Nichols, James L. *Confederate Engineers.* Confederate Centennial Studies. Edited by W. S. Stanley Hoole. Tuscaloosa, Ala., 1957.

EDWIN C. BEARSS

FORT STEDMAN, VIRGINIA.

This fort, located near Petersburg, was the site of a battle fought March 25, 1865, that was Gen. Robert E. Lee's last tactical offensive movement in the nine-and-a-half-month Petersburg campaign. Lee's plan was to find a weak point in the Federal line, punch through that portion of the enemy entrenchments, and force their abandonment. He could then shorten his line defending Petersburg and detach a force to go to Gen. Joseph E. Johnston's aid in North Carolina and stop his adversary, Maj. Gen. William Tecumseh Sherman. The troops could then return with Johnston and deal with the forces under Gen. Ulysses S. Grant.

General Lee entrusted the selection of the point of attack to Lt. Gen. John B. Gordon. Gordon chose the area between a section of the Confederate defenses known as Colquitt's Salient and the Union's Fort Stedman, where the lines were about 150 yards apart. The Ninth Corps under Maj. Gen. John G. Parke held this section of the Federal siege lines. The fort was named for Col. Griffin A. Stedman, Eleventh Connecticut Infantry, who had been killed near the site in 1864. The earthen structure was surrounded by a moat four feet deep and half full of water; it was thirteen feet from the bottom of the moat to the top of the parapet. To the north of the fort were the Ninth and Tenth Batteries; to the south the Eleventh and Twelfth Batteries, as well as Fort Haskell six hundred yards away.

General Lee committed Gordon's entire corps to the assault supported by reserves from Longstreet's and Hill's Corps. If they were successful, a body of cavalry was to be sent through the broken line and wreak havoc in the rear of the Federal army.

At 4:00 A.M. the attack began with ten thousand to twelve thousand infantry arranged in three compact columns, the cavalry being held in reserve. Hitting the Federal lines and breaking through, the Confederates captured Fort Sted-man, the adjacent Tenth Battery, and nine cannon, eleven mortars, and nearly a thousand prisoners (many escaped in the later stages of the battle), including Brig. Gen. Napoleon B. McLaughlin.

As the Confederates poured through the gap, one column moved north toward the Ninth Battery, and the other headed straight for the rear of the Federal army. The third was to move down the lines against Fort Haskell and capture the Eleventh and Twelfth Batteries. But heavy resistance at the fort caused the Confederate movement to falter and finally give way. At the other points of attack, the Southerners also lost their momentum.

Newly arriving Federal reinforcements in the field under Brig. Gen. John F. Hartranft stalled the Confederates around 8:00 A.M., and Gordon ordered a withdrawal. The Union loss amounted to 75 killed, 419 wounded, 523 missing; the Confederates, 1,600 killed and wounded, 1,900 captured. Four days later Grant began his final offensive movement, which culminated in the fall of Petersburg on April 3.

BIBLIOGRAPHY

Gordon, John B. *Reminiscences of the Civil War.* New York, 1911.
Hartranft, John F. "The Recapture of Fort Stedman." In *Battles and Leaders of the Civil War.* Edited by Robert V. Johnson and C. C. Buel. Vol 4. New York, 1888. Reprint, Secaucus, N.J., 1982.
Hodgkins, William H. *The Battle of Fort Stedman, March 25, 1865.* Boston, 1889.
Kilmer, George L. "Gordon's Attack at Fort Stedman." In *Battles and Leaders of the Civil War.* Edited by Robert V. Johnson and C. C. Buel. Vol. 4. New York, 1888. Reprint, Secaucus, N.J., 1982.
Trudeau, Noah Andre. *The Last Citadel: Petersburg, Virginia, June 1864–April 1865.* Boston, 1991.

CHRIS CALKINS

FORT SUMTER, SOUTH CAROLINA.

The scene of the opening battle of the Civil War, Fort Sumter was located on an artificial island inside the entrance to Charleston Harbor. A pentagon, with brick walls about three hundred feet long, forty feet high, and eight to twelve feet thick, the fort was still under construction in 1860. To it, on the night of December 26, Maj. Robert Anderson moved his garrison of U.S. troops from Fort Moultrie at the edge of the harbor entrance, where he and his men had been exposed to the threat of attack by South Carolinians.

Having declared their state an independent republic, the South Carolinians resented the presence of what was to them a foreign flag, and they looked upon Anderson's move to Fort Sumter as an act of aggression. They considered it another hostile act when, in January 1861, the Buchanan administration sent the unarmed merchant ship *Star of the West* with reinforcements for the fort. As the ship approached Charleston Harbor, South Carolina shore batteries opened fire and compelled it to turn back.

The Confederate government early established its policy with regard to the two principal forts remaining under Federal control in the seceded states. On February 15, 1861, the Provisional Congress in Montgomery secretly resolved that "immediate steps should be taken to obtain possession of Forts Sumter and Pickens . . . either by negotiation or force." President Jefferson Davis thereupon sent to Washington three commissioners—Martin J. Crawford, John Forsyth, and A. B. Roman—to try negotiation. He ordered P. G. T. Beauregard to Charleston to take command of the harbor and make preparations for the use of force.

In Washington the Confederate commissioners failed to get an audience with any member of the Lincoln administration, but Secretary of State William H. Seward communicated with them through a go-between. The commissioners thought it a great diplomatic victory for the Confederacy when Seward pledged that his government would not, without notice, undertake to change the situation at Sumter. As Commissioner Crawford reported, the Confederate States "were not bound in any way whatever to observe the same course" (but were left free to continue their preparations for attack). "We think, then, that the

policy of 'masterly inactivity,' on our part, was wise in every particular."

Such inactivity displeased Governor Francis W. Pickens and his fellow South Carolinians, who demanded immediate action. "The President shares the feeling expressed by you that Fort Sumter should be in our possession at the earliest possible moment," Secretary of War Leroy P. Walker assured Governor Pickens on March 1, but cautioned: "Thorough preparations must be made before an attack is attempted, for the first blow must be successful."

General Beauregard proceeded to extend and enlarge the batteries surrounding and targeting the fort. His preparations practically complete, he advised the Davis government on March 27 that the expulsion of Anderson from Sumter "ought now to be decided on in a few days." Davis gave Beauregard the following instructions on April 2: he should be ready to strike whenever the commissioners withdrew from Washington, and meanwhile he should cease to allow Anderson the privilege of buying groceries in Charleston.

On April 8 the Davis government heard from the commissioners that they had met a final "refusal" and considered their mission at an end. This news alone would have been sufficient to trigger an assault on Sumter, but even more ominous news arrived in Montgomery on the

INTERIOR OF FORT SUMTER. From a drawing by a Confederate engineer officer.

same day. A telegram from Beauregard said Governor Pickens had just received a message from President Abraham Lincoln to the effect that "provisions would be sent to Sumter peaceably, otherwise by force." Secretary Walker immediately replied to Beauregard: "Under no circumstances are you to allow provisions to be sent to Fort Sumter."

Davis and his cabinet decided not to wait for the arrival of Lincoln's expedition but, instead, to risk the onus of firing the first shot. On April 10 Walker on behalf of Davis ordered Beauregard to demand immediate evacuation of the fort and, if refused, to "reduce" it. Anderson the next day rejected the demand but said he and his men would be "starved out in a few days." Walker then authorized Beauregard to "avoid the effusion of blood" if Anderson would state a time for his withdrawal and would agree meanwhile not to fire unless fired upon. Beauregard sent James Chesnut, Roger A. Pryor, and two aides by boat to present this offer to Anderson after midnight. Anderson promised to hold his fire and to evacuate in three days—unless he should receive "controlling instructions" or "additional supplies." Chesnut and Pryor told him his reply was unsatisfactory and a bombardment would begin in an hour.

The bombardment began at 4:30 on the morning of April 12, 1861. Anderson was unable to make much of a response, completely outgunned as he was. He received no assistance from Lincoln's expedition, which proved a fiasco. The leading warship *Powhatan* had been misdirected to Fort Pickens, other vessels had been delayed by a storm, and the rest stood helplessly offshore. Cannon balls battered the brick walls of the fort while hot shot set fire to the wooden buildings inside. Anderson surrendered at noon on April 14. All his eighty-four soldiers and forty-three laborers had survived, but two men died as a result of a gun explosion during the surrender ceremonies.

Among Confederate leaders it had been an axiom that a clash at Sumter would induce Virginia and other states of the upper South and the border to secede. None of these states did so immediately, but Virginia, Tennessee, Arkansas, and North Carolina seceded in consequence of Lincoln's call for troops on April 15. Southerners generally rallied to the support of the Davis government. Northerners did the same with respect to the Lincoln administration. Most of them believed the Confederates had convicted themselves of war guilt, but the Confederates accused Lincoln of having deliberately provoked the attack. Davis, in *The Rise and Fall of the Confederate Government* (1881), still felt called upon to explain: "He who makes the assault is not necessarily he who strikes the first blow or fires the first gun."

In 1863, U.S. forces made two unsuccessful attempts to

FORT SUMTER, SOUTH CAROLINA. Interior view of the fort, April 14, 1861, after its evacuation by Maj. Robert Anderson. The north end of the two-tiered west barracks and the barbette of the adjacent north channel face are visible. NATIONAL ARCHIVES

retake Sumter and capture Charleston. The U.S. flag was not again raised over the fort until April 14, 1865, exactly four years after the surrender.

[*See also* Star of the West.]

BIBLIOGRAPHY

Current, Richard N. "The Confederates and the First Shot." *Civil War History* 7 (1961): 357–369.
Swanberg, W. A. *First Blood: The Story of Fort Sumter.* New York, 1957.

RICHARD N. CURRENT

FORT WAGNER, SOUTH CAROLINA.

Fort Wagner and Battery Gregg were the principal land defenses of Morris Island, which commanded the only approach for large vessels entering Charleston Harbor. The fort was an enclosed earthwork that extended entirely across a narrow point of the island and prevented the enemy from threatening Battery Gregg by land. Between July 10 and 18, the fort was assaulted by Federal forces. The successful defense by the Confederates manning the fort set back by months the Union's plan to capture Charleston.

In July 1863 a Federal army-navy force commanded by Brig. Gen. Quincy A. Gillmore and Rear Adm. John Dahlgren planned to seize Morris Island as a preliminary step in the effort to reduce the defenses of Charleston and ultimately capture the city. On July 10, Brig. Gen. George C. Strong successfully landed his brigade of 3,700 men upon Morris Island, despite resistance from the island's garrison. Strong lost 15 killed and 91 wounded. Confederate losses were 294.

On July 11, Strong ordered a daylight assault on Fort Wagner by three regiments. The fort had been reinforced the evening before, bringing its numbers up to approximately 1,200 defenders. Strong's attack was repulsed with the loss of 49 killed, 123 wounded, and 167 missing. The Confederate garrison lost 6 killed and 6 wounded.

Following this unsuccessful assault, heavy artillery was placed on the island. To cover the placement of the siege artillery, the Federal naval vessels subjected the fort to heavy bombardment on July 15–17. A second assault to capture the fort was planned for the evening of the eighteenth. To prepare the way for the infantry attack the fort was subjected to an extraordinarily heavy all-day bombardment by both Dahlgren's naval vessels and the land batteries. The garrison of the fort at this time consisted of 1,300 men, 13 heavy guns, and 1 light field battery. Despite the weight of the Federal bombardment, Confederate losses did not exceed 8 killed and 20 wounded.

At dusk the Federal infantry, consisting of Strong's and Col. H. S. Putnam's brigades, supported by Brig. Gen. Thomas G. Stevenson's brigade—altogether 6,000 men—

advanced upon the fort. Spearheading the assault was the Fifty-fourth Massachusetts, a black regiment under the command of Col. Robert G. Shaw. Although the Federals managed to gain a foothold in the fort, they were eventually driven out. General Strong was mortally wounded, Colonel Putnam was killed, and five out of Strong's six regimental commanders were killed or wounded. Union losses totaled 246 killed, 880 wounded, and 389 missing. The Confederate garrison, under the command of Brig. Gen. William Booth Taliaferro, suffered losses of 36 killed, 133 wounded, and 5 missing.

General Gillmore now abandoned the effort to capture Fort Wagner by direct assault and undertook siege operations to reduce the fort. By September 6, his forces had reached the ditch surrounding the fort and an assault on the fort was ordered for the seventh. The Confederates, however, abandoned the fort during the night. Losses during the siege operations for the Federals were 71 killed, 278 wounded, and 9 missing. Confederate losses through August 21 were 38 killed and 150 wounded.

BIBLIOGRAPHY

Bryan, E. K. "Defence of Fort Wagner." In *Histories of the Several Regiments and Battalions from North Carolina in the Great War, 1861–1865.* Edited by Walter Clark. Vol. 5. Goldsboro, N.C., 1901.
Twiggs, H. D. D. "The Defence of Battery Wagner." *Southern Historical Society Papers* 20 (1892): 166–183. Reprint, Wilmington, N.C., 1990.
U.S. War Department. *War of the Rebellion: A Compilation of the Official Records of the Union and Confederate Armies.* Washington, D.C., 1880–1901, Ser. 1, vol. 28, pts. 1–2.

D. SCOTT HARTWIG

FOSTER, THOMAS J.

(1809–1887), congressman from Alabama and colonel. Born July 11, 1809, at Nashville, Tennessee, Thomas Jefferson Foster moved to Lawrence County, Alabama, about 1830 and became a planter and slaveholder. He also engaged in manufacturing.

Before the war Foster was a Whig and a Unionist. But when war came, he served in the Confederate army as a colonel of the Twenty-seventh Alabama Infantry and assisted in the construction of Fort Henry. In 1861 he was elected to the First Confederate Congress, where he supported conscription and the administration of President Jefferson Davis. In 1863 he was reelected to a second term in the Confederate Congress and now opposed conscription. While in Congress he served on the Conference, Indian Affairs, Territories and Public Lands, Accounts, and other committees. He advocated economic development and financial stability for the Confederate government, endorsing all strong legislative policies except increased taxes. A slaveholder, he voted to arm and free slaves in 1865.

At the close of the war he returned to his plantation in Lawrence County. In 1865 he was elected to the U.S. House of Representatives under the Johnson plan of Reconstruction but was not seated. He moved to Kentucky in 1867 and died there on February 24, 1887.

BIBLIOGRAPHY

Owen, Thomas McAdory. *History of Alabama and Dictionary of Alabama Biography.* 4 vols. Chicago, 1921.

Thornton, J. Mills, III. *Politics and Power in a Slave Society: Alabama, 1800–1860.* Baton Rouge, La., 1978.

Wakelyn, Jon L. *Biographical Directory of the Confederacy.* Edited by Frank E. Vandiver. Westport, Conn., 1977.

Warner, Ezra J., and W. Buck Yearns. *Biographical Register of the Confederate Congress.* Baton Rouge, La., 1975.

SARAH WOOLFOLK WIGGINS

FRANCE. France responded to the outbreak of war in America with interests so varied and conflicting that they prevented the nation from pursuing a consistent policy toward the Confederacy. From the outset Emperor Louis Napoleon expressed sympathy for the Southern cause. Yet his deep involvement in European affairs had created potential enemies on the Continent, and any unilateral decisions that antagonized Washington would expose French commerce as well as the emperor's burgeoning Mexican venture to Northern retaliation. Napoleon had undertaken commitments in Mexico that he could not sustain. The process of intervention began in July 1861 when the Mexican government repudiated its international obligations. In the London Convention of October 30, Britain, France, and Spain, all harboring grievances against Mexico, agreed to occupy the country but not to interfere in its right to form its own government. Privately Napoleon, supported by Mexican monarchists, favored a European-controlled monarchy. A stabilized Mexico, Napoleon wrote on October 9, would attract European capital, increase European trade, supply European textile mills with cotton, and terminate both Mexican outrages and encroachments from the United States.

When in the spring of 1862 the French minister in Mexico, Dubois de Saligny, announced France's opposition to the Mexican government of Benito Juarez and its support for the Mexican monarchists, the British and Spanish forces withdrew. Thereafter the reinforced but isolated French army faced a hostile Mexican populace as well as effective Mexican guerrillas. Still Napoleon persisted in his misadventure. Confederate leaders concluded that Napoleon's massive defiance of the Monroe Doctrine would ultimately fail without the support of an independent South ready to accept a French vassal state in Mexico. For Napoleon,

however, salvation lay not in adopting the Confederate cause but in avoiding a unilateral confrontation with the United States. To escape that danger the French emperor required British support. This reality, operating in an atmosphere of sometimes immense cordiality between the French government and the Confederacy, sustained a recurring Confederate anticipation of French recognition even as it assured profound disillusionment at the end.

Confederate presumptions for success also rested on French perceptions of Southern military superiority and the alleged power of cotton. Such presumptions were not without merit. The French minister in Washington, Henri Mercier, believed from the outset that the South would emerge victorious and therefore deserved recognition. Then in September French foreign minister Antoine Édouard Thouvenel informed Mercier of the growing cotton famine in France. The cotton textile districts, he wrote, were facing disaster. Mercier responded by urging British and French recognition of the Confederacy and breaking of the blockade as soon as the public was prepared to assume the risks. When Mercier approached U.S. Secretary of State William H. Seward in late October with Thouvenel's demand for cotton, Seward retorted that France required Northern wheat more than Southern cotton. Any European intervention in the American contest, he warned, would produce both a wheat famine and war. As the year ended, pro-Southern sympathies in the French government as well as France's desire for cotton had failed to produce recognition or any defiance of the Federal blockade.

In late January 1862 James M. Mason and John Slidell, commissioners assigned to Britain and France respectively, reached London after having been taken from the British packet *Trent* and briefly held in the United States. Slidell continued to Paris to take up the questions of recognition and the blockade. For months the Confederacy had gathered evidence that the blockade was ineffective and therefore illegal by the standards embodied in the Treaty of Paris (1856). Thouvenel refused to defend the blockade but wondered why so little cotton reached European ports if the blockade was ineffective. Slidell acknowledged that owners of large cotton-carrying vessels preferred to avoid the risks of blockade running. Slidell concluded that French officials would challenge the blockade if Britain, with its greater maritime interests, would take the initiative. But British foreign minister Lord John Russell had already declared that any blockade was binding as long as some danger of capture existed. Russell's definition, Slidell complained, committed France to a paper blockade as long as the emperor refused to act independently.

Privately, French officials challenged the legality, even the morality, of the blockade. On April 11 William S. Lindsay, pro-Confederate member of the English Parliament, reminded Louis Napoleon in Paris that in three months the cotton famine in Britain and France would become intolerable. It was, moreover, Europe's acceptance of the blockade that unfairly compelled the South to fight without access to European manufacturers. The emperor offered sympathy and declared his willingness to send a fleet to the Southern coasts, but only if England would send an equal force. At the same time Mercier, with Seward's permission, traveled to Richmond and there, on April 16, sought to obtain from Secretary of State Judah P. Benjamin a firsthand estimate of the South's capacity and determination to win. Seward assumed that Mercier would find the South in disarray. Instead, Benjamin informed Mercier that Southerners would never dishonor themselves "by reuniting with a people for whom [they felt] unmitigated contempt as well as abhorrence." Benjamin reminded Mercier that the Federal blockade was ineffective, that he could name twenty ports where the United States had never stationed a warship. Mercier could only acknowledge to Thouvenel his embarrassment over French policy.

Slidell believed that the Confederate victories of June and July 1862, especially in Virginia, presented the opportune time to demand French recognition as a right won on the battlefield. Thouvenel, on July 23, advised Slidell to withhold his demand until additional Confederate victories would compel Britain to act. Confederate successes had raised the issue of European mediation to terminate the war. Slidell suggested to Thouvenel that the South would welcome mediation, but Mercier had warned Paris that any offer of mediation would merely antagonize the North and achieve nothing. Slidell reported to Benjamin on August 24: "We are still hard and fast aground here. Nothing will float us off but a strong and continued current of important successes in the field." Such victories remained elusive. Yet on October 28 the emperor welcomed Slidell to St. Cloud and declared his intention to propose a joint British-French-Russian mediation to end the war. The emperor declared his preference for a six-month armistice, with Southern ports open for commerce. In early November Louis Napoleon submitted his tripartite proposal to Britain and Russia only to have it rejected by both countries.

During subsequent months it became apparent, despite continued French promises of intervention, that France would not move without Britain. When the parliamentary debates of July 1863 revealed that the British ministry remained firm in its adherence to Northern demands, Benjamin and Slidell exerted renewed pressure on France to act alone; again they failed. Édouard Drouyn de Lhuys, the new French foreign minister, denied France's responsibility for Europe's acceptance of the blockade and repeated the plea that France was too vulnerable to defy the U.S. government without British support.

Benjamin expressed his final disillusionment with French policy in September 1864, complaining that the emperor had persistently exhibited a friendship for the South and yet, with equal persistence, had maintained open and cordial relations with the North. France had shown a minimum of hospitality to Confederate ships in French ports and had failed to deliver war vessels promised to the Confederacy. The emperor's subservience to the anti-Confederate policies of London and Washington, Benjamin concluded, had been total. French neutrality had favored the Union; the Confederacy could only submit in silence.

[*See also* Mexico; Monroe Doctrine; Trent Affair.]

BIBLIOGRAPHY

Blumenthal, Henry. *A Reappraisal of Franco-American Relations, 1830–1871.* Chapel Hill, N.C., 1959.

Carroll, Daniel B. *Henri Mercier and the American Civil War.* Princeton, 1971.

Case, Lynn M., and Warren F. Spencer. *The United States and France: Civil War Diplomacy.* Philadelphia, 1970.

Owsley, Frank Lawrence. *King Cotton Diplomacy: Foreign Relations of the Confederate States of America.* Revised by Harriet Chappell Owsley. Chicago, 1959.

Sears, Louis M. *John Slidell.* Durham, N.C., 1925.

NORMAN A. GRAEBNER

FRANKLIN AND NASHVILLE CAMPAIGN.

In early September 1864, after the close of the Atlanta campaign, the Confederate Army of Tennessee camped at Palmetto, Georgia, a few miles southwest of Atlanta. The army was exhausted and, like its opponents, needed to regroup before beginning the next round. While the soldiers rested, Southern leaders developed plans to pry the Federals out of Atlanta and to get them out of Georgia.

The Confederate strategy was hammered out between September 25 and 27 during a visit to the army by President Jefferson Davis. The chief executive and Gen. John Bell Hood, the army's commander, reasoned that operations against the railroad connecting the Federals occupying Atlanta with their base at Chattanooga, Tennessee, would compel them to withdraw northward to protect their line of supply. If all went well, the Southerners would eventually lure their enemy into an area where the Confederates could fight at an advantage. A Southern victory in North Georgia would go far to offset the past summer's defeats; if it came in time, it might also affect the 1864 election in the North.

In early October Hood moved into northwestern Georgia, striking eastward against the railroad as he went. His army—about 40,000 men—was divided into three infantry corps (commanded by Lt. Gen. Alexander P. Stewart and Stephen D. Lee and Maj. Gen. B. Franklin Cheatham), a cavalry corps (under Maj. Gen. Joseph Wheeler), and an independent cavalry division (under Brig. Gen. William Hicks Jackson). After doing extensive damage to the

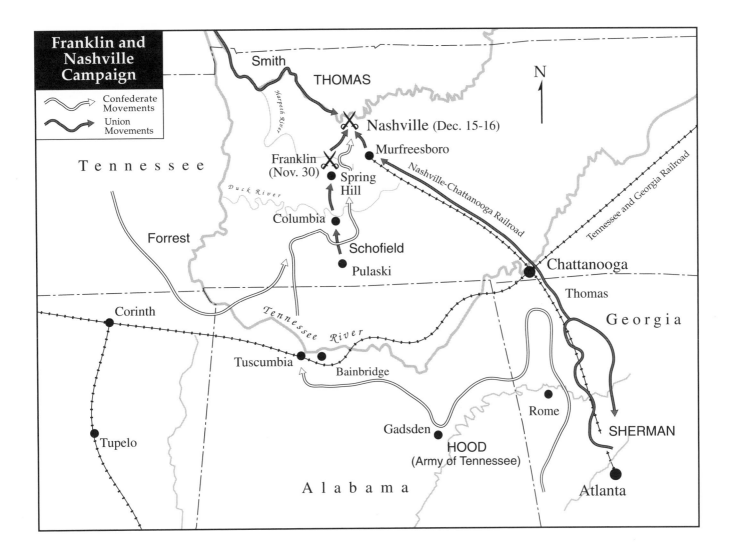

railroad, Hood moved west. He reached Gadsden, Alabama, on October 20.

The Federal army followed Hood, but one Northern corps was left to hold Atlanta. When Hood moved into Alabama, the Union commander, Maj. Gen. William Tecumseh Sherman, posted his army just west of Rome, Georgia. Sherman refused to be drawn farther westward. Instead, he soon detached part of his force to protect Tennessee and with the rest returned to Atlanta. On November 15 he marched off across Georgia for Savannah on the Atlantic coast.

Realizing that Sherman was not going to chase him across Alabama, and that it was unlikely he could move fast enough to head off the Federals in Georgia, Hood hatched the idea of marching into Tennessee. A threat to Nashville should force the Unionists to abandon Georgia. If it did not, the mere presence of a Southern army in middle Tennessee might confuse the Union plans. A Confederate victory in Tennessee would restore Southern morale and prestige. It

might even be possible, Hood fantasized, for the Confederates to win in Tennessee and then move to Virginia and join the army there for one great battle that would bring Confederate independence. Hood decided upon this scheme without consulting either the government or Gen. P. G. T. Beauregard, his immediate military superior. When informed of Hood's intentions, Beauregard insisted that Wheeler's cavalry be detached to oppose Sherman. To replace Wheeler, Beauregard promised Hood the cavalry of Maj. Gen. Nathan Bedford Forrest, then with Southern forces in Mississippi.

Execution of Hood's plan depended on speed. Every hour's delay gave the Unionists more time to prepare for his coming. Over the next several weeks a combination of poor planning and administration, logistical problems, and the need to link up with Forrest forced Hood to drift westward to Tuscumbia. Not until November 20 did Hood get all of his army across the Tennessee River, and on the twenty-first the Southerners started for middle Tennessee.

Maj. Gen. George H. Thomas commanded the Federals defending Tennessee. His force consisted of the Fourth Corps (Maj. Gen. David Stanley), the Twenty-third Corps (Maj. Gen. John M. Schofield), and assorted cavalry and garrison units. In all, there were about 65,000 Federal troops in the area, but many of them were posted along the railroad between Nashville and Chattanooga. Reinforcements from the Mississippi Valley and other points were on the way to Nashville. Thomas stationed Schofield with 30,000 men at Pulaski to observe Hood and delay his march while he assembled the rest of his force at Nashville.

When Hood moved forward, Schofield pulled back to the Duck River at Columbia. There the Southerners found him when they arrived on November 26. On the next day, the Federals crossed the river and destroyed the bridges, but they remained in position to block Hood's direct route to Nashville.

Hood decided to swing east of Columbia, cross the river at a ford, and then march northwest to Spring Hill where he would regain the road to Nashville. Historians have usually depicted Hood as maneuvering to cut Schofield off from Nashville and destroy his force. It seems more likely, however, that Hood was thinking only in terms of getting to Nashville ahead of Schofield, not in terms of destroying him.

Whatever his intent, Hood moved to execute it during the night of November 28–29. Forrest's cavalry, Cheatham, Stewart, and one division of Lee's corps marched off to swing around to Spring Hill. The rest of Lee's corps, almost all of the artillery, and the wagons remained in front of the Federals at Columbia.

By noon on November 29, Forrest's horsemen were near Spring Hill where they encountered small bodies of Northerners east of the town. Throughout the afternoon Confederate infantry arrived and deployed in the fields east of the road. Meanwhile, the Federals—aware of Hood's maneuver—were gradually pulling out of their river line and marching northward.

Confusion reigned among the Confederates. Units moved back and forth. The generals, without clear orders, did not know how their units were deployed, where they were, or what they were doing. Hood's staff—there was no chief of staff—simply broke down, and his control of the army dissolved. Messages from Hood were sometimes not delivered to corps commanders. Many reports from the field did not reach army headquarters. Hood made a few ineffective attempts to get some of his units onto the Columbia-Franklin road, but an almost total misunderstanding of how his army was aligned frustrated his efforts. (Hood believed that his men were deployed facing westward; they, in fact, faced to the north.) Finally, an exhausted Hood fell asleep in a nearby house. Confederate soldiers settled down for the night east of the road, and the Federals marched north to safety.

The Confederate breakdown at Spring Hill has never been satisfactorily explained. Some historians have thought that one or more of the Southern generals were drunk, under the influence of drugs, or off visiting some local ladies. More likely, Hood's own weaknesses as a commander (he typically did not ensure that his orders were obeyed), his poor administration of the army, his apparent lack of any definite plan, the absence of a functioning staff, and the fact that he had been up for more than twenty hours and was simply too tired to go on all combined to produce the chaos.

On November 30 Schofield had his men in position at Franklin while his engineers worked to prepare crossings over the Harpeth River. Hood's Confederates followed the Federals north. Late that afternoon Hood threw his army into a massive frontal assault on Schofield's position at Franklin. The Southerners overran an advanced Federal work and then continued on to smash into the very strong Union line. In places Hood's men broke through, but Northern reserves poured into the fight and eventually pushed the Southerners back. Many of the Confederates then rallied and attacked again and again. Some Federal officers reported a dozen separate attacks on their positions. Not until nine or ten at night did the fighting fade away. Schofield then crossed the river and continued his march to Nashville.

The Federals reported 2,326 men (of some 28,000 engaged) lost at Franklin. Hood lost about 5,000 (of 28,000), including twelve general officers and fifty-five regimental commanders. The leadership of the army had been shot away. Two Southern brigades were commanded after the battle by captains. One regiment numbered only thirty men.

Despite his heavy losses at Franklin, Hood decided on December 1 to follow Schofield northward. In truth, he had little choice. He obviously could not overtake Sherman who was far across Georgia, and to withdraw southward would be to abandon middle Tennessee, demoralize the army, and admit defeat. To remain at Franklin would not accomplish anything. Perhaps Hood could get reinforcements from the Trans-Mississippi; perhaps the Federals at Nashville would be content to wait out the winter; perhaps they would attack and give him and his men a chance to reverse the situation that had existed at Franklin. Nashville itself was too strongly fortified for the weakened Confederates to assault, but they could build their own works and perhaps hold them against an attack.

In early December Hood's crippled army deployed outside Nashville on a long east-west line to cover most of the major roads running south from the city. While the Southerners worked to fortify their position, Thomas continued to build up his army in the city. The Federals were joined by the Sixteenth Corps (Maj. Gen. A. J. Smith) as well as by some 5,200 men brought up from garrison posts in Tennessee and new troops shipped from the North. Thomas, a systematic

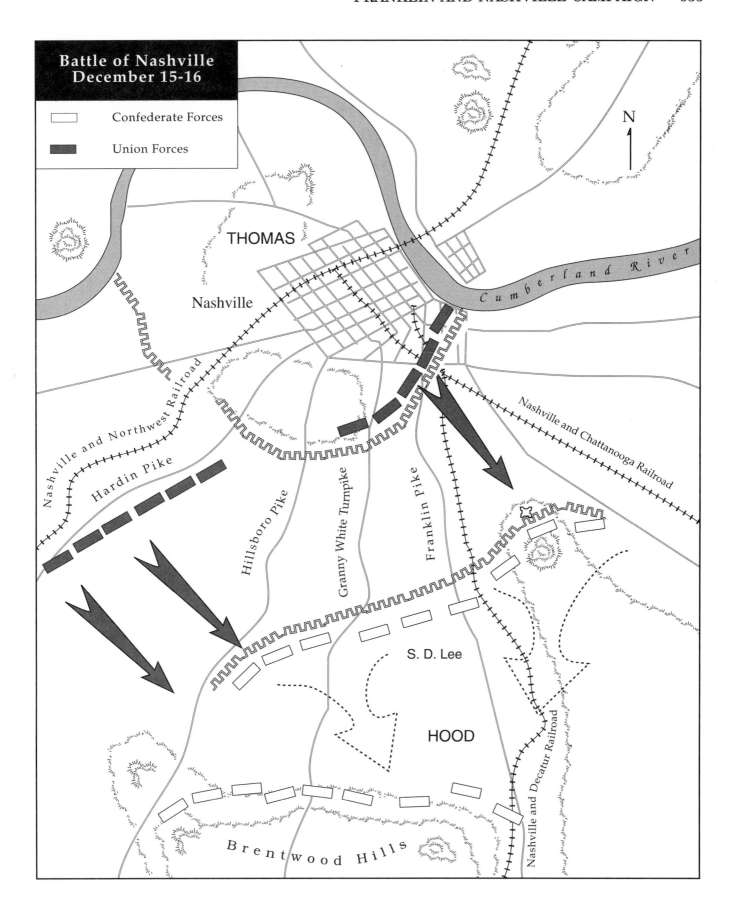

Battle of Nashville
December 15-16

Confederate Forces
Union Forces

N

THOMAS

Nashville

Cumberland River

Nashville and Northwest Railroad

Hardin Pike

Hillsboro Pike

Granny White Turnpike

Franklin Pike

Nashville and Chattanooga Railroad

S. D. Lee

HOOD

Nashville and Decatur Railroad

B r e n t w o o d   H i l l s

officer, wanted to prepare a force that would do a thorough job of wrecking Hood's army. Meanwhile, Hood made the Confederate situation even more desperate by sending off most of his cavalry and some infantry to Murfreesboro to operate against the Nashville-Chattanooga railroad.

The task of organizing the cavalry, and then bad weather, delayed the Federal attack until December 15. When Thomas struck, his plan was brilliant. He distracted Hood with an early probe against the right of the Confederate line and then launched an overwhelming assault against its left. Enveloped on their left, the Southerners fell back to a new, shorter line along the Brentwood Hills a few miles to the south.

On the afternoon of December 16, Thomas assaulted Hood's new line. While Union infantry attacked at several points, a massive artillery barrage pulverized the Southerners. Late in the day Northern cavalrymen were again able to envelope the Southerners' left, and the Confederates there found themselves under attack from three directions. At about 4:00 P.M., Hood's line collapsed, and his men fled southward.

For the next several days the Confederate army moved toward the Tennessee River with Union cavalry nipping at its heels. Lee's corps, the least beaten Southern unit (it had been on the Confederate right on December 16 and had not been involved in the debacle on the left of Hood's line), covered the retreat. Things were a bit easier for the Confederates after December 18 when they got across the Duck River at Columbia. On Christmas day the leading units reached the Tennessee near Bainbridge, Alabama, and by December 28 the last of Hood's men had crossed. The Confederates moved west to Corinth, Mississippi, and then south to Tupelo.

Thomas lost 2,562 men in the Battle of Nashville out of about 50,000 engaged. Hood had an estimated 23,000 troops in the battle. His losses are not known. The best estimates put his killed and wounded at about 1,500. The Northerners reported that they took 4,500 prisoners during the battle and while the Southerners were retreating to the Tennessee River. Doubtless, many other Confederates deserted and went to their homes. On December 31 Hood's army reported 18,708 officers and men "present for duty."

Hood's Franklin and Nashville campaign, in the words of one Confederate officer, was "a complete and disastrous failure." It was the worst-managed major military operation of the war. For all practical purposes, it destroyed the Army of Tennessee. Hood himself was relieved from command on January 23, 1865, and the army never again fought as a unit. Parts of it were sent off to help defend Mobile; other units set out for North Carolina to reinforce the Confederates there. Some arrived in time for the final skirmishes in the East; others were strung out all across Mississippi, Alabama, Georgia, and the Carolinas when the war ended.

BIBLIOGRAPHY

Connelly, Thomas Lawrence. *Autumn of Glory: The Army of Tennessee, 1862–1865.* Baton Rouge, La., 1971.

Cox, Jacob D. *The March to the Sea: Franklin and Nashville.* New York, 1889.

Daniel, Larry J. *Soldiering in the Army of Tennessee: A Portrait of Life in the Confederate Army.* Chapel Hill, N.C., 1991.

Hay, Thomas Robson. *Hood's Tennessee Campaign.* New York, 1929.

Horn, Stanley F. *The Decisive Battle of Nashville.* Baton Rouge, La., 1956. Reprint, Knoxville, Tenn., 1968.

McDonough, James Lee, and Thomas L. Connelly. *Five Tragic Hours: The Battle of Franklin.* Knoxville, Tenn., 1983.

Sword, Wiley. *Embrace an Angry Wind: The Confederacy's Last Hurrah: Spring Hill, Franklin, and Nashville.* New York, 1992.

RICHARD M. MCMURRY

FRAYSER'S FARM, VIRGINIA. One of the Seven Days' Battles on the Virginia Peninsula took place at Frayser's Farm, when Gen. Robert E. Lee sought to annihilate George B. McClellan's Army of the Potomac as it retreated toward the safety of a new base and the nearby Federal gunboats on the James River. Lee had already tried to destroy McClellan's forces as they drew back from their original goal of taking Richmond, but each time one or more of his subordinates had failed to fulfill his assignment and the Southerners had suffered heavy casualties while the Federals slipped away to new defensive positions.

On June 30, 1862, Lee again planned to strike the Union forces as they retreated. Following bloody fighting at Savage's Station, he decided to send the commands of Maj. Gens. James Longstreet, A. P. Hill, John B. Magruder, Benjamin Huger, and Thomas J. ("Stonewall") Jackson against the Federals in simultaneous assaults on their front, flank, and rear.

Once again, Lee's plan miscarried. Magruder's forces moved too slowly to be of any assistance in the fighting on the thirtieth. Huger spent precious time clearing the road on which he advanced of trees felled by the Federals, rather than ignoring the obstacles and proceeding without artillery and wagons. Inexplicably, Union artillery and sharpshooters prevented a usually aggressive Jackson from crossing White Oak Swamp. Even when some of his officers found fords suitable for the men to use, Jackson failed to make the effort, although the fighting raged only a few miles away. All these factors left Longstreet's and Hill's men to carry the brunt of the fighting at Frayser's Farm.

Longstreet opened the battle when he heard what he mistakenly believed to be a signal shot from Huger. Thinking that the attack was underway in that quarter, he sent his division and Hill's against the Union division of Brig. Gen. George A. McCall at about 4:00 P.M. The men cracked McCall's line, taking prisoners that included

McCall himself. But as the Southerners drove their counterparts back, Union troops under Maj. Gen. Joseph Hooker and Brig. Gens. Philip Kearny and John Sedgwick stemmed the attack. The fighting was severe, much of it hand to hand, as Longstreet's and Hill's men fought without the support of the other Confederate columns.

Although the bitter fighting raged into the night, the Federal line held. Other Union forces established new defensive positions at Malvern Hill, closer to the Army of the Potomac's base on the James, and McClellan once more avoided the fate Lee planned for him. The Battle of Frayser's Farm cost the attacking Confederates 3,615 casualties to the Federals' 2,853. But despite Lee's failure to destroy McClellan's army, he had succeeded in driving it farther from the Confederate capital at Richmond.

BIBLIOGRAPHY

Cullen, Joseph P. *The Peninsula Campaign, 1862: McClelland and Lee Struggle for Richmond.* Harrisburg, Pa., 1973.

Freeman, Douglas S. *Lee's Lieutenants: A Study in Command.* 3 vols. New York, 1942–1944. Reprint, New York, 1986.

Johnson, Robert U., and C. C. Buel, eds. *Battles and Leaders of the Civil War.* 4 vols. New York, 1887–1888. Reprint, Secaucus, N.J., 1982.

Robertson, James I., Jr. *General A. P. Hill.* New York, 1987.

Sears, Stephen W. *To the Gates of Richmond: The Peninsula Campaign.* New York, 1992.

BRIAN S. WILLS

FRAZER, JOHN WESLEY

FRAZER, JOHN WESLEY (1827–1906), colonel, acting brigadier general. Born January 6, 1827, in Harden, Tennessee, Frazer graduated from West Point in 1849 and served in the U.S. Army until he resigned his commission in March 1861 to become a lieutenant colonel in the Eighth Alabama Infantry of the Confederate army. After serving with that unit in Virginia for nearly a year, he was promoted to colonel of the Twenty-eighth Alabama Infantry, a regiment that he successfully led through Gen. Braxton Bragg's campaign of late 1862 in Kentucky and Tennessee in such battles as Munfordville (September 14–17), Corinth (October 3–4), and Murfreesboro (December 31, 1862–January 2, 1863).

Following a competent tour of duty with the Army of Tennessee, Frazer was appointed brigadier general on May 19, 1863, and commanded a brigade in the Department of East Tennessee. In August, Maj. Gen. Simon Bolivar Buckner was compelled to retreat by the superior forces of Union Maj. Gen. Ambrose E. Burnside. Frazer, as a result, was left behind with 2,500 mostly green Confederate troops to defend Cumberland Gap from Burnside's 25,000 Federals while the rest of the Southern army prepared for the Chickamauga campaign. Frazer bragged that he could hold the gap for a month; but in the face of such a superior force,

he was compelled to surrender his command on September 9. Outraged by his unconditional surrender, the Confederate government rejected his commission as brigadier general, and he languished in captivity at Fort Warren, Boston Harbor, until the end of the war.

After his release from Federal custody, Frazer became a planter in Arkansas for a short time. He then moved to New York City where he died on March 31, 1906.

BIBLIOGRAPHY

Cozzens, Peter. *No Better Place to Die: The Battle of Stones River.* Urbana, Ill., 1956.

Johnson, Robert U., and C. C. Buel, eds. *Battles and Leaders of the Civil War.* Vol. 2. New York, 1888. Reprint, Secaucus, N.J., 1982.

U.S. War Department. *War of the Rebellion: A Compilation of the Official Records of the Union and Confederate Armies.* Washington, D.C., 1880–1901. Ser. 1, vol. 17, pts. 1–2; vol. 20, pts. 1–2; vol. 30, pts. 2–4.

WARREN WILKINSON

FREDERICKSBURG CAMPAIGN

FREDERICKSBURG CAMPAIGN. The town of Fredericksburg, Virginia, at the falls of the Rappahannock River, which numbered 5,022 inhabitants in 1860, was the site of a victory for the Army of Northern Virginia on December 13, 1862, that must be reckoned its easiest major triumph of the war. Ambrose E. Burnside assumed command of the Federal Army of the Potomac on November 7 and at once determined to move it southeast toward Fredericksburg, hoping to interpose between Robert E. Lee and Richmond and thereby to gain either tactical or strategic advantages. Lee's army at the time was scattered in the lower Shenandoah Valley and in Piedmont Virginia, taking advantage of the harvest season while recuperating from the difficult Maryland campaign. Burnside promptly sought information about Southern strength around Fredericksburg by means of a cavalry reconnaissance. On November 8 Capt. Ulric Dahlgren, later notorious for a controversial raiding scheme around Richmond, led several dozen Union horsemen into the town. They surprised a handful of Confederate cavalrymen in Fredericksburg but found no other defenders.

The Federals advanced down the left bank of the Rappahannock toward Fredericksburg while Lee with forward elements of his army attempted to keep pace across the river. Burnside had divided his army into three "grand divisions," an innovation that did not survive his tenure in command. Gen. E. V. Sumner, leading the grand division at the head of the army, reached the heights opposite Fredericksburg on November 17. With most of Lee's regular infantry still two days away, Sumner looked across the river at a tiny Confederate detachment consisting of a few artillery pieces and a few hundred untested infantry. The shining opportunity for the Federals came to naught,

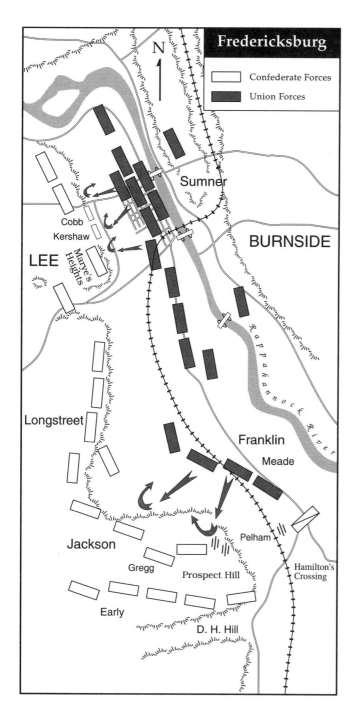

have been obliged to head southward another twenty miles to the next strong point. Burnside had called for a pontoon train with which to effect his river crossing, but it did not come for weeks. The orders that reached the train's operators had not conveyed any sense of urgency. Meanwhile the Federals had threatened to bombard the city of Fredericksburg on the premise that its cover was useful to Lee's army. The civilians evacuated the town in bitter cold weather amid haunting scenes of suffering that moved the Army of Northern Virginia to sympathy and eventually to an outpouring of donated funds to help support the refugees.

The bombardment of Fredericksburg finally came soon after the pontoons arrived. Early on December 11 Burnside sent engineer troops down to the river, which was more than four hundred feet wide, to build pontoon bridges at three points. The bridge builders had little difficulty at the crossing a mile below town; they eventually put down three spans there. The two crossing points in town proved to be far more dangerous for the engineers. Veteran riflemen of William Barksdale's Mississippi brigade held the waterfront in town, enjoying ample protection in basements and behind walls. The virtually unopposed crossing below town doomed any Confederate hope that the Federals could be held beyond the river permanently—indeed, why should they not be allowed into the city to try their luck on the killing plain beneath the heights where Lee's army waited in supreme confidence? Lee had left two divisions far downstream, however, and until D. H. Hill and Jubal Early could bring those troops up to lend a hand, the Confederates needed to buy some time. Barksdale's men provided a day's delay for that purpose.

Burnside's engineers pushed their first boats into the icy river (the thermometer read 24° at 7:00 A.M. in a nearby city), anchored them, and began to lay boards for the bridge flooring. Before they had reached midpoint in the stream, the growing light allowed the Mississippians to find them in their rifle sights and drive them away. After repeated costly and frustrating efforts, Burnside ordered that some 150 cannon on the heights above the river be fired on the town to clear away the opposition. Within an hour the artillery hurled several thousand rounds into Fredericksburg's buildings. "I believe," one of the Mississippians wrote, "there was not a square yard in the city which was not struck by a missile of some kind." After the guns ceased, the bridging teams attempted to resume work, but the Confederates met them with fire not at all diminished by the heavy shelling. The turning point at the river crossing came when three Northern regiments jumped into the pontoon boats and turned them into assault craft, crossing the river in the face of steady losses in order to drive away the Confederates and establish what apparently was the first literal bridgehead in American military history.

however, as they equivocated about crossing, even though a broad and rocky stretch of river at the north edge of town was readily negotiable.

Burnside arrived on the scene on November 19. So did Confederate Gen. James Longstreet. On the twentieth Lee reached Fredericksburg, and the Northern chance to take uncontested control of the strong ground west of town had vanished. With that position in Federal hands, Lee would

Barksdale's troops fell back reluctantly through the streets of Fredericksburg, contesting each block and ensuring the completion of their task. They had earned a full day for Lee to use in consolidating his position. The rest of the army, which had been watching Barksdale's men from the amphitheaterlike high ground around the city, cheered them as they came back from their hard day's work.

Burnside did not attack on December 12. He occupied the day in moving his troops across the river and laying plans. Those Federals in the city on the twelfth indulged in a carnival of looting and destruction of civilian property entirely unprecedented in the Virginia theater of the war. By 1864 such behavior would become a tacit Federal war policy, but in December 1862 it was new, and it embarrassed some Northern officers while outraging the Confederates who looked on helplessly. Their chance for revenge was not long in coming.

Lee's line at the foot of the high ground behind Fredericksburg ran for seven miles along irregular contours carved out by geological forces. Immediately west of the city a commanding ridge rose sharply from an open plain. Farther to the Confederate right the ground sloped up from the river much more gradually. On Lee's right center the ridge lay a good deal farther west than it did on his left or on his far right. As a result, a deep re-entrant angle in the line (a deep bulge swerved away from the attackers) created a zone in which Burnside could not consider attacking. Lee's position was really not vulnerable to frontal assault at all, but if one had to be made (and politicians and newspapers were pressuring Burnside to move), it would have to come against the shoulders of the re-entrant. Burnside determined to attack directly out of town against the ridge there and at the same time to move against Lee's far right near Hamilton's Crossing.

December 13 dawned foggy, but the mist cleared by midmorning and an Indian summer day (56° at 2:00 P.M.) burst upon nearly 200,000 soldiers approaching mortal combat. Lee had almost 80,000 men arrayed on his strong line and Burnside brought about 115,000 troops to battle. Gen. William B. Franklin, commanding on the Federal left, followed the army commander's vague orders about moving against the enemy by organizing an attack westward from the Bowling Green Road. His first alignment fell prey to one of the most famous individual feats of the war. Maj. John Pelham of Alabama and a small detachment moved rapidly from spot to spot firing a single cannon and managed by means of a daunting enfilade fire to confuse the Federal effort for nearly an hour.

When the Northern assault finally rolled forward, it came under intense artillery fire from Confederate guns emplaced on Prospect Hill, near the right of Stonewall Jackson's line. After extensive counterbattery fire, the Union attack went forward again. This time it found an unguarded point on the line, and a division of Pennsylvanians poured through. For the second consecutive battle Jackson had allowed a curious lethargy about defensive matters to land him in trouble. The Pennsylvanians, who were commanded by Gen. George G. Meade, penetrated deep into the Confederate position and mortally wounded Gen. Maxcy Gregg of South Carolina. The success of the breakthrough, however, was temporary and largely illusory. Jackson was holding the Confederate right with roughly one-half of Lee's strength, yet his line covered only about one-fifth of the army's front. That alignment resulted not from Confederate prescience but from simple good fortune. When Early and D. H. Hill brought their divisions back to the army's position from far downstream, using the time bought by Barksdale's defense of the riverfront, they piled them up behind their comrades in Jackson's corps. There was no time to juggle the entire front. Meade's men ran into more Southern reserves than they could hope to deal with, and soon the Northerners were obliged to retrace their steps under pressure from pursuing Confederates.

Franklin's brief success with Meade's division constituted the only marginally bright spot of the battle for the Union army. While Meade and his men advanced and retreated, their comrades several miles to the north had opened a series of attacks that turned into one of the most one-sided and hopeless butcheries of the war. The ridge just behind Fredericksburg included a stretch six hundred yards long through which the deep Sunken Road traversed its base. The road had a retaining wall of stone on the town side that became famous enough to be treated as a proper noun. Confederate infantry behind the Stone Wall enjoyed protection as thorough as any devised later in the war by military engineers. For a half-mile toward town from this ready-made fortress, the ground lay bare, broken only by a few fences and a half-dozen houses. A pronounced swale around a canal ditch offered the attacking Union soldiers a bit of cover, but the ditch was bridged poorly and in few places. Northerners moving across that bare plain would face terrible punishment from Confederate artillery on Marye's Heights (as the ridge above the road was known, after the family that owned part of it). The attackers might form under a little protection in the swale, but they would have to move toward the Stone Wall without cover of any sort. The only possible result would be a bloody disaster, with casualties in the thousands, the fatal multiplier being how many doomed brigades Burnside fed into the carnage.

That brief early winter afternoon, on one of the shortest days of the year, must have seemed an eternity to the thousands of Northern boys who took their turns lining up and then plunging bravely over the crest toward the Sunken Road, without a hope of success. Confederates in the road and on the hills behind it shot about eight thousand of the attackers without losing more than a thousand men. Gen.

Thomas R. R. Cobb of Georgia commanded the brigade that opened the battle defending the Sunken Road. He fell mortally wounded early in the action. Joseph B. Kershaw's South Carolinians joined the Georgians in the road, and other Southern units participated—almost unnecessarily—from nearby vantage points. When darkness put an end to the slaughter, no man of the attacking force had come close to the wall.

The Confederate command, apparently unaware of the degree of havoc wreaked upon their foe, expected a renewal of the attacks the next day. Burnside was of the same mind and even proposed leading a desperate assault in person, but wiser counsels prevailed. Southerners entrenched portions of their infantry line on December 14, the first such extensive field fortifications on a Virginia battlefield, but they found no occasion to use them until fighting resumed the following spring in the same location. Burnside recrossed his hard-won pontoon bridges under cover of a noisy storm on the night of December 15–16 and ended a campaign that had been an unmitigated disaster for the Union cause. Burnside had lost nearly thirteen thousand men while inflicting fewer than five thousand casualties on his enemy. The Battle of Fredericksburg closed the 1862 campaign in Virginia on an extremely high note for Lee's army and the South. For nearly five months the winter season would suspend active campaigning. When the war resumed in the spring of 1863, Lee's army would show tremendous confidence, based on its success at Fredericksburg, as it faced a new Federal commander.

BIBLIOGRAPHY

Allan, William. *The Army of Northern Virginia in 1862.* Boston, 1892. Reprint, Dayton, Ohio, 1984.

Freeman, Douglas S. *Lee's Lieutenants: A Study in Command.* Vol. 2. New York, 1943. Reprint, New York, 1986.

Henderson, George Francis Robert. *The Campaign of Fredericksburg.* London, 1886.

Scales, Alfred M. *The Battle of Fredericksburg.* Washington, D.C., 1884.

Whan, Vorin E., Jr. *Fiasco at Fredericksburg.* State College, Pa., 1961.

ROBERT K. KRICK

FREE BLACKS. *See* Free People of Color, *article on* Free Blacks.

FREEDOM OF THE PRESS. The Confederate Constitution in Article I stipulated that "Congress shall make no law . . . abridging the freedom of speech or of the press," and the government obeyed this mandate remarkably well for a society at war during most of its existence.

President Jefferson Davis, apparently proud and thin-skinned, admitted that he could not help feeling that "the public journals" were "generally partisan" and "venal." Yet he did not interfere with the press, and neither did the Confederate Congress, which discussed a sedition act in 1862 but never passed one.

Newspaper editors enjoyed so privileged a status in the Confederate States of America that they were exempted from conscription. In 1864, when the president urged passage of a law to allow military authorities to draft persons previously exempted, Congress resisted and the law was never passed. Presidential critics, of whom Davis had a great number by this late date, sometimes described the proposed legislation as an attempt to control the opposition press. In Davis's favor it should be noted that, according to the printed lists available, among the 302 civilian prisoners held by the War Department's authority in February 1863 while the writ of habeas corpus was suspended, not one was a newspaper editor, proprietor, or reporter.

Battles over press freedom in the Confederacy were fought regularly, resolving instance by instance the conflicting interests of generals in secrecy and of reporters in openness. Reporters were often banished from camps, but actual attempts at suppression of papers by generals were extremely rare, the only widely reported incident being Gen. Earl Van Dorn's order of July 4, 1862, for the Department of South Mississippi and East Louisiana. Van Dorn made it clear that the martial law being imposed by the order was "well defined to be 'the will of the military commander.' " He threatened to fine or imprison any editor who published information about troop movements or an article "calculated to impair confidence in any of the commanding officers" and would suspend publication of the offending newspaper. The hue and cry raised against Van Dorn in Congress was so great that the general apparently never enforced the part of his order dealing with the press.

Although many newspapers ceased publication because of Union occupation or economic hardship, only one, the *Knoxville Whig,* was shut down by government action or because of the actions of others. The paper's editor, William G. Brownlow, provided an intellectual beacon for eastern Tennessee Unionism, which inspired guerrilla bands, sabotage, and sedition. The paper ceased publication as early as October 24, 1861, and Brownlow fled to the mountains. Confederate forces arrested him, and he was indicted for treason. But the War Department, led by Judah P. Benjamin, who regarded such questions largely from the standpoint of public relations rather than constitutional rectitude, saw to it that Brownlow was banished to Union lines on March 3, 1862.

Although the Confederate press may have seemed sharp-tongued enough to the generals and politicians it regularly criticized, Southern editors in fact had long since compromised their ability to comment upon society. States such as Virginia and Louisiana enacted legislation in the 1830s that had essentially outlawed any criticism of slavery. Thus Southern editors may have known how to confine their freedom to an acceptable range of subjects.

Moreover, the absence of political parties in the Confederacy, generally regarded by historians as an institutional weakness, probably aided freedom of the press. In the North, where hundreds of papers were suppressed from time to time, the rigid partisan identification of the papers sometimes kept editors from closing ranks to protest interference with newspapers of the other party. In the Confederacy, newspapers could identify their peculiar interests as an industry well enough to form, in 1863, the Press Association of the Confederate States of America. Dozens of newspapers thus banded together to reach agreements with generals and Confederate authorities about reporters' access to news of the war.

[See also Censorship; Habeas Corpus; Newspapers.]

BIBLIOGRAPHY

Eaton, Clement. *The Freedom-of-Thought Struggle in the Old South.* Rev. ed. New York, 1964.
Mathis, Robert Neil. "Freedom of the Press in the Confederacy: A Reality." *Historian* 37 (August 1975): 633–648.

MARK E. NEELY, JR.

FREEMAN, THOMAS W. (1824–1865), congressman from Missouri. Freeman was born in Anderson County, Kentucky. He read law with G. W. Cavanah and John Draffin of Lawrenceburg, Kentucky, and practiced law in the state for two years before going to California where he established a successful criminal practice. Freeman, in 1851, migrated to Missouri and settled for a brief time in Osceola and then moved to Bolivar. He won election as a circuit attorney and served in that office until 1860, when he was elected to the state legislature as a Democrat.

A Breckinridge elector, Freeman strongly favored secession. Missouri's pro-Southern governor, Claiborne F. Jackson, sent him on a private mission to Texas and Louisiana before he was selected by the rump Neosho legislature as one of Missouri's representatives in the Provisional Congress. He also served in the First Congress. Although he was often absent from Congress, Freeman supported practically all of the Davis administration's policies, with the exception of the abjuration of old Confederate Treasury notes and Davis's desire to accept single volunteers. He served on the Enrolled Bills, Naval Affairs, and Territorial and Public Land committees. He lost the election to the Second Congress to Peter Singleton Wilkes.

Shortly after the war Freeman, at the age of forty, died from malarial fever while in St. Louis.

BIBLIOGRAPHY

Bay, W. V. N. *Reminiscences of the Bench and Bar of Missouri.* St. Louis, 1878.
Wakelyn, Jon L. *Biographical Dictionary of the Confederacy.* Westport, Conn., 1977.
Warner, Ezra J., and W. Buck Yearns. *Biographical Register of the Confederate Congress.* Baton Rouge, La., 1975.

JAMES W. GOODRICH

FREE MARKETS. The disruption of farming in the wartime South; inadequate transportation facilities; droughts, disease, and destruction; the voracious appetite of armies; and the Union blockade—all these caused the price of food to rise sharply in the South's urban centers. The poor of the cities suffered the greatest privations. To help feed them, some city governments supported the establishment of charity markets supplied by private individuals; other urban governments cooperated with benevolent organizations to provide food for the indigent; and still other cities appropriated public funds for poor relief.

One of the earliest and most extensive free markets subsidized by private contributions began in New Orleans. For instance, during the ten days it was open during December 1861, an average of 1,850 families received provisions daily. During March 1862 alone, $16,249 in donations paid for foodstuffs to distribute to the poor. After the city fell to Union forces, the Federals continued direct food relief for the indigent. Mobile, Alabama, also had a free market provided by private citizens. By March 1863 they had contributed $30,645 in cash to purchase food, including 6,000 bushels of corn, for distribution to the needy. Natchez, Mississippi, had two free markets supplied by private individuals; they were open two mornings a week so that the poor could draw rations of food.

In the capital of the Confederacy a rising tide of refugees swelled the ranks of the destitute. During December 1862, the Richmond City Council appropriated $20,000 to get the needy through the winter and the following year appropriated another $150,000. In late 1864, the council established a Board of Supplies to scour the countryside for food, transport it to Richmond, and provide for its storage and distribution. By the end of the war, the city government was cooperating with the Union Benevolent Society of Richmond to purchase and distribute food on a regular basis to 4,500 persons, but there was never enough to feed adequately all the people of the city.

In Charleston, South Carolina, beef that had sold for 15 cents per pound in 1861 cost $3 per pound by 1863, and corn sold for $225 a bushel. The city government was spending $10,000 monthly to feed about 3,000 poor people. But farmers balked at bringing food into the city when the bombardment began, and as refugees increased, rations had to be pared in half. To meet the needs of feeding the poor, the Charleston government created a Subsistence Committee, which sent agents into the countryside with public funds to buy produce. With the cooperation of the military authorities, the city council also contracted with the railroads to bring into Charleston thousands of pounds of rice, meal, peas, and potatoes, some of which was distributed to the poor.

The creation of free markets supported by both private donations and public expenditures in the South's major cities undoubtedly saved thousands from suffering and even starvation. It may also have prevented more food riots than occurred.

BIBLIOGRAPHY

Capers, Gerald M. *Occupied City: New Orleans under the Federals, 1862–1865.* Lexington, Ky., 1965.

Fraser, Walter J., Jr. *Charleston! Charleston!: The History of a Southern City.* Columbia, S.C., 1989.

Gates, Paul W. *Agriculture and the Civil War.* New York, 1965.

Thomas, Emory M. *The Confederate State of Richmond: A Biography of the Capital.* Austin, Tex., 1971.

WALTER J. FRASER, JR.

FREE PEOPLE OF COLOR.

[*This entry is composed of two articles that discuss the lives and contributions of free people of color in the Confederacy:* Free Blacks *and* Free Creoles of Color. *For further discussion of the role of free people of color in the Confederate armed forces, see* Army, *article on* African Americans in the Confederate Army, *and* Navy, *article on* African American in the Confederate Navy. *For discussion of creoles of European descent, see* Creoles.]

Free Blacks

For all practical purposes, the Confederacy was the most biracial society in North America from 1861 to 1865. Among the three tiers of this beleaguered community of whites, slaves, and free blacks, perhaps the last experienced the most complex and difficult lives in the shadow of bondage. A typical free black was either an African American ex-slave legally manumitted (either by a white person or through self-purchase) or someone born free, whose freedom was inherited through parents or some other antecedent, usually a white grandparent. Though most were "full-blooded blacks" (persons without white ancestry), a large number were mulattoes, persons of mixed black and white ancestry, sons and daughters of upper- or middle-class white men and free black or slave women.

According to the 1860 census, there were nearly 250,000 free blacks in the antebellum South, tenacious survivors in

Free Blacks in Future Confederate States in 1860

STATE	NUMBER	STATE	NUMBER
Alabama	2,690	North Carolina	30,463
Arkansas	114	South Carolina	9,914
Florida	932	Tennessee	7,300
Georgia	3,500	Texas	355
Louisiana	18,647	Virginia	58,042
Mississippi	773	**Total**	**132,760**

a sea of slavery whose numbers had increased by 12 percent (mulattoes by 2 percent) from the previous decade despite a combination of lower fertility, higher mortality rates, and prejudice. Their number in the seceded states was some 132,760. Forty-four percent of the Confederacy's free blacks resided in Virginia. The number in that state was exceeded only in the border state of Maryland, where 83,942 lived. Free blacks composed 1.4 percent; slaves, 35 percent; and whites, 60 percent of the Southern population. They were the most urbanized of African Americans; approximately 40 percent resided in towns and cities, and 15 percent of these dwelled in some of the Confederacy's largest municipalities: New Orleans, 10,689; Charleston, 5,478; Richmond, 2,576; Norfolk, 1,046; Mobile, 817; Savannah, 705; and New Bern, North Carolina, 689.

They functioned on the fringes of urban Southern society, living, working, and practicing traditional Judeo-Christian-American standards of morality and responsibility, yet maintaining their own identity. They recognized the limitations of their lives and the considerable power whites possessed over them. Free blacks quietly established and maintained networks of social, religious, educational, and benevolent organizations for mutual support, creating an outlying black-based economy and thus maintaining their quasi-independence. They worked chiefly as day laborers, farmhands, waiters, barbers, cooks, seamstresses, and nurses but also as mechanics, tailors, carpenters, hairdressers, bricklayers, clerks, blacksmiths, and wheelwrights. Treated as a third-rate, possibly subversive caste, free blacks were expected to know and obey state criminal codes concerning them, no matter how onerous or unfair. Georgia, Texas, and Virginia established legislative controls under which these blacks could voluntarily enslave themselves, an outgrowth of antebellum laws proposed or enacted for the enslavement of the Southern free black class. Similar wartime measures to force exile or enslavement upon them were contemplated but either failed to be passed or enforced; these were vigorously resisted by free blacks and their white allies.

Any black person was presumed to be a slave in the Confederate States of America unless he or she proved otherwise. As one of several obligatory survival skills, free blacks quickly learned to highlight their unique status by appending "f. c. p." (free colored person), "f. m. c." or "f. m. o. c." (free man of color), "f. n." (free Negro), "f. n. w." (free Negro woman), "f. w. c." (free woman of color), or "f. p. o. c." (free person of color) to their correspondence and legal documents. They were denied access to most public facilities or forced to accept separate, unequal accommodations. They were prohibited from selling or purchasing liquor, medicine, and firearms; from owning dogs, boats, and books or papers other than deeds or registers of their manumission; from purchasing train tickets, returning from visits to the North, or having sexual relations with whites. Their children, denied access to public education, were taught in underground schools, churches, and private homes by sympathetic whites and courageous blacks or were sent North.

As living reminders that not all African Americans were born to be slaves and as victims of the peculiar institution's oppressive customs, free blacks could not hold certain occupations or under most circumstances testify in court against whites who had assaulted or cheated them. Vigilante groups and citizen and home guard patrols monitored their movements. They were forbidden to hold meetings without the presence of whites or to have unsanctioned contacts with slaves. They were required to carry badges or passes at all times and were intimidated into remaining in their homes at night. They had few, if any, civil rights, and usually the greater their percentage in proportion to the white population in a given area, the more likely the communities were inclined to enact repressive measures, particularly in Virginia, Georgia, and North and South Carolina. Free blacks were expected to obey these laws and pay taxes, though they could not vote or hold public office.

Despite these limitations on employment, mobility, and residency, several became substantial owners of real estate, personal property, and slaves. One respected black Richmond resident, ex-slave Gilbert Hunt, owned slaves, a house, and associated property valued at more than two thousand dollars at his death in 1863. In the same city, several free blacks purchased four city lots worth four thousand dollars on behalf of their Union Burial Ground Society in 1864. Henderson Goings of Albemarle County, Virginia, was a prosperous farmer who owned seventy-five acres of land on which he grew corn, oats, potatoes, and wheat. There was a limited bilingual free black aristocracy in New Orleans, which distanced itself from non-French-speaking, non-slave-owning blacks and established schools for its children. Black slave owners were common in Louisiana and were known for being just as harsh toward slaves as white planters. Some of these men, Jordan Noble among them, raised companies of slave laborers on behalf of the South.

Mindful of their precarious status, most free blacks maintained a low public profile. Nevertheless, some deliberately identified with the Confederate cause (in some locales, up to 25 percent), though in practice they were more likely to be loyal to a particular town, county, or state rather than the Confederacy. This was a stratagem for survival, an effort to preserve their free status in the face of the pressures and suspicions of their white neighbors. Free black farmers, for example, sold crops and hired out their slaves to the government. One such family, the Ellisons of Charleston, earned nearly $24,000 between 1862 and 1864 from their agriculture.

Between January and July 1861 nearly three thousand free blacks in Tennessee, Virginia, South Carolina, and Georgia volunteered to serve the Confederacy, and South Carolina's blacks signed memorials attesting to their willingness to fight. Giles Price of Thomasville, Georgia, and John Rapier of Alabama publicly spoke and wrote on behalf of the South. Approximately eighty Savannah blacks offered to serve in any capacity for the duration of the war, and Joe Clark, a Columbus, Georgia, barber, sought official permission to raise a company of free blacks. Charlottesville, Virginia, free blacks offered their property and services to the town council and promised to faithfully serve anywhere in the state.

But not all free blacks were eager to embrace the cause of Southern nationhood. Some collaborated with and spied for Union forces. Plots of black insurrections were suspected, and minor outbreaks were suppressed throughout the region until the end of the war. Black pro-Union organizations across Virginia met during 1864 and 1865 to map out ways to undermine the Confederacy.

Compelled to use every resource, the Confederacy considered free blacks an integral component of its war effort, even though the drafting of slaves was extremely unpopular, its legality challenged by slaveholders as an infringement of their property rights. Free black volunteers, however, were sought and accepted for noncombatant military duty, and their numbers, though small in comparison to impressed slaves, released white males for the army. Louisiana, Georgia, Mississippi, South Carolina, and Virginia were among states that passed legislation for their employment and authorized their transfer to duty under the Confederate government. In February 1864, the Confederate Congress ordered free black men between the ages of eighteen and fifty to be impressed as laborers. Volunteers or conscripts, skilled or unskilled, these blacks received the same pay and rations as white soldiers and in many instances were organized at camps of instruction, formed into companies, and sent to fortifications, hospitals, factories, and similar facilities. Some were seized by press gangs or forced to pay 10 percent of their wages to extortionists to avoid conscription, fines, or imprisonment. A few even conspired with Confederate officers to substitute their slaves and shared the wages with the whites.

The most ironic development of military employment was the Confederacy's belated recognition of its need for black soldiers. Black military companies had been organized in Tennessee as early as April 1861; Louisiana and Alabama blacks served as militia members and marched in review with white regiments in February 1862; at the same time Virginia legislators tentatively discussed plans to enroll free black soldiers.

The Negro Soldier Law of March 13, 1865, called for the enlistment of 300,000 black troops, primarily slaves, to be formed into regiments, battalions, and brigades. Shortly before and after that time until the fall of Richmond, newspaper editorials and advertisements urged free blacks to enlist for the good of the nation. These solicitations hinted at postwar racial reforms and improved, albeit limited, black civil rights. Conceivably, there was a time when such appeals might have received an enthusiastic response from black Southerners, but by 1865 racial memories could not be so easily disregarded. An Atlanta free black was quoted in a January 1865 newspaper as refusing to enlist because he did not have a country nor had he ever had one. But crumbling logistics and near-exhaustion of resources on the eve of final Confederate defeat prevented implementation of this unprecedented entreaty.

Free black adroitness in maintaining a circumscribed freedom in the midst of slavery demonstrated a focused sense of purpose. White Confederates could have learned much about cultural endurance from them.

After Appomattox several free black families expected to wield political, religious, economic, and social leadership in the African American community. But they were out of touch with the black masses. As free blacks they had distanced themselves from slaves, curried favor with the white power structure, boasted of their antebellum freedom (as opposed to slaves "shot free" by the war, the Emancipation Proclamation, or the Thirteenth Amendment), or taken snobbish advantage of their privileged status in the antebellum South. When they sought to lead and speak on behalf of blacks, the freed people preferred the leadership of fellow ex-slaves, and having been a slave became a prerequisite for black-to-black political support. It would be a generation before Southern blacks could redefine themselves as a community embodying a collective history, trust, and self-preservation.

BIBLIOGRAPHY

Berlin, Ira, Barbara J. Fields, Thavolia Glymph, Joseph R. Reidy, and Leslie S. Rowland, eds. *The Destruction of Slavery.* Ser. 1, vol. 1 of *Freedom: A Documentary History of Emancipation, 1861–1867. Selected from the Holdings of the National Archives of the United States.* New York, 1985.

Blackerby, H. C. *Blacks in Blue and Gray: Afro-American Service in the Civil War.* Tuscaloosa, Ala., 1979.

Burnham, Philip. "Selling Poor Stephen." *American Heritage* 44, no. 1 (February–March 1993): 90–97.

Durden, Robert F. *The Gray and the Black: The Confederate Debate on Emancipation.* Baton Rouge, La., 1972.

Johnson, Michael P., and James L. Roark. *Black Masters: A Free Family of Color in the Old South.* New York, 1984.

Nelson, Bernard H. "Legislative Control of the Southern Free Negro, 1861–1865." *Catholic Historical Review* 32 (April 1946): 28–46.

Wesley, Charles Harris. *The Collapse of the Confederacy.* Washington, D.C., 1937.

Wiley, Bell Irvin. *Southern Negroes, 1861–1865.* New Haven, 1938.

Williams, George Washington. *History of the Negro Race in America from 1619 to 1880.* New York, 1882.

ERVIN L. JORDAN, JR.

Free Creoles of Color

In Louisiana and in the port cities of Alabama and Florida, native-born Catholic creoles of color of Latin European and African descent distinguished the lower South's free black population at the time of the Civil War. By 1860 New Orleans, with a free black population of 10,939 in an urban population of 170,024 (144,601 white; 14,484 slave), and Mobile, with 817 free blacks in a total population of 29,258 (20,854 white; 7,587 slave), possessed large, tightly knit communities of French- and Spanish-speaking creoles of color. In Florida, with 932 free blacks in a state population of 140,423 (77,746 white; 61,745 slave), most of the free black residents of the port cities of Pensacola, St. Augustine, Key West, and Jacksonville were either the creole descendants of the region's early Spanish and African inhabitants or West Indian émigrés.

These creoles, brought within United States borders by the Louisiana Purchase (1803) and the acquisition of West Florida (1810) and Florida (1819), prospered during the early decades of American rule. Acquiring a degree of recognition from the treaties with France and Spain and benefiting from the persistence of a relatively flexible tripartite racial order, free creoles exercised a comparatively high level of economic and social mobility. Creole artisans in New Orleans, Mobile, and Pensacola excelled in such varied occupations as cabinetmaker, tailor, shoemaker, mason, cigar maker, butcher, barber, and blacksmith. In New Orleans, highly educated free creoles of color pursued careers as architects, engineers, brokers, doctors, literary artists, and musicians, and in rural Louisiana, a few *gens de couleur* accumulated great wealth as slaveholding planters.

The presence of an intermediate class of free people of color proved inimical to the region's planter elite, however. Beginning in the 1840s, state legislators in Alabama and Florida enacted laws requiring free persons of color to choose a white guardian. By 1855 such guardians supervised the activities of over half of Mobile's free blacks. Finally, between 1858 and 1860 state legislatures throughout the lower South admonished free persons of color to choose their own masters and become slaves for life. Some creoles fled the rising tide of white oppression. In Pensacola the number of creole residents dropped precipitously from 350 in 1850 to 130 in 1860. In New Orleans the size of the free black population declined from 15,072 in 1840 to 10,689 in 1860.

Threatened with violence, expulsion, and confiscation of property after Louisiana seceded on January 26, 1861, the city's community of creoles of color mobilized to safeguard their community. In a defensive action, free black volunteers proffered their services to Confederate officials. In Mobile and in small creole enclaves in the outlying Louisiana parishes of Natchitoches, Pointe Coupée, and Plaquemines, free black leaders undertook similar measures. Though the Confederacy refused to enlist the men in the Regular Army, local officials in New Orleans and Mobile accepted the creole companies into their local militias. By November 1861 Louisiana Confederate Governor Thomas O. Moore had enrolled 1,500 free black soldiers in New Orleans in the First Native Guards, Louisiana Militia, and white officials inducted over 3,000 free black soldiers into the state militia units. However, officials assigned them neither arms nor supplies and confined their activities to company drills.

Within a year of their enlistment, the city's Native Guards militiamen confirmed Confederate fears of questionable black allegiance. In January 1862 authorities noted the free black regiment's high rate of absenteeism, and when Commodore David G. Farragut's naval bombardment forced the Confederates to evacuate the city in April 1862, the Native Guards refused to leave. Shortly after Gen. Benjamin F. Butler, the commanding officer of the Union army, occupied the city, the creole militiamen volunteered their services to the Union general. In August, Butler authorized the induction of the First Native Guards. By December, 3,122 free creoles of color and blacks filled three regiments of Louisiana Native Guards officered by both blacks and whites. At the Battle of Port Hudson in 1863, the desperate courage of creole officer André Cailloux and his fellow soldiers of the First and Third Native Guards helped to dispel doubts in the Union army and the United States regarding blacks' ability to fight.

Long before Cailloux and his colleagues enlisted in the Union army, however, the city's free creole intelligentsia had possessed a well-developed ideology of social and political radicalism. During the repression of the antebellum decades, slaveholding as well as nonslaveholding creoles of color developed an intense antagonism toward the governing planter elite. Disaffected activists tapped the ongoing current of political radicalism in nineteenth-century Europe and the Americas. In the city's romantic literary movement, some creole intellectuals, like thinkers in France and Haiti, channeled their discontent into their literary works. Others joined the spiritualist movement, a radical new religious sect whose origins lay in the French socialism of Charles Fourier. With the Federal occupation of the city, they launched an aggressive campaign for equal rights.

Simultaneous with the Native Guards' official induction into the Union army in September 1862, a cadre of influential creoles of color launched a French-language biweekly newspaper, *L'Union*. The editors of the paper condemned slavery, reviled the Confederacy, and urged their readers to support the Union cause. They immediately seized upon the issue of military service to demand equal citizenship. The predominantly creole First Native Guards, the paper insisted, already possessed a legitimate claim to citizenship in view of the role of the regiment's Haitian and Louisiana forebears in the American Revolution and the War of 1812. The paper's bold editorialists even criticized President Abraham Lincoln. Attacking his plan to colonize free blacks and freedmen in Central America, they urged the nation to adopt racial policies modeled after the emancipation and enfranchisement decrees of France's Second Republic.

In 1864, after Federal officials in New Orleans dismissed their demands for suffrage, creole leaders centered at *L'Union* redirected their efforts to Washington. In March their representatives met with the president. Though Lincoln evaded their request for the franchise, the men succeeded in laying their case before the nation. Their actions signaled the onset of a national campaign for black civil rights.

BIBLIOGRAPHY

Berlin, Ira. *Slaves without Masters: The Free Negro in the Antebellum South*. New York, 1974.

Blassingame, John W. *Black New Orleans, 1860–1880*. Chicago, 1973.

Hirsch, Arnold R., and Joseph Logsdon. *Creole New Orleans: Race and Americanization*. Baton Rouge, La., 1992.

Kolchin, Peter. *First Freedom: The Responses of Alabama's Blacks to Emancipation and Reconstruction*. Westport, Conn., 1972.

McPherson, James M. *The Negro's Civil War: How American Negroes Felt and Acted during the War for the Union*. New York, 1965. Reprint, Urbana, Ill., 1982.

CARYN COSSE BELL

FRENCH, SAMUEL G. (1818–1910), major general. Born November 22, 1818, in Gloucester County, New Jersey, French graduated from the U.S. Military Academy in 1843, fourteenth in a class of thirty-nine. Until 1856 he served in the artillery and quartermaster branches of the army, distinguishing himself in the Mexican War. When he resigned he was a captain.

From 1856 until 1861 French managed property he had purchased in Mississippi. In March 1861 he was appointed lieutenant colonel and chief of ordnance in the state army. On October 23, 1861, he was named a Confederate brigadier general and assigned to duty in the Virginia–North Carolina area, where he began construction of what eventually became the great fortifications of Richmond and Petersburg. On October 22, 1862, he was promoted to major general (with date of rank set at August 31).

In May 1863 he went to Mississippi to command a division in the force with which Gen. Joseph E. Johnston was trying to save Vicksburg. After the city fell, French continued in command of his division, which, in May 1864, was sent to Georgia to reinforce the Army of Tennessee.

French remained with his division until December 15, 1864, despite a worsening eye infection. He directed an unsuccessful attack on Union forces at Allatoona Pass in North Georgia (October 5) and participated in the Franklin and Nashville campaign. By mid-December his eye condition had become so serious he had to relinquish command. In the war's last days he served at Mobile, where he surrendered in April 1865.

After the war French settled in Florida. He died in Florida, April 29, 1910, and is buried in St. John's Cemetery, Pensacola.

BIBLIOGRAPHY

Davis, William C. "Samuel Gibbs French." In *The Confederate General*. Edited by William C. Davis. Vol. 2. Harrisburg, Pa., 1991.

French, Samuel G. *Two Wars: An Autobiography*. Nashville, Tenn., 1901.

RICHARD M. MCMURRY

FRIETCHIE, BARBARA (1766–1862), Unionist and subject of a poem by John Greenleaf Whittier. When Robert E. Lee's army entered Frederick, Maryland, in the fall of 1862, Barbara Frietchie was an ailing, ninety-six-year-old resident of that community. Frietchie died in December but was immortalized when Whittier's poem about her appeared in the October 1863 issue of the *Atlantic Monthly*.

In the Whittier tribute, Frietchie's flag flying outside her window incited the wrath of Thomas J. ("Stonewall") Jackson, who ordered his men to shoot the Union banner down. When Frietchie appeared at the window and demanded that the troops "shoot at this old gray head," instead, Jackson was shamed. "Who touches a hair of yon

BARBARA FRIETCHIE.   NATIONAL ARCHIVES

gray head," he said to his men, "dies like a dog! March on!"

Jackson did march through Frederick, a border town, on September 10, 1862, on his way to Harpers Ferry. Nonetheless, most contemporary and historical accounts suggest that the Confederate commander had no encounter with Frietchie, although there were flag-waving episodes involving some of the many Unionist residents of Frederick. Two days later, many of the townspeople turned out to cheer and wave flags when the Union troops entered Frederick, and it is believed that Barbara Frietchie was active during this patriotic demonstration.

Soon after the appearance of Whittier's poem, Southern commentators were quick to deny the story's authenticity. Confederates seem to have taken particular offense at the poem's cut at Jackson, recently killed at Chancellorsville and often lionized as a symbol of Southern chivalry. The implication that Jackson had ordered his men to fire on an old woman's house and was then shamed by the woman's fury apparently was especially galling to Confederate sensibilities.

BIBLIOGRAPHY

Cole, Adelaide. "Of Dame Barbara and Her Legend." *Indiana Social Studies Quarterly* 37 (1984): 54–57.

Quynn, Dorothy M., and William R. Quynn. "Barbara Frietschie." *Maryland Historical Magazine* 37 (September 1942): 227–254.

Seilheimer, George O. "The Historical Basis of Whittier's 'Barbara Frietchie.'" In *Battles and Leaders of the Civil War*. Vol. 2. Edited by Robert U. Johnson and Clarence C. Buel. New York, 1888. Reprint, Secaucus, N.J., 1982.

NINA SILBER

FROLIC. *See entry on the ship* Advance.

FRONT ROYAL, VIRGINIA.

This village in the northern Shenandoah Valley, at the confluence of the north and south forks of the Shenandoah River, was the site of a battle on May 23, 1862, that ruptured the strategic status quo and opened the way for Thomas J. ("Stonewall") Jackson's victorious Valley campaign. In a surprise attack at a point the Federals considered secure, Jackson inflicted nearly one thousand casualties on his foe while suffering only a few dozen himself.

Two months before the Battle of Front Royal, Jackson had suffered a tactical reverse at Kernstown that forced him to retreat south up the valley and take shelter in the mountain fastness of Swift Run Gap. He emerged at the end of April and made a circuitous march that led to the victory at McDowell on May 8. For the next two weeks Jackson gathered forces from various quarters and moved east and then north toward Strasburg, where Union Gen. Nathaniel P. Banks had entrenched his army. On May 21 Jackson swerved eastward from New Market and crossed Massanutten Mountain through the only gap along its fifty-mile length. The next day and into May 23 the Confederate column pressed steadily down the narrow subvalley running northward from Luray, heading toward an isolated Federal detachment guarding the railroad at Front Royal. As he neared his target, Jackson pointed his advance guard up the winding Snake Grade near Asbury Chapel, heading toward the Gooney Manor Road that curled along the western shoulder of the Blue Ridge. At the same time Southern cavalry swarmed across the south fork of the Shenandoah River at McKoy's Ford and rode northwest with the mission of breaking the rail line between Strasburg and Front Royal. The cavalry succeeded in its mission after a fight at Buckton Station that killed two promising young Southern officers.

Jackson's careful and devious approach along the mountainside enabled him to make a surprise appearance on the outskirts of Front Royal. When Confederates of the First Maryland Infantry, who had been chafing to leave the army at the expiration of their initial enlistments, learned that their counterparts of the Union First Maryland held Front Royal, they charged into the town. Gen. Richard Taylor's Louisiana brigade dashed into the streets with the Marylanders and soon put the vastly outnumbered Northern force to rout. The ecstatic townspeople who flocked into the streets posed as much impediment to the attackers as did the fleeing foe.

Federals set fire to the crucial bridges near town as they retreated, but pursuing Confederates, with Jackson in their midst leading by example, threw burning timbers into the river and forced their way across. The absence of his artillery, which was mismanaged by the army's chief of that arm, hampered Jackson's pursuit, but he pushed ahead with elements of the Sixth Virginia Cavalry. The mounted men brought the enemy to bay around a house and orchard less than three miles north of the bridge, near Cedarville. Jackson hurled his handful of cavalrymen against the new Federal concentration, exploiting the momentum his surprise had generated. The Southern horsemen galloped up the road four abreast and shattered the last resistance, but at the cost of heavier losses than their friends in the infantry had suffered all day; one color-bearer went down with more than twenty bullets in his body.

As his men rounded up the Federal survivors, Jackson began planning for operations designed to take advantage of the golden opportunity that his hard marching and carefully prepared surprise had won for him. The result was his major victory at the Battle of Winchester two days later.

BIBLIOGRAPHY

Allan, William. *History of the Campaign of Gen. T. J. (Stonewall) Jackson in the Shenandoah Valley of Virginia.* Philadelphia, 1880.

Hale, Laura Virginia. *Four Valiant Years in the Lower Shenandoah Valley.* Strasburg, Va., 1973.

Taylor, Richard. *Destruction and Reconstruction.* New York, 1879.

ROBERT K. KRICK

FROST, DANIEL MARSH

(1823–1900), brigadier general. Born near Schenectady, New York, Frost graduated from West Point in 1844, fourth of twenty-five cadets in his class. He served with the artillery in the Mexican War, winning a brevet for gallantry at Cerro Gordo. After the war, Frost saw action on the frontier as an Indian scout and served in Europe for a year before resigning his army commission in 1853 to engage in business in St. Louis. Intensely competent, Frost was on the Board of Visitors to the U.S. Military Academy, served one term in the Missouri State Senate (during which he framed an act creating the state's militia), and in 1858, as a brigadier general in that militia, led a brigade to southwestern Missouri to suppress border hostilities with Kansas Jayhawkers (antislavery guerrillas).

At the outbreak of the war in 1861, Frost sympathized with the South (his wife was from a slave-owning Maryland family) and openly favored the secession of Missouri, which voted to remain neutral. He prepared the state militia in and around St. Louis to oppose Federal troops stationed in the city. He urged the state's governor, Claiborne F. Jackson, to attack the Federal arsenal in St. Louis, which held the largest store of munitions in the slave states. Jackson ordered Frost to convene an encampment of the Missouri State Guard outside the city while he secured artillery from the Baton Rouge Arsenal (captured by Louisiana Confederates) to aid Frost's guardsmen in their proposed attack on the St. Louis Arsenal. On May 10, arsenal commander Nathaniel Lyon surrounded the encampment, forcing Frost to surrender it, which precipitated two days of rioting in St. Louis. Upon receiving his parole and exchange, Frost was appointed brigadier general in Confederate service.

Offered command of Missouri state troops at Elkhorn Tavern, Arkansas, in March 1862, Frost declined and watched the battle from a nearby position. He served for a brief time as inspector general under Braxton Bragg before assuming brigade command in the Army of the West. Frost fought at the battle at Prairie Grove in Arkansas, serving under Thomas Hindman, and succeeded him temporarily as division commander. After participating in the campaigns of Helena and Little Rock, he received news of his wife's banishment from their home near St. Louis, which caused him to leave the army in the fall of 1863.

Not having submitted a formal resignation, Frost took his family to Canada and was dropped from the official roll in December 1863 (though one source lists him as having been on "detached duty" as late as 1864). Following the war, Frost returned to his home in St. Louis County and there engaged in farming until his death.

BIBLIOGRAPHY

Duke, Basil W. *Reminiscences of General Basil W. Duke, C.S.A.* Garden City, N.Y., 1911.

Faust, Patricia, ed. *Historical Times Illustrated's Encyclopedia of the Civil War.* New York, 1986.

Johnson, Robert U., and C. C. Buel, eds. *Battles and Leaders of the Civil War.* 4 vols. New York, 1887–1888. Reprint, Secaucus, N.J., 1982.

Phillips, Christopher. *Damned Yankee: The Life of General Nathaniel Lyon.* Columbia, Mo., 1990.

Warner, Ezra J. *Generals in Gray: Lives of the Confederate Commanders.* Baton Rouge, La., 1959.

CHRISTOPHER PHILLIPS

FRY, BIRKETT DAVENPORT (1822–1891), brigadier general. One of the strengths of the Confederate army, particularly in the first months of the war, was its core of officers with military education and with combat experience during the Mexican War. Fry was such an officer who performed creditably with the Army of Northern Virginia.

Fry was born in Kanawha County, present-day West Virginia, on June 24, 1822, and attended both the Virginia Military Institute and West Point, though he graduated from neither academy. He practiced law, served as an officer during the Mexican War and later in a filibuster expedition to Nicaragua, and was living in Alabama when the Civil War began.

He was appointed colonel of the Thirteenth Alabama Infantry on July 19, 1861, and was slightly wounded in his first battle, at Seven Pines, in May 1862. He returned to the army for the Second Manassas and Sharpsburg campaigns, was severely wounded at the latter battle, and was wounded a third time at Chancellorsville. Fry succeeded to the command of his brigade on July 1, 1863, at Gettysburg and led it in Pickett's Charge two days later, when he was severely wounded and captured. In March 1864 he was exchanged and assigned to temporary brigade command, first under P. G. T. Beauregard and then Robert E. Lee. Fry, who had often been recommended for promotion, was appointed brigadier general on May 24, 1864. In August of that year he was assigned to command the post at Augusta, Georgia, where he remained until the end of the war.

Fry left the country for Cuba in 1865, but returned to Alabama in 1868. He lived in Alabama, Florida, and Virginia, was active in veterans' organizations, and died in Richmond on February 5, 1891.

BIBLIOGRAPHY

Fry, Birkett Davenport. "Pettigrew's Charge at Gettysburg." *Southern Historical Society Papers* 7 (1879): 91–93. Reprint, Wilmington, N.C., 1990.

Wheeler, Joseph. *Alabama.* Vol. 7 of *Confederate Military History.* Edited by Clement A. Evans. Atlanta, 1899. Vol. 8 of extended ed. Wilmington, N.C., 1987.

J. TRACY POWER

FUGITIVE SLAVE LAW. A revealingly unanswerable question illuminates blacks' influence on whites' history. Did fugitive slaves more disrupt the Union before 1860 or the Confederacy thereafter? During the Civil War, approximately one in six slaves fled to Union armies or territories. Approximately one in six of these runaways joined the Union's ultimately liberating army. The fugitives undermined the Confederacy's racial order, damaged its economic production, and swelled the ranks of its armed assaulters. Black runaways also created the Union's contraband problem, for although Lincoln's armies fought to secure obedience to Federal laws, which included the Fugitive Slave Law of 1850, could soldiers fight the slaveholders and also return slave property? Finally, the fugitives complicated the issue of the purpose of the war. A war effort at first aimed only at preserving the white people's Union came to need those 100,000 black soldiers. But would ex-slaves fight for exclusively white liberty? The 600,000 self-liberated fugitives, by raising these issues, helped cause a war initially fought on other grounds to spawn black emancipation.

Before the Civil War, too, black fugitives had disrupted white people's controversies. Without runaway slaves, the

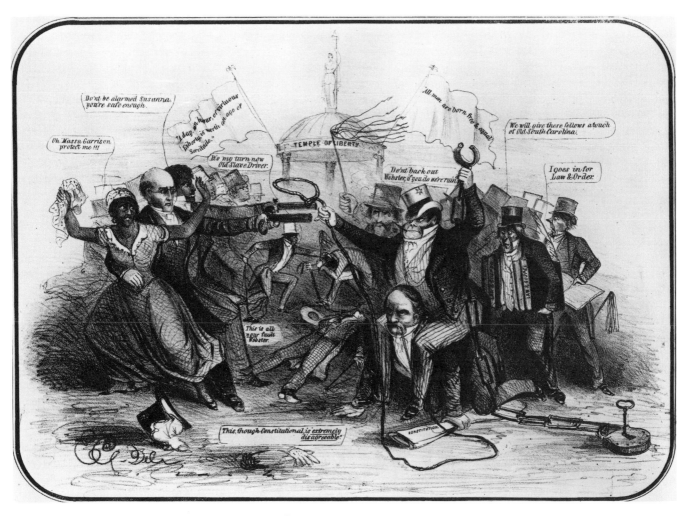

"PRACTICAL ILLUSTRATION OF THE FUGITIVE SLAVE LAW."   A satire of the antagonism raised by the passage of the law in 1850. Northern abolitionists, headed by William Lloyd Garrison, on left, protect slaves from the law's supporters, notably Daniel Webster, who crouches on all fours and is mounted by a slave catcher. The print has been attributed to New York artist Edward Williams Clay, but the signature, style, and political viewpoint are atypical of Clay. It is likely that the print was produced in Boston, a center of strong opposition to the Fugitive Slave Law in the early 1850s. Lithograph on wove paper, signed E. C. Del, 1850 or 1851.   LIBRARY OF CONGRESS

explosive fugitive slave issue would not have existed, and the equally explosive territorial expansion issue would have been more manageable. Southern expansionist drives were aimed, to a large degree, at deterring fugitive slaves. Southerners feared that if antislavery proponents controlled the other side of the slavocracy's borders, whether in Texas or Kansas or Florida, more slaves would flee toward freedom. If one can imagine a South without a fugitive slave problem, a much-longer-enduring antebellum Union becomes conceivable.

But this slaveholders' republic without fugitive slaves is ultimately unimaginable. American dreams of freedom inspired blacks, too, and flight was the slaves' most promising avenue to liberty. One black betrayer, by alerting whites to an insurrection plot, could destroy a group revolt, but a single fugitive could run as far as skill and luck allowed. A slave escaping from the border states, especially, shortened the long odds against successful flight and heightened the impact of the escape. Border blacks who freed themselves dampened the border South's not-so-great enthusiasm for slavery and challenged the North's not-so-serene compliance with the slaveholders. Successful fugitives could also become inspiring orators and writers, celebrating blacks' journey toward freedom, as did Frederick Douglass in his magnificent speeches and autobiography.

With the Fugitive Slave Law of 1850, the white establishment sought to abort the black slaves' major method of including themselves in white aspirations and history. An earlier Federal fugitive slave law, passed in 1793, had fallen victim to *Prigg v. Pennsylvania* (1842), wherein the U.S.

Supreme Court had declared that state authorities need not help enforce a Federal law. That Fugitive Slave Law depended on state enforcement, for few Federal judges and policemen yet existed.

The new Fugitive Slave Law, the South's major gain from the Compromise of 1850, established one-man bureaucracies. A commissioner, appointed by Federal judges, received total authority over runaway slaves; a commissioner could demand that any Northerner help capture alleged fugitives; and subsequently, a commissioner was judge and jury of last resort. Accused fugitives had no right to testify in their own behalf or to secure writs of habeas corpus. The commissioner was paid five dollars if he freed the alleged fugitive, ten dollars if he extradited the black to the South. Extra paperwork for extradition supposedly justified the extra payment, but many Northerners considered it a bribe—the symbol of an unspeakably despotic law.

In exchange for Northern acquiesence in allegedly despotic Federal machinery to return fugitives, Southerners agreed to the admission of free-labor California into the Union. After that Compromise of 1850 tradeoff, slaveholders demanded that their theoretical gain, the return of fugitive slaves, be realized. Contrary to popular myth, then and now, they largely received their due. Ninety percent of the 322 fugitives tried under the Fugitive Slave Law were remanded to their owners. But the other 10 percent made the headlines, and well-publicized stories of successful defiance weakened the law's deterrent effect on potential fugitives. The notoriety of the few who escaped the commissioners also poisoned Southern opinion of the North, just as the dispatching of blacks southward, without judge or jury, lowered the North's opinion of the South. Seldom has a law 90 percent successful so dismally failed.

Some famous exceptions to the usual, but ultimately less important, smooth return of fugitives included the rescue by Boston blacks in 1851 of Shadrack, a Virginia slave, from a courthouse; he was then sent to freedom in Canada. That same year a Syracuse mob rescued Jerry, a Missouri slave, from a police station, with the same eventual result: freedom in Canada. Also in 1851, a Maryland slaveholder, Edward Gorsuch, went with his son to Christiana, Pennsylvania, in pursuit of his fugitive slaves. A local black leader, William Parker, barricaded the fugitives in his house, with largely free blacks standing guard. When Gorsuch persisted, gunfire cracked, and the master was slain and his son badly wounded. The slaves got away to Canada, as did William Parker. Gorsuch's murderers remained at large.

A still more publicized fugitive slave incident involved a black returned to enslavement. In 1854, a Virginia fugitive, Anthony Burns, was arrested in Boston and ordered remanded to the South. Important intellectuals plotted to spring the literate slave from jail, but their plan failed and a policeman was killed. Fifty thousand angry Bostonians flooded the streets, demanding that Burns be freed. But at a cost of $100,000, a phalanx of policemen plus a U.S. infantry company and a detachment of artillery sliced a path through the protesters, and Anthony Burns set sail for Virginia. He soon voyaged back north, after Bostonians purchased his freedom.

Those huge numbers—$100,000, 50,000 Bostonians— did overwhelm in Southern memories the 290 slaves peaceably returned. Northern states' personal liberty laws also helped pave the Southern path toward secession. These laws affirmed that Northern state officials could not cooperate with Federal Fugitive Slave Law enforcers. Some personal liberty laws also reaffirmed free blacks' legal rights, including the right to secure a writ of habeas corpus. But states had no authority over Federal legal processes, and personal liberty laws never liberated a fugitive from a commissioner. The personal liberty laws chiefly served to express Northerners' sense of the Fugitive Slave Law: that it was outrageously un-American, and tyrannical, particularly in requiring all free citizens to hunt down a brave escapee from despotism. Southerners ultimately tried to secede in part from that insulting opinion. But secession and the Civil War only gave Northerners more power to aid more fugitives—a slaveholders' problem that no Union or Confederacy could solve.

[See also Compromise of 1850; Contraband; Dred Scott Decision.]

BIBLIOGRAPHY

Campbell, Stanley. The Slave Catchers: Enforcement of the Fugitive Slave Law, 1850–1860. Chapel Hill, N.C., 1968.
Galpin, W. Freeman. "The Jerry Rescue." New York History 43 (1945): 19–34.
Gara, Larry. The Liberty Line: The Legend of the Underground Railroad. Lexington, Ky., 1961.
Pease, Jane H., and William H. Pease. The Fugitive Slave Law and Anthony Burns. Philadelphia, 1975.
Slaughter, Thomas P. Bloody Dawn: The Christiana Riot and Racial Violence in the Antebellum North. New York, 1991.

WILLIAM W. FREEHLING

FULLER, THOMAS C. (1832–1901), first lieutenant and congressman from North Carolina. Born in Fayetteville, North Carolina, February 27, 1832, Fuller attended the University of North Carolina but left in 1851 without graduating to work for a Fayetteville merchant. He was admitted to the bar in 1856.

A Union Whig, he opposed a secession convention in 1861 but joined the First North Carolina Regiment (Lafayette Light Infantry) as a private after Abraham Lincoln's call for troops. He participated in the Battle of Big Bethel and attained the rank of first lieutenant. In November 1861, together with Joseph B. Starr, he raised a battery of light artillery and fought in several engagements in eastern North Carolina.

While still in active service, Fuller was elected as a Conservative to the Second Congress in 1863, defeating two secession Democrats. The youngest member, Fuller was also the least wealthy, owning no property according to the census of 1860. He seldom spoke on the floor of Congress and played only a minor role in policy-making, serving on the relatively unimportant Commerce and Patents committees. He was respected for his expertise on military affairs, however. Like most North Carolina Conservatives, he opposed the centralizing policies of the Davis administration, particularly in regard to conscription and the suspension of the writ of habeas corpus. He supported a negotiated peace and by 1865 had come to favor separate state action.

After the war, Fuller twice tried unsuccessfully for a seat in the U.S. Congress. Returning to his law practice, he became active in the affairs of the Conservative (later Democratic) party. In 1891 he was appointed a judge of the U.S. Court of Private Land Claims and served in that position until his death in Raleigh on October 20, 1901.

BIBLIOGRAPHY

Alexander, Thomas B., and Richard E. Beringer. *The Anatomy of the Confederate Congress: A Study of the Influences of Member Characteristics on Legislative Voting Behavior, 1861–1865.* Nashville, Tenn., 1972.
Ashe, Samuel A. *Biographical History of North Carolina.* 8 vols. Greensboro, N.C., 1905–1917.
Powell, William S. *Dictionary of North Carolina Biography.* 4 vols. to date. Chapel Hill, N.C., 1979–.
Warner, Ezra J., and W. Buck Yearns. *Biographical Register of the Confederate Congress.* Baton Rouge, La., 1975.

THOMAS E. JEFFREY

FUNERALS. The Civil War wrought a major change even in American funeral customs. Prior to the struggle, undertakers were cabinetmakers or hardware store owners who supplied casket, hearse, and team for the funeral service. Families of any means buried their deceased in wooden coffins; the less affluent wrapped the body in a blanket or sheet. Any viewing of the remains in the interval between death and burial was of short duration. Cooling boards and ice chests, in which ice was placed beneath the corpse as a temporary preservative, were sometimes used for prominent figures. The inadequacy of this practice, however, especially in the heat of summer, gave rise to a popular jingle: "Soon ripe, soon rotten; soon gone, but not forgotten."

Then came civil war, and with unprecedented numbers of men fighting, unprecedented numbers died. Grief-stricken families wanted the remains of their heroes, but how to transport the dead from battlefields to destinations hundreds of miles away was a major problem. The condition of the decomposing corpse when it finally reached home was of equal concern.

Two developments resulted. One was the rise of professional undertakers who handled remains in an orderly and knowledgeable fashion. Allied to this was the perfection of embalming through the arterial injection of fluid. The first embalming fluids had an arsenic base. They petrified rather than preserved (and hence were eventually outlawed by federal statute.) Nevertheless, with embalming and large-scale production of metallic, airtight coffins, it became possible in the Civil War to ship home untold numbers of fallen soldiers. Funeral services were held months after death, in either public or family cemeteries. Psalm-readings, prayers, sometimes a eulogy, and often one or more hymns comprised the usual burial service.

[*See also* Death and Mourning.]

BIBLIOGRAPHY

Habenstein, Robert W. *The History of American Funeral Directing.* Milwaukee, 1955.
Robertson, James I., Jr. "The Development of the Funeral Business in Georgia." *Georgia Review,* Spring 1959.

JAMES I. ROBERTSON, JR.

FUNSTEN, DAVID (1819–1866), colonel and congressman from Virginia. Born in Clarke County, Virginia, Funsten practiced law there after graduating from Princeton in 1838. After serving in the Virginia House of Delegates from 1844 through 1846 for Warren and Clarke counties, he moved to Alexandria in 1852. When the war began, Funsten took a commission as captain in the Eleventh Virginia Infantry and rose to the rank of colonel by 1862. He saw action at First Manassas, but a severe foot wound received at the Battle of Seven Pines disabled him from further military service. Funsten stood for election in 1863 to the House of Representatives. His easy victory entitled him to complete the unexpired congressional term of William Smith (who had become governor of Virginia) and to serve in the Second Congress.

Funsten was one of those increasingly numerous Confederate congressmen whose districts were entirely overrun by the other side. He was an extreme Confederate nationalist and advocated total war and the stern measures to carry it out, including conscription of free blacks and slaves, suspension of habeas corpus, and impressment of railroads and planters' surpluses. He proposed legislation for organizing disabled soldiers for the war effort.

Funsten returned to Alexandria after the war to reestablish his law practice but never recovered from his war wound. He died of pneumonia a day short of the first anniversary of Appomattox and was survived by his wife and nine children.

BIBLIOGRAPHY

Krick, Robert K. *Lee's Colonels: A Biographical Register of the Field Officers of the Army of Northern Virginia.* Dayton, Ohio, 1979.

Wakelyn, Jon L. *Biographical Dictionary of the Confederacy.* Edited by Frank E. Vandiver. Westport, Conn., 1977.

Warner, Ezra J., and W. Buck Yearns. *Biographical Register of the Confederate Congress.* Baton Rouge, La., 1975.

NELSON D. LANKFORD

G

GAINES' MILL, VIRGINIA. [*This entry discusses the battle of June 27, 1862. For discussion of the battle of May 31 through June 12, 1864, see* Cold Harbor.] Site of the third of the Seven Days' Battles fought on the outskirts of Richmond, Virginia, Gaines' Mill witnessed fighting between Robert E. Lee's Army of Northern Virginia and Union Maj. Gen. George B. McClellan's Army of the Potomac. The battle raged throughout most of the day of June 27, 1862, leaving the Confederates exhausted victors. Estimated casualties among the 57,018 Southerners numbered 8,751 dead, wounded, and missing; Federal losses totaled 6,837 killed, wounded, and missing out of 34,214 men.

On June 26, 1862, Lee had tried and failed to destroy Union Maj. Gen. Fitz John Porter's isolated Fifth Corps positioned north of the Chickahominy River, northeast of Richmond. The Battle of Mechanicsville, or Beaver Dam Creek, ended badly for the Confederates. Lt. Gen. Thomas J. ("Stonewall") Jackson's failure to arrive from the Shenandoah Valley in time to move behind and assail the enemy's flank left the attacking Confederates to falter before a well-entrenched enemy. Southerners took a great loss in casualties. That night, Porter withdrew to the southeast, closer to the remainder of McClellan's army. Lee followed in hot pursuit.

Near Gaines' Mill, south and east of New and Old Cold Harbor, Porter halted and turned to face the Confederates. His men soon formed a strong semicircular defense on a plateau behind Boatswain's Swamp just above the Chickahominy River. Federals dug themselves into the Virginia mud, south and east of a stream, and awaited the pursuing Confederates.

Soldiers of Gen. A. P. Hill's Light Division were the first to approach the Federal position, and they immediately formed into charging columns. Over the next several hours the brigades of Maxcy Gregg, William Dorsey Pender, Lawrence O'Bryan Branch, Joseph R. Anderson, James Jay Archer, and Charles W. Field stormed across the boggy swamp to assault the enemy lines. Each fell back before the deadly blaze of artillery and infantry gunfire.

At one point, Lee tried to divert the enemy's attention from its center by sending James Longstreet's division to the right of Hill's men. They too met with strong resistance and retreated to Confederate lines.

The bulk of Lee's army was on the field; only Jackson's fourteen brigades were absent. Jackson again was late, apparently directed down the wrong road, which almost brought his troops through Gaines' Mill. He countermarched four miles and finally arrived on the field around 3:00 P.M. But Jackson, hesitant to jump into the fray without knowledge of battle positions and plans, still waited and watched. Meanwhile the fight raged on with Confederate losses mounting and Union reinforcements on the way.

It was not until 7:00 that evening that all of Lee's men were in place and poised to move forward in one last coordinated assault. Four thousand fresh troops under Brig. Gen. John B. Hood and Col. Evander M. Law spearheaded a dramatic charge on the Union center. The remainder of Lee's army attacked on either flank. The fight grew hot and severe, and as darkness enveloped the field, Porter's men retreated. A last effort by the Federal cavalry to stem the tide of storming Confederates proved futile. Mounted men from the Fifth and Second U.S. Cavalry were easy targets for infantry rifle fire, and they soon turned to join the retreat. That night Porter again slipped farther south, this time to reunite with the rest of McClellan's withdrawing army.

The costly Southern victory had revealed disturbing problems in Lee's command structure. All-day delays, misinformation, inaccurate maps, garbled orders, and an overall lack of communication had greatly hindered Lee's ability to fight with his full strength against Porter's single corps.

Gaines' Mill again revealed the aggressive fighting spirit Lee had displayed at Mechanicsville. Over the next few days Lee would persist in his quest to destroy McClellan's army, but engagements at Savage's Station, Frayser's Farm, and Malvern Hill only resulted in more losses to Lee's army; he won no decisive victories. Nevertheless, Lee did succeed in forcing McClellan eventually to withdraw his massive army entirely from the peninsula. Not for another two years would a Union force come as close to threatening the Confederate capital.

BIBLIOGRAPHY

Catton, Bruce. *Mr. Lincoln's Army.* Garden City, N.Y., 1951.

Cullen, Joseph P. "Gaines's Mill." *Civil War Times Illustrated* 3, no. 1 (April 1964): 11–17.

Dowdey, Clifford. *The Seven Days: The Emergence of Lee.* Boston, 1964.

Freeman, Douglas S. *Lee's Lieutenant's: A Study in Command.* 3 vols. New York, 1942–1944. Reprint, New York, 1986.

LESLEY JILL GORDON-BURR

GAITHER, BURGESS S.

GAITHER, BURGESS S. (1807–1892), congressman from North Carolina. Born in Iredell County, North Carolina, March 16, 1807, Burgess Sidney Gaither briefly attended the University of Georgia, studied law, and became superior court clerk of Burke County. He served as a Whig in the North Carolina Senate (1840–1841; 1844–1845, as Speaker; and 1861), was district solicitor from 1845 until 1852, and twice ran unsuccessfully for the U.S. Congress.

A staunch Unionist, he opposed the calling of a secession convention and embraced disunion only after North Carolina actually seceded. He was elected without opposition to the First Congress and served on the Naval Affairs Committee. As chair of the committee to investigate the loss of Roanoke Island, Gaither submitted a critical report that led to the resignation of Secretary of War Judah P. Benjamin. Although opposed to conscription, the tax-in-kind, and the suspension of habeas corpus, he was generally more supportive of administration policies than other Whigs in his delegation. He was also one of the few prominent North Carolina Whigs to oppose peace negotiations. Reelected to the Second Congress in 1863 over peace candidate S. P. Smith, Gaither served on the Judiciary Committee and was one of only two North Carolinians who gave even occasional support to the administration. Continuing to urge a vigorous prosecution of the war, he was the only North Carolina congressman to advocate the arming of the slaves.

After the war, Gaither resumed the practice of law and was an unsuccessful candidate for Congress in 1868. He died in Morganton on February 23, 1892.

BIBLIOGRAPHY

Alexander, Thomas B., and Richard E. Beringer. *The Anatomy of the Confederate Congress: A Study of the Influences of Member Characteristics on Legislative Voting Behavior, 1861–1865.* Nashville, Tenn., 1972.

Ashe, Samuel A. *Biographical History of North Carolina.* 8 vols. Greensboro, N.C., 1905–1917.

Powell, William S. *Dictionary of North Carolina Biography.* 4 vols. to date. Chapel Hill, N.C., 1979–.

Wakelyn, Jon L. *Biographical Dictionary of the Confederacy.* Edited by Frank E. Vandiver. Westport, Conn., 1977.

Warner, Ezra J., and W. Buck Yearns. *Biographical Register of the Confederate Congress.* Baton Rouge, La., 1975.

THOMAS E. JEFFREY

GALVANIZED REBELS. *For detailed discussion of Southerners who fought for the Union, see* Tories. *For discussion of Northerners who fought for the Confederacy, see* Galvanized Yankees.

GALVANIZED YANKEES. Although the origin of the term *Galvanized Yankees* is obscure, it has two exactly opposite meanings—both are correct. The primary meaning refers to the 6,000 Southern soldiers who deserted the Confederate cause, joined the Union army as the First through Sixth Regiments, U.S. Volunteers, and spent the rest of the war fighting Indians on the western frontier. The second meaning refers to Northern soldiers who deserted the Federal army and joined the Confederate army, although these soldiers were sometimes referred to as "Galvanized Rebels."

Both groups of Galvanized Yankees were usually recruited from prisoner of war camps. There they chose to fight against their former flag rather than undergo the deprivation and possible death the camps offered. Many, however, changed uniforms only as a ruse to return to their former colors. Consequently, the Galvanized Yankee units experienced high desertion rates (one in seven) when they were in the vicinity of their former comrades. Desertion rates notwithstanding, the turncoat soldiers often fought well for their new country, as in the case of Northerners fighting for the South at Egypt Station, Mississippi, and of the U.S. Volunteer Regiments in the West.

[*See also* Tories.]

BIBLIOGRAPHY

Brown, D. Alexander. *The Galvanized Yankees.* Urbana, Ill., 1963.

Haw, Joseph R. "The Last of the C.S. Ordnance Department."

Confederate Veteran 34 (1926): 451. Reprint, Wilmington, N.C., 1985.

Laurie, Clayton. "Two-Sided Adventure." *Civil War Times Illustrated* 24 (June 1985): 40.

McLender, L. "About Some 'Galvanized Yanks.'" *Confederate Veteran* 13 (1905): 249. Reprint, Wilmington, N.C., 1985.

P. NEAL MEIER

GALVESTON, TEXAS.

GALVESTON, TEXAS. [*This entry includes two articles,* City of Galveston, *which profiles the city during the Confederacy, and* Battle of Galveston, *which discusses the military action there in 1863. See also Harriet Lane.*]

City of Galveston

In 1860 the second largest town in Texas contained a population of 7,307, including 2,688 European immigrants—a majority from Germany—as well as 1,178 slaves and 2 free blacks. On the eve of the Civil War, Galveston ranked as the major U.S. port on the Gulf of Mexico west of the Mississippi River and fifth among Southern seaports in trade. Despite some concern about the impact on commerce, a majority of voters in Galveston favored Southern Democrat John C. Breckinridge in 1860 and secession in 1861.

Once war began, Galvestonians volunteered for several military companies, including ones in Hood's brigade, Waul's legion, and Cook's artillery regiment. Confederates constructed fortifications and brought in cannon to defend the important island port. The first Union blockading ship appeared in July 1861. A Federal squadron of several vessels occupied the harbor on October 4, 1862, and Confederate troops retreated to the mainland. A counterattack by land and water on January 1, 1863, by Gen. John B. Magruder captured one warship, drove the others from the harbor, and reoccupied the town. The Union blockade resumed quickly and continued to the end of conflict in 1865. Despite the threat of a Federal force on the coast below Galveston in the fall of 1863, the port did not face another attack. Almost three hundred immigrants avoided conscription because they were foreign citizens and about fifty Unionists left with the Union navy.

Most Confederate blockade runners from Galveston escaped the Federal ships, but the use of smaller vessels and visits by fewer ships per year reduced the export of cotton by at least two-thirds. Several merchants moved their operations to Houston and focused on trade through Mexico. A few small rope and iron manufacturers continued in operation. Many middle- and upper-class families became refugees in Houston to escape possible shelling and occupation. Working men faced unemployment and shortages but received some aid from charitable groups organized primarily by women.

Citizens and Confederate officers held some dances and

MAP OF GALVESTON BAY.

HARPER'S PICTORIAL HISTORY OF THE GREAT REBELLION

celebrations. Yet the war disrupted social patterns in church services and schools on several occasions. Shortages, inflation, and the partial breakdown of local government led to thefts, the use of fences for firewood, and occasional violence. Confederate troops mutinied briefly in August 1863, and soldiers' wives protested the following summer over pay and food problems. Yellow fever caused more than 250 deaths in September 1864. Slavery also faced wartime changes as refugees took one-third of the bondsmen off the island. The Confederate army used slave labor to build fortifications. A few slaves escaped to the Union naval vessels, while the remainder welcomed the Union army on June 19, 1865, which became the popular date for celebrating emancipation in Texas.

Postwar Galveston recovered rapidly with trade nearing the prewar level by 1866. Its population had grown to 13,818 in 1870, which ranked the town first in Texas.

BIBLIOGRAPHY

Barr, Alwyn, "Texas Coastal Defense, 1861–1865." *Southwestern Historical Quarterly* 65 (1961–1962): 1–30.

McComb, David G. *Galveston: A History.* Austin, Tex., 1986.

ALWYN BARR

Battle of Galveston

In the early morning darkness of January 1, 1863, Confederates recaptured Galveston, the principal seaport on the Texas coast and key to the blockade of the western Gulf of Mexico. Its recapture provided a Confederate morale boost while denying the Union navy a base in the region. It also prevented a Union invasion of Texas from that city. Galveston continued to be an important blockade-running port for the rest of the war.

In October 1862, Union sailors and marines had seized the town after its Confederate garrison withdrew. Adm. David Farragut then requested that an army garrison be sent. On Christmas Day, a 260-man Union detachment composed of three companies of the Forty-second Massachusetts Infantry under Col. Isaac Burrell arrived to secure the town. Anchored off shore along the roadstead and in Galveston Bay were the gunboats of Commdr. William B. Renshaw's squadron, including USS *Clifton*, USS *Westfield*, USS *Sachem*, USS *Owasco*, USS *Corypheus*, and the revenue cutter USS *Harriet Lane*, as well as half a dozen coal tenders and troop transports.

Gen. John B. Magruder, the commander of the Department of Texas, used a surprise land-sea attack to retake the city. Magruder's battle fleet consisted of *Bayou City*, a river steamer, and *Neptune*, a coastal mail packet. Confederate shipworkers in Houston outfitted both vessels with bow cannons and piled cotton bales along the decks as makeshift armor. Accompanying the two cottonclads were two steamboats, *Lucy Gwinn* and *John F. Carr*, serving as wood tenders.

Magruder loaded his fleet with 300 volunteer sharpshooters to act as boarding parties. An additional 1,500 men, along with a dozen pieces of artillery, crossed over to Galveston Island on the night of December 31, 1862. At 4:00 A.M. on New Year's Day, Magruder ordered his troops to open fire. The Union fleet returned the fire with murderous ferocity, scattering the Texan gun crews. A Confederate infantry assault against the Forty-second Massachusetts also disintegrated. At dawn, Magruder aborted the attack.

Taking advantage of the distraction on shore, the Confederate naval forces attacked. Texan sharpshooters cleared the deck of *Harriet Lane* as a boarding party captured the ship. The Confederates then boldly sent a flag of truce to Commander Renshaw, ordering him to surrender his entire fleet. Mistaking the Confederate vessels for ironclad rams, Renshaw ordered his fleet out of Galveston Bay, abandoning the infantry on shore. His flagship, *Westfield*, was hard aground, and Renshaw ordered it destroyed; a premature explosion killed him and twelve crewmen.

Thirty Texans were killed, and another 130 were wounded in the Confederate victory. *Neptune* sank in shallow water and *Bayou City* was severely damaged. Union losses were 21 killed, 36 wounded, and 250 captured. In addition to taking *Harriet Lane* and causing *Westfield* to be scuttled, the Confederates captured three coaling vessels.

BIBLIOGRAPHY

Evans, Clement A., ed. *Confederate Military History*. 12 vols. Atlanta, 1899. Extended ed. in 19 vols. Wilmington, N.C., 1987–1989.

Hayes, Charles Waldo. *Galveston: A History of the Island and the City*. 2 vols. Austin, Tex., 1974.

Noel, Theophilus. *A Campaign from Santa Fe to the Mississippi: Being a History of the Old Sibley Brigade from Its First Organization to the Present Time; Its Campaigns in New Mexico, Arizona, Texas, Louisiana and Arkansas in the Years 1861–2–3–4*. Shreveport, La., 1865. Reprint, edited by Martin Hardwick Hall and Edwin Adams Davis. Houston, Tex., 1961.

DONALD S. FRAZIER

GANO, RICHARD MONTGOMERY (1830–1913), brigadier general. Born on June 17, 1830, in Bourbon County, Kentucky, Gano attended school at Bacon College in Harrodsburg, Kentucky, and Bethany College in Virginia. After studying at the Louisville University Medical School, he practiced medicine in Bourbon County. In 1859 he moved to Tarrant County, Texas, and was elected to the Texas legislature in 1860 and 1861.

When the Civil War began, he raised two companies of Texas cavalry at the request of Albert Sidney Johnston but did not join Johnston in time to participate in the Battle of Shiloh. P. G. T. Beauregard ordered Gano to report to John Hunt Morgan, and his squadron became the nucleus of the Seventh Kentucky Cavalry Regiment in Morgan's Brigade. Gano took part in Morgan's first Kentucky raid and fought

RICHARD MONTGOMERY GANO.　　　LIBRARY OF CONGRESS

at Tullahoma, but he became ill in June 1863 and returned home. In July he was placed in command of all the cavalry of the Texas state troops and in October reported to the Indian Territory. In the spring of 1864 Gano took part in the Camden campaign. Upon returning to the Indian Territory, he commanded cavalry in the fights around Fort Gibson and Cabin Creek in September 1864. He was promoted to brigadier general on March 17, 1865.

Following the war, Gano returned to Kentucky, but in 1866 moved back to Texas where he gave up his medical practice to become a minister in the First Christian church. He was still active in the church when he died on March 27, 1913, in Dallas, Texas.

BIBLIOGRAPHY

Brown, D. Alexander. *The Bold Cavaliers.* Philadelphia, 1959.
Wright, Marcus J., comp., and Harold B. Simpson, ed. *Texas in the War, 1861–1865.* Hillsboro, Tex., 1965.

ANNE J. BAILEY

GARDENHIRE, E. L.

GARDENHIRE, E. L. (1815–1899), congressman from Tennessee. After the war Governor William G. Brownlow of Tennessee branded Erasmus Lee Gardenhire a "bitter rebel," absolutely refusing to recommend him to President Andrew Johnson for executive clemency. Among Gardenhire's "sins" had been his avowed secessionism, his resignation from the Tennessee judicial circuit bench, and his November 1861 election as Fourth District representative to the First Congress. Appointed to the Claims, Elections, and Enrolled Bills committees, Judge Gardenhire, a prewar Democrat, was active in the House, attending daily, debating frequently, and rarely skipping a vote. From the opening day of the first session on February 18, 1862, to the close of the second session roughly eight months later, he was decidedly pro-administration, voting in favor of major conscription legislation, as well as the February 1862 measure suspending the writ of habeas corpus. During that same period he also introduced a bill requesting an investigation into the loyalty of certain Confederate officials in East Tennessee, to determine whether someone had "squandered Southern funds upon Lincoln favorites" in promoting "the cause of the despot."

On account of "urgent business," Gardenhire was absent during much of the next two sessions, missing nearly the entire month of April 1863, two weeks in December later that year, and the last fifteen days of the fourth session, which ended on February 17, 1864. Declining reelection to the Second Congress, he returned to his native Overton County, Tennessee, where he had taught school and practiced law before the war. Later he removed to White County, Tennessee, where he had briefly edited a newspaper and ran unsuccessfully for Congress in 1853. There is no evidence that he ever received an individual pardon from Johnson.

BIBLIOGRAPHY

Amnesty File. E. L. Gardenhire. Microcopy M1003, Roll 50. Record Group 94. National Archives, Washington, D.C.
Journal of the Congress of the Confederate States of America, 1861–1865. 7 vols. Washington, D.C., 1904–1905.
Speer, William S., ed. *Sketches of Prominent Tennesseans.* Nashville, 1888.
Warner, Ezra J., and W. Buck Yearns. *Biographical Register of the Confederate Congress.* Baton Rouge, La., 1975.

R. B. ROSENBURG

GARDNER, FRANKLIN

GARDNER, FRANKLIN (1823–1873), major general. Gardner was born in New York City, the son of Charles Gardner, who had served as the army's adjutant general during the War of 1812. Appointed to the U.S. Military Academy from Iowa, Gardner graduated seventeenth of thirty-nine in 1843. After serving in Florida during the Seminole War, he saw action in Mexico, for which he won two brevets for gallantry. He then received transfer to the frontier, where he engaged in Indian scouting and, in 1857, participated in the Utah campaign against the Mormons.

After marrying into the affluent Mouton family of Louisiana, Gardner tendered his services to the Confeder-

FRANKLIN GARDNER.   LIBRARY OF CONGRESS

ate army at the outbreak of the Civil War without having formally resigned his commission in the U.S. Army. He was dropped from rank on May 7, 1861, "for leaving . . . and abandoning his command." On March 16, 1861, Gardner received commission as lieutenant colonel in the Confederate army. After serving during the early war in Tennessee and Mississippi, he was promoted to brigadier general, to date from April 11, 1862. He participated in Braxton Bragg's invasion of Kentucky, commanding a brigade in Jones Withers's division of Leonidas Polk's corps. Promoted to major general in December 1862, he was transferred to Louisiana and was placed in command of the defenses at Port Hudson. Captured when the post surrendered following the fall of Vicksburg in the summer of 1863, Gardner was imprisoned until the following August, when he was exchanged and received assignment in the Department of Alabama and Mississippi. He served until war's end under Richard Taylor, engaging Federal cavalry units under James Wilson during his famous raid through those states into Georgia.

Gardner surrendered in May 1865 as part of the last active Confederate force east of the Mississippi River. He spent the remainder of his life as a planter near Vermillionsville, Louisiana.

BIBLIOGRAPHY

Faust, Patricia, ed. *Historical Times Illustrated's Encyclopedia of the Civil War.* New York, 1986.

Johnson, Robert U., and C. C. Buel, eds. *Battles and Leaders of the Civil War.* 4 vols. New York, 1887–1888. Reprint, Secaucus, N.J., 1982.

Warner, Ezra J. *Generals in Gray: Lives of the Confederate Commanders.* Baton Rouge, La., 1959.

CHRISTOPHER PHILLIPS

GARDNER, W. M. (1824–1901), brigadier general.

Confederate officers often paid a high price for entering combat at the head of their troops. Several promising leaders were killed at First Manassas, and many others were seriously wounded. One of the latter, who was disabled and never led troops in the field afterward, was Gardner.

William Montgomery Gardner was born in Augusta, Georgia, on June 8, 1824, and graduated from West Point in the class of 1846. He served as a lieutenant in the First U.S. Infantry during the Mexican War and rose to the rank of captain while serving on the frontier.

Resigning his commission when Georgia seceded, Gardner served as a staff officer before being appointed lieutenant colonel of the Eighth Georgia Infantry in June 1861. The next month, at First Manassas, he led the regiment while its colonel, Francis S. Bartow, commanded a brigade. Gardner was so severely wounded in the leg that he was

reported as killed and spent almost two years on leave recuperating. Gardner was appointed colonel to succeed Bartow, who had been killed at Manassas, and then was appointed brigadier general on November 14, 1861, while still absent at home.

Although he requested active duty, Gardner spent the rest of the war serving on courts of inquiry, reorganizing paroled units after Vicksburg, and commanding administrative departments in Florida and at Richmond. His most significant post-Manassas service was as commandant of military prisons east of the Mississippi River in 1864 and 1865, including a position as commander of military prisons in Richmond. After the war Gardner lived in Georgia and Tennessee. He died in Memphis on June 16, 1901.

BIBLIOGRAPHY

Compiled Military Service Records. William Montgomery Gardner. Microcopy M331, Roll 102. Record Group 109. National Archives, Washington, D.C.

Derry, Joseph T. *Georgia.* Vol. 6 of *Confederate Military History.* Edited by Clement A. Evans. Atlanta, 1899. Vol. 7 of extended ed. Wilmington, N.C., 1987.

J. TRACY POWER

GARLAND, AUGUSTUS HILL (1832–1899),

congressman from Arkansas and postwar governor, U.S. senator, and U.S. attorney general. Born June 11, 1832, in Tipton County, Tennessee, Garland was educated at St. Mary's College in Lebanon, Kentucky, and St. Joseph's College in Bardstown, Kentucky. While in school he was strongly influenced by his admiration for Henry Clay.

Returning to Washington, Arkansas, in 1852, Garland began reading law and formed a law firm with his stepfather, Thomas Hubbard, and worked for Simon T. Sanders, the county and circuit court clerk for Hempstead County. In 1856 he moved to Little Rock where his law practice became one of the most prestigious in the state.

The defeat of the American party candidates in the 1856 election left the Democratic party, led by the Johnson "Family," in control of Arkansas politics. When the 1860 election began, Garland participated in an opposition convention, assembling the group generally recognized as the successor to the Whig-American party coalition. In the national election that fall Garland was an elector for the Constitutional Union party.

At the January 1860 term of the Arkansas Supreme Court, Garland lost a series of appeals dealing with the taxation of swamp and overflowed lands, and he spent the summer preparing to carry his appeal to the U.S. Supreme Court. On the day after Christmas, he was enrolled as an attorney before the Court.

By the time Garland returned to Little Rock late in

AUGUSTUS HILL GARLAND.   LIBRARY OF CONGRESS

January 1861, the state was full of excitement over the coming election that would decide whether to call a secession convention. Garland immediately announced his candidacy for one of Pulaski County's two seats in the convention. With no time to publish his thoughts on secession, he declared that he agreed with the views of Joseph Stillwell, another candidate in Pulaski County.

Garland was a conservative Unionist. He opposed separate state secession and urged cooperation with the border states. He suggested calling a convention of all slaveholding states to adopt the Crittenden Resolutions. As the only cotton-growing state left in the Union, Arkansas would benefit from a monopoly on trade, he argued, and he urged the people to make the state one of the strongest in the Union instead of one of the weakest in the Confederacy.

In February the people of Arkansas voted to call a convention to consider the question of secession, but the convention had a strong Unionist contingent. Garland and Stillwell were elected by 550 votes over their secessionist opponents. The secession convention began on March 4, 1861, the same day that Abraham Lincoln was inaugurated. The Unionist leaders—Garland, his brother Rufus Garland, Hugh F. Thomasson, and W. W. Watkins—adopted a two-part strategy. They worked to defeat efforts to draw up a secession ordinance and suggested waiting to see what

Lincoln would do. After agreeing to submit the question of secession or cooperation to the voters, the convention adjourned on March 21.

The convention reconvened on May 6, however, in reaction to Lincoln's call for troops and immediately adopted a secession ordinance. Garland voted for the ordinance reluctantly in the hope of continuing to influence the course of events. Next the convention considered whom to send to the Confederate Congress. The first nomination went to former senator Robert Ward Johnson; the second to Garland. He was elected on the first ballot. While the convention turned to rewriting the state constitution, Garland headed for Montgomery to join the Provisional Congress. When he took his seat he was the youngest member of that body; he would become one of only twenty-eight men to serve in all three Congresses.

After Congress reconvened in Richmond, Garland was appointed to the Public Lands and the Finance committees. It was in committees that Garland built a reputation for hard work and scholarship. His first major motion was a resolution calling on the Finance Committee to investigate the expediency of declaring Treasury notes and bonds legal tender. This resolution was the beginning of a long controversy over legal tender that was never resolved. By the time discussion of the matter was dropped in 1864, notes were accepted as legal tender though they had never been designated as such.

Congress adjourned in August and Garland returned to Arkansas to seek election to the First Congress as a representative of the Third District. His main opponent was Jilson P. Johnson of Desha County, an early secessionist and part of the Johnson Family. Garland waged a vigorous campaign, and, certain he had won when the unofficial totals were announced, he left for Virginia for the final session of the Provisional Congress.

By the time he reached Richmond, Congress was already in session. Garland was appointed to the Judiciary Committee in addition to his other assignments, which was in keeping with his interest in constitutional law. During this session the committee was dealing with issues relating to the seizure of property. Resolutions introduced by Garland led this inquiry in two directions. He proposed allowing citizens whose goods or property had been confiscated by Federal authorities to recover their losses by seizing land owned by U.S. citizens, and amending the Sequestration Act to exempt the property of free blacks who had been forced to leave the slave states. Garland accepted the absolute right of a government to seize alien enemy property, but he sought to protect property owners from loss.

Meanwhile a problem had developed over the November election. Arkansas Governor Henry Rector had announced the results of the election on the basis of official returns sent to the secretary of state by the county clerks. According to these returns Garland had received 2,157 votes, Jilson Johnson, 2,125 votes, and four other candidates, fewer numbers of votes, giving Garland a plurality. But Johnson announced that he was contesting the election because of problems in the returns from Arkansas County. Garland at first ignored Johnson's challenge, but the House of Representatives accepted it and sent the matter to the Committee on Elections. The committee, deeply divided along party lines, was determined to work slowly and carefully. During the course of the controversy it issued a number of reports and asked the principals to provide evidence several times.

Although the status of his congressional seat was uncertain, Garland decided to run for the Senate. When Confederate senators were chosen in 1861, R. W. Johnson had used his influence as head of the Family to ensure his own selection, but he had drawn a short term and had to seek reappointment in 1862. Garland had gotten more votes than Johnson in the balloting for seats in the Provisional Congress, so he apparently felt the time was ripe to remove the Family from power.

Garland, Johnson, and a third candidate were invited to address the General Assembly. Garland, in his speech, put special emphasis on the financial difficulties facing the Confederacy, referring to the need to make notes and bonds legal tender and discussing a bill for new taxes. He then turned to the topic of ending the war. Garland argued that the cost of the war to both sides in men and money was such that it should end soon. He urged that the Confederacy stay ready for war but make an offer for peace. The final vote came two days later: Johnson received forty-six votes on the twelfth ballot, and Garland forty-two.

Garland had better luck with his congressional seat. When the third session of the First Congress convened in January 1863, more evidence concerning the contested election was sent to the Committee on Elections. Jilson Johnson, however, decided to withdraw his suit, the committee was dismissed, and Garland retained his seat.

He was now able to immerse himself in committee work. In addition to the Judiciary Committee, he was a member of committees on Enrolled Bills and on the Medical Department. He also served on various committees dealing with matters ranging from homesteads for disabled veterans to plans for retaliation against the United States for attempts to enforce the Emancipation Proclamation.

At the close of the First Congress, Garland sent a report to his constituents outlining major legislation and focusing on financial matters. The last part of the report was directed at boosting morale. Calling on civilians to support the government and the army, Garland mentioned in passing that he felt the conventions being held to organize a Unionist government for Arkansas were of no importance.

When the Second Congress convened in May 1864,

Garland was made chairman of the Committee on Territories and Public Lands and was again appointed to the Judiciary Committee. He also served on the Special Committee to Inquire into the Charges against W. R. W. Cobb.

The climax of Garland's summer came with his election to the Confederate Senate. Taking his seat in November 1864, Garland was appointed to the Committee on Post Offices and Post Roads. In the next month he introduced twelve bills, resolutions, and memorials on subjects ranging from the salaries of civil officers to limiting the number of slaves employed by the army.

Garland was increasingly concerned about the Confederacy's ability to maintain itself. His ideas on the economy reached final form in January 1865, when he offered a resolution calling for the Judiciary Committee to study the need for a Home Department. Such a department, he urged, should have broad powers for the development, management, and control of the South's internal resources. But the growing military crisis did not make an expansion of government powers attractive, and this resolution died in committee.

Garland brought to Congress his belief in constitutionalism and his faith in a strong central government. He supported the Davis administration on most issues. In letters to his constituents he always emphasized money and military matters and explained them in detail, for he felt these were the things of greatest interest to the people. But his own primary interests lay in two other areas—the suspension of the writ of habeas corpus and the establishment of a supreme court.

In 1862 Congress gave President Jefferson Davis the power to suspend the writ of habeas corpus and declare martial law in areas threatened by invasion. Although the law was applied sparingly nationwide, in Arkansas Gen. Thomas C. Hindman, and later Lt. Gen. Theophilus H. Holmes, exceeded this authority by issuing a series of directives curtailing the power of the civil authorities, establishing price controls, suspending the writ of habeas corpus, and declaring martial law. Garland was horrified.

With this firsthand knowledge of how martial law and suspension of habeas corpus could be misused, Garland was absolutely opposed to the extension of the law when it expired in February 1863. A new, more limited law for the suspension of habeas corpus was passed in February 1864. When the Second Congress convened in May, several members felt they had a mandate to repeal the law even though it was about to expire, and the matter was sent to the Judiciary Committee. The majority of the committee supported renewing the law, but in a minority report issued May 28, 1864, Garland and Burgess Sidney Gaither of North Carolina favored letting the law expire. Garland gave three major reasons the law should be allowed to lapse: first, the law allowed too much discretion about whom to arrest;

second, it violated judicial independence by allowing the president to appoint investigating committees for matters normally handled by the courts; and finally, it tended to lower civilian morale. Neither the majority nor the minority report recommended any action, and the law was allowed to expire.

The effort to establish a supreme court for the Confederacy also preoccupied Garland. The Judiciary Act of March 16, 1861, defined the powers of a supreme court, but its organization was suspended in July 1861, delaying its operation without destroying its proposed authority. Bills introduced in 1862 to organize the court never came to a vote.

In April 1863, in a report written by Garland, the House Judiciary Committee recommended the passage of the Senate supreme court bill, with an amendment to give the court appellate jurisdiction over state courts. Garland felt this jurisdiction was essential for the stability of the South in that it would ensure the equal enforcement of Confederate laws. Although his viewpoint was well received, the House postponed action on the bill and it died when Congress adjourned in January 1864.

By late 1864 Garland knew that the war had been lost. Disgusted with the Senate for spending its time and energies fighting with President Davis, Garland left Richmond in late February 1865 to return to Arkansas.

In May, Confederate Governor Harris Flanagin authorized him to confer with Federal authorities to arrange terms for the restoration of peace and order. Garland accepted the commission and went to Little Rock, where he met with Gen. J. J. Reynolds and Unionist Governor Isaac Murphy. When Garland presented Flanagin's plan for unifying the state, Reynolds and Murphy went as far as they could in being conciliatory. They agreed to give the army a chance to disband and promised not to arrest the Confederate civil officers unless ordered to do so. But they refused to recognize the county officers in southern Arkansas.

With the war over, Garland turned his attention to personal matters. He prepared an application for a pardon to be sent to President Andrew Johnson. He stressed that he had been elected to the Confederate Congress as a conservative, that he never called for harsh measures against the Unionists, and that he was always opposed by the secessionists. He included letters of recommendation written by an impressive array of prominent officials, all of whom backed his pardon as a way of securing conservative support for the government and as a step toward restoration of peace and order. The pardon was granted July 15, 1865.

Next Garland sought to reestablish his law practice. Among the matters needing attention was the case of *McGee v. Mathis,* and related cases, which he had filed with the U.S. Supreme Court during the December 1860 term.

When Garland checked the records in July 1865 he discovered that the cases were still on the docket. This posed a dilemma. He wanted to attend to the cases, but he could not take the Iron-clad Oath, which required all federal officeholders, including lawyers practicing in federal courts, to swear that they had neither supported nor served in any government that was opposed to the U.S. government.

In October 1865 Garland filed a petition asking that he be allowed to return to practice before the Court without taking the oath. The case, titled *Ex parte Garland,* challenged the oath's constitutionality. It was the first attempt by a Southerner to use the judicial system to ameliorate punishment of the ex-Confederates. In his petition Garland reminded the Court that he had been sworn as an attorney of the Supreme Court in December 1860 and that he had filed briefs and arguments in a number of cases that were pending when Arkansas seceded. He wanted to resume the duties he had taken on before the war, but he could not take the oath without committing perjury. He argued that all laws requiring an oath are repugnant to the Constitution and are therefore null and void; he further argued that if the oath was valid, his presidential pardon relieved him of having to take it. On January 14, 1867, the Court ruled that the law requiring the oath was unconstitutional. The decision restored to Garland, but only Garland, his right to practice before the Supreme Court without taking the oath. As a practical matter, other Southern lawyers could have petitioned the Court for readmission, basing their argument on Garland's victory; but the oath was quietly dropped to avoid the continuing litigation.

Garland now turned to the political arena. In 1868 he led Arkansas conservatives in an unsuccessful fight to prevent the ratification of a new constitution. He was also chairman of the Arkansas delegation to the Democratic National Convention. But as the final measures of Congressional Reconstruction were put into place, Garland withdrew from public affairs.

An adviser to Arkansas Democrats throughout Reconstruction, Garland returned to public life in 1874 when Joseph Brooks and his supporters tried to oust Elisha Baxter from the governor's office. During the Brooks-Baxter War which followed, Garland was a leader of the Baxter forces, devising a strategy that led to the reaffirmation of Baxter as the rightful governor and to the calling of a constitutional convention. When the new constitution was ratified, Garland was elected governor. Hampered by economic and political pressures, he reestablished conservative government and was the symbol of the end of Reconstruction in Arkansas.

In 1877 Garland was chosen for a seat in the U.S. Senate. While there he worked for legislation of both regional and national impact, including federal aid to education, relief for disaster victims, construction of a levee system, and establishment of a national health agency.

The high point of Garland's public life came with his appointment as U.S. attorney general in 1885. Long noted for his legal scholarship, he issued meticulously written opinions dealing with matters ranging from land patents to federal appointments. Garland returned to private life in 1889, establishing a law practice in Washington, D.C. On January 26, 1899, he died while arguing a case before the Supreme Court.

BIBLIOGRAPHY

Alexander, Thomas B., and Richard E. Beringer. *The Anatomy of the Confederate Congress: A Study of the Influences of Member Characteristics on Legislative Voting Behavior, 1861–1865.* Nashville, Tenn., 1972.

Dougan, Michael B. *Confederate Arkansas: The People and Politics of a Frontier State in Wartime.* University, Ala., 1976.

Kerby, Robert L. *Kirby Smith's Confederacy: The Trans-Mississippi South, 1863–1865.* New York, 1972.

Newberry, Farrar. *A Life of Mr. Garland of Arkansas.* N.p., 1908.

Thomas, David Y. *Arkansas in War and Reconstruction, 1861–1874.* Little Rock, Ark., 1926.

Woods, James M. "Devotees and Dissenters: Arkansas in the Confederate Congress, 1861–1865." *Arkansas Historical Quarterly* 38 (Autumn 1979): 227–237.

BEVERLY WATKINS

GARLAND, RUFUS K. (1830–1886), captain and congressman from Arkansas. Rufus King Garland, Jr., was a native of Tennessee, born on May 22, 1830. He moved to Arkansas as a child and settled in Hempstead County, where he became an attorney, prominent planter, and Methodist preacher. He was a Unionist in the secession crisis and was elected to the state secession convention as such. In the first session in March 1861, Garland succeeded in having passed a resolution stating that the people's preference was the perpetuation of the Union if the equal rights of all states could be guaranteed. In the second session he shifted his position to support secession after President Abraham Lincoln's call for volunteers to suppress the Southern states that had seceded.

Garland joined the Hempstead Hornets in the spring of 1861 and was elected captain. The unit was mustered into Confederate service at Mt. Vernon, Missouri, on August 17, as Company B, Fourth Arkansas Infantry (the South Arkansas Regiment). Garland led his company at the Battle of Elkhorn Tavern on March 7, 1862, and was cited in official reports for gallantry in rallying and encouraging his men and for assistance to his regiment's commander. Garland went with his regiment to Mississippi following the Confederate defeat at Elkhorn Tavern.

Garland's strong opposition to conscription led him into an open conflict with Gen. Earl Van Dorn while his unit was in Mississippi. The Conscription Act of April 16, 1862, declared that men already in the Confederate army would serve for a three-year term. The Fourth Arkansas was reorganized and new company elections were held. Garland refused to stand for reelection; when his men elected him anyway, he declared that he would neither accept a certificate of election nor discharge the duties of the position. Van Dorn ordered his arrest, but Garland was not held and was allowed to leave his regiment and return to Arkansas.

In 1863 Garland ran for Congress in the Second District. His opponent was Grandison D. Royston, the incumbent. Royston, who had been a strong supporter of President Jefferson Davis in Congress, refused to campaign actively. Garland, on the other hand, was extremely critical of the Confederate government and canvassed the district actively. He proposed an end to conscription, advocated the removal of Gen. Theophilus H. Holmes from command of the Confederate armies in Arkansas, and condemned Holmes's imposition of martial law in parts of the state to enforce conscription laws. He went so far as to suggest that it was time for the South to consider trying to obtain peace with the Federal government. Garland won the election easily.

At Richmond, Garland joined the anti-administration faction in the Second Congress. Although this group did not have a consistent majority, it was able to prevent the president from changing exemptions to the conscription laws and from suspending the writ of habeas corpus in 1865; it also delayed giving him authority to arm slaves. Garland voted with the president's opponents on all of these issues. Garland supported most measures designed to strengthen the armies in the field, however, including bills that would have increased taxes on agricultural products for the support of the armies. With his brother, Senator Augustus H. Garland, Congressman Garland left Richmond in early March, failing to attend the last days of the Second Congress.

In the years after the war Garland practiced law and preached. He ran unsuccessfully for governor on the Greenback ticket in 1882. He died on December 12, 1886.

BIBLIOGRAPHY

Dougan, Michael B. *Confederate Arkansas: The People and Policies of a Frontier State in Wartime.* University, Ala., 1976.

Shinn, David. *Pioneers and Makers of Arkansas.* Washington, D.C., 1908.

Thomas, David Y. *Arkansas in War and Reconstruction, 1861–1874.* Little Rock, Ark., 1926.

CARL H. MONEYHON

GARLAND, SAMUEL, JR. (1830–1862), brigadier general. A great-grand-nephew of James Madison, graduate of the Virginia Military Institute, and prominent lawyer, Garland organized the Lynchburg, Virginia, home guard in response to John Brown's raid on Harpers Ferry during the fall of 1859. A year and a half later the home guard became the Eleventh Virginia Infantry after Virginia seceded and civil war began. Elected colonel, Garland led the Eleventh Virginia through the early engagements at Blackburn's Ford, First Manassas, and Dranesville.

Historian Douglas Southall Freeman has speculated that the unexpected deaths of Garland's wife and infant son during the summer of 1861, combined with Garland's place as the last of a direct line, caused him to behave recklessly, disregarding danger. At the Battle of Williamsburg in May 1862, for example, Garland refused to leave the field, although he was painfully wounded. Promotion to brigadier general came a few weeks later. Garland and the brigade of North Carolinians he now commanded saw action at Seven Pines, Gaines' Mill, and Malvern Hill. D. H. Hill, J. E. B. Stuart, and Joseph E. Johnston all commended Garland for his bravery and fine leadership during these battles.

But Garland's recklessness soon caught up with him. On September 14, 1862, while his men fought to protect the Confederate flank at South Mountain, Garland fell dead at the head of his brigade. The Confederate army mourned the loss of such a promising young officer. Major General Hill in his report praised Garland as a "pure, gallant and accomplished Christian soldier . . . who had no superiors and few equals in service."

BIBLIOGRAPHY

Bell, Robert. *Eleventh Virginia Infantry.* Lynchburg, Va., 1985.

Freeman, Douglas Southall. *Lee's Lieutenants: A Study in Command.* Vols. 1–2. New York, 1942–1943. Reprint, New York, 1986.

Warner, Ezra J. *Generals in Gray: Lives of the Confederate Commanders.* Baton Rouge, La., 1959.

LESLEY JILL GORDON-BURR

GARNETT, MUSCOE RUSSELL HUNTER

(1821–1864), congressman from Virginia. Born into a wealthy Episcopalian family in Essex County, Virginia—his uncle was Gen. Robert M. T. Hunter—Garnett followed the accustomed path that led the talented sons of the state's antebellum gentry to politics and to ardent defense of state rights and the peculiar institution (slavery). In Garnett's case, this path of privilege led to the University of Virginia, legal practice in Essex County, secessionist writings (including an 1850 tract, *The Union, Past and Future*), activism in the national Democratic party, and election to the state's constitutional convention (1850–1851), to the Virginia House of Delegates (1853–1856), and to the U.S. House of Representatives (1856–1861). With fair complexion and a large head in proportion to his modest stature, Garnett impressed his colleagues as a brilliant speaker. He was quick to point out the differences, which he thought irreconcilable, between the Southern and Northern positions regarding the entry of Kansas into the Union, and he did everything he could to inflame passions in Congress when the secession crisis began.

A strident advocate in Congress of Southern rights, slavery, and the desirability of secession, Garnett predictably voted for disunion at the Virginia convention in 1861 and entered the Confederate House of Representatives in 1862. Although appointed to the Ways and Means Committee, he resigned from that post and instead was placed on the Committee on Military Affairs. In the legislature he often opposed the Davis administration and employed his financial expertise to oppose tax increases. Though he supported a vigorous prosecution of the war, he was defeated for reelection in 1863 by Robert L. Montague, largely by the soldier vote, which predominated in districts overrun by the Federal army. Near the end of his lame-duck term he contracted typhoid fever and died at his Essex County home.

BIBLIOGRAPHY

Garnett, James M. "Biographical Sketch of Hon. Muscoe Russell Hunter Garnett of Essex County, Virginia (1821–1864)." *William and Mary Quarterly,* 1st ser., 18 (1909–1910): 17–37, 71–89.

Wakelyn, Jon L. *Biographical Dictionary of the Confederacy.* Edited by Frank E. Vandiver. Westport, Conn., 1977.

Warner, Ezra J., and W. Buck Yearns. *Biographical Register of the Confederate Congress.* Baton Rouge, La., 1975.

NELSON D. LANKFORD

GARNETT, RICHARD BROOKE (1817–1863),

brigadier general. A member of Tidewater aristocracy, Garnett was born November 21, 1817, at the family mansion in Essex County, Virginia. In 1841 he and his cousin, Robert Selden Garnett, graduated in the same West Point class. Dick Garnett fought against the Indians in Florida and the West.

In May 1861, the handsome officer with blue eyes, wavy hair, and closely cropped beard accepted appointment as a Confederate major. Promotion to brigadier general in the Provisional Army came in November. When Gen. Thomas J. ("Stonewall") Jackson moved up to command of the Shenandoah Valley defenses, Garnett succeeded him at the head of the Stonewall Brigade.

His first battle, at Kernstown in March 1862, was Garnett's undoing. With his troops low on ammunition and Federals threatening both flanks, Garnett on his own sought to save his brigade by ordering it to fall back from the front. This withdrawal forced Jackson's whole force to abandon its position. Jackson promptly removed Garnett from command and initiated court-martial proceedings. They were never held because of the press of war. A staff officer who knew Garnett well remarked that he "was ever thereafter anxious to expose himself, even unnecessarily, and to wipe out effectually by some distinction in action, what he felt to be an unmerited slur upon his military reputation."

Garnett campaigned zealously to get a new command and soon was given a brigade in Gen. George E. Pickett's division. He led it well in the 1862 Sharpsburg campaign. On July 3, 1863, Garnett's brigade was in the front rank of the Pickett-Pettigrew charge at Gettysburg. Extremely ill, the general was wearing a heavy overcoat in spite of the heat. Garnett got to within twenty yards of the Federal lines when he disappeared in the gunsmoke and confusion. His riderless horse soon galloped toward the rear. Presumably, Federal soldiers stripped his dead body of its sword and other insignia before burying Garnett in one of the mass graves on the battlefield.

BIBLIOGRAPHY

Harrison, Walter H. Pickett's Men: A Fragment of War History. Gaithersburg, Md., 1987.
Pierce, John E. "The Civil War Career of Richard Brooke Garnett: A Quest for Vindication." M.A. thesis, Virginia Polytechnic Institute and State University, 1969.
Robertson, James I., Jr. The Stonewall Brigade. Baton Rouge, La., 1963.

JAMES I. ROBERTSON, JR.

GARNETT, ROBERT S. (1819–1861), brigadier general. Garnett, born in Essex City, Virginia, on December 16, 1819, was the first general officer of either the Confederate or Union armies to be killed during the Civil War. A graduate of West Point, class of 1841, he was a veteran of the infantry, artillery, and cavalry and served in both the Seminole and Mexican wars. He also served as assistant instructor of tactics at the U.S. Military Academy at West Point for three years. At Monterrey, Mexico, he was breveted captain for gallantry, and at Buena Vista, Mexico, major, for the same reason. Following the Mexican War, Garnett served as commandant of cadets at West Point. Returning home from a year's sojourn in Europe just prior to the secession of Virginia, Garnett, then a major in the Ninth U.S. Infantry Regiment, resigned his commission on April 30, 1861, and was assigned adjutant general of Virginia troops on the staff of Gen. Robert E. Lee.

While serving the Confederacy in northwestern Virginia (present-day West Virginia) with a small and undersupplied force of about four thousand men, Garnett was slowly but steadily compelled to fall back from his position first from Rich Mountain and then from Laurel Hill by the superior Union forces of Gen. George B. McClellan and Gen. William

Rosecrans. As he crossed his troops over the Cheat River at Carrick's Ford on July 13, 1861, Garnett, directing the fording, was mortally wounded in the back by Federal soldiers. His body and belongings were returned by Union officers. Garnett is buried in Greenwood Cemetery, Brooklyn, New York.

BIBLIOGRAPHY

Faust, Patricia L., ed. Historical Times Illustrated Encyclopedia of the Civil War. New York, 1986.
Freeman, Douglas S. Lee's Lieutenants: A Study in Command. 3 vols. New York, 1942–1944. Reprint, New York, 1986.
U.S. War Department. War of the Rebellion: A Compilation of the Official Records of the Union and Confederate Armies. Washington, D.C., 1880–1901. Ser. 1, vol. 2.

WARREN WILKINSON

GARROTT, ISHAM WARREN (1816–1863), Alabama secession commissioner and brigadier general. Born in Wake County, North Carolina, in 1816, Garrott graduated from the University of North Carolina in 1840, studied law, and moved to Marion, Alabama. He was an Alabama state legislator from 1845 to 1849 and a Breckinridge elector in 1860. A committed secessionist, Garrott was Alabama's secession commissioner to North Carolina.

With the assistance of Emund Winston Pettus, Garrott raised the Twelfth Alabama Regiment at Montgomery in September 1861 and was elected colonel. His first service was under Gen. Jones Mitchell Withers in the defense of Mobile in the fall of 1861. Transferred in February 1862 to Knoxville to join E. Kirby Smith's army, Garrott's regiment subsequently fought as part of Gen. Edward Dorr Tracey's brigade in the Kentucky campaign in the fall of 1862. That brigade was assigned to Mississippi in December as a reinforcement for John C. Pemberton's army, and it was here that Garrott's command saw its heaviest fighting. At Port Gibson on May 1, 1863, Garrott led his men into battle from the right flank of Gen. John Stevens Bowen's line. The Twelfth Alabama suffered heavy casualties of 272 men killed, wounded, and missing in the day's fighting. After another battle at Champion's Hill on May 16, 1863, Garrott's regiment retreated behind the Vicksburg defenses with the rest of Pemberton's command. On June 17, 1863, Garrott was killed on the skirmish line by a Union sharpshooter. His commission as a brigadier general, dated May 28, 1863, arrived just after his death.

BIBLIOGRAPHY

Brewer, Willis. Alabama: Her History, Resources, War Record and Public Men. Montgomery, Ala., 1972.
Powell, William S., ed. Dictionary of North Carolina Biography. Vol. 2. Chapel Hill, N.C., 1986.

WILLIAM L. BARNEY

GARTRELL, LUCIUS JEREMIAH (1821–1891), brigadier general and congressman from Georgia. Gartrell was born January 7, 1821, in Wilkes County, Georgia. He attended Randolph-Macon College (1838–1841) and the University of Georgia for one year, where his name appears as a matriculate but not as a graduate in the Class of 1843. Gartrell studied law in the office of Robert Toombs and was admitted to the bar in 1842. After one year in practice he became solicitor-general of the Northern Judicial Circuit, serving in that capacity from 1843 to 1847.

Beginning his political career in 1847, Gartrell was elected twice to the Georgia House of Representatives. He was a Whig of the extreme state rights wing and shortly switched over to the Democratic party. In the legislature of 1849 he was characterized as a "radical, prosouthern, proslavery leader" who introduced the celebrated "Southern Rights resolutions," which set forth the doctrine of state rights in relation to the pending settlement of the slavery controversy in Congress. When the moderate Democrats and Whigs formed a coalition Union party for the purpose of committing Georgia to Henry Clay's compromise proposal, Gartrell championed the extreme Southern rights view, stumping the state against his former law teacher Toombs, Alexander H. Stephens, and Howell Cobb.

Elected to represent his district in Congress in 1857, Gartrell became a strong advocate of secession, and when the Georgia delegation withdrew from Congress, he too resigned. His secessionist feelings led him to organize the Seventh Georgia Infantry Regiment in May 1861 at Atlanta. He was elected its first colonel. Assigned to Col. Francis S. Bartow's brigade of the Army of the Shenandoah, the regiment fought at First Manassas. Both Gartrell's sixteen-year-old son and Bartow were killed there. When Bartow fell from his horse, Gartrell caught him and Bartow died in his arms.

In November 1861, Gartrell easily won election to the Confederate House of Representatives. He resigned his commission in January 1862. In Congress Gartrell was chairman of the Committee on the Judiciary. He tried unsuccessfully to enable members of the Confederate cabinet to discuss on the floor of Congress matters relating to their departments. He was an ardent supporter of President Jefferson Davis and his administration, and in 1863 he caused a stir when he went before the Georgia legislature to praise Davis. In his legislative program, he proposed making Treasury notes legal tender, ending all military substitutions and exemptions, drafting employees in the executive departments, nationalizing the textile industry, and permitting the president to suspend the writ of habeas corpus when the public safety required it. He served until 1864 and did not seek reelection.

Gartrell was reappointed brigadier general to date from August 22, 1864. He returned to Georgia and organized four regiments of Georgia reserves known as Gartrell's Brigade, which he commanded until the end of the war. His men opposed Sherman's march into South Carolina, and it was their tenacious fighting in 1864 at Coosawhatchie that enabled Lt. Gen. William J. Hardee's Savannah garrison to withdraw, although nearly hemmed in by Sherman's soldiers. Wounded again during this attempt to stop Sherman, Gartrell was sent back to Augusta.

After the war, Gartrell resumed his legal career as a criminal lawyer in Atlanta. He was described by a contemporary as "a powerful robust man, full of animal spirits, and a ready debater." He played a prominent part in the state constitutional convention in 1877 and ran unsuccessfully against Alexander H. Stephens in 1882 for the Democratic gubernatorial nomination. Gartrell died in Atlanta April 7, 1891, and was buried in Oakland Cemetery.

LUCIUS JEREMIAH GARTRELL.   LIBRARY OF CONGRESS

BIBLIOGRAPHY

Coleman, Kenneth, and Charles Stephen Gurr, eds. *Dictionary of Georgia Biography.* Vol. 1. Athens, Ga., 1983.

Crute, Joseph H. *Units of the Confederate Army.* Midlothian, Va., 1987.

Faust, Patricia L., ed. *Historical Times Encyclopedia of the Civil War*. New York, 1986.

Warner, Ezra J., and W. Buck Yearns. *Biographical Register of the Confederate Congress*. Baton Rouge, La., 1975.

JOHN R. WOODARD

GARY, MARTIN WITHERSPOON (1831–1881), brigadier general. Born in Cokesbury, South Carolina, Gary entered South Carolina College in 1850, but was expelled in his junior year for participating in a student rebellion. He graduated from Harvard University in 1854 and returned to his native state, where he studied law and was admitted to the South Carolina bar the following year. Steeped in the politics of Southern nationalism, Gary was known as an ardent secessionist, and following his election to the South Carolina House of Representatives in 1860, he voted to convene a secession convention.

At the outbreak of war Gary resigned his commission in the state militia and volunteered for Confederate service in the Hampton Legion. Distinguished by his erect bearing, sharp features, and balding head, he became known as the "Bald Eagle" and rose in rank from captain to brigadier general. In temporary command of Hampton's Legion at First Manassas, he gained a reputation as a fierce warrior and led Confederate forces in numerous engagements including the Peninsular campaign, Second Manassas, Sharpsburg, Fredericksburg, and Petersburg. The last general officer to evacuate Richmond, he performed his final service for the Confederacy by escorting the fleeing entourage of President Jefferson Davis.

After the war, Gary resumed his legal and political career and became a leading figure in ending Reconstruction government and restoring the conservative regime to political power in South Carolina. Having revived a moribund Democratic party, he exploited racial tensions and used force and intimidation to disfranchise black voters. He was elected to the South Carolina Senate in 1876 and 1878. His path to the U.S. Senate, however, was blocked by moderate Democrats who rejected his racial extremism. Gary died in April 1881.

BIBLIOGRAPHY

Freeman, Douglas S. *Lee's Lieutenants: A Study in Command*. 3 vols. New York, 1942–1944. Reprint, New York, 1986.

Gary, Martin Witherspoon. Papers. Manuscript Division, South Caroliniana Library, University of South Carolina, Columbia.

Hollis, Daniel Walker. *South Carolina College*. Vol. 1. Columbia, S.C., 1951.

Sheppard, William Arthur. *Red Shirts Remembered: Southern Brigadiers of the Reconstruction Period*. Atlanta, 1940.

ROBERT T. BARRETT

GATLIN, RICHARD CASWELL (1809–1896), brigadier general. Gatlin was born in Lenoir County, North Carolina, on January 18, 1809. He attended the University of North Carolina and graduated thirty-fifth in his class from the U.S. Military Academy at West Point in 1832. Gatlin's military career prior to the Civil War spanned a wide area and included service against the Indians on the plains, the Seminoles in Florida, and the Mormons in Utah. He received a brevet for gallant and meritorious service in the Mexican War Battle of Monterrey and gained promotion to major in the regular army in February 1861.

Resigning his commission in the Fifth U.S. Infantry in May 1861, Gatlin accepted an appointment as adjutant general of North Carolina, with the rank of major general in the state militia and colonel in the Confederate army. He received a promotion to brigadier general in the Confederate army, to date from July 8, 1861, and an assignment to command the Department of North Carolina. As the officer with responsibility for the state's coastal defenses, he became the subject of much criticism following the Union capture of Fort Hatteras and the subsequent loss of New Bern to Federal forces under Brig. Gen. Ambrose E. Burnside. Gatlin was relieved of his command on March 19, 1862, and resigned his commission in September 1862. He continued to serve as adjutant general of North Carolina for the remainder of the war. After it ended, Gatlin immigrated to Arkansas, where he farmed until his death on September 8, 1896.

BIBLIOGRAPHY

Johnson, Robert U., and C. C. Buel, eds. *Battles and Leaders of the Civil War*. 4 vols. New York, 1887–1888. Reprint, Secaucus, N.J., 1982.

U.S. War Department. *War of the Rebellion: A Compilation of the Official Records of the Union and Confederate Armies*. Washington, D.C., 1880–1901. Ser. 1, vol. 4, pp. 573–579.

Warner, Ezra J. *Generals in Gray: Lives of the Confederate Commanders*. Baton Rouge, La., 1959.

BRIAN S. WILLS

GENTRY, MEREDITH POINDEXTER (1809–1866), congressman from Tennessee. Gentry was born September 15, 1809, in Rockingham County, North Carolina. As a child he moved with his parents to Williamson County, Tennessee, where his father purchased a farm. He attended neighborhood schools until fourteen; afterward he read widely.

Gentry became a leader in the Whig party soon after its formation, and in 1835 he was elected to the state legislature where he served two terms. In 1839, he was elected to Congress and served continually (with the exception of one term) until 1853. As a congressman, he established himself as an outstanding orator, and he was heard frequently in denunciation of the Mexican War, President James K. Polk's administration, and Democratic-sponsored measures generally. Becoming disillusioned with politics and Whig candidates for public office, he retired to his Williamson County farm in 1853. Two years later he came out of retirement to run for governor against incumbent Andrew Johnson but was defeated by 1,500 votes out of 130,000 cast.

With the approach of civil war, Gentry strongly opposed secession, but after Fort Sumter he championed the cause of the South. He was elected to the First Congress from the Sixth District in November 1861 and became a candidate for House Speaker. In Congress, he first urged an entirely volunteer army but later supported conscription. But his attendance at congressional sessions was poor, and he did not run for reelection. He returned home, sold his Williamson County farm, moved to Nashville, and died there on November 2, 1866. He was buried in Mount Olivet Cemetery.

BIBLIOGRAPHY

Bergeron, Paul. *Antebellum Politics in Tennessee.* Lexington, Ky., 1982.

Journal of the Congress of the Confederate States of America, 1861–1865. 7 vols. Washington, D.C., 1904–1905.

McBride, Robert, and Dan M. Robison. *Biographical Directory of the Tennessee General Assembly.* Vol. 1. Nashville, Tenn., 1975.

Temple, Oliver P. *Notable Men of Tennessee, from 1835 to 1875.* New York, 1912.

Warner, Ezra J., and W. Buck Yearns. *Biographical Register of the Confederate Congress.* Baton Rouge, La., 1975.

ROBERT E. CORLEW

GEORGIA. A record turnout in the 1860 election in Georgia gave Southern Democrat John C. Breckinridge a plurality of 51,893 votes, but Constitutional Unionist John Bell tallied 42,886 and Northern Democrat Stephen A. Douglas, 11,580. On January 19, 1861, a popularly elected convention voted to secede from the Union, and the initial narrow margin of 166 to 130 revealed again the ambivalence that had surfaced in the earlier presidential election. With a population of 1,057,286 (including 465,698 blacks of whom all but 3,500 were slaves) Georgia contributed approximately 120,000 troops to the Confederacy. That plus a booming agriculture centered around King Cotton, a rapidly expanding industrial base including many textile mills, and an extensive railroad network radiating out from the hub of Atlanta to the other growing cities of Savannah, Augusta, Macon, and Columbus made the Empire State of the South second only to Virginia within the Confederacy.

The state's political leaders adjusted quickly to the rush of events as a new order emerged. In Montgomery, Alabama, Georgians played a major role at the convention that established the new Confederate government. Howell Cobb presided over the assembly, which became the Provisional Congress, his younger brother Thomas R. R. Cobb played the major role in drafting the Confederate Constitution, Alexander H. Stephens became vice president of the new nation, and Robert Toombs accepted the post of secretary of state. Back home the state convention functioned as a legislature for a while and also formulated a new state constitution, again largely the work of Thomas Cobb. Governor Joseph E. Brown, an ardent secessionist, seized scattered Federal installations and mobilized troops and equipment, but he was less enthusiastic about cooperating with the new Confederate government, an ominous sign. Then on April 12 war erupted, and most of the upper South joined the Confederacy.

Governor Brown's Policies. Brown's call for volunteers on April 18 brought forth thousands of new troops, but equipment was scarce, and he tried to keep weapons from being carried out of the state by departing Georgia forces. This and his efforts to control military units and appoint their officers led to increasing clashes with Confederate officials.

Brown was loyal to the Confederacy, but he was more devoted to old Southern traditions like state rights, individual freedoms, and strict legalism, and he refused to subordinate them in the interest of the centralized war effort that was necessary for victory. Nevertheless Brown was an able administrator and a brilliant politician who understood his white constituents and rallied them to support Georgia's war effort, if not always the Confederacy's. Thus when he ran for an unprecedented third term in November he won easily, as he did again in 1863.

In April 1862 the Confederate government enacted the first national draft in American history, and Brown, convinced that it was unconstitutional, led the opposition. He tried to maintain control of all militia and other state troops, but the legislature gave him only limited support and the state supreme court sided with the Confederates. Grudgingly he yielded and rebuilt state forces with men too young or too old for the draft. Then each time the embattled Confederates later expanded the age limits of the draft, he waged the same struggle first to hold on to his own state army and then to rebuild it with older and younger recruits. He also granted draft exemptions to thousands of state employees, including militia officers, setting a precedent other states followed in their erratic enforcement of the unpopular conscription law.

Governor Brown also led his people's opposition to impressment, especially the requisition of slave laborers by the Confederate army. He blocked the imposition of martial law in Atlanta in 1862, as well as Confederate efforts to

FIRST FLAG OF INDEPENDENCE RAISED IN THE SOUTH.   Upon hearing of Abraham Lincoln's election, a public meeting held in Johnson Square, Savannah, adopted a resolution for a state secession convention. In this depiction, a crowd surrounds an obelisk bearing a banner with a coiled rattlesnake and the words "Our Motto Southern Rights, Equality of the States, Don't Tread on Me." The old City Exchange is visible behind. Originally, the lithograph contained a border on which was printed "The first Flag of Independence raised in the South, by the citizens of Savannah, Ga. November 8th, 1860." This copy was also inscribed with the words "Presented by Jos Pendergast to John Devereaux Nov 1960. J. P. helped to make the above Banner and himself painted the lettering thereon." The scene was drawn by Henry Cleenwerck and lithographed by R. H. Howell in Savannah, November 1860.   LIBRARY OF CONGRESS

control the state-owned Western and Atlantic Railroad the following years. He often criticized Confederate tax and blockade-running policies. His resistance to the Davis administration in Richmond peaked with attacks on arbitrary arrests and the suspension of the writ of habeas corpus, and early in 1864 he gained legislative backing on this issue. Brown sometimes cooperated with the Confederate government, but more often he was intransigent; increasingly the governor and the president engaged in bitter, hostile correspondence.

Brown had influential allies in his struggle against the Confederate government. Vice President Stephens, too, soon began to quarrel with the president, and by mid-1863 he was spending most of his time in Georgia denouncing the Davis "despotism." His brother Linton Stephens pursued the same policy in the state legislature. Robert Toombs

served only briefly as secretary of state and then as an army officer; by 1863 he too had returned to Georgia and joined the anti-Davis faction. These powerful politicians spearheaded the state rights crusade in Georgia, which increasingly undermined the Confederate war effort on the home front.

But Brown's main allies were the white masses whom he consistently championed. Early in the war he acted to supply Georgia troops with adequate clothing and equipment, and later he sent state agents far afield and even abroad with chartered steamships to acquire what was needed. He showed equal concern for the ordinary folks on the homefront. The governor ordered the state penitentiary to manufacture cotton cards so thread could be prepared for spinning, and he obtained and efficiently distributed scarce salt for preserving meat. He organized relief for the needy

GEORGIA'S LAST PREWAR DELEGATION TO THE U.S. CONGRESS.   This group attended the Thirty-sixth Session of the U.S. Congress, March 4, 1859, to March 3, 1861. They left after January 19, 1861, when Georgia passed its ordinance of secession. Pictured in the top row, from left to right, are Rep. John W. H. Underwood, Rep. Peter E. Love, and Rep. Lucius Jeremiah Gartrell. In the middle row, from left to right, are Rep. Martin J. Crawford, Sen. Robert Toombs, Sen. Alfred Iverson, and Rep. James Jackson. In the bottom row, from left to right, are Rep. Thomas Hardeman, Rep. John J. Jones, and Rep. Joshua Hill.

HARPER'S PICTORIAL HISTORY OF THE GREAT REBELLION

families of soldiers, and by the last two years of the war he had set up an extensive and expensive welfare system to assist the yeoman masses who bore the heaviest burdens of the war. Governor Brown pushed through the legislature a program of tax reforms, and he boosted food production by reducing cotton acreage and restricting distilling. Within Georgia, Brown ran an efficient operation with a special concern for the white masses, but he remained an ardent advocate of state rights and failed to channel the state's resources fully into the Confederate war effort.

Georgia's Economy. The state's resources were formidable. Its impressive prewar industries expanded rapidly if unevenly. Heavy industry boomed mostly in the fast-growing cities. The Confederates built a huge gunpowder mill in Augusta, and the railroad center of Atlanta had one of the few large rolling mills in the South. All five major cities had at least one arsenal, and growing towns like Athens, Dalton, and Rome also expanded operations, as all manner of military equipment was manufactured by Confederate and state plants and private factories fulfilling government contracts.

The state's large textile industry operated at full blast, but could not expand owing to a shortage of machinery. Shoe factories operated at full capacity, too, mostly fulfilling army contracts, but demand remained greater than supply. Iron production increased only a little.

Overall, Georgia's businesspeople, manufacturers, and managers worked effectively, though some profiteers helped fuel rampant inflation. Skilled and ordinary laborers, augmented by women and blacks, also performed well, but shortages of labor, capital, and machinery hindered all efforts to match the Northern industrial machine that was simply too powerful.

The state's prewar railroad system was quite extensive, and it ran well for several years. But no new lines were built, and overburdened equipment began to break down. Finally invading Union armies literally tore up the deteriorating system.

Overall Georgia's economy was sound in 1861, but the demands of the war were too great, and soon a ruinous inflation began to sweep through the land. Like the central government, Georgians relied too much on loans and not enough on taxes to finance the war, and soon the Confederacy, the states, banks, and even private businesses were pumping out floods of paper money, which became increasingly worthless. Hard money faded away, goods became scarce, and prices soared. By 1864 corn was selling in Atlanta for ten dollars a bushel and Irish potatoes for twenty dollars a bushel while soldiers at the front earned only eleven dollars a month!

Disaffection Increases. The snowballing inflation helped erode morale on the home front. Even in the early days of wartime enthusiasm, Unionism had persisted, especially in the hills of North Georgia where not even Governor Brown's political skills could restrain growing hostility to the war effort. As the war dragged on and casualties mounted and battles were lost, disaffection increased everywhere. Unpopular Confederate policies like conscription and impressment were magnified by the criticisms of the state's leaders. And always inflation worked its destructive way, convincing many Georgians that their world was out of control, that they might even lose the war. Moreover, the Emancipation Proclamation and the Union's increasing recruitment of black troops, mostly former slaves, prodded the South's most sensitive nerve.

More and more soldiers deserted the army to come home and look after their families, and a peace movement surfaced in western Georgia. Early in 1864, with William Tecumseh Sherman's huge army poised to invade North Georgia, a special session of the legislature denounced Confederate policies and toyed with the idea of peace negotiations. By the time Sherman captured Savannah at the end of 1864, many white Georgians had simply given up, as they watched their old way of life vanish.

The War's Impact on Blacks. Black Georgians, nearly half of the population, experienced the war very differently than whites. At the start they had no enthusiasm for secession and the new Confederacy. Indeed, during this formative period they endured a wave of terror, including lynchings, and the harsh slave code was made even more repressive.

Some slaves lived much as they always had, but as more and more white men marched off to war, many blacks found new opportunities. Some went with Confederate troops to the front as cooks, teamsters, and servants, and others were impressed to work on fortifications. Some were moved away from the threat of Union invasion, and others entered booming war industries. All this disrupted the slave system (and many black families) as change swept through the South.

Some blacks remained obedient, but others saw a new day dawning and became increasingly restless. Occasionally rumors of insurrection surfaced only to die out quickly. The few individual slaves who did strike out received summary treatment at the hands of courts or mobs. Many others ran away, a traditional method of resistance that greatly increased during the war. At first runaways headed in a steady trickle for the Union-held Sea Islands on the coast. Later they fled by the thousands to Sherman's invading army; he did not want them, but many stayed anyway. By then they knew that the North was winning and that its victory would mean the end of slavery. Many blacks became more assertive, discomfiting whites.

Although wartime privations hit blacks even harder than whites, many labored on under strict supervision. As in peacetime, they had no real choice; the slave system employed relentless and often brutal force. In agriculture, in new fields like hospital work and railroad and other transportation facilities, and especially in industry, slave laborers made a massive, indeed essential contribution to the South's war effort. At the same time traditional forms of resistance like loafing, stealing, and sabotage increased, as many blacks prayed for Union victory and helped the invading armies when they could. Like whites, black Georgians watched the old regime disintegrate as they struggled to survive in the rising chaos.

The desperate Confederate government moved to exploit black manpower fully in late March 1865 when it offered freedom for honorable service in the decimated ranks of its armies. The Union had been recruiting black Southerners for its armed forces since the spring of 1862 when field hands from the liberated Sea Islands along the South Carolina and Georgia coast were enlisted. Most of the Union's almost 200,000 black troops came from the North or from those areas of Dixie that were occupied before mainland Georgia. The Confederate decision to emulate the Northerners came far too late in the war—Robert E. Lee's army would surrender in less than three weeks—and, of course, Governor Brown and the legislature denounced the whole idea. White Georgia could not bring itself to make such a radical change even in the midst of total war.

Changing Roles of Women. Women on the home front also carried a heavy burden. With more and more men joining the army, they had to fill the gaps, and many for the first time actually managed farms and plantations. This was "man's work" and challenging enough in normal times, but wartime shortages and disruptions and the growing restiveness of the slaves multiplied the difficulties. Finally, women faced the ultimate horror—invasion and occupation by an enemy army.

But they persevered, ran things as normally as possible, and did what had to be done. The number of female teachers increased rapidly, and for the first time some white women like Madame M. C. Cazier of Savannah went to work as nurses in hospitals as far away as Richmond. Others got out old looms and spinning wheels to make clothing for their families and for soldiers, and some swelled the ranks of female wage earners in the booming factories. Women sponsored aid societies and wayside homes for the troops; they staged "starvation parties," plays, dances, bazaars, and other social events for the cause. Young women cut short their courtships amid a flood of wartime marriages that often ended suddenly on distant battlefields. A few belles partied through the war, or tried to, but most women faced up to the hard conditions. After the war many lived on as embittered spinsters and widows, passing their hatred on to later generations of Georgians who learned to say "Yankee" with a snarl.

As inflation steadily priced luxuries and then essentials out of reach, women had to improvise. They created substitute foods like coffee made from acorns, and occasionally they became so desperate for scarce items, especially food, that they banded together and looted government or private supplies in Atlanta, Augusta, Columbus, Macon, Milledgeville, and smaller towns. The increasing number of prostitutes reflected the general breakdown of law and order as the war dragged on.

Most women lived in isolated rural areas and faced intense loneliness. They worked hard, closed ranks with friends and kinfolk, became more active in their churches, and wrote letters to loved ones in the army. These sometimes lengthy and often unsophisticated letters concentrated on local affairs, often mixing humor and gossip with serious business matters, and they powerfully affected morale in the army. Some radiated optimism and patriotism, but gloomy or desperate letters encouraged desertion, which became a major problem as the war continued. Increasingly deserters, bushwhackers, and looters roamed through the countryside, and toward the end Sherman's soldiers sent thousands of citizens and slaves refugeeing into southwestern Georgia and other supposedly secure areas.

The Toll on Institutions. Georgians tried to maintain normalcy in the midst of the growing confusion. Many younger and older white men remained at home; many of draft age found it easy to avoid conscription by hiring a substitute or wangling a medical deferment or occupational exemption. They and black slavepower and white womanpower succeeded in carrying on much as usual—but only for a while.

Twelve daily urban newspapers and sixty smaller journals continued to publish with no real interference from authorities, and some carried Maj. Charles H. Smith's humorous Bill Arp stories, a running "cracker" commentary on the war that became a popular book in 1868. Early in 1863 publishers in Augusta organized the Press Association of the Confederate States to try to share resources and reduce costs, but as the war continued newspapers shrank in size and quality, and many finally faded away as Confederate Georgia crumbled. Book and magazine publishing experienced a similar decline, though Richard Malcolm Johnston during these years published his *Georgia Sketches* describing humorous events in the lives of ordinary folks. The thirteen-year-old Joel Chandler Harris, working as a printer's assistant on a plantation near Eatonton, first heard the African American folktales that later became the basis for his Uncle Remus stories.

Georgia's shaky education system faltered badly. Colleges closed as their students marched off to war, and the state's new white public education system collapsed as funds were shifted to wartime activities. Counties took up the slack as best they could, but many youngsters had no school to attend, and some ended the war little better educated than the children of slaves.

The state's churches were less devastated. Many ministers had opposed secession, but the great majority rallied around the war effort. Though they were draft exempt, some volunteered for combat, and others became hospital commissioners or chaplains in the army, which experienced periodic religious revivals. Ministers at home carried on their good works among increasingly distressed congregations, trying to boost morale. Some championed a liberalization of the slave code as the tide of battle turned against the South.

Military Events in Georgia. Ultimately, of course, the war was decided on the battlefield. Hundreds and then thousands of Georgia soldiers fell, but at first the carnage was far away in Virginia or the West. Then the Union navy began to blockade the coast, brushing aside a feeble Confederate "mosquito fleet" of a few riverboats. By March 1862 Union forces had occupied all the Sea Islands, and the following month their powerful new artillery overwhelmed Fort Pulaski at the mouth of the Savannah River, effectively sealing off the city of Savannah. In the summer of 1863 an amphibious attack destroyed the town of Darien, but five naval bombardments failed to demolish Fort McAllister, a new earth and stone fortification at the mouth of the Ogeechee River.

Probes along the coast continued as the Union blockade tightened, but the real threat to Georgia came from the interior. At first only a few raids threatened the vital Western and Atlantic Railroad running from Chattanooga to Atlanta, and in September 1863 a Southern victory at Chickamauga relieved the pressure. But then Ulysses S. Grant and Sherman took command of the Union forces.

Late in November at Lookout Mountain and Missionary Ridge, Union attacks sent the Confederate army reeling back into northwestern Georgia. Grant moved on to face Lee in Virginia, and in the spring of 1864, Sherman's army of nearly 100,000 men moved south along the Western and Atlantic Railroad toward Atlanta. Joseph E. Johnston's army of 55,000 men fought a series of delaying actions and even threw back the attacking Federals at Kennesaw Mountain near Atlanta with heavy losses. But always Sherman's troops flowed around the Southern flanks, and by summer Atlanta was besieged.

President Jefferson Davis replaced cautious Johnston with reckless John Bell Hood who squandered troops in poorly coordinated attacks and then marched north to escape encirclement. On September 2 Sherman's troops occupied Atlanta; only the fall of Richmond could have stunned the South more. In the North Abraham Lincoln's reelection in November was virtually assured, which in turn meant that the Union war effort would not falter.

Sherman sent sufficient troops after Hood's army to

REVIEW OF CLINCH RIFLES IN AUGUSTA, GEORGIA.

FRANK LESLIE'S ILLUSTRATED FAMOUS LEADERS AND BATTLE SCENES OF THE CIVIL WAR

finish it off later in Tennessee. Then he forced all remaining civilians to leave Atlanta and began planning his famous "march to the sea." During this crucial period Governor Brown furloughed ten thousand state troops to keep them out of Confederate control. He and Stephens at first rejected Sherman's peace feelers, but soon the governor was openly calling for peace as morale plummeted throughout the state.

On November 10, after burning most of what remained of battered Atlanta, Sherman cut all supply and communication lines and led 63,000 battle-hardened veterans into the heart of the state against only token resistance. Some expected him to follow the route of an earlier unsuccessful cavalry raid and head for Macon and Andersonville where 13,000 Union prisoners of war had already died in appalling squalor. But instead he followed the main rail line toward Savannah, tearing up track as he went. He relaxed discipline, spread his men over a forty-to-sixty-mile front, and ordered the destruction of bridges, mills, factories, salt supplies, and other resources. His men responded all too eagerly and despoiled homes and private property as well, though they generally refrained from murder and rape. On November 22 they entered the capital at Milledgeville, destroyed production facilities, and looted a little, but they did not damage government buildings, including the statehouse where they held a mock session of the legislature and rescinded the ordinance of secession (by a unanimous vote).

Concentrating their numbers more, they moved on in a southeastern direction along the Central of Georgia Railroad. A month later they approached Savannah as the ten-thousand-man Confederate garrison retreated northward. On December 22 Sherman and his troops marched triumphantly into the state's largest city, offering it to President Lincoln as a Christmas present. Old Savannah gave up without a fight; Confederate Georgia had had enough.

Georgians knew they were beaten, but the war dragged on for a few more months. After resting and refitting, Sherman's army headed north into South Carolina on February 1. The final blow in Georgia came from an entirely new direction. Only a few days after Lee surrendered at Appomattox, Union Gen. James H. Wilson and thirteen thousand crack cavalrymen slashed into western Georgia from Alabama, scattered Gen. Howell Cobb's few thousand militiamen, captured Columbus on April 16, and burned its many factories. Wilson's troopers rode on to capture Macon on April 20, and Governor Brown surrendered the last state troops early in May. Brown, Stephens, Cobb, and a few other Georgians were briefly imprisoned, but Toombs escaped to Europe.

One final Confederate drama remained to be played out in Georgia. President Davis had fled south from Richmond early in April, and the remnants of his government held its last official meeting at the well-to-do Georgia town of Washington not far from the Carolina border. Davis rode on farther south, hoping to carry on somehow, and Union troops captured him near Irwinville, Georgia, on May 10, only a few days before the last Confederate soldiers surrendered in Texas.

The war was finally over. White Georgians faced the bleak reality of total defeat. Black Georgians gained freedom, but the promise of equality soon turned to ashes. For generations all Georgians would be haunted by the awesome struggle of the war.

[*For further discussion of battles and campaigns fought in Georgia, see* Andrews Raid; Atlanta, Georgia, *article on* Atlanta Campaign; Chickamauga Campaign; Fort Pulaski, Georgia; March to the Sea, Sherman's. *For further discussion of Georgia cities, see* Atlanta, Georgia, *article on* City of Atlanta; Macon, Georgia; Savannah, Georgia, *article on* City of Savannah. *See also* African Americans in the Union Army; Georgia Military Institute; *and biographies of numerous figures mentioned herein.*]

BIBLIOGRAPHY

Boney, F. N. "War and Defeat." In *A History of Georgia.* Edited by Kenneth Coleman. Athens, Ga., 1991.

Bryan, T. Conn. *Confederate Georgia.* Athens, Ga., 1953.

DeCredico, Mary A. *Patriotism for Profit: Georgia's Urban Entrepreneurs and the Confederate War Effort.* Chapel Hill, N.C., 1990.

Escott, Paul D. "Georgia." In *The Confederate Governors.* Edited by W. Buck Yearns. Athens, Ga., 1985.

Hill, Louise B. *Joseph E. Brown and the Confederacy.* Chapel Hill, N.C., 1939.

Johnson, Michael P. *Toward a Patriarchal Republic: The Secession of Georgia.* Baton Rouge, La., 1977.

Lane, Mills, ed. *War is Hell: William T. Sherman's Personal Narrative of His March through Georgia.* Savannah, Ga., 1974.

Mohr, Clarence L. *On the Threshold of Freedom: Masters and Slaves in Civil War Georgia.* Athens, Ga., 1986.

Parks, Joseph H. *Joseph E. Brown of Georgia.* Baton Rouge, La., 1977.

Schott, Thomas E. *Alexander H. Stephens of Georgia: A Biography.* Baton Rouge, La., 1988.

Thomas, Emory M. *The Confederate Nation: 1861–1865.* New York, 1979.

F. N. BONEY

GEORGIA. The iron-hulled, brig-rigged cruiser *Georgia* measured 210 feet long, 27 feet in beam, 15 feet in depth of hold, 1,150 tons displacement, and 648 tons gross. Two boilers provided steam to steeple-type, geared condensing engines, yielding a trial speed of 13.66 knots. The ship was built in 1863 by Alexander Denny & Company of Dumbarton, Scotland. Confederate foreign purchasing agent Commdr. Matthew Fontaine Maury bought the vessel for the

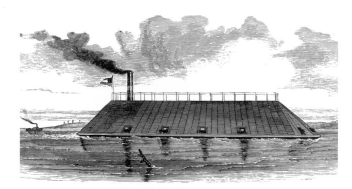

THE IRONCLAD RAM *GEORGIA*.   *FRANK LESLIE'S ILLUSTRATED FAMOUS LEADERS AND BATTLE SCENES OF THE CIVIL WAR*

Confederate navy using English shipowner Thomas Bold as cover. The aliases of *Japan* and *Virginian* enhanced secrecy during building. *Georgia* was armed from the tug *Alar* off Ushant, France, and commissioned CSS *Georgia,* April 9, 1863, by Commdr. William L. Maury. Armament consisted of two 10-pounder Whitworth guns, two 24-pounder guns, and a 32-pounder Blakely rifle.

Georgia cruised the north and south Atlantic Ocean against the Northern merchant fleet. On the coast of Morocco, *Georgia* fired on a large group of raiders attacking a shore party, an incident called the "Confederacy's only foreign war." During its cruise *Georgia* captured nine Union merchantmen. It burned the ships *Dictator, Constitution, Bold Hunter,* and clipper bark *Good Hope;* bonded the ships *Prince of Wales, George Griswold, City of Bath,* and *John Watt;* and allowed the bark *J. W. Seaver* to go free. *Georgia*'s cruise was cut short owing to the rapid fouling of its iron hull, which caused a dangerous loss of speed.

On May 10, 1864, *Georgia* was decommissioned, disarmed, and sold to a private Liverpool merchant for Mediterranean trade. USS *Niagara* captured it in international waters, and it was then condemned by a prize court and sold into U.S. service. Later sold to Canadian owners, *Georgia* continued in New England and Canadian maritime trade until lost on the coast of Maine in 1878.

BIBLIOGRAPHY

Lyon, David John. *The Denny List.* London, 1975.

Merli, Frank J. *Great Britain and the Confederate Navy, 1861–1865.* Bloomington, Ind., 1970.

Morgan, James Morris. *Recollections of a Rebel Reefer.* London, 1918.

Scharf, J. Thomas. *History of the Confederate States Navy.* New York, 1887. Reprint, New York, 1977.

Spencer, Warren F. *The Confederate Navy in Europe.* University, Ala., 1983.

KEVIN J. FOSTER

GEORGIA MILITARY INSTITUTE. In 1851 the Georgia Military Institute (GMI) opened its doors at Marietta as a private college. Based on the West Point model as modified by other Southern military colleges, notably the Virginia Military Institute and the South Carolina Military Academy, GMI's military system imposed a strict regimen upon the students, all of whom were required to be members of the school's corps of cadets. In 1858, the college's incorporators offered the school to the state of Georgia, which promptly accepted the offer. Within two years, Georgia Governor Joseph E. Brown was advocating increased enrollment at Georgia's military college, declaring, "We should not only arm our people but we should educate them in the use of arms and the science of war."

Shortly after the bombardment of Fort Sumter, the GMI cadets under the command of Superintendent Maj. Francis Withers Capers, former superintendent of Charleston's Citadel, trained recruits at Marietta's Camp Brown. In mid-June the cadets moved to Camp McDonald near Big Shanty, Georgia, and there helped train another group of raw recruits. Many cadets resigned at Camp McDonald and joined the regiments they had trained. Alumni of the institute served in all ranks of the Confederate army, and one, Pierce Manning Butler Young, rose to the rank of brigadier general.

With the exception of their training recruits and serving bridge guard duty in the wake of the 1862 theft of the locomotive General from Big Shanty by Andrews raiders, the war left the cadets undisturbed until 1864. There is some evidence that they were called to Resaca, Georgia, to bolster Gen. Joseph E. Johnston's lines and may have engaged Federal forces there on May 14, 1864.

In early June, the corps' 177 cadets were sent to guard the vital Chattahoochee River railroad bridge between Atlanta and Montgomery, Alabama. Upon their relief from this duty, the cadets joined the Georgia militia on Independence Day and moved with them into Atlanta's fortifications. On July 3, the Georgia Military Institute, now a Confederate hospital, was seized by Federal Maj. Gen. George H. Thomas for use as his headquarters. After witnessing the great battles around Atlanta, the cadets were transferred to the state capital of Milledgeville on August 20, having lost eight of their number to disease and enemy fire.

During Sherman's March to the Sea, the cadets were incorporated into a scratch battalion, which included convicts and guards from Milledgeville's state penitentiary. Falling back from the capital along the Georgia Central Railroad, this force, under the tactical command of Superintendent Capers, engaged the Federal advance at the Ogeechee and Oconee River railroad bridges. During these skirmishes, one cadet was killed and three were wounded.

By December 16, the corps was in the trenches around Savannah, Georgia. When Lt. Gen. William J. Hardee ordered the evacuation of the city on December 20, the cadets formed part of the army's rear guard. The corps finished the war on provost duty in Augusta, Georgia.

The Georgia Military Institute was burned by Federal forces on November 13, 1864, and was never rebuilt.

BIBLIOGRAPHY

Conrad, James Lee. "Training for Treason." *Civil War Times Illustrated* 30, no. 4 (September-October 1991): 52–57.

Holland, Lynwood M. "The Georgia Military Institute: The West Point of Georgia, 1851–1864." *Georgia Historical Quarterly* 43 (1959).

Temple, Sarah B. G. *The First Hundred Years: A Short History of Cobb County, in Georgia.* Atlanta, 1935.

Yates, Bolling C. *History of the Georgia Military Institute.* N.p., 1968.

JAMES LEE CONRAD

GEORGIA PLATFORM. The Georgia Platform was adopted in December 1850 by a special convention called to consider the state's response to the Compromise of 1850. The Platform announced that, although Georgia did not approve of the Compromise, the state would "abide by it as a permanent adjustment of this sectional controversy." It further specified that Georgia "will and ought to resist, even (as a last resort) to a disruption of every tie which binds her to the Union," any congressional act that repealed or altered the Fugitive Slave Law, that restricted or suppressed the slave trade, or that abolished slavery in the District of Columbia.

Since these were all matters settled by the Compromise, the effect of the Platform was to admit Georgia's acquiescence in the Compromise's principal provision, namely, the admission of California to the Union as a nonslaveholding state. It was this provision that had so excited the Southern states, since it upset the balance of slave and free states in the Senate. Many Southern political leaders feared that the Compromise represented an attempt to enact the Wilmot Proviso, which sought to ban slavery from territories acquired as a result of the Mexican War, and which had passed the House of Representatives but failed in the Senate.

By introducing the slavery question at the national level, the Compromise disrupted party lines in the South and began the formation of new alliances. In Georgia, Whigs, led by Robert Toombs, and Democrats, led by Howell Cobb, joined ranks to form the Constitutional Union party. Highly respected and safe on the slavery question, these men gave repeated assurances that the Compromise did not threaten slavery. They stood in opposition to fire-eaters led by Governor George W. Towns, who sought to precipitate secession of the Southern states. Though less vocal or numerous than in other states, especially South Carolina and Mississippi, the secessionists in Georgia posed a serious threat to the supporters of the Union in that state. And since Georgia was the first state to hold a convention to determine a position on the Compromise, all eyes were focused on Milledgeville when the convention assembled.

The position of "conditional Unionism" as articulated in the Georgia Platform quickly found support in the states of the upper South as well as in Alabama and Louisiana. Thus isolated, secessionists in South Carolina and Mississippi had little success in advancing their cause. The Georgia Platform thus lessened sectional tensions. It also stated clearly the consequences of further congressional interference with slavery, giving warning that any renewal of the slavery question would put the Union at risk.

[*See also* Compromise of 1850; Fugitive Slave Law.]

BIBLIOGRAPHY

Montgomery, Horace. *Cracker Parties.* Baton Rouge, La., 1950.

Shryock, R. H. *Georgia and Union in 1850.* Durham, N.C., 1926.

JOHN MCCARDELL

GERMANS. The second largest white ethnic group in the Confederacy was composed of German immigrants. There were 73,579 in the South on the eve of the Civil War; 20,000 were distributed over eight states and the remaining 53,000 resided in Texas, Louisiana, and Virginia.

The most striking features of the Germans in the Confederacy were their cultural resiliency and their success in the trades and the professions. German culture took firm hold primarily through music, theater, language, and fraternal organizations. Indeed, their community life succeeded in allowing the Germans to preserve their heritage in a foreign, and oftentimes hostile, environment. German culture persisted in the South through agricultural practices, food preparation, arts and architecture, family patterns, and religion. Most German immigrants to the Confederacy were simple people lured to America by the promise of land and wealth and not, contrary to popular belief, political refugees from the failed European revolutions of 1848.

In urban areas such as New Orleans, even successful German immigrants failed to avoid the antiforeign wrath of such groups as the Know-Nothings. Nevertheless, German immigrants mainly remained apart from other residents of urban areas or settled in the rural peripheries of the South such as Texas, Missouri, and Virginia. Some rural areas, particularly in places such as south-central Texas, became known as German belts where their large numbers and geographic isolation enabled the Germans to reconstruct their communal lives and their Old World folkways.

For the German immigrant, the quickest route to

acceptance lay in either heartily endorsing the white majority's opinions or, at the very least, remaining silent. But in Texas, the Germans openly opposed the Confederacy, an attitude that placed them squarely on a collision course with the remainder of the state. Most German Texans opposed slavery on principle and sincerely hoped that the institution would disappear. On one level, their opposition reflected the fact that the small German farmers in Texas had little land and capital and, hence, little use for slave labor. Beyond that, German intellectuals simply disliked the notions of slavery and disunion, as many had left Germany disgusted at the failure there to create a unified homeland.

For many Germans in Texas, slavery and disunion were disappointing contradictions to what America symbolized. To propagate such beliefs in the incipient Confederate States of America was, at best, blasphemous and, at worst, dangerous. This is precisely why some German Texans preached moderation. Ferdinand Lindheimer, editor of the *Neu-Braunfelser Zeitung,* cautioned his fellow Germans to avoid angering Confederate Texans by meddling in their affairs. Lindheimer argued that the controversy over slavery and secession was an old one and that the German newcomers simply did not have enough knowledge about it to form a valid opinion one way or the other.

But many Germans in Texas persisted in their opposition to the Confederacy, a stance that ultimately led to tragedy. On July 4, 1862, German Unionists from several Texas counties formed their own battalion. When news of their activities reached Confederate officials, these counties were declared in open rebellion and placed under martial law. Erroneously believing that they had been granted a safe-conduct, the German battalion left for Mexico. En route, on the morning of August 10, 1862, they were attacked by a Confederate force at what would become known as the Battle of Neuces. So thoroughly defeated were the German Unionists that no one even dared to gather the remains of the fallen soldiers until after the war. Only then were they transported to Comfort, Texas, where they were buried under an obelisk, which bears the inscription *Treie der Union* (loyal to the Union).

Gradually the Germans grew more cautious and at least gave the appearance of supporting the Confederates. Ironically, despite their disaffection, because of their sheer numbers, the largest number of foreign troops sent by Texas into battle were German.

Elsewhere in the South, a company of German residents was raised in Wilmington, and it fought for the Eighteenth North Carolina. Under the leadership of Col. John A. Wagener, another company of Germans, calling themselves the German Volunteers, was raised in Charleston. Germans also provided the manpower for the German Riflemen of the Fourth Brigade of the South Carolina Militia, the Palmetto-Schutzen, the Marion Rifles, the German Fusiliers, and the German Hussars, a company in the South Carolina Cavalry. South Carolina Germans also formed three companies in the artillery. Still other Germans fought valiantly for the Confederacy in companies raised in Georgia, Tennessee, Virginia, and Louisiana.

BIBLIOGRAPHY

Jordan, Terry G. *German Seed in Texas Soil: Immigrant Farmers in Nineteenth Century Texas.* Austin, Tex., 1966.

Lich, Glen E. *The German Texans.* San Antonio, Tex., 1981.

Lonn, Ella. *Foreigners in the Confederacy.* Chapel Hill, N.C., 1940. Reprint, Gloucester, Mass., 1965.

Silverman, Jason H. *Beyond the Melting Pot in Dixie: Immigration and Ethnicity in Southern History.* Lexington, Ky., forthcoming.

Silverman, Jason H. "Stars, Bars, and Foreigners: The Immigrant and the Making of the Confederacy." *Journal of Confederate History* 1 (1988): 265–285.

Wust, Klaus. *The Virginia Germans.* Charlottesville, Va., 1969.

JASON H. SILVERMAN

GETTYSBURG CAMPAIGN.

GETTYSBURG CAMPAIGN. Following the Union defeat at Chancellorsville in May 1863, Robert E. Lee sought approval from the Confederate government to mount an invasion of Maryland and Pennsylvania with his Army of Northern Virginia. The North was becoming increasingly despondent over the progress of the war with the repeated failures of the Northern armies and their attendant high casualties. Lee believed he could build momentum for the growing Northern peace movement by shifting his army to Northern soil and inflicting a defeat upon the Federal Army of the Potomac. Operations in Pennsylvania would also allow Lee to provision his army from the rich agricultural areas of Pennsylvania's Cumberland Valley, while relieving Virginia from the destructive presence of contending armies. Finally, Harrisburg, the Pennsylvania capital, could be threatened or perhaps temporarily captured, adding further embarrassment to the Lincoln administration and fuel for the peace movement.

Lee's proposal initially met with opposition in Richmond. There was concern over the security of the Confederate capital while Lee moved north. Some thought was also given to detaching elements of Lee's army to help break the siege of Vicksburg, Mississippi, by the Federal army of Ulysses S. Grant. It was also discussed whether Lee himself, with major elements of his army, should be shifted to Tennessee to mount an offensive against the Federal army under William Rosecrans. Lee's opinion ultimately prevailed, and it was agreed the invasion should take place. It was hoped that by taking the offensive in the east, the Federal forces threatening Vicksburg and Chattanooga would be forced to detach troops to drive Lee out of Pennsylvania.

In preparation for the invasion, Lee reorganized his army into three corps of approximately 20,000 men apiece. The

First Corps remained under Gen. James Longstreet's command. The Second Corps (Stonewall Jackson's old corps) was placed under Gen. Richard S. Ewell. The Third Corps, under Gen. A. P. Hill, was formed with elements of Jackson's old corps and with new troops from outside the army. The cavalry division, under Gen. J. E. B. Stuart, was reinforced to six brigades. Lee's total strength was approximately 75,000 men and 280 guns.

The leading elements of Lee's army left their camps near Fredericksburg, Virginia, on June 3. Ewell and Longstreet's corps led the way, screened by Stuart's cavalry, while Hill remained behind temporarily to observe and deceive the Federals.

The Union Army of the Potomac, under Gen. Joseph Hooker, was aware that Lee was on the move, but was uncertain of the Confederate's intentions. On June 9, he ordered his cavalry commander, Gen. Alfred Pleasonton, to conduct a reconnaissance in force, with 11,000 men, across the Rappahannock in the direction of Brandy Station. Pleasonton surprised the Confederate cavalry, and the largest cavalry battle of the entire war ensued. Although Stuart recovered from his initial surprise and forced Pleasonton back, the battle caused him great embarrassment. Stuart's losses were 523 out of approximately 10,000, while Pleasonton lost 837.

Brandy Station failed to check the movement of the Army of Northern Virginia, and the leading elements of the army entered the Shenandoah Valley on June 12. Hooker received definite intelligence concerning this on the thirteenth and promptly issued orders for his army to withdraw from the line of the Rappahannock and march north to a new point of concentration around the Centreville, Virginia, area.

While Hooker's army repositioned itself and Hill and Longstreet marched toward the Valley, Ewell's Second Corps arrived before Winchester, Virginia. Garrisoning Winchester was Gen. Robert Milroy's Second Division of the Eighth Corps, numbering approximately 9,000 men. Ewell launched a skillfully conducted attack late on the fourteenth and penetrated Milroy's defenses. That night, at 2:00 A.M., Milroy attempted to retreat but ran into a trap laid by Ewell. The Federals were routed and Milroy lost 4,443 men, most of whom were captured. Ewell's losses were 269.

Into Pennsylvania. On June 15, the leading elements of Lee's army entered Pennsylvania. By the twenty-fourth, Ewell's entire corps was bivouacked near Chambersburg, Pennsylvania. Hill's corps crossed the Potomac into Maryland on the same day with Longstreet's corps a day's march behind. In what proved to be one of the crucial decisions of the campaign, Lee gave discretionary orders to Stuart to take three of his brigades and march north, crossing the Potomac either east or west of the Blue Ridge Mountains, and eventually to take position on Ewell's right in Pennsylvania. Given the choice, Stuart chose to cut across the rear of the Federal army, crossing well east of the Blue Ridge.

Stuart's raid encountered numerous obstacles in its effort to circuit the Union rear. Powerful infantry columns forced him to make time-consuming detours in his march and an improved and aggressive Federal cavalry engaged him in several skirmishes that caused further delays and detours. Stuart captured a supply train of 125 wagons and 400 prisoners, but it was small compensation for Lee who was deprived of his best cavalry during the critical days of the campaign. Stuart would not rejoin the army until July 2.

By June 28, both Longstreet's and Hill's corps were camped in the vicinity of Chambersburg. Ewell's corps pushed farther east to threaten Harrisburg. Robert Rodes's and Edward Johnson's divisions occupied Carlisle, while Jubal Early's division marched to York, Pennsylvania. On the morning of the twenty-eighth, troopers of Albert Gallatin Jenkins's cavalry brigade advanced to within four miles of Harrisburg. This was to be the deepest Confederate forces penetrated into Pennsylvania, for Lee was forced to cancel the operations against Harrisburg and order Ewell to withdraw from his advanced positions owing to alarming news about the Federal army.

Without Stuart to provide him with timely and accurate information about the enemy, Lee was uncertain of the exact position of the Federal army. He believed it was still south of the Potomac. But on June 28 he was startled to learn through a spy, James Harrison, that the Federal army was massed in the vicinity of Frederick, Maryland, thirty miles south of Gettysburg. If the Federals moved west across South Mountain they would be on Lee's line of communications to Virginia. To prevent this, Lee issued instructions to bring about a concentration of his army east of the mountains in the vicinity of Cashtown, Pennsylvania, about ten miles west of Gettysburg. By positioning his army east of the mountains, Lee posed a threat to both Harrisburg and Baltimore, and he believed this would keep the Federals off his line of communications.

By the twenty-eighth, the Federal army was under new leadership. Hooker had resigned over differences with the War Department regarding the Harpers Ferry garrison. In his place Lincoln appointed Gen. George G. Meade to command. Meade pushed his 93,000 men north from Frederick on a broad front. The left brushed the Catoctin Mountains, while the right stretched nearly thirty miles east. Meade's plan was to cover Baltimore and relieve Harrisburg. When this was accomplished, he would seek battle on the most favorable terms. During the final days of June, Meade's numerous cavalry, which was skillfully screening the front of his advancing army, provided him with strong evidence that Ewell had withdrawn from Harrisburg and that Lee's army was concentrating west of Gettysburg. In response to this Meade shifted the weight of

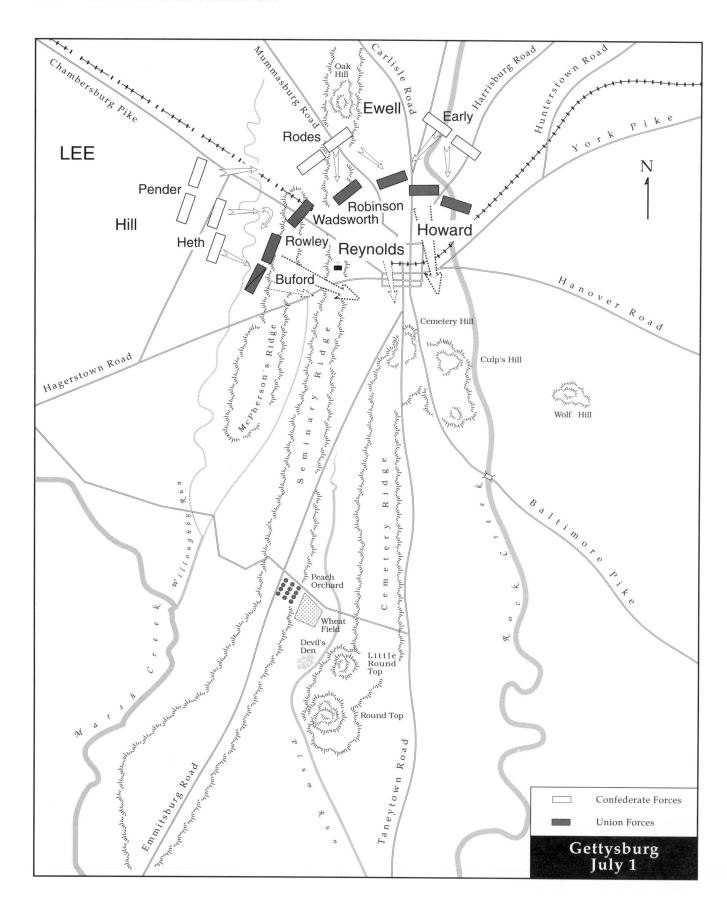

**Gettysburg
July 1**

Confederate Forces
Union Forces

his army to the left and began a gradual concentration of his army toward the Pennsylvania crossroads town. On June 30, John Buford's division of Federal cavalry marched to Gettysburg to secure the town and scout the region. They encountered a Confederate infantry brigade, which withdrew westward without an engagement.

The Confederate brigade belonged to Henry Heth's division of Hill's corps. Its commander reported the presence of Buford in Gettysburg, but Hill was skeptical. The Federal army was still believed to be in Maryland. Nevertheless, Hill planned to investigate. Heth and William Dorsey Pender's divisions, approximately 13,000 men, were ordered to march on Gettysburg on July 1. Their orders were to drive the Federal cavalry away but to halt if infantry was encountered. Lee did not want a general engagement to be precipitated with his concentration east of the mountains uncompleted.

The Federals also planned to move powerful forces to Gettysburg on July 1. Both the First and Eleventh Corps were under orders to march to Gettysburg to Buford's support, and four other corps were to move within supporting distance. The stage was set for the meeting of the opposing armies.

Day One. Contact was made at 5:30 A.M. on July 1 when the advance of Heth struck a picket post of Buford's division. Heth pushed on and encountered a dismounted line of Federal cavalry about two miles west of Gettysburg. Believing it was infantry, Heth deployed two brigades of infantry and pressed rashly ahead. About this time, Maj. Gen. John F. Reynolds, commander of the Union First Corps, arrived upon the battlefield. Exercising the discretion Meade had provided him, Reynolds decided to commit his First Corps and the Eleventh, as they arrived, to the engagement.

Between 10:30 and 11:00 A.M. a meeting engagement between Heth and James Wadsworth's division of the First Corps took place. Heth was soundly beaten, losing several hundred prisoners and the opportunity to seize Gettysburg cheaply. The Federals, although victorious, lost Reynolds, who was killed early in the fighting. They had, however, gained room and time to arrange a defense from which they could delay the Confederates and screen the strong defensive terrain that rose up south of Gettysburg.

Learning of Heth's contact with the enemy, Ewell diverted the march of Early and Rodes to approach Gettysburg from the north. At 1:30 P.M. the action was renewed with Rodes launching an uncoordinated attack upon the First Corps. Lee had arrived upon the battlefield and attempted to prevent the battle from escalating out of control. It was soon evident, however, that this was impossible, and at 2:30 P.M. he permitted Heth's division to advance to Rodes's support. Early arrived from the north and attacked around 3:00 P.M., inflicting a crushing defeat

upon the Eleventh Corps. Heth and Rodes had a more difficult time with the First Corps and lost heavily in their attacks. Late in the afternoon, Hill sent Pender in to relieve Heth and he and Rodes cleared the First Corps from their positions west of town. The Federals fell back in considerable disorder through Gettysburg to Cemetery Hill, immediately south of town, where they were rallied and reorganized by Generals O. O. Howard and Winfield Scott Hancock.

Hill's corps was too exhausted to attempt to complete the Southern victory by attacking Cemetery Hill. Lee therefore sent Ewell directions to carry the hill if it was "practicable" to do so. But Ewell had his own problems and was unable to mount an attack before night brought an end to the fighting. Out of approximately 42,000 men engaged, over 9,000 Federals and approximately 6,800 Confederates were casualties.

Although a Confederate tactical victory, the first day of fighting had been a strategic Union victory. The Federals had gained the advantage of position on ground they had selected. Lee, still without Stuart, was thrust into the role of the attacker, over ground he did not know. But battle had been joined, and Lee was determined to exploit his victory of July 1 by renewing the battle the next day.

Day Two. The early morning of July 2 was spent in reconnoitering the Federal position. Lee was uncertain how heavily the Federals had been reinforced during the night. They were found to be holding a horseshoe-shaped position, running from Culp's Hill to Cemetery Hill and down Cemetery Ridge, where Lee was told the Federal left flank rested. Upon this information he developed his battle plan. Longstreet was directed to take John Bell Hood's and Lafayette McLaws's divisions and conduct a covered march to gain a position that would place them upon the Union left flank. Their attack would be supported by Richard Heron Anderson's division of Hill's corps. It was believed at Lee's headquarters that these three divisions, numbering approximately 20,000 men, would crush the exposed Federal flank. Ewell's orders were to demonstrate against Culp's Hill and Cemetery Hill to pin the Federal defenders in place. If opportunity offered, however, he was given the discretion to deliver a full-scale attack. Longstreet was opposed to the operation and offered his opinion that the Confederates should attempt to outmaneuver the Federals to gain a position from which Lee could fight on the defensive. Lee was unmoved and the offensive was set in motion over Longstreet's objections.

Unknown to Lee, nearly the entire Army of the Potomac was in his front. By forced marches Meade had concentrated his army during the night. Only the Sixth Corps, thirty-five miles distant at Manchester, Maryland, was absent, and it was en route and expected by mid- to late afternoon. Meade had skillfully deployed his army to take advantage of the

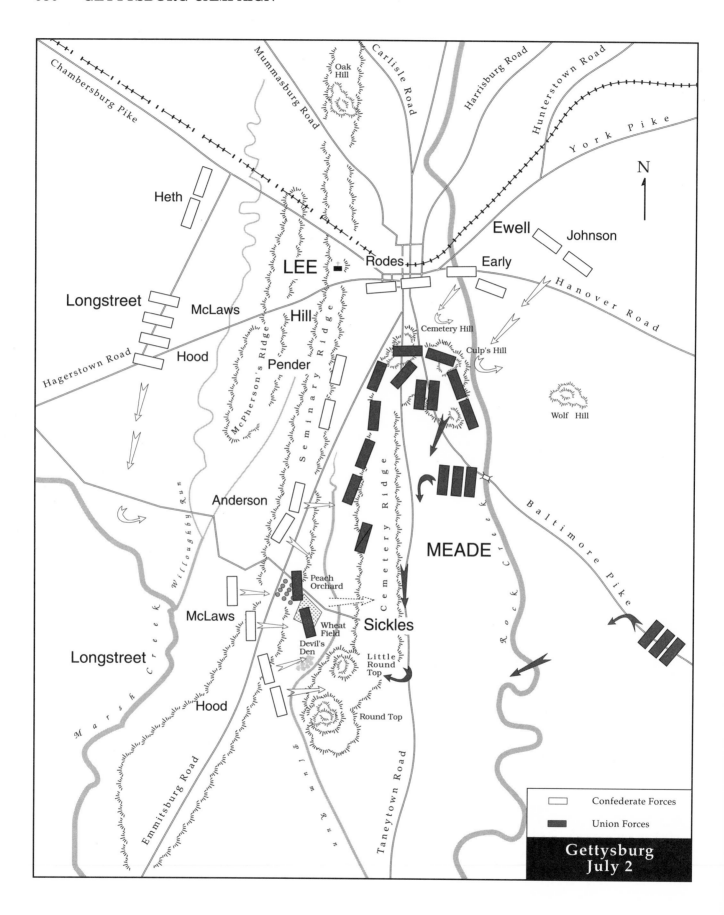

Chambersburg Pike

Mummasburg Road

Oak Hill

Carlisle Road

Harrisburg Road

Hunterstown Road

York Pike

N

Heth

Ewell   Johnson

LEE   Rodes   Early

Hanover Road

Longstreet   McLaws

Hill

Hood

Pender

McPherson's Ridge

Seminary Ridge

Cemetery Hill

Culp's Hill

Wolf Hill

Hagerstown Road

Willoughby Run

Anderson

Cemetery Ridge

Rock Creek

MEADE

Baltimore Pike

McLaws

Peach Orchard

Wheat Field

Sickles

Longstreet

Devil's Den

Little Round Top

Marsh Creek

Hood

Round Top

Plum Run

Emmitsburg Road

Taneytown Road

| | Confederate Forces |
| | Union Forces |

Gettysburg July 2

natural strength of the terrain. His left, contrary to the report of Lee's reconnaissance officers, rested not on Cemetery Ridge but on Little Round Top, nearly three-quarters of a mile south of where Lee believed the Federal flank to be. This sector of the Federal front was to be held by the Third Corps. But its commander, Gen. Daniel E. Sickles, was dissatisfied with his position and shortly after 2:00 P.M. he advanced his entire corps nearly one-half mile in advance of the army's general line. The line Sickles occupied extended for nearly one mile and formed a vulnerable salient angle at the Peach Orchard.

Longstreet's flank march occupied the entire morning and was further delayed when Longstreet discovered Sickles's corps in a completely unexpected position. Not until nearly 3:00 P.M. was Longstreet prepared to open his pre-assault bombardment. A sharp artillery duel ensued for nearly one-half hour. At 3:30, Longstreet's infantry stepped off. Devil's Den and Little Round Top were struck first. The efforts of Meade's chief engineer, Gen. Gouvenour K. Warren, managed to avert disaster on Little Round Top by seeing that infantry from the Fifth Corps were sent to its defense. They arrived not a moment too soon. The battle ebbed and flowed, but ultimately the Federals prevailed.

From Devil's Den the battle spread north to the Wheatfield and then the Peach Orchard. Meade hurried the Fifth Corps to Sickles's aid and stripped troops from elsewhere on his line. The heavy blows of Longstreet's and Anderson's brigades proved too much, however, and around 6:00 P.M. Sickles's line collapsed and streamed east in retreat. Uncommitted elements of the Fifth Corps, a division of the Twelfth Corps from Culp's Hill, and the Sixth Corps, which was beginning to reach the field, managed to stabilize the situation and check the victorious Confederates.

On Lee's left, Ewell had opened an artillery bombardment the moment he had heard the sound of Longstreet's guns. Federal guns responded and an hour-long duel ensued, the result of which was that Ewell's guns were completely silenced. Nearly two hours later Ewell sent his infantry forward. Johnson's division assailed Culp's Hill while two brigades of Early's division attempted to storm Cemetery Hill. Johnson's troops gained abandoned Federal entrenchments near the southern base of Culp's Hill, but the summit was defended by a brigade of New York troops who could not be dislodged. On Cemetery Hill, Early's brigades stormed up the hill, routing several regiments of the Eleventh Corps and getting in among some of the Federal artillery. But they were counterattacked by a brigade of the Second Corps and other Eleventh Corps regiments and driven off the hill. This action marked the end of the second day's fighting. At least 16,500 men or more were casualties.

After the war controversy developed over the cause of the Confederate failure to realize victory on July 2. Former Confederate Gens. William Dorsey Pendleton and Jubal Early selected James Longstreet as the scapegoat. Pendleton published an account affirming that Lee had actually instructed Longstreet to attack the Federals at daylight. Longstreet was also accused of deliberately dragging his feet out of opposition to Lee's plan during his corps flank march into position.

Although Longstreet did not support Lee's plan of attack and was guilty of a sulky and obstinate demeanor on July 2, Pendleton's and Early's charges were inaccurate and without substance. There was no early morning attack order, and although Longstreet's flank march was in some respects poorly managed, there is no evidence that Longstreet attempted to sabotage Lee's plan by delaying his corps march into position.

Day Three. Lee's confidence was unshaken by the failures of the second and he determined to continue the struggle on July 3. "The general plan was unchanged," wrote Lee. Longstreet, reinforced by George E. Pickett's division, which had been guarding wagon trains in Chambersburg, was to renew the attack, apparently at daylight. Johnson's division, heavily reinforced during the night, was to storm Culp's Hill at the same time. Stuart's cavalry, which had at last found the army, was instructed to march beyond the army's left flank and position itself to threaten the Federal rear.

Unfortunately for Lee, his plans were never realized. Meade seized the initiative and counterattacked on Culp's Hill at 4:30 A.M. Longstreet, who may have misunderstood what Lee wished, had prepared orders around sunrise for his corps to attempt to maneuver around the round tops and gain the Federal flank. Under the circumstances, concerted action was now impossible, and Lee was forced to modify his plan of attack. He now determined to launch a massive frontal assault designed to break the Federal center on Cemetery Ridge. A preattack bombardment by nearly 140 guns would cripple the Federal defenders, and then the divisions of Pickett and Pettigrew and one-half of Trimble's (slightly over 12,000 men) would advance over one mile of open ground and smash through the Union defenses. It was a bold, daring plan, and Longstreet, who was given the task of directing the attack, was adamantly opposed. Lee, however, was determined to make the effort, and Longstreet was compelled against his better judgment to carry out the plan.

At 1:00 P.M. the artillery cannonade opened. Between 80 and 100 Federal guns responded, and one of the largest artillery duels of the war ensued. Thick clouds of smoke covered much of the field and hindered the view of the artillerymen on both sides, causing gunners of both armies to overshoot their targets. After nearly one and one-half hours of intense firing, the Federal artillery ceased fire under orders to conserve their ammunition. By the time the

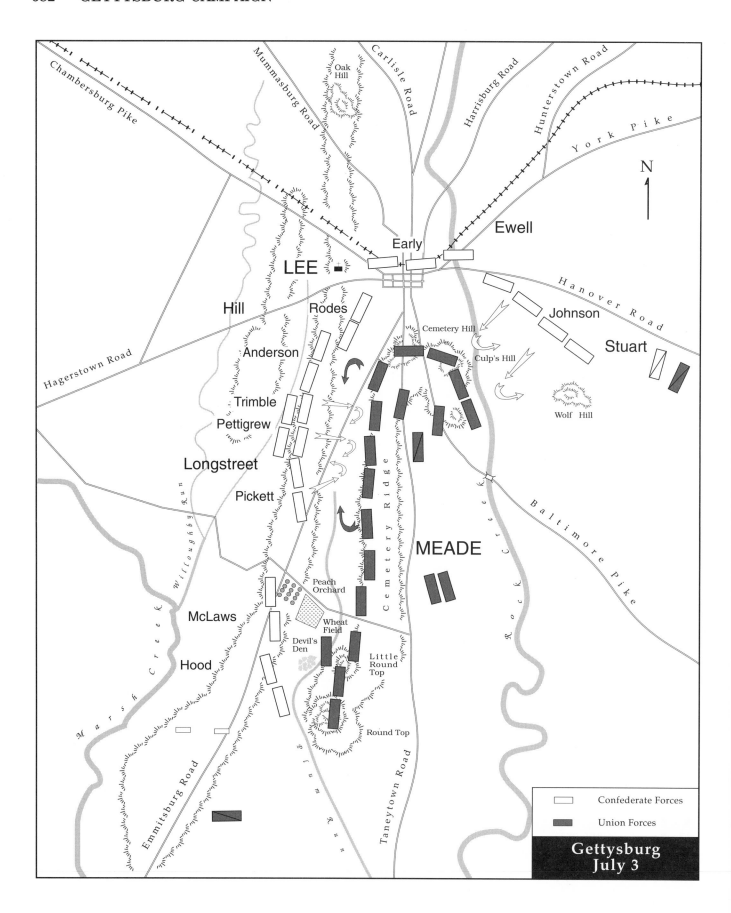

Gettysburg
July 3

Confederate Forces

Union Forces

bombardment stopped at 3:00, the Confederate artillery had exhausted its supply of long-range ammunition and was unable to support the infantry.

The Southern infantry emerged into view shortly after 3:00. Their perfectly preserved lines of battle extended for nearly one mile. The Federal artillery reopened at this time and inflicted terrible losses on the attackers but failed to check them. As the Southern infantry loomed nearer, the Federal infantry added its small-arms fire to the canister of the artillery and the Confederates fell by the hundreds. Federal infantry swung out on both Confederate flanks, which were exposed and unsupported, inflicting more losses and chaos. A small group of men, principally from Pickett's division and led by Gen. Lewis A. Armistead, managed to penetrate the Federal position briefly, but they were quickly overwhelmed. By 4:00 the attack had been repulsed with tragic loss. Between 5,500 and 6,000 Confederate soldiers were casualties, with perhaps as many as 1,000 being killed.

Elsewhere on the field, Johnson's division, after sustaining heavy losses, had retired from Culp's Hill by late morning. Stuart fared no better. His march east was detected, and powerful Federal cavalry units moved to engage him. Several miles east of town a cavalry action ensued that was indecisive, but it was successful in checking Stuart's forward progress.

The Army of Northern Virginia was spent and exhausted. Imperfect casualty figures give its losses at 4,427 killed, 12,179 wounded, and 5,592 missing. Its losses were undoubtedly higher, probably as many as 28,000. The Army of the Potomac had likewise suffered dreadfully: 3,155 killed, 14,529 wounded, and 5,365 missing.

Lee maintained his position on July 4 in hopes that Meade would attack him. He did not, and that night the army commenced its retreat under a heavy rain that helped slow the Federal pursuit. Lee's advance guard arrived at Williamsport, Maryland, on the sixth and discovered the Potomac swollen by rains and impassable. Lee entrenched his army on strong terrain and went to work building a pontoon bridge. Meade had brought his army up by the thirteenth and contemplated an assault, but called it off when the majority of his senior officers advised against it. That night, the pontoon bridge had been completed and the Potomac had fallen so that it was fordable, and Lee withdrew to Virginia. A rearguard action took place on the fourteenth between Buford's cavalry and elements of Heth's and Pender's divisions. The Confederates lost 719 prisoners and General Pettigrew, who was mortally wounded.

The Gettysburg campaign was over. On July 4, Vicksburg surrendered to Grant. The South, with its limited resources and manpower, was faced with a continuing struggle. The North's sagging morale was encouraged by the Union victories, and the peace movement lost its momentum.

Although Lee's army had survived to fight another day, it had suffered crippling losses from which it never fully recovered. One Confederate lieutenant may have summarized best what Gettysburg meant for the South when he wrote, "we gained nothing but glory and lost our bravest men."

[See also Brandy Station, Virginia; Winchester, Virginia.]

BIBLIOGRAPHY

Coddington, Edwin B. *The Gettysburg Campaign: A Study in Command.* New York, 1968.

Frassinito, William. *Gettysburg: A Journey in Time.* New York, 1975.

Freeman, Douglas S. *Lee's Lieutenants: A Study in Command.* 3 vols. New York, 1942–1944. Reprint, New York, 1986.

Hassler, Warren W., Jr. *Crisis at the Crossroads.* University, Ala., 1970.

Johnson, Robert U., and C. C. Buel, eds. *Battles and Leaders of the Civil War.* 4 vols. New York, 1887–1888. Reprint, Secaucus, N.J., 1982.

Pfanz, Harry W. *Gettysburg: The Second Day.* Chapel Hill, N.C., 1987.

Stewart, George R. *Pickett's Charge.* Boston, 1959.

Tucker, Glenn. *High Tide at Gettysburg.* Indianapolis, 1958. Reprint, Dayton, Ohio, 1988.

D. SCOTT HARTWIG

GHOLSON, SAMUEL JAMESON (1808–1883), brigadier general. Gholson was born in Madison County, Kentucky, on May 19, 1808, and as a child moved with his family to Alabama. After studying law and passing the bar, he relocated to Mississippi, where he became active in politics. He served in the Mississippi state legislature and was a member of the U.S. House of Representatives from 1836 to 1838. President Martin Van Buren appointed him a U.S. district judge in 1839, a post he held until 1861.

Gholson attended the Mississippi secession convention in January 1861 and when his state seceded, enlisted as a private. Elected captain of Company I, Fourteenth Mississippi Infantry, he was promoted to colonel and then brigadier general of state forces. He was wounded and captured at Fort Donelson, but returned to service under Maj. Gen. Sterling Price at Iuka and Corinth in the latter part of 1862. The following year Gholson was promoted to major general of state troops and a year later received a commission as brigadier general in the Confederate army to date from May 4.

As a brigadier general, Gholson commanded a cavalry brigade that operated in Alabama, Mississippi, and eastern Louisiana. In December 1864, while fighting at Egypt, Mississippi, he suffered a severe wound that required the amputation of his left arm.

Gholson returned to the state legislature in 1865 and

1866, serving as Speaker of the Mississippi House of Representatives. In 1878, he was again elected to the state legislature. Gholson died at his home in Aberdeen, Mississippi, on October 16, 1883.

BIBLIOGRAPHY

Bearss, Edwin C. *Forrest at Brice's Cross Roads.* Dayton, Ohio, 1979.

Biographical Dictionary of the American Congress, 1774–1984. Washington, D.C., 1984.

Henry, Robert Selph. *"First with the Most" Forrest.* Indianapolis, 1944.

Wyeth, John Allan. *Life of General Nathan Bedford Forrest.* New York, 1899. Reprint, Baton Rouge, La., 1989.

BRIAN S. WILLS

GHOLSON, THOMAS SAUNDERS (1808–1868), judge and congressman from Virginia.

Born in the southern Virginia town to which his family had given its name several generations before, Gholsonville, in Brunswick County, Thomas Gholson enjoyed a prosperous, provincial gentry upbringing. He graduated in 1827 from the University of Virginia, practiced law in his native county, and, in 1829, married his first cousin, Cary Ann Gholson. They had two children. In 1840 he moved to Petersburg where he made his name as an eloquent advocate. Gholson's prominence was attested by his appointment as visitor (trustee) of the College of William and Mary, president of the Bank of Petersburg, vestryman of Blandford Episcopal Church, and founder of the Petersburg public library.

Gholson accepted appointment in 1859 to the Fifth Judicial Circuit of Virginia. Although a partisan Whig, he was "ardently attached to the South and her institutions." He supported secession when the crisis came and continued as a judge in the Confederacy.

In 1863 he won election to the Second House of Representatives by defeating the incumbent, Charles Fenton Collier. He won by only twenty-seven votes, the margin of victory coming largely from the soldier vote. During the campaign Collier charged Gholson with continuing to hold court and drawing unfair advantage from that position. Gholson and his brother, also a judge, had had rancorous dealings before the war with Collier's family that led to a bitter exchange of accusatory pamphlets. With this history of bad blood between the families, it came as no surprise to the electors of Petersburg when Collier made his charge against the judge. Gholson stood his ground, refusing to sanction a recount, and Collier relented.

Gholson never became a leading figure in the legislature, though he consistently favored the strongest measures to prosecute the war effort. A member of the Judiciary Committee, he favored nationalization of industry and suspension of habeas corpus. He saw these as emergency measures necessary to win the war and did not hesitate to give the central government the additional powers the Davis administration sought.

Only when it came to arming the slaves did Gholson oppose the administration. In a speech in February 1865 he explained his reasons, all the while expressing his support for Davis and enjoining his colleagues "let us not forget our bleeding country." When Gholson opposed the belated attempt to use black men in the army, his argument inadvertently revealed the untenable plight of the slave owners: "You cannot fight white and black in the same army, without putting them on the same footing." His own solution was a vague if earnest effort to make conscription more efficient.

After the war Gholson decided to leave Petersburg in an effort to restore the heavy financial losses he had suffered. With his son-in-law, Col. Norman Stewart Walker, he founded a commission business handling cotton and tobacco in Liverpool. Gholson himself was the firm's agent in England. He died suddenly in Savannah on December 12, 1868, on his way back to Virginia.

BIBLIOGRAPHY

"A Note on Judge Thomas Saunders Gholson, President of the Petersburg Library Association." *Tyler's Quarterly Historical and Genealogical Magazine* 19 (1937): 84–86.

Wakelyn, Jon L. *Biographical Dictionary of the Confederacy.* Edited by Frank E. Vandiver. Westport, Conn., 1977.

Warner, Ezra J., and W. Buck Yearns. *Biographical Register of the Confederate Congress.* Baton Rouge, La., 1975.

NELSON D. LANKFORD

GIBSON, RANDALL LEE (1832–1892), brigadier general, U.S. congressman and senator.

Gibson was born September 10, 1832, in Woodford County, Kentucky. His family home was the plantation Live Oaks in Terrebonne Parish, Louisiana. After earning a law degree from the University of Louisiana, he served as military attaché with the American embassy in Spain and then opened a law practice and established a sugar plantation in Terrebonne Parish.

When the Civil War began, Gibson became aide-de-camp for Louisiana Governor Thomas O. Moore before being commissioned a captain in the First Louisiana Artillery in March 1861. In August 1861 he was promoted to colonel of the Thirteenth Louisiana Infantry, which he commanded at the Battle of Shiloh. There he assumed command of the Louisiana Brigade after its commander, Brig. Gen. Daniel Weisiger Adams, was wounded and lost his right eye. Gibson also fought at Perryville, Murfreesboro, and Chickamauga. Promoted to brigadier general on January 11,

1864, Gibson served in the Atlanta campaign and in Lieut. Gen. John Bell Hood's invasion of Tennessee. His military career ended with his command of the Louisiana Brigade in the defense of Spanish Fort, near Mobile, Alabama, in March 1865. During the fighting, Gibson's force of less than 2,000 lost 93 killed, 350 wounded, and 250 captured.

After the war, Gibson opened a law firm in New Orleans. He was elected to Congress in 1872 but was denied his seat by Radical Republicans. He was elected again to Congress in 1874 and served four terms. Gibson was instrumental in persuading President Rutherford B. Hayes to withdraw troops from Louisiana and end Reconstruction. In 1882 he was elected to the U.S. Senate and was reelected in 1888. He played a major role in founding Tulane University. Gibson died in Hot Springs, Arkansas, on December 15, 1892, and is buried at Lexington, Kentucky.

BIBLIOGRAPHY

Evans, Clement A., ed. *Confederate Military History.* 12 vols. Atlanta, 1899. Extended ed. in 19 vols. Wilmington, N.C., 1987–1989.

Johnson, Robert U., and C. C. Buel, eds. *Battles and Leaders of the Civil War.* 4 vols. New York, 1887–1888. Reprint, Secaucus, N.J., 1982.

KENNY A. FRANKS

GIFT, GEORGE W. (1833–1879) naval lieutenant.

By July 1861 when Gift rode east from California with Albert Sidney Johnston's party, he had already lived an adventurous life. Born March 1, 1833, in Polk County, Tennessee, he was a neighbor to Andrew Jackson and appointed in 1848 to the new Naval Academy by family friend James K. Polk. After service in the South Seas as a midshipman, he resigned in 1851 to join his father and brothers in California. He served in minor government posts and was, by turn, a ship captain, printer, banker, and surveyor in Washington Territory and Los Angeles County.

The range of Gift's service to the Confederate navy reflects both his versatility and his restless temperament: service on *New Orleans, McRea,* and *Louisiana* in defense of New Orleans, 1862; commander of a gun crew on the ironclad *Arkansas,* 1862; training gun crews and fitting out the gunboat *Chattahoochee,* 1862 and 1863; patrol duty aboard *Gaines* and *Baltic* in Mobile Harbor, 1863; an expedition to Canada with plans to join the Johnson Island expedition on Lake Erie, 1863; expeditions against the Union blockade at Apalachicola, Florida, and against *Underwriter,* 1864; mining Savannah Harbor, 1864; and in the same year service aboard the blockade runner *Ranger* and *Tallahassee, Chattahoochee, Savannah, Olustee,* and *Jackson.* Gift's initial success on *Arkansas* followed by failures in his later service reflect the general technical,

administrative, and tactical weaknesses of the Confederate navy.

After the war, Gift tried farming in Tennessee, managed the gasworks in Memphis, sailed to China, and finally relocated to California where he promoted tourism, railroads, and wineries as owner-editor of a Napa County newspaper. He died in Napa in 1879 just before his forty-sixth birthday.

BIBLIOGRAPHY

Castlen, Harriett Gift. *Hope Bids Me Onward.* Savannah, Ga., 1947.

Gift, Ellen Shackelford. Papers. Southern Historical Collection, University of North Carolina, Chapel Hill.

Turner, Maxine. *Navy Gray: A Story of the Confederate Navy on the Chattahoochee and Apalachicola Rivers.* Tuscaloosa, Ala., 1988.

MAXINE TURNER

GILLEM, ALVAN C. (1830–1875), Federal major general and military governor of Tennessee.

Born in upper middle Tennessee, Alvan Cullen Gillem graduated from the U.S. Military Academy in 1851. Over the next decade, he participated in actions against Florida's Seminole Indians (1851–1852) and performed garrison duties in Texas. On the Civil War's eve, Gillem was posted to Fort Taylor, Florida, where he pledged loyalty to the Union rather than his native state.

Gillem's friendship with Tennessee Senator Andrew Johnson had a strong impact on his Civil War career. Assigned to the western theater, he fought in the early Kentucky campaigns and then commanded the Army of the Ohio's quartermaster corps, seeing further action at Shiloh and Corinth. After the Battle of Shiloh, Maj. Gen. Don Carlos Buell cited Gillem's resourcefulness in securing transportation across the Tennessee River and thus contributing to the Union advance on the battle's second day.

After appointing Gillem Tennessee's military governor, Johnson designated him colonel of the Governor's Guard, which formed around the Tenth Tennessee Volunteers. Johnson later commissioned him Tennessee's adjutant general (June 1863) and pressured President Abraham Lincoln for his promotion to brigadier general of volunteers. From August 1863 to June 1864, he commanded troops guarding and repairing the vital railway link between Nashville and southern Illinois.

Throughout the late summer and fall of 1864, Gillem skirmished against residual Confederate forces in eastern Tennessee. He achieved his most notable success when he pursued and killed Confederate Gen. John Hunt Morgan at Greeneville on September 4, 1864. Two months later, Gillem's fortunes reversed when Confederate forces under Brig. Gen. John C. Breckinridge raided eastern Tennessee and trapped the Governor's Guards at Morristown. Gillem retreated to Knoxville with heavy losses: 150 men killed or taken prisoner, six cannons captured with 130 wagons and ambulances, and over 300 horses. Despite this defeat, his career advanced with Johnson's fortunes and he attained the rank of major general of volunteers in April 1865.

Gillem emerged as an important Reconstruction figure. In January 1865, he was elected vice president of the Tennessee convention reorganizing the civilian state government, served briefly in the state's General Assembly, and commanded the Military District of East Tennessee until September 1866. On January 8, 1868, President Johnson placed him over the Fourth Military District (Arkansas and Mississippi), where he pursued Reconstruction goals with far less vigor than his predecessor, Gen. Edward O. C. Ord. In so doing, he won the friendship of conservative white Southerners and the enmity of congressional Republicans. Immediately after Ulysses S. Grant's inauguration as president, Gillem was transferred to the Texas frontier. In his last command, he led troops against California's Modoc Indians (May 1873). Returning to Tennessee on sick leave, Gillem died in Nashville, December 2, 1875.

BIBLIOGRAPHY

Garner, James W. *Reconstruction in Mississippi.* New York, 1901.

Graf, LeRoy P., Ralph W. Haskins, and Paul Bergeron, eds. *The Papers of Andrew Johnson.* 8 vols. to date. Knoxville, Tenn. 1967–.

Register of Graduates and Former Cadets of the United States Military Academy, 1802–1965. Chicago, 1965.

Winston, Robert W. *Andrew Johnson: Plebeian and Patriot.* New York, 1928.

FRED ARTHUR BAILEY

GILMER, JEREMY FRANCIS (1818–1883), major general.

A native of North Carolina and a graduate of West Point, Gilmer was an engineer in the U.S. Army before the Civil War. He was chief engineer of the Army of the West in New Mexico during the Mexican War, supervising the erection of Fort Marcy at Santa Fe. From 1858 to 1861, he directed the construction of the defenses at the entrance of San Francisco Bay.

Gilmer resigned from the U.S. Army on June 29, 1861, and soon after volunteered his services to the Confederacy. As chief engineer of the Western Department, he served under Gen. Albert Sidney Johnston in Kentucky and Tennessee, overseeing the construction of defenses at Forts Henry and Donelson. He was with Johnston at Shiloh in April 1862 and was wounded in the second day of fighting. His superior abilities as an engineer did not go unnoticed, and in August 1862 Gen. Robert E. Lee appointed him chief engineer of the Army of Northern Virginia.

JEREMY FRANCIS GILMER.   NATIONAL ARCHIVES

In October 1862 Gilmer was appointed chief of the Engineer Bureau for the War Department, spending the majority of his time improving the defenses of Richmond and Petersburg. Transferred to the Department of South Carolina, Georgia, and Florida in August 1863, with the rank of major general, he directed operations in the defense of Charleston. He helped fortify Atlanta in 1864, but the lack of materials hindered his efforts. Thereafter, he returned to Richmond to resume his post as chief of the Engineer Bureau.

After the war, Gilmer worked in the railroad industry as an engineer and became president of the Savannah Gaslight Company. He died on December 1, 1883.

BIBLIOGRAPHY

Hill, D. H., Jr. *North Carolina.* Vol. 4 of *Confederate Military History.* Edited by Clement A. Evans. Atlanta, 1899. Vol. 5 of extended ed. Wilmington, N.C., 1987.

U.S. War Department. *War of the Rebellion: A Compilation of the Official Records of the Union and Confederate Armies.* Washington, D.C., 1880–1901. Ser. 1, vol. 11, pt. 3, p. 664; ser. 1, vol. 12, pt. 3, p. 944; ser. 1, vol. 28, pt. 2, p. 323; ser. 1, vol. 38, pt. 3, p. 664.

Wakelyn, Jon L. *Biographical Dictionary of the Confederacy.* Edited by Frank E. Vandiver. Westport, Conn., 1977.

MICHAEL G. MAHON

GILMER, JOHN A.

GILMER, JOHN A. (1805–1868), congressman from North Carolina. John Adams Gilmer's most significant contribution to the Confederacy was his effort to thwart its inception. By comparison, his role as a congressman during the last year of the war was quite secondary.

No Southern Unionist during the secession crisis faced so excruciating a dilemma as Gilmer, a member of the U.S. House of Representatives who lived in Greensboro, North Carolina. At the behest of New York Senator William H. Seward and his alter ego Thurlow Weed, President-elect Abraham Lincoln secretly invited Gilmer to serve in his cabinet. The offer was designed to show that Southerners had no reason to fear the new Republican president. Until a larger segment of Southern opinion became so persuaded, however, any individual Southerner who accepted a cabinet position would squander his political influence and destroy his political base. In the end, Gilmer refused the offer.

Gilmer lived in a distinctive part of the South. Although

JOHN A. GILMER.   LIBRARY OF CONGRESS

he himself owned more than fifty slaves, Guilford County and the adjacent North Carolina Piedmont were characterized by modest landownings and yeoman farming rather than plantation slavery. A substantial number of Quakers also lived there and opposed slavery on principle. These circumstances together with an eagerness for transportation improvements and a long-standing resentment of the eastern-dominated state government combined to give the Greensboro region a decided Whiggish orientation and a political outlook that had no room for Southern rights posturing.

A successful lawyer, Gilmer served in the state senate for several terms starting in 1846. There he promoted internal improvements, especially the North Carolina Railroad, and worked to expand the scope of public education. He took a strongly Unionist stance during the 1850 crisis. Defeated in an 1856 race for governor on the American party (Know-Nothing) ticket, he was elected to Congress in 1857.

Gilmer was among the handful of Southerners to vote with Republicans and Douglas Democrats in 1858 against the admission of Kansas as a slave state under the Lecompton constitution. Despite ferocious criticism of his Kansas vote by North Carolina Democrats, he won reelection in 1859. Gilmer gained a degree of national visibility in December 1859 when the Southern Opposition (or "South Americans" as the two dozen former Whigs in the House sometimes designated themselves) put his name forward as a candidate for Speaker of the House. He supported the 1860 presidential candidacy of John Bell, who was nominated by the Constitutional Union party. Lincoln, however, swept the North, provoking the states of the Deep South to secede.

Although not enthusiastic about offering a cabinet appointment to someone "who opposed us in the election," Lincoln judged that Gilmer was the most suitable of several Southern Unionists promoted by Seward and Weed. Gilmer, however, found the cabinet offer perplexing. It did indicate that Lincoln wanted to aid Southern Unionists. But Gilmer believed that the appointment by itself would not calm the uproar in the South and he dreaded the abuse he would face. Uncertain how to respond, Gilmer consulted confidentially with other antisecessionists. His predecessor in Congress, Edwin G. Reade, "strongly urged Mr. Gilmer to accept." Maryland Congressman Henry Winter Davis, the most audacious member of the Southern Opposition, emphatically agreed: it was "a matter of life or death."

Gilmer thereupon tried to persuade Lincoln and the Republican party to offer more substantive reassurances. The North Carolinian pointed out that "apprehensions of real danger and harm to them and their peculiar institution" had "seized" the people of the South. Gilmer considered a "generous and patriotic" concession on the vexing territorial issue the best way for Republicans to arrest the secession contagion. He believed that the compromise package proposed by Kentucky Senator John J. Crittenden would stop secession dead in its tracks.

Gilmer, who privately bewailed the unreasonable behavior of "my maddened brethren of the South," urged Republicans to treat Southern symptoms with an appropriate palliative. "Yield to them this useless and foolish abstraction of Congressional protection to slavery in the Territories," he implored Weed. In Gilmer's opinion, the North could safely grant to deluded Southerners "this silly boon for which they so furiously struggle," because the most stringent protection for slavery in the territories "would come as near making slave states, as the drying up of the Mississippi, could be secured by a law of Congress."

For Gilmer, the territorial issue was a "mere abstraction," created by extremists North and South. The North, he thought, had no need to prohibit slavery from an arid region to which it would never spread in any case. The South, however, was equally wrongheaded to fear that slavery in the states could not survive without Federal protection for slavery in the territories.

The impasse, even if rooted in misperceptions and political one-upmanship, had explosive potential. "We are in real trouble," Gilmer wrote to a friend in January 1861. "There is real danger at hand—I can't say that I have lost all hope, but . . . the prospects are gloomy in the extreme. I often shed tears in silence."

As much as any Republican, Gilmer blamed the immediate crisis on a conspiracy among Southern Democrats. Within the previous year, he charged, they had split their national party, falsely represented themselves as having no plans to disrupt the Union in the case of Lincoln's election, and then treacherously reversed themselves after the election to argue that disunion was the only way to preserve the peace and safety of the South. Their demand that Congress protect slavery in the territories seemed to Gilmer a transparent pretext, made in the expectation that the North would never allow it.

Unfortunately for Southern Unionists, Republicans gagged at the Crittenden Compromise's promise to protect slavery in all territory south of 36° 30′, now held or "hereafter acquired." They considered such language an open invitation to conquer new slave territory in the Caribbean and Latin America. Gilmer and the more flexible Southern Unionists thereupon indicated that they would accept the so-called border state plan, which prohibited either Congress or a territorial legislature from interfering with slavery in existing territory south of 36° 30′. This least dogmatic territorial compromise avoided both "protection" and "hereafter acquired."

Gilmer's speech to the House on January 26, 1861, stirred an emotional response. He implored his listeners to avert the "dreadful calamity" of civil war. More accurately than most of his countrymen, Gilmer foresaw that any clash of arms would so arouse the South as to make reunion impossible, except at the price of massive bloodshed. One reporter claimed never to have seen such an effect as was produced by this "honest appeal of a great heart." When Gilmer finished speaking, "dozens of Republicans and Southern Union men rushed forward to congratulate him." Conciliatory Republicans told reporters that "some compromise must be made to keep John A. Gilmer from being carried down by the secession tide."

Southern Unionists, attempting to reverse the drift of public opinion in their home states, mailed an unprecedented avalanche of pro-Union speeches and documents to citizens in the upper South. The effort was coordinated by Joseph C. G. Kennedy, head of the U.S. Census Bureau, and paid for by Gilmer, probably the wealthiest of the congressmen involved. A squad of twenty clerks addressed the mailings, which Union congressmen then franked for free delivery. Night after night, from the close of office hours until midnight, the mailing operation continued. Secessionists soon protested that "Gilmer and company," working with "the Census Bureau and the Black Republicans," were flooding the South with "submission and coercion speeches."

Elections held in the upper South in February 1861 demonstrated that Unionist efforts had an effect. Fewer than one-third of the delegates elected on February 4 to the Virginia convention favored secession. Virginia voters also specified by more than two-to-one that any action of the convention must be approved by popular referendum. The results in Tennessee on February 9 and North Carolina on February 28 added to secessionist woes. Voters in both states narrowly refused even to countenance the calling of a convention. Had either convention met, it would have been dominated by Union delegates.

Unfortunately for the Unionists, Lincoln and the majority of the Republican party continued to oppose any direct compromise on the territorial issue. That circumstance, together with indications that Lincoln planned to deliver a hard-line inaugural address, finally prompted Gilmer to refuse the cabinet post.

Seward, who was soon to become secretary of state in the new cabinet, scrambled to repair the growing breach between Lincoln and the upper South. The adroit New Yorker quietly persuaded a minority of Republicans in Congress to vote for a constitutional amendment guaranteeing the safety of slavery in the states. He then got Lincoln to endorse the amendment and to adopt a more peaceful and conciliatory tone in his inaugural address. Republicans in Congress also organized three new western territories without any language to prohibit slavery. Four days after Lincoln took office, Gilmer took a hopeful view. "What more," he asked rhetorically, "does any reasonable Southern man expect or desire?"

The North Carolinian dispatched a sheaf of letters to Seward, describing the desperation of secessionists in the upper South. Their "only hope," he noted, was that fighting might break out between the seceded states and the Federal government. In order to "avoid a collision," Gilmer advised, Lincoln should surrender the two remaining Federal outposts in the Deep South—Fort Sumter in the harbor of Charleston, South Carolina, and Fort Pickens, offshore from Pensacola, Florida. Allow the Deep South to remain "out in the cold for awhile." After it became plain that the upper South would not follow, the secession movement would self-destruct.

For several weeks from mid-March to early April, Southern Unionists such as Gilmer dared to believe that Lincoln had adopted a "let-alone" policy and that the great crisis had been surmounted. In fact, of course, Lincoln decided to try to hold Fort Sumter, notwithstanding the likelihood that Confederate forces would strike to wrest it from him. Doubtful that the Union could be restored peacefully, the new president judged that his options had narrowed to peaceable separation or war.

The accumulating evidence that the administration had decided to risk a confrontation threw Gilmer into a profound depression. "I am so deeply disturbed that my heart seems to melt within me," he wrote to Seward on April 11. "If what I hear is true that we are to have fighting at Sumter or Pickens, it is what the disunionists have most courted, and I seriously apprehend it will drive the whole South into secession."

Ten days later, his worst apprehensions fulfilled, Gilmer wrote a final letter to Seward. Its tone, unlike many other last letters sent North the week after the firing on Sumter, was not bellicose, but rather reflective and despairing. With his Union-saving hopes in ruins and his only son already serving in a Confederate volunteer company, Gilmer took a bleak view of the future. "All hope is now extinguished," he mourned. "As matters now stand, there is a United North against a United South, and both marching to the field of blood."

Gilmer was elected to the May 1861 convention that removed North Carolina from the Union. He voted with other Union Whigs to identify that action as an act of revolution rather than secession. Otherwise Gilmer played no conspicuous role in Confederate North Carolina until the midpoint of the war.

By the summer of 1863, however, following the catastrophic Confederate defeats at Vicksburg and Gettysburg, a groundswell of discontent swept the state. Antiwar sentiment flourished among the yeomen of the Piedmont, few of whom had favored secession in the first place. Conscription not only forced them to fight for a cause that many did not support; it also left nonslaveholding families without able-bodied males to perform farm work. Increasingly severe food shortages resulted.

Under the circumstances, original secessionists in North Carolina lost all political influence. Elections for the Second Congress, held in August 1863, produced the most militantly anti-administration delegation ever to represent any Confederate state. Nine of the ten, among them Gilmer, were former Union Whigs. Several, notably James T. Leach and George W. Logan, opposed all war measures and plainly would have welcomed restoration of the Union.

Although Gilmer necessarily stood in the anti-administration camp, his position in the context of the North Carolina delegation was more that of a pro-war moderate. He had close ties to Governor Zebulon Vance, a former colleague from the last fateful U.S. Congress before the war started. Vance walked a delicate tightrope. He sharply criticized Jefferson Davis for infringing on civil liberties and exceeding his authority as president. By so doing, however, Vance and like-minded conservatives worked to appease growing peace sentiment and thereby reconcile restless North Carolina to continued struggle for the Confederate cause.

During his tenure in Congress, which extended from May 1864 until shortly before the end of the war in March 1865, Gilmer attempted to develop more equitable tax laws and supply systems. The downward spiral of Confederate military fortunes inevitably thwarted his initiatives. Like other North Carolinians, Gilmer objected whenever the Davis administration moved to suspend the writ of habeas corpus. He also opposed arming slaves.

Gilmer did not support the resolution put forward by James T. Leach in November 1864, which indicated a readiness to abandon the quest for independence. He did, however, work to persuade Davis to send a delegation to the Hampton Roads conference of February 3, 1865. There Confederate spokesmen discovered that Lincoln and Seward insisted upon reunion as the basis for any settlement of the war. Shortly afterward, Gilmer proposed a dual government, or "diet," in which Union and Confederate congresses and executives would remain separate but function in a coordinated manner. His proposed halfway house between independence and reunion won scant support.

Gilmer estranged himself from the North Carolina peace faction, and even from his close friend and ally, Senator William A. Graham, when he went out of his way to give eleventh-hour public support to the continued military struggle. By sharing a platform on February 9, 1865, with Secretary of State Judah P. Benjamin, Gilmer identified himself with bitter-enders at a time when most North Carolinians were working behind the scenes for a negotiated surrender. Gilmer's position was made all the more awkward when Benjamin demanded enlistment of black soldiers.

The end of the war left Gilmer in "great distress," musing about uprooting to the free states in order to "begin life again.'' That did not happen. He remained in Greensboro, where he continued to provide his former slaves with food, clothing, farm implements, and medical care. Gilmer's ''extraordinary humanity and regard for his slaves'' was ''proverbial in his neighborhood.'' They were reported to be ''substantially free'' long before emancipation.

Gilmer's situation was complicated by politics. William W. Holden, who was appointed governor by President Andrew Johnson soon after the end of the war and who had earlier spearheaded the North Carolina peace movement, hoped to remain in power. Holden feared, however, that prominent Union Whigs such as Vance, Graham, and Gilmer might gain greater popular support because of their stronger Confederate credentials. Holden therefore persuaded Johnson to withhold pardons for his would-be rivals. Gilmer ''was once ultra right,'' Holden noted, ''but he went far astray'' during the war. Not until near the end of 1865 did Gilmer receive his pardon.

Conservatives did topple Holden, at least temporarily. He lost the election in November 1865 to former Whig Jonathan Worth, state treasurer during the Confederate period. Presently, however, Congress suspended the state governments organized under Johnson's auspices. Holden returned for another stormy tenure as governor in 1868 after enactment of the Reconstruction Constitution, which enfranchised blacks.

Gilmer traveled to Philadelphia in August 1866 to attend the National Union Convention, at which Conservatives from both North and South attempted unsuccessfully to devise a strategy to counter Republican Reconstruction policy. His health deteriorated by early 1867, however, and he died in May 1868.

Gerald W. Johnson, a native of Greensboro who became a well-known journalist and political commentator, wrote a perceptive biographical sketch of Gilmer in the 1920s. Although ''now unknown to all save a few specialists,'' Johnson observed, Gilmer was a tragic and appealing figure who had appeared briefly in ''the spotlight of history.'' Illuminated in the midst of a terrible storm, he was then ''lost in the night.''

BIBLIOGRAPHY

Alexander, Thomas B., and Richard E. Beringer. *The Anatomy of the Confederate Congress: A Study of the Influences of Member Characteristics on Legislative Voting Behavior, 1861–1865.* Nashville, Tenn., 1972.

Crofts, Daniel W. *Reluctant Confederates: Upper South Unionists in the Secession Crisis.* Chapel Hill, N.C., 1989.

Hamilton, J. G. deRoulhac, and Max R. Williams, eds. *The Papers of William Alexander Graham.* 7 vols. to date. Raleigh, N.C., 1957–.

Jeffrey, Thomas E. *State Parties and National Parties: North Carolina, 1815–1861.* Athens, Ga., 1989.

Journal of the Congress of the Confederate States of America, 1861–1865. 7 vols. Washington, D.C., 1904–1905.

Kruman, Marc W. *Parties and Politics in North Carolina, 1836–1865.* Baton Rouge, La., 1983.

Sitterson, Joseph Carlyle. *The Secession Movement in North Carolina.* Chapel Hill, N.C., 1939.

Yearns, Wilfred B. *The Confederate Congress.* Athens, Ga., 1960.

DANIEL W. CROFTS

GIRARDEY, VICTOR JEAN BAPTISTE

(1837–1864), brigadier general. Girardey was born June 26, 1837, in Lauw, France, and immigrated to Augusta, Georgia, with his family. After being orphaned at sixteen, he moved to New Orleans where he completed his education and afterward, in 1858, apparently returned to Georgia.

On October 12, 1861, he enlisted in Louisiana as a first lieutenant and aide-de-camp. When the colonel of the Third Georgia Infantry, Ambrose Ransom Wright, became brigadier general, Girardey was appointed his assistant adjutant-general with the rank of captain on June 21, 1862. He served in that capacity during the Seven Days' Battles around Richmond and received special recognition from Wright for his role in the Battle of King's School House on June 25. After the Chancellorsville campaign, Girardey was once again commended for his services. On the return from Gettysburg, at Manassas Gap, Captain Girardey successfully took command of the left of the brigade for which he also received recognition.

Girardey, on May 21, 1864, was transferred to the staff of Gen. William Mahone to serve in the same capacity he had under Wright. During the siege of Petersburg, in the Battle of the Crater on July 30, his help in organizing the Confederate counterattack earned him a quick promotion. He jumped to the grade of brigadier general with temporary rank, the only such instance in the Confederate army during the war. On August 16, thirteen days later, General Girardey was killed near Fussell's Mill on the Darbytown Road (Deep Bottom), while protecting the Richmond defenses. He is buried in Augusta, Georgia.

BIBLIOGRAPHY

Bernard, George S. *War Talks of Confederate Veterans.* Petersburg, Va., 1892.

Cavanaugh, Michael A., and William Marvel. *The Battle of the Crater: "The Horrid Pit" June 25–August 6, 1864.* Lynchburg, Va., 1989.

Derry, Joseph T. *Georgia.* Vol. 6 of *Confederate Military History.* Edited by Clement A. Evans. Atlanta, 1899. Vol. 7 of extended ed. Wilmington, N.C., 1987.

Horn, John. *The Destruction of the Weldon Railroad: Deep Bottom, Globe Tavern, and Reams Station, August 14–25, 1864.* Lynchburg, Va., 1991.

Warner, Ezra J. *Generals in Gray: Lives of the Confederate Commanders.* Baton Rouge, La., 1959.

CHRIS CALKINS

GIST, STATES RIGHTS (1831–1864), brigadier general. Gist was born in Union District, South Carolina, September 3, 1831. His father, an ardent disciple of John C. Calhoun, chose his son's unusual name to demonstrate his own political sentiments. After studying at South Carolina College and Harvard Law School, the young Gist practiced as an attorney. He also served in the South Carolina military forces and in 1861 was adjutant and inspector general of the state army.

Going to Virginia in 1861, Gist served as a volunteer aide-de-camp on the staff of Brig. Gen. Barnard E. Bee. At First Manassas (July 21), when all the officers of the Fourth Alabama Regiment became casualties, Gist took command of the regiment and directed it throughout the remainder of the battle.

Gist was back in South Carolina during the winter of 1861–1862, laboring to raise troops for the state. On May 20, 1862, he was appointed a Confederate brigadier general. For a year he served in the Carolina coast defenses.

Sent to Mississippi in May 1863, Gist commanded a brigade there and at the Battle of Chickamauga (September 20, 1863). In 1864 Gist commanded his brigade in the Atlanta campaign. Wounded there on July 22, Gist was absent from duty for about a month. At Franklin (November

ber 30), he was mortally wounded as he advanced with his men in the great Confederate charge on the Federal works. He died in a field hospital that night.

Gist was first buried in a nearby cemetery, but his body was later moved to Trinity Episcopal Church Cemetery in Columbia, South Carolina.

BIBLIOGRAPHY

Cisco, Walter Brian. *States Rights Gist: A South Carolina General of the Civil War.* Shippensburg, Pa., 1991.
Warner, Ezra J. *Generals in Gray: Lives of the Confederate Commanders.* Baton Rouge, La., 1959.

RICHARD M. McMURRY

GLADDEN, ADLEY HOGAN (1810–1862), brigadier general. Born in the Fairfield District of South Carolina, October 28, 1810, Gladden moved to Columbia, South Carolina, in 1830 and worked as a cotton broker. President John Tyler then appointed him postmaster of Columbia. Gladden's first military experience was with the militia in the Seminole uprisings. During the Mexican War, he served as a major and then lieutenant colonel of South Carolina's Palmetto Regiment. He was wounded in the assault on Belen Gate, and his service was considered distinguished. After the war, he settled in New Orleans, Louisiana.

In 1861 Gladden was appointed lieutenant colonel of the First South Carolina Infantry. Before he could serve, he was elected to the Louisiana secession convention and then appointed colonel of the First Louisiana Infantry. The regiment moved to Pensacola, Florida, where Gladden was appointed brigadier general to date from September 30, 1861. He commanded a brigade made up of the Twenty-first Alabama, Twenty-second Alabama, Twenty-fifth Alabama, Twenty-sixth Alabama, and the First Louisiana Infantry Regiments, and Felix Huston Robertson's Florida Battery.

In March 1862, at the request of Gen. Braxton Bragg, the brigade moved to Corinth, Mississippi, to reinforce the army of Gen. Albert Sidney Johnston, who planned to attack the Union forces at Shiloh. Just before the battle, Gladden's brigade was detached from Bragg's Second Corps and attached to William J. Hardee's. In the opening phases of the battle Gladden was wounded and he died in Corinth on April 12. He was buried in Mobile, Alabama.

BIBLIOGRAPHY

Connelly, Thomas L. *The Army of the Heartland: The Army of Tennessee, 1861–1862.* Baton Rouge, La., 1967.
Warner, Ezra J. *Generals in Gray: Lives of the Confederate Commanders.* Baton Rouge, La., 1959.

GEORGE A. REAVES III

STATES RIGHTS GIST.   LIBRARY OF CONGRESS

GLASSELL, WILLIAM T.

GLASSELL, WILLIAM T. (1834?–1879), naval officer. Born in Virginia, Glassell was appointed a midshipman in the U.S. Navy from the state of Alabama (March 15, 1848). Promoted to lieutenant in 1855, he was aboard USS *Hartford* off China when the Civil War broke out. When *Hartford* reached Philadelphia, Glassell declined to swear an additional oath of allegiance prescribed for Southerners, and was consequently imprisoned at Fort Warren and dropped from the U.S. service (December 6, 1861). Confederate authorities issued him a lieutenant's commission, arranged his exchange, and assigned him to CSS *Chicora* in the Charleston Squadron.

Glassell commanded his ship's forward division during the squadron's attack on the Union blockade (January 31, 1863). Intrigued by the army's experiments with torpedoes and mines, he requested and received assignment to a special command training to attack the blockading fleet's monitors.

On the night of October 5, 1863, Glassell and a crew of three in the diminutive torpedo boat *David* attacked the most powerful ship in the U.S. Navy, *New Ironsides*. The Confederates rammed a spar torpedo against the ironclad six feet beneath the waterline. The explosion threw a geyser of water over *David*, extinguishing its fires and leaving it immobile in a hail of small-arms fire. The Confederates abandoned ship. The pilot and fireman soon reboarded the drifting boat, relit the fire, and reached the safety of Charleston Harbor. Glassell, however, was captured and returned to Fort Warren. *New Ironsides*, initially thought undamaged, was leaking so badly that repairs kept it out of action until the last months of 1864.

Glassell, while in prison, was promoted to commander for his attack on *New Ironsides*. Exchanged in the last six months of the war, he returned to Charleston. On the evacuation of that city he was transferred to Richmond and assigned to command the ironclad *Fredericksburg* in the James River Squadron. With Richmond's evacuation, the squadron's personnel were reorganized as artillery and infantry, and Glassell commanded a regiment. He was paroled at Greensboro, North Carolina, on April 28, 1865. He died in Los Angeles, California, in 1879.

BIBLIOGRAPHY

DuBose, John W. "Lieut. William T. Glassell of Alabama." *Confederate Veteran* 24, no. 5 (1916): 193–195. Reprint, Wilmington, N.C., 1985.

Glassell, W. T. "Reminiscences of Torpedo Service in Charleston Harbor." *Southern Historical Society Papers* 4, no. 5 (1877): 225–235. Reprint, Wilmington, N.C., 1990.

Parker, William H. *Recollections of a Naval Officer*. New York, 1883. Reprint, Annapolis, Md., 1985.

Perry, Milton F. *Infernal Machines*. Baton Rouge, La., 1965.

Scharf, J. Thomas. *History of the Confederate States Navy*. New York, 1887. Reprint, New York, 1977.

MAURICE K. MELTON

GLENDALE, VIRGINIA. *See* Frayser's Farm, Virginia.

GLORIETA PASS, NEW MEXICO. The battle fought March 28, 1862, at Glorieta Pass marked the end of Confederate expansion in the Southwest and was the turning point in Brig. Gen. Henry Hopkins Sibley's attempt to seize New Mexico.

After defeating the main Union forces at Val Verde on February 21 and bypassing Fort Craig, Sibley planned to concentrate his 2,000 Texans near the last Federal outpost, Fort Union, in the northeast corner of the territory. A 200-man Confederate detachment remained at Albuquerque to watch movements by the Fort Craig garrison. A second force of about 350 men under Maj. Charles Pyron, occupied the capital. A third column, composed chiefly of some 800 foot soldiers under Lt. Col. William Read Scurry, took a circuitous route through the mountains, planning to rendezvous with Pyron near Glorieta Pass in the Sangre de Cristo Mountains east of Santa Fe.

On March 26, Pyron, proceeding with the plan, blundered into the vanguard of a 1,300-man army of mostly Colorado volunteers under Col. John Slough at the west end of Glorieta Pass known as Apache Canyon. Pyron, taken by surprise, saw a third of his troops captured, while the Federals lost less than a dozen before withdrawing. Scurry, alerted to Pyron's danger, led his men in a freezing night march and reached Apache Canyon the next morning.

On March 28, after a quiet day of waiting, the 1,300-man Federal force divided, with about 450 making a flank march over a rugged mesa to strike the Confederate rear while the balance marched down the pass. Scurry, unaware of the enemy plans, left a hundred-man detachment at the mouth of Apache Canyon to guard the wagons and led the remaining 950 Texans toward Slough's command in Glorieta Pass.

The two forces met at 11:00 A.M. near Pigeon's Ranch. The Federals were thrown back in confusion before taking position around the adobe ranch buildings. The battle was fought as a number of disjointed gun duels throughout the afternoon until Scurry ordered a three-pronged attack against the Union line around 4:00 P.M. The Confederates turned the Federal right, forcing the Colorado volunteers back to another line farther down the pass. The Confederates did not pursue; darkness ended the battle. Thirty-six Texans had been killed, 70 wounded, and some 25 captured; the Federals counted 38 killed, 64 wounded, and about 20 captured.

During the day, however, disaster had struck the Confederate rear. The Union flank detachment under Maj. John Chivington routed the Texan wagon guard at midafternoon, burning some ninety wagons and killing over eight hundred draft animals. The destroyed supplies constituted the bulk of the Confederate commissary and crippled Sibley's campaign.

On March 29, Scurry withdrew his force to Santa Fe, where Sibley and the rest of the army met him. After a week's delay, the Texans retreated, evacuating New Mexico Territory and Confederate Arizona forever by June.

BIBLIOGRAPHY

Alberts, Don E., ed. *Rebels on the Rio Grande: The Civil War Journal of A. B. Peticolas.* Albuquerque, N.M., 1984.

Colton, Ray C. *The Civil War in the Western Territories.* Norman, Okla., 1959.

Hall, Martin H. *Sibley's New Mexico Campaign.* Austin, Tex., 1960.

Josephy, Alvin M., Jr. *The Civil War in the American West.* New York, 1991.

DONALD S. FRAZIER

GODWIN, ARCHIBALD CAMPBELL (1831–1864), brigadier general.

Godwin was born in Nansemond County, Virginia, and grew up in Portsmouth. He went west during the California gold rush and engaged in ranching, mining, lumbering, and milling enterprises. In 1860, he lost the Democratic nomination for governor by an extremely narrow margin.

With the outbreak of the Civil War, Godwin returned to Virginia and was appointed a major by President Jefferson Davis. He became assistant provost marshal of Richmond, assigned to its prisons. In December 1861, to relieve Richmond's overcrowded jails, Godwin went to Salisbury, North Carolina, where he set up a new prison. He then organized the Fifty-seventh North Carolina Infantry, in which he was commissioned a colonel.

Standing six feet six inches, Godwin towered in height as well as ability. He performed well at Fredericksburg on December 13, 1862, when his regiment, bombarded by a large enemy force at the peak of battle, held the Confederates' extreme right with the help of Thomas J. ("Stonewall") Jackson. In May 1863, the Fifty-seventh North Carolina participated in the action around Chancellorsville. Dislodging the Union forces from their position on the turnpike out of Fredericksburg north of Marye's Heights, Godwin's regiment drove the enemy back and captured its objective. Although wounded, Godwin did not leave the field.

At Gettysburg, on July 1, Godwin's men routed the Union forces halfway up Cemetery Hill but were ordered to halt, thus losing the opportunity to fortify the hill for further battle. The next day, Godwin assumed command of Robert Frederick Hoke's brigade when its colonel was killed. Because of a lack of reinforcements, they were unable to hold Cemetery Hill. On July 3, Godwin's brigade supported Richard S. Ewell's right in an unsuccessful attack on Culp's Hill.

On November 7, 1863, Godwin was captured at Rappahannock Station and sent to Johnson's Island, where he remained until exchanged in mid-1864. Returning to his brigade, he was commissioned a brigadier general on August 5. He participated in the fighting in the Shenandoah Valley, including the Third Battle of Winchester on September 19, 1864. After rallying his men there to a better position, Godwin rode over the pike road to compliment Capt. John Beard for the steadiness of his regiment. Within Union cannon range, he was killed instantly when a shell fragment struck his head. He was buried in Winchester.

BIBLIOGRAPHY

Freeman, Douglas S. *Lee's Lieutenants: A Study in Command.* 3 vols. New York, 1942–1944. Reprint, New York, 1986.

Hatton, Clarence R. "Gen. Archibald Campbell Godwin." *Confederate Veteran* 28 (1920): 133–136. Reprint, Wilmington, N.C., 1985.

Johnson, Robert U., and C. C. Buel, eds., *Battles and Leaders of the Civil War.* 4 vols. New York, 1887–1888. Reprint, Secaucus, N.J., 1982.

SANDRA V. PARKER

GOGGIN, JAMES MONROE (1820–1889), major, acting brigadier general.

During the 1864 campaigns at Petersburg and in the Shenandoah Valley, as casualties increased in the officer corps of the Army of Northern Virginia, there were too few appropriate replacements available. In some instances staff officers were promoted to brigade command and found themselves leading troops in combat rather than performing administrative functions. Goggin, one such officer, served as a brigadier for four months before returning to staff duty.

Goggin was born in Bedford County, Virginia, on October 23, 1820. He attended but did not graduate from West Point, and he spent the antebellum years in various business pursuits in Texas, California, and Tennessee. Goggin's first Confederate service was as major of the Thirty-second Virginia Infantry, but he soon became assistant adjutant general of Lafayette McLaws's division (later commanded by Joseph B. Kershaw). As such he participated in all the major eastern campaigns from the Seven Days' Battles to the Shenandoah Valley campaign of 1864. He was repeatedly and enthusiastically recommended by several superiors for promotion to brigadier general.

Kershaw assigned him to a South Carolina brigade when its commander was wounded in October 1864, and Goggin won recognition and praise for his performance at Cedar Creek on October 19. Robert E. Lee and Secretary of War James A. Seddon nominated him for promotion and assignment to a Virginia brigade in December. Goggin's nomination, however, was canceled—apparently because of the return of the brigade's permanent commander—in March 1865. When he was captured at Sayler's Creek only three days before Appomattox, he was once again a major on Kershaw's staff.

After the war, Goggin lived in Texas and died in Austin on October 10, 1889.

BIBLIOGRAPHY

Compiled Military Service Records. James Monroe Goggin. Microcopy M331, Roll 108. Record Group 109. National Archives, Washington, D.C.

U.S. War Department. *War of Rebellion: Official Records of the Union and Confederate Armies*. Washington, D.C., 1880–1901. Ser. 1, vol. 21, pt. 1; ser. 1, vol. 43, pt. 1.

J. Tracy Power

GOODE, JOHN, JR.

GOODE, JOHN, JR. (1829–1909), colonel and congressman from Virginia. Born into a farming family near Liberty (now Bedford), in Bedford County, Virginia, Goode attended school in Connecticut before graduating from Emory and Henry College in his native state in 1848. Admitted to the bar three years later, he began a long legal practice in Bedford County. An Episcopalian and a Democrat, Goode won election to the Virginia legislature where he represented his county during 1852 and 1853.

As an ardent secessionist, Goode did not suffer the anguish of many Virginia politicians during the crisis of 1860–1861. He argued for disunion if Abraham Lincoln was elected, and when chosen to sit in the Virginia convention in 1861, he cast both votes for secession. Once the war began, Goode enlisted as a private soldier in the Second Virginia Cavalry and was wounded at the Battle of First Manassas. After Manassas he served as a volunteer aide on Jubal Early's staff.

Goode won election to both the First and the Second Congresses, on the first occasion without campaigning and while he was in camp with the army near Fairfax Court House. He recalled later how military service sufficed for a campaign. When his opponent made speaking tours through the district, "some friend of mine would arise in the audience and say 'Gentlemen, you must remember that Mr. Goode is also a candidate. . . . He cannot be here today because he is down at the front with the other boys in the army.' "

In the Congress Goode sat on the Commerce, Printing, Indian Affairs, Medical Department, and Enrolled Bills committees, as well as special committees. He became known as a staunch Davis man and one of the most effective Virginians in the Congress. Because he had been an army officer, he focused his energies in the legislature on strengthening the army and the war effort. Though usually undisturbed by doubts, he discarded his early opposition to conscription and became one of its strongest advocates. He also did not hesitate to urge stringent measures for ensuring adequate military supplies, including the impressment of production goods. On the question of using slaves in the army, Goode voted to arm them but would not consent to granting their freedom.

In March 1865, a few days before the Confederate Congress adjourned for the last time, Jefferson Davis sent a member of his staff to fetch Goode. Davis said he wanted Goode's opinion on the willingness of the people of Virginia "to submit to further demands upon them" for food and clothing for the army. Goode replied that he thought the people were prepared to make "still further sacrifices," but he preferred that Davis hear this opinion from others also and not just take his word for it. As a result, later that day Davis called all of Virginia's representatives together for a meeting with the cabinet and Robert E. Lee. According to Goode, there was, in the words diplomats use to describe a blunt exchange, "a full and free interchange of opinion." All in attendance agreed that the people of Virginia "would be found ready and willing to meet any requisitions." Lee explained the military situation to them but, according to Goode, did not "intimate in any manner whatever, that in his opinion the cause was lost."

Immediately after Appomattox, Goode went to Christiansburg and witnessed the disbanding of forces commanded by Gen. John Echols. He continued on to Greensboro, North Carolina, and found that Joseph E. Johnston had already surrendered to William Tecumseh Sherman. Goode called upon Johnston, who gave him the same advice he had given earlier that day to two other legislators—that members of the Confederate Congress should, as the general delicately put it, "remain in the background" until it was known what measures Washington would take regarding them. Goode decided to return home to Bedford "and await developments." The town was occupied by Federal troops, and he found no lack of legal work to engage him, but as there was no money in circulation, he had to accept bacon, chickens, and butter in payment.

In September 1865 he moved to Norfolk, "an entire stranger," with a view to practicing law there. He succeeded very well in his new home and made a name for himself, first as a criminal lawyer and then as a long-serving congressman. Retiring from Congress, he resumed the practice of law in Washington but retained his Virginia residency. He became president of the state bar association and won unanimous appointment as president of the constitutional convention of 1901–1902 that disfranchised those former slaves he had been willing to arm but not free. He died in

Norfolk on July 14, 1909, and was buried in his native Bedford County.

BIBLIOGRAPHY

Goode, John, Jr. *Recollections of a Lifetime.* New York and Washington, D.C., 1906.

Wakelyn, Jon L. *Biographical Dictionary of the Confederacy.* Edited by Frank E. Vandiver. Westport, Conn., 1977.

Warner, Ezra Jr., and W. Buck Yearns. *Biographical Register of the Confederate Congress.* Baton Rouge, La., 1975.

Yearns, Wilfred B. *The Confederate Congress.* Athens, Ga., 1960.

NELSON D. LANKFORD

GORDON, B. FRANK

GORDON, B. FRANK (1824–?), colonel and acting brigadier general. Gordon, born in Tennessee in 1824, moved with his family in 1831 to Lafayette County, Missouri. After participating in a "border protection" unit during the Bleeding Kansas period, Gordon joined the Missouri State Guard in 1861 and was appointed adjutant, First Brigade, Second Division.

While serving in the state guard Gordon fought in the Battle of Wilson Creek, where he was wounded. He transferred to Joseph O. Shelby's cavalry regiment and became major of the Fifth Missouri Cavalry in 1862. Elected lieutenant colonel of the regiment later that year, Gordon led his men into action during the Battles of Newtonia, Helena, and Little Rock. During part of the battle at Little Rock he was temporarily in command of Shelby's brigade. Gordon was promoted to colonel on December 15, 1863. He participated in Sterling Price's last raid and took command of the Missouri brigade after John Sappington Marmaduke was captured. Formally given command of the First Missouri Cavalry Brigade, Cavalry Corps, Trans-Mississippi Department, on October 25, 1864, Gordon served in this position until the end of the war.

Ten days before the Trans-Mississippi Department surrendered, Gen. E. Kirby Smith promoted Gordon to brigadier general in recognition of his service. After the war he served with Shelby in Mexico, returning to the United States in 1866. Gordon's life after the war is a mystery. He has no obituary in the *Confederate Veteran,* which began publishing obituaries in 1873. His name does not appear on the list of attendees at the reunion of Shelby's division in 1885. He is not recorded in the Missouri census of 1870. The implication of this combined evidence is that he died soon after his return from Mexico; however, he is not mentioned in *Published Missouri Obituaries: 1865–1872.*

BIBLIOGRAPHY

Edward, John N. *Shelby and His Men.* Cincinnati, Ohio, 1867.

Missouri Historical Company. *History of Lafayette County, Missouri.* St. Louis, Mo., 1881.

ROY R. STEPHENSON

GORDON, GEORGE WASHINGTON

GORDON, GEORGE WASHINGTON (1836–1911), brigadier general and U.S. congressman. Born October 5, 1836, in Giles County, Tennessee, Gordon was educated at Nashville's Western Military Institute. He was a surveyor from his 1859 graduation until the Civil War.

Serving as drill instructor for the Eleventh Tennessee Infantry Regiment, he became captain of Company I of that unit. When the regiment reorganized in May 1862, he was elected lieutenant colonel. Captured near Tazewell that summer, he was soon exchanged and rejoined his unit. In November he became colonel of the regiment. Captured again at Murfreesboro (December 31, 1862–January 2, 1863), he was back with his men for the battles of late 1863. When Brig. Gen. Alfred Jefferson Vaughn, Jr., was wounded during the Atlanta campaign, Gordon on August 16, 1864, was promoted to brigadier general to replace him.

After the fall of Atlanta, Gordon and his brigade went with the Army of Tennessee in the Franklin and Nashville campaign. Wounded and captured in the great charge at Franklin (November 30), Gordon was held at Fort Warren, Massachusetts, until July 24, 1865.

After the war Gordon practiced law in Memphis. He served as a state railroad commissioner, in the Federal Department of the Interior, as superintendent of Memphis public schools, in the U.S. House of Representatives (1907–1911, the last Confederate general to be a member of Congress), and as commander-in-chief of the United Confederate Veterans. Gordon died in Memphis August 9, 1911, and was buried there in Elmwood Cemetery.

BIBLIOGRAPHY

Hewitt, Lawrence L. "George Washington Gordon." In *The Confederate General.* Edited by William C. Davis. Vol. 3. Harrisburg, Pa., 1991.

Warner, Ezra J. *Generals in Gray: Lives of the Confederate Commanders.* Baton Rouge, La., 1959.

RICHARD M. MCMURRY

GORDON, JAMES BYRON

GORDON, JAMES BYRON (1822–1864), brigadier general. A businessman and farmer by trade, Gordon had briefly entered North Carolina politics in 1850 by serving a term in the state legislature. When his state went to war in 1861, he volunteered for the Wilkes County Guards, and shortly after, his fellow soldiers elected him lieutenant. Gordon became their captain when the Wilkes County Guards joined the Confederate army as Company B of the First Regular North Carolina troops.

In March 1862 Gordon became lieutenant colonel under Wade Hampton with whom he fought in many of the major battles in the eastern theater. Cavalry commander J. E. B. Stuart consistently praised Gordon's skills as a soldier and his ability to rally his men. Stuart and Gordon fought

JAMES BYRON GORDON.   LIBRARY OF CONGRESS

together during the Seven Days' Battles, Second Manassas, Stuart's daring raid into Pennsylvania in the fall of 1862, and the Confederate victories at Fredericksburg and Chancellorsville. At Gettysburg, Gordon and his men repelled a group of Union soldiers at Hagerstown as the Confederate army made its retreat.

Gordon's talents on the battlefield continued to earn him promotion; in September 1863, he became a brigadier general. Later that year he commanded his brigade in a skirmish with the enemy at Mine Run, where an enemy bullet shot his horse from under him. In May 1864, when the Army of the Potomac crossed the Rapidan to strike Robert E. Lee's army, Gordon and his men were the first to meet the rush of Federal troops. They fought Ulysses S. Grant's troops from the banks of the river to Spotsylvania Court House.

A week later, Gordon and his brigade helped repulse Philip Sheridan's attack on the Confederate capital. Although Richmond remained intact in 1864, Gordon lost his life in the struggle. He was wounded near Meadow Bridge, the day after the fight at Yellow Tavern, and died in Richmond May 18, 1864.

BIBLIOGRAPHY

Freeman, Douglas. *Lee's Lieutenants: A Study in Command.* 3 vols. New York, 1942–1944. Reprint, New York, 1986.

Hill, D. H., Jr. *North Carolina.* Vol. 4 of *Confederate Military History.* Edited by Clement A. Evans. Atlanta, 1899. Vol. 5 of extended ed. Wilmington, N.C., 1987.

Wakelyn, Jon L. *Biographical Dictionary of the Confederacy.* Edited by Frank E. Vandiver. Westport, Conn., 1977.

Warner, Ezra J. *Generals in Gray: Lives of the Confederate Commanders.* Baton Rouge, La., 1959.

JENNIFER LUND

GORDON, JOHN B. (1832–1904), major general, U.S. senator, and governor of Georgia. The descendant of Scottish immigrants and of a Revolutionary War soldier, Gordon was born in Upson County, Georgia, February 6, 1832, and for more than forty years was one of the most celebrated citizens of the state.

Gordon attended the University of Georgia but did not graduate. In 1854 he studied law in Atlanta and by the end of the year had passed his bar examination and was a partner in an established law firm. When the legal profession failed to provide the income he expected, Gordon moved to the state capital of Milledgeville in November 1855. There he obtained employment as a newspaperman covering the general assembly. By the end of the decade, however, he was in northwestern Georgia working with his father in developing coal mines.

Shortly after the bombardment of Fort Sumter, Gordon helped organize a company of volunteers from Georgia, Alabama, and Tennessee that styled itself the "Raccoon Roughs." On May 15 the company was mustered into Confederate service as part of the Sixth Alabama Infantry Regiment, with Gordon as major and his brother Augustus as captain. After training in Corinth, Mississippi, the regiment departed for Virginia. There it occupied the extreme right of P. G. T. Beauregard's line on July 21. While other regiments routed the Federals at First Manassas, however, the Sixth Alabama only waited, marched, and countermarched.

Gordon's rise in the command structure was spectacularly rapid. He was promoted to colonel on April 28, 1862; to brigadier, November 1, 1862; and to major general, May 14, 1864.

Gordon fought valiantly whenever his command was engaged. At Seven Pines, where he lost 60 percent of his troops, he was placed in temporary command of Robert Rodes's brigade when that officer was incapacitated by wounds. Gordon's brigade led Robert E. Lee's vanguard into Maryland in September 1862 and engaged the enemy at South Mountain. In the words of Rodes, Gordon fought in a "manner I have never heard or seen equalled during the

JOHN B. GORDON.   NATIONAL ARCHIVES

An officer who glimpsed Gordon riding a black stallion that day called the sight "the most glorious and inspiring thing . . . standing in his stirrups bareheaded, hat in hand, arms extended, and, in a voice like a trumpet, exhorting his men. It was superb, absolutely thrilling." Gordon did not consider his actions the next two days "of sufficient importance to mention."

At Spotsylvania, Gordon's men shouted their famous "Lee to the rear!" order to the commanding general while Gordon rode to the front of his troops and reestablished the Confederate line, thereby turning imminent disaster into victory.

In June 1864, Gordon's brigade was detached from the forces around Richmond and participated in Early's Shenandoah Valley campaign. Gordon's men helped drive David O. Hunter from the Valley and delivered a crushing blow to Lew Wallace at Monocacy on the aborted raid on Washington. Gordon then took part in the Battles of Third Winchester, Fisher's Hill, and Cedar Creek before rejoining Lee in the defenses of Petersburg.

His last major action occurred on March 25, 1865, when he directed a predawn attack on Fort Stedman, hoping to breach the Union lines and permit some of Lee's troops to escape to North Carolina and join Joseph E. Johnston. Initially, the attack carried the works, but lack of support and confusion in the darkness eventually doomed the venture. The thirty-three-year-old lawyer who possessed "the personality and genius for war" commanded the Second Corps on the retreat from Petersburg and surrendered at Appomattox.

Returning to Georgia, Gordon resumed the practice of law, this time in Atlanta, and entered Democratic politics. He lost a gubernatorial bid in 1868 but was elected to the U.S. Senate in 1873. Shortly after his reelection in 1879, Gordon resigned to enter the employ of a major railroad company. He served as governor from 1886 to 1890, after which the legislature again elected him to the Senate.

The popular soldier-statesman served as commander-in-chief of the United Confederate Veterans from the inception of the organization in 1890 until his death on January 9, 1904. He was buried in Oakland Cemetery, Atlanta.

war." D. H. Hill, the division commander, added: "Gordon excelled his former deeds at Seven Pines and in the battles around Richmond. Our language is not capable of expressing a higher compliment."

Gordon's brigade was in the thickest of the fighting at Sharpsburg, a battle in which the general was wounded five times, once in the head. Only a bullet hole in his hat prevented him from drowning in his own blood as he lay unconscious on the ground. He was nursed back to health by his wife, who had left their two sons with her mother-in-law in Georgia to accompany the general to the war. "I owe my life to her incessant watchfulness night and day," said Gordon, "and to her tender nursing through weary weeks and anxious months."

By the spring of 1863 the general, of "striking appearance and commanding presence . . . six feet tall, thin and straight as a rail but muscular and powerful of build," was back in action, commanding a brigade under Jubal Early at Chancellorsville. In the Gettysburg campaign, he led Early's column to York and Wrightsville. Rejoining the main Confederate force at Gettysburg, Gordon took an active part in the first day's engagement north and west of the town.

BIBLIOGRAPHY

Early, Jubal A. "Leading Confederates on the Battle of Gettysburg." *Southern Historical Society Papers* 4 (1877): 243–244, 254–258. Reprint, Wilmington, N.C., 1990.

Eckert, Ralph Lowell. *John Brown Gordon: Soldier, Southerner, American.* Baton Rouge, La., 1989.

Gordon, John Brown. *Reminiscences of the Civil War.* New York, 1903.

Ockenden, I. M. Porter. "Gordon, Commander in Chief, U. C. V." *Confederate Veteran* 12 (1904): 56–59. Reprint, Wilmington, N.C., 1985.

Tankersley, Allen P. *John B. Gordon: A Study in Gallantry.* Atlanta, 1955.

LOWELL REIDENBAUGH

GORGAS, JOSIAH (1818–1883), chief of ordnance of the Confederate army. Born July 1, 1818, at Running Pumps, Pennsylvania, Gorgas was the son of Joseph Gorgas and Sophia Atkinson. Appointed to the U.S. Military Academy in 1837, he graduated sixth in his class in 1841 and selected the Ordnance Corps for his service. His first assignment was to Watervliet Arsenal near Troy, New York. He traveled for a year in Europe (1845–1846) and then joined Gen. Winfield Scott's expeditionary force to Mexico. His good work in placing guns for the Vera Cruz siege and in servicing ammunition needs made Gorgas commander of the ordnance depot there. But a bout with yellow fever plus the tedious routine of the depot eroded much of the glamour of the Mexican War for him. A carper, he complained much about people and conditions, but his sound war service taught him, and several important superiors, something of his native competence in ordnance matters. Mexican service also introduced him to many younger officers who would work with and against him during the Civil War.

Gorgas's natural independence sometimes translated

JOSIAH GORGAS.   LIBRARY OF CONGRESS

into a resentment of superiors, and this involved him in a petty but lasting dispute with Secretary of State James Buchanan and Secretary of War William L. Marcy— a controversy that cost Gorgas a brevet promotion for Mexican services and hampered his entire U.S. Army career.

Routine ordnance duties throughout the 1840s and 1850s took Gorgas to installations in the Deep South and to scattered arsenals in the North. At Mount Vernon Arsenal in Alabama, he met Amelia Gayle, daughter of a former governor of Alabama. He and Amelia were married on December 26, 1853. She soothed the roughness of Josiah's personality, but could not heal the wound left by the dispute with Buchanan. She bore Josiah two sons (one, William Crawford, would be a conqueror of yellow fever) and four daughters.

Promotions were slow for this dark-haired soldier with steady eyes, a large nose, and a straight mouth hidden by a full beard. When the Civil War came, he was a captain in command of Frankford Arsenal in Philadelphia. At first Gorgas hesitated to join the new Confederate army, but continuing troubles with superiors pushed him at last to accept a commission (effective April 8, 1861) as major in the artillery of the Confederate States with assignment to the important duty of chief of ordnance. Gen. P. G. T. Beauregard, who knew him slightly, had urged his appointment on President Jefferson Davis. He proved one of the most effective of Davis's appointees.

The challenges facing Gorgas were staggering. The South had few manufacturing facilities, only one large foundry capable of casting heavy cannon (in Richmond, Virginia), and although each state had an armory, arsenals capable of repairing or making arms were few. Across the Confederacy Gorgas counted only 159,010 small arms of all kinds, about 3.2 million cartridges of various calibers, powder enough for another million and a half bullets, and an indeterminate amount of cannon powder. Close to 3 million percussion caps were counted, along with saltpeter and sulphur enough to make an additional 200 tons of powder. Supplies were scattered across different states; governors tended to guard their hoards with parochial jealousy.

Gorgas's first efforts were directed toward scavenging every battlefield, next toward creating or expanding existing industrial capacities, and finally toward the importation of all kinds of ordnance stores from the North and from Europe. He developed mineral resources through a Niter and Mining Corps. Various arsenals were overhauled and modernized; small ordnance shops were established in Tennessee, Mississippi, Virginia, and Texas. Gorgas hoped to create a centralized procurement and distribution plan that would rely on a few large works from which arms and munitions would be distributed to the railheads near field armies. But he soon realized that the rail system of the South inhibited such a centralized procurement plan, and without that luxury, he had to rely on decentralized distribution.

By 1862, Gorgas had turned his attention increasingly to blockade running as an essential source of cannons, powder, lead, copper, arms, and other ordnance needs. He successfully urged creation of a Bureau of Foreign Supplies to organize overseas purchasing. His efforts led to the purchase of blockade runners for his and other supply departments, and an efficient system of transshipment in Bermuda, Nassau, and Cuba. From 1861 to 1865 about 600,000 small arms reached the South. From December 1863 to December 1864, 1,933,000 pounds of saltpeter and 1,507,000 pounds of lead arrived.

Gorgas's programs succeeded. On April 8, 1864, he confided in his diary that

> it is three years ago today since I took charge of the Ordnance Department.... I have succeeded beyond my utmost expectations. From being the worst supplied of the Bureaus of the War Department it is now the best.... Where ... we were not making a gun, a pistol nor a sabre, no shot nor shell ... —a pound of powder—we now make all these in quantities to meet the demands of our large armies.

On November 19, 1864, he was promoted to brigadier general.

Gorgas performed logistical miracles to the end of the war. Perhaps his greatest strength was his judgment of subordinates. He picked able men to run his installations and to serve with the field armies, and he backed his men strongly. He and his department did more than any other supply agency to sustain the Confederacy.

After the war, failure in an iron-making venture at Brierfield, Alabama, led Gorgas to become, on July 1, 1869, head of the junior department of the nascent University of the South at Sewanee, Tennessee, and finally head of that institution (July 10, 1872). A stormy tenure there ended with his appointment in July 1878 as president of the University of Alabama. He enjoyed the town of Tuscaloosa and was a quick success with the faculty and student body. The Alabama move restored his self-confidence, but his happiness was brief. Illness forced Gorgas to resign the presidency in September 1879. Appointed librarian, he lived with his family on the university campus until his death on May 15, 1883.

BIBLIOGRAPHY

Vandiver, Frank E., ed. *The Civil War Diary of General Josiah Gorgas*. University, Ala., 1947.

Vandiver, Frank E. *Ploughshares into Swords: Josiah Gorgas and Confederate Ordnance*. Austin, Tex., 1952.

FRANK E. VANDIVER

GOSPORT NAVY YARD. Located across the Elizabeth River from Norfolk, Virginia, Gosport was the largest and best equipped naval yard in the United States in 1861. Norfolk was an important port and shipbuilding center from the colonial period, and Gosport was chosen as the site for a naval yard in the years after the War of 1812. In 1830 the navy opened its first stone dry dock at the yard. By 1861 the yard occupied a rectangular area about three-quarters of a mile long and a quarter of a mile wide. Yard facilities included a granite dry dock, two large ship houses, a third ship house under construction, riggers and sail lofts, sawmills, timber sheds, spar and mast storage sheds, foundries, machine shops, boiler shops, an ordnance magazine, and an ordnance laboratory. The Gosport Navy Yard also served as the storage site for over three thousand naval

BURNING OF THE GOSPORT NAVY YARD. April 20, 1861.

cannons, most important of which were some three hundred new Dahlgren shell guns.

Commandant of the yard in 1861 was Commo. Charles S. McCauley, a fifty-two-year-old navy veteran. Either under repair or anchored off the yard that spring were the sailing sloops *Plymouth* and *Germantown,* the brig *Dolphin,* ships-of-the-line *Delaware* and *Columbus,* and two frigates, *Columbia* and *Raritan.* Former ship-of-the-line *Pennsylvania* served as an unarmed receiving ship, and the ship-of-the-line *New York* was still on the stocks. The most important vessel at Gosport was the five-year-old steam frigate *Merrimack,* in dry dock for repairs. In March, the steam sloop-of-war *Cumberland* anchored off the yard.

In early April 1861, Federal Secretary of the Navy Gideon Welles, concerned over the fate of *Merrimack,* requested that McCauley make it ready for departure as quickly as possible. When McCauley replied that this would take a month, Welles ordered the U.S. Navy's engineer-in-chief, Benjamin F. Isherwood, to make the repairs. Isherwood went to Gosport with Commdr. James D. Alden, who was to command *Merrimack* when the repairs were finished; they arrived on April 14. He had *Merrimack* ready by the seventeenth, but McCauley refused to let him raise steam. Isherwood later charged that McCauley was drunk; other sources suggest that he was simply confused and indecisive.

Isherwood had *Merrimack's* boiler fires alight the next morning, but he could not persuade Commander Alden to sail the ship out in defiance of McCauley. Both officers returned to Washington. Secretary Welles promptly sent Commo. Hiram Paulding to relieve McCauley.

Although the gates into the yard were locked, a loud mob had gathered just outside them, convincing McCauley that thousands of Virginia troops were about to attack. On April 20 he ordered all the ships in the yard burned and scuttled. Upon his arrival, Paulding confirmed these orders and extended them to include the entire yard.

The destruction was not fully effective. Civilians and Virginia soldiers raced into the yard as soon as the defenders abandoned it and extinguished most of the fires. Although all the vessels at the yard, with the exception of *Cumberland* and *Pawnee,* were set afire, *Plymouth, Delaware,* and *Columbus* sank with little damage. Neither powder charges at the dry dock nor those at the powder magazine exploded. The sail loft, rigging loft, gun carriage depot, and two of the ship houses were totally burned, but all the other buildings were saved intact. Confederate naval authorities seized over a thousand guns, thousands of tons of supplies, and even uniforms from various storehouses within the yard, and recovered some four thousand shells from the harbor waters. Most important, in the undamaged dry dock, *Merrimack* sank with fire damage confined to its rigging and upper deck. Not only was the hull of the ship salvageable; within a watertight magazine below decks were over two thousand 10-pound cartridges.

Union forces recaptured the navy yard in May 1862. Despite extensive destruction of the yard's facilities by the retreating Confederates, the yard formed an important part of Union naval control of the Hampton Roads area for the remainder of the war.

BIBLIOGRAPHY

Beach, Edward L. *The United States Navy: 200 Years.* New York, 1986.

Wertenbaker, Thomas J. *Norfolk: Historic Southern Port.* Durham, N.C., 1931.

Still, William N., Jr. *Iron Afloat: The Story of the Confederate Armorclads.* Nashville, Tenn., 1971.

ROBERT S. BROWNING III

GOVAN, DANIEL CHEVILETTE (1829–1911),

brigadier general. Born in Northampton County, North Carolina, on July 4, 1829, Govan later attended the University of South Carolina, graduating in 1848. After participating in the California Gold Rush, he returned to Mississippi in 1852 and moved to Arkansas in 1860. A planter before the Civil War, Govan began his Confederate service as a lieutenant colonel in the Second Arkansas Infantry. Promoted to colonel, he commanded the regiment at Shiloh, Perryville, Kentucky, and Murfreesboro, Tennessee. He then took part in the engagement at Liberty Gap during the Tullahoma campaign, and in September 1863 he succeeded St. John Richardson Liddell in command of the brigade. The unit performed with distinction at Chickamauga, capturing hundreds of prisoners and several pieces of artillery when it repulsed a Federal attack during the first day of fighting. Govan fought at Missionary Ridge, and when the Confederate line gave way his brigade constituted part of the rear guard. In January 1864 he endorsed a petition circulated by Patrick Cleburne calling for the Confederacy to free some of its slaves and enlist them as soldiers. Promoted to brigadier general in December 1863, Govan led his brigade with skill and valor in the Atlanta campaign until he was captured at the Battle of Jonesboro on September 1, 1864. Exchanged three weeks later, he commanded his brigade at Franklin and Nashville. Wounded in the latter engagement, he returned to active duty in time to lead his men in the Carolinas campaign. He surrendered with Joseph E. Johnston at Greensboro on April 26, 1865.

After the war Govan returned to his Arkansas plantation and resumed farming. He died on March 12, 1911, in Memphis, Tennessee.

BIBLIOGRAPHY

McDonough, James Lee. *Chattanooga: A Death Grip on the Confederacy.* Knoxville, Tenn., 1987.

Spencer, James. *Civil War Generals.* Westport, Conn., 1986.

Tucker, Glenn. *Chickamauga: Bloody Battle in the West.* Dayton, Ohio, 1961.

Wakelyn, Jon L. *Biographical Dictionary of the Confederacy.* Edited by Frank E. Vandiver. Westport, Conn., 1977.

MICHAEL G. MAHON

GOVERNORS.

By 1860 all Southern states had governors elected by those citizens eligible to vote for members of the lower house of the general assembly except South Carolina, whose governor was elected by the assembly. All American governors under the first state constitutions had little authority, but the practical matter of efficient government compelled gradual change. By 1860 Southern governors had gained considerable independence from the legislatures, but they were not yet as powerful constitutionally. The power they had gained lay not so much in a strengthened executive branch as in their ability to curb legislative authority. The typical governor could delay legislation passed by the assembly but had little appointive power. It is true that every state that entered the Confederacy named the governor as its commander in chief, but this power was almost untested.

When the Confederacy began its war for independence, the old practice of decision making by legislatures proved inadequate. The citizenry had to be persuaded to make great sacrifices and consider defeat unthinkable; producers and merchants had to be induced to give the war their first priority; soldiers had to be supplied. A central government could provide the basic war measures and some methods of implementing them, but the South was not yet ready for this degree of central authority. And even if it had been, geography and the state of the economy would have prevented the imposition of much more centralism than actually occurred. To wage a successful war, the Confederate government had to have the full cooperation of the states. The extent of each state's cooperation can largely be measured by the actions of its governor.

Charisma and Leadership. In any struggle for independence against great odds, strong leadership is pivotal. All the first Confederate governors except John Letcher of Virginia had been secession leaders who obviously had the respect of their people. As their responsibilities increased during war, so did their visibility. How dedicated each of them was to victory offered guidance to their people, who usually responded to the war as their governor seemed to respond. With certain exceptions, then, the governors represented the collective sentiment of their constituents.

Twenty-eight men served as Confederate governors. Most were in their forties, and only Charles Clark of Mississippi and Harris Flanagin of Arkansas were Northern-born. All who were governor during secession were Democrats, and all but three of these had advocated secession upon Abraham Lincoln's election. In the last years of the Confederacy, when discontent was rampant, voters turned mainly to ex-Whigs and former Unionists. Most governors had been lawyers and half of them had college or university degrees. Most were politically experienced and six had had military experience. As a whole, they were quite representative of mid-nineteenth-century American political leadership.

Alabama, Florida, Louisiana, Kentucky, Mississippi, Tennessee, Texas, and Virginia began their Confederate years with governors clearly intent upon success. They made sound preparations for war, and when it came they acted decisively. They publicly sought to preserve state and individual rights, but also accepted the need for sacrifice. Possibly J. J. Pettus of Mississippi was overzealous in his support of wartime legislation, but he was reelected overwhelmingly; and Andrew B. Moore of Alabama had malcontents from the first whom he could not beguile. These eight governors were no better or worse managers than the other five original Confederate governors, but they had a symbolic quality that established their states' rapport with the Confederate war program.

The other secession governors failed to become charismatic pro-Confederate leaders. Joseph E. Brown of Georgia did so deliberately; Claiborne F. Jackson of Missouri was politically inept; John W. Ellis of North Carolina was too retiring; Francis W. Pickens of South Carolina was too inert; and Henry M. Rector of Arkansas was apparently too scatter-brained.

Only seven of the postsecession governors served long enough for their image to be of much consequence. John G. Shorter of Alabama and John Milton of Florida became governors early in the Confederacy and established themselves as protagonists of both state and nation. Henry W. Allen of Louisiana, Milledge L. Bonham of South Carolina, Francis R. Lubbock of Texas, and William ("Extra Billy") Smith of Virginia took office midway through the war. They were fair-minded, dedicated officials, and it would be difficult to imagine executives operating under such difficulties to have been more successful. None of them had a compelling personality, but all projected a grim determination that would be the last hope of the Confederacy. Zebulon Vance of North Carolina quickly became the paradigm of a state and individual rights fanatic, and both he and his state actually appeared to be anti-Confederate despite their enormous contributions to the war.

The quality of leadership of the eight remaining governors varied much but mattered little. The tenure of Henry T. Clark of North Carolina was very brief. Thomas H. Watts of Alabama served the last seventeen months of the war and made serious efforts at leadership, but by 1864 disaffection was so great that he seemed too pro-Confederate for Alabamans and too pro-Alabama for Richmond. Richard Hawes of Kentucky, Clark of Mississippi, and Thomas C. Reynolds of Missouri made valiant efforts to do something

Civil War–era Governors of Southern States[1]

STATE	GOVERNOR	DATES OF SERVICE[2]
Alabama	Andrew B. Moore	Dec. 1, 1857–Dec. 2, 1861
	John G. Shorter	Dec. 2, 1861–Dec. 1, 1863
	Thomas H. Watts	Dec. 1, 1863–Apr. 12, 1865[3]
Arkansas	Henry M. Rector	Nov. 15, 1860–Nov. 4, 1862
	Thomas Fletcher	Nov. 4, 1862–Nov. 15, 1862
	Harris Flanagin	Nov. 15, 1862–May 28, 1865[4]
	Isaac Murphy	*Apr. 18, 1864–July 3, 1868*
Florida	Madison S. Perry	Oct. 5, 1857–Oct. 7, 1861
	John Milton	Oct. 7, 1861–Apr. 1, 1865
	Abraham K. Allison	Apr. 1, 1865–Sept. 1865
Georgia	Joseph E. Brown	Nov. 6, 1857–May 9, 1865[5]
Kentucky	George W. Johnson	Nov. 20, 1861–Apr. 8, 1862
	Richard Hawes[6]	Apr. 8, 1862–spring 1865
	Beriah Magoffin	*Aug. 30, 1859–Aug. 18, 1862*
	James F. Robinson	*Aug. 18, 1862–Sept. 1, 1863*
	Thomas Elliott Bramlette	*Sept. 1, 1863–Sept. 3, 1867*
Louisiana	Thomas O. Moore	Jan. 23, 1860–Jan. 26, 1864
	Henry W. Allen	Jan. 26, 1864–June 6, 1865
	George F. Shepley[7]	*June 2, 1862–Mar. 4, 1864*
	Michael Hahn	*Mar. 4, 1864–Mar. 3, 1865*
	James Madison Wells	*Mar. 3, 1865–June 25, 1868*
Mississippi	J. J. Pettus	Nov. 21, 1859–Nov. 16, 1863
	Charles Clark	Nov. 16, 1863–May 22, 1865
Missouri	Claiborne F. Jackson	Jan. 3, 1861–Dec. 6, 1862
	Thomas C. Reynolds	Dec. 6, 1862–Apr. 1865
	Hamilton Rowan Gamble	*June 31, 1861–Jan. 31, 1864*
	Willard Preble Hall	*Jan. 31, 1864–Jan. 2, 1865*
	Thomas Clement Fletcher	*Jan. 2, 1865–Jan. 12, 1869*
North Carolina	John W. Ellis	Jan. 1, 1859– July 7, 1861
	Henry T. Clark	July 7, 1861–Sept. 8, 1862
	Zebulon Vance	Sept. 8, 1862–May 13, 1865
	Edward Stanly[7]	*May 26, 1862–Jan. 15, 1863*

constructive, but their states were largely in Federal hands. Flanagin of Arkansas, Andrew G. Magrath of South Carolina, and Pendleton Murrah of Texas took office near the end of the war and were both inactive in and sometimes obstructive to the war effort.

Cooperation with Richmond. Though the image that a governor projected was important to the morale of his state, what he did was even more important. There was a vast uncertainty regarding the proper course of action. Bred under state rights doctrine, he now had to accept the exigencies of war. Upon the enactment of Confederate laws on conscription, impressment, and suspension of habeas corpus, most governors protested automatically. Some—Brown of Georgia and Vance of North Carolina—complained so stridently that they were condemned more for their words than for their deeds. But after making their protests, and occasionally forcing slight compromises, the governors were generally cooperative.

An examination of the careers of the Confederate governors indicates that fifteen of them cooperated effectively with the war policies of the central government. Some were more nationalistic than their legislatures and suffered

Civil War-era Governors of Southern States[1]—cont'd

STATE	GOVERNOR	DATES OF SERVICE[2]
South Carolina	Francis W. Pickens	Dec. 14, 1860–Dec. 1862[8]
	Milledge L. Bonham	Dec. 17, 1862–Dec. 1864[8]
	Andrew G. Magrath	Dec. 18, 1864–May 28, 1865
Tennessee	Isham G. Harris	Nov. 3, 1857–Aug. 1863[9]
	Robert Looney Caruthers	Aug. 1863[10]
	Andrew Johnson[7]	*Mar. 3, 1862–Mar. 3, 1865*
	E. H. East[7]	*Mar. 3, 1865–Apr. 5, 1865*
	William G. Brownlow	*Apr. 5, 1865–Feb. 25, 1869*
Texas	Edward Clark	Mar. 16, 1861–Nov. 7, 1861
	Francis R. Lubbock	Nov. 7, 1861–Nov. 5, 1863
	Pendleton Murrah	Nov. 5, 1863– June 11, 1865
Virginia	John Letcher	Jan. 1, 1860– Jan. 1, 1864
	William ("Extra Billy") Smith	Jan. 1, 1864–May 9, 1865
	Francis H. Peirpoint[11]	*June 1861–Apr. 16, 1868*

[1]This table includes governors of state governments allied with the Confederacy as well as those allied with the Union. Names and dates in italics denote a Union alliance; those not in italics denote a Confederate alliance. Often a single state was represented simultaneously by a government allied with the Confederacy and a government remaining in, occupied by, or restored to the Union. Unless noted as a military appointee, all governors in this table were civilian executives.

[2]Dates of service vary widely in historical sources. The dates given here reflect the best available consensus based on various state records, state histories, military histories, and biographies. When an exact date is not given, no greater consensus is possible. Unless otherwise noted, the first date listed for each governor is the date of his inauguration.

[3]Date of the Union occupation of Montgomery, Alabama.

[4]Unaware that Confederate forces west of the Mississippi had surrendered on May 26, 1865, Flanagin continued to serve until at least May 28, the last date on record for his actions as governor.

[5]A Federal order for Governor Brown's arrest was issued on May 7, 1865, and carried out on May 9. President Andrew Johnson did not appoint a provisional governor until June 17.

[6]Hawes was elected and assumed the office of governor of the Provisional Confederate Government of Kentucky some time after George W. Johnson's death on April 8, 1862, and before late August of that year. The records containing Hawes's exact dates of service were lost at the end of the war.

[7]Union military governor; first date listed is date of appointment.

[8]Initial date is that of election by the state legislature.

[9]Although Harris called for a gubernatorial election to be held in August 1863, the winner of that election, Robert Looney Caruthers, never took office. According to the Tennessee Constitution, Harris technically remained governor until his successor, William G. Brownlow, qualified for the office.

[10]Month of the last Confederate gubernatorial election in Tennessee. Because of Union occupation of most of Tennessee, Caruthers was never inaugurated and never served.

[11]Peirpoint initially served as governor of Restored (or Reorganized) Virginia, a pro-Union government established by the Second Wheeling Convention, which elected Peirpoint governor some time after it convened on June 11, 1861. On May 9, 1865, the U.S. government recognized Peirpoint's as the sole, official government of Virginia.

politically for their zeal. These men were Smith and Letcher of Virginia, Pickens and Bonham of South Carolina, Perry and Milton of Florida, Moore and Shorter of Alabama, Moore of Louisiana, Pettus of Mississippi, Clark and Lubbock of Texas, Jackson of Missouri, George W. Johnson of Kentucky, and Isham G. Harris of Tennessee. Certain inevitable obstacles often hampered good execution of Confederate policies in a state, but within recognized limits these governors deserve good marks for nationalism.

Several others would like to have been more effective Confederates but were unable to do so. Ellis and Clark of North Carolina were too passive; Allen of Louisiana and Rector of Arkansas were cut off from Richmond by enemy occupation; Hawes and Reynolds were refugee governors. Five governors came to office when the war was already lost.

Watts of Alabama, Magrath of South Carolina, Murrah of Texas, and Charles Clark of Mississippi hoped to salvage something either by separate state action or by continuing the war in the Southwest, but none of their desperate efforts succeeded. Flanagin of Arkansas simply gave up and did nothing.

Only Brown of Georgia and Vance of North Carolina significantly hampered the war effort. Both were fanatical state righters and their constant carping undoubtedly fed the discontent developing in their states; both men willingly shouldered this resentment. Brown was the more destructive. Vance won the right to exempt state employees from military service and other, smaller victories, but on most matters he cooperated, albeit grudgingly. Brown differed with Richmond more, quarreled more violently, and won more victories over the central government.

Management. Equally important as charisma and the degree of cooperation with Richmond was a governor's executive ability. What power the Southern governors had acquired by 1860 was largely in negative control over legislation. But legislatures at this time were basically conservative, disliking taxation and preferring to interfere as little as possible in the state economy or the personal affairs of the citizens. This system could not operate effectively under the strain of constant demands from Richmond and ever-increasing problems at home. State governors now had to initiate virtually all the necessary legislation and to expand their power as commander in chief to unprecedented levels.

To exercise these new powers, governors often found themselves vying more with their own legislatures than with Richmond. The Florida and South Carolina legislatures even created a plural executive to diffuse executive power, though this worked badly in Florida and it soon returned to a single executive. But the need for emergency action usually prevailed. There would be a need for a law, the governor would specify what was needed, and generally the legislature would comply. Thus the national pattern also became the state pattern.

The first major duty of the governors was to raise volunteers for the Confederate provisional army. They had started doing so even before secession and soon had far more volunteers than the War Department could accept. The governors protested bitterly when so many volunteers were encamped at home at state expense; nevertheless, these men were available to Richmond at a moment's notice. Legislatures all wanted local defense forces and these the governors provided, though they never proved to be effective defenders.

One of the greatest contributions the states made, even under Brown and Vance, was in matériel for the army. The work in this area was ad hoc and improvisational. Governors found themselves suddenly saddled with a variety of duties without precedent: collecting weapons, manufacturing ammunition, negotiating contracts for the manufacture of all sorts of army needs, sending out purchasing agents and blockade runners to buy everything from meat to muslin, and begging clothing from churches and ladies' organizations. Moreover, they had to compete with Confederate purchasing agents. Selfish localism naturally dictated that one's own volunteers had first call upon such goods, leaving the War Department to outfit less fortunate soldiers.

All governors took seriously their position as commander in chief of state forces. They seized Federal installations on their own initiative, and those outside the main battle zones unwillingly took charge of their own defenses. They impressed slaves and free blacks for labor; they obtained from their legislatures or simply arrogated to themselves the right to restrict cotton planting, to arrest peace activists, to ban distilling, to restrict hoarding and speculation, and even to declare martial law. The governors of Georgia, South Carolina, and Texas even ventured into foreign diplomacy.

Some of the new policies were startlingly modern. All tried to allocate money or food to soldiers' families. Arkansas failed in this, but Georgia succeeded magnificently: its welfare expenditures dominated the state's budget for the last two years of the war. Salt was a vital preservative and every governor had carte blanche authority to acquire it. Cotton and wool cards were vital and scarce, and governors either imported them or ordered their manufacture. As unimportant as these efforts may seem, the home front could not have survived as long as it did without them.

To finance this work, conservative antebellum practices had to be abandoned. The financial history of each state shows regular demands by governors for appropriations and almost immediate responses by the legislatures in the form of fiat money and bond issues or new taxes. The Georgia state budget exceeded the state's appropriations for the entire decade of the 1850s. Refugee governors virtually carried their state treasury in their saddlebags and spent it at their own discretion. Thus with rare exceptions the governor asked and the legislature complied—an illustration of executive dominance during wartime. Obviously many of these expenditures were for military purposes, but events were creating such distress among civilians that for the first time in American history individual welfare was considered a government responsibility. The Civil War was indeed putting the Southern states and their governors through a revolutionary experience.

[*See also* State Rights; *biographies of particular governors; and entries on particular states.*]

BIBLIOGRAPHY

Escott, Paul D. *After Secession: Jefferson Davis and the Failure of Confederate Nationalism*. Baton Rouge, La., and London, 1978.

McMillan, Malcolm C. *The Disintegration of a Confederate State*. Macon, Ga., 1986.

Moore, Albert B. *Conscription and Conflict in the Confederacy*. New York, 1924.

Owsley, Frank L. *State Rights in the Confederacy*. Chicago, 1925. Reprint, Gloucester, Mass., 1961.

Ringold, Spencer. *The Role of State Legislatures in the Confederacy*. Athens, Ga., 1966.

Yearns, Wilfred B. *The Confederate Congress*. Athens, Ga., 1960.

W. Buck Yearns

GRACIE, ARCHIBALD, JR. (1832–1864), brigadier general. Born in New York City, December 1, 1832, Gracie received his early education in Germany. In 1854 he

graduated from the U.S. Military Academy (fourteenth of forty-six in his class). He served as a lieutenant in the Fourth and Fifth Infantry regiments until his resignation on May 3, 1856. He then lived in Mobile, Alabama, where he worked in his father's business and was active in the Washington Light Infantry, a local militia company.

Early in 1861, acting on orders from the Alabama governor, he helped seize the Mount Vernon Arsenal. He then became a captain in the Third Alabama Infantry. On July 12, 1861, he was promoted to major, and early the next year he helped raise and organize the Forty-third Alabama. Elected colonel of the regiment February 11, 1863, Gracie served with it in eastern Tennessee and northern Georgia until late 1863. On November 4, 1862, he was promoted to brigadier general.

Wounded in the arm on December 15, 1863, at Bean's Station, Tennessee, during the Knoxville campaign, Gracie recovered in time to rejoin his command in Virginia the following spring. He fought in the operations around Petersburg. At noon on December 2, 1864, while observing the Federal lines through a telescope, Gracie was killed by an exploding artillery shell. Upon hearing of his death, Gen. Robert E. Lee commented that Gracie had been a "bold, zealous & enterprising" officer.

Gracie is buried in Woodlawn Cemetery in New York City.

BIBLIOGRAPHY

Davis, William C. "Archibald Gracie, Jr." In *The Confederate General.* Edited by William C. Davis. Vol. 3. Harrisburg, Pa., 1991.

Warner, Ezra J. *Generals in Gray: Lives of the Confederate Commanders.* Baton Rouge, La., 1959.

RICHARD M. McMURRY

GRAHAM, MALCOLM D. (1827–1878), congressman from Texas. Graham was born July 6, 1827, in Alabama and moved to Texas in 1855. He settled at Henderson, Rusk County, where he was an attorney and politician. He served in the Texas Senate in 1857 and as attorney general from 1858 to 1860. He was an elector on the Breckinridge ticket in 1860 and a prominent advocate of secession. He was one of seventy-two men who signed a second address calling for the people to elect delegates to a state convention to address the threat posed to Southern rights by the election of President Abraham Lincoln.

In the spring of 1861, Graham volunteered for military service in a state unit, but he did not serve. In November 1861, he was elected to the House of Representatives of the First Congress. In the first session, he supported a majority of the measures sponsored by the Davis administration, including such controversial issues as conscription and suspension of the writ of habeas corpus. He ran for reelection in 1863 on his record and lost to Col. John R.

Baylor, a popular military officer who had campaigned as a critic of Davis.

In May 1864, Graham was appointed presiding judge advocate in the Trans-Mississippi Department, but was captured while trying to cross the Mississippi River on his way from Richmond to Texas. He was imprisoned at Johnson Island until he was exchanged in February 1865.

At the end of the war Graham returned to his native Alabama where he practiced law and was active in the Democratic party. He died in Montgomery, October 8, 1878.

BIBLIOGRAPHY

Alexander, Thomas B., and Richard E. Beringer. *The Anatomy of the Confederate Congress: A Study of the Influences of Member Characteristics on Legislative Voting Behavior, 1861–1865.* Nashville, Tenn., 1972.

Estill, Mary S., ed. "Diary of a Confederate Congressman." *Southwestern Historical Quarterly* 38 (April 1935): 270–301; 39 (July 1935): 33–65.

Lynch, J. D. *The Bench and Bar of Texas.* St. Louis, Mo., 1885.

Warner, Ezra J., and W. Buck Yearns. *Biographical Register of the Confederate Congress.* Baton Rouge, La., 1975.

CARL H. MONEYHON

GRAHAM, WILLIAM A. (1804–1875), governor of North Carolina, U.S. secretary of the navy, and congressman from North Carolina. William A. Graham enjoyed the broadest national reputation of any North Carolinian during the late antebellum era. Successively U.S. senator

WILLIAM A. GRAHAM.   LIBRARY OF CONGRESS

(1840–1843), governor (1845–1849), secretary of the navy in the cabinet of Millard Fillmore (1850–1852), and nominee for vice president on the Whig party ticket with Winfield Scott in 1852, Graham deplored North-South antagonism. Strongly antisecessionist in 1861, he struggled throughout the war and afterward to prevent the upheaval from becoming a full-scale assault on property and privilege.

Graham was a prominent lawyer. He was also a very large slaveholder, especially by the standards of North Carolina, where whites outnumbered blacks two to one. He held over fifty slaves at his home plantation in Orange County and several dozen others on absentee properties in the southwestern part of the state (where he had lived when young) and in adjacent South Carolina. Considered a paternalistic owner, Graham occasionally encountered sharp complaints from his overseers: "I have taken More from Your Negroes than I ever taken before and More Than I ever will A gain," one wrote. Graham's indulgence would "Spoil any Negro in the world."

As the Kansas controversy subsided in late 1858 and 1859, Graham hoped that "the flame of slavery agitation" would die down for want of new fuel. Political parties, he predicted, would have to "appeal to public sentiment on topics more expansive and general than opposition to, or zeal for the establishment of slavery in a territory." Graham looked equally askance at Northern alarms that slavery might soon be fastened upon the free states and at Southern claims that Free-Soilers hoped to ignite slave insurrections in the South. Neither could take place, he judged, "without a Revolution of the bloodiest character," an outcome "not desired by one man in a hundred of either section."

In 1860 Graham and like-minded Southern moderates created the Constitutional Union party, hoping thereby to reinvigorate the traditional Whig electorate and to exploit the rupture of the Democratic party. Never expecting to carry sufficient states to win an outright majority in the electoral college, Constitutional Unionists hoped instead that their candidate, former U.S. senator John Bell of Tennessee, would carry a number of Southern states and that the victory of fusion tickets in several Northern states would throw the election into the House of Representatives. There they anticipated that Union-saving dynamics, similar to those engineered by Henry Clay in 1820, 1833, and 1850, might dampen sectional animosity and set the stage for Bell's selection as president.

As that prospect faded and the Republican candidate, Abraham Lincoln, appeared likely to win, Graham warned the South against rashly disrupting the Union because it had lost the presidential election. Lincoln's election, even if "a calamity deeply to be deplored," posed no unmistakable danger. Only hostile actions would justify a drastic response. Lincoln's capacity to do harm would be limited, furthermore, because he would control neither Congress nor the Supreme Court.

The abrupt secession of seven Deep South states during the winter of 1860–1861, before Lincoln's inauguration, created an extraordinary crisis. Would the slave states of the upper South, among them North Carolina, follow the lead of the lower South? Or would they be able to arrange some sort of Union-saving compromise? For Graham and most other North Carolina Whigs, the only safe course lay in compromise.

In his view, secession meant war: "the idea that there will be no war because the Northern people will not fight is absurd." Graham also feared that war would have exactly the opposite effects than that which secessionists expected. Were the South to fight and lose, slavery would "certainly be abolished." Even were the South to fight and win, the exodus of runaway slaves from Virginia would become a torrent and the slave system of North Carolina would soon stand in jeopardy.

The possibility that Graham might play a key role in resolving the crisis became a topic of speculation during the secession winter. By appointing a prominent Southerner to his cabinet, Lincoln might indicate his commitment to peaceful compromise. As one of the best-known Unionists in the nonseceding slave states, Graham found his name mentioned repeatedly in newspapers. The prospect was not one he welcomed, nor was it one that would be offered. Lincoln and his managers did think the idea had promise, but they preferred to find a Southerner who currently held elective office. Lincoln's choice was John A. Gilmer, a congressman from Greensboro, North Carolina, and a close friend of Graham's. Gilmer, who regularly sought advice from Graham, agonized for two months before declining.

Graham did, however, participate vigorously in efforts to keep North Carolina in the Union. Nominated by antisecessionists in his home county to a state convention, Graham and his running mate, a Union Democrat, won overwhelming victories. Union strength proved so formidable that a narrow majority of voters statewide refused even to allow the convention to meet, fearing any process that might result in secession. Graham continued to advocate peaceful restoration of the Union. He had little hope that any successor government could secure "so much freedom, prosperity, and safety."

The clash at Fort Sumter and Lincoln's subsequent proclamation calling for 75,000 volunteer troops appalled Southern Unionists such as Graham. The proclamation came at a time "when the public mind in all the eight slave holding states that had not seceded, was settling down in the conviction that the forts were to be evacuated and repose was to be allowed." Rather than support a "war of conquest . . . against our brethren of the seceding States," Graham renounced the Union. "However widely we have differed from, and freely criticized the course taken by these States," they were "closely united with us, by the ties of kindred, affection, and a peculiar interest." At the same time, Graham confessed to "a painful sadness." Disunion was a catastrophe "that ought to have been prevented."

Graham could not avoid extensive involvement with the Confederate war effort. Five of his sons served in the army; all, miraculously, survived. Graham, elected in May 1861 to the convention that withdrew North Carolina from the Union, attempted unsuccessfully to present the state's action as revolution rather than secession (many former Unionists remained unconvinced that a state could secede from the Union). In December 1861, anticipating themes that reverberated in North Carolina for the duration of the war, Graham complained that a proposed loyalty oath and sedition law violated civil liberties. He made pointed reference to the plight of ten thousand Quakers, who had religious scruples against both sworn oaths and the bearing of arms.

The impact of the war increased in 1862. Federal troops occupied parts of eastern North Carolina. Heavy fighting in Virginia exacted a high price in blood and treasure, fueling increased demands for manpower and supplies. Confederate conscription and the suspension of the writ of habeas corpus raised fears about military despotism. Food shortages added to civilian miseries, as did soaring prices. Under the circumstances, former Unionists gained control over the state government, riding a wave of popular discontent against original secessionists.

Graham, who refused numerous suggestions that he himself run for governor, was one of an inner sanctum of prominent former Whigs who masterminded the landslide victory of former congressman Zebulon Vance, then an officer in the Confederate army. Proclaiming themselves "Conservatives," the erstwhile Unionists insisted that independence could be secured without sacrificing civil liberties or subordinating civilian government to military authority. Elected to the state senate in August 1862 at the same time Vance was chosen governor, Graham soon afterward was selected by the new legislature to fill one of the state's seats in the Confederate Senate. His term would not begin, however, until 1864.

Conservatives found it a burdensome task to maintain North Carolina's loyalty to the Confederacy. Following catastrophic defeats at Gettysburg and Vicksburg in the summer of 1863, dozens of peace meetings took place in the state to urge the opening of negotiations that might end the war. Support for a state convention, seen by some as a way to withdraw North Carolina from the Confederacy, grew during the subsequent winter and spring. The tendency of haughty Virginians and South Carolinians "to undervalue North Carolina" also stirred popular resentment.

Graham resisted admonitions to speak out against the growing peace movement. He also counseled Vance and others to maintain critical distance from the immensely unpopular Confederate government in Richmond. "The masses of the people are so wearied by the war," Graham privately observed, "that, if they can find candidates to represent their opinions, they may give us a delegation in Congress for unconditional peace." Graham himself saw no alternative to continued military struggle. He feared, however, that the war would, whatever its outcome, "destroy the institution of slavery" within two years.

So matters stood in May 1864 when Graham's term in the Confederate Senate began. There he and the delegation of Union Whigs from North Carolina compiled the most anti-administration voting record in the Second Confederate Congress. Graham's arrival in Richmond coincided with the bloodiest month of fighting in the entire war, as Robert E. Lee's Army of Northern Virginia tried desperately to blunt Ulysses S. Grant's offensives. North Carolina's relations with President Jefferson Davis reached a new low. Conscription of seventeen- and eighteen-year-olds and of men between forty-five and fifty eroded the already diminished supply of agricultural labor, raising the prospect of even more acute food shortages. Graham denounced renewed suspension of the writ of habeas corpus, regarded by many as a direct response to North Carolina peace sentiments and resistance to conscription. Such Confederate high-handedness "touched a nerve of exquisite sensibility" among people who had sacrificed prodigally for the Confederate cause. Conciliation, he advised, would secure more genuine loyalty than "force or terror."

Graham and like-minded North Carolina Conservatives aided Governor Vance, who overcame a challenge from William W. Holden to win reelection in August 1864. While continuing to give lip service to the cause of independence, Holden had shown greater readiness than other Conservatives to appease popular discontent with the war. Vance insisted that a state convention, favored by Holden, would throw North Carolina "into the arms of Lincoln" and force the state's soldiers "to fight alongside his negro troops in exterminating the white men, women and children of the South." The governor combined forthright support for continuation of the armed struggle with blunt criticism of the Davis government and of original secessionists. Vance's strong defense of habeas corpus did much to maintain his popularity.

Nothing, however, could reverse the crumbling military fortunes of the Confederacy. Just as Graham returned to Richmond in November 1864 for the reconvening of Congress, Lincoln won reelection, thereby frustrating lingering Southern hopes for negotiated independence. William Tecumseh Sherman then began his devastating march through Georgia. Soon John Bell Hood would lead the Army of Tennessee to destruction. Facing a desperate military emergency, Robert E. Lee and others proposed the enlistment of black troops, with promises of freedom to the recruits and their families. Graham would have none of it. Such "wild schemes" were "a confession of despair," illustrating that "military men are but poor Judges of the policy of a nation." Enrolling black soldiers would be "equivalent to a dissolution of the Confederacy."

Graham worked unsuccessfully behind the scenes during February and March 1865 to effect a negotiated surrender, recognizing the hopelessness of continued military resistance. He and John A. Campbell, former U.S. Supreme Court justice and assistant Confederate secretary of war, favored accepting Lincoln's apparent offer, made at the Hampton Roads conference of February 3, 1865, to provide amnesty and to restore property other than freed slaves. Campbell, one of three Confederate officials who had conferred with Lincoln, also understood him to say that the South could, by returning to the Union, block or delay general emancipation, as contemplated in the pending Thirteenth Amendment to the Constitution, which had already passed Congress. On March 2, 1865, Graham and two other members of the Senate met with President Davis to urge capitulation.

His counsels unheeded, Graham returned to North Carolina in mid-March 1865. He warned Governor Vance that Lee's army would be destroyed within thirty days and suggested that North Carolina should act unilaterally. As the governor vacillated, the Confederacy, by then reduced to a shrinking remnant of North Carolina and Virginia, fought to the bitter end. Two of Graham's sons were wounded in last-ditch hostilities around Petersburg.

Graham's postwar career was eclipsed by his profound disagreement with the Republican party's approach to Reconstruction. Selected by the state legislature for a U.S. Senate seat in November 1865, Graham and other members-elect from the ex-Confederate states were not allowed to take their seats. Although ready to protect black property rights and to allow for limited black testimony in court, Graham believed voting should be "jealously reserved to the white race." He thought that disabilities placed on former Confederate officeholders by Section III of the Fourteenth Amendment interfered with the right of voters to choose their own officials. Contemptuous of the Military Reconstruction Acts of 1867, he advised North Carolinians to remain under military rule rather than call a convention to write a new state constitution. Graham attended the National Union Convention in Philadelphia in August 1866 and was appointed to the board of the Peabody Educational Fund in 1867.

In a letter to Governor Vance written late in the war, Graham pronounced an epitaph on the efforts of "the conservative men, who opposed the revolution while there was a chance to avert it, but when it became inevitable, have nobly done their duty, in endeavouring to give it success." No North Carolinian stood higher in the estimation of his peers, but the profound challenges posed by secession, war, and Reconstruction swept him rudely aside.

BIBLIOGRAPHY

Alexander, Thomas B., and Richard E. Beringer. *The Anatomy of the Confederate Congress: A Study of the Influences of Member Characteristics on Legislative Voting Behavior, 1861–1865.* Nashville, Tenn., 1972.

Crofts, Daniel W. *Reluctant Confederates: Upper South Unionists in the Secession Crisis.* Chapel Hill, N.C., 1989.

Hamilton, J. G. deRoulhac, and Max R. Williams, eds. *The Papers of William Alexander Graham.* 7 vols. to date. Raleigh, N.C., 1957–.

Jeffrey, Thomas E. *State Parties and National Parties: North Carolina, 1815–1861.* Athens, Ga., 1989.

Journal of the Congress of the Confederate States of America, 1861–1865. 7 vols. Washington, D.C., 1904–1905.

Kruman, Marc W. *Parties and Politics in North Carolina, 1836–1865.* Baton Rouge, La., 1983.

Sitterson, Joseph Carlyle. *The Secession Movement in North Carolina.* Chapel Hill, N.C., 1939.

Yearns, Wilfred B. *The Confederate Congress.* Athens, Ga., 1960.

DANIEL W. CROFTS

GRANBURY, HIRAM BRONSON (1831–1864),
brigadier general. Granbury was born in Copiah County, Mississippi, and studied at Oakland College in Rodney, Mississippi. He moved in the early 1850s to Waco, Texas, where he practiced law and held the post of chief justice of the county court (an executive, not a judicial office).

He helped organize and was named captain of the Waco Guards, which became part of the Seventh Texas Infantry Regiment. In November 1861 he was elected major. Captured at Fort Donelson (February 1862), Granbury was soon exchanged, and on August 29, 1862, he became colonel of the regiment. For the rest of 1862 and most of 1863 he and his regiment were assigned to the Department of Mississippi and East Louisiana.

In the fall of 1863 Granbury's regiment went to Georgia to reinforce the Army of Tennessee. At Missionary Ridge (November 23–25) Granbury took command of the brigade when Brig. Gen. James Argyle Smith was wounded. Granbury's handling of the brigade at Ringgold Gap (November 27) on the retreat from Chattanooga won wide praise. On March 5, 1864, he was appointed brigadier general (with date of rank set at February 29).

Granbury commanded his brigade through the Atlanta campaign and in the Franklin and Nashville campaign. At the Battle of Franklin (November 30) he was killed leading his men in the great assault on the Federal works.

Granbury was buried at Franklin, but in 1893 his body

was moved to the Granbury Cemetery in Granbury, Texas—a town named for him.

BIBLIOGRAPHY

Hewitt, Lawrence L. "Hiram Bronson Granbury." In *The Confederate General*. Edited by William C. Davis. Vol. 3. Harrisburg, Pa., 1991.

Warner, Ezra J. *Generals in Gray: Lives of the Confederate Commanders*. Baton Rouge, La., 1959.

RICHARD M. McMURRY

GRAVES, WILLIAM A. (c.1830–1894), acting naval constructor. A lifelong resident of Norfolk, Virginia, Graves learned the shipbuilding trade under the tutelage of local shipwright William H. Hunter and then established his own prosperous yard on Water Street. Following the outbreak of the Civil War, Graves received contracts to build several warships for the Confederate navy, none of which was completed before the evacuation of the Hampton Roads area in May 1862. While so occupied he was appointed an acting naval constructor by Navy Secretary Stephen R. Mallory on March 22, 1862. After the loss of his Norfolk shipyard, Graves moved to Richmond and located a government yard opposite the one at Rocketts. There he designed and constructed the ironclad ram *Virginia II,* the most powerful warship built in the Confederacy. *Virginia II* entered service in the spring of 1864 as flagship of the James River Squadron. It took part in all the fleet's major actions before being destroyed by its crew upon the evacuation of Richmond on April 3, 1865.

Graves then commenced an unusual double-ended armored craft featuring twin screws, a rudder, and a ram on each end, and a short casemate containing only a single gun. This vessel was still under construction at war's end. Other of his wartime designs included the ironclad *Charleston* and similar types either built or contracted for at Savannah, Georgia, and on the Tombigbee River, Alabama; two classes of torpedo boats, one group of twelve under construction in 1864 at various sites in the South and another group of six to be fabricated in sections in Britain and shipped through the blockade; and a seagoing ironclad designed with John M. Brooke and intended for construction abroad.

After the war, Graves reestablished his Norfolk shipbuilding business, which he operated until his retirement in 1890. He died February 17, 1894, and is buried in Elmwood Cemetery.

BIBLIOGRAPHY

Still, William N. *Confederate Shipbuilding*. 2d ed. Columbia, S.C., 1987.

U.S. Navy Department. *Civil War Naval Chronology, 1861–1865*. Washington, D.C., 1971.

A. ROBERT HOLCOMBE, JR.

GRAY, HENRY (1816–1892), brigadier general and congressman from Louisiana. Born in Laurens County, South Carolina, Gray graduated from South Carolina College (now the University of South Carolina) and was admitted to the bar. He moved to Mississippi and served one term in its state legislature but soon left for Louisiana after an unsuccessful run for the U.S. Congress on the Whig ticket. In 1856 he was a presidential elector for James Buchanan and was elected to the Louisiana legislature. In 1859 he ran for the U.S. Senate on a secessionist platform but lost by a single vote to Judah P. Benjamin (future secretary of state of the Confederacy).

When Mississippi seceded, Gray returned to his former state and enlisted as a private, but Jefferson Davis—a personal friend—asked that Gray return to Louisiana and help raise a regiment instead. Elected a colonel of the Twenty-eighth Louisiana Infantry, he took his regiment to Mississippi in 1862 to join Gen. Richard Taylor in the Vicksburg campaign. In 1863 Gray fought against Nathaniel P. Banks in his first Red River campaign at the Battles of Irish Bend and Fort Bisland (April 12–14). Considerably outnumbered, the Confederate forces under General Taylor were forced to retreat, allowing Banks to advance as far as Alexandria, Louisiana. Taylor gave Gray and his regiment special praise in his report, stating that "no veteran soldiers could have excelled them in their conduct."

Gray also fought in the 1864 Red River campaign. In the effort to stop Banks's move to take Shreveport, Gray commanded one of the two brigades in Gen. Alfred Mouton's division stationed at Alexandria. In the initial stages of this campaign, the Union forces moved largely unopposed up the Red River valley as Taylor waited for badly needed reinforcements. Taylor established a defensive line at Mansfield with Gray commanding a brigade on the Confederate left. On April 8 Taylor ordered Mouton's division to lead the assault against the Union advance. The Confederate charge broke the Union offensive, and this marked Banks's farthest advance in the campaign. The next day (April 9) the two sides fought again at Pleasant Hill, but on this day the Confederate assault was repulsed. Gray, whose brigade served as the Confederate rear guard, again won Taylor's praise. Despite his repulse of the Confederates on the ninth, Banks began a long retreat back down the Red River.

Later in 1864, unbeknownst to Gray, he was elected to represent Louisiana's Fifth District in the Confederate Congress. He took his seat and became an outspoken critic of all Confederate peace overtures. He served on the Judiciary Committee and a special committee to enlarge the armed forces. While in Congress he was promoted to brigadier general, effective from the Battle of Mansfield. One source credits Gray's promotion, in spite of E. Kirby Smith's opposition, to his friendship with President Davis.

After the war Gray served one term in the Louisiana State Senate and then retired. He died on December 11, 1891, in Coushatta, Louisiana.

BIBLIOGRAPHY

Dimitry, John. *Louisiana.* Vol. 10 of *Confederate Military History.* Edited by Clement A. Evans. Atlanta, 1899. Vol. 13 of extended ed. Wilmington, N.C., 1987.

Kerby, Robert L. *Kirby Smith's Confederacy: The Trans-Mississippi South, 1863–1865.* New York, 1972.

Vandiver, Frank E. "Proceedings of the Second Confederate Congress." *Southern Historical Society Papers* 52 (1959): 1–500. Reprint, Wilmington, N.C., 1992.

THOMAS J. LEGG

GRAY, PETER W. (1819–1874), congressman from Texas. Peter Gray was a native of Virginia, born December 12, 1819. He was a resident of Houston, Texas, prior to the Civil War. An attorney and politician, he served in the Texas legislature from 1846 to 1847 and from 1852 to 1853, and as a district judge from 1854 to 1860.

In November 1861, Gray was elected to the House of Representatives of the First Congress. The congressman was a strong supporter of increasing the power of the Confederate central government and the measures of President Jefferson Davis. He backed government control of Southern railroads as well as the Conscription Act of 1862. He also actively supported legislation favorable to his state, pushing to keep open the cotton trade with Mexico and securing a branch of the Confederate Treasury in Texas.

In January 1863, Gray was at Galveston, Texas, where he served as a voluntary aide on the staff of Gen. John B. Magruder in the Battle of Galveston. The following summer he ran for reelection to the Congress but was beaten by Anthony Martin Branch who campaigned on a platform critical of Gray's support of Davis and the central government. Davis appointed Gray fiscal agent of the Trans-Mississippi Department in 1864.

At the end of the war Gray returned to Houston and practiced law. He died of tuberculosis on October 3, 1874.

BIBLIOGRAPHY

Lynch, James D. *The Bench and Bar of Texas.* St. Louis, Mo., 1885.

Warner, Ezra J., and W. Buck Yearns. *Biographical Register of the Confederate Congress.* Baton Rouge, La., 1975.

CARL H. MONEYHON

GRAYSON, JOHN BRECKINRIDGE (1807–1861), brigadier general. A native of Kentucky and an 1826 West Point graduate, Grayson was an early loss to the Confederacy. He was fifty-four years old when the Civil War began in April 1861, with thirty-five years of continual army experience behind him. He had served as an artillery and commissary officer in the Mexican and Seminole wars, earning two commendations in Mexico.

Grayson resigned from the U.S. Army on July 1, 1861, and in August received appointment as brigadier general in the Provisional Army of the Confederacy. His assignment was command of the newly created Department of Middle and Eastern Florida, headquartered in Tallahassee. Soon after his arrival in Florida, Grayson sent a highly critical report of the prevailing conditions to Confederate Secretary of War Leroy P. Walker. Citing a serious lack of personnel, supplies, and ammunition, Grayson warned, "As sure as the sun rises, unless canon powder, &tc can be sent to Florida in the next thirty days, she will fall into the hands of the North."

But General Grayson was in very poor health and lacked the energy to do much more than wire this report to Richmond. By early October witnesses described the veteran soldier as "enfeebled" and "nearly spent with consumption." On October 21, Grayson died of tuberculosis. His son, a member of the Washington Artillery, brought his father's remains to New Orleans for burial. Florida would not immediately fall to the North, but the Confederacy would never know how much Grayson could have contributed to the Southern drive for independence.

BIBLIOGRAPHY

Johnston, J. Stoddard. *Kentucky.* Vol. 9 of *Confederate Military History.* Edited by Clement A. Evans. Atlanta, 1899. Vol. 11 of extended ed. Wilmington, N.C., 1988.

Nulty, William H. *Confederate Florida.* Tuscaloosa, Ala., 1990.

Warner, Ezra J. *Generals in Gray: Lives of the Confederate Commanders.* Baton Rouge, La., 1959.

LESLEY JILL GORDON-BURR

GREAT BRITAIN. Prior to the Civil War, nineteenth-century relations between the United States and Great Britain were influenced by mutual resentments that had festered since the American Revolution and had been amplified during the War of 1812. Those historic antagonisms were reinforced by a series of crises that developed with disturbing regularity. Britain and the United States confronted disagreements over the Canadian rebellion, fishing and trade agreements, and disputed boundaries with Maine and Oregon. American efforts to annex California and Texas and control Central American nations brought the prerogatives of both countries into conflict and left the British with the impression that Americans were "most disagreeable fellows" at best. British officials and elements of the ruling gentry maintained a jaundiced view of Americans and harbored suspicions that the country was capable of all manner of international mischief.

The sectional crisis that led to the Civil War in 1860 fueled British fears that the country might resolve its internal problems through some form of international adventure. Britons and Canadians were both apprehensive about the fact that Americans openly expressed designs for the annexation of Canada to compensate for the loss of the Southern states. Those reservations appeared to be reinforced by President-elect Abraham Lincoln's choice of the aggressive William H. Seward as secretary of state. Seward was often outwardly antagonistic toward the British and had been a supporter of annexing Canada, which he considered "ripened fruit which must fall." Lord Lyons, British minister to the United States, reported that he thought that Seward would be "dangerous," as he frequently employed the Anglo-American relationship as "good material" for his brand of politics. Lyons considered Seward typical of American politicians of "second rate station and ability."

British perception of the Southern United States appears to have been somewhat different from the view held of the North. Though English evangelists soundly condemned the slaveholding South, many Britons felt a close, if only economic, relationship with the American Southeast. Southern cotton had become an essential element of the British textile economy, and manufacturing concerns found ready markets for industrial products in the agricultural South. The cotton-related industry in Great Britain had grown to approximately 80 million pounds sterling in the decade prior to the Civil War, and the mills of Lancashire and West Derbyshire consumed more than 2.5 million bales annually. By 1860 a large percentage of the British population was dependent upon the textile industry, and most recognized the implications of any disruption of the cotton trade. Unlike the general attitude toward the North, where problems with Canada were focused, British attitudes toward the South and Southern attitudes toward Britain were based on mutually beneficial economics and were characterized by a spirit of friendliness and even admiration.

Unfortunately for the Confederacy, that relationship began to deteriorate almost immediately after secession. In April 1861 President Lincoln proclaimed a blockade of Southern seaports. The blockade, designed to isolate the Confederacy politically and economically, threatened the cotton trade. A month later Queen Victoria issued a proclamation of neutrality. In spite of a highly antagonistic reaction in the North, the British proclamation assisted the United States: it forbade British subjects to engage in sympathetic activities on behalf of the Confederacy, forced recognition of the Union blockade, and prevented the fitting out of warships in British ports. The United States was quick to point out, however, that the declaration benefited the Confederacy by recognizing the South's status as a belligerent. That recognition undermined the United

States' position that the South's secession from the Union was an internal affair. It also provided a degree of protection for Confederate military personnel by making it difficult for the United States to treat them as criminals or pirates.

Although Victoria's proclamation proved to be important to Confederate survival, Southerners were convinced that Great Britain's need for cotton would ultimately lead to its supporting the Confederate cause. In response to the Union blockade the Confederacy declared a cotton embargo. Southerners shared a firm belief in King Cotton diplomacy. By starving the mills of Lancashire and West Derbyshire, the South could create sufficient economic and political pressure to force Great Britain to recognize the Confederacy and perhaps even provide military assistance. The *Charleston Mercury* summed up the argument in June 1861, reminding the South that "the cards are in our hands and we intend to play them out to the bankruptcy of every cotton factory in Great Britain and France or the acknowledgement of our independence."

The Confederate cotton embargo had a predictable impact on the British textile industry. In Lancashire the dwindling supply of cotton resulted in the closing of mills and the loss of thousands of jobs. That economic disaster resulted in considerable pressure to recognize the Confederacy and no small amount of interest in active British military intervention in America. But in spite of the pressure, British politicians stoically refused to be drawn into the conflict and even adopted measures designed to ensure that war materials were not shipped from Great Britain to either belligerent. Britain wanted no part of a war with the United States. The impact of the "cotton famine" would be nominal compared to the effect of an embargo on wheat from the United States. It would be cheaper to subsidize the cotton industry than to go to war and perhaps risk internal strife or revolution. In fact, while the cotton industry suffered, the woolen industry advanced. Shipbuilding, too, benefited from Confederate and speculative demands for British vessels. British resistance to involvement in American affairs was also based on the belief that the Confederacy could win its independence without assistance—a belief held until it was too late to provide assistance. For the Confederacy, King Cotton diplomacy proved to be a bitter disappointment, and British failure to recognize or assist the South elicited open expressions of resentment in the Confederacy.

Although the cotton embargo failed to have the desired political impact on Britain's policy toward the Confederacy, the Union navy provided an incident that almost achieved the Confederate political objective of provoking war between the United States and Great Britain. On November 8, 1861, Capt. Charles Wilkes forcibly removed newly appointed Confederate commissioners James Mason and John Slidell from the royal mail steamer *Trent* and took them as prisoners to Fort Warren in Boston Harbor. News of Mason's and Slidell's capture was received with public enthusiasm in the United States, but Britons were outraged by Wilkes's contempt for the sovereignty of a British vessel. The British press demanded release of the prisoners and an apology. The gravity of the *Trent* affair resulted in the creation of a War Committee in the cabinet. The committee mulled the options and after determining that Wilkes had acted illegally, considered preparing for war with the United States. Confederates were also indignant, but at the same time they were elated over the possible international consequences of Wilkes's actions. Southern newspapers reflected the general sentiment that the United States would not back down and that Britain would not stand for the violation of its neutrality. In spite of the high level of tensions between the United States and Great Britain, war was averted when Secretary of State Seward issued an apology and confirmed that Mason and Slidell would be released. The passions subsided, but the affair reinforced the British perception of Northern animosity.

The equitable resolution of the *Trent* affair was another disappointment for the Confederacy—a disappointment compounded by the reception that Mason and Slidell received, once they arrived in Europe. Slidell was able to gain a sympathetic audience with Napoleon III, but Lord John Russell refused to officially recognize Mason and treated his overtures with an indifference that surprised the Confederate State Department and angered Southerners. Throughout 1862 Mason attempted to achieve recognition for the Confederacy without success. Regardless of the impact of the Union blockade, the *Trent* affair, and the Confederate cotton embargo, Great Britain was not willing to be drawn into America's internal conflict. Although many Britons were openly sympathetic to the Confederate cause, the government refused to intervene. By the summer of 1862 the British refusal to recognize the Confederacy or its envoys had produced open resentment in the South. Southern newspapers called for the expulsion of British consuls residing in the Confederacy and the recall of Confederate commissioners in Great Britain. The *Richmond Enquirer* in April 1863 labeled Great Britain "our worst and deadliest enemy" aside from the United States. After being continually rebuffed by Lord Russell, Mason left London for Paris in August 1863, and the Confederacy broke off efforts to establish official relations with Great Britain.

Although Great Britain denied the Confederacy recognition, the South received valuable, if clandestine, assistance from the British. In spite of the declaration of neutrality, Confederate agents in Great Britain worked effectively to secure military supplies and equipment. To a great degree the industrial capacity of the Confederacy was enhanced by weapons and war matériel obtained from Great Britain in exchange for cotton and other marketable agricultural products. British shipbuilders supplied vessels for a variety of Confederate purposes. The majority were employed in running cargoes through the Union blockade. In spite of the efforts of the U.S. Navy, fast steamships maintained limited Confederate foreign commerce throughout the war. Other vessels were acquired to be fitted out as commerce raiders. Ships like *Alabama, Florida,* and *Shenandoah* put to sea from English shipyards and destroyed hundreds of U.S. merchant vessels.

"Dixie's Nurse." An illustrated sheet music cover for a comic song. The obese Britannia seated in the oval mocks classical reliefs and medallions. Signatures have apparently been scratched out of the lower portion of the oval. The print expresses Northern resentment over British support for the Confederate war effort. Lithograph, printed in black and brown-olive, on wove paper. Published in Philadelphia by Lee and Walker, 1865.

During the postwar arbitration of claims against Great Britain for the destruction inflicted by Confederate commerce raiders, it was estimated that British war matériel and unofficial support for the Confederacy extended the rebellion for as much as two years. Had it not been for the efforts of Charles F. Adams, U.S. minister to Great Britain, the amount of support would have undoubtedly been greater. Adams employed every device at his disposal to ensure the strict maintenance of British neutrality. Although he was not always successful, his efforts contributed significantly to frustrating Confederate diplomacy and procurement. His relentless pursuit of U.S. objectives at the Court of St. James was in no small way responsible for the lack of success registered by Confederate foreign policy and the ultimately unsatisfactory nature of relations with Great Britain.

[See also Alabama Claims; Anglo-Confederate Purchasing; Blockade, overview article; Propaganda; Trent Affair.]

BIBLIOGRAPHY

Adams, Ephram Douglass. Great Britain and the Civil War. 2 vols. New York, 1958.

Callahan, James Morton. Diplomatic History of the Southern Confederacy. Springfield, Mass., 1957.

Cullop, Charles P. Confederate Propaganda in Europe, 1861–1865. Coral Gables, Fla., 1969.

Ellison, Mary. Support for Secession: Lancashire and the American Civil War. Chicago, 1972.

Ferris, Norman B. Desperate Diplomacy: William H. Seward's Foreign Policy, 1861. Knoxville, Tenn., 1976.

Jenkins, Brian. Britain and the War for the Union. 2 vols. Montreal, Canada, 1974, 1980.

Owsley, Frank Lawrence. King Cotton Diplomacy: Foreign Relations of the Confederate States of America. 2d ed. Chicago, 1959.

Vanauken, Sheldon. The Glittering Illusion: English Sympathy for the Southern Confederacy. Washington, D.C., 1989.

GORDON WATTS

GREEN, MARTIN EDWIN (1815–1863), brigadier general. Green was born in Fauquier County, Virginia, in 1815. He moved with his bride in 1836 to Missouri, where he operated a steam sawmill in Lewis County with his brothers, one of whom, James, became a U.S. senator from Missouri. In the summer of 1861 he assumed leadership of the pro-Confederate minority in northeastern Missouri by organizing a cavalry company from a recruiting center near Monticello. He led his command in engagements at Athens, Missouri, on August 5 and at Shelbina on September 4, 1861. Avoiding pursuing Union forces under Gens. Stephen A. Hurlbut and John Pope, he safely got his recruits south of the Missouri River, where he linked up with a Confederate army commanded by Gen. Sterling Price.

Green's cavalry served under Price at the capture of Lexington on September 20, 1861, and at the Battle of Elkhorn Tavern, Arkansas, on March 7 and 8, 1862, a decisive Confederate defeat that effectively secured Missouri for the Union. On July 21, 1862, Green was commissioned a brigadier general. As the head of the Third Brigade in Price's army, he saw extensive action at Iuka, Corinth, and Hatchie Bridge, Mississippi, in the fall of 1862. During the Vicksburg campaign Green commanded the Second Brigade in Gen. John Stevens Bowen's division at Port Gibson on May 1, 1863. While surveying Federal lines from a Confederate parapet during the siege of Vicksburg, Green was killed by a sniper's bullet on June 27, 1863.

BIBLIOGRAPHY

Shoemaker, Floyd C. "The Story of the Civil War in Northeast Missouri." Missouri Historical Review 7 (1913): 63–75, 113–131.

Warner, Ezra J. Generals in Gray: Lives of the Confederate Commanders. Baton Rouge, La., 1959.

WILLIAM L. BARNEY

GREEN, THOMAS (1814–1864), brigadier general. Born in Amelia County, Virginia, Green moved to Texas in the 1830s. With the outbreak of the Civil War he was named a colonel in a regiment assigned to Henry Hopkins Sibley, Department of New Mexico. He participated in numerous battles in New Mexico and Texas including Galveston, Valverde, Glorieta Pass, and Las Cruces. After fighting to recapture Galveston on January 1, 1863, he received a vote of thanks from the Confederate Congress for his efforts. From April 12 through 14, 1863, Green commanded the Fifth Texas Mounted Volunteer Regiment in the Battles of Irish Bend and Fort Bisland. Gen. Richard Taylor commended Green for his spirited defense against numerous Union charges on April 13. Having assigned Green the rear-guard defense as they retreated, Taylor credited him with extricating the Confederate forces: "In truth he was the Ney of our retreat, and the shield and buckler of our little force." He was promoted to brigadier general in May 1863.

Taylor again called on Green to cover a Confederate retreat in the Red River campaign of 1864. While Taylor waited for reinforcements, Green was ordered to slow Nathaniel P. Banks's advance. The Union movement was stopped at Mansfield (April 8) and Pleasant Hill (April 9). After these battles, Banks withdrew, and Green, according to Taylor, "with his usual energy" harassed the Union rear guard. On April 12 Green was leading a cavalry charge against Union gunboats aground near Pleasant Hill Landing when he was killed. Taylor reported that the assault would have led to "the capture of the whole fleet but for the unfortunate fall of the noble Green."

BIBLIOGRAPHY

Arceneaux, William. *Acadian General: Alfred Mouton and the Civil War*. Lafayette, La., 1981.

Green, Thomas. "Battle of Atchafalya—Letter from General Thomas Green." *Southern Historical Society Papers* 3 (1877): 62–63. Reprint, Wilmington, N.C., 1990.

Hall, Martin Hardwick. *Sibley's New Mexico Campaign*. Austin, Tex., 1960.

THOMAS J. LEGG

ROSE O'NEAL GREENHOW. A portrait with one of her four daughters.   NAVAL HISTORICAL CENTER, WASHINGTON, D.C.

GREENHOW, ROSE O'NEAL (1815–1864), spy.

A popular Washington, D.C., hostess, the Maryland-born Greenhow joined the spy ring of Col. Thomas Jordan, Gen. P. G. T. Beauregard's adjutant general, as soon as the war broke out. Greenhow, whose late husband had worked for the State Department, assiduously mined her contacts in the U.S. government for military secrets that might be helpful to the Confederacy. Her greatest accomplishment came in the days before the Battle of First Manassas (July 21, 1861), when she sent cipher messages via secret couriers to General Beauregard, informing him of Gen. Irvin McDowell's marching orders and troop strength. Her information influenced Jefferson Davis to send Gen. Joseph E. Johnston to reinforce Beauregard; Johnston's men turned the tide of the battle.

On August 23, 1861, Greenhow was arrested by Allan Pinkerton, head of the Union army's secret service. Though incarcerated in her home, Greenhow managed, through visitors, to transmit information on Union forces to Jordan. She was transferred to Old Capitol Prison in January 1862 and paroled that June on the condition that she not return to the North during the war. In August 1863 Greenhow went abroad as an unofficial diplomat for the Confederacy in England and France; her prison chronicle, *My Imprisonment and the First Year of Abolition Rule at Washington*, was published in London that year. Greenhow drowned on October 1, 1864, when the British steamship carrying her back to the Confederacy ran aground off North Carolina. She was buried in Wilmington, North Carolina, on October 2, 1864, with full military honors.

BIBLIOGRAPHY

Greenhow, Rose O'Neal. *My Imprisonment and the First Year of Abolition Rule at Washington*. London, 1863.

Ross, Ishbel. *Rebel Rose: Life of Rose O'Neal Greenhow, Confederate Spy*. New York, 1954.

Sigaud, Louis A. "Mrs. Greenhow and the Rebel Spy Ring." *Maryland Historical Magazine* 41 (1946): 173–198.

ELIZABETH R. VARON

GREENSBORO, NORTH CAROLINA. The

future of Greensboro, North Carolina, as a transportation center was assured when the Confederacy completed the Piedmont Railroad in 1864 connecting it to Danville, Virginia. Greensboro had already benefited from the construction of the North Carolina Railroad in 1856, but traffic was limited to North Carolina. Opposition to allowing North Carolina goods to be sent out of state had created a fifty-mile missing link to the north. It would have been filled eventually, but by 1862 military necessity took precedent over those who had used their power and position to prevent construction.

When the war came, Greensboro was already ripe for change. In 1860 the corporate limits held some 350 people with about 1,500 more in the immediate vicinity. Guilford County had a population of 20,056—fourth in the state—of which 3,625 were slaves. The white population consisted of descendants of Scotch-Irish Presbyterians, German Lutherans, and English Quakers who had migrated to the area by the Great Valley Route prior to the Revolution. Religious affiliation was the chief determinant of differences among these people. There were twenty-nine manufacturing establishments in the county, but the future lay with the railroad, which Governor John Motley Morehead, a local resident, made sure came through Greensboro. He could not know how vital the tracks would become to the Confederacy as Greensboro became a major transfer point for men and supplies.

Greensboro was the seat of Guilford County, having been placed in its geographical center in 1808. A charter making it a town was granted in 1837, and its boundaries grew to one square mile. Retail activity centered on small establishments mainly providing for the needs of visitors to the courthouse. Manufacturing centered on gristmills, gun shops, spoke and handle factories, and leather fabricators. But by 1860 the most significant economic activity was railroading, which employed about twenty people. Power lay in the hands of lawyers and judges who retained control throughout the era of the Civil War and Reconstruction. Cultural life centered on churches and schools, particularly the Edgeworth Female Seminary and Greensboro College, which sponsored recitals and readings. The seminary served briefly as a military hospital. Blandwood, the home of Morehead, was a gathering place for the elite, and news was spread through the *Greensborough Patriot* until it lapsed in 1862. Its presses were then used to print grammar school textbooks presenting the Confederate point of view—a highly profitable business.

Most citizens supported secession at first, but by 1862 some had begun to have second thoughts as food shortages and increasing deaths eroded morale. Also, Greensboro was in the Quaker Belt of North Carolina, which was rife with dissension. Draft resisters and deserters found their way to the area and efforts to round them up only increased opposition to Richmond.

On the other hand, there were several training camps and a number of uniform and arms manufacturers in the vicinity. A company-sized unit, the Guilford Grays, was recruited in the area. In March 1865 wounded from the Battle of Bentonville were hospitalized in the Presbyterian church and other buildings. Although George F. Stoneman burned the railway bridge at Jamestown, he did not touch Greensboro, which was undamaged by the war. The North Carolina Railroad was operational again in a few weeks. As Jefferson Davis fled, he held his last cabinet meetings in a boxcar near the station on April 12 and 13, but he was not warmly received in the town. Rioting ensued as deserters and civilians sought food and clothing stored in the town. They were put down by loyal troops who were encamped around Greensboro awaiting parole. Gen. John M. Schofield's officers issued papers to 36,817 Confederates in Greensboro, making it their last point of military service.

BIBLIOGRAPHY

Arnett, Ethel Stephens. *Confederate Guns Were Stacked: Greensboro, North Carolina.* Greensboro, N.C., 1965.

Auman, William T. "Neighbor against Neighbor: The Inner Civil War in the Randolph County Area of Confederate North Carolina." *North Carolina Historical Review* 61 (1984): 59–92.

O'Brien, Gail Williams. *The Legal Fraternity and the Making of a New South Community, 1848–1882.* Athens, Ga., 1986.

Robinson, Blackwell P., and Alexander R. Stoesen. *History of Guilford County.* Greensboro, N.C., 1981.

Smith, O. Norris, ed. "The Civil War Decade in Greensboro, N.C., As Recorded in the Diary of Rev. J. Henry Smith, Pastor of the Presbyterian Church of Greensboro." Typescript, Greensboro Historical Museum Archives, 1989.

ALEXANDER R. STOESEN

GREENVILLE CONVENTION. *See* Knoxville and Greenville Conventions.

GREER, ELKANAH BRACKIN (1825–1877), brigadier general. Greer was born on October 11, 1825, at Paris, Tennessee, and fought in the Mexican War as part of Jefferson Davis's First Mississippi Rifles. In 1848 he moved to Marshall, Texas, where he was a fervent advocate of state rights and became grand commander of the Texas branch of the Knights of the Golden Circle. He took part in the Knights' plan to invade Mexico in 1860.

When the Civil War began, Greer organized the South Kansas–Texas Regiment (later the Third Texas Cavalry) and joined Ben McCulloch at Fort Smith. Greer fought at Oak Hills, Missouri, and was wounded slightly at Elkhorn Tavern, Arkansas. He was promoted to brigadier general on October 8, 1862, and in June 1863 was sent to the Trans-Mississippi Department where he became commandant of conscripts. Greer organized his department efficiently, but his methods of rounding up men for the army angered many, particularly those in political power. He clashed with state authorities, particularly Texas judges, when he alleged they issued too many exemptions from conscription to local residents. As a result, in November 1864 the Confederate government sent Brig. Gen. Francis Nicholls to replace him. E. Kirby Smith, who was pleased with Greer, tried to nullify the change but, in the end, relieved Greer in December 1864. In March 1865 Greer took command of the Texas Reserve Corps.

After the war he returned to Marshall and died while visiting his sister in Devall's Bluff, Arkansas, on March 25, 1877. He is buried in Elmwood Cemetery in Memphis, Tennessee.

BIBLIOGRAPHY

Heartsill, W. W. *Fourteen Hundred and 91 Days in the Confederate Army.* Jackson, Tenn., 1953.

Warner, Ezra J. *Generals in Gray: Lives of the Confederate Commanders.* Baton Rouge, La., 1959.

ANNE J. BAILEY

GREGG, JOHN (1828–1864), congressman from Texas and brigadier general. Born on September 28, 1828, in Lawrence County, Alabama, Gregg attended LaGrange

JOHN GREGG.   NATIONAL ARCHIVES

College in Alabama, served as a teacher, and read for the legal profession in Tuscumbia, Alabama. In 1854 he traveled to Texas and settled at Fairfield, where he won election to a district judgeship in 1856. By December 1860 Gregg had come to favor a Texas secession convention and became a delegate when it met in January 1861. In early February the state convention selected him as one of seven Texas representatives to the convention in Montgomery, Alabama, that organized the Confederate government and evolved into the Provisional Congress. Gregg served as chairman of the Claims Committee and as a member of the Accounts and Military Affairs committees. He contributed to the Confederate Constitution the concept that central government officeholders serving in a state could be impeached by that state's legislative body, but usually he favored a strong Confederate government. On trade he supported the limitation that cotton be shipped only from Confederate coastal ports to limit trade with Union states.

When fighting began in the summer of 1861, Gregg went back to Texas to enlist troops for the Seventh Texas Infantry. After official acceptance of his regiment in Marshall, Texas, by the Confederate army early in October, he led the troops across the Mississippi River in November to Hopkinsville, Kentucky. There he won election to the rank of colonel, as his regiment guarded railroads and river lines. As part of the Fort Donelson garrison defending Tennessee in February 1862, Gregg and his men fought against Gen. Ulysses S. Grant, but in the end surrendered. The colonel and other officers spent several months as prisoners of war, briefly at Camp Chase, Ohio, and, beginning in March, at Fort Warren, Massachusetts, before being exchanged in August.

Upon his return to active duty, Gregg was promoted to brigadier general, dated August 29, and was placed in charge of a Tennessee infantry brigade in northern Mississippi. During December 1862, Gregg and his men moved south where they helped defend Vicksburg against a strike down the Mississippi River by Gen. William Tecumseh Sherman in a clash along Chickasaw Bluffs. Gregg and his brigade temporarily moved on to support the Confederates holding Port Hudson on the Mississippi River in Louisiana. He then directed the small force that defended Raymond, Mississippi, in May 1863 against Grant's army, which had crossed the Mississippi River to encircle Vicksburg. Gregg, retreating to Jackson, became part of the army under Gen. Joseph E. Johnston that tried but failed to hold the town against a larger Federal force. Johnston and Gregg then sought unsuccessfully to relieve the Vicksburg garrison during June. By early fall Gregg and his brigade had been transferred to the Army of Tennessee under Gen. Braxton Bragg. At the Battle of Chickamauga in northwestern Georgia on September 19, Gregg was seriously wounded during an attack by the Confederates' left wing.

When Gregg resumed service in January 1864, the army appointed him to lead the Texas regiments, best known as Hood's Brigade, in the Army of Northern Virginia. During Grant's attack on the army of Gen. Robert E. Lee at the Wilderness in Virginia in early May, Gregg led a counterattack to restore the Confederate line. When Lee sought to join the advance, Gregg and his men feared for the life of their commander and refused to allow him past, shouting "Go back, General Lee!" A few days later Gregg's men fought hard to hold their trenches at Spotsylvania. After skirmishes at the North Anna River, Gregg directed his brigade in helping to throw back two Union attacks near Cold Harbor in June. Gregg's men occupied trenches at Bermuda Hundred for a time before they joined in the defense of Petersburg in July. Beginning the next month, Gregg directed the small garrison at Richmond that protected the Confederate capital from attack in September. When Lee ordered an attack on October 7, Gregg attempted to recapture part of the Confederate trenches east of Richmond and died at the front of an unsuccessful charge down the Darbytown Road. His body was returned to his wife, who buried him at Aberdeen, Mississippi.

BIBLIOGRAPHY

Gower, Hershel, and Jack Allen, eds. *Pen and Sword: The Life and Journals of Randal W. McGavock*. Nashville, Tenn., 1959.
McCaffrey, James M. *This Band of Heroes: Granbury's Texas Brigade, C.S.A.* Austin, Tex., 1985.
Miers, Earl Schenck. *The Web of Victory: Grant at Vicksburg*. New York, 1955.
Simpson, Harold B. *Hood's Texas Brigade*. 4 vols. Waco, Tex., 1968–1977.
Warner, Ezra J., and W. Buck Yearns. *Biographical Register of the Confederate Congress*. Baton Rouge, La., 1975.

ALWYN BARR

GREGG, MAXCY (1814–1862), secessionist and brigadier general. Gregg, born August 1, 1814, was a native of South Carolina who graduated from his state's university as covaledictorian. Beginning in the 1830s, he devoted himself to ardent support for the secession of South Carolina. Gregg served in the secession convention and received the state's highest military honor when it appointed him colonel of the First South Carolina Infantry. Although his military experience had been limited to a bloodless stint as a major of Mexican War volunteers, Gregg eagerly took to the field and diligently studied his new trade.

After the firing on Fort Sumter, Gregg led his regiment to Virginia, where it won a skirmish at Vienna on June 17. Expiration of the enlistments of his men left Gregg without a unit for a time, but he soon re-formed the First at full strength. Colonel Gregg still had not faced any major action when he received promotion to brigadier general on December 14, 1861. After spending the winter in the Pocotaligo region, Gregg led his brigade of five South Carolina infantry regiments through the 1862 campaigns in Virginia as part of A. P. Hill's division. The general and his men won respect during the Seven Days' Battles, but their highest contribution to the Confederacy came when they tenaciously held the army's far left at Second Manassas. At Fredericksburg on December 13, 1862, as a Federal breakthrough imperiled the Confederate position, Gregg rode in front of his men and was struck down by a bullet in the spine from which he died a few hours later. He stands out as one of the relatively few antebellum fire-eaters who proved both willing and able to back up his words on the war's battlefields.

BIBLIOGRAPHY

Daly, Louise Haskell. *Alexander Cheves Haskell*. Norwood, Mass., 1934.
Freeman, Douglas S. *Lee's Lieutenants: A Study in Command.* 3 vols. New York, 1942–1944. Reprint, New York, 1986.
Gregg, Maxcy. Papers. University of South Carolina, Columbia.
Krick, Robert K. "Maxcy Gregg." *Civil War History* 19 (1973): 3–23.

ROBERT K. KRICK

GREGG, WILLIAM (1800–1867), textile manufacturer. Gregg was one of the leading cotton textile manufacturers in the Confederate South. Although he began his career as a jeweler, he manifested an early interest in bringing cotton factories to the fields of the South, and he viewed secession and war as an opportunity for the region to develop its industry. He wrote numerous articles in *De Bow's Review* on the need for domestic manufacturing to sustain the Confederate cause. His own mill complex, located in Graniteville, South Carolina, became a key supplier for the Quartermaster Department. New equipment, installed before the outbreak of hostilities, and incentives to mill operatives to extend their shifts by two hours enabled the Graniteville Mills to produce at full capacity for the entire war.

As owner of the Graniteville Mills, Gregg took an active interest in every facet of their operation, especially during the war years. Gregg also endeared himself to locals by donating money and cloth to the needy of the area and by offering jobs and overtime pay to others.

Other Confederate industrialists recognized Gregg's path-breaking achievements in the development of Southern industry and rewarded him with the presidency of the Manufacturing and Direct Trade Association of the Confederate States. Gregg used the meetings of the association as a forum to encourage Southerners to look beyond immediate conditions and to plan for further industrial development after the war. In many ways, Gregg became the earliest exponent of the New South creed.

Confederate defeat found Gregg valiantly trying to refurbish his mills, and his death in 1867 was undoubtedly hastened by the rigors of rebuilding.

BIBLIOGRAPHY

Coulter, E. Merton. *The Confederate States of America, 1861–1865*. A History of the South, vol. 7. Baton Rouge, La., 1951.
Mitchell, Broadus. *William Gregg: Factory Master of the Old South*. Chapel Hill, N.C., 1928. Reprint, New York, 1966.

MARY A. DECREDICO

GRIFFITH, RICHARD (1814–1862), brigadier general. Griffith was born near Philadelphia, Pennsylvania, on January 11, 1814. He graduated from Ohio University at Athens, Ohio, in 1837 and moved to Vicksburg, Mississippi, soon after. Griffith taught school at Vicksburg until the outbreak of the Mexican War, when he enlisted in the First Mississippi Rifles under the command of Jefferson Davis. He was elected first lieutenant and served as regimental adjutant, establishing a close friendship with his commanding officer. After returning from Mexico, Griffith engaged in a wide range of occupations: banker, U.S. marshal, and state treasurer (serving two terms).

Shortly after Mississippi seceded from the Union, Griffith was elected colonel of the Twelfth Mississippi. On November 12, 1861, he became a brigadier general in command of a brigade of Mississippi regiments in Virginia under Maj. Gen. John B. Magruder. Griffith's troops remained in reserve at Seven Pines, but became actively engaged in the subsequent Seven Days' Battles. On June 29, 1862, while waiting with his troops in the reserve at the Battle of Savage's Station, Griffith suffered a mortal wound from a stray Union artillery round. Ironically, the artillery fire had little additional effect. Griffith died later that day in Richmond.

BIBLIOGRAPHY

Freeman, Douglas S. *Lee's Lieutenants: A Study in Command.* 3 vols. New York, 1942–1944. Reprint, New York, 1986.

Sears, Stephen W. *To the Gates of Richmond: The Peninsula Campaign.* New York, 1992.

U.S. War Department. *War of the Rebellion: A Compilation of the Official Records of the Union and Confederate Armies.* Washington, D.C., 1880–1901. Ser. 1, vol. 11, pt. 2, pp. 664, 750.

Warner, Ezra J. *Generals in Gray: Lives of the Confederate Commanders.* Baton Rouge, La., 1959.

BRIAN S. WILLS

GRIMES, BRYAN

(1828–1880), major general. A planter in Washington, North Carolina, before the war, Grimes entered Confederate service in 1861 as a major in the Fourth North Carolina. According to one observer, he had "unflinching hostility to all Yankees—Yankee notions—& Yankee sympathizers." His belief in the superiority of the Southern people propelled him in battle. He described some Northern prisoners in 1863 as "the lowest scum of the Yankee population." A reckless fighter, Grimes had seven horses shot from under him during the war.

Grimes distinguished himself during the 1862 Peninsular campaign, which earned him colonelcy of the regiment in June of that year. He saw action at South Mountain (September 14), Sharpsburg (September 17), and Fredericksburg (December 13). At Chancellorsville on May 3, 1863, Grimes handled his regiment superbly. His unit and the rest of Stephen D. Ramseur's brigade made a charge that was costly but cracked the enemy's line. He confirmed his superiors' high expectations at Gettysburg (July 1–3) and during the Overland campaign (May 4–June 12, 1864). A flawless performance at Spotsylvania on May 12 brought Grimes a brigadier general's commission seven days later.

BRYAN GRIMES.   LIBRARY OF CONGRESS

He also saw action in the Shenandoah Valley at Winchester (September 19), Fisher's Hill (September 22), and Cedar Creek (October 19). The death of Ramseur elevated Grimes to temporary command of a division after Cedar Creek. On February 23, 1865, his promotion became permanent when he was made a major general. Grimes was the organizer of the final Confederate assault at Appomattox on April 9, 1865, a reflection of his high standing in Robert E. Lee's army. Grimes spent the postwar years as a planter in North Carolina, where he was murdered by an assassin on August 14, 1880.

BIBLIOGRAPHY

Cowper, Pulaski, comp. *Extracts of Letters of Major-General Bryan Grimes to His Wife.* Raleigh, N.C., 1884. Reprint, Wilmington, N.C., 1986.

London, H. A. *Memorial Address on the Life and Services of Bryan Grimes.* Raleigh, N.C., 1886.

PETER S. CARMICHAEL

GUERRILLA WARFARE.

Historically, guerrilla wars are brutal, savage affairs waged by small groups of men among the mountains, forests, and swamps. The irregular conflict which occurred in the Confederate States of America during the years 1861 through 1865 was no exception. For pro-Confederate Southeners guerrilla warfare was a way of disrupting Northern invasion and occupation. Pro-Union Southerners, on the other hand, engaged in the "little war" to resist Confederate domination. Although it never achieved decisive military results, partisan activity enabled thousands of civilians behind the lines to strike at the enemy while retaining a semblance of their former peaceful lives.

Early Guerrilla Activity in the Border States. The first large-scale guerrilla actions took place on the western border even before the Civil War started. From May 24, 1856, when a group of abolitionists led by John Brown murdered five Southern settlers in Kansas, guerrilla warfare had raged on the frontier. Bands of Free-Soil and proslavery marauders burned, robbed, and killed in an effort to drive the other from "Bleeding Kansas." When war officially came in 1861, many on the Kansas-Missouri border were already veterans of irregular warfare.

Although Missouri, a slave state, remained technically in the Union, an active minority led by Governor Claiborne F. Jackson worked hard for secession. Consequently, hundreds of Kansas Unionists, fearful of being cut off from the North and nervous over a potential Confederate invasion, joined in bands and marched over the state line. Clad in blue and flying the U.S. flag, the Kansas jayhawkers showed virtually no restraint in their zeal to crush rebellion in Missouri. "Jayhawking" soon became synonymous with brigandage.

In the autumn of 1861, Senator James Lane led a small army of fellow Kansans into Missouri and left a trail of death and desolation in his wake. The climax came on September 23, when the jayhawkers looted and burned the city of Osceola. Smaller bands of Kansans led by James Montgomery, Marshall Cleveland, and others also roamed western Missouri, stealing slaves and livestock, burning homes, barns, and crops, and murdering any man who protested.

The most notorious gang of jayhawkers was that led by Charles Jennison. Composed largely of antislavery militants, horse-thieves, and common criminals, Jennison's regiment lent savagery to an already bloody border war. In addition to theft, arson, and murder, torture and probably rape joined the list. As a warning to others, Jennison personally sliced off the ears of his victims.

It was largely the vicious, indiscriminate forays of Jennison that finally compelled Federal authorities to force the jayhawkers from the border. By the winter of 1861–1862, however, much of western Missouri was a wasteland, and hundreds, perhaps thousands, of Missourians who might otherwise have remained loyal to the Federal government suddenly became bitter, and often active, enemies.

Although Missouri rebels made several thrusts into

QUANTRILL'S HEROES. Three of the notorious Missouri bushwhackers.   LIBRARY OF CONGRESS

Kansas in response to jayhawker raids, it was not until the following year, 1862, that full-scale guerrilla warfare reached the state. Led by William Clarke Quantrill, a twenty-four-year-old Ohio schoolteacher, Missouri partisans, called bushwhackers, launched a series of strikes into Kansas that all but paralyzed the state. On March 7, Aubrey was raided, in September, Olathe was looted, and a month later Shawnee was destroyed. Other bands as well as Quantrill's terrorized Unionists in Missouri, skirmished with cavalry patrols, and harassed Federal garrisons in the western part of the state. Although numerically superior, the Unionists were no match for the better-mounted, better-armed guerrillas. Hence, while blue-clad troops held the towns, colorfully dressed bushwhackers ruled the countryside.

Throughout the rest of Missouri a similar situation existed. In the northeast, Joseph Porter recruited hundreds of men and then laid ambuscades for his Federal pursuers.

Farther south, the dashing "Swamp Fox of the Confederacy," M. Jeff Thompson, operated in the bootheel of Missouri, surprising Northern patrols and sniping at Union gunboats on the Mississippi.

Across the river, the pattern was repeated. Although Kentucky was a slave state, most of its citizens remained neutral or loyal to the Union. As the regular conflict moved south, however, many of those left behind engaged in a bitter contest to gain control of the state. Unionist home guards, ill-disciplined and vengeful, scoured their communities testing the loyalty of neighbors and settling old scores. As a result, numerous bushwhacking bands sprang up.

In an attempt to tap the growing discontent behind enemy lines, both in Kentucky and elsewhere, the Confederate government legitimized guerrilla organizations by passing on April 21, 1862, the Partisan Ranger Act. Many guerrilla leaders, including Quantrill, officially enrolled their men. Federal commanders, however, refused to extend such recognition, and although there were exceptions, Southern partisans were to be hanged or shot when captured. "Pursue, strike, and destroy the reptiles" ran a typical Union decree.

In May 1862, Maj. Gen. John C. Breckinridge sent a number of men, including Adam Johnson, back into Kentucky to recruit troops for the Confederacy. After skirmishing with Federals in the streets of his hometown, Henderson, and surprising a Union detachment near Madisonville, Johnson led his recruits on a raid across the Ohio River. There, on July 18, he seized the arsenal at Newburgh, Indiana. Johnson's act spread panic across southern Indiana and neighboring Ohio. Throughout the summer Johnson remained in Kentucky, employing his men as guerrillas to burn bridges, attack garrisons, and eventually pin down enough Federal troops to facilitate the invasion later that year of a Confederate army led by Gen. Braxton Bragg.

Early Guerrilla Activity in the Deep South. Although most guerrilla activity was centered in the disputed border states and was waged largely by Confederate partisans, increasingly the Deep South became a scene of irregular Unionist operations. Stretching from the Ohio River to northern Georgia, the Appalachian Mountains rose like an island of discord in the heart of the new nation. Isolated and long ignored, many of the impoverished mountaineers of the region saw little to gain from secession and much to lose in a "rich man's war and a poor man's fight." After passage of the Confederate Conscription Act on April 16, 1862, with its numerous exemptions that favored the wealthy, their fears seemed justified.

The rugged Shelton Laurel region of North Carolina became a stronghold of anti-Confederate activity where deserters, draft dodgers, and Unionist guerrillas found refuge. After partisans made an unusually bold raid on nearby Marshall, January 8, 1863, Brig. Gen. Henry Heth, commander of the Department of East Tennessee, sent in a regiment. Subjected to sniper fire the moment they entered Shelton Laurel, the angered soldiers flogged and tortured several women to gain information. Then, on January 18, the troops rounded up over a dozen men and boys and shot them the following day. Though intended as a warning, the killings did little to curb mountain bushwhacking.

Elsewhere throughout the South, pockets of revolt and lawlessness materialized as the war dragged on. In the panhandle of Florida, gangs of deserters, criminals, and other "lay-outs" roamed the hardscrabble hills, raiding farms for food, loot, and liquor. On the west coast of the state, William Strickland led a band of freebooters who, emerging from their sanctuary in the swamps, spent the nights prowling nearby plantations and carrying off slaves, food, and plunder. In 1863, Strickland organized his gang into the Union Rangers, and in exchange for arms and equipment, he supplied Federal gunboats with food and information. Farther south, near Tampa, small bands of partisans sparred with Southern troops and drove off cattle intended to feed hungry Confederates to the north.

Although most Southerners had welcomed secession, many slaveless farmers in the uplands of Alabama and Mississippi, in the rural parishes of Louisiana, and in the German settlements of northern Texas had quietly opposed it. After passage of the Conscription Act, however, simple indifference to the Confederate cause in these regions often erupted into antigovernment violence. Secret societies sprang up, loyalist neighbors were threatened, and when enrollment officers tried to enforce the draft, they were chased, beaten, and sometimes killed. In Winston County, Alabama, Unionists worked to form their own Free State, and other Tories in the northwest corner of the state considered merging with the mountain regions of Tennessee and Georgia to create the nonslave commonwealth of Nickajack. When Col. A. D. Streight led a Federal cavalry raid through Alabama and Georgia in April 1863, companies of local Unionists eagerly served as guides.

Farther west, not only did pockets of pro-Union sentiment exist in the poorer parishes of Louisiana, but after the Federal capture of New Orleans early in 1862, pro-Confederate guerrillas also became active. When a Northern landing party was fired upon by a band of bushwhackers at Baton Rouge on May 28 of that year, Adm. David Farragut ordered his gunboats on the Mississippi to shell the town. Several months later Farragut's cannon also opened on Donaldsville for a similar occurrence. Organized gangs of criminals, runaway slaves, and deserters from both armies also preyed upon the state, robbing, raping, and murdering indiscriminately. One group operated from the Atchafalaya Swamp where the Teche region to the west and the Lafourche country to the east were equally accessible to their forays.

Like its neighbor to the south, Arkansas was also beset by guerrillas of both flags. In the east, Confederate bushwhackers led by James McGhee and Joseph Barton harassed traffic on the Mississippi and burned half a dozen Federal steamers. To the northwest, bands of Unionists clashed with Confederate partisans in the Ozark Mountains.

Similarly, guerrillas under John McNeill and John D. Imboden in rugged western Virginia fought savagely against both Unionist partisans and Federal troops.

William Clarke Quantrill. By the spring of 1863 Quantrill was on the minds of all Kansans. Because of his success the year before, the people of the state saw no reason to be optimistic about the coming summer. Already several ominous incidents had occurred, including a daring raid to Diamond Springs in May by Richard Yager's bushwhackers. Consequently, Federal Brig. Gen. Thomas Ewing, Jr., recently appointed to the border command, instituted a series of tough policies.

In an effort to prevent raids into Kansas, Ewing first established a system of stations along the state line. At each camp the general placed over one hundred well-armed and equipped cavalrymen. Next, Ewing recruited a number of spies who successfully infiltrated the partisan ranks. Fi-

nally, to deny support to the guerrillas, the general rounded up "several hundred of the worst" sympathizers in western Missouri and prepared to send them south. This last act would have tragic consequences. Hunted like animals themselves, the bushwhackers were outraged at the mistreatment and exile of their families and plotted retaliation. When a brick guardhouse collapsed in Kansas City on August 13, 1863, killing five of the women and children, their thirst for revenge mounted.

No place in America was more hated by Quantrill's followers than Lawrence, Kansas. Not only had the city served as a Free-Soil citadel during the 1850s, but the New England colony was also home to Senator James Lane, the jayhawker who had burned Osceola two years before. In addition, Lawrence was a sanctuary for runaway slaves and headquarters of the Red Legs, a gang of Unionist guerrillas.

One week after the prison disaster, on the morning of August 21, Quantrill and over four hundred bushwhackers, including Frank James and Coleman Younger, halted at the edge of Lawrence. Not only had Federal spies been unable to warn Ewing of the guerrillas' plans, but a captain commanding the border station at Aubrey, Kansas, offered no serious opposition when they crossed the state line. The officer also failed to send any word west. Hence, at 5:00 A.M. the three thousand people of Lawrence were asleep when Quantrill charged into the town. For the next several hours

Ruins of Lawrence, Kansas. After William Quantrill and his followers looted shops, razed the town, and killed over 150 of its citizens on August 21, 1863.

Harper's Pictorial History of the Great Rebellion

the guerrillas roamed Lawrence unhindered, robbing stores, burning homes, and murdering unarmed citizens. Although Senator Lane escaped and the Red Legs were absent that day, the second largest city of Kansas was in ashes and over 150 men and boys lay dead when the Missourians finally left. Thousands of Federal troopers and Kansas militiamen pursued the bushwhackers, but by skillful management Quantrill led his command to the woodlands of Missouri and safety the following day.

Four days after the massacre, on August 25, 1863, Thomas Ewing issued General Order No. 11. In part, the edict decreed that all Missourians residing in three of the counties bordering Kansas were to be expelled from the land and their crops and forage destroyed. Two weeks later the order had been carried out, as one officer put it, "to the letter." The suffering and hardship imposed on innocent and guilty alike were extreme, and Order No. 11 proved to be the harshest military act of the war aimed at a civilian population. Because most troops enforcing the edict were Kansans, it was also certain that the ensuing death and destruction in Missouri would equal, if not greatly surpass, that of Lawrence.

In mid-September, Ewing sent thousands of Federal cavalrymen on a massive sweep through the woodlands of western Missouri in a bid to crush the guerrillas. Several skirmishes occurred and a number of partisans were slain, but once again Quantrill eluded his pursuers.

On October 6, 1863, as he was passing through the southeastern corner of Kansas, Quantrill halted to attack the Union fort at Baxter Springs. Although several defenders were killed, the assault was soon repulsed. A short time later, however, the guerrilla leader encountered a Federal wagon train just north of the fort. Unaware of partisans in the area, Maj. Gen. James Blunt and his escort paused to watch the blue-clad bushwhackers, assuming they were troopers from the fort. Before Blunt realized his mistake, the guerrillas charged and quickly overwhelmed his command. Although the general and several of his men escaped, eighty-five others were killed, including the band musicians and James O'Neal, an artist for *Frank Leslie's Illustrated Newspaper*.

A wave of horror swept the North upon learning of the events in Kansas. For the first and only time the guerrilla war in the West overshadowed the battlefields of the East.

John S. Mosby. In January 1863, Confederate Gen. J. E. B. Stuart detached a private from his command, John S. Mosby, and directed him to take nine volunteers into Union-occupied northern Virginia and engage in irregular operations. Opposed to secession initially and an "indifferent soldier" at first, the twenty-nine-year-old Mosby, after joining Stuart's cavalry, had proven himself to be a daring trooper, courier, and scout. As a guerrilla leader, the former lawyer displayed a talent for war that soon became legendary. By the time his career ended he had achieved the rank of colonel and his field of operations, the region between the Blue Ridge and Bull Run mountains, had become known to friend and foe alike as "Mosby's Confederacy."

Immediately after crossing enemy lines, Mosby's tiny band went on the attack, harassing Union outposts, stealing horses, destroying equipment, and capturing surprised Federal soldiers by the score. On March 9, 1863, at Fairfax, Mosby gained national attention when he roused from bed and captured Brig. Gen. Edwin Stoughton. The embarrassment to the Union army was compounded when Mosby brazenly retreated with his prisoner in full view of the Federal fortifications at Centreville. The feat won Mosby a captaincy and enabled him to officially organize his growing company into the Forty-third Battalion of Partisan Rangers.

Later that month, near Chantilly, Mosby's Rangers were pursued by a force more than twice as large. Again, on April 1, while they were camped along the Potomac River, a similar Federal column surprised them. In each instance, however, the captain turned on his attackers, inflicting heavy casualties and taking more than a hundred prisoners.

In addition to hit-and-run raids and almost continuous skirmishing, the Virginia partisans burned bridges on the Orange and Alexandria Railroad and tore down miles of telegraph wire. On May 30, 1863, with the aid of a small fieldpiece, Mosby ambushed a locomotive near Manassas and set the cars on fire. As a result, Federal troops needed on front lines were detailed to guard railroads, patrol highways, and serve as escorts.

Unlike guerrillas in the West, Mosby's Rangers normally wore Confederate uniforms, paroled or sent their captives south, and generally conducted themselves according to the rules of warfare. But, as in the West, a large and sympathetic population in northern Virginia provided the guerrillas with food, shelter, information, and recruits. A wide variety of men were attracted to Mosby's company. Discharged veterans, soldiers on furlough, even convalescents, were drawn by the informal come-and-go nature of the command. Local farm boys from Virginia and Maryland were swept up by the romance associated with independent cavalry. A considerable number of deserters and freebooters also joined, lured by the prospect of easy plunder. Under Mosby's leadership, however, the conglomerates were honed into a highly effective fighting force.

Because of atrocities committed by bushwhackers in the West, as well as the penchant for plunder all guerrilla bands displayed, including Mosby's, powerful Southern voices were raised calling for a repeal of the Partisan Ranger Act, arguing that irregular warfare was barbaric, uncontrollable, and injurious to the cause. Even Robert E. Lee, whose own father had fought the British as a partisan,

GROUP OF MOSBY'S RANGERS. Photographed at Fairfax, Virginia, where they captured Brig. Gen. Edwin Stoughton on March 9, 1863. Col. Mosby is left of center in the middle row.   NAVAL HISTORICAL CENTER, WASHINGTON, D.C.

harbored doubts. Finally, in February 1864, the Confederate Congress revoked the act and a short time later Secretary of War James A. Seddon ended government sanction of all guerrilla groups—with two exceptions. Only John McNeill's partisans in western Virginia and Mosby's in the north were to remain officially recognized by Richmond.

In mid-May 1864, as Ulysses S. Grant pushed south on his great spring offensive against Lee, Mosby's men struck railroad bridges and supply trains in the Federal rear. Then when Confederate Gen. Jubal Early began a diversionary thrust toward Washington, Mosby joined him and soon succeeded in severing rail and wire communications between the U.S. capital and Harpers Ferry for two days.

Returning south, Mosby attacked a pursuing Union column at Mount Zion Church and all but annihilated it, taking over fifty prisoners and leaving another fifty dead and wounded. On the morning of August 13, as Union Gen. Philip Sheridan and his army were invading the Shenandoah Valley, Mosby and three hundred Rangers surprised a

section of his supply train near Berryville. Seventy-five wagons were seized or destroyed, almost a thousand head of livestock stolen, and over two hundred Federals taken prisoner.

Later, in an effort to construct another supply line for Sheridan's army, labor gangs set to work rebuilding the Manassas Gap Railroad. Mosby's men attacked furiously, tearing up rails, driving off work crews, even derailing two construction trains. Thousands of Federal troops soon arrived, however, making further raids suicidal. Nevertheless, in a brilliant counterstroke, Mosby raced north and struck Sheridan's "secure" supply line, the Baltimore and Ohio Railroad. On October 14, 1864, the guerrillas derailed a train near Harpers Ferry and stole $170,000 in U.S. payroll funds. Admitting defeat, the Federals suspended all work on the Manassas Gap Railroad.

Various stratagems were devised to crush Mosby. One plan called for the organization of an elite body of sharpshooters, armed with Spencer repeating rifles, to hound Mosby's trail until he was destroyed. On November

18, 1864, Mosby's lieutenant, Adolphus Richards, ambushed and wiped out the one-hundred-man unit. Another antiguerrilla tactic was to arrest the populace in Mosby's Confederacy and destroy their mills, barns, and crops. This caused terrible suffering, but Mosby continued to operate freely. An even more severe measure was the execution of captured Rangers. Although it proved the most difficult decision of his life, Mosby, in an effort "to prevent the war from degenerating into a massacre," ordered captured Federals hanged in retaliation. Summary executions on both sides then ceased.

On January 30, 1865, while visiting Richmond, Mosby was honored by the Confederate House of Representatives. A few days later the Senate paid a similar tribute, making the "Gray Ghost" the only partisan of the war accorded such recognition.

John Jackson Dickison. After the Federal occupation of eastern Florida early in the war, Capt. John Jackson Dickison of the Second Florida Cavalry withdrew his command across the St. Johns River. Although isolated and far from lines of support, Dickison chose to fight rather than retreat. Utilizing the swampy environment deftly, Dickison's company staged a series of amphibious assaults, sweeping up Federal pickets, scattering Union raiding parties, and returning runaway slaves. Although he seldom led more than a hundred men, the captain's ceaseless guerrilla attacks ultimately prevented the Northerners from extending their control over central Florida.

On the night of May 19, 1864, Dickison's men crossed the St. Johns and captured nearly sixty Federals at Welaka and Fort Gates. Several nights later, near Palatka, the guerrillas ambushed the Union gunboat *Columbine* as it was passing downriver, capturing or killing one hundred Federals and destroying the boat. Later that summer Dickison audaciously attacked a large Union force at Gainesville, killed, wounded, or captured over two hundred men, and then pursued the rest for miles. Once again, on the night of October 24, 1864, the Confederates surprised a Federal raiding party near Magnolia, inflicted heavy casualties, and chased the survivors into the swamps.

William Anderson. Probably no guerrilla anywhere waged war more ruthlessly than William Anderson, known to later generations as Bloody Bill. A native of Missouri, he was living in Kansas when the war began. In 1862, after Unionists murdered his father, Anderson returned to Missouri and joined the bushwhackers. When one of his sisters was killed in the Kansas City prison disaster the following year, the twenty-four-year-old guerrilla dedicated the remainder of his short life to the slaughter of Unionists. Several days after his sister's death, Anderson rode to Lawrence with Quantrill where he reportedly shot fourteen men in cold blood. Six weeks later he killed perhaps as many in the massacre at Baxter Springs.

On June 12, 1864, Anderson and his company, clad in blue uniforms, rode up to a fourteen-man Federal patrol near Kingsville, Missouri, and killed or captured all but two. The prisoners were shot, the bodies were stripped, and one man was scalped. Two days later the bushwhackers attacked a wagon supply train and killed eight more Federals. The following month Anderson's gang crossed the Missouri and in succession shot or hanged eight men and slashed the throat of a ninth. On July 15, Anderson raided Huntsville, Missouri, killed one man, and stole between $30,000 and $100,000. A week later the bushwhackers burned the railroad depot at Renick and pulled down miles of telegraph wire. The following day Anderson ambushed a Federal patrol, killed two, and then mutilated them.

Throughout the summer Anderson's gang roamed Missouri, burning bridges, bushwhacking patrols, and committing uncounted atrocities. Many, including Anderson himself, adorned their bridles with scalps. Some wore necklaces of human ears.

On September 27, 1864, Anderson and eighty bushwhackers, including Frank and Jesse James, raided Centralia, Missouri. Shortly before noon a train pulled into the station. Among those on board were over twenty Union soldiers, many returning home on furlough. The troops were stripped, lined up, and shot. With the depot and train in flames Anderson and his men rode south a few miles to a stand of timber where several hundred bushwhackers were camped. Shortly after Anderson left, over one hundred Union militiamen entered Centralia. Viewing the carnage and destruction, the militia immediately set off in pursuit. Aware of the Federals' presence, a squad of guerrillas lured them into ambush where they were surrounded and hopelessly outnumbered. The fight became a massacre in minutes. Those who surrendered were subjected to terrible torture. Some were clubbed to death, and others were pinned to the ground with bayonets. Wounded men had their throats cut and many were scalped. Some were beheaded. Throughout the ordeal, those waiting their turn were forced to watch. In all, over 150 Federals died at Centralia. "The war has furnished no greater barbarism," wrote a horrified Union general.

Other Guerrilla Activities Late in the War. Elsewhere throughout the South, because their loved ones had suffered death, injury, or outrage at the hands of Unionists, a number of guerrillas now waged remorseless vendettas. Sam Hildebrand stalked the forests of southern Missouri, dealing out death to dozens. Similarly, Champ Ferguson of Tennessee haunted the Cumberlands, shooting, stabbing, and mutilating Unionists wherever he found them. Before he was finally hanged, Ferguson claimed over one hundred victims.

The response to guerrilla warfare had also become more brutal. Unlike most commanders, who were content to simply shoot or hang captured bushwhackers out of hand, William Tecumseh Sherman believed the punishment should fit the crime. When torpedoes (land mines) laid along the track threatened to sever his rail communications as he fought south toward Atlanta in the summer of 1864, the general authorized his commanders to place prisoners in a car and pull it forward with a rope to test the track for additional mines. In the event no prisoners were available, suspected Southern civilians would do. "Make somebody suffer" summed up Sherman's response to partisans and their abettors.

By 1864, the situation in Kentucky verged on anarchy. Because of the Emancipation Proclamation and the Federal enlistment of black troops, slave owners loyal to the Union felt betrayed. Many who had formerly favored the Federal government now went to war against it. Guerrilla bands led by Ike Berry, Marcellus Clarke, and a score of others sprang up overnight. In an attempt to suppress the revolt, Maj. Gen. Stephen Burbridge issued a series of draconian laws, including confiscation of property and the execution of five guerrillas for every loyalist killed. Except for adding to the death and destruction, however, the acts accomplished little.

Of all the states that suffered from guerrilla warfare, however, none suffered more than Missouri. By 1864 few counties had been spared. Gangs of vengeful Unionist militia scoured the state, beating, torturing, and murdering Confederate sympathizers. Equally vicious bands of bushwhackers led by John Thrailkill, George Todd, and others roamed almost at will, ambushing Federal patrols, terrorizing the populace, and bringing life in Missouri to a standstill. Trains were attacked, stage lines stopped, and steamboats that braved the rivers subjected to almost constant sniper fire. To run the gauntlet on the Missouri, pilots in St. Louis asked and received a thousand dollars for a single trip to Kansas. Terrified Unionists fled their farms and huddled in garrisoned towns that, for all practical purposes, became little more than islands surrounded by vast killing fields. "The very air seems charged with blood and death," wrote a Kansas City editor.

The last significant guerrilla actions of the war occurred in Virginia. While Mosby was recovering from a serious wound, Adolphus Richards remained active throughout the winter. In addition to sparring with Federal patrols, Richards's men in late January 1865 destroyed a fifteen-car train on the Baltimore and Ohio near Ashby's Gap. An even more spectacular success came on February 21 when partisans under Jesse McNeill slipped into Cumberland, Maryland, and captured Union Gens. Benjamin Kelley and George Crook.

With the war reaching its climax in the spring of 1865 and the South facing imminent defeat, many, including Jefferson Davis, suggested that the Confederate army should disperse and wage guerrilla war. But General Lee forbade it. Drained by four years of desperate fighting, his nation in ruins, Lee ordered his men to lay down their arms and return home. With the partisans scattered in remote regions, it took weeks before some ceased operations. Many drifted home and tried with varying degrees of success to live normal lives. Others, fearing retaliation, moved elsewhere. A few, like Frank and Jesse James, either could not or would not surrender.

On April 21, 1865, twelve days after Lee's surrender, John Mosby disbanded his Rangers. Three weeks later, in one of the last skirmishes of the war, William Quantrill was shot near Bloomfield, Kentucky. Ironically, the career of perhaps the best-known partisan on either side was ended by Federal guerrillas.

The hatred engendered by the irregular war lingered long after hostilities ceased. Thousands who had never heard a cannon had been touched by the guerrilla conflict. The bitterness could be partly measured in the postwar years by the severity of Federal Reconstruction, and it could be seen in newspaper headlines describing bank robberies, train holdups, and murders committed by former bushwhackers. In the Appalachians, the Ozarks, and other regions, generations would be required to heal the wounds inflicted by the guerrilla war.

[See also Bleeding Kansas; Centralia Massacre; Chambersburg, Pennsylvania; Mosby's Rangers; and biographies of numerous figures mentioned herein.]

BIBLIOGRAPHY

Brownlee, Richard S. Gray Ghosts of the Confederacy: Guerrilla Warfare in the West, 1861–1865. Baton Rouge, La., 1958.

Castel, Albert. "The Guerrilla War." Civil War Times Illustrated 13 (October 1974): 4–50.

Castel, Albert. William Clarke Quantrill: His Life and Times. New York, 1962.

Fellman, Michael. Inside War: The Guerrilla Conflict in Missouri during the American Civil War. New York, 1989.

Goodrich, Thomas. Bloody Dawn: The Story of the Lawrence Massacre. Kent, Ohio, 1991.

Hall, James O. "The Shelton Laurel Massacre: Murder in the North Carolina Mountains." Blue & Gray 8, no. 3 (February 1991): 20–26.

Jones, Virgil Carrington. Ranger Mosby. Chapel Hill, N.C., 1944.

Paludan, Phillip S. Victims: A True Story of the Civil War. Knoxville, Tenn., 1981.

Siepel, Kevin H. Rebel: The Life and Times of John Singleton Mosby. New York, 1983.

Starr, Stephen Z. Jennison's Jayhawkers: A Civil War Cavalry Regiment and Its Commander. Baton Rouge, La., 1973.

Wert, Jeffry D. Mosby's Rangers. New York, 1990.

THOMAS GOODRICH

GUTHRIE, JOHN J.

GUTHRIE, JOHN J. (1815–1877), naval lieutenant. Born in Washington, North Carolina, April 15, 1815, Guthrie entered the U.S. Navy as a midshipman in 1834 after a one-year stint at West Point. During the Mexican

War he served on the blockade off Vera Cruz and was promoted to lieutenant in 1847. He participated in the Anglo-French War in 1856 and received the thanks of his native state for gallantry in combat. In late 1860 Guthrie served on the USS *Saratoga,* bound for slave patrol off western Africa. He led a successful assault on the slaver *Nightingale* loaded with nine hundred captives. As prize master, Guthrie freed the slaves in Liberia and then returned to New York on June 15, 1861, where he found the Civil War underway.

Guthrie entered the Confederate navy as a lieutenant in July. After service on the Rappahannock River defenses, he commanded in succession the steamer *Red Rover,* floating battery *New Orleans,* and steamer *Capitol* on western waters, and the floating battery *Arctic* near Wilmington, North Carolina. Ordered to the gunboat *Chattahoochee* on the Apalachicola River, Florida, in early 1863, he was in charge of that vessel when its boiler exploded the following May, killing or injuring many of its crew. In October Guthrie temporarily left naval service to command the blockade runner *Advance* for North Carolina. He made at least two successful round trips through the blockade before returning to the navy in April 1864. He commanded the Halifax, North Carolina, naval station for nearly a year and then served as a volunteer aide for Governor Zebulon Vance of North Carolina.

After the war Guthrie made his home in Portsmouth, Virginia. In 1875 President Ulysses S. Grant appointed him superintendent of life-saving stations from Cape Henry to Cape Hatteras. He died on November 25, 1877, attempting to rescue the crew of *Huron* off Nags Head, North Carolina. He is buried in Cedar Grove Cemetery, Portsmouth.

BIBLIOGRAPHY

Stewart, William H. *History of Norfolk County and Representative Citizens.* Norfolk, Va., 1902.

Turner, Maxine. *Navy Gray: A Story of the Confederate Navy on the Chattahoochee and Apalachicola Rivers.* Tuscaloosa, Ala., 1988.

A. ROBERT HOLCOMBE, JR.

HABEAS CORPUS. The so-called great writ of liberty, an order that can be given by any judge requiring authorities to produce prisoners in court and to explain the law by which they are held, was specifically protected by the Confederate Constitution. That document copied the language of the U.S. Constitution and stated in Article I, "The privilege of the writ of habeas corpus shall not be suspended, unless when in cases of rebellion or invasion the public safety may require it."

Despite military invasions by Federal forces in 1861 and considerable endangerment of public safety in certain areas of the Confederacy, President Jefferson Davis, who shared the customary American view that only Congress could suspend the writ of habeas corpus, did not act until the Confederate Congress on February 27, 1862, empowered him to suspend the writ in "such cities, towns and military districts as shall, in his judgment, be in such danger of attack by the enemy as to require the declaration of martial law for their effective defence."

Martial law had been imposed in the case of invasion only once in American history that anyone could remember—by Gen. Andrew Jackson at New Orleans in 1815. Though many Americans, North and South, held strong opinions on the subject, perhaps none possessed firm knowledge of the consequences of such action in a great civil war. Besides, suspending the writ of habeas corpus and imposing martial law were not the same thing (or, at least, are not so regarded by modern legal authorities who do not look upon suspension as an invitation to try civilians in military courts). The act of the Confederate Congress, which equated the two, was but a sign of general confusion on the subject. Moreover, military authorities had already arrested many civilians before the writ was suspended, and the second floor of the notorious Castle Thunder military prison in Richmond was reserved for civilians throughout the war.

As soon as he had the power, Davis used it, putting Norfolk and Portsmouth, Virginia, under martial law on the very day the bill became law. He then placed Richmond under martial law on March 1, 1862. Gen. John H. Winder, commander of the Department of Henrico, which included Richmond, quickly grew infamous for his attempts to rule the city. He outlawed liquor sales and recruited government detectives among Maryland refugees (he was from Maryland himself), who proved extremely unpopular with the Virginians.

The inevitable reaction by libertarians, state righters, factional opponents, and defeatists caused Congress to pass a bill on April 19, 1862, stipulating that the authorization would expire thirty days after the opening of the next legislative session. Indeed, the authority lapsed on September 17, 1862, but was renewed on October 13, to last until February 13, 1863. The reauthorization dropped mention of martial law but did not outlaw, limit, or clarify its use. The legislators allowed Davis's authorization to lapse in 1863, a congressional election year, and despite the efforts of ardent advocates of presidential authority like Mississippi Congressman Ethelbert Barksdale, habeas corpus remained a Confederate privilege for almost a year.

Habeas corpus served as a mini-judicial review in some instances, and nowhere more clearly than in controversies involving conscription. Any judge who thought conscription unconstitutional, and many did, could release civilians from enrollment or conscripts from military control with a habeas corpus writ. In the North, which retained active political parties throughout the war, these judges tended to come from the opposition Democratic party. In the Confederacy, such judges seem to have been concentrated within the boundaries of disaffected states, especially North Carolina. Another uncooperative state was Georgia, and Vice President Alexander H. Stephens proved to be more

Georgian than Confederate on this and many other issues and bitterly opposed suspension.

Defeatism and opposition to central authority flourished, and by late 1863 the need for reauthorization seemed acute to the president, who was especially worried about alleged disloyalty in North Carolina. His message to Congress of February 3, 1864, consisted of one long plea for a new bill authorizing suspension of the writ of habeas corpus. Davis mentioned a wide variety of cases where he deemed the power necessary: to suppress secret conspiracies and disloyal meetings, to keep judges from preventing generals from marching, to control desertion, to enforce conscription, to protect Richmond from spies, and to combat communication with the enemy. On February 17, 1864, Davis received what proved to be his last congressional authorization to suspend the writ. This authority had expired by August 1864, and numerous efforts to draft and pass another bill failed.

"The turning of the tide against the Confederacy," historian Frank L. Owsley concluded in 1925, coincided with the refusal of its Congress "to empower the President to suspend the writ of habeas corpus and to establish martial law." Owsley added "that after August 1, 1864, when the last act suspending the writ had expired, the fortunes of the South never rose again." More recent and specialized studies have chosen instead to praise Jefferson Davis and other Confederate authorities for their benign record on civil liberties. Virtually all authorities would agree that Davis was constitutionally more circumspect than Abraham Lincoln, who quickly assumed the authority and suspended the writ of habeas corpus in some areas less than two weeks after the firing on Fort Sumter and throughout the nation in certain kinds of cases for more than two years. By contrast, Davis always asked his Congress before suspending habeas corpus and enjoyed the authority to suspend for only some sixteen months of the war. Moreover, the Confederacy, though it allowed minor infractions to be punished by military courts in urban areas under martial law, never employed trials by military commission— essentially courts-martial for civilians—after disallowing a brief experiment with such justice in Texas. It was the use of these by the Lincoln administration that the U.S. Supreme Court roundly condemned in *Ex parte Milligan* in 1866.

Perhaps the most important writ of habeas corpus issued in Confederate history came from Judge James W. F. Allen of a Virginia circuit court. The writ was served on Gen. John D. Imboden's provost marshal, who was holding W. E. Coffman, a civilian from Rockbridge County sentenced to death by a court-martial in December 1863 for communicating with the enemy. Imboden would have ignored the writ, but the provost marshal had telegraphed the War Department immediately and Richmond authorities instructed obedience. This saved the Davis administration a potential martyr like Clement L. Vallandigham in the North and thus made favorable appraisals of the Confederacy's record on civil liberties much easier in later years.

How the internal security system actually operated in those periods when the writ of habeas corpus was suspended in the Confederacy simply is not known. While the Confederate Congress was considering the expiration of the suspension in February 1863, it demanded an account of civilian prisoners held by War Department authority, and the Davis administration submitted lists from prisons in Richmond and Salisbury, North Carolina. The government held 302 such prisoners at that time, and the total, adjusted for population differential, is proportionate with analogous numbers for the Lincoln administration in the same period. This suggests, despite the obvious dissimilarities in formal approach to this constitutional question, that actual practice in the Confederacy may have been roughly similar to that in the North. Moreover, those Confederate civilians most likely to be unsympathetic with the cause never enjoyed the privilege of the writ of habeas corpus: the slaves. The Union's president did not enjoy any such degree of control over millions of potentially disaffected persons in the North as the president of the Confederacy did over the slaves.

[*See also* Censorship; Freedom of the Press; Military Justice.]

BIBLIOGRAPHY

Alexander, Thomas B., and Richard E. Beringer. *The Anatomy of the Confederate Congress: A Study of the Influences of Member Characteristics on Legislative Voting Behavior, 1861–1865.* Nashville, Tenn., 1972.

Robbins, John B. "The Confederacy and the Writ of Habeas Corpus." *Georgia Historical Quarterly* 55 (Spring 1971): 83–101.

Robinson, William M., Jr. *Justice in Gray: A History of the Judicial System of the Confederate States of America.* Cambridge, Mass., 1941.

MARK E. NEELY, JR.

HAGOOD, JOHNSON (1829–1898), brigadier general and postwar governor of South Carolina. Hagood was born in Barnwell County, South Carolina, on February 21, 1829. He attended the Citadel (South Carolina Military Academy) in Charleston, graduating in 1847. Afterward he studied law and was admitted to the bar in 1850.

Before the war he served as a brigadier general of militia, and he became colonel of the First South Carolina Volunteers after his state's secession. He took part in the bombardment of Fort Sumter and was present at the Battle of First Manassas. Returning to South Carolina, he saw service around Charleston, particularly at Secessionville and Fort Wagner. His promotion to brigadier general came on July 21, 1862. His command remained along the coast in the defense of Charleston during its siege, only to be sent back to Virginia in spring 1864.

A portion of his brigade arrived in the Petersburg area on May 6, 1864, in time to fight against Gen. Benjamin Butler in the Bermuda Hundred Campaign. After the Battle of Drewry's Bluff, his men participated at Cold Harbor and in the fighting for Petersburg on June 16. On August 21, his brigade tried to regain the recently captured Weldon Railroad from the Federal forces, but it was unsuccessful, losing many prisoners. Gen. Beauregard commended Hagood as a "brave and meritorious officer" when he recommended him for promotion. His troops left the Petersburg front in December, when they were sent to the relief of Fort Fisher, North Carolina. He spent the final months of the war under Gen. Joseph E. Johnston, fighting at Kinton and Bentonville. The brigade surrendered at Greensboro on April 26.

After the war, Hagood was elected comptroller general of South Carolina on the 1876 Hampton ticket and was reelected in 1878. In 1880 he became governor of the state. He died on January 4, 1898, and is buried in Barnwell.

BIBLIOGRAPHY

Capers, Ellison. *South Carolina.* Vol. 5 of *Confederate Military History.* Edited by Clement A. Evans. Atlanta, 1899. Vol. 6 of extended ed. Wilmington, N.C., 1987.

Hagood, Johnson. *Memoirs of the War of Secession.* Columbia, S.C., 1910.

Hagood, Johnson. "Report of May 13, 1864." *Southern Historical Society Papers* 12 (1884): 119–122. Reprint, Wilmington, N.C., 1990.

Warner, Ezra J. *Generals in Gray: Lives of the Confederate Commanders.* Baton Rouge, La., 1959.

CHRIS CALKINS

HAHN, MICHAEL (1830–1886), Unionist, U.S. congressman, and Union governor of Louisiana. Like many other Louisiana Unionists, Hahn was born outside the South. He and his family emigrated from Germany to New Orleans in 1840 and resided among the city's established, though from a Southern perspective suspect, German immigrant community. Trained as a lawyer and eager to advance (and please), Hahn gravitated toward politics, serving on the New Orleans school board and as director of the public school system. He allied with a minority faction of the state Democratic party that was dedicated to national expansion and preservation of state rights within the Union.

During the early months of the 1860 presidential cam-
paign, Hahn emerged as a leading Unionist in the state, openly denouncing secession. But Louisiana's confederation with other seceding states silenced, at least for the moment, critics of Southern independence. Although many Unionists then left Louisiana, Hahn remained in New Orleans, keeping his Unionist sentiments to himself and making peace with Confederate officials.

With the arrival of Federal armies in 1862, Hahn reasserted his loyalty to the Union, organizing Union associations throughout the city. For his loyalty and service, he won the favor of the Lincoln administration. He served briefly in Congress in 1862 and 1863, returning to Louisiana convinced that Lincoln's moderate policies would restore a reconstructed Louisiana and South to the Union. He backed emancipation, endorsed Banks's well-regulated contract labor system, accepted a restricted black suffrage, and favored a generous reconciliation with the defeated Confederates. Elected governor in 1864, Hahn hoped to reestablish civil government and reconstruct Louisiana as Lincoln directed. He failed. Army generals in Louisiana distrusted the civilian government, and both conservatives and radicals in the state undermined the Hahn administration. Even Lincoln distanced himself from his Louisiana experiment.

Beleaguered at home and without political support, Hahn resigned as governor in 1865. Denied a seat in the U.S. Senate, he returned to Louisiana determined to achieve a moderate reconstruction, but the riot of 1866 destroyed that prospect. Though Hahn remained active in state politics for the rest of his life, he is remembered more for his conspicuous failures than for his continuous service and notable contributions.

BIBLIOGRAPHY

McCrary, James Peyton. *Abraham Lincoln and Reconstruction: The Louisiana Experiment.* Princeton, N.J., 1978.

Simpson, Amos E., and Vaughan Baker. "Michael Hahn: Steady Patriot." *Louisiana History* 13 (1972): 229–252.

Summers, Mark W. "The Moderates' Last Chance: The Louisiana Election of 1865." *Louisiana History* 24 (1983): 49–69.

Tregle, Joseph G., Jr. "Thomas J. Durant, Utopian Socialism, and the Failure of Presidential Reconstruction in Louisiana." *Journal of Southern History* 45 (1979): 485–512.

Tunnell, Ted. *Crucible of Reconstruction: War, Radicalism and Race in Louisiana, 1862–1877.* Baton Rouge, La., 1984.

TERRENCE W. FITZMORRIS

HALE, STEPHEN FOWLER (1816–1862), congressman from Alabama and lieutenant colonel. Born on January 31, 1816, in Crittenden County, Kentucky, Hale graduated from Cumberland University and taught school in Greene County, Alabama. In 1839 he graduated from the law school at Lexington, Kentucky, and opened a law office in Eutaw, Alabama. He served one term in the Alabama legislature and practiced law until the Mexican War broke out. He fought as the lieutenant of his company throughout the conflict. He resumed practicing law in Eutaw and returned in 1857 and 1859 to the legislature as a Southern rights Whig.

In 1861 he served as a commissioner to encourage secession sentiment in Kentucky before being elected a representative to the Provisional Confederate Congress, where he was a member of the Military Affairs, Judiciary, and Indian Affairs committees. He proposed legislation to protect slavery during the war and to ban payment of debts to Northerners. He did not stand for election to the First Confederate Congress but was chosen lieutenant colonel of the Eleventh Alabama Infantry. After the Battle of Seven Pines in 1862, he was briefly assigned to the Ninth Alabama regiment before returning to the Eleventh. He was wounded during the Battle of Gaines' Mill in June 1862 and died in Richmond, Virginia, on July 18.

BIBLIOGRAPHY

Owen, Thomas McAdory. *History of Alabama and Dictionary of Alabama Biography.* 4 vols. Chicago, 1921.

Thornton, J. Mills, III. *Politics and Power in a Slave Society: Alabama, 1800–1860.* Baton Rouge, La., 1978.

Wakelyn, Jon L. *Biographical Directory of the Confederacy.* Edited by Frank E. Vandiver. Westport, Conn., 1977.

SARAH WOOLFOLK WIGGINS

HAMMOND, JAMES H. (1807–1864), U.S. senator and Southern nationalist. Born in the frontier region of up-country South Carolina, Hammond graduated from South Carolina College in 1825, combined his classical education with the study of law, and was admitted to the South Carolina bar in 1828. He established a successful law practice and also edited the *Southern Times,* gaining recognition for his passionate support of state rights and nullification. The nullification controversy drew Hammond to the support of John C. Calhoun. Unlike the vice president, however, Hammond was unrestrained by the crosscurrents of national politics, and he became an uncompromising advocate of Southern nationalism.

In 1831 Hammond achieved social rank, wealth, and power by marrying Charleston heiress Catherine Elizabeth Fitzsimons. This led to a promising career in politics, which began in 1834 with his election to the Twenty-fourth Congress. Hammond asserted his leadership in defense of slavery by attacking the constitutionality of abolition petitions, but poor health forced his departure from the House of Representatives before the end of his term.

He returned to politics in 1842 as governor of South Carolina and reestablished his leadership in defense of Southern interests through his widely circulated letter on slavery to the Free Church of Glasgow. Near the close of his term, it became known that he had committed improprieties with his four nieces. In the face of a threatened public scandal, he retired from public life and returned to his Savannah River plantation.

In 1857 Hammond was elected to the U.S. Senate, where the following year he delivered his proslavery "Mud-sill" speech. He justified slavery as a feature of the natural order and declared "Cotton is King"—the South's best defense as well as its most effective weapon in preserving this "aristocratic civilization." His defiant rhetoric notwithstanding, Hammond came to regard secession and Southern independence with ambivalence and resigned from the Senate in November 1860 with misgivings. In poor health, he returned to South Carolina, where he turned his plantation lands to producing commodities for the war effort and, in his private correspondence, nursed his anger at the Confederate leadership.

Hammond's health continued to decline during the war, and he died at his plantation home, Redcliffe, in November 1864.

BIBLIOGRAPHY

Bleser, Carol, ed. *The Hammonds of Redcliffe.* New York, 1981.

Bleser, Carol, ed. *Secret and Sacred: The Diaries of James Henry Hammond, a Southern Slaveholder.* New York, 1988.

Faust, Drew Gilpin. *James Henry Hammond and the Old South: A Design for Mastery.* Baton Rouge, La., 1982.

Tucker, Robert Cinnamond. "James Henry Hammond, South Carolinian." Ph.D. diss., University of North Carolina, 1958.

ROBERT T. BARRETT

HAMPTON, WADE (1818–1902), lieutenant general, governor of South Carolina, and U.S. senator. Born in Charleston to a family of great wealth and distinction, Hampton spent his early years at Millwood Plantation and graduated from South Carolina College in 1836. He studied law, but returned to Millwood as a planter and also acquired vast land holdings in Mississippi.

Hampton considered public service more as an obligation than an opportunity and served in the South Carolina house of representatives from 1852 to 1857 without distinction. His election to the state senate in 1858, however, coincided with events that stirred him, and his was a voice for moderation and restraint amid a rising chorus calling for secession and Southern independence. Although the Hamptons were among the largest slaveholders in the South, he opposed reestablishing the African slave trade and believed that the South could resolve its differences within the Union. Nevertheless, when appealing for Southern unity

WADE HAMPTON. *HARPER'S PICTORIAL HISTORY OF THE GREAT REBELLION*

and respect for constitutional law, he declared from the floor of the state senate in December 1859, "Unless every patriot in our land strikes once more for the Constitution, I see not how the Union can be or should be preserved."

Hampton had little influence on the events that followed, and at the outbreak of war he resigned from the state senate and volunteered for Confederate service as a private soldier. Recognizing the power and influence of the Hampton name, Governor Francis W. Pickens instructed Hampton to raise a military command and secured for him the rank of colonel in the Confederate army. Hampton's call to arms was enthusiastically answered by the sons of the master class, and within days Hampton's Legion was formed.

Tall and powerfully built, Hampton epitomized the Southern ideal of a gallant warrior, and in his first engagement, in July 1861 at First Manassas, was praised for his contribution to the Confederate victory. Promoted to brigadier general the following year, he was successful in reducing the enemy threat in actions preliminary to Seven Pines. Hampton was heavily engaged in this battle and sustained a wound that forced him from command.

During his convalescence in South Carolina, he came to realize that the Federal advantages in both men and matériel were a fatal combination and became convinced that the South could not sustain a prolonged war. With this in mind, he returned to his command in June 1862

determined to press for an early victory and participated in the decisive stage of the campaign to sweep enemy troops from the approaches to Richmond. Maneuvering in the vicinity of White Oak Swamp, Hampton found himself behind the enemy's right flank and prepared to exploit this unexpected position. Gen. Thomas J. ("Stonewall") Jackson hesitated, however, and Hampton waited with growing anger and frustration as the advantage passed from Confederate hands and the main battle developed at Malvern Hill. Out of loyalty to Jackson, Hampton kept his counsel, but felt that a decisive defeat of the Army of the Potomac had been within their grasp and that they had lost a strategic opportunity.

While harassing the ensuing Union retreat from Virginia, Hampton was transferred to the cavalry, where he served as senior brigadier to Maj. Gen. J. E. B. Stuart. Stuart and Hampton were contrasts in temperament and leadership. Their military success masked their differences, which nevertheless broke through the surface when Hampton on one occasion wrote, "I suppose Stuart will as usual give all the credit to the Va. brigades. He praises them on all occasions, but does not often give us credit." Hampton fought at Sharpsburg in September 1862 and the following month returned with Stuart to Maryland, where they humiliated the Army of the Potomac with a series of bold maneuvers. After the Battle of Fredericksburg, Hampton led a series of daring raids behind enemy lines, which secured his fame as a leader of cavalry.

Hampton participated in some of the bloodiest fighting of the war during the spring and summer of 1863. In June he charged with his cavalry at Brandy Station, where his brother Frank was killed by enemy infantry. Less than a month later, Hampton sustained heavy losses to his command and was himself severely wounded in hand-to-hand fighting at Gettysburg. He expressed a tempered optimism when he wrote from the hospital at Charlottesville, "I am doing well. . . . Our army is in good condition after its horrible and *useless* battle." He returned to the field in November with a promotion in rank to major general and assumed divisional command of the cavalry under Stuart.

With the initiative shifting to the enemy, Hampton spent the early months of 1864 defending Confederate lines and recruiting fresh troops in his native state. In early May he was engaged in the Wilderness campaign when Stuart, protecting Richmond's outer defenses, was killed by enemy cavalry. With Stuart dead, Hampton reported directly to Robert E. Lee, and in August he was given overall command of the cavalry. Hampton reorganized his troops and led them in defense of Petersburg. It was during a heavy engagement in late October that his son, Preston, temporarily assigned to his staff, was fatally wounded while charging the enemy. This personal loss transformed the war for Hampton: he no longer hoped for an honorable peace but now sought to avenge his son's death.

In January 1865 Hampton was ordered to South Carolina to rally defenses against the threatened enemy invasion. Soon after his arrival, he was promoted to lieutenant general, one of only three general officers without formal military training to achieve this rank. Hampton, unable to deter the enemy advance, evacuated his troops to North Carolina, where he was among the last of the Confederate high command to surrender.

After the war, Hampton returned to South Carolina, where he led the efforts to defeat the Reconstruction government and restore the conservative regime to power. Rejecting the extremes of racial politics, he campaigned as a moderate Democrat and was elected governor in 1876 and again in 1878. After resigning the governorship, he was elected to the U.S. Senate, where he served from 1879 to 1891. Hampton died in April 1902.

BIBLIOGRAPHY

Cauthen, Charles E., ed. *Family Letters of the Three Wade Hamptons, 1782–1901*. Columbia, S.C., 1953.

Freeman, Douglas S. *Lee's Lieutenants: A Study in Command*. 3 vols. New York, 1942–1944. Reprint, New York, 1986.

Hampton, Wade. "What Negro Supremacy Means." *Forum* (June 1888): 383–395.

Sheppard, William Arthur. *Red Shirts Remembered: Southern Brigadiers of the Reconstruction Period*. Atlanta, 1940.

Wellman, Manly Wade. *Giant in Gray: A Biography of Wade Hampton of South Carolina*. New York, 1949.

ROBERT T. BARRETT

HAMPTON ROADS CONFERENCE. Held on the U.S. steamer *River Queen* off Fort Monroe at Hampton Roads, Virginia, on February 3, 1865, this four-hour conference between ranking officials of the Federal and Confederate governments failed to achieve any tangible

"THE TRUE PEACE COMMISSIONERS." A hostile Northern response to Confederate peace overtures and the efforts of Peace Democrats to reconcile with the South. Robert E. Lee and Jefferson Davis stand back to back in an attempt to ward off Northern officers. The officers pictured, from left to right, are Philip H. Sheridan, Ulysses S. Grant, David G. Farragut, and William T. Sherman. Lee and Davis cite the rhetoric of the 1864 Democratic National Convention in Chicago. Lithograph on wove paper, probably drawn by John Cameron. Published by Currier & Ives, New York, 1864.

LIBRARY OF CONGRESS

results despite hopes on both sides. President Abraham Lincoln and Secretary of State William H. Seward represented the United States; the Confederate delegation included Vice President Alexander H. Stephens, Senator Robert M. T. Hunter, and John A. Campbell, a former Supreme Court justice now serving as assistant secretary of war.

The meeting originated in a peace initiative proposed in late 1864 by Francis P. Blair to Lincoln, that both sides cease fighting and join forces against Napoleon III's troops in Mexico. Lincoln had no interest in this idea, but he was willing to talk to the Confederates and allowed Blair to explore the possibility. In several trips to Richmond, Blair secured Jefferson Davis's agreement for the conference. Though he held little hope for its success, Davis had political reasons of his own for sanctioning the meeting. He hoped what he regarded as the conference's inevitable failure would blunt the burgeoning peace movement in the Confederate Congress and in several states. The conference was almost aborted by a protracted disagreement on the diplomatic language of the Confederate commissioner's instructions. But Gen. Ulysses S. Grant's unabashed enthusiasm for the conference and his personal plea to Lincoln succeeded in removing this difficulty.

The mutually incompatible aims of both sides, not to mention the near-hopeless military situation of the Confederacy, guaranteed failure even before the talks began. Reunion and an end to the rebellion were for Lincoln sine qua non. Davis's instructions to his delegation spelled out its mission as "an informal conference" for "securing peace between the two countries." Stephens, who knew the only chance for the Confederacy was an armistice, tried several times to bring up Blair's Mexican plan. Lincoln rebuffed the suggestion each time, as well as Hunter's bid for an armistice. Nothing without reunion, he said. Blair's had been an unofficial mission.

Turning to the subject of slavery and the treatment of Confederate leaders, Lincoln promised leniency. He also held out the possibility of compensation—up to $400 million—to slave owners for their confiscated slaves. There would be no backing down on the Emancipation Proclamation: the courts would have to sort out tangled questions of its applicability that the Confederates raised. In any event, Seward said, the Thirteenth Amendment had just passed the U.S. Congress, thereby rendering such questions moot upon its ratification. Since both slavery and the rebellion were doomed, Lincoln urged the Confederates to lay down their arms and return to their former allegiance to save further bloodshed. On this note the conference ended.

The failure of the conference to achieve peace served the Davis administration in two ways. Southerners took Lincoln's insistence on reunion as a humiliating demand for unconditional surrender, and this rekindled momentarily a fierce war spirit across the ravaged Confederacy. The conference's failure also muffled the administration's many congressional foes.

BIBLIOGRAPHY

Kirkland, Edward Chase. *The Peacemakers of 1864.* New York, 1927.

McPherson, James M. *Battle Cry of Freedom: The Civil War Era.* New York, 1988.

Nicolay, John G., and John Hay. *Abraham Lincoln: A History.* Vol. 10. New York, 1890.

Stephens, Alexander H. *A Constitutional View of the Late War between the States: Its Causes, Character, Conduct and Results, Presented in a Series of Colloquies at Liberty Hall.* Vol. 2. Philadelphia, 1870.

THOMAS E. SCHOTT

HAMPTON-ROSSER CATTLE RAID. *See* Beefsteak Raid.

HAMPTON'S LEGION.

"Legions" were permitted and organized only in the early stages of the Civil War. A legion was a miniature army in that it contained all three military components: infantry, artillery, and cavalry. Ten such units existed in the Confederate armies. The most famous in the group was the South Carolina legion of Wade Hampton.

One of the wealthiest planters in the antebellum South, Hampton had known a life of splendid luxury. He was a state legislator and ardent Southern nationalist when the war began. Hampton promptly diminished his fortune by recruiting a legion that, if necessary, could fight independently. In less than a week after his initial call, thirty South Carolina companies volunteered for Hampton's unit. This was more than twice the number that could be accommodated. Hampton's Legion came to consist of six infantry companies, four cavalry companies, and a battery of artillery sporting six new and revolutionary Blakely guns.

The highest-born of the Palmetto State served as privates in such companies as the Columbia Zouaves and Edgefield Hussars. Officers came exclusively from the socially elite class. The legion also boasted a veritable platoon of black servants who prepared meals and attended to other tasks.

Hampton trained and splendidly equipped his unit at Camp Hampton, a few miles outside Columbia. The legion received a royal welcome upon its early summer arrival at Richmond, Virginia. One of its field officers boasted that the unit was "by all odds the finest looking and best drilled body of men that has left" South Carolina.

When battle became imminent at Manassas, Hampton speedily boarded his unit on a train and rushed northward.

The companies marched three miles from the railroad depot straight into the war's first major battle. Hampton's second-in-command, Lt. Col. Benjamin J. Johnson, was killed almost immediately. This left the legion with no experienced field officer. Federals enfiladed the Carolinians' position and soon had Hampton's force surrounded on three sides. Legion officers did not possess enough military knowledge to know when to retreat. Hence, the legion stubbornly maintained its position and fought gallantly until superior officers persuaded Hampton to retire to a less exposed sector. The unit suffered casualties of 121 of the 600 engaged. Among the wounded was Colonel Hampton, who barely escaped death when a bullet grazed his skull.

In November 1861, Hampton received promotion to brigadier general. His legion then became part of Gen. James Longstreet's division. It fought in the 1862 Peninsular campaign. The legion ceased to exist shortly thereafter when the infantry companies were merged with the brigade of Gen. John Bell Hood, the cavalry units became part of Col. Thomas Lafayette Rosser's command, and the artillery was redesignated as Hart's South Carolina Battery. Four officers in Hampton's Legion eventually became Confederate generals.

[See also Hampton, Wade.]

BIBLIOGRAPHY

Brooks, U. R., ed. Stories of the Confederacy. Columbia, S.C., 1912.

Heller, J. Roderick, III, and Carolyn A. Ayres, eds. The Confederacy Is on Her Way up the Spout: Letters to South Carolina, 1861–1864. Athens, Ga., 1992.

Wellman, Manly Wade. Giant in Gray: A Biography of Wade Hampton of South Carolina. New York, 1949.

JAMES I. ROBERTSON, JR.

HAND GRENADES AND LAND MINES.

The Civil War was a period of ordnance innovations that were quite controversial at the time. Mines, or subterranean torpedoes as they were known, were one such weapon. Called "infernal machines" by the Federals, these devices were developed by Gen. Gabriel J. Rains, a North Carolinian career army officer who left the Federal army to become chief of the Torpedo Bureau in Richmond. Rains had first used torpedoes as an antipersonnel weapon while serving in the Seminole War in 1840. He constructed the device using a standard spherical case artillery projectile in which he inserted a particularly sensitive friction primer of his own devising. Any disturbance of the primer caused immediate detonation of the torpedo. A significant number of artillery projectiles converted to torpedoes were employed during the Yorktown campaign in 1862. The weapon inflicted some Union casualties but had an even stronger psychological impact on advancing Federal troops.

CONFEDERATE CAST-IRON HAND GRENADE. The hole would be filled with powder and a paper fuse. Ruler shown for scale.

CIVIL WAR LIBRARY AND MUSEUM, PHILADELPHIA

As the war progressed, Rains developed a pressure-sensitive land mine fuse that was used successfully with 24-pounders and 10-inch spherical rounds. The primer of these fuses was designed to explode at the slightest pressure. The formula contained 50 percent potassium chlorate, 30 percent sulfuret of antimony, and 20 percent pulverized glass. The actual fuse was copper stock with a crushable dome over the igniter, all of which screwed into the body of a regular artillery shell. Although psychologically effective, mines and torpedoes never changed the outcome of a significant engagement and did not play the role they do today in modern warfare.

Grenades, a parallel development, also utilized Rains's fuses. Such a device was usually a small 6-pounder modified artillery shell thrown by hand. But there were much larger rampart grenades, which were rolled down a fortification. A. L. West developed another hand grenade based upon the Federal William F. Ketchum's patent device, which was produced in some quantity at the Augusta, Georgia, ordnance complex. And the Confederates also manufactured a 2.5-inch spherical grenade with an unsophisticated paper time fuse. Unlike some Federal grenades such as the Hanes, Confederate grenades were not particularly dangerous to handle. Their greatest problem was ineffective fusing that caused so many duds. Grenades have been evacuated in areas of prolonged siege operations such as Vicksburg, Mississippi, and Port Hudson, Louisiana, and in the Alabama River near the Selma Arsenal facilities, where they were dumped upon the approach of Federal forces toward the end of the war.

As in the case of torpedoes, the early grenades never realized their full potential during the Civil War. Both sides appreciated the concept of mines and grenades, but neither had the technological capabilities to manufacture the sophisticated fuses and detonators necessary to make these advanced weapons truly effective. Still, the development of mines and grenades foreshadowed the widespread use of similar but even more deadly weapons seventy-five years later.

[*See also* Rains, Gabriel J.; Torpedoes and Mines.]

BIBLIOGRAPHY

Dickey, Thomas S., and Peter C. George. *Field Artillery Projectiles of the American Civil War.* Atlanta, 1980.

Ordnance Bureau. *Field Manual for the Use of the Officers on Ordnance Duty.* Richmond, Va., 1862. Reprint, Arendtsville, Pa., 1984.

Perry, Milton F. *Infernal Machines.* Kingsport, Tenn., 1965.

Rains, Col. George W. *History of the Confederate Powder Works.* Newburgh, N.Y., 1882. Reprint, Wendell, N.C., 1979.

RUSS A. PRITCHARD

HANDICRAFTS. In the early nineteenth century, handicrafts played a vital role in Southern life, with professional and domestic craftspeople producing many of the goods needed by the populace. The region had few manufacturing plants, and the many farming settlements had only limited access to imported goods. Crafts traditions in the countryside were maintained largely by families rather than by the more urban system of formal apprenticeship; in addition, slaves were trained to make much of what was required on plantations.

By 1860 this situation had changed. There was more industry in the region and a greater amount of factory-made goods coming in from the North and overseas. But the war required factories to shift to military production, and the Union blockade reduced the flow of imported goods. Thus, the production of handicrafts, in some cases oriented to the war effort, again became important, especially for pottery and textiles.

Brothers-in-law William Ferguson and Jonathan Dial of Jackson (present-day Barrow) County, Georgia, potting in the Southern tradition of stoneware with alkaline (wood-ash– or lime-based) glazes, advertised in the January 28, 1863, *Southern Watchman* an expanded range of wares to fill the void in factory-made tablewares created by the blockade: "In addition to Jars, Jugs, and such other ware as we have formerly kept, we are now trying to supply the demand for other useful household articles. We are making Bowls and Pitchers, Dinner and Soup Plates, Cups and Saucers, Mugs, Coffee and Tea Pots, Bake Pans, [and] Chambers." An editorial endorsement of the operation in the same issue stated that it

is doing much to supply the people with a substitute for earthenware. . . . It is true they are not as smooth and handsome

as the articles we have been used to, but are decidedly better than none. This establishment and others of a like character, ought to be, it strikes us, exempt from conscription.

In Ferguson's case at least, the editor's plea seems to have been heeded, for the note beside his name in the 1864 militia census reads: "Potter. Exempted justice of peace." Another Georgia potter, Jesse Bradford Long of Crawford County, in his fifties when the war broke out, served as a home guard captain and produced wares such as chamberpots for Confederate hospitals, according to family tradition.

Women also contributed to the cause with their handiwork, making quilts for raffles to raise money for hospitals or such wartime needs as gunboats. One Alabama quilt raised a thousand dollars for the cause. Southern women took patriotic pride in returning to hand spinning and weaving, as expressed in the popular song "The Homespun Dress" (sung to the tune of "The Bonnie Blue Flag"):

> Hurrah! Hurrah!
> For the Sunny South so dear!
> Three cheers for the homespun dress
> The southern ladies wear.
> Now northern goods are out of date,
> And since Old Abe's blockade,
> We southern girls can be content
> With goods that's southern made.

In addition to civilian clothing, North Carolina women supplied much of the Confederacy's military fabric needs. African Americans supported plantation life by weaving, quilting, blacksmithing, brickmaking, carpentry, and making large field baskets. In Edgefield District, South Carolina, white-owned pottery shops depended on slave labor; Dave, a literate slave potter, inscribed poems of his own composition on food-storage jars as large as forty gallons. On the coastal rice plantations, West African–style rice-hulling mortars and coiled fanner baskets for rice winnowing were made.

Economic conditions following the war encouraged the continuation of such hand skills, especially in more remote sections. This trend was reinforced in the twentieth century by a handicrafts revival movement that opened up an outside market for Southern crafts.

[*See also* Soldiers' Aid Societies.]

BIBLIOGRAPHY

Burrison, John A. *Brothers in Clay: The Story of Georgia Folk Pottery.* Athens, Ga., 1983.

Roberson, Ruth H., ed. *North Carolina Quilts.* Chapel Hill, N.C., 1988.

Vlach, John M. *The Afro-American Tradition in Decorative Arts.* Cleveland, Ohio, 1978. Reprint, Athens, Ga., 1990.

JOHN A. BURRISON

HANLY, THOMAS B. (1812–1880), congressman from Arkansas. Hanly was born on June 9, 1812, in Nicholsonville, Kentucky. He was admitted to the bar and in 1833 migrated to Helena, Arkansas, where he opened a law practice and maintained a farm. Active in Democratic politics, Hanly served in the Arkansas House of Representatives from 1842 to 1843 and the Arkansas Senate from 1852 to 1855. In 1846 he was named a circuit judge and became an associate justice of the Arkansas Supreme Court in 1858.

An ardent supporter of secession, Hanly was a delegate to the Arkansas convention in May 1861, where he voted to take Arkansas out of the Union. Unlike many of his colleagues, he also supported submitting the secession ordinance to a vote of the people. Hanly was elected to represent the Fourth Congressional District of Arkansas in the Confederate Congress in 1861 and was reelected in 1863.

A staunch state rights proponent, Hanly opposed efforts in Congress to create a strong central government during his first term. He also vigorously opposed the Conscription Acts. He served on the Claims, Enrolled Bills, Post Office and Post Roads, Quartermaster's and Commissary, and Military Transport committees during his first term and the Impressments, Military Affairs, and Pay and Mileage committees during his second term. By the time Hanly entered his second congressional term in 1864, however, the plight of the Confederacy was so acute that he realized the need for a strong central government if the South was to survive. As a result he switched his allegiance and became a strong supporter of Jefferson Davis. As such he advocated doubling the agriculture tax, ending exemptions for the draft, and drafting slaves. Hanly in Congress was a bitter enemy of Henry S. Foote, a major critic of Davis.

Hanly remained in Richmond, Virginia, until Davis was forced to flee, and then he returned to Arkansas and reopened his law practice. Strongly opposed to Reconstruction, Hanly was elected to the state legislature in 1879. He died in Little Rock on June 9, 1880.

BIBLIOGRAPHY

Dougan, Michael B. *Confederate Arkansas: The People and Policies of a Frontier State in Wartime.* University, Ala., 1976.

Thomas, Davis Y. *Arkansas in War and Reconstruction, 1861–1874.* Little Rock, Ark., 1926.

Thomas, Davis Y. *Arkansas and Its People: A History, 1541–1930.* 4 vols. New York, 1930.

KENNY A. FRANKS

HANSON, ROGER (1827–1863), brigadier general. Roger Weightman Hanson was born August 27, 1827, at Winchester, Kentucky. At about age twenty he joined the Fourth Kentucky Volunteers and served in the Mexican War. Hanson returned to Winchester after the war and early in 1848 was seriously wounded in a duel. The wound damaged his right hip and left him with a peculiar gait the rest of his life. During his convalescence, Hanson studied law and was admitted to the Clark County bar. He joined the California gold rush briefly in 1849. Returning to Kentucky in 1850, he practiced law and was elected to the Kentucky legislature in 1853 and 1855. A conservative in politics, Hanson was a Fillmore elector in 1856 and a supporter of the Bell-Everett ticket in 1860.

When the Civil War broke out, he was enrolled as a colonel in the Kentucky State Guard. Entering Confederate service on September 3, he was commissioned colonel of the Second Kentucky Infantry. Hanson led his men to Camp Boone at Clarksville, Tennessee, where they formed the nucleus of Kentucky's famed Orphan Brigade. Hanson was captured at Fort Donelson on February 16, 1862, and was imprisoned at Fort Delaware, Maryland, until his exchange that fall. He fought briefly under Nathan Bedford Forrest at Nashville on November 5 and assisted in Gen. John Hunt Morgan's capture of the Federal garrison at Hartsville, Tennessee, on December 7, an action that resulted in the capture of over two thousand prisoners.

Hanson was promoted to brigadier general on December 13 and assigned to the command of the Kentucky (Orphan) Brigade of John C. Breckinridge's division. He and his men moved with the Confederate army to meet the advance of the Army of the Cumberland under William S. Rosecrans during the last week of December. Joseph Wheeler's cavalry successfully delayed the Federal advance long enough to allow Braxton Bragg's Army of Tennessee to concentrate at Murfreesboro. Late in the afternoon of January 2, 1863, Hanson and his six regiments, along with the rest of Breckinridge's division, were ordered to assault the Federal lines occupying the high ground northwest of town. Hanson fell mortally wounded at the head of his charging columns, struck by a Bormann fuse or similar object that shattered his left knee and tore through muscles, veins, and arteries. He was taken to the home of I. J. C. Haynes in Murfreesboro where he died on Sunday morning, January 4. Forbidden by the Federal commandant at Nashville to return the body to Kentucky, Hanson's widow arranged that the general be buried in that city until he could be moved. In November 1866 he was reinterred with full military honors in the Lexington, Kentucky, Cemetery.

BIBLIOGRAPHY

Thompson, E. P. *History of the 1st Kentucky Brigade.* Cincinnati, Ohio, 1868.

Warner, Ezra J. *Generals in Gray: Lives of the Confederate Commanders.* Baton Rouge, La., 1959.

TERRENCE V. MURPHY

HARDEE, WILLIAM J. (1815–1872), lieutenant general. Hardee was born October 12, 1815, on the troubled Georgia-Florida border, site of almost continuous warfare for more than a generation. Coming from a military family, he was expected to enter West Point, which he did in 1834. Upon graduation in 1838 he joined the Second Dragoons, serving briefly in Florida before going to France in 1840 to attend the Royal Cavalry School at Saumur. He returned to his regiment in 1842 and went with it to the Mexican border where, to his humiliation, he was captured in the first engagement of the war. He put this embarrassment behind him during Winfield Scott's march from Vera Cruz to the city of Mexico, being breveted twice for conspicuous service. Having been previously detailed as a special training officer for the Second Dragoons, Hardee continued this work, in

WILLIAM J. HARDEE. Pre–Civil War portrait in Union uniform.
THE SOLDIER IN OUR CIVIL WAR

which he excelled, at Carlisle Barracks after the war. Frontier duty in Texas followed, with Hardee engaging in several campaigns against Indian marauding parties.

In 1853 Secretary of War Jefferson Davis directed Hardee to prepare a system of light infantry tactics for the U.S. Army and Militia. Basing his work on a French manual born of the experience in the Algerian wars, Hardee completed his work early in 1855. His *Rifle and Light Infantry Tactics* became the standard by which Federal and Confederate soldiers trained and maneuvered. Service as senior major and chief training officer in Davis's hand-picked Second Cavalry followed. In 1856, he returned to West Point as commandant, an office he changed significantly.

Hardee resigned from the army in January 1861 and became colonel of the First Regiment of Georgia Volunteers. Davis called him to Montgomery in February where he worked with the president, Leroy P. Walker, and P. G. T. Beauregard to prepare an elaborate bill for the organization of the Confederate army. In March, Hardee, who had resigned from his Georgia post, became colonel of the First Regiment of Infantry. He commanded Fort Morgan, Alabama, until June, when he became a brigadier assigned to defend the Arkansas border and to organize troops there for service in the Confederate army.

Hardee remained in Arkansas until September 1861. He and Gideon Pillow participated in a poorly conceived invasion of Missouri, which failed for lack of transportation and cooperation. Hardee, however, managed to train and equip a splendid brigade of Arkansas troops. These men would become the heart of Hardee's division, his corps, and the Army of Tennessee. No finer troops existed in the Confederacy. Hardee also began the development of a group of subordinate officers who would excel in the war. His alter ego, Patrick Cleburne, headed the list.

Hardee's brigade crossed the Mississippi in September 1861, marching rather than being transported by water, and took position at Bowling Green, Kentucky, in October. That fall he vigorously trained his men, conducting marches and operations to the north and east. Hardee headed a division by this time, and in December 1861, he became commander of the Army of Central Kentucky.

Disasters at Mill Springs and Donelson that winter rendered Bowling Green untenable, and Hardee took the army south through Tennessee. At Shiloh he led a corps, the front line of Joseph E. Johnston's army, and fought well. In the Kentucky campaign that fall, Hardee, now a lieutenant general, led a wing. At Perryville he again performed well, spotting a gap in the center of the Union line and throwing Cleburne's division into it, a movement that broke the enemy right. At Murfreesboro, in December 1862, Hardee was at his best, leading a magnificent envelopment that crushed William S. Rosecrans's right wing.

Because of ongoing quarrels with Braxton Bragg, Hardee,

in August 1863, was transferred from the army to reorganize the exchanged men of the Vicksburg garrison. Thus he missed Chickamauga, where he was sorely needed. At Chattanooga, in November, Hardee's troops held off William Tecumseh Sherman's attacks and formed the defense behind which Bragg was able to extricate his army.

Offered command of the Army of Tennessee in December 1863, Hardee declined, believing Johnston better suited for that command. In the Atlanta campaign under Johnston, Hardee led his corps skillfully in successive actions. When John Bell Hood took command in July 1864, however, Hardee's corps turned to the offensive and wrecked itself in severe fighting at Peachtree Creek and Atlanta. Hardee performed poorly in the former battle, capably in the latter. At Jonesboro he led a beaten army against breastworks and failed. Relieved from the Army of Tennessee at his own request, over the pleas of Davis, Hardee took command of the Department of South Carolina, Georgia, and Florida and attempted to defend eastern Georgia against Sherman's army. He continued to organize resistance against Sherman as the latter pushed north into the Carolinas in early 1865. At Averasborough and Bentonville he fought well albeit with desperation. To the day the Army of Tennessee surrendered, Hardee demonstrated why the men he commanded and the Army of Tennessee regarded him as "Old Reliable."

Following the war Hardee tried plantation life and then moved to Selma, Alabama, where he became for several years president of the Selma and Meridian Railroad. He died in Wytheville, Virginia, November 6, 1873, on an annual family trip to White Sulphur Springs.

BIBLIOGRAPHY

Hughes, Nathaniel C., Jr. *General William J. Hardee, C.S.A.* Baton Rouge, La., 1965.
Pickett, William D. *Sketch of the Military Career of William J. Hardee, Lieutenant-General, C.S.A.* Lexington, Ky., 1910.

NATHANIEL CHEAIRS HUGHES, JR.

HARDEMAN, WILLIAM POLK (1816–1898),

brigadier general. Hardeman's was a life filled with conflict, commencing with service in the 1836 Texas Revolution, subsequent fighting with local Indian tribes, and then participation in the war with Mexico (1846–1848). Thereafter he farmed while taking a leading role in Texas secessionist politics, serving in the convention that took the state out of the Union.

He entered Civil War service as a captain in the Fourth Texas Cavalry, and saw his first action at Valverde, New Mexico, in February 1862. This led to his becoming colonel of the regiment by January 1, 1863, when he fought in the capture of Galveston, Texas. By the end of 1863 he was commanding a cavalry brigade in Louisiana, but the next year he rose to prominence during the Red River campaign in battles at Mansfield and Pleasant Hill. Department commander E. Kirby Smith pronounced Hardeman one of the three "best brigade commanders" in the Trans-Mississippi. He recommended Hardeman more than once for promotion to brigadier general, which finally came on March 18, 1865, one of the last generalcies handed out in the Confederacy. "Gotch" Hardeman finished the war in permanent brigade command, and though destined to serve in a backwater region of the conflict, he distinguished himself in leading the often unmanageable Trans-Mississippi cavalrymen.

Following the war, like many other Texans and thousands of ex-Confederates, he emigrated to Mexico, but eventually returned to Texas.

BIBLIOGRAPHY

Oates, Stephen B. *Confederate Cavalry West of the River.* Austin, Tex., 1964.
Roberts, O. M. *Texas.* Vol. 11 of *Confederate Military History.* Edited by Clement A. Evans. Atlanta, 1899. Vol. 15 of extended ed. Wilmington, N.C., 1989.

WILLIAM C. DAVIS

HARPERS FERRY, WEST VIRGINIA. [*This entry is composed of three articles:* Arsenal and Armory, *which discusses the establishment and contents of the U.S. installation;* John Brown's Raid, *which discusses the 1859 raid by abolitionist John Brown; and* Battle of 1862, *which discusses the battle won at the site by Thomas J. ("Stonewall") Jackson. For further discussion of the arms captured by Confederates at Harpers Ferry, see* Small Arms, *articles on* Captured U.S. Small Arms *and* Altered U.S. Small Arms.]

Arsenal and Armory

President George Washington recommended that Congress establish federal armories and arsenals to ensure adequate arms production for self-defense for the fledgling United States. Congress approved the legislation in 1794, and Washington selected Springfield, Massachusetts, as the site of the first national armory and Harpers Ferry, Virginia, as the site of the second. Washington favored Harpers Ferry because of the water power generated at the confluence of the Potomac and Shenandoah rivers; the abundance of raw materials, such as iron ore for gun barrels and timber for stocks; its location in Virginia, which would provide a Southern armory in Washington's home state and an economic boost to the Potomac valley; and its proximity to the new federal capital, located only sixty-two miles down the Potomac.

Production of small arms at Harpers Ferry did not begin until 1800, however, because of difficulties with land purchases and inadequate skilled labor to construct the factory and water power works. From 1800 to 1861, the armory produced over 620,000 rifles and muskets, with annual employment ranging between 250 and 425 workers. With the exception of the period from 1841 to 1854, when ordnance officers ran the Harpers Ferry establishment, a civilian superintendent managed the armory's overall operations, and a civilian master armorer supervised weapon designs and day-to-day production of the small arms. Both the armory (the factory complex where weapons were manufactured) and the arsenal (the warehouse for weapons' storage) fell under the auspices of the Ordnance Bureau, a branch of the government within the War Department under control of the secretary of war.

Harpers Ferry weapons accounted for numerous innovations in federal arms manufacturing. The 1803 model was the first military rifle produced at a federal armory, its handsome half-stock, octagonal barrel, and brass fittings reflecting the influence of Pennsylvania rifle artisans. Percussion technology replaced the antiquated flintlock with adoption of the 1842 model percussion smoothbore musket. The first percussion rifle produced by the government was the 1841 model "Mississippi" rifle. Improvement upon the individual percussion cap system occurred with development of the 1855 model rifle and 1855 model rifle-musket. These weapons utilized a Maynard primer system, which advanced a percussion tape onto the breech cone each time the weapon was cocked. Although the Maynard primer saved loading time by eliminating the fumbling percussion cap, the tape jammed easily and often was ruined by moisture; hence this system saw no use during the Civil War.

Interchangeable parts manufacturing also was pioneered at Harpers Ferry. John H. Hall, a Maine inventor who contracted with the government in 1819 to produce one thousand breech-loading rifles, developed a system of tools,

HARPERS FERRY, WEST VIRGINIA.   View of Harpers Ferry and the confluence of the Shenandoah and Potomac rivers. Photograph by James Gardner, July 1865.

NATIONAL ARCHIVES

machinery, and gauges in his rifle works along the Shenandoah River that "succeeded in establishing methods for fabricating arms exactly alike, and with economy, by the hands of common workmen." By developing precision machinery that produced uniform parts, Hall doomed craft-oriented production. His American System of manufacturing, he believed, "formed the taproot of modern industrialism."

Another Harpers Ferry invention that changed the character of warfare was the Burton bullet, better known as the minié ball. James H. Burton served as master armorer at Harpers Ferry from 1849 to 1854, and during his tenure, he perfected a hollow-based, conical-shaped lead bullet that expanded and gripped the rifling of a gun barrel upon discharge of the powder. Since the bullet was slightly smaller than the barrel's interior caliber, for the first time an infantryman could load a rifle as quickly as a musket (three times per minute). As a result, the Burton bullet antiquated the inaccurate musket and enabled the U.S. Army to adopt the much deadlier rifle as its primary small arm.

Despite these innovations at the Harpers Ferry armory, production consistently lagged behind its sister armory at Springfield. Reasons include persistent droughts, which reduced water power and shut down machinery; an infirm work force that was constantly battling disease; inept managers who practiced political patronage and promoted the regional economy above the national interest; and craft-oriented workers who resisted the introduction of machine technology. In an attempt to correct these problems, the Ordnance Bureau between 1841 and 1854 replaced the civilian superintendents with professional ordnance officers who rebuilt and retooled the armory, transforming it, according to historian Merritt Roe Smith, into one of the five "most progressive manufacturing establishments of its type" in the country.

Abolitionist John Brown eyed the Harpers Ferry armory for its products rather than for its progressive manufacturing. Approximately 100,000 weapons were stored at the arsenal in 1859—weapons Brown intended to seize and distribute throughout the South in an attempt to end slavery. On Sunday night, October 16, 1859, Brown and his eighteen followers captured the undefended armory and arsenal, but Brown failed to escape. Local militia soon surrounded the government buildings, and at dawn on October 18, U.S. Marines, under command of Lt. Col. Robert E. Lee, charged the armory fire engine house and captured Brown, ending the raid. Although Brown's men had removed a few guns, these were soon recovered, and the bullet-damaged armory buildings were quickly repaired.

Sixteen months following Brown's raid, Virginia seceded from the Union. Seizure of the Harpers Ferry armory and arsenal became a primary target of a group of secessionists led by former Virginia governor Henry A. Wise and including Turner and Richard Ashby, John D. Imboden, and former armory superintendent Alfred M. Barbour. On April 17, 1861, the date of Virginia's official secession vote, these secessionists received permission from Governor John Letcher to advance the state militia to seize the armory and arsenal. The following day, Barbour arrived in Harpers Ferry and announced Virginia's intention. His public pronouncement also warned Lt. Roger Jones and his small garrison of forty-five U.S. regulars guarding the federal property. Subsequently, Jones ordered gunpowder placed throughout the armory and arsenal buildings as he prepared for their destruction. At 10:00 P.M. on April 18, with three hundred Virginia militia only one mile from Harpers Ferry, Jones torched the federal property and withdrew his force into Maryland. The flames totally consumed the two arsenal buildings, destroying fifteen thousand small arms. Most of the armory was saved, however, as local residents extinguished the fires before much damage occurred.

With Harpers Ferry now located on the border between North and South, Virginia officials decided to dismantle the armory and ship its machinery south to Richmond, Virginia, and Fayetteville, North Carolina. Col. Thomas J. ("Stonewall") Jackson, who commanded at Harpers Ferry, superintended the transfer of most of the machinery. When the Confederates abandoned Harpers Ferry on June 15, 1861, the armory buildings were burned, leaving only brick skeletons as a reminder of the once-thriving small arms factory.

Federal armies occupied Harpers Ferry in 1862 and reroofed some of the armory buildings for quartermaster and commissary storage. The armory also housed Confederate prisoners and served as Gen. Philip Sheridan's primary supply depot during the 1864 Shenandoah Valley campaign. Following the war, the United States decided not to reestablish its armory at Harpers Ferry, and the property was sold at public auction in 1869.

BIBLIOGRAPHY

Imboden, John D. "Jackson at Harpers Ferry in 1861." In *Battles and Leaders of the Civil War*. Edited by Robert U. Johnson and C. C. Buel. Vol. 1. New York, 1887. Reprint, Secaucus, N.J., 1982.

Smith, Merritt Roe. *Harpers Ferry Armory and the New Technology*. Utica, N.Y., 1977.

Villard, Oswald G. *John Brown, 1800–1859: A Biography Fifty Years After*. New York, 1909.

DENNIS E. FRYE

John Brown's Raid

John Brown's attack on the Harpers Ferry armory and arsenal (October 16–18, 1859) sent shock waves throughout the North and South. In a violent attempt to rid the country of slavery, Brown chose Harpers Ferry as his initial

JOHN BROWN.   *HARPER'S PICTORIAL HISTORY OF THE GREAT REBELLION*

target because of the 100,000 weapons stored in the U.S. Arsenal. He planned to seize these rifles and muskets for his army of slaves—an army Brown would recruit, train, and use to conduct guerrilla warfare throughout the Southeast. Slaves emancipated by his forces would find safe refuge in the strongholds of the Appalachian Mountains, where Brown intended to establish his own nation, backed by a constitution that would guarantee freedom for all.

Brown launched his bold scheme on a dreary Sunday evening, October 16, 1859. At 10:00 P.M., he and eighteen followers began marching from the Kennedy farm, their isolated headquarters in Maryland five miles north of Harpers Ferry. By midnight, the raiders had possession of the armory and arsenal and the bridges leading into Harpers Ferry. With these initial targets secured, Brown sent raiding parties to seize hostages and slaves from prominent estates in the vicinity. One of these hostages was Lewis Washington, the great-grandnephew of George Washington, whom Brown wanted as a symbol of his revolution. In the opening hours, no shots had been fired and no opposition encountered. The attack had surprised the community and the U.S. government.

About 1:00 A.M., however, Heyward Shepherd, a free black baggage porter for the Baltimore and Ohio Railroad, panicked when confronted by Brown's men and was shot as he tried to escape. The gunfire awakened Dr. John W. Starry, who resided near the railroad; upon investigation, he

discovered Shepherd's mortal wound and learned of the raiders' intention to free the slaves. Brown's men then made a critical error. Instead of retaining Starry, they allowed him to slip away into the Monday morning darkness. Starry quickly galloped to nearby Charles Town, where he sounded the alarm and alerted local militia. Within hours, hundreds of militiamen from Virginia and Maryland were descending upon Harpers Ferry, blocking all avenues of escape for Brown and his men.

Brown compounded his problems by allowing an eastbound passenger train to proceed through Harpers Ferry. The conductor telegraphed notice of the raid, and word quickly arrived in Washington of the trouble. President James Buchanan then ordered a contingent of ninety Marines from the Washington Naval Yard to Harpers Ferry. Lt. Col. Robert E. Lee, at home on leave at Arlington, received instructions to proceed to the town and take command of the situation. Lt. J. E. B. Stuart, who delivered the War Department orders to Lee, accompanied the colonel. By the early morning of October 18, Marines had surrounded John Brown, now trapped within the small brick fire-engine house of the armory.

Just before dawn on the eighteenth, Lee sent Stuart to the barricaded doors of the engine house to demand Brown's surrender. Brown refused and then stated his terms of safe passage into Maryland and Pennsylvania for himself, his few remaining men, and his eleven hostages. Instructed not to parlay, Stuart backed away from the door and waved his hat, signaling the Marines to attack. The first attempts to beat down the doors with a sledgehammer failed. A dozen Marines then used a ladder as a battering ram, and a door was penetrated. Marine Lt. Israel Greene quickly dashed into the building and, confronting Brown, badly wounded him across the head and neck with his saber. Two raiders were bayoneted and killed; two others were captured. No hostages were injured during the attack.

The episode exacted a heavy toll. Ten of Brown's raiders had been killed or mortally wounded, including two of his sons. Four townspeople had died, including the Harpers Ferry mayor. One Marine had been mortally wounded during the attack on the engine house.

Brown was transported to Charles Town, the seat of Jefferson County, Virginia, where he was tried for murder, treason, and inciting slave insurrection. His trial commenced on October 27 and lasted over three days. A jury found him guilty of all charges, and on November 2, Judge Richard Parker sentenced him to be hanged. One month later, on December 2, 1859, with his gallows surrounded by thousands of Virginia militiamen, Brown was executed. Then the silence of the moment was broken by the voice of J. T. L. Preston of the Virginia Military Institute: "So perish all such enemies of Virginia! All such enemies of the Union! All such foes of the human race." Yet, just before his death, Brown had handed his jailer a note, with a prophecy:

"I, John Brown," it opened, "am now quite certain that the crimes of this guilty land will never be purged away but with blood."

Reactions to Brown's raid, the trial, and his execution propelled the country into a fervent emotional debate over the issue of slavery. Leading Southerners, alarmed by Brown's "direct stab at the peculiar institution" and dismayed by Northern support for Brown's overt violence, warned of the impending breakup of the Union. Jefferson Davis, speaking to the U.S. Senate, declared, "Have we no right to allege that to secure our rights and protect our honor we will dissever the ties that bind us together, even if it rushes us into a sea of blood?" The *Charleston Mercury* announced, "The day of compromise is passed.... The South must control her own destinies or perish." And the *Richmond Enquirer* dolefully noted, "The Harpers Ferry invasion advanced the cause of Disunion more than any other event . . . since the formation of the Government."

Influential Northerners, in contrast, praised John Brown as a martyr. Ralph Waldo Emerson described him as "the Saint" whose death made "the gallows glorious like the cross." Henry David Thoreau elevated him to "an angel of light," and Louisa May Alcott called him "Saint John the Just." Church bells throughout the North tolled in Brown's honor on his execution day, and public prayer meetings and gun salutes proclaimed a pro-Brown sentiment. Incensed by the Northern reaction, South Carolina invited the Southern states to a secession meeting, but the convention failed to materialize, in part because the governor of Texas declared the South Carolina response premature and certain to lead to the destruction of the Union.

John Brown and his failed thirty-six-hour raid upon Harpers Ferry drove the nation to the brink of civil war. His martyrdom in the North and the intense hatred for him in the South led a Kansas paper, the *Lawrence Republican,* to observe, "It is safe to say that the death of no man in America has ever produced so profound a sensation."

BIBLIOGRAPHY

Boyer, Richard O. *The Legend of John Brown: A Biography and a History.* New York, 1973.

Oates, Stephen B. *To Purge This Land with Blood: A Biography of John Brown.* New York, 1970.

Sanborn, Franklin B. *Life and Letters of John Brown.* Boston, 1885.

Villard, Oswald Garrison. *John Brown, 1800–1859: A Biography Fifty Years After.* Boston and New York, 1911.

DENNIS E. FRYE

Battle of 1862

Harpers Ferry was the site of a battle on September 13 through 15, 1862, in which Thomas J. ("Stonewall") Jackson captured 12,500 prisoners, the largest surrender of U.S. troops during the Civil War. Jackson's success at Harpers Ferry enabled Robert E. Lee to cease his withdrawal from Maryland and fight the Battle of Sharpsburg on September 17.

Robert E. Lee and the Army of Northern Virginia commenced the first invasion of the North on September 3, 1862, when thirty-five thousand bedraggled Confederates began splashing across the Potomac River at White's Ford northeast of Leesburg, Virginia. When the army arrived unchallenged at Frederick, Maryland, twenty miles north of the Potomac, Lee halted the advance to rest his troops and to monitor Northern reaction to his incursion into Union territory.

While at Frederick, Lee became particularly concerned about the fourteen thousand Federals who remained south of his army at Harpers Ferry and Martinsburg, blocking access to vital communication and supply lines into the Shenandoah Valley. To remove this threat from his rear, Lee on September 9 issued Special Order 191, a bold and complicated strategic move designed to eradicate the Union garrisons in the lower valley.

Special Order 191 divided the army into four parts. Three columns, comprising six divisions and totaling twenty-three thousand men, would march upon Harpers Ferry from three directions, seize the three mountains surrounding the town, and hence trap the Federals between the hills. Lee and the remainder of the army, meanwhile, would await reunion of the scattered Confederates at Boonsboro, Maryland, twenty miles north of the Ferry. Lee selected Maj. Gen. Thomas J. ("Stonewall") Jackson to direct the Harpers Ferry mission, and he allowed only three days for its completion.

Although the division of his army in enemy territory posed a hazard, Lee considered the risk minimal. His primary opponent, Maj. Gen. George B. McClellan and the Army of the Potomac, had moved cautiously and slowly toward Rockville, Maryland; but Lee considered this a defensive posturing for the protection of Washington and Baltimore, not an aggressive march toward the Confederates operating around Harpers Ferry. If and when McClellan appeared on the horizon, Lee intended to have his army reunited on a battleground of his choosing.

On Wednesday morning, September 10, implementation of Special Order 191 commenced. Maj. Gen. John G. Walker and his division of two thousand men waved farewell to Maryland and recrossed the Potomac into Loudoun County, Virginia, where eyes turned northwest toward their target—Loudoun Heights—a steep bluff overlooking Harpers Ferry from the south bank of the Shenandoah River. Maj. Gen. Lafayette McLaws and the seven thousand soldiers comprising his division, along with Richard H. Anderson's division, marched southwest from Frederick

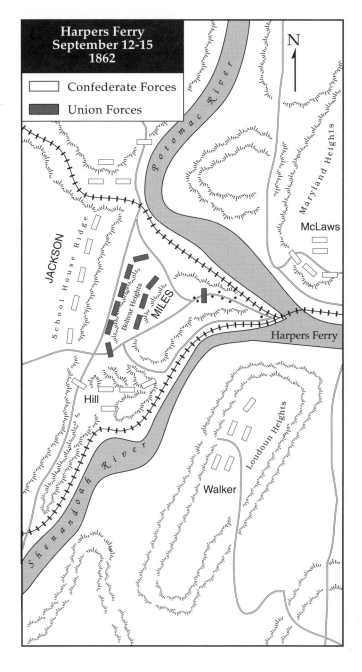

**Harpers Ferry
September 12-15
1862**

☐ Confederate Forces
▨ Union Forces

N

Potomac River

Maryland Heights

McLaws

JACKSON

School House Ridge

Bolivar Heights

MILES

Harpers Ferry

Hill

Loudoun Heights

Shenandoah River

Walker

The Federals knew they were coming. Col. Dixon S. Miles, commander of the Harpers Ferry garrison, had received scout reports and telegraph messages informing him of the danger. Consequently, at the outset of the invasion, Miles had deployed his forces in anticipation of a Confederate attack. But Miles had badly miscalculated. The fifty-eight-year-old West Point graduate believed an infantry attack against Bolivar Heights—a low-lying ridge one mile west of Harpers Ferry—would be the main Confederate target. Miles thus placed the bulk of his garrison, or nearly eight thousand men, upon Bolivar Heights. This number increased to ten thousand when the Martinsburg garrison arrived on September 12. Another poor judgment by the Harpers Ferry commander involved enemy artillery. Miles did not believe the Confederates could drag long-range cannon over a thousand vertical feet to the crests of Maryland and Loudoun Heights. Hence, the Union commander defended Maryland Heights with only two thousand men and placed no Federal soldiers on Loudoun Heights. Even if Maryland and Loudoun Heights fell to the Southern infantry, Miles considered these positions relatively harmless since Confederate small-arms fire from the ridge tops would be too far removed and isolated to cause damage to his garrison.

Miles's miscalculations proved fortunate for the Confederates, who were experiencing their own problems. River crossings and mountain gaps had slowed the Confederate march toward Harpers Ferry and had further debilitated infantrymen already suffering from lack of shoes and a paucity of food. In addition, Jackson's circuitous and fatiguing march through western Maryland and the lower valley encompassed fifty-one miles in seventy-two hours. Further complicating the situation were time constraints. Special Order 191 stipulated that the Harpers Ferry mission be completed by September 12, but the twelfth arrived and passed without any Confederates reaching jtheir targets. Because the Southerners had fallen behind schedule, McClellan's accidental discovery of Special Order 191 on September 13 further aggravated Lee's problems as the Federal commander boasted he had "all the plans of the Rebels" and would "catch them in their own trap."

Finally, on September 13, Confederates began taking their Harpers Ferry objectives. Walker occupied Loudoun Heights without firing a shot. Jackson's fourteen thousand men blocked escape from the west by settling upon School House Ridge, a linear rise paralleling the main Federal position on Bolivar Heights. The brigades of Joseph B. Kershaw and William Barksdale, both of McLaws's command, waged a six-hour battle on the crest of Maryland Heights before the Federals finally withdrew. By dusk on the thirteenth, Confederates completely encircled Harpers Ferry, and their artillerymen began clearing roads and

toward Maryland Heights, the high ridge dominating Harpers Ferry from north of the Potomac. Stonewall Jackson, with fourteen thousand men from his own division and the divisions of Richard S. Ewell and A. P. Hill, pushed west from Frederick. Jackson marched through Middletown and Boonsboro to Williamsport, where he crossed the Potomac and promptly frightened the Union garrison at Martinsburg into a hasty retreat south toward Harpers Ferry. From all directions of the compass, Confederates were tramping across the countryside in a three-pronged pincer movement directed at Harpers Ferry.

hauling artillery to the crests of Maryland and Loudoun Heights.

Union commander Miles, recognizing his predicament, desperately sent couriers searching for McClellan and assistance. McClellan responded on September 14 by attacking three gaps in South Mountain to "cut the enemy in two and beat him in detail." Confederate resistance stalled the Union advance, however, and provided Jackson with one additional day to conquer the Harpers Ferry position.

Confederate cannoneers began bombarding Miles's garrison at 2:00 P.M. on Sunday the fourteenth. Although the hail of shell demoralized the Federals, most found refuge in deep ravines, and few were injured by the ironstorm. To ensure a quick end to the siege, Jackson, during the night of the fourteenth, transferred fifteen guns to a plateau on Loudoun Heights to enfilade the ravines sheltering the Federals. Stonewall also ordered Hill's three thousand men to flank the Union left on Bolivar Heights by attaining a position on the Chambers Farm. With his garrison now outflanked and outgunned, Colonel Miles surrendered shortly after 8:00 A.M. on September 15.

The fruits of victory for Jackson included seventy-three pieces of artillery, thirteen thousand small arms, two hundred wagons, and 12,500 prisoners—the largest capitulation of U.S. troops during the Civil War. Jackson's loss included 39 killed and 247 wounded. The Confederate victory at Harpers Ferry temporarily halted General Lee's retreat from Maryland and allowed him to stand at Sharpsburg, where Jackson's forces reunited with the army on September 16 and 17.

BIBLIOGRAPHY

Frye, Dennis E. "Drama between the Rivers: Harpers Ferry in the 1862 Maryland Campaign." *Antietam: Essays on the 1862 Maryland Campaign.* Edited by Gary W. Gallagher. Kent, Ohio, 1989.

Frye, Dennis E. "Stonewall Attacks: The Siege and Capture of Harpers Ferry." *Blue and Gray Magazine* 5, no. 1 (1987): 7–27, 47–63.

U.S. War Department. *War of the Rebellion: A Compilation of the Official Records of the Union and Confederate Armies.* Washington, D.C., 1880–1901. Ser. 1, vol. 19, pts. 1–2.

Walker, John G. "Jackson's Capture of Harpers Ferry." In *Battles and Leaders of the Civil War.* Edited by Robert U. Johnson, and C. C. Buel. Vol. 2. New York, 1888. Reprint, Secaucus, N.J., 1982.

White, Julius. "The Capitulation of Harpers Ferry." In *Battles and Leaders of the Civil War.* Edited by Robert U. Johnson, and C. C. Buel. Vol. 2. New York, 1888. Reprint, Secaucus, N.J., 1982.

DENNIS E. FRYE

HARRIET LANE. The wooden, sidewheel U.S. Revenue Cutter Service steamer *Harriet Lane* measured 180 feet long, 30 feet in beam, and 12.5 feet in depth of hold and was 639 tons burden. Two boilers provided steam for the inclined, direct-acting engine, which assisted the brigantine sailing rig. The vessel was launched November 20, 1857, from the yard of Isaac Webb, engined by Allaire Works of New York. It was intended for revenue duty from the Port of New York and for cruises against slave ships. It also served with the U.S. Navy in the Paraguay expedition of 1858 and 1859.

Harriet Lane was sent to resupply Fort Sumter during the South Carolina secession crisis. While entering the harbor it stopped a ship bound for Charleston and fired the first shot of the war. The ship took part in the capture of Hatteras Inlet, North Carolina, April 1861. Transferred to the U.S. Navy on September 17, 1861, it fought in engagements on the Potomac and Mississippi rivers, and at Pensacola, Florida. It participated in the capture of Galveston, Texas, by Federal forces on October 4, 1862, and then served in the West Gulf Blockading Squadron.

On January 1, 1863, *Harriet Lane* was captured at Galveston in a brilliant attack planned by Maj. Gen. John B. Magruder. Confederate infantry forces retook the city while others aboard the cottonclad river steamers *Bayou City* and *Neptune* captured the majority of the Federal fleet in the bay. *Harriet Lane* was confiscated by the Confederate government and eventually sold to businessman T. W. House in early 1864. House converted it for blockade running by removing masts and armament and repainting the hull light gray. Renamed *Lavinia* and given Confederate registry, the ship escaped to Havana on April 30, 1864, and made at least one trip through the blockade. *Lavinia* was laid up at Havana because of financial problems when incendiaries under the pay of the Union consul set it afire. It sank on January 18, 1865. The wreck was raised after the war and converted into the merchant sailing ship *Elliott Richie*. It was abandoned off the Pernambuco River on May 13, 1884.

BIBLIOGRAPHY

Kern, Florence. *The United States Revenue Cutters in the Civil War.* Bethesda, Md., 1990.

King, Irving. *The Coast Guard under Sail: The U.S. Revenue Cutter Service, 1789–1865.* Annapolis, Md., 1989.

Pulsifer, F. H. "Reminiscences of the Harriet Lane." *Journal of the Coast Guard Association* 1, no. 1 (1917): 28–34.

Watson, William. *The Adventures of a Blockade Runner; or, Trade in Time of War.* London, 1892.

Yanaway, Philip. "The United States Revenue Cutter *Harriet Lane*, 1857–1884." *American Neptune,* July 1976, pp. 174–205.

KEVIN J. FOSTER

HARRIS, ISHAM G. (1818–1897), governor of Tennessee and U.S. senator. Harris ranks as one of the most

ISHAM G. HARRIS.   LIBRARY OF CONGRESS

significant figures in nineteenth-century Tennessee politics. He held public office for over five decades and played an influential role in shaping his state's history. Born on a farm in Franklin County, Tennessee, in 1818, Harris received a limited formal education. After teaching himself the law, he moved to Paris, Tennessee, opened a legal practice, and joined his brothers in a lucrative mercantile business. His marriage into a prominent planter family enhanced his standing in the community.

With the help of his father-in-law, Harris plunged into the political arena, working actively on behalf of Democratic candidates on all levels. A skilled orator and effective proponent of party issues, he easily won election to the state senate in 1847, using the issue of slavery to arouse voter support. Throughout his antebellum political career, Harris addressed other important issues such as banking, tariffs, and internal improvements, but defending slavery always was an integral part of his message.

Once in the Tennessee General Assembly, the senator lost no time in transferring the politics of slavery from the campaign trail to the legislative halls. A year later, Harris skillfully used the preservation of the peculiar institution and condemnation of northern abolitionists to win an overwhelming election to the U.S. Congress. The congressman's two-term record was not particularly distinguished, but without fail Harris sided with the South in every debate and roll call. Gerrymandered out of office by

a Whig-controlled legislature in 1851, Harris stayed away from politics for four years. He moved his growing family to Memphis and established himself as a leading attorney in the local bar. In 1855, Governor Andrew Johnson appointed him associate justice of the Tennessee Supreme Court.

After a brief stint on the bench, Harris reentered politics and easily won election for governor over a weak Whig opponent. Assuming office at a time of economic distress, he proposed legislation to reform state banking and restructure state currency. These measures, however, met with little success. Despite limited achievements in his first term, Harris was renominated and elected in a landslide victory for another term in 1859.

With the United States on the verge of disunion, Harris's second term proved far more eventful than his first. Early in the secession crisis, the Tennessee governor asserted his jealous regard for Southern state rights. During the 1860 presidential election, Harris campaigned tirelessly for Southern Democrat candidate John C. Breckinridge, insisting that voting for anyone else was a vote against Tennessee and the South. With the election of Abraham Lincoln and the subsequent secession of the lower Southern states, Harris began to openly question his state's future in the Union.

In January 1861, Harris called a special session of the General Assembly and recommended that the legislature submit a referendum to the people to vote for or against a secession convention. Although the convention was voted down overwhelmingly in February, the governor continued to advocate secession. After the firing on Fort Sumter, Harris issued an electrifying rejection of Lincoln's call for volunteers, proclaiming that "Tennessee will not furnish a Single Man for the purpose of Coercion but 50,000 if necessary for the defense of our rights and those of our southern brothers."

The governor then convened a special session of the General Assembly and rammed through ordinances declaring Tennessee independent and joining the state with the Confederacy. Harris had the ordinances submitted to the people in another statewide referendum on June 8. This time, with the exception of large numbers of dissenters in eastern Tennessee, the citizenry voted overwhelmingly to support secession.

Well in advance of the official vote, Harris committed his state to the Confederate cause. On May 1 (more than a month before the referendum) he appointed commissioners who signed an agreement with the Confederate government establishing a military league between Tennessee and the Confederate States and providing that Tennessee would immediately be under the "direction of the president of the Confederate States." He began raising and arming troops and constructing defenses to overcome the state's vulnerable geographic situation. Within a matter of weeks, the governor mobilized over 100,000 men and gradually turned them over to the Confederacy. The state army that Harris built eventually became the nucleus of the western Army of Tennessee. Internal divisions within the state continued to occupy the governor's time. At first he dealt leniently with the eastern Tennessee Unionists, but when his efforts met with little success, he clamped down sternly by arresting leaders and stationing more troops in the region.

By all measures, Harris performed brilliantly in overseeing the organization, equipping, and training of a large army under adverse conditions. Nevertheless, he made a fatal mistake in organizing the state's defensive lines. One of his earliest strategic moves was to commit state forces to the defense of the Mississippi River, while virtually ignoring the Tennessee and Cumberland rivers. Certain that Kentucky would remain totally neutral throughout the conflict, Harris argued that the only threat of invasion existed in the far west. Early in 1862, his short-sighted strategy had disastrous results. With the fall of Forts Henry and Donelson to a Union army under Ulysses S. Grant, Nashville was left wide open to capture. Harris ordered the evacuation of state government to Memphis.

For all practical purposes, Harris's governorship ended with the fall of Nashville. A handful of legislators who had followed him to Memphis drafted meaningless bills, but their efforts were futile. When Memphis surrendered to enemy forces in June, the governor once again fled and volunteered his services as an aide to the Confederate military. He became a member of the staffs of Albert Sidney Johnston, Braxton Bragg, Joseph E. Johnston, and John Bell Hood, serving in virtually every campaign of the Army of Tennessee until the end of the war. In late 1864, he was seriously considered for command of a cavalry brigade, but his refusal to relinquish his title as governor barred him by law from accepting the opportunity.

At war's end, Harris became a fugitive from justice. Pushed by Governor William G. Brownlow, the eastern-Tennessee-controlled General Assembly declared Harris guilty of treason and issued an award for his arrest. Two years later, however, the former governor was able to return to Memphis from exile in Mexico and England. He resumed the practice of law for several years, but the call of politics returned him to public office when he was elected to the U.S. Senate in 1877. Harris remained well entrenched in the Senate for twenty years, holding membership in several key committees. He consistently expressed the views of the Tennessee Bourbon Democrats, championing agrarian demands for paper money, free silver, bank reform, and tariff reduction. Along with the majority of Southern Democrats, he regularly supported measures restricting the rights and suffrage of African Americans. He died in Washington in June 1897 and was buried with full Confederate military honors in Memphis.

BIBLIOGRAPHY

Connelly, Thomas L. *Army of the Heartland: The Army of Tennessee, 1861–1862.* Baton Rouge, La., 1967.

Horn, Stanley F. "Isham G. Harris in the Pre-War Years." *Tennessee Historical Quarterly* 19 (1960): 195–207.

Watters, George W. "Isham G. Harris, Civil War Governor and Senator from Tennessee, 1818–1897." Ph.D. diss., Florida State University, 1977.

CHARLES F. BRYAN, JR.

HARRIS, NATHANIEL HARRISON (1834–1900), brigadier general.

Harris was born August 22, 1834, in Natchez, Mississippi. Educated in Louisiana, he practiced law in Vicksburg before the war. He raised a volunteer company there and led it to war in 1861 as its captain. Harris's company, part of the Nineteenth Mississippi Infantry, faced its first real fighting on May 5, 1862, at Williamsburg. The colonel of the Nineteenth lauded Harris in his report of the battle. Harris advanced from captain through the field-grade ranks of the regiment and became its colonel in the spring of 1863.

Colonel Harris won promotion to rank of brigadier general in February 1864. Perhaps the Mississippian's most distinguished service to the Confederacy came a few days into his first campaign as brigade commander, when he led his brigade into the maelstrom of the Bloody Angle near Spotsylvania Court House on May 12, 1864. For nearly twenty hours of intense fighting, often at hand-to-hand range, General Harris held his troops to their critical position. He commanded his brigade through the war's closing months near Petersburg. A disinterested Georgian who observed Harris's Brigade there called it "the grandest body of men that I ever saw." Harris and his men also performed spectacularly in one of their army's last-ditch struggles when they stubbornly held on inside Fort Gregg on April 2, 1865.

After the war, Harris practiced law and ran a railroad, among other things. He died in England, August 23, 1900, while on a business trip.

BIBLIOGRAPHY

Freeman, Douglas S. *Lee's Lieutenants: A Study in Command.* 3 vols. New York, 1942–1944. Reprint, New York, 1986.

Harris, Nathaniel H. *Movements of the Confederate Army in Virginia, and the Part Taken Therein by the Nineteenth Mississippi Regiment, from the Diary of Gen. Nat H. Harris.* Duncansby, Miss., 1901.

Roche, Thomas T. "The Bloody Angle." *Philadelphia Weekly Times,* September 3, 1881.

ROBERT K. KRICK

HARRIS, THOMAS A. (1826–1895), congressman from Missouri. Harris was born in Warren County, Virginia. During his youth, his family moved to Hannibal, Marion County, Missouri. In 1838 Harris participated in the Mormon war and a year later in the Missouri-Iowa boundary dispute. He won appointment to the U.S. Military Academy in 1843 but withdrew two years later to study law. In 1848, Harris gained a second lieutenancy in the Twelfth U.S. Infantry, but the war with Mexico ended before he saw action. He then pursued a military career in Venezuela. Harris returned to Hannibal in 1856 and served as city attorney from 1857 to 1859.

A Democrat, Harris in 1860 was elected a Marion County representative to the Provisional Confederate Congress. He also served in the First Congress. Usually supportive of the Davis administration, Harris served on the Conference and Military Affairs committees. Concerned about the well-being of Confederate soldiers, he did not favor a military draft. His support of Maj. Gen. Sterling Price eventually alienated Harris from Davis. Although he sought reelection in 1864, Harris, because of his reputation for carousing, lost to Nimrod Lindsay Norton.

After the war Harris tried a number of occupations in Missouri, Texas, and Louisiana before moving to Louisville, Kentucky, during the 1870s. He was appointed assistant secretary of state for Kentucky in 1880. His death occurred on April 9, 1895, in Pewee Valley, Kentucky.

BIBLIOGRAPHY

History of Marion County, Missouri. St. Louis, 1884.

Stevens, Walter B. *Missouri, the Center State, 1821–1915.* 5 vols. Chicago, 1915.

Wakelyn, Jon L. *Biographical Dictionary of the Confederacy.* Edited by Frank E. Vandiver. Westport, Conn., 1977.

Warner, Ezra J., and W. Buck Yearns. *Biographical Register of the Confederate Congress.* Baton Rouge, La., 1975.

JAMES W. GOODRICH

HARRIS, WILEY POPE (1818–1891), congressman from Mississippi. Harris, unlike most of his influential contemporaries, was a native Mississippian who could trace his lineage to Gen. Wade Hampton and George Washington. His father, once a wealthy Georgian, lost his property and died when Harris was only three years old. The boy was adopted by his uncle, for whom he was named. He attended the University of Virginia for two years and continued his study of law at Lexington, Kentucky. He practiced law in Mississippi from 1840 until 1847, when he was appointed circuit judge; subsequently he was elected to that same position and served until 1850.

In 1851 Harris was a delegate to a state convention called during the secession crisis of 1849–1851. The secession controversy had split Mississippi politicians into two camps—those favoring compromise and those like Jefferson Davis who wanted to protect slavery at any cost. Harris found himself caught in the controversy. At the convention, the majority advocated compromise, seeking to avoid any disruption of relations with the U.S. government. But Harris was a member of the minority who, though preferring to avoid secession, nevertheless declared it to be a "rightful remedy" if Southern demands were ignored and Northern policy was "pressed to a point deemed dangerous to the independence, and safety of the institutions of the States." Harris continued to believe that the Compromise of 1850 had produced only a "temporary repose" and, worse, had contributed to Northerners believing they could successfully "urge their policy to its extreme possibilities in the territories."

Harris served in the U.S. Congress from 1853 to 1855. During his tenure, he frequently warned of the growing power of the Federal government and of the diminishing strength of the states. He pointed out that the central government with an army, a navy, and vast revenues at its command was in a dominant position. Federal officials felt "more exalted" than state officials, and the shift in the balance of power was becoming dangerous.

In January 1861 Harris was a delegate to the constitutional convention that adopted the ordinance of secession. Reuben Davis, in his description of the convention, described Harris as "one of the most extraordinary men this State has ever produced." Davis wrote that Harris's name suggested to all Mississippians "the image of a tall, slender figure, crowned by a most intellectual head. Nature seems to have endowed him with all the qualities requisite in a great lawyer and a magnificent orator."

Looking back in later life to the troubled period of 1861, Harris in his unpublished autobiography described the thinking of Mississippi's leaders about the wisdom and justice of secession. Mississippians were divided between cooperation and secession. Harris clearly fit in the latter category, but his position was more thoughtful than that of the fire-eaters. In favoring secession, he felt that cooperationists were being indecisive, merely dragging out the inevitable with meetings and debate. He was certain that if Mississippi seceded, other states would follow, and he predicted two scenarios: one, that the border states would secede, thus preventing war "because the conquest of the slave States would be impossible," or two, the border states would not secede and instead would be "instruments of a settlement." Therefore, Harris expected no war. He also underestimated the North's determination and overestimated its dependence on cotton and commerce with the South. He believed the Northern people would "soon tire of a war which would entail such costly sacrifices." Harris admitted overlooking many considerations because of his "absorbing anxiety" over the consequences of secession.

Harris was chosen by unanimous vote on the first ballot to attend the Provisional Congress in Montgomery in 1861. While there, he scorned delay and proposed that the members dismiss preliminaries and move to a general election. He served on several committees, including Judiciary, Military Affairs, and Public Lands. One of his proposals was to impose a tax on slaves, which reflected his lack of sympathy with slaveholders; he himself had none. In his autobiography he commented that slave owners were unpopular as a class and "deserved to be unpopular." He wrote, "The ostentation at home and abroad drew upon them actual antipathy everywhere," adding that they "were generally ignorant, bigoted and intolerant of contradiction."

After his hard work at the Provisional Congress, it is surprising that he did not run for a seat in the regular Congress. Instead, he returned to the practice of law where he could exercise his legal expertise.

As he saw the North gain the advantage in the war, Harris began to hope for a peaceful settlement, but he realized "there could be no peace without the humiliation of the South." He wrote letters promoting the idea of some kind of "adjustment," but no one was interested. In the end he realized the South "had made a sad mistake."

During Reconstruction Harris was dismayed by the alienation and depression suffered by the state, which had neither a national nor a state government it could respect. "It is a dreary life we lead here," he wrote, "with a national government ever suspicious and frowning, imperious and hostile, and a home government feeble, furtive, false, and fraudulent." And he sought amelioration: "We are in a new world. . . . It is better that we hang a millstone about our necks than cling to these old issues."

BIBLIOGRAPHY

Alexander, Thomas B., and Richard E. Beringer. *The Anatomy of the Confederate Congress: A Study of the Influences of Member Characteristics on Legislative Voting Behavior, 1861–1865.* Nashville, Tenn., 1972.

Warner, Ezra J., and W. Buck Yearns. *Biographical Register of the Confederate Congress.* Baton Rouge, La., 1975.

RAY SKATES

HARRISON, HENRY THOMAS (1832–?), scout and spy.

A native of Tennessee, Harrison entered Confederate service in early 1861 as a civilian scout in northern Virginia and became a scout in Mississippi in 1862. He signed reports there as "H. T. Harrison, Secret Agent." One picture shows him in the uniform of a second lieutenant, holding a revolver and pointing to a simple numerical cipher printed on cardboard.

Called to Richmond in January 1863, he reported to Secretary of War James A. Seddon and was assigned to Gen. James Longstreet. While on temporary duty with Gen. D. H. Hill in North Carolina, Harrison was captured near New Bern by a Union patrol on March 21, 1863. He was released on April 13 when his complex cover story held up. No longer able to spy in North Carolina, he was sent back to Longstreet.

On June 2, 1863, Col. Moxley Sorrel of Longstreet's staff furnished Harrison with two hundred dollars in U.S. currency and ordered him to Washington to track Union troops as they set out to counter Robert E. Lee's invasion of Maryland and Pennsylvania. Harrison reached Longstreet near Chambersburg, Pennsylvania, on the night of June 28. As Longstreet wrote later, Harrison brought "information more accurate than a force of cavalry could have secured." This is generally credited with changing the disposition of Lee's army before the Battle of Gettysburg. During the last year of the war, Harrison was in New York City engaged in undisclosed clandestine activities.

In a letter from Baltimore, dated April 7, 1866, Harrison told his wife, Laura: "I write on the eve of a journey, and will not see you for some time, perhaps never." Later she learned that he was in the gold fields of Montana Territory. The last word of him there came in the spring of 1867. Thinking her husband dead, Laura remarried. After an absence of over thirty-four years, Harrison unexpectedly turned up on November 20, 1900, seeking to see his two daughters. Turned away, he went to Cincinnati. From there he wrote to Laura's brother in March 1901 that he was going to San Francisco. Then Harrison disappeared for good.

BIBLIOGRAPHY

Hall, James O. "The Spy Harrison." *Civil War Times Illustrated* 24, no. 10 (February 1986): 19–25.

Longstreet, James. *From Manassas to Appomattox.* Philadelphia, 1896. Reprint, Millwood, N.Y., 1985.

Longstreet, James. "Lee's Invasion of Pennsylvania." In *Battles and Leaders of the Civil War.* Vol. 3. Edited by Robert U. Johnson and C. C. Buell. New York, 1888. Reprint, Secaucus, N.J., 1982.

Sorrel, G. Moxley. *Recollections of a Confederate Staff Officer.* Edited by Bell Irvin Wiley. Jackson, Tenn., 1958.

JAMES O. HALL

HARRISON, JAMES EDWARD (1815–1875), brigadier general.

The older brother of Brig. Gen. Thomas Harrison, James was born in Greenville District, South Carolina. His family moved to Alabama, then to Mississippi, where he served two terms in the state legislature, and finally to Waco, Texas. In early 1861 he was appointed by Governor Edward Clark of Texas as a member of the commission to negotiate with the Five Southern Tribes.

Clark, fearing an Indian uprising with the removal of U.S. forces from Texas, hoped to ally the Indians with the South's cause. Afterward Harrison served as a member of the Texas secession convention.

When war broke out, he entered military service as a lieutenant colonel in the Fifteenth Texas Infantry. Harrison's brigade served primarily as a scouting and skirmishing force until 1863 when it was attached to Gen. Thomas Green. In the fall of that year Harrison fought in numerous actions in Louisiana (including Stirling's Plantation and Teche County), receiving General Green's praise for his gallantry. In late 1864 Harrison, with Jefferson Davis's backing, was again at work trying to establish a military alliance between the Confederacy and the southwestern Indians, especially the Commanches. He was promoted to brigadier general November 22, 1864. On June 2, 1865, Harrison served as chief of the commission to carry out the surrender terms between the District of Texas and the U.S. Army.

In the postwar period Harrison was prominent in Waco, Texas, serving as a trustee to Baylor University until his death in 1875.

BIBLIOGRAPHY

Roberts, O. M. *Texas*. Vol. 11 of *Confederate Military History*. Edited by Clement A. Evans. Atlanta, 1899. Vol. 15 of extended ed. Wilmington, N.C., 1989.

Walker, John C. "Reconstruction in Texas." *Southern Historical Society Papers* 24 (1896): 41–57. Reprint, Wilmington, N.C., 1991.

Wright, Marcus J., comp. *Texas in the War, 1861–1865*. Hillsboro, Tex., 1965.

THOMAS J. LEGG

HARRISON, JAMES THOMAS (1811–1879),

congressman from Mississippi. Harrison, a South Carolinian by birth, moved to Mississippi when in his twenties. While in South Carolina, he had studied law under James Louis Petigru, a staunch Unionist, and he set up a law practice now in Columbus, Mississippi. According to Joseph G. Baldwin in *Flush Times*, he was a preeminent lawyer who "could entangle Justice in such a web of law that the blind hussy could never have found her way out again if Theseus had been there to give her the clue."

Harrison avoided politics and even declined a seat on the Mississippi High Court of Errors and Appeals. Without his knowledge, he was selected as a delegate to the Provisional Congress in Montgomery, Alabama, in January 1861. Originally opposed to secession, he wrote to his wife while serving, "There will be no halting or backing down—no attempt at reconstruction." In Congress, Harrison followed the lead of Jefferson Davis and, though faithfully attending most sessions, offered few contributions of his own. His lack of enthusiasm may have reflected his lack of interest in political involvement.

After his term at the Provisional Congress, Harrison did not seek election to the regular Congress. Instead, he returned to his legal career for the remainder of the war. Apparently, however, some involvement in politics was unavoidable. He consented to serve as an adviser to Governor Charles Clark and was selected to defend Jefferson Davis if he were ever put on trial.

Immediately following the war, Harrison was elected to the U.S. Congress, but Congress refused to seat the Mississippians. Not until as late as 1870 was the state allowed a congressional delegation. Harrison was a member of the constitutional convention of 1865 and proposed the abolition amendment that was finally adopted after lengthy debate.

BIBLIOGRAPHY

Alexander, Thomas B., and Richard E. Beringer. *The Anatomy of the Confederate Congress: A Study of the Influences of Member Characteristics on Legislative Voting Behavior, 1861–1865*. Nashville, Tenn., 1972.

Warner, Ezra J., and W. Buck Yearns. *Biographical Register of the Confederate Congress*. Baton Rouge, La., 1975.

RAY SKATES

HARRISON, THOMAS (1823–1891), brigadier general. A daring soldier, Brig. Gen. Thomas Harrison led cavalry in the western Confederate armies. Born in Jefferson County, Alabama, he grew up in Mississippi before moving to Texas in 1843. During the Mexican War, Harrison returned to Mississippi and enlisted in Jefferson Davis's First Mississippi Rifles. After the war, he returned to Texas and entered politics as a representative in the state legislature, eventually settling in Waco. At the beginning of the Civil War, Harrison received a commission as captain of a militia unit, and he aided in the capture of Federal posts along the frontier. Later, his company enlisted in the famous "Terry's Texas Rangers," the Eighth Texas Cavalry, and he was elected major.

Harrison served with his regiment throughout the war, earning praise for his actions at Shiloh. He received promotion to colonel in November 1862 and had earned the sobriquet "Old Iron Sides" for his ability to escape injury in the midst of battle. The following year, Harrison took command of his brigade and served in Gen. Joseph Wheeler's cavalry corps throughout the remainder of the war. He was promoted to brigadier general on January 14, 1865. On March 10, Harrison received a slight wound at Monroe's Cross Roads, North Carolina, and left his brigade. He never resumed command. His brother, James Edward Harrison, was also a Confederate brigadier.

After the war, Harrison returned home to Waco, Texas, where he resumed his law practice. He served as district judge from 1866 to 1877. He died in Waco on July 14, 1891.

BIBLIOGRAPHY

Blackburn, James K. P. *Reminiscences of the Terry Rangers.* Austin, Tex., 1919.

Jeffries, C. C. "The Character of Terry's Texas Rangers." *Southwestern Historical Quarterly* 64 (1961): 454–462.

Sarrafian, Mary K. *The Harrison Family of Texas.* Waco, Tex., 1966.

DONALD S. FRAZIER

HART, NANCY (fl. 1862), Confederate guide and spy. Whether Nancy Hart actually lived is unknown; the story of her exploits may well be a legend. In any event, she is said to have lived in obscurity in the mountain district of West Virginia. She was a staunch supporter of the Confederacy and with the outbreak of the war volunteered her services to Thomas J. ("Stonewall") Jackson as a guide to lead his men along hidden mountain trails to surprise Federal garrisons. She proved so adept a guide that the Federals offered a reward for her capture.

In July 1862 Hart was captured at Summerville, West Virginia, by Companies A and F of the Ninth Virginia Volunteer Infantry commanded by Lt. Col. William C. Starr. At the time an itinerant photographer was at Summerville and persuaded Starr to allow him to photograph Hart. As the dark-haired young woman was positioned before the camera, her guards placed a military hat on her head. Somehow Hart managed to grab a guard's musket and kill him. Then she rushed outside, mounted Starr's horse, and galloped away to safety.

At 4:00 A.M. on July 25, Hart returned to Summerville along with two hundred Confederate cavalry under Maj. R. A. Bailey. The Southerners surprised Starr's men, seized the town, and captured Starr and several other members of his command. After burning two houses and a commissary storehouse and destroying two wagons, Hart and the Confederates withdrew taking with them several horses and mules as well as captured arms and ammunition.

BIBLIOGRAPHY

Miller, Francis T., ed. *The Photographic History of the Civil War.* 10 vols. New York, 1911.

U.S. War Department. *The War of the Rebellion: A Compilation of the Official Records of the Union and Confederate Armies.* Washington, D.C., 1880–1901. Ser. 1, vol. 12, pt. 2.

KENNY A. FRANKS

HARTRIDGE, JULIAN (1829–1879), Confederate and U.S. congressman from Georgia. Hartridge was born on Daufuskie Island, South Carolina, and grew up in nearby Savannah, the son of a prominent businessman. Educated at Brown University and Harvard where he studied law, he returned to Savannah and established a law practice in 1851. He served one term (1858–1859) in the Georgia legislature and was elected a delegate to the fateful Democratic convention of 1860, which met first in Charleston and then in Baltimore.

An ardent secessionist, Hartridge served as a lieutenant in a local unit, the Chatham Artillery, until he was elected to represent Georgia's First District in the Confederate House of Representatives in 1862, where he served two terms. As a congressman, he was a member of the Ways and Means Committee, the Commerce Committee, and the Committee on Illegal Seizures and Impressments. In his role on the latter, he joined his fellow Georgians in forcefully protesting President Jefferson Davis's conscription policies and pushed for abolishing state commissary impressments. On the whole, however, he gave rather strong support to the Confederate government.

At war's end, Hartridge and his family (which included nine children) were financially ruined, and he resumed his law practice. He actively opposed Republican rule in Savannah during Reconstruction and emerged as a prominent Democratic leader in Georgia, chairing the state convention of 1870, the state central committee, and the state delegation to the presidential nominating conventions of 1872 and 1876. He was elected to the U.S. Congress in 1874 and 1876, and died in Washington, D.C., toward the end of his second term in January 1879.

BIBLIOGRAPHY

Bell, Hiram P. *Men and Things: Being Reminiscent, Biographical, and Historical.* Atlanta, 1907.

Coleman, Kenneth, and Charles Stephen Gurr, eds. *Dictionary of Georgia Biography.* Vol. 1. Athens, Ga., 1983.

Knight, Lucian Lamar. *A Standard History of Georgia and Georgians.* Vol. 5. Chicago, 1917.

Northen, William W. *Men of Mark in Georgia.* Vol. 3. Atlanta, 1908. Reprint, Spartanburg, S.C., 1974.

JOHN C. INSCOE

HATTON, ROBERT HOPKINS (1826–1862), U.S. congressman and brigadier general. Hatton is a perfect example of a prewar Southern Unionist who cast his lot with the Confederacy and died in defense of a cause he had opposed adamantly. The son of an itinerant Methodist preacher, Hatton was born in Youngstown, Ohio, on November 2, 1826. Nine years later the family moved to Tennessee. After graduating from Cumberland University in Lebanon, Tennessee, in 1847, Hatton taught school for a while and then returned to Cumberland to study law. Admitted to the bar in 1850, Hatton opened a law practice in Lebanon.

During the next decade, Hatton devoted his energies to

A few days later Hatton and his men were in the thick of action at Seven Pines. Arriving on the battlefield on May 31, the Tennesseans ran into a fresh division of Union troops. Hatton was killed when his horse was shot from under him. Faced with withering fire, the Tennesseans retreated, carrying the body of their commander with them.

Buried initially in Richmond, Hatton's body was removed to Lebanon a year after the war. A statue of the general stands facing west in the courthouse square of Lebanon.

BIBLIOGRAPHY

Drake, James Vaulx. *Life of General Robert Hatton.* Nashville, Tenn., 1867.

Porter, James D. *Tennessee.* Vol. 8 of *Confederate Military History.* Edited by Clement A. Evans. Atlanta, 1899. Vol. 10 of extended ed. Wilmington, N.C., 1987.

Warner, Ezra J. *Generals in Gray: Lives of the Confederate Commanders.* Baton Rouge, La., 1959.

CHARLES F. BRYAN, JR.

ROBERT HOPKINS HATTON.   LIBRARY OF CONGRESS

elective politics. Initially a Whig, he shifted to the Know-Nothing (or American) party with the death of the Whig party in the mid-1850s and was elected to the Tennessee General Assembly in 1855. By all accounts, Hatton was a masterful public speaker, so much so that this relatively unknown politician was nominated by his party in 1857 to run against Democrat Isham G. Harris for governor. Despite a spirited campaign, Hatton was defeated in a landslide.

With increased recognition, however, Hatton was elected to Congress in 1859 and quickly established himself as a strong Unionist, working diligently in behalf of the Union well into the spring of 1861. Secessionists in his district castigated him for his stance, even threatening him with personal injury.

After the firing on Fort Sumter and Abraham Lincoln's call for volunteers, however, Hatton shifted his loyalties to the South. He raised a company of volunteers in May 1861 and was elected colonel of the Seventh Tennessee Infantry, which was brigaded with other regiments under the command of Gen. Samuel Read Anderson. In late summer the Tennessee troops were transferred to western Virginia and participated in the Cheat Mountain campaign. In February 1862 the Tennessee brigade joined Joseph E. Johnston's army at Fredericksburg. It participated in the month-long siege of Yorktown and served as the rear guard on the retreat to Richmond. When Anderson resigned from the army in May 1862, Hatton was appointed commander of the Tennessee brigade and promoted to brigadier general.

HAVANA. *See entry on the ship* Sumter.

HAWES, J. M. (1824–1889), brigadier general. Born in Lexington, Kentucky, in 1824, James Morrison Hawes was a West Point graduate, class of 1845. His service in the Dragoons during the Mexican War earned him the brevet rank of first lieutenant. After teaching cavalry and infantry tactics at West Point, he spent two years at Saumur, the French cavalry school, and was appointed to a frontier command.

He resigned from the U.S. Army on May 9, 1861, and volunteered for Confederate service. After his election as colonel of the Second Kentucky Cavalry, he joined the regular Confederate army in the summer of 1861 with a commission as major. At the request of Gen. Albert Sidney Johnston, Hawes was promoted to brigadier general in March 1862 and given command of the cavalry in the Western Department of the Confederacy. After the Battle of Shiloh in April 1862, Hawes asked to be relieved of his cavalry command so that he could head a brigade in John C. Breckinridge's division. In October 1862, he was assigned to the Trans-Mississippi Department in Arkansas where he commanded the Texas Brigade. During the Vicksburg campaign Hawes led his brigade against the Union position at Milliken's Bend, Louisiana, on June 7, 1863. The fighting was fierce but the Confederates were unable to push through the Union defenses west of the Mississippi River. His last command was in Texas where he was in charge of Confederate fortifications at Galveston Island.

After the war Hawes settled in Covington, Kentucky, where he was a hardware merchant until his death in 1889.

BIBLIOGRAPHY

Johnson, J. Stoddard. *Kentucky*. Vol. 9 of *Confederate Military History*. Edited by Clement A. Evans. Atlanta, 1899. Vol. 11 of extended ed. Wilmington, N.C., 1988.

Wakelyn, Jon L. *Biographical Dictionary of the Confederacy*. Edited by Frank E. Vandiver. Westport, Conn., 1977.

WILLIAM L. BARNEY

HAWES, RICHARD (1797–1877), major and Confederate governor of Kentucky. Born in Caroline County, Virginia, Hawes moved to Kentucky with his parents in 1810. A graduate of Transylvania University, he practiced law and engaged in hemp manufacturing. He served as a Whig in both the legislature and Congress. Hawes became a Democrat in the 1850s and supported John C. Breckinridge for president in 1860. He took a leading role during the secession crisis, serving as a member of the bipartisan legislative committee that recommended neutrality for the state. When that failed Hawes went with the Confederacy. Commissioned a major, he served briefly with Humphrey Marshall's command in eastern Kentucky.

When Provisional Governor George W. Johnson died on April 9, 1862, from wounds received at Shiloh, Hawes succeeded him. He had to lead a government-in-exile, however, for the Union controlled Kentucky. The situation changed when Confederate Gen. Braxton Bragg invaded the state in late August. After a quick trip to Richmond to secure assurances of support there, Hawes followed Bragg. In a ceremony held in the House chamber at Frankfort on October 4, he was formally installed as governor, but that afternoon Union artillery began shelling the town, and Hawes and Bragg abandoned the capital in haste. Hawes attempted to maintain a shadow government thereafter, sometimes in Richmond, more often with Kentucky troops in the Army of Tennessee, but he admitted in 1863 that he was "almost powerless." At war's end, he returned to Paris, Kentucky, and resumed his law practice. Elected to local judgeships, he continued on the bench until his death.

BIBLIOGRAPHY

Clift, G. Glenn. *Governors of Kentucky*. Cynthiana, Ky., 1942.

Connelly, Thomas L. *Autumn of Glory: The Army of Tennessee, 1862–1865*. Baton Rouge, La., 1971.

Harrison, Lowell H. "Kentucky." In *The Confederate Governors*. Edited by W. Buck Yearns. Athens, Ga., 1985.

WILLIAM E. PARRISH

HAWTHORN, ALEXANDER TRAVIS (1825–1899), brigadier general. A Yale graduate and Mexican War veteran, Hawthorn was elected lieutenant colonel of the Sixth Arkansas Infantry in June 1861. He became colonel after his commanding officer rode over a cliff and was killed.

Henry Morton Stanley, the future explorer and now an army private, described Hawthorn as "too vain of military distinction and the trappings of official rank." His troops, armed with obsolete flintlock muskets, "labored under great disadvantage" at the Battle of Shiloh, unable to get within range of their opponents. The resulting carnage left Hawthorn in command of a brigade of Alabama and Tennessee troops, but this organization was disbanded prior to the Battle of Perryville, Kentucky.

Transferred to the Trans-Mississippi Department, Hawthorn commanded a regiment at the Battle of Prairie Grove, Arkansas, December 9, 1862. This regiment became the nucleus of Hawthorn's Arkansas brigade, which spearheaded the assault on Fort Hindman, Arkansas, July 4, 1863, in a belated effort to relieve Federal pressure on Vicksburg. Although initially successful, the poorly coordinated attack faltered in the face of withering Federal fire. Hawthorn covered the Confederate retreat with only nine men.

Commissioned brigadier general on February 23, 1864, he was assigned to the Arkansas division of Maj. Gen. Sterling Price's army just prior to the Battle of Jenkins's Ferry, Arkansas, April 30, 1864, and served with it for the rest of the war. In May 1865, Hawthorn joined a cabal conspiring to replace the department commander, Gen. E. Kirby Smith, and continue the war west of the Mississippi. A month later, Union authorities reported that Hawthorn seemed "quite anxious" to take the amnesty oath.

After the war, Hawthorn was one of many ex-Confederates who emigrated to Brazil. Returning to the United States in 1874, he became a Baptist minister.

BIBLIOGRAPHY

"General A. T. Hawthorne [sic]." *Confederate Veteran* 7 (September 1899): 418–419.

Harrell, John M. *Arkansas*. Vol. 10 of *Confederate Military History*. Edited by Clement A. Evans. Atlanta, 1899. Vol. 14 of extended ed. Wilmington, N.C., 1988.

Stanley, Sir Henry Morton. *The Autobiography of Sir Henry Morton Stanley*. Edited by Dorothy Stanley. Boston and New York, 1909.

Thomas, David Y. *Arkansas in War and Reconstruction, 1861–1874*. Little Rock, Ark., 1926.

DAVID EVANS

HAYNES, LANDON CARTER (1816–1875), congressman from Tennessee. Probably the most influential Tennessean in the Confederate government, Haynes, a native of Carter County, Tennessee, graduated from Washington College (Tennessee) in 1838 and read law under the celebrated Unionist T. A. R. Nelson. Following a short stint as a Methodist minister and newspaper editor, Haynes launched his political career in 1845 by winning election as a Democrat to the Tennessee legislature, where his eloquence and political acumen catapulted him to the post of Speaker of the House just four years later.

By the 1850s, Haynes was recognized as a leader of the Democratic party in Tennessee. His canvass of the state as a Breckinridge elector in 1860 only enhanced his reputation as an ardent state rights man. This, and the fact that he was an "original" secessionist, paved the road to his selection by the General Assembly as Confederate senator in October 1861.

In the Senate, Haynes emerged as a champion of the pro-administration forces. Soon after Federal armies occupied most of Tennessee in early 1862, Haynes realized that the characteristics he had displayed in the state legislature—fiscal conservatism and extreme state rights—were hampering the Confederacy's fight for independence. Appointed to committees on Patents, Post Offices and Post Roads, Judiciary, Commerce, and Engrossment and Enrollment (which he chaired during the First Congress), Haynes cooperated with President Jefferson Davis to put Southern society on a wartime basis. Consistent with his newly found nationalism, he proposed and supported legislation that encouraged manufacturing, created productive tax laws, and facilitated impressment of private property. Although he disliked many of Davis's top appointments and feared that the war was being mismanaged, Haynes upheld the president's suspension of habeas corpus and worked to give the chief executive a strong conscription law. He resisted, however, all efforts to arbitrarily quash individual liberty and state rights at the expense of the war effort, jealously protecting freedom of speech and insisting on exemptions from the draft for state officials and the militia. The most notable legislation he introduced was the Twenty-Slave Law, which created discontent among nonslaveholders and those owning only a few slaves by exempting from the draft one person on a plantation where there were twenty or more slaves.

After the war, Haynes was arrested by Federal authorities but was eventually pardoned by President Andrew Johnson. Forced to flee East Tennessee by vengeance-seeking Unionists, he relocated in Memphis where he practiced law and made an unsuccessful bid for Congress in 1872.

BIBLIOGRAPHY

Bellamy, James W. "The Political Career of Landon Carter Haynes." M.A. thesis, University of Tennessee, 1952.
Caldwell, Joshua W. *Sketches of the Bench and Bar of Tennessee.* Knoxville, Tenn., 1898.
Journal of the Congress of the Confederate States of America, 1861–1865. 7 vols. Washington, D.C., 1904–1905.
Speer, William S. *Sketches of Prominent Tennesseans.* Nashville, Tenn., 1888.

W. TODD GROCE

HAYS, HARRY THOMPSON (1820–1876), brigadier general. Born on April 14, 1820, in Wilson County, Tennessee, Hays attended St. Mary's College in Baltimore. He then practiced law in New Orleans and became active in the Whig party. He fought with the Fifth Louisiana in the Mexican War.

When the Civil War began, Hays became a colonel of the Seventh Louisiana Infantry and fought at First Manassas and in Stonewall Jackson's 1862 Shenandoah Valley campaign with Richard Taylor's brigade. Hays was severely wounded at Port Republic but returned to duty at Sharpsburg. He had been commissioned a brigadier general on July 25, 1862, and succeeded Taylor as commander of the Louisiana brigade. Hays fought at Fredericksburg, Chancellorsville, and Gettysburg, but was seriously wounded again at Spotsylvania. After he recovered, Hays was transferred to the Trans-Mississippi Department in July 1864 where he searched for absentees from the Army of Northern Virginia until Robert E. Lee's surrender. No longer needed for this duty, he replaced William Robertson Boggs in command of the District of Louisiana. On May 10, 1865, E. Kirby Smith promoted Hays to major general, although this was not approved by Richmond.

HARRY THOMPSON HAYS.   NATIONAL ARCHIVES

After the war, Hays returned to New Orleans where he served as sheriff of Orleans Parish until Philip Sheridan removed him from the office in 1866. He later practiced law with Gen. Daniel Weisiger Adams. Hays died on August 21, 1876, and is buried in Washington Avenue Cemetery, New Orleans.

BIBLIOGRAPHY

Jones, Terry L. *Lee's Tigers: The Louisiana Infantry in the Army of Northern Virginia.* Baton Rouge, La., 1987.

Seymour, W. J. *The Civil War Memoirs of Captain William J. Seymour.* Baton Rouge, La., 1991.

ANNE J. BAILEY

HEALTH AND MEDICINE. [*This entry includes four articles that explore the state of medical care during the Confederacy:*

Sickness and Disease
Battle Injuries
Medical Treatments
Medical Training

For further discussion of medicine in the Confederacy, see Hospitals; Nursing. *For discussion of the organization of medical services in the Confederate army, see* Medical Department.]

Sickness and Disease

The spectrum of sickness and disease among military personnel was similar to that in the general population, both North and South. Disease prevention was hampered by the era's lack of understanding of the basis of disease (germ theory was unknown) and consequent ignorance of the importance of hygiene and antisepsis. Many symptoms, such as fever, diarrhea, and dysentery, were regarded as diseases and treated as such.

The civilian population in the South was subject to a variety of medical problems, some of which were unique to the region. Puerperal fever was often a complication following childbirth; it is now known to be caused by bacteria, but ignorance led to the death of new mothers. Malaria and yellow fever, both transmitted by mosquitoes, were common in much of the coastal south. Tuberculosis was found in cities where crowding existed but was more of a problem in the urban North. Lack of previous exposure would be fatal to soldiers crowded in camps. Common childhood diseases were not widespread in the largely rural population, and the absence of immunity led to serious problems for new recruits.

The military population, beset by constant fatigue, exposure, poor nutrition, inadequate clothing, lack of shelter, and deficient camp hygiene, was especially vulnerable to illness. A healthy fighting force required, above all, the exclusion of those who were unfit for the rigors of military life. But for a volunteer army motivated by patriotic fervor, there was great pressure to accept many who were unsuitable, and the difficulty of fielding sufficient numbers as the war continued increased such pressure.

In the primarily rural South, many men had not been exposed to the usual childhood diseases. Thus waves of measles with its complications of respiratory infections swept through the susceptible troops in their crowded camps of instruction. These measles epidemics were greatest early in the war. Many rural recruits also had not been immunized against smallpox. Although army medical authorities were familiar with vaccination and practiced it at various times and locations, this disease took a large toll.

Complicating the medical picture was the fact that many new recruits did not know the basic rules of hygiene. Further, ignorance of proper food preparation—evidenced by burned bread and greasy fried food—resulted in soldiers' suffering chronic indigestion, diarrhea, and abdominal pains.

A lack of proper clothing and shoes, especially in inclement weather, plagued the Confederacy throughout the war, as did its inability to transport sufficient nutritious food. Frequently, preserved meat was unfit to eat, vegetables were absent, and fresh beef a rarity. Outbreaks of scurvy occurred. Troops often had to drink impure water, teeming with pathogens, with disastrous results.

The most debilitating medical problems of Confederate soldiers were the intestinal disorders diarrhea (abnormally liquid and frequent bowel movements) and dysentery (loose, bloody bowel movements). These were caused by a variety of then unknown bacteria and viruses as well as inadequate and poorly cooked food. Improper placement of latrines with subsequent contamination of drinking water, coupled with a reluctance to use latrines, exacerbated the problem. Further, the general debility caused by these illnesses weakened many men and made them more susceptible to other illnesses. Given their myriad causes, diarrhea and dysentery were also extremely difficult to cure. Their incidence progressively increased during the war. They were responsible for more deaths than gunshot wounds, and more soldiers were discharged from the army because of them than because of battlefield injuries. An estimated 94,000 Confederates died from wounds; some 164,000 are believed to have died of disease.

Diarrhea and dysentery were treated with a variety of remedies, which shared the common effect of astringency in the hope of halting the watery intestinal discharge. Such treatment was almost entirely ineffective. A few physicians recognized that a well-prepared, balanced diet was helpful in some cases, but this was tried only in a few rear-echelon general hospitals.

Typhoid fever (a specific, bacterially caused disease), typhus fever (a group of diseases caused by the tick-borne *Rickettsia*), and "common continued fevers" (as they were called) were other major medical problems. Typhoid fever, which included gastrointestinal manifestations, killed at least a quarter of its victims. It was primarily a disease of new soldiers and was rarely seen in veteran armies because protective immunity developed. Typhus had among its effects aches and fevers. "Common continued fevers" were an ill-defined group of illnesses with some of the manifestations of typhoid.

Another transmissible disease, malaria, was endemic in the mid-nineteenth-century South. Now known to be caused by a mosquito-borne protozoan, the disease was then believed to be caused by "miasmas" arising from stagnant water. In the Southern coastal states during the warm months, there was an average of two reported cases of malaria for each soldier enrolled, indicating numerous recurrences of this debilitating illness. Quinine had been isolated from cinchona bark in 1822 and was known to be effective in the treatment of malaria. But adequate supplies of quinine were halted by the Federal blockade in late 1862. Various local remedies—such as turpentine and extracts of dogwood and willow bark—were reportedly partly effective.

Pneumonia, now known to be caused by a variety of bacterial and viral organisms, was considered a single disease and was treated variously by diet, whiskey, opium, and quinine when available. Respiratory diseases unexplainably were more prevalent among Confederate than Union soldiers; all other diseases were present in proportionate numbers in both armies. Pulmonary tuberculosis, rheumatism, and venereal diseases were among the other debilitating illnesses of which there was little understanding; thus, treatment for them was ineffective.

Confederate medical authorities labored heroically to deal with the medical problems of those under their care. But like their counterparts in the North, they were hindered by their lack of understanding of the cause of the diseases they were called upon to treat. Unlike their Union counterparts, they were also hampered by limited supplies of the medications they needed and the ever-tightening Federal blockade against imports.

BIBLIOGRAPHY

Adams, George W. *Doctors in Blue: The Medical History of the Union Army in the Civil War.* New York, 1952.
Cunningham, Horace H. *Doctors in Gray: The Confederate Medical Service.* Baton Rouge, La., 1958.
Medical and Surgical History of the War of Rebellion. 6 vols. Washington, D.C., 1875–1888. Reprinted as *The Medical and Surgical History of the Civil War.* Edited by James I. Robertson, Jr. 14 vols. Wilmington, N.C., 1990–1991.
Shryock, Richard H. "A Medical Perspective on the Civil War."
In *Medicine in America: Historical Essays.* Baltimore, 1966.
Steiner, Paul E. *Disease in the Civil War.* Springfield, Ill., 1968.
Wiley, Bell I. *The Life of Johnny Reb.* Baton Rouge, La., 1970.

HERBERT M. SCHILLER

Battle Injuries

Traumatic battle injuries and their treatment fall into the realm of surgical disease. Because few physicians in the Confederate army had any military surgery experience, they found Dr. J. Julian Chisolm's *A Manual of Military Surgery for the Use of Surgeons in the Confederate States Army* invaluable. Confederate Surgeon General Samuel Preston Moore continually ordered his surgeons to submit records of the outcome of their treatments and procedures, for it was only through review of such reports that advances in treatment could be maintained. But like their Union counterparts, Confederate surgeons disliked record keeping and understandably postponed the onerous task until they had treated the wounded. During active campaigning, intensive medical care might be required for days, and maintenance of accurate records was not possible. This, along with the fact that almost all the Confederate Medical Department's records were burned in Richmond in April 1865, has limited the study of Confederate battle injuries and treatment.

Wartime surgery was chiefly concerned with the repair of mangled bodies and the care of the infections that invari-

SHELTER FOR WOUNDED. It was usually necessary to throw together temporary shelters to accommodate the enormous flood of casualties after battles. This sketch depicts the aftermath of Sharpsburg.

HARPER'S PICTORIAL HISTORY OF THE GREAT REBELLION

ably followed wounds. Ether and chloroform anesthesia had been known since the 1840s; chloroform was much preferred and seems to have been readily available in the South during the war. Surgeons reported few deaths from its administration.

Most wounds were caused by the slow-moving lead conical minié ball, which, when entering the body, dragged fragments of skin and clothing with it and introduced contaminated, potentially infectious material. The soft ball would shatter any bone it struck and be itself distorted in shape. Should the ball continue farther it would produce massive tissue destruction. If it left the body, the gaping exit wound would be markedly disproportionate to the original size of the projectile.

Bullet wounds constituted approximately 93 percent of battlefield injuries; those from artillery projectiles, 6 percent; and those from sabers or bayonets, less than 1 percent. The anatomic distribution of bullet wounds was 71 percent in the extremities, 18 percent in the torso, and 11 percent in the head and neck.

The farther an injury from the trunk, the better the outcome: wounds to the extremities were rarely fatal; seven out of eight soldiers survived such injuries, albeit many with a missing or useless limb. Wounds in other parts of the body were more often fatal. Abdominal wounds had an overall fatality rate of 87 percent, and perforating injuries to the small intestine were invariably fatal. Wounds involving the colon showed up to 40 percent fatality, and those entering the peritoneal cavity but not damaging any abdominal organs were 25 percent fatal. Only 20 percent survived fracture of the pelvis. Penetrating thoracic wounds showed an overall fatality rate of 60 percent. Examination of bodies of men killed in action on battlefields has revealed that 82 percent of the mortal wounds were in the head, neck, or chest. Twelve percent of the fatalities resulted from abdominal injuries, and these were primarily a result of liver or aortic laceration with subsequent hemorrhage. Only 5 percent of the fatalities resulted from wounds of the extremities, and these too were the result of hemorrhage.

Hemorrhage among those who survived their initial wound and were brought to a field hospital was not a major problem. Those with major hemorrhage had already died on the field. Patients with hemorrhage were treated with tourniquets or compresses, although the former were frowned upon. Actually, of bleeding problems following traumatic wounds, only 10 percent occurred in the first twenty-four hours. During the "intermediary" period, from the first twenty-four hours until the onset of the inevitable wound infection, the incidence of bleeding complications would begin to increase. Hemorrhage would peak at the time of the "separation of the slough," when an area of infection and dead tissue would begin to separate from the underlying living tissue. During this dangerous time arter-

ies might reopen and bleeding resume when the dead tissue came away.

Surgical cases in which arteries had been tied also were subject to hemorrhage and suppuration. The cause of the hemorrhage was the removal of the suture around the vessel. In major surgery and amputations, the major arteries were tied off. Unsterile silk, linen, or cotton thread was used, and the ligature was left hanging out of the wound. Soaked with serum and blood, it was an excellent wick by which bacteria found their way into the swollen wound. During his daily rounds the surgeon would pull on the ligature to see if the artery had become shriveled and if the dead blood vessel would pull free; this usually meant that a firm blood clot had formed and the vessel had become sealed. Unfortunately, if such a clot had not formed, the end of the artery would pull free and hemorrhage would begin.

Controversy between preserving limbs or amputating them because of wound damage continued throughout the war. If the limb was badly damaged or had a compound fracture (one in which the bone protrudes through the skin) with splintering, immediate amputation was indicated. The risk of conservative treatment in such cases, with the

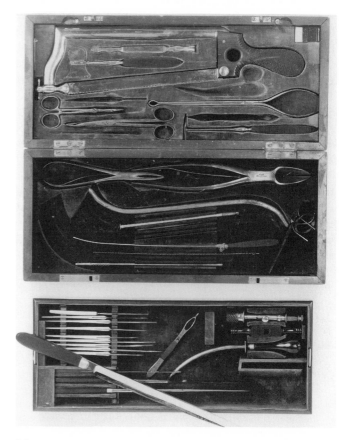

MAJOR AMPUTATION KIT. The standard kit on hand at battle sites and field hospitals.   CIVIL WAR LIBRARY AND MUSEUM, PHILADELPHIA

intervening probing for the bullet and fragments of bone, was development of one of the "surgical fevers" and at best a subsequently useless limb. Local excision of bone and soft tissue damage was more dangerous than amputation.

Debate over the proper amputation technique—whether or not to leave a flap of skin to cover the raw stump—continued throughout the war. The former involved tying the ends of arteries with the attendant risks. The latter was quicker but required removal of more of the limb. In cases of mass casualties after a battle, speed was critical, for the removal of damaged tissue, before it had time to become infected and gangrenous, was imperative. Dealing with any associated wound infections several days later seemed less of a problem.

In the 1860s bacteria were not known to cause infection; sterile technique was unknown. Postoperative infections associated with pus formation were seen so often in the healing of wounds, whether from injury or surgical treatment, that they were regarded as part of the healing process. These complications were known as "surgical fevers" and covered a spectrum of postoperative bacterial infections including erysipelas, pyemia, tetanus, osteomyelitis, and hospital gangrene. Hospital gangrene was almost invariably fatal. Its cause is unclear, but it seems to have resulted from a mixed infection by *Clostridium,* the bacteria that causes gas gangrene, and other bacteria associated with abscess formation. Pyemia ("blood poisoning") was invariably fatal and caused by widespread blood-borne infection. Soldiers in otherwise poor health—fatigued, malnourished, crowded, and depressed—were more susceptible to these complications.

Despite the state of medical information in 1860, Confederate surgeons seem to have been generally competent and achieved results equal to their Union counterparts.

BIBLIOGRAPHY

Adams, George W. *Doctors in Blue: The Medical History of the Union Army in the Civil War.* New York, 1952.
Chisolm, J. Julian. *A Manual of Military Surgery for the Use of Surgeons in the Confederate States Army.* 3d ed. Columbia, S.C., 1864. Reprint, Dayton, Ohio, 1983.
Cunningham, Horace H. *Doctors in Gray: The Confederate Medical Service.* Baton Rouge, La., 1958.
Wiley, Bell I. *The Life of Johnny Reb.* Baton Rouge, La., 1970.

HERBERT M. SCHILLER

Medical Treatments

Twentieth-century accounts of medical treatment during the Civil War make it sound like little more than a hodgepodge of folk remedies. Medical therapeutics in mid-nineteenth-century America was largely based on the medical properties of plants and was administered in elixirs, decoctions, ointments, poultices, and compounded powders and pills. There was, however, a scientific basis to much of the therapy, consistent with the state of medical knowledge in that era. Review of texts on therapeutics from the 1840s and 1850s reveals that more than two-thirds of the substances then considered effective were of vegetable origin.

These medicines, and other supplies, were plentiful in Southern cities at the beginning of the war, but they could not be expected to last long. Although supplies captured from the enemy provided an occasional bonanza, this was not a reliable source. Shortly after fighting began, the War Department sent Caleb Huse to Britain to serve as purchasing agent abroad. Although his primary charge was the obtaining of ordnance, part of his budget was for medical supplies. An office of the Medical Department was established at Nassau to coordinate the exchange of cotton and the collection of medical supplies to be brought in by blockade runners. Another source of needed medical supplies was the cotton-starved North. This government-sanctioned trade occurred along the Mississippi River, especially south of Memphis, but was erratic and produced only a little medicine. Individuals sympathetic with the Confederacy occasionally smuggled medicine across the changing borders, but such goods were few in number.

Early in the war the Medical Department established some eight depots under the supervision of physician medical purveyors who bought, stored, and distributed supplies. By war's end, such sites had increased fourfold. Many were located near ports of entry and near the manufacturing centers that arose throughout the Confederacy.

With external supplies unsure at best, it fell to the Confederate Medical Department to develop its own pharmaceutical laboratories. The nine major facilities were located in North and South Carolina, Georgia, Alabama, and Texas. Pharmacists and chemists staffed the facilities. Alcohol was distilled from grain, and white poppies were cultivated for gum opium, necessary for the production of morphine. Locally manufactured chloroform was plentiful. Many of the pharmaceutical facilities had their own botanical farms to supply needed medical plants.

Under the direction of Surgeon General Samuel Preston Moore, Francis P. Porcher, a teacher of materia medica and therapeutics (equivalent to today's pharmacology) in the then-closed medical school in Charleston, began his *Resources of the Southern Fields and Forests, Medical, Economical, and Agricultural,* which discussed the medical properties of over four hundred native plants. The book was referenced to dozens of other books of materia medica, some of them of recent publication. Copies of Porcher's book were sent to medical officers, and extracts were published in local newspapers to encourage the collection of needed plants.

Circuit riders from the medical depots collected plants and encouraged citizens to help. By the middle of the war, eight tons of herbal medicines had been prepared and thirty-two tons of roots and leaves awaited processing.

Among the illnesses thought to respond to herbal remedies were acute diarrhea and dysentery, which, depending on their severity, were sometimes treated with cathartics to speed the removal of the offending agent. Chronic disorders of the bowels were treated with products with astringent properties—for example, decoction of root of blackberry, dried bark of dogwood, sweet-scented water lily, ground root of cranesbill, root of marsh rosemary, pomegranate rind, tea of water pepper, syrup of unripe persimmons, tea of black alder bark and berries, decoction of white oak bark, and black oak galls. The problem in treating diarrhea and dysentery this way was that they were only symptoms of a variety of infectious and noninfectious diseases, not diseases themselves. Interestingly, most of the items mentioned by Porcher are included in George B. Wood's authoritative and contemporary *Treatise on Therapeutics and Pharmacology, or Materia Medica.* In short, these remedies were state of the art for their time.

Malaria was a disease whose true cause was unknown but that could be effectively treated with quinine, isolated from the bark of the cinchona tree. In the absence of quinine, the Medical Department recommended a mixture of dogwood, poplar, and willow bark mixed with whiskey. The use of these tree barks, separately or together, was recognized by Wood in his text. Scurvy was yet another disease whose cause, although not completely known, was felt to be related to a diet deficient in fresh fruit and meat. Confederate medical authorities recognized that sorrel eaten as a salad or in soup was a cure or preventive of scurvy. Other diseases or groups of diseases of uncertain cause were frequently grouped according to presenting signs and patient symptoms. Pneumonias, urethral discharges resulting from venereal diseases, pelvic pain, and the urinary burning of bladder infections were treated as if they were diseases themselves.

Civilians also suffered from problems in addition to those experienced by the men in uniformed service. Because adult males were absent from small farms, food production decreased, and the ability of families to earn money to purchase necessities, such as clothing and staples, became increasingly limited. Scarcity of food and increasing costs caused malnutrition in the women, old men, and children left behind. Public assistance by local government was largely unknown, although churches and some communities provided a small amount of relief for a few. The availability of medical care became increasingly limited by the absence of doctors and medicines needed by the military.

A large variety of remedies that experience had shown effective or that relieved certain symptoms of disease were available, and those used by the Confederate physicians differed little from those employed by their Union counterparts. Although these remedies seem curious today, they represented what was felt to be sound medical treatment, based on reports by reputable physicians in Europe and America during the previous fifty years. Some possessed merit; others did not. They did reflect, however, the trial-and-error observations recorded in medical journals and texts of the day. It would not be until the physiological changes that accompany particular diseases were understood that a more rational approach to medical treatment could be instituted.

BIBLIOGRAPHY

Blake, John B. "Women and Medicine in Ante-Bellum America." *Bulletin of the History of Medicine* 39 (March–April 1965): 99–123.

Cunningham, Horace H. *Doctors in Gray: The Confederate Medical Service.* Baton Rouge, La., 1958.

Medical and Surgical History of the War of Rebellion. 6 vols. Washington, D.C., 1875–1888. Reprinted as *The Medical and Surgical History of the Civil War.* Edited by James I. Robertson, Jr. 14 vols. Wilmington, N.C., 1990–1991.

Porcher, Francis P. *Resources of the Southern Fields and Forests, Medical, Economical, and Agricultural.* Charleston, S.C., 1863. Reprint, New York, 1970.

Wood, George B. *Treatise on Therapeutics and Pharmacology, or Materia Medica.* Philadelphia, 1856.

HERBERT M. SCHILLER

Medical Training

Medical training in the middle third of the nineteenth century varied greatly among the schools. In addition to the few university-affiliated schools, some of which maintained standards of educational excellence, proprietary schools abounded. These latter, run for profit and owned and operated by physicians, offered shortened instruction. The usual course of classroom lectures consisted of theory and practice (medicine), materia medica (pharmacology), chemistry, anatomy, surgery, and obstetrics. The course of instruction at good schools might last one year, while that at proprietary schools was much shorter, in some cases six weeks or less. Rarely was a school affiliated with a hospital; none offered much in the way of practical experience with patients. If clinical experience was obtained it was through apprenticeship to an established physician. State licensing boards did not exist. Most trained physicians were products of the proprietary schools and it was these men who staffed the medical corps.

Prior to the war there was little emphasis in the South on surgery and none on military medicine or surgery. Most Southerners seeking formal medical education attended schools in the North or abroad in preference to the Southern medical schools located in Charleston, Charlottesville, Augusta, Richmond, Mobile, and Nashville. The curriculum of these six schools was similar to that of the most prominent institutions in the Northeast; the course of instruction lasted about six months. As in the North, many proprietary schools also existed, producing marginal practitioners at best.

During the first months of the war, all the reputable Southern medical schools closed except the Medical College of Virginia. Located in Richmond, this school quickly adapted to wartime conditions. In addition to attending lectures, the students studied wounds and diseases firsthand in the numerous city hospitals as well as the field hospitals of the Army of Northern Virginia. During the course of the war, the Medical College of Virginia graduated four hundred students. But these new doctors and the existing physicians were hardly sufficient to care for the 600,000 Confederate soldiers mobilized during those years.

To provide some continuing education for military physicians, the Surgeon General's Office oversaw the publication of a medical journal as well as several texts on military surgery. And with the ever-tightening blockade preventing the importation of medicines, the surgeon general encouraged Francis P. Porcher to publish a medical botany in 1863 to provide guidance on the use of native herbs in the treatment of disease.

BIBLIOGRAPHY

Chisolm, J. Julian. *A Manual of Military Surgery for the Use of Surgeons in the Confederate States Army.* 3d ed. Columbia, S.C., 1864. Reprint, Dayton, Ohio, 1983.
The Confederate States Medical and Surgical Journal. 2 vols. Richmond, Va., 1862–1864. Reprint, Metuchen, N.J., 1976.
Cunningham, Horace H. *Doctors in Gray: The Confederate Medical Service.* Baton Rouge, La., 1958.
Porcher, Francis P. *Resources of the Southern Fields and Forests, Medical, Economical, and Agricultural.* Charleston, S.C., 1863. Reprint, New York, 1970.

HERBERT M. SCHILLER

HÉBERT, LOUIS (1820–1901), brigadier general. Born in Iberville Parish, Louisiana, Hébert was a cousin of Brig. Gen. Paul O. Hébert and brother-in-law of Brig. Gen. Walter H. Stevens. Part of the sugar planter aristocracy, he received a private education before graduating from Jefferson College in St. James Parish. Hébert attended West Point, graduating in 1845, third in a class of forty-one, but his military career was cut short when he resigned in 1847 to take over the family plantation. He was active in the state militia, a member of the state senate, the state's chief engineer, and served on the Board of Public Works.

When the war began, Hébert became colonel of the Third Louisiana Infantry. His adherence to strict military procedures initially made him unpopular, but he eventually won the men's respect. He fought at Wilson's Creek, Missouri, in August 1861, and was captured at Elkhorn Tavern, Arkansas, in March 1862. After being exchanged, Hébert was promoted to brigadier general on May 26, 1862, and joined Sterling Price's army in Mississippi. He fought at Iuka, Mississippi, in September 1862 and took command of Henry Little's division after Little was killed. In the fall of 1862 he took a brigade to join the defenders of Vicksburg, surrendering with the rest of the army on July 4, 1863. After a second exchange, Hébert was ordered to North Carolina where he commanded the heavy artillery around Fort Fisher and acted as chief engineer of the Department of North Carolina, remaining there until the war ended. His wartime record had been distinguished, although not particularly noteworthy.

Following the war Hébert worked as a newspaper editor and teacher. He died in St. Martin Parish on January 7, 1901, and was buried in Breaux Bridge.

BIBLIOGRAPHY

Shea, William L., and Earl J. Hess. *Pea Ridge: Civil War Campaign in the West.* Chapel Hill, N.C., 1992.
Tunnard, William H. *A Southern Record: The History of the Third Regiment Louisiana Infantry.* Baton Rouge, La., 1866. Reprint, Dayton, Ohio, 1970.

ANNE J. BAILEY

HÉBERT, PAUL O. (1818–1880), brigadier general. Born December 12, 1818, in Iberville Parish, Louisiana, Paul Octave Hébert attended Jefferson College where he graduated first in his class in 1836. He continued his distinguished academic career at West Point by graduating in 1840 first in a class of forty-two that included William Tecumseh Sherman and George H. Thomas. Hébert taught engineering at West Point but resigned in 1845 to become chief engineer of Louisiana. Although he had resigned from the army, he participated in the Mexican War as lieutenant colonel of the Third and Fourteenth Infantries, winning a brevet as colonel for gallantry at Molino del Rey. In 1852, only thirty-four years old, he was elected governor of Louisiana.

When the Civil War began, Hébert was commissioned colonel of the First Louisiana Artillery and on August 17, 1861, was promoted to brigadier general. He commanded the Department of Texas, the Galveston defenses, and the Subdistrict of North Louisiana during the Vicksburg campaign. His only action in battle was at Milliken's Bend, Louisiana, in June 1863, and in August he surrendered the town of Monroe to Federal soldiers rather than fight. On

PAUL O. HÉBERT.   LIBRARY OF CONGRESS

June 19, 1865, he relinquished the Department of Texas to the U.S. Army.

After the war Hébert was active in the Democratic party. He died in New Orleans on August 29, 1880, and is buried near Bayou Goula, Louisiana. He was a cousin of Gen. Louis Hébert.

BIBLIOGRAPHY

Bearss, Edwin Cole. *The Vicksburg Campaign.* Vol. 3. Dayton, Ohio, 1986.

Fay, Edwin H. *This Infernal War.* Austin, Tex., 1958.

ANNE J. BAILEY

HEISKELL, J. B. (1823–1913), congressman from Tennessee. The eldest of nine children of the editor and publisher of the *Knoxville Register,* one of the most respected and influential newspapers in the region, Joseph Brown Heiskell graduated from East Tennessee College (1840), read law under Finley Gillespie of Madisonville, and commenced his practice in Monroe County before relocating in Rogersville and marrying a daughter of John A. McKinney, a prominent member of the Rogersville bar. Like his father and uncle before him, Heiskell occupied a seat in the Tennessee legislature (1857–1859), where he chaired the committee that prepared the first legal code for the state.

A staunch Whig, Heiskell opposed secession but joined the rebellion after Abraham Lincoln's call for volunteers and ran on a pro-Confederate ticket for the Provisional Congress. Although he lost the August 1861 election for the First District of Tennessee by an overwhelming margin to Unionist T. A. R. Nelson, he was elected to the First Confederate Congress three months later, after the legislature had redistricted the state and many Unionists stayed away from the polls.

Taking his seat in Richmond on February 18, 1862, the opening day of the first session, Heiskell served continually and rarely missed a vote through the end of the second session in mid-October later that year. A member of the Judiciary and War Tax committees, he introduced as many as twenty-one bills and resolutions. Most had to do with fiscal matters, though one measure sought to facilitate the production of small arms, another called for an investigation of ordnance factories in Richmond, and another would have allowed draft exemptions to persons engaged in the manufacture of iron, lead, and copper, of whom there was a considerable number in upper eastern Tennessee.

During his first two sessions in office, Heiskell proved to be decidedly pro-administration, arguing and voting in favor of two conscription bills and the suspension of the habeas corpus writ. At the same time he firmly believed that it was the duty of the Confederate government to remunerate its citizens for losses sustained during the war, and he supported regulating by law the seizure and impressment of private property for the use of the military. Undoubtedly the most intriguing (and controversial) proposal introduced by Heiskell was his resolution of September 10, 1862, in which he advocated the taking of hostages in retaliation for the capture and imprisonment of Southern citizens and other noncombatants—that is, to arrest for the purpose of later exchanging not mere farmers and mechanics but "men prominent in their respective neighborhoods for their adhesion to the anti-slavery, black republican, anti-Christian government in Washington."

In the third and fourth sessions, from January 1863 to February 1864, Heiskell sponsored another twenty bills, distinguishing himself as one of the more active members of the Tennessee delegation, despite obtaining a leave of absence so that he could return home, where he served conspicuously as a voluntary aide-de-camp for Confederate forces in the area. Back in Richmond, Heiskell remained concerned about military affairs in eastern Tennessee, as witnessed by his calls for investigations of the Confederate disaster at Fishing Creek, Kentucky (in which his brother, Carrick W. Heiskell, then a captain of the Nineteenth Tennessee Infantry, had participated), and the operations of Gen. John S. Williams at Blue Springs, Tennessee. Perhaps the most curious measure he brought forward during this period was a January 1864 resolution that instructed the congressional doorkeeper to regulate the heating in the House "so as to preserve a temperature not higher than sixty-two degrees Fahrenheit." On major issues he generally stood by the president, voting in favor of a direct tax, the third Conscription Law, and the abolition of the practice of hiring substitutes for military service. He also assumed a hard-line position on a proposed prisoner of war exchange, approving (though in the minority) Jefferson Davis's refusal to recognize Gen. Benjamin F. Butler as a legitimate Federal exchange agent. Congress's vote on this issue prompted Heiskell's resignation in February 1864, some ten days before Congress adjourned.

Reelected unanimously to the Second Confederate Congress, Heiskell assumed increased responsibilities by serving on as many as five committees. Contrary to what has been written, he continued to play an active role in government, contributing ten additional pieces of legislation during the first session. For example, in May 1864, in the midst of the Wilderness campaign, he was the chief sponsor in the House of a bill authorizing President Davis to suspend the writ of habeas corpus and declare martial law in Richmond. Yet he also differed with Davis by criticizing the inequality of prices paid under impressment laws, complaining bitterly about the performance and abilities of the postmaster general, and, in his last recorded action in Congress, voting with the majority on June 14, 1864, against turning over control of the railroads to the Confederate military.

By the time Congress reconvened in November 1864 for what turned out to be its final session, Heiskell was in the enemy's hands, having been captured some three months earlier while at home. The details of his surrender are sketchy, but according to published reports it appears that he walked to meet the Federals before they entered Rogersville, prompting President Abraham Lincoln to question whether Heiskell "was scared and wanted to save his skin." The object of intense, high-level negotiations for a special prisoner exchange that never materialized, Heiskell remained confined in Camp Chase, Ohio, until the end of hostilities. In the meantime arrangements were made for his salary and mileage per diem to be drawn by his wife, Sarah, to help care for their five children.

Following the war, Heiskell moved to Memphis, where he reestablished his legal practice and was joined by his brother, Carrick, and fellow congressional colleagues Landon Carter Haynes and William G. Swan, among other eastern Tennessee émigrés. Although he was excepted from Andrew Johnson's amnesty proclamation of May 1865, there is no record that he requested a pardon or ever received one. Nevertheless, this unreconstructed Confederate who early in the war had vowed never to "affiliate with a people who are guilty of an invasion of [Southern] soil" eventually held public office again, serving as a delegate to the state constitutional convention in 1870 and as attorney general and court reporter of Tennessee (1870–1878), before rejoining his Memphis law firm. Interestingly, one of Heiskell's sons, Frederick, an 1872 graduate of Washington and Lee University, married a daughter of Senator Lucius Q. C. Lamar of Mississippi, a New South spokesman.

BIBLIOGRAPHY

Green, John W. *Law and Lawyers.* Jackson, Tenn., 1950.
Journal of the Congress of the Confederate States of America, 1861–1865. 7 vols. Washington, D.C., 1904–1905.
Thomas A. R. Nelson Papers. McClung Collection. Knox County Public Library, Knoxville, Tenn.
U.S. War Department. *War of the Rebellion: A Compilation of the Official Records of the Union and Confederate Armies.* Washington, D.C., 1880–1901. Ser. 1, vol. 39, pt. 2, pp. 299–300, 303.
Warner, Ezra J., and W. Buck Yearns. *Biographical Register of the Confederate Congress.* Baton Rouge, La., 1975.

R. B. ROSENBURG

HELM, BENJAMIN HARDIN (1831–1863), brigadier general. Born into a prominent Bardstown, Kentucky, family on June 2, 1831, Helm was a brother-in-law of Mrs. Abraham Lincoln (through his 1856 marriage to Emily Todd). He graduated from the U.S. Military Academy in 1851, ninth of forty-two in his class. On October 9, 1852, he resigned from the U.S. Army, in which he was a second lieutenant in the Second Dragoon Regiment. A "Southern rights Democrat," he practiced law, sat in the state legislature (1855–1856), and served as state's attorney (1856–1858).

At the beginning of the Civil War Helm declined an offered appointment as major (paymaster) in the Federal army. While Kentucky tried to remain neutral, he served as an assistant inspector general of the state guard. He was, however, a Confederate supporter, and as early as May 1861 he applied for a commission in the Southern army. He helped recruit the First Kentucky Cavalry Regiment for Confederate service and on October 19, 1861, was commissioned as the regiment's colonel.

Promoted to brigadier general March 14, 1862, Helm served in Mississippi and Louisiana until February 15, 1863, when he was assigned to command what had been

BENJAMIN HARDIN HELM.   LIBRARY OF CONGRESS

Brig. Gen. Roger W. Hanson's brigade in the Army of Tennessee. Helm was wounded on September 20, 1863, at the Battle of Chickamauga and died the next day. His body was first buried in Atlanta, Georgia, but in the 1880s it was moved to the Helm Cemetery in Elizabethtown, Kentucky.

BIBLIOGRAPHY

McMurtry, Robert G. "Confederate General Ben Hardin Helm." *Filson Club Historical Quarterly* 32 (1958): 311–328.

Warner, Ezra J. *Generals in Gray: Lives of the Confederate Commanders.* Baton Rouge, La., 1959.

RICHARD M. McMURRY

HELPER, HINTON ROWAN (1829–1909), abolitionist. Helper was born in the North Carolina up-country, the son of a small farmer. In the mid-1850s, after writing a book about his failed attempt to strike it rich in California's gold fields, he wrote *The Impending Crisis of the South: How to Meet It,* a 413-page tome that attacked slaveholders for forcing onto nonslaveholders a political economy that enriched the few while preventing economic development in the South as a whole. In the book, Helper called for uncompensated emancipation of all slaves and for their subsequent colonization outside the United States.

When the *Impending Crisis* was first published in New York in 1857, it provoked little stir in either the North or the South, much to Helper's disappointment. He therefore moved to New York and sought to market the work through a variety of schemes. All were unsuccessful, although he did manage to persuade Horace Greeley to give the book a favorable review in the *New York Tribune.* During the

presidential campaign of 1859, Greeley also raised $19,000 to pay for about 100,000 copies of a shorter edition of the book, *The Compendium of the Impending Crisis,* which was then distributed widely by the Republican party as a campaign document. The book, however, first came to national attention during the contest for Speaker of the House of Representatives in January 1860 when John B. Clark, a Democratic congressman from Missouri, presented a resolution calling *The Impending Crisis* "insurrectionary and hostile to the domestic peace and tranquility of the country." Clark argued that no one who endorsed its principles, as had Republican nominee John Sherman of Ohio, was "fit to be Speaker of this House." The ensuing controversy gave the Democrats, the minority party in the House, a means by which to brand the Republicans a party of disunion and thereby defeat Sherman's bid for the Speaker's chair. Thereafter, Southern Democrats pointed to *The Impending Crisis* as proof that the Republicans planned to abolish slavery immediately and destroy the South.

Helper realized little profit from *The Impending Crisis* or the controversy that it produced, however, and spent the remainder of his life working in poorly paying civil service jobs, serving as a collection agent for private debts, and writing four other unprofitable books, three of them violently racist in tone. He died by his own hand, bitter and virtually penniless, in Washington, D.C.

BIBLIOGRAPHY

Bailey, Hugh C. *Hinton Rowan Helper: Abolitionist-Racist.* University, Ala., 1965.

Helper, Hinton Rowan. *The Impending Crisis of the South: How to Meet It.* Edited by George M. Frederickson. Cambridge, Mass., 1968.

WAYNE K. DURRILL

HEMPHILL, JOHN (1803–1862), congressman from Texas. Hemphill was born in South Carolina on December 18, 1803. He moved to Texas in 1838 and became a prominent attorney, judge, and Democratic politician from Washington-on-the-Brazos. He served in the state constitutional convention in 1845 and was chief justice of the Texas Supreme Court from 1846 to 1858. In 1858 the state legislature elected him to the U.S. Senate.

In Washington, Hemphill was a strong spokesman for Southern rights. With other Southern senators, he openly resisted attempts to achieve a political compromise to the sectional problem following the election of President Abraham Lincoln. In response to efforts to submit the Crittenden Compromise to a popular vote, Hemphill joined with fourteen other Southern senators on January 5, 1861, and called for immediate secession and the meeting of a convention at Montgomery, Alabama, on February 15 to organize a confederacy. They agreed not to resign from the U.S. Senate, however, so that they could prevent the Republicans from taking action that might interfere with their efforts. On January 16, Hemphill joined with six other Southern senators in abstaining on a vote that practically killed the Crittenden Compromise. After Texas seceded on February 1, Hemphill left the capital, although he did not resign from the Senate. He was officially expelled from that body on July 11, 1861.

The secession convention at Austin elected Hemphill as one of Texas's seven delegates to the Provisional Congress. The Texas delegation arrived in Montgomery too late to take part in the writing of the Confederate Constitution or the election of officers. Nevertheless, Hemphill was an active member of the Congress. As an accomplished jurist, he devoted much of his attention to work on the House special committee charged with adapting the laws of the United States for use by the Confederacy. In November 1861, Hemphill ran for one of the Senate seats in the First Congress, but the Texas legislature elected Williamson S. Oldham instead. Hemphill died at Richmond while the Provisional Congress was still in session on January 4, 1862.

BIBLIOGRAPHY

Lynch, James D. *Bench and Bar of Texas*. St. Louis, Mo., 1885.
Warner, Ezra J., and W. Buck Yearns. *Biographical Register of the Confederate Congress*. Baton Rouge, La., 1975.

CARL H. MONEYHON

HENRY, GUSTAVUS ADOLPHUS (1804–1880), congressman from Tennessee.

Born in Scott County, Kentucky, October 8, 1804, Henry graduated in 1825 from Transylvania University of Lexington, where he developed a fast friendship with Jefferson Davis, also a student there. He studied law in Hopkinsville and practiced there until his removal to Clarksville, Tennessee, in 1833. Meanwhile he served in the Kentucky House of Representatives (1831–1833).

In Clarksville, Henry developed a law practice and several civic and commercial enterprises, including founding two insurance companies and serving as a trustee of two private schools. He was a vestryman and senior warden in the Episcopal church in Clarksville for many years.

But his prime interest was politics and he brought his affection for the Whig Henry Clay to Tennessee, the home state of the Democrat Andrew Jackson, Clay's nemesis. Some prominent politicians of the state formed the Whig party in opposition to Jackson and accepted Henry as a leader of the new party. Henry served as a Whig presidential elector in the 1840s and 1850s and was elected to the state house of representatives in 1851.

Henry became the Whig nominee for governor in 1853. The Whigs had won six of the last nine gubernatorial elections, but dissension in their ranks made their prospects dubious this time. Party leaders hoped that Henry—widely known as the "Eagle Orator" because of his skill as a debater and stump speaker—could heal party dissension and bring another victory. They were encouraged when Democrats nominated Congressman Andrew Johnson of Greeneville, who, though a skilled campaigner, lacked Henry's polish and refinement. But the Democrats, always strong in the central counties, won enough votes in the mountain area to carry the election. Johnson, out of 124,000 votes cast, won by a scant 2,000-vote majority.

Henry remained interested in politics, but with the decline of the Whigs in the 1850s his prestige and public appeal began to erode. Nevertheless, in 1860 he became actively involved in the presidential campaign and joined with many Whigs who, noting with apprehension the increasing sectional disharmony, tried to heal the breach by forming the Constitutional Union party. That group, the only national party now that Democrats had split along sectional lines, pledged its support for "the Constitution of our country, the Union of the states, and the enforcement of the laws," and joined forces behind the candidacy of former Whig senator John Bell of Tennessee. Henry participated in the Whig convention in Baltimore and returned to Tennessee to campaign for Bell. In the November elections Abraham Lincoln won, although Bell reaped the electoral vote of his home state—thanks in large measure to the work of Henry and other Whigs.

With the advent of secession and civil war, Henry followed a typical Whig pattern: he opposed secession but became a supporter of the Southern cause at the prospect of invasion and war. In May 1861, Governor Isham G. Harris, in an effort to woo other Tennessee Whigs, appointed Henry a commissioner to meet with Confederate leaders and enter the state of Tennessee into a "military league" with the South. These acts were preparatory to secession, and in the following month Tennesseans approved by a large majority union with the Confederacy. Henry then was chosen by legislators as one of the state's two senators.

As a senator, Henry attended sessions regularly and actively supported President Davis. One writer has described him as an "ultra nationalist"; as such, he, like other Tennesseans in Congress, had little sympathy for the state rights position voiced by some from the Deep South. As the war progressed and Southern military ranks thinned, he sponsored a bill to draft all able-bodied men between the ages of sixteen and sixty. He also proposed impressing all slaves if military leaders required them and repudiating two-thirds of the paper currency. He urged that the war be carried into enemy territory and, after 1862, that forces in large numbers be sent into Tennessee to reclaim that state.

He argued for greater unity within the military and wanted Robert E. Lee to be placed in full command of all the forces. During the war he continued to be heard not infrequently as the Eagle Orator; on one occasion, when he spoke in Richmond, Davis observed that in his "powerful speech" he exhibited "eloquence as inspiring as the notes of the bugle sounding the charge when the hosts are about to join in battle."

After the war Henry returned to the practice of law in Clarksville. He did not enter politics actively except for some behind-the-scenes work within the Democratic party. In 1874, at the age of seventy, he was chosen as chairman of the state Democratic convention. He died September 10, 1880, at Emerald Hill, his Clarksville home, and was buried in Greenwood Cemetery.

BIBLIOGRAPHY

Beach, Ursula. *Along the Warioto, or a History of Montgomery County, Tennessee.* Nashville, Tenn., 1964.

Bergeron, Paul. *Antebellum Politics in Tennessee.* Lexington, Ky., 1982.

McBride, Robert, and Dan M. Robison. *Biographical Directory of the Tennessee General Assembly.* Vol. 1. Nashville, Tenn., 1975.

Moore, John T., and A. P. Foster. *Tennessee: the Volunteer State.* Vol. 2. Nashville, Tenn., 1923.

Titus, W. P. *Picturesque Clarksville, Past and Present.* Clarksville, Tenn., 1887.

Warner, Ezra J., and W. Buck Yearns. *Biographical Register of the Confederate Congress.* Baton Rouge, La., 1975.

Journal of the Congress of the Confederate States of America, 1861–1865. 7 vols. Washington, D.C., 1904–1905.

Vandiver, Frank E. "Proceedings of the Second Confederate Congress." *Southern Historical Society Papers* 51–52 (1958). Reprint, Wilmington, N.C., 1992.

ROBERT E. CORLEW

HENRY AND DONELSON CAMPAIGN.

The Tennessee and Cumberland rivers in western Kentucky and middle Tennessee from February 3 through February 16, 1862, witnessed the creation of a vital link in the ultimate Union victory. Joint operations between land and naval forces on these rivers proved capable of surmounting Confederate position defense and indecisive leadership to capture Forts Henry and Donelson. In this campaign Ulysses S. Grant, together with his naval colleague Andrew Hull Foote, effected the first major penetration of the Confederacy in the West. Drawing upon antebellum perception of western rivers as valuable travel arteries of communication and commerce, Union authorities settled on the Mississippi valley with its tributary rivers like the Tennessee and Cumberland as the proper avenues of advance. The Confederate theater commander, Gen. Albert Sidney Johnston, was virtually powerless to blunt such an advance, although command mistakes on his part accelerated the opportunity.

Political, economic, and military strategic goals of the Lincoln administration in the West ultimately rested upon reopening western rivers. Johnston, whose responsibilities stretched from the Appalachian Mountains to beyond the Mississippi River, had neither men nor matériel to conduct a proper defense of such a vast area. He concentrated his poorly trained, mostly sick, and inadequately supplied force of forty thousand men at strong points like Columbus, Kentucky, on the Mississippi, and Bowling Green, Kentucky, astride the Louisville and Nashville Railroad. He relied upon two earthen fortifications, constructed by the Tennessee state government about twelve miles apart in frontierlike Stewart County, Tennessee, to hold where the twin rivers bisected his defense line. Inadequately sited, constructed haltingly by slave gangs and soldiers, neglected by the high command, Forts Henry and Donelson were overlooked by Johnston and senior Confederate officials until the moment of crisis. Yet these forts guarded the vital upper heartland where rich mineral and agricultural resources and important cities like Clarksville and Nashville, the Tennessee state capital and munitions center, lay directly behind Johnston's forward defenses. The rivers held the key to unlocking this treasure for the Union.

Northern ownership of most of the steamboat fleet on western rivers denied this resource to the Confederacy. But during the autumn of 1861 the Union government saw the merit in forging a gunboat flotilla. When teamed with steamboats as troop transports, the means of mounting a strike force to crack Johnston's line became apparent. Henry W. Halleck, Federal commander of the Department of Missouri, balked at first, fearing Johnston's perceived strength and the inadequacies of his own subordinates, and having misgivings about Grant. But Grant and Foote finally secured Halleck's grudging support for a rapid attack via the rivers.

The Union expeditionary force of fifteen thousand men, supported by seven gunboats, some armored, departed river staging areas like Cairo, Illinois, and Paducah, Kentucky, on February 3. Riding floodwaters of the swollen Tennessee, they moved virtually undetected to within striking distance of Fort Henry by February 6. Here, Kentuckian Lloyd Tilghman tried desperately to finish an uncompleted Fort Heiman on high ground across from a flooded Fort Henry and prepare his defenses. He was unprepared when Grant and Foote struck and only barely ordered his infantry to escape overland to Fort Donelson. Tilghman remained behind with a "forlorn hope" of about a hundred artillerymen to conduct an "honorable" defense against the gunboats. Meanwhile, Grant's soldiers became mired in the mud as his divisions under Generals John Alexander McClernand and Charles Ferguson Smith attempted to move on the forts by country roads.

Foote refused to be slowed by the army. Under orders from Grant to effect a coordinated attack, the gunboats pushed forward and engaged Tilghman's heavy seacoast fortress guns by early afternoon on February 6. The ensuing battle proved no contest. The Confederate gunners damaged several of the gunboats before virtually all their cannon were rendered inoperable and carnage was widespread among the gunners. Foote demanded unconditional surrender (the first rendering of that phrase) and Tilghman had no choice. Federal naval personnel simply rowed through the fort's sally port onto a flooded parade ground to take the Confederate's sword. Fort Henry cost the Union forces eleven killed, thirty-one wounded, and five missing. Tilghman suffered five killed and eleven wounded, with the rest of his force remaining at the fort captured.

The effect of the Union victory was electric. As Grant consolidated his position on the high ground around Fort Henry in preparation to moving on to Fort Donelson, the navy again took the initiative. A flotilla under Comm. S. L. Phelps raided 150 miles up the Tennessee River, cutting the railroad bridge above Fort Henry, spreading havoc along the way, and destroying quantities of war matériel. Before being stopped near Muscle Shoals, Alabama, this demonstration of Union naval power sent shock waves among Confederate military and the public alike. Lincoln's gunboats had

become a "superweapon." Meanwhile, on February 7, Johnston realized his Bowling Green position was no longer tenable and ordered a retreat to Nashville. He sent subordinates with their commands to cover his flank at Fort Donelson.

Johnston eventually dispatched John B. Floyd, Gideon Pillow, Simon Bolivar Buckner, and Bushrod Rust Johnson, together with upwards of eighteen thousand Confederates to defend Fort Donelson. His instructions were vague, but, in his mind at least, the army was to conduct a holding action long enough for the main Army of Central Kentucky to retire behind the Cumberland at Nashville. With Floyd (the most inexperienced of the generals) as senior commander, and none of the four a leader of first rank at this point in the war, the stage was set for disaster. Unit commanders and their men, while equally untried, were more combative, but with the exception of cavalry led by an unknown Tennessee colonel, Nathan Bedford Forrest, no Confederates contested Grant's march from Fort Henry on February 12. Union forces moved into position virtually without opposition, while Foote's flotilla steamed back down the Tennessee, up the Ohio, and thence up the Cumberland to help.

Action at Fort Donelson began on February 13. While awaiting Foote's arrival, Grant issued instructions to McClernand and Smith to move into position but avoid any

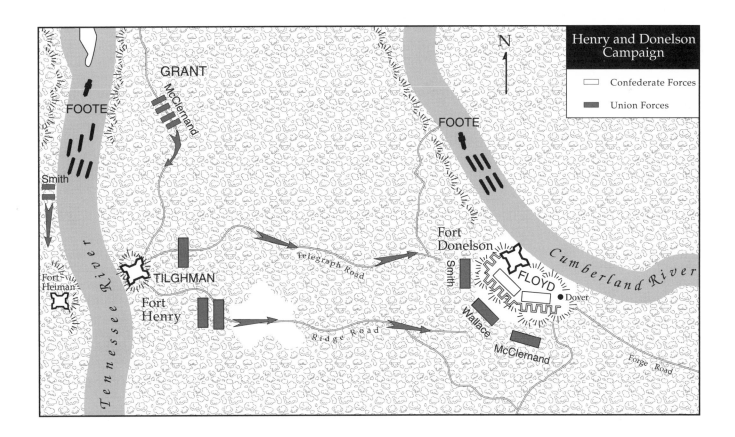

general engagement with the Confederates. Contrary to orders, both McClernand and Smith nudged forward in probing attacks that were repulsed. At one point, with the weather warm and balmy, dry leaves in front of a battery position caught fire, threatening Union wounded with horrible death. Their adversaries leaped from their rifle pits to help save them in a touch typical of later scenes in this war between brothers. By nightfall, Grant realized that Fort Donelson would be no easy repetition of the earlier victory. He ordered reserves forward from Fort Henry to form a third division under Lew Wallace and awaited Foote to make a naval attack the next day.

The youthful Union soldiers had jettisoned blankets and overcoats during the warm overland march from Fort Henry, but now the spring weather turned bitterly cold and blizzardlike overnight. Fires were forbidden on both sides, and everyone suffered. February 14 found two shivering armies capable of little more than sharpshooting and skirmishing. That afternoon, however, the Union navy approached Fort Donelson's two water batteries. This time the battle proved no contest for the gunboats. Confederate artillerists occupied commanding heights and had had weeks of training. Foote chose to run his ironclads close in toward the enemy guns, and the Southern gunners exacted a terrible toll. Virtually all the Union gunboats suffered damage, Foote was wounded, his flagship a shambles, and the myth of Lincoln's gunboats was shattered forever. Amid shouts of victory by the Confederates, their generals decided to escape the Fort Donelson trap.

At dawn the next day, Pillow's and Buckner's divisions went forward with a rush through the frozen countryside in an effort to beat back McClernand's division blocking the roads to Nashville and freedom. They succeeded handsomely. By noon not only was McClernand routed, but the roads lay wide open. Grant remained unaware of the impending disaster, having left headquarters that morning to consult with the wounded Foote aboard his flagship. McClernand's calls for help finally caused Lew Wallace to wheel his command into a blocking position to stymie the Confederate drive. Grant received word of the defeat and returned to rally his army. He told McClernand and Wallace, "Gentlemen, the position on our right must be retaken" and left it to them to accomplish the mission. Summoning his old West Point mentor, C. F. Smith, he explained that the Confederates had undoubtedly evacuated some of their lines to conduct the assault and ordered Smith to drive forward and capture the fort. More anxiously, he sent a dispatch to Foote saying that the army was in danger and asking for naval intervention.

Meanwhile, the Confederate generals dithered, argued, misread one another's concept of mission, and lost the initiative and hence the battle. Floyd and Buckner understood that once victory had been attained, the army would march off, leaving artillery and rear-area troops to the mercy of the enemy. Pillow demurred, wanting to hold Tennessee soil as long as possible and to evacuate the whole garrison. In the end, with the hour late and Union counterattacks beginning to press the tired Confederates, the four men decided to retire for the night, gather up supplies, wounded, artillery, and the like, and evacuate at dawn on February 16. But C. F. Smith's division had knifed forward and captured Buckner's outer defense line, thus

USS CARONDELET ATTACKING FORT DONELSON, FEBRUARY 13, 1862.   NAVAL HISTORICAL CENTER, WASHINGTON, D.C.

breaching Confederate fortifications and causing the Kentuckian to have grave reservations about further defense.

Confederate scouts searched for avenues of escape that night. Army doctors counseled that the men could not survive crossing frozen creeks and the long trek to Nashville. Buckner became gripped by battle fatigue and fears of Smith's division; Pillow urged continued resistance; Floyd vacillated. Time was wasted, and in a midnight council that has since defied understanding, a decision was made to surrender to Grant on the morrow. Forrest stalked angrily into the night, vowing to escape. Floyd and Pillow, fearing punishment at the hands of Union authorities, similarly deserted, passing command to Buckner in the famous opéra bouffe episode derided by subsequent generations. Floyd's three-thousand-man Virginia brigade, Pillow's personal staff, and uncounted hundreds of others evaded the Union dragnet over the days after the surrender. But when Buckner sent a flag of truce to his opponent that night, the Confederate fighting men became enraged and nearly mutinied at this betrayal by their leaders.

Eventually, Buckner met with his old army friend Grant in the hamlet of Dover, within Confederate lines. Grant demanded unconditional surrender, and Buckner, though aghast at such treatment from an old colleague, was powerless to refuse. Grant telegraphed Halleck later that day: "We have taken Fort Donelson and from 12,000 to 15,000 prisoners including Generals Buckner and Bushrod Johnson; also about 20,000 stand of arms, 48 pieces of artillery, 17 heavy guns, from 2,000 to 4,000 horses, and large quantities of commissary stores."

When this news reached Johnston at Nashville, he was shocked, since all previous news from the fort indicated victory. Nashvillians rioted and fled the city in droves, with Buell's army eventually occupying the capital on February 24. Johnston could provide no defense. Aided by Floyd, Pillow, and Forrest, his forces evacuated as much Confederate property as possible, but his retreat did not stop short of northern Alabama and Mississippi. Union forces stood poised to end the rebellion all over the upper South. But, as fatigued and battered in victory as the Confederates were in defeat, Grant's men could not move quickly. Moreover, their generals fell to bickering, and momentum slipped from their grasp. Johnston was able to regroup to fight another day.

Still, a Confederate field force was swept into Northern prison camps. Western and much of middle Tennessee as well as all of Kentucky were reclaimed for the Union. Hopes of early European recognition of the Confederacy were dashed, and Johnston's reputation as the South's greatest warrior was destroyed. The fall of Forts Henry and Donelson changed the war in the West overnight. Flagging spirits in the North were revived, and a deep wedge was driven into the South. The Southern home front began its wavering trend toward eventual collapse in a war of attrition.

BIBLIOGRAPHY

Connelly, Thomas L. *Army of the Heartland: The Army of Tennessee, 1861–1862.* Baton Rouge, La., 1967.
Cooling, Benjamin Franklin. *Forts Henry and Donelson: The Key to the Confederate Heartland.* Knoxville, Tenn., 1987.
Grant, Ulysses S. *Personal Memoirs.* Vol. 1. New York, 1885. Reprint, Cutchogue, N.Y., 1990.
Hamilton, James. *The Battle of Fort Donelson.* South Brunswick, N.J., 1968.
Simon, John Y., ed. *The Papers of Ulysses S. Grant.* Vol. 4. Carbondale, N.Y., 1972.

B. Franklin Cooling

HERBERT, CALEB C.

HERBERT, CALEB C. (1814–1867), congressman from Texas. Born in Virginia, Caleb Claiborne Herbert moved to Texas as a youth and became a resident of Eagle Lake, Colorado County. A planter and politician, he served in the Texas Senate from 1857 to 1859 and was a strong advocate of secession.

Herbert represented the Second Congressional District of Texas in the First and Second Congresses, where he was an active opponent of the Davis administration. In 1862 he opposed the first Conscription Act because he believed it was unconstitutional and feared it would leave Texas undefended. Herbert went so far as to argue that Texas should secede from the Confederacy before submitting to it. In 1863 he chaired a special committee that investigated the treatment of Union prisoners at Castle Thunder at Richmond and signed the minority report criticizing conditions in that prison as inhumane.

Herbert campaigned for reelection in the summer of 1863 on the basis of his opposition to the Davis administration's legislative program and was reelected. In the second session he continued his opposition to the central government. He was, for example, a strong opponent of efforts to enlist slaves in the Confederate army. Herbert's position in Congress was based primarily on his strong support of the concept of state rights rather than any antagonism toward the president or opposition to the war.

After the war Herbert returned to Texas. Although he was elected to the U.S. House of Representatives in 1865 and 1867, he was not seated on either occasion. He was killed in an accident on July 15, 1867.

BIBLIOGRAPHY

Estill, Mary S., ed. "Diary of a Confederate Congressman, 1862–1863." *Southwestern Historical Quarterly* 38 (1935): 270–301; 39 (1935): 33–65.
Yearns, Wilfred B. *The Confederate Congress.* Athens, Ga., 1960.

Carl H. Moneyhon

HEROES OF AMERICA.

A secret, underground, pro-Union organization (often called Red Strings because a piece of red string in a lapel or on a window or door served as a secret sign of membership) composed of militant Unionists, deserters, and draft dodgers—and to some extent, slaves and free blacks—the Heroes of America existed in North Carolina, Virginia, West Virginia, Tennessee, the District of Columbia, and possibly other states during the Civil War. Its main mission was to protect its members from Confederate authorities. The HOA also provided needy members with food and other necessities, maintained an underground railroad on which members could be spirited to the Union lines, encouraged disloyalty on the home front and desertion in the ranks of the Confederate army, fostered the formation of armed, anti-Confederate guerrilla units, provided military intelligence to Federal troops, and promoted class conflict in the Confederacy by inducing the poor to join by promising a postwar distribution of the property of wealthy planters.

During the war it was rumored that the HOA originated within Union lines and was introduced into the Confederacy by special Federal agents. But the balance of the evidence now available suggests that the secret society was founded in central North Carolina, probably in Davidson County (the environs of present-day Lexington), where so many of its known leaders lived. It likely had its roots in a secret underground association of approximately five hundred armed Unionists who mustered under the U.S. flag in Davidson and the adjoining counties of Forsyth, Guilford, and Randolph. Witnesses reported that this band of militant Unionists, headed by John Hilton of Davidson County, favored the "coercion policy of Lincoln" and were prepared to "strike for the old Union." In July 1861, Confederate troops aborted this threatened insurrection of disloyalists.

One of the main leaders and organizers of the HOA was Dr. John Lewis Johnson, a druggist and physician, who lived in the Abbotts Creek community in southern Forsyth County. Perhaps because he was pressured by Confederate authorities to volunteer for the army or face charges of disloyalty, he joined the ranks as a substitute in 1862. By 1863, Johnson was serving in a Confederate hospital in Raleigh. The Tarheel capital, where the Grand Council of the Heroes of America was first organized, thereafter became a center of HOA activity.

In the summer of 1863, William W. Holden, editor of the influential Raleigh *North Carolina Standard,* embarked on his campaign for peace. Holden and his Peace party followers—influenced by the movement of some Northern Democrats for peace and reunion with a constitutional guarantee of slavery for the returning Southern states—demanded that Confederate authorities, or the states acting in convention together, make a permanent peace with the North.

The HOA supported the peace movement. Johnson is on record as having taken part in a Peace party rally near Raleigh in July 1863. Many other disloyalists took part in peace meetings, especially in the central and western Piedmont. The U.S. flag was hoisted at peace meetings in Wilkes and Rowan counties.

The 1863 phase of the peace movement culminated in an insurrection of deserters and draft dodgers across the central counties in September. A brigade of Confederate troops was sent in to suppress the uprising. The Heroes of America, through a clever network of secret dugout caves, managed to conceal hundreds of the men from the hunters. When the troops left a neighborhood, the men in hiding emerged from their dens and returned to aid their families and to offer protection and support to those whose husbands or sons had been captured.

A raid by Confederate soldiers in September left Holden's press in ruins, but the redoubtable editor renewed his activities in January 1864. President Jefferson Davis reacted by suspending the writ of habeas corpus. Undaunted, Holden challenged the incumbent, Zebulon Vance, in the 1864 gubernatorial contest on a peace platform.

In July, as a tactic to cow Holden supporters, newspapers backing Vance exposed the Heroes of America to the public for the first time during the war. Prompted by a promise from Vance to be lenient with those who voluntarily came forward, dozens of men publicly confessed their membership in the society and asked pardon from the governor for allowing themselves to be "misled" into joining it. The press revealed the secret signs, passwords, and rituals of the HOA. Holden was accused of being a leader of the society. With most of his supporters fearing reprisals, including arrest for disloyalty, few showed up at the polls to vote for him, and Vance won by a landslide. After Holden's loss to Vance, the HOA ceased to play a role in the politics of Confederate North Carolina.

In October 1864, Johnson, who had been ordered to duty at the front (probably as punishment for his Peace party activities), decamped with a company of Confederate troops to the Federal lines. He then went to Washington, D.C., where he initiated into the HOA Daniel Reeves Goodloe (a Republican and abolitionist from North Carolina), Benjamin Sherwood Hedrick (a Patent Office examiner and native Tarheel who had been fired in 1856 from his professorship at the University of North Carolina for expressing pro-Republican and antislavery sentiments), and John G. Barrett (the commissioner of patents). A National Grand Council of the Heroes of America with Hedrick at its head was established in Washington. In 1870, Goodloe testified before a Senate committee that during the war Johnson had also initiated Abraham Lincoln and Ulysses S. Grant into the Heroes of America. If this is true, it is likely that Lincoln and Grant kept their membership quiet because the Republican party, alarmed at the tendency of many Southern Heroes to identify politically with the Northern Democrats, was wary of granting publicity to the Heroes of America or to the peace movement that many of them supported.

In the fall of 1864, an investigation by Confederate detectives revealed that the HOA was widespread and powerful in southwestern Virginia. An informant reported that the secret order had been introduced into the area in the fall of 1863 by one Horace Dean of North Carolina. Montgomery County alone was said to harbor eight hundred members, including the sheriff, several justices of the peace, and other local government officials. By the winter of 1864, bands of deserters and disloyal county officials, many of whom belonged to the HOA, controlled southwestern Virginia.

During the Civil War the Heroes of America played an important role in the demise of the Confederacy. At first composed solely of die-hard Unionists, the ranks of the order by midwar had become swollen by the addition of thousands of disaffected citizens, especially deserters and draft dodgers. Together, they spread dissension, disorder, and disloyalty in the army and on the home front.

[See also Holden, William W.; Johnson, John Lewis; Peace Movements; Unionism.]

BIBLIOGRAPHY

Auman, William T., and David D. Scarboro. "The Heroes of America in Civil War North Carolina." North Carolina Historical Review 58 (1981): 327–363.
Hamilton, J. G. de Roulhac. "The Heroes of America." Publications of the Southern History Association 40 (1907): 10–19.
Shanks, Henry T. "Disloyalty to the Confederacy in Southwestern Virginia, 1861–1865." North Carolina Historical Review 21 (1944): 118–135.
Tatum, Georgia Lee. Disloyalty in the Confederacy. Chapel Hill, N.C., 1934.

WILLIAM THOMAS AUMAN

HETH, HENRY (1825–1899), major general. Heth, born December 16, 1825, was a Virginian of distinguished lineage who graduated from the U.S. Military Academy in 1847 and served the U.S. Army well for the next fourteen years. After he joined his home state's forces upon secession, Heth spent the early part of the war primarily in western Virginia. As a brigadier general, he failed miserably at the Battle of Lewisburg in May 1862. Nonetheless, his friendship with Robert E. Lee earned him a field position with the Army of Northern Virginia in January 1863. Heth purportedly was the only officer in the army whom Lee addressed by his given name.

Heth commanded a brigade and temporarily a division at Chancellorsville, where he sustained a minor wound. A few weeks later, the Virginian advanced to the rank of major general and received permanent division command. On July 1, 1863, Heth achieved the dubious distinction of precipitating the epic fight at Gettysburg. His division stumbled into Federal troops that day and became so heavily engaged as to make disengagement impossible. During the battle he sustained his second wound in as many months.

Although Heth spent the last two years of the war as a solidly reliable division commander in the Army of Northern Virginia, he never advanced beyond mediocrity. His division fought well on virtually every field, but Heth rarely displayed strategic initiative. The highlight of his late-war career came at Reams's Station on August 25, 1864, when the general personally bore a battle flag at the head of his men as they carried a Union position. Heth surrendered his division at Appomattox.

After the war he held a variety of jobs. He died September 27, 1899, from the effects of Bright's disease. He is buried in Hollywood Cemetery, Richmond.

BIBLIOGRAPHY

Connolly, Thomas. An Irishman in Dixie. Columbia, S.C., 1988.
Morrison, James L., Jr., ed. The Memoirs of Henry Heth. Westport, Conn., 1974.

ROBERT E. L. KRICK

HIGGINS, EDWARD (1821–1875), brigadier general. Although he had spent over fifteen years at sea in the U.S. Navy and Merchant Marines, Higgins opted for land service when he joined the Confederate war effort. In April 1861 he became captain of the First Louisiana Artillery and then left to serve briefly on the staff of Maj. Gen. David E. Twiggs stationed at New Orleans. After Twiggs's removal, Higgins took command of a light artillery battery, but he soon resigned and left the Confederate army for a month, perhaps waiting for better use of his military experience.

In February 1862, he became lieutenant colonel of the Twenty-second Louisiana Infantry with orders to aid in the defense of Forts Jackson and St. Phillip below New Orleans. Higgins's men put up a stubborn resistance to Federal gunboats despite weeks of isolation and unpleasant conditions. When the disgruntled Confederates at Fort Jackson spiked their guns and organized a mutiny, Higgins remained at his post to await the imminent approach of the enemy. Capture and four months of imprisonment followed. After his exchange and promotion to colonel, he rejoined the Twenty-second Louisiana posted on the Mississippi near Vicksburg. Gen. John C. Pemberton later recalled Higgins's "gallantry, coolness and skill" while manning the heavy artillery batteries. When Vicksburg fell to the Union, Higgins was captured for the second time. Upon his exchange and return to the Confederacy in October 1863, he made brigadier general and took command of the batteries protecting Mobile Bay, but four months later, he was relieved from command.

Surviving records do not explain why the Confederate command could find no use for this experienced naval and army officer. The war ended with Higgins having failed to receive further orders for active duty. He returned to his birthplace at Norfolk, Virginia, to pursue a business career.

BIBLIOGRAPHY

Bergeron, Arthur W., Jr. "'They Bore Themselves with Distinguished Gallantry': The Twenty-second Louisiana Infantry." *Louisiana History* 13, no. 3 (1972): 253–282.

Porter, James D. *Tennessee.* Vol. 18 of *Confederate Military History.* Edited by Clement A. Evans. Atlanta, 1899. Vol. 10 of extended ed. Wilmington, N.C., 1988.

LESLEY JILL GORDON-BURR

HILL, A. P. (1825–1865), lieutenant general. Considered the finest division commander in Confederate service, and Lee's principal lieutenant in the last year of the war, A. P. "Little Powell" Hill has become the personification of the life and death of the Army of Northern Virginia. Both Robert E. Lee and Stonewall Jackson called for him on their deathbeds.

Ambrose Powell Hill was a product of Piedmont Virginia landed gentry. Born November 9, 1825, near Culpeper, he received a private education before his 1842 appointment to West Point. While on summer furlough from the academy in 1844, the tragedy of Hill's life occurred. He contracted gonorrhea. The disease's bacteria, unknown to anyone, lodged in his urinary tract and created strictures that eventually would bring debilitating illness.

An eight-month sick leave forced Hill to drop back a year at West Point. At his 1847 graduation, he stood fifteenth in his class. The new artillery lieutenant arrived too late in Mexico to see action. Seven years of duty assignments followed in Mexico, Texas, and Florida. In 1855 Hill transferred to the U.S. Coastal Survey Service in Washington. His 1859 marriage to Kitty Morgan McClung would produce four daughters.

With the outbreak of civil war, Hill became colonel of the Thirteenth Virginia. He saw no major action for a year. Nevertheless, his proven talents in organization, drill, and discipline led to his promotion on February 26, 1862, to brigadier general. His baptism in battle came on May 5 at Williamsburg. Hill's successful attack at a critical moment swept Union forces from his front, and he won praise as the most conspicuous brigadier on the field. On May 26, he received promotion to major general and command of the largest division (six brigades) in all of the Confederate armies.

A. P. HILL.   NATIONAL ARCHIVES

It was in the Seven Days' counteroffensive by Lee that the Powell Hill of history emerged. Directed to attack the Federal right flank in concert with Stonewall Jackson's forces, Hill grew impatient at Jackson's tardiness and assaulted on his own. His division took heavy casualties at Mechanicsville and equally severe losses the next day at Gaines' Mill. On June 30, the divisions of Hill and James Longstreet fought a bloody but inconclusive engagement with Federals at Frayser's Farm. Hill blamed all three defeats on Jackson's failure to provide necessary and expected support.

A post–Seven Days' argument with Longstreet resulted in the latter placing Hill under arrest. Lee intervened and transferred Hill to Jackson's command. An even stronger clash of wills developed. On August 8, Jackson criticized Hill for poor marching procedures on the move to intercept Gen. John Pope's advance. But Hill's timely arrival the following day in the Battle of Cedar Mountain was instrumental in the Southern victory. Similarly, Hill's steadfastness in beating back repeated Union attacks at Second Manassas elicited high praise.

By then, "Little Powell" was a familiar figure in the ranks. Five feet, nine inches tall, he weighed but 145 pounds. His curly hair was chestnut-colored and worn long. Hazel eyes flashed during battle or anger. Disdaining uniform and insignia, Hill customarily wore calico shirts—his favorite being bright red in color.

Lee's army was marching into Maryland on September 4, when Jackson's patience with Hill's casual marching style snapped. He placed Hill under arrest for insubordination. Hill obtained temporary release a week later and participated dutifully in the capture of Harpers Ferry. On September 17, in one of the most dramatic moments of the war, Hill's Light Division dashed into battle at Sharpsburg after a seventeen-mile forced march and saved Lee's army from almost certain destruction.

For seven months thereafter, Hill and Jackson waged an increasingly bitter exchange of charges and countercharges that did credit to neither man. An inexplicable gap in Hill's lines at the Battle of Fredericksburg added fuel to the controversy. The quarrel ended with Jackson's death following Chancellorsville. On May 26, 1863—a year to the day of his last promotion—Hill was assigned as a lieutenant general in command of the newly formed Third Corps in Lee's army. It was Hill's troops who opened the Battle of Gettysburg. Sickness limited the general's activities, and his debut as a corps commander was less than spectacular.

Hill partially redeemed himself on the retreat to Virginia with a smashing repulse of Federals at Falling Waters, Maryland. Yet on October 14, he suffered his worst defeat when he precipitately launched an attack against powerfully entrenched Federals at Bristoe Station. Hill was a central figure in Lee's attacks the following May against Ulysses S. Grant's army in the Wilderness. Illness then forced him to relinquish command for two weeks. Lingering effects from gonorrhea had produced a slow blocking of the kidneys.

The general prematurely struggled back to duty and performed badly in May 23 fighting at the North Anna River. With his health somewhat improved by the end of the month, Hill made a speedy arrival at Petersburg on June 18 and helped prevent that gateway city to Richmond from falling into Union hands. Throughout the long besiegement that followed, Hill commanded the southern half of Lee's defenses. He did so brilliantly. One high-ranking officer observed that from June 1864 through March 1865, "every Federal effort to break Lee's right was met and defeated by General Hill with promptness and without heavy loss on his part."

Victories, always against heavy odds, came after engagements at Jerusalem Plank Road, Weldon Railroad, the Crater, Reams's Station, Peeble's Farm, Jones's Farm, and Burgess's Mill. Lee relied heavily on the little general throughout the months of entrapment. Not once did Hill disappoint him.

These accomplishments came in spite of worsening health. Malfunctioning kidneys slowly produced uremia. For most of February and March 1865, Hill was unable to perform his duties. The general tried to regain his strength with rest at the James River estate of a kinsman. He painfully returned to the front only two days before Grant's all-out assault on April 2 against Lee's position. It was barely dawn that morning when Hill was fatally shot through the heart while trying to reestablish his lines. He is buried in Richmond beneath a statue to his memory.

A Richmond newspaper stated in 1864 that Hill was "the abiding strength and dependence of Lee's army." Gen. William Mahone later said of him: "A more brilliant, useful soldier and chivalrous gentleman never adorned the Confederate army."

BIBLIOGRAPHY

Hassler, William W. *A. P. Hill: Lee's Forgotten General.* Chapel Hill, N.C., 1979.
Pender, William Dorsey. *The General to His Lady.* Chapel Hill, N.C., 1965.
Robertson, James I., Jr. *General A. P. Hill.* New York, 1987.
Schenck, Martin. *Up Came Hill.* Harrisburg, Pa., 1958.

JAMES I. ROBERTSON, JR.

HILL, BENJAMIN H. (1823–1882), congressman from Georgia. Benjamin Harvey Hill was born into a modest farm family in Hillsboro, in Jasper County, Georgia, on September 14, 1823, the seventh of nine children. When he was ten, he moved with his family to Troup County in western Georgia's newly opened Creek Indian lands. He was the second of his family to attend college, entering the University of Georgia in 1841, where he proved to be far more of a scholar than his older brother who was also on campus at the time. Ben Hill graduated in three years at the head of his class. A year later he married Caroline E. Holt,

BENJAMIN H. HILL.   LIBRARY OF CONGRESS

of a politically and socially prominent Athens family. After admission to the bar, he moved to LaGrange, Georgia, and opened a law practice. His successful practice soon earned him a large estate and by 1860 fifty-seven slaves.

Hill took an active interest in politics and proved to be an accomplished orator, though his political career was characterized by repeated fluctuations in party affiliation and factional alignments, leading contemporaries and historians alike to judge him an opportunist. He first ran for office as a Whig and was elected to a single term in the Georgia legislature in 1851. As a Know-Nothing, he ran unsuccessfully for Congress in 1855 and for governor in 1857, losing the latter race soundly to a relatively unknown Democrat, Joseph E. Brown. But it was in the presidential campaign of 1856 that Hill first gained a statewide reputation. In his support of Millard Fillmore's attempt at presidential reelection, he clashed with two of the state's most prominent Democrats, Robert Toombs and Alexander H. Stephens, and challenged them to debates. His stinging attack on Stephens in a Lexington debate and on Toombs in their encounter the next day in Washington, Georgia, earned Hill widespread attention as a brash young "giant-killer." His insults led Stephens to challenge him to a duel, though Hill declined to fight the "frail invalid."

In 1859 Hill was elected to the state senate and from that platform became an increasingly outspoken Unionist. Though he threw his support to John Bell and his Constitutional Union party in the 1860 presidential election, he also pushed without much success a fusion scheme by which Georgia supporters of John Breckinridge, Stephen A. Douglas, and Bell would agree to throw their votes to the one who, on the eve of the election, looked most likely to defeat Abraham Lincoln.

In December he was elected by his Troup County constituents to represent their antisecessionist views at the state secession convention in Milledgeville. "May they who would destroy the Union in a frolic," he wrote on accepting his role as convention delegate, "have the wisdom to furnish our children a better." Still convinced that the South's grievances could be more effectively addressed within rather than outside the Union, Hill, along with Herschel V. Johnson, Alexander Stephens, and others, continued to argue against secession. Yet when a test vote he put forward for further negotiation indicated that the majority of the convention favored immediate secession, he capitulated, voting with the majority and signing the state's ordinance of secession. Yet he displayed his unhappiness over this turn of events openly, saying that he assisted with the dissolution of the Union as he "would bury a benefactor." This statement embittered some local secessionists who, in the midst of their celebration in Milledgeville, burned him in effigy.

Hill soon pledged his support for the new Confederacy, however, and was rewarded with election as one of Georgia's ten delegates to the Provisional Congress that met in Montgomery in February 1861. In November the Georgia legislature selected him as one of the state's two Confederate senators (along with Robert Toombs, who refused to serve), a position Hill continued to hold throughout the war. At age thirty-nine, he was that body's youngest member.

When Congress convened in Richmond in February 1862, Hill was named chairman of the Senate Judiciary Committee. From that position, he soon stirred dissension with his determined effort to establish a Confederate supreme court. Though the Constitution drawn up in Montgomery the year before authorized the creation of such a court, many state rights advocates in and out of Congress, including Governor Brown and other Georgia congressmen, opposed it as yet another effort toward centralizing on the part of the Davis government. Hill was vocal in the lively debate over the issue in March 1862, which led to a violent collision on the Senate floor with Alabama senator William Lowndes Yancey. In response to insults from Yancey, Hill hurled a glass inkstand at him, grazing his cheekbone. Further infuriated when Yancey calmly ignored this blow from behind, Hill rushed at him with a chair but was restrained by other senators. Though Hill's persistence eventually led to the bill's passage in the Senate in 1863, it was buried in the House and a Confederate supreme court never materialized.

On this and on other matters, Hill was a particularly vocal adherent to Jefferson Davis and his administration and cultivated the perception that he was the president's spokesman in the Senate. Davis referred to him as "Hill the faithful" and once said of him, he "stood by me when all others forsook our cause. . . . His pen and voice were on my side when I most needed them. They were equal to ten thousand bayonets—and I will not forget his services." Two other much-debated issues on which Hill demonstrated his loyalty to presidential policy were conscription and suspension of the writ of habeas corpus. In both cases, his support took the form of direct attacks on Governor Brown.

The matter of conscription was the first to seriously distance President Davis from Brown. Davis felt the need for mandatory military service of white male citizens as early as the spring of 1862 and pushed the first Conscription Act through Congress in April. Brown at first refused to cooperate and wrote of his strenuous objections to Davis throughout the summer. When a second act extending the age limit of conscripts to forty-five was passed in September, Brown became defiant and turned to his legislature in an effort to secure a state law opposing it. In messages to the General Assembly of Georgia he condemned the president's actions as unconstitutional and a direct denial of the states' right to protect their own territory and citizens. Hill spent much of the fall in Georgia as an unofficial emissary of Davis, attempting to counteract the effects of the governor's charges. When Brown continued to defy the act after his own state supreme court upheld its validity, Hill went before the state legislature on December 11 and delivered an incendiary speech in which he defended both the need and the legitimacy of conscription and attacked Brown for the irrationality of his arguments against it and for undermining the war effort.

Three acts by Congress between February 1862 and August 1864 gave President Davis the prerogative to suspend the writ of habeas corpus. Although these measures were widely condemned by Georgians, including Brown, Ben Hill again proved fully supportive of this presidential privilege, insisting that it was a necessary war measure and as such did not violate a citizen's constitutional rights.

These clashes created such enmity between Senator Hill and Governor Brown that when Brown ended his third term in 1863, several of his political enemies, including Alexander Stephens, felt Hill was the natural challenger for the gubernatorial race that year. But Hill, recognizing Brown's continued popularity among Georgians and not wanting to risk his own influential position in Richmond, declined the opportunity to oppose him. Hill did exert his influence to keep Robert Toombs, as outspoken a critic of Davis as Brown was, from winning the state's second Senate seat. Herschel V. Johnson, far less hostile to the Confederate administration, easily defeated Toombs, much to Hill's satisfaction. Hill's biographer called Johnson's victory "the last great victory of Hill for the administration."

Hill's staunch loyalty to the administration wavered briefly in the face of the peace movement that was gaining momentum in the spring of 1864. He opposed a resolution by the vice president's brother, Linton Stephens, that Georgia as a single state could initiate peace negotiations with the Union government. But he was more conciliatory on this issue than he had been on others and reasoned with Stephens that such a plan would be effective only if undertaken by the Southern states acting together through a convention. Nothing came of such proposals, as Georgians became preoccupied with their defense against William Tecumseh Sherman's invasion.

Hill returned home from Richmond and took an active and highly visible role in rallying morale, as in a speech in Macon in which he urged continued resistance to Sherman, who he warned planned to exterminate Georgians and repopulate the state with "Yankees." On behalf of the Confederate War Department, he traveled to the southwestern part of the state to urge planters there to give up much-needed cotton and other supplies they were hoarding for army use. At Davis's request, Hill constantly urged Georgia draft evaders and deserters to come forward in the Confederacy's great hour of need; his persistence was such that he aroused animosity among some yeomen in the state and criticism from state newspapers.

When Sherman himself made overtures of peace to Georgia officials in October 1864, Hill convinced Jefferson Davis that nothing short of a presidential appearance in the state could counteract peace sentiment in Georgia. Davis made the trip accompanied by Hill, and despite controversial statements by the president blaming Confederate troops for their failure to defend Atlanta adequately, nothing came of Sherman's attempts to negotiate with state officials.

Hill was also influential behind the scenes at the Hampton Roads conference on February 3, 1865. Lincoln and William H. Seward met aboard a steamer off the Virginia coast to discuss peace terms with a Confederate commission headed by Vice President Alexander H. Stephens. When Governor Brown urged the Georgia legislature to back a Southern convention to negotiate a peace settlement, Hill, alarmed that Stephens might tell Lincoln of this proposal, intervened and persuaded his fellow Georgian not to pass along Brown's idea at the conference. Though nothing came of the conference (the Union leaders would consider nothing short of unconditional surrender), Hill maintained that it had served a valuable purpose in that it silenced the Southern peace movement and strengthened resolve for a fight to the finish. He undertook a speaking tour of the state in which he attempted to rally Georgians to renewed support for the war effort. Defeatism was rampant enough at that point to make his campaign a failure and himself a target of ridicule and hostility, but it also earned Hill a postwar reputation as having been "the last to accept secession, and the last to accept defeat." On March 11, 1865, in his hometown of LaGrange, he delivered one of his most moving appeals, which is thought to have been the final speech made by a Southerner on behalf of the Confederacy.

After Robert E. Lee's surrender at Appomattox a month later, Hill returned home, where he took great satisfaction in the fact that most of his former slaves chose to stay with him. In May, Federal authorities came to his home, arrested him and Confederate naval secretary Stephen R. Mallory who was visiting him at the time, and took both to New York, where they were imprisoned at Fort Lafayette. Hill remained a prisoner for over two months until his parole by President Andrew Johnson in July.

Hill retired from public life until 1867, when he moved to Athens, Georgia, and emerged to deliver a series of well-publicized and widely circulated speeches denouncing the recently passed Reconstruction Act and the entire Southern policy of the Radical Republicans. He urged Georgians to defy the policy and harshly condemned those Southerners who cooperated with Reconstruction measures. He maintained that such actions by Congress were unconstitutional and urged President Johnson to block enforcement. In December 1867, he was unanimously elected president of a conservative convention held in Macon, where he lashed out at black suffrage policies and vowed that Georgians would "not be brought under the dominion of the Negro." His rhetoric over the next three years became particularly critical of the "cowardly" cooperationism of former governor Joseph Brown and of current governor Rufus Bullock, whom he labeled a "stupid express agent." His newspaper column "Notes on the Situation" in the *Augusta Chronicle and Sentinel,* published regularly during this period, gained him national attention.

Then suddenly in December 1870, Hill switched sides and announced his acquiescence to Reconstruction policy and urged his fellow Georgians to do likewise. Continued opposition, he maintained, was futile and a misuse of political energies that could be diverted to other, more pressing issues. This unexpected flip-flop on Hill's part was probably related to his recent membership in the Western and Atlantic's leasing company, which forced him to make peace with the Northern radicals who controlled the company. The man so recently hailed for his courage in speaking out against what many Georgians viewed as despotic rule was now denounced as a turncoat and a traitor and once again seen as a mere opportunist. His involvement with the company, as much as his political sellout, so offended Georgia conservatives that he was ostracized from state politics for the next five years.

In the meantime, he also embraced the New South cause and became one of its earliest spokesmen, long before Henry Grady began touting the same message. Hill gave what many consider his most effective speech before University of Georgia alumni in 1871, when he extolled the merits of modernized agriculture, more efficient use of natural resources, and a more broadly based educational system.

After moving to Atlanta in 1872, Hill reentered the political fray and was elected to Congress from the Ninth District in 1875. He quickly reasserted himself as a defender of Southern rights when in January 1876 he confronted James G. Blaine, the congressman from Maine seeking the Republican presidential nomination that year, on the floor of the House of Representatives. After Blaine "waved the bloody shirt" with insulting remarks about Jefferson Davis and his responsibility for the atrocities at the Andersonville prison, Hill rose and made a stirring and well-received defense of Davis, demanding that "this reckless misrepresentation of the South stop right here." Hill was elected to the U.S. Senate in January 1877 and served in the office he had so long coveted until a painful malignancy on his tongue rendered him speechless (for one of the era's most accomplished orators, an irony not lost on his contemporaries). It led to throat cancer in 1881 and death at home in Atlanta on August 16, 1882.

BIBLIOGRAPHY

Bryan, T. Conn. *Confederate Georgia.* Athens, Ga., 1953.

Coleman, Kenneth, and Charles Stephen Gurr. *Dictionary of Georgia Biography.* Vol. 1. Athens, Ga., 1983.

Conway, Alan. *The Reconstruction of Georgia.* Minneapolis, Minn., 1966.

Hill, Benjamin Harvey, Jr. *Senator Benjamin H. Hill of Georgia: His Life, Writings, and Speeches.* Atlanta, 1891.

Knight, Lucian Lamar. *Reminiscences of Famous Georgians.* 2 vols. Atlanta, 1907.

Pearce, Haywood J., Jr. *Benjamin H. Hill: Secession and Reconstruction.* Chicago, 1928.

Yearns, Wilfred B. *The Confederate Congress.* Athens, Ga., 1960.

JOHN C. INSCOE

HILL, BENJAMIN JEFFERSON

HILL, BENJAMIN JEFFERSON (1825–1880), brigadier general. Born June 13, 1825, near McMinnville, Tennessee, Hill was educated in local schools. He entered the mercantile business and was elected to the state senate in 1855.

Hill joined the Confederate army and was appointed colonel of the Thirty-fifth Tennessee Infantry Regiment October 7, 1861, to rank from September 11. (For the war's first two years the regiment was designated the First Tennessee Mountain Rifle Regiment or the Fifth Tennessee.) Hill and his regiment fought in the Army of Tennessee during 1862 and 1863. Both the commander and his men often received praise for their bravery.

On February 3, 1864, Hill was relieved from command of the regiment and assigned as provost marshal general of the Army of Tennessee. He served in that capacity until relieved on August 24. On November 30, 1864, he was promoted to brigadier general. It was intended that he raise recruits for the army in Tennessee during the Franklin and Nashville campaign, but, in fact, he commanded a cavalry force. It seems likely that the instructions for recruiting service did not reach him until after the Confederates were driven from Tennessee. In the closing months of the war he commanded a cavalry brigade in Mississippi and Alabama.

After the war Hill resumed his mercantile pursuits in McMinnville and then practiced law there. He died in McMinnville January 5, 1880, and is buried there in the city cemetery on South High Street.

BIBLIOGRAPHY

Hewitt, Lawrence L. "Benjamin Jefferson Hill." In *The Confederate General.* Edited by William C. Davis. Vol. 3. Harrisburg, Pa., 1991.

Warner, Ezra J. *Generals in Gray: Lives of the Confederate Commanders.* Baton Rouge, La., 1959.

RICHARD M. MCMURRY

HILL, D. H. (1821–1889), lieutenant general. Born July 12, 1821, in the York District, South Carolina, Daniel Harvey Hill was the youngest of eleven children. Boyhood illnesses left him with a pain-racked spine for most of his life but did not prevent him from pursuing a military career.

Hill entered the U.S. Military Academy at West Point in 1838, graduating twenty-eighth of fifty-six in the class of 1842. As a brevet second lieutenant, he was assigned to the First Artillery in August 1842, was transferred to the Third Artillery on October 20, 1843, and was promoted to full second lieutenant on October 13, 1845. During the war with Mexico, he served first under Zachary Taylor at Monterrey and then with Winfield Scott in the Mexico City campaign. Conspicuous bravery earned Hill promotion to first lieutenant on March 3, 1847, with brevets as captain for Contreras and major for Chapultepec.

Hill resigned from the army February 28, 1849, and settled into life as an educator. He served as professor of mathematics at Washington College, Virginia (1848–1854), and Davidson College, North Carolina (1854–1859). The opening of the Civil War found Hill as superintendent and professor of mathematics and artillery at the North Carolina Military Institute.

Elected colonel of the First North Carolina on May 11, 1861, Hill repulsed inept Federal charges at the Battle of Big Bethel Church, south of Yorktown, Virginia, on June 10. This effort won him promotion to brigadier general, to date from July 10, 1861, and assignment to improve defenses in North Carolina. Hill returned to Virginia on November 16 to serve under Gen. Joseph E. Johnston. As

D. H. HILL.   NATIONAL ARCHIVES

a major general, to date from March 26, 1862, Hill led a division under Johnston at Williamsburg (May 5, 1862) and Seven Pines (May 31–June 1), and under Gen. Robert E. Lee at Mechanicsville, Gaines' Mill, and Malvern Hill (June 26–July 1, 1862). From July through August, he left Lee's army to command the Department of North Carolina but did not enjoy the experience. Before rejoining the Army of Northern Virginia on September 2, Hill helped build up the defenses in the Richmond-Petersburg area that would become important in the latter stages of the war.

With a combative personality that served better on the battlefield than off, Hill increasingly alienated those who controlled his advancement. None doubted his courage or leadership: he often exposed himself to fire just to settle his men. His fighting spirit and willingness to place himself in danger made him popular with the soldiers in his command, but his carping rankled fellow officers and superiors who called Hill a "croaker" because of his despondent talk and tactless complaining. In battle reports, the North Carolinian criticized superiors—including Lee—for mismanaging the spring 1862 battles around Richmond.

Although the repercussions of such challenges would not become fully apparent until late 1863, Hill's personality may have made him an inviting target for those who wanted either to slight his abilities or to find a convenient scapegoat. In the Maryland campaign of 1862, he was incorrectly accused of having lost the Confederate battle plan (Special Orders No. 191) that fell into Union hands. Hill also received less than his due for employing his minimal force to delay the advance of the Army of the Potomac over South Mountain near Boonsborough on September 14, 1862. At Sharpsburg, his division stood up well in the horror of what became called the "Bloody Lane."

Yet when Lee reorganized the army in October, he did not see Hill as having potential for corps command. Lee believed him "an excellent executive officer" with not "much administrative ability. Left to himself he seems embarrassed and backward to act." Poor health, coupled with the sting of not receiving promotion to lieutenant general, caused Hill to submit his resignation from the army on January 1, 1863. Thomas J. ("Stonewall") Jackson, Hill's brother-in-law, was among those who persuaded the North Carolinian to remain in the service.

Hill subsequently accepted an appointment as a corps commander under Braxton Bragg in the Army of Tennessee, where he contributed to the Confederate victory at Chickamauga (September 19–20, 1863), but he shortly became embroiled in a bitter dispute with his commander. Bragg had alienated many of his chief officers, who signed a petition calling for the general's dismissal. Bragg incorrectly blamed Hill as the petition's author. President Jefferson Davis supported Bragg against Hill, who became the only officer relieved from command. The experience cost him promotion to lieutenant general, which Davis declined to put through for confirmation, and caused some unfairly to equate Hill with the missed opportunities of the Chickamauga campaign.

Hill spent the remainder of the war trying to clear his record and win meaningful command, but he managed only a series of relatively minor positions. Beginning on May 5, 1864, Hill became a volunteer aide to General P. G. T. Beauregard, serving in whatever capacity was most needed. This included commanding a division for several days, going to Lynchburg to help organize the defense against Union Maj. Gen. David Hunter, and returning to the Richmond-Petersburg area to perform duties as inspector general of trenches. Occasionally, other officers requested Hill's services, but he lacked the support of Davis and Bragg, who had since become military adviser to the president. Hill ended his military career first as commander of the District of Georgia in mid-January 1865 and then under Johnston in North Carolina. He fought at Bentonville (March 19–20) and surrendered with Johnston's forces at Durham Station on April 26.

After the war, Hill remained in North Carolina and published a monthly magazine, *The Land We Love,* from 1866 to 1869 and a weekly newspaper, *The Southern Home.* The gap between him and Lee widened as Hill refused to accept blame for the lost order or to back down from criticism of his former commander. After 1877, Hill returned to a college campus, this time serving as the president of Arkansas Industrial University (the future University of Arkansas) until 1887 and then the Middle Georgia Military and Agricultural College in Milledgeville from 1885 to 1889. He died of cancer while in Charlotte, North Carolina, on September 24, 1889, and was buried in Davidson College Cemetery.

BIBLIOGRAPHY

Bridges, Hal. *Lee's Maverick General: Daniel Harvey Hill.* New York, 1961. Reprint, Lincoln, Nebr., 1991.

Freeman, Douglas S. *Lee's Lieutenants: A Study in Command.* 3 vols. New York, 1942–1944. Reprint, New York, 1986.

Johnson, Robert U., and C. C. Buel, eds. *Battles and Leaders of the Civil War.* 4 vols. New York, 1887–1888. Reprint, Secaucus, N.J., 1982.

WILLIAM ALAN BLAIR

HILTON, ROBERT B. (1821–1894), congressman from Florida. Hilton, born in Virginia, moved to Savannah, Georgia, in the mid-1840s and began his life-long affiliation with newspapers. He moved to Florida in 1848 and became the editor of the *Tallahassee Floridian.* He was also a lawyer and a prominent Democrat who supported the secession movement in 1861.

Hilton enlisted as a private in the army at the outset of the war but was elected to the Confederate Congress in 1861 as representative of Florida's Second Congressional District and served for the duration. He was a member of the Military Affairs Committee for both of his terms, and of the Inauguration, Patents, Post Office and Post Roads, and War Tax committees during his first term. During his second term, he served on the Conference, Elections, and Territories and Public Lands committees. In 1863 he sponsored a bill to exempt a small number of overseers, fearing that slaves were not being properly supervised. In 1865, he served on the special committee that recommended additional taxes be collected, and that state governors greatly reduce the number of military exemptions being granted; he also strongly supported the promotion of Gen. Robert E. Lee to commander in chief of the Confederate armies.

Hilton was an ardent supporter of the war and at the end of the conflict he had lost everything. He returned to Tallahassee and continued to work as an attorney and editor until his death on January 10, 1894.

BIBLIOGRAPHY

Groene, Bertram H. *Ante-Bellum Tallahassee.* Tallahassee, Fla., 1971.

Sifakis, Stewart. *Who Was Who in the Civil War.* New York, 1988.

Wakelyn, Jon L. *Biographical Dictionary of the Confederacy.* Edited by Frank E. Vandiver. Westport, Conn., 1977.

Warner, Ezra J., and W. Buck Yearns. *Biographical Register of the Confederate Congress.* Baton Rouge, La., 1975.

ARCH FREDRIC BLAKEY

HINDMAN, THOMAS C. (1828–1868), major general. Born on January 28, 1828, in Knoxville, Tennessee, Thomas Carmichael Hindman graduated from Princeton in 1846. He served in the Mexican War in the Second Mississippi Infantry where he was recognized for bravery. After the war he practiced law in Mississippi and served a term in the state legislature before moving to Helena, Arkansas. Hindman, barely over five feet tall with long curling locks, was a colorful character who often wore pink kid gloves and ruffled shirts. He made many political enemies and was wounded by a would-be assassin in the 1850s. He was elected to Congress in 1858 and 1860, but did not serve the latter term.

Hindman advocated Arkansas's secession and, when the war started, raised the Second Arkansas Infantry. He was promoted to brigadier general September 28, 1861, and major general April 14, 1862, following Shiloh. When the Trans-Mississippi Department was established in May 1862, he took command and remained there until July. As head of the department he was an efficient but somewhat tyrannical commander, a fact that hastened his removal.

When replaced, he was given command of the District of Arkansas and led the Confederates at Prairie Grove. Transferred east, he commanded a division in the Army of Tennessee where he became identified with the anti–Braxton Bragg group. He was wounded at Chickamauga, but returned to fight at Chattanooga and was later partially blinded at Kennesaw Mountain. Unable to fight anymore, he moved to Mexico for three years. On September 28, 1868, he was killed at his home in Helena by an unknown assassin, probably for his vocal stand against Reconstruction. He is buried in Maple Hill Cemetery.

BIBLIOGRAPHY

Connelly, Thomas L. *Autumn of Glory: The Army of Tennessee, 1862–1865*. Baton Rouge, La., 1971.
Ferguson, John L. *Arkansas in the Civil War*. Little Rock, Ark., 1964.

ANNE J. BAILEY

HISTORIOGRAPHY. *See* Bibliography and Historiography.

H. L. HUNLEY. The Confederate submarine *H. L. Hunley* was the first undersea warship to sink an enemy vessel in combat. Despite the importance of the act and the fame that resulted, many details of the submarine's history are uncertain. The submarine was the last in a series of privateer submersibles built by a consortium of investors and engineers in New Orleans, Louisiana, and Mobile, Alabama. To reward private initiative, the Confederacy offered prize money equaling 20 percent of the value of any Union warship sunk. The submarine partners planned to earn prize money sinking Federal warships.

The partners originally included James R. McClintock and Baxter Watson, machinists and engineers; Robert Ruffin Barrow, financier; and Horace L. Hunley and Henry J. Leovy as surety on the privateer bond. The men first built a submarine called *Pioneer* in New Orleans in 1862. The submarine received a privateering commission but apparently never saw action before being destroyed when the city fell.

Hunley, McClintock, and Watson moved to Mobile, Alabama, and built another submarine there. The machine was constructed in the shop of Thomas B. Lyons and Thomas W. Parks and may have been named *American Diver*. Hunley financed the construction of the hull and research to develop an "electro-magnetic engine" to propel it. An effort to produce an electric engine for it failed, and instead a hand-operated crank turned by four men was installed. *American Diver* was lost, without loss of life, in rough seas off Fort Morgan in an attempted attack on the Federal fleet.

Hunley lost little time in building another submarine. He retained one-third interest and sold the remainder to E. C. Singer, R. W. Dunn, B. A. Whitney, and J. D. Breaman. Constructed as a larger version of *American Diver,* the new submarine was propelled by nine men, with one man steering and controlling depth and the other eight turning a crank propeller. The new vessel apparently was first called *Fish Boat*, but was later renamed *H. L. Hunley*. The boat was described as about thirty feet long, four feet wide, and five feet deep. The submarine would sink an enemy ship by passing beneath it and allowing a towed explosive "torpedo" to detonate against the ship's side. Control of the towed

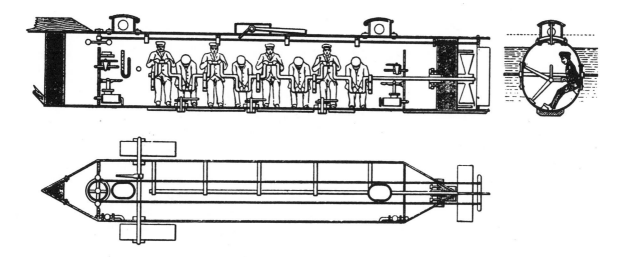

H. L. HUNLEY. Cutaway plan by William A. Alexander, 1863. NAVAL HISTORICAL CENTER, WASHINGTON, D.C.

torpedo proved too uncertain, and it was later mounted on a spar projecting beyond the bow.

H. L. Hunley was tested at Mobile and then sent by railroad flatcar to Charleston, South Carolina. Large Union naval targets, and chances for helping the Confederacy and earning prize money, were more plentiful off that port. McClintock, operating as skipper, took the submarine on several trips against the blockaders off Charleston Harbor but failed to meet the enemy. In late August 1863, the Confederate government seized the submarine and replaced the crew with naval volunteers from the ironclads *Chicora* and *Palmetto State,* under Lt. John A. Payne. On August 29, 1863, while learning to operate the submarine, Payne accidentally sank it, killing five men.

The sub was raised and repaired and placed under Horace Hunley and Lt. George E. Dixon of the Twenty-first Alabama Volunteers. The two men trained another naval crew in September, but a second accidental sinking on October 15 killed Hunley and seven crewmen. Dixon persuaded Gen. P. G. T. Beauregard to allow another attempt against the steam sloop USS *Housatonic.* The sub was raised a second time, refitted, and a new crew trained. On February 17, 1864, Dixon and a mixed navy and army crew attacked *Housatonic.* The torpedo sank the blockader but may have also sunk *Hunley.* The submarine did not return from its raid and has never been found.

Two modern reconstructions of *Hunley* have been built by local groups working with city museums and technical schools, one in Charleston in 1966 and 1967, and one in Mobile in 1990. Each is located at the city museum. They were based primarily on a painting by Conrad Wise Chapman, now in the Museum of the Confederacy at Richmond, and on somewhat hazy recollections of the builder and various witnesses. No contemporary plans are known to exist. Both modern ships were of welded construction with simulated rivet detailing. Neither should be termed an exact replica, but a conjectural reconstruction, as accurate as research and modern techniques allowed at the time of its construction.

BIBLIOGRAPHY

Duncan, Ruth H. *The Captain and Submarine CSS H. L. Hunley.* Memphis, Tenn., 1965.

Kloeppel, James E. *Danger beneath the Waves: A History of the Confederate Submarine H. L. Hunley.* College Park, Ga., 1987.

Perry, Milton F. *Infernal Machines: The Story of Confederate Submarine and Mine Warfare.* Baton Rouge, La., 1965.

Robinson, William Morrison. *The Confederate Privateers.* New Haven, Conn., 1928.

U.S. Naval War Records Office. *Official Records of the Union and Confederate Navies in the War of the Rebellion.* Washington, D.C., 1894–1927. Ser. 1, vol. 15, pp. 229, 231, 238, 327–337, 366–367, 528, 592; ser. 1, vol. 16, p. 427; ser. 2, vol. 1, pp. 104, 256.

KEVIN J. FOSTER

HODGE, BENJAMIN LOUIS (c. 1824–1864),

colonel and congressman from Louisiana. Born in Tennessee, Hodge was one of Louisiana's wealthiest men before the war. Little is known of his background, but by 1860 Hodge's estate was valued at over one hundred thousand dollars. He was one of Louisiana's most successful attorneys, owned business property in Shreveport, and had interest in plantations and two steamboats. A Whig, he served several terms in the state legislature and was a presidential elector for John Bell.

As a delegate to the Louisiana secession convention in 1861, Hodge voted for secession. Following an unsuccessful run for the Louisiana senate in 1861, he volunteered as colonel of the Nineteenth Louisiana Infantry. Plagued by illness, he resigned his commission on May 29, 1862. In 1863, Hodge placed fourth in the Louisiana gubernatorial race. He served briefly as presiding judge of the Trans-Mississippi Department's military court, but stepped down in 1864 to take his congressional seat, which he won in an uncontested race.

Hodge attended one session of Congress. Although he held no committee posts, Hodge voted regularly and advocated higher taxes and the regulation of foreign commerce. Unlike his predecessor, Henry Marshall, Hodge exhibited strong support for the Davis administration. He died August 12, 1864, near Shreveport.

BIBLIOGRAPHY

Warner, Ezra J., and W. Buck Yearns. *Biographical Register of the Confederate Congress.* Baton Rouge, La., 1975.

Yearns, Wilfred B. *The Confederate Congress.* Athens, Ga., 1960.

Wakelyn, Jon L. *Biographical Dictionary of the Confederacy.* Edited by Frank E. Vandiver. Westport, Conn., 1977.

KEVIN S. FONTENOT

HODGE, GEORGE BAIRD (1828–1892), acting

brigadier general and congressman from Kentucky. Hodge was born in Fleming County, Kentucky, in April 1828. The son of a prominent planter, he attended briefly the Mayville Seminary in Kentucky and then the U.S. Naval Academy at Annapolis, where he graduated in 1845 and was commissioned a midshipman. He remained in the navy until 1851, when he resigned as a lieutenant. Hodge then studied law and opened a practice in Newport, Kentucky, where he also became active in politics. In 1852 he ran unsuccessfully for the U.S. Congress as a Whig. He then joined the Democratic party, winning a seat in the Kentucky state legislature in

1859, which he held until 1861. He was also an elector on the John C. Breckinridge ticket in 1860.

At the beginning of the Civil War, Hodge, a staunch state rights advocate, was sympathetic to the Southern cause, but only reluctantly supported secession. He served as a member of the Executive Council of the provisional government of Kentucky in 1861. He also enlisted in the Confederate army as a private under Gen. Simon Bolivar Buckner. Kentucky's secession governor, George W. Johnson, appointed Hodge to represent Kentucky in the Provisional Confederate Congress. Then in January 1862 Hodge was elected to represent northern Kentucky's Eighth Congressional District in the First Congress.

Hodge alternated his time between the army and the Congress, but he preferred life in the military and the contributions he could make there. He was soon promoted to captain because of his family and political connections and was made adjutant general on Breckinridge's staff. Hodge was able to improve his standing after showing gallantry at the Battle of Shiloh, resulting in his promotion to major on May 6, 1862. He continued as Breckinridge's adjutant general, and exactly one year later he attained the rank of colonel.

With this promotion, Hodge first served for a short time as inspector general at Cumberland Gap. He then commanded William Preston's cavalry under Maj. Gen. Joseph Wheeler and Brig. Gen. Nathan Bedford Forrest. Moving through eastern Tennessee, this brigade took part in the Chattanooga operations and, after fighting at Chickamauga, rode in Wheeler's raid of northern Georgia in October 1863. Hodge's actions in these campaigns brought special commendation from Wheeler and labeled him a cavalry hero. For his efforts, Hodge was appointed brigadier general on November 20, 1863, but the Senate failed to confirm the rank.

Throughout this period, Hodge had continued to hold his congressional seat, although he was seldom present. When he was there, he frequently offered and supported firm military legislation. His voting record on conscription was strong, and in February 1863 Congress passed a resolution he had proposed calling for all captured black Union soldiers to be held until they could be returned to their masters. Captured freedmen were to be "sold into perpetual bondage, for the purpose of raising a fund to reimburse citizens of the Confederacy who have lost their slave property." As a representative from a Union-occupied district, Hodge also supported other stern economic measures as necessary for the Confederacy to survive. His continual absence from the House, however, did not allow him to work as effectively as he could have to obtain relief for his home state. Remaining in his cavalry command, he decided not to run for election to the Second Congress in the fall of 1863.

In August 1864 Hodge's name was resubmitted for promotion to brigadier general, but once again it went unconfirmed by the Senate. Nevertheless, he was assigned to head the District of Southwest Mississippi and East Louisiana. Under him the command began to deteriorate, bringing complaints of poor leadership from his critics. In January 1865 Hodge was brought up on formal charges of incompetency and cowardice. Although he successfully defended his record against these accusations, Forrest requested that he relinquish his command of the district and relieved him in March, ordering him to Richmond for special assignment. The disillusioned Hodge refused to go and remained in Meridian, Mississippi, where on May 10, 1865, he surrendered and was paroled as a brigadier general.

After the war, Hodge reopened his law practice in Newport, Kentucky, and once again became involved in politics. In 1872 he was an elector on Horace Greeley's presidential ticket. He was elected to the state senate a year later as a Democrat and served there until 1877, when he moved to Longwood, Orange County, Florida, to become a farmer. He died there on August 1, 1892.

BIBLIOGRAPHY

Alexander, Thomas B., and Richard E. Beringer. *The Anatomy of the Confederate Congress: A Study of the Influences of Member Characteristics on Legislative Voting Behavior, 1861–1865.* Nashville, Tenn., 1972.

Davis, William C. *Breckinridge: Statesman, Soldier, Symbol.* Baton Rouge, La., 1974.

Henry, Robert S. *"First with the Most" Forrest.* Indianapolis, Ind., 1944.

Yearns, Wilfred B. *The Confederate Congress.* Athens, Ga., 1960.

ROBERT F. PACE

HOGG, JOSEPH LEWIS (1806–1862), brigadier general. Born in Georgia on September 13, 1806, Hogg moved to Tuscaloosa County, Alabama, twelve years later. There he studied law and developed an interest in politics. In 1839 Hogg moved to Texas, where he began a law practice. He also became active in politics and was elected to the Republic of Texas Congress. During the Mexican War, Hogg served as a private in one of the Texas regiments. Afterward he was elected to the state senate.

In 1860 Hogg was elected to the state secession convention, where he voted in favor of secession. He then accepted a commission as a colonel of state troops and was given the job of organizing the force into regiments. On February 14, 1862, Hogg was commissioned a brigadier general in the Confederate army.

Hogg was ordered to Corinth, Mississippi, and arrived shortly after the battle of Shiloh. He soon fell victim to dysentery, however. He died on May 16, 1862, in Corinth and is buried in the Confederate section of the Corinth Cemetery. It is believed that he never had a chance to wear his general's uniform. Hogg's son became governor of Texas and his granddaughter, Ima Hogg, was active politically in the state for many years.

BIBLIOGRAPHY

Roberts, O. M. *Texas.* Vol. 11 of *Confederate Military History.* Edited by Clement A. Evans. Atlanta, 1899. Vol. 15 of extended ed. Wilmington, N.C., 1989.

Warner, Ezra J. *Generals in Gray: Lives of the Confederate Commanders.* Baton Rouge, La., 1959.

GEORGE A. REAVES III

HOKE, ROBERT FREDERICK (1837–1912), major general. Hoke was born in Lincolnton, North Carolina, May 27, 1837, and was educated in the local schools and at the Kentucky Military Institute. He was only seventeen when, following the death of his father, he was placed in charge of family industries that included a cotton mill and ironworks.

At the start of the war Hoke enlisted as a private in Company K, First North Carolina Infantry. He was a second lieutenant at Big Bethel in which he was cited by D. H. Hill for "great coolness, judgment and efficiency." He was promoted to captain shortly thereafter and received three more promotions within nine months: to major of the Thirty-third North Carolina, November 27, 1861; to lieutenant colonel of the same regiment, January 17, 1862; and to colonel of the Twenty-first North Carolina, August 5, 1862.

Hoke's vigorous repulse of Meade on the Confederate right at Fredericksburg evoked high praise from Jubal Early, who recommended Hoke for promotion, saying, "He is an officer of great energy and industry. . . . He displayed the most conspicuous gallantry . . . and the ability to command of a very high order." Hoke received his brigadiership on April 23, 1863, to date from January 17.

Wounded at Chancellorsville, Hoke missed the Gettysburg campaign. Late in the year he was transferred to North Carolina where he further distinguished himself by capturing the strongly fortified town of Plymouth, a victory that was regarded by some as one of the most brilliant of the war. A telegram from Jefferson Davis congratulated Hoke and concluded, "You are promoted to be a Maj. Genl."

Hoke returned to Virginia in the summer of 1864. He helped P. G. T. Beauregard bottle up Benjamin Butler at Drewry's Bluff and resisted strongly Ulysses S. Grant's attacks at Cold Harbor. By early 1865 Hoke was back in North Carolina serving under Joseph E. Johnston. His final action was at Bentonville. He surrendered and was paroled at Greensboro, May 1, 1865.

The general then returned to the family businesses and served as a director of the North Carolina Railroad Company. He died in Raleigh, July 3, 1912, and was buried there.

BIBLIOGRAPHY

Compiled Military Service Records. Robert Frederick Hoke. Microcopy M331, Roll 129. Record Group 109. National Archives, Washington, D.C.

Hill, D. H., Jr. *North Carolina.* Vol. 4 of *Confederate Military History.* Edited by Clement A. Evans. Atlanta, 1899. Vol. 5 of extended ed. Wilmington, N.C., 1987.

Warner, Ezra J. *Generals in Gray: Lives of the Confederate Commanders.* Baton Rouge, La., 1959.

Wright, E. A. "Tribute to Maj. Gen. Robert F. Hoke." *Confederate Veteran* 20 (1912): 570–571. Reprint, Wilmington, N.C., 1985.

LOWELL REIDENBAUGH

ROBERT FREDERICK HOKE.   NATIONAL ARCHIVES

HOLCOMBE, JAMES P. (1820–1873), congressman from Virginia, diplomat, and secret service agent. A native of Powhatan County, Virginia, Holcombe came from a background unlikely for an ardent secessionist. The eldest son of an antislavery doctor who freed his bondsmen and moved to Indiana, Holcombe attended Yale and studied law at the University of Virginia. Like his father, he moved to the Midwest, where he wrote legal treatises, but he later returned to Virginia and eventually taught law at the university in Charlottesville. A Presbyterian, Holcombe and his wife, Ann Selden Watts, had six children.

Holcombe resigned his professorship in 1861 and harnessed his oratorical skills and state rights advocacy to win election to Virginia's secession convention. Elected to the House of Representatives (1862–1864), he bent his state rights principles to the harsh demands of war, even supporting heavy taxation and government intrusion into the economy. After standing down from his congressional seat, Holcombe went in early 1864 to Nova Scotia to sort out claims involving the capture of the Federal ship *Chesapeake* by unauthorized Southern privateers and to organize the return of Confederate soldiers in Canada.

He pursued the latter objective indifferently until new, more aggressive Confederate commissioners arrived. With one of these, Clement C. Clay, Holcombe was drawn into the shadowy machinations of the Confederate intelligence service. He helped Clay begin a correspondence with Horace Greeley, ostensibly about peace negotiations but in fact designed to encourage Northern opposition to Lincoln. When he returned to Richmond, he urged Secretary of State Judah P. Benjamin to expand efforts to disrupt Northern morale. Among other schemes, he advocated promoting anarchy in the North to persuade the northwestern states to secede from the Union.

After the war he ran a private school, first on his Bedford County farm and later at Capon Springs, West Virginia, where he died.

BIBLIOGRAPHY

Gaines, William H., Jr. *Biographical Register of Members, Virginia State Convention of 1861, First Session.* Richmond, Va., 1969.

Tidwell, William A., with James O. Hall and David Winfred Gaddy. *Come Retribution: The Confederate Secret Service and the Assassination of Lincoln.* Jackson, Miss., 1988.

Warner, Ezra J., and W. Buck Yearns. *Biographical Register of the Confederate Congress.* Baton Rouge, La., 1975.

NELSON D. LANKFORD

HOLDEN, WILLIAM W.

HOLDEN, WILLIAM W. (1818–1892), newspaper editor, politician, and postwar governor of North Carolina. During the 1850s Holden, as editor of the Raleigh *North Carolina Standard,* was the most powerful political leader in the state. Largely owing to his efforts the Democratic party had emerged by 1850 as the dominant political organization in the state.

At the end of the decade Holden found himself at a disadvantage in a struggle for control of the Democratic party with Governor John W. Ellis, a strong Southern rights proponent. Although Holden had long advocated Southern rights on the slavery issue and had in theory supported the right of a state to secede from the Union, as a delegate to the Democratic National Convention at Charleston in 1860 he was appalled by the fervor for secession among delegates from the lower South. This experience, along with his rival Ellis's sectional stance, swung Holden toward a Unionist position during the crucial 1860 presidential campaign. After Abraham Lincoln's election he filled the columns of the *Standard* with appeals for a watch-and-wait policy toward the new president. He almost single-handedly organized the Union party of early 1861, which defeated at the polls a call for a state convention to determine North Carolina's position in the secession crisis.

Holden's watch-and-wait policy ended with the firing on Fort Sumter and Lincoln's call for seventy-five thousand troops to suppress the rebellion in the South. He served as a delegate to the convention that on May 20 took North Carolina out of the Union. He voted for the secession ordinance and proclaimed that North Carolina should give her "last dollar and her last man" to win Confederate independence. He later insisted, however, that his signing of the secession document "was the saddest and most reluctant act" of his life.

Hardly had North Carolina joined the Confederacy than Holden found reason to attack the Democratic administration in Raleigh. He charged that Governor Ellis and his successor, Henry T. Clark, were derelict in their preparations for war and that they had ignored former Unionists in their appointments to military positions. Holden soon organized a caucus of "conservatives" in the state convention to oppose the original secessionists who controlled the state executive branch and the legislature.

In early 1862 the fall of Roanoke Island, New Bern, and adjacent areas gave Holden ample ammunition to assail the Democrats. He also began to lump the Davis administration in Richmond with his foes at home, charging that the Confederate government had done nothing to save the state from the Lincolnites and had discriminated against North Carolinians in its appointments to office. When the Confederate Congress passed the Conscription Act in April 1862, Holden denounced the law as oppressive and unconstitutional, but he did not call for resistance to it. He organized the Conservative party to resist encroachments against the rights of North Carolinians and secured the nomination of Zebulon Vance for governor. Primarily owing to the efforts of Holden, who conducted a masterful campaign through the columns of the *Standard,* the Conservatives dealt the so-called Confederate party a stunning defeat in the 1862 election.

Whig Conservatives, the largest element in the new administration, never completely trusted Holden and were uncomfortable with his leadership of the Conservative party. The Raleigh editor's continuing assaults upon old secessionists and his unrelenting criticism of Confederate policies particularly appalled Governor Vance and Senator William A. Graham. Holden even threatened to lead the state out of the Confederacy if the Davis administration did not cease its anti–North Carolina bias and respect the rights of the people. Many staunch Confederates charged, with some justification, that Holden was giving aid and comfort to the enemy and encouraging desertions from the army, a charge that he vehemently denied.

When the carnage of the war reached a new high in mid-1863, he called for negotiations to "arrest this awful evil." He advocated a peace that would "preserve the rights of the sovereign states and the institutions of the South [slavery]." In response to his call, "peace meetings" were held throughout North Carolina, precipitating a bitter debate that threatened Confederate intervention and a civil war within the state. Finally, at the urging of Vance and Graham, Holden in September called off the peace rallies, a few days before Georgia troops, passing through Raleigh, sacked the office of his newspaper.

In early 1864 Holden proposed that a state convention be called to initiate, along with other Southern states and in cooperation with Confederate authorities, negotiations with the Lincoln government before it was too late to save the South. When the Davis administration suspended the writ of habeas corpus, mainly in reaction to events in North Carolina, Holden announced his candidacy for governor against Vance, who opposed the state convention movement. Holden suffered a humiliating defeat in the August election, which occurred at a time when Lincoln's defeat at the polls appeared imminent and Confederate independence assured.

After the war Holden was appointed provisional governor of North Carolina by President Andrew Johnson. In 1866 he became disenchanted with Johnson and his plan of Reconstruction. He cast his lot with the Republicans in Congress, and when military Reconstruction was imposed upon the South, he announced his support for black political rights. He assisted in the organization of the Republican party in North Carolina and was elected governor in 1868. After the Democratic Conservatives captured control of the legislature in 1870, he was impeached and removed from office. Retiring to private life, he died in Raleigh in 1892.

BIBLIOGRAPHY

Barrett, John G. *The Civil War in North Carolina.* Chapel Hill, N.C., 1963.

Hamilton, J. G. de Roulhac, and Max R. Williams, eds. *The Papers of William Alexander Graham.* 8 vols. to date. Raleigh, N.C., 1957–.

Harris, William C. *William Woods Holden: Firebrand of North Carolina Politics.* Baton Rouge, La., 1987.

Kruman, Marc W. *Parties and Politics in North Carolina, 1836–1865.* Baton Rouge, La., 1983.

Raper, Horace W. "William W. Holden and the Peace Movement in North Carolina." *North Carolina Historical Review* 31 (1954): 493–516.

Yates, Richard E. *The Confederacy and Zeb Vance.* Tuscaloosa, Ala., 1958.

WILLIAM C. HARRIS

HOLDER, WILLIAM DUNBAR

HOLDER, WILLIAM DUNBAR (1824–1900), colonel and congressman from Mississippi. Holder, born in Tennessee, moved in 1839 to Mississippi when he was fourteen years old. While living in Pontotoc, Holder was appointed U.S. district clerk and later became a deputy U.S. marshal. In 1853 he was elected to the Mississippi legislature but did not seek reelection after serving one term.

In April 1861 he organized an infantry company, which entered Confederate service with the Seventeenth Mississippi Infantry. Holder served as a captain of Company C and after participation in the battles at Manassas, Leesburg, and Chickahominy, was promoted to colonel in 1862. At Malvern Hill, Holder was wounded; a rifle ball shattered his left thigh. After he had recovered somewhat, he led his company at Chancellorsville. At Gettysburg he was again seriously wounded, shot through his abdomen.

When Reuben Davis resigned from the Second Congress in 1863, Holder succeeded him. At first, Holder opposed higher taxes, the arming of slaves, and increased government control, but the South's military setbacks and deteriorating political and economic situation forced him to agree to desperate measures. Not a strong supporter of Jefferson Davis, Holder wanted the Congress to have more influence in running the Confederacy. He introduced bills to ameliorate the sorry conditions of enlisted men. About a month before Congress adjourned for the last time, Holder resigned—apparently in frustration over the course of events. After the war he engaged in farming and returned to public service in 1886 as deputy state auditor.

BIBLIOGRAPHY

Alexander, Thomas B., and Richard E. Beringer. *The Anatomy of the Confederate Congress: A Study of the Influences of Member Characteristics on Legislative Voting Behavior, 1861–1865.* Nashville, Tenn., 1972.

Warner, Ezra J., and W. Buck Yearns. *Biographical Register of the Confederate Congress.* Baton Rouge, La., 1975.

RAY SKATES

HOLLIDAY, FREDERICK WILLIAM MACKEY

HOLLIDAY, FREDERICK WILLIAM MACKEY (1828–1899), colonel, and Virginia congressman and postwar governor. Born into a prosperous family in Winchester, Virginia, Holliday returned to his hometown after graduating from Yale College and studying law at the University of Virginia. He served as commonwealth attorney in Winchester from 1849 until the war. Despite his favorable impressions of the North gleaned while living in

Connecticut, Holliday became increasingly troubled by perceived threats to the Southern way of life. By 1860 he was convinced that disunion would likely be the only honorable course for Virginia to pursue after Abraham Lincoln's inauguration. He was defeated for election to the Virginia secession convention of 1861 but saw himself vindicated with secession in April.

Holliday became captain of a Frederick County volunteer company when war broke out and rose to the rank of colonel of the Thirty-third Virginia Infantry in the Stonewall Brigade. He saw action at First Manassas, Jackson's Shenandoah Valley campaign, and the Seven Days' Battle. Holliday won praise from superiors for his "coolness" under fire at the Seven Days' and for a "truly providential" escape from injury. He was not so fortunate later that year: at Cedar Mountain he lost an arm on August 9, 1862, and retired from active service.

In 1863 he stood for election against incumbent congressman Alexander R. Boteler and won. In Congress he served on the Quartermaster's and Commissary Department and Claims committees. He generally supported the Davis administration and took an interest in employment of disabled soldiers like himself. He struggled to keep the Confederate cause alive to the end. As late as March 18, 1865, he proposed a resolution urging Congress to redouble its energy "to the maintenance of our great cause and to the prosecution of the war to a successful issue."

After the war Holliday returned to the law and Democratic politics and was elected governor of Virginia in 1877. He died in Winchester on May 20, 1899.

BIBLIOGRAPHY

James Tice Moore. "Frederick William Mackey Holliday: Paradoxical Patrician." In *The Governors of Virginia, 1860–1978*. Edited by Edward Younger and James Tice Moore. Charlottesville, Va., 1982.

James Tice Moore. "Of Cavaliers and Yankees: Frederick W. M. Holliday and the Sectional Crisis, 1845–1861." *Virginia Magazine of History and Biography* 99 (1991): 351–388.

Wakelyn, Jon L. *Biographical Dictionary of the Confederacy*. Edited by Frank E. Vandiver. Westport, Conn., 1977.

Warner, Ezra J., and W. Buck Yearns. *Biographical Register of the Confederate Congress*. Baton Rouge, La., 1975.

NELSON D. LANKFORD

HOLLINS, GEORGE N. (1799–1878), naval officer.

Born in Baltimore on September 20, 1799, Hollins entered the U.S. Navy as a midshipman in 1814. After serving aboard USS *Erie* in its attempt to raise the British blockade of Chesapeake Bay, he was transferred to USS *President*. Captured at Bermuda, Hollins remained a prisoner of war until the conclusion of hostilities. He received a presentation sword for his performance during the Algerian war in 1815. He subsequently served aboard several vessels, attaining the rank of lieutenant in 1828, commander in 1841, and captain in 1855; his only action was the bombardment of Greytown, Nicaragua, in 1854.

When Hollins submitted his resignation in 1861, the Navy Department rejected it and ordered his arrest. Avoiding capture, Hollins reached Montgomery, Alabama, in March, where he advised Confederate officials about creating a navy. Appointed a commander, Hollins gained fame by capturing USS *St. Nicholas* in the Potomac River on July 29. Eleven days later he received orders to assume command of the James River defenses. He was reassigned on July 31 to command the New Orleans Naval Station and defeated the Federal blockading squadron in October. Promoted to flag officer, Hollins received orders in December to take his fleet up the Mississippi River to support the Confederate defenses at Columbus, Kentucky.

In April 1862, he abandoned New Madrid, Missouri, took his fleet to Memphis, and requested permission to proceed with the vessels to New Orleans. When Secretary of the Navy Stephen R. Mallory refused, Hollins abandoned his fleet and traveled to New Orleans aboard *McRae* against orders. Hollins believed, correctly, that the real threat to the Crescent City was the Union fleet below Forts Jackson and St. Phillip. For this action, Mallory demoted Hollins to captain and ordered him to proceed to Richmond immediately. Instead of opposing Union Flag Officer David Farragut at the forts, Hollins sat on a court of inquiry investigating midshipmen. He saw no further action.

After the war, Hollins returned to his native Baltimore, where he died on January 18, 1878.

BIBLIOGRAPHY

Hollins, George N. "A Daring Exploit." *Southern Historical Society Papers* 24 (1896): 88–91. Reprint, Wilmington, N.C., 1991.

Pratt, Fletcher. *Civil War on the Western Waters*. New York, 1956.

Sweetman, Jack. *American Naval History: An Illustrated Chronology of the U.S. Navy and Marine Corps 1775–Present*. Annapolis, Md., 1984.

LAWRENCE L. HEWITT

HOLLY SPRINGS, MISSISSIPPI. Located

thirty-five miles southeast of Memphis, Tennessee, on the Mississippi Central Railroad, this northern Mississippi town was the site of a raid by Confederate Gen. Earl Van Dorn on December 20, 1862. As a result of this raid, Gen. Ulysses S. Grant was forced to abandon his drive down the Mississippi Central Railroad aimed at capturing Vicksburg, Mississippi. The Union lost 1,500 men captured and over $1,500,000 in destroyed supplies.

In the fall of 1862, Gen. Ulysses S. Grant drove south from Tennessee into Mississippi. He established a supply

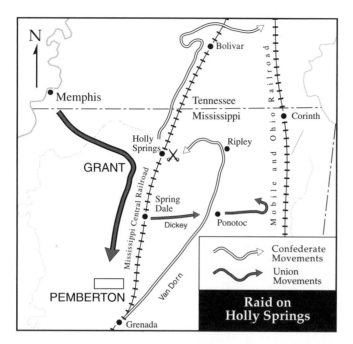

Raid on Holly Springs

base at Holly Springs, planning to use the facilities of the Mississippi Central to support his drive. As part of his advance, Grant ordered his cavalry under the command of Col. Theophilus L. Dickey to raid the Mobile and Ohio Railroad. Dickey, with eight hundred men, moved out of Spring Dale, Mississippi, on December 14.

Lt. Col. John Griffith commanded the Texas Cavalry Brigade in Gen. John C. Pemberton's army at Grenada, Mississippi. He recommended that Pemberton concentrate the cavalry under the command of Gen. Earl Van Dorn in order to raid Grant's supply base at Holly Springs. Pemberton agreed and on December 12, he placed Van Dorn in charge of a cavalry force made up of brigades commanded by Colonels Griffith, William H. Jackson, and Robert McCulloch. Griffith commanded the Sixth, Ninth, and Twenty-seventh Texas Cavalry; Jackson's force was made up of Mississippi and Tennessee cavalry; and McCulloch commanded the First Mississippi Cavalry and the Second Missouri Cavalry. The total force was approximately 3,500 men.

Van Dorn informed the three brigade commanders of the raid, emphasizing that their only chance of success was absolute secrecy—they were to tell their men nothing. The brigade commanders, knowing they faced a long ride, weeded out any troopers and horses that would not be able to keep pace.

On the evening of December 17, Van Dorn and his men moved out of Grenada along the Ponotoc road. Many of the men thought they were after Dickey's column, known to be along the Mobile and Ohio Railroad. Van Dorn, however, wanted to avoid Dickey's column, if possible. But in spite of his efforts, the Union force brushed the rear of the Southerners.

When he left Ponotoc, Van Dorn avoided any road leading directly toward Holly Springs, hoping this deception would lead the Northerners into believing he planned to strike into Tennessee. The men went into camp on the evening of the eighteenth, still ignorant of their objective. That afternoon Van Dorn had sent one of his men ahead to scout the town, and he reported back late that evening that the garrison had no knowledge of the approaching column.

While Van Dorn conferred with his brigade commanders, the men ate and fed their horses. The column then countermarched along the Ripley road until it came to the Holly Springs turnoff. As the Confederates approached the town, they posted guards at every farmhouse to ensure that no one warned the Federals they were coming. Van Dorn also increased the pace of the column. He wanted to reach Holly Springs ahead of any Northern scouts.

About 10:00 P.M. on the nineteenth Van Dorn halted for a final briefing. He also separated Griffith's Brigade from the main force and sent it along a side road that would bring it into Holly Springs from a different direction. When it became apparent that the columns would reach the town before daylight, Van Dorn ordered the commanders to stop five miles away and await sunrise. An hour before dawn, the men moved out in columns of four with guns loaded, but uncapped. McCulloch's brigade led on the main road. The First Mississippi and First Missouri of this brigade were to attack the Union cavalry. The Second Missouri had orders to dismount and attack any infantry they encountered. The Texans were to charge from the east and mop up any Federals around the depot. In addition, Griffith had orders to set up a roadblock south of town. Jackson was to approach from the north to cut off any Northerners escaping in that direction.

When Dickey had brushed against the Southerners close to Ponotoc, he had sent scouts to report their presence to Grant, but owing to a misunderstanding, the scouts did not depart immediately. Dickey did not discover this until later. When he did, he sent other scouts to Grant, but they were too late. Luckily, Grant had received word from other sources that raiders were on the loose. He warned his depot commanders to keep a sharp lookout. When Col. Robert C. Murphy, commander at Holly Springs, received this message, he ordered his cavalry commander to be ready to join a pursuit column. Murphy had under his command the 101st Illinois Infantry, detachments of the Twentieth and Sixty-second Illinois, and six companies of the Second Illinois Cavalry.

On the morning of the twentieth an African American informed Murphy that 5,000 Confederates were advancing on Holly Springs along the Ripley road. Murphy tried to order the crews manning two trains at the depot to alert the garrisons north and south of the town, and he set the infantry to work building barricades out of cotton. It was too late.

Van Dorn's men captured the Union pickets without firing a shot. With the pickets captured, Griffith's Confederates were able to surprise the Northerners at the depot and capture them after firing only a few shots. Among their prisoners was Colonel Murphy. McCulloch's First Mississippi then charged to the fairgrounds where the Union cavalry camped. The First Missouri followed, mopping up elements of the 101st Illinois. At the fairgrounds they surrounded the Union cavalry and, after a hard fight, forced them to surrender. With this action, Holly Springs was in Confederate hands. In addition to the supplies captured, they paroled 1,500 Northern soldiers. Van Dorn set up pickets, knowing that Grant would learn of his location the minute he cut the telegraph wires. After allowing his men to reequip with the best supplies, Van Dorn ordered the rest destroyed. Grant's wife and several other Union women who were in the town were not harmed.

At 4:00 P.M. the Confederates rode out of Holly Springs, their work completed. The destruction of the Holly Springs supply base, along with Nathan Bedford Forrest's raids in western Tennessee, forced Grant to abandon his advance down the Mississippi Central Railroad. This delayed the capture of Vicksburg for six months.

BIBLIOGRAPHY

Bearss, Edwin C. *Decision in Mississippi.* Little Rock, Ark., 1962.

Dupree, J. G. "The Capture of Holly Springs, Mississippi." *Mississippi Historical Society* 4 (1901): 49–61.

Hartje, Robert G. *Van Dorn: The Life and Times of a Confederate General.* Nashville, Tenn., 1967.

GEORGE A. REAVES III

HOLMES, THEOPHILUS H. (1804–1880), major

general. Born November 13, 1804, in Sampson County, North Carolina, Theophilus Hunter Holmes graduated from West Point in 1829, forty-fourth out of forty-six. He earned a brevet for gallantry in the Seminole War and a second one in the Mexican War. He resigned from the Federal army in April 1861.

Commissioned a brigadier general in the Confederate army that June, he commanded the troops at Fredericksburg and was promoted to major general in October. He led a division during the Seven Days' Battles but was criticized for his actions at Malvern Hill. On July 16, 1862, he was given command of the Trans-Mississippi Department, replacing the efficient but unpopular Thomas C. Hindman. Holmes was a poor choice for the position and frequently used his personal friendship with Jefferson Davis as an excuse for disregarding orders. Known as the "Old Granny General," Holmes was frequently ill, and some suspected that he had "softening of the brain." He proved unequal to his task and in February 1863 was replaced by E. Kirby Smith. In March 1863 Holmes was assigned to command

THEOPHILUS H. HOLMES.   LIBRARY OF CONGRESS

the District of Arkansas, including the Indian Territory and Missouri. In an attempt to relieve Vicksburg, Holmes unsuccessfully assaulted Helena, Arkansas, on July 4, 1863. Early the next year he learned that several Arkansas politicians were working for his removal. Rather than face dismissal Holmes resigned on March 16, 1864, and the next month he was placed in command of North Carolina reserves.

He died near Fayetteville, North Carolina, on June 21, 1880, and is buried there.

BIBLIOGRAPHY

Bailey, Anne J. *Between the Enemy and Texas.* Fort Worth, Tex., 1989.

Castel, Albert. "Theophilus Holmes: Pallbearer of the Confederacy." *Civil War Times Illustrated* 16 (1977): 10–17.

Kerby, Robert L. *Kirby Smith's Confederacy: The Trans-Mississippi South, 1863–1865.* New York, 1972.

Park, Joseph H. *General Kirby Smith, C.S.A.* Baton Rouge, La., 1954.

ANNE J. BAILEY

HOLT, HINES (1805–1868), congressman from Geor-

gia. Born in Baldwin County and raised in neighboring

Putnam County, Holt graduated from the University of Georgia in 1824. He studied law and settled in Columbus, Georgia, then a frontier river town. He spent the rest of his life there and became one of Columbus's most prominent attorneys and wealthiest planters. Holt was elected to Congress as a Whig in 1841, where he served a single term. He actively campaigned for the Know-Nothing party in the mid-1850s and traveled around the state to oppose Democrat Joseph E. Brown's gubernatorial candidacy in 1857.

A Unionist in 1860, Holt attended the state Constitutional Union convention in Milledgeville to support John Bell's presidential candidacy that year. Too old for military service, he served as a representative of Georgia's Third District in the First Confederate Congress. In that position, he actively pushed for peace negotiations and, along with Henry S. Foote of Tennessee, introduced the first official peace proposal in Congress in September 1861. In it, he called for a Confederate delegation to be sent to Washington to negotiate a just and honorable peace. But the measure was tabled by a decisive vote and never discussed on the House floor. In 1862, Holt unsuccessfully sought legislation authorizing Confederate government purchases of staple crops, particularly cotton. He resigned his seat later that year and was replaced by Porter Ingram. Though he returned to private life in Columbus, he continued to serve Governor Brown in an occasional advisory capacity for the rest of the war. Holt was elected to the state constitutional convention that met in November 1865, the last public office he held before his death in Milledgeville in 1868.

BIBLIOGRAPHY

Northen, William W., ed. *Men of Mark in Georgia.* Vol. 3. Atlanta, 1908. Reprint, Spartanburg, S.C., 1974.

Worseley, Etta Blanchard. *Columbus on the Chattahoochee.* Columbus, Ga., 1951.

Yearns, Wilfred B. *The Confederate Congress.* Athens, Ga., 1960.

JOHN C. INSCOE

HOLTZCLAW, JAMES THADEUS

HOLTZCLAW, JAMES THADEUS (1833–1893), brigadier general. Born in present-day Henry Hotze County, Georgia, on December 17, 1833, Holtzclaw spent his youth in Lafayette, Georgia, before moving to Montgomery, Alabama in 1855. A practicing attorney in Montgomery at the start of the Civil War, he began his military service as a lieutenant in the Montgomery True Blues and by May 1862 commanded the Eighteenth Alabama Infantry as a colonel. Wounded in the fighting at Shiloh, he recovered to take charge of the regiment, now stationed at Mobile. He fought at Chickamauga and Chattanooga, taking temporary command of the brigade in the fighting at Lookout Mountain. Upon the recommendation of Gen. Joseph E. Johnston, the War Department promoted Holtzclaw to brigadier general on July 7, 1864, and assigned him command of Henry DeLamar Clayton's former brigade. In the Atlanta campaign he participated in the fighting at Rocky Face Mountain, Resaca, New Hope Church, and Jonesboro. He arrived too late to take part in the Battle of Franklin, and after fighting at Nashville his brigade acted as rear guard during the retreat. Transferred to the District of the Gulf, he and his brigade spent the last months of the war protecting the forts at Mobile. He surrendered with Richard Taylor on May 4, 1865. After the war Holtzclaw returned to Montgomery and resumed his law practice. Active in Democratic state politics, he was serving as a state railroad commissioner when he died in Montgomery on July 19, 1893.

BIBLIOGRAPHY

Spencer, James. *Civil War Generals.* Westport, Conn., 1986.

U.S. War Department. *War of the Rebellion: A Compilation of the Official Records of the Union and Confederate Armies.* Washington, D.C., 1880–1901. Ser. 1. Vol. 31, pt. 2, pp. 720–732; vol. 49, pt. 2, pp. 1128, 1187, 1283; vol. 52, p. 634.

Wakelyn, Jon L. *Biographical Dictionary of the Confederacy.* Edited by Frank E. Vandiver. Westport, Conn., 1977.

MICHAEL G. MAHON

HONOR. Winston Churchill once claimed that the Civil War was the last to be fought among gentlemen. The concept of honor played a salient part in the war as well as in its causes and aftermath. Although a Northern concept of honor can be identified, the Southern version has caught the historical imagination. Indeed, some scholars consider the Southern code of honor, as it is often called, a foundation stone of regional distinctiveness and cultural continuity to the present day—even though the ethic has shrunk under the influences of national homogenization over the past fifty years.

For most of American history, the Southern people, white and black, were largely agrarian folk. They were scattered in small communities across an enormous and still underdeveloped countryside. As a result, white Southerners of the Civil War era were more likely to adhere to the precepts of honor than contemporary Northerners, whose economy and social life had become rather urbanized. According to an older generation of scholars, the Southern white male was alleged to have demonstrated a sensitivity to personal insult, a romantic notion of cavalier virtues and valor, a devotion to proper manners and the dictates of hospitality, a colorful deference toward women, and a sense of rugged individualism. The 1932 edition of the *Encyclopedia of the Social Sciences* encapsulated this commonly held view. The writer explained, "Honor represents a strong personal sense of socially accepted dignity or socially expected conduct.'' Margaret Mitchell's *Gone with the Wind* (1935) was the most popular literary work to bathe that sentiment in pleasing nostalgia.

Historians have lately applied a more anthropological and psychological definition of honor to the Southern ethic. They claim that the Southern code involved much deeper social, racial, and political issues than simply ballroom manners or horseback tournaments in imitation of scenes from Walter Scott's novels. The sociology of honor embraces internal and external features. Thus, the ethic may serve as a mediator between individual and group aspirations and the judgment of the watching world. Anthropologist Julian Pitt-Rivers observes that ''honor felt becomes honor claimed, and honor claimed becomes honor paid.'' In other words, a white Southerner's sense of identity was directly linked to public recognition.

In the Southern patriarchal and agrarian order, hierarchies of diverse forms shaped social relations—male over female, personal prosperity over poverty, respected lineage over family obscurity, education over illiteracy, age over youth, and, above all, white over black. These moral polarities were strictly observed. A gentleman of refined family origins, learning, and wealth expected to have his status confirmed by the community. In the lower ranks of society, men assumed their distinctive places in the social and racial order. Yet they insisted upon a rough egalitarianism to create what might be called a ''people's timocracy,'' that is, the notion that virtually *all* white men and their womenfolk had a claim for respect. The well-born and wealthy could not be too lordly without risking retaliation for encroaching on the dignity of inferiors, and even the lowliest white woodchopper deemed himself superior to any black, slave or free.

If a white male Southerner did not attain public notice of his claim to status, the resulting stain of contempt could scarcely be tolerated. Rejection meant, in a phrase, ''social death,'' a stripping of independence, the stigma of shame, which was the very opposite of honor. Violence might well ensue as the only means of reasserting one's self-regard.

In contrast to the Southern view was the Northern concept of honor. The commercial and industrial revolution that so energized the economy prepared the North for a more institutional approach to the question of honor. Under the inspiration of a revised, New Testament theology, an inner voice of caution and self-discipline—the conscience—was supposed to animate the Northerner. Unlike shame, guilt did not involve public exposure and therefore was less ruinous to self-regard. Pursuing the dictates of conscience, Northerners were likely to believe, was the essence of liberty. Their definition of liberty, unlike the Southern variety, did not include a right to enslave others. In contrast to the face-to-face style of Southern exchange, the Northern code of behavior stressed obedience

to law and reliance upon the written word. Nor could Northerners understand why Southerners demanded community consensus, enforced at times by mob action in the suppression of dissent. The South's decision to leave the Union appeared as a childish, impulsive act soon to be repented, not the act of an aggrieved and honorable people.

For the Northerner, honor was perceived as duty to God and Union. The concept also incorporated the idea of personal dignity. A Northern gentleman, it was assumed, would not demean himself to notice insult, certainly not to the extremity of engaging in a duel. As Northerners saw the matter, ritual violence was a vestige of barbarism. Abrasive or brusque conduct should not entail receipt of a blow or a note to demand a lethal exchange of gunfire. Ex-Confederate General Nathan Bedford Forrest, for instance, after the war issued a challenge to a Northerner who disputed his status as a gentleman. Forrest's adversary simply ignored the summons.

On a collective scale, too, honor had sectional meanings. White Southerners became increasingly disaffected within the Union for precisely the same reasons that they might react to an indignity on an individual level. Only so long as white Southerners thought their adversaries recognized their moral and political parity were many willing to remain in the Union. Throughout the first half of the century each sectional dispute had weakened that allegiance. First the abolitionists provoked fury in the South. Then antislavery politicians echoed the radicals' charges that slaveholders fell below the standards of civilized, Christian society. When Northern congressmen strenuously objected to a draconian fugitive slave bill in 1850 and posed unwelcome conditions for its passage, for instance, a secessionist fire-eater declared, ''We cannot stay in the Union any longer with such dishonor attached to the terms of our remaining.'' The admission of Kansas as a slave state concerned ''a point of honor,'' declared Representative Preston Brooks of South Carolina in 1856. Soon afterward, during the Kansas debate, he illustrated his convictions. On the Senate floor, he inflicted nearly murderous blows on the head of antislavery Senator Charles Sumner of Massachusetts. Not only had Sumner attacked the Southern way of life, he had also questioned the loyalty of South Carolina troops in the Revolutionary War and personally insulted Brooks and his cousin Andrew Butler. Brooks's allies excused his conduct, claiming that Senator Sumner did not merit the option of a duel but had to be thrashed. Dueling required a social and moral equality of the parties; a horsewhipping or caning appropriately addressed the provocations of an underling.

For many in the lower South, the election of ''Black Republican'' Abraham Lincoln in the fall of 1860 was a calculated outrage against the South. Its leaders had long threatened disunion under such circumstances, but much to Southern chagrin, Northern politicians disregarded the warning. When Lincoln gave his mobilization order after the fall of Fort Sumter in April 1861, upper South whites were convinced that he sought to deprive them of their freedom and their honor. Both threats, the reasoning went, obliged them to unite with their kindred in the lower slave states. Throughout the secession crisis of 1860 and 1861, fire-eaters accused Southern Unionists of abject cowardice. Submission to Northern rule was an invitation to perpetual enslavement and loss of manhood, they claimed.

Honor also played a role in the conduct of the war itself. Historian Grady McWhiney argues that a singular stress upon martial valor, theatrical bravado, and even recklessness distinguished a number of Confederate leaders. J. E. B. Stuart, John B. Magruder, Thomas J. ("Stonewall") Jackson, Nathan Bedford Forrest, even Robert E. Lee, were among them. Statistics on casualties under circumstances of both offense and defense, however, do not bear out the charge of Southern rashness in battle. On the other hand, at the beginning of the war, Northern military caution was pronounced. It was partly attributable to anxieties that Southern bellicosity was greater than the martial zeal of city-dwelling and self-confessedly "effete Yankees." That myth later dissolved. Yet, from start to finish, Southern women expected and indeed insisted that their defenders pledge themselves to "the law of Knightly honour and chivalry," as Catherine Edmonston of North Carolina put it.

In the organization of the Southern army, the strictures of honor found a place as well. No doubt its mandate inspired enlistments and generally aided morale. To refuse to fight or to return home early, some believed, would leave a stain upon the family escutcheon. But it could have a negative impact, also. When, as sometimes happened, a Southern officer was voted out of command by his troopers, he usually resigned his commission. He considered the removal a defacement of his honor. William Faulkner's great-grandfather's election defeat as a colonel inspired the novelist to fictionalize the incident in *The Unvanquished*. In another area of military life, punishments included ways to strip a soldier of his dignity by subjecting him to the ridicule and execration of fellow troopers. Shaving heads, standing on whiskey barrels, riding rails, wearing a sign labeled "thief," or whippings of varying severity were among the devices to shame an offender. Northern officers also sometimes subjected their miscreants to humiliating penalties of this sort.

Honor, which has always been considered an essential inspiration in military life, was especially apparent in the upper ranks of command. Throughout the war, some egocentric Southern generals disputed their location on seniority lists. They disobeyed commands given by alleged inferiors and repudiated other signals of implied inferiority, occasionally with disastrous repercussions. When, for instance, Jefferson Davis placed Joseph E. Johnston fourth on the list of five full generals, the irate Virginia West Pointer

protested. The ranking "seeks to tarnish my fair fame as a soldier and a man," he wrote. The alleged affront denied him the symbolic meaning of his "father's Revolutionary sword," bequeathed "without a stain of dishonor." Johnston's *amour propre*, as well as that of his high-strung commander in chief, severely damaged the relations of the two leaders when cooperation was vital to Confederate success.

Honor also helped assuage the humiliation of defeat. To lose the struggle by no means chastened white Southerners into heartfelt submissiveness. Repudiation of Confederate debts, even emancipation could be rationalized as war casualties. But not so Republican attempts to invest the freed people with equal protection of the law. Likewise, Federal occupation and then Congressional Reconstruction seemed a conspiracy to debase the conquered whites by rendering white men virtually powerless in comparison with the former slaves. Reaction to such interferences even received sexual expression. Robert Dabney of Davidson College, for instance, warned that under the new regime, former Confederates were "subjugated to every influence from without, which can be malignantly devised to sap the foundation of their manhood, and degrade them into fit material for slaves." He therefore called upon the women to help rouse Southern men to resist the baleful consequences. God had not favored the South, Dabney and others reasoned, as punishment for the Old Testament sins of debauchery, haughtiness, and greed. Slaveholding and disunionism—both honorable and justifiable—were no more condemned by God, Dabney was persuaded, than by the whites themselves.

Thus, the Southern ethic of honor, with its emphasis upon familial, rank-conscious values, assisted in the coming of the war and provided a rationale for continuing white oppression of blacks. That habit of mind, which justified bloody violation of federal and state criminal law, eventually helped in the overthrow of Reconstruction governments and the return of ex-Confederates to positions of power.

To be sure, the ascriptions of honor, particularly regarding race, colored attitudes above the Mason-Dixon Line as well as below it. Copperhead Democrats in the North defended Southern mores. Nor did all Southerners subscribe wholeheartedly to the venerable and primitive code as briefly sketched here. Instead, some adopted, to a degree, the Christian code of conscience and guilt and rejected reliance upon honor and shame. Nonetheless, honor played a major, but elusive role in the tragic history of mid-nineteenth-century America.

[*See also* Class Conflict; Dueling; Sumner, Caning of.]

BIBLIOGRAPHY

Adams, Michael C. C. *Our Masters the Rebels: A Speculation on Union Military Failure in the East, 1861–1865*. Cambridge, Mass., 1978.

Greenberg, Kenneth S. *Masters and Statesmen: The Political Culture of American Slavery.* Baltimore, 1985.

Hattaway, Herman, and Archer Jones. *How the North Won: A Military History of the Civil War.* Urbana, Ill., 1983.

McWhiney, Grady, and Perry D. Jamieson. *Attack or Die: Civil War Military Tactics and the Southern Heritage.* University, Ala., 1982.

Pitt-Rivers, Julian. "Honor." In *International Encyclopedia of the Social Sciences.* Vol. 6. Edited by David L. Stills. New York, 1986.

Smith, T. V. "Honor." In *Encyclopedia of the Social Sciences.* Vol. 7. Edited by R. A. Seligman. New York, 1932.

Wyatt-Brown, Bertram. *Southern Honor: Ethics and Behavior in the Old South.* New York, 1982.

Wyatt-Brown, Bertram. *Yankee Saints and Southern Sinners.* Baton Rouge, La., 1985.

BERTRAM WYATT-BROWN

HOOD, JOHN BELL (1831–1879), lieutenant general. Born in Owingsville, Bath County, Kentucky, on June 1, 1831, Hood spent his boyhood years in neighboring Montgomery County. His parents were descendants of pioneer stock and solid members of Kentucky society. His father attended medical school, and though he did not take a degree, he opened a practice in Bath County. After the

JOHN BELL HOOD.   NATIONAL ARCHIVES

members of his family moved to Montgomery County in 1835, their fortunes were reversed when Hood's maternal grandfather died and left them 225,000 acres of land and a sum of cash. As a result young Hood thereafter led a comfortable life.

Hood won appointment to West Point on February 27, 1849, and graduated in 1853, finishing forty-fourth in a class of fifty-two. He was appointed brevet second lieutenant in the Fourth U.S. Infantry and was stationed in the West. Later, he was transferred to a detachment of dragoons and appointed second lieutenant in the Second U.S. Cavalry. The dragoons were stationed in Texas, and it was at this time that Hood formed his lifelong attachment to the Lone Star State, especially appreciating its rough pioneer spirit. Although he spent relatively few years there, he came to identify strongly with Texas. For the most part his duties on the frontier were uneventful, though he was once wounded while campaigning against the Indians.

With the secession of Texas, Hood resigned his commission in the U.S. Army on April 17, 1861, and headed east to Richmond, where he volunteered his services to the Confederate government. Assigned to the rank of captain and then major, Hood rose rapidly in command until he was given charge of the newly organized Fourth Texas Infantry, which he whipped into shape with stiff discipline and organization. As a young officer, Hood was a splendid physical specimen. He stood six feet, two inches, was broad at the shoulders, narrow at the hips, and had a full head of blondish auburn hair with a provocative off-color cowlick. He had a long, lean face and great sad eyes of a hypnotic blue.

His service record with the Confederate army in the East, especially after First Manassas and the Peninsular campaign, reads like a history of the Army of Northern Virginia. He quickly established a reputation as a fighting general and demonstrated that quality on many fields. Hood served with distinction at Williamsburg, the Seven Days' Battles (especially at Gaines' Mill), Second Manassas, Sharpsburg (Antietam), and Fredericksburg. He missed the Confederate victory at Chancellorsville in May 1863, but fought at Gettysburg where he was severely wounded in the left arm. Although he recovered sufficiently to resume command, he never regained the full use of his arm. Hood was promoted to brigadier general to rank from March 3, 1862, and to major general to rank from October 10, 1862.

At times brilliant as a brigade and divisional commander, Hood was always a fierce fighter. Robert E. Lee regarded Hood's men as shock troops to be used in the most desperate situations, and at that assignment they never failed. Hood fought with an intensity he passed on to his men. His unit, though he commanded it for less than six months, was known throughout the war as Hood's Texas Brigade and was composed mostly of Texans who came east at the beginning of the war.

In the fall of 1863, Lee transferred an entire corps of his army, including Hood, to Tennessee, where it joined the Army of Tennessee under the command of Braxton Bragg in an attempt to defeat the Federal army under William S. Rosecrans. This move ended Hood's association with Lee and the army in the East. Hood's command arrived from Virginia in time to participate in the greatest battle fought in the West, Chickamauga, where Hood lost his right leg. Not expected to recover from his wound at first, he survived, but was never the same physically and perhaps emotionally. Recovery was slow, but by early winter of 1864 he was fit to return to duty.

Promoted to lieutenant general on February 1, 1864, with date of rank set at September 20, 1863, Hood was ordered to return to the Army of Tennessee as a corps commander under Bragg, a man whom he neither liked nor trusted. Hood's association with the army in Tennessee became a tapestry woven of intrigue, defeat, humiliation, and near-annihilation. Shortly after Hood's return to the army, Joseph E. Johnston replaced Bragg as commander, largely as a result of a series of squabbles within the high command. Hood was directly involved and was accused of having undermined his old commander in an attempt to ingratiate himself with his superiors. Johnston, consequently, never quite trusted Hood, and Hood returned the favor by continuing the criticism he had leveled at Bragg. When Johnston was relieved from command of the Army of Tennessee, Hood succeeded him on July 17, 1864. He was promoted to full general with temporary rank on July 18, 1864.

Having begun the war commanding about a thousand men, Hood now found himself in charge of an entire army numbering many thousands. Though he had succeeded at the previous level, he was not equal to his new task. Against the advice of many, Hood attacked William Tecumseh Sherman's army in a series of battles around Atlanta, and he continued these assaults until he had seriously crippled his army. Successive losses at Peachtree Creek, Ezra Church, and Jonesboro cost Hood the fighting edge of his army as well as the city of Atlanta, which was evacuated on September 1. Instead of attempting to block Sherman's March to the Sea, Hood turned north into Tennessee to threaten Sherman's rear and cut his line of supply and communication. Sherman, however, refused to take the bait and turn northward, leaving Hood instead to contend with Federal troops under John M. Scofield and George H. Thomas (both classmates of Hood's at West Point).

In a series of rash and ill-prepared battles, Hood succeeded in nearly destroying what was left of his army. After much maneuvering through middle Tennessee, he attacked the well-entrenched Federals under Scofield at Franklin on November 30, 1864. Despite staggering losses and the demoralization of much of his army, Hood pushed his troops on to Nashville where he deployed and awaited attack from both Scofield and Thomas. When it came, the Federal assault was delivered with such weight of numbers and ferocity that it was over in a matter of hours. Confederate military history records no rout more thorough than that sustained by Hood at Nashville. A despondent Hood was now relieved from command at his own request. In May 1865 he surrendered at Natchez, Mississippi, having never been returned to command.

As a soldier, Hood was without peer in the Confederate army as a leader at the brigade and divisional levels. He was able to inspire his men and make them follow him despite the odds. His troops, man for man, were judged perhaps the best combat troops in the Army of Northern Virginia. Above the divisional level, however, Hood was a failure. As an administrator, he lacked the most basic of skills, and as a strategist he was rash, impulsive, and inappropriately aggressive. To be sure, he suffered from physical handicaps after the loss of his arm and leg, although to his credit, he never used this as an excuse for failure. Hood demonstrated both distressing traits—shifting responsibility to subordinates and intriguing against superiors, to name but two—and attractive qualities—courage, dash, devotion to an ideal, gallantry, and charm. In the end, however, it was his inability to recognize his own weaknesses and to make realistic adjustments to the changing circumstances of war that brought about his downfall.

After the war, he made his home at New Orleans where he engaged in the cotton business and married Anna Marie Hennen. Shortly before Gettysburg, Hood met and fell deeply in love with Sally ("Buck") Preston, daughter of John S. Preston of South Carolina. After at least two refusals of marriage, Sally finally agreed to an engagement, despite strenuous objections from her family. This was after Chickamauga. By the time the Franklin and Nashville disaster had come and gone, so had their relationship. The union between Hood and Sally Preston was never consummated and the two parted company at war's end never to see each other again. His business thrived and his family lived well. Yet for all his apparent happiness, Hood spent the remaining years of his life writing his war memoir, *Advance and Retreat*, which was full of apologies, bitterness, and hostility. Before Hood found a publisher for the book, a final calamity befell him. In 1878 and 1879 a yellow fever epidemic in New Orleans forced the closing of the cotton exchange and brought ruin to a number of local businessmen, Hood among them. He lost his wife and a daughter to the fever in August 1879, and on August 30, he too died of the disease. He left behind heavy debts and ten orphaned children for whom no financial provision had been made. Friends had his memoirs published and sold for the benefit of the children. Hood was laid to rest in Matairie Cemetery, New Orleans.

BIBLIOGRAPHY

Dyer, John. *The Gallant Hood.* Indianapolis, 1950.

Freeman, Douglas S. *Lee's Lieutenants: A Study in Command.* 3 vols. New York, 1942–1944. Reprint, New York, 1986.

McMurry, Richard M. *John Bell Hood and the War for Southern Independence.* Lexington, Ky., 1982.

O'Connor, Richard. *Hood: Cavalier General.* New York, 1949.

Warner, Ezra J. *Generals in Gray: Lives of the Confederate Commanders.* Baton Rouge, La., 1959.

TERRENCE V. MURPHY

HOOD'S TEXAS BRIGADE. This brigade was organized on November 1, 1861, at Dumfries, Virginia, from thirty-two volunteer infantry companies recruited in Texas. The original brigade included the First, Fourth, and Fifth Texas Infantry and the Eighteenth Georgia Infantry. These three Texas regiments were the only units from that state to serve in Robert E. Lee's Army of Northern Virginia.

In all, Hood's Texas Brigade fought in thirty-eight engagements. After the Battle of Seven Pines on May 31, 1862, the eight infantry companies of Hampton's South Carolina Legion were added to the brigade. The Texans became famous at the Battle of Gaines' Mill on June 27. In this battle, the brigade was credited with breaking the Union line and putting the enemy to flight. The unit continued its heavy fighting at Second Manassas and Sharpsburg. In October 1862, the Third Arkansas Infantry replaced the Eighteenth Georgia and Hampton's Legion, giving the brigade its final organization. As part of Lt. Gen. James Longstreet's corps, the unit fought at Gettysburg, Chickamauga, and Knoxville. At the Battle of the Wilderness, the brigade stemmed the Federal assault at the Widow Tapp farm, earning the unit lasting glory but at the cost of half its men. The Texas Brigade participated in the battles around Petersburg before surrendering with Lee's army at Appomattox.

The brigade holds a number of records for its staggering loss rate. In six major battles—Gaines' Mill, Second Manassas, Sharpsburg, Gettysburg, Chickamauga, and the Wilderness—the unit lost 3,470 killed, wounded, or missing. The most terrible period for casualties, however, came early in the brigade's career when it suffered 1,780 casualties in the eighty-three days between Gaines' Mill, June 27, 1862, and Sharpsburg, September 17, 1862. Through recruitment and replacements, an estimated 4,500 men served in its ranks. At Appomattox, only 476 were left to surrender.

Regiments within the brigade also suffered record losses. The First Texas Infantry is credited with having the highest percentage loss for a Confederate unit on a single day: 82.3 percent. Over 150 men of this regiment fell in twenty minutes of heavy fighting in Miller's Cornfield at Sharps-burg. Overall, the brigade lost 64.1 percent casualties for the day, ranking it third of any brigade in the war for a single day's loss.

During the war, Hood's Texas Brigade was commanded by several officers. The original commander was Louis T. Wigfall, who resigned to join the Confederate Senate early in 1862. He was replaced by Brig. Gen. John Bell Hood, a West Point graduate and veteran of the Texas frontier. Hood received promotion to division command in midsummer, leaving Col. William Tatum Wofford in command of the brigade. Brig. Gen. Jerome Robertson led the brigade through the fall of the year and throughout 1863. Then Brig. Gen. John Gregg commanded the brigade until his death at Darbytown Road on October 7, 1864. Command then fell to a succession of regimental officers including Col. C. M. Winkler, Col. Fredrick S. Bass, and Col. Robert H. Powell.

BIBLIOGRAPHY

Fletcher, William A. *Rebel Private, Front and Rear.* Beaumont, Tex., 1908. Reprint, Washington, D.C., 1954.

Polley, J. B. *Hood's Texas Brigade.* New York, 1910.

Simpson, Harold B. *Gaines' Mill to Appomattox.* Hillsboro, Tex., 1963.

DONALD S. FRAZIER

HORSES AND MULES. Together with the vehicles they pulled, horses and mules played a much larger role in the Civil War (but have received much less attention) than railroad trains or riverboats. Mounts were indispensable for cavalry, and draft animals for gun carriages, supply wagons, and ambulances. Besides their military uses, horses and mules were necessary for civil transportation and farm production, for which purposes oxen also served.

Possessing an inferior railroad system, the Confederate States depended on horses and mules to an even greater extent than did the United States. To Confederates, this seemed a matter of little concern at first, for suitable animals then appeared to be plentiful. In 1860 the South, consisting of the fifteen slave states, had less than 40 percent of the people but 45 percent of the horses, 90 percent of the mules, and 52 percent of the oxen in the country as a whole. Southern saddle horses were reputed to be superior to Northern horses in quality as well as quantity. Southerners prided themselves on their knowledge of horseflesh, their skill at breeding and training, and their general horsemanship.

Not all this livestock remained available to the Confederacy, however. Among the Southern states, Missouri was first and Kentucky second in the raising of horses, and Kentucky led in the production of mules. Though the Confederacy claimed both Missouri and Kentucky, it no longer had easy access to either of the two states after the first year of the war. Much of the output of other important breeding states—notably Virginia, Tennessee, Louisiana, and Texas—was lost as the Union armies advanced and the area under Confederate control shrank.

Even at the outset the Confederacy was deficient in the production of certain items necessary for the employment of horses and mules—feed, vehicles, and other manufactures. Concentrating on such profitable crops as cotton and tobacco, Southerners depended largely on Northern farms for hay. They looked to Northern factories for most of their wagons and carriages; the rest, those of local manufacture, often used wheels and other mass-produced parts that came from the North.

During the first two years of the war, the existing supply of horses was steadily depleted. Many were killed in battle, worn out by hard usage, or felled by disease, especially during an epidemic that caused severe losses to the Army of Northern Virginia (as well as the Army of the Potomac) in September 1862. Many of the surviving animals were in poor condition. They suffered from shortages of hay and fodder, veterinary surgeons and hospitals, and facilities for winter care. Emaciation was particularly to be seen in the areas of frequent campaigning, where the contending armies used up all the forage.

By the summer of 1863 the Confederacy faced a crisis, the "sources for the supply of horses and mules being well-nigh exhausted in the Confederate States," as the quartermaster general was informed. Jefferson Davis referred to him a proposal to "introduce horses and mules from Mexico, California, and Europe." The quartermaster general replied that several hundred mules had been purchased in Texas and were "awaiting a safe opportunity" to cross the Mississippi River. It was questionable whether they would be of much use, however, for they were "generally small." Horses from Mexico, California, Texas, and New Mexico might be useful for the cavalry "if very judiciously selected," but wild mustangs would be "entirely useless." As for obtaining horses from Europe, that was "certainly impracticable." It became impracticable also to bring many from west of the Mississippi, once the Federals had captured Vicksburg and Port Hudson and taken control of the river.

"For the future I see nothing left us but to procure animals from the enemy's country," an officer advised the quartermaster general in July 1863. The quartermaster general sent funds with Robert E. Lee's army for the

ARMY WAGON TRAIN.

HARPER'S PICTORIAL HISTORY OF THE GREAT REBELLION

purchase of horses during the Pennsylvania campaign, hoping to get as many as two thousand in Maryland. Instead, Lee left behind quite a few of his own horses when he returned from Gettysburg. John Hunt Morgan obtained some remounts during his 1863 raid into Indiana and Ohio, and he gathered a large herd from Federal stables during an 1864 raid into Kentucky. Other forays into enemy territory brought in as many as a thousand at a time. Still, the total captured fell far short of the requirements, and the numbers were offset by losses to Federal raiders. According to William Tecumseh Sherman, his foragers collected fifteen thousand mules and a great many horses just during the march from Atlanta to Savannah.

Originally the Confederate government bought animals, feed, vehicles, and equipment in the open market. As inflation worsened, however, the government began to seize these along with other goods from the owners, paying them less than market prices. An "average figure" of $350 was set in 1863 for first-class artillery and wagon horses and $300 for first-class mules. For wagons with iron axles, a higher price was allowed than for the more primitive kind with wooden axles. Rates were also set for the hire of teams, wagons, and drivers and for the labor of baling hay and fodder and shelling and bagging corn.

To tighten its control over the supply of animals and vehicles, the Confederate government centralized its system of procurement and distribution in 1863. The inspector general of field transportation was henceforth to take charge of "all inspections, purchases, impressments, and issues of field transportation (including artillery horses)." The Confederacy was to be divided into districts in each of which an officer was to "control the subject." Thus competition from state purchasing and impressment agents would be reduced if not eliminated. The Mississippi governor, who had impressed 619 horses for his state's service, now agreed to turn them over to the Confederate government, which was to pay the state for their use and reimburse it for any losses.

While the government procured draft animals for the army, cavalrymen had to provide their own mounts. The owner was paid forty cents a day for the use of his horse and was reimbursed if the animal was killed in action—but not if it was captured, disabled, diseased, or worn out. The man would have to find his own remount or be transferred to the infantry or the artillery. Many more cavalry horses were disabled or worn out than were killed, and the owners were hard put to pay for replacements. A man might have difficulty buying another horse even if his first one died in action, for with scarcity and inflation the purchase price became much higher than the reimbursement, which was based on the original evaluation. Davis himself pointed out: "it may thus not unfrequently happen that the most efficient troops, without fault of their own—indeed, it may

be because of their zeal and activity—are lost to the cavalry service."

The government was responsible for equipping the cavalry horses but was not always able to equip them adequately. The saddles, inferior to the McClellan saddles of the U.S. cavalry, often proved "ruinous to the backs of horses." There came to be a "want of horseshoes and horseshoe nails, forges, and transportation therefor," as well as a shortage of blacksmiths. During Lee's Pennsylvania campaign "many valuable horses were lost owing mainly to the want of shoes."

The scarcity of horses, mules, feed, equipment, and vehicles had grave consequences for the Confederacy. Its cavalry, far better than the Union's in the beginning, deteriorated from 1863 on. To save horses for the field artillery, the Confederates more and more substituted mules for other hauling, but still had to eliminate some artillery as well as a number of transports and ambulances. Civil transportation and the economy suffered as impressment officers took the best horses, mules, and vehicles for the military and left farmers and planters with rickety carts and wagons and decrepit, if any, teams. Oxen meanwhile became less available as draft animals, since owners often had to slaughter them for food. In 1865 the head of the Bureau of War, Robert G. H. Kean, listed seven "causes of the failure of Southern independence," the fifth of which was the following: "Want of horses for transport and artillery; country stripped by impressment of horses, which straightway perished for want of forage; this want due to defective transportation by railroad and wagon, and limited supply in any given area of country."

BIBLIOGRAPHY

Ramsdell, Charles W. "General Robert E. Lee's Horse Supply, 1862–1865." *American Historical Review* 35 (1930): 758–777.
Vandiver, Frank E. *Rebel Brass: The Confederate Command System.* Baton Rouge, La., 1956.
U.S. War Department. *War of the Rebellion: A Compilation of the Official Records of the Union and Confederate Armies.* Ser. 4, vol. 2. Washington, D.C., 1900.

RICHARD N. CURRENT

HOSPITALS. The Confederacy at the outbreak of the Civil War had no well-established system of hospitals to care for its sick and wounded soldiers. Few hospitals existed in the prewar South because most nineteenth-century Americans cared for sick family members at home. Hospitals, or almshouses as they were frequently called, were regarded as asylums for the indigent. For the working poor, the newly arrived immigrant, and the merchant seaman, the few antebellum hospitals offered a level of health care previously unavailable to those who did not have home care. The

United States maintained no general military hospitals before 1861, and the few marine hospitals located in the South's port cities and towns could not begin to meet the medical needs of the Confederacy.

The Confederate government established a Medical Department in February 1861 but failed to foresee the need for

Hospitals in the Confederacy (1864)

LOCATION		NUMBER OF HOSPITALS
ALABAMA		
Montgomery		6
Mobile		4
Other Towns		13
	Total	23
FLORIDA		4
GEORGIA		
Macon		11
Marietta		3
LaGrange		4
Newnan		4
Columbus		3
Griffin		4
Other Towns		21
	Total	50
MISSISSIPPI		3
NORTH CAROLINA		
Wilmington		3
Raleigh		3
Salisbury		3
Other Towns		12
	Total	21
SOUTH CAROLINA		
Columbia		3
Charleston		5
Other Towns		4
	Total	12
TENNESSEE		2
VIRGINIA		
Richmond		11
Lynchburg		6
Petersburg		8
Other Towns		14
	Total	39

SOURCE: *Confederate States Medical and Surgical Journal* 1 (October–November 1864): 152, 176.

an organized hospital system until after First Manassas. When newly appointed Surgeon General Samuel Preston Moore arrived in Richmond in July 1861, he faced the overwhelming task of providing care for the large numbers of sick and wounded soldiers who had streamed into the Confederate capital. Soldiers were placed in temporary hospitals set up in tobacco warehouses, churches, barns, hotels, schools, and other large buildings, and many were cared for in private homes. Fearful that widespread epidemics might result from housing patients in crowded and poorly ventilated facilities, Moore embarked on an aggressive building scheme in the summer of 1861. The Provisional Congress appropriated fifty thousand dollars for this purpose in August. Moore advocated the construction of pavilion-style general hospitals. These facilities consisted of three to five divisions of individual ward buildings designed to accommodate about six hundred patients each. The wards were constructed from undressed pine planks and included many windows and doors for maximum ventilation.

Private Facilities. While the Confederate Medical Department developed its system of general hospitals, private citizens and charitable organizations provided much of the care for soldiers away from the front. Some forty-four private hospitals were organized in Richmond in the weeks after First Manassas. The citizens of Memphis formed the Southern Mothers' Society and established a hospital that served the western army until June 1862. In Alabama, a group of Montgomery women opened the Ladies Hospital or Soldiers' Home in the early months of the war. The Nashville Hospital Association, organized by a committee of local women, administered the Gordon Hospital in the Tennessee capital.

In July 1861, Sally L. Tompkins opened and equipped at her own expense a private hospital in the home of Judge John Robertson of Richmond. When the Confederate Congress passed legislation requiring military control of all hospitals housing soldiers, Tompkins appealed to President Jefferson Davis to continue her role as administrator of the Robertson Hospital. Davis, impressed by the hospital's exceptional record of returning men to the field, ensured its continuance by commissioning Tompkins a captain in the cavalry. Other private hospitals, however, though equally successful at nursing men back to health, were not extended the same privilege, and most were closed or absorbed into the Confederate Medical Department by 1863.

Staff Organization. General hospitals were administered by a surgeon-in-charge who served as the chief medical officer and oversaw the prudent management of the hospital fund. This fund, created from moneys generated by the commutation of rations, was used to purchase food and other supplies for soldiers. The surgeon-in-charge, assisted by surgeons serving as division heads, also dealt with desertion, drunkenness, gambling, and other disciplinary problems among the patients. Congress authorized one assistant surgeon or contract surgeon for every seventy patients, but hospitals seldom had a full complement of physicians. Surgeons were also assisted by hospital stewards, clerks, and ward masters who handled routine duties such as cleaning wards, managing supplies, and maintaining records.

Hospital surgeons provided emergency medical treatment and operated on the wounded, primarily amputating limbs following military engagements. But the vast majority of their time was spent treating the sick with the primitive and sometimes lethal therapeutics of the era. On the other hand, they were well aware of the importance of good diet to the healing process and did their best to see that patients were properly nourished. Unfortunately, however, Confederate hospitals often lacked the foodstuffs necessary, and patients faced the same daily rations no matter what their prescribed diet.

Combating Poor Conditions. In spite of the tremendous strides made by the Confederate Medical Department in organizing a hospital system during the first year of hostilities, it failed to meet the needs of the army. A shortage of beds was not the only problem facing the system. A congressional investigating committee found inadequate medical supplies, surgical instruments, food, nurses, transportation facilities, and record-keeping practices in the military hospitals.

Congress passed key legislation in 1862 and 1863 to alleviate the problems. The most significant was the Act to Better Provide for the Sick and Wounded of the Army in Hospitals. This statute, enacted after an extensive debate on the merit of female nurses, allowed the appointment of hospital matrons. As early as August 1861 the Provisional Congress had authorized hospital attendants, but these hired nurses and cooks, mostly freed or enslaved African Americans, along with volunteer nurses, convalescing soldiers, and members of various Catholic orders, had failed to provide adequate nursing care. The new legislation authorized for each hospital two matrons, two assistant matrons, and two ward matrons per ward. The chief matron had authority "over the entire domestic economy of the hospital," and the assistants supervised laundry and patients' clothing. Ward matrons prepared beds, monitored food preparation, and administered medicines. A number of prominent women accepted appointments as matrons, including Phoebe Yates Pember, chief matron of the Georgia Division of Chimborazo Hospital; Emily Mason, matron of Winder Hospital; Mary Pettigrew, matron of the Virginia Division of Chimborazo and of hospitals in Raleigh; Juliet Opie Hopkins, matron of the Alabama Division of Chimborazo; Louisa Cheves McCord, matron of hospitals in South Carolina; and Ella King Newsom, Kate Cummings,

Mrs. William P. Gilmer, and Fannie Beers, matrons of hospitals serving the Army of Tennessee. Nevertheless, Confederate society never regarded hospital employment as respectable work for women.

In the spring of 1863, Congress ordered the establishment of "way hospitals" at railroad junctions and in major towns to supplement the small hospitals established by private citizens. Enterprising men and women in South Carolina organized the first wayside hospitals in the Charleston and Columbia depots of the South Carolina Rail Road Company during the summer of 1861. These facilities provided care for soldiers on medical furlough.

The legislation that authorized matrons also required the Medical Department to assign soldiers to hospitals according to their home states. In theory, this would group soldiers with the same manners and customs together and enable officers to locate the hospitalized sick and wounded more readily. It was also meant to facilitate the distribution of provisions sent by the various state governments and relief associations for particular groups of soldiers. In reality, this practice was difficult to follow and was often ignored by the surgeons.

Medical conditions in the hospitals were as satisfactory as could be expected given the Confederacy's shortage of medical supplies and physicians. Congress monitored conditions throughout the war, and the early reports were quite favorable, although Congress considered closing Richmond hospitals for a thorough cleaning in 1863. The lack of cleanliness and prevalence of contagious disease proved to be formidable foes for hospital personnel. Soldiers followed the same poor sanitary practices in the hospitals that had turned their camps into cesspools. Conditions were particularly bad following battles, when the hospitals were filled to capacity and the stench of rotting flesh permeated the air. These conditions, combined with the era's limited understanding of the nature of illness, made the hospitals virtual breeding grounds for disease. To combat the situation, surgeons attempted to separate the sick from the wounded, particularly the erysipelas and gangrene patients, and the surgeon general issued numerous directives concerning hospital conditions.

Eastern Hospitals. Chimborazo Hospital, one of the largest and most famous of Confederate general hospitals, was constructed on a high plateau overlooking the James River just east of Richmond. This pavilion-style facility served as the prototype for other general hospitals. Dr. James Brown McCaw of Richmond accepted the post of commandant in October 1861 a few weeks before the hospital admitted its first patients. Chimborazo, a complex of 120 buildings including soup houses, icehouses, kitchens, mess halls, morgues, bathhouses, a bakery, and a brewery, operated as a self-sufficient post. Its five divisions accommodated about 600 patients each. McCaw, an innovative and efficient administrator, purchased food and supplies unavailable through military channels and acquired two canal boats to transport the purchases to the hospital via the James River and Kanawha Canal. Almost 78,000 patients were hospitalized at Chimborazo during the course of the war, including 17,000 treated for battle wounds.

Other major hospitals in Richmond included Jackson, Howard's Grove, Stuart General, Louisiana General, and Winder. The Winder Hospital opened in April 1862 under the command of Surgeon Alexander G. Lane. The hospital, spanning 125 acres on the western outskirts of Richmond, was organized into six divisions; its capacity of 4,800 patients made it the largest facility in the Confederacy. Winder had a dairy, icehouse, extensive gardens, and a highly productive bakery. Like Chimborazo, it maintained two canal boats. Winder admitted some 76,000 patients, treating 64,683 with the loss of 3,259 soldiers between its opening and March 1, 1865. A fire in January 1864 and the general decline in the Richmond hospital census resulted in its temporary closing in 1864.

Petersburg and Lynchburg also served as hospital centers for the army in Virginia, along with facilities in Charlottesville, Danville, and Liberty where an eight-hundred-bed hospital was situated adjacent to the Virginia and Tennessee Railroad. North Carolina, South Carolina, and Florida maintained hospitals modeled after Virginia facilities.

Western Hospitals. In the latter part of the war, Chattanooga and Atlanta served as medical centers for the western army. Samuel Hollingsworth Stout, one of eight medical directors of hospitals in the Confederacy, was largely responsible for the development and success of the hospital program in the West. A medical pioneer, Stout designed wards with just two rows of bunks to reduce the amount of "impure gases generated by patients," which were thought to affect others. He ordered his subordinates to barter and forage on a regular basis, to plant gardens, and to build bakeries. Stout acquired a printing press to print forms for his hospitals and saved funds for the purchase of food and supplies.

Chattanooga's hospitals served as the models for others in the western theater. Academy, Foard, Gilmer, and Newsom hospitals were relocated prior to the Battle of Chickamauga, with their original organization intact. By 1863, the western hospitals were constantly being moved south in the face of the advancing Union forces. To Stout's credit, he selected the best sites for the hospitals, areas of high elevation adjacent to railroads in localities where the citizens could provide supplies. Like their counterparts in the East, however, Stout's western hospitals were hampered by the vagaries of the Confederate transportation system and the inability of the commissary and quartermaster to keep up with the mobile hospitals.

The hospital system in the Trans-Mississippi was small in comparison to the operations maintained by Stout for the Army of Tennessee and the large network in the eastern theater. The Medical Department maintained general hospitals in Shreveport, Louisiana; Little Rock, Arkansas; and Houston and Galveston, Texas. These facilities proved inadequate in the latter years of the war. Military and civil authorities established field hospitals, converted hotels, and enlarged existing state institutions to accommodate the increasing number of sick and wounded following the escalation of hostilities in the far West.

Specialized Facilities. The Medical Department organized a number of specialized hospitals in Georgia, including the Empire Hospital in Macon for gangrene patients, the Ophthalmic Hospital in Athens for patients with eye disorders, the Polk Hospital in Macon for hernia patients, and a hospital in Kingston for severe venereal disease cases. Tuberculosis patients were treated in Richmond's General Hospital Number 24, and separate wards were established at Howard's Grove for smallpox patients. The Louisiana Hospital in Richmond provided facilities for mental patients toward the end of the war. In February 1865, Congress established orthopedic hospitals "for the exclusive treatment of cases of old injuries and deformities from gun shot wounds."

The Confederates also established special hospital facilities in their prisons for Union soldiers. Located in tobacco warehouses or factory buildings, these small facilities were staffed and administered much like the general hospitals. Members of the Provisional Congress inspected prison hospitals early in the war and declared that Union soldiers were receiving adequate care and sustenance. Prison hospitals continued to offer satisfactory medical care until the cessation of prisoner exchanges. But, as the Confederacy's fortunes waned, so did conditions in prison hospitals.

The Final Record. After the initial medical crises in both the East and the West, the Confederate Medical Department had built a large and generally efficient hospital system. By 1864, the department was operating 154 facilities in eight states. Among the innovations were the design of the pavilion-style hospital, forerunner of the modern general hospital; the organization of the mobile hospital, prototype for future military medical units; and the development of specialty hospitals. The Confederate hospital experience demonstrated the importance of good nursing care and allowed women to enter the workplace. Most important, it helped change Southerners' perceptions about hospital care. Men who had never before been in a hospital learned they could be nursed back to health in one. It would not be until after Reconstruction that modern hospitals emerged on a large scale across the United States, but the Civil War had hastened the movement.

[See also Health and Medicine; Medical Department; Nursing.]

BIBLIOGRAPHY

Chisolm, J. Julian. *A Manual of Military Surgery for the Use of Surgeons in the Confederate States Army.* 3d ed. Columbia, S.C., 1864. Reprint, Dayton, Ohio, 1983.

Cullen, Joseph P. "Chimborazo Hospital." *Civil War Times Illustrated* 19 (January 1981): 36–42.

Cumming, Kate. *Kate: The Journal of a Confederate Nurse.* Edited by Richard B. Harwell. Baton Rouge, La., 1959.

Cunningham, Horace H. *Doctors in Gray: The Confederate Medical Service.* Baton Rouge, La., 1958.

Medical and Surgical History of the War of Rebellion. 6 vols. Washington, D.C., 1875–1888. Reprinted as *The Medical and Surgical History of the Civil War.* Edited by James I. Robertson, Jr. 14 vols. Wilmington, N.C., 1990–1991.

Pember, Phoebe Yates. *A Southern Woman's Story: Life in Confederate Richmond.* Edited by Bell I. Wiley. Jackson, Tenn., 1959.

Peters, Joseph P. "Confederate Hospitals during Civil War Days." *Southern Hospitals* 34 (January 1966): 21–25.

Straubing, Harold E., ed. *Bullets, Bandages, and Beans: Personal Narratives by Hospital Workers in the U.S. Civil War.* Canton, Ohio, 1991.

JODI KOSTE

HOTCHKISS, JEDEDIAH

HOTCHKISS, JEDEDIAH (1828–1899), major and topographer. A native of Windsor, New York, Hotchkiss, who became known as "mapmaker of the Confederacy," spent his youth in the North and was educated at the Windsor Academy. In 1847, after a year of teaching, he set

JEDEDIAH HOTCHKISS.   LIBRARY OF CONGRESS

out on a walking tour through the Cumberland Valley into western Virginia and the Shenandoah Valley. Attracted by the beauty of the region, Hotchkiss accepted a position as tutor for the Daniel Forrer family in Staunton. Eventually this family school evolved into the Mossy Creek Academy, a widely known school for boys. In 1858 Hotchkiss organized the Loch Willow School at Churchville, which he operated until the Civil War began.

When the war came, Hotchkiss closed his school and volunteered his services to his adopted homeland. Because of his self-taught mapmaking skills, he made a nearly unique contribution to the Confederate military effort. At the outset of the war, generals on both sides demanded maps, and few were available. The historian T. Harry Williams has noted that, as in many areas, the North had the advantage in mapmaking skills and resources but that the South produced some very capable mapmakers; he called Hotchkiss "possibly the foremost mapmaker of the war."

Hotchkiss drew maps for Gen. Robert S. Garnett before the Battle of Rich Mountain in western Virginia in July 1861 and witnessed the Confederate defeat there. Afterward Hotchkiss became ill and retired for several months to recuperate at home. By March 1862 he felt fit again and sought a position on the staff of Lt. Gen. Thomas J. ("Stonewall") Jackson of the Second Corps, Army of Northern Virginia. Jackson made Hotchkiss his topographical engineer and set him the task of making a map of the Shenandoah Valley from Harpers Ferry to Lexington. Henceforth, Hotchkiss carried out reconnaissance and drew maps for the general until Jackson's death in May 1863. Thereafter he performed the same services for Gens. Richard S. Ewell and Jubal Early until the end of the war.

Hotchkiss sketched most of the maps while on horseback, using different colored pencils to note the chief characteristics and peculiarities of the terrain as well as troop positions, roads, and residences. The sketches were often critical in the planning of military operations by Jackson, Ewell, and Early. Hotchkiss knew the ground and usually guided the generals unerringly as they planned their moves. In a sense, his eyes were the eyes of the Second Corps. Hotchkiss also kept a journal, which is one of the most useful of Civil War military diaries because of his staff role with the leading figures directing the Confederate military efforts in Virginia.

After the war Federal authorities in Virginia ordered Hotchkiss to surrender his maps. Hotchkiss carried his protest against confiscation of the maps to Washington where he obtained a private conference with Ulysses S. Grant. Grant agreed that Hotchkiss should retain the maps and offered to pay him for copies of selected maps that might have future military use.

Hotchkiss knew the maps had great historical value, and

he hoped to use them himself to illustrate accounts of the war. Indeed, his maps appeared in many books. In 1867 a New York firm published *The Battlefields of Virginia.* Written with William Allan, who had been chief of ordnance for the Second Corps, the account drew upon Hotchkiss's maps and journals and official records of both sides to summarize the major battles in Virginia from Fredericksburg to Chancellorsville. The book also included a firsthand account of Stonewall Jackson's death penned by his doctor, Hunter McGuire. Hotchkiss corresponded with many writers who drew upon both his maps and his memories. Among these were early Jackson biographers John Esten Cooke and the Englishman G. F. R. Henderson. In the early nineties, he supplied more than 120 maps to the editors of the *Atlas to Accompany the Official Records of the Union and Confederate Armies.* Hotchkiss worked for many years on a military history of the war in Virginia, which was published in 1899 as part of Clement A. Evans's series *Confederate Military History.*

With his intimate knowledge of the Army of Northern Virginia, Hotchkiss became a popular lecturer on the Civil War. Using chalk to illustrate his talks, he fascinated audiences in the North and South, often lecturing on "Reminiscences of Stonewall Jackson's Campaign in the Valley of Virginia." He also turned his geographical knowledge and mapmaking skills to other advantage. Known by 1890 as the "Father of Booms," Hotchkiss as author, lecturer, geological authority, editor of an industrial journal, and friend of Northern and English investors was one of Virginia's most persistent advocates of industrialism in the late nineteenth century.

Hotchkiss's maps and journals on the Civil War remained in private hands for nearly fifty years after his death in 1899, but in 1948, the Library of Congress acquired the materials.

BIBLIOGRAPHY

LeGear, Clara Egli, comp. *The Hotchkiss Map Collection.* Washington, D.C., 1951.

McDonald, Archie P., ed. *Make Me a Map of the Valley: The Civil War Journal of Stonewall Jackson's Topographer.* Dallas, Tex., 1973.

Roper, Peter. *Jedediah Hotchkiss: Rebel Mapmaker and Virginia Businessman.* Shippensburg, Pa., 1992.

Thomas, Jerry B. "Jedediah Hotchkiss, Gilded Age Propagandist of Industrialism." *Virginia Magazine of History and Biography* 84 (1976): 189–202.

JERRY BRUCE THOMAS

HOTZE, HENRY (1833–1887), propagandist abroad. This Swiss-born journalist is commonly regarded as the most effective Confederate agent in Europe. Immigrating to the United States as a young man, Hotze became a citizen, joined the staff of the *Mobile Register* in 1855, and served as secretary of the U.S. legation in Brussels in 1858 and 1859. His experience and demeanor suited him for a distinctive role.

Commissioned as a commercial agent of the Confederate State Department on November 14, 1861, Hotze was dispatched to London to organize a propaganda campaign to create a climate favorable to recognition and assistance. Through envoy James M. Mason, he made many contacts in the city's social clubs. He wrote pro-Southern speeches for sympathetic members of Parliament and posted Confederate placards throughout the streets. Cultivating the leading newspaper writers, Hotze found the pages of London's principal papers open to him. Because of his subtlety and moderation, the young publicist became far more influential than his counterpart Edwin de Leon, who ultimately proved a heavy-handed embarrassment to the Confederacy in France.

Hotze's most effective instrument was the *Index,* a weekly journal he founded in May 1862 and edited until August 1865. Its circulation was only 2,250, but it reached opinion makers in the British establishment. So impressive was Hotze's work that his budget was quickly raised from a grudging $750 to $10,000 and eventually to $30,000.

By 1864, however, Hotze had become disillusioned about prospects for victory and increasingly strident in defense of slavery. His influence dissipated. Embittered after the war, he refused to return to America. He died in Zug, Switzerland, in 1887.

[*See also* Index.]

BIBLIOGRAPHY

Cullop, Charles P. *Confederate Propaganda in Europe, 1861–1865.* Coral Gables, Fla., 1969.

Oates, Stephen B. "Henry Hotze: Confederate Agent Abroad." *Historian* 27 (February 1965): 131–154.

JAMES J. HORGAN

HOUSE, JOHN F. (1827–1904), congressman from Tennessee and captain. A descendant of the Dabneys of Virginia, House attended Transylvania University before graduating from Cumberland University in Lebanon in 1850. He first read and practiced law in his hometown of Franklin, Tennessee, but then moved to Clarksville, which he later represented in the state legislature (1853–1855). A staunch Unionist and a Bell-Everett elector in 1860. House came to support secession after the firing on Fort Sumter and Abraham Lincoln's call for volunteers.

Elected to represent Tennessee's Eighth District in the Provisional Congress in Richmond, House took his seat on August 12, 1861, and served continually until closing day,

February 13, 1862. A member of the Finance Committee, he introduced a total of ten bills, including one to increase the pay of enlisted men and two others (some three months before the fall of Forts Henry and Donelson) to construct a half dozen ironclads and gunboats for the defense of the Cumberland and Tennessee rivers. He also chaired a committee to investigate fraud and abuse in the Commissary Department.

Not seeking election to the Regular Congress, House entered the Confederate military and served as aide-de-camp on the staff of Gen. George Earl Maney at Murfreesboro, Chickamauga, and Missionary Ridge, and during the Atlanta campaign. For the remainder of the war he held an appointment as a judge advocate for the military court in northern Alabama.

Paroled at Columbus, Mississippi, on May 18, 1865, House returned to Clarksville. He soon applied for a special pardon from President Andrew Johnson but did not receive it until December 27, 1866. Active in state politics after the war, House was a delegate to the Democratic National Convention in 1868, a Horace Greeley supporter in 1872, and a member of Congress (1875–1883), before returning to his law practice in Clarksville.

BIBLIOGRAPHY

Amnesty File. John F. House. Microcopy M1003, Roll 49. Record Group 94. National Archives, Washington, D.C.

Journal of the Congress of the Confederate States of America, 1861–1865, 7 vols. Washington, D.C., 1904–1905.

Speer, William S., comp. *Sketches of Prominent Tennesseans.* Nashville, Tenn., 1888.

Warner, Ezra J., and W. Buck Yearns. *Biographical Register of the Confederate Congress.* Baton Rouge, La., 1975.

R. B. ROSENBURG

HUGER, BENJAMIN (1805–1877), major general. Most high-ranking officers in the Confederate army were graduates of West Point and professional soldiers, and many had combat experience as officers during the Mexican War. Some of them who earned their reputations in Mexico proved inadequate for higher command during the Civil War. Huger was one of those officers who were found wanting.

Huger was born in Charleston, South Carolina, on November 22, 1805, and graduated from West Point in the class of 1825. He served in the artillery, specializing in ordnance, and acted as chief of ordnance to Winfield Scott in Mexico. Huger rose to the rank of colonel and spent most of his antebellum career commanding various arsenals.

He resigned his commission after the firing on Fort Sumter and entered Confederate service as a colonel. Promotions to brigadier general and major general followed

BENJAMIN HUGER. Pre–Civil War portrait in a Union uniform.
NATIONAL ARCHIVES

on June 17 and October 7, 1861. Huger commanded the Department of Norfolk from May 1861 to May 1862, when he was assigned to a division under Joseph E. Johnston. He commanded it at Seven Pines and under Robert E. Lee during the Seven Days' Battles, but his performance was undistinguished. He was widely criticized both in and out of the army after these campaigns for being slow and failing to support other units. Though he requested a court of inquiry, none was ever convened.

He was transferred from field command in the Army of Northern Virginia to various administrative positions and spent most of the war as chief of ordnance in the Trans-Mississippi Department, from July 1863 to May 1865.

Huger farmed after the war in Virginia and died in Charleston, South Carolina, on December 7, 1877.

BIBLIOGRAPHY

Capers, Ellison. *South Carolina.* Vol. 5 of *Confederate Military History.* Edited by Clement A. Evans. Atlanta, 1899. Vol. 6 of extended ed. Wilmington, N.C., 1987.

Compiled Military Service Records. Benjamin Huger. Microcopy M331, Roll 134. Record Group 109. National Archives, Washington, D.C.

J. TRACY POWER

HUMES, WILLIAM YOUNG CONN (1830–1882), brigadier general. Born in Abington, Virginia, Humes attended the Virginia Military Institute, graduating second in the Class of 1851. He studied law in Knoxville,

Tennessee, and opened a law office in Memphis in 1858.

In June 1861 Humes became a lieutenant in Col. John Porter McCown's Artillery Corps of Tennessee. Promoted to captain on November 8, he was placed in command of two artillery batteries on Island Number 10 during the operations from March 3 to April 7, 1862. Humes became a prisoner of war when the Confederate troops surrendered.

Exchanged in September, Humes commanded an infantry battalion in Maj. Gen. Sterling Price's Army of the West and then was ordered to Mobile, Alabama. On March 15, 1863, Maj. Gen. Joseph Wheeler named Humes his chief of artillery and promoted him to major. After demonstrating "great gallantry" in Tennessee, Humes was promoted to brigadier general to date from November 16 and was assigned a cavalry brigade. He participated in all engagements of the Atlanta campaign and accompanied Wheeler into northern Georgia and middle Tennessee in the fall of 1864. Humes's brigade then harassed Maj. Gen. William Tecumseh Sherman's March to the Sea, engaging the enemy several times. In January 1865 Humes was given command of a division in Wheeler's cavalry corps and was recommended for promotion to major general, although the promotion was never carried out. Humes was paroled when Gen. Joseph E. Johnston's army surrendered to Sherman.

After the war, Humes returned to his Memphis law practice. He died on September 11, 1882.

BIBLIOGRAPHY

Barrett, John G. *Sherman's March through the Carolinas*. Chapel Hill, N.C., 1956.

Castel, Albert. *General Sterling Price and the Civil War in the West*. Baton Rouge, La., 1968.

Connelly, Thomas L. *Autumn of Glory: The Army of Tennessee, 1862–1865*. Baton Rouge, La., 1971.

Dyer, John P. *"Fightin' Joe" Wheeler*. Baton Rouge, La., 1941.

ROBERT F. PACE

HUMPHREYS, BENJAMIN GRUBB (1808–1882), brigadier general and Reconstruction governor of Mississippi. Because of his mother's death when he was nine, Humphreys left Mississippi to spend his early school years in Kentucky and New Jersey. In 1824 he returned home and worked briefly as a store clerk. A year later, he was appointed to West Point, where he joined the class of Joseph E. Johnston, Robert E. Lee, and other Civil War figures. Despite a good record, Humphreys, after a Christmas riot, was expelled from the academy along with thirty-eight others. He then became overseer of his father's plantation in Claiborne County and at the same time studied law. He was elected in 1838 to the state house of representatives and in 1839 to the state senate. In 1846 he bought land on the banks of the Yazoo River in Sunflower County, and after clearing it for cultivation, he moved there with his family.

When war erupted, Humphreys joined the Sunflower Guards and was elected captain. After being commissioned colonel on September 11, 1861, he was assigned to the Twenty-first Mississippi Regiment, First Mississippi Brigade, Army of Northern Virginia. The brigade was commanded by Brig. Gen. William Barksdale. In June 1863 Humphrey's regiment moved north into Pennsylvania with Robert E. Lee's army. At the Battle of Gettysburg, Humphreys's Twenty-first Regiment was heavily engaged. On the second day the brigade, fighting as a part of Longstreet's Corps, attacked the Union left; General Barksdale was killed in the attack. As the only Mississippi field officer not killed or wounded, Humphreys assumed command of the brigade. In September 1864 Humphreys, now a brigadier general, led the Mississippi Brigade to Georgia and participated with Longstreet in the defeat of the right wing of Rosecrans's army at Chickamauga. Humphreys commanded his brigade in the siege of the Union army at Chattanooga and fought through November and December in difficult conditions with few rations and supplies in the campaign against the Federal works at Knoxville. In May 1864 Humphreys's brigade, now back with Lee's army in Virginia, participated in the Wilderness campaign. He also fought with Jubal Early in the Shenandoah Valley. In September at Berryville, Virginia, Humphreys received a gunshot wound that disabled him for the remainder of the war.

After the war, Humphreys was elected governor of Mississippi in October 1865 despite the fact that he had not been pardoned by President Andrew Johnson. Humphreys, calling himself "an unpardoned rebel," sought to renew his allegiance to the United States and to show the victors that the days of the fire-eating secessionists were over. Because of his high rank in the Confederate army, President Johnson only reluctantly sent a pardon, but Humphreys was inaugurated.

In office, he supported a moderate position in the legislative debate on the freedmen question and criticized attempts to reconstitute slavery through restricting the rights of the ex-slaves. The bill that passed was more moderate than the one promoted by extremists, but it did severely restrict the rights of ex-slaves and eventually became the basis for the Mississippi Black Code.

Because of his opposition to Military Reconstruction, Humphreys was removed from office in 1867. Gen. Irwin McDowell, who commanded the Mississippi district, then appointed Union Gen. Adelbert Ames provisional governor, but Humphreys refused to vacate his office. Faced with his intransigence, a detail of soldiers forcibly evicted him and took over the statehouse. Even after his ejection from the capitol, the governor and his family continued to occupy part of the executive mansion until they were finally marched out between a file of military guards.

In 1868, under the new Republican constitution, Humphreys again ran for the governorship. The voters elected him but rejected the new constitution, which proscribed the rights of many Confederates. As a result, the state continued to be governed by a military governor.

BIBLIOGRAPHY

Rainwater, Percy Lee, ed. "The Autobiography of Benjamin Grubb Humphreys." *Mississippi Valley Historical Review* 20 (1934): 231–255.

Roland, Dunbar. *History of Mississippi: The Heart of the South.* Vol. 2. Chicago, 1925. Reprint, Spartanburg, S.C., 1978.

RAY SKATES

HUNLEY, HORACE (1823–1863), inventor and businessman. Born in Sumner County, Tennessee, on December 29, 1823, Hunley graduated from the University of Louisiana in 1849. He represented Orleans Parish in the state legislature from 1848 to 1849 and was admitted to the bar in 1849. Hunley then began a law practice and had become a successful sugar factor and cotton planter at a plantation in Lafourche Parish by 1857. On April 1 of that year, Hunley was appointed corresponding clerk at the U.S. Customs House in New Orleans. On May 8, 1860, he was promoted to special collector for the port. As a Confederate government agent, Hunley led an expedition on board the Lighthouse Service schooner *Wm. R. King* in search of two vessels carrying arms for the Confederacy. He sailed on June 10, 1861, to the coasts of Yucatan and Cuba, failed to find the supply ships, and returned to Berwick Bay on July 1.

In March 1862 Hunley acted as surety for the bond of a submarine privateer named *Pioneer.* The Confederate government offered a bounty of 20 percent of the value of any Union warship sunk by a licensed privateer. It was hoped that the little *Pioneer* might sink some of the Union vessels off the Mississippi and earn money for its owners. But when New Orleans fell to the Union, the submarine was lost without a chance to prove itself. Hunley and several of his partners fled to Mobile, Alabama, where they soon built a second submarine, *American Diver,* financed by Hunley. The sub foundered with no loss of life while being towed down the bay for an attack on the blockade fleet.

Hunley continued to act as a government agent while financing experimental submarines. A third submarine, named *H. L. Hunley* (sometimes called *Fish Boat*), was soon completed and carried to Charleston, where crew training began. Hunley was traveling but kept himself informed about the submarine by correspondence. After an accidental sinking caused the death of five men, Hunley was convinced that the boat had been mishandled. He personally led another crew of seven that was drowned when the sub flooded on the morning of October 15, 1863. Hunley was buried on November 8 with the other victims in a plot called "Hunley Circle" in Magnolia Cemetery in Charleston. The submarine named for Hunley proved that his idea worked, but it did not long survive him. *H. L. Hunley* sank the Union blockader USS *Housatonic* but did not return from its triumphant voyage.

[*See also entry on the submarine* H. L. Hunley.]

BIBLIOGRAPHY

Duncan, Ruth H. *The Captain and Submarine CSS H. L. Hunley.* Memphis, Tenn., 1965.

Kloeppel, James E. *Danger beneath the Waves: A History of the Confederate Submarine H. L. Hunley.* College Park, Ga., 1987.

Perry, Milton F. *Infernal Machines: The Story of Confederate Submarine and Mine Warfare.* Baton Rouge, La., 1965.

Robinson, William Morrison. *The Confederate Privateers.* New Haven, Conn., 1928.

KEVIN J. FOSTER

HUNTER, ROBERT M. T. (1809–1887), secretary of state, congressman from Virginia, and commissioner to the Hampton Roads peace conference. The second Confederate secretary of state was born April 21, 1809, at Mount Pleasant in Essex County, Virginia. After graduating from the University of Virginia in 1828, he studied law and was admitted to the Virginia bar in 1830.

From 1834 to 1837 Hunter served in Virginia's House of Delegates. Though elected as an independent, he allied himself with the anti-Jackson state rights Whigs. As an opponent of Old Hickory, he voted against legislative efforts to instruct Virginia's senators to support Thomas Hart Benton's expunging resolution and opposed Virginia's endorsement of the specie circular. On the other hand, to the dismay of the Whigs, he refused to endorse state internal improvements or the enlargement of banking establishments.

In 1837 Hunter, running as a "Sub-Treasury, Anti-Clay, state rights Whig," was elected to the U.S. House of Representatives. To the distress of the national Whigs, he consistently supported Martin Van Buren's subtreasury plan. Hunter's peculiar political independence proved advantageous after the Twenty-sixth Congress convened in December 1839. When the House deadlocked over the election of a Speaker, each party saw enough of its own principles in the Virginian to elect him as a compromise candidate, and at the age of thirty, Hunter became the youngest man ever to fill the position. But by attempting to act as a nonpartisan Speaker, he pleased neither party

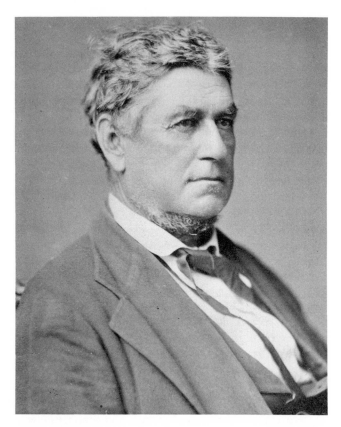

ROBERT M. T. HUNTER. Portrait made during Hunter's tenure as secretary of state.   NAVAL HISTORICAL CENTER, WASHINGTON, D.C.

and let pass an opportunity to build a base of political support.

During the presidential campaign of 1840, Hunter issued a public letter stating that he would support neither President Martin Van Buren nor the Whig, William Henry Harrison, in the autumn election. Virginia Whigs were offended at what they considered yet another act of rebellion from a renegade who was nominally in their party. In 1841, when Hunter sought reelection with the endorsements of both parties, the Whigs repudiated him. Local Democrats nominated Hunter and he retained his seat in Congress, but he had effectively ended his association with the Whig party. The Whigs retaliated by voting him out of office in 1843.

In the race for the presidency in 1844, Hunter, acting with a group of Virginia colleagues, tried to engineer a victory for John C. Calhoun by attempting to change the rules of the national nominating convention to favor minority candidates. Although they failed to win the nomination for Calhoun, they managed to deny Van Buren the party's nod. Instead, dark horse James K. Polk was nominated for and won the White House.

In March 1845, Hunter returned to the House of Representatives, where he led the fight for the retrocession of Alexandria County (later Arlington County) from the District of Columbia to Virginia. In 1847 the Virginia legislature sent Hunter to the U.S. Senate. As chairman of the Senate Finance Committee, he steered through Congress the tariff of 1857.

During the crisis over the settlement of the Mexican Cession, Hunter stood in opposition to the Clay compromise proposals. He ultimately voted for the Fugitive Slave Law and the organization of New Mexico and Utah; he opposed the admission of California, the abolition of the slave trade in the District of Columbia, and the settlement of the boundary dispute between Texas and New Mexico. After the death of Calhoun during the compromise debate in March 1850, Hunter, along with Jefferson Davis of Mississippi and Robert Toombs of Georgia, took over the direction of the Southern Democrats. The three came to be known as the "Southern Triumvirate."

Hunter was widely mentioned as a possible Democratic nominee for president in 1860, and his native state supported him when the party convened in Charleston. After a deadlock developed, however, and the delegates reconvened in Baltimore, Hunter threw his support to John C. Breckinridge, the eventual nominee of the Southern branch of the party.

As conditions deteriorated after the election of Abraham Lincoln, Hunter was one of three senators from the border states chosen to sit on the Committee of Thirteen that ultimately proposed the Crittenden Compromise. In an attempt to defuse the situation at Fort Sumter, on January 2, 1861, he introduced a resolution that would have required the president to retrocede any fort, dockyard, arsenal, or other such Federal installation upon proper application by a state legislature or convention. In response to Republican obstinacy, Hunter joined his senatorial colleague James M. Mason and eight Virginia congressmen in calling for a convention to avert sectional crisis by redrawing the Constitution.

Hunter presented his own proposals for restructuring the Federal government in a speech before the Senate on January 11, 1861. In a plan derived directly from principles enunciated by John C. Calhoun during the debate over the Compromise of 1850, Hunter called for constitutional amendments declaring that Congress had no power to abolish slavery in the states, the District of Columbia, or Federal dockyards, forts, and arsenals and that Congress could not abolish, tax, or obstruct interstate slave trade. He demanded a constitutional guarantee that fugitive slaves would be restored to their rightful owners or that the state providing refuge would compensate the slave owner for his lost property. To prevent a president from fomenting insurrection and circumventing the Constitution through patronage, Hunter called for a dual executive. One president would be elected from each section. While one president served in the White House for four years, the other would sit as president of the Senate; at the close of four years, they would switch offices. No bill could be passed without the consent of both.

He also proposed restructuring the Supreme Court. The chief executive from each section would appoint five justices. These justices would have the power to call before them any state that did not fulfill its constitutional obligations, including the return of fugitive slaves. If a state were found guilty, the rights of its citizens would be abrogated, and any other state in the Union could tax their property or commerce.

Hunter's plan had no support, and he resigned his Senate seat in March. After the Old Dominion seceded from the Union, the Virginia secession convention named Hunter one of its five delegates to the Provisional Confederate Congress, then meeting in Montgomery. Once he had taken his seat, he lobbied intensely for the removal of the Confederate capital to Richmond or another Virginia city.

After the resignation of Robert Toombs, Hunter accepted appointment as secretary of state, a post he held from July 24, 1861, until February 22, 1862. One of his first acts was to adopt the principles of the Paris Conference of 1856 governing privateering, neutral flags, and blockades. Refusing to recognize a paper blockade, he insisted that blockades must be effective to be in force.

Displeased with the progress that the three Confederate commissioners to Great Britain—A. Dudley Mann, Pierre A. Rost, and William Lowndes Yancey—were making in winning recognition for the Confederacy, Hunter recalled Yancey and reassigned Mann and Rost. He dispatched his old colleague James M. Mason to England with instructions to stress that the Confederacy would offer low tariffs to the industrial giant. Mason was directed to recall to the British that they had in the past extended diplomatic recognition to other break-away nations, including the South American colonies that declared independence from Spain, and Greece when it declared itself free of the rule of the Ottoman Empire. Hunter sent John Slidell to France with similar instructions. Both representatives were seized from the British mail packet *Trent* shortly after the ship departed Havana on November 8. Although Hunter and other members of the administration hoped that the *Trent* incident would offer Britain an excuse to declare war on the United States, the English did not seize the opportunity. Hunter initiated a mission to Spain that proved similarly unsuccessful.

A slow and ponderous man, Hunter might have made an admirable secretary of state in ordinary times, but he was not suited for policy-making in a revolutionary emergency. In February 1862 he yielded his post as head of the State Department and then took a seat in the Confederate Senate,

where he was elected president pro tem. He continued to dabble in diplomatic affairs by serving on the Foreign Relations Committee; he also sat on the Conference and Finance committees.

In the Senate, Hunter took a keen interest in the Confederacy's financial woes, especially attempts to limit inflation. Recognizing the need to restrict the amount of unsecured paper money, he preferred selling Treasury bonds below par over issuing depreciated currency. At one point he proposed that each taxpayer, in exchange for a bond, should contribute one-fifth of his total income to the Confederate government to finance the war; this measure failed to pass the House. During the next session, Hunter proposed a tax-in-kind, which was enacted. He also introduced a bill on January 23, 1863, gradually reducing interest rates on Treasury bonds from 8 percent to 6 percent and limiting the amount of bonds the secretary of the Treasury could issue monthly to $50 million. The miserable condition of the Confederacy's finances by March 3, 1865, forced Hunter to defend his economic vision in the Senate, where he blamed the failure to halt rampant inflation on "impaired publick confidence."

As 1864 closed, Hunter objected to a bill exempting cargoes of vessels owned by individual states from restrictions on imports and exports; he feared that all trade would pass from the national government to the states. Instead, he proposed lifting all restrictions on importation. He also offered an amendment to a bill to provide supplies to the army that would have allowed commanding generals to impress whatever supplies they required for the use of their armies.

In general Hunter supported the Davis administration until the matter of freeing and arming the slaves came up in February 1865. Hunter opposed the move as unconstitutional and a blatant violation of state rights, but he was forced to vote in support of the measure because of strict directions to do so from the Virginia General Assembly.

Early in 1865, Francis Preston Blair, a political colleague of Hunter's since the Jacksonian period, appeared in Richmond to urge a meeting between the warring sides to conclude a peace. Blair warned that if the conflict continued much longer, the United States would be forced to overwhelm the South by offering its forfeited lands to the people of Europe. Under Blair's initiative, a peace conference was arranged for February 3 on board the steamboat *River Queen* in Hampton Roads. Davis commissioned Hunter, Vice President Alexander H. Stephens, and Assistant Secretary of War John A. Campbell to meet with Lincoln and Union Secretary of State William H. Seward. The Confederate commissioners were instructed by Davis to begin discussing "the issues involved in the existing war, and . . . securing peace to the two countries."

Stephens expected to improve the Southern bargaining

position by suggesting that the two sections reunite to revive the Monroe Doctrine and force Napoleon III out of Mexico, although Hunter thought this a feeble suggestion. Lincoln refused to negotiate on any basis other than reunion and abolition, although he held out a small hope that the abolition might be a compensated one. He also categorically refused to discuss anything further while the South was in arms. Hunter reminded Lincoln that Charles I had treated with the Parliamentarians during the English Civil War. According to the Virginian, the president "laughed, and said that 'Seward could talk with me about Charles I, he only knew that Charles I had lost his head.'" Hunter could not accept such "an absolute submission both as to rights and property, . . . a submission as absolute as if we were passing through the Candine forks," and the conference broke up.

Although he believed the South's defeat was inevitable, Hunter returned to Richmond and in a public address urged greater prosecution of the war. In March, however, after a consultation with Robert E. Lee on the military situation, he seized an opportunity to seek a cease-fire during which questions about slaveholders' property rights and the status of the rebellious states could be answered. On this occasion, he worked with William A. Graham, John A. Campbell, James L. Orr, and William C. Rives to introduce a resolution in the Confederate Senate calling on Davis to propose through Lee an armistice to reestablish peace and union and to settle whether the seceded states would retain their former rights and privileges if they returned to the Union. Sympathetic members of the Senate, however, determined that Davis's mind was set against suing for peace and that the resolution would do no good. They had not acted on the peace resolution when Congress adjourned for the last time.

At the conclusion of the war, Ulysses S. Grant called for Hunter's arrest, and he was imprisoned in Fort Pulaski, Georgia, until January 1866. During Hunter's incarceration, Benjamin F. Butler took great delight in devastating the Virginian's lands in Essex County. Upon being paroled, Hunter returned to Fonthill, his 3,100-acre plantation near Lloyds, Virginia, and again took up farming and the practice of law.

In 1867 and 1868 Hunter served as a delegate to Virginia's Underwood convention. He supported the resulting new state constitution minus its two clauses that disfranchised all former state and local Confederate officials and that required a loyalty oath as a qualification for public office. (As a result of a compromise engineered by the Committee of Nine, these two clauses were separately voted on by the electorate and defeated.) Under the new order, he served as state treasurer beginning in 1874 and grappled with the problem of the payment of Virginia's enormous prewar debt. He was defeated for reelection in January 1880 by one of William Mahone's Readjuster candidates.

As vice president of the Southern Historical Society, Hunter engaged in heated public correspondence with Jefferson Davis over the reasons for the calling of the Hampton Roads peace conference and the policy of conscripting and emancipating blacks. The dispute was made all the more bitter because the point of contention was so small. Davis maintained he had agreed to the meeting only because Blair had asked for it and produced a corroborative letter from Judah P. Benjamin to back his argument. Hunter stressed the public pressure to bring the war to an end because of the rapidly diminishing resources of the South and backed his recollection of the peace conference with letters from the other two commissioners. Hunter also produced an account of the "Origin of the Late War," published in 1876 in the *Southern Historical Society Papers,* which defended the South's decision to secede as the only possible response to repeated Northern aggression. At the urging of Calhoun's children, he gave serious consideration to writing a full-scale biography of the South Carolinian to enshrine his principles and protect his memory but decided that such a work from his hand would hurt rather than help his former mentor and colleague.

In his declining years, Hunter was named collector of the port of Tappahannock by Grover Cleveland. Two years later, on July 18, 1887, he died at Fonthill and was interred in the family cemetery at Elmwood.

BIBLIOGRAPHY

Ambler, Charles Henry, ed. *Correspondence of Robert M. T. Hunter, 1826–1876.* In *Annual Report of the American Historical Association for the Year 1916.* Washington, D.C., 1918.

Crow, Jeffrey J. "R. M. T. Hunter and the Secession Crisis, 1860–1861: A Southern Plan for Reconstruction." *West Virginia History* 34 (1972–1973): 273–290.

Davis, Jefferson. "The Peace Commission: Letter from Ex-President Davis." *Southern Historical Society Papers* 3 (1876–1877): 208–214. Reprint, Wilmington, N.C., 1990.

Fisher, John E. "The Dilemma of a States' Rights Whig: The Congressional Career of R. M. T. Hunter, 1837–1841." *Virginia Magazine of History and Biography* 81 (1973): 387–404.

Hitchcock, William S. "Southern Moderates and Secession: Senator Robert M. T. Hunter's Call for Union." *Journal of American History* 59 (1972–1973): 871–884.

Hunter, Martha T. *A Memoir of Robert M. T. Hunter.* Washington, D.C., 1903.

Hunter, Robert M. T. "Origin of the Late War." *Southern Historical Society Papers* 1 (1876): 1–13. Reprint, Wilmington, N.C., 1990.

Hunter, Robert M. T. "The Peace Commission of 1865." *Southern Historical Society Papers* 3 (1876–1877): 168–176. Reprint, Wilmington, N.C., 1990.

Hunter, Robert M. T. "The Peace Commission: Hon. R. M. T. Hunter's Reply to President Davis' Letter." *Southern Historical*

Society Papers 4 (1877–1878): 303–318. Reprint, Wilmington, N.C., 1990.

Simms, Henry H. *Life of Robert M. T. Hunter: A Study in Sectionalism and Secession.* Richmond, Va., 1935.

SARA B. BEARSS

HUNTON, EPPA (1822–1908), brigadier general and U. S. congressman. Born September 22, 1822, in Fauquier County, Virginia, Hunton practiced law before the war. He entered Confederate service without benefit of an advanced education and with no military experience other than service in the militia as an officer. His political connections, however, won him a commission as colonel of the Eighth Virginia Infantry on May 8, 1861. He led his raw regiment at First Manassas and then arose from a sickbed in his Prince William County home to command the Eighth at nearby Ball's Bluff in October 1861. After sick leave that extended through most of the war's first winter, Colonel Hunton took charge of his brigade at Gaines' Mill when Gen. George E. Pickett (whom Hunton disliked intensely) fell wounded.

Eppa Hunton led the Eighth Virginia at Second Manassas and Sharpsburg and took it to Suffolk early in 1863. At Gettysburg on July 3, Hunton went into the charge on horseback and suffered a severe wound in his right leg. The next month he was promoted to brigadier general. For nine months General Hunton and his brigade garrisoned the post at Chaffin's farm near Richmond. He rejoined Robert E. Lee's army in time for Cold Harbor and then occupied a relatively quiet position near the Howlett house during the long siege of Petersburg. Hunton's command fought steadily during the last weeks of the war before the general fell into Northern hands at Sayler's Creek.

Hunton rebuilt his law practice and his fortune after the war and served four terms in the U.S. Congress before his death in Richmond on October 11, 1908. His blunt and opinionated *Autobiography*, which is among the rarest and most desirable of Confederate books, has made more fame for Hunton than have his deeds.

BIBLIOGRAPHY

Freeman, Douglas S. *Lee's Lieutenants: A Study in Command.* 3 vols. New York, 1942–1944. Reprint, New York, 1986.

Hunton, Eppa. *Autobiography.* Richmond, 1933.

Keith, James. *Addresses.* Richmond, 1917.

ROBERT K. KRICK

IMBODEN, JOHN D. (1823–1895), brigadier general. Born near Staunton, Virginia, on February 16, 1823, John Daniel Imboden practiced law in Staunton and represented that district for two terms in the Virginia legislature prior to the war. As a conspirator in the plot to capture the Harpers Ferry armory and arsenal, Imboden's first military operation occurred on April 19, 1861, less than 30 hours after Virginia's secession, when the captain marched his Staunton Artillery into Harpers Ferry.

Following his promotion to brigadier general on January 28, 1863, Imboden conducted his most famous campaign. From April 20 to May 27, 1863, Imboden, in cooperation with Brig. Gen. William Edmondson ("Grumble") Jones, marched his command of 3,400 men through northwestern Virginia to destroy railroad bridges and collect horses, mules, and cattle for the Confederacy. Imboden's route carried him 400 miles in 37 days. Torrential spring rains and mud slowed their progress, but his force destroyed eight railroad bridges, captured over $100,000 worth of Federal animals and supplies, and rounded up 3,100 cattle.

Imboden returned to the valley, and his next notable exploit was the surprise and capture of an entire Federal regiment, or nearly five hundred men of the Ninth Maryland Infantry, at Charles Town, on October 18, 1863. Imboden's final campaign occurred during the summer and fall of 1864, when he led his cavalry brigade in operations with Lt. Gen. Jubal Early. Typhoid fever forced the general from active duty to a prison command in Aiken, South Carolina, when he finished out the war.

During the postwar period, Imboden helped develop the coal mining industry in southwestern Virginia. Following his death on August 15, 1895, he was buried in Richmond.

BIBLIOGRAPHY

Imboden, John D. "Stonewall at Harpers Ferry in 1861." In *Battles and Leaders of the Civil War.* Edited by Robert U. Johnson and C. C. Buel. Vol. 1. New York, 1887. Reprint, Secaucus, N.J., 1982.

Imboden, John D. "Reports of Brig. Gen. John D. Imboden, April 29–June 1, 1863." In *War of the Rebellion: A Compilation of the Official Records of the Union and Confederate Armies.* Ser. 1, vol. 25, pt. 1. Washington, D.C., 1889.

JOHN D. IMBODEN.   LIBRARY OF CONGRESS

Warner, Ezra J. *Generals in Gray: Lives of the Confederate Commanders*. Baton Rouge, La., 1959.

DENNIS E. FRYE

IMPERIALISM. Imperialism played a role in the origins of the Confederate States of America. When dis-Unionists argued the case for secession, they sometimes voiced predictions that an independent Southern nation would grow into a vast empire for slavery—that the new country would extend its domain and institutions southward into Mexico, Central America, the islands of the Caribbean Sea, and even the farthest reaches of South America. Such pronouncements, in many instances, were merely rhetoric designed to persuade Southerners that the potential benefits of secession outweighed its risks. However, Article IV, Section 3, of the Confederate Constitution, with its provision that the Confederacy could acquire new territory and that slavery was to be legal in such acquisitions, suggested that the new nation might follow an imperialistic course.

Confederate imperialism derived from the Southern expansion movement of the 1850s, when many Southerners reached the conclusion that American extension into Latin regions would benefit their section. They looked southward for new slave states that would enhance their political power in Washington. They also anticipated other advantages from southward expansion, including plantation opportunities, the elimination of northern Mexico as a haven for fugitive slaves, wealth from control of isthmian transit routes, improved Southern trade with the Pacific coast and Asia, and an outlet for the surplus black population of the upper South. Virginian Matthew Fontaine Maury, who as superintendent of the U.S. Naval Observatory helped plan an expedition by two U.S. naval officers to explore the Amazon River, hoped that Virginia planters would one day take their slaves to Brazil, thus relieving his state of the danger of race war. Some Southern expansionists anticipated that U.S. acquisition of the Spanish colony of Cuba, which already had slavery, would enhance the competitive position of the South's sugar planters in world markets: since U.S. acquisition of the island would terminate the African slave trade to Cuba, labor costs there, and thus the price of Cuban sugar, would rise.

Southern pressure for America's territorial and commercial expansion southward influenced American diplomacy. President Franklin Pierce completed the Gadsden Purchase from Mexico and tried to pressure Spain into selling Cuba. President James Buchanan sought land cessions from Mexico, asked the U.S. Congress to authorize an American protectorate over Mexican Chihuahua and Sonora, supported the efforts of the Louisiana Tehuantepec Company to procure transit concessions across Mexico's isthmus, and

tried to purchase Cuba. Southern politicians, diplomats, and entrepreneurs played key roles in these projects. From 1849 to 1860, the slave states provided much of the leadership, manpower, and support for the era's illegal filibustering (that is, private, military) expeditions. The most important of these expeditions attacked Cuba, Mexico, and several of the states of Central America. Native Tennessean William Walker conquered and ruled Nicaragua in the mid-1850s. Even though Walker had no intention of seeking Nicaragua's annexation to the United States, many Southerners rallied to his cause, especially after he legalized slavery there in September 1856.

Prominent Southern radicals became involved with the filibusters. Edmund Ruffin met with Walker during the Southern Commercial Convention at Montgomery, Alabama (1858). William Lowndes Yancey, C. A. L. Lamar, Roger A. Pryor, Albert Gallatin Brown, and John A. Winston aided filibusters in a support capacity. Mississippi secessionist John A. Quitman agreed to lead a filibuster army against Spanish forces in Cuba. Such contacts between notorious radicals and the filibusters attracted attention from the nation's press. This publicity, combined with the secrecy that necessarily cloaked planning for illegal military expeditions, gave rise to charges by antislavery Republicans, Southern anti-imperialists, and foreign observers that the whole tropical expansion movement was part of a secessionist conspiracy. The Knights of the Golden Circle, a filibuster organization that aspired to create a new slave empire with Cuba at its center and embracing the Deep South, most of the border slave states, Central America, the West Indies, and parts of Kansas and South America, conformed to this conspiracy interpretation. Southern imperialism, however, was less an agenda for separate nationhood than a program to avert the necessity of a separate nation. It enjoyed broad public support throughout the South, especially in the Gulf states. Important Southern politicians who did not favor immediate secession, including Jefferson Davis, Alexander H. Stephens, John Slidell, and Judah P. Benjamin, advocated slavery's southward extension and worked toward that end, sometimes in collaboration with the filibusters.

The frustration of Southern imperialism intensified the alienation of the slave states from the Union and thus became a contributing cause to Southern secession. Northern Presidents Pierce and Buchanan, though willing to acquire territory through diplomatic channels, enforced U.S. neutrality statutes against filibustering expeditions. Their efforts prevented Quitman's planned strike against Cuba in 1854 and 1855, and contributed to Walker's downfall in Nicaragua in 1857 and his inability to reconquer that country in the years that followed. Antislavery Republicans in Congress opposed legislation to facilitate the purchase of Cuba. Many Southerners interpreted Northern obstruction of tropical expansion projects as evidence that the South's population was being reduced to second-class status within the Union; Northern hostility to slavery's southward extension appeared an indictment of their way of life. One of the last prewar efforts to resolve sectional strife, the so-called Crittenden Compromise, addressed these perceptions. This proposal (December 1860) would have reinstated the Missouri Compromise line and extended it to the Pacific Ocean, protecting slavery in any territory "hereafter acquired" south of the 36°30' parallel latitude—a seeming invitation to slavery's future thrust into the tropics. President-elect Abraham Lincoln and the Republican party rejected the plan.

Had the Confederacy established its independence, it likely would have attempted expansion into the tropics. Warfare with the North, however, precluded such initiatives. Confederate armies did invade vulnerable areas of the Union with hopes of incorporating those areas into the new nation. But Confederate penetration of the New Mexico Territory and the states of Kentucky, Missouri, and Maryland was hardly an example of imperialism—which implies rule over subject peoples. The Confederacy made part of New Mexico into the Confederate territory of Arizona, under the expectation of eventual statehood, and recognized Missouri as its twelfth state. Southern imperialism, with its dream of a vast slave empire, died at the beginning of the Civil War.

[*For further discussion of Southern efforts to acquire additional territory, see* Expansionism. *See also* Crittenden Compromise; Cuba; Mexico; Nicaragua.]

BIBLIOGRAPHY

Barney, William L. *The Road to Secession: A New Perspective on the Old South.* New York, 1972.

Brown, Charles H. *Agents of Manifest Destiny: The Lives and Times of the Filibusters.* Chapel Hill, N.C., 1980.

Genovese, Eugene D. *The Political Economy of Slavery: Studies in the Economy and Society of the Slave South.* New York, 1967.

May, Robert E. *The Southern Dream of a Caribbean Empire, 1854–1861.* Baton Rouge, La., 1973.

McCardell, John. *The Idea of a Southern Nation: Southern Nationalists and Southern Nationalism, 1830–1860.* New York, 1979.

Rauch, Basil. *American Interest in Cuba: 1848–1855.* New York, 1948.

Walker, William. *The War in Nicaragua.* Mobile, Ala., 1860. Reprint, Tucson, Ariz., 1985.

ROBERT E. MAY

IMPRESSMENT. The Confederacy's need for supplies prompted the Congress to enact an impressment law on March 26, 1863. As with other initiatives passed in an effort to obtain goods for the war effort, the Impressment Act created severe dissension on the home front.

The act established state boards of commissioners throughout the South. President Jefferson Davis and the state governors were each entitled to appoint one person to the board. This board served two functions: it mediated disputes between impressment agents and the individual whose property was to be impressed, and it fixed prices for goods set to be impressed by government agents. The board published the list of prices frequently so as to keep in step with fluctuations on the markets. Still, the lists rarely reflected the prevailing market price.

Local impressment agents administered the law. They traveled throughout the South and surveyed the stocks of farmers, merchants, and others with products deemed necessary for the government. The agent and the farmer or merchant would assess the value of the property chosen for impressment. The individual whose property was impressed was either paid in full in Confederate scrip at the time or was issued a certificate entitling him to payment upon redemption later.

Apparently, the civilian population voiced little opposition to the impressment measure until the summer of 1863. Then the floodgates of protest opened. With the nation reeling from the military debacles at Gettysburg and Vicksburg, and with Confederate currency rapidly depreciating in value, Southerners were less than pleased to see impressment price lists that set prices well below market values. These rates—which were often 50 percent below the market price for the good—infuriated farmers and small businessmen alike who were squeezed by inflation and government demands. It came to be assumed that if the government impressed your goods for the army's use, you would take a loss. Southerners were also bothered by the haphazard way impressment agents enforced the law. Moreover, the burden of impressment was not distributed equally: those living near the Confederate field armies or near transportation depots were hit hardest. Similarly, Southerners were preyed upon by fake impressment agents who used counterfeit certificates as licenses to steal from neighbors. These were real problems, but for many, what irked them most about the law was its wastefulness: too often impressed foodstuffs, supposedly destined for the field armies, rotted at depots because agents failed to obtain transportation prior to the impressment or because transportation could not be found.

From the beginning of the war, military authorities also impressed slaves to work on fortifications or to serve as teamsters, nurses, or cooks. As with the impressment of foodstuffs and other supplies, this impressment was administered by local military authorities—Congress did not regulate impressment procedures until the 1863 law. After 1863, Congress insisted that the impressment of slaves and military goods conform to the laws of the state where the slave was impressed.

The owners of impressed slaves were paid thirty dollars a month or whatever wage may have been agreed upon in advance. In the event the impressed slave was killed while working for the government, the owner was entitled to be reimbursed in full. Masters nonetheless were often resistant to allowing impressment agents to spirit off their slaves. Planters found that impressed slaves were not treated well and were kept past the time specified in the government contract. In addition, the government was slow to pay, and when it did, it always paid in worthless Confederate currency. In short, many owners found impressment to be an economic liability. Nonetheless, military authorities found slave labor to be imperative for the war effort, especially as the tide turned against the Confederacy. By February of 1864 the government wanted to hire a minimum of twenty thousand slaves; if the slave owners did not volunteer their chattels, the government reserved the right to impress them.

Scholars have been unable to calculate the amount of goods impressed. Authorities on the Confederate financial system, however, have speculated on the amount. Since Treasury notes were issued largely to pay for impressed goods, the amount of notes issued during the course of the Impressment Act's existence provides a rough estimate of what impressment brought to the Confederate government. Over $500 million worth of vouchers and notes were still unpaid as late as March 1865.

The unpopularity of the impressment system and the inequities it represented almost preordained its demise. By the end of the war, the Impressment Act was a dead letter, and the government found itself forced to pay for goods at market prices.

BIBLIOGRAPHY

Ball, Douglas B. *Financial Failure and Confederate Defeat.* Urbana, Ill., 1991.
Coulter, E. Merton. *The Confederate States of America, 1861–1865.* A History of the South, vol. 7. Baton Rouge, La., 1950.
Todd, Richard Cecil. *Confederate Finance.* Athens, Ga., 1954.

MARY A. DeCREDICO

INDEX. The *Index* was a newspaper published weekly in London from May 1, 1862, to August 12, 1865. Founded by Henry Hotze, chief Confederate propagandist, it was an outgrowth of his successful program to recruit and educate a corps of British writers. The *Index* gave them extra employment, income, and education in Southern affairs. But it did much more. As a central repository it created a virtual monopoly in collection, distribution, and control of Southern news.

This monopoly in turn enabled Hotze to achieve his greatest goal—to create a journal not for popular or mass circulation but for a select readership composed of the English cabinet, members of Parliament, leaders in banking, industry, and commerce, and editors of the nation's most influential publications.

To put the Southern case most effectively before his intended audience and win and retain their confidence, Hotze made the *Index* thoroughly English in style and appearance and ensured that its content, while pro-Southern, was credible and restrained. Hotze never wavered despite the impatience of some Southerners with his moderate approach.

Since Confederate propaganda did not persuade Britain to intervene, Hotze's paper might be dismissed as an innovative but failed experiment. But this was not the case. The *Index* achieved all its expectations and became the centerpiece of Confederate propaganda in Great Britain. Historian Douglas S. Freeman was right when he declared that "the *Index* must have been one of the most effective of all organs of propaganda before the period of the [First] World War."

BIBLIOGRAPHY

Cullop, Charles P. *Confederate Propaganda in Europe, 1861–1865.* Coral Gables, Fla., 1969.
Owsley, Frank L. *King Cotton Diplomacy: Foreign Relations of the Confederate States of America.* 2d ed. Revised by Harriet C. Owsley. Chicago, 1959.

CHARLES P. CULLOP

INDIANS. Native Americans who lived in the Confederate States of America and in Indian Territory possessed common cultural traditions. These ranged from a mixed economy of agriculture and hunting, to a villagelike settlement pattern, to a profound respect for the supernatural. Extensive interaction with Europeans, including intermarriage, had dramatically altered these traditional ways of life of the Southern Indians. Well before 1861, many of the tribespeople had adopted Euro-American clothing and housing styles, engaged in plantation-style agriculture that included slave labor, welcomed formal education, and adopted Christianity.

The most notable of the Southern Indians were the so-called Five Civilized Tribes—the Choctaws, Chickasaws, Creeks, Seminoles, and Cherokees. These people's ancestral domains extended from the Great Smokey Mountains westward to the Mississippi River, and from the Tennessee River southward to the Gulf of Mexico. The cultural transformation within their communities was particularly dramatic after 1800. The syllabary of the great Sequoyah (which enabled the Cherokees to achieve literacy in their own language), the adoption of a written constitution and code of laws by the Cherokees and the Choctaws, and a general acceptance of slavery illustrated the nature and extent of the change.

Little of this impressed Southern whites, however. The tribes possessed lands that were both fertile and mineral-rich, lands they wanted for their own use. They brought pressure upon the government of the United States to remove the Southern Indians from their ancestral homes, preferably beyond the Mississippi River. Although considered as early as 1801, removal did not become a clear national policy until 1830 when President Andrew Jackson secured congressional approval of the General Removal Act. In the decade that followed, the Five Civilized Tribes were forced to leave their homelands and take up new ones in Indian Territory. But not all of the Indians made the move; some avoided it by taking refuge in isolated hills or swamps, where they remained in virtual obscurity until removal pressures subsided. Thereafter and during the era of the Confederacy, these remnant bands lived lives of economic deprivation, political disfranchisement, and social alienation.

With their population of 50,000, the Five Civilized Tribes held title to virtually all of Indian Territory. The Quapaws, Senecas, and Seneca-Shawnees occupied small reservations in the northeast corner. Originally natives of Arkansas, 450 Quapaws were removed to Indian Territory after 1834. A Northern people, the Senecas of Sandusky ceded their Ohio lands in 1832, after which some 275 of them moved to Indian Territory. The same year a mixed band of 252 Senecas and Shawnees, also from Ohio and known as Eastern Shawnees, followed them, arriving only a few months later.

In the southwestern quadrant of Indian Territory, some 2,000 Native Americans lived in 1861 on lands leased from the Choctaws and Chickasaws. Plains Indian in cultural characteristics, these included the Wichitas and affiliated tribes, Caddos, Comanches, and Absentee Shawnees, among others. The Wichitas were the original occupants of the area, indeed of all of Oklahoma, and the Caddos were recent arrivals (1859) from Louisiana via Texas. The Penateka Comanche band came with the Caddos out of Texas, as did the Absentee Shawnees, although other Absentee bands had lived along the Canadian River since the 1830s.

With a reserve in Kansas, the Osage Indians were not technically an Indian Territory tribe. But for centuries they had seen themselves as sovereigns over the region, hunting where they wished and terrorizing anyone who objected. Peace and stability in the territory required the cooperation of the Osages.

Although there were Chickahominy Indians in Virginia, Lumbees in North Carolina, Catawbas in South Carolina, and Tunicas and Houmas in Louisiana, when the Confederate States government thought of Indian peoples they thought primarily of the tribes of Indian Territory. Recognizing the strategic necessity of drawing them into the Confederacy's orbit, the Provisional Congress in March 1861 resolved to send a commissioner to the territory to negotiate treaties of alliance. Accordingly, President Jefferson Davis appointed Albert Pike, a native of New England and now a prominent Arkansas lawyer, as commissioner to all the Indian tribes west of Arkansas. Legislation passed in May "for the protection of certain Indian tribes" became the substance of Pike's instructions. The Richmond government expected to secure the support of the Indians because of their Southern background, the military withdrawal of the United States from the territory, and Washington's failure to pay the tribes for their land.

Pike's first stop was Park Hill, the governmental center of the influential Cherokee Nation, where he arrived in early June 1861. There he found the tribe divided in its support of the Confederacy and Chief John Ross intent upon preserving a neutral course. Pike respected Ross's position and moved on to North Fork Town in the Creek Nation where, on July 10, he signed a treaty with the Creeks despite considerable opposition among the fullbloods. Unanimous in their support of the South, the Choctaws and Chickasaws signed two days later; a divided Seminole Nation signed on August 1. In these treaties the Confederates assumed all the financial obligations of the old treaties with the United States, made explicit pledges that the Indians' land would not be organized into official territories, guaranteed slavery, granted procedural rights in Confederate courts, and gave the tribes the privilege of sending delegates to Congress. For their part, the Indians agreed to become allies of the South in the current conflict.

From North Fork Town, Pike moved farther west to negotiate with the tribes of the Wichita Agency. On August 12 he signed one treaty with the Wichitas, Caddos, and affiliated tribes, and another one with the nonreservation Plains Comanches. The treaties encouraged the tribes "to prepare to support themselves, and live in peace and quietness," all under the laws and protection of the Confederate States.

While Pike was treating with the Plains tribes, he received word that the Cherokees were finally willing to negotiate with the Confederacy. The defeat of Union forces at Wilson's Creek in Missouri (August 10), the increasing belligerency of mixed-ancestry Cherokee slaveholders, the desire to retain the unity of the tribe, and the attractive offers made by Pike had caused Chief Ross to abandon his neutral posture. The treaty signed on October 7 was similar to those signed in June by the other four of the Five Civilized Tribes.

Pike used the occasion of the Cherokee treaty to negotiate with the neighboring Quapaws, Senecas, Eastern Shawnees, and Osages. Signed on October 2 and 4, these treaties recognized the four tribes as wards of the Confederate government and parties to the existing war, guaranteed slavery (which none of them practiced), and committed the Richmond government to generous annuities. These treaties, along with those signed by the Five Civilized Tribes and the Plains tribes, brought Pike's mission to a successful close. With only minor modifications, all of the treaties were ratified by the Confederate Congress.

It was one thing for the Richmond government to secure treaties of alliances with the tribes of Indian Territory, but it was something else again to carry out the provisions of the treaties. To facilitate that task the Confederate Congress authorized the establishment of a Bureau of Indian Affairs within the War Department (March 1861), the creation of a regional superintendency (April 8, 1862), and the appointment of six tribal agents. Jefferson Davis appointed David Hubbard of Alabama as the first commissioner of Indian affairs. Hubbard was followed by S. S. Scott (1862–1863) and R. W. Lee (1864).

Political squabbling prevented the appointment of a superintendent, but agents were selected. Serving rather consistently in their posts during the course of the war were John Crawford as Cherokee agent, Douglas Hancock Cooper as Choctaw and Chickasaw agent, Israel G. Vore as Creek agent, J. J. Murrow as Seminole agent, J. L. Harmon as agent for the Plains tribes, and A. J. Dorn as agent for the Osages, Quapaws, Senecas, and Seneca-Shawnees. Preoccupation with war and the scarcity of resources, however, left the Bureau of Indian Affairs largely a paper organization.

The treaties with the Five Civilized Tribes gave each the right to send one nonvoting delegate to sit in the Confederate House of Representatives at Richmond. Elias C. Boudinot took his seat as the Cherokee representative on October 2, 1862; Robert McDonald Jones acted as the Choctaw-Chickasaw delegate after January 17, 1863; and Samuel Benton Callahan, a trusted white man, represented the Creeks and Seminoles beginning May 30, 1864. The three introduced legislation affecting Indian Territory and participated in debate, but like the Bureau of Indian Affairs, their impact upon Confederate-Indian relations was negligible.

The treaties with the Five Tribes also called for the creation of a postal system. The postmaster general of the Confederacy, John H. Reagan of Texas, sought to meet those commitments by maintaining the thirteen routes and twenty-nine offices formerly established by the United States. Most of his plans were stillborn, however, because Indian Territory was early dominated by military events. Apparently only the routes and offices paralleling Red River remained in operation after 1863. Even then most mail was generated by military personnel and dispatched by courier to post offices in Texas or Arkansas.

Although never officially recognized by the Richmond government, tribal people other than those in Indian Territory contributed to the Confederacy. Most notable was a 400-man eastern Cherokee battalion attached to North Carolina's Thomas Legion, which engaged in several sharp skirmishes guarding the western approaches to the state. The 180-man First Mississippi Choctaw Infantry Battalion helped defend Vicksburg in 1863, but during the course of the battle it was captured by Union troops and met an uncertain fate. The Alabama and Koasati peoples in Louisiana also raised a Confederate unit.

Historians have often debated why remnant Indian groups in the Southern states and larger tribes in Indian Territory should have fought on behalf of the very people who had dispossessed them of their ancestral lands only thirty years before. There is no clear answer. Economic, cultural, and family ties provide a partial explanation. Important too in Indian Territory were the activities of Southern sympathizing tribal agents and border state pressure groups. Less tangible but just as significant was the remarkable ability of the Southern Indian tribes to use history to their advantage—in this case agreeing to forget the trauma of removal in order to win firmer recognition of tribal sovereignty. In retrospect the move was not particularly prudent, but it was an independent one. Alliance with the Confederacy was above all, then, an expression of independence.

[*See also* Elkhorn Tavern, Arkansas; Indian Territory; Wilson's Creek Campaign; *and articles on particular Indian tribes and numerous figures mentioned herein.*]

BIBLIOGRAPHY

Brown, Walter L. "Albert Pike, 1809–1891." Ph.D. diss., University of Texas, 1955.

Foreman, Grant. *The Five Civilized Tribes.* Norman, Okla., 1934. Reprint, Norman, Okla., 1982.

Hudson, Charles. *The Southeastern Indians.* Knoxville, Tenn., 1976.

McNeil, Kenneth. "Confederate Treaties with the Tribes of Indian Territory." *Chronicles of Oklahoma* 42 (1964–1965): 408–420.

Wilson, T. Paul. "Delegates of the Five Civilized Tribes to the Confederate Congress." *Chronicles of Oklahoma* 53 (1975): 353–366.

W. David Baird

INDIAN TERRITORY. With boundaries roughly identical to those of present-day Oklahoma, Indian Territory in 1861 was an unofficial designation for that area assigned by treaty to Native American tribes who had been removed to it from their eastern ancestral domains in the 1820s and 1830s. Those with the largest tracts were the Choctaws, Chickasaws, Creeks, Seminoles, and Cherokees—

the so-called Five Civilized Tribes. In the northeastern corner the Quapaws, Senecas, and Shawnees occupied much smaller tracts, and in the southwest the Wichitas, Caddos, Absentee Shawnees, and Comanches inhabited lands leased from the Choctaws and Chickasaws. Some 3,000 to 4,000 Indians from the territory enlisted in the Confederate army during the Civil War. It was also the site of numerous skirmishes and battles.

Indian Territory in 1860 was only sparsely populated. Best estimates place the total number of Indians at just under 53,000, or less than one person per square mile, with the Cherokee, Choctaw, and Creek nations having the largest populations. The western two-thirds of the territory was virtually uninhabited, with the Plains tribes numbering no more than 2,000 people. Living among the Indians were some 3,000 mostly Southern-born whites and 8,376 black slaves, nearly 60 percent of whom were held by the Cherokees and Choctaws.

The sectional debate that raged in the United States during the 1850s was only dimly reflected in Indian Territory. Slavery was the focus of much discussion and the cause of tribal division, but the phrase "state rights" was meaningless. Yet tribal leaders were seriously disturbed by Republican rhetoric during the presidential campaign of 1860 that proposed expropriation of tribal lands for white settlement. When Abraham Lincoln was elected, the Indians expected the worst. Trusted advisers and friends confirmed and played upon their fears.

Many tribal leaders, therefore, welcomed the formation of the Confederate States of America. Cherokees of mixed ancestry led by Stand Watie organized the Knights of the Golden Circle to advance the Southern cause and to counteract the Keetoowahs, an antislavery society of fullbloods influenced by missionaries. Choctaw Robert M. Jones, a large slaveholder, argued that opponents of Southern secession should be hanged. That the destiny of Indian Territory lay with the Confederacy seemed clear when, in early May 1861, U.S. troops abandoned Forts Washita, Arbuckle, and Cobb along the western frontier and withdrew to Kansas.

In the summer and fall of 1861, the Five Tribes and the Quapaws, Senecas, Shawnees, Osages, Comanches, Wichitas, and affiliated tribes all signed treaties of alliance and entered new bureaucratic relationships with the Confederacy. Simultaneously, the Richmond government organized a separate military department for Indian Territory commanded by Brig. Gen. Albert Pike (subsequently by William Steele, Samuel Bell Maxey, and Douglas Hancock Cooper) and composed of both Indian and non-Indian, largely Texas, regiments. Indian units and their officers were recruited from members of the Five Civilized Tribes. By 1864 they formed one division of three brigades (a Cherokee, a Choctaw-Chickasaw, and a Creek-Seminole,

commanded respectively by Stand Watie, Tandy Walker, and D. N. McIntosh). The Indian division had a reported strength of 3,260, but the effective fighting force was surely less than 1,000.

Not everyone in Indian Territory supported a Confederate alliance. Among its opponents was the Creek fullblood and slaveholder Opothleyahola and some 7,000 of his followers, all of whom proclaimed loyalty to the old treaties with the United States. In late 1861, 1,400 Confederate Indian and Texas troops commanded by Cooper engaged in three sharp battles with the dissidents (Round Mountain on November 19, Chusto-Talasah on December 8, and Chustenahlah on December 25) in an effort to force them into submission. Although one of Cooper's fullblood Cherokee regiments deserted en masse at Chusto-Talasah, the Confederate onslaught forced the Creek leader to retreat from Indian Territory and seek refuge in Kansas.

By early 1862, therefore, Confederate Indian troops controlled all of Indian Territory. That position of strength soon deteriorated, especially after the defeat of Southern forces at Elkhorn Tavern, Arkansas (March 6–8, 1862). Although based entirely upon circumstantial evidence, subsequent charges by Federal officers that Cherokee soldiers scalped the dead demoralized Indian Territory units. Following the battle, General Pike retreated with much of his command deep into the Choctaw Nation (twenty miles north of Texas) where he built defensive positions. He directed the Cherokee and Creek-Seminole regiments to patrol the Kansas border and along the Arkansas River.

The victory at Elkhorn Tavern encouraged the Union command to invade Indian Territory from Kansas in June 1862. Organized by Col. William Weer, the so-called Indian Expedition included eight white units and two Indian military units as well as several thousand returning refugees. Weer's troops pushed virtually unopposed a hundred miles south to Fort Gibson. At nearby Park Hill, Cherokee Chief John Ross welcomed the Union troops as liberators; and deserters from John Drew's Cherokee Confederate regiment, who had not been paid in months, volunteered for service, enough to organize the Third Indian Home Guard Regiment. Despite this reception and bright prospect, a failure of leadership and rumors of a counterattack caused the Union troops to withdraw back to Kansas, taking Chief Ross and as many as two thousand Cherokee refugees with them.

Southern forces were unable to capitalize upon the collapse of the Indian Expedition. Among the Cherokees two tribal governments vied for legitimacy, one recognizing John Ross as chief and the other acknowledging Stand Watie. There was not much more stability in the Confederate command. General Pike, unable to get requested supplies and believing his authority undermined, resigned

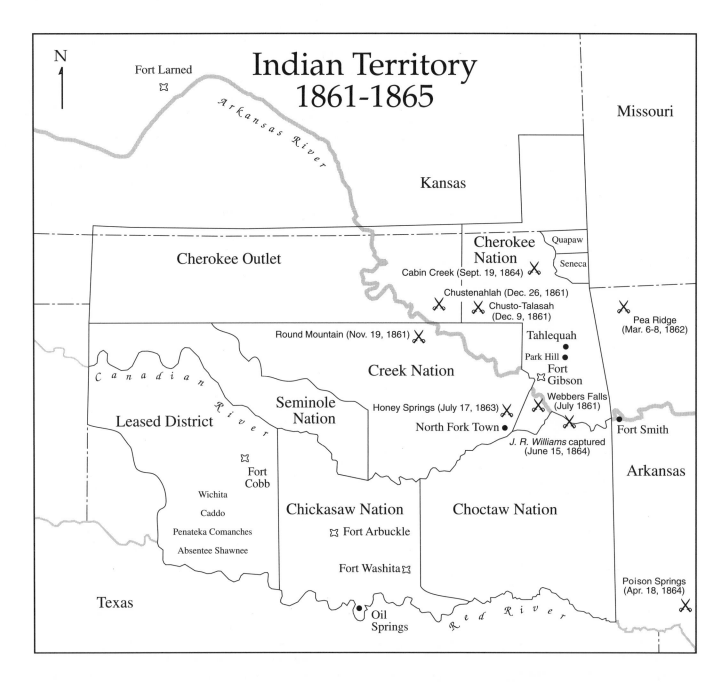

N

Indian Territory
1861-1865

Fort Larned

Arkansas River

Missouri

Kansas

Cherokee Outlet

Cherokee Nation

Quapaw

Seneca

Cabin Creek (Sept. 19, 1864)

Chustenahlah (Dec. 26, 1861)

Chusto-Talasah (Dec. 9, 1861)

Pea Ridge (Mar. 6-8, 1862)

Round Mountain (Nov. 19, 1861)

Tahlequah

Park Hill

Creek Nation

Fort Gibson

Canadian River

Seminole Nation

Honey Springs (July 17, 1863)

Webbers Falls (July 1861)

North Fork Town

Leased District

Fort Cobb

J. R. Williams captured (June 15, 1864)

Fort Smith

Arkansas

Wichita

Caddo

Penateka Comanches

Absentee Shawnee

Chickasaw Nation

Fort Arbuckle

Choctaw Nation

Fort Washita

Texas

Oil Springs

Red River

Poison Springs (Apr. 18, 1864)

in protest, only to be arrested by his subordinate and successor, General Cooper. The resulting chaos reduced Confederate military activity in Indian Territory to isolated raids and private justice.

Southern forces were in no position to challenge seriously a second Union invasion that began in April 1863. An Indian brigade composed of three loyalist regiments and commanded by Col. William A. Phillips occupied Fort Gibson with only minimal opposition. Three months later, Maj. Gen. James G. Blunt led a three-thousand-man force down the Texas Road and across the Arkansas River to attack five thousand Confederates commanded by General Cooper camped at Honey Springs. After a sharp battle on July 17, the poorly supplied Southern troops retreated from the field. They ultimately found safety in camps along Red River, where they were shortly joined by some fifteen thousand family members who abandoned their homes rather than suffer the wrath of Union forces that now controlled the northern two-thirds of Indian Territory.

Honey Springs was the decisive battle of the Civil War in Indian Territory. Thereafter Confederate operations were guerrilla-like activities designed to interrupt Union supply lines to Fort Blunt (old Fort Gibson). On such "scouts" Gen. Stand Watie and his First Indian Brigade were most effective, especially in capturing the steamer *J. R. Williams* (June 15, 1864) and, in conjunction with Texas troops commanded by Brig. Gen. Richard Montgomery Gano, a supply train of three hundred wagons at Cabin Creek (September 19, 1864). Less effective but more terrorizing were forays by Col. William Quantrill into the northeast corner of Indian Territory. Col. Tandy Walker's Second Indian Brigade gave more respectable support in the Confederate victory at Poison Springs, Arkansas (April 18, 1864).

The fall of Richmond and the capitulation of Gen. Robert E. Lee in April 1865 made further resistance of Confederate Indian troops in Indian Territory futile. On May 26, Lt. Gen. E. Kirby Smith surrendered the white Confederate command in Indian Territory, and the three tribes most tenacious in their commitment to the South surrendered through their chiefs: the Choctaws on June 19, the Cherokees on June 23, and the Chickasaws on July 14. Stand Watie, who acted on behalf of the Cherokees, was the last Confederate general to surrender.

The military contribution of Indian Territory to the Confederate war effort was marginal. Despite the place of the territory in its grand strategy, the Confederate high command never allocated sufficient resources to Indian and non-Indian troops operating there. In December 1863, at least one thousand of the Five Tribes enlistees were without guns of any kind, and those that were armed were generally not present in camp, often composing as little as 25 percent of the aggregate force. Without arms, discipline, or training, Indian troops fought bravely but with only minimal effect.

The tribes of Indian Territory paid dearly for their participation in the Civil War. The conflict left some of them so divided that factional disputes plagued their communities a century later. For them the war was an internecine struggle, with pro-Southern tribespeople devastating the property of their pro-Northern kinsmen, and vice versa. By 1865, there were few structures in Indian Territory that had not been torched at least once. And there were virtually no cattle, some 300,000 of them having been driven off by white entrepreneurs from Kansas or Arkansas.

Estimates that the tribes suffered losses of as much as one-third of their populations seem much too high. Yet we do know that 1,018 of the 3,530 Indians who enlisted in Union regiments died during their service. Assuming a higher loss among Confederate troops and an even greater number of deaths among noncombatants, Indian Territory may have lost as much as 20 percent of its Indian population, or 10,000 individuals.

An even greater cost was the loss of nationhood. Declaring that acceptance of Confederate alliances had abrogated all existing treaties, U.S. officials demanded that Indian Territory tribes negotiate new ones. Signed in 1866 and 1867, these required substantial land forfeitures, consent to the construction of railroads across tribal domains, and participation in an intertribal government, among other things. Put differently, the treaties were designed to open up Indian Territory to alien economic and political interests. The subsequent invasion culminated fifty years later in the loss of the Native Americans' land base and national identity and in the creation of the state of Oklahoma.

[*See also* Copperheads; Elkhorn Tavern, Arkansas; Indians; *and articles on particular Indian tribes and numerous figures mentioned herein.*]

BIBLIOGRAPHY

Doran, Michael F. "Population Statistics of Nineteenth Century Indian Territory." *Chronicles of Oklahoma* 53 (1975–1976): 492–515.

Franks, Kenny A. *Stand Watie and the Agony of the Cherokee Nation.* Memphis, Tenn., 1979.

Gaines, W. Craig. *The Confederate Cherokees: John Drew's Regiment of Mounted Rifles.* Baton Rouge, La., 1989.

Grayson, G. W. *A Creek Warrior for the Confederacy: The Autobiography of Chief G. W. Grayson.* Edited by W. David Baird. Norman, Okla., 1988.

Rampp, Lary C., and Donald L. Rampp. *The Civil War in Indian Territory.* Austin, Tex., 1975.

W. DAVID BAIRD

INFANTRY. During Gen. Philip Sheridan's victorious 1864 Shenandoah Valley campaign, a veteran Federal officer noted that, though outnumbered and repeatedly defeated, the Confederate infantry often inflicted more casualties than they took. They were better shots, he decided, than his own men and more skilled in taking cover, fighting like Indians or hunters. Also, in emergencies their regiments could move rapidly in an apparently disorderly swarm without losing their cohesion, offering less of a target than the orderly ranks the Federals tried to maintain. (It must be noted that this difference was most pronounced in the eastern theater, in actions between the Army of Northern Virginia and the Army of the Potomac; in the west, where Federal soldiers often had much the same civilian backgrounds as their opponents and Federal leadership was more aggressive, it was less evident.)

Several major factors contributed to this combat efficiency of the Confederate infantry. The government wisely attempted to keep its existing regiments filled with volunteers and conscripts rather than allowing them to dwindle away from battle casualties and sickness while raising more new regiments (as was done in the North for political reasons). Mixed in with veterans under experienced officers, these replacements quickly learned both the formal and the practical aspects of soldiering. The combat efficiency of Confederate infantry regiments therefore remained generally constant, as compared to the U.S. forces, which were a mixture of badly under-strength veteran units and fat newly raised regiments, green as gourds from colonel to drummer boy.

Organization

The basic Confederate infantry organization was the regiment. Its organization was practically identical with that of a U.S. regiment: ten companies (each consisting of three officers and approximately ninety-five enlisted men); a small regimental headquarters (colonel, lieutenant colonel, major, adjutant, quartermaster, surgeon, assistant surgeon, sergeant major, quartermaster sergeant, commissary sergeant, hospital steward, and two "principal musicians"); and sometimes a band. The major noticeable difference between the two sides was that each Federal regiment had its own chaplain.

During the first year of the war, the Confederate infantry included a number of odd units—separate companies and battalions (formations with three to eight companies), and so-called legions. These last were inspired by famous Revolutionary War formations, such as "Light-Horse Harry" Lee's legion of light infantry and light dragoons, which had proven highly effective in the irregular warfare waged in the Southern states. Probably the outstanding Civil War example was Hampton's Legion—organized, uniformed, armed, and equipped by Wade Hampton of South Carolina—an eight-company battalion of infantry, four companies of cavalry, and two of artillery. It soon proved impossible, however, to employ such legions as units in large-scale warfare. Hampton therefore recruited his infantry up to regimental strength and transferred the cavalry and artillery to regiments of their respective arms. Some separate battalions remained in existence throughout the war, but many of them were added to existing regiments or combined to form new ones.

A varying number of regiments—usually four or five—formed a brigade, a basic tactical formation at this time. Brigades were made up of regiments from the same state (a notable exception in the Army of Northern Virginia was its lone Arkansas regiment, which was lumped into its Texas Brigade); whenever possible they were commanded by an officer from that state. Brigades were frequently identified by name—usually that of the commander under which it originally won distinction—rather than by its number. Thus the Virginia Brigade, which Gen. Thomas J. Jackson led at First Manassas, was known as the Stonewall Brigade for the rest of its much-battered existence. The Texas Brigade referred to itself as Hood's Texans even after John Bell Hood had left the Army of Northern Virginia. Sometimes the practice became confusing: at Gettysburg,

for example, McGowan's Brigade was first commanded by J. Johnston Pettigrew and then by J. K. Marshall; Archer's Brigade was led by Birkett Davenport Fry. A different type of nickname was that adopted by some Kentucky troops after the Federal occupation of their home state—the Orphan Brigade.

Until the winter of 1862–1863 the Army of Northern Virginia's infantry brigades might include a company of artillery, a practice that continued for approximately a year more in the western Confederate armies.

Several—usually four or five—brigades of infantry, with several companies of artillery, constituted an infantry division. (In contrast, until February 1863 most Federal divisions also included a regiment or more of cavalry.) An average of four infantry divisions and additional artillery made up a corps; several corps (with cavalry, reserve artillery, engineers, and service troops) formed an army. Thanks to the Confederate practice of keeping existing infantry regiments as near full strength as possible, their infantry formations usually were stronger than their Federal equivalents; a Confederate infantry brigade of 1862 through 1864 could put approximately as many rifles into line as a whole Federal division. Only when the Confederate conscription could no longer furnish sufficient replacements did their infantry units dwindle away like the veteran Federal regiments.

Though most of the Confederate states raised separate battalions of sharpshooters, there is little evidence that many of these were trained, armed, or employed as such. Instead, like other separate battalions, they frequently were later consolidated to form standard infantry regiments. However, during the 1864 campaign many infantry brigades of the Army of Northern Virginia organized 180-man corps of picked soldiers for outpost service, sniping, and patrolling. These corps were divided into four-man groups, each of which lived and fought as a team. These organizations proved highly useful, especially for fighting in thick woods such as the Wilderness.

Mounted infantry were infantrymen given horses or mules for greater mobility; they moved mounted, but dismounted to fight. In the East they appeared largely in the more irregular Confederate forces in the Shenandoah Valley, but in the West they were relatively common. Though useful in raids and in advance or rearguard actions, especially in broken country, Confederate mounted infantry had two major weaknesses. Being armed with unhandy, long muzzle-loading muskets, it was relatively helpless if caught while mounted by Federal cavalry: dismounted, with every fifth man detailed to hold horses, it seldom could stand off attacks by superior numbers of enemy infantry for any great length of time—a mission that Federal mounted infantry units armed with Spencer repeating rifles could accomplish handily.

Clothing and Equipment

Though the first year of the war saw gentlemen's companies with smart uniforms, elaborate camp equipment, and black body servants for each private, the average Confederate infantryman of 1861–1862 could be only sketchily equipped. This became something of a virtue for he soon preferred to travel light. Knapsacks (packs) were discarded as too cumbersome; most soldiers substituted the traditional American "horseshoe roll," rolling their blankets up lengthwise (inside an oilcloth or rubber blanket if they had one), slinging it over the left shoulder, and fastening its ends together behind the right hip. Extra articles of clothing could be rolled up inside the blanket. Alternatively, the soldier might make a short roll of his blanket and sling it across the middle of his back on a narrow strap or thong. A shortage of suitable material made blankets a difficult item to procure. Northern observers reported Confederates using varicolored quilts or strips of carpet, the latter sometimes with a central slit cut in them so they could be worn as ponchos. Captured U.S. blankets and civilian ones in all colors were also common.

The haversack (a plain canvas bag, roughly a foot square, with a flap cover and often a removable inside bag for small articles) slung at the soldier's left hip held his rations and few personal possessions. Over it would hang his canteen. His leather cartridge box with its forty rounds of ammunition usually was worn on the waist belt, handy to his right hand; between it and the belt buckle was a small leather pouch for percussion caps. The bayonet was carried in a leather scabbard suspended from a frog on the left side of the waist belt, under the haversack and canteen.

Confederate equipment as a whole showed great variety—prewar militia issue, obsolete U.S. material found in seized arsenals, different European models smuggled in through the blockade, captured material, and various domestic manufactures. Soldiers frequently added two practical items, a large tin cup and a "side" (bowie) knife, which was more of a tool than a weapon. Some veterans claimed that Confederate infantrymen tended to discard their bayonets (which were seldom actually bloodied in combat) and even their cartridge boxes and cap pouches, preferring to stuff cartridges and caps into their pockets. Considering the limited pocket space the Confederate jacket and trousers provided, this last story should be regarded with suspicion.

Recent research, confirmed by contemporary photographs, indicates that the Confederate infantryman was, contrary to received tradition, generally well supplied with clothing. Quartermaster Department records show a steady issue of clothing, if not smart uniforms, to the troops. Perhaps the Army of Northern Virginia's most ragged period was during the Second Manassas and Sharpsburg campaigns of August through September 1862, when its first locally procured uniforms (especially shoes) were wearing out and the Quartermaster Department was just beginning to develop an efficient supply system. By 1865 raggedness reemerged in troops from states such as Florida, which could not provide adequate support. Other states, such as North Carolina, however, had a surplus of uniforms on hand in 1865. Clothing supply for the Confederate western armies was less reliable but appears to have been generally adequate. America was rough campaigning country: after a few weeks in the field new uniforms would be showing heavy wear and tear.

The standard infantry uniform was a gray forage cap, a short, single-breasted gray jacket, sky-blue trousers, and heavy shoes. Naturally there were many variations, especially in the shades of gray cloth available. A frequent substitute for gray was "butternut," yellowish-brown shades obtained by dyes made from walnut hulls and copperas. Trousers were often gray or butternut, instead of blue, and many soldiers replaced their issue caps with soft slouch hats of many patterns. The showy zouave uniforms of 1861 soon disappeared, though one or two Louisiana regiments may have retained theirs for some time. The Second Alabama and Fourth Arkansas infantry in 1863 wore reddish homespun and broad-brimmed wool hats. The Forty-seventh Georgia had uniforms of blue-striped brown ticking. Requiring uniforms in a hurry before the Battle of Shiloh, the Second Texas received undyed clothing which reminded them of shrouds. Some prisoners taken in 1863 had English-manufactured jackets and overcoats of excellent dark-blue cloth. In the Wilderness in 1864, a North Carolina brigade in new uniforms of unusually dark gray were mistaken for Yankees and shot up—along with Lt. Gen. James Longstreet—by another Confederate unit.

Shoes were a major problem. Imports from England were gradually throttled, and domestic production was seriously hampered by a shortage of leather. By 1863 shoes were being made with canvas uppers, which came apart in wet weather. By 1864 some unfortunate infantrymen were receiving shoes with iron-bound wooden soles. In consequence, dead or captured Northerners were frequently stripped of their footgear.

Parts of Federal uniforms, which might also be taken from captured supply depots, were commonly worn. Although sky-blue trousers were regulation for Confederates, the use of blue coats and overcoats was considered a violation of the laws of warfare, and Confederate commanders usually ordered such articles redyed or discarded. It could result in unfortunate incidents. A. P. Hill's attack on the Federal left flank at Sharpsburg probably owed part of its success to the fact that his men had replaced their tattered outfits with blue uniforms they had just captured at Harpers Ferry, and the Federals could not readily distinguish friend from foe.

THE SUMTER LIGHT GUARDS. Company K, 4th Regiment, Georgia Volunteer Infantry, April 1861.   LIBRARY OF CONGRESS

The general appearance of Confederate infantry was marred by a thriftless element that neglected its clothing and equipment, preferring to go ragged rather than care for it or carry a change of shirts and underwear. A good many of them (like some Federal soldiers) seem to have had a personal aversion to soap and water; in 1864 a Federal cavalryman described prisoners from the Eighth South Carolina Infantry Regiment as having the aroma of aged billy goats. Ironically, such men became the "ragged rebels" of Confederate tradition—supposedly the epitome of the Confederate infantryman and one of the South's most beloved myths.

Weapons

The Confederate infantryman's standard weapon was the rifle-musket, a long-barreled, muzzle-loading, percussion-ignition, rifled weapon that fired the so-called minié ball.

Besides the rifle-musket, there was the rifle, a weapon with a shorter, heavier barrel, usually equipped with a sword bayonet. The Confederates also had a few special sharpshooters' rifles, the most prized of which seems to have been the short, English-manufactured, caliber .45 Whitworth. When fitted with a telescope sight, it was reportedly accurate up to eight hundred yards.

The first Confederate infantry organized in 1861 were haphazardly armed with weapons taken from seized U.S. arsenals in their territory, those already in the possession of their state militias, and whatever could be purchased in Europe or the Northern states before hostilities began. (It is estimated that approximately 600,000 small arms were brought into the South by blockade runners.) Such sources were later supplemented by the hastily developed Confederate arms industry and by captured weapons.

Though some Confederate infantry, especially in the

West, were initially armed with flintlock muskets, smooth-bores, shotguns, and hunting rifles, by late 1862 and early 1863 the average Confederate infantryman had received a modern rifle-musket or rifle. The English-made caliber .557 Enfield rifle-musket and short rifle were reportedly the most popular, but various U.S. models—either captured or Southern-manufactured—were also common. Some one hundred thousand good Austrian Lorenz caliber .54 rifle-muskets added variety. It should be noted that Federal infantry were not much better armed than the Confederates during the war's first two years; even in 1863, at Vicksburg and Gettysburg, some Federal soldiers turned in their obsolete smoothbore muskets and replaced them with captured rifle-muskets.

In general, these weapons were accurate at up to six hundred yards and could kill at one thousand. Their percussion firing mechanism functioned even in bad weather, which had left the flintlock musket useless except as a long handle for its bayonet. Their major weakness was a comparatively slow rate of fire. A fresh, well-trained soldier with a clean rifle-musket could fire three rounds a minute, but as continued firing fouled its barrel the rate of fire would drop to two rounds a minute, or less.

Tactics

The rifle-musket's increased range and accuracy forced considerable changes in tactics. American officers—Confederate and Federal—whose last combat service had been in 1846 and 1847 against Mexican troops armed with smoothbore flintlock muskets with an effective range of barely two hundred yards, now found themselves in a new, far more deadly sort of war. Artillery could no longer attempt to unlimber within three hundred yards of enemy infantry and demolish it with canister without quickly taking prohibitive losses. Cavalry charges against unbroken infantry became next to impossible, and infantry attacks were risky, costly affairs. In short, the infantryman with his rifle-musket dominated the battlefield; the effectiveness of his fire led to the increasing use of field fortifications.

Both opponents began the war with the same drill manuals and the same tactics, modifying the latter to fit the improvements in infantry weapons. If the changes seem slow and insufficient to modern readers, it must be remembered that it probably was late 1862 before the majority of infantry on either side had modern rifle-muskets and the need for change became apparent. Also, the rifle-musket's relatively slow rate of fire made it necessary to use masses of men in both the attack and the defense. At Fredericksburg, Robert E. Lee's defensive line in the Sunken Road at the foot of Marye's Heights was four men deep, each line firing in turn and then passing to the rear to reload. An attacking army normally expected heavy losses

and so commonly adopted deep formations, to be certain of getting enough men into its objective to hold it against counterattacks. At Shiloh in 1862, Confederate Gen. Albert Sidney Johnston's initial attack on the Federal left flank was delivered by two corps, one behind the other, with two more corps held in column as reserves. At Gettysburg, the right flank of Pickett's charge was three brigades deep; at Atlanta in 1864, John Bell Hood formed his brigades with their regiments in column (one behind the other), thus giving them a depth of eight to twelve men.

The common formation used by an infantry regiment in action throughout the war was the "line of battle"—its companies abreast in a two-deep line, with the regimental colors in the center. One company usually would be deployed as skirmishers from one hundred to three hundred yards in front of their regiment, depending on the terrain. In wooded or broken country, this skirmish line would be strengthened, sometimes with half the regiment being so engaged. During prolonged fighting in such areas, whole regiments might be deployed in heavy lines of skirmishers, individual soldiers taking cover and firing at will.

A typical infantry division attack formation was in three lines, each composed of one or more brigades. (The composition of each line would be based on the number of brigades present, their relative strength, and the tactical situation.) The leading brigade would be in line of battle, its regiments advancing abreast, preceded by one or two lines of skirmishers who probed forward to locate and develop the enemy position. The second line, also deployed in line of battle, followed approximately 250 yards behind. The third line might be similarly deployed or held in "column of fours" for rapid movement to a point of danger or opportunity.

Once hostile contact was made, the first line pushed up to absorb the skirmishers and attacked. This seldom was a dashing bayonet charge; instead it often broke down into an "advance by rushes," elements of the first line working forward, sometimes gradually, from one bit of cover to the next, with pauses to build up the fire superiority to cover the next rush. If the first line stalled, the second line would be fed in to restore the momentum of the attack, followed if necessary by the third line. The assaulting force, at the moment of collision with the enemy, would thus consist of two or three lines merged into one heavy, disorderly wave, the individual regiments badly intermixed. Only forceful personal leadership by officers and noncommissioned officers of all grades could keep it under the necessary minimum of control to ram the attack home. Even then, it might fail, especially if the enemy had had time to entrench and so was sheltered from infantry and artillery fire.

Perhaps the most marked tactical feature of the Civil War was the employment of hasty entrenchments, made of whatever materials were available. These were little used before late 1863, but after experiencing the protection afforded by sunken roads at Fredericksburg and Sharpsburg and stone farm fences at Gettysburg, the average soldier on both sides concluded that it was wise to dig in. Through 1864 and 1865, unless utterly exhausted, troops in the vicinity of the enemy, even if they were under orders to attack, would habitually entrench as soon as they halted, using their tin cups, halves of discarded canteens, and knives.

In action, infantry officers of all grades had to be quick to detect gaps in the enemy's front and to maintain tight contact with the friendly units to their front and flanks. A gap of any size between units might allow the enemy to wedge into their front and roll up their line in both directions, while an open flank not covered by alert patrols was an invitation to disaster, troops in line formation being very vulnerable to attacks from the flank and rear.

Though his war ended in defeat, the Confederate infantryman had won an outstanding reputation for hard fighting, swift marching, endurance amid hardships, and sheer pugnacity. He nevertheless had remained a thorough individualist, much given to straggling, unauthorized foraging, absence without leave, and general indiscipline.

Officers whom the Confederate infantryman trusted could lead him against any danger. But such trust was hard-earned, the Southern infantryman being persnickety and demanding of his officers. He disliked strict West Pointers (particularly for officers below the grade of general), regarded men from other states as unreliable foreigners, and scorned any tendency toward pomp and circumstance. Above all, he expected nothing less from every officer, whether new lieutenant or general, than unhesitating, outstanding courage and personal leadership. Both victory and defeat killed or disabled large numbers of such officers; eventually it became impossible to replace them with men of equal courage and competence. A British observer concluded that Confederate infantry could accomplish wonders—but at a cost the South could not afford.

[See also Civil War, article on Strategy; Field Fortifications; Small Arms; Uniforms, article on Army Uniforms.]

BIBLIOGRAPHY

Coggins, Jack. Arms and Equipment of the Civil War. Garden City, N.Y., 1962.
Comminger, Henry S. The Blue and the Gray. Vol. 1. New York, 1950.
Department of Military Art and Engineering, U.S. Military Academy. Supplemental Material: Weapons of the Civil War and Organization and Tactics. West Point, N.Y., 1959–1960.
Elting, John R. American Army Life. New York, 1982.
Freeman, Douglas S. Lee's Lieutenants: A Study in Command. 3 vols. New York, 1942–1944. Reprint, New York, 1986.
Todd, Frederick P., ed. American Military Equipage. Vol. 2. Providence, R.I., 1977.
Watkins, Sam R. Co. Aytch. New York, 1962.
Wiley, Bell I. The Life of Johnny Reb. New York, 1943. Reprint, Baton Rouge, La., 1986.

JOHN R. ELTING

INFLATION. During the four short years of its existence, the Confederacy was plagued by a classic case of hyperinflation. This inflation destroyed the value of the government's currency and its credit and thus its capacity to supply its armies. Ultimately it contributed heavily to the destruction of the civilian population's morale and to the Confederacy's defeat.

The causes of this inflation included a bloated currency and public concern regarding the ultimate worth of the Richmond government's Treasury notes. This feeling was accentuated by the Union ban against the circulation of Confederate money in territory under Federal control. Inflation was also strongly influenced by the malfunctioning of the internal transportation system, military impressments, and the Federal blockade.

At the time the Confederate government was established in February 1861, the circulating medium of the eleven states of the Confederacy amounted to approximately $85 million in bank notes and $46 million in gold, silver, and copper coins. Three years later, before the Forced Funding Act of February 17, 1864, ordered the holders of Treasury notes to buy bonds or else have their money declared worthless, the currency of the country was approximately $1.115 billion, consisting of $900 million in Treasury notes, $125 million in bank notes, and $90 million in state, local government, and private scrip. Thus the currency was 8.5 times its prewar size. This growth was caused not only by massive government expenditures (greatly increased by the inflation) but also by the failure to regulate the circulation of $215 million worth of competing currencies. Inflation was further promoted by the absence of effective and timely internal taxes to sop up the excess currency.

The value of the currency and the inflation were affected by a number of factors over which the government had only varying degrees of control. For example, Union military victories followed by Federal rules prohibiting the circulation of Confederate notes in occupied territory caused such notes to be sent to the regions still under Richmond's control. Thus by 1864, with at least a third of its land area and people under occupation, the real increase in the currency in the area remaining under Confederate control was more nearly 11, not 8.5, times the prewar circulation.

The inflation was reflected in the price of gold expressed in paper money and the prices of domestic and imported goods. So far as the gold value of paper money was concerned, Treasury notes were at par with gold during much of 1861. Confederate money enjoyed a considerable advantage over other currencies because it circulated without discount or exchange charges throughout the whole country. By the beginning of 1862, however, five gold dollars commanded six in Treasury notes. In January 1863, a gold dollar was worth three paper dollars, and by early 1864, the ratio had risen to about 1–20, with rates as high as 1–40 being posted west of the Mississippi River, where the residents had long held a strong aversion to paper money.

The gold premium advanced most quickly during times of Union victories and more slowly during periods when the tide of battle favored the Confederates. The premium declined only twice, first in mid-1864, when a forced funding act and the recall of old notes of exchange for new ones temporarily reduced the size of the currency. The second occasion was in March 1865, when the Treasury sold its gold coin for Treasury notes in order to pay the Army of Northern Virginia. Just before the capture of Richmond, in March 1865, the ratio was around sixty Treasury dollars to one in gold.

The prices for such imported goods as coffee, which could not be easily restocked because of the blockade, increased very rapidly. Southern merchants, denied Northern credits, had not been able to stock up with imported or Northern goods and supplies of these were soon exhausted. By January of 1864, the premium on such goods was 41 times prewar prices, nearly twice the gold premium. The differential would have been even higher except that many people could no longer afford such luxuries and had to do without or use local substitutes. After the "New Plan" regulating imports and exports went into effect on February 17, 1864, there was a modest decline in prices. But prices resumed their rise, reaching 88–1 after Wilmington was captured in early 1865.

The prices of domestically made goods up until the second half of 1863 grew more rapidly than the gold premium. By April 1863, domestic goods were priced 6.25 times higher than in 1861, whereas the gold premium in paper was only 4.5. Thereafter, the prices of domestically made goods, chiefly food, declined when compared with gold, so that by January 1865, the gold-to-paper ratio was 1–53, whereas the domestic price index was only 38.5 times the prewar level.

This apparent anomaly can be attributed to a number of factors. Domestic food production rose, so more food was available. On the other hand, the breakdown in the railroad system made it difficult to move surpluses from where they were produced to where they were needed. In addition, the military impressment officers seized produce at artificially low prices before it could reach the cities, so that food prices were artificially raised in urban areas.

Wages and salaries, particularly of those working directly or indirectly for the government, were seldom raised and never on a scale sufficient to keep pace with inflation. This inflicted severe economic hardship on many people, thus further undermining public morale, particularly among soldiers, many of whom deserted.

Confederate government efforts to retard or reverse the inflation proved inadequate and sometimes harmful. The plan to limit the currency by making Treasury notes fundable into bonds failed because the Treasury did not take the needed measures to make the interest payable in coin.

Because taxes were low, were levied late, and favored the planters, the government's fiscal revenues were inadequate to reduce the currency. Treasury efforts to reduce expenses and inflation by levying taxes-in-kind and by impressing provisions at artificially low prices only fueled inflation by encouraging nonproduction, hoarding, and speculation. The supply of food produced or marketed near cities or the armies declined, thereby further increasing the shortages and high prices.

Similarly, the three-year delay in enacting regulations governing foreign trade encouraged high-priced luxury imports, provided no incentive to import necessities, and drew off badly needed foreign exchange. This negligence further promoted economic disintegration. Inflation, like so many other difficulties, was a problem for which the Confederates did not have timely or adequate remedies.

[See also Bonds; Bread Riots; Counterfeiting; Currency, An Overview; New Plan; Speculation; Taxation.]

BIBLIOGRAPHY

Lerner, Eugene. *Money, Prices and Wages in the Confederacy, 1861–1865.* Chicago, 1954.

Schwab, John C. *The Confederate States of America, 1861–1865: A Financial and Industrial History of the South during the Civil War.* New York, 1901.

DOUGLAS BALL

INGRAHAM, DUNCAN N. (1802–1891), naval officer. The son of a Revolutionary War naval hero, Ingraham entered the U.S. Navy as a midshipman at age nine. He gained national prominence while commanding the sloop of war *St. Louis* by rescuing a Hungarian revolutionary with U.S. ties, who was being held aboard an Austrian warship.

With the secession of South Carolina, Captain Ingraham tendered his resignation (February 4, 1861) and received commissions in the South Carolina and Virginia navies and then in the Confederate navy (October 23, 1862, to date from March 26, 1861). After serving briefly as chief of the Bureau of Ordnance and Hydrography, Ingraham was assigned in November 1861 to command the squadron in his hometown, Charleston. By October 1862 the squadron consisted of the ironclads *Palmetto State* (flagship) and *Chicora,* and four small wooden gunboats.

Ingraham had a reputation for bold action and personal courage. But his junior officers considered him too cautious, a view shared by Gen. P. G. T. Beauregard, who commanded the coast's defenses. Beauregard incorporated Ingraham's squadron into his coastal defense command and prodded the captain into action.

In the early hours of January 31, 1863, Ingraham's ironclads crossed the Charleston bar and attacked the blockading fleet in the Atlantic. The flagship surprised and rammed one blockader (USS *Mercedita*) while *Chicora* exchanged fire with several others. But the ironclads were too slow to give chase, and the Federals withdrew from danger. Beauregard and Ingraham proclaimed the blockade broken, but the U.S. Navy's ships returned to station and Charleston remained sealed.

On March 28, 1863, Navy Secretary Stephen R. Mallory, in an effort to generate more action with younger commanders, removed Ingraham from command afloat and assigned him to the naval station ashore. He commanded the Charleston station for the rest of the war.

Ingraham remained a resident of the city until his death on October 16, 1891.

BIBLIOGRAPHY

Bradlee, Francis B. C. *A Forgotten Chapter in Our Naval History: A Sketch of the Career of Duncan Nathaniel Ingraham.* Salem, Mass., 1923.

Melton, Maurice. *The Confederate Ironclads.* South Brunswick, N.J., 1968.

Parker, William H. *Recollections of a Naval Officer, 1841–1865.* New York, 1883. Reprint, Annapolis, Md., 1985.

Scharf, J. Thomas. *History of the Confederate States Navy.* New York, 1887. Reprint, New York, 1977.

Still, William N. *Iron Afloat: The Story of the Confederate Armorclads.* Nashville, Tenn., 1971.

MAURICE K. MELTON

INGRAM, PORTER (1810–1893), congressman from Georgia. Though born into a poor farming family in Vermont, Ingram was educated at Yale University and taught school in New York State from the time of his graduation in 1831 until he moved to Georgia in 1836. He settled first in Harris County and then, in the mid-1840s, in Columbus where he established a law practice with Martin J. Crawford, a partnership that lasted for over twenty-five years. Ingram became a city court judge in the mid-1850s.

Though an active Democrat and successful planter, Ingram initially opposed secession. He was among the Muscogee County representatives to Georgia's secession convention in January 1861, where he was among the minority supporting the cooperationist platform. But once Georgia committed itself to the Confederacy, Ingram became a loyal supporter. In late 1862, he replaced Hines Holt as representative of the state's Third District in the Confederate Congress. He served on the Committee for Medical Departments. Ingram, who was at home in the spring of 1865, was part of the local home guard unit that defended Columbus during James Wilson's Union cavalry raid from Alabama in April. Ingram was elected to the state constitutional convention that met in Milledgeville in November 1865, but retired from political life afterward. He resumed his law practice in Columbus, where he continued to live until his death in 1893.

BIBLIOGRAPHY

Northen, William W., ed. *Men of Mark in Georgia.* Vol. 3. Atlanta, 1908. Reprint, Spartanburg, S.C., 1974.

Wakelyn, Jon L. *Biographical Dictionary of the Confederacy.* Edited by Frank E. Vandiver. Westport, Conn., 1977.

Worseley, Etta Blanchard. *Columbus on the Chattahoochee.* Columbus, Ga., 1951.

JOHN C. INSCOE

IRISH. As the largest white ethnic group in the Confederacy, with a population of 84,763 in the South on the eve of the Civil War, the Irish were zealous supporters of secession and the Southern war effort. For example, when Governor Thomas Moore of Louisiana called for volunteers to defend his state, the Irish responded in overwhelming numbers. The *New Orleans Daily Delta* reported that all foreign-born in the city were eager soldiers, but "as for our Irish citizens—whew! they are 'spilin' for a fight' with Old Abe."

Indeed, the Irish had many motives for enlisting. Many objected to what they perceived as the problack attitudes of Northerners. Too, many Irish laborers, particularly those on construction gangs, regarded soldiering as an exciting alternative to their usual work. And one of the few means available to the Irish immigrant to gain acceptance and assimilation was to join the majority. "The moment the immigrant donned his uniform," one scholar wrote, "he ceased to be only a foreigner, an outsider. He was [now] a comrade-at-arms."

This should not be surprising, however. The rural Irish became the urban Irish in the Confederacy. Irish poverty drew them to the towns where they could find work in transportation and on the docks. In Charleston, South Carolina, Irish immigrants crowded into the area near the city's wharves and warehouses. Savannah's and Augusta's working class immigrants were largely Irish and competed for space with blacks in their city's poorest neighborhoods. In Mobile and Richmond this situation was repeated as it was in urban areas throughout the Old South. Consequently, too many Southerners ignored the value in the diversity of the Irish neighborhoods and saw only disease and disorder. They lumped the Irish into one large lower class irrespective of differences in caste or condition. Indeed, Southerners often regarded the Irish as among the "worst elements" and treated them accordingly.

Thus, for many Irish the only way out of such work as digging ditches, repairing levees, building roads, and loading and unloading cargoes was through the military. For other Irish, success in drayage, taxi service, hotel employment, or on police forces had not brought social acceptance. The Irish swelled the ranks of the police forces in New Orleans, Memphis, Charleston, and Savannah until Know-Nothing administrations reduced the size and Irish presence in their police departments.

For many Irish then, enthusiastic adoption of the Confederacy and its cause brought about the long-sought-after Southern approval. And Southern newspapers continually spoke to the importance of the Irish joining in the Confederate effort. The *New Orleans Daily Delta* commented that "our Irish friends . . . are daily proving that they are entirely with the true men of the South." So enthusiastic about the Confederate cause were the Louisiana Irish that in nearly every state regiment there were two or three companies composed primarily of Irish. New Orleans even had its own Irish brigade. Other Louisiana Irishmen, mostly from the wharves and alleys of New Orleans, fought in Virginia as members of the Louisiana Tigers, reputedly the "roughest battalion in the army."

For the Irish in other Southern states, the situation was similar. In Texas, eighteen Irish settlers signed the Texas ordinance of secession, and Irish soldiers filled the muster rolls of Texas regiments. Texas also had its all-Irish regiment—the Davis Guards, or the "Fighting Irishmen," as they were better known. Like the Louisiana Tigers, they were mostly in their twenties or younger and came directly off the docks and wharves, in this case, of Houston and Galveston. At the Battle of Sabine Pass in September 1863, the forty-three Irishmen of the Davis Guards repulsed a Federal fleet, captured two gunboats, and took over three hundred prisoners without losing a man themselves. So impressed with their efforts was the Confederate Congress that it passed a resolution of thanks to the Davis Guards; the city of Houston raised $3,000 for them and erected a monument at Sabine Pass in their honor.

Louisiana and Texas were not exceptional. Some 30,000 Irish-born Southerners in all fought for the Confederate army, and Irish units were raised in eight of the eleven states of the Confederacy. Five generals were Irish-born: Patrick Cleburne, Joseph Finegan, Walter Paye Lane, and Patrick Theodore Moore. "Strange people these Irish!" reflected Gen. Richard Taylor, commander of the Louisiana

Tigers. "Fighting every one's battles, and cheerfully taking the hot end of the poker, they are only found wanting when engaged in what they believe to be their national cause. . . . As Argyle's to the tartan, my heart has warmed to an Irishman."

[*See also* Louisiana Tigers.]

BIBLIOGRAPHY

Flannery, John Brendan. *The Irish Texans.* San Antonio, Tex., 1980.
Lonn, Ella. *Foreigners in the Confederacy.* Chapel Hill, N.C., 1940. Reprint, Gloucester, Mass., 1965.
Niehaus, Earl F. *The Irish in New Orleans, 1800–1860.* Baton Rouge, La., 1965.
Silverman, Jason H. *Beyond the Melting Pot in Dixie: Immigration and Ethnicity in Southern History.* Lexington, Ky., forthcoming.
Silverman, Jason H. "Stars, Bars, and Foreigners: The Immigrant and the Making of the Confederacy." *Journal of Confederate History* 1 (1988): 265–285.

JASON H. SILVERMAN

IRONCLADS. The development of iron armor protection for warships in the second quarter of the nineteenth century was prompted when the perfection of the naval shell gun rendered obsolete the wooden man-of-war. Ironclad warships were successfully tested in combat during the Crimean War (1854–1856), and by 1861 most of the major European powers had armor-plated ships in service or under construction.

In the newly formed Confederacy, Navy Secretary Stephen R. Mallory quickly realized that limited resources prevented the South from equaling the U.S. Navy in conventional warships. Believing that invulnerability would overcome disparity in numbers, Mallory initiated an ambitious program of acquiring armored fighting ships. After first receiving funds in May 1861 to purchase an armored ship in Europe, he determined to build an ironclad in the Confederacy. This decision led to the conversion of the fire-gutted hull of the U.S. steam frigate *Merrimack* into the ironclad *Virginia* based on plans formulated by Lt. John Mercer Brooke, Naval Constructor John L. Porter, and Chief Engineer William P. Williamson. Large and unwieldy, with a draft far too great for coastal waters, *Virginia* nevertheless served as the prototype of Confederate ironclads. Its ram bow and sloped wooden casemate covered with laminated iron plate became distinctive features of virtually every such vessel constructed in the South.

The ironclad designs immediately following the conversion of *Virginia* reflected an offensive policy initially advocated by Mallory. Exemplified by *Mississippi* and *Louisiana,* they were large and heavily armed, mounting ten or more guns, and were intended to operate on the high

CSS *Manassas*. Artwork by R. G. Skerrett, 1904.

seas and break the Union blockade. In 1862 Mallory shifted to a defensive strategy that resulted in ironclads far better suited to the South's shallow harbors and inland rivers. Characterized by the first of the type, the *Richmond* class, these vessels were comparatively smaller and more maneuverable, carried fewer guns, and drew less water than their predecessors.

A second design adopted in 1862 was intended specifically for construction at inland sites far from sources of skilled shipwrights. With a shallow-draft, flat bottom, and simplified hull form, this class, epitomized by *Albemarle*, was meant to be easily constructed by untrained laborers.

As the war progressed, combat and operational experience caused evolutionary changes that resulted in improved models like *Virginia II* and *Columbia*: casemates became shorter but carried heavier armor, purpose-built steam machinery was provided, increasing use was made of pivot guns to provide a more flexible armament arrangement, and large-caliber Brooke smoothbores and spar torpedoes supplemented the Brooke rifles previously adopted as the standard shipboard gun. Late in the war officials approved the construction of a turreted monitorlike vessel at Columbus, Georgia, but work on it never commenced.

About fifty armored warships were laid down in the Confederacy. Of these, approximately twenty-two saw service. Another five were contracted for in Europe, but only one, *Stonewall*, reached Confederate hands. Sometimes considered failures because of their inherent lack of seaworthiness, poor speed, and unreliable machinery, these

craft nevertheless served the Confederacy well. Credibly armed and armored, their mere presence frequently tied down Federal ships and men needed elsewhere. Often, they inspired "ram fever," an exaggerated fear of their capabilities, which reduced the offensive spirit of some Union officers. When operating in conjunction with land defenses such as those at Charleston, Savannah, and Mobile and on the James River, Confederate ironclads frequently played important roles in delaying or thwarting naval attacks.

[*See also* Rams *and entries on the ships* Albemarle, Arkansas, Jackson, Nashville, Neuse, Stonewall, Tennessee, Tuscaloosa, Virginia, *and* Web.]

BIBLIOGRAPHY

Baxter, James P., III. *The Introduction of the Ironclad Warship.* Cambridge, Mass., 1933. Reprint, Cambridge, Mass., 1968.

Durkin, Joseph T. *Confederate Navy Chief: Stephen R. Mallory.* Chapel Hill, N.C., 1954. Reprint, Columbia, S.C., 1987.

Still, William N. "Confederate Naval Policy and the Ironclad." *Civil War History* 9 (June 1963): 145–156.

Still, William N. "Confederate Naval Strategy: The Ironclad." *Journal of Southern History* 27 (August 1961): 330–343.

Still, William N. *Iron Afloat: The Story of the Confederate Armorclads.* 2d ed. Columbia, S.C., 1985.

A. ROBERT HOLCOMBE, JR.

IRONCLAD TEST OATH OF LOYALTY. *See* Oath of Allegiance.

ISLAND NUMBER 10. *See* New Madrid and Island Number 10.

IUKA, MISSISSIPPI. Twenty-two miles east of Corinth, Mississippi, on the Memphis and Charleston Railroad, Iuka was the scene of the attempt by Gen. Ulysses S. Grant to crush Gen. Sterling Price's command on September 19, 1862. The attempt was a failure, but as a result of the fighting Price did not join Braxton Bragg's Confederate army in Kentucky. Instead, he joined Gen. Earl Van Dorn's attempt to capture Corinth, Mississippi.

When Gen. Braxton Bragg invaded Kentucky in the summer of 1862, he left the corps under the command of Price to control northern Mississippi and to keep Grant from sending troops north. If the Union evacuated Nashville, Price was to move into middle Tennessee.

To support Gen. Don Carlos Buell's command, Grant sent three of his five left-flank divisions to Kentucky. This forced him to contract his line across northern Mississippi, and he abandoned everything east of Corinth.

On September 14th, Price occupied Iuka as the first step toward Tennessee. Discovering Grant's two divisions under Gen. William Rosecrans were still in northern Mississippi, he paused. While he waited, Price received word from Van Dorn that he was now under Van Dorn's orders, and Van Dorn wanted to concentrate against the Union forces at Corinth.

In the meantime, Grant was planning to destroy Price's corps, and he sent Rosecrans southwest of Iuka with two divisions numbering 9,000 men. Gen. E. O. C. Ord moved out of Corinth with 8,000 men to attack Price from the west. Price had 15,000 men in two divisions to oppose a force totaling 17,000. The plan was for Ord to attract Price's attention, and while Price prepared to meet the threat from the west, Rosecrans would attack from the south. When Ord heard the sound of Rosecrans's guns, he would attack; between them, they would crush Price.

The operation started out according to plan, although problems forced a delay of one day. Ord moved into position to the northwest of Iuka, and Price concentrated his men against him. Price's scouts served him well, however, by reporting the Union advance from the south along the Bay Springs Road. In response, Price ordered Gen. Henry Little to move Gen. Louis Hébert's brigade to meet this threat. Hébert marched south along the Bay Springs Road and encountered the advancing Union forces. He deployed the Third Texas Cavalry dismounted as skirmishers. They collided with the Twenty-sixth Missouri and forced them to give ground. The Confederates then advanced two guns of Clark's Missouri Battery, and Hébert deployed the rest of his brigade in line of battle. The Twenty-seventh Texas Cavalry was dismounted on the right with the Fourteenth and Seventeenth Arkansas, Third Louisiana, and the Fortieth Mississippi. The St. Louis Artillery anchored the Southern left.

While Hébert deployed his line, Price decided to send Col. John Martin's brigade to his support. Little and Price himself accompanied this unit. Martin used the Thirty-seventh Alabama and the Thirty-sixth Mississippi to support Hébert's left. The Thirty-seventh and Thirty-eighth Mississippi supported the Confederate right. With these troops in position, the Southerners attacked. They faced the brigades of Col. John B. Sanborn and Gen. Jeremiah Sullivan of Gen. David Stanley's division, deployed in two lines.

The Union left broke under the Southern attack. Confederates silenced the Eleventh Ohio Battery and captured their guns. Before the Northern line completely collapsed, Rosecrans sent in Col. Joseph A. Moore's brigade of Gen. David Stanley's Second Division. Only the Eleventh Missouri followed him, however. Stanley diverted the Twentieth Illinois to the extreme right and put the Forty-seventh Illinois in a blocking position astride the road.

With the coming of darkness, the fighting stopped. Just before this, Price had decided that the enemy was much stronger than he had thought, and he ordered General Little to bring up his other two brigades. Before he could accomplish this task, Little was killed, and Hébert took command of the division. Price first ordered Hébert to prepare the division for battle the next day. But concerned about the possibility of an attack by Ord's forces, Price changed his plans and moved out of town to join Earl Van Dorn for the assault on Corinth.

Ord occupied the position the Southerners abandoned, but he did not attack during the day. He heard no sound of the firing, and he thought the smoke from the battle was the town burning. The next day Rosecrans prepared to resume the battle, but when he advanced, he found the town of Iuka evacuated by the Confederates. Only the wounded and sick remained.

BIBLIOGRAPHY

Bearss, Edwin C. *Decision in Mississippi.* Little Rock, Ark., 1962.

Foote, Shelby. *The Civil War: A Narrative.* 3 vols. New York, 1958–1974.

Johnson, Robert U., and C. C. Buel, eds. *Battles and Leaders of the Civil War.* 4 vols. New York, 1887–1888. Reprint, Secaucus, N.J., 1982.

GEORGE A. REAVES III

IVERSON, ALFRED (1829–1911), brigadier general. Born in Clinton, Georgia, the son of a U.S. senator, Alfred Iverson, Jr., fought in the Mexican War, became a lawyer and railroad contractor, and then joined the First U.S. Cavalry. In March 1861 he became a captain in the

Provisional Army of the Confederate States. At Wilmington, North Carolina, Iverson almost singlehandedly recruited the Twentieth North Carolina Infantry and became its colonel. Iverson's men participated in the Seven Days' Battles in Virginia, capturing at Gaines' Mill a Federal battery whose fire had been enfilading Confederate positions.

Although wounded at Gaines' Mill, Iverson participated in the Battles of South Mountain and Sharpsburg, commanding the brigade of Brig. Gen. Samuel Garland, Jr., who was killed early in the fighting. Promoted to brigadier general on November 1, 1862, Iverson led his men successfully at Fredericksburg and Chancellorsville. On July 1, 1863, however, the Union First Corps ravaged his brigade at Gettysburg. Upon seeing this devastation, Iverson "went to pieces" and was sent to Rome, Georgia, to relieve Maj. Gen. Henry Rootes Jackson as commander of state forces.

On February 29, 1864, he was given a brigade in Maj. Gen. Joseph Wheeler's cavalry corps. He redeemed his reputation on July 27 near Macon, Georgia, by capturing Union Maj. Gen. George Stoneman and seven hundred of his troopers—one of the greatest cavalry victories of the war.

Iverson surrendered in April 1865. After engaging in business in Georgia, he was a Florida orange grower until his death on March 31, 1911.

BIBLIOGRAPHY

Derry, Joseph T. *Georgia*. Vol. 6 of *Confederate Military History*. Edited by Clement A. Evans. Atlanta, 1899. Vol. 7 of extended ed. Wilmington, N.C., 1987.

Freeman, Douglas S. *Lee's Lieutenants: A Study in Command*. Vol. 2. New York, 1943. Reprint, New York, 1986.

Palfrey, Francis Winthrop. *The Antietam and Fredericksburg*. New York, 1882. Reprint, Wilmington, N.C., 1989.

Stackpole, Edward J. *The Fredericksburg Campaign: Drama on the Rappahannock*. Harrisburg, Pa., 1957.

Wheeler, Richard. *Sword over Richmond: An Eyewitness History of McClellan's Peninsular Campaign*. New York, 1986.

ROBERT F. PACE

J

JACKMAN, SIDNEY D. (1828–1886), colonel and acting brigadier general. Jackman, a native of Kentucky, was born March 21, 1828. His family moved to Missouri, where he became a supporter of the Southern cause.

During the early part of the war, Jackman led a group of irregulars in western Missouri that bedeviled the Union occupation forces by ambushing small Federal units and conducting night raids on Federal installations. In 1863 he raised a regiment of Missouri refugees designated the Seventh Missouri Infantry (Mounted), and was elected its colonel. Later that year he was authorized to increase the unit to brigade size, which he apparently accomplished by November, since "Jackman's brigade" appears in the records as part of Joseph O. Shelby's command. During Sterling Price's last, ill-fated invasion of Missouri this brigade participated in much of the hard fighting that Price's army encountered. The brigade dissolved during the retreat back to Arkansas, although it was maintained on the books as a brigade organization, and Jackman continued in command until the end of the war. Jackman's brigade was recruited during 1863 and 1864 from Missouri refugees in Arkansas. When, returning from the Missouri debacle, many of the men observed the plight of their families in Arkansas, they simply left the army to care for them. Others used this pretext to leave. The unit lost nearly 50 percent of its strength due to desertion. Gen. E. Kirby Smith, on Trans-Mississippi Department orders, promoted Jackman to brigadier general on May 16, 1865, but since the Confederate government had already collapsed, the promotion was never made official.

After the war Jackman made his home in Hayes County, Texas, and served in the Texas legislature for one term. He was appointed to a Federal position by the Cleveland administration and was so serving when he died June 2, 1886. He was buried in Kyle, Texas.

Jackman was an effective recruiter and many records testify to his successful service in Shelby's command as a hard-fighting, hard-riding cavalry commander. On more than one occasion during Price's 1864 retreat from Missouri, his brigade was responsible for saving Shelby's forces from destruction.

BIBLIOGRAPHY

Darr, John. "Price's Raid into Missouri." *Confederate Veteran* 9 (1903): 361–362. Reprint, Wilmington, N.C., 1985.
Edwards, John N. *Shelby and His Men*. Cincinnati, Ohio, 1867.
Grover, George S. "The Price Campaign of 1864." *Missouri Historical Review* 6 (1912): 167–181.
Oates, Stephen B. *Confederate Cavalry West of the River*. Austin, Tex., 1961.

ROY R. STEPHENSON

JACKSON, ALFRED EUGENE (1807–1883), quartermaster and brigadier general. With his experience as a successful storekeeper and dealer of produce and manufactured goods, Alfred Jackson was a natural for the position of quartermaster in the Confederate army. As a young man, Jackson farmed a small tract of land along the banks of the Nolichucky River in Tennessee. By 1861, he had expanded his farm into a substantial business with extended trading networks throughout the South. He owned stores, mills, and factories from North Carolina to the Mississippi River, as well as boats and wagons to transport his goods.

In 1861, Jackson joined the Confederate army as a major and became quartermaster under Gen. Felix K. Zollicoffer. After Zollicoffer died in January 1862, Jackson became paymaster in Knoxville for a year. He got his first taste of actual soldiering in 1863. In February he was appointed brigadier general and took command of an infantry brigade under Gen. Daniel Smith Donelson. His assignment was to patrol eastern Tennessee and search for enemy raiding parties in the area.

Jackson's troops engaged primarily in small battles. Their greatest victory occurred in September 1863 when they took part in a struggle at Telford's Depot and captured 350 Union soldiers during the melee.

Jackson resigned from active service in November 1864. During the course of the war he had lost both his fortune and his business. After leaving the army, he went back to tending a small farm in Tennessee.

Several sources erroneously list Jackson with the nickname "Mudwall," which properly belonged to William Lowther Jackson.

BIBLIOGRAPHY

Porter, James D. *Tennessee.* Vol. 8 of *Confederate Military History.* Edited by Clement A. Evans. Atlanta, 1899. Vol. 10 of extended ed. Wilmington, N.C., 1987.

Warner, Ezra J. *Generals in Gray: Lives of the Confederate Commanders.* Baton Rouge, La., 1959.

JENNIFER LUND

JACKSON, CLAIBORNE F. (1806–1862), governor of Missouri. Born in Fleming County, Kentucky, Claiborne Fox Jackson moved to Missouri when he was twenty, settling in Arrow Rock. He became involved in the mercantile business and banking while also actively pursuing a career in politics. He served in the Missouri House of Representatives from 1836 to 1848 and in the state Senate from 1848 to 1852. Here he allied himself with Senator Thomas Hart Benton, the longtime leader of Missouri Democratic politics, and became a leader in the Central Clique, a group of politicians who dominated affairs at Jefferson City.

In the aftermath of the Mexican War, Jackson became an ardent champion of the extension of slavery into the new territories, drafting resolutions to that effect in the legislature. This led to his break with Benton, who refused to support that issue. The resultant split kept Missouri Democratic politics in turmoil throughout the 1850s, although the Democrats managed to retain the governorship. Jackson tried to play a conciliatory role during this period and was rewarded by being named the state's first banking commissioner in 1857 while also serving as state Democratic chairman. Thomas L. Snead, who was his aide during the Civil War, described Jackson as "tall, erect and dignified; a vigorous thinker, and a fluent and forcible speaker, always interesting, and often eloquent ... with positive opinions on all public questions, and the courage to express and uphold them."

In 1860 Jackson became the consensus candidate of the party for governor, something he had long sought. Almost immediately he was confronted with the split in the national Democratic party. Although sympathetic to the Breckinridge wing of the party, he realized that his best chance for election came from remaining loyal to the regular Douglas Democrats, a move that proved successful.

At his inauguration on January 3, 1861, however, Jackson revealed his true sentiments by warning that Missouri would have to join the slaveholding states in secession if the North tried coercion in any form against those who were leaving the Union. He asked the General Assembly to call a convention to determine Missouri's future course while also seeking a strengthening of the state militia.

In the days that followed, Jackson worked actively to prepare the militia for the future possibility of secession. He sent his lieutenant governor, Thomas C. Reynolds, to Washington to confer secretly with Southern leaders there as to the best course of action. The legislature approved his recommendation for a convention, but when it met on February 28 it adopted a course of strict neutrality, taking a wait-and-see attitude with regard to any future action. Following the firing on Fort Sumter, President Abraham Lincoln requested four thousand three-month volunteers from Missouri. Jackson rejected this call for Missouri troops as "illegal, unconstitutional and revolutionary; in its objects inhuman and diabolical." At the same time he met secretly with Southern sympathizers in St. Louis to determine the best course of action to secure the U.S. arsenal in that city with its sixty-thousand-stand of arms.

Calling the legislature into special session, Jackson sought unprecedented powers over the state militia while also ordering that organization into week-long statewide encampments the first week of May. This latter move served as a coverup for an attempt to seize the U.S. arsenal at St. Louis as the militia established Camp Jackson on the outskirts of that city. That plot was thwarted by decisive action on the part of Capt. Nathaniel Lyon, in command of the facility, who ringed the arsenal's approaches with a series of defensive positions. Meanwhile Jackson sent secret emissaries to President Jefferson Davis at Montgomery and to the recently seceded state of Virginia seeking aid. Davis responded by forwarding two 12-pound howitzers and two 32-pound guns from the arsenal at Baton Rouge, which arrived at Camp Jackson disguised as "Tamaroa marble." On the final day of the encampment, Lyon surrounded Camp Jackson with ten thousand men and forced the surrender of the militia. While Lyon marched his prisoners to the arsenal, rioting broke out, and twenty-eight persons were killed.

The legislature now promptly passed Jackson's militia

bill, giving the governor expanded powers. Jackson appointed Sterling Price to head a reorganized "Missouri State Guard." Missouri quickly became an armed camp as the new organization moved forward. Price arranged a truce with the Union forces in St. Louis, now commanded by Gen. William S. Harney. But this broke down after ten days as rumors circulated that Jackson was continuing to strengthen his forces in the interior of the state. A *New York Herald* reporter, visiting Jefferson City, found Confederate flags much in evidence.

When Lyon replaced Harney, he made it clear in a personal confrontation with Jackson and Price at St. Louis on June 11 that he intended to assert Union authority over the entire state. Jackson now called for fifty thousand volunteers to defend the state and abandoned Jefferson City, retreating to a more defensible position at Boonville as Lyon moved up the Missouri River to occupy the capital. Following a brief skirmish at Boonville in which Lyon quickly dispersed state guardsmen led by Jackson, the governor and Price retreated to southwest Missouri to reorganize their forces.

Jackson, accompanied by former senator David Rice Atchison, hastened to Richmond in mid-July where he secured an agreement from Jefferson Davis to pay Missouri troops in the field as soon as the state seceded. Returning to New Madrid, which the Confederates had recently occupied, Jackson learned that he had been deposed by a reconvened state convention and replaced with a pro-Union provisional government. Undaunted, he issued a proclamation on August 5 declaring Missouri a free and independent state under authority presumably given him by the legislature. Returning to Memphis, Jackson discovered that the Confederate Congress had appropriated $1 million for Missouri troops cooperating with its armies.

Hastening through Arkansas, Jackson learned that Price had defeated a Union force under Lyon at Oak Hills, Missouri, and moved on to Lexington. There Jackson rejoined him and called the legislature to meet at Neosho to formally withdraw Missouri from the Union. Unable to hold their position at Lexington, the State Guard retreated once more into southwest Missouri. A rump session of the state legislature met at Neosho on October 28 and passed an ordinance of secession. Jackson's emissaries in Richmond promptly signed an alliance with the Confederacy whereupon the legislature made provision for Missouri's representatives in the Confederate Congress and authorized the governor to issue $10 million in defense bonds to underwrite the cost of Missouri's war effort. Jackson now traveled to New Orleans to secure arms for the State Guard. He also managed to float the recently authorized defense bond issue.

Union forces under Gen. Samuel R. Curtis had meanwhile pushed Price out of Missouri. Jackson rejoined Price in time for the Battle of Elkhorn Tavern in early March. Thereafter he established a temporary capital at Camden, Arkansas. Sometime during the winter he managed to bring his wife and family south, together with twenty handpicked slaves. They were settled on a farm in Red River County, Texas. In July 1862, Jackson conferred with his fellow governors in the Trans-Mississippi at Marshall, Texas, and cooperated with them in dealing with problems in that theater. That fall he established reception camps along the Missouri-Arkansas border for those Missouri recruits wishing to join Confederate forces.

In mid-November 1862 Jackson contracted pneumonia and died at Little Rock after a confinement of several weeks. Though one might question the practical wisdom of Jackson's actions in 1861, he did pursue against overwhelming odds a course he believed was best for his state and the South. Certainly he was deeply attached to both.

BIBLIOGRAPHY

Kirkpatrick, Arthur R. "Missouri's Secessionist Government, 1861–1865." *Missouri Historical Review* 45 (January 1951): 124–137.

Knox, Thomas W. *Camp-Fire and Cotton-Field: Southern Adventure in Time of War.* Cincinnati, Ohio, 1865.

Parrish, William E. *A History of Missouri.* Vol. 3. Columbia, Mo., 1973.

Parrish, William E. "Missouri." In *The Confederate Governors.* Edited by W. Buck Yearns. Athens, Ga., 1985.

Snead, Thomas L. *The Fight for Missouri from the Election of Lincoln to the Death of Lyon.* New York, 1888.

WILLIAM E. PARRISH

JACKSON, HENRY ROOTES (1820–1898), brigadier general. Born in Athens, Georgia, June 24, 1820, Jackson graduated from Yale in 1839. He settled in Savannah and followed a varied career that included stints as a lawyer, Federal district attorney, colonel in the Mexican War (Georgia volunteers), editor, judge, diplomat (in Austria), delegate to presidential nominating conventions, presidential elector, and secession convention member.

Appointed a Confederate judge, Jackson soon resigned that office. On June 4, 1861, he was named brigadier general in the army. He served in western Virginia with the Army of the Northwest until he resigned December 2, 1861. Jackson was then appointed major general to command a division of Georgia state troops. When those troops were absorbed into Confederate service, he was left without a command. For a brief period he was attached to the staff of Maj. Gen. W. H. T. Walker.

On September 21, 1863, Jackson was reappointed a brigadier general, and until mid-1864 he commanded troops on the South Atlantic coast—mostly in the Savannah area defenses. He then joined the Army of Tennessee and commanded a brigade until he was captured December 16 at Nashville.

After the war Jackson resumed his Savannah law practice. During the first administration of Grover Cleveland, he was minister to Mexico. He died in Savannah May 23, 1898, and is buried there in Bonaventure Cemetery.

BIBLIOGRAPHY

Bergeron, Arthur W. "Henry Rootes Jackson." In *The Confederate General*. Edited by William C. Davis. Vol. 3. Harrisburg, Pa., 1991.

Warner, Ezra J. *Generals in Gray: Lives of the Confederate Commanders*. Baton Rouge, La., 1959.

RICHARD M. McMURRY

JACKSON, JOHN KING (1828–1866), brigadier

general. Born in Augusta, Georgia, Jackson was educated at the Richmond Academy near that city and at South Carolina College (later the University of South Carolina), where he graduated with honors in 1846. After passing the bar in his home state, he practiced law in Augusta and served in a local militia unit, the Oglethorpe Infantry, of which he was elected captain.

At the outbreak of the war, Jackson was named lieutenant colonel of Augusta's volunteer battalion, and in May he received a colonel's commission in the Fifth Georgia Volunteer Regiment of Infantry. He commanded the post at Pensacola, Florida, until the following January, when he received promotion to brigadier general and was ordered to Grand Junction, Tennessee, to organize troops for the Shiloh campaign. In that battle, Jackson commanded a brigade in Braxton Bragg's corps and continued to serve under Bragg at Perryville and at Murfreesboro, Tennessee.

In 1863, Jackson directed communications between Chattanooga and Tullahoma, Tennessee, and then commanded brigades under Leonidas Polk at Chickamauga and under William J. Hardee at Missionary Ridge and during the Atlanta campaign. Prior to the Battle of Atlanta, Jackson was transferred to command of the District of Florida and participated in the defense of Savannah, Georgia. During the final months of the war, he was in charge of supply depots in the Carolinas.

Following the war, Jackson resumed his law practice in Augusta. On a visit the following year to Milledgeville, Georgia, he developed pneumonia and died. He is buried in an unmarked grave in Augusta's City Cemetery.

BIBLIOGRAPHY

Faust, Patricia, ed. *Historical Times Illustrated's Encyclopedia of the Civil War*. New York, 1986.

Johnson, Robert U., and C. C. Buel, eds. *Battles and Leaders of the Civil War*. 4 vols. New York, 1887–1888. Reprint, Secaucus, N.J., 1982.

Warner, Ezra J. *Generals in Gray: Lives of the Confederate Commanders*. Baton Rouge, La., 1959.

CHRISTOPHER PHILLIPS

JACKSON, THOMAS J. ("STONEWALL")

(1824–1863), lieutenant general. Stonewall Jackson ranks among the most brilliant commanders in American history. Even though his field service in the Civil War lasted but two years, his movements continue to be studied at every major military academy in the world. He was an artillerist who excelled in infantry tactics, a devout Christian merciless in battle, a man of eccentricities but one motivated by an inflexible sense of duty. Jackson's death at the midway point of the war was the greatest personal loss that the Confederacy suffered. Many writers then and now insist that had he lived, the outcome of the South's attempt at independence might have ended differently.

No general ever rose from humbler beginnings. Jackson was born January 21, 1824, at Clarksburg deep in the mountains of what is now West Virginia. Although Jacksons were longtime residents of the area, his father was a struggling attorney with mounting debts. Jackson was only two years old when the father and an infant sister died of typhoid fever. For four years the widow and three children were virtual wards of the town. Mrs. Jackson remarried, but her new husband was unable financially to care for the children. They were sent individually to live with relatives. Jackson's mother died a year after the breakup of the family.

The lad grew up under the care of an uncle who ran lumber and grist mills in Lewis County, south of Clarksburg. Jackson developed into a sturdy youth accustomed to hard work and outdoor activities. The absence of parents also made him withdrawn and introspective in personality. Local tutors, plus a love of reading, provided him with a limited education.

Jackson went to the U.S. Military Academy in 1842 only after the first appointee from his congressional district decided not to pursue a military education. Few cadets ever entered West Point with less scholastic preparation than Jackson. Moreover, the mountain lad was introverted, awkward, and lacking in social graces. He made few friends during the four years at the academy. Using impassivity as a protection, Jackson concentrated all of his energies on learning. Determination, patience, and hours of studying by day and night accomplished his goal. Rising from near the bottom of his class at the start, Jackson ranked seventeenth of fifty-nine cadets at his 1846 graduation.

War had already been declared with Mexico when Jackson entered the army as a lieutenant in the Third U.S. Artillery.

THOMAS J. ("STONEWALL") JACKSON. An 1851 portrait.

He proceeded at once to Mexico. His battery saw no action for six months, and Jackson openly despaired of getting into battle. In March 1847, however, he participated in the assault on Vera Cruz; other engagements followed, with Jackson cited for gallantry at Contreras and Chapultepec. By the end of the war, Jackson held the rank of brevet major. None of his West Point classmates had done as well in Mexico.

Jackson returned to the States and reported for duty at Fort Hamilton on Long Island, New York. By then he had developed an increasing interest in religion. (In Mexico, he had had several discussions about Catholicism with the bishop of Mexico City, but found the services too formal.) In September 1848, Jackson received baptism and attended a number of communions at an Episcopal church adjacent to Fort Hamilton. His duties as assistant quartermaster and occasional member of courts-martial left Jackson free to pursue his fondness for reading. History was his favorite subject. Jackson also maintained a steady correspondence with his beloved sister, Laura, who was married and lived in Beverly, Virginia. He continued through the years to make periodic visits to this only surviving member of his immediate family.

Apprehensions over health were an ongoing concern to Jackson. Chronic discomfort, especially with his stomach, liver, and kidneys, soon convinced him that his troubles were punishment from God for his sins. Jackson sought relief from several New York physicians. When hydrotherapy seemed to ease his pain, Jackson became an ardent devotee of water treatments and thereafter regularly visited spas whenever possible. He likewise made physical exercise a part of his daily routine. Although many of his problems may have been the result of hypochondria, his weak eyesight and poor hearing were real and plagued him after his Mexican service.

In December 1850, Jackson's company transferred to Fort Meade in the remote interior of Florida. The artillerist uncharacteristically became embroiled in arguments with his commanding officer, Maj. William H. French. Jackson was soon under arrest for accusing French of having an affair with his maid. Meanwhile, Jackson had received an offer to become professor of artillery tactics and optics at the Virginia Military Institute in Lexington, Virginia. The academy was small, having been in existence barely a dozen years; nevertheless, it offered Jackson both a challenge and a change of scenery. He resigned his army commission and reported to the institute on the eve of the 1851–1852 school year.

"The Major" spent a fourth of his life at VMI. Only three months after his arrival in Lexington, Jackson joined the Presbyterian church and rapidly became one of the most devout Calvinists of his age. He found solace in constant prayer and strength through an inflexible faith. He attended every service at the Lexington Presbyterian Church. To the amusement of the congregation, Jackson slept through at least part of every service. He always sat bolt upright, his back never touching the pew. In that way, Jackson said, the pain of discomfort was punishment for his disrespectful naps.

Jackson's name and that of VMI are permanently intertwined—but not because of the professor's classroom performance. He was too skilled in artillery principles to be able to present it effectively. Having no background in the other subjects he taught—acoustics, analytical mechanics, astronomy, and physics—Jackson was forced to study as he taught. Memorizing lectures the night before he gave them, he was unable to expand upon or deviate from presentations. A question from a cadet, and Jackson could only repeat verbatim what he had previously said on the subject.

At the same time, the professor was a disciplinarian who tolerated nothing less than absolute attention and response from cadets in class. Jackson was personally responsible for the expulsion of a half-dozen cadets from VMI. At least two of them challenged him to duels; one threatened to kill him on sight. Cadets called him "Major Jackson" to his face. Behind his back, he was "Tom Fool," "Old Blue Light," "crazy as damnation," "the worst teach that God ever made," and similar derogations.

Giving credence to many of those disparagements were a

number of eccentricities that Jackson regularly exhibited. He would often thrust his arm into the air without warning and then make several pumping motions with it (in order to make his blood circulate better, he explained). Jackson on occasion would forget to eat; he seemed always wrapped in inner concentration; his reticence sometimes led him to stare in darkness at a blank wall; he ate only foods he disliked; he walked with exaggerated strides; on the few occasions when he laughed, Jackson threw back his head, opened his mouth widely, and emitted no sound whatsoever. He was unquestionably a "town character," Lexingtonians said with a shake of their heads.

On the other hand, Jackson displayed a number of qualities that impressed those who knew him well. Devotion, duty, and determination were his bywords. He was honest to a fault, extremely conscientious, and pleasant in the confines of small, private gatherings; his dependability won friends just as his piety won respect. In the latter years of the 1850s, Jackson organized and taught a black Sunday School class for slaves and freedmen, in open defiance of a Virginia law that forbade blacks from congregating in public.

Jackson married twice, both times to daughters of Presbyterian ministers. His first marriage, to Elinor Junkin of Lexington in 1853, ended when she died in childbirth fourteen months later. In 1857 he married Mary Anna Morrison of Davidson, North Carolina. That union, extraordinarily bound by Christian love, produced one surviving daughter.

Thoughts of a possible civil war began with Jackson in December 1859, when he and part of the VMI cadet corps were among the witnesses at the execution of abolitionist John Brown. Jackson remained a strong Unionist until he thought his beloved Virginia threatened by Federal coercion. At the secession of his state, he dutifully offered his services to the Confederacy. He left Lexington on April 20, 1861, never again to see his adopted town.

When Jackson and a contingent of cadets arrived in Richmond to serve as drill instructors for thousands of recruits gathering for military service, the ex-professor hardly resembled an impressive soldier. It had been fourteen years since Jackson had last seen combat. He was then thirty-seven, five feet, ten inches tall, with extended forehead, sharp nose, thick beard, and high-pitched voice. Unusually large hands and feet were the extremities of a 170-pound frame. Jackson rode a horse awkwardly, body bent forward as if he were leaning into a stiff wind. His uniform for the first year of the war consisted of battered kepi cap pulled down almost to his nose, the well-worn blue coat of a VMI faculty member, and boots that reached above his knees.

Appearance was deceiving. Jackson swept into war with cool professionalism and complete confidence in himself.

Something else was there that molded Jackson into an outstanding general. He reduced his burning faith to military logic. The great national catastrophe that had descended was a trial ordained by God to test the faith of man. Therefore, as Jackson viewed it, the Civil War was a religious crusade to regain the Almighty's favor. Christian faith and the Confederate cause were, for Jackson, one and the same. He proved to be demanding, steel-cold, even pitiless, in the field because he was fighting on the order of Joshua, Gideon, and other commanders of Old Testament fame.

His field dispatches, official reports, and home correspondence all contained references to "the blessings of God" and "an all-wise Providence." At the height of one of his greatest victories, Jackson turned to an aide and exclaimed joyfully: "He who does not see the hand of God in this is blind, sir, blind!"

Appointed a colonel of infantry on April 27, 1861, Jackson's first orders were to return to the Shenandoah Valley and take command of gaudily dressed militia and inexperienced volunteers rendezvousing at Harpers Ferry. The new commander assumed his duties with a stern and heavy hand. Units theretofore accustomed to parades underwent hours of daily drill; incompetent officers were sent home; all liquor in the town was poured into the streets; artillery emplacements and picket posts quickly ringed the area. Jackson taught the ignorant, corrected the errant, and punished the insubordinate. An officer who returned to Harpers Ferry after Jackson took command stated in wonder: "What a revolution three or four days had wrought! I could scarcely realize the change."

In less than a month, fresh troops swelled the Confederate garrison to such a size that Gen. Joseph E. Johnston assumed command. Jackson's accomplishments, however, bore personal dividends. On June 17, 1861, he was promoted to brigadier general and given a brigade of five infantry regiments from the Shenandoah Valley. His first duty as a general was to help destroy railroad property at nearby Martinsburg. ("If the cost of the property could only have been expended in disseminating the gospel of the Prince of Peace," Jackson observed.) On July 2, Jackson and one of his regiments easily repulsed a Federal probe near Falling Waters, Virginia.

The most famous nickname in American history came to Jackson and his brigade on July 21 at Manassas. When a Union army moved into Virginia to seize the railroads at Manassas Junction, the forces of Johnston and P. G. T. Beauregard combined to resist the advance. The all-day battle was actually a collision between two armed mobs seeking to become armies. Jackson's brigade was posted back of the crest of Henry House Hill, an eminence that commanded the Confederate left. In early afternoon Federals broke through the first lines of the defenders and

THOMAS J. ("STONEWALL") JACKSON. This portrait by George W. Minnes, from the Mathew Brady collection, was taken two weeks before Jackson's death on May 10, 1863.

swept up the hill in anticipation of victory. Jackson ordered his men to the hilltop. Gen. Barnard E. Bee, seeing the force in position, shouted to his faltering South Carolina troops: "Look, men! There stands Jackson like a stone wall! Rally behind the Virginians!"

Stonewall Jackson's line held fast in hours of vicious combat. A late-afternoon counterattack by fresh Confederate regiments sent exhausted Federals in retreat toward Washington. The South had gained a victory and found a hero.

In the next three months, Jackson and his Stonewall Brigade lay quietly encamped near Centreville. Promotion to major general (retroactive to August 7) came with orders in November for Jackson to take command of the defenses of the Shenandoah Valley. He established his headquarters at Winchester, organized his small force, and obtained the use of Gen. W. W. Loring's small Army of the Northwest. On New Year's Day, 1862, Jackson embarked on an expedition to clear Federals from nearby railroad stations and Potomac River crossings. Owing primarily to sleet storms and wretchedly cold weather, the ensuing Romney campaign achieved little but underscored Jackson's always-present determination to strike the enemy.

Jackson returned with his men to Winchester after ordering Loring's troops to remain in the field at Romney. Loring complained to the War Department. Secretary of War Judah P. Benjamin ordered Jackson to recall Loring. Jackson did so and then submitted his resignation from the army because of what he regarded as unwarranted interference with his authority. Governor John Letcher and other friends succeeded in persuading Jackson to remain in command. Secretary Benjamin yielded, and Loring was transferred elsewhere.

This affair demonstrated that like all mortals of unswerving purpose, Jackson was convinced of his own infallible judgment. "Old Jack," as his troops affectionately called him, was nevertheless exceedingly contentious with many of his immediate subordinates. These prickly relationships—with such officers as Gens. Turner Ashby, Richard Brooke Garnett, Charles S. Winder, and A. P. Hill—often marked, and marred, Jackson's career. He was never apologetic about wounding the pride of others. "Through life," Jackson insisted, "let your principal object be the discharge of duty."

His greatest achievement was the 1862 Shenandoah Valley campaign. That spring, Jackson's responsibilities were twofold: to block any Union advance into the valley, and to prevent Federals there and at Fredericksburg from reinforcing George B. McClellan's army moving on Richmond. When Jackson began his offensive, a Federal officer later commented, the Confederate general "began that succession of movements which ended in the complete derangement of the Union plans in Virginia."

Rebuffed at Kernstown on March 23, Jackson retired up the valley. He appeared suddenly at McDowell on May 8 and sent a Federal force in retreat. Then his "foot cavalry" marched rapidly northward down the valley. On May 23, Jackson overpowered the Federal garrison at Front Royal, drove the main Federal army from Winchester two days later, and then fell back when three Federal armies totaling 64,000 soldiers began converging on Jackson's 17,000 Confederates. On June 8 and 9, Jackson inflicted defeats on his pursuers at Cross Keys and Port Republic. He had thwarted every Union effort made against him. He did so through a combination of hard marches, knowledge of terrain, unexpected tactics, singleness of purpose, heavy attacks concentrated at one point, and self-confidence arising from the belief that God was on his side.

Jackson shifted his army to Richmond to assist Robert E. Lee in the counterattack against McClellan. "Old Jack's" role in the Seven Days' Battle was critical and became controversial. He failed to make his expected June 26 arrival at Mechanicsville and the battle that exploded there; he was also late the next day in reaching the field at Gaines' Mill. On June 30, whether from fatigue or lack of directives from Lee, Jackson remained inactive at White Oak Swamp while conflict raged a few miles away at Frayser's Farm. It was a less-than-sterling performance by the general who had brilliantly whipped Union armies in the Shenandoah Valley.

Thereafter, Jackson won new laurels with every engagement he fought. On August 9, at Cedar Mountain, he defeated the vanguard of Gen. John Pope's army. Later that month, Jackson executed the flank movement for which he became both feared and famed. He swung his men almost sixty miles around Pope's right, captured the main Federal supply depot in the rear of Pope's army, launched an attack of his own at Groveton, and then held off Pope's army at Second Manassas until Lee's forces arrived and sent the Union forces reeling in defeat. In Lee's Maryland campaign the following month, Jackson's troops overwhelmed the large Federal garrison at Harpers Ferry before rejoining Lee's army for the Battle of Sharpsburg. Jackson successfully withstood heavy Federal assaults throughout that morning and gave affirmation to the nickname "Stonewall."

Reorganization of the Army of Northern Virginia came in the autumn. On October 10, 1862, Jackson was appointed lieutenant general and placed in command of half of Lee's forces. Jackson spent weeks polishing his corps: reshuffling officers, replenishing men and supplies, and personally seeing that religious services, Bibles, and tracts were present in the ranks. A widening disagreement with one of his division commanders, A. P. Hill, overshadowed much of that period.

Jackson's forces repulsed with comparative ease a major

Federal assault at the December Battle of Fredericksburg. Four months of inactivity followed, in which Jackson oversaw the preparation of his 1862 battle reports, worked hard at enkindling a deeper religious spirit in his soldiers, and knew genuine happiness when Anna Jackson visited her husband with the five-month-old daughter he had not seen.

Spring 1863 brought a new advance from the Federal army. In the tangled confusion of the Virginia Wilderness, Jackson performed his most spectacular flanking movement. A twelve-mile circuitous march brought Jackson and 28,000 men opposite Gen. Joseph Hooker's unprotected right. Late in the afternoon of May 2, Jackson unleashed his divisions in an attack that drove routed Federals some two miles before darkness brought the battle to a standstill. Jackson was anxious to continue pressing forward. For the only time in the Civil War, he rode out to make a personal reconnaissance of the enemy's position. He was returning through thick woods to his own lines when Confederates mistook the general and his staff for Union cavalry and opened fire.

Three bullets struck Jackson. One shattered the bone in his left arm below the shoulder. Following amputation of the limb, Jackson was taken to the railhead at Guiney's Station for possible transfer to a Richmond hospital. Pneumonia rapidly developed. Jackson had always expressed a desire to die on the Sabbath. Around 3:15 on Sunday afternoon, May 10, 1863, he passed away quietly after saying: "Let us cross over the river and rest under the shade of the trees."

The general is buried beneath his statue, the centerpiece in Stonewall Jackson Cemetery, Lexington, Virginia.

[See also Loring-Jackson Incident.]

BIBLIOGRAPHY

Chambers, Lenoir. Stonewall Jackson. 2 vols. New York, 1959.
Henderson, G. F. R. Stonewall Jackson and the American Civil War. 2 vols. London, 1898.
Jackson, Mary Anna. Memoirs of "Stonewall" Jackson, by His Widow. New York, 1892. Reprint, Dayton, Ohio, 1976.
Robertson, James I., Jr. The Stonewall Brigade. Baton Rouge, La., 1963.
Vandiver, Frank E. Mighty Stonewall. New York, 1957. Reprint, Texas A & M University Military History Series, no. 9. College Station, Tex., 1988.

JAMES I. ROBERTSON, JR.

JACKSON, WILLIAM HICKS (1835–1903), brigadier general. Born at Paris, Tennessee, Jackson, nicknamed "Red" for his hair entered West Point in 1852 and graduated near the bottom of his class. Resigning his commission on May 26, 1861, he entered Confederate military service as a captain of artillery. On November 7, as an aide to Brig. Gen. Gideon Pillow, Jackson participated in the Battle of Belmont. He was severely wounded while leading a successful counterattack against the forces of Brig. Gen. Ulysses S. Grant.

On March 18, 1862, Jackson was promoted to colonel and given command of the Seventh Tennessee Cavalry. He conducted reconnaissance in northwestern Tennessee in April, and from June through September raided railroads in use by Federal forces in western Tennessee and northern Mississippi. His troopers fought at the Battle of Corinth (October 3–4) and served as a rear guard during the retreat to Ripley. On October 16, 1862, Maj. Gen. Earl Van Dorn appointed Jackson chief of cavalry for the newly organized Army of West Tennessee. In December, he participated in Van Dorn's raid upon Grant's supply depot at Holly Springs, Mississippi, which led to the latter's withdrawal from the state. Jackson was promoted to brigadier general on December 29.

In January 1863, Van Dorn's cavalry corps was transferred to middle Tennessee to protect the left flank of Gen. Braxton Bragg's Army of Tennessee. Operating out of Columbia, Jackson commanded a division under Van Dorn. He participated in the Battle of Thompson's Station on March 5 and in late May assisted Gen. Joseph E. Johnston in his effort to lift the siege of Vicksburg. Following its surrender, Jackson and his troopers covered Johnston's withdrawal to Morton, Mississippi, and successfully thwarted a Federal attempt to seize Canton in October.

In February 1864, Jackson's division harassed William Tecumseh Sherman's raid on Meridian, Mississippi, striking at his foraging parties. In his official report, Maj. Gen. Stephen D. Lee noted Jackson's "good conduct and soldierly qualities" during the campaign. The Tennessee brigadier general joined Johnston in northern Georgia on May 17 and operated on the left flank of the Army of Tennessee from May 20 to the evacuation of Atlanta. In November, Jackson's division, under Maj. Gen. Nathan Bedford Forrest, took the lead in Gen. John Bell Hood's invasion of middle Tennessee. He engaged Federal troops at Thompson's Station and at the Battle of Franklin. He was away with Forrest raiding Federal rail lines during the Battle of Nashville, but rejoined Hood's army to safeguard its withdrawal to Alabama at the year's end.

Jackson finished the war conducting cavalry operations under Forrest in the Department of Alabama, Mississippi, and East Louisiana. He was paroled on May 18, 1865, and returned to western Tennessee to manage his father's cotton plantations. Upon his marriage in 1868, Jackson joined his father-in-law in breeding thoroughbred horses at Belle Meade near Nashville. He also served as president of the National Agricultural Congress and the Tennessee Bureau of Agriculture. Jackson died at Belle Meade in 1903.

BIBLIOGRAPHY

Bearss, Edwin C. "William Hicks Jackson." In *The Confederate General*. Edited by William C. Davis. Vol. 3. Harrisburg, Pa., 1991.

Porter, James D. *Tennessee*. Vol. 8 of *Confederate Military History*. Edited by Clement A. Evans. Atlanta, 1899. Vol. 10 of extended ed. Wilmington, N.C., 1987.

Warner, Ezra J. *Generals in Gray: Lives of the Confederate Commanders*. Baton Rouge, La., 1959.

ALAN C. DOWNS

JACKSON, WILLIAM LOWTHER "MUD-WALL"

(1825–1890), brigadier general. Born February 3, 1825, Jackson was—like his second cousin, the famous "Stonewall"—a native of Clarksburg, in what is now West Virginia. Jackson gained admittance to the bar in 1847 and rose through political ranks from commonwealth attorney to the Virginia House of Delegates, lieutenant governor, and judge of an eight-county district. An imposing figure, Jackson stood six feet tall, weighed two hundred pounds, and had deep red hair and whiskers.

One of the most popular men in northwestern Virginia in 1861, Jackson resigned from the bench and enlisted as a private. He quickly became colonel of the Thirty-first Virginia and participated in the disastrous campaign of Gen. Robert S. Garnett. Jackson then served on his cousin's staff until April 1863, when he went inside Federal lines and recruited a regiment that became the Nineteenth Virginia Cavalry. Jackson saw action in the Jones-Imboden raid, Jubal Early's march on Washington, Sheridan's Shenandoah Valley campaign, and numerous small cavalry engagements. On December 19, 1864, after temporarily commanding units as large as a division, Jackson received promotion to brigadier general.

He returned to West Virginia after the war and found himself disbarred because of his Confederate service. Jackson moved to Louisville, Kentucky, where he won repeated elections to the bench. He died March 24, 1890, and is buried in Louisville's Cave Hill Cemetery.

During the war the judge was dubbed "Mudwall" in order to distinguish him from his better-known cousin, Stonewall Jackson. Yet one of his compatriots took offense at the nickname. "There was not a more polished gentleman nor a more gallant and competent officer in the Confederate army," he stated.

BIBLIOGRAPHY

McNeil, John A. "The Imboden Raid and Its Effects." *Southern Historical Society Papers* 34 (1906): 294–312. Reprint, Wilmington, N.C., 1991.

White, Robert. *West Virginia*. Vol. 2 of *Confederate Military History*. Edited by Clement A. Evans. Atlanta, 1899. Vol. 3 of extended ed. Wilmington, N.C., 1987.

Warner, Ezra J. *Generals in Gray: Lives of the Confederate Commanders*. Baton Rouge, La., 1959.

JAMES I. ROBERTSON, JR.

JACKSON, MISSISSIPPI.

[*This entry includes two articles,* City of Jackson, *which profiles the city during the Confederacy, and* Battle of Jackson, *which discusses military actions there.*]

City of Jackson

Located on the Pearl River in the center of the state, 44 miles from Vicksburg and the Mississippi River to the west and 93 miles from Meridian to the east, Jackson, Mississippi, was the state capital and a railroad, commercial, and manufacturing center at the beginning of the Civil War. In 1860 its population stood at 3,798 people (2,178 whites, 1,601 slaves, and 19 free blacks). Among the whites were Germans, Irish, Italian, and French.

As the state capital, Jackson was the site of the Mississippi secession convention of January 1861. Mississippi was the second state to secede from the Union, its ordinance citing the protection of slavery as the reason for its action. As the delegates voted in the chambers of the House of Representatives in what today is called the Old Capitol, citizens crowded the lawn outside. The announcement of the 84–15 vote for separation caused wild cheering and the presentation of a blue silk flag with a single white star to the president of the convention. The scene so inspired an Irish actor named Harry McCarthy, the story goes, that later that same day he wrote the song "The Bonnie Blue Flag." The lyrics were printed in a local newspaper, and he sang it to an enthusiastic audience that night at the concert hall.

Governor J. J. Pettus immediately began making war preparations for the city, acquiring, for example, some heavy artillery. There was a rush of men to arms, and in the enthusiasm, church bells were melted down for cannon. By the summer, however, many Jacksonians had come to believe that the war would be short and criticized Pettus's activities. In these early months, in fact, life in Jackson continued little changed from its prewar rhythm. The circus and the famous Christie's Minstrels made their annual visits in 1861. Commercial activity on State Street continued. The hotels remained full, shops and stores were busy, and functions at the concert hall attracted large audiences. The Baptist, Catholic, Christian, Episcopal, Methodist, and Presbyterian churches were filled on Sundays, and the five elementary schools remained open. The train ride on the Southern Railroad between Jackson and Vicksburg took two hours and forty-five minutes, excellent time by contemporary standards. The buying and selling of slaves continued, though whites worried about a war-inspired increase in runaways. The city's major newspaper, the weekly *Jackson Mississippian,* advertised the availability of "negro dogs" for five dollars an hour or twenty dollars per capture. As the war progressed, the newspaper also printed notices of deserters from the Confederate army.

Early war rumors had Jacksonians edgy. In the summer and fall of 1862 the city became a Confederate and state command center for logistics, coordination of railroads, mobilization of slaves for construction of defenses, and deployment of state troops. John C. Pemberton arrived in the fall of 1862 to coordinate the Confederate war effort against Ulysses S. Grant's activities to the north and Nathaniel P. Banks's threat from the south. Rifle pits and forts were built to the north, west, and south of the city, the Pearl River protecting the east. Grierson's Raid through the eastern part of the state in the spring of 1863 cut the railroads between the city and Meridian to the east and Louisiana to the south. The raid also encouraged the mobilization of all able-bodied men and the institution of daily drill. Military authorities took over business property surrounding the capitol.

The war first came home to Jackson during Grant's Vicksburg campaign of 1863. After marching down the west bank of the Mississippi River, Grant crossed over to the east side near Bruinsburg and quickly placed his troops between Pemberton's forces, now in Vicksburg, and Joseph E. Johnston's, recently arrived in Jackson. Grant first turned his army against Jackson and from May 14 through 16, 1863, drove the Confederate forces from the city. He then ordered William Tecumseh Sherman to destroy Jackson's war-related facilities and the railroads tying the city to Vicksburg and the rest of the state. After Vicksburg's capture on July 4, Grant ordered Sherman back to Jackson to evict Johnston again, and he did further damage between July 17 and 23, 1863. On his way to Meridian in early 1864, Sherman passed through Jackson once more from February 5 through 7.

Union occupations of the city caused Governors J. J. Pettus and Charles Clark to move the state government to safer locations. Thus, while Jackson remained Mississippi's capital throughout the war, it housed the state government for only a brief time from May 1863 until the Confederate surrender in the spring of 1865. During Sherman's second visit to Jackson in July 1863, however, a group of prominent citizens held a meeting with delegates from nearby towns in the hopes of creating a new government and returning to the Union. Sherman was cooperative, but the movement never gained widespread popular support.

With the coming of the enemy, life in Jackson underwent substantial change. Destruction was so widespread that the city gained the title "Chimneyville." In reality, the damage was inflicted primarily on factories, warehouses, and railroads. Many structures remained standing, including the capitol building. Fighting in the environs resulted in the presence of Confederate wounded and deserters. Many

Jacksonians left the city for safer residence, and during Union sieges, some people lived in tents along the Pearl River. Economic activity was severely curtailed, and goods of all sorts were in short supply. Food was scarce, age-old coffee substitutes were revived, and homespun clothing appeared. As inflation made unbacked Confederate paper money increasingly worthless, money became a major problem for the state government and its citizens.

When the fighting ended in the spring of 1865, Jackson was restored as capital of a state impoverished by the ravages of war. Its population in 1866 stood at 3,406 people, 425 fewer whites and 113 more blacks than in 1860. Mississippi underwent a mild Reconstruction and provided leadership in the South's postwar restoration of white conservative rule.

BIBLIOGRAPHY

Bettersworth, John K. *Confederate Mississippi: The People and Policies of a Cotton State in War Time.* Baton Rouge, La., 1943. Reprint, Philadelphia, 1978.

Bettersworth, John K. "The Home Front, 1861–1865." In *A History of Mississippi.* Edited by Richard Aubrey McLemore. 2 vols. Jackson, Miss., 1973.

Jackson. Vertical File. Mississippi Department of Archives and History, Jackson.

Ranlett, S. A. "The Capture of Jackson, Mississippi." In *Civil War Papers Read before the Massachusetts Commandery of the Military Order of the Loyal Legion of the United States.* Boston, 1900.

Russell, William Howard. *My Diary North and South.* New York, 1954. Reprint, Philadelphia, 1988.

JOHN F. MARSZALEK

Battle of Jackson

During the Vicksburg campaign, Gen. Ulysses S. Grant considered the capture of Jackson, Mississippi, a strategic objective not because it was the state's capital but because of its location. If the Union army controlled Jackson, it would hold the high ground between the Yazoo and Big Black rivers, from which it could attack Vicksburg from the east. Defended by Gen. John C. Pemberton's forces, Vicksburg was a crucial site on the Mississippi, and Jackson could be a stepping-stone to its capture. Jackson was also a major railroad junction.

At the end of April 1863, Grant occupied Grand Gulf, twenty-eight miles south of Vicksburg at the mouth of the Big Black River. With him was a force of 24,000 men. On May 8, Gen. William Tecumseh Sherman joined him, swelling the number of men to 40,000. Grant was now able to move with three corps—Gen. James B. McPherson's, Gen. John A. McClernand's, and Sherman's. On May 11, Sherman's corps, accompanied by Grant, was briefly detained by a burning bridge and a skirmish with William Wirt

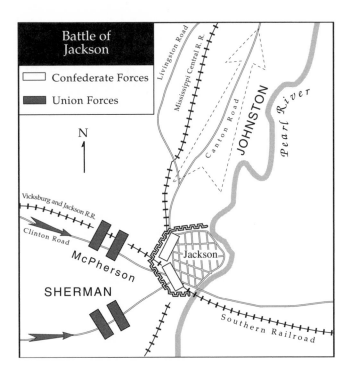

man's corps was ordered to remain in Jackson for twenty-four hours to destroy railroads and Confederate supplies. Jackson suffered heavy damage; Union troops destroyed railroad tracks and much public and private property. As Sherman wrote, "Jackson, as a railroad center or government depot of stores and military factories, can be of little use to the enemy for six months." Disorder reigned and wanton destruction, even of the Catholic church, followed. Sherman blamed the unjustified acts on "bad rum" drunk by his troops. On May 16, while Johnston's forces were moving to join Pemberton to defend Vicksburg, Sherman's corps set out quickly for that city.

Immediately after the fall of Vicksburg on July 4, the victorious Grant, instead of celebrating, ordered Sherman back to Jackson, which he felt was crucial to protect the Mississippi River from Confederate interference. After Vicksburg, "I did want rest," Sherman wrote, "but I ask nothing until the Mississippi River is ours, and Sunday and 4th of July are nothing to Americans till the river of our greatness is free as God made it."

On July 5, Sherman, with eleven infantry divisions, moved against Johnston, positioned near the Big Black River. Johnston, who believed Sherman's force to be double his, fell back to Jackson behind heavy entrenchments, which, anchored on the Pearl River both north and south, ringed the town. Skirmishes failed to turn Sherman away. And on July 12, the Confederates bombarded his troops with heavy-caliber, long-range artillery. The Federal troops were repulsed. They lost about 500 men and three battle flags. Despite this success, Johnston feared that Sherman would surround the city with his superior numbers. To Jefferson Davis, he wrote, "The enemy . . . is evidently making a siege which we cannot resist." On July 16, during the night, the Confederates quietly abandoned Jackson undetected by Sherman or his men. Johnston crossed the Pearl River, burning bridges behind him. His losses had been lighter than Sherman's—Confederate casualties (killed, wounded, and missing) were 600; Union casualties were 1,132. Low casualties notwithstanding, discipline and desertions were problematic, and Johnston had felt defeat was inevitable. Retreat was to him the wisest course. Sherman did not pursue Johnston because of "the intense heat, dust, and fatigue" of his troops. He wrote that the 30,000 men retreating with Johnston would probably "perish by heat, thirst, and disappointment."

Sherman's troops moved into Jackson on July 17. Sherman assigned Gen. Frank P. Blair's division to guard private property and prevent looting—a mission that Blair apparently failed to perform with much energy. Jackson was again sacked, plundered, and burned. Sherman condemned the lack of discipline "that reflects discredit on us all," but he hastened to add that the conduct was "confined to a few men." On July 24, the Federal troops once again moved out of Jackson.

Adams's brigade. At the same time, McPherson's corps met Gen. John Gregg's brigade at Raymond, a few miles from Jackson. Expecting a small enemy force, Gregg, with only 2,500 men, instead had to fight a force three times the size of his own. Nevertheless, Gregg held his ground for more than four hours. When he heard that Union reinforcements were on the way, Gregg ordered withdrawal to Jackson. The Confederates suffered about 500 killed or wounded; the Union forces, about 400. When Gen. Joseph E. Johnston, Pemberton's immediate superior, arrived in Jackson from Tennessee to witness the Confederate retreat and to find the enemy with no significant obstacle between it and Vicksburg, he lamented, "I am too late."

On the next day, May 14, the Federal troops under Sherman and McPherson moved on Jackson. Sherman's corps came up the Mississippi Springs Road from Raymond, while McPherson's advanced on the Clinton Road. During a heavy rainstorm, a battalion of sharpshooters and artillery fire delayed their progress long enough for the Confederates to remove supplies, for Johnston had already decided to abandon the city without a fight. The Union forces had a fairly easy entry; one of Sherman's units located an unmanned line of entrenchments, and his men came unopposed up the railroad from the south. The Confederates had even failed to burn a critical bridge that provided easy access into town. Johnston's Confederates evacuated northward up the Canton Road. Estimates put the Union casualties at 300; the Confederate at less than 400.

After spending the night of May 14 in Jackson, Grant and McPherson's corps moved quickly toward Vicksburg. Sher-

Jackson was occupied two more times during the war. On the evening of February 5, 1864, Federal troops on their way to Meridian entered the town after clashing with the cavalrymen under Gen. William Wirt Adams and Col. Peter Starke, who could do little against Sherman's 20,000 men. The troops left the next day. In early July 1864, Sherman, still trying to eliminate danger from the feared Gen. Nathan Bedford Forrest, sent Union forces under the command of Gen. Henry Slocum from Vicksburg to keep reinforcements from getting to Forrest. Slocum's forces occupied Jackson, although only briefly, for a fourth time on this mission.

BIBLIOGRAPHY

Grant, U. S. *Personal Memoirs of U. S. Grant.* Edited by William S. McFeely. New York, 1982.

Sherman, William T. *Memoirs of William T. Sherman.* Edited by William S. McFeely. New York, 1984.

U.S. War Department. *War of the Rebellion: A Compilation of the Official Records of the Union and Confederate Armies.* Washington, D.C., 1880–1901. Ser. 1, vol. 24, pts. 1–3.

RAY SKATES

JACKSON. The shallow-draft ironclad ram *Jackson* measured 225 feet in length, 59 feet in beam, and 10 feet in depth of hold. Its armored casemate consisted of a two-foot thickness of pine and oak covered with four inches of rolled iron plate. Two inches of iron protected the waterline and exterior decks. Within the casemate were four 7-inch and two 6.4-inch Brooke rifles.

Laid down as *Muscogee* in late 1862 at the navy yard in Columbus, Georgia, Lt. Augustus McLaughlin commanding, the vessel was initially constructed as a 190-foot-long recessed paddlewheel ironclad. Several failed launching attempts the following year resulted in modifications to the vessel's structure while still on the stocks. Beginning in the spring of 1864 the casemate was reduced in length to decrease weight, and the hull was lengthened to increase buoyancy and accommodate a twin-propeller arrangement in lieu of the center paddlewheel. After being renamed for the capital of Mississippi, *Jackson* was successfully launched into the Chattahoochee River December 22, 1864.

Fitting out further delayed *Jackson*'s completion, and it was still unfinished when Federal troops under Gen. James H. Wilson captured Columbus April 16, 1865. Set afire the following day by its captors, *Jackson* drifted about thirty miles below the city where it grounded on a sandbar and burned to the waterline. During the Civil War centennial the ironclad's hull was retrieved and placed in the Confederate Naval Museum in Columbus.

BIBLIOGRAPHY

Sellers, Tom. "The Raising of the *Muscogee*." *Civil War Times* 9 (January 1962): 6–8.

Turner, Joel. "The Saga of the *Muscogee*." *Georgia Magazine* 6 (February–March 1963): 16–19.

Turner, Maxine. *Navy Gray: A Story of the Confederate Navy on the Chattahoochee and Apalachicola Rivers.* Tuscaloosa, Ala., 1988.

A. ROBERT HOLCOMBE, JR.

JAMES BROTHERS. Frank James (1842–1915) and Jesse James (1847–1882) were Missouri Confederate guerrillas and legendary postwar bandits. Farm boys from Clay County, of Kentucky stock, Frank and Jesse James, along with several of their youthful neighbors, fought during the Civil War against what they considered to be a Union invasion. Frank joined William C. Quantrill in 1862, and Jesse joined William ("Bloody Bill") Anderson two years later. Neither boy attained leadership status. In July 1865, Frank surrendered to Union forces in Kentucky, where he had ridden with Quantrill. According to unreliable folklore, Jesse, with a bullet in his lung, finished his Civil War in Nebraska, where he was nursed back to health by his mother.

As early as 1867, the James brothers began their far more notable and lengthy postwar careers as bank and train robbers. Jesse was shot down in 1882 by Robert Ford, a young gang subordinate. Later that year, Frank surrendered to the law, was tried and acquitted of murder, and spent the remaining thirty-two years of his life living peacefully if marginally by riding in minor Wild West shows and starting horses at the Kansas City racetrack.

Even during their lifetimes, the James brothers were turned by sensationalistic newspapermen into the legendary social bandits they remain. Supposedly robbing from rich banks and railroads and giving to the poor, the James brothers consciously wrapped themselves in Robin Hood's mantle, the better to dispel the record of their actual vicious cold-bloodedness, first as guerrillas and later as gangsters.

BIBLIOGRAPHY

Brownlee, Richard S. *Gray Ghosts of the Confederacy: Guerrilla Warfare in the West, 1861–65.* Baton Rouge, La., 1958.

Fellman, Michael. *Inside War: The Guerrilla Conflict in Missouri during the American Civil War.* New York, 1989.

Settle, William A., Jr. *Jesse James Was His Name: or, Fact and Fiction concerning the Careers of the Notorious James Brothers of Missouri.* Columbia, Mo., 1966.

MICHAEL FELLMAN

JAMES RIVER SQUADRON. Created in the spring of 1862, the James River Squadron served as a crucial part of the Confederate defenses on the James River below Richmond until its vessels were destroyed by their own crews in the spring of 1865.

THE REBEL IRON-CLAD FLEET FORCING THE OBSTRUCTIONS IN JAMES RIVER.—[Sketched by A. R. Waud.]

IRONCLAD FLEET IN THE JAMES RIVER. The ships *Fredericksburg, Richmond*, and *Virginia* forcing obstructions on January 23, 1865.   NAVAL HISTORICAL CENTER, WASHINGTON, D.C.

Aware of the possibility of a Federal attack up the James River, the Confederates built a number of shore batteries along the river and supplemented them with several small civilian steamers converted into gunboats. The first of these was the gunboat *Patrick Henry,* a former river steamer commanded by Capt. John R. Tucker. Added later was the former screw-tug *Teaser,* armed with a single 32-pound gun. In early 1862, with the ironclad CSS *Virginia* nearing completion, Secretary of the Navy Stephen R. Mallory combined the vessels on the James River to form the James River Squadron commanded by Flag Officer Franklin Buchanan aboard *Virginia.* Buchanan's squadron was supplemented by the addition of the wooden gunboats *Jamestown, Raleigh,* and *Beaufort,* which escaped to the James River after the Federal capture of Roanoke Island in the Carolina sounds. The unarmored vessels supported *Virginia* during its epic struggle with USS *Monitor.* In May, after the Confederates were forced to abandon Norfolk and scuttle *Virginia,* the remaining vessels took refuge above the batteries and river obstructions at Drewry's Bluff. Several were stripped of their armament for additional shore batteries. The remaining gunboats joined the shore batteries in repelling a Union foray up the river on May 15, 1862.

Aside from minor raiding sorties, the squadron partici-

pated in no major operations during the rest of 1862 or 1863. Capt. French Forrest, former Confederate commander of the Gosport Navy Yard, succeeded Buchanan as squadron commander and played a role in having *Patrick Henry* turned into the home of the Confederate Naval Academy in October 1863. Although the Federals captured *Teaser* in late 1862, the strength of the squadron was increased by the addition in 1862 of the ironclad *Richmond* and in 1863 the ironclads *Fredericksburg* and *Virginia II.* Like *Richmond,* these newer ironclads were shallow-draft, casemated vessels. They mounted four guns in varying calibers and configurations, but typically two of these were large-shell guns and two were large-caliber rifled pieces. Along with the ironclads, the wooden gunboats *Nansemond, Hampton,* and *Drewry* and the small steam launches *Torpedo, Scorpion, Wasp,* and *Hornet* had joined the squadron by the start of 1864. The gunboats were armed with a variety of cannons, but the launches had only a single spar torpedo apiece for armament.

With a nucleus of three strong ironclads, the James River Squadron was the most powerful group of vessels ever assembled by the Confederacy. Disappointed by Forrest's apparent lack of initiative, Mallory replaced him with Commdr. John K. Mitchell in January 1864. By this time, however, the Federals had effectively blocked the river just above City Point with a combination of submersible mines and sunken hulks. Led by the ironclads, Mitchell's squadron fought a series of engagements in the summer of 1864, driving off Union working parties and assisting in the defense of shore installations. When flooding carried away some of the river obstructions in January 1865, Mitchell seized the chance to attack the Federal supply city at City Point. In the darkness, though, both *Virginia II* and *Richmond* ran aground and came under fire from Union shore batteries. Supported by the wooden gunboats and *Fredericksburg,* the stranded vessels eventually got free. *Virginia II,* however, was damaged and the small gunboat *Drewry* was blown up after being abandoned by its crew. Mitchell's foray thus failed, as did a bold attempt in early February to put the small launches on wheels and move them overland to attack the Union ships at City Point.

On February 18, 1865, Rear Adm. Raphael Semmes, former captain of *Alabama,* took command of the squadron. Morale was low. Many officers and men served as gunners ashore. Semmes and the squadron were powerless to prevent the fall of Richmond, and on April 3 he ordered the ships scuttled to prevent capture. With the remaining crewmen, Semmes fled inland to Danville, Virginia. There the remnant of the James River Squadron dissolved on May 1 after receiving word of the surrender of Gen. Joseph E. Johnston. Among the last to surrender were the naval cadets of *Patrick Henry.* After serving as guards of the final gold supply of the Confederacy, the young officers were given forty dollars a piece and sent home.

[*See also entries on the ships* Patrick Henry *and* Virginia.]

BIBLIOGRAPHY

Gibbons, Tony. *Warships and Naval Battles of the Civil War.* New York, 1989.
Johnson, Robert U., and C. C. Buel, eds. *Battles and Leaders of the Civil War.* 4 vols. New York, 1887–1888. Reprint, Secaucus, N.J., 1982.
Scharf, J. Thomas. *History of the Confederate States Navy.* New York, 1887. Reprint, New York, 1977.
Still, William N., Jr. *Iron Afloat: The Story of the Confederate Armorclads.* Nashville, Tenn., 1971.

ROBERT S. BROWNING III

JEFFERSON DAVIS. The brig *Putnam* was built in Baltimore, probably in 1845, and registered in New Orleans. Measuring 187 tons, *Putnam* was built for speed and subsequently entered the illegal African slave trade under the name *Echo.* The brig was captured off Cuba on December 21, 1858. The Africans aboard were freed and sent to Liberia, and the brig was condemned and sold by the Charleston U.S. District Court in January 1859. *Putnam* reentered legal trade under its original name.

After the outbreak of the Civil War, the new owners applied for a privateering commission and permission to name the vessel *Jefferson Davis* on May 7, 1861. Both requests were granted and the brig was armed with one 18-pound pivot, two 32-pound, and two 24-pound broadside guns. Capt. Louis M. Coxetter, an experienced coastal mariner, commanded the ship, with a crew of ten officers and about sixty men from Charleston.

On July 6 about three hundred miles off the Delaware coast, the privateer captured the brig *John Welsh* with a valuable cargo of sugar. The brig's crew was removed to the *Davis* and a prize crew was sent on board in what became the standard pattern for handling prizes. That afternoon the *Jefferson Davis* captured the schooner *Enchantress,* and the next day it captured the schooner *S. J. Waring.* The ship *Mary Goodell* and brig *Mary E. Thompson* were captured on July 9 and turned into cartels to relieve the privateer of prisoners. These two vessels hurried to port, however, and warned the Union of the danger offshore.

Jefferson Davis then turned south on reaching Narragansett shoals and captured the bark *Alvarado* on July 21. After a stop in San Juan, Puerto Rico, the privateer captured the schooner *Windward* and the hermaphrodite brig *Santa Clara* on August 5. The ship *John Caver,* carrying coal for the U.S. Navy, was then captured and burned. While attempting to return home on August 18, 1861, *Jefferson Davis* grounded and wrecked on the bar at St. Augustine, Florida. Its nine captures, four of which successfully entered Confederate ports, made *Jefferson Davis* the most successful privateer of the war.

BIBLIOGRAPHY

The Jeff. Davis Piracy Case: Full Report of Trial of William Smith for Piracy as One of the Crew of the Confederate Privateer Jeff. Davis. Philadelphia, 1861.
Robinson, William Morrison, Jr. *The Confederate Privateers.* New Haven, 1928.
Scharf, J. Thomas. *History of the Confederate States Navy.* New York, 1887. Reprint, New York, 1977.

KEVIN J. FOSTER

JEMISON, ROBERT (1802–1871), congressman from Alabama. Born near Augusta in Lincoln County, Georgia, on September 17, 1802, Jemison was the son of a wealthy planter. In 1807 the family moved to Twiggs County, Georgia, where Jemison spent his childhood. (He added Junior to his name to distinguish himself from an uncle for whom he was named.) He studied at Mount Zion Academy in Hancock County, Georgia, under Dr. Nathan S. S. Beman, the stepfather of William Lowndes Yancey, who later became Jemison's political opponent during the Alabama secession crisis. Afterward Jemison enrolled at the University of Georgia and then read for the law. He abandoned a legal career, however, and entered the family plantation business.

In 1821, the Jemison family moved to Alabama and in 1826 settled in Pickens County, where Jemison played a major role in developing his father's plantation holdings. Ten years later Jemison settled in Tuscaloosa, Alabama, and began his own planting enterprise. By 1860, he was a wealthy planter in his own right and owned more than ten thousand acres scattered among six plantations. In addition, he invested in a sawmill, a flouring mill, and a toll bridge and held a mail contract, which he distributed through a stagecoach line. Jemison's ventures became so successful that he was one of the business and financial leaders of the pre–Civil War South. In 1862 he completed a classic antebellum Southern mansion in Tuscaloosa. The structure survived the war and was restored as the Friedman Memorial Library.

Jemison was active in Alabama politics as a Whig for twenty-six years. He was elected to the state senate in 1837 and then to the Alabama House of Representatives in 1841, 1844, 1845, 1847, and 1849. He was reelected to the Alabama Senate in 1851 and held that seat for twelve years. His financial genius was recognized by his fellow legislators, and he became an expert in the state's banking and public financial affairs. He served as chairman of the Committee on Finance and Taxation and in 1847, as head of the General Assembly's Ways and Means Committee, he restructured the state's revenue system, enabling Alabama to sustain the public credit and continue to function during a series of disastrous bank failures. He also was active in Southern railroad development and led the way in creating an insane asylum at Tuscaloosa.

During the secession crisis, Jemison was an outspoken Unionist and served as a delegate from Tuscaloosa to the state secession convention in January 1861. He was the candidate of the moderates in the state for chairman of the convention, but his bid was thwarted by those demanding immediate withdrawal from the Union. Nevertheless he continued to oppose Yancey's demand for immediate secession by arguing on the floor of the convention that if the South left the Union a reign of terror like that of the French Revolution would sweep through the region. For a while it appeared that Jemison's opposition to secession would at least postpone Alabama's withdrawal from the Union, but in the end his plea was ignored, and on January 11 the convention decided on secession. After voting against the ordinance of secession, Jemison refused to sign it, but he did pledge his support to a sovereign Alabama and later the Confederacy.

Although his opposition to secession was well known, it apparently did not detract from his political popularity in the state, for in 1862 he was elected unanimously as president of the Alabama Senate. When Yancey died the next year, Jemison was elected by the General Assembly on December 28 to complete his term in the Confederate Senate.

Jemison's career in the Senate was tainted by his farewell speech to the Alabama General Assembly. Because he promised to work for an honorable peace between the Confederacy and the Federal government, he was not well received by the secessionists in the Confederate Congress. Jemison was assigned to the Naval Affairs and the Claims committees in the First Congress, the Post Office Committee in the Second Congress, and to the Finance Committee in both Congresses.

As a senator Jemison introduced very few pieces of legislation and refused to support a total war effort against the North. Instead he argued for stronger local defense measures that would allow the Southern states to protect themselves. He supported extending conscription to all white males between sixteen and sixty years of age, but insisted that they remain under state control instead of being formed into a national army capable of undertaking offensive operations against the North. He also opposed efforts by the central government to finance an offensive war and to assume control over transportation and production facilities. By June of 1864, Jemison was so unpopular with other members of the Confederate government that he ceased to attend Senate sessions and returned to Alabama to salvage what he could of his business operations, much of which was destroyed by Federal troops during the fighting. Although he did not attend sessions, he continued to hold his seat until the end of the war.

In 1865, Jemison joined the Democratic party. He retired from politics, however, and concentrated on developing the Northeast and Southwest Railroad, which built the Alabama and Chattanooga Railroad, and served as president of the enterprise from 1865 to 1869. He died in Tuscaloosa on October 16, 1871, and was buried in the family cemetery at Northport, Alabama.

BIBLIOGRAPHY

Brewer, W. *Alabama: Her History, Resources, War Record, and Public Men from 1540 to 1872.* Montgomery, Ala., 1872.

Evans, Clement A., ed. *Confederate Military History.* 12 vols. Atlanta, 1899. Extended ed. in 19 vols. Wilmington, N.C., 1987–1989.

Garrett, William. *Reminiscences of Public Men in Alabama.* Atlanta, 1872.

Warner, Ezra J., and W. Buck Yearns. *Biographical Register of the Confederate Congress.* Baton Rouge, La., 1975.

KENNY A. FRANKS

JENKINS, ALBERT GALLATIN (1830–1864),

congressman from Virginia and brigadier general. Jenkins was born November 10, 1830, at Greenbottom, Cabell

ALBERT GALLATIN JENKINS.   NATIONAL ARCHIVES

County, Virginia (now West Virginia). Educated at Marshall Academy, Jefferson College, and Harvard Law School, he practiced law in western Virginia and served in the U.S. Congress from 1857 to 1861.

After leaving Congress that year, Jenkins enlisted recruits for the Border Rangers (a Virginia militia group) and was elected captain of the unit on May 20. Three other cavalry units recruited from western Virginia were also placed under his command. Their first recorded expedition took place in June, when they rode to Point Pleasant on the Ohio River and seized a number of Union sympathizers.

On July 16 at the Battle of Scary Creek, Kanawha County, West Virginia, Jenkins commanded the Border Rangers, which carried the flag for the battle. After early fighting and a retreat, Jenkins rallied with Capt. James M. Corns and the Sandy Rangers to capture the field. They took Col. Charles A. DeVilliers of the Eleventh Ohio Volunteers and Col. William E. Woodruff of the Second Kentucky and his staff prisoner. Jenkins incurred a slight wound.

Jenkins was appointed aide to Gen. John B. Floyd with the rank of colonel on August 24 and formed the Eighth Virginia Cavalry from the Border Rangers, Sandy Rangers, and other cavalry units. His commission as lieutenant colonel of the Eighth Cavalry was dated September 24, 1861. In November Jenkins with his cavalry unit and Col. John Clarkson with the Wise Legion Cavalry staged a surprise raid on Camp Paxton, a Union recruitment camp at Guyandotte. There they captured about a hundred recruits and marched them to the railhead at Newbern, Virginia.

In early 1862 Jenkins was elected to the First Confederate Congress and resigned his field commission on February 20. He served as a member of the standing committees of Printing and of Territories and Public Lands.

Jenkins, after receiving an appointment as brigadier general of cavalry, resigned from Congress on August 5 and assumed command of forces in Monroe County. He and 550 cavalrymen then embarked on a five-hundred-mile raid through West Virginia. On September 4 he and his men crossed the Ohio River and became the first force to raise the Confederate flag on Ohio soil.

Jenkins, during the winter of 1862–1863, helped organize the Sixteenth and Seventeenth Virginia Cavalry regiments encamped near Salem. By spring, he commanded the Cavalry Brigade of the Army of Western Virginia, headquartered at Dublin under Maj. Gen. Samuel Jones. The Jenkins Brigade consisted of five Virginia cavalry regiments and three battalions. Jenkins made another raid into western Virginia in March. Leading companies of the Eighth and Sixteenth Cavalries, he rode to Hurricane Bridge in Putnam County where he attacked a small fort defended by three companies of U.S. infantry. After several hours and few casualties, Jenkins broke off and moved on to Point Pleasant. There his cavalry attacked a Union force barricaded in the courthouse before withdrawing deeper into Virginia.

Jenkins and his brigade, part of the vanguard of forces moving into Pennsylvania that June, gathered cattle and horses around Chambersburg to supply the Confederate army. On June 28 he and his men were on the hills surrounding Harrisburg, the state capital. Before they could take the town, however, Jenkins received orders to move to Gettysburg. They arrived there on the afternoon of July 1 and were assigned to guard prisoners. While scouting enemy positions the next day, Jenkins was wounded in the head. He was cared for at a house in Gettysburg until the Confederates retreated into Virginia, where he spent a number of weeks recuperating.

Some sought that fall to have Jenkins promoted to major general. A petition to this end was sent to the Confederate secretary of war and was marked to "file for consideration when there is a division to which an appointment can be made."

Jenkins resumed command of his brigade by January 1864 and set about recruiting and organizing cavalry troops in western Virginia and West Virginia. He was appointed cavalry commander of the Department of Western Virginia with headquarters in Dublin that spring.

When Federal forces under Gen. George Crook threatened the Virginia and Tennessee Railroad and Confederate stores at Dublin in May, Col. John McCausland moved his brigade to defensive positions on Cloyds Mountain. Jenkins arrived there on the night of May 8 and assumed command. The next morning, he changed the Confederate positions over the objections of McCausland and others.

During the ensuing Federal attack, Jenkins ordered a charge by the Forty-fifth Virginia regiment and Beckley's Battalion, which penetrated Federal lines but was repulsed. As the Confederates were retreating, Jenkins rode forward to rally them, but a musket ball struck him in the left arm and he fell from his horse. He was captured after the Confederates retreated further to New River Bridge. On May 13, Federal surgeons, after consulting with Confederate surgeons, amputated his arm. But eight days later, he suffered a secondary hemorrhage, supposedly when an orderly knocked loose a ligature used to clamp off an artery. Jenkins died early in the morning of May 21, 1864.

In February 1866 Jenkins's body was moved to the family cemetery at Greenbottom, West Virginia. In 1891, he was again reinterred by the United Confederate Veterans in the Confederate plot in Spring Hill Cemetery, Huntington, West Virginia, where he rests today.

One of the Richmond newspapers in 1863 described Jenkins as being "about five feet ten inches high, well formed and of good physique; dark hair, blue eyes, and heavy brown beard; pleasing countenance, kind, affable manners, fluent and winning in conversation, quick, subtle and argumentative in debate." He was an experienced debater and dynamic public speaker.

BIBLIOGRAPHY

Dickinson, Jack L. *Eighth Virginia Cavalry.* Lynchburg, Va., 1986.

Dickinson, Jack L. *Jenkins of Greenbottom: A Civil War Saga.* Charleston, W. Va., 1988.

Geiger, Joe. *Civil War in Cabell County, West Virginia.* Charleston, W. Va., 1991.

Lowry, Terry. *The Battle of Scary Creek.* Charleston, W. Va., 1982.

Rosanna Blake Confederate Collection. Morrow Library, Marshall University, Huntingon, W. Va.

JACK L. DICKINSON

JENKINS, MICAH (1835–1864), brigadier general.
Jenkins was born on Edisto Island, South Carolina, December 1, 1835, the son of a planter who traced his ancestry to Welsh nobility. After graduating at the head of his class from the South Carolina Military Academy in 1854, Jenkins helped establish the King's Mountain Military School at Yorkville, which flourished until the start of the war.

In 1861 Jenkins was instrumental in organizing the Fifth South Carolina Infantry, one of the first state regiments to enter Confederate service, and was elected colonel. After conspicuous service at First Manassas, Jenkins organized the Palmetto Sharpshooters, handpicked riflemen from three other state regiments. Jenkins commanded a brigade at Seven Pines and, according to D. H. Hill, "rendered more service than any two engaged."

Jenkins was ordered to South Carolina in July 1862 to round up conscripts. Promoted to brigadier later that month, he was severely wounded at Second Manassas while commanding Richard Heron Anderson's old brigade. As he was being borne from the field, Robert E. Lee rode up and told Jenkins: "I hope yet to see you one of my lieutenant generals."

Jenkins's battlefield exploits engendered many recommendations for his promotion. John Bell Hood praised him for his "great gallantry and ability . . . his untiring energy and constant attention to his command." James Longstreet called him "one of our most distinguished Brigadiers," and Arnold Elzey said he was "one of the most gallant & meritorious officers in the service."

When Longstreet was sent west in 1863, Jenkins's brigade was transferred to Hood's division but reached Chickamauga too late to take part in the battle. He played a prominent role in the operations in eastern Tennessee before returning to Virginia in early 1864.

On May 6, the second day of the Battle of the Wilderness, Jenkins was riding with Longstreet. He had just told his chief that he felt "assured that we will put the enemy back across the Rapidan before night," when he was toppled from his saddle by friendly fire. He died a short time later and was buried in Charleston, South Carolina. Interestingly, Jenkins was wounded mortally in much the same manner and the same vicinity as Stonewall Jackson the previous year.

BIBLIOGRAPHY

Capers, Ellison. *South Carolina.* Vol. 5 of *Confederate Military History.* Edited by Clement A. Evans. Atlanta, 1899. Vol. 6 of extended ed. Wilmington, N.C., 1987.

Compiled Military Service Records. Micah Jenkins. Microcopy M331, Roll 140. Record Group 109. National Archives, Washington, D.C.

Thomas, John P. *Career and Character of General Micah Jenkins, C.S.A.* Columbia, S.C., 1903.

Warner, Ezra J. *Generals in Gray: Lives of the Confederate Commanders.* Baton Rouge, La., 1959.

LOWELL REIDENBAUGH

JEWS. "Be loyal to the Union," New York's Samuel M. Isaacs, editor of the *Jewish Messenger,* wrote in April 1861. "Stand by the flag. . . . You are doing your duty, and acting well your part on the side of liberty and justice." The Jewish community in Shreveport, Louisiana, however, had little taste for either the Union or the flag that Isaacs had in mind. In response to Isaacs's call, they resolved "that we . . . scorn and repel your advice, although we might be called Southern rebels; still, as law-abiding citizens, we solemnly pledge ourselves to stand by, protect, and honor the flag, with its stars and stripes, the Union and Constitution of the Southern Confederacy with our lives, liberty and all that is dear to us." And then they canceled their subscription to Isaacs's publication.

American Jews had become divided over the issues of slavery and state rights no less than had everyone else in the country, and they had exhibited attitudes and loyalties that were no more or less sectional than those of others. For Southern Jews, whether newly arrived immigrants or native-born, loyalty to the Confederacy was a matter of personal gratitude and cultural affinity. Nowhere else in the United States had Jews been offered the opportunity to participate so fully as equals in society. In large cities and small towns alike, Jews had achieved a more genuinely integrated status with their neighbors than in any other part of America. As a consequence, Jews had acclimated themselves to Southern values, had become imbued with Southern traditions, and therefore had become committed to the struggles and fortunes of the Confederacy. Some Jews were slave owners, some were slave traders, and still others offered defenses of slavery. As war clouds gathered, however, the issue of slavery was transcended by that of devotion to the region. "Now, we of the South seeing that public opinion, the law of the land at the North are against all that we hold valuable, seeing that . . . our enemies have triumphed and that the government is about to pass into the hands of those who hate us and our institutions," Solomon Cohen, a Jewish leader of Savannah who was to lose a son in the war, wrote in 1861, "feel that prudence and self-defense demand that we should protect ourselves, even while there is ruption of every tie that binds us to the union that we have loved so well."

At least two-thirds of Southern Jews were recent immigrants, yet there was little distinction in the feeling of identification with the South between them and native-born Jews; nor was there between the religious traditionalists and the adherents of Reform Judaism; or between the religious, nonreligious, and converted; or between landowner, peddler, merchant, politician, and intellectual. Thus, it is not surprising that in Montgomery, Alabama, Rabbi James Gutheim, who had arrived in the country in 1843, asked from his pulpit for divine "favor and benevolence [for] our beloved country, the Confederate States of America. May our young Republic increase in strength, prosperity and renown."

Once war broke out, most Jews heeded the call of their region. Gratz Cohen, who was to die in battle, reflected the mood of most Southern Jews with a poem that exhorted his fellow students at the University of Virginia to action; one of the stanzas read:

> Go, for your soldier brothers need you at their side;
> Go, fight as we have fought and die as we have died.
> If need there be, a thousand deaths were better than
>   disgrace;
> Better that every man should die than live a conquered
>   race.

Two Jewish U.S. senators, David Levy Yulee of Florida and Judah B. Benjamin of Louisiana, who had struggled to bring their respective territories into the Union, joined the exodus of Southern statesmen from Washington to Montgomery and worked equally hard to bring their states into the Confederacy. Jewish manufacturers transformed their shops into armories. The Haiman brothers of Columbus, Georgia, became the Confederacy's largest manufacturer of swords and pistols. Others such as Nathan Lazarus went abroad to England as emissaries and purchasers for the Confederacy. Jewish women's organizations participated in collection drives for local troops and their families. Jews joined the armed forces in a far larger proportion of their numbers than did Jews in the North. Although some Jews, like other Southerners, enlisted because of a fifty-dollar enlistment bounty and a belief that the duration of the war would be a short "breakfast spell," most joined out of a sense of patriotism. There were instances of Southern Jews enlisting as entire families: the five Moses brothers of South Carolina, the six Cohen brothers of North Carolina, the three Levy brothers of Louisiana, and the three Levy brothers of Virginia.

Jews not only served in the ranks; they were elected and appointed as noncommissioned and commissioned officers, some receiving battlefield appointments. One Georgia company, the Macon German Artillery, was affectionately called the "Jew Company" because its soldiers had elected Nathan Bindswanger as its commanding officer. Jews held staff positions in both field and government commands: David Camden De Leon, a hero of the Mexican War, became the first surgeon general of the Confederate forces; Levy Myers Harby, another hero of the Mexican War, commanded the port of Galveston; Lionel Levy served as judge advocate of the Confederate forces; J. Randolph Mordecai was assistant adjutant general; Abraham C. Myers was quartermaster general; Raphael Moses was commissary general for Georgia Governor Joseph E. Brown after having served on Thomas J. ("Stonewall") Jackson's staff; and Judah P. Benjamin, sometimes called the "brains of the Confederacy,'' served successively as the Confederacy's attorney general, secretary of war, and secretary of state.

A complete and accurate roster of Jews who fought for the Confederacy does not exist. Their numbers were sufficiently large, however, that at one point the secretary of war hesitated to grant Jewish soldiers leaves for religious holidays in fear that many field commands would be disrupted. These troops encountered far less official discrimination than did their Union counterparts. Jewish Confederate soldiers found it easier to celebrate their religious festivals in camp or to take advantage of special furlough orders, which Robert E. Lee and other generals issued.

Nevertheless, prejudice occasionally appeared throughout the war. The agitation was particularly virulent during the early days when charges were made throughout the Confederacy that Jewish traders and peddlers were guilty of profiteering and price-gouging, and were responsible for the spread of counterfeit money. Yet Jewish civilians and soldiers, with the support of many non-Jews, felt secure enough to mount effective protests against such hysteria.

The experiences of Jews in the war forged a camaraderie with those who had fought for the common cause. It was usually sufficient to silence the loudest prejudiced voice, for such war experiences assured local non-Jewish residents that among them were men, Jews notwithstanding, who had defended and would continue to defend the South against the desecration of its soil and the deprivation of its liberty. In both a wartime and a postwar South, struggling for an identity by glorifying its past and honoring its struggle, that was no small recommendation for accepting the Jews into their midst, for reassessing malicious stereotypes of Jews, and for preparing the way for those Jews who in the following decades were to immigrate into the South.

[See also Benjamin, Judah P.; Myers, Abraham C.]

BIBLIOGRAPHY

Hermann, Isaac. *Memoirs of a Confederate Veteran.* Lakemont, Ga., 1979.

Korn, Bertram. *American Jewry and the Civil War.* New York, 1961.

Korn, Bertram. "Civil War Centennial: Southern Issue." *American Jewish Archives* 13 (April 1961).

Korn, Bertram. *Jews and Negro Slavery in the Old South.* Elkins Park, Pa., 1961.

Pember, Phoebe. *A Southern Woman's Story: Life in Confederate Richmond.* Jackson, Tenn., 1959.

Robbins, Peggy. "The Fighting Minority." *Civil War Times Illustrated* 31, no. 2 (May–June 1992): 38–43.

Schmier, Louis. "An Act Unbecoming." *Civil War Times Illustrated* 23, no. 6 (October 1984): 20–25.

Wolf, Simon. *The American Jews as Patriot, Soldier, and Citizen.* New York, 1895.

LOUIS E. SCHMIER

JOE BROWN'S PIKES. At the outbreak of the Civil War, the Confederacy suffered acute shortages of weapons, and state and national officials concocted various schemes to remedy the problem. The governor of Georgia, Joseph E. Brown, proposed the use of pikes to arm Southern troops. The advent of firearms had rendered the pike obsolete, but some armies continued to use the weapon for ceremonial purposes. Pikes were easy to produce and conjured the image of Greek or Swiss phalanxes cutting their way to victory.

In the spring of 1862, with the Confederate States facing a critical shortage of small arms, Maj. Gen. Thomas J. ("Stonewall") Jackson suggested to the governor of Virginia that recruits be supplied with pikes as their principal weapon. Gen. Robert E. Lee approved the idea and requested that a thousand be forwarded to Jackson as early as possible. Subsequently, Lee wrote that pikes were in production and said he would approve their requisition.

Although the shortage of arms subsequently eased, with stocks on hand supplemented by weapons captured from the Federals, some leaders, most notably Governor Brown, continued to advocate the production and use of pikes. He ordered the manufacture of thousands of them for his Georgia state troops.

Production of the weapons included several modern versions of the style of pike used by the Swiss to cut the bridle reins of charging cavalrymen, who would then be easy targets for more conventional weapons. Other variations appeared, such as a pike with a collapsible blade, which was apparently a safety feature for times when the pike was not in use. Most of these weapons were locally manufactured and designed for Georgians. Thus this style came to be labeled "Joe Brown's Pikes."

BIBLIOGRAPHY

Lord, Francis A. *Civil War Collector's Encyclopedia: Arms, Uniforms, and Equipment of the Union and Confederacy.* New York, 1963.

Wiley, Bell Irvin. *The Life of Johnny Reb: The Common Soldier of the Confederacy.* Indianapolis, 1943.

BRIAN S. WILLS

JOHN BROWN'S RAID. *See* Harpers Ferry, *article on* John Brown's Raid.

JOHNSON, ADAM RANKIN ("STOVE-PIPE") (1834–1922), brigadier general. Johnson, a Kentucky native, moved to Texas at the age of twenty and worked as a surveyor, army guide, and mail contractor. In 1861 he joined Nathan Bedford Forrest as a scout. When Fort Donelson fell to Federal forces, he escaped and began small guerrilla raids behind Union lines. On July 17, 1862, with a force of thirty-five men, he captured his hometown of Henderson, Kentucky. The next day Johnson won the sobriquet "Stovepipe" by seizing the Federal arsenal at Newburg, Indiana, through a ruse. He mounted a charred log and a stovepipe on wagon wheels. Manned and stationed on the opposite shore of the Ohio River, they looked from a distance like cannon. Johnson left eight of his thirty-five men on the Kentucky side of the Ohio River to pretend to man the "cannon." With the others, he crossed the river and occupied the unguarded arsenal. The Union officer appeared and surrendered with his few men. Johnson had loaded over 250 rifles in wagons to transport to the river when a force of home guards formed in line. He pointed to the "cannon" and threatened to shell the town if attacked. The home guards retreated and allowed Johnson's men to row away, under the protection of a log and stovepipe.

On August 13, 1862, Johnson was commissioned colonel in command of the Tenth Kentucky Partisan Rangers, and in December 1862, his regiment joined Gen. John Hunt Morgan's cavalry division. Commanding a brigade during Morgan's Indiana-Ohio raid, he with three hundred men eluded capture on July 19, 1863, by swimming the deep ford of the Ohio River at Belleville, West Virginia. Promoted to brigadier general as of June 1, 1864, he was raiding in Trigg County, Kentucky, on August 23 when he suffered a wound that left him blind.

After the war Johnson went into business, primarily real estate, and founded the town of Marble Falls, Texas. He died at Burnet, Texas, October 20, 1922.

BIBLIOGRAPHY

Ballard, Michael B. " 'Stovepipe' Johnson Raids Indiana: Deceived in Newburgh." *Civil War Times Illustrated* 21, no. 7 (1982): 22–26.

Johnson, Adam Rankin. *The Partisan Rangers of the Confederate States Army.* Louisville, Ky., 1904.

JAMES A. RAMAGE

JOHNSON, ANDREW (1808–1875), military governor of Tennessee, and vice president and president of the United States. Johnson, the only member of the U.S. Senate from a seceding state to remain loyal to the Union, was born the son of a Raleigh, North Carolina, innkeeper whose death left the family in poverty. Bound out as an apprentice tailor, Johnson learned his trade and the rudiments of reading and writing at the shop. He broke his apprenticeship articles after three years, ultimately settling in Greeneville, Tennessee, where he practiced his trade and became active in local politics. Between 1829 and 1842 Johnson served as alderman and then mayor of Greeneville and as a state legislator. From 1843 to 1853 he served in Congress.

ANDREW JOHNSON.   NATIONAL ARCHIVES

Johnson cultivated a reputation as a radical Democratic representative of the workingmen, artisans, and small farmers who predominated in the hilly country of eastern Tennessee. As he sought statewide office, however, Johnson became a strong advocate of the rights of slaveholders in the Union. A united Democratic party elected him governor for two terms (1853–1857) and then to the U.S. Senate in 1857, where he took a firm proslavery stand. In the presidential election of 1860 he supported the Breckinridge-Lane ticket of the proslavery wing of the Democratic party. Nonetheless, Johnson was not comfortable in the extreme proslavery camp. He did not agree that a state had a constitutional right to secede, and it would become clear that he bore a powerful emotional attachment to the Union.

When the states of the Deep South began to secede after the election of Abraham Lincoln to the presidency, Johnson took a much firmer pro-Union stand than most upper South and border-state congressmen. As Southern senators resigned their seats, he assailed them and was bitterly denounced in return. His course was controversial in Tennessee, where he emerged as the leading Unionist, but it made him a hero in the North and gave him a national reputation.

Johnson defeated his state's secessionists at first, but he could not dam the wave of secessionism that swept Tennessee after the firing on Fort Sumter and Lincoln's call for troops. Johnson was driven from Tennessee and took an active role in devising war measures in the Senate.

By 1862 Union forces had occupied Nashville and surrounding areas of central Tennessee. Hoping to make the state an example that would undermine support for the Confederacy among reluctant secessionists, Lincoln made Johnson a brigadier general of volunteers and appointed him military governor of the state, with instructions to establish a loyal civil government to take its place in the Union.

Johnson immediately set to work creating a political organization to serve as a vehicle for restoration, but a variety of factors frustrated his efforts. Unlike eastern Tennessee, central Tennessee was firmly secessionist. The few Unionists were conservative Whigs, deeply committed to slavery and suspicious of the radically Democratic Johnson. Only after sullen resistance did central Tennesseans obey orders requiring all who had aided the rebellion to take oaths of loyalty or to promise to desist from disloyal action. Despite eastern Tennessee's strategic importance, Johnson was unable to persuade the Union military commanders in Tennessee to secure a political base for loyalism by liberating his home region. Nor could he get Lincoln or the War Department to intercede. The commanders proved unwilling even to commit the resources necessary to make Nashville itself secure militarily. Few people were willing openly to espouse Unionism when Confederate troops might return at any time. Moreover, the commanders refused to recognize Johnson's final authority over matters of civil government, insisting that they retain ultimate control of law enforcement and other matters of military concern. Bickering took up a good deal of Johnson's energy.

The uncertain future of slavery also inhibited the establishment of a Unionist political organization. Johnson himself had defended slavery, and he doubted he could secure much support for antislavery Unionism in Tennessee. When runaway slaves gathered around the Union military encampments in Tennessee, Johnson favored using them as military laborers but opposed organizing them as fighting units. But proslavery Unionists turned out to be lukewarm in their condemnation of disloyalty and reluctant to act to restore loyal government. Johnson gravitated toward more radical Unionists, who began to attack slavery and to demand that only ardent Unionists participate in the restoration process. After Lincoln issued the preliminary Emancipation Proclamation in the fall of 1862, Johnson endorsed emancipation in Tennessee and the recruitment of African Americans as soldiers. With this, conservative Unionists repudiated both Johnson and Lincoln. The divisions among Unionists, who probably remained a minority in central Tennessee, rendered establishment of a Unionist government impossible.

In December 1863 Lincoln took reconstruction matters into his own hands, promulgating proclamations offering amnesty to Southerners who took an oath of loyalty and outlining a procedure whereby they could restore civil governments whenever their number equaled 10 percent of the 1860 presidential electorate in their states. Lincoln's proclamations galvanized Johnson into action, but he insisted upon a more rigorous oath and a more limited electorate. As a result his efforts sputtered once more.

As he attempted to restore Tennessee's state government on a radical basis, Johnson also undertook extensive speaking tours in the North to help Union election campaigns. He proved a popular political attraction and reconfirmed his position as the leading Unionist of the South. As such, and because he was more radical than Lincoln and a Democrat, Johnson seemed an ideal running mate for Lincoln in 1864. The party convention nominated him in June and he was elected in November.

Johnson was determined to complete restoration of the state government before ascending to the vice presidency in March 1865. An irregularly chosen constitutional convention met in January and proposed amendments to the state constitution that abolished slavery and made key state offices appointive by the governor. These were to be submitted to the people for ratification, with election of a governor and state legislature to follow. On February 22, 1865, 25,000 voters—compared to 145,000 who had voted in the 1860 presidential election—ratified the amendments almost unanimously. Johnson resigned his military commission and governorship on March 3, 1865, and was inaugurated vice president of the United States the following day.

Johnson succeeded to the presidency upon the death of Lincoln on April 15, 1865. As president, he undertook a more lenient program of Reconstruction than he had followed as military governor. Where Lincoln had not already appointed provisional governors, Johnson issued proclamations doing so. The governors were to appoint temporary state officials and to recommend persons for appointment to Federal offices. They were to call constitutional conventions, insisting only on the abolition of slavery, nullification of ordinances of secession, and repudiation of Southern war debts. By an amnesty proclamation Johnson pardoned nearly all Confederates who would take a loyalty oath. Pardoned Confederates were permitted to participate in the Reconstruction process and often took leading roles in the reestablished governments.

As president, Johnson opposed extending voting privileges to black Americans, vetoed Federal legislation to protect their civil rights, and worked to defeat the Fourteenth and Fifteenth Amendments to the Constitution. The bitter conflict Johnson's course engendered with the Republican-controlled Congress led to his impeachment in

1868. He was acquitted by one vote and served out his term, retiring in 1869. In 1875 he was again elected senator from Tennessee, but he died the same year.

BIBLIOGRAPHY

Hall, Clifton R. *Andrew Johnson: Military Governor of Tennessee.* Princeton, 1916.

Maslowski, Peter. *Treason Must Be Made Odious: Military Occupation and Wartime Reconstruction in Nashville, Tennessee, 1862–1865.* Millwood, N.Y., 1978.

Trefousse, Hans L. *Andrew Johnson: A Biography.* New York, 1989.

MICHAEL LES BENEDICT

JOHNSON, BRADLEY TYLER (1829–1903), brigadier general. Johnson graduated from Princeton University in 1849 and was admitted to the Maryland bar in 1851. A leader in the state Democratic party, Johnson fervently worked for self-determination in Maryland. His sense of honor and devotion to his state led him to form a militia company in his hometown of Frederick, Maryland, which became part of the First Maryland Infantry. Johnson was elected major and later was promoted to lieutenant

BRADLEY TYLER JOHNSON.   NATIONAL ARCHIVES

colonel (July 1861) and to colonel (March 1862). The First Maryland fought at First Manassas, served under Gen. Thomas J. ("Stonewall") Jackson during the 1862 Shenandoah Valley campaign, and participated in the Seven Days' Battles. In August 1862, the unit was mustered out of service, and Johnson joined the staff of Stonewall Jackson.

Johnson was assigned temporary command of Gen. John Robert Jones's brigade during Second Manassas and acted as provost marshal of Frederick in the Sharpsburg campaign. He next served on a military court in Richmond. In November 1863, Johnson assumed command of the Maryland Line and in June of the next year was promoted to brigadier general to replace Gen. William E. ("Grumble") Jones, who was killed in the Battle of Piedmont. In Gen. Jubal Early's raid on Washington in July 1864, Johnson led an aborted attempt to liberate Confederate prisoners at Point Lookout, Maryland. Johnson and Gen. John McCausland led the raid on Chambersburg, carrying out Early's orders to burn the town. After Johnson's brigade was routed at Moorefield, West Virginia, in August, he and McCausland disputed responsibility for the disaster. Johnson requested a court of inquiry, but none was ever convened. Johnson's brigade participated in the 1864 Shenandoah Valley campaign, and in November, he was relegated to command a prison at Salisbury, North Carolina, where he served until the close of the war.

After the war, Johnson practiced law in Richmond and served in the Virginia state senate. He wrote and spoke frequently on the war, demonstrating his eloquence, humor and passion for the South. Johnson died at Amelia, Virginia, and is buried in Loudon Park Cemetery, Baltimore.

BIBLIOGRAPHY

Goldsborough, William W. *The Maryland Line in the Confederate Army.* Baltimore, Md., 1900. Reprint, Gaithersburg, Md., 1987.

Hartzler, Daniel D. *Marylanders in the Confederacy.* Westminster, Md., 1986.

Johnson, Bradley T. *Maryland.* Vol. 2 of *Confederate Military History.* Edited by Clement A. Evans. Atlanta, 1899. Vol. 2 of extended ed. Wilmington, N.C., 1987.

Newman, Harry Wright. *Maryland and the Confederacy.* Annapolis, Md., 1976.

Warner, Ezra J. *Generals in Gray: Lives of the Confederate Commanders.* Baton Rouge, La., 1959.

JOHN E. OLSON

JOHNSON, BUSHROD RUST (1817–1880), major general. A native of Belmont County, Ohio, Johnson was born October 7, 1817, and graduated in 1840 from the U.S. Military Academy. For the next seven years Johnson served with the Third U.S. Infantry. He took part in the Seminole and Mexican wars and, for six months following the fall of

Mexico City, served as depot commissary at Vera Cruz. He resigned from the army in October 1847 and took a teaching position at the Western Military Institute in Georgetown, Kentucky. For four years (1851–1855) he doubled as a teacher and superintendent. During the same period he held commissions in the militia of Kentucky (1849–1854) and Tennessee (1854–1861).

Commissioned a colonel at the start of the war, Johnson was promoted to brigadier, January 24, 1862, and was in command of the garrison at Fort Henry when it fell in February 1862. He was captured in that action but escaped a few days later when the Federals took over Fort Donelson. Johnson was severely wounded at Shiloh, but he recovered in time to take part in Braxton Bragg's invasion of Kentucky. At Chickamauga, Johnson was the first to spot a gap in the Union line and exploit it fully "with the coolness and judgment for which he was always distinguished," according to D. H. Hill.

While Johnson was with James Longstreet in eastern Tennessee, influential friends stumped for his advancement. Alexander P. Stewart reported that he had "utmost confidence in his fitness" to command a division. Longstreet affirmed that Johnson "has courage, skill and ability to an eminent degree. . . . I have found him always ready, with able suggestions, and the desire to execute them." Simon Bolivar Buckner extolled Johnson's "gallantry and ability." Patrick Cleburne and B. Franklin Cheatham added their voices to the clamor for a major general's commission, which came on May 21, 1864.

The Ohioan transferred to Virginia for the spring campaign of 1864. He opposed Benjamin Butler's assault on the Richmond and Petersburg Railroad and took part in the engagement at Drewry's Bluff, where he captured the enemy's guns but lost more than one-fourth of his division. After commanding South Carolina troops at the Battle of the Crater, Johnson saw his division shattered at Sayler's Creek and was without a command when he surrendered at Appomattox.

Johnson returned to Tennessee and became chancellor at the University of Nashville. He also arranged to conduct a collegiate department at the Montgomery Bell Academy as a preparatory school. When a depression forced that institution to close its doors in 1874, Johnson moved to Brighton, Illinois, where he died on September 12, 1880. He was buried in nearby Miles Station. A century later, however, his remains were exhumed and reburied next to those of his wife in Nashville, Tennessee.

BIBLIOGRAPHY

Compiled Military Service Records. Bushrod Rust Johnson. Microcopy M331, Roll 141. Record Group 109. National Archives, Washington, D.C.

Cummings, Charles M. *Yankee Quaker, Confederate General.* Rutherford, N.J., 1971.

Porter, James D. *Tennessee.* Vol. 8 of *Confederate Military History.* Edited by Clement A. Evans. Atlanta, 1899. Vol. 10 of extended ed. Wilmington, N.C., 1987.

LOWELL REIDENBAUGH

JOHNSON, EDWARD (1816–1873), major general. Born in Virginia, Johnson graduated from West Point in 1838 and then served in the Sixth U.S. Infantry for twenty-three years. During the war with Mexico he was twice brevetted for bravery.

Johnson resigned from the U.S. Army in June 1861 and was soon appointed colonel of the Twelfth Georgia Infantry. For the next year he served west of Staunton, Virginia, in the Allegheny Mountains, where he became known as "Allegheny" Johnson. His conduct was conspicuous in the actions at Greenbrier River, Allegheny Mountain, and McDowell. In the latter engagement, on May 8, 1862, Johnson, encouraging his men with a club instead of a sword, went down with a wound in the foot. He spent the next year recovering in Richmond.

Johnson returned to duty as a major general commanding the Stonewall Division in the Army of Northern Virginia. He actively led the division at Second Winchester, Gettysburg, Mine Run, the Wilderness, and Spotsylvania. On May

EDWARD JOHNSON.   NATIONAL ARCHIVES

12, 1864, the Union Second Corps assaulted his position at Spotsylvania's Bloody Angle, capturing the general and some 2,500 of his men. He was sent to Charleston and was exchanged in August. After his release "Allegheny" served as a division commander in the Army of Tennessee. On December 16, 1864, he was again captured following the Confederate defeat at Nashville. He remained a prisoner until July 1865.

Following the war Johnson returned to Virginia, engaged in farming and participated in civic organizations. "Allegheny," who never married, left behind little personal correspondence. He was buried in Hollywood Cemetery, Richmond.

BIBLIOGRAPHY

Adams, Charles R., ed. *A Post of Honor: The Pryor Letters, 1861–63.* Fort Valley, Ga., 1989.
Cullum, George W., ed. *Biographical Register of the Officers and Graduates of the United States Military Academy.* 2 vols. New York, 1868.
Hotchkiss, Jed. *Virginia.* Vol. 3 of *Confederate Military History.* Edited by Clement A. Evans. Atlanta, 1899. Vol. 4 of extended ed. Wilmington, N.C., 1987.

MICHAEL J. ANDRUS

JOHNSON, GEORGE W.

JOHNSON, GEORGE W. (1811–1862), Confederate governor of Kentucky. Johnson was born near Georgetown, Kentucky, on May 27, 1811. He received his law degrees at Transylvania University but decided to farm rather than practice law. In addition to a prosperous bluegrass farm, Johnson acquired a thousand-acre cotton plantation in Arkansas. A wealthy slaveholder, noted for his lavish hospitality, he was elected to the state house of representatives in 1838, 1839, and 1840. Although he supported John C. Breckinridge for president in 1860, he denied that Abraham Lincoln's election justified secession. As secession began, Johnson argued that if Kentucky joined the South the sections would be too evenly balanced to fight.

Johnson supported Kentucky's neutrality until it ended in September 1861. To avoid arrest, he joined Gen. Simon Bolivar Buckner in Bowling Green as a volunteer aide. Johnson was a leader in the Russellville convention of October 29 and 30 that planned a sovereignty convention to meet there on November 18. That body declared Kentucky to be "a free and independent state," established a provisional government that was admitted into the Confederacy on December 10, 1861, and elected Johnson governor.

Johnson could do little to create a viable government before Albert Sidney Johnston withdrew from Kentucky in February 1862. At Shiloh on April 6 Johnson served as a volunteer aide, but that evening, despite his age and a crippled arm, he insisted on enlisting as a private in the Fourth Kentucky Infantry. Fatally wounded the next day, he died on a Federal hospital ship on April 8. He was buried in Georgetown.

BIBLIOGRAPHY

Coffman, Mrs. William H., comp. "Letters of George W. Johnson." *Register of the Kentucky State Historical Society* 40 (October 1942): 337–352.
Duke, Basil W. *Reminiscences of General Basil W. Duke, C.S.A.* Garden City, N.Y., 1911.
Harrison, Lowell H. "George W. Johnson." In *Kentucky's Governors, 1792–1985.* Edited by Lowell H. Harrison. Lexington, Ky., 1985.
Harrison, Lowell H. "George W. Johnson and Richard Hawes: The Governors of Confederate Kentucky." *Register of the Kentucky Historical Society* 79 (Winter 1981): 3–39.

LOWELL H. HARRISON

JOHNSON, HERSCHEL V.

JOHNSON, HERSCHEL V. (1812–1880), Georgia governor, Democratic vice presidential candidate, congressman, and president of Georgia's constitutional convention. Herschel Vespasian Johnson was among Georgia's most influential antebellum politicians. As Stephen A. Douglas's vice presidential running mate in 1860, he played a central role in the secession crisis as one of the Deep South's

HERSCHEL V. JOHNSON.   LIBRARY OF CONGRESS

strongest Unionist voices, while consistently advocating state rights policy before and during the Civil War.

Johnson was born on September 18, 1812, in Burke County, Georgia, the son of a modest planter. He was educated at private schools, including the Monaghan Academy in Warrenton, Georgia, and in 1831 entered the University of Georgia, graduating in 1834 in a class that included Alexander H. Stephens, who became a lifelong friend and close political ally. Johnson married Ann F. Polk, the daughter of a Maryland Supreme Court justice, a niece of President James K. Polk, and a cousin of Bishop (and later Confederate general) Leonidas Polk.

Johnson studied law for a year in Augusta, where he opened a successful practice after passing the bar in 1835. Four years later, he used his earnings to purchase a large Jefferson County plantation called Sandy Grove, which he managed while practicing law in a new partnership in nearby Louisville, Georgia. It was in Louisville that Johnson first became involved in politics, and in 1840, at the age of twenty-eight, he was approached by local Democrats to run for Congress. He declined but made a strong impression as an effective stump speaker when campaigning for the Democratic nominee that year, for his own unsuccessful bid for Congress in 1843, and for his wife's uncle, James K. Polk, in the presidential election of 1844. Johnson's hard-hitting oratory had by then attracted statewide attention. Though he lost a gubernatorial bid in 1847, the man who defeated him, Governor George W. Towns, appointed him to fill the remaining year of Walter T. Colquitt's vacated U.S. Senate seat. During his brief term in Washington, Johnson made several speeches on the Senate floor in which he took strong pro-Southern stands on the Mexican War, on Texas's admission to the Union, and on slavery's protection from any interference from Congress, either in states where slavery existed or in present or future territories.

Johnson returned from Washington in March 1849 and in July was elected to a four-year term as superior court judge of the Ocmulgee District. As an outside observer of the sectional crisis that erupted the following year over California's bid for statehood, he continued to maintain a hard-line defense of state sovereignty and argued that any new territory should be divided equally into slave and nonslave states. He initially opposed the terms of the Compromise of 1850 and challenged fellow Georgian Howell Cobb's conciliatory stance in Congress. Only when disruption of the Union seemed the likely alternative did he reluctantly accept the compromise.

In 1853, with his judicial term drawing to a close and encouraged by Georgia Democrats' support the year before for nationalist presidential nominee Franklin Pierce for whom he had actively campaigned, Johnson ran for governor. He was elected by a narrow margin over Whig candidate Charles J. Jenkins, author of the Georgia platform of 1850. During his two terms as governor (1853–1857), Johnson retreated from his earlier fire-eating stance and moved to a more moderate position on sectional issues. He supported Stephen Douglas's Kansas-Nebraska Act in 1854, having much earlier advocated its principle of popular sovereignty as the determinant of a territory's status in regard to slavery. Its failure disappointed him greatly, and he was quite vocal in denouncing the ensuing violence on the part of extremists on both sides. Though he remained staunch in his commitment to state rights principles, he became more outspoken in his opposition to secession or any other threat to national unity.

Johnson retired to Sandy Grove at the end of his second term as governor in November 1857, to preside over what by 1860 amounted to over 3,600 acres of land and 117 slaves. He vowed that his political career was behind him, but his decision proved short-lived when the presidential election three years later brought the sectional crisis to a critical juncture. Johnson was convinced that Stephen Douglas offered the only hope for a Democratic candidate with viable appeal on both sides of the Mason-Dixon Line. He attended the party's convention in Charleston and worked hard to maintain party unity and gain the nomination for the Illinois senator. Though his efforts proved futile at the abortive convention, Johnson impressed enough delegates there to win their nomination as Douglas's vice-presidential running mate when the Democrats met again in Baltimore. Johnson accepted the nomination reluctantly as his "patriotic duty." The party had by then split, with the Southern wing nominating John C. Breckinridge as its presidential candidate in yet another convention. Most Georgia Democrats aligned themselves with this movement and were critical of Johnson's refusal to do likewise. Johnson was in fact the only Georgian still present at the "national" convention when Douglas won the nomination.

In an unpublished autobiography, Johnson described the reception that awaited him when he returned to Georgia after the convention. In the towns and villages he passed through on the train, "crowds would gather at the windows to get a glance at the man . . . who deserved the gallows, for alleged treason to the rights of the South, who, as they supposed, had abandoned his friends and his hearthstone, for the poor price of the Vice-Presidency." Throughout a speaking tour of the state, he was greeted with hostility and resentment and was told by friends and former political associates that his present linkage with Douglas "was fatal to all my future prospects and would not only consign me to obscurity, but to political infamy." He also made an extensive campaign tour through the northern and midwestern states, traveling over four thousand miles between New York and Iowa. There he faced a more favorable, if guarded, reception than that at home.

Though never as optimistic as Douglas that Northern commitment to the Union could carry their ticket to victory over Abraham Lincoln, Johnson was sorely troubled by the election's outcome and its aftermath. Despite his loss of support within Georgia, he traveled around the state in late November and December urging Georgians not to follow the rash course of South Carolinians in seceding. Though he was consistent in his insistence that the Southern states had a constitutional right to secede, he was equally adamant that Lincoln's election alone was not enough justification to do so. He preached the logic of a wait-and-watch policy of taking no action until the new president assumed office late in March and had a chance to negotiate a settlement of the crisis.

As a delegate to Georgia's secession convention in Milledgeville in January 1861, Johnson urged delay and proposed a stopgap measure of having delegates from all Southern states, both in and out of the Union, meet in Atlanta in February and draw up their own terms to present to Lincoln and to Congress as an alternative to secession. Up until this point, Johnson had been closely aligned with fellow cooperationists Benjamin H. Hill and Alexander H. Stephens. Though Hill encouraged him to continue pushing for the measure whenever the opportunity for a vote on it came up, Stephens felt the lengthy list of demands and conditions it included was completely unworkable and refused to support it, which led to a temporary rift between Johnson and the soon-to-be Confederate vice president. Nevertheless, when the measure was put to a vote as "Johnson's Substitute" to Eugenius Aristides Nisbet's ordinance of secession, minority support for it proved surprisingly strong. In one of a series of votes on January 19, Johnson's proposal received 133 votes as opposed to 164 for Nisbet's move for immediate secession.

Once Georgians had voted themselves out of the Union, Johnson, like most other Unionists, pledged his support for the new Confederacy. Yet he remained pessimistic regarding its chances for survival, writing soon afterward that "I felt that the State of Georgia would soon be launched upon a dark, uncertain and dangerous sea. I was never so sad before." He once again retired to his plantation, too old for military service and too unpopular for elective office. "I think my public career is ended," he confided to Alexander Stephens, then at the Confederacy's Provisional Congress in Montgomery. "My adhesion to Douglas and the North was fatal."

But Johnson's retirement plans proved as premature then as they had in 1857. In November 1862, the state legislature elected him to replace John W. Lewis in the Confederate Senate. A year later he was reelected for a full term, so that he served in Richmond from January 16, 1863, until the war's end.

Throughout his wartime congressional career, Johnson remained consistent in adhering to his state rights principles. He opposed conscription, the suspension of the writ of habeas corpus, and the establishment of a Confederate supreme court. He even took the radical step of proposing an amendment to the Confederate Constitution that would have authorized the right of peaceful secession of an individual state from the Confederacy. He was strongly criticized for this move in Georgia newspapers, particularly the *Savannah Republican.* He later explained to this newspaper that the purpose of the proposal was not to encourage secession, which he felt should never be more than a last resort. But in the event that such extreme action was felt necessary, he said, the "object of the amendment is to sheath forever the sword of civil war. . . . The aggrieved State may withdraw without the shedding of fraternal blood and take her position among the family of nations to work out her destiny as best she can." After stirring much controversy, Johnson was forced to withdraw the bill on a procedural technicality, and the issue was never raised again.

Despite his considerable political stature before the war, Johnson was not a dominant force in the Confederate Congress. As he later explained in his autobiography, "I did not pretend to make myself prominent in the Senate, because I found that my views were so averse to the policy of the administration, and the effort to enforce them so hopeless, that I contented myself with giving my views mildly and in few words and in voting according to the convictions of my judgment."

Perhaps more surprising than his relatively passive role in the Senate was the staunch loyalty to Jefferson Davis that Johnson maintained behind the scenes, revealed primarily through his correspondence with Davis's far less supportive vice president. Johnson journeyed from Richmond to Milledgeville in November 1863 for the primary purpose of thwarting a meeting of Georgia legislators openly hostile to the president. He subsequently wrote to Stephens, "Differing as I do from the President in several particulars, yet I am satisfied that a warfare on his administration will be disastrous. It will discourage the army; divide the people at home and weaken the energies of the country. One revolution at a time is enough."

Johnson chided Stephens on his involvement in the efforts among Georgians to undermine and discredit President Davis. In a series of letters in March 1864, he denounced the vice president's lengthy absences from Richmond and his failure to use his position to constructively shape or influence administration efforts. Johnson accused his friend of advocating impeachment proceedings against Davis and denounced his measures as foolhardy and misguided. "You are the Vice President & . . . a part of the Executive branch of the Government," he wrote. "How deeply to be lamented that holding that relation you should feel it to be your duty to avow your hostility to & advise the Legislature to array the States against the Government! Nothing has yet occurred which fills me with so much gloom and sadness. . . . From Gen'l [Robert] Toombs and Gov. Brown I expected rashness—I did not expect it of you."

Johnson played an ambivalent role in the peace movement that emerged in 1864. He was one of the few senators active in efforts that were much more conspicuous among members of the lower house. In June 1864, he was part of a coalition of congressional peace advocates that, in the wake of Confederate victories at Spotsylvania and in the Wilderness, sought to lobby both houses of Congress to initiate negotiations with the Lincoln administration to end the war with Southern independence intact. But resolutions introduced by the coalition's spokesmen to send peace commissioners to Washington were soundly rejected by both houses.

After Atlanta's fall two months later, however, as the prospect of Georgians negotiating a separate peace with William Tecumseh Sherman was discussed, Johnson showed little enthusiasm for such an initiative. Despite rumors that Sherman had approached both him and Governor Joseph E. Brown to discuss terms for Georgia's reentry into the Union, Johnson denied any serious consideration of the option. In an open letter to "Several Gentlemen of Middle Georgia" on September 25, 1864, he maintained that "there can be no peace upon any honorable terms so long as its present rulers are in power." Far from inspiring the Federal government with a sense of justice or magnanimity, he said, any Southern peace sentiments in the wake of Atlanta's fall and Richmond's imminent capture by Ulysses S. Grant would be construed "as intimidation on our part and would stimulate and intensify the war spirit of the North." He advised his fellow Georgians that such a "confession of overthrow" could lead to no better than terms of unconditional surrender, which he knew they were not yet ready to concede.

In December 1864, Sherman's troops overran Johnson's Sandy Grove plantation, ransacking but not destroying it. By the war's end, Johnson could take little satisfaction in his prescience four years earlier regarding its outcome and the disastrous effects on the South, for he was among those facing financial ruin as he returned home in April 1865 to resume his law practice and rebuild his plantation.

But again, his attempt to return to private life was interrupted by political responsibilities. When the state constitutional convention met in Milledgeville in October 1865, Johnson was chosen as its president. Under the terms of its short-lived Constitution, the legislature met in January 1866 and elected Johnson and Stephens, recently released from prison, to the U.S. Senate. The lack of proper repentance implied by the quick conversion of these high-ranking Confederate officials into Federal officeholders compelled the Radical Republican Congress to bar their entry and deny them their seats. Johnson reacted with a combination of relief and resentment at this indignity. He wrote Stephens that he had had no desire to go to Washington and found the one "prospect of relief" in the fact that "for the present, I can play Senator and also stay at home & attend to my profession." In response to Stephens's musings over whether to relinquish the office to a Georgian less offensive to Northern sensibilities, Johnson urged him to stand firm. "They have elected you with full knowledge of your objections & your ineligibility (according to Radical tests). Therefore, keep me company in the agreeable task of staying at home, until we can be allowed to take our seats."

That time never came, and Johnson's political career, in effect, was over. He practiced law and managed his plantation, and though deeply resentful of Radical Republican rule in the state, he refrained from speaking out against it, despite frequent invitations to do so. In 1873 Governor James M. Smith appointed Johnson to the superior court judgeship of Georgia's middle circuit, a position he accepted despite increasingly poor health in order to alleviate his continued financial hardship. He served in that position until his death at Sandy Grove on August 16, 1880.

BIBLIOGRAPHY

Bryan, T. Conn. *Confederate Georgia*. Athens, Ga., 1953.

Conway, Alan. *The Reconstruction of Georgia*. Minneapolis, Minn., 1966.

Flippin, Percy Scott. *Herschel V. Johnson of Georgia: State Rights Unionist*. Richmond, Va., 1931.

Flippin, Percy Scott, ed. "From the Autobiography of Herschel V. Johnson." *American Historical Review* 30 (January 1925): 311–336.

Johnson, Michael P. *Toward a Patriarchal Republic: The Secession of Georgia*. Baton Rouge, La., 1977.

Knight, Lucian Lamar. *Reminiscences of Famous Georgians*. Vol. 2. Atlanta, 1908.

Mellichamp, Josephine. *Senators from Georgia*. Huntsville, Ala., 1876.

Phillips, Ulrich Bonnell. *Georgia and State Rights*. Washington, D.C., 1902. Reprint, Yellow Springs, Ohio, 1968.

JOHN C. INSCOE

JOHNSON, JOHN LEWIS (1818–1900), a founder and leader of the secret pro-Union organization, the Heroes of America. A native of Philadelphia, Johnson studied medicine there and in North Carolina and then worked as a physician in Virginia and as a druggist in North Carolina. When the war broke out, he was trying to set up a medical practice in Abbott's Creek (present-day Union Cross),

North Carolina, a small community located about nine miles southeast of Winston (present-day Winston-Salem), the seat of Forsyth County.

Johnson, a Moravian, lived in the heart of one of the most disaffected areas in the Confederacy. Central North Carolina contained the largest concentration of antislavery Moravians, Quakers, and Wesleyan Methodists in the South. The populace, composed mostly of die-hard anti-secession Whigs, voted by large majorities against the holding of a state secession convention in February 1861.

That summer the central counties witnessed the growth of an anti-Confederate underground organization numbering in the hundreds whose members secretly drilled under the U.S. flag and vowed that secessionists would soon "feel the rope." Confederate troops suppressed a threatened uprising among the Unionists in July. The next spring saw a resurgence of Unionist activity in reaction to the passage of state and national draft laws. So-called peace meetings were held in Davidson and Randolph counties at which leaders called for peace and reunion. Severe reprisals were mounted against the agitators: many were sent to prison without trial, and others were forced into the ranks of the Confederate army.

It was against this backdrop of violence and intimidation that Johnson and his son Chapman joined the Confederate army as substitutes, enrolling in the Forty-eighth North Carolina Regiment on July 5, 1862. Johnson was assigned to serve as an assistant to the regimental surgeon. At forty-four years of age in 1862, Johnson was not liable to the draft. He may have entered the service to avoid imprisonment for his Unionist activities or to promote the Union cause by secretly recruiting members for the Heroes of America from among Confederate troops.

Whatever his motive, while serving in the Army of Northern Virginia, Johnson was captured by the Federals, probably during the Sharpsburg campaign, and was paroled on September 22, 1862. After participating in the Battle of Fredericksburg in December, he was assigned to serve as a druggist in a military hospital in Raleigh, the capital of North Carolina. While stationed there, Johnson probably played a leading role in the founding of the Grand Council of the Heroes of America, for it was in Raleigh that the council was organized.

Johnson was an avid supporter of the Unionist peace movement that erupted on the political scene in North Carolina in July 1863. William W. Holden, its leader, was editor of Raleigh's *North Carolina Standard* and allegedly a member of the Heroes. Johnson took part in a peace meeting in Wake County on July 23, 1863, giving credence to the charge by loyal Confederates that disloyal influences were behind the peace movement.

During the 1864 gubernatorial contest, pro-Confederate newspapers tried to discredit the Peace party by associating its leaders with the Heroes of America. A justice of the peace in Richmond County, in recanting his connection with the society, told newsmen that he had heard the Heroes of America had originated within Union lines and had been "communicated to our people by a surgeon named Johnson." It is more likely that the secret order originated in central North Carolina. Whatever the case, Johnson clearly played a leading role in founding and propagating the Heroes in the state.

Johnson's service in a regiment at the front was probably punishment for his activities. On October 15, 1864, he decamped a company of Confederate soldiers to the Union lines, a feat referred to by his deriders after the war as "Johnson's Raid." Upon crossing the lines, Johnson went to Washington, D.C., where he and Benjamin Sherwood Hedrick established the National Grand Council of the Heroes of America. Hedrick was chief of the Division of Chemistry, Metallurgy, and Electricity at the U.S. Patent Office and a native Tarheel who in 1856 had been fired from his post as a professor at the University of North Carolina because of his antislavery, pro-Republican sentiments.

Daniel Reeves Goodloe, another North Carolina expatriate who lived in Washington during the war, testified to a Senate committee in 1870 that Johnson (probably in late 1864) initiated Goodloe, Hedrick, and Joseph Barrett, the commissioner of pensions, into the Heroes. Goodloe also testified that Johnson had told him that he had earlier initiated President Abraham Lincoln and Gen. Ulysses S. Grant into the secret order, although proof of this has yet to be uncovered. At war's end, Johnson was attending medical lectures in Cincinnati, Ohio, where he was living with his son Chapman, who had deserted from the Confederate army.

Johnson and his family paid a high price for their loyalty to the United States. Three of his sons were incarcerated in Confederate prisons in Richmond where two of them died. That one was an infant of only ten months implies that Mrs. Johnson too was arrested and imprisoned by Confederate officials.

After the war, the Republican party rewarded Johnson for his loyalty to the Union by appointing him an assistant assessor with the Internal Revenue Service in North Carolina. During Congressional Reconstruction, he led in the reactivation of the Heroes of America, which served as a vehicle for organizing and controlling the native white Unionist (i.e., scalawag) vote for the Republican party in the state. Johnson spent the remainder of his life in Forsyth County, practicing dentistry (he attended dental school in Philadelphia after the war) and engaging in farming. He died at his daughter's house in Winston-Salem of a stroke and was buried in the cemetery at the Moravian church in Union Cross.

[*See also* Heroes of America.]

BIBLIOGRAPHY

Auman, William T., and David D. Scarboro. "The Heroes of America in Civil War North Carolina." *North Carolina Historical Review* 58 (1981): 327–363.

Goodloe, Daniel Reeves. Testimony. *Senate Report*. 42d Congress, 1st sess., February 18, 1871.

Hamilton, J. G. de Roulhac. "The Heroes of America." *Publications of the Southern History Association* 40 (1907): 10–19.

WILLIAM THOMAS AUMAN

JOHNSON, ROBERT W.

(1814–1879), congressman from Arkansas. Robert Ward Johnson was a native of Kentucky, born July 22, 1814. He moved to Arkansas in 1821 and was a prominent antebellum politician, serving in the state legislature (1847–1853), the U.S. House of Representatives (1847–1853), and the U.S. Senate (1853–1861). A Democrat, Johnson was the leader of the political faction within the state known as the Family, a name derived from the familial connections among many of its more prominent members. He was an important advocate of secession in 1860 and returned from Washington, D.C., after the election of Abraham Lincoln to push the state along that course.

The secession convention selected Johnson as one of five delegates to the Provisional Congress in May 1861, and the state legislature sent him to the Confederate Senate (1862–1865). There he was a supporter of President Jefferson Davis throughout the war, although he advocated policies that would give more autonomy to the Trans-Mississippi region. He chaired the Committee on Indian Affairs and was active in efforts to develop a policy that would guarantee Indian support for the Confederacy. He did not return to Richmond for the last session of Congress in 1865, and at the war's end he considered moving to Mexico. He had gotten as far as Texas in his flight, when he decided to ask for a presidential pardon.

After receiving the pardon from President Andrew Johnson, his distant relative, he returned to Jefferson County, Arkansas, where he resumed planting and politics. In 1868 he moved to Washington, D.C., where he practiced law with former Confederate general Albert Pike. In 1877 he returned to Little Rock, where he remained until his death on July 26, 1879.

BIBLIOGRAPHY

Hallum, John. *Biographical and Pictorial History of Arkansas*. Albany, N.Y., 1887.

Shinn, J. H. *Pioneers and Makers of Arkansas*. Washington, D.C., 1908.

Warner, Ezra J., and W. Buck Yearns. *Biographical Register of the Confederate Congress*. Baton Rouge, La., 1975.

CARL H. MONEYHON

JOHNSON'S ISLAND PRISON.

In October 1861, Lt. Col. William Hoffman, the U.S. commissary general of prisoners, examined the Lake Erie islands for a prison site and selected as the most practicable a three-hundred-acre island in Sandusky Bay, some two-and-three-quarters miles from Sandusky, to which prisoners could be brought by rail and from which they could be moved by boat. On the island, half of which Hoffman leased from its owner and namesake, Leonard B. Johnson, there was a forty-acre clearing on which Hoffman had buildings for guards and prisoners erected. For the latter there were ultimately thirteen two-story barracks in a fifteen-acre enclosure surrounded by a high plank fence with platforms for guards and two blockhouses with small cannons. At this early stage of the Civil War, the U.S. authorities thought that Johnson's Island would hold all their prisoners.

The prison almost immediately began to be used mainly for officer prisoners up to the rank of general, with the first arriving on April 10, 1862. The highest number held before the commencement of regular exchange was 1,462 at the end of August 1862. After a temporary reduction, exchanges broke down and the total rose to 2,763 by the end of 1863 and to a peak of 9,423 by January 1865.

Throughout most of its existence, Ohioans administered Johnson Island. When creating the prison, Hoffman arranged for the appointment of William S. Pierson as commander. Though lacking military experience, Pierson was a former mayor of Sandusky and able to administer what began as a small institution. He became major of the locally recruited Hoffman Battalion, ultimately enlarged to the 128th Ohio Volunteer Infantry Regiment, which made up the core of the guard force. In January 1864, Brig. Gen. Henry D. Terry took command, bringing with him five additional regiments for guards. Complaints of indiscipline and bad physical conditions continued under Terry as they had under Pierson. On May 8, 1864, the adjutant general of Ohio, Charles W. Hill, took command for the remainder of the war. He instituted a thorough cleaning of the buildings and grounds.

Part of the explanation for the filth on the island was that the rock that underlaid the scant topsoil impeded drainage and made it difficult to dig adequate sinks (latrines). Pure wells were also hard to provide and pumping water from the lake was not always feasible, especially in winter. Winter exacerbated the problems because, though the island was very like a resort in summer, it was brutal in the cold season, especially for prisoners accustomed to a Southern climate and furnished with insufficient blankets and clothing. In 1864 when the Union authorities in retaliation for alleged Confederate mistreatment of Union prisoners reduced rations and cut off most purchases from the sutler and the delivery of gift boxes, prisoners began to complain of severe hunger. Indicative of the reality of their suffering was the organization of a "rat club" for hunting, eating and selling rats to other prisoners. Far more common diversions were theatricals, handcrafts, reading, classes, and religious services.

Inevitably, escape was a preoccupation of the prisoners. Attempts at tunneling were almost never successful, but it was sometimes possible to deceive the guard at the gate or to scale the wall at night and then cross to the mainland on winter ice. Even then, rewards posted for escapees often induced recapture; still, a few prisoners reached Canada and were able to run the blockade into the Confederacy.

Some other escaped prisoners became involved in attempts by Confederate agents in 1864 and 1865 to launch irregular attacks on the United States, to encourage insurrection, and especially to free Confederate prisoners from Northern camps. A rescue of the Johnson's Island prisoners and a conspiracy among the inmates to aid the effort had been rumored in 1863, and the Federals had begun to mount cannons in earthworks and to station near the island the ship *Michigan,* the only armed vessel on the Great Lakes. Confederate agents in Canada plotted to capture the vessel and free the prisoners. They sent an escaped prisoner to prepare the way and, in September 1864, sent a party headed by John Yeats Beall, an acting master in the Confederate navy, which captured two lake steamers. But Beall's crew lost heart before trying to seize *Michigan,* and he was later captured out of uniform on U.S. soil and hanged for violation of the laws of war. Thus failed the most formidable raid on Johnson's Island.

In 1865, first the resumption of exchange and then the end of the war rapidly emptied the prison. In September, the handful of remaining prisoners was transferred. By the following June, the buildings had been sold and the post abandoned. Parts of the site were used for orchards, quarrying, and summer resorts. In the mid-twentieth century a causeway was built to connect the island and the shore. Though remnants of the fortifications remain, the only publicly owned memorial is the cemetery whose 206 graves attest to the fact that this prison for officers was less fatal than many. A statue of a Confederate soldier gazes toward the South.

BIBLIOGRAPHY

Barrett, John G., ed. *Yankee Rebel: The Civil War Journal of Edmund DeWitt Patterson.* Chapel Hill, N.C., 1966.
Frohman, Charles E. *Rebels on Lake Erie.* Columbus, Ohio, 1965.
Hesseltine, William B. *Civil War Prisons: A Study in War Psychology.* Columbus, Ohio, 1930. Reprint, New York, 1964.
Shriver, Philip R., and Donald J. Breen. *Ohio's Military Prisons in the Civil War.* Columbus, Ohio, 1964.

FRANK L. BYRNE

JOHNSON, THOMAS (1812–1906), congressman from Kentucky and colonel. Kentuckian Thomas Johnson served only a few days in the Provisional Congress and played at best an insignificant role in the government of the new Southern republic. Born in Montgomery County, Kentucky, Johnson prospered as a farmer and merchant in Mount Sterling, Kentucky, in the antebellum years. His trade in livestock throughout the South enabled him to garner sizable wealth. Johnson's obvious influence in the commonwealth led to his appointment as major general in the militia.

Late in 1861 the Provisional Government of Kentucky appointed Johnson to the Provisional Congress from the Sixth District. He was a member of the Military Affairs Committee during his brief tenure. Johnson wholeheartedly supported the Davis administration's initial steps in establishing a central government. Declining to run for election to the First Congress, Johnson in late 1862 returned to Kentucky and recruited the Second Battalion of Kentucky Mounted Rifles. This unit distinguished itself in October 1863 in raids against Union Gen. William S. Rosecrans's forces in Tennessee and Alabama, and in April 1864 in a skirmish on Puncheon Creek, Magoffin County, Kentucky. Johnson served as colonel until his capture in April 1865.

After Appomattox, Johnson came back to Mount Sterling and reestablished his profitable mercantile operations. In 1876, he was elected to the Kentucky House of Representatives and served from 1878 to 1882 in the Kentucky Senate.

BIBLIOGRAPHY

Quisenberry, A. C. "The Alleged Secession of Kentucky." *Register of the Kentucky State Historical Society* 15 (1917): 15–32.
Wakelyn, Jon L. *Biographical Dictionary of the Confederacy.* Edited by Frank E. Vandiver. Westport, Conn., 1977.
Warner, Ezra J., and W. Buck Yearns. *Biographical Register of the Confederate Congress.* Baton Rouge, La., 1975.

JOHN DAVID SMITH

JOHNSON, WALDO (1817–1885), lieutenant colonel and congressman from Missouri. A Virginia-born lawyer and resident since 1842 of Osceola, Missouri, Johnson served in the First Missouri Mounted Volunteer Regiment in the Mexican War and later, briefly, in the Missouri House of Representatives and as a state circuit judge.

With the coming of the secession crisis in early 1861, Johnson was appointed as one of Missouri's commissioners to the Washington peace conference, which met in February of that year in an unsuccessful attempt to work out a compromise solution between North and South. Returning to Missouri, Johnson was elected the following month to the

U.S. Senate. This came about largely because he was viewed as being more of a Union man, or at least less virulently secessionist, than the previous incumbent senator, James S. Green. Therein, however, the state legislature proved to have been mistaken and it expelled him in January 1862 for his secessionist sympathies—Johnson had enlisted in Missouri's Confederate forces. As lieutenant colonel of the Fourth Missouri Infantry Regiment he saw action at the Battle of Elkhorn Tavern, Arkansas, in March 1862, and was twice wounded. Aside from combat duty, Johnson was also detailed to carry on recruiting activities and was selected in December 1863 by Missouri's Confederate government in exile to fill one of the state's seats in the Confederate Senate in Richmond.

There Johnson, a spokesman for Western interests, supported a 50-percent property tax to fund the war. He was critical of cabinet members Judah P. Benjamin and Christopher G. Memminger, then secretaries of state and treasury, and he supported the effort to shift control of the war from the president and Gen. Braxton Bragg to Gens. Robert E. Lee, P. G. T. Beauregard, and Joseph E. Johnston.

After the war and a brief exile in Canada he returned to Osceola, where he practiced law until his death. Johnson was buried in Kansas City.

BIBLIOGRAPHY

McElroy, John. *The Struggle for Missouri.* Washington, D.C., 1909.
Meyer, Duane G. *The Heritage of Missouri.* St. Louis, 1970.
Snead, Thomas Lowndes. *The Fight for Missouri: From the Election of Lincoln to the Death of Lyon.* New York, 1886.

STEVEN E. WOODWORTH

JOHNSTON, ALBERT SIDNEY (1803–1862),

general. Johnston, a distinguished soldier of three republics, was born February 2, 1803, in Washington, Kentucky, and was educated in private schools and at Transylvania University. He graduated from the United States Military Academy in 1826, standing eighth in his class.

Johnston had an unusually versatile military career. He served in the Black Hawk War as adjutant to the commanding general, as senior general, and, later, as secretary of war of the Republic of Texas, as a staff officer in the Battle of Monterrey in the Mexican War, as paymaster of U.S. troops stationed in the frontier forts of Texas, as colonel of the elite Second Cavalry Regiment, and as the commander of the U.S. force sent to quell the incipient Mormon rebellion in Utah Territory.

Upon the secession of his adopted state, Texas, Johnston resigned his U.S. commission and joined the Confederacy. His former fellow cadet and now close friend, Jefferson Davis, immediately appointed him a full general in the army

ALBERT SIDNEY JOHNSTON.   NATIONAL ARCHIVES

of the Confederacy and placed him in command of the western theater of operations. Heavily outnumbered and indecisive in his early moves, Johnston lost Forts Henry and Donelson in February 1862 to a Federal offensive led by Brig. Gen. Ulysses S. Grant, thereby opening the region to Union penetration along the Tennessee and Cumberland rivers. But Johnston redeemed himself two months later by concentrating his forces at Corinth, an important rail center in northern Mississippi, and surprising Grant in the Battle of Shiloh, April 6 and 7. Johnston was killed the first day of the engagement while his lines were still advancing. He was buried in the Texas State Cemetery in Austin.

BIBLIOGRAPHY

Johnston, William Preston. *The Life of General Albert Sidney Johnston.* New York, 1878.
Roland, Charles P. *Albert Sidney Johnston: Soldier of Three Republics.* Austin, Tex., 1964.
Schaller, Frank. "A Review of the Life and Character of the Late General Albert Sidney Johnston, C.S.A." In *The Spirit of Military Institutions.* Edited by Auguste F. Marmont. Columbia, S.C., 1864.

CHARLES P. ROLAND

JOHNSTON, GEORGE DOHERTY (1832–

1910), brigadier general. Born in Hillsboro, North Carolina,

May 30, 1832, Johnston soon moved with his father to Alabama. He was educated by private tutors and at Howard College and Cumberland University where he studied law. He practiced in Marion, Alabama, and dabbled in local politics, serving as mayor and in the state legislature.

He became a lieutenant in the Fourth Alabama Infantry Regiment in 1861 and was then commissioned major of the Twenty-fifth Alabama. Johnston and his regiment were with the Army of Tennessee through the last years of the war. He was made lieutenant colonel in April 1862 and colonel in June 1863. He served with the Army of Tennessee in all of its major battles, winning special praise for his performance in the Battle of Atlanta (July 22, 1864); on July 26, 1864, he was promoted to brigadier general. He received notice of his promotion on July 28, and three hours later he was seriously wounded at Ezra Church. The wound forced him to use crutches for several months, but he was with his men in the Franklin and Nashville campaign. In early 1865 he briefly commanded a division in the Carolinas campaign.

After the war Johnston resumed his law practice. He served as commandant of cadets at the University of Alabama, as superintendent of the South Carolina Military Academy (The Citadel), on the U.S. Civil Service Commission, and in the Alabama State Senate. He died in Tuscaloosa, Alabama, December 8, 1910, and is buried in Greenwood Cemetery there.

BIBLIOGRAPHY

Jones, Terry L. "George Doherty Johnston." In *The Confederate General*. Edited by William C. Davis. Vol. 3. Harrisburg, Pa., 1991.

Warner, Ezra J. *Generals in Gray: Lives of the Confederate Commanders*. Baton Rouge, La., 1959.

RICHARD M. MCMURRY

JOHNSTON, JOSEPH E. (1807–1891), general.

Johnston was the son of Peter Johnston, a distinguished soldier in the command of "Light-Horse Harry" Lee in the War for Independence. From this association came a long friendship between the two veterans' sons—Joseph E. Johnston and Robert E. Lee.

Joseph Eggleston Johnston was born February 3, 1807. When he was four the family moved from Prince Edward County, Virginia, to the southwestern part of the state, near Abingdon, where Peter Johnston was a circuit judge. Both the new location and the family's kinships gave young Joseph ties to what was to become a powerful, informal network of prominent Confederates called the "Abingdon bloc."

Johnston graduated from the U.S. Military Academy in 1829, thirteenth in a forty-six-man class. His friend Robert

JOSEPH E. JOHNSTON.   NATIONAL ARCHIVES

E. Lee stood second. For most of the rest of his life Johnston would place behind Lee, and there are hints that, despite their friendship, Johnston experienced twinges of jealousy toward his more distinguished classmate.

Except for a few months when he was employed as a civil engineer, Johnston remained in the service until he resigned in 1861 to join the Confederacy. Johnston's story for those thirty-two years was the usual one of a career military officer whose assignments took him from New York to Florida to Mexico. Meanwhile, he steadily made his way up through the grades of the army's hierarchy while acquiring a reputation as a brave, competent officer. Commissioned into the Fourth Artillery as second lieutenant in 1829, Johnston served in the Mexican War and was named lieutenant colonel of the First Cavalry in 1855. Wounded in the wars against the Seminole Indians in Florida and in the Mexican War, he won frequent praise for heroism.

In 1860 Johnston's career took an upward turn when the position of quartermaster general of the army became vacant. Johnston was selected for the coveted post, which carried with it promotion to the staff grade of brigadier general. He was now both a brigadier general (staff grade) and a lieutenant colonel (permanent grade). For once, he had surpassed Lee, who remained a lieutenant colonel. On April 22, 1861, Johnston resigned to go with Virginia into the Confederacy.

When Johnston reached Richmond, he found Robert E. Lee a major general in command of the state army. The governor named Johnston to the same grade. Soon, however, the state decided that it needed but one major general, and Johnston was reduced to brigadier general.

Displeased with his demotion in the state army, Johnston transferred to Confederate service as a brigadier general (then the highest grade in that army). Johnston was sent to command the Southern forces gathering at Harpers Ferry, Virginia. He was to organize and train the troops and defend the town. Almost immediately, however, Johnston concluded that Harpers Ferry could not be held. After a brief squabble with the government, he evacuated the town and fell back to Winchester.

In July Johnston took his army to reinforce the Confederates at Manassas. There, in the first great battle of the war, the South won a victory. As the senior officer present, Johnston commanded the victors, and after the battle, he remained in command of all Confederate troops in the area.

In September Johnston fell into a row with the Southern government about his rank. He and four other officers had been named to the new grade of full general. Confederate law stipulated that former army officers joining the Confederacy would be ranked within each grade by the relative rank they had held in the U.S. Army. Johnston believed he would be ranked by his staff grade of brigadier general and would therefore be the highest-ranking Confederate officer. To his dismay, he found himself ranked fourth, after Samuel Cooper, Albert Sidney Johnston, and Lee.

President Jefferson Davis later justified the placement on the grounds that Johnston was ranked by his permanent grade of lieutenant colonel, not by his staff grade of brigadier general. The reasons for Davis's decision are unknown. Some historians have speculated that Davis and Johnston had long been personal enemies or that their wives had engaged in a dispute of some sort. Others have argued that Davis had supported another candidate for the quartermaster general vacancy in 1860 and used the matter of Confederate rank to strike back at Johnston. It is also possible that Davis simply distrusted Johnston's abilities and wanted to make sure that he would never exercise command over Albert Sidney Johnston or Lee.

Whatever the reason for this action, Davis's decision was unfair to Johnston and probably illegal. Cooper was ranked by his staff grade. (Cooper, however, was in a staff position in both armies; the others were in command of troops in the Southern army.) Fair and legal or not, Davis's decision stood. It was wise because it meant that Johnston would never be in position to hamper Lee. The real problem, of course, was that Confederate law made no provision for the different types of grade that existed in the U.S. Army.

Throughout the winter of 1861–1862 Johnston carried on an increasingly bitter correspondence with Davis and other officials about his rank, the organization and supply of his army, and the general war policy that the Confederacy should follow. As the differences between the general and the president grew more heated, many of Davis's political and military enemies realized that Johnston made a good point man for their attacks on the administration. Increasingly Johnston became identified with the opponents of the president. At the same time Davis began to lose whatever confidence he had in Johnston's ability to handle an army.

On May 31, 1862, at the Battle of Seven Pines, Johnston was seriously wounded. Because he would be incapacitated for some months, Davis on June 1 named Lee to take his place. Lee soon won such a string of victories that there would never be a question of any other officer commanding the main army in Virginia.

Johnston was able to return to duty in November. By then the South had suffered several disasters in the area between the Appalachian Mountains and the Mississippi River then known as "the West." Davis decided to send Johnston to the West as an overall commander for Confederate forces in Tennessee and Mississippi. The president hoped that Johnston would be able to coordinate those two armies and, by transferring troops from one to the other, combine their resources to defeat a Union threat to either.

Unfortunately for the Southerners, the Federals were strong enough to mount simultaneous operations against more than one point, and the Confederates were usually unable to ascertain what their enemy was doing. Johnston lacked faith in Davis's scheme to shift troops around to defeat the enemy, and he was unwilling to assume responsibility for ordering such movements. Instead, Johnston offered the impracticable proposal of shifting troops from west of the Mississippi to help defend Vicksburg.

The result was a disaster for the South. By mid-May one Confederate army was cooped up in Vicksburg, Mississippi, and was slowly being starved into surrender. Davis ordered Johnston to Mississippi to assume personal command of the effort to raise the siege. Johnston was either unable or unwilling to take any meaningful action, and on July 4 the city and its army surrendered.

From the Confederate point of view the Vicksburg campaign was a debacle from start to finish. As soon as it was over, Davis and Johnston fell into an unseemly squabble over who was responsible for the loss of the city, its army, and enormous quantities of invaluable railroad equipment. Johnston, his wife, his staff officers, and his political and military friends exchanged letters among themselves in which they expressed the belief that Davis's hatred for Johnston had become so great that the president would do anything to disgrace him. It is hard to escape the belief that the Johnston coterie was becoming at least mildly paranoid about the government's attitude toward the general. Johnston also made available to Davis's critics, such as Senator Louis T. Wigfall, information about the campaign that they were able to use in their attacks on the president.

For several months after the loss of Vicksburg, Johnston was in what amounted to exile in Mississippi. There Davis doubtless would have been glad for him to remain. In December 1863, however, Davis had to find a new commander for the Army of Tennessee, the Confederates' major military force in the West. After considering several alternatives, he had to name Johnston to the post because there was no better choice. At the end of the year Johnston reached Dalton, Georgia, and assumed his new command.

By May 1864 Johnston had done a creditable job of rebuilding the strength and morale of the Army of Tennessee. The old mistrust of the government remained, however, and he and the Richmond authorities were never able to agree on a plan for the summer's campaign. Davis wanted Johnston to advance and reestablish Confederate control over Tennessee. Johnston thought he was not strong enough for such an offensive move. Johnston also believed that Davis was withholding supplies and reinforcements. He would not tell the government what he intended to do, and he constantly complained about whatever suggestions were made to him.

When the Federals advanced against Johnston at Dalton, he was unable to hold his position and fell back into the heart of Georgia. By mid-July, Johnston had backed his army south to Atlanta. He had lost more than twenty thousand men, given up valuable territory in North Georgia, abandoned the right bank of the Chattahoochee River (thereby exposing the great Confederate industrial complex in central Alabama), demoralized many of his soldiers, and thrown some Southern political figures into a near panic. The government was still in ignorance of whatever plans he may have had to defend Atlanta.

In mid-July, Davis, his patience finally exhausted, removed Johnston from command of the army and replaced him with Gen. John Bell Hood. Johnston, with a small group of loyal officers, retired to Macon, Georgia. For seven months he and his wife traveled about the fast-shrinking Confederacy while his political allies continued their assaults on the Davis administration for its handling of the war in general and its treatment of Johnston in particular.

In February 1865 Davis recalled Johnston to active service—mostly at the request of Lee who had been named general-in-chief of the Confederate armies. Johnston was ordered to assume command of troops in the Carolinas and halt the advance of a Union force that had marched across Georgia and was heading north toward Virginia. The effort was hopeless, and on April 26 in North Carolina, Johnston surrendered his army.

In the years after the war Johnston lived in Virginia, Alabama, and Washington, D.C. He worked in the transportation ("express") business, as a railroad president, and later as a commissioner of railroads. From 1879 to 1881 he served in the U.S. House of Representatives from Virginia. He devoted much of his time and energy to writing. His chief work, *Narrative of Military Operations Directed during the Late War between the States,* was published in 1874. Like almost all Civil War generals' memoirs, it is self-serving and presents a one-sided view of events. Johnston died March 21, 1891. He was buried in Baltimore.

Johnston's reputation has probably changed more drastically than that of any other Confederate general. For decades historians who based their work on postwar memoirs praised his military abilities. Recent writers, using more reliable sources, have revised that opinion, and as a result his reputation has precipitously declined.

BIBLIOGRAPHY

Connelly, Thomas L. *Autumn of Glory: The Army of Tennessee, 1862–1865.* Baton Rouge, La., 1971.

Connelly, Thomas L., and Archer Jones. *The Politics of Command: Factions and Ideas in Confederate Strategy.* Baton Rouge, La., 1973.

Jones, Archer. *Confederate Strategy from Shiloh to Vicksburg.* Baton Rouge, La., 1965.

Lash, Jeffrey N. *Destroyer of the Iron Horse: General Joseph E. Johnston and Confederate Rail Transport, 1861–1865.* Kent, Ohio, 1991.

McMurry, Richard M. "'The Enemy at Richmond': Joseph E. Johnston and the Confederate Government." *Civil War History* 27 (1981): 5–31.

Symonds, Craig L. *Joseph E. Johnston: A Civil War Biography.* New York, 1992.

Woodworth, Steven E. *Jefferson Davis and His Generals: The Failure of Confederate Command in the West.* Lawrence, Kans., 1990.

RICHARD M. McMURRY

JOHNSTON, ROBERT

JOHNSTON, ROBERT (1818–1885), congressman from Virginia. Born in Rockbridge County, Virginia, Johnston followed a career in the law. He began practice in Clarksburg (now in West Virginia) in 1842 after studying under John White Brockenbrough and attending Washington College, both in Lexington. Johnston married and served in the Virginia House of Delegates from 1855 to 1858. He expressed strong secessionist opinions during the crisis of 1860–1861 and became a leader of the State Rights party. Nevertheless, he was not a member of the Virginia convention of 1861. He was elected to the Provisional Congress, however, even though he did not seek the post.

His district was part of West Virginia when it was formed in 1863, but the votes of refugees and soldiers returned Johnston to both the First and the Second Congresses.

In the legislature Johnston's committee assignments included Post Office and Post Roads, Currency, Accounts, States Claims, and Quartermaster's and Commissary Departments. He was not a leading member of the legislature, but in his voting he supported most of the stern measures the Davis administration proposed for prosecuting the war. He thought the war emergency justified suspension of habeas corpus, impressment of slaves, sharp increases in taxation, and deference to the president's wide-ranging authority.

After the war Johnston settled in Harrisonburg, Virginia, where he returned to the practice of law. He also served as a judge from 1881 until his death on November 6, 1885, in Rockingham County.

BIBLIOGRAPHY

Wakelyn, Jon L. *Biographical Dictionary of the Confederacy.* Edited by Frank E. Vandiver. Westport, Conn., 1977.

Warner, Ezra J., and W. Buck Yearns. *Biographical Register of the Confederate Congress.* Baton Rouge, La., 1975.

NELSON D. LANKFORD

JOHNSTON, ROBERT DANIEL (1837–1919),

brigadier general. A significant characteristic of Civil War armies was that they were primarily volunteer forces, and the majority of their officers had little or no prior military education or service. Many such men in the Army of Northern Virginia were adequate at best. Others, such as Robert Daniel Johnston, became highly regarded officers by the war's end.

Johnston was born March 19, 1837, in Lincoln County, North Carolina, was educated at the University of North Carolina, and studied law at the University of Virginia. He entered Confederate service as a captain in the Twenty-third North Carolina Infantry, and was appointed lieutenant colonel at the age of twenty-three in May 1862.

Wounded at Seven Pines soon after his promotion, Johnston returned for the Sharpsburg campaign in September and was praised for his leadership there in the Bloody Lane. Johnston was promoted to colonel after Chancellorsville and commanded his regiment at Gettysburg in July 1863, being severely wounded in the latter battle. Continuing to win recognition from his superiors, he was promoted to brigadier general on September 2, 1863, and commanded a North Carolina brigade until the war's end. After being wounded a third time, at Spotsylvania in May 1864, Johnston distinguished himself in the Shenandoah Valley campaign later that year. He was on detached duty at Roanoke when the war ended.

After 1865 Johnston practiced law in North Carolina and was a banker in Alabama; he was one of the last surviving Confederate generals when he died in Winchester, Virginia, on February 1, 1919.

BIBLIOGRAPHY

Compiled Military Service Records. Robert D. Johnston. Microcopy M331, Roll 142. Record Group 109. National Archives, Washington, D.C.

Hill, D. H., Jr. *North Carolina.* Vol. 4 of *Confederate Military History.* Edited by Clement A. Evans. Atlanta, 1899. Vol. 5 of extended ed. Wilmington, N.C., 1987.

J. TRACY POWER

JOMINI, HENRY (1771–1869), military tactician.

The Baron Antoine Henri Jomini, a premier historian and theorist of the Napoleonic Wars, was considered in Europe and America to be a leading authority on military tactics. His most famous work, *Summary of the Art of War* (1838) was translated from the French by O. F. Winship and E. E. McLean and published in New York City in 1854. It was adopted as a textbook at West Point and studied by many of the future military leaders of the Civil War.

According to Jomini, there was no substitute for the offensive. When forced onto the defensive, a commander must retake the offensive as quickly as possible. "The best of all for an army which awaits the enemy defensively," Jomini wrote, "is to know how to retake the initiative when the moment has arrived for doing so with success." He also argued strongly for bayonet attacks and traditional close-order formations to maintain tactical offensive operations.

Jomini's theories undoubtedly had an influence on military tactics early in the Civil War. Henry W. Halleck's work, *Elements of Military Art and Science,* considered by officers of the time to be a classic, borrowed much of its contents from Jomini. In addition, J. E. B. Stuart adopted many of his successful cavalry tactics from Jomini's writings. But Napoleonic tactics quickly proved disastrous in the face of the massed firepower brought about by the innovations in arms that appeared during the Civil War. As early as 1860 Joseph E. Johnston recommended that the *Summary of the Art of War* be dropped as a textbook at West Point.

Military historians still argue over Jomini's impact on Confederate military strategy. His supporters point to P. G. T. Beauregard as the most famous of Jomini's students in the Southern military and maintain that through Beauregard, Jomini influenced the strategy of Jefferson Davis. After the war, however, Beauregard criticized Jomini's tactics and stated that he had never owned the Frenchman's book.

BIBLIOGRAPHY

Connelly, Thomas L., and Archer Jones. *The Politics of Command: Factions and Ideas in Confederate Strategy*. Baton Rouge, La., 1973.

Jomini, Antoine Henry. *Summary of the Art of War*. Translated by O. F. Winship and E. E. McLean. New York, 1854.

McWhiney, Grady, and Perry D. Jamieson. *Attack and Die: Civil War Military Tactics and the Southern Heritage*. University, Ala., 1982.

KENNY A. FRANKS

JONES, ARNOLD ELZEY. *See* Arnold Elzey.

JONES, CATESBY

JONES, CATESBY (1821–1877), naval officer. Born April 15, 1821, in Fairfield, Virginia, Catesby ap Roger Jones entered the U.S. Navy as a midshipman in 1836. He was promoted to lieutenant in 1849 and remained in that rank until he left the service in 1861. His career in the U.S. Navy was characterized by the normal ship-to-shore rotation. In the 1850s he worked with Lt. John A. Dahlgren in experiments with naval ordnance. This experience would result in his appointment to similar work in the Confederate navy.

Upon the secession of Virginia, Jones resigned his commission and was appointed a captain in the Virginia State Navy. On June 10, 1861, he was commissioned a lieutenant in the Confederate navy and assigned to command naval batteries on Jamestown Island. Jones's experiments with the effect of naval gunfire on sloping iron armor led to his appointment as executive officer of the ironclad CSS *Virginia*. As second in command he participated in the March 8, 1862, engagement in which USS *Cumberland* and *Congress* were destroyed by *Virginia*. When Capt. Franklin Buchanan was wounded, Jones assumed the command and was in charge the following day when the Confederate armorclad fought USS *Monitor*. He resumed the position of executive officer when Buchanan's replacement took command.

After the destruction of *Virginia* in early May 1862, Jones commanded, successively, river batteries at Drewry's Bluff on the James River near Richmond, the wooden gunboat *Chattahoochee* on the Chattahoochee River near Columbus, Georgia, and the naval ordnance works at Charlotte, North Carolina. On May 9, 1863, he was ordered to take charge of the Confederate Naval Iron Works at Selma, Alabama. Under his direction this facility cast more than a hundred large naval guns. Jones commanded the ironworks until they were captured by Union forces on April 2, 1865.

After the war Jones established residence in Selma and formed a partnership with John M. Brooke and Robert D. Minor, fellow Confederate naval officers, to purchase war supplies in the United States for foreign governments. The

CATESBY JONES.   NAVAL HISTORICAL CENTER, WASHINGTON, D.C.

company was never successful despite extensive travel by Jones in the United States and a trip to Peru. On June 20, 1877, Jones died after being shot by a neighbor over a quarrel between their children.

Jones was highly respected by his peers both in the Confederate and the U.S. navies. Adm. David Dixon Porter remarked after the war that he had regretted the loss of only two officers from Union service, Jones and Brooke.

BIBLIOGRAPHY

Mabry, W. S. *Brief Sketch of the Career of Captain Catesby Ap R. Jones*. Selma, Ala., 1912.

Still, William N., Jr. *Iron Afloat: The Story of the Confederate Armorclads*. Columbia, S.C., 1986.

WILLIAM N. STILL, JR.

JONES, DAVID RUMPH "NEIGHBOR"

JONES, DAVID RUMPH "NEIGHBOR" (1825–1863), major general. A South Carolinian, West Point graduate, Mexican War veteran, and husband of

Zachary Taylor's niece, "Neighbor" Jones provided consistent but unspectacular service to the Confederacy from the firing on Fort Sumter until his death in early 1863. As P. G. T. Beauregard's chief of staff in Charleston, Jones is reputed to have pulled down the U.S. flag over Fort Sumter after the fort's surrender.

At First Manassas, Jones commanded a brigade on the Confederate right and therefore saw little important action. But during the eventful summer of 1862, as a division commander in the Army of Northern Virginia, he participated in all the major Virginia actions. After unsuccessful efforts at Savage's Station and Malvern Hill during the Seven Days' Battles, Jones seized Thoroughfare Gap during James Longstreet's march to Second Manassas. On August 30, at Second Manassas, his division participated in taking Chinn Ridge and then led the final, unsuccessful Confederate assaults against Henry Hill, suffering heavy casualties in the process. At Sharpsburg, Jones's division defended the army's right, delaying the Federals at Burnside Bridge for several hours. Later that day, in the face of overwhelming numbers, Jones's men resisted the Union drive toward Sharpsburg long enough for A. P. Hill's division to arrive from Harpers Ferry and drive the Federals back. For this he received the commendation of both Robert E. Lee and Longstreet.

Soon after Sharpsburg, Jones was debilitated by heart disease. This affable, well-liked Carolinian died from the ailment in Richmond on January 15, 1863. He was buried at Hollywood Cemetery.

BIBLIOGRAPHY

Capers, Ellison. *South Carolina.* Vol. 5 of *Confederate Military History.* Edited by Clement A. Evans. Atlanta, 1899. Vol. 6 of extended ed. Wilmington, N.C., 1987.

Freeman, Douglas S. *Lee's Lieutenants: A Study in Command.* 3 vols. New York, 1942–1944. Reprint, New York, 1986.

Warner, Ezra J. *Generals in Gray: Lives of the Confederate Commanders.* Baton Rouge, La., 1959.

JOHN J. HENNESSY

JONES, GEORGE W. (1806–1884), congressman from Tennessee. Described by one of his colleagues, Henry S. Foote, as being "the wisest framer of bills the world ever knew," Jones moved with his family from his native Virginia at an early age to Fayetteville, Tennessee. He worked as a saddler's apprentice before embarking on a political career, which carried him from the Lincoln County courthouse to both houses of the Tennessee legislature (1835–1841) and eventually the U.S. House of Representatives (1843–1859). While in Washington, Jones earned a reputation for favoring economy and simplicity in government, for opposing heavy taxation, and for being a stickler on constitutional matters: all traits he later clearly exhibited in the Confederate Congress.

A Douglas Democrat in 1860, Jones opposed secession until Abraham Lincoln's call for volunteers, when he was, as he put it, "bourn down, along and into the terrible current which was sweeping through the Country." In November 1861 he defeated Lee M. Bentley in the race for Tennessee's Seventh District in the First Confederate Congress. As chairman of the Committee on Rules and Officers of the House, Jones fulfilled his role well. From February 18, 1862, the day he took his seat, until January 23, 1863, when he at his own request was excused from duty on the Rules Committee, Jones often indicated when a colleague's actions were "not in order" or when a particular measure posed a "constitutional question." Moreover, as a member of the House Committee on Ways and Means, Jones sought to eliminate wasteful spending. For example, he opposed the continuance of the Confederate Patent Office, calling it "a stupendous fraud," like its U.S. model; he argued against the publication of the proceedings of the Provisional Congress on the grounds that it was too costly; and he kept close reins on congressional salaries and postage rates and other such expenditures. On the other hand, he introduced in March 1862 a resolution authorizing the secretary of war to send gold to Confederate military personnel while they were in Northern prisons, and he favored providing disability payments to honorably discharged Confederate veterans.

During his two-year term in office, Jones introduced more than five dozen bills and resolutions, making him one of the most active members of the Tennessee delegation. He consistently voted against conscription measures (though he favored ending the practice of hiring substitutes), saw no need for the passage of sequestration laws, and opposed as unconstitutional the declaration of martial law. In addition, he was critical of congressional investigations of the military and the executive branch, warning that if his fellow members did not cease their condemnations of the Davis administration, then "history would record that this was the most inefficient branch of Government existing in this revolution." At one point, having become exasperated with the inaction of Congress, Jones uttered sotto voce: "If the House would adjourn and not meet anymore, it would benefit the country."

But it was during an April 1863 House debate over the motto for the Confederate seal, which featured an equestrian engraving of George Washington, that Jones is best remembered. He objected to Alexander R. Boteler's proposed *Deo duce vincemus* ("God being our leader, we will conquer"), because he claimed that he did not know what it meant. Instead, Jones suggested "Liberty and Independence," explaining that he preferred a motto that all who were fighting could understand when they saw it. His substitute was narrowly defeated, and the motto *Deo vindice* ("God vindicates") was ultimately adopted.

Refusing to be a candidate for reelection, Jones left Richmond in February 1864 for Georgia and eventually Charlotte, North Carolina, where he spent the last ten months of the war "quite retired and rather isolated from the immediate noise and bustle of the times." Pardoned by his longtime friend, President Andrew Johnson, in June 1865, Jones returned to Tennessee but did not hold elected office again, except for serving as a delegate to the state constitutional convention in 1870. Eight years later he delivered an oration at the unveiling of the monument erected to Johnson's memory.

BIBLIOGRAPHY

Amnesty File. George Washington Jones. Microcopy M1003, Roll 49. Record Group 94. National Archives, Washington, D.C.

Journal of the Congress of the Confederate States of America, 1861–1865. 7 vols. Washington, D.C., 1904–1905.

Speer, William S., comp. *Sketches of Prominent Tennesseans.* Nashville, Tenn., 1888.

Warner, Ezra J., and W. Buck Yearns. *Biographical Register of the Confederate Congress.* Baton Rouge, La., 1975.

R. B. ROSENBURG

JONES, HENRY COX

JONES, HENRY COX (1821–1913), congressman from Alabama. Born on January 23, 1821, in Franklin County, Alabama, Jones graduated from La Grange College in 1840 and was admitted to the bar in 1841. Jones was elected probate judge of Franklin County in 1841, a position he held until 1843, when he resigned to take a seat in the Alabama House of Representatives. He was reelected to the House in 1844 and in 1853 was elected to the Alabama Senate. In 1856 he moved to Florence, Alabama, where he continued to practice law. In 1860 he was a presidential elector pledged to Stephen A. Douglas and in 1861 represented Franklin County in the Alabama secession convention. A Unionist, he refused to vote for or to sign the ordinance of secession. Nevertheless, he was elected to the Provisional Congress of the Confederacy and served for one year. He was a member of the Claims, Indian Affairs, Patents, and Pay and Mileage committees. He objected to enlarging the power of the Confederate central government and opposed additional uses of the militia, taxes, loans, and executive powers. During the war he manufactured cottons and woolens and after the war resumed his law practice in Florence. In 1876 he was a presidential elector pledged to Samuel Tilden. Jones died in Florence on June 20, 1913.

BIBLIOGRAPHY

Owen, Thomas McAdory. *History of Alabama and Dictionary of Alabama Biography.* 4 vols. Chicago, 1921.

Wakelyn, Jon L. *Biographical Directory of the Confederacy.* Edited by Frank E. Vandiver. Westport, Conn., 1977.

Warner, Ezra J., and W. Buck Yearns. *Biographical Register of the Confederate Congress.* Baton Rouge, La., 1975.

SARAH WOOLFOLK WIGGINS

JONES, J. B.

JONES, J. B. (1810–1866), writer. Born in Baltimore on March 6, 1810, John Beauchamp Jones grew up in Kentucky and Missouri. He became a successful novelist—his *Wild Western Scenes* (1841) sold 100,000 copies—but he achieved greater recognition as a journalist. In the 1840s Jones settled near Philadelphia where he wrote many novels portraying frontier society and in 1857 established the *Southern Monitor,* a weekly journal that defended Southern rights within the Union.

In *Secession, Coercion and Civil War* (1859) Jones sought to temper the passions of secession, but the Fort Sumter crisis caused him to move to the new Confederate capital at Montgomery. Here he was hired by the War Department as a clerk and began to compose his important diary. "At fifty-one I can hardly follow the pursuit of arms; but I will write and preserve a diary of the revolution. . . . To make my diary full and complete as possible is now my business," he wrote on April 29. He made almost daily entries until April 19, 1865. Early the next year *A Rebel War Clerk's Diary* was published in two volumes—his supreme achievement, the most consulted and quoted primary source for events in wartime Montgomery and Richmond.

Jones's *Diary* presents portraits of Jefferson Davis and other leaders that are among the best contemporary likenesses in Civil War literature. His daily record of activities in the War Office, under five secretaries and numerous bureau chiefs, colonels, and generals, provides much of the inner history of the Confederacy. Also important to social and economic historians are his observations on inflation and the daily prices of necessities; military historians value his faithful reports of weather conditions.

From Jones's pages one can discern the pain and privations of the common people, the self-interest and narrowness of politicians and military men, and the anguish accompanying a failing cause. Using terse, direct language, often colored by anger, stereotypes, and prejudice, Jones is a personal and lively chronicler. He lacks the literary qualities of Mary Boykin Chesnut, however, and the objectivity and deeper perception of Robert Garlick Kean, whose diary, *Inside the Confederate Government,* was published in New York in 1957. Jones's style—tough and combative—masks the fears of a father of a large family eking out survival on a small salary in Richmond's wildly inflationary economy.

With the fall of Richmond, Jones moved back to Philadelphia, where he oversaw the publication of his book. In October 1865 he gave testimony in the Henry Wirz trial in Washington, defending the commandant of Andersonville from charges of willful neglect and starvation of Union prisoners of war (and defending the Confederate administration as well). Soon after, he succumbed to declining health and died in Burlington, New Jersey, on February 4, 1866, while the *Diary* was in press. It enjoyed a large publication and has been reprinted, in whole or part, at least three times. A modern scholarly edition is a major need of Confederate historiography.

BIBLIOGRAPHY

Freeman, Douglas S. *The South to Posterity.* New York, 1939. Reprint of revised edition, Wilmington, N.C., 1983.

Jones, J. B. *A Rebel War Clerk's Diary at the Confederate States Capital.* 2 vols. Philadelphia, 1866. Revised ed. by Earl Schenck Miers. New York, 1958.

JOHN O'BRIEN

JONES, J. R. (1828–1901), lieutenant colonel. Born March 12, 1828, in Harrisonburg, Virginia, John Robert Jones graduated from the Virginia Military Institute in 1848. He taught school in Virginia, Maryland, and Florida until the outbreak of the war.

On January 6, 1861, under orders from the governor of Florida, Jones commanded a company that seized the U.S. arsenal at Apalachicola. In April, Jones returned to Harrisonburg and organized a unit that became Company I of the Thirty-third Regiment, Virginia Infantry. His company was on detached duty in Winchester during First Manassas. Appointed lieutenant colonel on August 21, 1861, Jones participated in Jackson's 1862 Shenandoah Valley campaign and was cited as "distinguished" at Kernstown on March 23. In April, he led a successful expedition to quell a militia insurrection in Rockingham County.

Appointed brigadier general by Thomas J. ("Stonewall") Jackson, June 25, 1862, Jones took command of the Second Brigade in Jackson's division. Although approved by Robert E. Lee and Jefferson Davis, the promotion was never confirmed by the Senate. Wounded on July 1, 1862, at Malvern Hill, Jones retook command of his brigade in September. From September 7 to December 12, 1862, he commanded Jackson's division. He participated in the capture of Harpers Ferry and was wounded again at Sharpsburg. Afterward, he was detailed to gather stragglers in the Valley.

On December 13, 1862, while commanding the Second Brigade at Fredericksburg, Jones reportedly was cashiered for "getting behind a tree." Cowardice charges were preferred in February 1863, but a court-martial board acquitted him. After commanding his brigade at Chancellorsville on May 2, 1863, Jones left the field that night with an "ulcerated leg." Replaced by Brig. Gen. John M. Jones, he resigned from the army. He was captured as a civilian by Union forces at Smithburg, Pennsylvania, July 4, 1863, and remained a prisoner of war until July 24, 1865.

After the war, Jones was a commissioner in chancery of the Rockingham County Circuit Court and a businessman in Harrisonburg. He died there on April 1, 1901.

BIBLIOGRAPHY

Freeman, Douglas S. *Lee's Lieutenants: A Study in Command.* 3 vols. New York, 1942–1944. Reprint, New York, 1986.

Warner, Ezra J. *Generals in Gray: Lives of the Confederate Commanders.* Baton Rouge, La., 1959.

DALE F. HARTER

JONES, JOHN M. (1820–1864), brigadier general. John Marshall Jones was born in Charlottesville, Virginia, July 26, 1820. He graduated from the U.S. Military Academy in the class of 1841. His social style at West Point earned him the nickname "Rum" Jones. During his twenty

JOHN M. JONES.   NATIONAL ARCHIVES

years in the U.S. Army, Jones advanced only to the rank of captain. He did not participate in the Mexican War, but did see extensive active duty in the West.

For the first two years of the Civil War, Jones served in staff roles under John B. Magruder, Richard S. Ewell, and Jubal Early, at low rank for one of his education and experience. Trouble with alcoholism bedeviled "Rum" Jones, but by May 1863 Robert E. Lee, thinking that Jones had conquered his problem, dramatically promoted him all the way from lieutenant colonel of staff to brigadier general of the line. The new brigadier took over a sturdy brigade in Thomas J. ("Stonewall") Jackson's old division and led it competently at Gettysburg until he was wounded in the thigh near enemy lines on Culp's Hill. By October, Jones was back at the head of his brigade during the Bristoe campaign. At Mine Run on November 27, 1863, the general suffered another wound, this time in the head.

Jones's Brigade faltered under a tremendous Federal onslaught at the beginning of the Battle of the Wilderness on May 5, 1864. According to McHenry Howard, Jones was shot from his horse and killed when, "apparently disdaining to fly," he sat "gazing at the approaching enemy." His career was distinguished by triumph over personal difficulty, followed by competent performance in some of the most famous actions of the Army of Northern Virginia.

BIBLIOGRAPHY

Brown, G. Campbell. Manuscript memoir. Tennessee State Archives, Nashville.

Freeman, Douglas S. *Lee's Lieutenants: A Study in Command.* 3 vols. New York, 1942–1944. Reprint, New York, 1986.

Howard, McHenry. *Recollections of a Confederate Soldier and Staff Officer under Johnston, Jackson, and Lee.* Baltimore, 1914. Reprint, Dayton, Ohio, 1975.

Compiled Military Service Records. John Marshall Jones. Microcopy M331, Roll 144. Record Group 109. National Archives, Washington, D.C.

ROBERT K. KRICK

JONES, JOSEPH (1833–1896), physician and medical researcher. A native of Liberty County, Georgia, and son of a Presbyterian minister and planter, Jones attended South Carolina College before graduating from Princeton in 1853. Avidly interested in scientific research, young Jones selected medicine as a profession, graduating from the medical department of the University of Pennsylvania in 1856. Upon graduation he chose a teaching career rather than private practice because it would give him more opportunities to pursue his beloved research. Thus, before the Civil War, Jones briefly taught chemistry at the Savannah Medical College, natural science at the University of Georgia, and chemistry and pharmacy at the Medical College of Georgia.

An ardent secessionist and Southern partisan, Jones served six months as surgeon of the Liberty Independent Troop, a Liberty County militia unit (October 1861–March 1862). In June 1862, he became a contract (civilian) physician at the Confederate general hospital in Augusta, Georgia. While working there, he began to research the diseases prevailing in the Southern armies. In November Jones passed the examination for surgeon in the Confederate army, but instead of being ordered to a regiment or hospital, he was given the unique assignment of continuing and extending his research from the base of his home in Augusta.

During the course of the war, Jones conducted research in South Carolina and in Richmond, Charlottesville, and Lynchburg, Virginia, as well as in Augusta, the coastal area, the Army of Tennessee hospitals in and near Atlanta, and the prison camp at Andersonville in Georgia. At each location he copied the hospital records, assembling statistics on the prevalence of various diseases in the armies, in addition to examining patients and observing changes in their physical condition as a result of the progress of their disease. He attempted to gain additional information by distributing extensive questionnaires to Confederate medical personnel, but few of these physicians were able to respond because their time was so fully occupied in treating casualties.

In addition to investigating malaria, tetanus, and pneumonia, Jones was particularly interested in studying typhoid fever and hospital gangrene. At Andersonville he sought to discover the reasons for the terrible mortality among the prisoners confined there. With the aid of his secretary, Louis Manigault, Jones prepared at least four lengthy reports for Surgeon General Samuel Preston Moore on the results of his research. His report on Andersonville is considered the best description of the abysmal conditions at that prison camp and led to his being called as a witness at the trial of prison commandant Henry Wirz in October 1865.

After the war Jones briefly taught pathology at the Medical College of Nashville, but then spent the rest of his very productive career at the University of Louisiana (Tulane) as professor of chemistry and clinical medicine (1868–1894).

BIBLIOGRAPHY

Breeden, James O. *Joseph Jones, M.D.: Scientist of the Old South.* Lexington, Ky., 1975.

Cunningham, H. H. *Doctors in Gray: The Confederate Medical Service.* Baton Rouge, La., 1958. Reprint, Gloucester, Mass., 1970.

Jones, Joseph. *Medical and Surgical Memoirs.* 3 vols. New Orleans, 1876–1890.

Myers, Robert Manson, ed. *The Children of Pride: A True Story of Georgia and the Civil War.* New Haven, Conn., 1972.

GLENNA R. SCHROEDER-LEIN

JONES, ROBERT MCDONALD (1808–1873), congressional delegate of the Choctaw and Chickasaw nations. A Choctaw of mixed ancestry, Jones was born in Mississippi, educated in Kentucky, and became wealthy in Red River County of the Choctaw Nation, owning general merchandise stores, plantations, and over two hundred slaves. He headed the Choctaw and Chickasaw negotiators who signed a treaty with the Confederacy in 1861. Although winning election as delegate of the two Indian nations to the Confederate Congress in October 1861, he did not take office until January 17, 1863; he served until June 1864.

Jones's first action as a nonvoting member of the Confederate House of Representatives was to introduce a bill compensating one of his own commercial firms for supplies furnished the Choctaw Volunteers. He offered one other bill, which the House adopted, to appropriate funds to print additional copies of the *Report of the Commissioner of Indian Affairs* for the use of Confederate-allied tribes. The bulk of the Choctaw delegate's time in Richmond was spent trying to look after his constituents' wartime needs. Especially irksome were the continual interruptions in the flow of arms and munitions from the Confederacy to Indian Territory where his fellow Indians fought.

Although Jones and the two other delegates representing the Five Civilized Tribes had little practical impact on the course of the Civil War, their presence in the Confederate Congress showed that Indians were able and willing to participate as more than passive wards of white governments.

BIBLIOGRAPHY

Abel, Annie. *The American Indian as Participant in the Civil War.* Cleveland, Ohio, 1919.
Wilson, Terry P. "Delegates of the Five Civilized Tribes to the Confederate Congress." *Chronicles of Oklahoma* 53 (1975): 353–366.

TERRY P. WILSON

JONES, SAMUEL (1819–1887), major general. A product of Virginia landed gentry, Jones was born December 17, 1819, at the Woodfield family estate in Powhatan County. In 1841 he graduated from the U.S. Military Academy. His pre-1861 career included duty at various frontier posts, five years as a member of the West Point faculty, and a three-year assignment as assistant to the judge advocate of the army. Jones had a reputation as a gentleman and professional soldier, always alert and dignified.

On April 27, 1861, he resigned his commission and was immediately appointed major of Confederate artillery. His service as Gen. P. G. T. Beauregard's chief of artillery in the First Manassas campaign brought quick promotion to brigadier general. Jones commanded the Department of Florida until his March 19, 1862, appointment as major general and divisional commander in Tennessee. He saw only limited field service before his reluctant acceptance, in December 1862, of command of the military Department of Southwestern Virginia. His area included the major iron, lead, and salt mines of the Confederacy.

Jones's little army was ineffectual in stopping numerous Federal raids into his department. His civilian and military critics were many and loud, and on February 11, 1864, Gen. Robert E. Lee relieved him from command. Jones then headed military departments in South Carolina, Georgia, and Florida. He surrendered to Union forces May 10, 1865, at Tallahassee.

From 1866 to 1880 Jones engaged in farming near Mattoax, Virginia. He spent his remaining years as a War Department clerk in Washington, D.C. Jones died July 31, 1887, at Bedford Springs, Virginia. He is buried in Richmond's Hollywood Cemetery.

BIBLIOGRAPHY

Burton, E. Milby. *Siege of Charleston, 1861–1865.* Columbia, S.C., 1982.
Hotchkiss, Jed. *Virginia.* Vol. 3 of *Confederate Military History.* Edited by Clement A. Evans. Atlanta, 1899. Vol. 4 of extended ed. Wilmington, N.C., 1987.
Warner, Ezra J. *Generals in Gray: Lives of the Confederate Commanders.* Baton Rouge, La., 1959.

JAMES I. ROBERTSON, JR.

JONES, THOMAS MCKISSICK (1816–1892), congressman from Tennessee. Jones was born December 16, 1816, in Persons County, North Carolina, and moved with his parents to Pulaski, Tennessee, as a small child. After attending local schools, he enrolled at the University of Alabama and, later, the University of Virginia.

Jones studied law in the offices of two attorneys and, after serving as a captain in the Seminole War of 1836, returned to Pulaski where he set up a law practice that continued for more than fifty years. He also served at various times as president of the Nashville and Decatur Railroad, a director of the Pulaski-Columbia-Elkton Turnpike, and a director of two Pulaski banks.

Always interested in politics, Jones served Pulaski as mayor off and on for much of his adult life. Soon after beginning law practice he became a leader in the Democratic party and in 1844 was an elector on the national Democratic ticket. He campaigned widely for James K. Polk, especially liking Polk's stand for territorial expansion. Jones served in the state legislature and was a regular delegate to the state Democratic convention for many years; in 1856 and 1860 he was a delegate to the Democratic National Convention. When his party divided along sectional lines in 1860, he adhered to the Southern Democrats and met with that group at Charleston where he played a leading role in the selection of John C. Breckinridge as the party's nominee.

As was true of the vast majority of middle Tennesseans prior to Abraham Lincoln's inauguration, he opposed secession and urged his fellow Democrats to follow suit. But after Lincoln's determination to employ force against the Confederate states became known, Jones joined with many others in the June 1861 referendum in endorsing secession.

Soon after Tennessee seceded, Jones was elected to the Provisional Congress from the Seventh District and took the initiative in that body to protect soldiers' interests. He urged higher pay and exhorted civilians to make the necessary sacrifices to afford troops the best equipment available. He had three sons—Calvin, Charles, and Thomas—who served in the Confederate army.

As the Federals tightened the noose around Tennessee in 1862 and 1863, Jones apparently became discouraged with Confederate prospects, and he did not seek reelection to the First Congress. But as a member of the Provisional Congress, he attended sessions regularly and introduced several measures. One sought to raise the pay of private soldiers and another to supervise the manufacture of gun powder and small arms in the Confederate states.

When his congressional term expired, Jones returned to his home in Pulaski where he remained until Federal troops invaded the town and took him into custody. He was permitted to appeal to military governor Andrew Johnson, a fellow Democrat he had respected for many years and supported in his gubernatorial bids of 1853 and 1855. Johnson paroled him on the condition that he cease all communication with the Congress and the Southern military leaders. He soon joined the Confederate forces, however—not as a soldier but as a "camp follower"—and remained with the troops until the war's end.

Jones returned to law practice in Pulaski immediately after the war and was elected to the constitutional convention of 1870. There he played an important role in the revision of the basic law. In 1872, he became judge on the criminal court and a few years later on the Court of Arbitration for Middle Tennessee, created to settle land claims. Later he served on several occasions as a special judge of the state supreme court.

Judge Jones was active in the Masonic Order and in the Episcopal church in Pulaski. At the time of his death he owned a farm of nearly a thousand acres and, according to one contemporary account, had "accumulated a very handsome fortune." In 1860 he had held fifty-four slaves and a farm valued at $91,500. He was buried in the Maplewood Cemetery in Pulaski.

BIBLIOGRAPHY

Caldwell, Joshua W. *Sketches of the Bench and Bar of Tennessee.* Knoxville, Tenn., 1898.
Journal of the Congress of the Confederate States of America, 1861–1865. 7 vols. Washington, D.C., 1904–1905.
McBride, Robert, and Dan M. Robison. *Biographical Directory of the Tennessee General Assembly.* Vol. 1. Nashville, Tenn., 1975.
Moore, John T., and A. P. Foster. *Tennessee: the Volunteer States.* Vol. 2. Nashville, Tenn., 1923.
Speer, William S., ed. *Sketches of Prominent Tennesseans, Containing Biographies and Records of Many of the Families Who Have Attained Prominence in Tennessee.* Nashville, Tenn., 1888.
Warner, Ezra J., and W. Buck Yearns. *Biographical Register of the Confederate Congress.* Baton Rouge, La., 1975.

ROBERT E. CORLEW

JONES, WILLIAM EDMONDSON "GRUMBLE"

(1824–1864), brigadier general. Sour-visaged, belligerent, fully deserving of his nickname "Grumble," Jones lived a short and stormy life. He was born May 3, 1824, in southwestern Virginia's Washington County. An 1848 graduate of West Point, he had nine years of duty at frontier posts stretching from Texas to Washington Territory. The death of his bride in an 1852 shipwreck left Jones permanently embittered. In 1857 he resigned from the army and became a semirecluse on his Glade Spring farm.

Virginia's secession led Jones to organize a mounted company that became part of the First Virginia Cavalry. He soon succeeded J. E. B. Stuart as colonel of the regiment and later commanded the equally renowned Seventh Virginia Cavalry. On September 19, 1862, Jones received promotion to brigadier general and command of the Laurel Brigade. Gallant conduct at Brandy Station in June 1863 brought Jones additional fame. His piercing eyes, long beard, high-pitched voice, penchant for profanity, and farmer's attire in battle made him an easily recognizable general.

Long-standing enmity between Jones and Stuart soon reached the explosive stage. In October, Jones was court-martialed from the Army of Northern Virginia and sent to command the isolated Department of Southwest Virginia and East Tennessee. He performed well in the Knoxville campaign and later at the Battle of Cloyds Mountain, Virginia. On June 5, 1864, in a sharp fight at Piedmont with Gen. David Hunter's Federals, Jones was struck in the forehead by a bullet and killed instantly. He is buried in the Glade Spring Presbyterian Church cemetery.

"Grumble" Jones was a hard-fighting and thoroughly dedicated soldier. He won a reputation as "the best outpost officer" in Robert E. Lee's army. Yet a running feud with his superior officer proved to be his downfall.

BIBLIOGRAPHY

Blackford, William W. *War Years with Jeb Stuart.* New York, 1945.
"'Grumble' Jones." *Civil War Times Illustrated* 7 (June 1968): 35–41.
Thomas, Emory M. *Bold Dragoon: The Life of J. E. B. Stuart.* New York, 1986.

JAMES I. ROBERTSON, JR.

JONES COUNTY, MISSISSIPPI. According to legend, in 1864 the pro-Union populace of Jones County, Mississippi, formed a revolutionary government, adopted a declaration of independence, and formally seceded from Mississippi and the Confederate States of America. This new nation called itself the Republic (or Confederacy, or Kingdom) of Jones. When Mississippi and the Confederacy subsequently attempted to enforce their sovereignties in the county, the Republic of Jones organized its own army and navy and declared war on its parent states. The Republic of Jones, so the story goes, maintained its exist ence until the defeat of the Confederacy the following year. For the past century and a quarter, this tale has been retold regularly in the national press and entertainment media.

The facts behind this legend indicate that the epithet "Republic of Jones" did, indeed, originate in events that occurred in 1864 in Jones County, Mississippi, but the history of the matter differs quite sharply from the legendary accounts. By 1864, Jones County, Mississippi, had been known whimsically for more than a generation as "The Free State of Jones" because of its geographical remoteness, its lack of formal government and social amenities, and the independent, uninhibited lifestyle of its pastoral citizens. Like other frontier counties, Jones had little share in the cotton and slave economics and politics of the state, and most of its scattered population opposed secession. Nevertheless, when war came, the three thousand white people of Jones County provided two full companies and parts of six others to Southern armies.

Because of its isolation and sparse population, Jones County during the war became a haven for Confederate army deserters, some of whom banded together to plunder the local citizens and resist capture by Southern troops. In early 1864 Sherman's march to Meridian drove the Confederate army briefly from the state. Thinking that Federal troops had come to southeastern Mississippi to stay, some of the deserters sought to justify their robberies, assaults, evictions, and even killings of local citizens by representing such crimes as political acts. There is little to suggest, however, that the mass of these stragglers were any more ideologically committed to the Union than they were to the Confederacy.

In mid-1864 Confederate efforts to quell deserter free-booting in Jones County inspired the newspaper *Courier*, of Natchez, a town long since under Union occupation, to lampoon the idea of secession by claiming that the rustic pineywoodsmen of the Free State of Jones had seceded from Mississippi just as that state had seceded from the Union. A month later, this burlesque was taken up by the *New Orleans Daily Picayune*. The spoof was then taken literally by elements of the Northern press, which portrayed the military policing in Jones County as Confederate attempts to suppress a civilian political revolt. In time, these different versions of the story merged with Jones County oral tradition to produce the modern legend of the Republic of Jones.

BIBLIOGRAPHY

Leverett, Rudy. *Legend of the Free State of Jones.* Jackson, Miss., 1984.

Montgomery, Goode. "Alleged Secession of Jones County." *Publications of the Mississippi Historical Society* 8 (1904): 13–22.

Natchez Courier, July 12, 1864.

New Orleans Daily Picayune, July 17, 1864.

New York Tribune, August 1, 1864.

RUDY LEVERETT

JORDAN, THOMAS (1819–1895), brigadier general. Born September 30, 1819, at Luray, Virginia, Jordan graduated in 1840 from West Point. One of his roommates at the academy was William Tecumseh Sherman. Jordan saw service in both the Seminole and the Mexican wars. He was captain and assistant quartermaster upon his May 21, 1861, resignation from the army.

Throughout the Civil War, Jordan held staff assignments. As adjutant general of Gen. P. G. T. Beauregard's Confederate army at Manassas, Jordan established the spy apparatus in Washington whereby Rose O'Neal Greenhow

THOMAS JORDAN. LIBRARY OF CONGRESS

kept Beauregard informed of Federal movements. Jordan got his brigadier's promotion effective April 16, 1862, following duty with Gen. Albert Sidney Johnston at Shiloh. Staff service with Gen. Joseph E. Johnston in the West preceded Jordan's return to Beauregard during the siege of Charleston. Thereafter, stated a fellow officer, Jordan became "the all-powerful adjutant general" to the French Creole.

No one was more aware of this than Jordan. He came to regard himself as Beauregard's alter ego. Such an attitude did not endear him to associates. Mary Boykin Chesnut referred to him in her diary as "querulous, faultfinding"; a South Carolina newspaperman termed Jordan "the obnoxious colonel."

His postwar years were stormy. Late in 1865, in a defense of Beauregard, Jordan wrote a blistering article in which he criticized the military policies of President Jefferson Davis. An embarrassed Beauregard repudiated the attack. Jordan the following year became editor of the *Memphis Appeal* and then coauthored a biography of Gen. Nathan Bedford Forrest. Beginning in 1869 Jordan supported an insurrection in Cuba. He ultimately became commander of the revolutionaries, with a $100,000 reward offered by Spain for his capture. Jordan returned to America and edited a financial magazine in New York until his November 27, 1895, death. He was buried in Mount Hope Cemetery near Hastings-on-Hudson.

BIBLIOGRAPHY

Hotchkiss, Jed. *Virginia.* Vol. 3 of *Confederate Military History.* Edited by Clement A. Evans. Atlanta, 1899. Vol. 4 of extended ed. Wilmington, N.C., 1987.

Warner, Ezra J. *Generals in Gray: Lives of the Confederate Commanders.* Baton Rouge, La., 1959.

Williams, T. Harry. *Beauregard: Napoleon in Gray.* Baton Rouge, La., 1954.

JAMES I. ROBERTSON, JR.

JUDICIARY. The Confederacy's judicial system was a subject of controversy from the start, and Congress never established in full the system called for by the new nation's constitutions. In a departure from the Federal system, circuit courts were never created. Subsequently, bitter divisions over principle and personalities prevented organization of both a supreme court and a court of claims, which had been planned. The court of claims would have heard lawsuits against the Confederate government in the same way that the U.S. Court of Claims—established in 1855—handled suits against the U.S. government. Nevertheless, a judicial system resting on state courts and Confederate district courts functioned without paralyzing confusion or variances in rulings. State courts, following precedents established in the U.S. system, customarily upheld the powers of the central government.

The judicial clauses of the Provisional Constitution sought to continue cases interrupted by secession by extending judicial powers to all cases in law and equity arising under the laws of the United States. (Most Southern states had both law courts and courts of equity; the latter, following English practice, supplemented law courts by applying general principles of justice in circumstances not covered by the law.) But other features, beyond this practical provision, soon occasioned controversy. The Provisional Constitution called for a single judicial district in each state, which meant that the number of district courts that had existed under the United States was reduced by more than half. This undesirable situation produced the only amendment made to either Confederate constitution, when in May 1861 Congress received the authority to define districts as it deemed appropriate.

The Provisional Constitution also called for a supreme court, and the Judiciary Act of March 16, 1861, envisioned that this high court would exercise appellate jurisdiction over state courts—a disturbing idea to many. The supreme court was to consist of all the district court judges assembled together. Experience in the states had shown that this was not a satisfactory procedure, and observers pointed out that western judges would have difficulty traveling to Richmond in a timely manner. Consequently, on July 31, 1861, Congress suspended the supreme court until it could be organized under the Permanent Constitution.

Battles over the role of the judiciary grew more heated as the Provisional Congress debated a permanent Constitution. To radical state rights thinkers in the Congress, the court system had been one of the chief engines of centralization and usurpation under the United States. One senator declared that if John Marshall's abilities had not made the U.S. Supreme Court so powerful, the Union would still be in existence. Questions of state versus Confederate authority presented themselves in almost every clause of the section on the judiciary, and changes adopted for the Permanent Constitution foreshadowed subsequent controversy.

First, state rights radicals, in March 1861, succeeded in eliminating the jurisdiction of Confederate courts over disputes between citizens of different states. Failing in several other limitations of central authority, they attacked the most important point: appellate jurisdiction for the Supreme Court over decisions rendered in state courts. On this point the radicals nearly prevailed, but a divided delegation from Florida denied them a majority, and thus the Permanent Constitution called for a supreme court that was not explicitly restricted and crippled as the state rights men wished. Battles over the nature of the court, however, would continue in the First Congress.

Another change made to Article III of the Provisional Constitution eliminated language giving the Confederate judiciary power over all cases of law and equity. This deletion respected state rights, since Louisiana and Texas operated under the Roman legal tradition, which lacked separate courts of equity. The distinction between law and equity, however, remained for most of the states, and Congress could have given its district courts power over cases of law and equity there. Instead it eventually prevented them from entering cases of equity wherever "plain, adequate remedy may be had at laws."

The Permanent Constitution called for a court of claims, but Congress never established one. In the absence of that court the executive departments, the Board of Sequestration Commissioners, and the district courts handled the relevant work. Provision was made for a court of admiralty to sit in Key West, but since the Confederacy never controlled that city, the admiralty court never became a reality.

In accordance with the Permanent Constitution, President Jefferson Davis asked the First Congress on February 25, 1862, to establish a supreme court. Although Congress considered the matter in 1862 and 1863, it failed to act. Soon after Davis's request, bills were introduced calling for a supreme court consisting of one chief justice and three associate justices. Senator Benjamin H. Hill of Georgia argued that a government without a supreme court would be "a lame and limping affair," but both houses let the matter drop without a vote in 1862. The next year Hill proposed a similar bill, and the conflicts that had stalled consideration came out into the open.

Supporters of a supreme court argued that the nation needed clarity and consistency in its laws and sought to allay concerns that there would be a usurpation of state power within the Confederacy. On that point, however, many legislators—led by men such as Clement C. Clay, William Lowndes Yancey, Louis T. Wigfall, and Robert W. Barnwell—were extremely sensitive. The key question was whether a supreme court would be free to enforce Confederate law as the supreme law of the land. Without appellate jurisdiction over state courts, a supreme court was superfluous, yet appellate jurisdiction seemed likely to Clay to "favor the consolidation of the government." Yancey warned that it would "chain" the states to central authority. According to historian W. Buck Yearns, all but four senators wanted a supreme court, but only six of them were willing to grant the appellate jurisdiction that would make it meaningful.

Politics and personalities also played a role in the battle over a supreme court. With elections approaching in 1863, some congressmen were reluctant to go on record as giving the central government any additional power. Other congressmen thought they knew who would be appointed to the court if it were established, and their opposition to certain individuals became opposition to the court. Tennessee's representative, Henry S. Foote, asserted that he would "never consent to the establishment of a supreme court of the Confederate States so long as Judah P. Benjamin shall continue to pollute the ears of majesty Davis with his insidious counsels." Others feared that Assistant Secretary of War John A. Campbell, a former justice of the U.S. Supreme Court and a very able lawyer, would become chief justice and promote central power in the Confederacy just as John Marshall had done in the United States. In the end, the Senate passed a bill for a watered-down supreme court, but the House let the matter drop, and the Confederacy had to proceed without the highest court called for by its Constitution.

Confederate district courts were organized and judges appointed. Under the Judiciary Act they were instructed to follow state laws and state court practices as well as enforce Confederate laws. But they were often busy with traditional civil and criminal matters and especially with habeas corpus cases involving soldiers seeking to avoid military service. Because the Confederate judicial system was so weak and truncated, it was the state courts that proved to be most influential.

In a striking irony, the Davis administration turned to and relied upon state courts to uphold the powers of the central government. No issue presented the question of central versus state power more sharply or elicited more angry threats from governors than conscription. On this question President Davis and several state governors thoroughly debated the powers of the Confederacy and brought strongly opposed viewpoints into the open. In the absence of a supreme court, Davis took the contested questions into state courts, where Confederate authority was affirmed.

In September 1862, Governor Joseph E. Brown of Georgia thundered against the second conscription act, charging that it struck down Georgia's "sovereignty at a single blow." Brown even declared that "no act of the government of the United States prior to the secession of Georgia" had been so injurious to constitutional liberty, and he obtained resolutions from his legislature to support him. In similar fashion South Carolina's governor and executive council insisted that any man exempted by state law from the militia was also exempt from conscription and threatened to issue a "countervailing order" against any Confederate conscription officer who tried to enroll such individuals.

In response Jefferson Davis was unbending on principle and conciliatory on procedure. He defended the constitutionality of the conscription law at length to Governor Brown, and he bluntly wrote South Carolina's leaders that "if a State may free her citizens at her own discretion from the burden of military duty, she may do the same in regard to the burden of taxation, or any other lawful duty, payment or service." That would deny the Confederacy the right "to enforce the exercise of any delegated power and would render a Confederacy an impracticable form of Government." Yet Davis also promised the Palmetto State's leaders that he would release any soldier whose exemption was upheld by South Carolina courts, and he assured Senator Benjamin Hill that he relied "on the decision of the Supreme Court of Georgia to remove the difficulties."

In these two states, as well as in Virginia, Alabama, Texas, Florida, and Mississippi, President Davis won his tests of the constitutionality of conscription. In Georgia the decision of the state supreme court was unanimous and was greeted by spectators with an outburst of applause that forced the chief justice to call for order. The decision of the Texas Supreme Court declared that the "power to raise and support armies is an express constitutional grant to the Congress of the Confederate States, and there is no limitation as to the mode or manner of exercising it. . . . When Congress calls for the military service of the citizen . . . the right of the State government must cease or yield to the paramount demand of Congress." Thus state courts upheld the supremacy of Confederate law on a vital question and continued to do so. Although individual judges, such as Richmond Pearson of North Carolina, sometimes caused much concern, the South's judicial system proved to be "fragmented in structure but centralized in substance," in the words of historian Emory Thomas.

There were undoubtedly several reasons for this surprising outcome. The facts that the administration's measures were necessary and that opponents offered no alternatives may have had some influence. Perhaps more salient was the fact that the permanent Constitution authorized Congress to "make all laws which shall be necessary and proper for carrying into execution" the powers granted to the national legislature. The power to make war and the power to raise and support armies were among those grants of authority. Even in a confederation whose members were historically jealous of state prerogatives and state sovereignty, the logic of having a central government to wage war against external enemies remained clear.

In addition, the judges who staffed the courts of the Southern states had learned their law in the judicial system of the United States. They, as well as the attorneys general of the Confederate States, referred to past decisions in U.S. history for guidance and often cited decisions of U.S. courts as precedents. Although Southern jurists may have believed that the Federal government had usurped state authority, they were not unfamiliar with the idea of a central government supreme in its defined sphere. The crisis of war surely called out for such a government in the South. It was

fortunate for the Confederacy that the absence of a supreme court did not greatly multiply the problems under which it already labored.

[See also Conscription; Crime and Punishment; Habeas Corpus; State Rights.]

BIBLIOGRAPHY

Coulter, E. Merton. *The Confederate States of America, 1861–1865.* A History of the South, vol. 7. Baton Rouge, La., 1950.
Escott, Paul D. *After Secession: Jefferson Davis and the Failure of Confederate Nationalism.* Baton Rouge, La., 1978.
Moore, Albert Burton. *Conscription and Conflict in the Confederacy.* New York, 1924.
Robinson, William M., Jr. *Justice in Grey.* Cambridge, Mass., 1941.
Thomas, Emory M. *The Confederate Nation, 1861–1865.* New York, 1979.
Yearns, Wilfred B. *The Confederate Congress.* Athens, Ga., 1960.

PAUL D. ESCOTT

JULIO, E. B. D. (1843–1879), artist. Probably the most popular work of art made of Robert E. Lee in his lifetime was the large folio copper engraving *The Last Meeting of Lee and Jackson* by New Orleans artist E. B. D. Julio. The print (engraved by Frederick W. Halpin in New York in 1872) did not make its appearance until 1873, three years after Lee's death, but it was based upon a painting by Julio that had won Lee's approbation. It subsequently became a familiar symbol of the Lost Cause, proudly displayed in Southern homes in the difficult post–Civil War years.

Its creator was a landscape painter born on the island of St. Helena. He studied in Paris before immigrating to America in 1860, and then in Boston before moving on to St. Louis in 1864 because of his strong Southern sympathies. By 1870 he had a studio in New Orleans. In these years Julio painted landscapes but portraiture soon caught his attention. Often these were oil paintings over large-scale photographs. This blend of photography and painting became the means for the making of his best-known work, the double portrait of Lee and Jackson completed in 1869.

Julio depicted in dramatic form the meeting of the two Confederates on the eve of the Battle of Chancellorsville. Working from accounts by veterans of the Army of Northern Virginia, he created an accurate depiction of the scene: the two generals seated on their horses, Traveler and Little Sorrel, with attending staff officers, during the early morning of May 2, 1863. For the faces of his subjects, he chose an 1866 Brady photograph of Lee, a civilian likeness to which he added the necessary change of uniform and black felt hat. For Jackson, he used an 1863 profile portrait by Richmond photographer D. T. Cowell. Similarly, Julio drew from wartime photographs for the staff officers seen in the background: Cols. Walter Taylor and Charles Marshall, aides to Lee, and Alexander S. Pendleton, aide to Jackson.

The finished painting, almost nine by seven feet, was a striking image, one that conveyed much of the personal appeal and strengths of the two generals. In 1873 it appeared in its engraved medium and was soon copied in pirated lithographs and photographs, and widely used as an illustration in books and magazines. The painting was initially offered as a gift to Lee, who declined it, feeling that the young artist needed the sale of such an important picture. It was eventually acquired by a Confederate veteran in New Orleans, where it remained for several generations.

Julio had little luck with his subsequent career. He planned to paint other Confederate subjects, indeed to become "the historical painter of the South." He was in correspondence with a number of ex-Confederate leaders, including Jefferson Davis and members of the Lee family, to this end. But poor health interfered. In 1874 he studied again in Paris, and the following year journeyed to Kingston, Georgia, in search of better health and climate. He died there at age thirty-six.

BIBLIOGRAPHY

Bundy, David S., comp. *Painting in the South: 1564–1980.* Richmond, Va., 1983.

Neely, Mark E., et al. *The Confederate Image: Prints of the Lost Cause.* Chapel Hill, N.C., 1987.

Pennington, Estill Curtis. *The Last Meeting's Lost Cause.* Spartanburg, S.C., 1988.

JOHN O'BRIEN

JUNETEENTH. June 19 (or "Juneteenth") is observed by African Americans in Texas to commemorate the official emancipation of slaves in the Lone Star State following the end of the Civil War.

Although Gen. Robert E. Lee capitulated to Gen. Ulysses S. Grant at Appomattox Courthouse on April 9, 1865, the Trans-Mississippi Department did not surrender until June 2, and a shortage of transport vessels delayed for over two weeks the arrival of Union forces in Texas. On June 19, 1865, Gen. Gordon Granger landed in Galveston and proclaimed the freedom of the state's slaves. Subsequently, African Americans in Texas have celebrated June 19 annually as their true emancipation day.

During the late nineteenth century, the typical Juneteenth celebration was a day-long event commencing with a parade complete with brass bands and representatives of the leading African American churches, fraternal orders, and social clubs. A barbecue, speeches, sporting events, and dancing (sometimes concluding with an evening ball) would follow.

Although the popularity of the celebration diminished after World War II, it never completely died out. Employers complained that many of their African American employees used Juneteenth as an excuse to take the day off, and some civil rights activists preferred that their constituents pay more attention to contemporary efforts to gain full equality. The growing interest in African American history during the late 1960s and early 1970s fueled public recognition for Juneteenth commemorations. In 1972, the Texas legislature passed a resolution proclaiming June 19 to be a "holiday of significance to all Texans and, particularly, to the blacks of Texas." As such, this event fosters community spirit among blacks and also serves as a source for racial interaction in communities throughout the state.

BIBLIOGRAPHY

Barr, Alwyn. *Black Texans: A History of the Negroes in Texas, 1528–1971.* Austin, Tex., 1973.

Rice, Lawrence D. *The Negro in Texas, 1874–1900.* Baton Rouge, La., 1971.

Watriss, Wendy. "Celebrate Freedom: Juneteenth." *Southern Exposure* 5 (1977): 80–87.

JAMES M. SORELLE

K

KANSAS-NEBRASKA ACT. In 1854, Congress passed the Kansas-Nebraska Act, repealing part of the 1820 Missouri Compromise. That previously sacrosanct agreement had divided Federal territories acquired in the Louisiana Purchase (1803) at the 36°30' geographic line, with slavery permitted southward (including south of the slave state of Missouri) but prohibited northward (including west and north of Missouri) whenever Congress authorized settlement of these areas. In 1824, Illinois, to Missouri's east and outside the Louisiana Purchase area, banned slavery after a historic struggle. In 1846, Iowa, carved out of Louisiana Purchase territory to Missouri's north, extended the 36°30' ban from the territorial to the statehood stage by entering the Union as a free-labor state. If Congress had authorized settlers to enter the Louisiana Purchase territory to Missouri's west without repealing the 36°30' proscription of slavery, Missouri, with only 10 percent of its population enslaved, would have been guaranteed a third nonslaveholding neighbor.

In 1854, Missouri's very powerful Senator David R. Atchison warned several equally powerful Southern Democrats, living with him in a Washington, D.C., boarding-house, that slavery in Missouri could not then endure. Its neighbors would both inspire Missouri slaves to flee and stimulate Missouri's 88 percent majority of nonslave-holders to rout the slaveholders. Congress, declared Atchison, must instead repeal the 36°30' ban when opening the area for settlement. Then, he promised, Missouri slave-holders would seize their western hinterlands and consolidate their regime.

The final form of the Kansas-Nebraska Act, drawn to Atchison's specifications, repealed the Missouri Compromise ban on slavery in Kansas Territory, located west of Missouri, and in Nebraska Territory, located north of Kansas Territory. The majority of settlers in each, decreed

Congress, would decide slavery's fate. An area previously reserved for one section was here turned into a prize for the winner of an endurance race, involving which section would send more settlers to the two territories.

Most Northerners loathed having to compete for an area previously declared theirs. Congress nevertheless passed the minority section's law, for first Atchison's boarding-house mates, then almost all Southern Democrats, and then most Southern Whigs supported the Missourian—and because Northern Democrats could not then defy Southern Democrats. Particularly, Illinois Senator Stephen A. Douglas, the Northern Democrats' congressional leader, wished to open Kansas and Nebraska Territories to settlers, for he wanted whites and railroads to develop the West. He also hoped to win the presidential nomination of a revitalized Democratic party. These objectives required Southern Democrats' support, and the price of their support was legislation that allowed settlers rather than congressmen to determine a locality's institutions—precisely Douglas's popular sovereignty principle. So after Southern Democrats insisted, Douglas made repeal of the Missouri Compromise his cause, as did President Franklin Pierce, another Northern Democrat.

The ensuing law helped inspire the rise of Douglas's Illinois rival, Abraham Lincoln, and more broadly, the rise of the Democratic party's new rival, the Republican party. The Kansas-Nebraska Act also provoked armed combat in what became known as Bleeding Kansas. Although pro-slavery Missourians reached that pre–Civil War battle-ground first, more antislavery Northerners ultimately arrived. Yet in 1857 and 1858 Southerners demanded that Douglas support the admission of Kansas into the Union under the Kansas proslavery minority's proposed Lecomp-ton constitution, which protected slavery. When Douglas balked at this defiance of what the majority of Kansans wanted, Southerners blamed him for the congressional decision that rejected the Lecompton constitution. After Douglas won the Democratic party's presidential nomination in 1860, most Southern Democrats seceded from the party. With the Democrats split, the Republican Lincoln won the presidency, and a Southern Confederacy beckoned.

[*See also* Bleeding Kansas.]

BIBLIOGRAPHY

Freehling, William W. *Secessionists at Bay, 1776–1854*. Vol. 1 of *The Road to Disunion*. New York, 1990.

Johannsen, Robert W. *Stephen A. Douglas*. New York, 1973.

Nichols, Roy F. "The Kansas-Nebraska Act: A Century of Historiography." *Mississippi Valley Historical Review* 43 (1956): 187–212.

Rawley, James A. *Race and Politics: "Bleeding Kansas" and the Coming of the Civil War*. Philadelphia and New York, 1969.

Roy, P. Orman. *The Repeal of the Missouri Compromise*. Cleveland, 1909.

WILLIAM W. FREEHLING

KEEBLE, EDWIN A. (1807–1868), congressman-from Tennessee.

Long a Democratic wheelhorse in Murfreesboro, Tennessee, where he was mayor for nearly two decades prior to the outbreak of hostilities, Keeble was elected without opposition in August 1863 to represent Tennessee's Sixth District in the Second Congress. A planter of substantial means and an active secessionist, Keeble spent the first two years of the war in the Tennessee (Confederate) House, serving as Speaker. Finally taking his seat in Richmond on May 2, 1864, he was appointed to the Judiciary Committee and generally was a Davis supporter throughout his term, which ended on March 18, 1865.

During his brief tenure Keeble spoke out on or introduced only three bills or resolutions: one, during his first full month in office, in which he endorsed a congressional investigation into frauds suspected to have been committed in the Commissary and Quartermaster departments in Richmond; a second, in January 1865, amendatory of a bill authorizing the reorganization and consolidation of the Confederate army; and a third, on the day before final adjournment, in which he proposed pardoning all deserters and other soldiers who were absent without official leave and allowing them to return to their former commands unmolested.

After the war Keeble returned to Murfreesboro, where on July 12, 1865, he applied for executive amnesty from President Andrew Johnson, with whom he had long been acquainted. He was pardoned two months later.

BIBLIOGRAPHY

Amnesty File. Edwin A. Keeble. Microcopy M1003, Roll 50. Record Group 94. National Archives, Washington, D.C.

History of Rutherford County, Tennessee. Chicago, 1886–1887.

Journal of the Congress of the Confederate States of America, 1861–1865. 7 vols. Washington, D.C., 1904–1905.

Warner, Ezra J., and W. Buck Yearns. *Biographical Register of the Confederate Congress*. Baton Rouge, La., 1975.

R. B. ROSENBURG

KEITT, LAWRENCE (1824–1864), congressman from South Carolina and colonel.

Keitt, one of South Carolina's most outspoken advocates of secession, was elected to the U.S. House of Representatives in 1852. While in Congress, he twice resigned his seat. In 1856, he accompanied fellow South Carolinian Preston Brooks to the U.S. Senate chamber where Brooks beat Senator Charles Sumner senseless. During the fray, Keitt used his own cane to keep away others who tried to come to Sumner's defense. A special House committee recommended expelling Brooks and censuring Keitt. When Northern congressmen couldn't muster the votes to expel Brooks, they turned their wrath on Keitt. He was censured and promptly resigned his seat. In a special election, the voters of his district turned out in record numbers and voted overwhelmingly to return him to Congress.

By the summer of 1860, with Abraham Lincoln's election a certainty, Keitt was in the forefront of those calling for South Carolina's secession. Like Robert Barnwell Rhett, Sr., he was strongly radical on the question and had little

LAWRENCE KEITT.   *HARPER'S PICTORIAL HISTORY OF THE GREAT REBELLION*

patience for cooperationists and none for Unionists. Some have interpreted his behavior as a reaction to the murder of his ill brother by slaves in Florida. His speeches and correspondence do contain numerous references to slave insubordination, plots, and conspiracies.

Keitt was in Columbia when news of Lincoln's election came. He was a popular figure in the state capital and was serenaded by the excited crowds. On at least one occasion, in response to the clamor, he addressed a throng gathered outside his hotel. Elected a delegate to South Carolina's secession convention, he resigned his seat in Congress the day the convention met in Columbia.

In the convention, he remarked that he had "been engaged in this movement" since the day he first embarked on a political career. And when the ordinance of secession was adopted, he said that he was pleased that the convention had "carried the body of this Union to its last resting place, and now we drop the flag over its grave." When the convention was preparing its "Declaration of the Immediate Causes which Induce and Justify the Secession of South Carolina," Keitt was among those who refused to shy away from the question of slavery as a primary cause. "It is," he said, "the great central point from which we are now proceeding." He was defeated in a bid to be one of the commissioners to confer with the government in Washington over the status of Federal property in South Carolina, but he was elected to be one of the state's eight delegates to the Montgomery convention.

Keitt, like Rhett, found in Montgomery that his reputation had preceded him. For most of his political career he had played a negative role. After years of criticizing the existing central government, he found it difficult to participate in creating a new one for the Confederacy and seldom spoke. According to Alexander H. Stephens, Keitt said his wife had advised him "to keep his mouth shut and his hair brushed." Whether because of his reputation as an obstructionist or his wife's admonition, he played only a modest role in the convention.

Keitt was named to a five-person committee to draft the rules governing the convention. Other than that, his contributions centered on efforts to amend the proposed constitution. He led the South Carolina delegation's attempts to eliminate the three-fifths clause for taxes and representation. South Carolina was willing to pay more taxes (it could well afford to) in return for a larger congressional delegation. Initially, the amendment passed, but later the convention reversed itself and the three-fifths clause remained. He also supported an amendment giving Congress the authority to reopen the slave trade, a measure that was defeated.

In the maneuvering for the presidential election, Keitt and James Chesnut torpedoed Rhett's candidacy. Keitt and W. W. Boyce strongly favored Howell Cobb of Georgia and worked for his election. With persuasion, the South Carolina delegation went for Jefferson Davis, but Boyce and Keitt were openly reluctant. On the evening of the election, a crowd gathered at the Exchange Hotel to serenade Vice President Stephens. He spoke to the jubilant crowd, and then Keitt was called upon to make some remarks. As a radical secessionist he assured the assemblage that the new government was in good hands with Davis and Stephens. Above all else, he noted, the Union was dead!

Back in South Carolina's convention, Keitt argued against ratification of the Confederate Constitution. He was part of a very small minority, however, and when the vote was taken, both he and Rhett were recorded as voting yes.

Upon his return to Montgomery for the second session of the Provisional Congress, Keitt resumed his role as government critic. Later, en route to Richmond with the Chesnuts, he pronounced "Jeff Davis a failure—and his cabinet a farce." Needless to say, it did not take long for these Davis loyalists to spread the word. By July, Richmond gossips were already talking about the "coalition against Davis." Keitt and Boyce were rumored to be among the leaders "of the party forming against Mr. Davis."

Lawrence Keitt was an unhappy man. As one of the earliest and most ardent secessionists, he had expected to become a power broker in the new government. His reputation as something of a Hotspur and his impolitic criticism of Davis doomed him to a minor role at best. Realizing the futility of his situation and dreaming of military glory, the congressman refused to stand for election to the First Congress.

Back home, he raised a regiment of eight hundred men, the Twentieth South Carolina Volunteers. He was elected colonel, and from mid-January to March 1862, he organized and trained the unit. Keitt was excited about being in uniform and wrote glowing letters to his wife, Sue. In June 1862, when John C. Pemberton reorganized the Department of South Carolina, Georgia, and Florida, Keitt was given command of the defenses of Sullivan's Island in Charleston.

Four months later, Davis replaced Pemberton with P. G. T. Beauregard. The new commander enhanced Keitt's command to include the area between the Cooper and South Santee rivers. It was a difficult area to defend. The coast was riven with innumerable inlets, creeks, and tidal marshes. Most of the white population had abandoned the area. Keitt wanted to divide his command to defend several potential invasion sites, but Beauregard ordered him to keep his forces concentrated in the Charleston area. In May and June 1863, the Twentieth South Carolina was chasing Union raiding parties south of the port city.

On July 18, Union troops attacked Fort Wagner on Morris Island. Following the failure of the Fifty-fourth Massachusetts to take the Confederate position, a six-week siege commenced. On August 1, Fort Wagner was added to Keitt's command. He visited the island on several occasions to view the ever more successful Union attempts to breach the works. On September 5, he sent a message to Beauregard from Fort Wagner that the fortifications were no longer tenable. Beauregard told him to hold. The situation was desperate. Union sappers (specialists in field fortifications) were literally at what was left of the walls. Constant shelling kept the defenders in their bombproofs. When they ventured out to try to repair the parapets or get some fresh air, they usually became casualties. On September 6, Keitt wrote, "The retention of the post after to-night involves the sacrifice of the garrison." He added that if he could not withdraw his forces, he intended to assault the enemy at first light the next day. Late in the afternoon, Beauregard agreed to the abandoning of Wagner.

As soon as darkness fell, Keitt began evacuating his men. He remained with the rear guard and was among the last Confederates to leave Morris Island early on the morning of September 7. The withdrawal was done so stealthily that as close as the Union forces were, they did not realize it had taken place. There were only a few glitches. The powder magazines failed to blow up because of faulty fuses, and two barges of men were captured. Nevertheless, it was a successful operation and more than one thousand men were saved for further Confederate service. Beauregard commended him for his actions. With Sullivan's Island now within reach of Federal guns, the Twentieth South Carolina was moved to Mount Pleasant on the mainland opposite the city.

In the fall of 1863, Keitt, who had long dreamed of becoming a general officer, decided to take matters into his own hands. He obtained leave and journeyed to Richmond to press his case in person. He was on a quixotic quest. He had never tempered his early criticism of Davis and continually expressed such sentiments as "to be a patriot, you must hate Davis," or, "His [Davis's] imbecility has been as mischievous as treachery." Such comments circulated in government circles and further damaged what was already a lost cause. Nor did Keitt's champions—Major General Pemberton and Congressmen Boyce and Louis T. Wigfall—help matters. All were known Davis critics. In addition, the superintendent of conscription reported that the number one violator of the Conscription Act of 1862 was Col. Lawrence M. Keitt. Keitt accepted volunteers in excess of his unit's authorized strength. This was a clear violation of the law that was designed to raise as many men as possible for front-line units. The South Carolinian tap-danced on this issue and maintained that he had done nothing illegal.

In his meeting with Davis and War Department officials, Keitt agreed to raise a second regiment (this one to be cavalry) in the hopes that this would bring him a star. Back home he found recruiting far more difficult in late 1863 than it had been eighteen months earlier. The promotion was not forthcoming. The president, through channels, always found a reason to say no. Keitt seemed to accept that but was offended that Davis had neither the good manners nor the manly courage to answer him personally.

In May 1864, the Twentieth South Carolina was ordered to Virginia. Twice, Keitt loaded his men on trains only to have his order rescinded and his unit sent to James Island to repel possible Union advances. After a week of this uncertainty, the tired and exhausted unit boarded railroad cars for the northern front. On May 30, Keitt met with Davis and asked that the Twentieth South Carolina be assigned to Kershaw's Brigade. The president granted his request, and much to his surprise and delight, Keitt found himself the senior colonel in the brigade. As such, he became its acting commander. Keitt was pleased, but the brigade's veterans "felt and saw at a glance" Keitt's "inexperience and want of self-control."

The Army of Northern Virginia was maneuvering near Cold Harbor. On June 1, Keitt was directed to do a reconnaissance of the area along the brigade's front. Instead he formed his entire brigade along an old road. He ordered the line to advance. Astride his iron-gray charger with saber held high, the brigade's acting commander led the charge. The left side of the line broke under Federal shelling. In trying to rally his troops, Keitt was an inviting target for enemy marksmen. Felled by a musket ball in the liver, he lingered a day and died on June 2.

At Cold Harbor, Colonel Keitt's inexperience and impetuousness resulted not only in his own death but also in that of many brave men of Kershaw's Brigade. Historian Douglas S. Freeman singled out Keitt in the introduction to his third volume of *Lee's Lieutenants:* "The competent Generals who escaped bullets and disease were hampered in almost every action by some man who, like Keitt at Cold Harbor, . . . was unable to meet the exactions of the field." It's a scathing indictment of the secessionist who sought glory on the battlefield and found only death.

Keitt's body was returned to South Carolina, and he was buried in Orangeburg during a downpour of rain. There were the usual tributes in the press, but one contemporary source was noticeably silent. Although in South Carolina at the time of Keitt's death, Mary Boykin Chesnut makes no mention of it in her famous diary. Earlier she had written that Keitt was "quick as a flash. No one gets the better of him." And when he was in Richmond in 1863 lobbying for promotion: "Our old tempestuous Keitt breakfasted with us yesterday. I wish I could remember half of the brilliant things he said." "Quick," "tempestuous," "brilliant," are words that capture the spirit of the man who was in the vanguard of the movement to break up the Union. They are a fitting epitaph.

BIBLIOGRAPHY

Burton, E. Milby. *The Siege of Charleston, 1861–1865.* Columbia, S.C., 1970.

Cauthen, Charles Edward. *South Carolina Goes to War, 1860–1865.* Chapel Hill, N.C., 1950.

The Correspondence between the Commissioners of the State of South Carolina to the Government at Washington and the President of the United States; together with the Statement of Messrs. Miles and Keitt. Charleston, S.C., 1861.

Dickert, D. Augustus. *History of Kershaw's Brigade, with Complete Rolls of Companies, Biographical Sketches, Incidents, Anecdotes, Etc.* Newberry, S.C., 1899.

Herd, Don Elmer, Jr. "Chapters from the Life of a Southern Chevalier: Lawrence Massillon Keitt's Congressional Years, 1853–1860." M.A. thesis, University of South Carolina, 1958.

Merchant, J. Holt, Jr. "Lawrence M. Keitt, South Carolina Fire-Eater." Ph.D. diss., University of Virginia, 1976.

Woodward, C. Vann, ed. *Mary Chesnut's Civil War.* New Haven, 1981.

WALTER B. EDGAR

KELL, JOHN MCINTOSH (1823–1900), naval officer. Born and raised in coastal McIntosh County, Georgia, Kell entered the U.S. Navy as a midshipman in 1841. After participating in operations in California during the Mexican War, he graduated from the Naval School in 1848. That same year Kell was court-martialed for disobeying an order he considered illegal. Lt. Raphael Semmes, USN, served as his legal counsel. Although judged guilty and dismissed from the service, Kell was reinstated in 1850.

Resigning his commission as lieutenant after Georgia's secession, Kell was appointed to the Georgia navy. He commanded the steamer *Savannah* off the Georgia coast. Then, when Semmes became captain of the commerce raider *Sumter,* he requested Kell as his first lieutenant and executive officer. Less than a year later, Kell served in the same capacity aboard *Alabama,* built in England especially for the purpose of commerce raiding. As executive officer of *Sumter* and *Alabama,* Kell was responsible for daily operations, including the disciplining of a largely mercenary crew. He was a hard taskmaster, but the men developed a respect (some, even affection) for their "luff." Kell played a

JOHN MCINTOSH KELL ABOARD CSS *ALABAMA.* Lieutenant Kell, in background, and Captain Raphael Semmes, standing by *Alabama*'s 110-pounder rifled gun. Photographed at Capetown, South Africa, August 1863.   NAVAL HISTORICAL CENTER, WASHINGTON, D.C.

leading role during the dramatic battle with USS *Kearsarge* off Cherbourg, France, June 19, 1864. After the defeated *Alabama* sank, Kell escaped capture by being brought to England aboard the English yacht that rescued him. Kell ended his naval service commanding the ironclad *Richmond* of the James River Squadron. He was home sick in Georgia when the war ended.

After years of farming at Sunnyside, Georgia, Kell was appointed adjutant general of Georgia in 1886, a position he held until his death.

BIBLIOGRAPHY

Delaney, Norman C. *John McIntosh Kell of the Raider Alabama.* University, Ala., 1973.

Kell, John McIntosh. *Recollections of a Naval Life, Including the Cruises of the Confederate States Steamers Sumter and Alabama.* Washington, D.C., 1900.

Semmes, Raphael. *Memoirs of Service Afloat during the War between the States.* Baltimore, 1869. Reprint, New York, 1987.

NORMAN C. DELANEY

KELLY, JOHN HERBERT (1840–1864), brigadier general.

Kelly, a native of Alabama, resigned from the U.S. Military Academy on December 29, 1860, and later accepted a commission as second lieutenant in the Confederate army, assigned to Fort Morgan. Appointed to the staff of Gen. William J. Hardee, he became an assistant adjutant-general with the rank of captain on October 5, 1861. Promoted to major and assigned to command the Ninth Arkansas Battalion, he led frontal assaults with gallantry at Shiloh. On May 5, 1862, he was appointed colonel of the Eighth Arkansas Infantry, the regiment he commanded at Perryville and Murfreesboro. At Chickamauga, on September 20, 1863, he commanded a brigade in Gen. James Longstreet's advance on Gen. George H. Thomas at Snodgrass Hill. His horse was shot from under him and 303 of his 852 men were killed or wounded, but he captured and held the position. He was promoted to brigadier general on November 16, 1863. At twenty-three he was the youngest brigadier general then in the army. He then commanded a division in Gen. Joseph Wheeler's cavalry corps in the Atlanta campaign. During a raid on William Tecumseh Sherman's communications near Franklin, Tennessee, he was mortally wounded in a skirmish on September 2, 1864, and died a few days later.

BIBLIOGRAPHY

Kelly, Maud McLure. "John Herbert Kelly: The Boy General of the Confederacy." *Alabama Historical Quarterly* 9 (Spring 1947): 9–112.

Tucker, Glenn. *Chickamauga: Bloody Battle in the West.* Indianapolis, 1961.

JAMES A. RAMAGE

KELLY'S FORD, VIRGINIA.

During this battle, fought on November 7, 1863, the Army of Northern Virginia lost 2,023 soldiers and Federal troops sustained 264 casualties while forcing the Confederates to retreat farther southward into Virginia.

As the Confederate army prepared to bivouac for the winter, President Abraham Lincoln pressured Gen. George G. Meade to strike the retreating Southerners before the onset of winter complicated maneuvers. From his headquarters near Warrenton, Meade formulated a plan to attack Robert E. Lee's troops on the banks of the Rappahannock River.

The summer campaign of 1863, culminating in the horror of Gettysburg, had weakened the Army of Northern Virginia. More recently, the upset at Bristoe Station in October 1863 had further troubled General Lee. He began moving his cold and weary army back toward the Rappahannock, settling along the southern bank of the river near Kelly's Ford in early November.

The topography of the area around Kelly's Ford strongly favored an enemy approaching from the North. The high northern bank made defense from the southern position perilous at best. To hinder any Union attempts to cross the river, Robert Rodes placed the Second North Carolina Regiment close to the shore. Its fire would allow the rest of the army to get into a defensible position farther from the northern bank. Jubal Early and Rodes had positioned their divisions on the southern side of the river in a line that reached for miles on either side of Kelly's Ford. Guarding against a surprise attack, Harry Thompson Hays's brigade manned a number of rifle pits on the northern bank of the Rappahannock. Hays's troops maintained ties to the rest of the army by way of a pontoon bridge located several hundred yards above the remains of the Orange and Alexandria Railroad crossing.

The morning of November 7, Federal troops advanced on Kelly's Ford. As they clashed with the Second North Carolina, Rodes sent in the Thirtieth North Carolina for support. But this unit panicked and sought cover in some abandoned buildings. In the confusion, Union troops captured both regiments, and by midafternoon the Northerners had forced their way across the river. There they exchanged fire with Richard E. Anderson's division until dark, ultimately pushing the Southerners back into their trenches.

On the opposite bank, reports that the Federals were heading north toward the bridgehead prompted Early to reinforce Hays and his men. He sent a large segment of Robert F. Hoke's brigade, under the command of Archibald C. Godwin in Hoke's absence, to help Hays's men defend the rifle pits.

As darkness descended on the battle, the firing diminished. Because a nocturnal attack was unprecedented, Lee did not believe that the Union would move on his army that night. With Hays and Godwin holding the redoubts on the northern bank, Lee made plans to attack the Union army at Kelly's Ford the next morning.

In the evening, however, during a cold rain, the Fifth and Sixth Federal army corps, under the direction of Gen. John Sedgwick, initiated an attack at the bridgehead. On the southern side of the river, Early watched in dismay as only a few Confederates managed to escape. Early had lost 1,674 men and four guns.

Dislodged from their position on the northern bank and with a substantial force of Union troops already across the river, the Confederates could no longer hold Kelly's Ford. They retreated that night to a position between Culpeper Courthouse and Brandy Station. The next morning Lee moved the army to more favorable ground south of the Rapidan. Despite his victory at Kelly's Ford, Meade succeeded in gaining only an insubstantial amount of ground. As 1863 came to a close, the Northern commander failed to achieve the blow to the Southern army that Lincoln so desperately wanted.

BIBLIOGRAPHY

Freeman, Douglas S. *Lee's Lieutenants: A Study in Command.* 3 vols. New York, 1942–1944. Reprint, New York, 1986.

Graham, Martin F., and George F. Skoch. *Mine Run: A Campaign of Lost Opportunities, October 21, 1863–May 1, 1864.* Lynchburg, Va., 1987.

U.S. War Department. *War of the Rebellion: A Compilation of the Official Records of the Union and Confederate Armies.* Washington, D.C., 1894–1927. Ser. 1, vol. 29, pp. 553–635.

JENNIFER LUND SMITH

KEMPER, JAMES LAWSON (1823–1895), major general. A native of the Virginia Piedmont, Kemper was born June 11, 1823, in Madison County. He graduated in 1842 from Washington College in Lexington, saw limited service in the Mexican War as a captain of Virginia volunteers, and then established a law practice in his home area. Elected five times to the Virginia General Assembly, Kemper also chaired the state committee on military affairs and was president of the board of visitors of the Virginia Military Institute. In 1861 he resigned as Speaker of the House of Delegates to enter the Confederate army.

Appointed colonel of the Seventh Virginia, he led the regiment from First Manassas through Seven Pines. On June 3, 1862, Kemper received a brigadier's commission and took command of a Virginia brigade formerly led successively by James Longstreet, Richard S. Ewell, and A. P. Hill. That unit became part of George E. Pickett's division. Kemper won praise for gallantry at Second Manassas and Sharpsburg. A man of "solid qualities and sound judgment," he became known for high-flown oratory before and after battles.

JAMES LAWSON KEMPER.   NATIONAL ARCHIVES

On July 3, 1863, Kemper and his troops were on the extreme right in the first line of the Pickett-Pettigrew attack at Gettysburg. Kemper was captured after being shot in the groin. Subsequently exchanged, he was unable to resume field service. Kemper was promoted to major general on September 19, 1864, and commanded Virginia's reserve forces for the remainder of the war.

He resumed his law practice in Madison County, became a postwar orator of renown, and in 1874 was elected governor of Virginia. After his April 7, 1895, death in Orange County (where he is buried), a eulogist said of Kemper: "A Virginian, he loved his State with all the force of an ardent and earnest nature."

BIBLIOGRAPHY

Hotchkiss, Jed. *Virginia.* Vol. 3 of *Confederate Military History.* Edited by Clement A. Evans. Atlanta, 1899. Vol. 4 of extended ed. Wilmington, N.C., 1987.

Riggs, David F. *Seventh Virginia Infantry.* Lynchburg, Va., 1982.

"The Southern Cause." *Southern Historical Society Papers* 30 (1902): 366–368. Reprint, Wilmington, N.C., 1991.

JAMES I. ROBERTSON, JR.

KENAN, AUGUSTUS HOLMES (1805–1865), congressman from Georgia. Kenan was born in Montpelier,

Georgia, near Milledgeville. Educated in New York, he was admitted to the Georgia bar in 1825. He settled in Milledgeville, then Georgia's state capital, where he became one of the state's leading criminal lawyers. In 1835, Kenan raised a cavalry company that fought in the Seminole War in Florida. He stayed on afterward to serve on the staff of Gen. Winfield Scott, with whom he became good friends. After his return to Milledgeville, he played an active role in instigating Cherokee removal from the state and served several terms in the state legislature.

Although he held a few slaves as house servants, Kenan opposed slavery in principle and never invested in land or slaves as did most men in his position. A lifelong Whig, he was an ardent Unionist when the issue of secession was raised. As the representative of Baldwin County at the state's secession convention in January 1861, he voted against secession on thirteen occasions, and though he signed the final ordinance for the sake of unity, he threw away the pen with which he had signed it. Nevertheless, once Georgia entered the Confederacy, Kenan's support was unwavering. He was one of nine delegates representing Georgia at the constitutional convention in Montgomery, Alabama, and served in both the Provisional and the First Confederate Congresses, where he became a close friend and supporter of Jefferson Davis. Though he lost his bid for reelection to Clifford Anderson in 1863, he remained a loyal spokesman for Davis. This led to tensions between Kenan and Governor Joseph E. Brown, who called him "the stooge of Mr. Davis." At war's end, the governor tried unsuccessfully to block Kenan's request for a presidential pardon, which President Andrew Johnson granted him just three weeks before his death in Milledgeville on June 16, 1865.

BIBLIOGRAPHY

Bonner, James C. *Milledgeville: Georgia's Antebellum Capital.* Athens, Ga., 1978.

Cook, Anna Maria Green. *History of Baldwin County, Georgia.* Anderson, S.C., 1925.

Northen, William W., ed. *Men of Mark in Georgia.* Vol. 3. Atlanta, 1908. Reprint, Spartanburg, S.C., 1974.

JOHN C. INSCOE

KENAN, OWEN RAND (1804–1887), congressman from North Carolina.

Kenan represented North Carolina's Third Congressional District in the First Congress. A wealthy planter whose three sons all fought for the Confederacy, Kenan was one of the few legislators from North Carolina who gave strong support to the Davis administration and its programs.

Kenan was born on March 4, 1804, at Kenansville, in Duplin County, North Carolina, into a wealthy family who grew cotton and tobacco. After a brief time studying medicine, Kenan became an attorney and began practicing in Kenansville. As time went on, however, he devoted himself primarily to managing his large plantation. In 1860 he possessed an estate valued at $87,000.

From 1834 to 1838 Kenan served as a Democrat in the lower house of the North Carolina General Assembly, but thereafter he was not active in politics until the secession crisis. He became a strong secessionist after Abraham Lincoln's election and campaigned for the Confederate House of Representatives on a platform promising full cooperation with the Confederate government. His prominence in local society helped him defeat two opponents.

Kenan lived up to his pledge, joining with William Lander to furnish the only strong support from North Carolina for vigorous wartime legislation. Kenan had little to say in debates and offered few proposals, but he interested himself in the defense of his state's coastline and supported the Davis administration reliably. His record shows especially strong support for economic legislation and for proposals to suspend the writ of habeas corpus. In two areas—the forced funding of Treasury notes and the tax-in-kind—Kenan put local interests above the administration's program, opposing both these measures because he feared they would damage his productive agricultural district. Kenan declined to seek reelection in 1863 but denied at that time that there was serious discontent in North Carolina.

After the war he remained out of politics and died at his home on March 3, 1887.

BIBLIOGRAPHY

Alexander, Thomas B., and Richard E. Beringer. *The Anatomy of the Confederate Congress: A Study of the Influences of Member Characteristics on Legislative Voting Behavior, 1861–1865.* Nashville, Tenn., 1972.

Powell, William S., ed. *Dictionary of North Carolina Biography.* Vol. 3. Chapel Hill, N.C., 1988.

Warner, Ezra J., and W. Buck Yearns. *Biographical Register of the Confederate Congress.* Baton Rouge, La., 1975.

Yearns, Wilfred B. *The Confederate Congress.* Athens, Ga., 1960.

PAUL D. ESCOTT

KENNEDY, JOHN DOBY (1840–1896), brigadier general and U.S. diplomat.

The son of a Scottish immigrant father, Kennedy was born at Camden, South Carolina, January 5, 1840. He attended South Carolina College for two years and then read law and was admitted to the bar shortly before the start of the Civil War.

In 1861 Kennedy enlisted as a captain in Company E, Second South Carolina Infantry, under Joseph B. Kershaw. At First Manassas, he was struck by a stray rifle ball. When Kershaw was promoted to brigadier in February 1862, Kennedy succeeded him as colonel of the regiment.

Kennedy participated in the Peninsular and Seven Days' campaigns before he was incapacitated by fever following Savage's Station. He helped capture Maryland Heights in the reduction of Harpers Ferry in September 1862, and his regiment was the first of the brigade to rush to the relief of Thomas J. ("Stonewall") Jackson at Sharpsburg. In this engagement Kennedy drove the enemy in his front but was painfully wounded in the charge. It was one of fifteen times during the war that he was hit by enemy fire. At Fredericksburg his brigade helped repel Union assaults on Marye's Heights.

When Kershaw was promoted to major general in May 1864, he vigorously urged Kennedy's promotion to brigadier. Kershaw called his subordinate "a brave and accomplished officer, an excellent disciplinarian, well informed, moral and patriotic. . . . [He] has managed his Regiment with judgement and skill in many battles, has been often wounded; three times severely. . . . [He] has always been faithful and devoted to his duties." Kennedy received his promotion on February 8, 1865, while in South Carolina serving in Lafayette McLaws's division of Alexander P. Stewart's corps. Following his surrender to the Federals, Kennedy was paroled at Greensboro on May 1, 1865.

Kennedy returned to Camden where, after several years as a planter, he resumed the practice of law. In December 1865 he was elected to Congress but was denied his seat when he refused to take the Ironclad Oath. Kennedy served in the state legislature for two years, as lieutenant governor from 1880 to 1882, and presidential elector on the Democratic ticket in 1884. From 1886 to 1889 he was consul general at Shanghai by appointment of President Grover Cleveland. He died of a stroke at Camden, April 14, 1896, and was buried there.

BIBLIOGRAPHY

Capers, Ellison. *South Carolina*. Vol. 5 of *Confederate Military History*. Edited by Clement A. Evans. Atlanta, 1899. Vol. 6 of extended ed. Wilmington, N.C., 1987.

Compiled Military Service Records. John Doby Kennedy. Microcopy M331, Roll 147. Record Group 109. National Archives, Washington, D.C.

Warner, Ezra J. *Generals in Gray: Lives of the Confederate Commanders*. Baton Rouge, La., 1959.

LOWELL REIDENBAUGH

KENNER, DUNCAN F. (1813–1887), congressman from Louisiana and diplomat.

By birth and circumstance Duncan Farrar Kenner was a child of the Old South. Temperament and history made him a father of the New South. Born to a wealthy and influential Southern family, Kenner possessed all the advantages of the ruling class. He attended private academies in New Orleans, graduated from Miami College in Ohio (the alma mater of several Confederate generals and politicians), studied law with John Slidell, traveled widely throughout the northern United States and Europe, grew rich planting sugar cane and breeding horses, and maintained these advantages by serving in the Louisiana legislature.

Though among the largest and wealthiest slaveholders in Louisiana, Kenner, like scores of other Southerners, had mixed feelings about slavery. Uncertain of its permanent and tangible benefits to the South, he considered slavery a generally wasteful, unproductive institution that impeded the economic development of the South and exaggerated its dependence on an unsympathetic, increasingly hostile North. Kenner's experiences sustained these impressions. He saw firsthand the expansive and productive character of the Northern free labor economy, and he recognized that both Northern and European sentiment had turned against slavery.

Despite his reservations, Kenner chose to defend slavery and to work toward the creation of an independent Southern republic dedicated to its preservation. Though he did not participate in the Louisiana secession convention, he endorsed its actions and represented Louisiana at the Montgomery convention. For Kenner, unlike his friend Judah P. Benjamin, secession was no mere contrivance that held promise of reconstructing the Union along lines favorable to the slaveholding South. It was, rather, a genuine expression of Southern independence and an opportunity to create a Southern republic. At the Montgomery convention, Kenner called for expedient, resolute action in establishing the new nation. He proposed that the convention act as a provisional congress, authorized to create a confederation of states and to adopt a constitution defining its character and governing its affairs.

Without much debate and with little hesitation, the delegates adopted Kenner's proposal. The Provisional Congress focused its efforts on establishing a permanent government, creating executive departments, defining their powers, and regulating their operations. On several issues Kenner was a visible and assertive nationalist. He advocated the creation of an active national government, patterned on the United States and endowed with sufficient powers to guarantee Southern independence and forge a national identity. He favored the selection of a nationalist president (the entire Louisiana delegation endorsed Jefferson Davis from the beginning), opposed the right of secession for the states of the new confederation, called for the adoption of a protective tariff, promoted government subsidies for railroad improvement, advocated strict confiscation and sequestration laws, and urged the development of a more diversified economy.

In the constitutional convention and permanent Congress, Kenner was less conspicuous and, to some degree, less assertive. For reasons most Southerners understood and applauded, the convention rejected his proposals establishing a protective tariff and other high tax measures aimed at the agricultural South. On the issue of slavery, Kenner, like all delegates, was an ardent supporter of the rights of masters. The Montgomery convention gave slavery a prominent place in the Confederate Constitution, referring to it by name, guaranteeing its protection in the territories, and permitting its unrestricted transportation throughout the Confederate states. Kenner agreed with these provisions, though apparently he believed they provided inadequate protection against the encroachment of government. He offered an amendment to the Constitution restricting Congress's authority over slavery and augmenting the rights of property in slaves. And though the convention defeated Kenner's particular proposal, the Confederate Constitution limited severely the government's authority and opportunity to "impair" the rights of Southern masters.

During the first weeks of the war, Kenner, like many congressmen, seemed absorbed with the routine of government, apparently content to let Jefferson Davis determine national policy and conduct national affairs. As chairman of the Ways and Means Committee, Kenner devoted himself to committee assignments, concentrating on matters of public debt and financing. But he had no illusion about the tenacity of the Lincoln government and its commitment to the preservation of the "old" Union. And he was convinced that victory in the war would be neither swift nor complete. From the beginning, Kenner pressed for both military preparation, including a limited conscription, and European recognition. After Federal armies occupied southeastern Louisiana in 1862, including Kenner's congressional district, he called for an even more vigorous prosecution of the war and a more audacious foreign policy. In Congress he opposed the many exemptions granted from military service, including the infamous Twenty-Slave Law, urged the impressment of slaves for military purposes, and endorsed the suspension of the writ of habeas corpus. In private discussions with his friend Secretary of State Benjamin and with President Davis, he recommended the use of all economic and diplomatic resources, including the emancipation of slaves, to end the political stalemate and gain independence.

The Federal occupation of Louisiana, the collapse of chattel slavery in the sugar parishes, and the reemergence of Unionism among whites convinced Kenner that the Confederacy could not win its independence or establish a national identity on the battlefield. The South would never gain its independence unless it obtained European recognition and massive financial and military assistance. Its unbending commitment to slavery barred any legitimate hope of securing foreign recognition and forcing the Lincoln government to submit to Southern independence. Kenner

maintained that emancipation should be seen strictly as a wartime measure, designed to secure recognition and independence. He insisted as well that Confederate emancipation was not an invitation for foreign mediation or an overture for reunification with the Union. And, as the Federal contract labor system and free-state movement in Louisiana indicated, emancipation did not imply abandoning white supremacy.

At the insistence of Benjamin and Davis, Kenner kept these sentiments to himself. President Davis considered them unwarranted, though Secretary of State Benjamin thought them merely premature. Kenner's proposals took on greater relevance in the last weeks of the war. Late in 1864, following Lincoln's disheartening reelection and in the wake of massive Confederate desertions and casualties, Secretary Benjamin persuaded President Davis to send Kenner to Europe. Davis gave Kenner near plenary power to negotiate recognition in exchange for limited, gradual emancipation.

After weeks of exhausting travel, Kenner arrived in Europe, eager to complete his mission and confident of its success. The Confederate emissaries, especially John Slidell and James M. Mason, did not share Kenner's enthusiasm or confidence. In the context of events, their pessimism was justified. The principal European powers, particularly France and Great Britain, were never convinced that an independent Southern republic was in their best interests. Despite its pretensions and expectations, the Confederacy had few relevant economic and cultural ties with Europe—certainly none that justified diplomatic recognition and a permanent division of the American Union. And though slavery was an important diplomatic issue, by 1865 the issue had lost its relevance. The British government recognized Lincoln's commitment to a disciplined, workable emancipation that would not disrupt production, risk investment, or unnecessarily divide Northern public opinion. The British cabinet concluded that recognition would only prolong the war, jeopardizing investment and threatening the destruction of the Union.

Kenner's mission also ignored domestic political circumstances. The Lincoln government was committed to a thorough restoration of the Union. It rejected mediation and discounted recognition, pursuing instead military victory and permanent emancipation. The Confederacy too dismissed mediation, demanding recognition, financial assistance, and permanent slavery. The mission did not fail because the South had lost the war. Military victory belied both recognition and emancipation. The Kenner mission failed because it denied the fundamental reality of the war: the Southern states had abandoned the Union and formed the Confederacy to preserve slavery. Southern independence and national identity were impossible without slavery.

With the final defeat of Confederate forces, Kenner reasserted his allegiance to the Union and returned home to Louisiana. He also returned to public life, serving as a state senator and advocate of the New South. He wanted the North to leave the South alone to deal with its immense economic and social problems. "Our people desire no further agitation, discord, or revolutions," he wrote to Governor James Madison Wells. "We desire nothing but peace and the opportunity to repair our shattered fortunes."

BIBLIOGRAPHY

Alexander, Thomas B., and Richard E. Beringer. *The Anatomy of the Confederate Congress: A Study of the Influences of Member Characteristics on Legislative Voting Behavior, 1861–1865.* Nashville, Tenn., 1972.

Bauer, Craig A. "The Last Effort: The Secret Mission of the Confederate Diplomat, Duncan F. Kenner." *Louisiana History* 22 (1981): 67–95.

Blumenthal, Henry. "Confederate Diplomacy: Popular Notions and International Realities." *Journal of Southern History* 32 (1966): 151–171.

Brauer, Kinley J. "British Mediation and the American Civil War: A Reconsideration." *Journal of Southern History* 38 (1972): 49–64.

Brauer, Kinley J. "The Slavery Problem in the Diplomacy of the American Civil War." *Pacific Historical Review* 46 (1977): 439–469.

Price, Grady Daniel. "The Secret Mission of Duncan F. Kenner, Confederate Minister Plenipotentiary to Europe in 1865." M.A. thesis, Tulane University, 1929.

Warner, Ezra J., and W. Buck Yearns. *Biographical Register of the Confederate Congress.* Baton Rouge, La., 1975.

Yearns, Wilfred B. *The Confederate Congress.* Athens, Ga., 1960.

TERRENCE W. FITZMORRIS

KENNESAW MOUNTAIN, GEORGIA.

The Confederate victory at Kennesaw Mountain on June 27, 1864, was a setback in Union Maj. Gen. William Tecumseh Sherman's Atlanta campaign. But though a tactical success for the Southerners, it proved a strategic reverse for Confederate Gen. Joseph E. Johnston.

Johnston, after delaying Sherman's 100,000-man army across sixty miles of northern Georgia, took a blocking position with 65,000 men across Lost, Pine, and Brushy mountains. He opened communications with Richmond officials to bring cavalry forces from Mississippi to cut the Union railroad supply line, a plan later disapproved by President Jefferson Davis.

Sherman resumed his advance on June 8, deploying his superior numbers farther toward his right than Johnston could defend with a lesser force. On June 14 Lt. Gen.

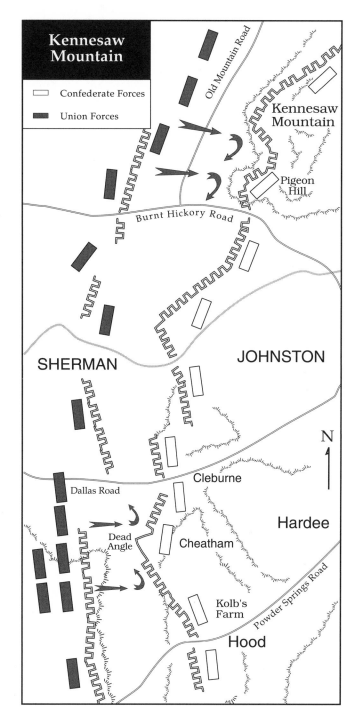

Leonidas Polk was killed on Pine Mountain. Threatened with envelopment at Lost Mountain, Johnston withdrew his left wing behind Mud Creek, but Union pressure at a salient in the center held by Lt. Gen. William J. Hardee led Johnston to withdraw his army on the night of June 18–19 to a previously selected position astride Kennesaw Mountain. In an arc-shaped line west of Marietta, the Confederates protected the Western and Atlantic Railroad, their supply link with Atlanta.

Advancing, Sherman made contact along the Confederate front while extending to his right to threaten the railroad. Two Union corps reached the vicinity of Kolb's farm on June 21. Johnston reacted by transferring Lt. Gen. John Bell Hood's corps of eleven thousand from right to left. Hood exceeded Johnston's orders and attacked on June 22, suffering severe losses. Although defeated at Kolb's farm, Hood extended the flank beyond Sherman's reach.

Believing his foe to be stretched thin, Sherman abandoned flanking maneuvers for a direct attack. His plan for destroying Johnston's army called for deceptions on either flank while two strikes pierced the center. Johnston remained confident.

At 8:00 A.M., June 27, Sherman's plan went into effect following an artillery bombardment. A feint attack at the north end of Kennesaw Mountain produced negligible results. In the meantime, three Union brigades numbering 5,500 men moved to attack the mountain's southerly spur, called Pigeon Hill. The Federals easily overran the skirmish line but soon became pinned down at close range on the hill's slope. Heavy Confederate fire coming from strong earthworks held by Maj. Gen. Samuel G. French's division paralyzed this assault.

Two miles farther south, the main Union attack of eight thousand infantry got started an hour behind schedule. The Federals charged in five dense brigade columns. Fighting from behind earthworks the Confederate divisions led by Maj. Gens. Patrick R. Cleburne and Benjamin F. Cheatham inflicted frightful losses on the attackers. Savage hand-to-hand fighting took place at a projecting salient called the "Dead Angle." Although two Union brigades simultaneously assaulted the angle's apex and south flank, Cheatham's soldiers bravely held fast, repulsing them. The battle was over by noon. Sherman was personally chagrined by the result. He lost three thousand men compared to Johnston's one thousand.

When Sherman later learned that a subordinate's movement around the Confederate's south flank had gained a favorable position, he reverted to his flanking maneuvers. On July 2 Johnston withdrew from Kennesaw Mountain to Smyrna, satisfied with having delayed Sherman for nearly a month and inflicted disproportionate losses.

BIBLIOGRAPHY

Cox, Jacob D. *Atlanta.* New York, 1881. Reprint, Dayton, Ohio, 1987.

Kelly, Dennis P. *Kennesaw Mountain and the Atlanta Campaign.* Atlanta, 1991.

Symonds, Craig L. *Joseph Johnston: A Civil War Biography.* New York, 1992.

Womack, Robert J. *Call Forth the Mighty Men.* Bessemer, Ala., 1987.

DENNIS KELLY

KENTUCKY. Although John C. Breckinridge, the Southern Democratic candidate for president in 1860, was a favorite son, Kentucky voters favored John Bell, the Constitutional Union candidate. Republican Abraham Lincoln received only 1,364 votes in the state of his birth. With an 1860 population of 1,155,684 (919,484 whites, 225,483 slaves, 10,684 free blacks, 33 Indians), Kentucky provided some 100,000 soldiers to the Union, including the Home Guard, and between 25,000 and 40,000 to the Confederacy. Over 20,000 of the Union soldiers were blacks.

Sentiment was badly divided in the commonwealth when the war began. Slavery was an obvious tie with the South, the Kentucky Resolutions of 1798 and 1799 had enunciated the doctrine of state rights, and the Mississippi River trade had forged strong economic bonds. Many Kentuckians had Southern backgrounds, and the state's culture bore a Southern flavor. Yet Kentucky had a strong nationalistic tradition, and Henry Clay and John J. Crittenden had become famous as compromisers who sought mutually acceptable solutions to the sectional crises. Railroads were changing transportation patterns, and Kentucky was becoming more closely associated with the North.

Political Developments. On May 20, 1861, the pro-Southern governor Beriah Magoffin declared Kentucky's neutrality after rejecting both Union and Confederate requests for troops following the attack on Fort Sumter. A select group of six political leaders tried to formulate a policy for state defense, but it failed when Unionists would not accept Magoffin on a special board to manage state preparedness.

Two elections during the summer of 1861 demonstrated that the Unionists had a clear majority. In the congressional campaign Unionists such as A. M. Starling effectively charged that the Confederacy would destroy the lucrative slave trade by reopening the African slave trade and that the South wanted "Kentucky to stand between her & danger, to be her battleground." Unionist candidates won nine of ten seats, losing only in the extreme western end of the state. After the state legislative election on August 5, Unionists had 76–24 and 27–11 margins in the house and senate, more than enough to override gubernatorial vetoes.

Lincoln moved cautiously, for, as he wrote, "I think to lose Kentucky is nearly the same as to lose the whole game." Recruiting camps outside the state, such as Camp Joe Holt in Indiana and Camp Boone in Tennessee, welcomed Kentuckians who were eager to fight, and clandestine agents operated within the state. After the August election Unionists established Camp Dick Robinson in Garrard

County, and Lincoln refused to remove it.

War came to Kentucky in early September 1861 when Confederate Gen. Gideon Pillow seized Columbus on the Mississippi River. Gen. Ulysses S. Grant quickly occupied Paducah, and rival forces moved into the northern and southern portions of the state. The General Assembly ordered only the Confederates to withdraw, but that directive was ignored.

Gen. Albert Sidney Johnston, given command of Confederate forces west of the Appalachian Mountains, established a line across southern Kentucky with key positions at Cumberland Gap, Bowling Green, Forts Henry and Donelson on the Tennessee and Cumberland rivers, and Columbus. Gen. Robert Anderson, the hero of Fort Sumter, became the Federal commander in the state, but he soon gave way to Gen. William Tecumseh Sherman, who was in turn replaced by Gen. Don Carlos Buell. Numerous skirmishes occurred, but neither army was prepared to fight, and each commander was convinced that he was greatly outnumbered.

Confederates held meetings in Russellville in late October and mid-November and established a provisional state government that was admitted into the Confederate States of America on December 10, 1861. Its capital was Bowling Green, but its jurisdiction extended no farther than Confederate troops advanced. This government withdrew with the Confederate army in mid-February 1862. When Governor George W. Johnson, a wealthy Scott County farmer, was killed at Shiloh, the ten-man council selected lawyer Richard Hawes as his successor. The Confederate government returned briefly with Braxton Bragg and E. Kirby Smith in the late summer, 1862, and Hawes was installed at Frankfort. But he soon left the state with the Confederate army, and for the rest of the war the Confederate government of Kentucky was in exile.

Although Governor Magoffin carefully executed orders from the legislature, Unionists did not trust him, and many of his powers were removed. In August 1862 he resigned, and James F. Robinson completed his term. In 1863 Union Democrats nominated Thomas E. Bramlette who easily defeated Charles A. Wickliffe, the regular Democratic candidate, for governor. Both parties distanced themselves from the Lincoln administration, which had become more unpopular because of the Emancipation Proclamation, even though it did not apply to Kentucky. In the 1864 presidential election, Lincoln, running on a Union party ticket, was decisively defeated in the state by Gen. George B. McClellan.

During the last two years of the war Bramlette claimed with some justification that Kentucky was being treated as if it were a Confederate state. He was especially incensed by the Union decision to use black troops. John J. Crittenden had spoken for many Kentuckians when he declared, ''I would rather see our young men brought home as corpses than see them saved by such unsoldierly means,'' but the war's insatiable demands for manpower forced adoption of the policy. Col. Frank L. Wolford, commander of the famed First Kentucky Cavalry (U.S.), was dismissed from service for his outspoken opposition, and in the spring of 1864 Bramlette nearly broke with the national administration. The Reverend Robert J. Breckinridge, believed to be the Kentuckian with the most influence with Lincoln, helped prevent an open rupture. Kentucky began black enlistments, for slaves as well as freemen, in April 1864. Slaves who served became free, and after March 3, 1865, their wives and children were also freed. Loyal masters were supposed to receive $300 from the Federal government for each slave lost. Slaves had been assessed at $107,494,527 in 1860; the figure in 1864 was only $34,179,246. Kentucky had stubbornly rejected Lincoln's efforts to introduce compensated emancipation, and the discredited institution lingered in the state until adoption of the Thirteenth Amendment to the Federal Constitution in December 1865.

Military Action in Kentucky. The first battle of significance in Kentucky came at Mill Springs (Logan's Crossroads) toward the eastern end of Johnston's line. On January 19, 1862, Gen. George H. Thomas defeated a Confederate force that attacked him under the command of Generals George B. Crittenden and Felix K. Zollicoffer. Zollicoffer was killed when he rode into the Union lines, and the Confederate casualties of 519 were double the Union losses. Most of the Confederates escaped across the flooded Cumberland River.

More critical were the early 1862 losses of Forts Henry and Donelson. Anticipating that the battle for Kentucky would be fought in the Bowling Green area, Johnston did not visit the forts, and he allowed a confused command situation to develop there. Fort Henry on the Tennessee River fell to Andrew H. Foote's Union navy gunboats on February 6. Ten days later Grant acquired the nickname ''Unconditional Surrender'' when Simon Bolivar Buckner, his West Point classmate and friend, surrendered some seventeen thousand men at Donelson. With the two great rivers open to Federal gunboats, Johnston abandoned Kentucky and withdrew south of the Tennessee River to protect his supply lines. The Battle of Shiloh, fought on April 6–7, 1862, in which both Johnston and George Johnson were killed, should have been fought in Kentucky.

The Confederates made another major invasion of the state in the late summer of 1862. Gen. E. Kirby Smith almost annihilated a Union force of 6,500 near Richmond on August 30 and soon occupied Lexington and Frankfort. Then he scattered his forces across the bluegrass and made little effort to cooperate with Braxton Bragg, who headed a larger invading force. Bragg did not reach Glasgow until September 14, and when he delayed at Munfordville to force the surrender of some 4,000 Unionists, General Buell reached Louisville before Bragg could threaten it. Smith and Bragg did not coordinate their efforts, and when Kentucky's largest battle of the Civil War was fought at Perryville on October 8 the Confederates used only some 15,000 troops, one-third of the number in the state. The Confederates made gains in savage fighting, but they had secured few enlistments in Kentucky, and Bragg and a council of war decided to withdraw. After some unkind remarks about cowardly Kentuckians, Bragg became the Confederate officer most hated by Kentuckians, especially those fighting under his command.

During the rest of the war Kentucky was held by Union forces except for occasional Confederate raids, most notably those led by John Hunt Morgan. His spectacular incursions embarrassed Union commanders who failed to intercept him and resulted in considerable damage to Union facilities. The destruction of the massive railroad trestles on the Louisville and Nashville Railroad line near Elizabethtown was especially damaging. Other Confederates entered the state from time to time. Occasionally, a unit would remain in the commonwealth for a few weeks, recruiting men and horses and allowing some of the troops to visit briefly with their families. Such raids pinned down a substantial number of Federal troops who tried to defend key points against sudden attacks.

Of course, many Kentuckians on both sides fought outside the state, practically all of them in the armies west of the mountains. The most famous Confederate unit was the "Orphan Brigade," the First Kentucky Brigade. Of the many Federal units, Wolford's "Wild Riders" of the First Kentucky Cavalry was one of the best.

During the last two years of the war guerrillas spread destruction across the state and brought about savage repressive measures from harried Union commanders. "Sue Mundy" (Jerome Clarke) and William Clarke Quantrill were among the most infamous. Public reaction to the repressive measures reinforced the opposition to emancipation and the use of black troops, so that a War Department official reported in 1864 that "a large majority of Kentuckians are today undoubtedly disloyal." A more tactful general, John M. Palmer, replaced Gen. Stephen G. Burbridge on February 10, 1865, but there were few changes in Union policy. There was some truth to the later assertion that Kentucky joined the Confederacy after the war was over.

The Home Front. Despite guerrilla depredations, Kentucky did not suffer the economic destruction visited upon several Southern states. But losses were heavy whenever large military units passed through an area. Fences became firewood, horses and mules volunteered for military service, chickens and hogs disappeared, vegetables and fruit were devoured. The Shaker communities at Pleasant Hill and South Union were hurt severely by visits from both armies. On the other hand, the war provided markets for almost anything that could be raised or manufactured, and many Kentuckians benefited from the boom. The farm price index (1860 = 100) rose as high as 210 in 1864, and since the general price index increased only to 182, farmers on the average profited from the war economy. The decline in manpower led to a reduction of 4 million acres in croplands. Nonagricultural wages rose more slowly than prices, and the average worker lost close to a third of real purchasing power by 1865. Louisville was by far the state's largest city and manufacturing center, and its position on the Ohio

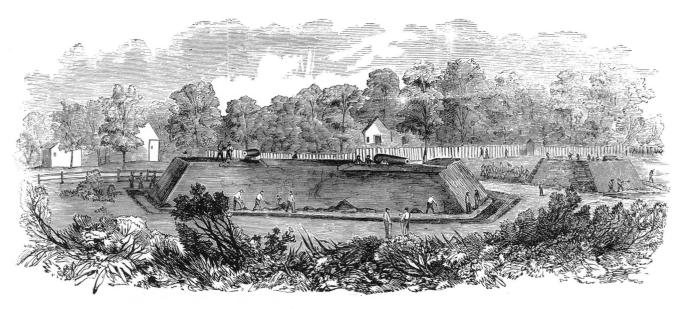

EARTHWORKS AT PADUCAH. Batteries built by Federal troops.

THE SOLDIER IN OUR CIVIL WAR

River and as a terminus for the Louisville and Nashville Railroad contributed to its prosperity.

The Civil War affected nearly every aspect of life in the state. The educational system that had made real progress during the 1847–1853 administration of School Superintendent Robert J. Breckinridge lost ground and was ill prepared to deal with postwar problems, including education for the blacks. Slavery's extinction created complex social and economic problems with which the state was not prepared to cope. The differences among Kentuckians brought strains and often divisions to many institutions and may have contributed to some of the famous postwar feuds. Harriet Means of Ashland wrote that "I would not *dare* to give a large party now for fear the ladies would all get into a free fight." It is impossible to measure the loss of the thousands of men who were killed or maimed in the conflict, or who died from disease, or who were never able to adjust to the postwar era.

For most Kentuckians, the Civil War was one of the most traumatic experiences in their lives; later, some of them gave it a romantic gloss that became part of the Kentucky heritage. As for the state, slavery was ended, realistic limits were set to state rights, and an alliance was forged with the Southern Democratic party. Although other factors were also involved, postwar Kentucky was never as important nationally as it had been before 1861.

[*For further discussion of battles and campaigns fought in Kentucky, see* Henry and Donelson Campaign; Kentucky Campaign of Bragg; Mill Springs, Kentucky; Morgan's Raids; Paducah, Kentucky; Shiloh Campaign. *See also biographies of numerous figures mentioned herein.*]

BIBLIOGRAPHY

Connelly, Thomas L. *Army of the Heartland.* Baton Rouge, La., 1967.

Connelly, Thomas L. *Autumn of Glory.* Baton Rouge, La., 1971.

Coulter, E. Merton. *The Civil War and Readjustment in Kentucky.* Chapel Hill, N.C., 1926.

Harrison, Lowell H. *The Civil War in Kentucky.* Revised edition. Lexington, Ky., 1988.

Harrison, Lowell H. "The Civil War in Kentucky: Some Persistent Questions." *Register of the Kentucky Historical Society* 76 (January 1978): 1–21.

Johnston, J. Stoddard. *Kentucky.* Vol. 9 of *Confederate Military History.* Edited by Clement A. Evans. Atlanta, 1889. Vol. 11 of extended ed. Wilmington, N.C., 1988.

McDowell, Robert Emmett. *City of Conflict: Louisville in the Civil War.* Louisville, 1962.

Speed, Thomas. *The Union Cause in Kentucky.* New York, 1907.

LOWELL H. HARRISON

KENTUCKY CAMPAIGN OF BRAGG. On
June 20, 1862, Gen. Braxton Bragg superseded Gen. P. G. T. Beauregard as commander of the Western Department of the Confederate States. Bragg immediately began rebuilding the army of 45,000 men camped near Tupelo, Mississippi, and preparing it to take the offensive. The Federal armies concentrated at Corinth, Mississippi, were about to move farther south. Bragg planned to strike the enemy wherever the Federal army was most vulnerable.

By July, the massive Union army had separated into its various components and now threatened the lower South on a number of fronts. At Corinth, a 60,000-man force under Ulysses S. Grant began operations against Vicksburg and northern Mississippi. Maj. Gen. Don Carlos Buell took an additional 54,000 men into northern Alabama, heading east to threaten the vital rail junction at Chattanooga, Tennessee.

Confederate Maj. Gen. E. Kirby Smith, commander of the Department of East Tennessee, had 13,000 men to oppose Buell's advance. On June 27, Bragg sent him John Porter McCown's division of 3,000 men. Bragg still debated where he should make his move: he seemed to favor an attack on Corinth but was concerned that the loss of Chattanooga would split the Confederacy. By July 22, he had decided.

The successful transfer of McCown's men, accomplished in only six days, had convinced Bragg that a massive shift of his army from Tupelo to Chattanooga was possible. Buell continued to move slowly east. By quickly joining Kirby Smith, Bragg reasoned, the combined Confederate army

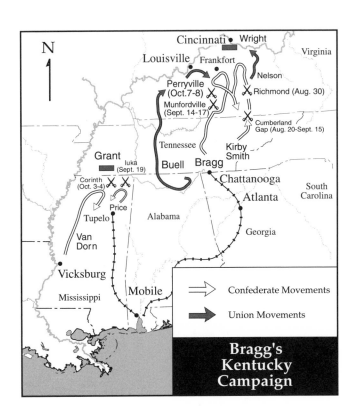

Bragg's Kentucky Campaign

could slip into middle Tennessee ahead of Buell's army and threaten the Union line of supply and communications. This, in turn, would cause both Buell and Grant to withdraw to the north, where each army could be defeated in turn. In preparation for his move, Bragg divided the army. He left 16,000 men at Tupelo under Maj. Gen. Sterling Price to operate in conjunction with Maj. Gen. Earl Van Dorn's 16,000 men at Vicksburg. Together, they would invade western Tennessee.

On July 23, the remaining infantry units of Bragg's army loaded onto train cars at Tupelo to begin their odyssey to Chattanooga. The journey took the troops over 776 miles on six railroads on a widely circuitous route via Mobile, Alabama, and Atlanta, Georgia. Different track sizes caused frequent transfers between trains, and the army had to cross Mobile Bay on ferries. While the foot soldiers moved by rail, the artillery, wagons, and cavalry took an overland route. When the lead elements of Bragg's Army of Mississippi arrived in Chattanooga on July 29, Buell was still miles away. Bragg had successfully moved men farther and faster than troops had ever been moved before and had united two Southern armies whose direct line of communications the enemy had severed. He was now in position to reverse the course of the war. Once middle Tennessee had been retaken, Bragg planned to invade Kentucky.

But while Bragg regrouped his army at Chattanooga, the entire plan changed. Detailed to take Cumberland Gap, Kirby Smith commanded a separate department and remained somewhat independent. He moved his 16,000 men into siege positions and then was advised by his cavalry chief, Col. John Hunt Morgan, that Kentucky was eager to join the Confederacy. After receiving two additional brigades from Chattanooga and leaving 9,000 men to besiege the 8,000-man Union force at Cumberland Gap, Kirby Smith decided to invade Kentucky regardless of Bragg's intentions.

On August 30, 6,000 Confederates attacked and destroyed a Union force of 6,500 new recruits at Richmond, Kentucky. Federal Maj. Gen. William ("Bull") Nelson attempted to rally the inexperienced soldiers, but Confederate troops quickly poured around their flanks, routing them. The Federals, many of whom had been in the army only a week, lost 206 killed, 844 wounded, and more than 4,000 captured. Kirby Smith's veterans had 78 killed and 372 wounded. After taking Lexington, Kirby Smith confidently named his force the "Army of Kentucky."

Bragg, fearful that his colleague was taking too big a risk, decided to support the invasion of Kentucky by positioning the Army of Mississippi between Buell's Federals and Kirby Smith's Confederates. As the Union Army of the Ohio retreated north toward Nashville, Bragg moved his 20,000 men via Carthage, Tennessee, and Glasgow, Kentucky, to reach the Green River first. On September 14, the 4,000-

man Union garrison of heavily fortified Munfordsville, Kentucky, repulsed advanced units of the Southern army. Three days later, after the rest of the Confederates moved up, the Federals surrendered.

While Bragg's army was entrenching around Munfordsville, Buell slipped past them to the west, eventually reaching Louisville, Kentucky. Here Buell received some 30,000 reinforcements while yet another 45,000-man Union force began growing at Cincinnati under Maj. Gen. Horatio Wright. Bragg, in turn, attempted to join Kirby Smith at Bardstown. Instead, he found the Army of Kentucky positioned from Cumberland Gap to Lexington. The Union garrison of Cumberland Gap, commanded by Brig. Gen. George Morgan, made an epic retreat across rugged terrain, avoiding Kirby Smith's columns. As a result, the Army of Kentucky remained dispersed and of little use to Bragg. In all, only 48,776 scattered Confederates now faced 137,282 Federals.

With Confederate forces dispersed and Union armies growing and concentrating, Bragg moved to make the best of his precarious situation. Despite optimistic predictions, Kentuckians were reluctant to join the Southern army. After placing Maj. Gen. Leonidas Polk in charge of the army, Bragg moved to Frankfort to set up a Confederate state government. He planned thereafter to enforce the national Conscription Acts and draft recruits into the ranks to defend the new Confederate state from Federal reconquest.

On October 2, Brig. Gen. Patrick Cleburne reported Federal movements from Louisville toward Frankfort. Bragg ordered Polk to move his troops north and to fall upon the enemy flank in conjunction with an attack by Kirby Smith's troops. Instead, citing superior scouting reports of enemy intentions and strengths, Polk retreated to Danville, maintaining the split in Confederate forces. Four converging Union columns of Buell's rested and refitted army, unopposed by Polk, then moved to block Bragg's line of retreat from Kentucky.

With his army still split, Bragg had no choice but to abandon his state capital and its new government and take command of his army in the field. Unsure of where Buell would strike, Confederates concentrated at both Danville and Versailles. On October 7, Maj. Gen. William J. Hardee reported Federals attacking his outposts at the small town of Perryville. Bragg ordered Polk to move quickly to reinforce Hardee, rout what he assumed was an enemy detachment at dawn, and then join Kirby Smith.

Instead, Polk hesitated. Bragg assumed command on October 8 and at 2:00 P.M. blindly launched his attack with 16,000 men against the assumed portion of the Federal army at Perryville. In reality, Buell had nearly 25,000 on the field and another 32,000 men within easy marching distance. The Confederates were at first wildly successful, driving Maj. Gen. Alexander McCook's Union corps before them. After their initial shock, however, the Federals rallied. At 4:00 P.M., Brig. Gen. Philip Sheridan counterattacked, driving in the Confederate left before withdrawing around nightfall. Tactically a draw, the Battle of Perryville had been costly. Bragg had committed all of his 16,000 troops on hand there; nearly 3,100 men had been killed, wounded, or captured—a loss of almost 20 percent. Buell had, however, used only half of his men. About 25,000 of his 61,000 men fought at Perryville, of which nearly 3,700 became casualties.

The Battle of Perryville and the fall of the embryonic Confederate government in Kentucky convinced Bragg that his campaign was futile. Van Dorn and Price, recently defeated at the Battles of Iuka on September 19 and Corinth on October 4, could not support the Kentucky invasion. Coordinating two armies—Bragg's and Kirby Smith's—had proven difficult. In addition, lack of citizen support and dwindling supplies complicated the Southerner's task. On October 13, after rendezvousing with Kirby Smith, Bragg marched his army out of Kentucky.

Bragg's Kentucky campaign was the only serious offensive threat to Northern territory posed by the western Confederate armies. If Bragg had been successful, the state of Kentucky would have been added to the Southern nation. The Union armies in Tennessee would have been withdrawn, and the Ohio River would have become the front line. Instead, the Confederates met defeat. Grant remained free to operate in Mississippi against Vicksburg. Buell, because of his slow pursuit of the retreating Confederates, was replaced by Gen. William Rosecrans, who ably led the newly designated Army of the Cumberland against Bragg in Tennessee. The invasion of Kentucky proved to be the high point for the western Confederates; afterward, the Richmond government changed the name of Bragg's force to the Army of Tennessee.

[*See also* Munfordville, Kentucky; Perryville, Kentucky.]

BIBLIOGRAPHY

Buell, Don Carlos. "East Tennessee and the Campaign of Perryville." In *Battles and Leaders of the Civil War.* Edited by Robert U. Johnson and C. C. Buel. Vol. 2. New York, 1888. Reprint, Secaucus, N.J., 1982.

Connelly, Thomas L. *Army of the Heartland: The Army of Tennessee, 1861–1862.* Baton Rouge, La., 1967.

Coulter, E. Merton. *The Civil War and Readjustment in Kentucky.* Chapel Hill, N.C., 1926.

Hawke, Paul. "Perryville, Kentucky." In *The Civil War Battlefield Guide.* Edited by Francis H. Kennedy. Boston, 1990.

McWhiney, Grady. *Braxton Bragg and Confederate Defeat.* Vol. 1. New York, 1968. Reprint. Tuscaloosa, Ala., 1991.

Morgan, George W. "Cumberland Gap." In *Battles and Leaders of the Civil War.* Edited by Robert U. Johnson and C. C. Buel. Vol. 2. New York, 1888. Reprint, Secaucus, N.J., 1982.

Wheeler, Joseph. "Bragg's Invasion of Kentucky." In *Battles and*

Leaders of the Civil War. Edited by Robert U. Johnson and C. C. Buel. Vol. 2. New York, 1888. Reprint, Secaucus, N.J., 1982.

DONALD S. FRAZIER

KERSHAW, JOSEPH B. (1822–1894), major general.

Descended from forebears prominent in military and political arenas, Kershaw was born at Camden, South Carolina, January 5, 1822. His grandfather, also named Joseph, had emigrated from England and played an active role as a colonel in the Revolutionary War. His father, John, served several terms as mayor of Camden, was a county judge, a member of the state legislature, and a one-term member of Congress.

Orphaned at seven, Joseph Kershaw attended local schools and the Cokesbury Conference School in the Abbeville District. Leaving after a brief period there, Kershaw went to Charleston where he clerked in a dry goods store. The job paled quickly, and he returned to Camden, read law, and was admitted to the bar in 1843. At the start of the Mexican War Kershaw wore the uniform of a first lieutenant with the DeKalb Rifle Guards of his hometown. His stay in Mexico was cut short by a fever that forced his early return to Camden where he resumed his law practice and was elected to the state legislature in 1852.

Kershaw was a member of his state's secession convention and in February 1861 was elected colonel of the Second South Carolina Infantry, which he had recruited. The regiment occupied Morris Island during the bombardment of Fort Sumter. Kershaw led the regiment at First Manassas as part of Milledge L. Bonham's brigade. Promoted to brigadier general, February 13, 1862, and given command of the brigade following Bonham's resignation, Kershaw fought in the Peninsular campaign and Seven Days' Battles and helped capture Maryland Heights during the reduction of Harpers Ferry. While defending the Sunken Road at Fredericksburg, he displayed "great coolness and skill," in the words of E. Porter Alexander. The South Carolinian also fought with distinction at Chancellorsville. On the second day at Gettysburg, as Lafayette McLaws's division embarked on its assault against Little Round Top, Kershaw appeared "cool, composed and grand, his steel-gray eyes flashing the fire he felt in his soul," wrote D. Augustus Dickens, brigade historian.

Transferred west with James Longstreet in September 1863, Kershaw arrived at Chickamauga in time to help crush the Federal right flank. He also participated in the Knoxville campaign before the corps was recalled to Virginia.

On May 6, 1864, Kershaw was riding with Longstreet and Micah Jenkins through the Wilderness when a mistaken volley from William Mahone's troops across the Plank Road ripped through the group. As his men prepared to return the fire, Kershaw dashed to the head of the column, shouting "They are friends!" His prompt action averted further bloodshed, although Longstreet was severely wounded and Jenkins was killed.

On May 18, shortly after he took part in the Battle of Spotsylvania, Kershaw was promoted to major general. He joined Jubal Early in the Shenandoah Valley campaign of 1864 but was ordered back to Richmond in September. While en route to the capital, he received news of Early's defeat at Winchester. He hastened back to the valley where he opened the attack at Cedar Creek. Kershaw eventually moved into the defenses of Petersburg and marched westward in April 1865. He was captured at Sayler's Creek and imprisoned at Fort Warren until August 12.

Returning to his law practice in Camden after the war, Kershaw was elected to the legislature in 1865 and became president of the senate. In later years he was elected judge of the Fifth District, a position he held until failing health intervened. He was appointed postmaster of Camden in 1893 and died April 13, 1894. He was buried in Quaker Cemetery, Camden.

BIBLIOGRAPHY

Alexander, E. Porter. "The Battle of Fredericksburg." *Southern Historical Society Papers* 10 (1882): 455. Reprint, Wilmington, N.C., 1990.

Capers, Ellison. *South Carolina.* Vol. 5 of *Confederate Military History.* Edited by Clement A. Evans. Atlanta, 1899. Vol. 6 of extended ed. Wilmington, N.C., 1987.

Dickert, D. Augustus. *History of Kershaw's Brigade.* Dayton, Ohio, 1976.

McLaws, Lafayette. "Gettysburg." *Southern Historical Society Papers* 7 (1879): 88–90. Reprint, Wilmington, N.C., 1990.

Warner, Ezra J. *Generals in Gray: Lives of the Confederate Commanders.* Baton Rouge, La., 1959.

LOWELL REIDENBAUGH

KEYES, WADE (1821–?), interim attorney general. An Alabama Democrat, Keyes was assistant attorney general throughout the war and attorney general ad interim from October 1863 to January 1864. He proved a dependable workhorse for the Department of Justice and helped defend the powers of the Confederacy's central government.

Born into wealth in Mooresville, Alabama, Wade Keyes studied at LaGrange College in Georgia and the University of Virginia. He practiced law in Kentucky and Florida before moving to Montgomery, Alabama, in 1851, where he became chancellor for the Southern Division of the state in 1853. Keyes authored two legal treatises and was well connected with Alabama politicians, but apparently he was not ambitious for a higher appointment.

After Thomas H. Watts resigned as attorney general, Jefferson Davis ignored a demand from the *Charleston Mercury* that he redesign the entire cabinet. Instead he appointed Keyes attorney general ad interim until he could select George Davis of North Carolina as Watt's successor. In five other periods Keyes was actually in charge of the department while the attorney general was absent—two months in the fall of 1861; Christmas holidays, 1861; October and November 1862; August 1863; and September and October 1864.

Keyes wrote twenty-three opinions that often cited precedents established by U.S. courts. A representative opinion (on distillation of liquor for the army) held that a state "cannot punish as an offense an act which the Confederate Government has the power to authorize and which is done under its authority." When the war ended Keyes returned to Alabama to practice law.

BIBLIOGRAPHY

Patrick, Rembert W. *Jefferson Davis and His Cabinet.* Baton Rouge, La., 1944.

U.S. War Department. *The War of the Rebellion: A Compilation of the Official Records of the Union and Confederate Armies.* Washington, D.C., 1880–1901. Ser. IV, vol. 3, pp. 876–879.

Wakelyn, Jon L. *Biographical Dictionary of the Confederacy.* Edited by Frank E. Vandiver. Westport, Conn., 1977.

PAUL D. ESCOTT

KILPATRICK-DAHLGREN RAID. This raid, named for Union Gen. Judson Kilpatrick and Col. Ulric Dahlgren, began on February 28, 1864, with the avowed purpose of freeing Union soldiers held in Richmond's Libby Prison and Belle Island. Over the next four days, 4,000 handpicked Federal cavalrymen clashed with a scattered force of 500 Southern soldiers and home guard units to the west and north of Richmond. In the end, the Federals lost 340 men, 583 horses, and much equipment and never reached close proximity to either of the two prisons.

In mid-February 1864 Union intelligence reported that the Confederate capital's meager defenses left it especially vulnerable to a cavalry raid. The boisterous and ambitious Judson Kilpatrick sought the approval of President Abraham Lincoln for a surprise raid that would free prisoners and wreak havoc on the Confederate capital. Lincoln gave his enthusiastic support, hoping that Kilpatrick would bring some positive results to the Union war effort.

On the night of February 28, Kilpatrick set out with his men toward Ely's Ford on the Rapidan River. Included in his force was young Ulric Dahlgren. The earnest son of navy officer John Dahlgren was to lead a detachment of cavalry across the James River and attack from the south, while Kilpatrick's main force entered the city from the north. Gen. Robert E. Lee had predicted such a raid four months earlier and was well prepared for this one. As sleet and rain

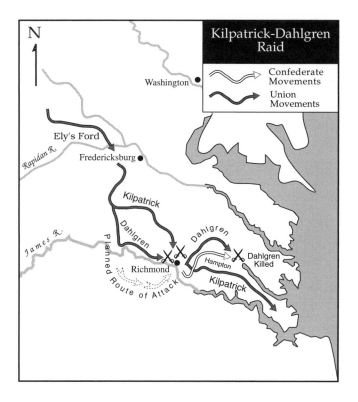

simply freeing prisoners. The papers detailed Federal intentions to burn the city and kill Jefferson Davis and his cabinet. Richmond newspapers soon published the papers, and Southerners were outraged. They demanded an investigation and explanation from Federal authorities. Union officials first claimed that the papers were forgeries and later admitted only to Dahlgren's guilt.

The extent of Union involvement in the plans to burn Richmond and kill Confederate civilian leaders remains unclear. But in March 1864, the mere allegation of such dark intentions was enough to strengthen Southern resolve to persevere in the war.

[See also Dahlgren Papers.]

BIBLIOGRAPHY

Dahlgren, John. *Memoir of Ulric Dahlgren.* Philadelphia, 1872.
Jones, V. C. *Eight Hours before Richmond.* New York, 1957.
Riggs, David F. "The Dahlgren Papers Reconsidered." *Lincoln Herald* 83 (1981): 658–667.
Thomas, Emory M. "The Kilpatrick-Dahlgren Raid—Part I and II." *Civil War Times Illustrated* 16–17 (February–April 1978): 4–9, 26–33.

LESLEY JILL GORDON-BURR

fell in torrents, Confederate spies spread the word of the Union plans and alerted city defenses of the enemy approach. By the time Kilpatrick's men arrived, the Confederates were ready.

Federals first sensed trouble soon after Dahlgren split away from Kilpatrick's main force on February 29. Kilpatrick unexpectedly met strong resistance five miles north of Richmond. After fighting several hours, he withdrew to the east and then, after hesitating, turned to resume battle. Maj. Gen. Wade Hampton and his small force of three hundred cavalrymen came from behind. In the ensuing darkness Kilpatrick's exhausted men doggedly fought the Confederates, but the Union general's fighting spirit was gone and he again turned to retreat eastward toward Federal lines.

Meanwhile, Dahlgren with his detachment of five hundred men found the James River swelled from the recent rains. When Dahlgren tried instead to enter Richmond from the west, he met stiff resistance from G. W. Custis Lee's local defense brigade. This force of armory workers and government clerks blocked Dahlgren's planned approach. In the confused retreat, Dahlgren and one hundred of his men became separated. Trying to reach the safety of Union lines, Dahlgren stumbled upon an ambush in King and Queen County. He was killed instantly, and most of the remaining Federals surrendered.

Papers found on Dahlgren's body by a teenaged boy revealed that the raiding cavalrymen planned more than

KING, WILLIAM H.

KING, WILLIAM H. (1839–1910), colonel and acting brigadier general. King, born June 10, 1839, at Cullondenville, Georgia, trained in medicine and law at Americus, Georgia, between 1846 and 1853. After making a trip to Texas in 1856, he moved to Cass County in that state in 1860.

On October 15, 1861, King joined the Confederate army and was appointed to the rank of major and quartermaster of Henry E. McCulloch's division (later John H. Walker's division). In 1862 he transferred to the Eighteenth Texas Infantry Regiment and was elected lieutenant colonel and then commander with an accompanying promotion to colonel. He led this regiment during the Red River campaign and was wounded at Mansfield. A competent and effective commander, he, along with his unit, was cited by Gen. Thomas Neville Waul and General Walker for bravery. Gen. E. Kirby Smith promoted King to brigadier general and on May 11, 1864, when Waul resigned, placed him in command of the Second Brigade of Walker's division. When Walker was transferred, King took temporary command of his division from July 17 to September 2, when Maj. Gen. John Horace Forney, the new division commander, arrived.

During King's short tenure as commander, the division was ordered across the Mississippi to support Confederate forces in the Trans-Mississippi region, but two popular captains opposed the crossing and urged their troops to go home. They were court-martialed and executed for treason. President Jefferson Davis then halted the projected movement, deeming it too risky an operation, and the division returned to western Louisiana. King's appointment to brigadier general was never confirmed by the Confederate government; although the reason was unstated, it is possible that the mutiny and executions had an effect on the decision.

King resumed brigade command after Forney's arrival and served in that capacity until the end of the war. Afterward, he practiced law and was elected mayor of Sulphur Springs, Texas. He later was elected to the state legislature and then was appointed adjutant general of Texas (1881–1891). King died in Sulphur Springs in 1910.

BIBLIOGRAPHY

Blessington, James P. *Campaigns of Walker's Texas Division*. New York, 1875.

Fitzhugh, Lester N., comp. *Texas Batteries, Battalions, Regiments, Commanders, and Field Officers, Confederate States Army, 1861–1865*. Midlothian, Tex., 1959.

Roberts, O. M. *Texas*. Vol. 11 of *Confederate Military History*. Edited by Clement A. Evans. Atlanta, 1899. Vol. 15 of extended ed. Wilmington, N.C., 1989.

ROY R. STEPHENSON

KING COTTON. *See* Cotton; Diplomacy; Textile Industry.

KIRKLAND, WILLIAM WHEDBEE (1833–1915), brigadier general. When the war began, Kirkland was colonel of the Eleventh North Carolina Volunteers, later designated the Twenty-first North Carolina. He fought at First Manassas and the following spring participated in Thomas J. ("Stonewall") Jackson's Shenandoah Valley campaign. Wounded at the First Battle of Winchester, he recovered to become chief of staff to Patrick Cleburne during the Murfreesboro campaign. He returned to active service with his old regiment at Gettysburg, taking part in the first two days of fighting. Promoted to brigadier general in August 1863, Kirkland commanded a brigade in the fighting at Bristoe Station where he was wounded a second time. In 1864 he participated in the fighting at the Wilderness and Spotsylvania before being wounded once again at Cold Harbor. Assigned to the command of another brigade in August 1864, he served under James Longstreet at Richmond, taking part in the attack on Fort Harrison in October 1864. Transferred to North Carolina in December, Kirkland assisted in the defense of Fort Fisher by forcing back the Federal advance under the command of Benjamin Butler. Later, when the Confederates abandoned the fort and withdrew to Wilmington, he commanded the rear guard and directed events in the fighting at Wise's Fork. He fought

at Bentonville and surrendered with Joseph E. Johnston on April 26, 1865. Kirkland fought with honor and distinction throughout the war and gained the respect of all who knew him.

After the war, Kirkland had a career as a private businessman.

BIBLIOGRAPHY

Freeman, Douglas S. *Lee's Lieutenants: A Study in Command*. 3 vols. New York, 1942–1944. Reprint, New York, 1986.

Hill, D. H., Jr. *North Carolina*. Vol. 4 of *Confederate Military History*. Edited by Clement A. Evans. Atlanta, 1899. Vol. 5 of extended ed. Wilmington, N.C., 1987.

U.S. War Department. *War of the Rebellion: A Compilation of the Official Records of the Union and Confederate Armies*. Washington, D.C., 1880–1901. Ser. 1, vol. 27, pt. 2, p. 489; ser. 1, vol. 29, pt. 1, p. 433; ser. 1, vol. 29, pt. 2, p . 701; ser. 1, vol. 47, pt. 1, pp. 956, 1056, 1088, 1091.

MICHAEL G. MAHON

KNIGHTS OF THE GOLDEN CIRCLE. *See* Copperheads.

KNOW-NOTHING PARTY. *See* American Party.

KNOXVILLE AND GREENEVILLE CONVENTIONS. The Knoxville Convention of May 30 and 31, 1861, and the Greeneville Convention of June 17 through 20, 1861, represented eastern Tennessee Unionists' challenge to the state's secession crisis. Although they failed to prevent Tennessee's alliance with the Confederacy or to establish a separate pro-Union state, they gave powerful voice to anti-Confederate sentiment, provided leadership for those opposed to the Southern cause, and required the Confederate government to allocate precious resources to Tennessee's mountain districts. Because of its dependence upon the strategically vital East Tennessee and Virginia Railroad to carry troops from the Deep South to the eastern theater of war, the Confederacy had to retain the region regardless of its inhabitants' expressed wishes.

A people with scant commitment to slavery or commercial agriculture, eastern Tennesseans had long felt alienated from planter-dominated middle and western Tennessee. On February 9, when the entire state had voted against Governor Isham G. Harris's call for a secession convention, eastern Tennesseans with a negative vote of 81 percent were far more emphatic than western Tennesseans at 65 percent and middle Tennesseans with only 51 percent. But the bombardment of Fort Sumter and Abraham Lincoln's subsequent call for volunteers galvanized the Tennessee legislature to declare separation from the Union on May 6 and to schedule a plebiscite for June 8.

Reacting to this in mid-May, fifteen prominent Knox County Unionists, including William G. Brownlow and Oliver Perry Temple, met in Temple's law office and called for a Union convention. Whigs in politics, they found common cause with their longtime Democratic party foe Senator Andrew Johnson. Emboldened by editorials in Brownlow's *Knoxville Whig* and Johnson's passionate rhetoric, over 400 delegates assembled at Knoxville's Temperance Hall on May 30 and 31 and chose Congressman Thomas A. R. Nelson as their presiding officer. Though a nondelegate, Johnson addressed the convention, which thereafter passed resolutions condemning the June plebiscite, urging Tennesseans to reject secession, and empowering Nelson to convene a second convention should events warrant.

On June 8, middle and western Tennesseans overwhelmingly endorsed secession, but eastern Tennesseans rejected it by a 68 percent vote. Arguing that the referendum had been won by force and fraud, Nelson called a second convention at Greeneville on June 17, but only 285 delegates gathered. Some earlier supporters had reluctantly accepted the plebiscite's verdict, and others—most notably Andrew Johnson—had fled the state. Transient Confederate troops constantly threatened the delegates, and a passing Louisiana regiment ate the conventioneers' breakfast. Nonetheless, the convention entertained truculent proposals advocating armed resistance and eastern Tennessee statehood, but eventually it passed calmer resolutions expressing an "earnest desire" that eastern Tennessee remain neutral territory and requesting the Nashville government to allow the region separate statehood. Not surprisingly, the convention's three-man commission to the Tennessee legislature found an unsympathetic audience.

Whatever the conventions' lack of success, they served notice of eastern Tennessee's resistance to joining the Confederacy. Over thirty thousand of its inhabitants would enroll in Union regiments, others fought as guerrillas, and when Ambrose Burnside's Union army marched into the region in 1863, his soldiers were greeted as liberators.

BIBLIOGRAPHY

Bryan, Charles F., Jr. "A Gathering of Tories: The East Tennessee Convention of 1861." *Tennessee Historical Quarterly* 34 (Spring 1980): 27–48.
Campbell, Mary E. R. *The Attitude of Tennesseans toward the Union, 1847–1861.* New York, 1961.
Henry, J. Milton. "The Revolution in Tennessee, February, 1861 to June, 1861." *Tennessee Historical Quarterly* 18 (Summer 1959): 99–118.
Queener, Verton M. "East Tennessee Sentiment and the Secession Movement, November, 1860–June, 1861." *East Tennessee Historical Society's Publications,* no. 20 (1948): 59–83.
Temple, Oliver Perry. *East Tennessee and the Civil War.* Cincinnati, Ohio, 1899.

FRED ARTHUR BAILEY

KNOXVILLE CAMPAIGN. Located on the Holston (now Tennessee) River in eastern Tennessee, Knoxville was the object of an unsuccessful Confederate siege against Federal forces in the fall of 1863. While Gen. Braxton Bragg was investing Chattanooga during that period, he requested that President Jefferson Davis order Gen. James Longstreet, with whom Bragg could not get along, to assault the Union Army of the Ohio in Knoxville. The Federals, numbering about 12,000 infantry and 8,500 cavalry under Gen. Ambrose Burnside, had been quartered there since taking the city on September 2. Bragg's intention was not only to get rid of Longstreet but also to divert Northern concentration from Chattanooga.

Although furious with Bragg for splitting the Confederate command, Longstreet had no choice but to follow orders, and on November 5, he started his 17,000-man force north. The journey was difficult, and eight days later, they had traveled only sixty miles, reaching the town of Sweetwater. There the general had expected rations and supplies, but they were not forthcoming. Berated by Bragg for taking too much time, and with his troops exhausted, hungry, and ragged, Longstreet pushed on nevertheless.

Realizing that Longstreet was approaching, Burnside sent a force of 5,000 troops to confront him. Burnside knew he could not defeat the superior number of Confederates, but he wanted to keep Longstreet busy so that he could not return to Chattanooga and assist Bragg's army when the Federals there attacked those troops. Longstreet, on November 13, ordered three brigades of Gen. Joseph Wheeler's cavalry to take and hold the heights across from Knoxville on the southern bank of the Holston River. Wheeler, after being slowed by two regiments of Federal horsemen, arrived at the river on November 15, but found the heavily armed heights impregnable. With no chance of victory, he and his troopers rode back to rejoin Longstreet.

In the meantime, the Southern infantrymen were thirty miles southwest of Knoxville fording the Little Tennessee River at Loudon, when Longstreet received word that the Union troops were a few miles east of him across the river and seemingly retreating to Knoxville. Longstreet headed for Lenoir's Station, about eight miles northeast of Loudon, hoping to cut them off. But the Federals moved quicker, and by the time Longstreet arrived in Lenoir on November 16, they were gone.

Longstreet nevertheless pressed on hard, hoping to destroy Burnside's troops at the crossroads of Campbell's Station, fifteen miles southwest of Knoxville. Learning of a shortcut, Longstreet sent Gen. Lafayette McLaws's division

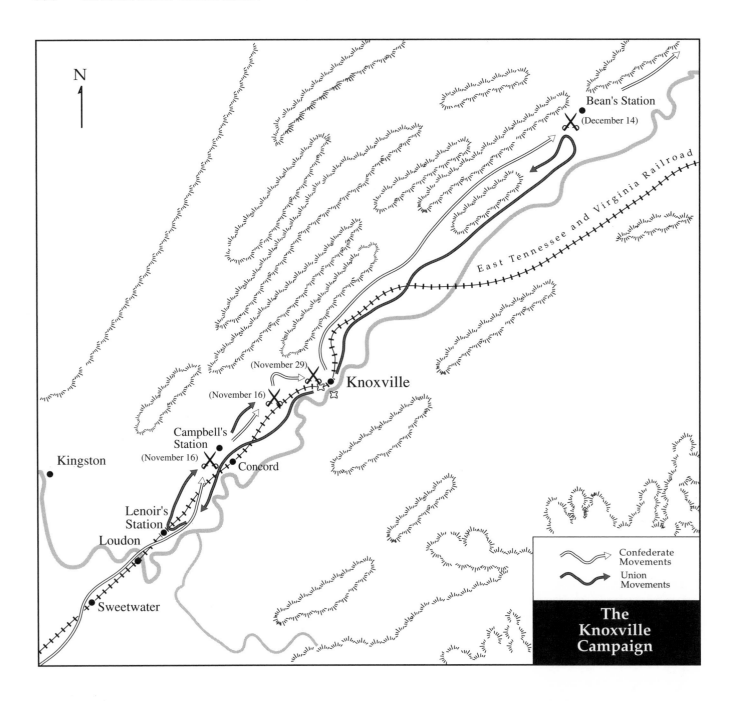

N

Bean's Station
(December 14)

East Tennessee and Virginia Railroad

(November 29)

Knoxville

(November 16)

Campbell's
Station
(November 16)

Concord

Kingston

Lenoir's
Station

Loudon

Sweetwater

Confederate
Movements

Union
Movements

**The
Knoxville
Campaign**

forward on that route, while the division of Gen. Micah Jenkins pressed the Federals from the rear. But Burnside discovered the Confederate plan and rushed forward a division to outrun McLaws to Campbell's Station. The Federals arrived first, taking up defensive positions along the Kingston and Concord roads. The Confederate attacks that day were poorly coordinated and gained nothing, and as a result, Burnside's soldiers, protected by some seven hundred Federal cavalry acting as a rear guard, were able to withdraw after dark. Making a forced march along the Kingston Road, the Union infantrymen retired to Knoxville.

Right behind the Federals followed Longstreet's men. Approaching the city, the Confederates routed a Federal cavalry force commanded by Gen. William Sanders. Sanders was killed, the only Southern-born Union general to meet that fate in the Civil War. Taking up positions around Knoxville, Longstreet laid siege to the town.

Capt. Orlando Poe, Burnside's chief engineer, had built stout defensive forts and earthworks around Knoxville's eastern, northern, and western perimeter; the Holston River covered the southern side. In the northwestern corner of these defenses was located a strong work known as Fort Sanders. Longstreet determined to attack there, but after a couple of aborted assaults, he briefly shelved Sanders as an objective. After being reinforced with two brigades numbering about 2,600 men under Gens. Bushrod Rust Johnson and Archibald Gracie, Jr., however, on November 29 Longstreet decided to strike the fort at dawn.

Prior to the attack, the ground in front of the fort had been reconnoitered by the Confederates, but they failed to realize that a ditch surrounding Sanders was between six and eight feet deep. Added to that, the fort's walls at ground level were thirteen feet high and sloped forty-five degrees, making an average total of twenty difficult feet that had to be climbed before the attackers could gain access to the interior of the work. And if those conditions were not enough to ensure failure, cold, wet weather had covered the earth of the fort with ice.

Unaware of what lay in store for them, the Confederate attack proceeded as scheduled—and met with disaster. With Longstreet's soldiers caught in the ditch, Federals on the fort's parapets slaughtered them mercilessly. One Union officer even lit the fuses of cannon balls and rolled them down into the tightly bunched gray ranks, creating havoc. Recognizing unqualified defeat after twenty minutes of fighting, Longstreet called off the assault. Confederate losses in that short battle amounted to 129 killed, 458 wounded, and 226 missing, while the Federals lost 5 killed and 8 wounded.

During the fight, Longstreet received a telegram from Jefferson Davis informing him that Bragg's forces had been routed at Chattanooga and ordering him to abandon Knoxville and reinforce Bragg. Longstreet, though, with the intention of keeping Federal reinforcements from harassing Bragg's army, stayed in the Knoxville area until the night of December 4, when he withdrew to the northwest. A Federal pursuit engaged in—and lost—one last battle with the Confederates at Bean's Station, Tennessee, on December 14. This action effectively ended the siege of Knoxville.

Total losses for the siege were 1,142, exclusive of cavalry, for the Confederates out of approximately 20,000 engaged, and 693 for the Union out of about 12,000 infantry effectives. The Confederacy suffered an even greater check to its cause as a result of splitting the forces at Chattanooga, thereby ensuring major defeats there and at Knoxville.

BIBLIOGRAPHY

Johnson, Robert U., and C. C. Buel, eds. *Battles and Leaders of the Civil War.* Vol. 3. New York, 1888. Reprint, Secaucus, N.J., 1982.

Longstreet, James. *From Manassas to Appomattox.* Philadelphia, 1896. Reprint, Bloomington, Ind., 1960.

Seymour, Digby Gordon. *Divided Loyalties: Fort Sanders and the Civil War in East Tennessee.* 2d ed. Knoxville, Tenn., 1990.

U.S. War Department. *War of the Rebellion: A Compilation of the Official Records of the Union and Confederate Armies.* Washington, D.C., 1880–1901. Ser. 1, vol. 31, pts. 1 and 3.

WARREN WILKINSON

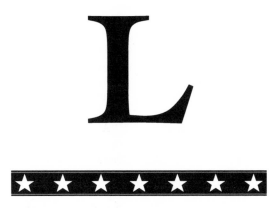

L

LABOR. [*This entry includes two articles that discuss the workers on the Confederate home front and battlefront, the conditions under which they labored, and their contributions to the Confederacy:* An Overview *and* Skilled Labor. *See also* African American Forgeworkers; Bread Riots; Civil Service; Farming; Inflation; Mining; Naval Ordnance Works; Plain Folk; Plantation; Powder Works; Sailors; Shelby Iron Company; Shipyards; Slavery; Soldiers; Textile Industry; Tredegar Iron Works.]

An Overview

Making war entails hard work on the part of civilians and soldiers alike. The Confederacy's war effort differed fundamentally from the Union's in that it mobilized slaves as well as free persons. As Confederate leaders often boasted, slavery provided both the rationale for the rebellion and the practical means for achieving victory. With slave laborers producing the goods that sustained soldiers as well as civilians, white men could focus upon the fight. At home and afield, in service and out, residents of the Confederate states shouldered the heavy burden of war.

The Battlefront. The dangerous work of combat fell almost without exception upon men and disproportionately upon the small farmers and laborers who constituted the bulk of the white population. The job paid little, and the amenities were few. Soldiers ran a comparatively high risk of occupational injury or death, from microbes as well as minié balls. Even apart from the hazards of combat, soldiers performed arduous duty virtually on a daily basis.

The work began with basic training, where fresh recruits endlessly practiced using firearms and moving in tactical formations of several dozen to several thousand men. Soldiers in cavalry and artillery units had to perfect similar skills, coordinating the movements of animals with those of men. Artillerists also worked on positioning, sighting, and firing cannon. In all, despite times of comparatively light duty—even downright boredom—soldiers in both armies viewed training as hard work.

Whether or not soldiers saw marching in the same light, they understood that when the walking stopped, work would begin: clearing brush and trees, pitching camp, constructing shelter. Some of these tasks, like cooking, tidying the living area, and washing and mending clothes, were traditionally women's work. Others, like digging fortifications, currying horses, and loading and unloading wagons, were traditionally slaves' work. Soldiers who possessed artisan skills ranging from blacksmithing to shoemaking often continued to ply their trades while in service. And, through need if not predilection, most soldiers became expert tinkerers, fashioning natural materials and broken or abandoned equipment into useful articles.

Slaves, too, worked in direct support of field armies, for the most part as personal servants, cooks, and laborers. During the first year of the war, slaves attended owners in the enlisted ranks as well as in commissioned offices. Over time, however, only officers retained their servants; the slaves of private soldiers either returned home or found employment with the army. They cooked for their owners' bunkmates or for entire companies of soldiers; they worked as teamsters or laborers for the quartermaster or subsistence departments; they tended the sick and wounded or buried the dead for the medical corps.

Most slaves in Confederate employ, however, did the heavy, disagreeable, and often dangerous work of moving earth and trees to construct fortifications, roads, and bridges. Commanders who anticipated Federal attack routinely impressed slaves from surrounding plantations to serve in labor battalions. Impressment orders usually obligated masters to furnish 10 percent of their able-bodied adult slaves, with tools and rations, for thirty days' service.

Impressed slaves often worked under hard-driving overseers. If the intensity and regimentation of such labor offered slaves little opportunity for rest, at times the confusion provided cover for escape, as the "contrabands" who in May 1861 approached Union Gen. Benjamin F. Butler's lines at Fortress Monroe, Virginia, testified. Over time, masters as well as slaves devised strategies to avoid impressment. Nonetheless, impressed slaves labored prodigiously; extant earthworks on battlefields across the South bear mute testimony to their diligence.

The Home Front. The war reshaped labor on the home front no less than on the war front. From the start of the war, Confederate military strategists had comfortably assumed that plantation slaves working in their accustomed ways would raise food enough for soldiers and civilians alike. But industrial self-sufficiency was another matter, given the paucity of the antebellum infrastructure. Entrepreneurs, artisans, and laborers would need to contribute their respective skills and energies to produce the arms and ammunition; the flour and pork; the clothing and other textiles; the saddles, harnesses, and other leather products; the wagons, gun carriages, and other wood products—in short, the innumerable necessities of modern warfare. In the best of times, reallocation of material and human resources would have been difficult; the Union blockade and the success of Federal armies beginning in the spring of 1862 compounded the difficulty.

In the circumstances, shopkeepers and artisans in the luxury trades had to adjust. Carriage makers could fashion caissons as well as phaetons, and clocksmiths could make and repair small arms as well as timepieces. Other artisans likewise contributed their skills to the war effort, working either in private establishments with government contracts or in the numerous facilities established and operated by the Confederate government throughout the South.

For various reasons, ordnance establishments assumed pride of place among these works. The Ordnance Department employed thousands of metalworkers, molders, and men skilled in the use of machinery to cast cannon and shot, make and repair small arms, and fabricate ammunition. Thousands of carpenters and brickmasons made additions and repairs to existing structures. These skilled workers represented such a valuable component of the civilian labor force that conscription legislation pointedly exempted them from military service. Many an artisan—native-born Southerners as well as German and Irish immigrants—availed himself of the exemption, in some cases for reasons of Unionist politics, in others for family considerations. Still others believed they best served the cause by remaining at their workbenches.

Both private and government employers paid skilled workers well, but as the war progressed, rising inflation undercut the artisans' wages. Beginning in 1863, skilled workers protested against their losing battle with the high cost of living. In various cities of the Confederacy, typographers and telegraphers struck for higher wages; by 1864 workers in every branch of government service from the post office to the Ordnance Department were doing the same, as were both skilled and unskilled workers employed by government contractors.

Although skilled workers did not monopolize popular opposition to inflation—as the well-known women's bread riots of 1863 demonstrate—the workers' protests were significant for several reasons. First, the work stoppages and slowdowns threatened production of vital war matériel. Second, the attack on inflation had potentially broad appeal among the Confederate citizenry. Third, even if the protest did not ultimately address larger political questions, officials feared that it might. Accordingly, they squelched strikes by drafting the strikers into military service.

Women in the Work Force. Although not subject to conscription, southern women were drawn into the vortex of war in countless ways. Even before the first shot had been fired, the wives and daughters of black belt planters and women from the urban commercial and professional classes formed societies to knit socks and sew uniforms and flags for their men. After the fighting began, they also practiced a strict domestic economy aimed at achieving self-sufficiency in necessities and at conserving scarce resources. With similar fervor, some women of the upper classes went to work as clerks and bookkeepers in private shops and government offices, though traditional opposition to work outside the home limited such employment. Accordingly, upper-class women tended to focus their energy on volunteer services as nurses, schoolteachers, and members of committees to relieve the suffering of soldiers' families.

Slave women had to accommodate to their owners' new concerns, without, however, sacrificing their perspective on unfolding events or their ultimate objectives. In the short run, this accommodation meant additional hours of spinning and weaving after housework was completed. In the long run, it entailed even greater contributions to the orderly functioning of households. But, ironically, as mistresses became increasingly dependent upon their slaves, the slaves became less dependent upon them.

On yeoman farms and in urban tenements, women could ill afford the luxury of voluntary labor for the public good. With few if any slaves at their command, farm women assumed new agricultural chores to supplement their customary dairying, cooking, housekeeping, and child-rearing. Whereas farm women in the North faced similar challenges, they contended with no comparable dearth of work animals and, indeed, benefited from a proliferation of mechanical inventions to compensate for the shortage of workers.

Southern women of the urban working classes also struggled for subsistence, but within the context of earning sufficient wages for necessities and rent. By removing the men, conscription severely reduced the earning power of working class households. Although the resulting shortage of men created job openings for women and children, soaring inflation reduced the purchasing power of their earnings. The well-known bread riots of 1863 hint at urban women's mounting frustration with these circumstances, but, despite the protests, conditions got worse instead of better.

Agricultural Work. Confederate agriculture could scarcely have escaped the reallocation of men and resources. Both yeoman farms and slave plantations experienced the effect, but in different ways and with different—though equally profound—results. On the farms the combination of conscription and the Confederate tax-in-kind created a subsistence crisis, which the most determined exertions of the soldiers' wives and children could not alleviate. During 1864 and 1865, growing numbers of soldiers deserted to assist their families. Arriving home, they often found little if any food, fields grown over in weeds, and wagons and stock confiscated. In many cases, they labored in vain to reverse the deterioration that had occurred in their absence. Many had little alternative but to mortgage their land for the means of subsistence, thereby committing their future to commercial agriculture in order to liquidate their debts. The long-term consequences of these new patterns played themselves out through the rest of the nineteenth century.

Slave Labor. As the war dragged on, both private employers and Confederate authorities of necessity turned to slaves to meet their production goals. In time, the Niter and Mining Bureau as well as the Ordnance, Quartermaster, Subsistence, and Medical departments employed large numbers of slaves. Most of these men and women, hired from their masters by the year, worked as laborers, although men with skills in the building or mechanical trades worked in their specialties. Some evidence also suggests that employers promoted unskilled slaves into jobs of skill or responsibility as the need arose. By the end of the war, such slaves had managed to bargain for various perquisites not enumerated in the initial agreements of hire; these included extensive travel privileges and cash payments for overtime work.

On the plantations, the shift from staples to foodstuffs altered field routines and, as a result, larger patterns of employing slave laborers. The absence of military-age men decreased supervision, despite provisions for one exemption per each twenty slaves (later modified to one exemption per each ten slaves). On many plantations, slaves worked essentially on their own, with little or no oversight by owners or overseers. They raised grains and vegetables, in most circumstances more fearful of Confederate tax-in-kind officials than of Northern soldiers.

On the plantations where masters or overseers remained in control, slave-grown foodstuffs provided subsistence for families, black and white, and a surplus for tax purposes and exchange in local markets. Even in the midst of war, plantation slaves were capable of producing bountiful harvests, as Federal armies repeatedly learned, perhaps none more appreciatively than that of William Tecumseh Sherman. If soldiers in the trenches at Petersburg endured maddening hunger, the fault lay with the transportation system rather than the plantation system.

By itself, the shift from staples to cereals guaranteed an aggregate decrease in the amount of labor performed by plantation slaves, a pattern that continued into the postwar years. But slaves in large portions of the South ceased laboring altogether on behalf of the Confederacy by fleeing from their owners. Some 500,000 escaped to Union-occupied areas of Tennessee, the Mississippi valley, the Carolina low country, and the Chesapeake Tidewater. Other slaves fled to Union armed forces wherever they operated, upsetting the balance of power between masters and slaves throughout the Confederacy. The system of plantation labor was far different in December 1864 from what it had been in December 1860. Though still the foundation of agricultural production, it was chipping badly around the edges.

These changes in turn dramatically affected Confederate labor policy during the closing months of the war, in no respect more so than in the matter of enlisting slave men into military service. Despite the continuing need for slaves to work in fields and factories, and despite the obvious irony of relying upon slaves to resuscitate the struggle on behalf of perpetuating slavery, Confederate leaders felt that the exhaustion of white manpower left no other choice. Critics of the policy contended that the short-term objective of prolonging the fight subverted the original purpose of the war: if slaves were fit for combat, then they were not fit for slavery. Appomattox settled the debate.

In sum, the Civil War significantly altered traditional labor relations in the South even before emancipation thoroughly revolutionized them. Not just masters and slaves experienced the consequences. With white women plowing, white men cooking, black women supervising big houses, and black men bearing arms, it was clear how profoundly war could change the course of human events.

BIBLIOGRAPHY

Berlin, Ira, et al., eds. *Freedom: A Documentary History of Emancipation, 1861–1867.* 4 vols. to date. Cambridge, England, 1982–.

Brewer, James H. *The Confederate Negro: Virginia's Craftsmen and Military Laborers, 1861–1865.* Durham, N.C., 1969.

Coulter, E. Merton. *The Confederate States of America, 1861–1865.* A History of the South, vol. 7. Baton Rouge, La., 1950.

Eaton, Clement. *A History of the Southern Confederacy.* New York, 1954.

Escott, Paul D. *After Secession: Jefferson Davis and the Failure of Confederate Nationalism.* Baton Rouge, La., 1978.

Thomas, Emory. *The Confederacy as a Revolutionary Experience.* Englewood Cliffs, N.J., 1971.

Wiley, Bell Irvin. *The Life of Johnny Reb: The Common Soldier of the Confederacy.* Baton Rouge, La., 1943.

Wiley, Bell Irvin. *Southern Negroes, 1861–1865.* New Haven, 1938.

JOSEPH P. REIDY

Skilled Labor

Despite the popular enthusiasm generated by secession, the success of the Confederacy depended upon creating an industrial infrastructure capable of prosecuting war against an economic powerhouse. In comparison with the rest of the nineteenth-century world, the Confederacy had little cause for shame. Railroads spanned the region, iron foundries dotted the Appalachians and its foothills, and workshops of considerable variety and output flourished in the interior as well as along the coast. But for the Confederacy to win the war it would have to sustain itself in manufactures; therefore, the existing infrastructure would have to be expanded and integrated. Confederate government officials, working largely through the War Department's assorted bureaus, laid the plans for this effort. Skilled workers transformed the designs into reality.

Every Confederate state boasted both free and slave artisans. The former practiced trades whose origins lay in colonial times if not earlier: they fashioned wood, metal, leather, and other raw materials into items for use in homes, farms, and businesses. Blacksmiths and related iron-workers were an especially distinctive group, with growing importance in the nascent industrial economy. As railroads spread from the 1830s until the start of the war, these blacksmiths and ironworkers labored in mills and workshops building, repairing, and operating machinery of increasing complexity and sophistication. A small but noteworthy number of these metalworkers were free men of color. In Charleston and New Orleans, in particular, their ironwork set a standard for artistry as well as craftsmanship.

Other skilled workers were slaves. These included plantation blacksmiths, carpenters, coopers, and jacks-of-all-trades, as well as a host of urban craftsmen. Although most urban slave artisans were building tradesmen—carpenters and masons, in particular—others worked in the specialties that catered to the needs of urban populations. Some worked with iron and other metals of potential use to the military.

As war clouds gathered, civilians and government officials contemplated how to achieve industrial self-sufficiency. Foundries throughout the region would produce the lighter work, and such establishments as the Atlanta Rolling Mill and the renowned Tredegar Iron Works in Richmond would handle the heavy work, which in addition to rails and ordnance soon also included armor plate for warships.

Confederate planners calculated the need for additional industrial productivity beyond that represented by extant facilities. Rather than rely entirely upon private enterprise, they envisioned a direct government role. The chief architect of this plan was Josiah Gorgas, head of the Ordnance Department. Under his direction, the government began manufacturing cannons, small arms, and ammunition at sites across the South.

From start to finish, managers of workshops both private and government-sponsored faced a shortage of skilled workers. Recognizing this, lawmakers designing the conscription law that took effect in spring 1862 exempted pilots, telegraph operators, printers, and employees of railroads, riverboat companies, mines, furnaces, and foundries. By the fall of 1862, as the impact of conscription upon industrial production became clearer, lawmakers expanded the protected list.

In addition to the well-known provisions covering overseers for every twenty slaves, the revised guidelines exempted millers, tanners, saltmakers, shoemakers, blacksmiths, wagon makers, charcoal makers, and employees of wool and cotton factories, paper mills, and government arms-making facilities. In practice, the conscripts were selected from among all men of eligible age, and then those deemed eligible for exemption were detailed on special service to remain in their civilian occupations. Conscription officers reviewed each case periodically, returning to his unit each man whose skills were no longer required on the home front.

Artisans generally favored the exemptions out of a variety of motives ranging from personal to political. The needs of their families often loomed large. Certain craftsmen plied trades essential to the well-being of their communities. Among individual artisans throughout the Confederacy and among organizations of certain tradesmen in the cities of the upper South, lingering Unionism explains the popularity of exemption. Whether their Unionism was rooted in opposition to slavery, or family ties to the Union, such men were less than enthusiastic arms-bearers in the Confederate cause. In fact, when pressed into service against their will, such men often crossed over the lines to the Northerners.

Artisans detailed from the army faced certain particular burdens. Legislation of spring 1863 had limited the pay of men on detached service to the regular soldier's pay plus a ration. Such soldier-artisans often found themselves working alongside paroled Federal prisoners or foreign-born men earning several times that amount. Only in mid-1864 did new legislation allow for higher wages, to the satisfaction of the men but the consternation of their employers.

For artisans no less than other Confederate civilians, inflation undercut the purchasing power of their wages, however high. Skyrocketing prices also sapped morale. As early as 1863, certain skilled workers—telegraphers and typographers, in particular—began striking for increased wages to keep pace with the rising cost of living. In 1864, such stoppages became routine in government-operated as well as privately owned facilities. So rampant were these actions and so potentially disruptive to production that Confederate authorities adopted a policy of breaking strikes by drafting the strikers. Workers often resorted to individual acts of defiance—expressed most frequently by desertion—to protest the government's failure to control the cost of necessities.

In the circumstances, shop superintendents turned increasingly to boys, women, and slaves to meet production targets. They promoted semiskilled operatives into skilled positions, hoping that experience would prove an adequate teacher. They employed women to fill vacancies left by men. And they relied especially upon slave laborers to perform both skilled and semiskilled work. Statistics from Tredegar indicate the magnitude of these changes. On the eve of the war, the company's main facility employed approximately 1,000 white men and fewer than 100 slaves, but by late 1864, there were roughly 200 slaves and 400 white men at work there. At the latter date, slaves made up roughly half of the 2,000 persons employed in all the company's facilities.

In the end, state-sponsored industrialization both drew out skills latent within the Southern population and focused that talent with remarkable efficiency and effect. Skilled laborers helped lay the foundation for postwar industrial development, which for various reasons, both economic and political, fell short of the potential that had been drawn out by the exigencies of war.

BIBLIOGRAPHY

Brewer, James H. *The Confederate Negro: Virginian's Craftsmen and Military Laborers, 1861–1865.* Durham, N.C., 1969.

Dew, Charles B. *Ironmaker to the Confederacy: Joseph R. Anderson and the Tredegar Iron Works.* New Haven, 1966.

Escott, Paul D. *After Secession: Jefferson Davis and the Failure of Confederate Nationalism.* Baton Rouge, La., 1978.

Moore, Albert Burton. *Conscription and Conflict in the Confederacy.* New York, 1924.

Vandiver, Frank E. *Plowshares into Swords: Josiah Gorgas and Confederate Ordnance.* Austin, Tex., 1952.

JOSEPH P. REIDY

LAIRD RAMS. Two iron-hulled, steam-powered ironclad warships were built by the firm of John Laird and Sons of Birkenhead, United Kingdom, for James D. Bulloch, chief Confederate naval purchasing agent in Europe. The ships, considered among the most formidable naval weapons of their time, incorporated some of the ideas of Capt. Cowper Coles of the Royal Navy, a leading designer of ironclads.

Built between April 1862 and August 1863, they displaced 1,423 tons (light); they measured 224.5 feet long, 42.5 feet in beam, and 15.5 feet in depth of hold. A two-cylinder, horizontal direct-acting engine of 1,450 indicated horsepower drove a single screw propeller. Auxiliary power was provided by their bark sailing rig. Their two polygonal turrets were designed to carry two nine-inch, 220-pounder Armstrong guns. These turrets were protected by 5-inch iron armor over 22-inch teak and iron backing. The raised, armored forecastle and poop were designed to carry two 32-pounders, and the hull was covered with iron plate armor, which tapered from 4.5 inches at midship to 3 inches at the bow and 2 inches at the stern.

Their intended names in the Confederate navy were CSS *North Carolina* and CSS *Mississippi,* and great things were expected of them. Bulloch believed that they might have a "conclusive" answer to "the question of the blockade"—they could take the war to the coastal cities of the North.

The distinguishing feature of these vessels was a heavy iron beak, a ram, that projected forward about seven feet from the bow. The introduction of steam propulsion to warships had revived an ancient tactic of sea war by transforming such ships into formidable battering rams, allowing them to sink an enemy vessel by smashing its hull. Naval officers considered the rams to be among the most powerful weapons of sea war, but for the most part these vessels did not perform as well as expected.

Such ships, however, posed a special challenge to existing definitions of neutrality. Bulloch suspected that, in the aftermath of the *Alexandra* trial (which held that British firms could build ships for the Confederacy so long as those ships were not equipped with armaments while in Britain), the crown might reconsider its neutral obligations and take steps to prevent the departure of the rams. He therefore arranged their sham sale to the French firm of Bravay and Company of Paris, ostensibly for a future sale to the Egyptian navy. To enhance the subterfuge, the ships were given the cover names of *El Tousson* and *El Monassir.* This clandestine operation did not fool the British ministers, however. As the rams neared completion in late 1863, the government seized them while it conducted an extensive investigation in Paris and Cairo and came to the conclusion that the departure of these ships would not be in the national interest. And so, in May 1864, the Admiralty— "with a law suit in one hand and the valuation in the other"—made an offer to Bravay that the firm could not refuse. The rams thus became the property of the Royal Navy and were commissioned HMS *Scorpion* and HMS *Wivern.* They served the Queen's navy with no particular distinction until the early years of the twentieth century.

In addition to their intrinsic interest as secret weapons and technological innovators, the Laird Rams had another aspect of importance. They set off a crisis in Anglo-

American affairs. The United States wanted Great Britain to stop the ships from leaving Liverpool, but British internal law did not clearly require the government to do so. The situation forced Lord John Russell and his cabinet colleagues into a reappraisal of their neutral obligations. As the British debated their correct course in the matter, the American minister, Charles Francis Adams, wrote his famous—and much misunderstood—"this is war" note to the Foreign Office. In it he threatened a rupture of diplomatic relations between the two countries if Britain did not cease its "warlike" activity—that is, its supposed complicity in constructing a Confederate navy and allowing the rams, vessels equipped for war, to join that navy. The crisis brought on by the rams drove the British to confiscate those ships and to impose greater restrictions on Bulloch's procurement efforts. Russell's decision effectively thwarted Confederate efforts to build a navy in British yards. September at Birkenhead, no less than July at Gettysburg, doomed the South.

[See also Alexandra; Laird Shipyards.]

BIBLIOGRAPHY

Bulloch, James Dunwoody. The Secret Service of the Confederate States in Europe: or, How the Confederate Cruisers Were Equipped. 2 vols. New York, 1884. Reprint, New York, 1959.

Jones, Wilbur D. The Confederate Rams at Birkenhead. Tuscaloosa, Ala., 1961.

Merli, Frank J. "The Confederate Navy." In In Peace and War: Interpretations of American Naval History, 1775–1984. Edited by Kenneth J. Hagan. 2d ed. Westport, Conn., 1984.

Merli, Frank J. Great Britain and the Confederate Navy, 1861–1865. Bloomington, Ind., 1970.

Parkes, Oscar. British Battleships, 1860–1950: A History of Design, Construction, and Armament. Hamden, Conn., 1971.

Spencer, Warren. The Confederate Navy in Europe. University, Ala., 1983.

KEVIN J. FOSTER and FRANK J. MERLI

LAIRD SHIPYARDS. The William Laird and Sons Company was founded by John Laird, Jr., and William Laird, who had a history of successful construction of merchant and military ships. Located on the English River Mersey, across from the harbor of the city of Liverpool, the company was one of the earliest shipyards to build iron ships and by 1842 had built forty-four. In 1839 it constructed the iron paddle packet Dover for the British navy and in 1842 the iron paddle frigate Guadalupe for the Mexican government. At 788 tons Guadalupe was the largest iron vessel that had ever been constructed.

During the American Civil War the Lairds contracted with Confederate navy agent James Dunwoody Bulloch for the construction of Alabama and two ironclad rams. The Alabama contract was signed on August 1, 1861, and the ship was completed on June 15, 1862. The shipbuilders, following Bulloch's design, constructed a unique vessel for its day: it was powered by both steam and sail, and it had a device to lift the propeller out of water when under sail only, large storage areas for provisions to enable the ship to stay at sea for long periods of time, passages for the passing of ammunition to the deck guns, and a condenser to convert seawater into drinking water.

During its cruise of twenty-three months under Capt. Raphael Semmes, the ship destroyed more enemy vessels than any other ship in naval history. Its destructive cruise raised the question of British culpability, which in turn led to the Geneva Arbitration Tribunal that in 1873 ordered Great Britain to pay $15.5 million to the United States for failure to prevent delivery of the ship to the Confederate navy.

The two ironclad rams Bulloch contracted for were formidable ships designed to operate in the shallow American coastal and river waters in order to raise the Union blockade and even to lay siege to certain Northern cities. The ships were 230 feet long, 42 feet at the extreme width, with a draft fully loaded of 15 feet. Made of wood with iron siding, they were powered by both sail and steam. Their most distinctive feature was a seven-foot iron ram protruding from the bow below the water level.

Largely because of the destructive Alabama cruise, the British government had become sensitive to Washington complaints and to reports submitted to it by the U.S. consul in Liverpool. Before the rams were completed, the British government seized them in 1864, thus preventing delivery to the Confederate navy. The Laird rams served well and long in the British navy as Scorpion and Wivern. Because the British domestic law to impose its neutrality on British subjects was outdated, the Lairds were not punished, despite the later decision of the Geneva tribunal.

The William Laird and Sons Company still operates on the Mersey River and maintains a Confederate museum that concentrates on Alabama and the Laird rams.

[See also Alabama Claims; Laird Rams; and entry on the ship Alabama.]

BIBLIOGRAPHY

Baxter, James Phinney. The Introduction of the Ironclad Warship. Cambridge, Mass., 1933. Reprint, Hamden, Conn., 1968.

Bulloch, James D. The Secret Service of the Confederate States in Europe; or, How the Confederate Cruisers Were Equipped. 2 vols. Liverpool, 1883. Reprint, New York, 1959.

Spencer, Warren F. The Confederate Navy in Europe. University, Ala., 1983.

Spencer, Warren F. "Ships for the South: James D. Bulloch, Confederate Agent in Europe." In Divided We Fall: Essays on Confederate Nation Building. Edited by John M. Belohlavek and Lewis N. Wynne. Saint Leo, Fla., 1991.

Summersell, Charles Grayson. *CSS Alabama, Builder, Captain, and Plans.* University, Ala., 1985.

WARREN F. SPENCER

Treasury Department Records. Gazaway B. Lamar. Record Group 366. National Archives, Washington, D.C.

STEPHEN R. WISE

LAMAR, GAZAWAY B. (1798–1874), businessman and operator of blockade runners. Born in Richmond County, Georgia, October 2, 1798, Lamar became one of the most respected businessmen in the South. With operations centered in Augusta and Savannah, Lamar was an early champion of iron-hulled, steam-propelled merchantmen. He brought to Savannah in sections the British-built sidewheeler *John Randolph,* the nation's first iron-hulled steamship, and the iron-hulled, paddlewheel steamer *Chatham.* During the Civil War the *Chatham* was used as a transport before being captured in December 1863 while trying to run the blockade.

Lamar was also a financial backer of the Republic of Texas and in 1845 moved to New York where he operated the Bank of Republic. Just before Georgia seceded, Lamar purchased ten thousand muskets and shipped them to Savannah. After the firing on Fort Sumter, he returned to Savannah and became president of the Bank of Commerce and was later elected president of the Confederacy's Bank Convention.

During the war Lamar continued to work in the banking industry and also became actively involved in blockade running. His first venture centered on the paddlewheel steamer *Nina,* but the little packet foundered while returning to the Confederacy. Undaunted, Lamar formed the Importing and Exporting Company of Georgia, which operated six British-built blockade runners under a charter from the state of Georgia. In an attempt to soften the blockade for his vessels, Lamar contacted New York politician and Southern sympathizer Fernando Wood to help bribe Union officers to allow his ships to reach Savannah. Nothing came of this, but Lamar's vessels had successful careers operating between Bermuda and Wilmington.

When Savannah was occupied, Lamar considered the war over and took the oath of allegiance. He tried to retain his property, especially the cotton owned by his company, but it was seized by Federal authorities. He was later arrested for attempting to bribe Federal officials and confined briefly in Washington, D.C., until released by President Andrew Johnson. Lamar then retained Benjamin Butler, and eventually a large amount of his property was recovered by his heirs after his death on October 5, 1874.

BIBLIOGRAPHY

Coddington, Edwin B. "Activities and Attitudes of a Confederate Businessman: Gazawy B. Lamar." *Journal of Southern History* 9 (February 1943): 3–36.

LAMAR, L. Q. C. (1825–1893), framer of Mississippi's ordinance of secession, lieutenant colonel, diplomat, U.S. congressman, and Supreme Court judge. Lucius Quintus Cincinnatus Lamar, a native of Georgia, graduated from Emory College at Oxford, Georgia, in 1845. He married the daughter of Augustus Baldwin Longstreet, president of Emory College. When Longstreet resigned to become the president of the University of Mississippi, Lamar followed, taking a job as a mathematics professor despite his legal education and his preference for the law.

By 1851, Lamar had become an advocate of state rights, speaking out publicly in opposition to California's admission as a free state and earning a reputation as an eloquent and forceful speaker. Lamar was elected from Mississippi to the U.S. House of Representatives in 1857 and reelected in 1859. By this time, he was a vigorous spokesman for Southern interests, though he denied being a secessionist. As a delegate to the Charleston Democratic National Convention in 1860, Lamar sided with moderate Southern Democrats, opposing Southern withdrawal over the issue of territorial rights. Yet when the representatives of the Southern states withdrew, Lamar joined them. The election of Abraham Lincoln convinced him that secession was inevitable, and he began planning for a Southern nation.

L. Q. C. LAMAR.   *HARPER'S PICTORIAL HISTORY OF THE GREAT REBELLION*

He resigned his seat in Congress and as a member of Mississippi's secession convention drafted the ordinance of secession.

At the beginning of the war, Lamar helped raise a regiment and became a lieutenant colonel. He insisted that the time for speeches and statesmanship was over. He was, nonetheless, depressed over the prospects of a long and bloody war, and while encamped at Richmond, he began to suffer attacks that left him temporarily unconscious and paralyzed on one side. After recuperating in Mississippi, he returned to Richmond and fought in the battle at Williamsburg, taking command of his regiment upon the death of Col. C. H. Mott. One-fifth of the regiment's men were casualties. Afterward, Lamar suffered another attack and was again forced to return home.

In late 1862 Lamar was appointed a special commissioner to seek Russian recognition of the Confederacy. He traveled as far as London and France, where he was received and entertained as a diplomat. The Confederate Senate realized, however, that Russia was unlikely to recognize a nation that advocated slavery. It did not confirm Lamar's commission, and he returned to Richmond.

Near the end of 1863, Lamar was sent by the Davis administration to Georgia to quell growing opposition to Confederate policies. Again, he suffered the poor health that would recur the rest of his life. In December 1864 he was commissioned judge advocate of the military court of the Third Army Corps, Army of Northern Virginia.

After the war, although disfranchised, Lamar worked in Mississippi to promote conciliation, and in 1866 he returned to the university as a professor of ethics, metaphysics, and law. In 1870, during Republican rule, Lamar was forced to resign his professorship and to return to the practice of law.

The remainder of his life proved to be the most important and productive of his career. Pardoned from the disabilities imposed on Confederate officials, he served in the U.S. House of Representatives from 1872 to 1877 and in the U.S. Senate from 1877 to 1885. In 1885 he became President Grover Cleveland's secretary of the interior, and in 1888 Cleveland appointed him to the Supreme Court. He served until 1892 and died a year later.

BIBLIOGRAPHY

Cate, Wirt Armistead. *Lucius Q. C. Lamar: Secession and Reunion.* Chapel Hill, N.C., 1935.

Mayes, Edward. *Lucius Q. C. Lamar: His Life, Times, and Speeches.* Nashville, Tenn., 1896.

RAY SKATES

LAMKIN, JOHN TILLMAN (1811–1870), captain and congressman from Mississippi. Lamkin moved from his native state of Georgia, where he practiced law, to Texas in

an unsuccessful effort to improve his fortunes. Next he moved to Louisiana, where he learned accounting, and finally to Mississippi in 1838, where he passed the bar. His law practice in Marion and Pike counties led to his election in 1841 as district attorney, a position he held for four years.

Lamkin opposed secession, but when Mississippi left the Union, he felt obligated to support his state. He sought election to the First Congress but was defeated by John Jones McRae, an enthusiastic secessionist. He then volunteered for military service, raised a company—the Holmesville Guards—and was elected captain. His company became part of the Thirty-third Mississippi Regiment. While serving in Virginia, he wrote, "The time has come when every man who has a spark of patriotism in his bosom should promptly volunteer his services." But in 1863, when disenchantment with the conflict was setting in, he was elected to the Second Congress, ousting the fire-eater McRae. In the Congress Lamkin seems to have foreseen inevitable defeat and sought to ameliorate the consequences, voting for all peace resolutions. He favored military exemptions and protection of private property. Apparently giving up hope, Lamkin resigned his seat a month before Congress adjourned.

He returned home to discover adverse financial consequences caused by the war, but before he could recover, he suffered a lengthy illness and died in 1870.

BIBLIOGRAPHY

Alexander, Thomas B., and Richard E. Beringer. *The Anatomy of the Confederate Congress: A Study of the Influences of Member Characteristics on Legislative Voting Behavior, 1861–1865.* Nashville, Tenn., 1972.

Warner, Ezra J., and W. Buck Yearns. *Biographical Register of the Confederate Congress.* Baton Rouge, La., 1975.

RAY SKATES

LANDER, WILLIAM (1817–1868), congressman from North Carolina. North Carolina's William Lander made a name for himself as one of the strongest secessionists in his state and on that record won election to the First Congress. He supported the Davis administration firmly but soon discovered that he was out of line with the increasingly critical or disaffected feelings in his state. For this reason, he served only one term.

Born in Ireland in 1817 to parents who belonged to the Church of England and later the Methodist church, Lander grew up in Lincolnton, North Carolina. After attending Lincolnton Academy and Cokesbury College, in South Carolina, Lander read law and was admitted to the bar in 1839. His phenomenal memory and oratorical skills brought him a flourishing practice, and he also operated a small farm and owned ten slaves in 1860. He held posts as county solicitor and district solicitor and was elected to the state legislature for one term in 1852.

Lander made his political reputation in 1860 and 1861 when he led North Carolina Democrats who walked out of the party's second Baltimore convention rather than acquiesce in the nomination of Stephen A. Douglas. Speaking for "a very large majority of our delegation," Lander condemned "the unjust course that has been pursued" and then helped other southern Democrats nominate John C. Breckinridge for president. Shortly thereafter Lander engaged in a well-publicized debate with Zebulon Vance in which Lander criticized the Bell-Everett Constitutional Unionist ticket as anti-Southern and predicted that secession might soon be justified. He was a secessionist by early 1861, well ahead of opinion in North Carolina, but the outbreak of war made voters more sympathetic to his position, and in November he was elected to the House of Representatives.

Serving on the Patents, War and Tax, and Quartermaster's committees, Lander established a record of active support for the Davis administration. He gave strong backing to conscription, suspension of the writ of habeas corpus, and the government's economic controls. One of his few concessions to state interests was an unsuccessful amendment requiring that conscripts be called first from the states that had furnished the least manpower.

By 1863 Lander's strong support for the war effort and the Confederate government bore little resemblance to feeling back home, and he lost his bid for reelection to a peace candidate. Lander resumed his law practice in Lincolnton and died on January 6, 1868.

BIBLIOGRAPHY

Alexander, Thomas B., and Richard E. Beringer. *The Anatomy of the Confederate Congress: A Study of the Influences of Member Characteristics on Legislative Voting Behavior, 1861–1865.* Nashville, Tenn., 1972.

Journal of the Congress of the Confederate States of America, 1861–1865. 7 vols. Washington, D.C., 1904–1905.

Powell, William S., ed. *Dictionary of North Carolina Biography.* Vol. 3. Chapel Hill, N.C., 1988.

Warner, Ezra J., and W. Buck Yearns. *Biographical Register of the Confederate Congress.* Baton Rouge, La., 1975.

PAUL D. ESCOTT

LAND MINES. *See* Hand Grenades and Land Mines.

LANE, JAMES (1833–1907), brigadier general. The grandson of a sergeant in the War of 1812 and son of a Virginia militia colonel in the Civil War, Lane was born at Mathews Court House, Virginia, July 28, 1833.

JAMES LANE.   LIBRARY OF CONGRESS

After an early education in private schools, Lane entered Virginia Military Institute as a sophomore in 1851. He graduated in 1854, ranking second in a class of fourteen. Three years later he graduated from the University of Virginia and returned to VMI as an assistant professor. Subsequently, Lane taught at the Florida State Seminary and the North Carolina Military Institute in Charlotte.

Elected major of the First North Carolina Volunteers at the start of the war, Lane saw service on the peninsula where he was wounded twice. He also led the scouting party that brought on the victory at Big Bethel. Lane was elected lieutenant colonel of the regiment in September 1861. The choice was immensely popular, for, wrote a newspaper correspondent, "he possesses the necessary qualifications to make an officer the idol of his men, viz.: theory and practice of military science, firmness in discipline, with the affable manners and sociality of a gentleman." When Lane was elected colonel of the Twenty-eighth North Carolina shortly thereafter, the officers of his old command presented him a sword, saddle and bridle, and two pieces of silver plate.

Within a week after Lawrence O'Bryan Branch fell at Sharpsburg, Lane sought the help of Gens. Joseph R. Anderson and Henry A. Wise and Secretary of War George Wythe Randolph in obtaining a brigadier's commission and permanent command of the brigade. Anderson assured Jefferson Davis that Lane was "an intelligent and accomplished officer, and one who devotes himself to his duties." Lane received his coveted promotion on November 1, 1862, but it was not confirmed until April 23, 1863.

Lane's brigade fought at Fredericksburg, Chancellorsville, and Gettysburg. At Chancellorsville, the Eighteenth North Carolina of Lane's brigade mistakenly fired at General Thomas J. ("Stonewall") Jackson, inflicting wounds that led to his death on May 10, 1863. At Spotsylvania his troops checked the Federals after the breakthrough at the Bloody Angle until reinforcements arrived. The young general suffered a severe thigh wound at Cold Harbor and surrendered at Appomattox.

Upon returning home after the war, Lane found his parents in want and the plantation desolate. He borrowed $150 to make a fresh start and for seven years taught in private schools. He taught at Virginia Polytechnic Institute and the Missouri School of Mines before becoming a civil engineering professor at Alabama Polytechnic Institute. He died at Auburn, Alabama, September 21, 1907, and was buried there.

BIBLIOGRAPHY

Compiled Military Service Records. James Henry Lane. Microcopy M331, Roll 152. Record Group 109. National Archives, Washington, D.C.

Hill, D.H., Jr. *North Carolina*. Vol. 4 of *Confederate Military History*. Edited by Clement A. Evans. Atlanta, 1899. Vol. 5 of extended ed. Wilmington, N.C., 1987.

Lee, Charles C. "The First North Carolina Volunteers." *Southern Historical Society Papers* 19 (1891): 245–246. Reprint, Wilmington, N.C., 1990.

LOWELL REIDENBAUGH

LANE, WALTER PAYE (1817–1892), brigadier general. Lane, a native of Ireland, immigrated with his family to Ohio in 1821. Answering the call of Stephen F. Austin for volunteers for the Texas Revolution, Lane moved there in March 1836. He fought at San Jacinto in April as part of Capt. Henry W. Karnes's cavalry company and was rewarded for his bravery with promotion to second lieutenant. Lane remained active in Texas military operations and later fought in the war with Mexico, rising to the rank of major.

Upon the secession of Texas, Lane was elected lieutenant colonel of the South Kansas–Texas Cavalry, which was later renamed the Third Texas Cavalry. The unit first saw combat under the command of Gen. Ben McCulloch at Wilson's Creek. In his report of this battle Col. Elkonah Greer, commanding the Confederate brigade to which Lane's regiment was attached, remarked that even after his

horse was shot from under him Lieutenant Colonel Lane continued to fight. In December 1861 Lane and his regiment were dispatched with Col. James McIntosh's brigade to the Indian Territory to break up a gathering of Indians hostile to the Confederacy. On the twenty-sixth they attacked and destroyed the encampment. In March, again under Greer's command, Lane fought gallantly at the Battle of Elkhorn Tavern.

Transferred east of the Mississippi, Lane, his unit now dismounted, saw action under the command of Gen. P. G. T. Beauregard outside Corinth, Mississippi; both Lane and the unit were noted in a special order. Transferred back to the Trans-Mississippi, Lane, now commanding a brigade, participated in the Confederate victory at Bayou Lafourche. In the 1864 Red River campaign, his brigade under his capable leadership won laurels at Pleasant Hill and Mansfield, Louisiana. Gen. E. Kirby Smith recommended Lane for promotion to brigadier general in October 1864, and his commission was signed by President Jefferson Davis on March 17, 1865.

Lane disbanded his brigade and returned to Texas after the Trans-Mississippi Department surrendered. He became a merchant in Marshall, Texas, and died there on January 28, 1892.

Lane has been described by his peers as a man of extraordinary bravery: "Wherever the fighting was thickest he could be found." An outstanding cavalry commander, his unit was one of the few not dismounted to supplement the infantry in 1864.

BIBLIOGRAPHY

Lane, Walter P. *The Adventures and Recollections of General Walter P. Lane*. Austin, Tex., 1970.

Roberts, O. M. *Texas*. Vol. 11 of *Confederate Military History*. Edited by Clement A. Evans. Atlanta, 1899. Vol. 15 of extended ed. Wilmington, N.C., 1989.

ROY R. STEPHENSON

LANIER, SIDNEY (1842–1881), poet, critic, and musician. Sidney Clopton Lanier's importance for the Confederacy was at least as great after his death as before. Born in Macon, Georgia, and educated at Oglethorpe, Lanier volunteered for the local regiment, the Macon Volunteers, just before graduation in the spring of 1861. He was first posted to Norfolk, Virginia, with his regiment. He saw his first action at Drewry's Bluff in 1862 and survived the Seven Days' Battles later that summer and Chancellorsville in 1863. He served in the Signal Corps at Fort Boykin and aboard blockade runners based in Wilmington, North Carolina. He was captured in November 1864 and spent several months in Federal prison camps. He bribed his way out in February 1865.

Lanier's health, never robust, was ruined by the war and imprisonment. He died of the effects of consumption in 1881. Because of his relatively brief life, his frail health, and his popular poems and orations, he became, after his death, the "Keats of the Confederacy." His suffering, anecdotes of his flute playing under extreme hardship (in prison, in camp between actions), his extremely romantic philosophy (a blend of German and Oriental idealism and mysticism), and his proto-Agrarian political essays (e.g., "The New South," 1880) combined to make Lanier the focal point of cultural reconstruction in the South. Hamilton Wright Mabie wrote of Lanier after his death:

> Lanier was distinctively a national poet—one who felt the stir of the vast movement of coordination which did not begin with the close of the war, but which revealed itself then for the first time, and who expressed in the depth and largeness of his poetic conception neither the sentiment of New England nor of the South, new or old, but of that America which is to be also much larger, more significant, more influential, richer in appeal to the imagination than the provinces of which it is composed.

BIBLIOGRAPHY

Mabie, Hamilton Wright. "The Poetry of the South." *International Monthly* 5 (1902): 200–223.
Mims, Edwin. *Sidney Lanier.* Boston, 1905.
Rubin, Louis D., Jr. "The Passion of Sidney Lanier." In *William Elliott Shoots a Bear: Essays on the Southern Literary Imagination.* Baton Rouge, La., 1975.
Starke, Aubrey Harrison. *Sidney Lanier: A Biographical and Critical Study.* Chapel Hill, N.C., 1933.

MICHAEL KREYLING

LATANÉ, WILLIAM. *See* Burial of Latané.

LAW, EVANDER MCIVOR (1836–1920), brigadier general. There was an unfortunate tendency among many Confederate generals to engage in bitter disputes with their fellow officers. Some feuds, such as that between Joseph E. Johnston and P. G. T. Beauregard, are well known. Another bitter and less familiar feud, between two talented and ambitious young brigadiers, involved Evander McIvor Law and Micah Jenkins.

Law was born at Darlington, South Carolina, on August 7, 1836, and graduated from the Citadel in the class of 1856. He taught, along with Jenkins, at Kings Mountain Military Academy in South Carolina and then moved to Alabama. In early 1861 Law entered Confederate service and soon became lieutenant colonel of the Fourth Alabama Infantry. He was severely wounded at First Manassas and after his recovery was promoted to colonel.

He commanded a brigade from the Seven Days' Battles through the Sharpsburg campaign, was frequently praised by superiors, and was appointed brigadier general on October 13, 1862. Law commanded John Bell Hood's division admirably at Gettysburg after Hood was wounded; he led it again when Hood was wounded at Chickamauga. When temporary command of the division went to Jenkins, who ranked Law by three months, their rivalry was so intense that corps commander James Longstreet appointed a third officer to replace Hood. Longstreet preferred charges against Law, but they were dropped. Law commanded his brigade until he was severely wounded at Cold Harbor in 1864. He never returned to the Army of Northern Virginia but commanded a cavalry brigade in the Carolinas campaign of 1865.

After the war, Law was active in education and in the United Confederate Veterans. He was one of the last surviving Confederate generals when he died at Bartow, Florida, on October 31, 1920.

BIBLIOGRAPHY

Law, Evander McIvor. "From the Wilderness to Cold Harbor." In *Battles and Leaders of the Civil War.* Edited by Robert U. Johnson and C. C. Buel. Vol. 4. New York, 1888. Reprint, Secaucus, N.J., 1982.
Law, Evander McIvor. "On the Confederate Right at Gaines's Mill." In *Battles and Leaders of the Civil War.* Edited by Robert U. Johnson and C. C. Buel. Vol. 2. New York, 1888. Reprint, Secaucus, N.J., 1982.
Law, Evander McIvor. "The Struggle for 'Round Top.'" In *Battles and Leaders of the Civil War.* Edited by Robert U. Johnson and C. C. Buel. Vol. 3. New York, 1888. Reprint, Secaucus, N.J., 1982.
Wheeler, Joseph. *Alabama.* Vol. 7 of *Confederate Military History.* Edited by Clement A. Evans. Atlanta, 1899. Vol. 8 of extended ed. Wilmington, N.C., 1987.

J. TRACY POWER

LAWTON, ALEXANDER R. (1818–1896), brigadier general, quartermaster general, and U.S. ambassador to Austria. A graduate of West Point (1839) and Harvard University Law School (1843), Lawton before the war was a lawyer in Savannah, Georgia, president of a railroad, state legislator, militia colonel, and ardent secessionist. Acting on the orders of Governor Joseph E. Brown, he commanded the First Georgia Militia Regiment when it seized Federal Fort Pulaski at Savannah before Georgia had seceded.

When war broke out, Lawton was promoted to brigadier general (April 13, 1861) and directed the defense of the Georgia coast. In June 1862, commanding a Georgia brigade, he joined Thomas J. ("Stonewall") Jackson in the Shenandoah Valley. Lawton fought in the Seven Days' Battles and replaced Richard S. Ewell when he was wounded at Second Manassas. Although badly wounded at

ALEXANDER R. LAWTON.   LIBRARY OF CONGRESS

Sharpsburg while in command of Ewell's division, he returned to service in May 1863.

President Jefferson Davis appointed Lawton, over his strong objections, quartermaster general in August 1863. (Lawton replaced Col. Abraham C. Myers, whose wife supposedly had called Mrs. Varina Davis a "squaw" because of her dark complexion.) In his new post he was to provide Confederate soldiers with uniforms, shoes, nonordnance equipment, and transportation, a virtually impossible task in the inflation-wracked and politically divided Confederacy. His efficiency diminished by state governors who controlled vital war matériel, Lawton nevertheless increased by thousands the number of uniforms and blankets sent to the Army of Northern Virginia. In a January 1865 letter to the Confederate Congress he reported, "The Army has been fully provided."

After the war, Lawton entered Georgia state politics. In 1887, President Grover Cleveland appointed him ambassador to Austria. He died in New York and is buried in Savannah.

BIBLIOGRAPHY

Coulter, Merton E. *The Confederate States of America, 1861–1865.* A History of the South, vol. 7. Baton Rouge, La., 1950.

Eaton, Clement. *A History of the Southern Confederacy.* New York, 1954.

Vandiver, Frank E. *Rebel Brass: The Confederate Command System.* Baton Rouge, La., 1956.

Weinert, Richard P. *The Confederate Regular Army.* Shippensburg, Pa., 1991.

P. NEAL MEIER

LEACH, JAMES MADISON (1815–1891), lieutenant colonel and congressman from North Carolina. James Madison Leach fought for the Confederacy in 1861 and represented North Carolina in the Second Confederate Congress. As a determined foe of the policies of President Jefferson Davis, Leach gave voice to much of the discontent and restiveness with war measures that characterized his state. Although he supported demands for peace, on occasion he differed with his outspoken cousin, Congressman James T. Leach, over the latter's peace proposals.

Born on January 17, 1815, at his family's plantation in Randolph County, North Carolina, James Madison Leach attended Caldwell Institute in Greensboro and the U.S. Military Academy. He then studied law under an older brother and, after obtaining his license in 1842, opened a practice in Lexington, where he resided the rest of his life. A remarkably effective advocate, Leach was renowned as a defense lawyer and is said to have prevailed in seventy of seventy-one murder cases, losing only the first case he handled.

Throughout his life he was a strong proponent of education and internal improvements. Elected to the North Carolina House of Commons in 1848 as a Whig, Leach promoted education and supported the Railroad Act of 1849, which committed the state to building the North Carolina

JAMES MADISON LEACH.   NATIONAL ARCHIVES

Railroad. Leach served in the state legislature for ten years and then ran for the U.S. House of Representatives against a Democratic incumbent, winning election by a large majority.

As the secession crisis grew, Leach took a consistent stand against secession. As soon as Abraham Lincoln called for volunteers to put down the rebellion, however, he changed his stance. He canceled a tour on which he was speaking against secession and rushed home to raise a company of volunteers. Chosen as captain of his company, Leach became lieutenant colonel upon organization of the Twenty-first Regiment, North Carolina Troops. He fought at First Manassas and saw other action in Virginia before he resigned on December 23, 1861.

By 1863 discontent with the war had become pronounced in North Carolina, and the state elected new congressmen in eight out of ten districts. Five of the newcomers were avowed peace candidates. When one of these, Congressman-elect Samuel H. Christian, died in March 1864, Leach ran for the seat and won easily on a pledge that he would seek peace with independence.

In the Second Congress Leach developed a record as a foe of all administration programs. He gave his approval to resolutions declaring that Secretaries Judah P. Benjamin, Christopher G. Memminger, and John H. Reagan were incompetent, and he voted to override every presidential veto. Opposition to the suspension of the writ of habeas corpus was one of his special causes. On December 5, 1864, Leach introduced a resolution declaring "that the privilege of the writ of *habeas corpus* is one of the great bulwarks of freedom, and that it ought not to be suspended except in extreme cases . . . that the people of this Confederacy are united in a great struggle for liberty, and that no exigency exists justifying its suspension." Later that year and in January 1865 he tried unsuccessfully to win the House's approval of this statement. Leach's efforts prompted a North Carolina captain to declare that the congressman "has thrown more obstacles in the way of my arresting deserters . . . than any ten men in this County." Leach also fought Jefferson Davis's proposal to arm and emancipate Southern slaves, offering an amendment to prohibit the government from arming the slaves, mustering them into Confederate service, or "at any time" using them as soldiers.

James M. Leach urged the government to initiate peace negotiations, and by April 1865 he believed that North Carolina should pursue separate state negotiations on its own. But he drew a distinction between his support for peace and that of his colleague and cousin James T. Leach. On November 25, 1864, James M. Leach refused to support his cousin's peace resolutions (which won only three votes) and, to the delight of the *Richmond Examiner,* told the House "that there was no member from North Carolina

who desired peace upon any terms [other] than eternal separation from the North."

Many of Leach's other efforts in Congress seemed designed to relieve his constituents from the heavy demands of the Confederate war effort. He worked to exempt from the tax-in-kind tenant farmers and nonslaveholders who "produce no surplus, but only a support." Similarly he called for the exemption of "such number of mechanics and artisans as shall be indispensably necessary to carry on the mechanical and industrial pursuits of the country." In January 1865 Leach tried unsuccessfully to exempt in each county one blacksmith and one miller for every two thousand people and one tanner and one shoemaker for every four thousand residents. He presented memorials from slaveholders concerned about the health of their impressed bondsmen, but he also sought repeal of the exemption for those who owned or managed fifteen or more slaves.

After the Civil War Leach rebuilt his fortune through successful legal work and remained active in politics. During Presidential Reconstruction he served in the North Carolina Senate from 1865 to 1868 and became a leader among the conservatives who opposed Congressional Reconstruction. Leach chaired the committee that denounced the proposed Fourteenth Amendment and urged its rejection. As a Conservative (later Democrat) Leach won election to Congress in 1870 and 1872 but declined to run a third time. He worked for the Democratic party in the 1876 and 1880 elections and returned to his state's General Assembly as a senator in 1879. Leach died on June 1, 1891, and was buried in Hopewell Church Cemetery.

BIBLIOGRAPHY

Alexander, Thomas B., and Richard E. Beringer. *The Anatomy of the Confederate Congress: A Study of the Influences of Member Characteristics on Legislative Voting Behavior, 1861–1865.* Nashville, Tenn., 1972.

Hamilton, J. G. de Roulhac. *Reconstruction in North Carolina.* New York, 1914.

Journal of the Congress of the Confederate States of America, 1861–1865. 7 vols. Washington, D.C., 1904–1905.

Powell, William S., ed. *Dictionary of North Carolina Biography.* Vol. 3. Chapel Hill, N.C., 1988.

"Proceedings of the Confederate Congress." In *Southern Historical Society Papers.* 51–52 (1958–1959). Reprint, Wilmington, N.C., 1992.

PAUL D. ESCOTT

LEACH, JAMES T. (1805–1883), congressman from North Carolina. James T. Leach of North Carolina served in the House of Representatives of the Second Congress of the Confederate States. Elected in 1863 as an avowed peace candidate, Leach quickly became one of the most energetic and determined foes of Jefferson Davis's administration.

His career illustrates the Confederacy's difficulty in establishing firm loyalty to a new government and reflects the extremes of discontent that developed in response to the South's plight. Leach's actions in Congress also reveal the kinds of issues that aroused opponents of the government.

Born in 1805 into a prominent family in Johnston County, North Carolina, James Thomas Leach studied first law and then medicine, earning a diploma from Jefferson Medical College in Philadelphia. He returned home and practiced medicine, and occasionally some law, for the rest of his life. Marrying Elizabeth Willis Boddie Sanders in 1833, Leach built his home on his family's Leachburg Plantation and gradually purchased the parcels of land inherited by his brothers and sisters. By 1860 he owned and managed a large plantation with forty-seven slaves. It is said that his policy in acquiring slaves was to purchase only those who wished to earn their freedom. He encouraged self-improvement among his white neighbors, also, by opening a free school in his home and later building schoolhouses nearby. He took orphaned boys and destitute women into his house and urged improved farming methods upon his neighbors.

In prewar politics Leach was an old-line Whig. He served one term in the North Carolina Senate (1858–1860), during which he became an ally of State Treasurer Jonathan Worth, a conservative who possessed a keen empathy for common farmers and cared little about the territorial issues that were dividing the nation. During the secession crisis Leach took a staunchly pro-Union position. He argued vigorously against secession, opposing that step even after Abraham Lincoln called for volunteers in April 1861. These pro-Union convictions cost Leach reelection to the state legislature.

In 1863 Leach ran for the Confederate House of Representatives as one of several disaffected North Carolina peace candidates. Campaigning in his district against three strong supporters of the Confederate government, Leach denied the right of secession and openly pledged himself to seek "a just, honorable and lasting peace." He won election easily. His broadside to "Fellow-Citizens of the Third Congressional District," published in September 1863, immediately placed him among the leadership of the peace movement in the Second Congress.

In Richmond, Leach was appointed to the committees on Post Offices and Post Roads and on Territories and Public Lands, but he devoted most of his energy to larger questions of policy. He spoke out against "reckless legislation . . . endorsed by the President and the mighty strides now making toward a military despotism." To Leach there was "too much of brass button and bayonet rule in the country," and he declared that the central government should "leave the execution of some of its laws to the people at home." In May 1864 he condemned suspension of the writ of habeas corpus and introduced a resolution "declaring the supremacy of the civil over the military law." He also introduced resolutions denouncing secret sessions and "defining the rights of the States in furnishing soldiers."

Leach was solicitous of the needs of his constituents, seeking to increase the pay of soldiers and to "exempt soldiers' families from the payment of the tithes [tax-in-kind] when there is not more than is necessary for the comfortable support of the family." But his primary initiatives in the House were three joint resolutions, offered in May 1864, November 1864, and January 1865, in favor of peace negotiations. His resolutions of May 23, 1864, condemned the usurpations of the United States but called for the appointment of commissioners to seek a ninety-day armistice. The second set of resolutions, presented on November 25, 1864, frankly called the South's decision to secede because Lincoln had won the presidency a mistake, declaring that that decision had brought a train of "fearful consequences not contemplated by those who advocated" secession. Although these resolutions proposed that the South enter peace negotiations when the United States recognized the "reserved rights of the States" and guaranteed the "rights of property," they received only three votes (from Leach and two other North Carolina representatives). On January 23, 1865, Leach offered his last set of peace resolutions, which blamed the United States for violations of the federal Constitution, cruelty, and "acts of wantonness," but nevertheless sought an armistice. On March 1, 1865, he offered resolutions approving the appointment of Robert E. Lee as general-in-chief and recommending that "he be invested with powers to treat for peace." Two weeks later he alone opposed the House's concurrence in a Senate resolution that pledged Southerners to fight on to independence rather than accept dishonorable peace terms.

Leach fought the Davis administration to the end of his time in office, blasting the president's proposal to arm slaves and promise them the reward of freedom. Such a policy, Leach raged, "would be wrong in principle, disastrous in practice, an infringement upon the States' rights, an endorsement of the principle contained in President Lincoln's emancipation proclamation, an insult to our brave soldiers and an outrage upon humanity." During his term Leach criticized cabinet officers, opposed the administration's economic proposals, sought to broaden exemptions, and voted to override every presidential veto.

After the Civil War Leach became an ally of William W. Holden and late in 1866, when conservatives were denouncing the proposed Fourteenth Amendment, joined in a call for a new Reconstruction government in North Carolina. He remained active in local affairs and became a dedicated prohibitionist, resigning from his position as county commissioner in 1875 rather than certify anyone as a "qualified" barroom operator. Leach died on March 28, 1883, and was buried in the family cemetery near Mount Zion Church in Johnston County, North Carolina.

BIBLIOGRAPHY

Alexander, Thomas B., and Richard E. Beringer. *The Anatomy of the Confederate Congress: A Study of the Influences of Member Characteristics on Legislative Voting Behavior, 1861–1865*. Nashville, Tenn., 1972.

Hamilton, J. G. de Roulhac. *Reconstruction in North Carolina*. New York, 1914.

Journal of the Congress of the Confederate States of America, 1861–1865. 7 vols. Washington, D.C., 1904–1905.

"Proceedings of the Confederate Congress." *Southern Historical Society Papers* 51–52 (1958–1959). Reprint, Wilmington, N.C., 1992.

Yearns, Wilfred B. *The Confederate Congress*. Athens, Ga., 1960.

PAUL D. ESCOTT

LEAD. A Confederate government of highly limited resources often had to utilize blockade runners and contracts with private firms in order to obtain badly needed war supplies. Lead was among the most vital of these commodities. Without it, weapons had no ammunition.

So scarce was lead in the wartime South that soldiers would collect bullets from battlefields and send them to arsenals in the rear to be melted down and recast. Southern officials issued appeals requesting citizens to strip their homes of all lead articles such as pipes, roofs, window weights, and common utensils. Blockade runners did a brisk business in lead importation: over 1.5 million pounds entered the Confederacy by this means in one thirteen-month period.

Small lead mines existed in eastern Tennessee and Arkansas. But as Col. William Broun of the Confederate Ordnance Department later stated: "Our lead was obtained chiefly, and in the last years of the war entirely, from the lead mines at Wytheville, Va. The mines were worked night and day, and the lead converted into bullets as fast as received. The old regulation shrapnel shells were filled with leaden balls and sulphur. The Confederacy had neither lead nor sulphur to spare, and used instead small iron balls and filled with asphalt."

Wytheville's state-owned mines had supplied George Washington's army with bullets in the American Revolution. After the new nation came into being, Virginia sold the mines to two Austin brothers. (Stephen F. Austin, the "Father of Texas," was a son of one of the owners.) The mines at Wytheville—the quarries themselves were at Austinville, seven miles away—were a thriving business when civil war came.

Of the three types of lead mined there, sulphuret (or "blue ore") was the most abundant. It was either crystalline or granular in structure and easily recognizable from the carbonate and oxide varieties of lead. The C.S. Niter Corps monitored production, with Gen. Josiah Gorgas of the Niter and Mining Bureau in overall charge of operations. When conscription drained manpower from the mines, Confederate officials impressed slaves to continue the work. Output at the Wytheville mines averaged about 80,000 pounds monthly. In all, these mines produced 3,283,316 pounds of lead for the Confederacy.

By 1864 Union officials regarded the Wytheville quarries as the most important target in southwestern Virginia. Federal raiding parties went into action as soon as the Virginia and Tennessee Railroad and nearby points were secured. Gen. William W. Averell made a stab at Wytheville on May 11 but was driven off by Confederate cavalry under Gen. John Hunt Morgan. On December 17, several mounted regiments of Gen. George Stoneman's force captured the mines, poured oil on the equipment, and set fire to the works before returning to their base.

Persistent miners repaired the damage and, on March 22, 1865, resumed operations. Confederates managed to repulse an April 5 attempt by Federals to seize the mines. Two days later, however, a heavier assault by Union cavalry routed the defenders. The lead works were destroyed a second time, only two days before Robert E. Lee's surrender at Appomattox.

In all the Confederacy consumed 10 million pounds of lead in the manufacture of the 150 million cartridges used by its armies.

[*See also* Niter and Mining Bureau.]

BIBLIOGRAPHY

Marvel, William. *Salt, Lead and Rail*. Lynchburg, Va., 1992.

Vandiver, Frank E. *Ploughshares into Swords: Josiah Gorgas and Confederate Ordnance*. Austin, Tex., 1952.

Walker, Gary G. *The War in Southwest Virginia, 1861–65*. Roanoke, Va., 1975.

JAMES I. ROBERTSON, JR.

LEADBETTER, DANVILLE (1811–1866), brigadier general. Leadbetter was born at Leeds, Maine, on August 26, 1811, and graduated from West Point third in the class of 1836. First assigned to the artillery, Leadbetter subsequently was transferred to the engineers. As an engineer officer, Leadbetter served in New York, on the Pacific Coast, and, in the early 1850s, in Mobile, Alabama. After a number of years in Mobile, Leadbetter adopted the town as his own. He resigned his commission in the army in 1857 and accepted a commission as lieutenant colonel and chief engineer in the militia of the state of Alabama. He was placed in command of Fort Morgan.

With the outbreak of hostilities in 1861, Leadbetter cast his lot with his adopted state. He was named one of the first majors in the Confederate Engineer Bureau in March 1861 and was sent to Richmond to take charge of the bureau in August. In the late spring of 1862, after a field command in northern Alabama not far from Chattanooga, Leadbetter was ordered to return to Mobile to superintend the strengthening of the defenses of Mobile Bay. Although still chief of the Engineer Bureau, Leadbetter's distance from the capital at Richmond finally caused him to be replaced. On February 27, 1862, he was elevated to the rank of brigadier general in the Confederate service.

General Leadbetter was transferred to Chattanooga again after Gen. Braxton Bragg's Army of Tennessee routed the Union army at Chickamauga. Leadbetter was named chief of the engineer department of the Army of Tennessee, and he helped lay out Bragg's siege lines along Missionary Ridge.

When Gen. James Longstreet's corps was sent to Knoxville, Leadbetter, following in the vanguard of Brig. Gens. Bushrod Rust Johnson's and Archibald Gracie's brigades, was directed to provide engineering assistance to Longstreet; Leadbetter had been stationed at Knoxville at one time and knew the area. After a three-day reconaissance in front of Knoxville, Leadbetter decided that an attack on Fort Sanders could succeed. The assault was launched but proved to be a disaster.

After Knoxville, Leadbetter served on the staff of Gen. Joseph E. Johnston when Johnston took over command of the Army of Tennessee, but by war's end, Leadbetter was back in his beloved Mobile.

To avoid being captured, Leadbetter escaped to Mexico and then journeyed to Canada. He died in Clifton, Canada, on September 26, 1866. His remains were subsequently returned to Mobile, where he was buried.

BIBLIOGRAPHY

Nichols, James L. *Confederate Engineers*. Tuscaloosa, Ala., 1957.
Wheeler, Joseph. *Alabama*. Vol. 7 of *Confederate Military History*. Edited by Clement A. Evans. Atlanta, 1899. Vol. 8 of extended ed. Wilmington, N.C., 1987.

KENT MASTERSON BROWN

LEE, EDWIN GRAY (1836–1870), colonel and acting brigadier general. Lee was born at Leeland, near Shepherdstown, Virginia, May 27, 1836. Nicknamed Ned, this distant kinsman of Robert E. Lee and future son-in-law of Gen. William N. Pendleton attended the Hallowell School in Alexandria and graduated from William and Mary, after which he practiced law.

At the beginning of the war Lee was commissioned a second lieutenant in the Second Virginia Infantry. He was an aide to Thomas J. ("Stonewall") Jackson at Harpers Ferry and saw action at First Manassas. When the army was

reorganized in the spring of 1862, Lee was elected lieutenant colonel of the Thirty-third Virginia. He regarded the grade as unsatisfactory inasmuch as he was superior to John F. Neff, who was chosen colonel. He threatened to resign but, on the counsel of Alexander Pendleton, his brother-in-law, and others, he eventually agreed to serve in the subordinate role. At Cedar Mountain, Lee had the rare distinction of commanding his superior officer, Colonel Neff, who had been placed under arrest by Charles S. Winder over a minor policy matter and had gone into battle without his sword or authority.

Following the death of Neff at Second Manassas, Lee commanded the Thirty-third at Fredericksburg. Ill health, caused by the hardships of military life, forced Lee to resign in December 1862. He was recommissioned a colonel a few months later and given duty in Richmond.

In June 1864, Lee was assigned to Staunton, Virginia, with orders to organize local troops for defense of the Shenandoah Valley. He was appointed brigadier general on September 20, 1864. Two months later he was given a six-month leave of absence because of failing health. His nomination to the grade of brigadier was rejected by the Senate on February 24, 1865, although he apparently continued to appear on the rolls at that rank until the end of the war.

Shortly before the surrender, Lee and his wife, Susan, ran the blockade and went to Montreal on a secret mission for the government. Returning to the United States in 1866, he continued to struggle against the ravages of lung disease. He died at Yellow Sulphur Springs, Virginia, August 24, 1870, and was buried in Lexington.

BIBLIOGRAPHY

Hotchkiss, Jed. *Virginia*. Vol. 3 of *Confederate Military History*. Edited by Clement A. Evans. Atlanta, 1899. Vol. 4 of extended ed. Wilmington, N.C., 1987.
Lee, Susan P. *Memoirs of William Nelson Pendleton*. Philadelphia, 1893.
Levin, Alexandra Lee. *This Awful Drama: General Edwin Gray Lee, C.S.A., and His Family*. New York, 1987.
Warner, Ezra J. *Generals in Gray: Lives of the Confederate Commanders*. Baton Rouge, La., 1959.

LOWELL REIDENBAUGH

LEE, FITZHUGH (1835–1905), major general, postwar governor of Virginia, and U.S. diplomat. Born at Clermont, in Fairfax County, Virginia, Fitz Lee was the grandson of Henry ("Light Horse Harry") Lee and great-grandson of George Mason. Lee attended the U.S. Military Academy from 1852 to 1856, while his uncle, Robert E. Lee, was superintendent. Graduating forty-fifth out of forty-nine, he excelled in horsemanship. His equestrian skills

FITZHUGH LEE.   NATIONAL ARCHIVES

earned him a position with the Second U.S. Cavalry in Texas. For two years, he served on the frontier fighting Comanches, where he received a critical wound to his lungs that nearly cost him his life. He returned to West Point as an instructor in 1860.

In May 1861, Lee resigned from the U.S. Army and returned to Virginia. In September, after serving as adjutant to Brig. Gen. Richard S. Ewell during the Battle of First Manassas, he received a commission as lieutenant colonel of the First Virginia Cavalry. Lee led scouting and raiding parties against the Federals picketed in northern Virginia and often left taunting notes for former comrades in the U.S. Army.

Serving under Maj. Gen. J. E. B. Stuart, he received high praise from his commander and was promoted to colonel in the spring of 1862. He joined Stuart for the Ride around McClellan during the Peninsular campaign and was cited for his "zeal and ability." In July, Lee was promoted to brigadier general in command of the Second Brigade. He continued to serve with the Army of Northern Virginia, seeing limited action at Second Manassas and Sharpsburg. During the winter of 1862–1863, he made successful hit-and-run attacks against the Federal army.

On March 17, 1863, one of Lee's taunting messages drew a response from Gen. William Averell, who launched a raid across the Rapidan River at Kelly's Ford. Fitz Lee's small command outside of Culpeper, Virginia, drove the larger invading force across the river for a marginal victory.

At Chancellorsville, Lee's reconnaissance provided key information that the Federal right flank was "in the air" and vulnerable to an attack. This prompted the renowned

flank attack led by Gen. Thomas J. ("Stonewall") Jackson on May 2 that resulted in the Confederates' strategic victory. In September, Lee was promoted to major general commanding the Second Division of the cavalry corps.

In 1864, Lee distinguished himself at Spotsylvania, Yellow Tavern—where he assumed command after Stuart was mortally wounded—and Trevilian's Station. During the battle at Winchester on September 19, Lee received a serious wound to his thigh, which kept him out of service until January 1865. At Five Forks, Lee's military reputation was tainted when his attendance at the notorious shad bake (a fish fry given by a fellow officer some distance from his force's position) resulted in his absence from the battle front. He redeemed himself by delaying Gen. Philip Sheridan's pursuit of the retreating Army of Northern Virginia.

After the war, Lee tried farming at his home, Richlands, in Stafford County, Virginia, but he soon turned to politics and was elected governor of Virginia in 1886. He was the U.S. consulate general in Havana, Cuba, from 1896 to 1898. During the Spanish-American War, Lee served as a major general in the U.S. Army. He died on April 29, 1905, in Washington, D.C., and was buried in Hollywood Cemetery in Richmond, Virginia.

BIBLIOGRAPHY

Bond, Frank. "Fitz Lee in the Army of Northern Virginia." *Confederate Veteran* 6, no. 9 (1898): 420–423. Reprint, Wilmington, N.C., 1985.

Nichols, James A. *General Fitzhugh Lee: A Biography.* Lynchburg, Va., 1989.

Warner, Ezra J. *Generals in Gray: Lives of the Confederate Commanders.* Baton Rouge, La., 1959.

KAREN G. REHM

LEE, GEORGE WASHINGTON CUSTIS

(1832–1913), major general. Born September 16, 1832, at Fort Monroe, Virginia, the first child of Mary Custis Lee and Robert E. Lee, Custis Lee spent much of his life coping with the burden of his father's fame. At West Point he graduated first in the class of 1854, exceeding his father's record (second in the class of 1829). Commissioned in the Corps of Engineers (like his father), Custis Lee served on several construction projects before resigning May 2, 1861, in response to the secession of Virginia.

Lee secured a place on the military staff of President Jefferson Davis and spent most of the war in Richmond. Rewarded with promotions for faithful service, Lee became a brigadier general on June 25, 1863, and a major general on October 20, 1864.

By turns eager for command in the field but unsure of his capacity to lead in combat, Lee was often ill during the war. He remained on Davis's staff because the president wanted

GEORGE WASHINGTON CUSTIS LEE.   NATIONAL ARCHIVES

him and because his father needed him. The elder Lee relied upon his son to express his views to the president and to keep him informed about policies and politics within the administration.

Lee finally did command a reserve regiment of industrial workers on the retreat from Richmond, but had to surrender himself and his men at Sayler's Creek on April 6, 1865. After the war Lee taught engineering at the Virginia Military Institute in Lexington. Following his father's death, Custis Lee became president of Washington and Lee University from 1871 to 1897. He died on February 18, 1913.

BIBLIOGRAPHY

Freeman, Douglas S. *R. E. Lee: A Biography.* 4 vols. New York, 1934–1935.
Nagel, Paul C. *The Lees of Virginia: Seven Generations of an American Family.* New York, 1990.

EMORY M. THOMAS

LEE, ROBERT E. (1807–1870), general. Born at Stratford, Westmoreland County, Virginia, on January 19, 1807, Lee was the fourth of five children (the third son) of Ann Hill Carter Lee and Henry ("Light-Horse Harry") Lee. Two children of Harry Lee's first marriage also lived with the family. Robert Lee did not remain very long at Stratford. His father had been a hero in the Revolution, governor of Virginia, and a member of Congress; but by the time of Robert's birth, Lee's fortunes were in serious decline. Harry Lee's debts forced him into prison in 1809 and compelled the family to move to Alexandria, Virginia, in

1810. Then in 1812 Harry Lee sustained serious injuries in Baltimore helping an editor defend his newspaper against a mob outraged over editorials opposing the War of 1812. In May 1813, he sailed away to the Caribbean, ostensibly to recoup his fortune and recover his health, leaving family and creditors behind. Light-Horse Harry Lee died on Cumberland Island, Georgia, in 1818 without having seen his family again.

Ann Lee raised her children in very modest circumstances and tried to teach them standards of conduct in the hope that they would avoid their father's mistakes. After attending schools in Alexandria, Robert Lee managed to secure an appointment to West Point. Rather suddenly he left the company of his mother and sisters, for whom he had cared during his adolescence, and in 1825 entered the exclusively male society at West Point.

His mother's precepts, his academic background, and his quick, precise mind all served Lee well at West Point. He finished second in the class of 1829 and garnered not one demerit during his four years at the academy. Lee's success earned him an appointment in the Engineer Corps at a time when the U.S. government was willing to support public projects. His first assignment was at Cockspur Island in the Savannah River preparing the foundation of what much later became Fort Pulaski.

Approximately a month following his graduation from West Point, Ann Lee died, and Robert Lee began his career in the military with a small inheritance (about ten slaves) and roots in his extended family. Although Lee made friends in Savannah, he spent his leaves in northern Virginia increasingly in the company of Mary Custis, the only child of Mary Fitzhugh Custis and George Washington Parke Custis, the adopted son of George Washington. Lee was extraordinarily handsome then, and throughout his young manhood and middle age people called him the best-looking man in the army. He was about five feet, ten or eleven inches tall, with a fit, medium build and nearly perfect posture. A guest at his son's wedding in 1859 claimed that Lee outshone the entire company, and those who saw him on horseback insisted that he appeared even more imposing riding than afoot.

Mary Custis and Robert Lee married in July 1831 at Arlington, the Custis estate just across the Potomac from Washington. The young couple began life together in officers' quarters at Fort Monroe, Virginia, Lee's second duty assignment. They had seven children between 1832 and 1846. The Lees and their children often lived at Arlington while Lee served in the Engineer Department in Washington, and Mary Lee remained with the children at Arlington when duty called Robert Lee to St. Louis and later to the Mexican War.

Lee served on the staff of Winfield Scott during the campaign from Vera Cruz to Mexico City in 1847. He

ROBERT E. LEE. Lee's first sitting in wartime, his only sitting in the field, and his best-known portrait. Photograph by Charles DeForest Fredericks, early 1864.   NATIONAL ARCHIVES

became a member of Scott's "little cabinet," his inner circle of advisers, and Lee's talent, energy, and daring were especially conspicuous at Cerro Gordo and Chapultepec. He emerged from the war with Scott's unabashed admiration and the brevet (temporary) rank of colonel.

In 1852 Lee returned to West Point as superintendent, and in 1855 he transferred from staff assignments to command of cavalry troopers on the Texas frontier. When his father-in-law died in 1857, Lee began a protracted leave as executor of Custis's estate.

Custis had dabbled in many enterprises and had done none of them very well. Unfortunately for Lee, Custis had not done a very good job of making his will either. So Lee attempted to unsnarl affairs associated with Custis's estate, a task he never quite completed in his lifetime.

Lee was still working at Arlington in October 1859 when reports of a slave insurrection sent him hurriedly to Harpers Ferry in command of a detachment of marines. He confronted John Brown and a few of his followers barricaded in a fire engine building with thirteen hostages. The situation was tense, but Lee managed to capture Brown and put down his raid without harming Brown's hostages.

In 1860 Lee returned to Texas and duty, having had his fill of farming on his father-in-law's estates. In February 1861, he returned to Arlington in response to the secession crisis. He rejected an opportunity to command the principal field army charged with suppressing the rebellion, choosing

instead to offer his services to Virginia and the Southern Confederacy. Lee resigned his commission in the U.S. Army on April 20, 1861, and on April 23 accepted command of the armed forces of Virginia. In this capacity Lee organized the mobilization of Virginia troops and on June 10 surrendered his men and equipment to the Confederate government for the national army and navy. Thereafter Lee served as informal adviser to President Jefferson Davis and remained for the most part in the new capital at Richmond.

On August 31, 1861, Lee became a full general in the Confederate army. By this time he was in western (present-day West) Virginia attempting to unscramble egos and thwart a Union campaign in the Kanawha Valley. Lee failed in both undertakings and returned to Richmond on October 31. Less than a week later Davis sent Lee to command the Department of South Carolina, Georgia, and Florida and to confront Federal incursions along the Southern coast.

Lee arrived in South Carolina on the very day a Federal combined arms force captured Port Royal. Subsequently he worked to contain the enemy invasion and to organize the defense of the coastal region. He concluded that the Confederacy lacked the ships, men, and guns to defend the barrier islands and so contracted the chain of defensive positions up rivers to sites where the guns available would have some chance of stopping Union gunboats. Lee's plans were sound, but his design forced coastal residents to flee inland with their slaves and thus made refugees of some rich and powerful Confederates.

In March 1862, Davis recalled Lee to Richmond and made him, in effect, his chief of staff. Lee was again an adviser while others commanded armies. He did perform a valuable service as buffer between the president and Joseph E. Johnston, who commanded the primary Confederate army in Virginia. In the process of countering Union Gen. George B. McClellan's Peninsular campaign, Davis and Johnston seemed overconcerned about personal prerogatives, and Lee was able to filter some of the vitriol out of communications between the two men. Otherwise, though, Lee worked hard at thankless tasks while McClellan's blue host came steadily closer to Richmond.

Then on May 31, 1862, Johnston committed his army to what became the Battle of Seven Pines, and as the inconclusive fighting wound down, Johnston was seriously injured. On June 1 Davis gave Lee command of Johnston's army and in so doing placed Lee in charge of the Confederacy's tottering fortunes.

Lee withdrew the army into the outskirts of Richmond and ordered the men to prepare elaborate field fortifications. So in the public mind, Lee became "the King of Spades" as well as "Granny Lee" for his supposed overcaution. Lee, however, was already making plans that were anything but defensive and cautious. He reorganized

Johnston's army and renamed it the Army of Northern Virginia—all while in the face of the enemy. He sent J. E. B. Stuart and the cavalry to scout McClellan's right flank, a reconnaissance that became known as Stuart's "Ride around McClellan" because he circled the entire Federal army. Lee shifted divisions of troops to attack the Federal right flank and summoned Thomas J. ("Stonewall") Jackson's Shenandoah Valley army to strike the Federal rear. The result of these actions was the Seven Days' Battles (King's School House, Mechanicsville, Gaines' Mill, Frayser's Farm, White Oaks Swamp, and Malvern Hill) from June 25 through July 1, 1862. After the nearly constant and always bloody fighting, the Federals lay inert under cover of their gunboats at Harrison's Landing on the James River, twenty-three miles from Richmond. Lee was suddenly a hero, and the Confederacy seemed saved. But Lee was frustrated: he had wanted not merely to drive the enemy away but to destroy McClellan's army altogether.

The Seven Days' Battles began a year of success for Confederate arms. Lee continued to seek his enemies' destruction and marched to the old battlefield at Manassas to strike the forces of John Pope. While Jackson fixed Pope's attention and fended off Federal attacks, Lee maneuvered James Longstreet and the other half of the Confederate army to strike Pope's flank. Second Manassas was a resounding Confederate victory, but still less than Lee's dream of annihilating a major Union army.

In the hope of fighting a decisive battle on Northern soil, Lee led his army into Maryland as part of a dual offensive in that state and in Kentucky. En route, however, a copy of Lee's invasion order fell into Union hands and under the eyes of McClellan, who was once more in command of the primary Union army in the East. Lee scrambled to reconcentrate his forces while McClellan moved cautiously to strike Lee's divided command. The armies met at Sharpsburg, Maryland, across Antietam Creek, and the battle became the bloodiest single day of the war. The Army of Northern Virginia barely survived a tactical draw, but Lee abandoned his invasion and retreated back into Virginia.

The campaigns of 1862 in Virginia concluded on the Rappahannock River at Fredericksburg on December 13. Ambrose E. Burnside, next to command the Federal Army of the Potomac, attacked Lee's army entrenched south of the city. The result was a massacre of Federal troops, who never breached Lee's lines.

The spring of 1863 brought a new Federal commander to challenge Lee. Joseph Hooker attempted to sweep across the Rappahannock and strike Lee's flank and rear. Lee set most of his army in motion to meet Hooker, and the armies collided in a sparsely settled region near a crossroads called Chancellorsville. Then Lee learned that Hooker's flank was unsecure, and he dispatched Jackson with his entire corps to envelop the Federals. Jackson's attack was devastating,

but in the wake of the success, Jackson himself fell, accidentally wounded at the hands of some of his own troops. With J. E. B. Stuart in charge of Jackson's corps, Lee was able to unite the two wings of his army and press Hooker severely. But even at Chancellorsville in what many consider Lee's greatest battle, the Army of Northern Virginia was unable to destroy the Army of the Potomac.

Still hoping for a climactic victory, Lee once more marched north, this time into Pennsylvania. He met the Federals and the new commander George G. Meade at Gettysburg. On July 1, 1863, the Confederates captured the town and drove their enemies onto Cemetery Hill and Ridge. But Richard S. Ewell, in command of one of Lee's three corps, stopped, following to the letter Lee's orders against a general engagement before the entire army arrived. The next day, July 2, Longstreet's corps sought the Federal left flank, found it, and fought a desperate but drawn battle at Little and Big Round Tops and within Devil's Den. Late in the day Stuart arrived with news of his raiding, but with no reliable reconnaissance reports of the strength and disposition of Meade's army. Nevertheless, Lee determined to attack again—to make one last attempt at a battle of annihilation. He decided to try to break the center of the Federal lines on Cemetery Ridge.

Pickett's Charge was a debacle reminiscent of Malvern Hill. Lee took the risk because he believed he had to in order to achieve victory. He had come too far, worked too hard, to shrink from what he perceived to be the moment of truth. He lost.

After the Army of Northern Virginia had limped back into northern Virginia in August, Lee submitted his resignation to the president. He pointed out that he had been ill the previous spring (likely with the heart disease that eventually killed him) and had never really recovered. He argued that because he had not been successful, the president should install another in his place. Davis declined to accept the resignation and told Lee that he knew no one better to command the army.

Lee, however, was still unwell. He was compelled to conduct his abortive Bristoe Station campaign (October 9–22) from a wagon instead of horseback. Yet Bristoe Station and Mine Run, which followed in November, demonstrated that Lee was still intent on victory and still capable of stratagems designed to lay waste his enemy.

Throughout the winter of 1863–1864 Lee labored to conserve his resources and himself. He ordered rigorous inspections throughout his army to ensure that men and equipment would be ready for the spring and to emphasize the need to husband their dwindling supplies. His new opponent was Ulysses S. Grant, now commander in chief of Union armies. Grant elected to exercise his far-flung command from a headquarters in Meade's army opposite Lee.

ROBERT E. LEE. This April 20, 1865, photograph by Mathew Brady was taken under the back porch of Lee's home near Richmond, Virginia, shortly before Lee became president of what is today known as Washington and Lee University.   NATIONAL ARCHIVES

During the first week of May in 1864 Grant crossed the Rapidan River and plunged into an area known locally as the Wilderness. Lee let the Federals cross the river and waited to strike until the Wilderness compelled the Federals to disperse their superior numbers and even the odds. From a tactical perspective Lee won in the Wilderness; but Grant did not withdraw and lick his wounds as other Union commanders had done. Grant put his army in motion, east and south, to try to force his way between Lee and Richmond. Lee was just resourceful enough to block Grant's march at Spotsylvania Court House. There the armies again came to grips, and again Grant recoiled and resumed his drive to the east and south. Lee continued his canny counterpunching until the armies came near Cold Harbor, very close to the site of the fighting two years before at Gaines' Mill. Then Grant tried to break through the center of Lee's long line and failed disastrously.

In the wake of Cold Harbor, however, Lee lost his enemy: Stuart was dead, and his cavalry was unable to determine Federal intentions. When Grant's army reappeared, it was south of the James marching on Petersburg, a crucial railroad junction south of Richmond. Inspired fighting and blind luck held Petersburg long enough for Lee to reinforce the defenders. Then Lee again became the "King of Spades." He used trenches to compensate for his inferiority in numbers and held his lines around Petersburg and the line of forts north of the James, east of Richmond, for the next nine and a half months.

Both commanders attempted to break the trench stalemate. For his part Lee dispatched Jubal Early to Lynchburg, down the Shenandoah Valley, and to the outskirts of Washington in hopes of fighting Federals outside of prepared fortifications. And Lee attempted to break the Federal lines and trap his enemies in their holes on several occasions. Ultimately, though, he was himself trapped in a war of attrition that he had worked to avoid. Eventually, on April 1, 1865, Lee's lines became too thin and too short; he had to evacuate his works and Richmond on April 2.

The Army of Northern Virginia survived in flight for only one week. On April 9, 1865, Lee surrendered to Grant at Appomattox Courthouse. The Confederacy lived little longer than Lee's army.

In peace Lee stood for sectional reconciliation. He accepted the presidency of Washington College in Lexington, Virginia, and attempted to educate a new generation of Southerners to cope with an altered reality in the South. He established a balance in the curriculum between the traditional classical education and the more practical disciplines in science and engineering. He introduced elective courses and supplanted the many rules governing student conduct with one: students should conduct themselves as gentlemen. In Lee's mind conducting oneself as a gentleman was essentially a matter of selfless concern for other people. "The great duty in life," he once wrote, "is the promotion of the happiness and welfare of others."

Even as he lived, Lee became a legend. Southerners needed Lee to prove that good people can and do lose and to demonstrate that success in battle or elsewhere does not necessarily denote superiority. Lee became something of a Christ figure for the defeated Southern Confederates.

Cardiovascular troubles, probably dating from the war period, increasingly plagued Lee in Lexington. During the spring of 1870 he took an extended trip into the Deep South, ostensibly for his health, more likely as a farewell tour. Because he knew or sensed that he was dying, he agreed to sit for a portrait and pose for a statue, acts he had loathed in the past, during the summer of 1870.

Then one evening in the fall Lee came home late from a vestry meeting and suffered a stroke as he attempted to bless his supper. He lingered a time in a passive state, and on October 13, 1870, he died.

[See also Arlington House; Army of Northern Virginia; Lee Memorial Association; Lee Monument Association.]

BIBLIOGRAPHY

Connelly, Thomas L. The Marble Man: Robert E. Lee and His Image in American Society. New York, 1977.

Dowdey, Clifford. Lee. Boston, 1965.

Dowdey, Clifford, and Louis H. Manarin, eds. The Wartime Papers of R. E. Lee. Boston, 1961.

Freeman, Douglas S. R. E. Lee: A Biography. 4 vols. New York, 1934–1935.

Lee, Robert E. [Jr.]. Recollections and Letters of General Robert E. Lee. Garden City, N.Y., 1924.

Sanborn, Margaret. Robert E. Lee. 2 vols. Philadelphia, 1966–1967.

EMORY M. THOMAS

LEE, STEPHEN D. (1833–1908), lieutenant general. Lee was born September 22, 1833, at Charleston, South Carolina. His mother died when he was quite young, and he and a sister were raised by their financially unsuccessful physician father. Stephen was named for one of his uncles, who ran a military boarding school where Stephen received all of his early formal education. Appointed to West Point, he graduated in 1854, seventeenth out of forty-six.

Lee spent nearly seven years on active duty in the U.S. Army. He saw combat in Florida during the Third Seminole War and along the Kansas-Missouri border. Lee impressed his superiors with his organizational and administrative capabilities. The young Lee displayed no deep concern for politics, but his sentiments were unquestionably proslavery and thoroughly Southern.

At the outset of the Civil War, Lee was appointed a captain in South Carolina's regular artillery service. He served during the Fort Sumter episode as an aide-de-camp to Brig. Gen. P. G. T. Beauregard. The ensuing year constituted the high point of his practical military education. He emerged distinguished from the mass of other junior officers, reflecting and always infusing professionalism. Above all else, he had a certain air of competence. Some observers perceived him to be dashing and inspiring, and many were impressed with his ingenuity and his courage. Although he was bold in combat—some critics later would say he was audacious to a fault—he never attracted notice for any oddity.

Lee rose eventually to become a lieutenant general at thirty, the youngest man in the war to attain that rank. He did not attain independent command until 1863 and oversaw only small bodies of troops until August 1864. Lee commanded an artillery battery during late 1861 and an artillery battalion in the Peninsular campaign. He briefly headed the Fourth Virginia Cavalry early in mid-1862 and won notice as an artillery commander at Second Manassas and at Sharpsburg. Lee defeated William Tecumseh Sherman at Chickasaw Bayou, helped with the defense of Vicksburg, and commanded all the cavalry in Mississippi in late 1863 and early 1864. He rose to military department command, the only one of Nathan Bedford Forrest's superiors to work well with that eccentric genius. He finally attained a corps command with the Army of Tennessee.

Late in the war Lee married a Mississippi woman and thereafter lived in his wife's home, which is now a museum and historical pilgrimage headquarters. After the war Lee worked as an insurance salesman, served in the Mississippi senate, and headed the A. & M. College of Mississippi. He was deeply committed to and involved with the establishment and early management of the Vicksburg National Military Park and helped found the United Confederate Veterans, which he served as commander in chief during the last four years of his life. He died May 28, 1908, and is buried in Friendship Cemetery, Columbus, Mississippi.

BIBLIOGRAPHY

Davis, William C., ed. *The Confederate General.* Vol. 4. Harrisburg, Pa., 1991.

Hattaway, Herman. *General Stephen D. Lee.* Jackson, Miss., 1976.

HERMAN HATTAWAY

LEE, WILLIAM HENRY FITZHUGH (1837–1891), major general and U.S. congressman. Born May 31, 1837, to Mary Custis Lee and Robert E. Lee at Arlington, "Rooney" Lee attended Harvard, inspired a damning passage in classmate Henry Adams's *Autobiography* ("the Southerner has no mind"), and left without graduating to accept a direct commission in the U.S. Army in 1857. Lee resigned his commission in 1859 to marry and become a farmer at White House on the Pamunkey River in Virginia.

After Virginia seceded, Lee enlisted in the Confed-

WILLIAM HENRY FITZHUGH LEE.   LIBRARY OF CONGRESS

erate army, initially as a captain of cavalry. He served with W. W. Loring in western (present-day West) Virginia during the summer and fall of 1861. By early 1862 he was at Fredericksburg in command of the Ninth Virginia Cavalry. He led this regiment on J. E. B. Stuart's Ride around McClellan in June 1862 and served with Stuart in the Army of Northern Virginia thereafter. Promoted to brigadier general for bravery at South Mountain, Lee participated in raids and reconnaissance during the period in which Confederate cavalry dominated in the East. Then at Brandy Station on June 9, 1863, Lee suffered a wound in his leg and was captured soon after while he recuperated at his wife's home near Richmond.

Imprisoned at Fort Monroe and Fort Lafayette until exchanged in March 1864, Lee afterward resumed active service. On April 23, 1864, he became at the age of thirty-six the youngest major general in the Confederate army. By the time his father surrendered at Appomattox, Lee was second in command of cavalry in the Army of Northern Virginia.

After the war Lee rebuilt his farm and his life. His first wife had died while he was a prisoner of war, and in 1867 he remarried. Lee became president of the Virginia Agricultural Society, state senator (1875–1878), and U.S. congressman (1886–1891). Likely the most successful of the Lee children, Rooney Lee died October 15, 1891.

BIBLIOGRAPHY

Freeman, Douglas S. *R. E. Lee: A Biography.* 4 vols. New York, 1934–1935.

Thomas, Emory M. *Bold Dragoon: The Life of J. E. B. Stuart.* New York, 1986.

EMORY M. THOMAS

LEE MEMORIAL ASSOCIATION. The Robert E. Lee Memorial Association is a nonprofit organization that owns and operates Stratford Hall Plantation, Lee's birthplace in Westmoreland County, Virginia. It was formed in 1929 under the leadership of Mrs. Charles D. Lanier to purchase Stratford. The Great House and outbuildings at Stratford were restored under the direction of noted architect Fiske Kimball. The all-female governing board has a member from each state of the Union, the District of Columbia, and Great Britain. A leading benefactor and board member was Mrs. Alfred I. duPont, in whose honor a research library was named at its inception in 1980.

Stratford was built by Thomas Lee about 1738. Two signers of the Declaration of Independence, Richard Henry Lee and Francis Lightfoot Lee, grew up there. A later resident was General Lee's father, Henry ("Light Horse Harry") Lee, the brilliant Revolutionary War cavalry leader. His wife, Ann Hill Carter Lee, gave birth to their fourth son, Robert Edward, at Stratford on January 19, 1807. Lee lived at Stratford for only three and a half years, however. The plantation was sold by the Lee family in 1822 and remained in other private hands until purchased by the association.

The mission of the association today is to preserve and interpret Stratford and to educate the public on the historical significance of Robert E. Lee and other family members. In 1981 the association initiated an annual summer seminar for history teachers. It sponsors special events and annual open houses on General Lee's birthday and July 4. Special tours include one on Children's Days. Others concern architecture, the farm, gardens and decorative arts.

[*See also* Lee Monument Association.]

BIBLIOGRAPHY

Armes, Ethel. *Stratford Hall: The Great House of the Lees.* Richmond, Va., 1936.

Dill, Alonzo T., and Mary Tyler Cheek. *A Visit to Stratford and the Story of the Lees.* Stratford, Va., 1986.

Nagel, Paul C. *The Lees of Virginia: Seven Generations of an American Family.* New York, 1990.

C. VAUGHAN STANLEY

LEE MONUMENT ASSOCIATION. The Lee Monument Association, which played an important role in ensuring the prominent place of Robert E. Lee among the heroes of the Lost Cause, first organized in 1870 shortly after the general's death. At the behest of Jubal Early,

veterans of the Army of Northern Virginia met in Richmond, resolved to erect a monument to Lee in the former Confederate capital, and began a regionwide fund-raising campaign. Initially the association competed with similar groups, including the Lee Memorial Association that dedicated a statue to Lee at Washington and Lee University in 1883.

In 1886, Virginia Governor Fitzhugh Lee, a veteran and nephew of the Confederate commander, reorganized the Lee Monument Association under a board composed of state officials and representatives from Richmond's Ladies' Lee Memorial Association, which had raised more money than any other group. With Fitzhugh Lee's leadership and contributions from Early and Lee Camp, a newly formed Confederate veterans' group in Richmond, the reorganized Lee Monument Association raised the remainder of the necessary funds. Its board selected a sculptor, Frenchman Jean Antoine Mercié, chose a site on the edge of one of Richmond's growing suburbs, and dedicated the statue's base in 1887. Three years later, on May 29, 1890, a crowd of over 100,000 gathered to watch the unveiling of Mercié's

UNVEILING OF THE LEE MONUMENT, RICHMOND, VIRGINIA. Dedicated May 29, 1890, and unveiled by Gen. Joseph E. Johnston, assisted by Gens. Fitzhugh Lee and Wade Hampton. The only inscription on the statue is "LEE."   ELEANOR S. BROCKENBROUGH LIBRARY, THE MUSEUM OF THE CONFEDERACY, RICHMOND, VIRGINIA

majestic mounted Lee and to celebrate not only the general but the Confederacy. Later, when statues to other Confederate leaders were erected near that of Lee, Richmond's Monument Avenue became a major shrine to the Lost Cause.

[*See also* Lee Memorial Association.]

BIBLIOGRAPHY

Connelly, Thomas L. *The Marble Man: Robert E. Lee and His Image in American Society.* New York, 1977.

Foster, Gaines M. *Ghosts of the Confederacy: Defeat, the Lost Cause, and the Emergence of the New South, 1865 to 1913.* New York, 1987.

GAINES M. FOSTER

LEESBURG, VIRGINIA. *See* Ball's Bluff, Virginia.

LEISURE.

In the Confederacy leisure put to the test the difficult relationship between a culture for men and a culture for the religious, both male and female. Male culture existed wherever men gathered and tended to be confrontational and potentially violent; religious culture was centered in the home and church and tended to be more harmonious and to respect the notion of the special purity of women. The culture of white Southerners existed in a state of balanced tension, with men indulging their forms of recreation in masculine areas and then generally respecting the norms of religious culture when they were near the home or the church.

The experience of the war intensified the aggressive side of male culture. The obvious need to take pride in fighting ability, the free time, the demands on the men to prove themselves to one another, the absence of women, and the tensions about forthcoming battles meant that soldiers carried a fighting spirit into their leisure time. Heavy drinking and profanity gave a masculine flavor to most recreations at the front, and almost anything became more exciting when soldiers turned it into a competition. Men in the camps experienced an exaggerated version of the normal cycles of aggressive masculine recreation and more straitlaced religious morality. In many camps, visits to prostitutes, drunkenness, and gambling—especially with cards and dice—prevailed for several months at a time. Some searched so hard for ways to gamble that they staged races and fights with lice. But then religious revivals reminded the soldiers that they believed the behavior of male culture to be ultimately sinful. The glorification of home and motherhood that revealed itself in the most popular song of the Confederate troops—"Home, Sweet Home"—had much to do not only with loneliness and the possibility of early death but also with the guilt so many young men felt

about violating the behavior that was expected of them in their homes and churches.

The shared experience of team sports in the camps helped unify the troops. Along with relieving boredom, the sports created a sense of community and shared purpose. Such sports as football and baseball had far fewer rules than their present versions; they allowed recreation within the changing settings and frequent interruptions of camp life. Some of the wartime sports offered opportunities for competing visions of the class structure of the South. Both gander-pulling and ring-and-lance tournaments, for example, offered exciting horseback spectacles, the former by wringing the neck of a goose suspended in the air, and the latter by hooking rings with a lance. Gander-pulling, a democratic activity that made a sport of the dramatic destruction of poultry, could be played by any farm boy with a horse. The tournament, however, involved conscious aspirations to elitist recreation. Upper-class "knights" took the names of their plantations or styled themselves after characters from Sir Walter Scott; the winner had the honor of crowning a queen. Tournaments became extremely popular immediately after the war, as wealthy Southerners searched for ways to connect their part in the Confederacy to a historic upper class.

On the home front, activities white women had long considered part of their responsibilities took on new moral gravity. Visits among women became not just social functions but also ways to tend to the sick and console those with relatives who had died. Writing letters became a way to remind men at the front of the importance of home life.

Sewing in groups, traditionally an important activity in which women combined their commitment to the domestic economy with the pleasures of conversation, took on new meanings of patriotism and sacrifice. Many women turned circles of friends into sewing organizations, often in association with churches. Sewing for the soldiers became such a patriotic responsibility that the term *famous knitter* became, as historian George Rable has written, "a stock encomium for these heroines of the home front." With the demand high for sacrifice at home, white women made a point of dressing with fewer concerns for fashion and imported fabrics. Diarist Mary Chesnut argued in 1861 that "true patriotesses would be willing to wear the same clothes until our siege was raised."

This ideal of sacrifice helped turn many recreations into patriotic events. Raffles of food; bazaars to sell food, clothing, and jewelry; concerts and theatricals—all traditional functions of the wealthy—gained a new sense of high purpose when they raised money for the Confederacy. And whites on the home front tried, not always successfully, to turn the need to limit spending and celebrating at Christmas into a patriotic form of religious self-denial.

The most important aspect of leisure in the slave

community was the celebrations of emancipation. After they had seized the possibilities wartime dislocations created for frequent movement, freed slaves in 1865 went into towns and cities to verify that they were in fact free. Some of the larger celebrations numbered over ten thousand people for events that mixed music (some of it religious), parades, politics, and sometimes alcohol. In Athens, Georgia, freed slaves danced around a liberty pole before whites tore it down at night. Very soon African Americans turned these celebrations into yearly holidays, especially the so-called Juneteenth celebrations still popular in many towns and cities.

[See also Juneteenth.]

BIBLIOGRAPHY

Chesnut, Mary Boykin. *Mary Chesnut's Civil War.* Edited by C. Vann Woodward. New Haven, Conn., 1981.

Faust, Drew Gilpin. "Christian Soldiers: The Meaning of Revivalism in the Confederate Army." *Journal of Southern History* 58 (February 1987): 63–90.

Litwack, Leon F. *Been in the Storm So Long: The Aftermath of Slavery.* New York, 1979.

Ownby, Ted. *Subduing Satan: Religion, Recreation, and Manhood in the Rural South, 1865–1920.* Chapel Hill, N.C., 1990.

Rable, George C. *Civil Wars: Women and the Crisis of Confederate Nationalism.* Urbana, Ill., 1989.

Wiggins, William H. *O freedom! Afro-American Emancipation Celebrations.* Knoxville, Tenn., 1987.

Wiley, Bell Irvin. *The Life of Johnny Reb.* Indianapolis, Ind., 1943.

TED OWNBY

LEON, EDWIN DE (1818–1892), diplomat. After graduation from South Carolina College, Edwin de Leon changed his plans for a legal career and became instead a journalist. While editing the *Southern Press* in Washington, he was appointed consul general to Egypt, a position he held from 1854 to 1860.

After South Carolina seceded, de Leon returned to the South and volunteered for Confederate service. Jefferson Davis, a close friend, sent him to France to promote the Southern cause in the European press and to propagandize Confederate successes. Davis gave de Leon a fund of $25,000 from the Treasury to work toward gaining recognition of the Confederacy by France and England. De Leon had some success; several French newspapers began to champion the Confederacy. But his enthusiastic advocacy of slavery and his criticism of the French undermined his effectiveness.

De Leon alienated himself from several important Confederates including Secretary of State Judah P. Benjamin. On his way to Europe, de Leon opened and read some confidential letters from Benjamin to John Slidell, the Confederate representative to France. Later, a letter written by de Leon to Davis, attacking Benjamin and Slidell, was intercepted and published in the *New York Daily Tribune.* Benjamin's displeasure with de Leon led in 1864 to the end of de Leon's diplomatic career.

De Leon had spent his life savings on the Confederacy, and after his Southern career ended, he remained in Europe and Egypt, working as a writer. He published *The Khedive's Egypt* in 1872 and *Under the Stars and Crescent* in 1879. In 1886 he published *Thirty Years of Life in Three Continents.* De Leon spent his final years in the United States and died in New York City in 1892.

BIBLIOGRAPHY

Sifakis, Stewart. *Who Was Who in the Confederacy.* New York, 1988.

Simonhoff, Harry. *Jewish Participants in the Civil War.* New York, 1963.

RAY SKATES

LESTER, GEORGE N. (1824–1892), captain and congressman from Georgia. George Nelson Lester was born in Abbeville, South Carolina, on March 13, 1824. Four years later, the family moved to Gwinnett County, Georgia. He studied law and was admitted to the bar in 1843 at the age of eighteen. He then moved to Cumming in Forsyth County and established a successful law practice there. In the early 1850s, he moved to Marietta, Georgia. In 1858 Lester was elected to the General Assembly representing Cobb County. Reelected in 1860, he was named chairman of the House Judiciary Committee, the body that initiated the secession process for the state following Abraham Lincoln's election.

Once Georgia was out of the Union, Lester organized a company from Cobb County and led it as part of Georgia's Forty-first Regiment under the command of Col. Charles A. McDaniel. This regiment saw action in the Kentucky campaign of 1862. At the Battle of Perryville in October, McDaniel was killed and Lester seriously wounded; he eventually lost his right arm. He returned to Marietta and, once recovered from his wound, served with the Georgia State Reserves. In October 1863, he was elected to represent the state's Third District in the Second Congress. He supported the current military force and discouraged any tampering with its organization or leadership. Yet he also demonstrated a genuine commitment to the home front situation. He introduced legislation to exempt men from conscription whose labor was considered vital to production and opposed further conscription or confiscation measures that would hamper morale and survival at home. By early 1865 he was committed to peace and resigned his congressional seat upon hearing of the failure of the Hampton Roads peace conference in February 1865.

Lester returned home and resumed his law practice. He

was appointed commissioner of the newly established Bureau of Immigration, but he chafed at interference by Republican administrators and soon resigned. He spent a number of years as a judge on the Blue Ridge Circuit of North Georgia and remained active in state politics. In 1890, he was elected state attorney general, but suffered a paralytic stroke before he took office. He died on March 30, 1892.

BIBLIOGRAPHY

Northen, William J., ed. *Men of Mark in Georgia.* Vol. 3. Atlanta, Ga., 1908. Reprint, Spartanburg, S.C., 1974.

Warner, Ezra J., and W. Buck Yearns. *Biographical Register of the Confederate Congress.* Baton Rouge, La., 1975.

JOHN C. INSCOE

LETCHER, JOHN (1813–1882), governor of Virginia. Letcher grew up in the comfortable middle class in Lexington, Virginia, in the Shenandoah Valley. Optimistic and gregarious, he became a lawyer and for a while edited a local newspaper. Politics was his real calling, and Letcher gradually rose as a moderate Jacksonian Democrat. As a delegate to the state convention of 1850–1851, he helped write a more liberal constitution for Virginia, and in return the voters in his district elected him to Congress for four consecutive terms from 1851 to 1859. There he was a moderate conservative as the South came under increasing pressure from the rising Republican party. In 1859 he won the governorship in a close contest with the disintegrating Whig party.

On January 1, 1860, forty-six-year-old Letcher and his large family moved into the governor's mansion in Richmond to begin his four-year term as the nation stumbled toward civil war. Still a moderate, he championed "prudence and moderation . . . conciliation and compromise" and only grudgingly went along with increased military preparations. In the November presidential election he supported Stephen A. Douglas, the Northern Democratic candidate, and after Abraham Lincoln's victory, he unsuccessfully resisted the calling of a state convention. Only after war erupted, Lincoln called for troops, and the Virginia convention voted to secede did Letcher lead his state out of the Union and into the new Confederacy.

Now Governor Letcher was the wartime leader of the most powerful state in the Confederacy; he had a new role to play. Working frantically to mobilize Virginia for total war, Letcher performed efficiently, and even many secessionists conceded that he was finally doing well. He appointed Matthew Fontaine Maury and other able men to his Advisory Council, and aware of his own lack of military experience, he often followed their suggestions. Letcher appointed Robert E. Lee to command the Virginia forces,

and among the many other officers he commissioned was Thomas J. Jackson, soon to be known as "Stonewall."

Virginia's rapid mobilization produced more volunteers than weapons, but even so the governor loaned some scarce equipment to other states. A practical man, he knew the Southern states had to cooperate to win. Even more important, he realized that they would have to close ranks behind the Confederate government, which was now moving to Richmond. Letcher's confidence in President Jefferson Davis encouraged his cooperation with the Confederates as did the presence of massive Federal forces on Virginia's borders. But mainly common sense told him that old concepts of state rights, individual freedoms, and strict legalism would have to yield to the immediate demands of the war effort. This pragmatic acceptance of Confederate leadership was the hallmark of his administration.

Soon the war became a grinding battle of attrition, and the Confederacy in April 1862 acted to hold its one-year volunteers in the ranks and to mobilize able-bodied civilians by enacting the first national draft in American history. A storm of protests arose, and some states never fully cooperated with this radical but necessary measure. In private correspondence with other Southern governors Letcher denounced the new draft as unnecessary and unconstitutional, naively assuming that each state would effectively mobilize its own manpower, but he also advised his fellow governors to support Confederate conscription for the duration of the war and only then to challenge it in the courts. Again Letcher followed a win-the-war-first policy, and publicly he ordered Virginia officials to enforce the new draft.

He also cooperated with Confederate call-ups of Virginia's rapidly dwindling militia forces, despite protests from affected counties. Uneasy about vulnerable areas of the state, he backed a small, independent state force, the Virginia State Line, which did not accept men eligible for the draft. Despite Confederate complaints the governor uncharacteristically continued to support this inept little "army" until the legislature disbanded it in February 1863.

Letcher wanted the Line to protect vital saltworks in the southwestern part of the state. The South needed this essential preservative, and Virginia had some of the main sources. In the fall of 1862 the legislature passed the problem of fair distribution at reasonable prices on to the governor and gave him sweeping new powers. Letcher became the salt czar of Virginia, but he failed to establish an efficient statewide system. He hesitated to seize uncooperative saltworks and to fix prices, and he often got tangled in red tape. Early in 1863 the legislature transferred his powers to another state agency, but the salt program continued to falter.

At every level Southerners had difficulty establishing sweeping new administrative policies, and they failed to control inflation. Governor Letcher often denounced "speculators" and "extortioners," but neither he nor the legislature nor any Confederate officials could long check soaring prices that were undermining the South's economy.

Letcher also failed to prevent the Northwest's secession from the state of Virginia, but this too was a problem beyond his or the Confederates' control; the Unionists in that region were too powerful. He also failed to rouse his people with stirring oratory; his speeches were usually loaded with tedious accumulations of facts and statistics.

Clearly he had weaknesses as a popular leader, but he seldom wavered in his selfless support of the Confederate war effort, even as attacks on the Davis administration escalated. Letcher tolerated Confederate impressment of civilian property, a practice he detested and had hesitated to employ in his salt program. Even the impressment of slaves, which infuriated many planters, gained the resigned support of the governor who wanted above all to win the war.

Letcher's continuing cooperation with the Confederates became increasingly unpopular with the conservative people of Virginia. The legislature moved from complaints to actual investigations of his salt program, his support for impressment, and especially his call-ups of militia units. Letcher defended himself ably—he was handling difficult programs that were vital to the war effort—and he was never officially censured. Nevertheless, the legislators' message was clear: do not be so quick to put Confederate needs before the traditional rights and privileges of Virginians.

An experienced politician, Letcher understood, and he did ease up a little, but basically he continued to support President Davis's administration. During 1863, the last year of his governorship, the Confederates and to a lesser extent the Virginia legislature took over many of Letcher's responsibilities as he planned to continue his career by running for the Confederate Congress in his old congressional district. His supporters conducted a brief campaign, but on May 28 he lost to the incumbent. The voters had spoken: Letcher had been too much a Confederate and not enough a Virginian. Shaken by this first major defeat at the polls and economically hurt by the raging inflation in Richmond, he completed his term of office, still hoping that President Davis and General Lee could achieve victory.

Early in January 1864 Letcher and his family returned to Lexington where he continued to support the Confederate war effort as a private citizen. In June a Union army briefly occupied Lexington, and the Northern troops destroyed a few mills and salt supplies, the Virginia Military Institute, and Letcher's home—another crude but clear recognition of his service to the Southern cause.

Early in the spring of 1865 the battered Confederacy finally collapsed, and on May 17 Letcher was arrested and taken to Washington where he remained in prison for almost seven weeks. Paroled on July 10, he returned to Lexington, championed sectional reconciliation, and resumed the practice of law. In the mid-1870s he served a term in the state legislature, but his health declined rapidly. On January 26, 1882, he died at home, once again an American, a Southerner, and a Virginian.

BIBLIOGRAPHY

Boney, F. N. "Governor Letcher's Candid Correspondence." *Civil War History* 10 (1964): 167–180.

Boney, F. N. *John Letcher of Virginia: The Story of Virginia's Civil War Governor.* University, Ala., 1966.

Boney, F. N. "John Letcher: Pragmatic Confederate Patriot." In *The Governors of Virginia: 1860–1978.* Edited by Edward Younger and James Tice Moore. Charlottesville, Va., 1982.

Boney, F. N. *Southerners All.* Macon, Ga., 1990.

Boney, F. N. "Virginia." In *The Confederate Governors.* Edited by W. Buck Yearns. Athens, Ga., 1985.

Dabney, Virginius. *Virginia: The New Dominion.* New York, 1971.

Thomas, Emory M. *The Confederate Nation: 1861–1865.* New York, 1979.

F. N. BONEY

LETTERS. *See* Diaries, Letters, and Memoirs.

LEVENTHORPE, COLLETT (1815–1889), brigadier general of state troops and colonel in the Confederate army. Possibly the tallest general officer in the Confederacy, six-foot, six-inch Collett Leventhorpe was born May 15, 1815, at Exmouth, England. He was educated at Winchester College and, at seventeen, commissioned an ensign in Her Majesty's Fourteenth Regiment of Foot. As captain of grenadiers he saw service in Ireland, the West Indies, and Canada. In 1842 he resigned and immigrated to North Carolina.

At the outbreak of the Civil War, Leventhorpe offered his services to his adopted state. When the Thirty-fourth North Carolina was organized, he was unanimously chosen its colonel. In December 1861 he was given command of a brigade comprising four North Carolina regiments.

In April 1862, Leventhorpe was placed in charge of the Eleventh North Carolina, formerly the First Regiment. He commanded the district of Wilmington for several months before being replaced by Thomas Lanier Clingman. An outbreak of yellow fever prevented Clingman from assuming command immediately, however, and Leventhorpe retained his position until ordered to the Blackwater.

Leventhorpe returned to North Carolina in January 1863. Subsequently transferred to J. Johnston Pettigrew's brigade, Leventhorpe was severely wounded in the first day's fight at Gettysburg. Captured on the retreat from

Pennsylvania, he was imprisoned at Point Lookout for nearly nine months.

In April 1864, Leventhorpe reported that his left arm and hand were "almost useless from the effects" of the wound. At the same time he noted that he had been suffering "for nearly three years from severe inflammation of the eyes resulting from an accident."

Leventhorpe, who had been appointed a brigadier of state troops earlier, was commissioned a brigadier in the Confederate States Army, to date from February 3, 1865. The promotion was confirmed on February 18, but on March 6, Leventhorpe rejected the commission, saying: "I am under obligation to the Governor of North Carolina to organize the state troops now assembling in Raleigh, and I am not able, consistently with this duty, to accept the command in the Confederate Service with which I am honored." He expressed his "thanks and regret."

Leventhorpe devoted his postwar years to business enterprises. He made several trips to England, resided in New York for a time, and eventually returned to North Carolina, where he died December 1, 1889. He was buried in the Episcopal Cemetery in Happy Valley near Lenoir.

BIBLIOGRAPHY

Compiled Military Service Records. Collett Leventhorpe. Microcopy M331, Roll 156. Record Group 109. National Archives, Washington, D.C.

Hill, D. H., Jr. *North Carolina*. Vol. 4 of *Confederate Military History*. Edited by Clement A. Evans. Atlanta, 1899. Vol. 5 of extended ed. Wilmington, N.C., 1987.

Johnson, Edward. "The Gettysburg Campaign—Official Reports." *Southern Historical Society Papers* 6 (1878): 259–260. Reprint, Wilmington, N.C., 1990.

Warner, Ezra J. *Generals in Gray: Lives of the Confederate Commanders*. Baton Rouge, La., 1959.

LOWELL REIDENBAUGH

LEWIS, DAVID PETER (1820–1884), Alabama congressman and Reconstruction governor. Lewis was born in Charlotte County, Virginia. There is no record of his actual birthdate. His gravestone records his age as sixty-five at the time of death, but the census of 1860 listed him as being thirty-seven that year. While he was a child, his parents moved to Madison County, Alabama. Lewis was college-educated, and after reading for the law in Huntsville, Alabama, he was admitted to the bar. Lewis opened a private law practice in Lawrence County and became a well-known lawyer in the hill country of northwestern Alabama. He never married.

An opponent of secession, as were many of the citizens of northern Alabama, Lewis was elected to represent Lawrence County in the Alabama convention of 1860 that was called to decide the issue of secession. The gathering convened at Montgomery on January 7, 1861, and remained in session for four days. At the convention Lewis voiced the objection of the minority of Alabamians, who were concentrated in the northern counties, to immediate secession. Lewis urged that withdrawal from the Union be delayed to await the calling of a Southern convention, which would allow the Southern states to act in unison. When the vote on immediate secession was taken, he voted against it, but signed the ordinance of secession once it was approved on January 11. Because he consented to sign the ordinance Lewis was elected without opposition by the convention to the Provisional Congress of the Confederate States of America, which convened at Montgomery on February 4, 1861. Lewis arrived to take his seat four days later and was assigned to the Indian Affairs and the Patents committees. His Unionist viewpoint, however, allowed him to attend only a few days of the gathering before he resigned his seat on April 29, stating that it would not be "convenient" for him to serve any longer.

Lewis did not enter active politics again until 1863 when Governor John G. Shorter appointed him a judge on the Alabama Circuit Court. During this same time a mini–civil war erupted in northern Alabama as deserters and brigands from both armies concentrated in the region. The bitterness between the Unionists of northern Alabama and the secessionists of southern Alabama erupted into guerrilla warfare. Homes and public buildings were burned, crops were destroyed, and murders became commonplace. Local control broke down and the region was overrun with tories, pro-Northern Southerners, and lawless bands calling themselves "Angels of Destruction." Lewis's pro-Union sympathies were well known, and as the chaos spread, he resigned his judgeship after only a few months and fled northward for safety. Lewis found sanctuary behind Union lines in Federal-controlled Nashville, Tennessee, where he remained until the end of the Civil War.

Lewis returned to Huntsville in 1865, resumed his law practice, and once again became involved in Alabama politics. In July 1868 he represented Alabama Democrats at the Democratic National Convention in New York City. For reasons he never publicly revealed, however, he abandoned the Democratic party and became a Republican. In doing so he allied himself with the scalawags. Hated by white Southerners of the period, scalawags were local supporters of Radical Republican administrations during Reconstruction. They were kept in power by newly enfranchised blacks, the disenfranchisement of many whites who had supported the Confederacy, and Northern troops.

In Alabama the scalawags lost the support of many of the white Unionists who had opposed secession in 1861, and some of the scalawags themselves refused to cooperate with the carpetbaggers, as Northerners who came South during

Reconstruction and gained positions of power were called. As a result the Republicans split in the 1870 gubernatorial election, allowing Democrat Robert B. Lindsey to be elected.

Determined to regain the governor's office, the Radical Republicans nominated Lewis as governor in 1872 to oppose Thomas H. Herndon. With the support of freedmen and the railroad lobby, Lewis won, but the Democrats gained control of both houses of the state's General Assembly. Lewis realized that the Republicans could do little if the Democrats controlled the legislature and with the help of Lewis E. Parsons, the presidentially appointed provisional governor of Alabama following the Civil War, he organized a rival Republican-dominated legislature called the "Courthouse Legislature." Among the last actions taken by Lindsey before he surrendered the chief executive office to Lewis, however, was to recognize the Democrat legislature, which was called the "Capitol Legislature," as the properly elected General Assembly. Lewis refused to deal with it, deferring instead to the decisions of the Courthouse Legislature until the attorney general of the United States upheld Lindsey's original decision.

Lewis's term of office was characterized by some of the worst problems of Radical Reconstruction as state spending outpaced tax revenue. In addition, the activities of the Ku Klux Klan increased as whites resorted to terrorism to prevent the freedmen from exercising their constitutional rights. Lewis's was the last administration under Radical Reconstruction in Alabama and he was defeated in his 1874 bid for reelection. Afterward Lewis returned to Huntsville and his legal practice. He died there on July 3, 1884, and was buried in Maple Hill Cemetery in Huntsville.

BIBLIOGRAPHY

Brewer, W. *Alabama: Her History, Resources, War Record, and Public Men from 1540 to 1872.* Montgomery, Ala., 1872.

Moore, Albert B. *History of Alabama and Her People.* 3 vols. Chicago, 1927.

Owen, Thomas M. *History of Alabama and Dictionary of Alabama Biography.* 4 vols. Chicago, 1921.

Pickett, Albert J. *History of Alabama and Incidentally of Georgia and Mississippi from the Earliest Period.* Birmingham, Ala., 1900.

Saunders, James E. *Early Settlers of Alabama.* New Orleans, 1899.

Woolfolk, Sarah Van V. "Five Men Called Scalawags." *Alabama Review* 17 (January 1964): 45–55.

KENNY A. FRANKS

LEWIS, DAVID W. (1815–1885), congressman from Georgia. Lewis was born in Hancock County, Georgia, on October 24, 1815, the son of a prominent planter. He was educated at the University of North Carolina and the University of Georgia, where he graduated in 1837. He served as Governor George R. Gilmer's private secretary from 1837 to 1839 and then studied law and opened a practice in Sparta in 1843. He soon acquired a large plantation and several hundred slaves.

Lewis's involvement in state politics began in 1845 when he was elected to the first of ten terms representing Hancock County in the Georgia General Assembly. In 1858, he was named a trustee of the University of Georgia and served in that position until his death. Though he began his political career as a Whig, he joined the Democratic party when, by the early 1850s, its commitment to slavery became apparent.

Lewis was also active in agricultural reform efforts, helping to found the Hancock County Planters' Club and the Georgia State Agricultural Society. He was secretary of the Southern Central Agricultural Society and editor of its quarterly publication.

Lewis was a staunch advocate of secession and was elected to represent Georgia's Fifth District in the First Congress in November 1861. Like most other Georgia representatives, he proved a more loyal supporter of Jefferson Davis's administration than of Governor Joseph E. Brown's and was considered by some to be Davis's staunchest ally from the Georgia delegation. His only major departure from nationalist policy was his introduction of bills protecting planters and their property from possible abuse by Confederate army agents and procurement officials. In his reelection bid in October 1863, he was soundly defeated by former Confederate senator John Troupe Shewmake, who challenged Lewis on a strong state rights platform.

Lewis's reputation as both agricultural and educational reformer led to his appointment by Governor Rufus Bullock in 1869 to head a committee to plan a statewide system of public education for Georgia (at that point still nonexistent). In 1873, he was named the first president of the newly established North Georgia Agricultural College in Dahlonega, a land-grant college founded under the Morrill Act of 1862. Lewis spent the rest of his life attempting to build a solid foundation for this college located in a poverty-stricken mountainous region, and in most respects, he succeeded in doing so. North Georgia College was unique in that it was the only such college to admit women, and Lewis's daughter Willie was its first female graduate. On December 28, 1885, while still president, Lewis died in Dahlonega.

BIBLIOGRAPHY

Cain, Andrew W. *History of Lumpkin County for the First Hundred Years, 1832–1932.* Dahlonega, Ga., 1979.

Coleman, Kenneth, and Charles Stephen Gurr, eds. *Dictionary of Georgia Biography.* Vol. 2. Athens, Ga., 1983.

Northen, William J., ed. *Men of Mark in Georgia.* Vol. 3. Atlanta, 1908. Reprint, Spartanburg, S.C., 1974.

Wakelyn, Jon L. *Biographical Dictionary of the Confederacy.* Edited by Frank E. Vandiver. Westport, Conn., 1977.
Warner, Ezra J., and W. Buck Yearns. *Biographical Register of the Confederate Congress.* Baton Rouge, La., 1975.

JOHN C. INSCOE

LEWIS, JOHN W.

LEWIS, JOHN W. (1801–1865), congressman from Georgia. Lewis was born in Spartanburg, South Carolina, on February 1, 1801. Though his father died while he was still an infant, he was well-educated and became a physician. His practice was short-lived, however. He became caught up in the evangelistic revivalism that swept through up-country South Carolina and in 1832 became an ordained Baptist minister. Lewis preached in Greenville until 1840, when he moved to Canton in the North Georgia mountains, where he served as pastor of several churches and established a series of profitable iron furnaces and mills.

In 1844, twenty-three-year-old Joseph E. Brown moved to Canton to teach at the local academy and later that year moved into Lewis's home to tutor his children. Lewis became a benefactor, even a father figure, to the future governor. In 1846, he loaned Brown the funds for his education at Yale and, when he returned, gave him farmland in the area. Lewis himself became involved in a number of business ventures, including railroads. When Brown was elected governor in 1857, he appointed Lewis superintendent of the state's Western and Atlantic Railroad, then plagued by financial mismanagement. Lewis undertook sweeping changes in the railroad's operations, but resigned after a mild disagreement with Brown in the midst of the latter's 1861 reelection campaign.

Lewis had always had a keen interest in politics, and as a Democrat, he had served briefly in the South Carolina legislature and in the Georgia Senate from 1845 to 1848. He was an avid secessionist in 1861 but was defeated in his bid to represent his North Georgia district in the First Congress. When Robert Toombs refused to accept his election by the legislature to the Confederate Senate in November 1861, Governor Brown appointed Lewis to fill the seat until the legislature reconvened and elected another senator. Lewis served in Richmond only two months in 1862, where he, like Brown, maintained a strong state rights position and opposed Davis administration policies regarding conscription, taxation, and the creation of a supreme court.

Before leaving the Senate, Lewis had accepted Brown's request that he serve as state agent to East Tennessee and Virginia to acquire much-needed salt for Georgia. Lewis leased a portion of the saltworks in Saltville, Virginia, and for about a year and a half produced salt to be transported to Georgia and sold to citizens at cost.

He returned home to Canton in 1864 and died there in June 1865.

BIBLIOGRAPHY

Parks, Joseph H. *Joseph E. Brown of Georgia.* Athens, Ga., 1977.
Wakelyn, Jon L. *Biographical Dictionary of the Confederacy.* Edited by Frank E. Vandiver. Westport, Conn., 1977.
Warner, Ezra J., and W. Buck Yearns. *Biographical Register of the Confederate Congress.* Baton Rouge, La., 1975.

JOHN C. INSCOE

LEWIS, JOSEPH HORACE

LEWIS, JOSEPH HORACE (1824–1904), brigadier general. A prominent prewar Whig in Kentucky, Lewis practiced law until 1857, and made a failed bid for Congress in 1860. He was an early and ardent supporter both of the Confederacy and of the movement to see Kentucky join with the seceded states. He raised the Sixth Kentucky Infantry, which was formally enlisted on November 19, 1861, with Lewis as colonel, and immediately assigned to the First Kentucky Brigade, later called the "Orphan Brigade."

Lewis led his regiment in virtually all of the brigade's battles, starting with Shiloh, and then on to Vicksburg, Baton Rouge, Murfreesboro, and Chickamauga. At the last, when brigade commander Ben Hardon Helm received a mortal wound, Lewis, as senior colonel, took over the brigade and retained command for the balance of the war.

Promoted to brigadier general on October 1, 1863, Lewis led the brigade at Missionary Ridge in November but saw little fighting. Following the winter in Dalton, Georgia, he led his men through the Atlanta campaign. Lewis was a stern disciplinarian, but he was also jealous of the honor and reputation of his command, asserting that "every man in the Kentucky Brigade is a *hero!*" He also persistently lobbied with other prominent Kentuckians to have his command mounted so he could lead it back into Kentucky, in the vain belief that he could rally the Bluegrass State for the Confederacy.

Following the brigade's near-destruction at Jonesboro on September 1, 1864, Lewis did finally see parts of it turned into mounted infantry, which he led in the final operations resisting William Tecumseh Sherman in South Carolina. He surrendered on May 7, 1865.

He returned to the law, then spent six years in Congress before becoming chief justice of the Kentucky Court of Appeals. He died July 6, 1904.

BIBLIOGRAPHY

Davis, William C. *The Orphan Brigade.* New York, 1980.
Johnston, J. Stoddard. *Kentucky.* Vol. 9 of *Confederate Military History.* Edited by Clement A. Evans. Atlanta, 1899. Vol. 11 of extended ed. Wilmington, N.C., 1988.

WILLIAM C. DAVIS

LEWIS, LEVIN M. (1832–1887), brigadier general. Lewis, born January 6, 1832, in Maryland, entered the ministry and was ordained to preach in Missouri in 1855. In response to Governor Claiborne F. Jackson's call for volunteers in April 1861, Lewis helped organize and was elected colonel of the Third Missouri Cavalry. After the Battle of Elkhorn Tavern (March 7–8, 1862) Gen. Earl Van Dorn cited him for his intelligence gathering. When the Third Missouri mustered out of service after its term of enlistment, Lewis joined Company A of the Sixteenth Missouri Infantry at Mayville, Arkansas, and in June was elected its captain. In December he was promoted to lieutenant colonel of the Sixteenth Regiment and in January 1863 became its colonel.

In the fighting around Helena, Arkansas, on July 4, 1863, Colonel Lewis was wounded and captured while leading a charge. He was held at Johnson's Island until September 1864. He rejoined his unit in November near Camden, Arkansas, as a brigadier general and was assigned command of Mosby Monroe Parsons's brigade after Parsons was promoted to divisional command. Lewis commanded the unit until it surrendered at Shreveport, Louisiana, on May 23, 1865.

After the war Lewis became pastor of the First Methodist Church in Dallas, Texas. Suffering from poor health, he followed his doctor's advice and moved to California in 1887. He died in Los Angeles on May 28 that same year.

BIBLIOGRAPHY

Moore, John C. *Missouri.* Vol. 9 of *Confederate Military History.* Edited by Clement A. Evans. Atlanta, 1899. Vol. 12 of extended ed. Wilmington, N.C., 1988.

Werry, Adolphus. *History of the First Methodist Church of Dallas, Texas, 1846–1946.* Dallas, Tex., 1947.

ROY R. STEPHENSON

LEWIS, WILLIAM GASTON (1835–1901), brigadier general. Lewis was born at Rocky Mount, North Carolina, September 3, 1835, a descendant of Revolutionary War veterans. He was educated at Lovejoy's Military School at Raleigh and graduated from the University of North Carolina at the age of nineteen. He taught school in Florida and North Carolina and spent a year as a government surveyor in Minnesota. From 1858 to 1861 he was an assistant engineer involved with the construction of the Wilmington and Weldon Railroad.

On April 18, 1861, Lewis enlisted for six months in Company C, First Regiment, North Carolina Troops, and was appointed a third lieutenant. He took part in the Battle of Big Bethel, the first sizable clash of arms in Virginia. Promoted to first lieutenant to date from September 7, 1861, he was mustered out of service with the First Regiment in November. On January 17, 1862, Lewis was

appointed major of the Thirty-third Regiment and distinguished himself at the Battle of New Bern on March 14. Promoted to lieutenant colonel, he was transferred to the Forty-third Regiment. Lewis fought all three days at Gettysburg and served at Bristoe Station and Mine Run before returning to North Carolina in the spring of 1864 to assist with the capture of Plymouth. Placed in command of Robert Frederick Hoke's old brigade, Colonel Lewis led his men in the Second Battle of Drewry's Bluff on May 16. He conducted a slashing attack against the right flank of Maj. Gen. Benjamin Butler's Army of the James, helping repulse its thrust toward Richmond. Fifteen days later Lewis was appointed brigadier general to date from May 31. Lewis and his brigade participated in Early's Washington raid and the 1864 Shenandoah Valley campaign, and fought in the trenches at Petersburg. During the retreat to Appomattox, he was severely wounded on April 7, 1865, at Farmville and was captured.

After his parole, Lewis resumed his practice as a civil engineer in North Carolina and served for thirteen years as the state engineer. Lewis died at Goldsboro, January 7, 1901, and was buried there.

BIBLIOGRAPHY

Faust, Patricia L. *Historical Encyclopedia of the Civil War.* New York, 1986.

Jordon, Weymouth T., Jr., and Lewis H. Manerin. *North Carolina Troops, 1861–1865: A Roster.* Vols. 3, 4, and 10. Raleigh, N.C., 1971, 1983, 1985.

Warner, Ezra J. *Generals in Gray: Lives of the Confederate Commanders.* Baton Rouge, La., 1959.

JOHN R. WOODARD

LIBBY PRISON. In March 1862, the Confederates required the Richmond, Virginia, firm of Libby and Son, ship chandlers and grocers, to vacate its premises so that it could be used to hold prisoners. The Libbys left behind their business sign, which gave their name to one of the Confederacy's better known prisons. Located on Cary Street with the James and Kanawha Canal and the James River itself in the rear, it was a brick building about 300 feet long and 103 feet deep. Although it seemed to be one structure, interior brick walls divided it into thirds. It had three floors plus a basement. Barred windows, many of them unglazed, provided ventilation. City water drawn from the James provided for drinking and washing and also flushed primitive water closets, a rare amenity in Civil War prisons.

Libby's commander during most of the war was Thomas P. Turner. A Virginian who had attended but not completed both West Point and Virginia Military Institute, he began as a lieutenant and ended as a major. He also supervised other Richmond prisons. The jailer under him was an enlisted

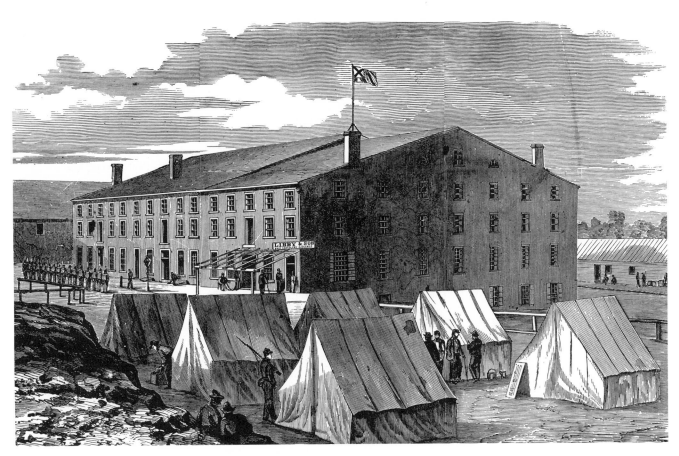

LIBBY PRISON, RICHMOND, VIRGINIA. Sketch from a photograph.   *FRANK LESLIE'S ILLUSTRATED FAMOUS LEADERS AND BATTLE SCENES OF THE CIVIL WAR*

man, the unrelated Richard R. Turner. A prewar overseer, Dick Turner was a large, often angry and violent man whom most prisoners came to despise and in their recollections often confused with his superior. Prisoners also tended to dislike the officious clerk, Erasmus Ross. The staff came to include blacks captured from the Union who were made to do cleaning and other menial work. The guards were drawn from local military companies.

Because of its division into several parts, it was possible to segregate several types of prisoners within Libby. At first a few political prisoners were held there, but soon it was used exclusively for prisoners of war. Although some privates were occasionally held in certain rooms later in the war, the Confederates used Libby almost entirely as an officers' prison. Because the headquarters of the Richmond prisons was in the building, many men who were being taken elsewhere were brought in to be registered, and thus a large number of prisoners later recalled having been "in Libby." During the war perhaps 125,000 prisoners actually stayed in Libby, of whom about 40,000 to 50,000 were held for a prolonged time.

The prison was most crowded between May 1863, when regular exchange of officers ceased, and May 1864, when the Confederates transferred most of the officers, using Libby

thereafter mainly for transients. During the congested period, over three thousand officers complained of lack of space, cold, vermin, and short rations. Most of the officers, however, had access to money with which they purchased additional comforts, and their hardships never approximated those of the enlisted men imprisoned at Richmond nor did more than a handful die. Nonetheless, because many were highly literate they were able to circulate their understandable complaints about their imprisonment and quickly made Libby infamous.

Unhappy prisoners sometimes escaped individually, and on February 9, 1864, 109 made the Civil War's best known escape through a tunnel, with 48 being recaptured. Correctly believing that some of the others had been helped by sympathizers in the city, the Confederates attempted to stop signaling through hand gestures and cloths by shooting at prisoners who appeared at windows. In March 1864, in an effort to intimidate the prisoners and prevent an uprising in support of the Kilpatrick-Dahlgren raid on Richmond, the Confederates buried several hundred pounds of gunpowder in the basement. They later claimed that since they had informed the prisoners, this was simply a bloodless warning, but the Federals effectively featured it in their propaganda during and after the war. At the war's end, the

United States used Libby for a time to confine Confederates, including Dick Turner. After reverting to commercial uses, the building was dismantled in 1888 and 1889, reerected as a museum in Chicago, and later demolished. There are remnants of it still in that vicinity.

BIBLIOGRAPHY

Byrne, Frank L. "Libby Prison: A Study in Emotions." *Journal of Southern History* 24 (1958): 430–444.
Byrne, Frank L. "Prison Pens of Suffering." In *Fighting for Time.* Vol. 4 of *The Image of War, 1861–1865.* Edited by William C. Davis. Garden City, N.Y., 1983.
Hesseltine, William B. *Civil War Prisons: A Study in War Psychology.* Columbus, Ohio, 1930. Reprint, New York, 1964.
Parker, Sandra V. *Richmond's Civil War Prisons.* Lynchburg, Va., 1990.

FRANK L. BYRNE

LIDDELL, ST. JOHN RICHARDSON (1815–1870), brigadier general.

Born September 6, 1815, near Woodville, Mississippi, Liddell attended West Point in 1833 but was discharged the next year "for deficiency in studies." His father bought him a plantation in Catahoula Parish, Louisiana.

When the Civil War began, Liddell served on William J. Hardee's staff at Bowling Green and in 1862 became a courier for Albert Sidney Johnston. He commanded an Arkansas brigade at Corinth and was promoted to brigadier general July 17, 1862. Liddell commanded a brigade in the Kentucky campaign, fighting at Perryville. He also led a brigade at Murfreesboro and in the Tullahoma campaign. He headed a division in W. H. T. Walker's Reserve Corps at Chickamauga but was back to brigade command at Chattanooga. By his own request he was transferred to the Trans-Mississippi Department in December 1863 and fought in the Red River campaign. In July 1864 he returned east of the Mississippi and commanded the District of the Gulf. He was captured at Fort Blakely on April 9, 1865.

Liddell's war reminiscences are a valuable record of the campaigns. He wrote, "The life of a soldier . . . was so exciting and agreeable that it often . . . made me think that war had too many natural charms for the peace of man." After the war, personal differences sharpened between Liddell and his neighbor Charles Jones, a former Confederate lieutenant colonel. On February 14, 1870, Jones and his two sons killed Liddell on a steamer in the Black River. He is buried on his Catahoula Parish plantation.

BIBLIOGRAPHY

Hughes, Nathaniel C., ed. *Liddell's Record.* Dayton, Ohio, 1985.
Winters, John D. *The Civil War in Louisiana.* Baton Rouge, La., 1963.

ANNE J. BAILEY

LILLEY, ROBERT DOAK (1836–1886), brigadier general.

Born in Greenville, Virginia, on January 28, 1836, Lilley attended Washington College and worked as a survey equipment salesman before the Civil War. He entered the Confederate service in the spring of 1861 as captain of the Augusta Lee Rifles, later incorporated into the Twenty-fifth Virginia Infantry. Stationed in northwest Virginia during the early stages of the war, Lilley fought in the engagements at Rich Mountain, Greenbrier River, Allegheny Mountain, and McDowell. Thereafter, as part of Jubal Early's brigade, he participated in the Shenandoah Valley, Seven Days', Second Manassas, Sharpsburg, and Fredericksburg campaigns. His bold leadership at Cedar Mountain and Second Manassas elicited praise from Early, and in January 1863 he was promoted to major. After temporary duty in western Virginia under John D. Imboden, Lilley rejoined the army in time for the Gettysburg campaign. He participated in the Mine Run campaign and later fought at the Wilderness and Spotsylvania. Promoted to brigadier general in May 1864, he commanded a brigade when Early marched on Washington. In the fighting at Stephenson's Depot on July 20, 1864, he was shot three times and taken prisoner. Recaptured four days later, he recovered to command the reserve forces in the valley until the close of the war. He participated in the engagement at Waynesboro in March 1865. In May he tried unsuccessfully to raise new recruits to go south and continue the struggle.

After the war Lilley worked at Washington College (later Washington and Lee University). He died in Richmond, Virginia, on November 12, 1886.

BIBLIOGRAPHY

Gallagher, Gary W. *Stephen Dodson Ramseur: Lee's Gallant General.* Chapel Hill, N.C., 1985.
Hotchkiss, Jed. *Virginia.* Vol. 3 of *Confederate Military History.* Edited by Clement A. Evans. Atlanta, 1899. Vol. 4 of extended ed. Wilmington, N.C., 1987.
Spencer, James. *Civil War Generals.* Westport, Conn., 1986.
U.S. War Department. *War of the Rebellion: A Compilation of the Official Records of the Union and Confederate Armies.* Washington, D.C., 1880–1901. Ser. 1. Vol. 27, pt. 2; vol. 29, pt. 1; vol. 43, pt. 2; vol. 46, pt. 3.

MICHAEL G. MAHON

LINCOLN, ABRAHAM.

[*This entry is composed of two articles,* Image of Lincoln in the Confederacy, *which discusses Confederates' views of the Republican ticket in the 1860 presidential election and of Abraham Lincoln himself, and* Assassination of Lincoln, *which discusses John Wilkes Booth's plot to assassinate Lincoln. For further discussion of Confederates' views of Lincoln, see* Election of 1860 *and* Republican Party. *For further discussion of the plot to assassinate Lincoln, see* Booth, John Wilkes, *and* Espionage, *articles on* Confederate Secret Service *and* Confederate Military Spies.]

Image of Lincoln in the Confederacy

The presidential election of 1860 did little to educate voters of the South about Abraham Lincoln, the Republican candidate. The campaign was waged in the North as a contest between Northern Democrats and Republicans, and in the South, between Southern Democrats and Constitutional Unionists; little dialogue between the sections occurred. The distorted image of Lincoln as an abolitionist (which he had never been) carried over into the Confederacy. Once war broke out, Confederates added to this core image of radicalism the usual scurrilous allegations made by one belligerent about the other.

The Confederates' descriptions of Lincoln in the press and popular literature mostly constituted perverse opposites or antic caricatures of his genuine traits. A teetotaler, Lincoln was assumed by Confederates to be a habitual inebriate. Although he had little formal education, their depiction of him as an ignorant illiterate would repeatedly be refuted by public letters and speeches of memorable eloquence and clarity. Lincoln may have seemed a coward to swaggering and militant secessionists because of his unfortunate decision to heed advisers' fears of assassination and to travel in secret through Baltimore to Washington for his inauguration in 1861. Yet from youthful tests of physical strength on the frontier to reckless exposure to enemy fire when Confederates neared Washington in 1864, Lincoln proved generally oblivious to problems of personal safety. Likewise, to depict Lincoln as a corrupt profiteer, as Confederates occasionally did, was to run counter to his consistent personal honesty in money matters. All such images were quite off the mark.

A more durable accusation focused on alleged atrocities committed by Union soldiers in the South during the war. Jefferson Davis himself initiated this tactic even before First Manassas. On July 20, 1861, the Confederate presi-

"THE GREAT EXHIBITION OF 1860." A sardonic comment on the Republican Party's antislavery position. At left is abolitionist editor Horace Greeley, grinding his New York *Tribune* organ as Abraham Lincoln prances to the music on a wooden rail labeled "Republican Platform." Lincoln is tethered to Greeley's index finger and his jaws are clamped shut, a reference to the Republican effort to de-emphasize the slavery issue during the 1860 campaign. At right stand Henry J. Raymond of the *New York Times* (with ax) and James Watson Webb of the New York *Courier and Enquirer*, both friendly to the Republican cause. William H. Seward stands in the background holding a wailing black infant. Lithograph on wove paper, probably drawn by Louis Maurer. Published by Currier and Ives, New York, 1860.

dent jeered at Lincoln's recent message to the U.S. Congress and denounced to the Congress in Richmond as "rapine" the destruction of "private residences in peaceful rural retreats," the "outrages [i.e., rapes] committed on defenseless females by soldiers," and the "deliberate malignity" of denying medicines to "the sick, including the women and children" by declaring them contraband of war—in short, "waging an indiscriminate war upon . . . all, with a savage ferocity unknown to modern civilization." William Tecumseh Sherman's image would come to bear the brunt of these accusations, levied from 1861 to this day in the South, while in the end Lincoln's would by and large escape them.

One Confederate accusation, also raised early by Jefferson Davis, would stick: that the North's president was a tyrant who crushed civil liberties and rode roughshod over the U.S. Constitution. This charge, consistent with Southern antebellum complaints about Northern policies, also served Davis well, as historian Paul Escott has shrewdly observed, in keeping the focus of the Confederate citizenry on preserving white liberty from Northern aggression rather than on defending black slavery, an institution whose profits were not enjoyed equally by all classes of Southern citizens. Finally, unlike the demonic pieces of character assassination and popular billingsgate, this charge had some substance. Denouncing Lincoln's arrogation to himself of the power to suspend the privilege of the writ of habeas corpus, Davis said in the summer of 1861, "We may well rejoice that we have forever severed our connection with a government that thus tramples on all the principles of constitutional liberty."

When Lincoln announced the preliminary Emancipation Proclamation on September 22, 1862, he fulfilled Southern fears of his abolitionism. On this issue popular vituperation could hardly be distinguished from the criticism by high-ranking Confederate officials. Virtually all regarded it as a monstrous and criminal invitation to slaves to murder their masters. Davis said in his January 12, 1863, message to Congress, that the document "encouraged [slaves] to a general assassination of their masters," but he added the sophisticated argument that emancipation would mean "extermination" of the black race in America, as they would surely die out in hopeless competition with the allegedly superior white race.

Eventually Davis himself embraced emancipation (as a reward for black military service), but the desperate idea came too late in Confederate history to be put into effect. Davis's increasing difficulties in quelling dissent, desertion, and draft resistance also led him to adopt a policy on civil liberties that Confederate critics in the press likened to Lincoln's. In other words, Davis and Lincoln came to fight the war in similar ways, as historian David Donald pointed out in 1978, using conscription and avoiding realistic taxation. Yet to this day most historians retain images of Davis and Lincoln as opposites.

The notion, born of Lincoln's reputation for personal charity and forgiveness, that Lincoln would not have reconstructed the Southern racial order had he lived contained genuine power to soften Lincoln's image in the South after the war was over. Eventually, Davis's reputation would fall, even among Southerners, and Lincoln's would rise.

In truth, the Confederate view of Lincoln contained little beyond what Northern Democrats said of Lincoln during the Civil War. For example, Roger B. Taney's decision in *Ex parte Merryman,* declaring Lincoln's suspension of the writ of habeas corpus illegal, became Confederate propaganda when it was reprinted in Jackson, Mississippi, and New Orleans during the war. And *Abraham Africanus I,* a political pamphlet published in New York in 1864, would have found a welcoming audience in the Confederacy. Only the intensity of feeling against Lincoln was greater among Confederates than among his determined Northern critics—and even the intensity was finally matched by John Wilkes Booth and his little band of Confederate sympathizers.

BIBLIOGRAPHY

Davis, Michael. *The Image of Lincoln in the South.* Knoxville, Tenn., 1971.

Donald, David Herbert. *Liberty and Union: The Crisis of Popular Government, 1830–1890.* Boston, 1978.

Escott, Paul D. *After Secession: Jefferson Davis and the Failure of Confederate Nationalism.* Baton Rouge, La., 1978.

MARK E. NEELY, JR.

Assassination of Lincoln

"Damn the rebels! This is their work," exclaimed U.S. Secretary of the Navy Gideon Welles when he first learned of Lincoln's assassination. Many other Northerners naturally leaped to the same conclusion, and President Andrew Johnson issued a proclamation on May 2, 1865, offering rewards for the arrest of Jefferson Davis along with Jacob Thompson, Clement C. Clay, Beverly Tucker, and George N. Sanders, identified as "rebels and traitors . . . harbored in Canada," for conspiring to procure the murder of President Lincoln. These prominent Confederates escaped prosecution, but the military trial of Booth's co-conspirators and Maryland associates was guided by the theory that the assassination was a Confederate plot.

That now seems very unlikely, though many persons active at one time or another in the Confederate cause were involved with John Wilkes Booth, the actor who shot Lincoln and who identified himself as "a Confederate . . . doing duty *upon his own responsibility.*" Booth's original

PRIVATE BOX, FORD'S THEATRE. Box where Abraham Lincoln was assassinated, April 14, 1865.   NATIONAL ARCHIVES

notorious as a haunt of Confederate agents. In Maryland and Washington he recruited for his political crime two former Confederate soldiers, Samuel Arnold and Michael O'Laughlin; an escaped Confederate prisoner of war, Lewis Payne; a Confederate spy, John H. Surratt; and at least two other men.

By the time he gathered the conspirators, Booth had lost his opportunity (he planned to capture Lincoln as he rode to the Soldiers Home, where the president slept during Washington's hot summer months). When he decided instead to kidnap Lincoln from a theater—the president's appreciation of drama was well known—several men dropped out of Booth's plot. Very late he decided on assassination rather than kidnapping. He shot the president on April 14, 1865, and Payne gravely wounded Secretary of State William H. Seward. Apparently the conspirators hoped, by killing high government officials, to bring about a change that would yet save the Confederacy.

Booth escaped for a time after the murder and was aided by the Confederate spy Thomas A. Jones of Maryland, who years later wrote a book about these experiences. A Union cavalryman finally shot the assassin dead against orders.

Attempts by the U.S. War Department to implicate Confederate officials stumbled conspicuously in 1866 when a congressional committee discovered that government witness Sanford Conover and others had given perjured testimony. The cooling of Civil War passions caused further decline in belief in the existence of a Confederate assassination plot. Gradually, the theory triumphed that the crime was entirely Booth's inspiration, and even his pro-

idea, hatched in the overheated election summer of 1864, was to kidnap Lincoln, take him to Richmond, and perhaps exchange him for Confederate prisoners of war. Late in the year Booth visited Montreal, where he stayed in a hotel

BRIDGE ACROSS THE EASTERN BRANCH OF THE POTOMAC. After the assassination of Abraham Lincoln, John Wilkes Booth and David Herold escaped over this bridge and fled toward Anacostia, Virginia. The photograph was taken in 1862.   NATIONAL ARCHIVES

Confederate political motivation was soft-pedaled by (unconvincing) assertions that he was a deranged actor whose career was faltering.

Eventually some sentimentalists emphasized the expressions of dismay heard in the states of the Confederacy at the time of Lincoln's assassination. In truth, plenty of joy was also expressed in the South, and there exists no systematic, statistical evaluation of the evidence for Southern feelings about the murder of the Confederacy's nemesis, Abraham Lincoln.

BIBLIOGRAPHY

Davis, Michael. *The Image of Lincoln in the South.* Knoxville, Tenn., 1971.

Hanchett, William. *The Lincoln Murder Conspiracies.* Urbana, Ill., 1983.

Tidwell, William A., with James O. Hall and David Winfred Gaddy. *Come Retribution: The Confederate Secret Service and the Assassination of Lincoln.* Jackson, Miss., 1988.

MARK E. NEELY, JR.

LITERATURE. [*This entry is composed of two articles,* Literature in the Confederacy, *which discusses literature written in the South during the Confederacy, and* The Confederacy in Literature, *which discusses depictions of the Confederacy in literature written after the Civil War.*]

Literature in the Confederacy

Writing during the Civil War focused on the war itself and its ramifications, for the topic not only offered opportunities to established authors to develop and expand traditional themes, methods, and subject matter but also opened the way for fresh materials and approaches from new writers as well. William Gilmore Simms, Paul Hamilton Hayne, Henry Timrod, and other well-known authors continued to contribute poetry, essays, lectures, and fiction to Southern periodicals and newspapers, and such relatively new names as James Ryder Randall, Francis Orray Ticknor, and Abram Joseph Ryan began to appear in various publications. Over the four years of the war a respectable body of belles lettres made its way into print.

In the beginning, getting into print was not too difficult. One of the first calls, along with the demand for troops to fight the war, was for a literature to explain, defend, and celebrate the new nation. There had been summonses for a Southern literature since the 1840s, but the establishment of a Confederate government in 1861 led immediately to the realization that the new nation must have its own literature soon. And nowhere was this need better encapsulated than in Timrod's odes "Ethnogenesis" (February 23, 1861) and "The Cotton Boll" (September 3, 1861). These poems posit a laureatelike speaker who celebrates the new nation's past and present and prophesies a future for it in which its mission—not unlike that perceived by the United States after World War II—is to share its "mighty commerce" and many "blessings" with "mankind."

The country's purpose defined, Simms, Hayne, John Esten Cooke, John R. Thompson, and other writers of standing celebrated battles and leaders in verse on Fort Sumter, Manassas, Vicksburg, Gettysburg, Petersburg, and Richmond and on P. G. T. Beauregard, J. E. B. Stuart, Thomas J. Jackson, Robert E. Lee, and Jefferson Davis. Relative newcomers like Randall, Ticknor, Margaret Junkin Preston, and John Williamson Palmer joined the chorus. Palmer's poems, and many others, were often attributed to anonymous sources, and his best-known lyrics, "Stonewall Jackson's Way" (1862) and "In Martial Manner" (1863), made their own way without benefit of the poet's reputation.

Eloquent and patriotic poetry could readily be printed in magazines and newspapers in the early days of the conflict, but by 1864, after paper, personnel, and equipment shortages and the failure of publishers to pay contributors or of subscribers to pay for subscriptions, the number of periodicals was reduced drastically. Despite the popularity of verse in newspapers, few volumes of it were published during the period, although John H. Hewitt's *War: A Poem with Copious Notes, Founded on the Revolution of 1861–1862* (1862), Theophilus Hunter Hill's *Hesper, and Other Poems* (1861, 1863), Joseph H. Martin's *Smith and Pocahontas: A Poem* (1862), William M. Martin's *Lyrics and Sketches* (1861), and Preston's *Beechenbrook* (1865) were exceptions. Much of this poetry dealt with themes and material familiar to and widely accepted by both poets and readers.

Prose, on the other hand, could not always be so readily exchanged among newspapers as verse could. Accordingly, fiction, especially novels, more frequently appeared in book form. Serial fiction and short stories, their natural popularity notwithstanding, were usually in limited supply. Over the life span of the Confederacy, for example, fewer than thirty novels were printed or reprinted, including Augustus Baldwin Longstreet's *William Mitten* (1864), James Dabney McCabe, Jr.'s, *Aide-de-Campe* (1863), and Augusta Jane Evans's *Macaria* (1864), the most popular of all Confederate novels, and one that was written to support the Confederacy. It was characterized by the author as "the bodyguard for the liberty of the Republic." Several novels were republished—Nathaniel Beverly Tucker's *Partisan Leader* (1862), for instance. Some editions of English novels appeared, such as Charles Dickens's *Great Expectations* (1863), George Eliot's *Silas Marner* (1863), and William Makepeace Thackeray's *Adventures of Philip* (1864), as well as translations of a few German and French novels. Victor Hugo's *Les Misérables* (1863–1864) was a particular favorite of Confederate soldiers. Also available were books of humorous tales and sketches, including George W. Bagby's *The Letters of Mozis Addums to Billy Ivvins* (1862), Richard Malcolm Johnston's *Georgia Sketches* (1864), and H. O. Judd's *Look Within for Fact and Fiction* (1864), and some drama was published, such as J. J. Delchamps's *Love's Ambuscade* (1863), McCabe's *The Guerrillas* (1863), and William Russell Smith's *The Royal Ape* (1863).

Few of the more significant Southern writers published books during the period of the Confederacy, however. Hayne and Thompson, for example, collected their poems and attempted to send them to England for publication, but the manuscripts were lost in the blockade. Simms contributed one backwoods novel, "Paddy McGann," to the *Southern Illustrated News* in 1863, but it did not appear in book form until a century later. Cooke's *Life of Stonewall Jackson* was brought out by Ayres and Wade in Richmond in 1863, but his newspaper sketches of his experiences in the war were not published as a book until 1867 and his novels on the war did not begin to appear until it was over. Indeed, much good writing during the period—both poetry and prose—was neither collected nor put into book form until later, much later in the case of Randall's *Poems* (1908), Simms's *Paddy McGann* (1972), Mary Boykin Chesnut's *Diary* (1905), and William J. Grayson's *Autobiography* (1990).

Confederate publishers were scattered throughout the new nation in Raleigh, Nashville, Columbia, Charleston, Augusta, Macon, Atlanta, and New Orleans. Both West and Johnston, and Ayres and Wade, were based in Richmond, S. H. Goetzel and Company in Mobile, and Burke, Boykin, and Company in Macon. Evans and Cogswell in Charleston was one of the largest firms, but despite a prewar list that included several of Simms's novels and plays, it published little belles lettres during the war. By 1863 shortages led to books being bound in wallpaper and printed on crude wrapping paper. Many firms failed under such conditions.

Magazines and newspapers faced the same hardships. Few of the journals (almost a hundred at the beginning of the war) lasted until the cessation of hostilities. The best of them were short-lived and by 1864 could seldom pay their contributors. In May of that year, for example, Hayne sought with partial success to barter his verse for medicine with Ayres and Wade, publishers of *Southern Illustrated News* (1862–1865), who owed him $180 for contributions printed since January.

The plight of newspapers by this time was even more serious. Paper could seldom be found and printing equipment could not be kept repaired sufficiently to publish regularly. With the loss of territory resulting from the war, many papers folded or were forced to move their offices from place to place, as in the well-known flight of the *Memphis Appeal* from its original base to towns in Mississippi, Alabama, and Georgia, a situation that led it to be referred to frequently as the "Moving Appeal."

The literature of the Confederacy, as may be expected, achieved mixed results. Limited by time and the pressure of events, writers found it difficult to sustain works of any length. Simms's "Paddy McGann," Longstreet's *William Mitten,* and Evan's *Macaria* are not important novels in an aesthetic sense, and the short fiction by Bagby, Johnston, and others was hardly any more significant. The best prose on the war appeared later in novels and tales by Sherwood Bonner, George Washington Cable, Cooke, Joel Chandler Harris, Grace King, Mary Murfree, and Thomas Nelson Page, among others, and in history, biography, and diaries by Chesnut, Cooke, King, and Page. The greatest achievement in the period's literature, however, was the short poetry the war inspired. Randall's "Maryland, My Maryland," Palmer's "Stonewall Jackson's Way," and Ticknor's "Little Giffin" express patriotic fervor and have the right touch, and Timrod's lyrics are clearly the ultimate accomplishment of Confederate literature. His "Ethnogenesis," "The Cotton Boll," "A Cry to Arms," "Carolina," "Spring," "Christmas," "The Unknown Dead," and the memorial "Ode" (1866) represent a body of poetry on the war excelled only by the Northerners Walt Whitman in *Drum-Taps* (1865) and Herman Melville in *Battle-Pieces* (1866). Not a massive literary achievement, assuredly, but one not unworthy of the Lost Cause.

[*See also* Broadsides; Cooke, John Esten; Diaries, Letters, and Memoirs; Evans, Augusta Jane; Lanier, Sydney; Magazines; Newspapers; Timrod, Henry.]

BIBLIOGRAPHY

Hubbell, Jay B. *The South in American Literature, 1607–1900.* Durham, N.C., 1954.

London, Lawrence F. "Confederate Literature and Its Publishers." In *The James Sprunt Studies in History and Political Science.* Edited by J. C. Sitterson. Chapel Hill, N.C., 1959.

McKeithan, Daniel M., ed. *A Collection of Hayne Letters.* Austin, Tex., 1944.

Moore, Rayburn S., ed. *A Man of Letters in the Nineteenth-Century South: Selected Letters of Paul Hamilton Hayne.* Baton Rouge, La., 1982.

Muhlenfeld, Elisabeth. "The Civil War and Authorship." In *The History of Southern Literature.* Edited by Louis D. Rubin, Jr., et al. Baton Rouge, La., 1985.

Oliphant, Mary C. Simms, et al., eds. *The Letters of William Gilmore Simms.* 6 vols. Columbia, S.C., 1952–1982.

Parks, Edd Winfield, and Aileen Wells, eds. *The Collected Poems of Henry Timrod: A Variorum Edition.* Athens, Ga., 1965.

Parrish, T. Michael, and Robert M. Willingham, Jr., comps. *Confederate Imprints: A Bibliography of Southern Publications from Secession to Surrender.* Austin, Tex., 1987.

Sears, Stephen W., ed. *The Civil War: A Treasury of Art and Literature.* New York, 1992.

RAYBURN S. MOORE

The Confederacy in Literature

In his bitter requiem for the fallen Confederacy, "The Conquered Banner," Father Abram J. Ryan predicted that "its fame on brightest pages, / Penned by poets and by sages, / Shall go sounding down the ages." But even the unreconciled bard might have been amazed by the extent to which his prophecy was fulfilled, for the fact is that for well over a century the clash between the Confederacy and Union became the single most popular event in American history for fiction writers and poets.

The first to appear were those, on both sides of the struggle, who had lived through it. Among immediate postwar Southern poets, only Sydney Lanier saw much active combat; his first book, a little-known novel called *Tiger-Lilies* (1867), recorded his life as soldier and prisoner of war. More successful was John Esten Cooke, who as an active participant and staff officer had gained an insider's view. Beginning in 1866 with *Surry of Eagle's-Nest,* Cooke devoted seven novels to the course of the war. But he avoided depicting the horrors of combat and instead focused on portraying heroes like Robert E. Lee, J. E. B. Stuart, and Thomas J. ("Stonewall") Jackson as avatars of the Cavaliers who, in regional myth, had fathered the Southern nation. Realism in fiction was not the mode of the day. When a Northern veteran, John W. De Forest, attempted to set down the bloodiness of battle in scenes in *Miss Ravenel's Conversion from Secession to Loyalty* (1867), he knew that readers would shrink from such gross depiction. But his novel, which also retroactively championed abolitionism, was the most faithful to actuality of any long fictional work before Stephen Crane's *The Red Badge of Courage* (1895).

Whether viewed as gallant defenders of their homeland or as Johnny Rebs, the Southern armies, for most readers, *were* the Confederacy; the domestic scene, by comparison, was thin material. But, as the scars of battle faded, writers of the defeated South embarked on a campaign of regional justification that swept the North as well. By 1888, Albion W. Tourgée, who had described his disillusioning experiences during Reconstruction in *A Fool's Errand* (1879), charged that American writing, particularly that class called "local color," had become "not only Southern in type but distinctly Confederate in sympathy." The prevailing mood was romantic nostalgia. Now that the South presented no military danger, its quixotic attempt to establish an aristocratic empire could take on the special glamour reserved for lost causes. The primary promulgator of this romanticized history was Thomas Nelson Page, whose *In Ole Virginia* (1887) and other works portrayed a vanished world of grace and honor.

Less lofty in social status were the dialect tales of Joel Chandler Harris, which replaced the image of the black as the pious and suffering Uncle Tom with the sly and engaging Uncle Remus; for the first time the rich oral tradition of black people found its way into popular writing. Harris's many other books also dealt with the middle Georgia region, most notably *Tales of the Home Folk in Peace and War* (1898). A countertrend soon became observable in the work of George Washington Cable. Though he had served as a Confederate cavalryman, Cable became increasingly liberal in his views about the plight of the freed blacks. He had gained wide popularity with his tales of Louisiana creoles; but when he turned to direct social criticism of the region in such books as *Dr. Sevier* (1884) and *John March, Southerner* (1894), he was treated as an apostate.

By the 1890s, the historical romance had become the dominant genre throughout the nation. The spate of newer romancers drew heavily upon types their predecessors had established—the Southern belle, the chivalrous young officer, the cantankerous old father, the faithful black retainer—and their settings were often the tall-pillared plantation home as well as the field of battle. But their plots grew more melodramatic, and the love interest became central to reader appeal. Typical of this school was Mary Johnston, whose *The Long Roll* (1911) features a Confederate captain who fights both for the cause and for the hand of his lady. Another staple plot is pivotal to Thomas Dixon's *The Southerner* (1913), whose heroine is loved by two brothers who espouse opposite sides. Dixon is also responsible for the most blatant example of the racism that could not be entirely eradicated from many Southerners' memories, *The Clansman* (1905), which furnished the plot for D. W. Griffith's *The Birth of a Nation* (1915). Even writers who were better known for other work turned to the Southern romance; examples are Winston Churchill's *The Crisis* (1901) and Upton Sinclair's *Manassas* (1906). One author, however, soon had enough of the moonlight-and-magnolia ambience; Ellen Glasgow, proclaiming that "what the South needs is blood and irony," soon proceeded to give it both, though her only novel that directly deals with the Confederacy is an early one, *The Battle-Ground* (1902).

The 1920s and 1930s saw the rise and flowering of what has been dubbed the "Southern Renaiscence"—a remarkably wide-ranging and acute reexamination of the legacy of the region's past. Chief among these poets, novelists, and critics were John Crowe Ransom, Donald Davidson, Robert Penn Warren, Cleanth Brooks, Merrill Moore, Andrew Lytle, and Allen Tate. These were the "inheritors"—those who by birth, ancestry, and early residence had roots deep in the Southern experience. They were hardly uncritical defenders, but they saw a decline of once-valued moral and ethical imperatives in a modern world of materialism and commercialism—views they set forth in their manifesto *I'll Take My Stand* (1930). These ideas also became themes in the literature they produced. Notable examples are the novels of Warren, particularly the Cass Mastern section in *All the King's Men* (1946), *Band of Angels* (1955), and *Wilderness* (1961). Characteristic, too, of this newer historical awareness are Andrew Lytle's *The Long Night* (1936) and Caroline Gordon's *None Shall Look Back* (1937). Allen Tate, a biographer of Stonewall Jackson and Jefferson Davis, also produced a novel, *The Fathers* (1938), an antisentimental inquiry into the moral ambiguities of the Civil War. This attitude is also central to his poem "Ode to the Confederate Dead" (1936), in which a modern man, pausing at a cemetery, ponders his relationship to the past which these buried soldiers had represented. The war is also recalled in Donald Davidson's "Lee in the Mountains" (1938); here the great general, now a college president in Virginia, reflects on his battles and his hopes for mercy and justice for his compatriots.

The greatest writer of the Renaiscence was, of course, William Faulkner, whose centrality to American writing about the South can only be suggested here. The great-grandson of a Confederate colonel, Faulkner was obsessed by all periods of Southern history, but the complex reasons for the South's defeat are central to the body of his work. A key text here is the novella "The Bear" (in *Go Down, Moses*, 1942), in which Ike McCaslin renounces his inheritance of the family plantation because of what he perceives as the human misuse of God-given land and the further curse put upon it by slavery. Among the works more directly dealing with the Confederacy are *Absalom, Absalom!* (1936), *The Unvanquished* (1938), and a number of short stories.

The 1930s and succeeding decades saw a continuation of the historical romance. Escapist reading about a vanished and glamorous past was undoubtedly the main reason for their popularity. A few, however, were characterized by a more careful portrayal of historical events and greater attention to the central fact of slavery and the legacy it had left. A representative selection would include Hervey Allen's *Action at Aquila* (1938), John Peale Bishop's *Many Thousands Gone* (1931), James Boyd's *Marching On* (1927), DuBose Heyward's *Peter Ashley* (1932), MacKinlay Kantor's *Andersonville* (1955), Joseph Stanley Pennell's *The History of Rome Hanks* (1944), a trilogy by T. S. Stribling (*The Forge*, 1931, *The Store*, 1932, *Unfinished Cathedral*, 1934), Ben Ames Williams's *House Divided* (1947), and Stark Young's *So Red the Rose* (1934). In a class by itself, because of its astonishing continued worldwide popularity both as book and film, is Margaret Mitchell's *Gone With the Wind* (1936). More recent examples are Shelby Foote's *Shiloh* (1952) and John Jakes's best-selling trilogy: *North and South* (1982), *Love and War* (1984), and *Heaven and Hell* (1987).

Whatever readers are looking for—from mere light entertainment to a desire to know more about the South

and the nation it created—the Confederacy shows no present signs of dying as a subject for literature.

[*See also* Cooke, John Esten; Lanier, Sydney.]

BIBLIOGRAPHY

Aaron, Daniel. *The Unwritten War.* New York, 1973.

Bain, Robert, Joseph M. Flora, and Louis D. Rubin, Jr. *Southern Writers: A Biographical Dictionary.* Baton Rouge, La., 1979.

Bridges, Emily. *The South in Fiction.* Chapel Hill, N.C., 1948.

Hubbell, Jay B. *The South in Southern Literature, 1609–1900.* Durham, N.C., 1954.

Lively, Robert A. *Fiction Fights the Civil War.* Chapel Hill, N.C., 1957.

Wilson, Edmund. *Patriotic Gore.* New York, 1962.

J. V. RIDGELY

LITTLE, LEWIS HENRY

LITTLE, LEWIS HENRY (1817–1862), brigadier general. Henry Little was born March 19, 1817, in Baltimore, Maryland, the son of a congressman. In 1839 he received a direct commission in the U.S. Army and served with distinction during the Mexican War, in which he was brevetted captain for bravery and meritorious conduct at Monterrey. He resigned his commission on May 7, 1861, to enter Confederate service. Commissioned as a major of artillery, Little soon became attached to Gen. Sterling Price's command as a colonel and assistant adjutant general. During the Battle of Elkhorn Tavern, Arkansas, he distinguished himself while leading a brigade. For his intrepid actions General Price and Gen. Earl Van Dorn recommended his promotion to brigadier general, which he received on April 16, 1862.

During the evacuation of Corinth, Mississippi, Gen. Braxton Bragg assigned Little to command a division, and his unit fought at the Battle of Iuka, September 19, 1862. While he was sitting on his horse talking with Price, Little was hit in the forehead by a minié ball and died instantly. He was buried by torchlight that night. His remains were later moved to Baltimore for permanent interment.

BIBLIOGRAPHY

Castel, Albert. *General Sterling Price and the Civil War in the West.* Baton Rouge, La., 1960.

Johnson, Bradley T. *Maryland.* Vol. 2 of *Confederate Military History.* Edited by Clement A. Evans. Atlanta, 1899. Vol. 2 of extended ed. Wilmington, N.C., 1987.

ROY R. STEPHENSON

LITTLE ROCK, ARKANSAS

LITTLE ROCK, ARKANSAS. On the eve of the Civil War, Little Rock, Arkansas's capital city and a transient point for westward-moving settlers, counted 3,727 permanent residents. Its 2,874 whites, most of whom were born in the United States although many had migrated from Europe, were augmented by 853 slaves. Arriving in 1861, the New York–born schoolteacher Ralph L. Goodrich appreciated the city's upper class of Southern-born planters and merchants together with "bustling Yankee[s] who [had] thrown aside [their] repulsion to slavery." Rawboned backwoodsmen dressed "in homespun and Kentucky jeans," the "turbulent, troublesome Irish," and Germans who believed that liberty coexisted only "with socialism" mixed with these prominent citizens. Their city, located on the western fringe of Southern civilization, had developed a highly stratified society characterized by class and race.

A wealthy core of planters, prominent government officials, merchants, attorneys, and other professionals enjoyed the perquisites of society's favored class. No more than 10 percent of the white working population, this upper class owned 87 percent of the city's total wealth; and indeed, the ten richest individuals husbanded 44 percent of their town's affluence. This class remained virtually closed to the foreign-born: only 5 percent had originated outside the country, 70 percent were native Southerners, and 25 percent hailed from Northern states. Two of this last group—the New York–born William Woodruff, Sr., and the Massachusetts-born Albert Pike—would play significant roles in the coming war. Woodruff, a land agent and founder of the *Arkansas Gazette,* became the city's best-known proponent of the Confederate cause; and Pike, a successful attorney and accomplished poet, not only became an important general but also wrote a popular version of the Southern anthem "Dixie."

Minor professionals (government bureaucrats and less affluent attorneys, merchants, and others) supported this upper class. Native whites dominated this group with the foreign-born becoming more significant toward the social

pyramid's base. Only 25 percent of the minor professionals were foreign immigrants; their numbers rose to 41 percent among artisans and 49 percent in the laboring class. Germans filled the ranks of carpenters, cabinetmakers, tailors, shoemakers, and gunsmiths; the Irish gravitated to the less skilled activities of common laborers.

Although a river port, Little Rock had but tenuous contacts with the larger world, for in dry seasons the Arkansas River shallows blocked steamboat transportation. The Memphis and Little Rock Railroad was only two-thirds completed in 1860, and the telegraph did not arrive until January 1861. Anticipating these completions and the resulting economic boom, land speculators and building contractors prospered. State government furnished some employment, and on the city's outskirts stood a Federal arsenal and the state penitentiary. Although streets remained unpaved and sewage disposal nonexistent, a degree of modernity arrived in August 1860 when a coal-gas system illuminated public buildings and the city's main avenues.

The community's cultural life formed around education, journalism, religion, and the theater. In 1855, Little Rock instituted a public school system that provided a meager education for its less affluent inhabitants. Wealthier citizens sent their children to prestigious academies: Mrs. Richards' Young Ladies Institute, the Little Rock High School for Young Ladies, Edward Souter's Classical School for Young Gentlemen, and Mr. Matthew's Private Academy. St. John's College, founded by the Grand Lodge of Arkansas Masons, opened in 1859. Throughout the 1850s, the state capital supported several newspapers, but by 1860 the *Arkansas Gazette* dominated, forcing out all rivals but one. Four churches—Episcopal, Methodist, Presbyterian, and Baptist—served white Protestants, and one Baptist congregation catered to black worshipers. An Irish bishop, two Irish priests, and twelve Irish nuns ministered to the city's

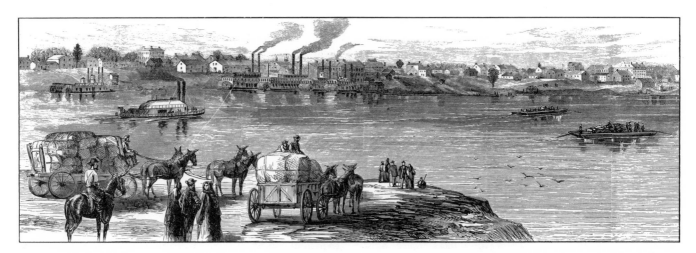

LITTLE ROCK, ARKANSAS.

HARPER'S PICTORIAL HISTORY OF THE GREAT REBELLION

Catholics. The community's small theater presented secular entertainment with itinerant players, and numerous drinking shops slaked the citizens' thirst.

The Civil War disrupted Little Rock's evolution from a frontier community to a settled urban center. Shortly after Abraham Lincoln's election, the state's newly inaugurated governor proclaimed that should "any of the Southern states . . . deem it necessary to declare independence" Arkansas would give "active support." Sensing danger, Federal authorities ordered seventy-five soldiers of the Second U.S. Artillery into Little Rock's arsenal. When on January 30, 1861, Arkansas's solicitor general was granted the honor of sending the city's first telegram, he grasped the opportunity to warn the state's eastern regions of the arsenal's threat. Eight hundred armed men, most from Helena-area militia units, arrived on February 5 and besieged the post for a week. Unable to communicate with his superiors and unwilling to commence hostilities, the arsenal's commander deeded the facility to the governor and withdrew his command to St. Louis. Following Fort Sumter's bombardment and Lincoln's subsequent call for volunteers, a secessionist convention, already assembled in Little Rock, declared for the Confederacy on May 6.

In spite of the city's worth as the state's political center and headquarters of the Trans-Mississippi Department, Confederate authorities in Richmond considered Little Rock of little strategic importance and so dispatched less glittering worthies—Thomas C. Hindman and Theophilus H. Holmes—to protect the region. The fall of Memphis and the subsequent investment of Vicksburg further diminished the city's military value. Recognizing this, in March 1863, E. Kirby Smith, the new Trans-Mississippi commander, shifted his headquarters to Louisiana.

The Confederate years had a profound impact on the city's social life. Initially a large percentage of its young males left for military service; they were soon replaced by a transient mélange of political opportunists, refugees, drifters, and temporarily assigned soldiers. Social order declined, public drunkenness increased, and prostitution became a serious problem. As wounded soldiers flowed into the city, Little Rock quickly developed into a convalescent center. By 1863, social class conflict loomed. The *Arkansas Gazette* gloomily complained that prominent citizens' sons avoided military service and that the foreign-born, especially the Germans, failed to support the Confederate cause.

Vicksburg's surrender in July 1863 doomed Little Rock. Only the Arkansas River's chronic low water prevented the city's immediate besiegement, and the long-awaited Union thrust was delayed until early fall. On September 10, Frederick Steele's small Union army entered Little Rock, having met only light resistance from local militia. The city thereafter was the headquarters for Union military activities in the state.

Regardless of any emotional ties to the Confederacy, the city prospered under Union control. Trade, which had languished under the Confederacy, revived, stimulating goodwill between citizens and occupiers. In spite of this fortuitous development, however, two unhappy incidents marred the restoration of Federal rule. In the first, Steele ordered the expulsion of William Woodruff, Sr., for his blatant Confederate partisanship. In the second, Steele hanged a youthful spy, David Dodd, a popular seventeen-year-old telegraph operator. The general proposed clemency on condition Dodd reveal his accomplices, but the youth chose martyrdom and paid the penalty on January 8, 1864.

Union occupation reoriented Little Rock's social development. The state penitentiary now held Confederate prisoners of war, St. John's College became a Federal hospital, and black and white refugees flooded the city. By May 1864 an estimated 2,650 ex-slaves had congregated in the capital, seeking protection from their former masters, hoping for employment, and needing charity. In response, Northern humanitarians established Arkansas's first school for blacks. Anti-Confederate whites also sought asylum; harassed by Confederate bands ranging the countryside, these refugees arrived destitute. In the first three months of 1865, Steele's successor in the Little Rock command persuaded two thousand of them to accept transportation to Northern havens; he housed seven hundred others—mainly indigent women and children—on a small farm confiscated from a Confederate supporter.

Little Rock emerged from the Civil War profoundly changed. The Negro population rose from 23 percent in 1860 to 43 percent in 1870, and newly enfranchised freedmen regularly elected four blacks to the city's eight-man council. Much to the consternation of former Confederates, they controlled urban affairs through an alliance with German Republicans. When white conservatives regained power in 1875, they immediately gerrymandered the council districts, negating black influence. Prostitution remained a Civil War legacy. Virtually nonexistent prior to the conflict, it germinated during the war and flourished afterward. Well into the twentieth century, Little Rock retained a justified reputation as a place where "ladies of the evening" catered to the taste of all, from the most distinguished politician to the humblest boatman.

Apart from such questionable commerce, however, Little Rock prospered. The Memphis and Little Rock Railroad's completion in 1869 assured the city's importance as a transportation center and encouraged a steady population growth throughout the century's balance. Secure in its status as Arkansas's first city, Little Rock assumed the ambience of a successful Southern community until the Central High School desegregation crisis of 1957 reminded the nation of the Civil War's unfinished business.

BIBLIOGRAPHY

Huff, Leo E. "The Memphis and Little Rock Railroad during the Civil War." *Arkansas Historical Quarterly* 23 (1964): 260–270.

Lester, Jim, and Judy Lester. *Greater Little Rock.* Norfolk, Va., 1986.

O'Donnell, William. *The Civil War Quadrennium: A Narrative History of Day-to-Day Life in Little Rock, Arkansas, during the War Between the States, 1861–1865.* Little Rock, 1985.

Richards, Ira Don. *Story of a Rivertown: Little Rock in the Nineteenth Century.* Little Rock, 1969.

Ross, Margaret. *Arkansas Gazette: The Early Years, 1819–1866.* Little Rock, 1969.

FRED ARTHUR BAILEY

LOCOMOTIVE CHASE. *See* Andrews Raid.

LOGAN, GEORGE WASHINGTON (1815–1889), congressman from North Carolina. Logan established a consistent record as a Unionist, an opponent of the Confederate administration, an advocate of peace negotiations, and a postwar Republican. As a representative from western North Carolina's Tenth Congressional District, he reflected the substantial Unionism and disaffection with the Confederacy that existed among his constituents.

Born in Rutherford County, North Carolina, on February 22, 1815, Logan received his education at local academies and at home. After moving to the town of Rutherfordton, he held a series of judicial offices and became clerk of the county court in 1841. Resigning that position in 1849, he studied law under Richmond Pearson and subsequently opened a practice. From 1855 to 1856 Logan was county solicitor, and for a period after 1858 he edited the *Rutherfordton Enquirer.* He also farmed, owned eleven slaves in 1860, and was active in the state militia. Politically, Logan was an old-line Whig and an admirer of Henry Clay.

Logan actively opposed secession, and he never gave strong support to the Confederacy. The growing peace movement in North Carolina in 1863 brought him back into office after a peace convention in his district nominated him to oppose incumbent Congressman Allen Turner Davidson. Observers believed, probably with good reason, that the votes of "disaffected and disloyal men" gave Logan a decisive majority. His opponents charged that he was a leader of the Red Strings (or Heroes of America), a secret, pro-Union organization that had a considerable following in western North Carolina.

In the Second Congress Logan consistently supported calls for an armistice and for the opening of peace negotiations. He steadfastly pursued these positions even when he was in a decided minority, as on November 25, 1864, when only two representatives joined him in voting for James T. Leach's resolutions on peace, or on December 2, 1864, when only thirteen were willing to consider controversial peace resolutions offered by Tennessee's Henry S. Foote.

On other issues Logan gave the Confederate administration virtually no support. He strongly opposed impressment, conscription, taxes, suspension of the writ of habeas corpus, and the use of slaves as soldiers. Through various amendments that he proposed, Logan also sought to shield his constituents from the increasing demands of the Confederacy. He favored exempting from conscription farmers and mechanics who were over forty-five and had eight dependents, and he proposed an exemption for one tanner, blacksmith, shoemaker, and miller "in each and every territory of eight miles square." He successfully offered an amendment to exempt soldiers' families and disabled soldiers from the tax-in-kind.

After the war Logan won election to North Carolina's constitutional convention of 1865 and to the legislature of 1866–1867. He joined the Republican party and fought vigorously against Conservatives or Democrats, planters, and even eastern interests in his own party. In 1868 he became a superior court judge and soon distinguished himself as an implacable foe of the Ku Klux Klan in Cleveland, Rutherford, and nearby counties. Democratic lawyers protested that he was hostile to them, partial to black citizens, and incompetent; the Democratic legislature of 1871–1872 considered impeaching him but did not do so. Defeated by a Democrat in 1874, Logan retired to private life and died at his home in Chimney Rock on October 18, 1889.

BIBLIOGRAPHY

Alexander, Thomas B., and Richard E. Beringer. *The Anatomy of the Confederate Congress: A Study of the Influences of Member Characteristics on Legislative Voting Behavior, 1861–1865.* Nashville, Tenn., 1972.

Journal of the Congress of the Confederate States of America, 1861–1865. 7 vols. Washington, D.C., 1904–1905.

Powell, William S., ed. *Dictionary of North Carolina Biography.* Vol. 3. Chapel Hill, N.C., 1988.

"Proceedings of the Confederate Congress." *Southern Historical Society Papers* 51–52 (1958–1959). Reprint, Wilmington, N.C., 1992.

PAUL D. ESCOTT

LOGAN, THOMAS MULDRUP (1840–1914), brigadier general. Thomas Logan was bright and ambitious. In 1860 he graduated at the head of his class from South Carolina College and joined the Confederate army as a private in Company A of the Hampton Legion, Washington Light Infantry, to defend his state. He swiftly gained the attention of both his comrades and his superiors for his daring while on reconnaissance missions and for his abilities as a skirmisher.

Logan moved quickly up the Confederate ranks. After participating in the capture of Castle Pinckney and the bombardment of Fort Sumter, his company elected him as its first lieutenant. Following the Battle of First Manassas, he received promotion to captain. While fighting at Gaines' Mill during the Seven Days' Battles, he received a wound that forced him to ride to the confrontation at Second Manassas in an ambulance. The next month, however, he was back in the field fighting the tragic battle at Sharpsburg, where his performance earned him a promotion to major.

In 1864 Logan survived yet another wound to become the youngest brigadier general then in the Confederate army. During the final days of the war, his brigade fought in the North Carolina campaign. At Bentonville, Logan and his troops were nearly cut off from the body of the main army; only Logan's quick thinking and skill as a soldier saved his men from immediate disaster. The next month, he surrendered with Gen. Joseph E. Johnston.

Following the war, Logan built a fortune in the railroad business and urged peaceful reconciliation with the North.

BIBLIOGRAPHY

Capers, Ellison. *South Carolina.* Vol. 5 of *Confederate Military History.* Edited by Clement A. Evans. Atlanta, 1899. Vol. 6 of extended ed. Wilmington, N.C., 1987.

Reception of General T. M. Logan, Ex-Captain W.L.I. Volunteers, Company A, Hampton Light Infantry. Charleston, S.C., 1875.

Warner, Ezra J. *Generals in Gray: Lives of the Confederate Commanders.* Baton Rouge, La., 1959.

JENNIFER LUND

LOGAN'S CROSS ROADS, KENTUCKY.
See Mill Springs, Kentucky.

LOMAX, LUNDSFORD LINDSAY (1835–1913), major general. Lomax was born November 4, 1835, in Newport, Rhode Island, where his father was stationed as an army major of ordinance. Young Lomax received his early education in Virginia, the family home state. He graduated in 1856 from West Point, joined the Second U.S. Cavalry, and saw frontier service against the Indians until his April 2, 1861, resignation from the army.

Lomax received a captain's commission and spent the first two years of the Confederacy in the West on the staffs of Gens. Ben McCulloch, Earl Van Dorn, and Joseph E. Johnston, respectively. In the spring of 1863, at the urging of his lifelong friend, Fitzhugh Lee, Lomax came east and accepted the colonelcy of the Eleventh Virginia Cavalry.

LUNDSFORD LINDSAY LOMAX.   LIBRARY OF CONGRESS

Solid performances at Brandy Station and Gettysburg brought July 23, 1863, promotion to brigadier general. Most of Lomax's remaining service was in the Shenandoah Valley. After elevation to major general on August 10, 1864, he commanded Jubal Early's cavalry in the second Shenandoah Valley campaign. On March 29, 1865, Lomax succeeded Early in command of what was left of the Valley District.

He became a postwar farmer in Fauquier County and married a cousin of Gen. William H. Payne. In 1885 he began a four-year tenure as president of what is now Virginia Tech. He spent the next six years aiding in the compilation of the U.S. War Department's *Official Records of the Union and Confederate Armies.* In later years, as a commissioner of the Gettysburg battlefield park, Lomax played a leading role in the erection of the dominant Virginia monument across from Cemetery Ridge. He died May 28, 1913, and is buried in Warrenton, Virginia.

BIBLIOGRAPHY

Armstrong, Richard L. *Eleventh Virginia Cavalry.* Lynchburg, Va., 1989.

Hotchkiss, Jed. *Virginia.* Vol. 3 of *Confederate Military History.* Edited by Clement A. Evans. Atlanta, 1899. Vol. 4 of extended ed. Wilmington, N.C., 1987.

"Maj. Gen. L. L. Lomax." *Confederate Veteran* 21 (1913): 450. Reprint, Wilmington, N.C., 1985.

JAMES I. ROBERTSON, JR.